D0466424

THAT
INFERNAL
LITTLE
CUBAN
REPUBLIC

THAT INFERNAL LITTLE CUBAN REPUBLIC

the UNITED STATES *and the* CUBAN REVOLUTION

LARS SCHOULTZ

The University of North Carolina Press
Chapel Hill

This book was
published with the
assistance of the
William R. Kenan Jr.
Fund of the University
of North Carolina
Press.

Designed by Kimberly Bryant
Set in Arnhem and Sveva
by Tseng Information Systems, Inc.
Manufactured in the United States of America

The paper in this book meets the guidelines for
permanence and durability of the Committee on
Production Guidelines for Book Longevity of the
Council on Library Resources.

The University of North Carolina Press has been a
member of the Green Press Initiative since 2003.

Library of Congress Cataloging-in-Publication Data
Schoultz, Lars.
That infernal little Cuban republic : the United States and
the Cuban Revolution / Lars Schoultz.
p. cm.
Includes bibliographical references and index.
ISBN 978-0-8078-3260-8 (cloth : alk. paper)
1. United States—Foreign relations—Cuba. 2. Cuba—
Foreign relations—United States. 3. United States—
Foreign relations—1945–1989. 4. United States—Foreign
relations—1989– 5. Presidents—United States—History—
20th century. 6. Cuba—History—Revolution, 1959–
7. Cuba—Politics and government—1959–1990. 8. Cuba—
Politics and government—1990– I. Title.
E183.8.C9S375 2009
327.7307291—dc22
                                        2008036714

13 12 11 10 09 5 4 3 2 1

I am so angry with that infernal little Cuban republic that I would like to wipe its people off the face of the earth. All we have wanted from them was that they would behave themselves and be prosperous and happy so that we would not have to interfere. And now, lo and behold, they have started an utterly unjustifiable and pointless revolution.

—*President Theodore Roosevelt, 1906*

CONTENTS

THAT
INFERNAL
LITTLE
CUBAN
REPUBLIC

INTRODUCTION
NEIGHBORS

Imagine living in a neighborhood where the family across the street irritates you. It's a wide street, fortunately, so most of the time you can simply ignore them, but every so often they do something annoying—your kids go over to play with theirs and wobble back home with the marijuana giggles, or these neighbors welcome some out-of-town houseguests who are clearly up to no good, placing you nervously on guard until you see them leave. Or what about that morning when you awoke to discover that a few of their many children had pitched a tent in your front yard, complaining they can no longer endure living at home? They apparently intend to stay forever.

Then imagine that you try not to let all this bother you. You understand that these neighbors haven't had your advantages. They come from different stock—a "tropical" people, outwardly cheerful but hopelessly emotional and pathologically frenetic, investing most of their energy in billowy arm-waving and oral pyrotechnics. Style is fairly insignificant, of course, but when combined with the irresponsible behavior, it all adds up, sometimes to the point where you simply cannot take any more. That's when you march across the street to set them straight. Usually, you don't have to do anything more than raise your voice—they know the consequences when you get angry, so they quickly promise to behave better. Yet can they? Probably not without your help, which requires lots of solid advice and sometimes a modest loan but also makes you feel good. After you've set them on the right path, you always return home with a sense of genuine accomplishment.

Then imagine you do this once too often.

WHAT HAPPENED NEXT was called the Cuban Revolution. Of course, the revolution involved much more than shooing the Yankees back across the street, but this book focuses on the U.S.-Cuban relationship. It examines how the United States deals with a difficult neighbor. The story focuses on the island's revolutionary generation, which grew to maturity in a country characterized by widespread deprivation, extreme inequality, and extraordinary corruption. And, unfortunately, many Cubans of that generation were convinced that the United States bore much of the responsibility for the problems that faced them. The first chapter of this book explains what the dean of historians of Cuba meant when he wrote that "almost any comprehensive history of Cuba is, of necessity, a discourse on U.S.-Cuban relations."[1]

This initial chapter also introduces Washington's mental image of Cuba, focusing on the widespread expectation that the United States would act as a guardian of the less-developed peoples of the Caribbean but emphasizing that the root of this hegemonic presumption was a benevolent disposition and an unshakable belief that proximity to the United States was the region's singular good fortune. Or, as an assistant secretary of state asserted in 1916, "Nature, in its rough method of uplift, gives sick nations strong neighbors."[2] Three months later the United States sent several hundred soldiers to lift up what was then Cuba's sickest province, Camagüey, where they stayed for five years.

The trouble *really* began several decades later, in 1959, when a group of rebels ousted a perfectly acceptable dictator and proceeded to cause more trouble than anyone could have imagined. "There was something on Cuba every five minutes," complained an exasperated secretary of state, Christian Herter, and while he and President Dwight D. Eisenhower at first tried to be accommodating, they soon lost patience and began planning the Bay of Pigs invasion. "There is a limit to what the United States in self-respect can endure," Eisenhower said when he announced the closing of the U.S. embassy, and when he handed John F. Kennedy the keys to the White House three weeks later, Eisenhower also passed along an admonition: "We cannot let the present government there go on."[3]

That was in 1961. Twenty years later, Eisenhower and Kennedy were both dead and buried, yet Fidel Castro was boasting that "we will still be here in *another* 20 years." Not if incoming U.S. president Ronald Reagan and his new secretary of state, Alexander M. Haig Jr., had anything to say about the matter. During the 1980 campaign, Reagan had proposed a blockade of Cuba, and now, at the first meeting of his national security team, Haig proposed going one step further: an invasion. Finding little support for the idea, the secretary pulled his principal deputy aside and gave him his first assignment: "I want to go after Cuba, Bud. I want you to get everyone together and give me a plan for doing it."[4]

That was in 1981. Twenty years later, Ronald Reagan was dying of Alzheimer's disease and Alexander Haig was a semiretired consultant padding around his Northern Virginia office in Hush Puppies, while George W. Bush had slipped on the presidential wingtips and was promising no letup: "I've got a plan to spread freedom," he told a 2004 campaign audience, "not only in the greater Middle East but also in our own hemisphere, in places like Cuba." But the second President Bush, like his nine immediate predecessors, had been obliged to focus on more important problems. He did not even mention the island in a wide-ranging foreign policy speech near the end of his tenure, and in reply to a question from the audience, he indicated that he was leaving the island's fate to divine intervention: "One day the good Lord will take Fidel Castro away."[5]

IMAGINE NOW, on the revolution's golden anniversary, that your grandchildren ask you to explain U.S. policy during the half century after 1959. On a basic level, the answer is easy: We have been attempting to protect our interests. Specifically, Washington's policy has reflected first the economic concerns of U.S. investors, then—and much more important—the security concerns of U.S. defense managers, and finally the electoral concerns of U.S. politicians, who have eagerly sought the support of Cuban Americans, some of whom are wealthy campaign contributors and several hundred thousand of whom vote in the crucial state of Florida. It's that simple—an ever-varying mixture of economic, security, and domestic political interests—and if you think it will be enough of an explanation for your grandchildren, read no further.

But you'll miss what makes this relationship so intriguing: underlying these everyday interests is an *ideology*, a set of tightly integrated beliefs that controls the way powerful countries like the United States have traditionally thought about smaller neighboring countries like Cuba. At the most rudimentary level, this book is simply a case study in an intellectual tradition stretching back to the fifth century, B.C., when Thucydides, chronicling the conflicts among Greek city-states, captured perfectly the bedrock principle of what we today call realism: the strong will do what they want, and the weak will accept what they must. Realism is a part of our ideology—an important part.

Were Thucydides explaining U.S. policy toward the Cuban Revolution, he would begin with some basic data:

	United States	Cuba	Cuba as % of United States
Area	9,826,630 sq. km.	110,860 sq. km.	1.1
Population	301 million	11 million	3.7
Gross Domestic Product	$13,860 billion	$51 billion	0.4

Here, Thucydides would emphasize, is a modest island with an economy *1/250th* the size of its wealthy, continent-wide neighbor, which has used a substantial portion of its fabulous wealth to create the most powerful military in the history of the human race. And that raw strength has given politicians such as Vice President Richard Nixon the ability to tell voters that "the United States has the power, and Mr. Castro knows this, to throw him out of office," and it has given cabinet members such as Alexander Haig the ability to ask President Reagan for a simple green light: "You just give me the word and I'll turn that f—— island into a parking lot."[6]

What Thucydides would have difficulty explaining—and what makes traditional realism an incomplete theory—is this: When the Cubans refused to accept what they must, their leaders were not thrown out of office and their island was not turned into a parking lot. This gives rise to the question that makes relations with this modest island fascinating for casual observers and especially relevant for theorists: How have Cubans managed to get away with it? For decades, the answer was that Cuba balanced U.S. power by enlisting the support of a rival superpower, but that answer, which was never more than partially correct, takes us only to about 1990, when the Soviet Union withdrew its support. A complete answer has to include the constraints that the modern world now imposes on the exercise of power.

This book accents the most elemental constraint, the need to maintain a sense of proportion, and emphasizes that it is not simply a good idea; it is mandatory. This constraint arose as humans became increasingly aware of the costs attached to every benefit, especially in international relations, where the potential costs have risen in lockstep with technology. For chronic but not acute aggravations such as Cuba, superpowers are now especially wary of the opportunity costs, and a simple list of all the other issues confronting any superpower like the United States is sufficient to explain why Richard Nixon did not employ U.S. power to throw Castro out of office (in fact, Nixon largely ignored Cuba when he finally claimed the presidency), why President Reagan declined to endorse Secretary Haig's parking-lot solution, why President Bush left Cuba to the good Lord, and why presidential adviser Arthur Schlesinger Jr. said this about the one president who seemed to spend more time than any other on Cuba: "Castro was not a major issue for Kennedy, who had much else on his mind."[7] It took JFK's best and brightest only three months—until the Bay of Pigs—to discover that Cubans were going to fight back. We could certainly make them accept what they must, but not with a couple of thousand Cuban exiles; we would have to do it ourselves, with the U.S. Marines, and they might indeed have to turn the island into a parking lot. Victory would be ours, but at an especially exorbitant price in the currency that might matter most, world opinion.

So what was Plan B? After a few years of what we today would call state-sponsored terrorism—of sabotaging power plants, torching sugar fields, and arming assassins—U.S. policymakers slowly reached a consensus that Cuba was not all that important and that the logical course of action was to back off. During the Kennedy era, "I used to get a call from McGeorge Bundy or one of his assistants every day about something," recalled the State Department's principal Cuba officer, but then "under Johnson, the calls dropped down to probably once a week, and then maybe once every two weeks or once a month." Inexperienced in foreign affairs, Lyndon Baines Johnson had waited only a few days after inheriting the White House to seek advice from the widely respected chair of the Senate Committee on Foreign Relations, J. William Fulbright, who warned against doing anything dramatic. "I'm not getting into any Bay of Pigs deal," Johnson interrupted to agree. "No, I'm just asking you what we ought to do to pinch their nuts more than we're doing."[8]

Nut-pinching has been U.S. policy ever since.

Why? Because even a superpower's resources are limited, and LBJ, like every one of his successors, had better ways to spend his political capital. Instead of ramping up Operation Mongoose, JFK's effort to overthrow the island's government, President Johnson initially chose to focus on domestic issues—a month after consulting with Fulbright, LBJ went before a joint session of Congress to declare the War on Poverty and to press for passage of the Civil Rights Act of 1964. Thus distracted, Johnson had little time for

Cuba, especially as his administration's foreign policy eyes began to focus on Indochina. National security adviser McGeorge Bundy soon was encouraging everyone to face reality. "The chances are very good that we will still be living with Castro some time from now," he said; "we might just as well get used to the idea."[9] Thucydides never would have said that.

In our time, only an administration misjudging the Cubans as an easy takedown (as JFK's did) or an administration underestimating the costs in political capital (as Jimmy Carter's did) would invest heavily in an island such as Cuba. All the rest have done what they felt they had to do to protect the ever-changing U.S. economic, security and political interests, but all have done so on the cheap, never treating Cuba as a problem requiring decisive action. "Of course the United States could turn the island into a parking lot," they seemed to say, especially after the end of the Cold War, "but it might distract the country from more important problems" such as combating terrorism or resolving the domestic issue du jour. In a world packed to overflowing with threatened interests and an unlimited number of domestic problems, small islands are simply not that important. Realists have to be realistic.

This moderation is a fascinating aspect of modern realism. When your grandchildren ask you to explain it, you can use Cuba. There is no better example of how we are obliged to control ourselves—and, therefore, of how today's foreign-policy-making process actually works.

BUT THERE IS MORE to the "Cuba" ideology than moderated realism. An additional part was largely hidden during the three decades when Washington justified its hostility by pointing to the revolutionary government's alignment with the Soviet Union. But then the Cold War ended, and the geostrategic shell cracked apart to reveal the existential core of the ideology underlying Washington's compulsion to march across the street and set everything straight: the United States simply could not stand aloof while the Cuban government misbehaved. Specifically, for the past two decades, we have been determined to do something to protect Cubans' human rights. Thus, when the Cold War ended and the United States needed new laws about Cuba, we gave them "human rights" titles, beginning with the 1992 Cuban Democracy Act and the 1996 Cuban Liberty and Democratic Solidarity Act.

This was nothing new. Cold and hot wars come and go, but what remains constant is the belief that Cubans, like most of the people who live beneath the United States, will benefit from our humanitarian legislation. Cubans are Hispanics and blacks, imperfect leaves on two stunted branches of the human species—not simply underdeveloped, but probably underdevelopable left to their own devices and given their origin. Or, as a U.S. ambassador wrote from Havana in the late 1940s, just as Cuba's revolutionary generation was reaching adulthood, "Many of them possess the superficial charm of clever children, spoiled by nature and geography—but under the surface they combine the worst characteristics of the unfortunate admixture and interpenetration of Spanish and Negro cultures—laziness, cruelty, inconstancy, irresponsibility, and inbred dishonesty."[10]

It is probably a sign of progress that U.S. diplomats no longer write such sentences, but today's political correctness makes it more difficult to identify and examine this aspect of the ideology underlying U.S. policy. Perhaps that explains why it is so common to argue that today's focus on human rights is only a ruse—that human rights offers a convenient rationale for a policy dictated by post–Cold War domestic politics, dictated specifically by the need to curry favor among the Cuban Americans who detest the Cuban Revolution, several hundred thousand of whom live in a state with twenty-seven electoral votes. Don't tell this to your grandchildren—it's wrong. Anyone who watched George W. Bush snatch the White House from Al Gore in 2000 understands how important Florida can be, but elections, like wars, come and go, while Washington's civilizing mission remains a constant. Florida had only five electoral votes and there was no such thing as a Cuban American voter in 1901, when Congress passed the Platt Amendment granting the United States the right to march across the street whenever it wanted "for the maintenance of a government adequate for the protection of life, property, and individual liberty."[11]

Today this part of the ideology—a civilizing mission—remains largely hidden, embedded in a human rights context. Only occasionally does direct evidence of its existence pop to the surface, generally in an unscripted comment such as when a reporter asked the first President Bush if he intended to engage Fidel Castro now that the Soviet threat had disappeared. "What's the point of my talking to him?" Bush replied. "All I'd tell him is what I'm telling you, to give the people the freedom that they want. And then you'll see the United States do exactly what we should: Go down and lift those people up."[12] President Bush's immediate predecessor, Ronald Reagan, always answered that Cuba first had to end its alliance with Moscow, but here in 1991 how effortlessly a three-decade-long policy justified by the need to contain communism was replaced by a policy based on a conviction that Cubans' lack of freedom triggered an obligation to help, to uplift. Washington's new policy was to insist that the island's government be less repressive of its citizens' human rights.

Revealing as it may have been, President Bush's comment was a rarity—rare because it sounds bad to our postcolonial ears. Today we no longer feel comfortable about uplifting underdeveloped peoples, about the white man's burden. Now we have to examine behavior and then *infer* the commitment to a civilizing mission. This examination consumes a good many of the pages that follow, including a discussion of Washington's most recent plan for Cuba's uplifting, unveiled in 2004 by the President's Commission for Assistance to a Free Cuba. It identified six major areas where Cubans could benefit from U.S. assistance, the first and most important of which was in selecting their leaders. This has been an especially consistent part of Washington's policy toward Cuba, stretching back to 1901, when Governor-General Leonard Wood, writing from Havana, put his proconsular finger squarely on the problem: "No one wants more than I a good and stable government, of and by the people here, but we must see that the right class are in office."[13]

That also sounds presumptuous to us, so now we use a euphemism: "Hastening Cuba's Transition" is the title of Chapter 1 of the plan President Bush unveiled; it specified sixty-two steps the United States intended to take to oust Cuba's current repressive leaders. Then, after they have been replaced by the right class of people, it will be on to the uplifting: Chapter 2, "Meeting Basic Human Needs"; Chapter 3, "Establishing Democratic Institutions"; Chapter 4, "Establishing the Core Institutions of a Free Economy"; Chapter 5, "Modernizing Infrastructure"; and Chapter 6, "Addressing Environmental Degradation." And since some of the island's volatile residents might refuse to watch quietly while the United States sets everything straight, the plan also contains a still-classified security appendix, the gist of which is probably captured by an unclassified sentence indicating that some part of the U.S. government—the Pentagon?—will be standing by if needed "to keep all schools open during an emergency phase of the transition in order to keep children and teenagers off the streets."[14]

The unspoken conceptual framework—the mentalité—of the Commission for Assistance to a Free Cuba is that only a few die-hard revolutionaries and perhaps some immature adolescents would want to live in today's Cuba if, with Washington's help, they could meet basic needs, establish both democratic institutions and a free economy, build a modern infrastructure, and even tackle the problem of environmental degradation.

Since this is so obvious, simply to decline Washington's offer of uplifting is to set off an alarm: Why are Cubans behaving in an irrational way?

Cold War geopolitics at first dictated "communism" as the answer—it is impossible to work through the archives of the Eisenhower and Kennedy years and fail to be impressed by how genuinely worried everyone was. It was not simply a convenient justification for our hostility. In the apocalyptic version then common in the United States, communism threatened us with death and destruction, probably not with a direct attack but by slowly undermining vulnerable allies, one by one, until the United States stood alone in a hostile world. Then Nikita Khrushchev would have his way. "We will bury you," he had boasted in 1956, just as Cuba's rebels were planning their campaign against Fulgencio Batista's army. And, we need to remind ourselves, that was not said by someone whose best shot was to fly hijacked airliners into skyscrapers, however horrible that was. Khrushchev's finger rested on a nuclear button.[15]

With Moscow intent on depositing the Free World in the dustbin of history, the United States had to be particularly vigilant in the Caribbean, where physical proximity would make a communist beachhead especially threatening. Central Intelligence Agency (CIA) director Allen Dulles insisted that the United States could not allow the establishment of such a beachhead: "As the evidence of a communist attempt at takeover is uncovered, it is vital to deal with it before it has permeated the society which it is attacking. . . . The longer one waits the more drastic must be the medicine. It is like cancer."[16] Cuba was far too close for comfort, and the island's new leaders were declining every well-intentioned offer of uplifting; instead, they made no secret of their intention to reform Cuban society without Washington's assistance and to do so in the broadest sense of the word—to "re-form" more or less everything, including many things belonging to powerful U.S. citizens who liked their belongings just as they were.

When U.S. diplomats brought these investors' concerns to the attention of the new Cuban government, the country's leaders insisted that the United States respect their sovereign right to reform their own society: "The Cuban people are anxious to live in peace and harmony with the Government and the people of the United States," Cuba's revolutionaries said in a formal diplomatic note, "and they are also desirous of intensifying their diplomatic and economic relations, but on the basis of mutual respect." Thucydides did not believe in mutual respect between unequals, and the obvious asymmetries between the United States and Cuba led Washington's realists to believe they could do whatever they wanted. But then came the cold shower we call the Bay of Pigs, and thereafter a reasonable sense of proportion mandated caution. A final solution by U.S. forces—an invasion— would have "grave political dangers to our position throughout the Western hemisphere," the State Department warned JFK in 1961.[17] The world had changed since the Peloponnesian Wars, and by the mid–twentieth century, the leader of the Free World was not allowed to select the parking-lot option without incurring significant costs. Moscow used that approach for *its* neighbors, like Hungary, and U.S. citizens saw the difference as their trump card. And so Washington selected nut-pinching—an embargo that would make life as miserable as possible for everyday Cubans. Strangle the island's economy and eventually the regime would collapse; in the interim, Washington could focus on its many more important problems.

So far it has not worked, and your grandchildren will probably want to know if it ever will. Change is certain to come, but you should point out that the future is for others to narrate; for now, you can explain why the United States doggedly pursued one of the most unproductive policies in the history of U.S. foreign relations—a policy that has included everything from a CIA assassination plot featuring a ballpoint pen rigged with a hypodermic needle so fine that Fidel Castro would not notice he was being injected with poison (1963) to a U.S. Interests Section in Havana with a Times Square–style streaming electronic ticker running across its facade. The State Department uses the ticker to acquaint Cubans with the wisdom of representative U.S. thinkers such as rocker Frank Zappa: "Communism doesn't work because people like to own stuff" (2006).

You can talk until you are blue in the face about how every country protects its economic, security, and political interests and about how a half century of hostility really did not cost very much, but your grandchildren will find it difficult to understand what your elected representatives could have been thinking when they used even a modest part of your taxes to pay for the ballpoint pen and the ticker and everything that came in between. There is no quick answer. First you will have to tell them about the Cuba that existed before 1959, which explains why there was a revolution and helps explain why the revolution seemed so unwilling to accommodate Washington. Then you can mention Thucydides, but quickly point out how two millennia of amendments to his version of the law of the jungle have constrained superpowers; they now have to maintain a sense of proportion about small neighboring countries. They always have much larger fish to fry, and always with a limited supply of political capital. Tell your grandchildren that superpowers sometimes do not get along with their small neighbors, but that does not mean you can turn their property into a parking lot. Most important, try to place all this in a long-term perspective, just as Fidel Castro did in a 1974 interview: "We cannot move, nor can the United States. Speaking realistically, someday some sort of ties will be established." After all, he pointed out, "We are neighbors."[18]

It is next to impossible to make them believe that
we have only their own interests at heart
—Governor-General Leonard Wood, 1901

1

HERITAGE

Exactly when Cubans began to irritate the United States remains an unsettled question, but it was in the nineteenth century and perhaps as early as the 1820s, when the village of Regla in Havana's harbor became a resale shop for pirates who had plundered U.S. shipping. That forced Secretary of State John Quincy Adams to stop more important work (he was just getting started on the Monroe Doctrine) and instruct his envoy in Madrid to lodge a formal complaint. "It is surely within the competency of the government of Cuba to put down that open market," he wrote, but he clearly had no intention of relying on Spain's colonial authorities: U.S. Marines had already been sent to do the job, landing six times along the Cuban coast, and they would land again six months later and once more in early 1825, making Cuba the site of eight of the first nine deployments of U.S. forces in what we today call Latin America.[1]

These events were hardly worth mentioning when compared to what occurred when an unsuccessful ten-year struggle for Cuban independence broke out just prior to Ulysses Grant's 1868 election, and Hamilton Fish had barely managed to warm the secretary of state's chair before some members of Congress began to argue that the war offered the United States an opportunity to seize the island. With the administration focused on domestic reconstruction and with the State Department concentrating on how to react to the Senate's rejection of the *Alabama* claims treaty with Great Britain, the last thing on Secretary Fish's mind during his first month in office was the acquisition of a Caribbean island, but he, too, had to stop his more important work to muster the administration's forces in Congress. Responding to his call, one ally in the House of Representatives made fun of "the 'manifest destiny' men [who] would make American citizens alike of the Esquimaux toward the north pole and the naked natives of the tropics." Another stood up to argue against "a further introduction of the African element by annexation," followed by agreement from a third: "We have enough of inferior races in our midst without absorbing and not assimilating the Creoles and blacks of Cuba."[2]

With annexation quashed, Fish still had to reply to Spain's complaints that U.S. citizens were aiding Cuba's rebels — "the departure of various filibustering expeditions in broad day-light, and unmolested, from New York and other federal ports," the Spanish claimed.[3] The initial response to Madrid was handled by an assistant, but then the rebels purchased a U.S. steamship, the *Virginius*, that dodged around the Caribbean carrying supplies and messages until the Spanish finally captured it and summarily executed the ship's captain and thirty-six crew members, most of them U.S. citizens. As would be the case today, the dead sailors' relatives descended on their representatives in Congress, demanding revenge and restitution. Legislators, in turn, proposed everything from a full investigation to a declaration of war, and the secretary of state again had to drop everything and prepare two lengthy reports to mollify Congress. This, the *Virginius* incident, was only the most grievous of many, and Fish soon concluded that close ties with Cuba would be an "unmitigated calamity."[4]

After ten years the Cuban rebellion faltered, although enough sporadic violence continued into the 1880s for U.S. consul Adam Badeau to urge caution when Washington, intent on expanding exports, began to consider an agreement to liberalize trade with Spanish Cuba. Badeau admitted that he was torn: on the one hand, he asked, why bother to establish closer relations with an island where Spain's corrupt rule was leading to "the misery and anxiety of all, condemned alike to poverty and ruin"; on the other hand, was not facilitating trade a consul's primary responsibility? In the end, he came down in favor of an agreement, concluding that U.S. merchants would "extend to the country and its inhabitants the advantages of contact with the higher civilization, the greater energy, the purer morality of America."[5]

There the matter rested until 1895, when the New York–based Cuban Revolutionary Party issued a new call for independence, and soon Antonio Maceo, José Martí, and Máximo Gómez had returned to lead the fight against Spanish colonialism. As usual, Grover Cleveland's State Depart-

ment was preoccupied by a much larger problem—the Venezuelan boundary dispute with Great Britain—but Secretary of State Richard Olney soon
was approached by a U.S. investor, said to be "one of the largest landed
proprietors of Cuba, a man of great wealth" and clearly a rebel sympathizer.
After their meeting, Olney sent the president a lengthy memo arguing that
the rebels "have a right to ask, I think, that we inform ourselves upon the
point, whether they are merely gangs of roving banditti, or are a substantial
portion of the community revolting against intolerable conditions."[6]

The British soon expressed a willingness to negotiate an end to the
Venezuelan dispute, and Olney was free to give Cuba more attention. He
composed a lengthy diplomatic note describing the disruptive effect of
the conflict on U.S. economic interests and the dangers faced by U.S. citizens residing in Cuba, and he warned Madrid that "the United States can
not contemplate with complacency another ten years of Cuban insurrection." The Spanish replied with a conciliatory message expressing a willingness "to adopt such reforms as may be useful or necessary," but only
after the rebels had laid down their arms. Spain's envoy noted tactfully that
the rebels would do so more quickly if "all the people of the United States
. . . will completely cease to extend unlawful aid to the insurgents."[7] Little
more was said during President Cleveland's ten remaining months in the
White House, but in his final message to Congress he cautioned that "it
can not be reasonably assumed that the hitherto expectant attitude of the
United States will be indefinitely maintained." His solution was "a measure
of home rule . . . while preserving the sovereignty of Spain."[8]

The McKinley administration thus inherited what has remained a recur-
ring problem of U.S. relations with its Caribbean neighbors: instability was
both damaging U.S. economic interests and arousing U.S. humanitarian
concern. While refusing to be swept up by the rising clamor for action, the
new president accepted the platform on which he had run—"The United
States should actively use its influence and good offices to restore peace"—
and in late 1897 a combination of Washington's pressure and the insurgents' successes convinced the Spanish government to put reform before
pacification.[9] McKinley responded with guarded optimism; Spain "should
be given a reasonable chance," he wrote in his first annual message, but
if the reforms failed, "other action by the United States will remain to be
taken."[10]

McKinley was also doing his best to calm a rising generation of U.S. politicians intent on picking up where the pre–Civil War advocates of Manifest
Destiny had left off. By the mid-1890s, these jingoes had largely taken over

the Republican Party, and with a colonial war just over the southern horizon, jingo leader Theodore Roosevelt saw his generation's opportunity to do what civilization demanded—earlier, he had characterized the Mexican-American War of the 1840s as an example of nature's guiding principle: "It was inevitable, as well as in the highest degree desirable for the good of humanity at large, that the American people should ultimately crowd out the Mexicans. . . . It was out of the question that the Texans should long continue under Mexican rule; and it would have been a great misfortune if they had. It was out of the question to expect them to submit to the mastery of the weaker race." Now, eight years later, just as Cuba's war for independence was resuming, Roosevelt picked up the same pen to write that "all the great masterful races have been fighting races, and the minute that a race loses the hard fighting virtues, then, no matter what else it may retain, no matter how skilled in commerce and finance, in science or art, it has lost its proud right to stand as the equal of the best. Cowardice in a race, as in an individual, is the unpardonable sin."[11]

Roosevelt's charge up San Juan Hill suggests that this was more than a politician's bluster; it was his creed. "The truth is he believes in war," concluded William Howard Taft. "He has the spirit of the old Berserkers."[12] And Roosevelt was not alone. As the Cuban insurrection was getting under way, Senator Henry Cabot Lodge reminded citizens that the United States had a proud heritage "of conquest, colonization, and territorial expansion unequalled by any people in the nineteenth century"—and, he added, "we are not to be curbed now."[13] A Civil War hero who had watched friends die in combat, the older McKinley disagreed: in his first annual message to Congress he rejected the growing chorus pushing to annex Cuba, and at about the same time he told a former secretary of state that "these people will have a different view of the question when their sons are dying in Cuba."[14]

Meanwhile, Cuban émigrés were doing their best to support the jingoes. Former President Cleveland recalled being "time and again threatened by frenzied men and women with dire calamities to be visited upon myself and children because of what they saw fit to assert was my enmity to the Cuban cause,"[15] but most Cuban leaders in the United States were much more sophisticated; in particular, the leaders of the New York–based junta focused their lobbying on the media, virtually writing the war news for a number of major dailies. One such story exploded in the headlines at a critical moment in early 1898, when the junta destroyed the credibility of the Spanish minister in Washington, Enrique Dupuy de Lôme, who in a private letter characterized President McKinley as "a pandering politician." There are various explanations of how the letter found its way into the hands of the junta's legal counsel, Horatio Rubens, but there is no doubt that Rubens gave it to the *New York Journal*, which published a facsimile of the letter on its front page.[16] Understandably offended, McKinley demanded the envoy's recall, and a week later, Spain had only a chargé in Washington when the USS *Maine* exploded in Havana's harbor.

Cuba's New York junta developed its partnership with jingo journalism soon after a young Californian purchased the ailing *New York Journal* in 1895 and promptly launched a circulation war with Joseph Pulitzer's *New York World*. Like Pulitzer, who needed no instruction in sensationalism, William Randolph Hearst sought to capture the mass market of unsophisticated readers by dramatizing the news with little regard to the accuracy of the stories he printed—Senator George Norris was not far off the mark when he characterized the Hearst organization as "the sewer system of American journalism."[17] Searching for copy that would excite their readers, Hearst and Pulitzer locked their sights on the colonial war in Cuba, converting the rebellion into a modern-day morality play, with daily reports of pitched battles, fictional and real, often supplemented by first-person accounts of questionable authenticity, all focusing on Spanish abuse of liberty-loving Cubans and, when possible, on Spanish slights to U.S. virility—"Does Our Flag Protect Women?" was a characteristically inflammatory headline, subtitled "Indignities Practiced by Spanish Officials on Board American Vessels. Refined Young Women Stripped and Searched by Brutal Spaniards While Under Our Flag on the Olivette." And that was only the headline; readers who turned the page could find a Frederic Remington drawing of Spanish officials leering at a naked young Cuban woman and reporter Richard Harding Davis demanding that the president retaliate: "War is a dreadful thing, but there are things more dreadful, and one of them is dishonor."[18]

Did this type of coverage encourage the march to war? Opinion polling had not yet been invented, but we know that the public was paying attention, since Hearst, Pulitzer, and their imitators sold more papers as they published more news about Spanish atrocities in Cuba—the *Journal* saw its circulation jump from thirty thousand in 1895 to four hundred thousand in 1897, and it became the first U.S. newspaper to sell a million copies in a single day after the *Maine* sank in Havana's harbor, when the paper devoted an average of eight pages to the tragedy every day for a week, turning this single incident, probably an accident, into that generation's equivalent of the 9/11 attack on the World Trade Center.

Both the public and their elected officials undoubtedly recognized that much of this news was fabricated or exaggerated beyond recognition, but that was not the point. Rather, as Senator Orville Platt observed, the coverage was affecting public opinion: "The newspaper rot about what is going on there, though published one day and contradicted the next, seems to stir up all the aggressive spirit in the minds of the people." By the time war finally erupted, even McKinley's pacific predecessor, Grover Cleveland, had been convinced that the Spaniards were "the most inhuman and barbarous cut-throats in the world."[19]

All of this pressure—jingoism, Cuban lobbying, yellow journalism—may have dragged the nation into war, but it is at best an incomplete explanation, as Louis A. Pérez Jr. has emphasized, for the McKinley administration also had concrete concerns about endangered U.S. economic interests. These interests had been growing since the eighteenth century, when New England traders began exchanging salted cod (*bacalao*) for molasses, and this trade had expanded significantly in the nineteenth century, when investors were searching for raw materials to fuel a rapidly industrializing economy. By the 1890s, the U.S. consul in eastern Cuba reported that U.S. companies were shipping up to fifty thousand tons of iron ore a month and that further expansion was anticipated since "the ore of these mines is among the richest in the world." President Cleveland was not exaggerating when he told Congress that "our actual pecuniary interest in [Cuba] is second only to that of the people and government of Spain," and this fact, Pérez argues, remained on McKinley's mind two years later when he cited "endangered American interests" as one of the reasons for declaring war.[20]

BUT WE ARE GETTING AHEAD OF OURSELVES. As they opened the files to brief themselves on the conflict they inherited after the 1896 election, the new administration's officials discovered two themes tightly woven into the fabric of U.S.-Cuban relations. The first was a presumption of ownership, a presumption based on geostrategic principles and captured perfectly by secretary of state John Quincy Adams when he wrote of Cuba and Puerto Rico as "natural appendages to the North American continent," insisting that "the annexation of Cuba to our federal republic will be indispensable to the continuance and integrity of the Union itself." And inevitable: "There are laws of political as well as of physical gravitation, and if an apple severed by the tempest from its native tree, cannot choose but fall to the ground, Cuba, forcibly disjoined from its own unnatural connection with Spain, and incapable of self-support, can gravitate only towards the North American Union, which by the same law of nature cannot cast her off from its bosom."[21] An aging Thomas Jefferson was telling President James Monroe the same thing: Cuba's "addition to our confederacy is exactly what is wanting to round our power as a nation." A few months later, Jefferson wrote again: "I have ever looked on Cuba as the most interesting addition which could ever be made to our system of States. The control which, with Florida Point, this island would give us over the Gulf of Mexico, and the countries and isthmus bordering on it, as well as all those whose waters flow into it, would fill up the measure of our political well-being."[22]

But Jefferson's and then John Quincy Adams's generations were willing to leave well enough alone, and neither would move to acquire Cuba as long as the island remained a possession of Spain, an increasingly impotent European power. When these leaders slowly faded out of the picture, however, a new generation, emboldened by a successful war against Mexico, decided that the apple was ripe. The issue arose during an 1848 debate over a proposed military occupation of the Yucatán, which focused on preempting British expansion. "We have seen Great Britain year after year extending her naval stations, until, by a line of circumvallation, she almost surrounds the Gulf of Mexico," complained Mississippi's Jefferson Davis, who saw Mexico's Yucatán Peninsula and Cuba as "the salient points commanding the Gulf of Mexico, which I hold to be a basin of water belonging to the United States. Whenever the question arises whether the United States shall seize these gates of entrance from the south and east, or allow them to pass into the possession of any maritime Power, I am ready, for one, to declare that my step will be forward, and that the cape of Yucatán and the island of Cuba must be ours." John Calhoun agreed: "It is indispensable to the safety of the United States that this island should not be in certain hands. If it were, our coasting trade between the Gulf and the Atlantic would, in case of war, be cut in twain, to be followed by convulsive effects."[23]

Some of this geostrategic hand-wringing focused on the possibility that Spain might cede Cuba to a major European power, but most of it was a subterfuge for a southern effort to acquire more slave states. The Civil War ended that effort, however, and reconstruction and industrialization occupied the nation's attention until the next generation of expansionists began to worry, as did Senator Lodge in 1895, that "England has studded the West Indies with strong places which are a standing menace to our Atlantic seaboard. We should have among those islands at least one strong naval station, and when the Nicaragua canal is built, the island of Cuba

... will become to us a necessity." And, he added, helping to create a coalition between security concerns and economic interests, Cuba was "still sparsely settled and of almost unbounded fertility."[24] With the demand for sugar, tobacco, and industrial raw materials growing daily, many people conceived of Cuba as a beggar sitting on a golden throne—"the soil is a marvel of richness," a U.S. consul reported in early 1897, and "if all the land suitable to the growth of sugar cane were devoted to that industry, it is estimated that Cuba might supply the entire Western Hemisphere." As for its mineral wealth, the U.S.-owned iron mines represented only the tip of the iceberg: "There are numerous underdeveloped mines of equal value in this region."[25]

Cuba's strategic location and its value to the U.S. economy may be sufficient to explain why late-nineteenth-century jingoes extracted a declaration of war from doubters like McKinley, but their task was made easier—*much* easier—by the second theme the new administration's officials found in the files they inherited: Cuba's 1.6 million residents needed uplifting. For a century, northern visitors had noted what a U.S. consul described in 1848: "the listless, timid character of the population, great distrust of each other, and fear of loss of property, and risque of life," characteristics "unworthy of those who are capable of a love of liberty." Cubans, he continued, "are not animated by those high impulses of Patriotism which prompt to great, daring, and generous undertakings"; on the contrary, "the Creoles have an abiding conviction of their utter incapacity for self government, a conviction which must be felt by any one who has had opportunities of studying or even observing their character." As in politics, so in economics. "In the hands of an industrious, thrifty and *go-ahead* population, Cuba would blossom like the rose," wrote a visiting Yankee businessman just before the Civil War. But "now it is a garden growing wild, cultivated here and there in patches, but capable at least of supporting in ease a population of ten times its present number." Not just any population, however: "What is needed here is an infusion of blood and nerve of a more enterprising and sterner race of men."[26]

President Millard Fillmore would not be tempted. He conceded that "were this island comparatively destitute of inhabitants, or occupied by a kindred race, I should regard it, if voluntarily ceded by Spain, as a most desirable acquisition." But given its current population, "I should look upon its incorporation into our Union as a very hazardous measure."[27]

Kentucky senator John Crittenden reused Fillmore's argument seven years later, when Congress was considering a bill to authorize Cuba's pur-

chase to protect the nation's southern flank: "Tell me that Cuba is necessary, absolutely necessary to the preservation of this Government! Why, sir,
my national pride as an American revolts at the idea. . . . I do not want to see
our Anglo-Saxon race; I do not want to see our American tribe, mingled up
with that sort of evil communication." Maryland senator Anthony Kennedy
was equally repelled by the thought of "a wholesale naturalization of five or
six hundred thousand Cubans, utterly ignorant of the institutions of this
country, utterly unfit to exercise the rights of a republican government."
Once again, much of this talk had a subtext—Crittenden and Kennedy were
abolitionists determined to prevent the South from acquiring more slave
territory, and both knew nothing about Cuba and probably had never met
one of its inhabitants. But the Civil War was two decades in the past when
someone who knew plenty of Cubans, U.S. consul Adam Badeau, characterized the island's residents as "a heterogeneous and foreign people, unused to republicanism and many of them either to civilization or Christianity."[28]

So when Cubans rekindled their war for independence a few years later,
the first challenge facing the acquisition-oriented jingoes was to reassure
the public, as Senator Lodge did, that "among the principal military officers
there are only three of negro blood," while the rest were "white men, and
of good family and position." They could control their uncivilized people
much as southern elites had learned to control their societies after Reconstruction. Perhaps. Or perhaps Lodge lacked the knowledge needed to make
such a judgment. At the same time the jingoes were puffing up the rebels as
white, liberty-loving patriots, a sugar magnate who lived on the island was
warning Grover Cleveland's secretary of state that the insurgency was built
on "the Negro element, together with adventurers from abroad."[29]

WHOEVER THEY WERE, they needed help, or so the jingoes eventually—
but not immediately—convinced President McKinley. For his initial policy
in 1897, he returned to the pre–Civil War effort to purchase Cuba but found
the Spanish unwilling to give up their colony; instead, Madrid granted
Cubans substantial home rule, just as President Cleveland had suggested.
That action only prompted Havana's Tories to protest: "Mobs, led by Spanish officers, attacked to-day the offices of the four newspapers here advocating autonomy," reported Consul-General Fitzhugh Lee in the early days of
1898. "Excitement and uncertainty predominates everywhere," he reported
in one of several similar cables, including one urging that "ships must be
sent."[30] McKinley's response was to move the battleship *Maine* from Key

West to Havana's harbor, where it sat quietly at anchor until the night of 15 February, when an explosion tore open the ship's hull, sending it to the bottom of the harbor and killing 260 U.S. sailors.

"The Whole Country Thrills with War Fever," trumpeted the *New York Journal*, and this time it may not have been exaggerating. Senator Orville Platt complained privately that "those who have been clamoring for liberty and freedom and war, have worked up a spirit in the country that something must be done and done quickly to stop the condition of things in Cuba." Then he publicly declared that "when, by accident or design, the good ship *Maine*, with its American sailors on board, was blown into the air, and its sailors found a grave in the harbor of Habana, there was no power on earth that could prevent the war." Others shared Platt's position: "I have no doubt at all that the war would have been averted had not the *Maine* been destroyed in Havana harbor," wrote Senator Shelby Cullom. "The country forced us into it after that appalling catastrophe." Even the long-resisting Democrats were ready to fight, with McKinley's 1896 opponent, William Jennings Bryan, finally agreeing that "the time for intervention has arrived. Humanity demands that we shall act."[31]

The war was over in three months. U.S. casualties were light (about three hundred dead), citizens at home were elated, and Theodore Roosevelt was on the fast track to the White House. Meeting in Paris, U.S. and Spanish negotiators quickly hammered out a peace treaty stipulating that Cuba "is, upon evacuation by Spain, to be occupied by the United States."[32]

Now began the first civilizing mission. "Acceptance of a practical protectorate over Cuba seems to me very like the assumption of the responsible care of a madhouse," wrote the U.S. minister from Madrid, warning McKinley that the island's substantial nonwhite population, its bitter divisions between *peninsulares* and creoles, and its history of inept government and official corruption pointed to the need for U.S. control. Cubans are "generally of little good," wrote one army general, and "no more capable of self government than the savages of Africa. The average Cuban is of a very low order of mankind . . . [a] mixture of Spanish, Indian, Italian and negro, and he inherits the bad qualities of all."[33] But the congressional war resolution—a declaration known as the Teller Amendment—had specifically rejected annexation, and McKinley acknowledged this commitment to Cuba's independence in his year-end annual message to Congress, but only after order had been restored and a government created.[34]

Doing so took until 1902. The transition might have been quicker had the jingoes not been determined to annex Cuba. They had accepted the

Teller Amendment only reluctantly, and now, lacking the votes to rescind it, they tried a different tactic: working through the like-minded governor-general of Cuba, Leonard Wood, they sought to convince the Cubans to request annexation. That should not be difficult, Wood told Roosevelt: "Clean government, quick decisive action and absolute control in the hands of trustworthy men, establishment of needed legal and education reforms and I do not believe you could shake Cuba loose if you wanted to." Roosevelt assured Senator Lodge that "in two or three years they will insist on being part of us."[35]

But General Wood soon discovered that Cubans could not be convinced so quickly to become part of the United States, and he needed to extend the transition period. "We are going ahead as fast as we can," he wrote to McKinley in 1900, "but we are dealing with a race that has steadily been going down for a hundred years into which we have got to infuse new life, new principles and new methods of doing things. This is not the work of a day or of a year, but of a longer period." At this point, it was easy to understand why José Martí had warned that "the scorn of our formidable neighbor who does not know us is our America's greatest danger."[36]

Wood's letter arrived in Washington at a moment when McKinley's thoughts were turning to reelection, and the rival Democrats were already making political capital out of his administration's rapidly escalating counterinsurgency problem in the Philippines, another part of the spoils seized from Spain. Seeking to balance that quagmire with progress in Cuba, the president ordered Wood to accelerate the transition. Accepting his instructions, Wood drew up the first U.S. plan for Cuba's transition to democracy. Its initial step was to disenfranchise that part of the Cuban population that had gone furthest downhill—by decree, he eliminated the voting rights of two-thirds of Cuba's adult males, and Secretary of War Elihu Root sent his congratulations when he learned that whites so greatly outnumbered blacks in the truncated electorate: "When the history of the new Cuba comes to be written the establishment of popular self-government, based on a limited suffrage, excluding so great a proportion of the elements which have brought ruin to Hayti and San Domingo, will be regarded as an event of first importance."[37]

The wisdom of McKinley's decision to push toward Cuban independence became apparent after the rival Democrats wrote a platform identifying imperialism as "the paramount issue of the campaign." The Republican platform responded by conceding Cuban independence and arguing that the struggle against Aguinaldo's Philippine rebels was a selfless effort "to confer the blessings of liberty and civilization upon all the rescued peoples."[38] Then, in a contest that soon moved away from imperialism to a number of unrelated issues, in 1900 the Democrats lost more heavily than in 1896, and the victors now claimed a mandate for the continued occupation of the Philippines (which lasted until 1946) and for the protectorate they were about to impose on Cuba.

When General Wood had gaveled Cuba's first constituent assembly to order—not coincidentally, one day before the U.S. presidential election—he could see that Washington's first effort at democracy building had run into trouble: Cubans had elected the wrong individuals. "The dominant party in the Convention to-day contains probably the worst political element in the Island." Since this body would write Cuba's first constitution and since the U.S. election was over, Wood's first reaction was to press for a delay, promising "that at the next municipal elections we shall get hold of a better class of people." He also reopened the issue of keeping the island, citing the concerns of local property owners, who, he reported, "are very reluctant to see a change of government, unless it be annexation to the United States." But the Philippine insurgency remained a nagging front-page problem, and the Republican platform had made an unambiguous commitment to Cuban independence, so the jingoes turned to their fallback position—the Platt Amendment, named after Connecticut Senator Orville Platt, chair of the Senate Committee on Relations with Cuba. It prohibited the withdrawal of U.S. troops until the Cubans had granted the United States the constitutional right to intervene for "the maintenance of a government adequate for the protection of life, property, and individual liberty."[39]

Cuba's constituent assembly initially refused to append the amendment to the country's new constitution. "It is next to impossible to make them believe that we have only their own interests at heart," Wood told Roosevelt, brushing opponents aside by noting that they were "led by a little negro of the name of Juan Gualberto Gomez; a man with an unsavory reputation both morally and politically." Following Washington's instructions, Wood announced that the U.S. occupation would continue until the amendment was accepted.[40] Seeing no alternative, the Cubans capitulated.

In return, Wood presided over Cuba's first transition to democracy, then sailed for home. Shortly before leaving, he wrote to assure Roosevelt, now president after McKinley's assassination, that "there is, of course, little or no independence left Cuba under the Platt Amendment." Such had been the plan all along, as Senator Platt noted in a reassuring letter to a major U.S. investor on the island: "The United States will always, under the so-called Platt Amendment, be in a position to straighten out things if they get seriously bad." A century later, Fidel Castro offered much the same interpretation: with the Platt Amendment, he said, the United States "converted the country into a neo-colony."[41]

ROOSEVELT'S REPUBLICANS congratulated themselves in their 1904 party platform—"We set Cuba free"—but the president clearly spoke too soon when he wished that every country washed by Caribbean waters "would show the progress in stable and just civilization which with the aid of the Platt amendment Cuba has shown since our troops left the island." Barely a year later, the fraudulent reelection of President Tomás Estrada Palma provoked an armed uprising by the opposition, and the rebels were soon poised to seize power, leading U.S. consul Frank Steinhart to cable frantically from Havana, "*Absolutely confidential*. Secretary of state, Cuba, has requested me, in name of President Palma, to ask President Roosevelt [to] send immediately two vessels; one to Habana, other to Cienfuegos; they must come at once. Government forces are unable to quell rebellion."[42]

An exasperated Roosevelt confided to a friend, "I am so angry with that infernal little Cuban republic that I would like to wipe its people off the face of the earth," but that was not his official response. Sensing that the U.S. public was growing weary of Caribbean adventures (including his recent takeover of the Dominican Republic), Roosevelt told Steinhart that "perhaps you do not yourself appreciate the reluctance with which this country would intervene." Fine, replied Estrada Palma, telling the consul that he, his vice president, and his cabinet were determined to resign, "and therefore the prevailing state of anarchy will continue unless the United States Government will adopt the measures necessary to avoid this danger." Noting that "disgust with the Cubans is very general," Senator Lodge gave Roosevelt a green light from Congress ("The general feeling is that they ought to be taken by the neck and shaken until they behave themselves"), but the president, his eyes on the upcoming off-year election, decided instead to send Secretary of War William Howard Taft to negotiate a settlement, warning him to "remember that we have to do not only what is best for the island but what we can get public sentiment in this country to support."[43]

Reaching Havana, Taft cabled that "the situation is most serious. The Government controls only coast towns and provincial capitals. Anarchy elsewhere." He had worried from the beginning that something like this would occur—when Cubans had balked at accepting the Platt Amendment five years earlier, Taft had written that "the trouble in Cuba is just beginning, and the lack of wisdom in the Teller Resolution is beginning to show itself." Now, in 1906, Taft quickly concluded that Estrada Palma's electoral fraud had its origin in Cuba's Hispanic culture: "The Spanish American, or one educated in the Spanish political school, has no idea of impartiality, and if he is an election officer, regards it as a duty to cheat for his party." Thus predisposed, Taft indeed discovered fraud when his ship docked in Havana. He realized that electoral fraud was to be found elsewhere, but what distinguished the Cubans was their knack for blowing a little fraud out of proportion—the insurrection "could not have occurred in a country in which the common and ignorant people are not as easily aroused." In his view, "the whole thing demonstrates the utter unfittness of these people for self govt."[44]

With nine U.S. warships anchored in Havana's harbor, Roosevelt's envoy printed a few reams of letterhead reading "Office of the Governor, Republic of Cuba, Under the Provisional Administration of the United States," and set about running the country. Taft had struggled to avoid this takeover, wrote a disgusted Roosevelt, but neither the secretary of war nor anyone else could ever "tell when those ridiculous dagos would flare up over some totally unexpected trouble and start to cutting one another's throats." That was Roosevelt's assessment in a private letter to his son; to the public he explained that "I am doing my best to persuade the Cubans that if only they will be good they will be happy. I am seeking the very minimum of interference necessary to make them good."[45]

Taft also conceived of the takeover as a generous effort, and not the first: "The record of the nine years since the beginning of the Spanish War, looked at from an impartial standpoint, is on the whole an unblemished record of generous, earnest effort to uplift these people, to help them on the way to self-government, and to teach them a higher and better civilization." One way to do so would be to acquaint Cubans with their shortcomings: "Perhaps you will pardon me if I invite your attention, as an educated and intelligent audience, to some of the difficulties of your people," Taft began in a speech celebrating the reopening of the University of Havana. These difficulties were many, but the most significant problem was that "the young Cubans who are coming forward into life are not sufficiently infused with the mercantile spirit." Put simply, "What you need here among the Cubans is a desire to make money."[46]

The U.S. occupation was intended to be brief, with President Roosevelt instructing the War Department that "our business is to establish peace and order on a satisfactory basis, start the new government, and then leave the island." With Taft eager to return to Washington (his presidential aspirations might not survive a lengthy Caribbean sojourn), these tasks were assigned to a new governor-general, Charles Magoon, an ideal choice, noted an associate, since the overweight Nebraska attorney exhibited "the gentle nature which so often accompanies vast bulk." Magoon believed that the Platt Amendment had contributed to the rebellion by giving "the business class" (a term he used interchangeably with "Cubans fully capable of good judgment") the freedom to ignore politics, but he shared the common view that Cuba's fiery Hispanic culture constituted the underlying problem: "Like all other people of Spanish origin they are hot blooded, high strung, nervous, excitable and pessimistic."[47]

Like Roosevelt, Magoon reserved such observations for his private correspondents, leaving a less circumspect army colonel to put his finger on the problem in an article for the nation's most popular magazine: "A basic difference that accounts for much that we criticise in Cuban character," he wrote, "is the fault of the Cuban's raising and training his children from birth to manhood to know not discipline."

> This accounts for the Cuban emotionality and impracticability, their excitability and anger when opposed in any way, their wild rushing into revolutions where everything does not go to suit them, their lack of poise in government and public affairs. It makes them want to gratify every whim or desire; it takes from them the power of self-denial. It makes them ready to pay any price in money or anything else, except self-control, for whatever they desire. It keeps them children.

And, ipso facto, "it makes it necessary for a neighbor to take them in hand, control, direct and manage their government and public policy." Genuine improvement would therefore be slow, Magoon reported to the president, for "we cannot change these racial characteristics by administering their Government for two years or twenty years."[48]

As an alternative to a time-consuming attempt to transform Cuban culture, Magoon tried to constrain "their wild rushing into revolution" by strengthening Cuba's institutions, creating the Advisory Law Commission, composed of nine carefully chosen Cubans and three U.S. citizens and chaired by Colonel Enoch Crowder, an army attorney. They prepared the second U.S. transition plan—an array of administrative reforms including a thoroughly revised electoral code that expanded suffrage to nearly all adult males and established proportional representation to encourage the loyal participation of minority parties. But the commission still had the nagging worry that hotheaded Cubans might fail to implement its plan and therefore concluded that an army was needed for those times when the police were unable to handle the island's turbulent residents. Leonard Wood had reached the same conclusion five years earlier but had been rebuffed when he requested a permanent U.S. military presence to serve as "the moral force to hold these people up to their work until the decent element assumes its normal position in the government of this island." Now that Cubans had demonstrated their unruly character, however, Taft hoped that Crowder "will have sense enough to lay the foundation of an army that will suppress future resorts to violence." The Advisory Law Commission accordingly created a new permanent army whose leaders were selected and trained by U.S. officers.[49]

With his reforms accomplished, Magoon then called for elections, and in early 1909 he handed Cuba's presidential sash to José Miguel Gómez. Like Wood seven years earlier, Magoon then sailed for home.

Cubans subsequently reaccustomed themselves to having U.S. soldiers patrol their streets. In mid-1912, the marines briefly returned to quash a complex Afro-Cuban labor and political dispute in Oriente Province. The same year, however, Gómez turned the government over to Mario García Menocal, whose fraudulent reelection in 1916 prompted the 1917 "February Revolution," which, from the U.S. perspective, could not have occurred at a worse moment—soon after Germany had resumed unrestricted submarine warfare and immediately after Britain had handed Washington an intercepted telegram from German foreign minister Arthur Zimmermann. The cable instructed the German ambassador in Mexico City to seek a military alliance with Mexico, offering as an incentive "the territory lost by her in a prior period in Texas, New Mexico, and Arizona."[50] Heaven only knew what the Germans might be offering Cuba.

If a heightened concern over the nation's undefended southern flank were not enough of a problem, it was compounded by the lobbying of U.S. investors, who had been rushing into Cuba after a 1903 treaty gave the island's sugar preferential access to the rapidly expanding U.S. market. Now, as the February Revolution began to disrupt the harvest, John Foster Dulles, a young attorney with New York's Sullivan and Cromwell, boarded the *Congressional Limited* for Washington, and on the return trip he wrote a note to thank his uncle, Secretary of State Robert Lansing, for taking the time to listen to the problems facing Sullivan and Cromwell's clients ("companies which own a very large number of sugar estates in the

Island of Cuba") and to repeat the request Dulles had made during his visit: "It would be highly desirable to have a United States vessel appear, if only for a short time, in the Manati harbor" on Cuba's northeastern coast.[51] Two companies of marines were promptly dispatched to Camagüey and Oriente Provinces, including the port of Manatí, ostensibly to protect U.S. sugar interests but in effect to free up the Cuban troops García Menocal needed to suppress the February Revolution. One company of 350 U.S. Marines remained in Camagüey for five years.

Logic suggests that these troops should have departed after the German threat had been eliminated and after U.S. investors had been reassured, but President Woodrow Wilson also had a civilizing mission; his general policy, as he told a British envoy, was "to teach the South American republics to elect good men."[52] Initially preoccupied by the Mexican Revolution and an ambitious domestic policy agenda, Wilson left the details of Cuba's education to Secretary of State William Jennings Bryan, but, as the State Department's principal legal officer observed, Bryan seemed unable "to give consecutive thought or really intelligent consideration to anything brought before him." Compounding this problem was Bryan's team of inexperienced Democrats, including Boaz Long, a stockbroker who felt that his party loyalty merited something more important than the backwater appointment as U.S. minister to El Salvador. In 1918, seeking to attract the attention of Bryan's replacement, Lansing, Long proposed "extending our influences over these less favored people with the idea of educating them and regulating and improving their agricultural and commercial development, and making them good citizens of a democracy."[53]

President Wilson and Secretary Lansing were thinking just that about the obstreperous Cubans, so they promoted Long to the U.S. legation in Havana, where he was joined by Enoch Crowder, now an army general and back for a second attempt to make Cubans behave properly. When the two envoys reported that their suggestions were being ignored, the Wilson administration again invoked the Platt Amendment, keeping Long as minister but naming Crowder the president's "Personal Representative on Special Mission" and warning that troops would also be sent unless García Menocal "assumes a receptive attitude in respect to the advice and just recommendations which the President has instructed General Crowder to convey to him."[54]

In 1921, Warren Harding's new Republican administration accepted Long's resignation but continued Wilson's mission, promoting Crowder to ambassador and instructing him to pressure the new administration of

Alfredo Zayas to launch a crusade for clean government. Crowder produced draft legislation covering essential reforms (many of them strikingly similar to reforms required by the 1996 Helms-Burton Act), which he handed to the Cubans as numbered memoranda.[55] Implementation was difficult, and backsliding always remained a problem, but in time a modus vivendi was established: Washington helped the Cuban government obtain loans from New York bankers, and Cubans played along with what came to be known as Crowder's "Moralization Program."

Many U.S. officials judged this eight-year civilizing mission a success, and some considered it a model for nearby countries. In 1928, seeking support for a similar intervention in Nicaragua, Senator William Bruce asked his colleagues to "think of our intervention in Cuba. This is absolutely one of the finest things in human history." Although few Caribbean-basin neighbors seemed to appreciate this effort, Washington dismissed their opposition with a father-knows-best response: "If the United States has received but little gratitude, this is only to be expected in a world where gratitude is rarely accorded to the teacher, the doctor, or the policeman, and we have been all three. But it may be that in time they will come to see the United States with different eyes, and to have for her something of the respect and affection with which a man regards the instructor of his youth and the child looks upon the parent who has molded his character."[56] So lectured a State Department instructor to incoming Foreign Service officers in 1926, the year Fidel Castro was born.

Crowder's crowning achievement had been the 1924 election of Zayas's replacement, Gerardo Machado, later nicknamed the Butcher of Las Villas, in part because that was his hometown profession and in part because of the methods he used to maintain his grip on power—what one U.S. envoy referred to as Machado's "pathological obsession that only repressive measures, culminating in acts of hideous cruelty, could stifle the opposition."[57] But he was Washington's man in Havana, as he went out of his way to demonstrate in 1928 when with one classic sentence he introduced the only sitting U.S. president ever to visit Cuba:

> Intense is our joy and complete our faith in the future destinies of our hemisphere when, gazing over this hall, adding brilliancy to this transcendental occasion, we behold the illustrious person of His Excellency Calvin Coolidge, Chief Executive of the greatest of all democracies; head of the great people whom Cuba had the honor of seeing at her side in her bloody struggle for independence, which she enjoys without limitation,

as stated in the joint resolution of April 20, 1898, honorably applied and inspired by the same ideals set forth in the ever famous Declaration of Independence of North America, liberty's greatest monument and gospel of rights of man and countries.[58]

Such words captured perfectly the tenor of U.S.-Cuban relations in the 1920s, and U.S. officials appreciated not only the sentiment but also the stability Machado brought to the island, which encouraged U.S. investors. As a result, no one in Washington wanted him to retire when his term expired. "I have been getting the utmost cooperation from Machado on everything I have asked of him," reported ambassador Noble Judah soon after the president's fraudulent reelection, and this assessment pleased Herbert Hoover's secretary of state, Henry Stimson, who confided to his diary that the Machado government "was not the government that we should care for in America, but that it seemed to be in full control of Cuba; that it was popular with the Army, and that was the main thing in Latin-American countries."[59]

Franklin Delano Roosevelt inherited this policy at a time when the depression had severely weakened Machado's grip on power. "The Cuban situation is getting worse," warned a member of FDR's transition team; "in the near future the [State] Department may be involved." Any U.S. involvement would now have to exclude the marines, however, because the thinking of the new administration's principal Latin Americanist, Sumner Welles, once an ardent interventionist, had evolved to accommodate Latin Americans' increasingly vocal opposition to intervention: helping with a draft of Roosevelt's inaugural address, Welles suggested a flat prohibition on "the dispatch of the armed forces of the United States to any foreign soil whatsoever," a suggestion that became the defining characteristic of the Good Neighbor policy.[60]

The last thing FDR wanted was an early test of this novel policy, but how could it be avoided? "Politically Cuba may, in theory, be independent," *The Nation* editorialized, but "economically she is a vassal, and her economic bondage and political control are today inextricably linked. Machado is not the representative of a free Cuban people, but the *administrador* of American financial feudalism." Fearful that instability triggered by the severely depressed economy might lead to the demand for yet another U.S. intervention, the new president postponed Welles's appointment as assistant secretary of state and sent him instead to Havana, where the envoy quickly pinpointed the problem: "a detestation of the President's person which is unparalleled." Welles recommended the withdrawal of recognition, and with his encouragement the Cuban army promptly forced Machado from power, naming a former Cuban ambassador to Washington, Carlos Manuel de Céspedes, as interim chief executive.[61]

Welles had been promoting the U.S.-born Céspedes for more than a decade—in 1921, Welles had told Crowder that Céspedes would make an ideal president because of his "amenability to suggestions or advice which might be made to him by the American Legation." But the problem, as General Crowder had argued in response, was that the new Cuban president, "through sheer weakness of character"—a reference to Céspedes's rumored homosexuality—"is negligible in any kind of a political crisis."[62] Sensing this weakness, the army's noncommissioned officers, led by Sergeant Fulgencio Batista, escalated a pay dispute into a rebellion and replaced Welles's favorite with a reform-oriented university professor, Ramón Grau San Martín. The indignant envoy asked Washington for "a temporary landing of possibly a thousand men," admitting that the literal-minded might consider this armed intervention a violation of the Good Neighbor policy but warning Secretary of State Cordell Hull that Batista's rebellious confederates "who are in close touch with Communist leaders in Habana may resort to desperate measures if they become sufficiently drunk."[63]

As an aide confided to his diary, Secretary Hull "is slow in making up his mind, sometimes, it has seemed to me, in situations that call for rapid action. But his judgment is far better than Sumner's. Sumner, on the other hand, will move like a shot in all situations."[64] True to this portrayal, Hull put off a decision until he could consult with others; then, for reasons related primarily to the principle of nonintervention, the main item on the agenda at an upcoming foreign ministers' conference in Montevideo, he refused Welles's request for troops. Unwilling to concede, Welles waited until Hull had sailed for Uruguay and then appealed directly to the president, a family friend. Roosevelt held firm against a takeover, but he refused to recognize Grau's government, encircled the island with every available warship (thirty in all), and then sent Welles back to Havana to plot the government's overthrow, this time by forging an alliance with Batista, who in four months had risen from sergeant to colonel and army chief of staff.[65]

Batista was soon president, and Cuban-American relations were cordial and quiet during the remaining years of the Roosevelt administration. Symbolic of the Good Neighbor policy was the 1934 abrogation of the Platt Amendment, for which Batista reciprocated by offering Cuba's full cooperation when Caribbean stability became a significant concern during

World War II. "We can ask for things and get them practically over the telephone," wrote ambassador Spruille Braden, recently transferred from Bogotá; "the American Ambassador here is in a completely unique position, and if I breathe out of one nostril harder than the other it may provoke a political crisis." Accordingly, Welles asked FDR to roll out the red carpet for the Cuban chieftain's 1942 state visit, "since the overthrow of Batista might plunge the Island during this critical period into chaos." A highlight of the trip was Batista's speech to the House of Representatives, which emphasized the two nations' "common ideals of democracy."[66]

During these years, Fidel Castro's generation was passing from adolescence to adulthood. Decades later, Castro told diplomat Wayne Smith, "I came to power with some preconceived ideas about the United States and about Cuba's relationship with her. In retrospect, I can see a number of things I wish I had done differently [but] we would not in any event have ended up as close friends. The U.S. had dominated us too long. The Cuban Revolution was determined to end that domination."[67]

While a large part of the world struggles with the grim problems of hunger and security, the Cubans are still enjoying war-born prosperity and the carnival comparsas *revived early this month have filled the streets with thousands of weirdly-costumed dancers whose gyrations are reminiscent of their primitive forbears. The philosophy of 'mañana'—that tomorrow will somehow take care of itself—still seems to permeate all thoughts and activities from high officialdom down.*
    —*U.S. Embassy to Department of State, 1946*

2

PRELUDE THE TRUMAN YEARS

Cuba's revolutionary generation reached adulthood in the late 1940s, when the island was enjoying a prosperity unseen since the Dance of the Millions decades earlier. U.S. embassy officials reported that the economy was being driven not only by sugar but also by the return of visits from the neighbors—tourists were pouring into Havana "via 28 Pan-American flights per day and the Hotel Nacional, full for the second time in its history, began charging a minimum of $19 a day for rooms to relieve the guests of their war profits."[1] Cuban politics had not improved nearly as much, but Ambassador Spruille Braden had been upbeat when he reported soon after his arrival in 1942 that "the venality in public office in Cuba is regrettable but explainable, and I am even sanguine that, given time by judicious handling, we can assist in bringing about a tremendous betterment."[2] Braden was the type of take-charge envoy regularly posted to small Caribbean countries by senior officials who were themselves focused on far larger problems. And while he was a political appointee, not a career Foreign Service officer, Braden's broad Latin American experience dated from the 1920s in Chile, where he had worked with his father's copper company, married a Chilean, and learned fluent Spanish. In 1933, when FDR entered office, Braden was a young but stalwart Democrat, eager for a diplomatic appointment. His immediate designation as a delegate to the inter-American conference at Montevideo and then as the U.S. representative on the Chaco Peace Commission only whetted his appetite; Braden's first ambassadorship came in

1939, to Colombia, and then shortly after Pearl Harbor he was transferred to Havana, where he spent nearly all of World War II. Dean Acheson aptly described Braden as a "bull of a man physically and with the temperament and tactics of one, dealing with objects of his prejudices by blind charges, preceded by pawing up a good deal of dust." One of Braden's successors in Cuba, Philip Bonsal, noted that "his sensitivity to Cuban susceptibilities was not great," while Arthur Schlesinger Jr. added that the envoy "perfectly fulfills their idea of what a Yankee should be like."[3]

In Havana, Braden had two responsibilities. The first—not difficult—was to assist the war effort. Cuba had declared war on Japan a day after the United States did so, and in early 1942 outgoing ambassador George Messersmith left Braden a briefing memo indicating that "the Cuban Government and people are one hundred percent with us in the war and their measures of cooperation are whole-hearted and complete. . . . You will find President Batista understanding and helpful in the best of dispositions with respect to us."[4] Among his other contributions, Batista mimicked the U.S. wartime internment policy by imprisoning on the Isle of Pines several hundred residents with ties to the Axis; the United States paid for their subsistence. Cuban police also allowed the embassy's legal attaché to interview suspicious passengers arriving from Europe; he forwarded his interrogation reports to FBI headquarters in Washington, which identified suspected Axis sympathizers to be interned.[5]

Batista also allowed the U.S. military to use Cuban territory. A U.S. contractor quickly improved several airfields and constructed another at San Antonio de los Baños (it remains unclear who decided it should be called "Batista Field"), from which U.S. aircraft scoured the Caribbean in search of the Nazi submarines that were sinking ships loaded with essential bauxite from the Guianas. With one notable exception, jailing Cuba's German nationals was almost certainly misguided—the overwhelming majority were no more of a threat than the interned Japanese Americans living in the United States—but the submarines were a significant problem; in the worst month of the war, May 1942, the Germans sank three ships per day in Caribbean and East Coast waters.[6]

In late 1942, Germany pulled its U-boats out of the area, leaving stability as the only wartime goal of U.S. policy in the Caribbean. Understandably, U.S. officials wanted the region quiet so that they could focus their attention elsewhere, and they also had to ensure that nothing impeded the northward flow of Latin America's food and raw materials. Here Cuba also helped, providing the Allies with a steady stream of whatever it had available, beginning immediately after Pearl Harbor, when President Batista agreed to sell the United States all of Cuba's sugar at low prices: a U.S. envoy reported that "Braden and I encountered some tough bargaining and had to agree to various concessions"—Washington promised to continue selling Cuba adequate supplies of rice, flour, and lard—"but in a remarkably short time we had an agreement to buy Cuban sugar at 3.25 cents a pound (this was later increased to 3.50 cents). If Batista had insisted on holding out and demanding all the traffic would bear, he could have had several times that amount." One embassy official included in his memoir a chapter that, he hoped, "may serve to remind historians how much the United States and its allies owe to the man who was president of Cuba during World War II."[7]

Ambassador Braden's second responsibility, this one self-assigned and much more difficult, was to ensure that Cuba held a clean election in 1944. At one point, the envoy reported that he was nearing failure, primarily because "democracy, as it has been experienced in Cuba, is far from the real thing. On the contrary its workings have been filled with corruption, abuse and inefficiency." Batista had been freely elected in 1940, but that was only another example of Cubans' tendency to make poor choices. "Batista and his gang would like to free themselves from such few shackles as the Cuban creole democracy imposes," Braden reported, "and which prevent their unbridled acquisition of even more complete power and greater wealth." Here Braden was picking up the view of his predecessor, George Messersmith, who had noted in 1940 that Batista's "principal interest is to be in power for the material advantage which it gives him."[8] Braden agreed—"Corruption has never before been so rampant, so organized, and so profitable for those at the top"—and warned that this behavior "can only lead eventually to serious internal trouble in Cuba, which may gravely prejudice our relations." A few months later, he added that "the unparalleled dishonesty of the Batista Administration is not only destructive of democracy in this country but inevitably must prejudice Cuban-American relations." Democracy, then, was in Washington's own interest: "To permit Batista to establish himself as the Trujillo of Cuba would be a negation of everything for which we are fighting this war and would constitute an appeasement for which we would pay dearly in the future."[9]

And so the ambassador stepped into the political ring. He first ordered local U.S. businessmen to stop paying bribes to the government and then began to condemn Batista in one speech after another; an upper-level State Department official soon was warning Secretary of State Cordell Hull about tension between Braden and Batista.[10] When the Cuban president informally requested the envoy's recall in 1943, Braden sent Hull a twenty-four-page single-spaced defense indicating that "the Cuban Government's charges are preposterous and absolutely without foundation. I have not intervened in Cuban internal affairs, I have not reiterated widely and in an improper manner my low opinion of the Government. I have not publicly characterized the recent electoral elections as fraudulent. I have not in any way, shape or manner incited the Opposition against the Government." All he had done, Braden continued with a half-truth, was "to put a stop to our nationals, corporate and individual, paying graft, bribing Cuban officials and intervening in the internal political affairs of Cuba," and he had only done so in an effort to reduce "the persistence and growth of the unbelievable corruption which is sapping the moral and physical strength of this country."[11]

Reluctant to recall Braden without a formal request from the foreign minister, Secretary Hull instead told Cuba's ambassador to Washington that the best approach would be to "let the normal transfers among our diplomats take care of the situation." Always sensitive to Washington's wishes, Batista decided not to exercise his formal option to declare Braden persona non grata.[12]

Although Braden soon entered the history books as a ham-handed diplomat, primarily because of his ill-advised 1945–46 vendetta against Argentina's Juan Perón, he also deserves to be recognized as a champion of democracy—clumsy to be sure, but well intentioned. Many other diplomats of the era should be remembered for the same reason: the promotion of democracy had become a major feature of U.S. policy during World War II, and at Washington's initiative, all four wartime inter-American conferences had gone on record as favoring democracy. The conference resolutions were limited to declaring the hemisphere's "adherence to the democratic ideal," and covariation is not causation, but Washington's democratic rhetoric coincided with a slow but significant shift away from dictatorship throughout Latin America and probably nudged the transition along.[13] Such certainly held true for Cuba, where in 1944 Batista reluctantly yielded to the tenor of the times and to the constitutional prohibition on immediate reelection by supervising an election that everyone considered fair (and that his handpicked successor lost). Fidel Castro had just turned eighteen when Batista turned the government over to his principal rival, Ramón Grau San Martín.

With the election behind him, an elated Ambassador Braden informed Washington in late 1944 that President Grau was not only determined "to exercise the powers of the government as a public trust for the good of the Cuban people" but also "fired up with a zeal to improve the lot of the average Cuban." Braden's enthusiasm continued into early 1945 ("a splendid record for his first three months"), but just barely, and by mid-January the honeymoon was over. Braden wrote that Grau "simply does not have what it takes to succeed as President." The specific problem? "An egolatric stubbornness," which meant that the new Cuban president was disinclined to accept the envoy's advice—"to ignore wise counsels and to stand on his opinion once formed, irrespective of how faulty it may be."[14] And the rest of his government was as bad as ever: Cuban politicians were hotheads, the embassy reported, emphasizing their "volatile nature" and "low boiling point," which, again, often led to an irrational reluctance to accommodate reasonable requests. "My experience of fourteen years in dealing with Cubans, including nearly eight years of service in Habana, convinces me that nothing whatever is obtained from the Cuban Government merely because the request is just and legitimate." So wrote Ellis Briggs, a career officer who thought it "high time that Cuba grows up" and was pleased with a transfer to Chile, since "the few Chileans I had met were excellent people, not gaily irresponsible like the Cubans."[15]

Henry Norweb found the same set of problems when he replaced Braden in mid-1945—"chronic administrative inefficiency," "gangster-student-fanatics," and especially "the corrupt and hard-boiled grafting clique heading up to the First Lady." Typical embassy dispatches from the Norweb era began with a discussion of the "gradual relapse of the political scene into the conventional Cuban irresponsibility, venality and intermittent violence," then pointed out that little improvement would result from removing one or two bad apples from the barrel, since nine out of ten Cuban politicians "would fit better into a Rogues' Gallery than a roster of responsible public servants. Many of them possess the superficial charm of clever children, spoiled by nature and geography—but under the surface they combine the worst characteristics of the unfortunate admixture and interpenetration of Spanish and Negro cultures—laziness, cruelty, inconstancy, irresponsibility and inbred dishonesty."[16]

Fate had dealt Cuba a poor hand during the era of European colonization, and now, in the mid–twentieth century, the embassy reported that "it is idle but not irrelevant to speculate what might have been the status of this bountiful island community had it been settled by colonists from the British Isles, Scandinavia, French Canada or even China." Instead, adventurers from Spain and slaves from Africa had produced a society where "compromise, in the century-old Anglo-Saxon sense, is unfortunately impossible." So, Ambassador Norweb concluded, "the real determinants of Cuban political life for the foreseeable future will probably be the success or failure of assassin's bullets"—a grim prognosis, he admitted, but "it seems less than honest to report that there appears to be anything either in the Cuban character or in our present policy towards Cuba and the other Caribbean peoples that would augur the future establishment of an honorable and constructive member of the family of nations in this rich island." His depressing conclusion: "Moral deterioration seems permanent."[17]

THESE ENVOYS' REPORTS defined the Cuba that Harry Truman inherited in the spring of 1945, when FDR died. Born in 1884, Truman as a young man exhibited the racial prejudices of his generation, writing to Bess Wallace about a conversation with his uncle Will, who had said "that the Lord made a white man from dust, a nigger from mud, then threw up what was left and it came down a Chinaman. He does hate Chinese and Japs. So do I." How much of this racial venom poisoned Truman's evaluations of non-Anglo Caucasians is unknown—his only other surviving statement regarding Latin Americans is a letter urging his wife's brother to reconsider Mexican vacation plans in "Greaserdom"—but it would be a mistake to use his youthful correspondence to characterize the thinking of this midcentury president. Truman grew as he aged: he campaigned in Harlem, the first presidential candidate to do so; he ordered the desegregation of the U.S. armed forces; and he proposed a comprehensive civil rights program that included the desegregation of interstate transportation and the strengthening of voting rights—all pioneering moves in their day, and all far beyond the mental horizon of Congress, which refused to consider even the most uncontroversial of Truman's proposals, that lynching be made a federal crime. To many people's surprise, the man FDR left behind to define the immediate postwar era was much more than an artless midwestern haberdasher; Harry Truman was a principled social democrat. "I am asking for equality of opportunity for all human beings," he wrote to his friend Ernie Roberts a few months before the 1948 election. "If that ends up in my failure to be reelected, that failure will be in a good cause."[18]

Truman had been vice president for only three months when FDR died, but the new president knew that his generation no longer had the luxury of rekindling the prewar internationalist-isolationist debate. By 1934, the year Truman won a seat in the Senate, the Great Depression had shifted the debate's focus away from the abstract question of preventing war through world organization (Should the United States participate in the League of Nations?) to the immediate and very concrete issue of domestic economic recovery through increased trade: How can the government encourage foreigners to purchase U.S.-made goods? In 1933, the answer had been a flood of reciprocal trade agreements, the first of them with Cuba. And then, for those isolationists who remained unconvinced by depression-era arguments in favor of expanded commerce, Pearl Harbor had buried forever the notion that the United States could retreat behind its own borders. The attack also suggested that the nation's leaders should take another stab at global cooperation to prevent war.

This emerging internationalist vision received a permanent structure in the months immediately prior to FDR's death, first by the 1944 Bretton Woods and Dumbarton Oaks conferences and then by the San Francisco conference, which began two weeks after Truman became president. By creating a set of facilitating institutions, including the International Monetary Fund, the World Bank, the General Agreement on Tariffs and Trade, and of course the United Nations, these conferences hot-wired the process of global integration. Then, by taking the lead in operating these institutions, Truman's generation of victorious internationalists defined what it meant to be a great power in the mid–twentieth century.

Given these responsibilities, Truman and his four secretaries of state had no time for Latin America, let alone tiny Cuba. Completely overwhelmed by the problems of postwar Europe, they turned responsibility for U.S. policy toward Latin America over to Spruille Braden, newly named assistant secretary of state for Latin American affairs. After his success in Cuba, Braden had become the leader of a group of envoy-advocates promoting democracy in Latin America, but he never enjoyed a completely free hand. First, he had to contend with popular culture, for just beneath the nation's thin veneer of cosmopolitan leaders was a parochial population educated by writers such as John Gunther, whose series of "Inside" books (*Inside Europe*, *Inside Latin America*, and so forth) were perennial best sellers in the early postwar era. In a 1941 article, Gunther summarized Cuba's first four decades of independence: "After the Spanish-American War and our withdrawal from the island, a succession of feeble governments had attempted to rule. Poverty and squalor; the instability caused by mixed blood; flaming political corruption; laziness, greed among the rich; revolutionary agitation by the students—this was the background."[19] Democracy certainly could not thrive in such a climate.

Braden and his modest coterie of democracy advocates might have been able to ignore outsiders, but Gunther's thinking was also common in official Washington, as a member of the State Department's policy planning staff illustrated in his memoir: "When candid and not saying what he thinks a visiting American would like to hear, the average Asian or Latin-American laborer, farmer, or businessman will confide: 'We need a strong hand governing us.'"[20] Or, as one 1939 State Department memorandum had pointed out, dictators were unavoidable in Latin America: "The United States supports, legally and financially, such men in power as are widely recognized to be dictators holding their power by force. In the present stage of cultural and political development of some of the republics this is not only inevitable but perhaps the only way toward stability which can be realistically envisaged." Spruille Braden's wartime response was that "this apparent divergence in what we declare we are fighting for and our alleged benevolent attitude towards reactionary powers has mystified and baffled some of our more genuine friends in Latin America."[21]

Unfolding world events would not favor Braden's position, but in the immediate postwar period his view was briefly dominant—after all, the envoy had convinced Batista to hold a clean election, and Washington's reaction to his success had been to unleash like-minded envoys on other Latin American dictatorships, including Brazil and especially Argentina, to which Braden had been transferred from Havana for a brief period before being named assistant secretary. Even the president was enlisted in the effort; in April 1946, Truman told the Pan American Union that "the peoples of the Americas have a right to expect of the Pan American system that it show its validity by promoting those liberties and principles which the word 'democracy' implies." Warned in advance that his audience was primarily concerned with economic development, Truman threw in a sentence agreeing that "the danger of war will never be completely wiped out until the economic ills which constitute the roots of war are eliminated," but he then returned immediately to his central theme: "Democracy is the rallying cry today for free men everywhere in their struggles for a better life."[22]

But the promotion of democracy in Cuba or anywhere else in the region now had to compete with two more important issues—Latin America's demand for economic development and Washington's rapidly growing fear of communist expansion. At war's end, Latin American leaders feared that demand for their exports would dry up and that their economies would go into a tailspin, and they well remembered how the depression had aroused enormous public dissatisfaction leading to the downfall of nearly every one of the region's governments in the early 1930s. Cuba's experience had been typical: the price of sugar had dropped to a half cent a pound during the depression, far below the cost of production, and Gerardo Machado soon was living in exile.[23] In 1945 the pressures were even greater, with Latin America at the dawn of what would soon be called the Revolution of Rising Expectations. Mexico's Lázaro Cárdenas and Argentina's Juan Perón had led the way, and "all across Latin America the ancient oligarchies—land-holders, Church, and Army—are losing their grip," wrote a young Arthur Schlesinger Jr. "There is a ground swell of inarticulate mass dissatisfaction on the part of peons, Indians, miners, plantation workers, factory hands, classes held down past all endurance and now approaching a state of revolt."[24]

Fearful that the cousins of Argentina's *descamisados* might produce Juan Peróns throughout the region, Latin American elites began pressing for U.S. assistance with economic development. Mexico's foreign secretary told a member of the U.S. delegation to the 1945 Chapultepec conference that "the way to the heart of the masses is through raising the standard of living," and the conferees not only adopted the Economic Charter of the Americas calling for greater economic cooperation but also created the Inter-American Economic and Social Council to promote the region's development. Latin Americans also brought this message to San Francisco, where the United States agreed to a conference before the end of 1945 to implement Chapultepec's economic charter.[25]

The press of postwar events in Europe and Spruille Braden's consuming dispute with Argentina delayed any inter-American conference until mid-1947. By the time this conference was held at Rio de Janeiro, the Cold War had seized center stage in U.S. foreign policy, and the meeting was thus titled the Inter-American Conference for the Maintenance of Continental Peace and Security. The conference got under way with three major topics on the crowded diplomatic table—democracy, economic development, and anticommunism—and with the unspoken position among senior U.S. officials that the first two were relatively unimportant and had to go.

The first to be shoved aside was democracy, which had become an unwelcome and unnecessary distraction. This dispute had reached a climax in early 1946, when the State Department published its famous Blue Book (*Consultation among the American Republics with Respect to the Argentine Situation*), in which Assistant Secretary Braden accused Perón of being a fascist dictator. As the word "consultation" suggested, one purpose of the Blue Book was to enlist Latin American backing in the campaign for democracy in Argentina, and the obliging anti-Peronist government of neighboring

Uruguay proposed that Western Hemisphere nations take collective action to restore democracy whenever it might be replaced by dictatorship. Even in the abstract, Uruguay's proposal would have aroused substantial opposition among intervention-sensitive Latin American governments, but here it was interpreted correctly as a thinly veiled attack on Argentina. Now at the height of its campaign against Perón, the United States quickly expressed its support of the Uruguayan initiative, as did Cuba, Venezuela, and four Central American governments, but they all qualified their endorsements, while the rest of Latin America flatly rejected the idea. Mexico replied that "the principle of non-intervention, one of the most highly valued results of inter-American cooperation, must not be violated in any way."[26]

Mexico's response led to Braden's pink slip. It came shortly after President Truman traveled to Mexico City to prepare the ground for the upcoming Rio conference, which he hoped would formally align all of Latin America on Washington's side in the emerging Cold War. Truman sought to secure Mexico's support, and he did so with a flair that stunned even his critics, first by taking the unprecedented step of laying a wreath at the monument to Mexico's Niños Héroes, the revered military cadets who died defending their capital from Winfield Scott's invading army. (Truman wrote in his diary that he almost wept during the tribute, which "really set off the visit. They had it coming.") Then it was Mexico's turn to impress the president with a party: he wrote, "Fiesta! Oh my what a show. Never saw anything like it and never expect to again. 60000 in the Stadium and twice as many outside. Dinner with the President at his house. Three Ex-Presidents present. A grand time. Music and everything. To bed at 1 A.M. What a time!" Sandwiched in between was an address to the Mexican Congress, where Truman insisted that "the good-neighbor policy specifically includes the Doctrine of Nonintervention." Implicitly distancing himself from Braden, Truman argued that "a strong nation does not have the right to impose its will, by reason of its strength, upon a weaker nation. The wholehearted acceptance of this doctrine by all of us is the keystone of the Inter-American system. Without it we could not exist as a community of good neighbors. It is a binding commitment."[27] After his trip to Mexico and just before the Rio conference, Truman fired Braden.

That removed democracy and left anticommunism and economic development on the table at Rio, with Mexico again insisting that development was the "only sound basis for hemisphere peace."[28] Traveling to Rio to address the conference, President Truman responded by giving his "solemn assurances that we in Washington are not oblivious to the needs of increased economic collaboration within the family of American nations and that these problems will be approached by us with the utmost good faith and with increased vigor." But then he let the other shoe drop: at precisely the moment when sixteen European countries were meeting in Paris to draw up a U.S.-financed reconstruction program, Truman told the Latin American leaders at Rio de Janeiro that "our resources are not unlimited" and that the United States was obliged "to differentiate between the urgent need for rehabilitation of war-shattered areas and the problems of development elsewhere."[29]

That left only security on the table at Rio, where conferees produced the Cold War's first mutual security pact, the Inter-American Treaty of Reciprocal Assistance, which specified that "an armed attack by any State against an American State shall be considered as an attack against all the American States and, consequently, each one of the said Contracting Parties undertakes to assist in meeting the attack."[30]

By this time, George Kennan had sent his Long Telegram from Moscow, Winston Churchill had given his Iron Curtain speech in Missouri, and Truman had gone before a joint session of Congress to request aid for Greece and Turkey, setting the rationale for U.S. economic aid programs for the next four decades: "The seeds of totalitarian regimes are nurtured by misery and want. They spread and grow in the evil soil of poverty and strife. They reach their full growth when the hope of a people for a better life has died. We must keep that hope alive."[31] Truman's speech had been followed almost immediately by Kennan's "X" article in *Foreign Affairs*, which argued for the containment of communism "by the adroit and vigilant application of counter-force at a series of constantly shifting geographical and political points," and not long thereafter, Braden's successor as assistant secretary of state for Latin America was telling a New England audience that "the basic situation in the hemisphere today is this. The 21 American states together face the challenge of Communist political aggression against the hemisphere."[32]

The allegiance of Latin American military leaders became Washington's trump card in this contest, and military aid became the administration's understandable response to the perception of a communist challenge. But this case had not been easy to make in war-weary 1946, the year Truman asked Congress to pass the Inter-American Military Cooperation Act. Testimony by General Dwight D. Eisenhower and Admiral Chester Nimitz convinced the House Committee on Foreign Affairs, which reported the bill unanimously, but the full House did not act before adjournment; in the

Senate, Truman's proposal did not even receive a hearing by the Committee on Foreign Relations.[33] When the bill was resubmitted to the next session of Congress, both committees killed it.

As late as 1949, Congress still refused to authorize a cent for Latin America in the $1.3 billion Mutual Defense Assistance Act. The outbreak of the Korean War bolstered the arguments of military aid proponents, however, and in May 1950, a month before the shooting began, the National Security Council warned that "Communists in Latin America have the capability of severely weakening any war effort of the United States by interfering with the source and transit of strategic materials, by damaging vital installations, and by fomenting unrest and instability." Then came the punch line: "In the event of war, the main deterrent to execution of this capability is the ability of the security forces of the Latin American nations." Although a young member of the House named John F. Kennedy argued that aid was unnecessary because Latin America was "not in the line of the Soviet advance," the Mutual Security Act of 1951 contained thirty-eight million dollars in military aid for Latin America; the following year, the number jumped to fifty-two million dollars, and it grew every year thereafter.[34]

As a concession to those who feared that this military aid would help dictators repress their own citizens, eligibility for these funds required contracts—mutual defense assistance agreements—specifically guaranteeing that the U.S. training and equipment would be used only for hemispheric defense. Thirteen Latin American governments promptly signed on, among the first of them the Cuban government of Carlos Prío Socarrás, which initialed an accord on 7 March 1952. Three days later Prío was overthrown by Fulgencio Batista.[35]

FAIRLY ELECTED IN 1948 to replace Grau San Martín, Prío had inherited a corruption-as-usual banana republic—or so thought the U.S. embassy. In 1947, just before the end of a four-year assignment in Havana, the embassy's second secretary, H. Bartlett Wells, had produced a long memorandum warning that "no Cuban is guided by any system of restraints in his political, social, or perhaps even commercial conduct." Looking over a list of emerging political leaders, he commented that "all these young people got where they did though concerted insubordination. It would be fair to say that organized indiscipline has become . . . a fetish of Cuban public life."[36] Wells's analysis was reinforced a year later by an even more elaborate embassy report that focused on how "the magnified sense of honor of the Spaniards has degenerated in Cuba into excessive and ridiculous vanity."

Officials in Washington should not be misled by the fact that "Cubans individually give the impression of an alert people. This may be attributed to a marked Cuban tendency to bluffing." Nor should U.S. leaders be startled by the fireworks that accompany everyday life: "Cubans are prone to be extremely nervous, which, coupled with a tendency to stomach and liver disorders, frequently make them short-tempered and excitable. Ordinarily the gesticulating and shouting of Cubans carrying on a friendly discussion gives the American observer the impression that extreme violence is imminent."[37]

President Prío was just another banana on this bunch: "clever and astute but lacking in intellectual integrity," according to one early embassy evaluation.[38] "People expect little of him," a new ambassador reported in 1948, but "perhaps, with an eye to a possible second term in 1956, Prío will try to satisfy as best he can the people's longing for an efficient and honest administration. If he should make appreciable progress in that direction, the Cuban people would be surprised—and so would this Embassy."[39] U.S. envoys were equally worried about Prío's cabinet: "They are not, by and large, particularly intelligent, well educated or conscientious"; the new prime minister, Tony de Varona, was "slippery," treasury minister Antonio Prío (the president's brother) was "known to be venal," and education minister Aureliano Sánchez Arango was "left of center, unstable." Even Minister of State Carlos Hevia, an Annapolis graduate, received only faint praise: "Honest, correct, highly respected . . . but, unfortunately, poor administrator." When Prío was ousted four years later, the ambassador's postmortem emphasized how "the early idealism of the group, to the extent that it existed, had degenerated in many cases into personal self-seeking and license."[40]

But U.S.-Cuban relations had been excellent during the Prío years, which began with the new leader's state visit to Washington in December 1948, soon after his inauguration. As a special gesture, Truman sent Air Force One to pick up Prío in Havana, and the president was waiting at the airport when the new Cuban leader arrived. This unusually warm welcome reflected the fact that Prío's inauguration had occurred at one of the darker moments of the Cold War, a few months after Prague fell behind the Iron Curtain and almost immediately after Moscow began the Berlin blockade. For years, the embassy had been warning that communists might seek "to inflame the easily aroused nationalism of the Cubans against the United States and to create, for their own purposes, an Ireland on our doorstep," and Prío had earned high praise for his anticommunist efforts while serving as Grau's minister of labor.[41]

But the goodwill generated by Truman's welcome was soon over-shadowed by the unfortunate behavior of three U.S. sailors who climbed onto José Martí's statue in Havana's Parque Central and, perched on his shoulders, relieved themselves of the liquids accumulated during an evening of revelry. The Prío government quickly stepped in to help dampen public outrage, first by adopting a "boys will be boys" interpretation of the episode and then by having the foreign minister accompany the U.S. ambassador at a wreath-laying apology; thereafter, the embassy reported that only "communists and front organizations continue strong anti-American agitation following incident."[42]

Prío was especially cooperative with Washington's effort to contain communism. In mid-1950, after speaking with the Cuban leader about repressing Cuba's communists, embassy officials asked Washington to send down a copy of U.S. legislation aimed at subversives "and any other pending legislation directed at eliminating Communists from Strategic jobs," plus "details of the recent action taken against Communists by United States maritime workers [that] would be useful in discussing the problem of Communist workers with local labor leaders." At about the same time, Prío's ambassador in Washington asked that the United States assign an expert on communism to the U.S. embassy to help the Cuban government combat subversive activities, a request that launched the CIA's partnership with Cuba's new Buró de Represión Anti-Comunista.[43]

"One thing should always be remembered regarding President Prío," summarized ambassador Robert Butler near the end of his tenure: "whenever we have asked him anything regarding Cuban foreign policy he has always stated that Cuba will follow United States' leadership which, I feel, is very commendable. We couldn't ask for anything more in this regard."[44] The State Department reported that Cuba had downgraded its relations with Moscow, that Cuba almost always voted with the United States in the United Nations, and that Cubans were friendly to the United States. When chided by Prío for waiting two months to present his credentials in late 1951, the new U.S. ambassador explained that "I hadn't bothered him so far because we really had no problems of significance."[45]

The bilateral agenda during the Prío years therefore consisted primarily of minor commercial disputes ranging from the treatment of U.S. accounting firms (a turf squabble with their Cuban competitors) to the difficulties U.S. businesses encountered when they wanted to dismiss employees (the "unfair and irresponsible practices of labor") to the tariff on ammoniated superphosphate. Such humdrum issues of daily diplomacy throughout the late 1940s and early 1950s were either resolved or quietly brushed under the carpet with the explanation that a solution was impossible given Cuba's "political immaturity."[46] To the extent that disputes existed, one official reported, they were "due in no small measure to: (1) a spirit of nationalism fanned by extremists and a vocal communist minority; (2) a psychological feeling of inferiority on the part of a small and comparatively underdeveloped country lying next to a large, powerful and highly developed neighbor; and (3) the low moral and ethical standards of the Cuban governing classes."[47]

SINCE CUBANS' SHORTCOMINGS lay in their diminutive size and their unsavory culture and not in any particular set of leaders, the Truman administration had no reason to oppose Fulgencio Batista's seizure of power in March 1952. Eight years earlier, he had retired to his residence in Daytona Beach after handing power to Grau San Martín, but Batista's taste for political power had remained undiminished, and in 1948 he had won a seat in the Cuban Senate. Just before returning home, Batista was asked if he might be interested in running for the presidency in 1952. "You never can tell," he replied. "Who knows what will happen in the next four years?"[48]

Anyone familiar with Batista knew—of course he was interested. But as the campaign for the June 1952 election got under way, the embassy reported that "his chances now do not look too promising," and an opinion poll gave him less than 15 percent of the vote, a very distant fourth, even after the suicide of the leading candidate, Eduardo (Eddy) Chibás.[49] Recognizing his pending defeat, Batista turned to his core constituency, the Cuban army, and on 10 March he overcame his popularity problem by pointing a gun at President Prío. The *Gaceta Oficial* then published a proclamation notifying Cubans that the Constitution of 1940 had been suspended and reprinted Batista's message informing Cubans that something called a Revolutionary Junta had "decided that I should assume the office of chief of state and that I should take charge of organizing and directing the executive and legislative powers, all their powers and functions resting in me."[50]

The embassy interpreted Batista's coup as simply one more example of the country's immature political culture: "Cubans have got into the position of thinking that Government is an institution which deals out favors and privileges to people. Until Cubans learn that discipline and sacrifice are a necessary part of democracy, the upsets such as just occurred will be inevitable." Batista encouraged this evaluation by emphasizing the Prío administration's corruption and by promising to remain in office only until public confidence had been restored, when he would cede power to the winner of a fair election. "Whether the new group under Batista will be any better is a question," reported a skeptical U.S. envoy. "Governments in Cuba are made up of Cubans."[51]

Batista had immediately sought Washington's support: the coup began before dawn on 10 March, and by 7:00 A.M. he had rousted a U.S. military attaché and asked him to "tell the Ambassador I am 100% in accordance with his wishes. All agreements are in effect." By noon, Batista's adviser, Burke Hedges, was at the U.S. ambassador's door with the same message. For guidance, the embassy turned to Washington, where Assistant Secretary of State Edward Miller initially believed that "the Cubans seem to be headed for a terrific mess." He told Ambassador Willard Beaulac that "our attitude should be one of aloofness." Then the United States asked Batista for three things: some indication that there would soon be constitutional continuity (that is, an election), a promise of friendly treatment of U.S. investors, and a tougher attitude toward communism.[52]

None of these requests posed a problem. First, an election had already been promised "at the earliest possible moment," and Batista soon pinpointed the third Sunday of November 1953.[53] Second, investors were reassured—the embassy had already reported "a rising tide of confident expectation" among business leaders, but just to be certain, Beaulac quizzed Batista's new minister of state, Miguel Angel de la Campa: "I asked Dr. Campa whether he had anything to say on the treatment of private capital. I said I had in mind the situation deriving from Article 77 of the Constitution which made it nearly impossible for a company to discharge a man." The minister refused to be pinned down on this specific issue, but he pointed out "that business men were among the most enthusiastic supporters of the new regime."[54]

Third, Batista provoked a break in relations with Moscow, which Washington accepted as a step in the right direction but thought it not quite far enough, since local communists also posed a problem. During Batista's 1940–44 presidency, communist Lázaro Peña had led Cuba's labor movement, ten members of the communist Popular Socialist Party had sat in the Congress, and the FBI had worried that Havana had become "the center of extensive Communist activities."[55] Ambassador Beaulac now "reminded Campa that General Batista used to have close relations with the Communists. I asked whether we might expect that these close relations would continue. Dr. Campa said that the Provisional Government and he himself would do what could be done under the law to eliminate the freedom and privileges which the Communists were now enjoying in Cuba."[56]

"All our conditions for recognition have been met," cabled a reassured ambassador, recommending recognition, and at this point senior officials paused from their more important work to give Cuba five minutes of their attention: Secretary of State Dean Acheson asked President Truman for permission to recognize Batista, citing the new government's reassuring public and private statements with regard to all three preconditions. Edward Miller, the assistant secretary who had initially counseled aloofness, now wrote to a colleague that "from the cold-blooded standpoint of U.S. interests, we have nothing to worry about Batista who is a proven friend of ours and who might possibly be tougher on the commies than Prio was." The British ambassador reported to London that "Beaulac feels that if this had to happen Batista was the best material for the job."[57]

On 27 March, the Truman administration recognized Batista's dictatorship, and the next morning's newspapers featured the picture of a smiling Ambassador Beaulac handing the formal memorandum of recognition to Cuba's new minister of state. The United States was not the first government to recognize Batista—it was the seventeenth—but Washington's imprimatur was clearly crucial, and a much-relieved Batista told the press that "no one can ignore the significance of the friendly decision of the American Government in terms of the maintenance of relations of affection and business." Herbert Matthews met with Batista ten days later: "He was glad we had recognized him so quickly," the journalist wrote in his notes. "It meant a lot."[58] The Canadian ambassador shared this view, reporting to Ottawa that when Washington recognized Batista, "his government breathed an almost audible sign of relief. It was now over the shoals into the calm waters of international respectability."[59]

SO HERE WAS CUBA ONCE AGAIN—a Caribbean country run by a dictator who had promised to suppress communists, to welcome U.S. investors, and if possible to cover his naked military rule with a modest veil of electoral legitimacy. To solidify diplomatic relations, the Truman administration sent its highest-ranking Latin Americanist on a goodwill visit to Havana. "I deeply appreciate your receiving me," wrote assistant secretary of state Edward Miller in his thank-you note to Batista. "Having followed your illustrious career for 20 years and having known of the friendship which you have always had for my country . . . , it was a special pleasure at last to have met you in person." But it was also true, as the embassy reported a few days after the coup, that "Cuba has been set back many years in its development of constitutional processes."[60] Among the individuals suffering a setback was a young lawyer who until the coup had been making his first try for election to Cuba's Chamber of Deputies, Fidel Castro.

The Cubans are good people. They are very sensitive and easily aroused, but I have a feeling that they would listen to reason. The Cubans look upon us as big brothers.

—Senator Allen J. Ellender, December 1958

3

AROUSAL THE EISENHOWER YEARS, 1953–1958

Perhaps the easiest way to start an argument with Cuban-Americans who left the island around 1960 is to say that Cuba was "under-developed" in the years immediately before the revolution. Nonsense, they will reply, Cubans had made impressive progress in the half century since independence, and they have data to back them up. In the 1950s, Cuba's income per capita was among the highest in Latin America, and this wealth had spread beyond the mansions that continued to spring up in Havana's western suburbs: in health care, prerevolutionary Cuba had Latin America's lowest infant-mortality rate; in education it was tied for second for the region's highest literacy rate; and in secondary indicators of development such as television sets or newspaper sales per capita, Cuba was far ahead of the rest of Latin America and indeed much of Europe. "Undeniably there was poverty and there were social inequities," admitted one Havana-based U.S. lawyer, "but where not? The fact is that Cuba had a larger and more substantial middle class than any country in Latin America and one of the highest if not the highest standards of living of any semi-tropical or tropical country in the world." Years later, a longtime U.S. resident of prerevolutionary Cuba told President Gerald Ford, "I know the island [and] it was a paradise before Castro arrived on the scene."[1]

But all these assessments depended on perspective. A 1950 World Bank study mission reported that "living levels of the farmers, agricultural laborers, industrial workers, storekeepers, and others, are higher all along the line than for corresponding groups in other tropical countries and in nearly all other Latin American countries," but Cuba's per capita income at midcentury was only about half that of Mississippi, the poorest U.S. state. And while Cuba may have been doing well by Latin American standards, it was quickly losing its advantage—the World Bank reported that Cuba's postindependence growth spurt had come in the first quarter of the century, and the economy had subsequently made relatively little progress. There was also the thorny question of distribution: Cuba may have had a large middle class by Latin American standards, but that may have said more about Latin American standards than about Cuba's middle class. "Any figure for average *per capita* income is rather fictitious," the World Bank warned, "especially where—as in Cuba—there is a very wide gap between the incomes of a relatively few high-income receivers at the top and the mass of income receivers."[2]

This gap between the haves and the have-nots was especially obvious in the countryside, where a survey sponsored by the Agrupación Católica Universitaria found that "people are living in conditions of stagnation, misery, and desperation that are difficult to believe." The data reported in the 1953 census were also discomforting: it was not that inside toilets were found in only 3 percent of rural homes, but that more than half of all rural dwellings had neither an inside nor an outside toilet—the residents simply used the bushes. Two-thirds of rural dwellings had dirt floors; 9 percent had electricity; 2 percent had running water. As a result, the Cuban countryside constituted a public health nightmare, with the World Bank estimating that between 80 and 90 percent of rural children were infested with intestinal parasites, generally acquired by walking barefoot in animal feces; the fecal worms then work their way up through the bloodstream to lodge in the intestines, where they live on food intended to nourish the child.[3]

And to make the situation seem almost hopeless, education, the primary route to improvement, was closed to most of Cuba's rural population. Less than a quarter of age-eligible rural children attended school, and only about 40 percent of the adult rural population could read, four times the urban illiteracy level. The World Bank was also concerned about urban children, less than half of whom attended school and, again, especially about the absence of progress: "The general trend in the school system as a whole has been one of retrogression. A smaller proportion of the school-age children are enrolled today than a quarter of a century ago; the number of hours of instruction has been cut; the quality and morale of the teaching and supervisory force have gone down." The bank argued that "unless and until drastic improvements are effected, the Cuban people cannot hope effectively to develop their country," concluding, "It is impossible to be optimistic."[4]

Everyone agreed that Cuba's socioeconomic situation was rooted in sugar. More than half of Cuba's cultivated land was planted in cane, nearly a third of the nation's workforce was employed in the sugar industry, and from one-quarter to one-third of the national income came directly from sugar, which also accounted for slightly more than 90 percent of the total value of Cuba's exports in the 1950s. Yet most sugar workers were employed only during the harvest, which lasted ninety-four days in 1953, the year Dwight Eisenhower entered the White House.[5] Summing up Cuba's sugar-based economy in the early postwar period, the U.S. embassy's commercial attaché painted a bleak picture: "Cuban farmers and their families with few exceptions are undernourished, inadequately clothed, illiterate or semi-literate, readily susceptible to a variety of diseases, and at the mercy of country merchants and middlemen whose prices are what the traffic will yield and whose interest rates are generally exorbitant. Some optimist described rural Cubans as being happy and hopeful people. He did not explain why."[6]

What could be done to alleviate these problems? The U.S. commercial attaché argued against the panacea touted by development experts — distributing land to peasants — because "the average non-land-owning Cuban farmer and ranch hand is an indolent, ignorant, unambitious individual who is content with his apparently sad lot because he is too stupid and shiftless to try to improve it."[7]

There was no argument about Cuban politics. Everyone agreed that the two principal political constants of the mid–twentieth century were corruption and the presence of Fulgencio Batista, whose March 1952 coup — his fifth — had come a few months before the Republicans nominated Eisenhower as their presidential candidate. "Ethical standards in government are very low," reported the State Department in 1953, and Philip Bonsal, who would soon return as ambassador but had already spent several years in Cuba in the 1920s and 1930s, wrote in his memoir, "I know of no country among those committed to the Western ethic where the diversion of public treasure for private profit reached the proportions that it attained in the Cuban Republic." Visiting Havana a month after Batista's 1952 coup, journalist Herbert Matthews agreed: "The trouble seems to be that politics is a career to make money in, and just about nothing else. . . . The cynicism with which politics is regarded by all concerned would be horrifying to anyone with civic ideals, but there has never been anything else here and they have been given little reason or hope for anything different. This is politics as a spoils system and nothing else."[8]

The evaluations of Cuba's dictator were mixed. "Maybe Batista has a number of faults that I haven't recognized," wrote one of his defenders, "but after twenty years of friendship, he still seems to me to be an exceptionally nice fellow." Most U.S. officials held a different view; since the mid-1930s, they had been filing report after report characterizing the Cuban chieftain as ruthless and corrupt. But few complained about the way he ran Cuba; as the Canadian ambassador reported, "From the United States point of view, Cuba is an example of how their policy toward small, friendly countries works at its best." When disputes arose, more often than not they were brushed aside with a you-know-those-Cubans remark—"Their actions are sometimes influenced by a sense of inferiority, which promotes exaggerated nationalism," commented one State Department official in 1953. As a U.S. ambassador later acknowledged, Batista certainly kept his hand in the till, but he immediately qualified his remark with "I don't think we ever had a better friend. . . . He was doing an amazing job."[9]

What most pleased Eisenhower-era officials was the Cuban chieftain's ability to keep the island quiet by putting a lid on politics. When the election he suspended in March 1952 was finally held in late 1954, no one was surprised to see Batista garner 87 percent of the popular vote: all his various rivals had withdrawn, charging fraud. The embassy tried to place the results in the best possible light, labeling the opposition's charges "unconvincing," "flimsy," and "pure obstructionism," but it was difficult to put a positive spin on a one-candidate race, and everyone knew what lower-level U.S. embassy officials had regularly reported after the 1952 coup: "Despite efforts to win popular support, the regime is unpopular."[10]

No one in U.S. official circles cared. By this time, Washington's early postwar policy of promoting democracy had been not simply forgotten but openly rejected, with Treasury Secretary George Humphrey telling the National Security Council that U.S. officials should "stop talking so much about democracy, and make it clear that we are quite willing to support dictatorships of the right if their policies are pro-American."[11] So no one raised an eyebrow a few months later when Cuba was included in Vice President Richard Nixon's 1955 goodwill tour of the Caribbean and Central America. "His continuance in office is probably a good thing from the standpoint of the U.S.," reads the briefing memo handed Nixon on the eve of his departure; Batista "is friendly to the U.S., admires the American Way of Life, and believes in private enterprise."[12] Nixon therefore used his toast at a state dinner in Havana to compare Batista to the most revered public figure in U.S. history: "This month we, in the United States, are celebrating the birthday of Abraham Lincoln," he began:

> As we celebrate his birthday we think of the fact that he is a man who has done much for our country and he is a symbol to every young American that regardless of his background, however humble it may be, he may someday be the president of his country. And it seems to me that our President-elect, President Batista in Cuba, is also a symbol of that with the people of Cuba. A man of humble background, but a man who has been a leader of his country in the past and who now comes again to the Presidency to lead his country to even greater things in the future.

"Warmest congratulations occasion your inauguration," telegraphed the vice president two weeks later. "My wife joins me in personal regards to you and Mrs. Batista."[13]

In a few years, nearly everyone would agree that the United States had erred in cozying up to Batista, but doing so seemed logical in the mid-1950s. Here was a small, powerless neighbor, and who would have dreamed that the dictator's domestic opposition would mushroom into a genuine social revolution or that a revolution, should one occur, would be hostile to the United States? Indeed, everyone believed exactly the opposite: as the Canadian ambassador wrote in 1953, "the Cubans cannot afford to be on any but the best terms with the United States," and before seizing power, Batista had personally assured U.S. embassy officials that "the Cuban people, as is logical, are, and always will be, aligned with the friendly country of the United States."[14]

The proof of this pudding was Batista's several decrees restricting communist activities, and in mid-1953 the State Department listed thirteen specific steps the Cuban leader had taken to attack domestic communists. One was that "Communist headquarters and publishing establishments have repeatedly been raided, and in some cases damaged"; another was that "Communists and Communist sympathizers have repeatedly been arrested." The State Department was also pleased by Batista's consistent assistance in international forums, especially the United Nations, where the embassy noted that "Cuba has supported our UN delegation to an extent perhaps unsurpassed by any other country in the hemisphere"—this at a time when Washington's representative to the world body worried "that if we did not have the Latins with us in the voting processes in the UN, the United States would simply have to get out."[15]

ANTICOMMUNISM WAS THE FOUNDATION of the Eisenhower administration's embrace of Batista, but Hispanic stereotyping was a substantial building block. Vice President Richard Nixon began his report on his 1955 tour with the observation that "Latinos had shown a preference for a dictatorial form of government rather than a democracy," and given that preference, Nixon found Batista "a remarkable man." Similar statements are laced throughout the documents produced by State Department officials during the Eisenhower years—from a lower-level analysis referring to "the Latin penchant for *personalismo*" to the president telling British prime minister Harold Macmillan that "the average Cuban sugar worker wants to receive his earnings in cash and go to the store, buy a white *guayabera*, white shoes, a bottle of rum and go to a dance." John Foster Dulles believed that for these "tropical" people, the only thing required of Washington was to "pat them a little bit and make them think you are fond of them."[16]

This stereotyping meshed perfectly with the prevailing view of Latin America's insignificance. In 1946, just weeks after George Kennan had sent his Long Telegram from Moscow and at a time when it seemed probable that Republicans would soon regain the White House, publisher Henry Luce offered John Foster Dulles the pages of *Life* magazine to discuss foreign policy. Focusing on the emerging Cold War, Eisenhower's future secretary of state accepted Kennan's view of Moscow's relentless expansion, adding nuance by dividing the Soviet worldview into three zones—inner, middle, and outer—and by arguing that the Soviets were at the moment consolidating their power in the inner zone surrounding Russia; biding their time in the middle zone, which included the oil-rich Middle East and Western Europe; and ignoring Latin America, which fell into the outer zone. Given these priorities, it is unsurprising that President Eisenhower never mentioned Latin America in his fifty-seven-page oral history about working with Dulles, whose neglect was shared by Congress. After a fact-finding Caribbean trip in 1957, Senator George Aiken reported that "the West Indies includes dozens of islands big and small. No single country has problems important enough for us to keep that country in our consciousness."[17]

"Some of our Latin friends felt rather shut out from things," recalled one of Dulles's assistant secretaries, "but only in the sense of not having opportunities to sit down with him for long periods of time and to chat about all manner of things. He was a very busy man. He didn't waste his time, and he didn't want other people to waste it either." Dulles's principal Latin Americanist recalled that "he did have a sense of appreciation of the problems — social and economic — in Latin America. But he didn't go around talking about them all the time."[18] Instead, Dulles tended to lump Latin America together with the thirty new nations created in Asia and Africa during the Eisenhower years and to interpret all their problems in terms of the global balance of power, writing that these new states in the outer zone were engaged in "a tremendous surge in the direction of popular government by peoples who have practically no capacity for self-government and indeed are like children in facing this problem. . . . Many of the Latin American states are leaping ahead to irresponsible self-government directly out of a semi-colonial status. This presents the Communists with an ideal situation to exploit."[19]

This process seemed to be occurring in Guatemala when Dulles became secretary of state in 1953. U.S. policy was clear: "Our purpose should be to arrest the development of irresponsibility and extreme nationalism and their belief in their immunity from the exercise of US power."[20] The principal question at the time was how exactly to achieve this goal, and to answer that question the administration turned to retired general James Doolittle, who agreed to chair a study group. Its 1954 report argued that "long-standing American concepts of 'fair play' must be reconsidered." "We are facing an implacable enemy whose avowed objective is world domination by whatever means and at whatever cost. There are no rules in such a game. Hitherto acceptable norms of human conduct do not apply. . . . We must develop effective espionage and counterespionage services and must learn to subvert, sabotage and destroy our enemies by more clever, more sophisticated and more effective methods than those used against us."[21]

In practical terms, this approach meant that the Eisenhower administration would support traditional dictators such as Fulgencio Batista, to whom ambassador Arthur Gardner had presented his credentials a few months before an Organization of American States (OAS) meeting in Caracas in 1954 that had been called to condemn a reform-oriented Guatemalan government threatening U.S. economic interests and leaning far to the left. After the ceremony, Gardner reported that Batista "stood on the balcony and waved goodbye as we left"; then he went inside and issued a press release declaring his government to be in favor of discussing communist intervention at the upcoming Caracas conference. As the embassy reported to Washington, Batista's move "places the Cuban Government squarely on the side of the United States in its dispute with the Communist-ridden regime in Guatemala."[22] Within a few months, the CIA had arranged for a group of disgruntled military officers to overthrow Guatemala's elected government.

Now, after Guatemala, the challenge was to stabilize a rambunctious people. In an earlier era, the United States could simply send in the marines, but in the 1950s John Foster Dulles had to weigh the cost of violating the fundamental tenet of the Good Neighbor policy—no armed intervention. To maintain anticommunist stability in these insignificant outer-zone countries that were, as he said, "leaping ahead to irresponsible self-government," the solution was to rely on Latin America's military. That was the thinking behind the Mutual Security Act of 1951, which authorized the agreements that the Truman and Eisenhower administrations signed with thirteen Latin American governments in the early 1950s. As with the other twelve, the agreement with Cuba stipulated that the United States would provide military training and hardware and that Cuba would use it to defend the Free World from communism.

U.S. officials at first said they sought to "reduce to a minimum the diversion of U.S. forces for the maintenance of hemisphere security," but at a 1956 National Security Council meeting, the president "expressed doubt as to whether much could be expected by way of capability and missions for the armed forces of the Latin American countries," and Dulles added that the United States "would be better off if it by itself undertook to protect the sea lanes of communication and the Panama Canal." Alarmed by this line of thinking, which would logically lead to a cut in military aid, the representative of the Joint Chiefs of Staff, Admiral Arthur Radford, jumped in to explain that the references to Latin America fighting off invaders had been inserted to please Congress; the *real* reason the Pentagon wanted to strengthen Latin American militaries, he said, was so they would have the skills and weapons to repress domestic communists. Reporting from Havana two years later, the chief of the U.S. Military Assistance Advisory Group noted that he had been working with Batista's military on four specific missions, and "they all affect the internal security of Cuba."[23]

NO SENIOR EISENHOWER administration official foresaw how this type of military cooperation might have negative repercussions. Undeterred by Batista's 1952 coup and Cuba's conversion from a civilian democracy to a military dictatorship, the Department of Defense acted as if nothing had happened and proposed sending a seven-member military assistance advisory group to Havana. U.S. embassy officials understood the problem, however, and voiced their opposition, noting that thirty-eight U.S. military personnel already were stationed in Cuba and that "every one is aware of the support which the Cuban armed forces have received from our own armed forces before and since the *coup d'etat.*" Ambassador Willard Beaulac repeatedly emphasized that "the presence of this large number of American military personnel is very noticeable to persons in Cuba," and he again reminded Washington that "it is essential that our military help to Cuba be provided in the most discreet manner possible," since everyone in Havana knew that Cuba's military leaders "are more interested in affecting and controlling the domestic political situation and in improving their own personal finances than they are in cooperating in measures of continental defense."[24] The embassy sent Washington another warning in mid-1953, a few weeks after a group of anti-Batista rebels had assaulted the Moncada army barracks at Santiago: "The arms supplied by the United States to Batista's Government are regarded by a segment of the population as weapons to attack rather than defend democracy and to maintain an oppressive regime in power."[25] Washington ignored every one of these messages.

Ambassador Beaulac was soon transferred to Argentina—ostensibly a promotion to a more prestigious embassy, but one that was also motivated by the need to make room for Arthur Gardner, a wealthy Ohio industrialist who ultimately proved to be among the least-successful envoys in U.S. diplomatic history. One foreign service officer later observed that Gardner "displayed an unnecessarily florid and spectacular cordiality to Batista and his officials," and Cuban opposition leader Tony de Varona called Gardner "Batista's best publicity agent," but Gardner was a deeply committed Republican partisan and a friend of President Eisenhower since their service together in World War I.[26]

While Gardner had hoped for a European embassy, accepting Cuba only as a consolation prize, the new ambassador quickly plunged into action, immediately reversing the embassy's opposition to an enlarged U.S. military presence in Cuba. Just before Beaulac departed for Argentina, the Batista government had asked to purchase an exceptional array of materiel ranging from mortars and hand grenades to rocket launchers and anti-tank guns, and Gardner's embassy endorsed all of the purchases.[27] And the hardware was probably not as significant as the training: 692 Cuban soldiers took advanced courses at U.S. facilities during the 1950s, and the Pentagon's administrative support was also considerable, with Admiral Arleigh Burke reporting that "the U.S. Naval mission runs the entire supply operation of the Cuban Navy."[28]

The supporting memos accompanying the embassy's aid requests never mentioned the dictatorial nature of the Batista government; typical was a 1955 request from the embassy's air force mission, which argued that "inasmuch as the incumbent administration is friendly to the U.S. beyond all doubt, it is believed to be [in] our best interests to continue to contribute to the internal security of Cuba." The following year, Ambassador Gardner wrote that the U.S. military aid program "does not, in the opinion of the embassy, contain any significant political or economic implications."[29]

Similar comments accompanied other forms of aid. The FBI continued to build up Cuba's military intelligence service, the Servicio de Inteligencia Militar (SIM), which it had been training since World War II, and when the SIM seemed unable or unwilling to focus on Washington's principal concern—Cuba's communists—CIA director Allen Dulles urged Batista to create a second secret police unit, the Buró de Represión Anti-Comunista (universally known by its acronym, BRAC), which was "twinned" with the U.S. Central Intelligence Agency. "May I say, Mr. President, what a great honor and pleasure it has been to meet and talk with you," wrote CIA director Allen Dulles after a visit with Batista. "I trust we will be in a position to assist you and your country in our mutual struggle against the enemies of Freedom." Turning specifically to the BRAC, Dulles added that he was "honored that your Government has agreed to permit this Agency to assist in the training of some of the officers of this most important organization," and the CIA soon had an officer working full time in BRAC's offices. The CIA also sent inspector general Lyman Kirkpatrick to Havana to tell Cuban officials that "we would be glad to assist in training and providing guidance to the BRAC."[30] But in 1958, Kirkpatrick had to make another trip to Havana, prompted by a highly critical embassy report characterizing the Bureau as "weak and ineffective, poorly staffed, and with its attention directed more to ferreting out the political opponents of the government than to keeping down communist activities."[31] Kirkpatrick disagreed (he wrote in his memoir that "Batista appeared to be following to a letter all of the suggestions that had been made"), but he clearly missed the central point that Kennedy administration officials would soon find obvious: BRAC "became simply another organ of repression," and it did not help the U.S. image to be associated with its depredations. Only much later did Allen Dulles acknowledge that "in some cases, especially in South America, a dictator has later taken over an internal security service previously trained to combat Communism and has diverted it into a kind of Gestapo to hunt down his local political opponents. This happened in Cuba under Batista."[32]

Weapons and training were important, but nothing was more significant than U.S. diplomatic support during the four years (October 1953 to June 1957) when Ambassador Gardner represented not only the interests of his own country before the Cuban government but also those of Fulgencio Batista before the U.S. government. During the ambassador's first month in Havana, he asked Cuba's minister of state to provide a list of Batista's accomplishments, which Gardner then sent to *New York Times* editorial writer Herbert Matthews. "I hope that he may select some of them so that he can give Batista a pat on the back in his next editorial," Gardner reported. The envoy also became a partisan in Cuba's one-candidate 1954 election campaign, informing the State Department that Batista was the "only one man qualified as a true administrator." Gardner recognized that the Cuban dictator was not sufficiently popular to win a fair election, but as the campaign heated up, he sought permission to decorate Batista's military commander with the Legion of Merit, writing to the secretary of state that "my staff and I all feel very strongly that General [Francisco] Tabernilla definitely deserves the award." Such support continued until the end of Gardner's tenure; two months before returning home, he telephoned Washington to say that "Batista represents the best there is in Cuba and that there would be chaos without him."[33]

And the ambassador was not alone. As Cuba's election campaign was getting under way, the State Department's chief of protocol asked Mamie Eisenhower to give a luncheon in honor of Batista's wife. Why? Because "the political situation in Cuba is delicate" and Batista "faces strong political opposition. Cubans are exceptionally sensitive to United States attitudes and the lack of a warm reception in Washington for Señora de Batista would be seized upon and used by the opposition as another weapon against the Batista administration." A few months later, when an editor of the *Washington Star* asked the Eisenhower administration for its prepublication comment on a mildly critical article, the State Department requested that something be added about "President Batista's policy of suppressing Communism and crippling the activities of Communists."[34]

But Gardner was about to leave, since ambassadors who acquire their posts through patronage are expected to submit their resignations after one presidential term. Worried that no one could be more complaisant, Batista had his ambassador to Washington plead for continuity. Gardner, too, wanted to stay, and he telephoned assistant secretary of state R. Richard Rubottom Jr., whose notes indicate that Gardner argued that his departure "would be an everlasting shame," and, the notes continue, Gardner added one of those Cold War comments that seems incomprehensible today: "Some people might think his leaving would show that the US Government does not support dictatorships."[35] But there are many campaign contributors and few embassies, and the president finally had to ease Gardner out to make room for the chair of Florida's Republican Party finance committee, Earl Smith.[36] Gardner reappeared briefly in 1960 when a Senate committee conducted hearings to determine what had gone wrong in Cuba. He argued that Batista had been a perfect ally—"I don't think we ever had a better friend."[37]

AT THE SAME TIME, an insurrection was getting under way. In mid-1955, Fidel Castro had been released from prison after serving less than two years of a fifteen-year sentence for leading an armed attack on the Moncada army barracks on 26 July 1953. Castro had first come to the attention of U.S. officials several years earlier, in a 1947 report on university student activism. At that time the embassy had classified the eighteen-year-old Castro as "a typical example of a young Cuban of good background who, because of lack of parental control or real education, may soon become a full-fledged gangster." The embassy reported precisely that after the Moncada incident, passing along to Washington the Batista government's view of Castro as "a university student–gangster."[38]

Castro had moved to Mexico after his release, and in late 1955 he had traveled to the United States to raise money among the anti-Batista exile community, telling a Tampa audience that "if the tyrant of Cuba does not resign, revolution will come to the 'Pearl of the Antilles' and blood will be spilled." A local newspaper praised Castro's "three hours of verbal bombardment against Batista, who rules with a hand of steel and who quenches his thirst with the blood of Cubans who desire liberty and democracy. Even the two members of the FBI present at the meeting seemed to be impressed by his passionate appeal and eloquence."[39]

The FBI attended Castro's speech because Batista had protested Castro's presence in the United States, and when Castro's tourist visa expired, he returned to Mexico.[40] There he gathered eighty-two anti-Batista activists, and in late November 1956, just after Dwight Eisenhower's reelection, the rebel force set out by sea for southeastern Cuba. On 2 December, they landed near Niquero, on Cuba's southeastern coast, an event of sufficient importance for the embassy to telephone the State Department's Cuban desk officer at his Washington home on a Sunday. He was told that all of the rebels had been killed.[41]

That was not quite accurate. Twelve of the eighty-two rebels had escaped into the Sierra Maestra, and while the Cuban government promptly announced that the survivors had also been killed or captured, it probably knew otherwise. Three months later, the *New York Times* settled the issue by publishing a series of three articles by Herbert Matthews, the first of which featured a large front-page picture of Castro, very much alive.[42] Working through Felipe Pazos, a former (and future) central bank president and a foe of Batista, the rebels had asked the *Times* reporter in Havana, Ruby Hart Phillips, to visit the Sierra. As she subsequently wrote, "A woman would be too conspicious [*sic*], especially an American," so she asked NBC correspondent Edward Scott if he wanted to go. Scott demurred, thinking that doing so would lead to his expulsion from Cuba, so Phillips contacted her New York office to suggest Matthews, a veteran reporter who spoke Spanish and was now one of the newspaper's editorial writers.[43]

Matthews reported that the Cuban rebel was not only alive but thriving. "Thousands of men and women are heart and soul with Fidel Castro," not simply because of his message—his "strong ideas of liberty, democracy, social justice, the need to restore the Constitution, to hold elections"—but also because of his charisma: "The personality of the man is overpowering. It was easy to see that his men adored him and also to see why he has caught the imagination of the youth of the island. Here was an educated, dedicated fanatic, a man of ideals, of courage and of remarkable qualities of leadership."[44]

The embassy conceded that Matthews probably had seen Castro ("or at least someone he thought was Castro") but criticized the reporting: Matthews "has emphasized the negative features of the situation, appears overly impressed by the romantic nature of his experiences, exaggerates the size and importance of the Castro movement and its supporters, and uses colorful and extreme phraseology." Embassy officials believed that Batista had the situation under control but agreed that Castro had considerable support among the country's youth ("much of it from the better classes") and that he was "an unusual man"—but in a negative sense: "dedicated, fanatical, impractical, possibly megalomaniac. There is reason to believe that he is exceptionally ambitious. He pictures himself as the great Cuban leader of the present generation." Overlooking the fact that Batista had closed the electoral route to power, the embassy observed that the rebels "seem to prefer violence to negotiation, bullets to ballots. The rest of their program is nebulous. They seem socialistic and nationalistic, and have talked vaguely of agrarian reform, socialization of profits, industrialization of Cuba by Cubans, and the like. They are hell-bent on change."[45]

Matthews telephoned the State Department about another matter on the same day this lengthy report arrived from the embassy, and Assistant Secretary Rubottom seized on the opportunity to gently criticize the journalist: "I said that it seemed to me his series of articles would build Castro up into a hero somewhat beyond his real proportions." Matthews responded that Rubottom would be "amazed at his supporters among all walks of Cuban life," and the journalist appears to have turned some heads, because at about this time the State Department began a slow reappraisal of Batista's value to Washington. The Canadian ambassador in Havana soon reported to Ottawa that "the strain on Cuban relations with the United States had been mainly the work of Herbert Matthews."[46]

If the articles had this impact, they did so primarily because they assuaged Washington's worry that the rebels might be communists. Matthews emphasized that "communism has little to do with the opposition to the regime. There is a well-trained, hard core of Communists that is doing as much mischief as it can and that naturally bolsters all the opposition elements. But there is no communism to speak of in Fidel Castro's 26th of July Movement." As one senior senator recalled years later, this reporting had disarmed Washington: "Matthews' stories that [Castro] was a Robin Hood helping the poor, fooled this committee, caused the State Department to disregard the reports which they had about Castro being a Communist, and accepting him in that favorable light."[47]

But Matthews was not finished. He also added a comment that would be especially encouraging to the rising generation of U.S. officials who were coming to perceive a new flowering of democracy in Latin America. Castro's struggle was "more than an effort by the outs to get in and enjoy the enormous spoils of office"; rather, it represented a sea change in which "the old, corrupt order in Cuba is being threatened." Then came the policy-relevant punch line: "It is disturbing to find the opposition, which contains some of the best elements in Cuban life, is today bitterly or sadly anti–United States." But how could the opposition possess anything except animosity, Matthews added, when U.S. policy helped a tyrant repress the island's population? "While I was there, seven tanks were delivered in a ceremony headed by Ambassador Gardner. Every Cuban I spoke with saw the delivery as arms furnished to General Batista for use in bolstering his regime and for use 'against the Cuban people.'"[48]

Returning to the Sierra Maestra in mid-1957, Matthews filed another front-page story, this one telling of the rebels' progress since February. By now Castro had earned "an extraordinary place in the hearts and minds of Cubans and has caused the Government's accusations of criminality and communism to be ridiculed. . . . Fidel (no one ever calls him anything else) is worshiped here in Oriente Province." This time, Matthews's reporting prompted Rubottom to send Secretary Dulles a memorandum acknowledging the growing strength of Castro's rebels, who, Rubottom said, had developed "the almost universal support of the people of the surrounding area."[49]

In this context, a new U.S. ambassador paid his first visit to Santiago, the principal city of the surrounding area, doing so only eighteen hours after Santiago police had ambushed and murdered Frank País, an underground 26th of July leader. Ambassador Earl Smith was driven from the airport to the city hall, where, after alighting from his car, he reported, "women broke police ranks and surrounded me shouting and gesticulating." Smith could see that the women were upset, but since he spoke no Spanish, he did not understand what they were saying. The din followed him inside, where, he reported, the "ceremony was repeatedly drowned out by noise and shrieks, scuffling, shouting and singing of Cuban national anthem from plaza in front." Outside, the women were "repeatedly manhandled and threatened with drawn weapons by police, who found themselves unable to control [the] situation. At one stage, fire hoses were turned on demonstrators, who disregarded the wetting. [Santiago police chief José] Salas Cañizares was observed personally beating women with his pistol." After watching about two hundred of the women being trucked off to jail, the new ambassador issued a press statement asking that they be released, asserting that "any form of excessive police action is abhorrent to me."[50]

Smith's statement represented a clear violation of the norm that diplomats do not comment publicly on the internal political affairs of the country to which they are accredited, and the State Department demanded an explanation. Eager to defend his action, Smith replied that "in view of what I and members of my party had just witnessed, I consider my statements to have been moderate." Clearly pleased by the evidence that Ambassador Smith might alter Arthur Gardner's policy of casting a blind eye toward Batista's abuses, the embassy's career officers rose to his defense. "The Ambassador felt that after being a witness to this sorry display of brutality he could not ignore it," wrote one political officer to a colleague in State's Latin American bureau; "I suspect that he made many friends for the U.S.

when he deplored the use of excess force." Rather than censure the new envoy, he continued, "it is extremely important that the Department give every backing to Ambassador Smith at this point. The slightest insinuation of disagreement would be unthinkable."[51]

But Smith, a Palm Beach stockbroker, was no rebel sympathizer, and he never again publicly disapproved of Batista's excesses. Just a few months later, Undersecretary of State Christian Herter wrote that "our present appraisal of [Smith's] performance has improved very greatly." Herter continued, "In his first few days there he did get himself into difficulties, partly I think because of a reaction to his predecessor who had gone overboard rather one-sidedly in the other direction. Now Ambassador Smith has had two long and very satisfactory conferences with Batista and has apparently gotten back into the good graces of the latter gentleman."[52]

Indeed, Smith quickly fell victim to the dictator's charms, becoming one of Batista's principal supporters. Nonetheless, Smith's protest statement had nudged an inch or two wider the door Matthews had cracked open; Washington now was aware that all was not normal in Cuba, and embassy reports began emphasizing the number of police patrolling the streets, the press censorship, and the growing air of unease. Just days after the Santiago brouhaha, the embassy reported that a general strike was possible.[53]

This cable traffic was not being read in a vacuum. Dictators were falling in Latin America—the era soon became known as the Twilight of the Tyrants—and most of the region's political leaders were paying increased attention to economic development. It was both a hopeful and a worrisome time, and Washington became paralyzed. If dictators were out of fashion, what did that imply for U.S. policy? One answer came from President Eisenhower's brother, Milton, who after two Latin American fact-finding missions confirmed what a 1953 National Security Council (NSC) report had captured: "Our postwar policies of rebuilding a sound Europe gave rise to [Latin] American charges that the United States, friendly to them only during the war years, was again neglecting them. Latin Americans felt that they should at least have received a larger share of aid."[54]

Although several years passed before this message sank in, by early 1957 President Eisenhower had been convinced by his brother's argument in favor of an active U.S. role in Latin America's economic development.[55] And, as luck would have it, the same *New York Times* front page that carried the first of Matthews's articles had also featured a second major story: "2 Studies Bid U.S. Start 20-Year Plan For Economic Aid." Both studies essentially concluded that enlightened self-interest required the U.S. government to supplement the normal market forces of trade and investment in order to spur economic growth in developing societies.[56]

These findings ran counter to the view of Treasury Secretary George Humphrey: three years earlier, just after Milton Eisenhower's first report, an unidentified NSC official had been sent to feel out Humphrey on an aid program: the answer was a definite "No." "He is utterly convinced that a soft policy and a policy of winning Latin America by spending money on them is not the way to go about it. He believes the way to control Latin America is by a tough hard-hitting policy which would envisage, if necessary, the use of force." But that was in 1954; now, in early 1957, a few weeks after Fidel Castro's U.S. newspaper debut and the unveiling of the two studies favoring aid, the president wrote Humphrey a personal note underscoring that "protection of our own interests" required more than lecturing Latin Americans about how to attract private investment. "We must at the same time understand that the spirit of nationalism, coupled with a deep hunger for some betterment in physical conditions and living standards, creates a critical situation."[57]

With his influence waning (and the economy in recession), Humphrey soon resigned, clearing away the principal obstacle to fresh thinking about Latin America. But while Milton Eisenhower had clearly captured a bit of the president's attention, little sense of urgency had arisen—this was the outer zone, after all, and in late 1957 John Foster Dulles reported that "we see no likelihood at the present time of communism getting into control of the political institutions of any of the American Republics." This confirmed one former ambassador's observation that "Mr. Dulles was so preoccupied with other areas of the world that perhaps he did not recognize the tremendous importance of the Latin American area, and events there were swept under the rug."[58]

As a result, nothing concrete had changed in U.S. policy before Vice President Richard Nixon set out on his 1958 South American goodwill tour. Nixon had been criticized for meeting primarily with military dictators during his 1955 visit to the Caribbean and Central America—the trip where he had compared Batista to Abraham Lincoln—so the State Department now instructed its South American embassies to diversify his itinerary, noting that the vice president "is anxious to meet man on street."[59] U.S. officials arranged such a meeting at the first stop, in Montevideo, where Nixon participated in a spirited but civil exchange with a group of Uruguayan students. But after attending Arturo Frondizi's inauguration in Buenos Aires and making brief stopovers in Paraguay and Bolivia, the vice president faced a group of rock-throwing protesters in Lima, one of whom, Nixon later reported, "let fly a wad of spit which caught me full in the face." Next came uneventful stops in Ecuador and Colombia, but Nixon then flew to Caracas, where, five months earlier, Venezuelans had finally freed themselves from the decadelong clutches of Colonel Marcos Pérez Jiménez. As a final symbolic slap in the face of Venezuela's democrats, the Eisenhower administration had recently opened the nation's doors to both Pérez Jiménez and his detested secret police chief, Pedro Estrada—"as vicious a man hunter as Hitler had ever employed," in historian Hubert Herring's apt characterization.[60]

Within minutes of Nixon's arrival, the Caracas embassy sent Washington the first of several flash cables reporting that "a large and unfriendly crowd met the Vice President and his party at the airport." That was an understatement. Nixon later recalled that at the airport, "hundreds of people were there on the balcony spitting down on us as we stood listening to their national anthem." Then, the embassy's cables continued, on the way into town, Nixon's motorcade was blocked by a group "made up of ruffians and riffraff and it was in an ugly mood. The mob closed in on the vehicles in which the vice president and his party were traveling, and the Venezuelan police escort ran. The windows were broken out of the car in which Mr. Nixon was riding," and as a *Life* photographer snapped pictures for next week's cover, the enraged demonstrators spent the next fourteen minutes spitting on the vice president of the United States of America.[61]

Nixon's driver eventually nudged his limousine through the protesters, jumped the highway median, and raced down the wrong side of the divided highway to the U.S. ambassador's residence, where the vice president remained sequestered until he left for a hero's welcome at home. President Eisenhower led the forty thousand federal employees who received time off from work to greet Nixon at the airport, and another eighty-five thousand lined the vice president's motorcade route to the White House.

The minutes of Nixon's report to the NSC indicate that he began by telling everyone that "we should all get clearly in mind that the threat of Communism in Latin America was greater today than ever before in history," and the Caracas embassy reported that "undoubtedly the attack on the Vice President was organized by the Communists."[62] In a 1962 book, Nixon noted that "not all the rioters, of course, were Communists. But this misses the major point: there can be no doubt that the riots were Communist-planned, Communist-led, and Communist-controlled." Nixon added that "it made me almost physically ill to see the fanatical frenzy in the eyes of teenagers—boys and girls who were very little older than my twelve-year-old daughter, Tricia. My reaction was a feeling of absolute hatred for the tough Communist agitators who were driving children to this irrational state." Just about everyone agreed, with lower-level State Department bureaucrats informing Secretary Dulles that "the pattern of organizations and of slogans in all cases points to Communist inspiration and direction."[63]

But then the House Committee on Foreign Affairs decided to solicit the views of a broader circle. State Department representatives had the opportunity to speak first, and they explained that the anti-Nixon demonstrations represented a small minority and did not reflect broader Latin American opinion. Then came the dissenting view, offered by former Costa Rican president José Figueres: "People cannot spit on a foreign policy, which is what they meant to do." Of course, he agreed, "spitting is a despicable practice, when it is physically performed. But what about moral spitting? When your Government invited Pedro Estrada, the Himmler of the Western Hemisphere, to be honored in Washington, did you not spit on the faces of all Latin American democrats?" In November 1954, Dulles had held a fete in honor of Estrada as a gesture of appreciation for the calm streets during the OAS meeting in Caracas the preceding March. Estrada had led Venezuela's secret police from 1951 to 1958, during which time he purchased a home in a Washington suburb and obtained a multiple-entry visa, which he used to effect his hasty departure. Holding no such visa, Pérez Jiménez had fled first to Trujillo's Dominican Republic, but three months before Nixon's visit, the United States had allowed the deposed dictator to move to Miami.[64]

Figueres's message was reinforced by another Latin American democrat, Brazilian president Juselino Kubitschek, who wrote to President Eisenhower to suggest that "the hour has come for us to undertake jointly a thorough review of the policy of mutual understanding of this Hemisphere," emphasizing that "the problem of underdevelopment will have to be solved." Then came a similar message from a third leading Latin American democrat, Argentina's Arturo Frondizi: "The hour of concrete decisions has come," he warned a joint session of Congress during his 1959 state visit to Washington. "You cannot remain indifferent to the fact that millions of individuals lead a life of hardship in the American Continent. The situation of these fellow human beings is not only a challenge to our common ideals of human solidarity, but is also a source of danger to the security of the hemisphere. To leave an American country in stagnation is as dangerous as an attack coming from an extra-continental power." Sandwiched between the Nixon trip and the Frondizi visit was a third fact-finding mission by President Eisenhower's brother, this one to Panama and Central America. "Now I must add a note of urgency," Milton Eisenhower reported, just before Senator Frank Church warned that "when our own Vice President is mobbed in South America, I think it is time for us to wake up to the fact there is something seriously amiss."[65] Latin America now had everyone's attention.

SO WHAT WOULD the tiring Eisenhower administration do about Cuba? In early 1958 the embassy had warned that "the revolutionary elements are disorganized, splintered and lack a program with public appeal. If Batista were assassinated, there is no responsible group to take over the government. Vandalism, chaos and bloodshed would surely ensue." Then, just before Nixon's trip, the State Department added that within the rebel ranks "there is little about its top leadership to inspire confidence that it would show the qualities of integrity, moderation, and responsibility which will be needed to restore order and tranquility to Cuba. Although the evidence available to the Department does not confirm the Cuban government's charge that Castro is a communist, it does suggest that he is immature and irresponsible." So in mid-1958, a few weeks after the attacks on Vice President Nixon, State's Latin American bureau concluded that "the major danger insofar as U.S. position in Cuba is concerned would appear to be a successful revolution by the forces of the 26th of July movement." But months earlier, the embassy had reported that the Batista government had been unable to halt the rebellion and that "there is little possibility that it can do so in the near future."[66]

These developments alarmed those U.S. officials who, like Milton Eisenhower, were coming to think of dictators as roadblocks to the "deradicalization" of Latin America through economic development. For Cuba, these officials voiced their concerns regarding the specific issue of weapons, almost all of which were either purchased from U.S. vendors or given to Batista by the U.S. government. This raised a delicate political issue, since the Mutual Security Act required—and the 1952 U.S.-Cuba Mutual Defense Assistance Agreement specifically stipulated—that U.S. arms and training were only for "the defense of the Western Hemisphere" and that Cuba could not "devote such assistance to purposes other than those for which it was furnished."[67]

The amount of grant military assistance plan (MAP) aid was fairly insignificant, with Cuba scheduled to receive only about half a million dollars in the fiscal year that began in mid-1958 and with more than 90 percent of that to be used for training. But training is fairly inexpensive, and the numbers had added up: by mid-1958, the embassy reported that three out of every four members of Batista's air force had received U.S. schooling, as had almost all of the Cuban navy, and that U.S.-trained officers in the Cuban army "occupy key positions and are indispensable."[68]

There was no debate about whether Batista was using his U.S.-trained personnel to fight the rebels—everyone knew he was. When the rebels first landed, he had dispatched a MAP-supported company to reinforce the army's Oriente garrisons and then had sent an entire battalion into the Sierra Maestra; both units "were MAP equipped and the best trained of Cuban troops," the embassy reported. A few months later, embassy officials added that these units constituted "the crack force of the infantry. From 75 to 90 percent of its officers have received MAP training." Moreover, all of their equipment had been provided by the U.S. government. Obviously unaware of the use critics could make of these cables, Ambassador Smith added that the "battalion has been actively engaged in fighting with armed rebels."[69]

In early October, Washington sent what Smith should have interpreted as a warning: "There seems to be no doubt that Cuba has violated . . . the Mutual Defense Assistance Agreement." But Smith repeated his blunder, unself-consciously informing Washington that the misuse was continuing. One cable mentioned that "army has used substantial amount MAP-supplied and supported equipment past several months in campaign against rebel force," while another reported that the U.S.-trained Cuban air force "is frequently engaged in activities in support of Sierra Maestra operations"—this at a time when every one of the technicians who kept Batista's planes in the air had been trained by the U.S. Air Force.[70]

With these cables, the embassy had, willy-nilly, taken itself off the hook by informing the State Department of Cuba's violation of the Mutual Security Act. Now Washington had the problem.* The hint of a decision had

---

*Since nearly all outgoing cables were drafted by officers of the embassy's political section and teletype-signed "Smith," it is difficult to be certain that the ambassador agreed with (or even saw) all of them. In his memoir, the embassy's most junior officer, Wayne Smith, noted that Ambassador Smith insisted on editing outgoing cables to suit his policy preferences, but Wayne Smith also observed that two savvy professionals in the embassy's political section, John Topping and William Bowdler, often disagreed sharply with Ambassador Smith, while the British ambassador characterized his U.S. counterpart as "not particularly intelligent." In such a situation, it is entirely possible that the cables were sent without the

already come in early 1957, when both the embassy and the State Department had agreed that it would be unwise to license the sale of napalm, an especially sensitive item, but U.S. commercial arms dealers subsequently won the next few rounds, gaining approval of export licenses for machine guns, pistols, and military communications equipment.[71]

When an obscure member of Congress complained, the State Department replied that Cuba had made a commitment to use the equipment only for hemispheric defense. But then an influential Republican senator, George Aiken, returned from a fact-finding trip to report that Batista's opposition charged that U.S. arms were keeping the dictator in power. At that point, the *New York Times* sent another reporter to the Sierra Maestra, and after two weeks with the rebels, Homer Bigart resurfaced in Havana to tell the embassy the same thing. The embassy in turn notified Washington that the rebels "complained bitterly of grants and sales by the United States of military equipment."[72]

So State Department officials called in Cuban ambassador Miguel Angel de la Campa and handed him a diplomatic note expressing displeasure over the misuse of U.S. military aid, but the message was coated with a thick sugar glaze: "It was explained to the Ambassador that it was unfortunate that the alleged violations of the agreement left us no recourse but to make it the subject of the note that we had handed him which indeed was couched in the friendliest terms possible under the circumstances." Beneath the sweet coating was a harsh reality, however: Batista might run out of bullets. A few days later, the State Department reversed an earlier decision to permit the export of twenty armored cars and small arms.[73]

The issue quickly came to a head. Almost a year before the rebels had launched their insurgency, the Batista government had requested a price quotation for the routine purchase of five thousand M-1 rifles. An offer had been made by a U.S. arms merchant and accepted by the Cuban government, and licenses had been issued for the export of one thousand of the rifles in 1956 and two thousand in 1957. The remainder were sitting on a dock in New York, and the arms dealer now requested an export license

---

ambassador's awareness that he was sending incriminating evidence. It is certainly difficult to read these dispatches today and not conclude that they were intended to provide bureaucratic allies in Washington with the ammunition they needed to halt military aid. See A. S. Fordham to Selwyn Lloyd, 25 June 1958, AK1902/1, FO371/132189, PRO; Wayne S. Smith, *The Closest of Enemies: A Personal and Diplomatic Account of U.S.-Cuban Relations since 1957* (New York: Norton, 1987), 30.

for them from the State Department's Office of Munitions Control.[74] As required, the office sought approval from the Latin American bureau, which until now had agreed to most sales.

Not this time. As the request was being considered, the elected president whom Batista had deposed, Carlos Prío Socarrás, was indicted along with eight other exiles for conspiracy to violate the Neutrality Act. An outspoken critic of U.S. policy, Prío had for years been under FBI surveillance, and after determining that he was aiding the rebels, the State Department had unsuccessfully petitioned the Immigration and Naturalization Service to revoke his asylum or, if that was not possible, to reduce his influence among anti-Batista Cuban exiles by removing him from Florida.[75] In the wake of Prío's indictment, another of the Senate's most influential members launched a withering criticism of continuing U.S. military aid: "A military dictatorship can buy arms or have arms given it by the United States, but a constitutionally elected President is put in jail for trying to assist in the overthrow of that government," complained Senator Mike Mansfield. "Do you think that is the kind of policy that is likely to help this country keep its reputation of devotion to freedom among the people of Latin America?" The State Department promised to review the decision. Hoping, perhaps, that his audience was ignorant of the circumstances surrounding Cuba's 1954 election, Assistant Secretary Rubottom added that Batista "has been the constituted President under the laws of Cuba," but Rubottom did not fool an annoyed Senator Wayne Morse: "Do you think the election was somewhat different than a Russian election? They have elections over there in Russia, too."[76]

A week later, the Cuban rebels announced a twenty-two-point plan of action, and Batista's immediate reaction was to suspend constitutional guarantees and initiate a new round of press censorship. "Sales of arms to dictatorial governments is already under fire in both branches of Congress," wrote State's Latin American bureau, asking the secretary of state to authorize an arms embargo. "Failure to halt the shipment [of the two thousand rifles] would, if it became known publicly, subject us to a rash of criticism from a large sector of the Cuban and American public, and the U.S. press." Dulles agreed, but representative Adam Clayton Powell still found time to amplify the chorus by providing an eyewitness report of how U.S.-supplied weapons were being used: on a recent visit to Cuba, he had seen three adults "mutilated beyond recognition and in a crude crib a child about 3 or 4 years old with a bayonet pinning it down through the stomach." Powell demanded that the United States "get out and get out at once."[77] Four days later, the State Department announced the arms embargo.

As Herter, the acting secretary of state, later explained to President Eisenhower, "We could not continue to supply weapons to a government which was resorting to such repressive measures."[78] But just as the State Department had sugarcoated its 3 March warning, Ambassador Smith now twice assured Cuban foreign minister Gonzalo Güell that there was no change in the friendly U.S. attitude, blaming the embargo on the administration's need to counter criticism from Congress and the press. Smith then tried to reverse Dulles's decision, warning Washington that "continued suspension of arms shipments at this critical juncture in Cuban affairs would weaken the Cuban Government and possibly lead to its downfall, probably with attendant violence and risk to American lives and property." When that traditional argument did not work, he pulled the Cold War arrow out of his quiver, reminding officials in Washington that "whenever US has requested cooperation and assistance in our stand against world Communism [the Cuban government] had never been found wanting."[79]

As Smith's effort to resume arms shipments unfolded, he found a powerful ally in the Department of Defense, which placed the embargo on the agenda for one of its regular meetings with State Department officials. Admiral Arleigh Burke, the chief of naval operations, began by complaining that Dulles's decision "had cancelled valid contracts with a free government." Moreover, he continued, Cuba had now contacted him about purchasing PT boats, and he wanted to send a positive response. When the State Department held firm to its embargo decision, Admiral Burke again complained that State was interpreting the 1952 mutual defense agreement with Cuba "too literally." And he enlisted the assistance of the army chief of staff, Maxwell Taylor, who told State Department officials that he "was surprised by the position we were taking."[80]

At the same time, Ambassador Smith repeated his warning that communists would be the only beneficiaries of the arms cutoff. In particular, Smith urged reconsideration of an export license for ten jet trainers, and this time he seemed to have gained a victory: in mid-June, the State Department agreed that the planes were not combat equipment and approved the export license. But at almost exactly this time, the Cuban rebels began kidnapping U.S. citizens and scattering them among the rebel forces in an apparent effort to lessen the chances of attack by Batista's air force. On one day, the rebels kidnapped eleven U.S. citizens working at the Moa Bay Mining Company, and on the next they captured twenty-four U.S. Navy personnel riding a bus near Guantánamo. On 2 July, after an additional forty-three U.S. citizens had been kidnapped in Oriente Province, the State Department reversed its 19 June decision to export the airplanes.[81]

After the U.S. consul in Santiago had secured the hostages' release, Batista tried to pressure the United States by withdrawing Cuban guards from the water supply for the U.S. Navy base at Guantánamo, which was located four miles outside the base boundary. Since sabotage could cause a genuine crisis—the on-base tanks held only one day's supply of water—U.S. Marines briefly (28 July–1 August) entered Cuba to secure the pipeline, but they were withdrawn when the embassy convinced Batista to restore the Cuban guards. At the same time, Ambassador Smith resumed his effort to obtain the jet trainers for Batista's air force, while State's Rubottom countered that the "sale of the T-28s would get us into deep trouble with the Cuban opposition, liberal elements in the hemisphere and the United States, and those Senators and Congressmen who have been making much ado of our policy toward dictatorial governments."[82] Secretary Dulles sided with Rubottom, and the debate ended—almost: in July and September, Ambassador Smith sent lengthy cables arguing that the only beneficiaries of the arms cutoff "could well turn out to be the Communists," and while visiting Washington in late November, he approached the British ambassador, who reported to London that "Smith, in confidence, encouraged Britain to continue to deliver arms to Batista while he tries . . . to change United States policy."[83]

While no U.S. arms were legally exported to Cuba after March 1958, the military advisers remained, and the following May they exchanged three hundred five-inch rocket heads for a different type from stocks at Guantánamo, with both the embassy and the State Department defending the action by noting that the navy had delivered the wrong type of rocket heads in January 1958, before the arms embargo had gone into effect, and felt obliged to correct the mistake.[84] Less deadly but equally damaging politically was the public relations support: on 16 December 1958, barely two weeks before Batista's capitulation, the *Havana Post* published a photograph showing the smiling commander of the Guantánamo base sipping coffee with the commander of the Cuban navy. Even better publicized was a luncheon sponsored by the U.S. military missions in Cuba in honor of Colonel Tabernilla, who had recently been promoted.[85]

Representative Charles Porter condemned these meetings as identifying the United States "with the forces of a police state," and Tony de Varona, the prime minister of the government Batista had overthrown, complained to an influential U.S. senator that Cubans could see that the United States wanted to keep Batista in power because "high praises, mammoth banquets, and meritorious medals have been bestowed on Cuba's worst scoundrels." The administration shrugged off this criticism, but Porter's complaint merely echoed what the U.S. consul in Santiago had been saying for a year—that the Cuban army "applies its own system of justice which is swift, effective and without appeal. As a daily occurrence bodies of young men are found hanged or lying along the roadside with as many as 40 bullet holes." And, consul Park Wollam continued, this brutality was working in favor of the rebels, helping the 26th of July Movement to grow "from an annoying thorn in the side of the Batista Government to a slowly spreading cancerous tumor."[86]

Far from the fighting, the embassy continued to curry Batista's favor, with Ambassador Smith going out of his way to assure Cuba's dictator that the embassy was on his side: "I told Batista I was gratified and impressed by his sincerity, his desire to be fair, and his willingness to cooperate and that I would so report to my government." Smith continued his effort to breathe life into a dying dictatorship to the very end, telling a New York audience in late 1958 that "Batista is an intelligent man, a courageous man, with a firm chin and a ready smile." As this statement suggests, the most striking feature of Smith's brief diplomatic career was the vast distance separating his perceptions at the time from what hindsight has demonstrated was the Cuban reality. In mid-1958, for example, he urged Cuban prime minister Gonzalo Güell to end the insurgency by "giving Castro a large sum of money and making him a senator." Two months later, Smith reported not only that "both Fidel and Raúl [Castro] are mentally unbalanced," but—mother of offenses—that "when Raúl was attending Havana University there was talk that he was homosexual." A month later, Smith told Washington that Fidel Castro had "a syphilitic inheritance."[87]

The ambassador was not alone. Also sticking with Batista to the end was Senator Allen J. Ellender, an unreconstructed Democrat from Louisiana and chair of the powerful Committee on Agriculture, which passed on sugar legislation, a position that led him to make a fact-finding visit to Havana less than three weeks before the rebel victory. While there, reporters asked him about an earlier comment endorsing renewed military assistance:

QUESTION: "Senator, may I quote you as saying that you are in favor of selling arms to Batista?"
ANSWER: "Well, I really don't see any reason why not."

QUESTION: "In Civil War?"

ANSWER: "Well actually, I don't see any fighting, do you? My understanding is that there are bandit groups which are against constituted authority. In that case, I see no reason not to aid the Government. . . . Constituted authority ought to be respected."

A lower-level embassy official characterized Ellender's comments as "regrettable," and the senator's personal diary was more candid: "What makes
it difficult for Batista is, of course, his unpopularity. He is despised." But
Washington had to choose, he argued, between an unpopular but friendly
dictator and an unfamiliar rebel leader, adding that "it is risky for us to
merely stand by and let these things happen," since "it is certain that conditions will get worse, and I doubt that a successor to Batista, chosen in
the heat of battle, will be any improvement in the long run." Rather than
worry further, the senator concluded that nothing much could go wrong:
"The Cubans are good people. They are very sensitive and easily aroused,
but I have a feeling that they would listen to reason. The Cubans look upon
us as big brothers."[88]

By this time the end was near. Months earlier, in April, the rebels' call
for a general strike had fizzled, prompting a more confident army to launch
an offensive against Castro's forces, but it took until July for Batista's army
simply to enter the foothills of the Sierra Maestra, and that was as far as
the president's forces got: the rebels soon seized the offensive, and by early
August the army had withdrawn. With the collapse of the offensive and, as
one junior embassy official later wrote, with popular rejection of Batista "so
strong that one could feel it in the air," the only certainty was his defeat.
State's Bureau of Inter-American Affairs echoed this view: "The Batista Government will terminate, by peaceful or violent means, probably the latter,
sometime between now and February 1959," the date set for the inauguration of a new president.[89]

IF SO, THEN THE QUESTION BECAME whom to support as Batista's replacement. Until mid-1958, the U.S. government perceived three principal
alternatives to the 26th of July Movement: the student-led Revolutionary Directorate, which had been seriously weakened by an ill-fated attack on the
presidential palace in March 1957; the second guerrilla front in the Escambray Mountains, led by Eloy Gutiérrez Menoyo and a U.S. citizen, William
Morgan; and the Civic Resistance, led by José Miró Cardona, a prominent
lawyer. But defeat of Batista's offensive by the 26th of July Movement greatly

enhanced its relative power among these competing groups, and in mid-July they signed an agreement naming Fidel Castro commander in chief of all rebel forces.[90] By that time, nearly every U.S. official was worried that power seemed to be falling into the rebels' hands, although some officials worried more than others. Among the least concerned were those in the State Department's Bureau of Intelligence and Research, who concluded that "although the Cuban Government has consistently charged that 26th of July Movement is penetrated and influenced by communism, little evidence exists to prove these allegations." The CIA agreed, while State's Latin America bureau was "greatly concerned about the character of the leadership of the July 26 Movement" but admitted that "our information is not as conclusive as we would like."[91]

Convinced that it was better to be safe than sorry, the State Department launched a search for an alternative to either Batista or Castro, an undertaking that by this time, of course, was easier said than done. It was especially unrealistic to believe that a viable successor to Batista might emerge from the elections scheduled for 3 November, since they were to be held under the most unfavorable conditions imaginable—with a full-blown civil war raging in the eastern third of the island, with constitutional guarantees (including freedom of expression and the right of assembly) suspended, and with three candidates contending for the votes of the few Cubans willing to go to the polls. A week before the election, the State Department acknowledged the obvious—"The weakness of the presidential candidates and the unpopularity of the regime and distrust over how it will handle the elections all combine to produce an apathetic and cynical Cuban electorate." On Election Day, the Santiago consulate estimated voter turnout at less than 5 percent, and even Ambassador Smith noted that "not too many Cubans went to the polls." Batista's handpicked candidate may have won, but the CIA concluded that "his election under the present chaotic internal conditions can seem little more than a sham." The British ambassador reported that the victor, Andrés Rivero Agüero, represented a continuation of the Batista regime, and acting secretary of state Christian Herter told President Eisenhower that "any hopes that the elections might ease the tensions in Cuba were dashed by the circumstances under which they were held."[92]

By this time (November 1958), the CIA had already made contact with various anti-Castro groups, but as both Thomas Paterson and Julia Sweig have ably demonstrated, these contacts came to naught. "Confusion, uncertainty, disarray, and dismay gripped the highest echelons of the U.S.

government," wrote Paterson, and up to the last days of 1958, "the United States was still haplessly attempting to locate a credible anti-Castro third force." With the embassy unable to identify any alternative to the 26th of July Movement, in an act of total desperation, the chief of the CIA's Western Hemisphere division, Colonel J. C. King, traveled to Havana with businessman William Pawley, whose long experience in Cuba apparently recommended him as a secret envoy. Two years after the visit, Pawley told a Senate subcommittee, "I was selected to go to Cuba to talk to Batista to see if I could convince him to capitulate, which I did. I spent 3 hours with him on the night of December 9." The rudimentary plan, he said, was for the Cuban dictator to take up exile in his home at Daytona Beach, while the United States "would make an effort to stop Fidel Castro from coming into power."[93]

But while Batista sent two of his children to the United States, he otherwise seemed not to be moving, so Ambassador Smith was instructed to call on Güell: "It is my unpleasant duty," Smith said, "to inform the President of the Republic that the United States will no longer support the present government of Cuba." Güell took Smith to see Batista, and the ambassador spent two and a half hours telling him the same thing. Meanwhile, the rebel forces were moving quickly, with the British ambassador reporting that the eastern third of the island was effectively in their hands.[94]

These events prompted a National Security Council meeting two days before Christmas, apparently an attempt by U.S. officials to brainstorm ways to stop the 26th of July Movement from coming to power. Herter brought a very tentative memo for the president indicating that "the communists are utilizing the Castro movement to some extent, as would be expected, but there is insufficient evidence on which to base a charge that the rebels are communist dominated." Not everyone agreed. After listening to the discussion, the director of the U.S. Information Agency asked why the United States should attempt to prevent a rebel victory, and Allen Dulles responded with the CIA's assessment: "The Communists appear to have penetrated the Castro movement, despite some effort by Fidel to keep them out." After Vice President Nixon "pointed out it would be undesirable to take a chance on Communist domination of Cuba," Herter summarized: "the undesirability of a Castro regime appeared to be unanimous." The next day President Eisenhower told his national security adviser that "he had not known until the NSC meeting that the view of the U.S. Government was that of wishing to oppose Fidel Castro" and "expressed a feeling that for one reason or another the main elements of the Cuban situation had not been presented to him." The president clearly had forgotten being briefed at four recent NSC meetings, and he must not have read a late-November special national intelligence estimate.[95]

Christmas came and went, and on 30 December, a reporter for the *Miami Herald* saw more police patrols than usual but found Havana otherwise quiet as the tourist season was getting under way—"You get the impression that even a battle might be postponed for a party of well-heeled American visitors." But he did not know that on 26 December, Tabernilla, the army chief of staff, had been rebuffed when he asked Ambassador Smith to approve the formation of a junta to save Cuba from Castro; the reporter also did not know that the State Department was telegraphing one final "No" to Ambassador Smith's last request for an end to the arms embargo. As Batista's pilot was warming up his engines for a flight to the Dominican Republic, Rubottom was spending the final day of 1958 at a closed hearing of the Senate Committee on Foreign Relations, telling the few senators in attendance that Batista's ouster was supported by Cubans "who are, we are absolutely certain, not Communists at all" but warning that "this kind of revolution, of course, is made to order for the Communists."[96]

Nations stand up and greet one another. "What are we?" is the mutual question, and little by little they furnish answers.
—José Martí, Nuestra América, *1891*

I hope the boy intends to do what's right.
—Former President Harry Truman, *1959*

4

WATCHING AND WAITING THE EISENHOWER ADMINISTRATION, 1959

At dawn on 1 January, Radio Rebelde warned "Santiago de Cuba: You are still not free." Batista had fled a few hours earlier, the announcer continued, but he had left the government in the hands of military officers who "want to prohibit the entry into Santiago of those who have freed the country. The history of 1895 will not be repeated. This time our rebels will enter Santiago de Cuba." Within hours, Batista's military had capitulated, and Fidel Castro told a wildly cheering audience in Santiago's Parque Céspedes exactly what his radio announcer had meant: "This time, fortunately for Cuba, the revolution will truly achieve power. It won't be as in 1895, when the Americans came at the last hour and took over the country."[1]

So there it was, in the first speech on the first day: a negative comment about the United States. But few Americans were paying attention; more important was the departure of many Republicans from Washington. With the U.S. economy in recession, the November 1958 off-year election had been a disaster for the president's party—not a simple loss but an unvarnished calamity, with the Senate going from a Democratic majority of 2 seats to one of 30 seats, the largest such shift in the Senate's history, and with the House going from a Democratic advantage of 33 seats to one of a staggering 130 seats. With Democrats' thoughts surging ahead to the 1960 presidential race, the new Congress that assembled in Washington the same week that Batista left Cuba was not going to be docile. The sledding might be especially rough in the Senate Committee on Foreign Relations, where ninety-two-year-old Theodore Francis Green was stepping down as chair in favor of J. William Fulbright, a brilliant, energetic legislator and more than a match for anyone the increasingly lame Eisenhower administration might send his way.

Then, just as Fidel Castro was moving into the Havana Hilton and the newly elected Democrats were settling into their seats on Capitol Hill, John Foster Dulles underwent a second operation for stomach cancer; by May he was dead. In April, the foreign policy mantle was formally draped over the shoulders of Deputy Secretary Christian Herter, an experienced politician from the progressive wing of the Republican Party. When compared to Dulles, Assistant Secretary R. Richard Rubottom Jr. found Herter "a softer man, a sweeter man."[2] He was also a severe arthritis sufferer who regularly used crutches to ease his constant pain while coping with a variety of exceptionally complex problems, most of them in truly important places: the final year of fighting in Cuba had coincided with the U.S. invasion of Lebanon, with the communist Chinese shelling of the Nationalist islands of Matsu and Quemoy, with ominous communist advances in Laos, and now, in early 1959, with renewed Soviet threats to Berlin that so alarmed the chair of the Joint Chiefs of Staff that in January he warned a secret session of the Senate Committee on Foreign Relations, "We must hold Berlin at all costs, even to general war."[3] Obliged to focus on these conflicts, Secretary Herter was in Geneva negotiating with the foreign ministers of Britain, France, and the Soviet Union when he was called back to Washington for Dulles's funeral. Immediately thereafter, President Dwight D. Eisenhower flew off for a hastily scheduled visit to Britain and France, obliged to consult with his two principal NATO allies about Nikita Khrushchev's upcoming visit to Washington.

Not much time remained available for little Cuba. With Western Europe's security in play and other East-West issues occupying whatever room remained at the top of the foreign policy agenda, Cuba's significance to Washington rested squarely on one question: Where did it stand on the Cold War? On our side, senior State Department officials told President Eisenhower. The island's new government "appears free from Communist taint and there are indications that it intends to pursue friendly relations with the United States." CIA director Allen Dulles told a closed-door session of the Senate Committee on Foreign Relations that Fidel Castro did not have communist leanings.[4]

With recognition came a new ambassador: Earl Smith was ordered to resign so that Washington's principal representative in Cuba could at a minimum be someone who understood Spanish. Smith did not go without a fight, and the president was reluctant to fire him, but after three days of back-and-forth, Eisenhower authorized Herter to order Smith to resign.[5] His replacement was a man with all the right credentials: Cuba was even part of Philip Bonsal's intellectual lineage, since his father had received the Pulitzer Prize for his coverage of the Spanish-American War. The young Philip had learned Spanish when his family lived in the Philippines; he had then received his secondary education in Switzerland and a 1924 degree from Yale. His first job, with the International Telephone and Telegraph Company, landed him back in Cuba, and when the market crashed in 1929, he entered the Foreign Service and was again posted to Havana as vice consul. Bonsal subsequently rose steadily up the career ladder, becoming ambassador to Colombia in 1955 and Bolivia in 1957, both difficult posts. "Working for him was a distinct pleasure," wrote one of his junior associates, recalling Bonsal as "an astute diplomat, a man of moderate instincts, and a gentleman in every sense of the word." Herbert Matthews told Fidel Castro that Bonsal was a perfect choice.[6]

With their new ambassador in place in Havana, senior officials adopted a "watch and wait" approach that has been criticized ever since. The watching first focused on Fidel Castro's almost-daily speeches, beginning with a 13 January appearance before the Havana Lions Club, where the new Cuban leader referred to the Platt Amendment as "an injustice imposed on the generation that struggled for independence — the law that took away our independence." Not every U.S. official had heard of the 1901 amendment that had converted Cuba into a protectorate, but they all understood when Castro switched to the present tense: "The Cuban Revolution is being criticized in the United States," he complained, and he wondered aloud why the critics had not been a little more concerned about Batista's assassins; instead, he continued, "there was an American mission in Cuba teaching the criminals." A week later, he complained to the largest audience in Cuban history about "a barrage of defamation" coming from the Washington. His emphatic response: "I do not have to give an account to any U.S. Congressman." The crowd roared its approval.

Castro was referring to congressional criticism of the executions that were occurring. This was not revenge, he replied; it was simple justice. The accused had received fair trials, so, "I tell those Congressmen that, aside from the fact that *Cuban affairs are none of their business*, that we are executing the tyrant's henchmen to obtain peace, and we are executing the butchers so that they cannot murder our children again tomorrow." Contrasting the executions to the U.S. bombing of Japan, the Cuban leader predicted the number would not exceed 400—"that is about one for every 1,000 men, women, and children murdered at Hiroshima and Nagasaki."[7] The cheering was so loud Castro had to ask his audience to quiet down.

He reserved particular criticism for U.S. military aid to Batista's dictatorship. A few days before his 13 January speech, he had responded to a journalist's query by casually remarking that it would be a "courtesy" for Washington to withdraw its military missions, but at the Lions Club he converted military aid into a major issue: "This country has the same rights as others to govern itself, to freely plan its own destiny, and to do things better and more democratically than others who talked about democracy and then sent Batista Sherman tanks. . . . There's no law that requires us to keep those who were teaching our soldiers to kill Cubans."[8]

State Department officials worked overtime to prepare their flat rejection of this criticism, but clearly it was true.[9] The U.S. military advisers had been integrated into Cuba's three military branches, with U.S. Army and Air Force personnel sharing offices with Batista's forces at Camp Columbia and U.S. Navy advisers doing the same at the Cuban navy headquarters in the port of Havana. The number of U.S. advisers had doubled as the rebel threat grew, from fourteen to twenty-eight over the course of 1958, and the embassy had repeatedly informed Washington that these advisers were helping the government's forces. Batista's military certainly thought the advisers were doing so: in a memo written twelve days before the regime's collapse, one of Batista's officers summarized the emergency aid he had received during the preceding two weeks from the U.S. Army advisers: "The six officers of the Mission have dedicated all their energy to carry out an analysis" of three topics: "1. To raise to the maximum the morale of our soldiers. 2. To contain the progress of the enemy. 3. To defeat the enemy."[10]

In early 1959, however, even well-informed citizens knew next to nothing about the U.S. military advisers stationed in friendly countries around the world, and the bias was overwhelmingly in favor of believing public officials when they defended the United States against charges of wrongdoing. These officials were themselves in denial—the Department of State's most detailed description of the last years of the Batista government, a candid internal document never intended for public eyes, asserted that "the U.S. was aware of the dictatorial nature of the Batista regime from its inception. It was careful never to express approval of the regime *per se*." To this day, the U.S. government has never admitted that it actively and enthusiastically supported the Batista dictatorship. When confronted with the issue, the most common response has been a flat denial, such as that of Richard Shifter, the George H. W. Bush administration's assistant secretary of state for human rights, who told Congress a generation later, "I don't believe, first of all, that the relationship between the United States Government and Batista was really that close."[11]

But some U.S. officials probably understood Castro's criticism, and many of them subsequently acknowledged the problem. In retirement, for example, President Eisenhower switched his evaluation of Batista from "nice guy" to "self-enriching and corrupt dictator."[12] And regardless of whether one chose to side with Castro or the State Department, there was certainly no reason to bicker over this issue: in late January the United States offered to withdraw its advisers. Cuba immediately accepted.[13]

Then it was back to watching and waiting and to listening to predictions that little could go wrong. On 2 January, the day after Castro's Parque Céspedes speech, U.S. Army intelligence experts warned that Cuba's new leaders "will probably be initially critical of the United States," but "with the economy of the island greatly weakened and the treasury probably empty, any new Government will probably have to face realities and seek closer relations with the United States."[14] This analysis fit well with the long-prevailing view from Washington, voiced best by Senator George Aiken, who reported after his late-1957 fact-finding trip to Cuba that "the Cubans know and cherish the fact that we assisted them to attain independence. They see the evidence on every side of our investment in their economic future. American businessmen in Cuba today sense no resentment against the large measure of United States economic participation in Cuba." With Sears Roebuck operating stores in seven Cuban cities and Woolworth in ten, the ubiquitous U.S. presence led Aiken to conclude that "it is difficult to conceive of the possibility that any new regime would be unfriendly to the United States."[15] The embassy agreed, arguing in late 1958 that "it is improbable that a Government actively unfriendly to the United States could exist for any length of time," while the consul in Santiago also helped dampen concern about Castro's harsh words by emphasizing that they were for local consumption, since "many Cubans have always had an inferiority complex with respect to the United States." The embassy agreed, noting that "Castro is obsessed these days with keeping his personal popularity coefficient high, which partly explains his appeals to latent anti-Americanism of uninformed masses."[16]

But other voices almost immediately took a darker view. By early February, the CIA was worrying about "the relative youth and inexperience of a great many top leaders" and in particular about Fidel Castro's reluctance "to buckle down to the responsibilities of his position as Commander in Chief of the Armed Forces." An embassy official also reported that "the physical and mental exhaustion of both Castro and [President José] Miró [Cardona] was an important factor in the erratic behavior of both. He notes that Castro is under sedation and close medical attention." Castro's behavior in those early days also mystified visiting U.S. congressman Adam Clayton Powell. "He's just gone to hell," he told journalist Herbert Matthews. "He is on benzedrine; still keeps on his 21 and 22 hour days, but the problem is to find him. He disappears, completely, for two days at a time." The embassy agreed that "Castro has led the new Cuba into a critical attitude toward the United States," but, the report continued, "this feeling is not deep-seated, and will give way in time to a general desire based largely on self-interest, for good relations with the United States." What was required at this point was "patience, goodwill, and cooperation."[17]

At the same time, Cuba's new government proceeded with the execution of Cubans accused of severe abuses during the Batista era. While the exact number is still debated—probably between five hundred and a thousand—there has never been any question about the shock effect of these executions on the U.S. public: some of the executions were televised, showing images of a solitary man standing in front of a wall, then his body jerking into a *V* as his arms and head flew forward and his midsection was pushed backward by a half dozen bullets. *Time* magazine thought the executions reflected Hispanic culture ("the Latin capacity for brooding revenge and blood purges"), and the CIA's Allen Dulles simply shrugged his shoulders: "When you have a revolution, you kill your enemies. There were many instances of cruelty and oppression by the Cuban army, and they certainly have the goods on some of these people. Now there probably will be a lot of injustice. It will probably go much too far, but they have to go through this."[18] One unnamed State Department official wanted to delay Ambassador Bonsal's arrival in Havana "to show the new regime that we are in no hurry about this as the country is repelled by the actions of the new government," but that was a minority view; more typical was the opinion of representative Charles Porter following a two-day visit to Cuba in mid-January: he told his House colleagues that the trials and executions were fair and that "Fidel Castro and his friends who seek to bring democracy to Cuba need and deserve our sympathy, or forbearance, and support." And, he added, Castro "is not anti–United States at all."[19]

There were also troubling personnel decisions. In mid-January, Castro named his brother, Raúl, as his successor, and the embassy reported that Raúl, one of the two leading radicals in the revolutionary government, "has at no time to the Embassy's knowledge shown any noticeable friendliness toward the United States."[20] Raúl had also worried Representative Adam Clayton Powell: Fidel was impressive, he recalled years later, but "his brother, Raul, seemed always to be sneaking around. Much smaller than Fidel, his tiny, glittering eyes somehow gave me the impression of a rat."[21] During an April meeting of the National Security Council (NSC), President Eisenhower commented "that Raúl Castro must certainly be a Communist. If not, said Mr. [Allen] Dulles, he was at least very close to being one." Worse yet was the other leading radical, Che Guevara, whom one State Department intelligence officer described as "a truly sinister character," "definitely anti-American and . . . acting like a Communist." Moreover, Matthews noted some months later, Guevara "is beyond question the most intelligent man in the Cuban government."[22] Cuba's new Fundamental Law had granted Guevara "native-born" citizenship, making him eligible for any government position.

And then, of course, there was the question of Fidel's role in the new Cuban government. On 6 January, Castro had announced that voting would be postponed for at least eighteen months; on 28 February he extended the delay to two years; and on 9 April he explained that for suffrage to be effective, Cuba first had to eliminate "unemployment, illiteracy and misery." On 30 January, the constitution had been suspended, replaced by a new Fundamental Law of the Republic that assigned all legislative, executive, and judicial powers to the president and his cabinet.[23] On 1 January, Castro had told his Parque Céspedes audience, "Personally I am not interested in power nor do I envisage assuming it at any time," but a few weeks later he said he would agree to be president "if the people demand it of me some day in the future." By mid-February, Castro had been promoted from commander of the armed forces to prime minister, replacing Miró Cardona, the moderate former dean of the University of Havana's School of Law, and then the Fundamental Law lowered the minimum age for president to thirty, which had the obvious effect of overcoming a constitutional impediment that Castro himself had identified in his 1958 *Coronet* magazine article: "I am, at 31, far too young to be eligible for the presidency."[24]

All these early concerns did not keep U.S. officials from attempting to cooperate, however. The first concrete opportunity came in mid-February, when a delegation from Cuba's Banco Nacional arrived in Washington for talks with the International Monetary Fund (IMF) and with U.S. officials. Two years of fighting had taken its toll on the economy, and the Eisenhower administration offered to help arrange an IMF standby agreement and to provide an immediate line of credit from the U.S. Treasury. Perhaps more important, the February visit gave Washington officials their first opportunity to talk with their new Cuban counterparts, moderate in their business suits and shaven faces, a sharp contrast to the pyrotechnics coming from Havana. The State Department informed Senator Fulbright that the visitors were "responsible Cuban financial technicians."[25]

After this visit, U.S. officials began to view the revolutionary government as a fragile coalition of three factions: a group of radicals led by Che Guevara and Raúl Castro; a second group, led by Fidel Castro, that, while volatile and left-leaning, was "oriented primarily towards moderation and the establishment of a prosperous democratic Cuba with honest government"; and a third "more mature, moderate group," characterized by the officials visiting Washington—"men of integrity and competency, friendly to the U.S. and moderate in their political and economic viewpoints."[26]

The task at hand was to nudge the volatile, in-between leftists closer to the mature moderates, and that meant nudging Fidel Castro. Everyone had immediately recognized that his political power rested on personal magnetism. "In these modern times the Western Hemisphere has seen nothing comparable to Fidel Castro," Herbert Matthews wrote in his field notes during a visit six weeks after Batista fled. "In fact, he is a unique phenomenon in hemispheric history." In public speaking, his voice "is appealing and arresting, partly because of naturally skillful gestures and a mobile face whose range of expression would be the joy of any actor. He never reads his speeches and never falters. His ideas are clear and his expression of them simple and eloquent, without rhetoric, without the artificial inflections of the elocutionist. The result is invariably that he holds his audience always interested and sometimes spellbound." In one-on-one encounters, "Fidel really loves people as people. It is not the baby-kissing, handshaking activity of a politician but a genuine, simple pleasure and interest. This was part of the secret of the unanimous support he got from the guajiros and also a reason why his soldiers worship him."[27]

Such an assessment was difficult to fathom in Washington, where a decade of McCarthyism had cleansed the foreign policy bureaucracy of imagination and initiative, making it especially congenial for personalities the polar opposite of Castro's: bland white males in gray flannel suits, many of whom seemed to consider any sign of life beyond breathing an indicator of poor breeding. One of the gray suits was worn by CIA director Allen Dulles, who warned a February NSC meeting that "the new Cuban officials had to be treated more or less like children. They had to be led rather than rebuffed. If they were rebuffed, like children, they were capable of doing almost anything." Later in 1959, he told the British ambassador that Castro "had a streak of lunacy in his make-up" and that the CIA was doing its best to generate an internal Cuban opposition to the rebel government but, unfortunately, "the crop had been quite good this year and in these primitive countries where the sun shone, the demands of the people were far less than in more advanced societies."[28] But while the embassy agreed that "Castro is impetuous and emotional," it argued that he could be nudged: "There is some reason to believe that Castro is not as anti-American as he sounds in his public pronouncements."[29]

This assessment came in mid-February. The embassy's willingness to tolerate emotionalism and other Hispanic frailties soon was exhausted, and by mid-March, its description of a Castro television appearance indicated a clear concern:

> Castro in his standard uniform of rumpled fatigues, radiating health and boundless energy, hunched over the table as he talks, waving arms and hands, with the eternal cigar always at hand. Words pour from him like a ceaseless torrent. He appears literally capable of talking forever, on any subject under the sun. He is a dynamic, forceful speaker, with that rare quality of fixing and swaying his audience regardless of the contents of his words. His language was careless and informal. He spoke with tremendous vitality and rapidity. At one point he was timed at over three hundred words per minute. He was somewhat incoherent.

Many U.S. observers simply interpreted Castro's style as par for the Hispanic course, but then the embassy turned to substance. Although Castro touched on almost every imaginable topic during this four-hour extravaganza, most of his negative comments focused on Cuba's northern neighbor; basically, the embassy reported, "he feels that the United States is to blame for everything that is or has been wrong with Cuba since 1898." Only a few weeks earlier, the embassy would have attributed this criticism to a combination of Castro's youthful immaturity and Hispanic bloodlines or interpreted it as a device to sway his unsophisticated audience. Now bureaucrats construed his statements as accurately representing his beliefs, and "there can be little doubt that his basic attitude toward the United States is one of distrust and unfriendliness." The embassy warned Washington to "get used to the feeling of walking gently around the edges of a volcano that is liable to burst forth with sulphurous fumes at the slightest provocation."[30]

While the public executions, the anti–U.S. rhetoric, and Castro's strange behavior made watching and waiting difficult, communism had been Washington's principal worry from the beginning. Noting that many communists had lost their lives fighting the Batista tyranny, on 9 January Che Guevara had suggested that they had earned the right to participate openly in Cuban political life, and three days later, the government legalized the communist Popular Socialist Party, banned since 1952. On 13 January, Fidel Castro announced that Cuba, a Rio Treaty ally, intended to assume a new position in international affairs, equidistant between the United States and the Soviet Union, and then he floored U.S. observers with the comment that "I honestly have no faith in the OAS." Washington considered the Organization of American States a regional symbol of anticommunist solidarity; Castro considered it a waste of time: "It decides nothing. The whole thing is a lie, it is all fiction, it fundamentally does not fill any role."[31]

By mid-March, the watch-and-wait advocates had begun to lose their credibility and a schism began to emerge, with Rubottom still willing to be patient but the assistant secretary for economic affairs, Thomas Mann, warning that inaction was dangerous: "Whether extremism of the Castro type spreads will depend in large measure on our ability to demonstrate to other Latin American countries that anti-Americanism, demagoguery and administrative irresponsibility doesn't pay; that we are not so afraid of international communism that we are powerless to react."[32] Siding with Mann were the acting secretary, Herter, who told Senator Fulbright that the State Department was "concerned and distressed over the apparent resurgence of the communists in Cuba," and the CIA director, Dulles, who warned the NSC that "while the Castro regime could not be described as Communist-dominated, it was nevertheless true that the Communists have penetrated into various organizations such as labor unions, the armed forces, and others. They have a potential for even greater penetration in the future." By mid-April, the embassy was also warning Washington that communists were "successfully infiltrating various sectors of public life."[33]

IN THIS EDGY CONTEXT, Fidel Castro accepted an invitation from the American Society of Newspaper Editors to address its spring meeting in Washington. Clearly annoyed that Castro had accepted the invitation without checking with the U.S. embassy, a breach of protocol that Herter also considered "singularly bad behavior," President Eisenhower's first reaction was to deny the Cuban prime minister a visa, but both Herter and Allen Dulles argued that a denial would be unwise, since anti-Castro sentiment was stirring in Cuba and the administration should be careful not to do anything that would discourage its growth. Rather than exclude Castro, Eisenhower jumped at the State Department's suggestion that he exclude himself—he took off for a round of golf at Augusta, Georgia, leaving his subordinates to determine how much official attention to give the Cuban leader.[34] They decided that the assistant secretary, Rubottom, should meet Castro when he arrived on 15 April, that Secretary of State Herter should host a luncheon in his honor, and that Vice President Nixon and congressional leaders should meet with him at the Capitol.

Castro was pleasantly surprised by his warm public reception, repeatedly telling his finance minister, "They're *Americans*, and they like me, Rufo!" One of the participants in the Herter luncheon recalled that it went well: "There was a lot of kidding, a lot of jokes. Castro has a sense of humor, and so did Herter and Rubottom, and they were making cracks back and forth." His 2.5 hour exchange with the newspaper editors, all of it in English, was warmly received, with the *New York Times* reporting that "when he entered the ballroom, the applause was light and almost awkward. After he had finished, there was prolonged clapping." He also received good reviews for his Sunday appearance on *Meet the Press*, where in weaker English he emphasized the need for rapid improvement in the living standards of Cuba's poor and attempted to defuse the issue of delaying elections, replying to one query with his own question about the 1906 U.S. takeover of Cuba: "Why United States intervention in 1906 endured three years? Why did you need three years [before holding an election]?" When the moderator asked, "I want to know where your heart lies in the struggle between communism and democracy," Castro replied, "Really, same as democracy. Democracy is my ideal. . . . I am not Communist. I am not agreed with communism. There is no doubt for me between democracy and communism."[35]

The evaluations were mixed. After Castro met with members of the Senate Committee on Foreign Relations and the House Committee on Foreign Affairs, Senator Russell Long told reporters, "I feel reassured about a number of matters," and Representative James Fulton added his approval: "I was neutral and suspicious before, but today I was very favorably impressed. I think we should help him." Herter was more ambivalent, reporting to Eisenhower that Castro was "a most interesting individual, very much like a child in many ways, quite immature regarding problems of government." The Cuban leader spoke in English, "with restraint and considerable personal appeal," but when he switched to Spanish, he "became voluble, excited, and somewhat 'wild.'" President Eisenhower was reminded of what he had heard about Arabs—"When they begin to speak, a kind of accumulated emotional frenzy develops."[36]

But Nixon reported that Castro "has those indefinable qualities which make him a leader of men. Whatever we may think of him he is going to be a great factor in the development of Cuba and very possibly in Latin American affairs generally."[37] The State Department agreed: "It would be a serious mistake to underestimate this man. With all his appearance of naiveté, unsophistication, and ignorance on many matters, he is clearly a strong personality and a born leader of great personal courage and conviction." No one should be deceived, however: "The Castro who came to Washington was a man on his best behavior"; his actions in Cuba had clearly demonstrated that "he does not have the same idea of law and legality as we have in the United States. He appears to confuse the roar of mass audiences with the rule of the majority in his concept of democracy." After reading this memorandum, President Eisenhower decided to continue watching and waiting, writing on the bottom line: "File. We will check in a year!!"[38]

ENTER THE PRIVATE SECTOR. Castro's 1953 *History Will Absolve Me* had been worrisome, not only pledging to carry out an agrarian reform in a country where U.S. investors owned a significant amount of land but also promising workers 30 percent of the profits of all large firms, many owned by U.S. citizens, plus the outright nationalization of the U.S.-owned public utilities, which, Castro had promised, would be required to "return to the people the unlawful excess that they have been charged in their rates." But the rebel leader's subsequent statements had been reassuring; writing in *Coronet* magazine in early 1958, he had not only promised to compensate landowners for any property they might lose but had also emphasized that the agrarian reform would focus on peripheral lands tilled by tenant farmers, not on sugar estates, and while "the extension of government ownership to certain public utilities—some of them, such as the power companies, U.S.-owned—was a point of our earliest programs," he now wrote that those ideas had been shelved: "Let me say for the record that we have no plans for the expropriation or nationalization of foreign investments."[39]

And so it seemed. After meeting with local U.S. business leaders on 6 January, an embassy official cabled Washington that "they were unanimously of view that present government was much better than they had dared hope"; from the other end of the island, the U.S. consul reported that Santiago's business community was optimistic. These dispatches echoed a front-page story in the *Wall Street Journal* that used interviews to capture business sentiment: "This revolution so far has been the most pleasant surprise in years," said one official of a U.S. sugar company, while the manager of a U.S.-owned hotel added, "I've never seen such well-behaved fellows. We have not even had an ash tray stolen. They even make their own beds." A U.S. banker also saw a bright future—"The way their troops have behaved so far certainly throws dust on the fear that they are a bunch of Communists"—and another U.S. businessman needed only four words to capture what appeared to be the private-sector consensus: "They're just nice kids."[40]

But by the time of Castro's April visit to Washington, the Cuban government had enacted substantial reforms to benefit Cuba's less privileged citizens at the expense of investors. Rents had been lowered up to 50 percent, for example, and Revolutionary Law 122 had canceled the March 1957 telephone rate increase, sending a loud alarm through the New York headquarters of the International Telephone and Telegraph Company.[41] Vice President Nixon had picked up immediately on the trade-off that seemed to characterize the Cuban leader's thinking: "He said over and over that a man who worked in the sugar cane fields for three months a year and starved the rest of the year wanted a job, something to eat, a house and some clothing and didn't care a whit about whether he had freedom along with it."[42] Castro's message was that hungry peasants who had been waiting since 1940 for a promised agrarian reform should not be asked for more patience.*

---

*Article 90 of the Constitution of 1940 had prohibited latifundio but did so without specifying the amount of land that could be owned by a single individual or corporate entity. The constitution simply stated, "Se proscribe el latifundio" and "La Ley señalará el máximo de extensión que cada persona o entidad pueda poseer."

Nine days after his return to Havana, the Cuban government announced a genuine agrarian reform. Basically, large landholdings were prohibited, as was small tenant farming. The maximum size of a landholding was limited to thirty *caballerías* (about one thousand acres), with the exception of sugar, rice, and cattle lands, which could be up to one hundred *caballerías* (about thirty-three hundred acres). Article 6 prohibited tenant farming, and Article 11 prohibited sharecropping. Article 12 permitted landholdings by corporations, the typical form of U.S. ownership, but after a year, all the shareholders of any landowning corporation had to be Cuban citizens. Article 15 stipulated that only Cubans could acquire rural property in the future, and Article 12 also specified that anyone who owned shares in a corporation that grew sugarcane could not at the same time be a shareholder of a corporation that processed the cane into raw sugar, a provision that would deprive processors of about two million acres.[43] In short, U.S. investors would lose their land.

The first major expropriations occurred in late June, when 2.4 million acres of cattle land were nationalized in Camagüey province, as was all the sugar acreage owned by companies operating processing mills (*centrales*). For Camagüey, this represented two-thirds of the entire province, or an area about the size of Rhode Island and Delaware combined, and much of it was owned by U.S.-based corporations, including 40,000 acres held by the family corporation that also owned the largest single piece of private property in the United States, the King Ranch of Texas. King president Robert Kleberg had seen the expropriation coming and had already requested the assistance of his senior senator, majority leader Lyndon Johnson, who checked with the State Department and advised Kleberg to watch and wait. "No one is quite sure just how the Cuban government is going to interpret the law," he wrote, but "we are following the Cuban matter closely."[44]

Four days later, the Cuban government nationalized Kleberg's property, and the aggrieved investor fired back a blistering five-page memorandum, not to complain about losing his land but to argue that "Cuba is being dominated and run by agents of Soviet Communism." The Agrarian Reform Law was not what Castro claimed it to be—an effort to change an unjust landowning structure and reduce foreign control; rather it was "a clear-cut action to destroy democratic processes in Government, usurp individual freedom, and cripple the flow of investment capital." The action reverberated far beyond Cuba; it was "a deliberate Communist effort to block the flow of American capital to all Latin-America, create eventual chaos and soften the hemisphere for Communism." Johnson and cookie pushers in the State Department might want to watch and wait, but Kleberg wanted action: "The United States Government cannot allow this to happen."[45]

The Texas cattle baron did not confine his lobbying to the most powerful member of the U.S. Senate. He had already sought assistance from Treasury Secretary Robert Anderson, and the day before the nationalization he complained to Secretary of State Herter that for compensation purposes, Cubans were valuing the expropriated land "at ancient and absurd levels"; quite obviously, "the Castro land reform movement was Communist-inspired." Kleberg stopped dealing with these lower-level officials when the expropriation occurred the next day; instead, he headed straight to the Oval Office, where he asked President Eisenhower to suspend the Cuban sugar quota, to seize all Cuban assets in the United States, to order a display of naval power in the Caribbean, and finally to "announce that in 1898 we fought to free Cubans from tyranny—we will not stand by now and allow Communism to permanently destroy this freedom."[46]

Few U.S. investors enjoyed this type of access, of course, and even fewer had the president and the secretary of state exchanging sympathetic memos about "Bob" and his problems, but others had friends of their own. At the same time that Kleberg was seeking protection for his cattle lands, Lawrence Crosby was pulling the levers of power on behalf of U.S. sugar interests. Both as the president of a trade group (the Cuban-American Sugar Council) and as the vice chairman of the Atlántica del Golfo Sugar Company, Crosby had no trouble gaining an appointment with Thomas Mann, the assistant secretary of state for economic affairs, who then ushered Crosby into the office of undersecretary Robert Murphy, where the sugar baron emphasized that the agrarian reform would destroy the Cuban sugar industry.[47] Crosby returned to Washington in September with nine other sugar executives, including the vice president of the United Fruit Company, who, like Kleberg, warned State Department officials that the land takeover would have a demonstration effect on the rest of Latin America. The other executives agreed, with the president of the Francisco Sugar Company arguing that "if Castro succeeds unchallenged, no respect for contracts will follow throughout the area. Mr. [Huntington] Howell [of the West Indies Sugar Company] agreed with him, declaring that the situation is desperate and that they are being nibbled to pieces. Mr. [John A.] Nichols [president of the Cuban American Sugar Company] declared that agrarian reform is only a part of the gloomy picture," and no one believed the worst was over: Cuban officials "are watching the American firms like a cat watches mice."[48]

"I had a two-hour discussion last Thursday with Mr. Nic[h]ols," wrote the State Department's Cuba desk officer in early August. "It was clear that he expects the U.S. Government to see to it that the *status quo* is not too drastically altered." The Cuba files in the Eisenhower Library are packed with similar memoranda describing encounters with worried investors, and they were not conversations with lobbyists but with executives occupying the very pinnacle of corporate power.[49] At times the investors came in phalanxes, as with a late 1959 delegation from the National Foreign Trade Council, including such political heavyweights as the chairman of the board of United Fruit, the president of American and Foreign Power Company, and the treasurer of Standard Oil of New Jersey. Meeting with C. Douglas Dillon, a Wall Street investment banker then serving as acting secretary of state, their message was blunt: "If Castro stays in power, all American investments in Cuba are doomed."[50]

CLEARLY OUT OF TOUCH with this Washington lobbying, the embassy's initial evaluation of the land reform law had been surprisingly positive. After canvassing both domestic and foreign investors, the embassy cabled that sugar interests might suffer, but many members of the business community "feel that in [the] long run [the] program may be of great benefit to Cuba."[51] And in Washington most career officials now accepted the need for a moderate agrarian reform — it would shortly become a cornerstone of the Alliance for Progress — but they could not have disagreed more with the radical law enacted by Cuba's new revolutionary government. The precise reason for this disagreement will never be known, but part of the explanation surely lies in the conservative tenor of the times, and part lies in their daily confrontations with angry investors and their equally indignant congressional representatives. As the State Department's Cuba desk officer, Robert Stevenson was involved in all of these meetings, and they wore him down. In late June, he cabled Ambassador Bonsal that "everyone here is very discouraged at the failure of the Cubans to show any real interest in discussing a more moderate approach on land reform." Bonsal urged Stevenson to hold the line: "Our problem, as I see it, is to avoid being swept off our feet either by screams coming from New York and Texas or by [Castro's] semi-hysterical observations aimed at us over television here."[52] But at exactly the same time, Secretary Herter was telling the NSC that frightened U.S. business interests "were now clamoring for U.S. economic action against the Castro regime" and telling President Eisenhower that Kleberg's situation "is indeed most vexatious and frus-

trating, and I sympathize deeply with him."[53] And Kleberg was a registered Democrat.

Would sympathy lead to action? The secretary of state's job has always
been to protect and promote U.S. interests abroad, including the interests
of individual and corporate citizens, but the nation's diplomats are more
than the handmaidens of industry; they are bound by both tradition and
training to determine not only whether aggrieved investors have legitimate
concerns that require the U.S. government to seek redress but also whether
competing U.S. interests should be afforded a higher priority. Rarely has
this burden of judgment been greater than in Cuba after the fall of Batista,
for the problem was structural: given the magnitude of U.S. investments,
no Cuban government could make any significant change in the Cuban
economy without affecting U.S. interests.[54]

The situation involved not merely making one judgment or a few but
thousands, and the State Department did not automatically side with U.S.
investors. In early 1960, a memo from the policy planning staff even recommended that an officer be assigned to determine which U.S. investors
"have been exploitive and have drained off high profits while paying low
wages"; then, "if we find that returns have often been very high, it will be
good ammo for the policy of not bleeding too hard for the United States
corporations. High returns on foreign investments justified by high risks
are incompatible with a high degree of United States Government protec-
tive action."[55] Later in 1960, the embassy sent Washington a highly critical evaluation of prerevolution U.S. investors: "Engulfed in their profitable
business ventures, comfortable living and pleasure-seeking, they generally
ignored the pressures building up. They looked for stability and found it in
Batista."[56] By implication, they had gotten what they deserved.

That said, U.S. envoys in Havana had begun efforts to protect U.S. investors almost immediately after Castro's takeover, in mid-January 1959, when
the embassy expressed concern over newly imposed import restrictions,
and in early March, Ambassador Bonsal had placed these restrictions at the
very top of the agenda for his first meeting with Foreign Minister Roberto
Agramonte.[57] These initial efforts appear to have been largely pro forma,
however; the State Department's efforts on behalf of U.S. investors began
in earnest only with the May announcement of Cuba's Agrarian Reform
Law. On 1 June Ambassador Bonsal met with Agramonte to emphasize the
need for compensation; he raised the issue again the next day with Finance
Minister Rufo López-Fresquet. The State Department subsequently handed

Cuba's ambassador in Washington a formal diplomatic note requesting payment.[58]

The Cuban government never denied that compensation was required, but the Agrarian Reform Law defined "proper compensation" as equal to the assessed tax value as of October 1958, which was about 20 percent of market value, and this compensation was to be paid not in cash but in twenty-year government bonds yielding an annual interest no higher than 4.5 percent. The United States acknowledged Cuba's right to expropriate property, but Washington's reading of international law was that compensation should be prompt (within six months), adequate (full market value), and effective (in convertible currency). That position was never realistic, however; Cuba had no money to pay U.S. investors for their cattle land or to compensate those next in line—the U.S. sugar investors who had lost thirty-one mills and almost two million acres, about 7 percent of Cuba's total land.[59]

On 12 June, the day after Cuba's ambassador in Washington received the U.S. note requesting compensation, Ambassador Bonsal had one of his rare meetings with Prime Minister Castro. The encounter apparently was cordial, with Castro expressing an understanding of the U.S. position but emphasizing his government's inability to pay cash. Calling land reform "a matter of life or death," he argued that it could not be postponed until the government's reserves permitted compensation in dollars.[60] Then, three days later, came Cuba's formal reply to Washington's 11 June note, and its tone was far harsher. Once again comparing the Cuban situation with U.S. actions in occupied Japan, Minister of State Raúl Roa pointed out that "the United States Government, in promoting agrarian reform in Japan, ordered the transfer of the properties of landowners to their occupants within a period of four months, establishing as the form of indemnification the issuance of Agrarian bonds earning 3.5 percent interest and payable in annual installments over a period of twenty-five years." Cuba was doing better (twenty-year bonds at 4.5 percent), and that was the best it could manage: Batista had looted the treasury, and the revolutionary government "found itself with empty coffers and is proceeding accordingly."[61]

In the end, most U.S. corporate executives followed the lead of the chair of the board of Atlántica del Golfo Sugar Company, which lost more than four hundred thousand acres; he informed his stockholders that the Cuban government had seized the company's assets "without regard to Cuban law or traditional civilized practices" and linked his company's fate to the nation's security: "Failure to negotiate a just and adequate rate of compensation and to effect prompt settlement shall constitute the final proof that the government of Fidel Castro is unalterably committed to the collectivization of the Cuban economy, the imposition of a Soviet-style political system, Cuba's isolation from the Free World community of nations and an alliance with the Communist bloc." The president of the Compañía Azucarera Vertientes-Camagüey made no such linkage; he simply told his stockholders that they had lost everything. Robert Kleberg had no need to write a similar letter to his stockholders, since they were primarily members of his family; he simply filed a $3.1 million claim with the U.S. Foreign Claims Settlement Commission.[62]

AS CUBA'S REFORMS were alienating U.S. investors, Castro's anti-American rhetoric was taking an independent toll on the limited amount of patience possessed by everyday U.S. citizens. This generation had struggled through the depression and then fought World War II, which left the United States the undisputed leader of what everyone was now calling the Free World. The Archie Bunkers of 1959 could not have cared less about Robert Kleberg's fortune, but they heartily disliked Castro's incessant carping about the injustices the United States had heaped on Cuba. If these people thought at all about the region, they considered their country a benevolent big brother to its smaller Caribbean siblings—as did Admiral Arleigh Burke, who, when asked why the navy paid Cuba so little to rent its base at Guantánamo, replied that in addition to the rent, "of course we had provided Cuba with its freedom."[63] These everyday citizens would be interested to hear what the candidates proposed during next year's election campaign.

Meanwhile, former president Truman continued to urge patience, telling a Columbia University audience in April to watch and wait—"Let's see if he intends to install free government in Cuba. . . . I hope the boy intends to do what's right"—and advising *New York Times* readers in July that "Fidel Castro is a good young man, who has made mistakes but who seems to want to do the right thing for the Cuban people and we ought to extend our sympathy and help him." Truman's view was shared by the nation's most influential newspaper columnist, Walter Lippmann, who cautioned that "the wiser course and the more practical one is to be patient and relaxed. . . . The thing we should never do in dealing with the revolutionary countries in which the world abounds is to push them behind an iron curtain raised by ourselves."[64]

But this advice was published just after the resignation of Foreign Minister Roberto Agramonte and four other Cuban moderates, and the next day Pedro Díaz Lanz, commander of the rebel air force, fled Cuba. Two weeks later he was in Washington, warning a Senate subcommittee that Fidel Castro was a communist. The House held no similar hearing, but its members nonetheless ratcheted up the rhetoric, with South Carolina's Mendel Rivers telling his colleagues that "Castro hates this Government like the Devil hates holy water" and Tennessee's Carroll Reece asserting that Cuba "is being run by Communists." This thinking filtered into a midyear special national intelligence estimate: Castro "has little sense of the practical consequences of his impulsive attitudes and actions," it asserted, warning that "the most dangerous aspect of this situation of radical change is the opportunity it gives to the Communists."[65]

Then two weeks later another moderate, President Manuel Urrutia, was obliged to resign. His career-ending blunder had come during a 13 July television appearance during which he voiced concern about the growing strength of Cuba's communists. Four days later, Castro took advantage of the same medium to announce his resignation as prime minister because of differences with President Urrutia; specifically, Castro complained, Urrutia was worrying needlessly since the revolution was following a third position between the East and West. Having said this, there was no reason for Castro to state the obvious: if Urrutia wanted to criticize communism, he also should criticize capitalism. Better yet, he might want to say nothing at all, as befits a figurehead. The humiliated Urrutia resigned and Castro named a longtime member of the communist Popular Socialist Party, Osvaldo Dorticós, as Cuba's new president.

His appointment threw the fat into the fire. Two weeks earlier, Ambassador Bonsal had insisted that he was "not prepared at this time to submit a finding that revolutionary government is heading in direction of Communism"; now, with Dorticós's appointment, the embassy had to acknowledge the obvious—that "Castro is more definitely committed than ever to public position of non-persecution of communists."[66] Bonsal continued to advise forbearance, but John Calvin Hill Jr., a recent arrival in the State Department's Bureau of Inter-American Affairs, found that position silly. "I want somebody who knows how Communism is behind the Iron Curtain," Rubottom had told the deputy undersecretary responsible for personnel assignments, "so, he assigned to me a fellow named John Hill who had been in Guatemala, and who before Guatemala had been in Rumania."[67] For several crucial years—from late 1951 to early 1955—Hill had led the U.S. embassy's political section in Guatemala, and from mid-1958 until mid-1960 he sat next door to Rubottom, serving primarily as the assistant secretary's "communism" expert and focusing on Cuba.

As Rubottom recalled, Hill "opened up a lot of things to me that I had not been aware of prior to that time." Hill's enlightenment led Rubottom to question Ambassador Bonsal's analysis. In distinct contrast to the embassy's claim that the revolution reflected the aspirations of most Cubans, Hill argued that the only Cubans who supported the revolution were a "minority of the middle class constituting young radical students and ex-students and intellectuals, almost always Marxist—Nationalist—and anti-American oriented and sometimes also of Communist coloration." Cuba desk officer Stevenson recalled that "we all thought there might be a possibility of working with the Castro government, except for John Calvin Hill, God rest his soul. He was the only one."[68]

But Hill was not the only apprehensive U.S. official to gain Rubottom's ear. Another was Whiting Willauer, a political appointee then serving as U.S. ambassador to Costa Rica and, like Hill, one of the officials who had helped engineer the overthrow of Guatemala's Arbenz government in 1954. Willauer and the legendary Claire Chennault had founded China's Civil Air Transport—later Air America—and then secretly sold it to the CIA. With Willauer serving as the airline's president, Air America had maintained its cover by flying regular commercial flights while assisting the French and anticommunist groups with airdrops in Indochina, especially Laos. In early 1954, Willauer's very special skills at covert airborne support were needed in Central America, and he had been named ambassador to Honduras, arriving in Tegucigalpa in March 1954, three months before the Honduras-based offensive by Colonel Carlos Castillo Armas against Guatemala's democratic government. Now, in late April 1959, several months before Urrutia's ouster, Ambassador Willauer told Rubottom that the situation in the Caribbean "is going to get much worse very rapidly unless the Communist beachhead in Cuba is liquidated."[69]

Given his continuous access to the assistant secretary, Hill also probably alerted Rubottom to the congressional testimony of another cold warrior, Spruille Braden, the former anti-Batista ambassador to Cuba who now, having seen the bearded alternative, had decided that Batista had been not so bad after all: "Batista was, if you please, a bad boil or an ulcer, not a malignancy of some kind. An ulcer is bad and disagreeable but now you have a cancer that will kill Cuba." Braden told a Senate subcommittee, "I pray with all my heart, body, and soul, that the Communists and their most useful tool to date, Fidel Castro, may be ejected from their control of Cuba." He was especially worried about a revolutionary spillover across the Windward Passage to Hispaniola, where vehemently anticommunist dictator Rafael Trujillo still governed the Dominican Republic. If he were to be overthrown, as Castro promised, then "Haiti goes completely. That poor little country is defenseless anyway, but you have the Negro population there which under Communist domination would be very serious."[70]

WITH U.S. INVESTORS clamoring for action and with the administration's own cold warriors warning of a communist takeover, the slide from watch-and-wait to active opposition began to accelerate. As Washington's trees began to lose their leaves and Cuba's sugar mills began to prepare for the harvest, the embassy warned that in Cuba "we may be approaching [a] showdown between different groups supporting Castro and struggling for his approval."[71] It came in mid-October, triggered by Florida-based counterrevolutionary forces who launched a series of air attacks on Cuban sugar mills.

Cuba's immediate response came on 16 October, when the Ministry of National Defense was dissolved and replaced by a new Ministry of the Revolutionary Armed Forces, with Raúl Castro as its commander—"a disturbing development," reported Ambassador Bonsal, suggesting "further expansion of control of extremists at [the] expense [of] moderates." A week later came the resignation of one of the revolutionary government's highest-ranking moderates, Major Huber Matos, the military commander of Camagüey province. Matos sought to protest the military reorganization and the general direction of the revolution, but his resignation came at precisely the moment U.S.-based exiles dropped incendiary bombs on sugar mills in three different raids. Then on the day of the third raid, just after Matos's resignation, the former head of Castro's air force, who had fled Cuba in June, Pedro Díaz Lanz, flew over Havana, dropping antirevolutionary leaflets. The unsuccessful attempt to shoot him down left two bystanders dead and forty-five wounded.[72] The next day a Florida-based aircraft strafed a passenger train in Las Villas.

The Cuban government then announced the formation of a People's Militia and called for a mass rally in front of the Presidential Palace, where Castro lashed out at the United States. The embassy reported that this 26 October speech "listed virtually all local American interests as items which were not in the interests of Cuba. He talked of controlling utilities and of new mining and petroleum laws. He got approval from audience for reestablishment of revolutionary tribunals. He got approval of execution of

Matos and others. He repeatedly mentioned Cuban people fighting to last man in caves and tunnels if necessary to repel foreign invasion." And, the embassy noted, the "crowd was with him to the last man."[73]

The State Department dismissed every one of Castro's charges as "utterly unfounded"—the Díaz Lanz flight, for example, had come from one of Florida's many small, unguarded airstrips. Foreign Minister Raúl Roa replied that "the Cuban people know, from bitter experience, that if the Government of the United States sets in motion its formidable system of vigilance and defense it is almost impossible to conspire in its territory, traffic in arms, leave its ports illegally, or take off in airplanes without proper papers."[74] "Every Cuban from Fidel downward is convinced that the United States is not making the efforts that should be made to prevent these bombings," Herbert Matthews told his editors, and "I agree entirely with the Cubans on this point." So did Secretary Herter, who complained to both the Department of the Treasury and the attorney general, and more than a hundred federal agents were sent to Florida in what proved to be a futile attempt to stop the flights.[75]

"I don't know exactly what the difficulty is," President Eisenhower had told a press conference two days after Castro's 26 October speech. "After all, their principal market is right here, their best market. You would think they would want good relationships." Roa had an answer to that, too: "Undoubtedly, the United States is an excellent customer for Cuba, but it is just as true that Cuba is a much better customer of the United States."[76]

Those searching for the straw that broke the camel's back can find it in Castro's 26 October speech. A few days later, Ambassador Bonsal told finance minister López-Fresquet, "I had come to the reluctant conclusion that I was now accredited to an unfriendly Cuban Government." A key moderate, López-Fresquet seemed ready to throw in the towel, telling Bonsal "that developments of recent weeks represented a definite triumph for the radical 'Sierra' element of the Government (especially Raul Castro and Che Guevara)" and that "Castro's temperament and tactics closely resemble those of Hitler." The State Department had already been debating a change in U.S. policy, and the consensus that had emerged in September was best captured by Assistant Secretary Rubottom: "Perhaps we erred in not striking back earlier." Castro's 26 October speech a month later removed the "perhaps."[77] A corner had been turned; the watching and waiting was over.

On 5 November, Secretary Herter handed President Eisenhower a revised policy proposal for Cuba. Patience, goodwill, and cooperation had failed: "There is no reasonable basis to found our policy on a hope that Castro will voluntarily adopt policies and attitudes consistent with minimum United States security requirements and policy interests." Since "the prolonged continuation of the Castro regime in Cuba in its present form would have serious adverse effects on the United States position in Latin America and corresponding advantages for international Communism," Herter requested permission to begin "a step-by-step development of coherent opposition." The president initialed his approval on 9 November, and a few days later the British ambassador reported to Whitehall about a conversation with Allen Dulles in which the CIA director said that "something might be made of an opposition consisting of elements outside, and inside, Cuba. But the time for that had not yet come, though for our most confidential information, he was already making some contact with these people for possible future use."[78]

The embassy had also given up. Shown a copy of Secretary Herter's policy proposal, the chief of the embassy's political section responded immediately that "long continuation of the Castro Government . . . is not something which would be in our best interests." Ambassador Bonsal cabled his concession the same day: "My previous view of Castro as highly emotional individual yet generally rational and often cold-bloodedly and cynically playing the demagogue replaced by opinion that evident cynicism goes hand in hand with definite mental unbalance at times." Predicting that Cuba's revolutionary government would not last long—"months rather than years"—Bonsal urged restraint only because open U.S. opposition would inflame nationalist sentiment.[79]

Embassy officials then sat down and prepared a three-count indictment. The first charge was that the revolutionary government was threatening Washington's leadership of Latin America by engaging "in a concerted, malicious, and cynical attack on the United States." As Rubottom later recalled, at this point "it didn't make much difference whether Castro was a Communist or not. He was . . . bitterly hostile to the United States," and that hostility compromised inter-American solidarity on Cold War issues. The embassy noted that Castro not only "rejects the concept that hemisphere defense under U.S. leadership is necessary" but also "favors a greater role for Latin America, if possible under Cuba's leadership, in world affairs, though not as a component part of the Western community of nations but rather as an independent force, associated closely with the Afro-Asian bloc."[80]

The second charge in the embassy's indictment was economic irresponsibility: the regime had "adopted sweeping socio-economic measures that may cause serious damage to the economy." It might be difficult to convince a Cuban jury to convict on this charge, however, because, as a State Department report noted two weeks later, "in the eleven months that Castro has been in power the standard of living of low-income groups appears, on the basis of available statistics, to have improved." If the charge of economic irresponsibility were to stick, then, the revolution's reforms had to be linked to graver crimes. One referred back to the first count: Cuba's reforms threatened U.S. economic interests throughout Latin America. As Rubottom warned acting secretary of state Douglas Dillon in a year-end conversation, "If Cuba gets by with the actions she is taking against American property owners, our whole private enterprise approach abroad would be in serious danger."[81]

The indictment's crucial third count was a capital crime: sedition. Within Cuba, "great freedom has been allowed the local Communist party, and the Castro regime has itself shown a striking affinity for some Communist ideas and practices." Outside Cuba, the revolutionary government had shown a "friendly attitude toward Communist countries, including Communist China."[82]

No attempt was made to separate the first count (undermining U.S. policy) from the third (communism)—to do so would have been unthinkable in Cold War Washington, where security was conceptualized as a question of balancing power and where international relations was often compared to a playground seesaw. For an imbalance to occur, it was not necessary that a nation defect to the other side; all that was needed to upset the balance was for one participant, even a lightweight one, to opt out of the game.[83] In this symbolic sense, a neutral Cuba would have the same effect on U.S. security as a communist Cuba.

On 13 January, at the very beginning of the revolution, Fidel Castro had suggested that Cuba would adopt a position equidistant from the United States and the Soviet Union. Like everyone else in Washington, the members of the House subcommittee responsible for Latin America had been astounded by this decision to jump off the seesaw: "We, together with other free nations, are engaged in a titanic battle against totalitarian communism to preserve the fundamental freedoms which we all cherish. We hope Latin Americans share our ideological objectives. Witness our shock when it was recently reported that the Revolutionary Government of Cuba planned to be neutral." As an example of what this decision meant, U.S. officials cited Roa's September speech to the U.N. General Assembly, which focused on the use of force in international relations and criticized the behavior of the United States (for Guatemala), China (for Tibet), and the Soviet Union (for Hungary). And this criticism was nothing when compared to the votes—fifty-four of them in that year's General Assembly, with Cuba voting in opposition to the United States thirty-nine times.[84] One of those thirty-nine votes was Washington's litmus test: Would the mainland communist government or Taiwan represent China? Cuba abstained.

Now uncertain about what should be done to change the course of the Cuban Revolution, Ambassador Bonsal simply warned Washington about what *not* to do: "Drastic measures by the United States to show its displeasure with some aspects of the regime, such as reduction of the Cuban sugar quota, would be more likely to aggravate anti-American attitudes than to diminish them." U.S. officials should not forget, he continued, that "Castro continues to enjoy the support of the masses." That support prompted Calvin Hill to question Cubans' judgment: arguing that normal human beings break off abusive relationships, he told Rubottom that there was something wrong with the island's population—"a marked emotional reluctance among many Cubans to face up to the fact that their union with Castro is turning out badly."[85]

A DIFFICULT YEAR WAS ALMOST OVER. "I have been received here with great cordiality," Ambassador Bonsal had written from Havana soon after his arrival in February; "my reception has certainly been as warm and cordial as anyone could wish." Bonsal was never insulted or otherwise mistreated, but by year end his reports clearly showed the strain of daily disappointment, especially his disappointment with Fidel Castro. "World history since the end of World War II in particular means nothing to him. The fact, for instance, that our country of 160 million, Cuba's nearest neighbor, has made and is making immense sacrifices on behalf of the defense of the free world against the aggressive forces of international communism apparently is wasted on him." But Bonsal continued to recognize Castro as a very special man. "We are certainly confronted with one of the most remarkable leaders of men in modern times," he continued. Castro "possesses extraordinary mental and physical powers. I do not know of anyone in my now rather long period of active Foreign Service who has made a deeper impression on me. He is a man in whom many millions believe with all their hearts."[86]

As Bonsal was composing this year-end report in Havana, the members of the NSC were going around the table in Washington and voicing their own disappointments. Secretary Herter called Cuba "a first-rate headache," Vice President Nixon said that Castro's government "was being driven toward Communism," and deputy CIA director Richard Bissell noted that "only one top official now in the Cuban Government was without some sort of communist affiliation." Meanwhile, the Office of Naval Intelligence was reporting that "the outlook for improved Cuban-US relations diminishes daily," and Assistant Secretary Rubottom was writing that the United States "could no longer tolerate the continued harassment of American property owners in Cuba, the failure of that government to seek a friendly solution to the problem of expropriation, and the vicious, unjustified attacks by the Castro government on the United States." The year's final national intelligence estimate concluded that "the outlook for US relations with Cuba is dark."[87]

*We no longer believe in your philosophy of exploitation
and privilege. We no longer believe in your philosophy
of gold, the gold you rob from the work of other peoples.
We no longer are willing to submit to the orders of your
ambassadors. We no longer are disposed to follow in
tow your reactionary policy, which is the enemy of
human progress.*
—Fidel Castro, August 1960

*We who in living memory rescued the island from
medieval bondage; we who have given order, vitality,
technical wisdom and wealth are now being damned
for our civilizing and cooperative virtues!*
—Senator Karl Mundt, August 1960

5

1960 THE YEAR OF PUSHING AND SHOVING

"We will bury you." So Nikita Khrushchev had boasted in late 1956, and a year later the Soviet Union had won the race into space. When the United States placed a satellite in orbit two months later, a relieved Fulgencio Batista cabled President Eisenhower that the Cuban leader, for one, had never doubted "the security which is found in American resources and its scientific capacity to surpass the achievements being made by the Russians." But nearly everyone else conceded that the Russian word "Sputnik" now identified the cutting edge of space technology, and that fact alone almost guaranteed that the 1960 election would focus on America's fading global supremacy. "Most informed people agree that the Soviets are ahead of us technologically," warned General James Gavin, who popularized the term "missile lag," and the Eisenhower administration's public response, intended to reassure, had the opposite effect; in early 1960 the grandfatherly president reluctantly acknowledged that "the Soviets have made some very spectacular achievements" and then followed with a lame admonition—"I don't think that we should begin to bow our heads in shame." His next sentence sounded even more defensive: "Our country is not asleep, and it is not incapable of doing these things."[1]

Then why weren't the Republicans doing them? Clearly aware of the issue being handed him on a silver platter, Democratic presidential candidate John Kennedy reminded voters a few months later that "the first passengers to return safely from a trip to outer space were named Strelka and Balka, not Rover or Fido or Checkers." Not content to drag Vice President Richard Nixon's dog into the debate, Kennedy also made fun of his rival's well-publicized kitchen debate at a U.S. trade exhibit in the Soviet Union, telling a campaign audience that the best Nixon "could do in that Moscow kitchen was to wag his finger in Mr. Khrushchev's face and say: 'You may be ahead of us in rocket thrust, but we're ahead of you in color television.'" Then, in the next sentence, came Cuba: "He tells us now that economic aid to Cuba and Latin America five years ago would have prevented the rise of Castro—but he neglects to say that he was there five years ago and didn't do anything about it."[2] In this election year, Cuba was about to become for the Republicans what the loss of China had been for the Democrats eight years earlier—a political albatross.

IN CUBA, the new year began as the old one had ended, with more bad news for U.S. investors—the expropriation of another seventy thousand acres of U.S.-owned sugar lands, half belonging to the United Fruit Company, whose executives maintained exceptionally close ties to the Eisenhower administration. Focusing on Cuba's promise to pay in bonds rather than cash, the U.S. protest note on 11 January was delivered to Cuban authorities just as counterrevolutionary exiles were escalating their occasional bombing of Cuban targets into a concerted effort to destroy the sugar harvest, hitting several sugar mills the day after the note's delivery. A week later, an airplane dropped four bombs on Havana, while another dropped incendiary white phosphorus on a Las Villas sugar mill; the next week, Camagüey was hit by five aerial bombings and Oriente by another three. Since all of the attacks had been launched from Florida, it was Cuba's turn to lodge a protest, which Fidel Castro delivered in a blistering public attack on 18 January, lashing out at both the counterrevolutionaries and their supporters, which he vaguely identified as "international oligarchies" and "foreign tyrannies." Asked about Castro's charge, a seemingly puzzled President Eisenhower told reporters, "We don't know really the foundation of these accusations."[3]

That assertion is difficult to believe. Months earlier, immediately after the exiles' first aerial leafleting of Havana, Assistant Secretary of State R. Richard Rubottom Jr. had requested a coordinated effort by state and federal authorities to stop any further flights, calling them a needless complication for U.S. policy. Secretary of State Christian Herter had taken Rubottom's request to the president, who then assured reporters that Attorney General William P. Rogers was "using every kind of reinforced means he can to make sure that there is no violation of this kind." That was news to the attorney general, who asked the president at a meeting of the National Security Council (NSC) to explain "what our policy was with respect to stopping anti-Castro elements preparing some action against Cuba from American territory." Here, away from the TV cameras, Eisenhower was not puzzled; the meeting's minutes indicate that he immediately cut off any discussion: "The President said it was perhaps better not to discuss this subject. The anti-Castro agents who should be left alone were being indicated."[4] The flights kept occurring; Cuba kept protesting.

Ambassador Philip Bonsal had spent much of 1959 receiving these protests and passing them to Washington, regularly adding his view that the attacks were inflicting grave damage on U.S.-Cuban relations. Now a worried embassy again cabled that "regardless of origin of aircraft, large portion of public convinced they come from United States." Two days later came a second cable, reporting that "twin engine aircraft painted white with red stripes flew over general area of Centrals Adelaida and Punta Alegre beginning about 1530 yesterday, dropping incendiary bombs and starting extensive fires. . . . Consulate Santiago reports officials of Cuban American Sugar company have called to say that same or another unidentified aircraft appeared about ten o'clock this morning, attempting to start fires in Chaparra Delicias area." The Eisenhower administration issued its standard denial of any responsibility, but on 18 February a plane exploded while trying to bomb the España *central*, and when documents found in the wreckage revealed the pilot to be a U.S. citizen, Robert Ellis, the administration finally launched a concerted effort to halt the flights. The president issued an executive order conferring extraordinary powers on the attorney general to seize arms and aircraft, he called General Elwood Quesada out of retirement to lead a government-wide effort to stop the raids, and at a cabinet meeting he instructed all federal agencies to help interdict and prevent the illegal flights.[5]

The Federal Aviation Administration promptly created a flight information center in Miami and began contacting aircraft rental agencies throughout the Southeast to request cooperation, but results were slow in coming: on 21 February, another plane bombed the Havana suburbs of Regla and Cojimar; on 23 February, planes dropped white phosphorus on harvested cane in Matanzas and Las Villas; on 24 February a similar attack occurred on the Trinidad *central*; on 2 March white phosphorus was dropped for a second time on the Washington *central* in Las Villas and on the Chaparra and Delicias *centrales* in Oriente; on 8 March more bombs were dropped in Las Villas; on 2 April Havana and Matanzas were bombed; and on 23 April bombs fell on several *centrales* around Bauta.[6]

The embassy also requested that the most notorious perpetrators be moved out of striking distance, a request championed by Rubottom, who wrote to Herter that "many Cubans find it increasingly hard to reconcile our professions of friendship for the Cuban people with the continued presence in Florida of persons commonly regarded in Cuba as butchers guilty of unspeakable atrocities against the Cuban people. Bonsal on numerous occasions has expressed his opinion that the presence of these individuals adds to the difficulties of his task and has recommended that the Department make every effort to remove them from the area." Rolando Masferrer soon became one of the few major exile figures to be ordered by the Immigration and Naturalization Service to stay out of Florida and at least 150 miles from the coast of any other state bordering the Gulf of Mexico, but the ban was overturned a few months later by the U.S. District Court in Miami.[7]

Although it wanted the flights stopped, the embassy considered the Cuban government's protest language "arrogant, insolent and provocative," and Rubottom agreed. In January, he recalled Bonsal "in view of the stepped-up campaign of calumny against the United States Government by the Government of Cuba which had descended to the point of insulting and derogatory public statements by Prime Minister Castro." Rubottom insisted that the recall "is required in order to maintain the dignity and prestige of the United States Government (which is a particularly important concept in Latin American eyes)."[8]

When he arrived back in the nation's capital, Bonsal discovered that any decision about U.S. policy toward the Cuban Revolution was being complicated enormously by U.S. officials' inability to understand Fidel Castro's popularity. He was clearly popular; as Vice President Nixon had noted after their meeting a year earlier, Castro "has those indefinable qualities which make him a leader of men," and Nixon was not alone in his evaluation; everyone could see what the Canadian ambassador saw in early 1960: the revolution's "principal asset is the undoubted devotion to Castro of the great majority of the people. Devotion is not too strong a word; anyone who has seen and heard the reaction of a Cuban crowd when Castro appears on a balcony is left in no doubt at all that the unlettered multitude regards him quite simply and sincerely as a Messiah."[9]

Washington has always had trouble understanding this type of leadership. The U.S. political system to date had specialized in producing very white men in very dark suits whose politics were calculated to attract the modal voter, who above all else was strongly averse to anything radical, such as a beard. Given this preference for muted, moderate politics, the initial U.S. reaction to Castro's ebullient personality had been to label his charismatic appeal as an indicator of Cubans' immaturity; Cuban politics differed from U.S. politics because Cubans differed from the solid voters of Peoria. In Cuba, "the amorphous mass representing the lower classes has characteristically been on the side of whoever was in power," the embassy reported, with "the 'intellectual' issues of human rights, representative government, free enterprise, etc., having little bearing on their reactions." Instead, Cubans were said to be "guided largely by their emotions and full-stomach psychology." At about this time, Rubottom told his colleagues that "until Latin Americans, and especially Cubans, can approach politics with reason, we will always have problems in Cuba and elsewhere."[10]

Fidel Castro was a perfect example of what such a political culture could produce, and his "foreign tyrannies" speech on 18 January had been mild when compared to a television appearance two days later, where the Cuban leader spent five hours firing salvo after salvo at every subject that displeased him, touching at one point on Spanish dictator Francisco Franco. Within minutes, the program's startled viewers saw a furious Spanish ambassador storm into the TV studio to demand an apology, prompting Castro's heated defense of his accusation. With the two men close to blows, the studio director wisely took the program off the air; when it resumed a few minutes later, a calmer Castro explained that the Spanish ambassador had been escorted back to his embassy and given twenty-four hours to leave Cuba — subject, of course, to the agreement of President Osvaldo Dorticós, who was seated in the studio audience. Dorticós nodded his approval. Castro then wondered aloud whether Cuba's ambassador to Spain should be recalled; Dorticós thought that was a good idea, too.[11]

Peoria had never seen anything like this, and the State Department's Bureau of Intelligence and Research was having trouble deciding whether Castro was a reflection of Cuban culture or just plain crazy. In one early 1960 report, the bureau took both views, beginning on the former tack by arguing that Castro had "a typical Latin temperament" and then, two pages later, characterizing the Cuban leader as "a vain egocentric with a decided messianic complex which some observers believe borders on paranoia." Eisenhower preferred the latter interpretation, as Bonsal discovered when he briefed the president in late January. But both men agreed that "we should not punish the whole Cuban people for the acts of one abnormal man," and early 1960 was not yet time for an open condemnation. Eisenhower was therefore more diplomatic at a press conference the next day, telling reporters, "We are not going to be party to reprisals or anything of that kind" in response to Castro's 18 January criticism of foreign tyrannies.[12]

IN LATE FEBRUARY, Cuba finally responded to the 11 January U.S. note protesting the uncompensated seizure of U.S. property by proposing the creation of a commission to discuss the two nations' differences, including compensation, with the only condition that the United States take no hostile action during the discussions.[13] Washington's prompt rejection of this proposal reflected the fact that Cuba had already taken hostile action: on 4 February, the first deputy chair of the Council of Ministers of the Soviet Union, Anastas Mikoyan, had arrived in Havana with a scientific, cultural, and technical exhibition, and before departing he signed an agreement to purchase about 20 percent of Cuba's sugar crop for each of the next five years.[14]

The impact on Washington was profound. Senator Fulbright's Committee on Foreign Relations immediately held a closed-door hearing at which the State Department reported that the Soviet purchase had been negotiated at world market prices, about half the price paid by the United States, but that Mikoyan had also offered Cuba a one-hundred-million-dollar credit, half for the purchase of Soviet machinery and petroleum. Even more worrisome were Moscow's agreement to send unspecified but ominous-sounding "technicians" to Cuba and an announcement that the two countries would soon resume diplomatic relations, which they did in early May. "A great propaganda victory for the USSR," is how the CIA characterized the accord; now "there is little hope we can work out a satisfactory relationship with the Cuban Government."[15]

The Soviet trade agreement unified Washington. CIA officials had predicted something similar, and its occurrence gave them an upper hand over the dwindling group advocating patience, whose members now threw in the towel. Assistant Secretary Rubottom conceded that "for all practical purposes Castro could be in the employ of the Soviet Government," and a few days later Undersecretary Livingston Merchant made the State Department's change of heart official, informing the NSC that the Cuba problem had become "the most difficult and dangerous in all the history of our relations with Latin America, possibly in all our foreign relations."[16] And this statement was made *before* Mikoyan's visit.

Now how should the United States respond? Just after Mikoyan left Cuba, the State Department's director of policy planning instructed a staff member to walk down to the fourth floor and pick the brains of the Latin American bureau. He came back empty-handed: "The general view within ARA is one of defeatism, that nothing can be done until a new Administration takes a fresh look at our Latin American policy with a view to making departures from existing attitudes and policies."[17]

That was not helpful. A new administration was a political eternity away, events were moving rapidly in Cuba, and asserting that nothing could be done was simply unacceptable. Something *had* to be done, even if the Bureau of Inter-American Affairs had decided to take itself out of the game, and the policy vacuum was quickly filled by men such as Admiral Arleigh Burke, the chief of naval operations, who recommended that the United States "assist rebel groups covertly to overthrow the present government." He had no difficulty convincing his colleagues on the Joint Chiefs of Staff, who together recommended that the United States "initiate now a program of positive action to re-establish a stable, friendly, non-communist government in Cuba."[18]

Two days later, on 4 March, the French freighter *La Coubre*, carrying a shipload of Belgian arms, exploded in Havana's harbor, killing seventy-five Cuban dockworkers. "This was sabotage and not an accident," asserted an outraged Fidel Castro at the funeral, placing responsibility for the blast squarely on Washington: "Aircraft piloted by criminal mercenaries take off from the United States, and that government, which is so concerned with preventing us from getting arms, has been unable to prevent these flights." The U.S. goal was obvious, he said: "They want us to be defenseless. And why do they want us to be defenseless? So that they can force us to yield, so that they can subjugate us." Warning that "anybody who attacks us should know quite clearly that the Cubans of today are not the Cubans of 1898 and 1899," Castro pledged that "this generation will fight to the last drop of blood."[19]

Castro's comment about Washington "preventing us from getting arms" referred not to the Belgian arms or to the U.S. arms embargo that had begun the previous October but to a highly public U.S. effort to convince Britain to turn down Cuba's request to purchase Hawker Hunter jet fighters. The

United States clearly did not want to see jet fighters anywhere in the region, but CIA director Allen Dulles had a special reason to halt this particular sale, telling the British ambassador that "he hoped that any refusal by us to supply arms would directly lead to a Soviet bloc offer to supply. Then he might be able to do something."[20] Eager to export, the British needed a substantial amount of arm-twisting, but in the end they agreed to Washington's request. The Cuban government complained bitterly that "the Government of the United States has the right to refuse to grant export licenses for arms and other implements of war to whomever it pleases, but what it cannot do is use its influence with other governments, on the pretext of cooperating in the maintenance of peace in the Caribbean area, to prevent a friendly government from acquiring, for purely defensive reasons, the aircraft it needs."[21]

The episode demoralized many State Department moderates. The Cuba desk officer recalled that after Cubans blamed the United States for the explosion, "from then on, there really was no talking," and the embassy informed Washington that no hope remained of establishing a satisfactory relationship with the revolutionary government. Dulles said the same thing to the NSC, and after a brief discussion, national security adviser Gordon Gray summarized the new U.S. policy: "Our objective is to bring another government to power in Cuba." The problem, he continued, was that "there is no apparent alternative."[22]

The CIA had been developing one. A product of the agency's Western Hemisphere Division, led by Colonel J. C. King, the plan had its genesis six weeks before the explosion, at a 13 January meeting of the NSC subcommittee responsible for covert action—the 5412 Committee—where Dulles suggested that "covert contingency planning to accomplish the fall of the Castro government might be in order." Between that mid-January meeting and Castro's early March funeral outburst, King's division prepared "A Program of Covert Action against the Castro Regime," which Dulles presented to President Eisenhower and his principal advisers in mid-March.[23] Budgeted at a modest $4.4 million for the first eighteen months, it was a four-part effort to launch a propaganda offensive, to create a civilian opposition outside Cuba, to set up an anti-Castro underground within Cuba, and to develop a military force outside Cuba that would land at the Bay of Pigs thirteen months later. The president needed no convincing but merely emphasized the need to keep the plan secret: "Everyone must be prepared to swear that he has not heard of it." One way to ally suspicion was to send Bonsal back to Cuba ("as good a cover as we could have," said Herter), but just one more aggressive comment by the Cubans and he would be recalled again, never to return: "This is the last effort at reasonableness."[24]

The propaganda offensive began immediately, with the CIA not only purchasing time on commercial radio stations whose broadcasts reached Cuba from the United States, Guatemala, and Venezuela but also installing its own radio station on the Swan Islands off the coast of Honduras, with plans to place another in the Bahamas and a third on a ship anchored off Cuba. The agency also began producing a U.S. version of the Cuban magazine *Avance* for airdropping into Cuba, while a CIA-controlled group inside Cuba was already printing counterrevolutionary broadsides. The offensive also included Latin American lecture tours by Cuban exiles, and when President Dorticós and Foreign Minister Roa visited six Latin American capitals in May, the CIA arranged for "every manner of unpleasant and embarrassing question to be thrown at them."[25]

At the same time, Secretary Herter outlined "an accelerated program to prepare Latin American public and governmental opinion to support the United States in possible OAS action." The goal was to ready Latin Americans for a resolution similar to the 1954 Caracas Declaration, which had justified the U.S.-supported invasion of Guatemala by dissident military forces. Since U.S. officials again planned to base their proposed OAS resolution on the collective-defense provision of the 1947 Inter-American Treaty of Reciprocal Assistance, they immediately began preliminary discussions with every Rio Treaty ally, revealing an outline of the U.S. plan to nineteen Latin American governments, some of whose abilities to keep secrets have never been much better than Washington's. Not surprisingly, Cuban authorities soon learned of the effort, and Castro's reaction was to abrogate the Rio agreement—"We do not feel bound by this treaty," he announced in late March. The White House responded that "it would be difficult to overstate the amazement and concern with which we view this statement."[26]

U.S. INVESTORS CONTINUED to add their concerns to the policy discussions. According to Julius Shepard, owner of the Hotel Capri, "When [Castro] came in, the first thing he did was order me to accept 200 soldiers, house and feed them in the hotel, with the promise that I would be reimbursed. This went on for several months, until my iceboxes and refrigerators were empty." Although Shepard obviously could not use the occupied rooms for paying customers, "I had to meet the payroll, regardless, but when I finally told them I did not have any money, they said, 'You go to Miami and get some money,' and like a fool, I did." After more than a year,

on the afternoon of May 11, 1960, an official of the Cuban revolutionary government, accompanied by two armed soldiers entered the Hotel
Capri, the hotel I began building in 1957 and which opened in November
1958, and demanded the keys to my apartment, my office, and my safe,
saying that everything now belonged to the revolutionary government of
Cuba. I was told I could leave the country, but I must take nothing with
me, since it no longer belonged to me. Being unable to obtain transportation that night, my family and I stayed until the next day when we
were able to get air travel reservations.

As a final indignity, "I was charged $30 for spending the night in my own
hotel."[27]

Shepard's experience was far from unique; Cuba was the largest uncompensated nationalization in U.S. history. A similar story was told by the
Mississippi-based Karpark Corporation, which never received a dime for
the seven thousand parking meters it had recently installed in Havana—a
$686,000 loss—and the meters themselves could not be repossessed since
the Cubans, unaccustomed to paying for on-street parking, had destroyed
every one of them in the celebration following Batista's departure. A similar
tale was told by Frederick Swetland, a rancher from the Isle of Pines, who
reported that "we got our silver out and we got out some of our books and
everything else we left behind, including the dog."[28]

The State Department was the first contact for many of these aggrieved
investors, including the general manager of the Miami-based Dixie Export
Company, whose two-hundred-thousand-dollar inventory in a Havana
warehouse had been confiscated. As he later complained to President
Eisenhower, all he received from State Department officials was "a vast
amount of press releases and such statements as 'our government, through
its regular channels, is abreast of the situation in Cuba.' As losers we find
such statements to be far from consoling and certainly not indicative of
some government action worthy of the strongest nation on earth." Other
investors did what Walter Reynolds did when the Cuban government seized
his bat guano fertilizer company—they went to their congressional representatives, who, in turn, demanded the State Department's assistance. The
result was innumerable telephone calls such as that from Senator James O.
Eastland, who dialed Rubottom in early April to say that he "totally dis-
agrees with our Cuban policy"—"it is appeasement down there and a lot of
others up here [on Capitol Hill] feel the same."[29]

What impact did such a call from one of the Senate's most powerful members have? It probably helped solidify the administration's hostility, but that hostility would have existed anyway, and Eastland's action certainly had no effect on immediate tactics: in mid-1960, the State Department instructed Ambassador Bonsal to stop seeking compensation for U.S. investors because "it would set us back if he attempted any reconciliation effort at this time."[30] Upset investors and members of Congress nonetheless kept prodding: one list of proposed sanctions handed to State Department officials by the private-sector Business Advisory Council contained eight recommendations, including a cut in Cuba's sugar quota and a program to assist "opposition elements to over-throw the Castro regime." Replying that he was not ready for such drastic action, Rubottom agreed that "we should plan to throw the economic book at the Cubans."[31]

And a weighty book it was. It included a number of minor but nonetheless damaging moves such as recalling the Department of Agriculture's on-site inspectors who provided expedited entry of Cuban fruits and vegetables into the United States. The State Department also terminated the small Point Four technical assistance missions in agriculture and civil aviation and immediately thereafter complained publicly about Cuba's "calculated campaign to misrepresent and denigrate the special economic relationships between our two countries."[32]

This was only the warm-up for the first eyeball-to-eyeball dispute, which developed out of Cuba's need to refine the Soviet petroleum it had obtained in Mikoyan's February trade agreement, and it triggered one of those interesting cases of the government seeking help from the private sector, not vice versa. In late April, officials from Standard Oil of New Jersey (Esso) had asked State Department officials for help with an unrelated problem of its Cuban subsidiary, which had imported and refined crude oil and then sold it to Cuban consumers, who paid in pesos; the company wanted the Cuban central bank to convert those pesos into dollars, but the bank was refusing to do so. The State Department could offer little assistance; in the course of the meeting, however, Esso executives mentioned that "they might be requested by the Cuban Government to run Russian crude through their Cuban refinery," intimating that a plan to handle that problem was being prepared elsewhere in Washington.[33]

This information was news to the State Department, and two days later national security adviser Gordon Gray filled in acting secretary of state Douglas Dillon: "There is a special activity proceeding under the chairmanship of Bob Anderson with which you may or may not be familiar," he wrote. Six weeks earlier, at the 17 March White House meeting launching the CIA's four-part assault on the Cuban Revolution, Treasury Secretary Robert Anderson, a Texas oil executive, had suggested a fifth measure: "If we were to cut the Cubans off from their fuel supply, the effect would be devastating on them within a month or six weeks." While the Mikoyan trade agreement appeared to make such a cutoff more difficult, the Soviet crude oil would need to be refined in Cuba's three facilities, all of them owned and operated by foreigners—Esso and Shell in Havana and Texaco in Santiago.[34]

The issue came to a head in mid-May, an especially difficult time. On 1 May, the Soviets had shot down a U-2 spy plane, and fifteen days later Nikita Khrushchev had walked out of a Paris summit after President Eisenhower refused to apologize for the spying. The next day, Cuba's Banco Nacional notified the three companies that operated oil refineries on the island that the country would soon be taking possession of a substantial amount of Soviet crude oil, which the refiners would be required to accept as payment for debts owed the companies by the Cuban government. Texaco was selected to begin with a boatload of Soviet crude that had already arrived.[35]

The bank's directive meant that Texaco would be stuck with even more wads of Cuban pesos when it retailed the refined Soviet oil, but local managers of the three oil companies were willing to be flexible—Esso's Cuba manager told Bonsal that he saw no alternative to refining the Russian crude, and he was especially reluctant to antagonize the shipment's formal owner, the Banco Nacional, whose recently appointed president, Che Guevara, controlled the hard currency that Esso wanted in exchange for its Cuban pesos. Guevara, of course, was known for his dislike of foreign investment, on one occasion characterizing it as "a great business for the investor, but a bad business for the country" and on another arguing that "private foreign capital comes here only for profit and does nothing for the people of Cuba."[36]

Given the issue's delicacy, local refinery managers sought instructions from their home offices, giving Anderson the opportunity he had been seeking—he asked two assistant secretaries of state (Rubottom and Thomas Mann) to travel to New York to urge senior company executives not to refine the Soviet crude. As requested, the home offices promptly instructed their local managers to refuse the oil, then waited for the other shoe to drop as a furious Castro told a Cuban television audience that the companies' refusal was "a concrete act of aggression." In Washington, the talk was equally tough; at a special NSC meeting just three days before the Republican National Convention, Vice President Nixon argued that U.S. airlines serving Cuba should be ordered not to use the Soviet oil, and he became adamant when Secretary Herter seemed lukewarm to the idea: "The time has come to take strong, positive action to avoid becoming labeled 'Uncle Suker' throughout the world."[37]

Then the shoe dropped: on 28 June, Prime Minister Castro signed Decree 188 ordering Texaco to process the waiting boatload of Soviet oil. After warning Washington that the situation was "pretty hopeless," Bonsal watched as Texaco refused to obey the decree and the Cuban government immediately took over management of the refinery. Then came Resolutions 189 and 190, ordering Esso and Shell to refine the oil Texaco had rejected. When they also refused, the Instituto Cubano de Petróleo "intervened" their facilities as well.[38]

The refusal to refine the Soviet oil dramatically increased Moscow's influence in Cuba—as one Kennedy administration official would remark several years later, "We forced the Russians to pick up the tab in Cuba [and] the consequences of the decision may not have been thought out."[39] That was not the view at the time, when everyone at an NSC meeting seemed eager to strike back: Eisenhower asked for advice about when (not whether) to sever diplomatic relations, Undersecretary of State Dillon responded with a manly jousting metaphor ("We had entered the lists. We can only lose or win; it was important that we win."), and Anderson observed that "the American people are beginning to wonder how much roughing up and how much abuse we can accept." Fortunately, he continued, the Texaco plant would need spare parts within a month, and he intended to pressure European suppliers not to provide them. In the interim, the administration limited its public response to a sharply worded diplomatic protest, calling the takeover one more example of the "relentless economic aggression by the Government of Cuba designed to destroy Cuba's traditional investment and trade relations with the free world."[40]

CUBA'S ACHILLES HEEL was not petroleum, however, but sugar—or, more precisely, Cuba's preferential access to the U.S. sugar market. This access had its origin in a 1902 treaty granting the fledgling republic's exports a 20 percent tariff reduction, making Cuban sugar inexpensive relative to that of other foreign producers. Then came the 1934 Sugar Act, whose principal purpose was to protect depression-era U.S. growers by restricting the entry of foreign sugar.[41] The act directed the Department of Agriculture to establish a target price for domestic sugar that would ensure a profit for U.S.

growers and then to calculate how much to restrict both domestic acreage and the entry of foreign sugar to raise the price to that level, with the foreign supply regulated by assigning a quota to each producing country.

Under the Sugar Act, about 55 percent of all U.S. consumption was satisfied by domestic producers, and 45 percent was satisfied by foreigners, with about 70 percent of the foreign quota going to Cuba. The island's share represented about a third of the entire U.S. sugar market between 1934 and 1960, with sugar representing about 80 percent of the value of Cuban exports, dwarfing the second-leading export, tobacco, which accounted for about 7 percent. One-third of Cuba's labor force was employed in the sugar industry. As the Canadian ambassador reported in 1953, "The mainspring of Cuba's foreign policy is the necessity to sell her sugar abroad in order to live." And, as the King Ranch's Robert Kleberg laid out the scenario when he visited the State Department in mid-1959, "If Cuba were deprived of its quota privilege, the sugar industry would promptly suffer an abrupt decline, causing widespread further unemployment. The large numbers of people thus forced out of work would begin to go hungry. They would then readily perceive the catastrophic nature of Castro's program, and that would mean the end of Castro politically."[42]

Career officials spent the following months debating among themselves whether a quota cutoff would have the effect Kleberg predicted, with a worried William Wieland, the director of State's Office of Caribbean and Mexican Affairs, capturing the consensus: "We would be taking an irrevocable step which would certainly injure and could indeed destroy, the source of Cuba's livelihood." In early 1960, the discussions became increasingly pointed, in part because of Cuban behavior but primarily because the Sugar Act was up for renewal. The previous renewal had been for four years and, as one official noted, "We would not want an extension for 4 years which would guarantee Castro's U.S. market."[43] Ambassador Bonsal had previously opposed a quota cut, arguing that it "would, in my judgment, prove disastrous not only for our relations with Cuba but also to our relations with other Latin American countries," but Mann responded that "there are cogent economic reasons for making a reduction in Cuba's quota." Most career officials remained on the fence, with one undecided economic officer writing that "my major difference with Mr. Mann was this: Mr. Mann would start cutting Cuba's quota right away. My difference with Wieland is that apparently he would never cut the quota."[44]

This ambivalence was not apparent at senior levels, where the hardliners had become overwhelmingly dominant, and the White House therefore proposed legislation to extend the Sugar Act for only one year and to grant the president authority to cut Cuba's quota for 1960 and 1961.[45] Although Congress had never before ceded this authority, the legislators' election-year response was never in doubt—two quota-cutting bills had been introduced even before the administration's proposal reached Congress, and they became the first effort by Congress to insert interest-group politics (the protection of domestic sugar producers) into Washington's policy toward revolutionary Cuba: one bill from a representative of sugar-beet-growing Idaho proposed giving part of Cuba's quota to domestic producers, and a second proposed eliminating the quota entirely. Both were quickly discarded in favor of the administration's proposal, which reached the House floor the day after Texaco's refinery was seized. Sensing a financial opportunity for his cane-growing constituents, Representative Robert Sikes told his colleagues that to replace Cuban supplies "the great State of Florida can tremendously expand its sugar production"; he then yielded the floor to another member from Florida, who argued that "we cannot sit idly by exercising patience and forbearance in the face of threats made by a Communist puppet"—and, incidentally, he urged the House to "give every consideration to expanding and enlarging our domestic sugar industry." With the feeding frenzy under way, he yielded the floor to yet a third Florida representative, who argued that the United States should "use hard economic sanctions—and in the sugar field they are powerful—to show we will not be clobbered by a tiny nation made free by us." Then it was time for the Rocky Mountain beet growers to weigh in, led by Wyoming representative Keith Thompson: "Cuba lives off our sugar purchases," he reminded his colleagues, and "it is time to apply Teddy Roosevelt's policy of 'speak softly but carry a big stick.'"[46]

While parochial economic advantage clearly generated much of the enthusiasm for cutting Cuba's quota, there was no shortage of support from representatives whose districts grew no sugar. "I am a patient man, but I am also an American," began Rhode Island's Silvio Conte; with the sugar quota "we are, in effect, supporting the rapid growth of international communism at our very doorstep." South Carolina's Mendel Rivers asked his colleagues to "think of what is happening—Castro's communism—both must be destroyed," arguing that a quota cut was too light a rap on the knuckles: "We should, if necessary, and, if conditions demand it, occupy Cuba." One obscure Delaware representative, elected by a razor-thin margin in 1958 and now facing a stiff challenge, elbowed his way into the well of the House, eager to document a get-tough attitude: "If Cuba's splendid people understand they must sell their sugar or their economy will be destroyed they will themselves find a way to deal with the present misleaders and fomenters of hatred." Democratic House speaker John McCormack made certain to put Republican Albert Quie on the record: "There was no member of [the agriculture] committee, Republican or Democrat, that was soft on Castro, was there?" "Not one," Quie responded. With that, the House voted 396–0 to authorize the president to cut Cuba's quota.[47]

The Senate quickly followed suit, and on 6 July President Eisenhower cut Cuba's sugar quota. Before leaving his desk at the end of the day, he wrote in his diary, "Approved emergency sugar act and after 2 long conferences today, issued official proclamation and accompanying statement. Have warned all to be alert to Cuban reaction." When the next day's *New York Times* editorialized that "the die is cast and there is no question that the United States, Cuba and Latin America are entering a new era," President Eisenhower took the time to write to the newspaper's publisher that "the piece reflects my views exactly."[48]

TWO WEEKS EARLIER, Castro had warned Cubans that "they are adopting there a law against our economy," promising a quick reaction. Then he told a radio and television audience that "if we can lose our sugar quota, part of our quota, they can lose part of their investments; [if] we can lose all our sugar quota, they can lose all their investments." A defiant Castro then promised to follow through on the day President Eisenhower cut the quota, although Ambassador Bonsal was relieved to report that there was nothing in his speech, "violent and disagreeable as it was, to indicate an intention on his part to resort [to] mob or goon squad action against Americans." But, he continued, "I rather get impression that at this stage he will use special powers in recently approved legislation to seize American property in retaliation."[49]

The recent legislation was Law 851 empowering the government to nationalize the property of U.S. citizens. Written in anticipation of the quota cut and explicitly retaliatory, it provided for compensation with thirty-year bonds at 2 percent interest, paid from a fund created by one-quarter of the proceeds from U.S. sugar purchases in excess of 3 million tons per year at prices over 5.75 cents per pound. If these purchases did not occur in any year, then Cuba's payment for that year would not simply be deferred but canceled. (During the 1950s, the United States had purchased on average 2.6 million tons per year at prices slightly below 5.75 cents.)[50]

Implementation began with a flourish: a Castro speech four days after the quota cut that criticized the United States as "the country that wants to destroy us, that wants blood to run down our streets, that wants to destroy our cities, that wants to spread mourning, death and ruin on our land." That said, more shoes began to drop. The initial focus was on expropriating firms that had already been intervened—twenty-eight large U.S. companies valued at slightly less than a billion dollars, including the Cuban Electric Company (majority-owned by the American and Foreign Power Company), the Cuban Telephone Company (an International Telephone and Telegraph subsidiary), the U.S.-owned oil refineries plus a smaller Sinclair operation, and twenty-two sugar refineries whose surrounding acreage had already been lost to the agrarian reform. Over the next few months, Law 851 served as the legal basis for the nationalization of nearly all remaining nonresidential U.S. property in Cuba.[51]

Cuba also lodged a formal complaint with the U.N. Security Council, charging that the quota cut and other moves constituted economic aggression. President Eisenhower told Secretary Herter that "if the Cubans can make a case against us that will have any weight with the other nations of the world, then he could only conclude that he does not know what the terms 'right' and 'wrong' mean." Then the president left for a vacation and Vice President Nixon hit the campaign trail, so national security adviser Gordon Gray called to ask the secretary of state to chair an upcoming NSC meeting: "There might be something on Cuba," he said. An exasperated Herter replied that "there was something on Cuba every five minutes."[52]

Meanwhile, Cuban foreign minister Raúl Roa opened the U.N. debate by accusing the United States of aggression, and U.S. ambassador Henry Cabot Lodge ended it by telling the Security Council that "unnecessary though it most certainly seems to me, let me here and now give him this assurance, heaped up and overflowing: The United States has no aggressive purposes against Cuba." Unwilling to acknowledge planning for the Bay of Pigs invasion but also clearly trying not to tell an outright lie, Herter chose his words carefully when reporters asked about the Cuban complaint: "I have never talked with the President about military intervention in Cuba." Delicately picking his way through an ethical minefield, Herter added, "We have a very solemn obligation under the Charter of the United Nations not to take aggressive action against any member of the United Nations."

The Security Council shelved Cuba's complaint, accepting the U.S. suggestion that the matter be referred to the Organization of American States. Senator Karl Mundt was upset by the entire proceeding: "We who in living memory rescued the island from medieval bondage; we who have given order, vitality, technical wisdom and wealth are now being damned for our civilizing and cooperative virtues!"[53]

The real surprise came from the other side of the world, when Nikita Khrushchev told a Moscow audience that "Soviet artillerymen can support the Cuban people with their rocket fire if the aggressive forces in the Pentagon dare to launch an intervention against Cuba." The president instantly replied "in the most emphatic terms that the United States will not be deterred from its responsibilities by the threats Mr. Khrushchev is making." But the next day Che Guevara warned Eisenhower to think twice — "We are defended by one of the most powerful military forces in history" — while Khrushchev proceeded to compare the United States to a vulture that "snatches the last crumb out of the mouths of the dying children and old folk just to grow fat and rich." He told reporters that "the Monroe Doctrine has had its day, has outlived itself, has died a natural death, so to speak. Now the remains of that doctrine ought to be buried, the way any dead body is buried, so that it won't poison the air with its putrefaction."[54]

"What did they expect?" asked Castro a week later. "For us to kneel down and wait to be killed? For us to renounce all help in this world, so we will remain alone, without a quota, and easy victims of aggression. What do they want? For us to place our necks under the Yankee axe and tell our mighty northern neighbor: 'You can go ahead now, and let the axe fall'?"[55]

THE PROBLEM NOW FACING Cuba's leaders was not simply that the United States held lots of axes (on the day of the quota cut, President Eisenhower instructed advisers to begin "looking forward to subsequent steps") but also that Khrushchev's 9 July statement had converted whatever was left of a bilateral dispute into a highly public test case of U.S. leadership of the Free World, with the secretary of defense warning about "a disturbing tendency on the part of smaller nations to seek to involve the Soviet Union in their problems in the hope of playing East against West. If we do not follow through with respect to Cuba, we may be encouraging similar behavior by other countries."[56]

These words were unmatched by immediate actions. Recruitment for the Bay of Pigs was now under way, of course, but it was secret. With no concrete steps forthcoming, the White House was back on the defensive soon after the quota cut, and Khrushchev's "rocket" comment prompted a wave of constituent letters to the vacationing president: "For God's sake stop fishing and golfing and get back to Washington and prepare aggressive action against Castro," cabled one New Yorker; another ordered Eisenhower to "stop playing golf and go back to work and tell Mr. K. that America is not afraid." And, the writer added, "I was your campaign manager in West Chester County in 1952. I am a Republican. I am very much afraid that you are disappointing your many friends."[57]

By this time both major parties had held their nominating conventions, and the administration was now busy beating off repeated demands for tougher action from nervous Republican legislators. In one meeting, a vulnerable senator proposed a blockade, but the president urged Republican members of Congress to exercise restraint, pointing out "that if the United States does not conduct itself in precisely the right way vis-a-vis Cuba, we could lose all of South America." Yet he had told the NSC months earlier that "it might be necessary to blockade Cuba yet," and Treasury Secretary Anderson had argued that the United States had to be "prepared to go all the way." Now, with the election on the near horizon and Khrushchev's 9 July statement striking Washington like a thunderbolt, these flakes of random suggestion began to turn into a blizzard of concrete proposals. In late July, the Pentagon handed the State Department a lengthy list of possible moves—everything from freezing Cuba's U.S. bank accounts to cutting the telecommunications cable between Havana and Moscow. Secretary Herter replied that he was already working on most of them.[58]

State was especially eager to muster the support of U.S. allies. When the CIA reported that it had been unable to convince Greek owners to halt the use of their ships to transport Soviet petroleum, Herter persuaded the president to write to British prime minister Harold Macmillan for help "not only with respect to British tankers, but in influencing other tanker-owning countries." Macmillan replied sympathetically: "Castro is really the very Devil," he wrote, and he later assured Eisenhower, "I know, and fully sympathize with, your purpose—the unseating of Castro," but he also expressed reservations, worrying first that Washington had no plan ("I am not very clear how you really mean to achieve this aim") and second that hostile acts might turn Castro into a martyr.[59] Macmillan was saying that he had cooperated once by refusing to sell Cuba jet fighters and had done so at considerable domestic political cost; with regard to a broader trade embargo, Britain would cheer quietly from the sidelines but would not lift a finger.

Other friendly governments also "had not been as cooperative as they might have been," Allen Dulles reported, and even if they were to cooperate, the world surplus in ships was working to Cuba's advantage. Treasury's Anderson kept up the pressure, urging Eisenhower to remind NATO allies "that we have given billions of dollars to them for mutual security, and that it is important for NATO to align itself with us" by helping to tighten the screws on Cuba. In particular, Anderson felt, "it was inconceivable that the Canadians would not cooperate," but when given a green light to apply pressure, he found Ottawa reluctant to support economic sanctions; instead, the northern neighbors favored "patient forbearance." The Canadian foreign office was frank with Anderson's emissary, who reported that "they could not imperil the free right of their banking institutions and businesses to take up any slack that might be created by U.S. economic sanctions. Altogether, it was a very disturbing conversation."[60]

Then the administration turned to its Latin American allies. In 1938, the twenty-one independent countries of the Western Hemisphere had met in Lima and, recognizing that occasional conferences were ill-suited to the faster pace of the times (the final act of one conference typically called for another in five years), created a new diplomatic mechanism, a "meeting of consultation of ministers of foreign affairs," that could be called at any time.* Three such meetings had been held during World War II, and each had been fairly cooperative, but the 1954 Caracas meeting that tacitly gave Washington permission to overthrow the democratic Guatemalan government (technically, an international conference of American states and not a meeting of consultation) had left many Latin Americans worried about a return to the big-stick policy of an earlier era. Such was the situation in 1960, when the U.N. Security Council turned Cuba's complaint over to the OAS, prompting the Eisenhower administration to propose a meeting of consultation in San José, Costa Rica.

By this time, Washington's purpose had become obvious—to do to Cuba what the 1954 meeting had done to Guatemala—and as an alternative, Mexico, Brazil, and nonmember Canada offered to mediate the dispute. The United States declined the offer, with Rubottom advising Herter that withdrawal of the sugar quota was already damaging Cuba's economy and that negotiations would help Castro just as he was beginning to weaken.

---

*The concept of a meeting of consultation was incorporated into both the 1947 Rio Treaty and the 1948 OAS Charter, and a meeting of consultation subsequently could be called under two separate treaties. The Rio Treaty allowed a meeting only to address an armed attack or a threat to the peace; a resolution adopted by such a meeting required a two-thirds vote and required all members to impose any approved sanctions, with the exception that each state remained free to determine whether to accept a resolution calling for the use of military force. The OAS Charter allowed a meeting to consider urgent problems, but the foreign ministers had the power only to recommend and not require sanctions.

To soften this refusal to accept mediation and to avoid the taint of "another Guatemala," the United States had to mollify several democratic Latin American leaders who were more concerned about Rafael Trujillo than about Cuba—the Dominican dictator was widely accused of supporting a coup against Venezuela's President Rómulo Betancourt and, after that effort failed, of being the mastermind behind a car bombing that wounded the Venezuelan leader.[61]

Secretary Herter had already warned the president that Trujillo's despotism "may soon create a situation like that in Cuba where the opposition is taken over by wild radicals," and in April the two U.S. leaders had discussed promoting a coup. At a mid-May White House meeting, "Mr. Rubottom said that Trujillo is involved in all sorts of efforts all over the hemisphere to create disorder. The President commented that Castro is also, and he would like to see them both sawed off." In June, therefore, the administration decided to propose not one meeting but two, held consecutively: first a meeting of consultation would focus on the Dominican Republic; it would then adjourn, and a second meeting would focus on Cuba. Eisenhower accepted this pairing as the cost of Latin American cooperation, telling aides that "until Trujillo is eliminated, we cannot get our Latin American friends to reach a proper level of indignation in dealing with Castro."[62]

By endorsing both meetings, the Eisenhower administration had signaled its decision to distance itself from Trujillo, leaving the State Department free to throw its energy into preparing the case against Cuba, an effort that began with the release of an exceptionally detailed document accusing the revolutionary government of a variety of sins but focusing on its close relationship with communists and its dictatorial behavior. Fidel Castro replied with a speech the embassy characterized as a "gutter-type attack . . . remarkable for its disregard for established institutions and the amenities of international life." The Cuban leader was especially critical of Washington's attempt to round up Latin American support, noting that "our enemies are used to threatening countries, they are used to trampling on the sovereignty of nations and issuing orders"; in contrast, he held up the example of Cuba, where "there are no Yankee soldiers commanding our armies anymore."[63]

When a reporter asked about Castro's comments, President Eisenhower appeared mystified: "Cuba has been one of our finest friends. We were the ones that conducted the war that set them free. And when they got in trouble, we had an occupation, back about 1908, and again we set them on their feet, and set them free." Although he had just been updated on progress for the Bay of Pigs invasion, the president insisted that "we have not tried to throw out someone we didn't like, or anything like that."[64]

The first of the two San José meetings focused on the charge that Trujillo had tried to kill Betancourt, the Venezuelan president. Since everyone found the evidence compelling, the foreign ministers quickly agreed to an immediate break in diplomatic relations and a partial suspension of trade, then adjourned.[65] The meeting about Cuba began the next day. Nelson Rockefeller had advised Herter to permit a longer intermission—a transition that would allow Latin American leaders to make speeches expressing the "hopes and aspirations of their people"—and had encouraged the secretary of state to make a similar speech, sending along some suggested language that, he confessed, was "warm and human, which may sound corny but is the kind of thing the Latins love." The Massachusetts Yankee had little time for diplomatic foreplay, however, and after a couple of pro forma introductory sentences, Herter plunged in with the indictment: "The leaders of the Soviet Union and Communist China have made abundantly clear their determination to exploit the situation in Cuba as a means of intervening in inter-American affairs. Their purpose is to break the bonds of inter-American solidarity, sow distrust and fear among the peoples of the American hemisphere, and thereby prepare the way for political control of the New World."[66]

Such charges were easy to document. On the same day as Herter's speech, Fidel Castro told a Havana audience, "We will be friends of the Soviet Union and of the Chinese People's Republic because they have shown they are our friends." Then he spoke directly to the United States: "You have attacked and wish to destroy us." Why, he asked? Because "we no longer believe in your philosophy of exploitation and privilege. We no longer believe in your philosophy of gold, the gold you rob from the work of other peoples. We no longer are willing to submit to the orders of your ambassadors. We no longer are disposed to follow in tow your reactionary policy, which is the enemy of human progress." The OAS proceedings in San José constituted nothing other than one more example of this "false Pan Americanism with which you wish to cloak the system of oppression and abuse, the system of domination that you have introduced among the divided peoples of America."[67]

"Castro has burned his bridges," Secretary Herter telephoned the president from Costa Rica, but his aides knew better—their informal conversations with intervention-sensitive delegates revealed a widespread fear that the United States was preparing to take action against Cuba. Just days earlier, South Carolina's Olin Johnston had stood up on the Senate floor and suggested that "Castro should be seized and dealt with as an international criminal," offering his view that "a few marines could do the job."[68] This congressional bluster had been supplemented by an ill-timed State Department announcement that third countries could no longer buy Cuban sugar with U.S. aid funds, which hinted at Washington's intention to curtail third-country trade with Cuba, a move that would be deeply resented in Latin America, especially Mexico. As a result, no support could be found among meeting participants for a resolution containing a direct reference to Cuba.[69]

That was not an insurmountable problem (the 1954 Caracas declaration had accomplished its purpose without naming Guatemala), so the United States settled for what came to be known as the Declaration of San José, in which the OAS condemned "the intervention or the threat of intervention"—a pointed reference to Khrushchev's 9 July "rocket" comment—"by an extra-continental power in the affairs of the American republics." Latin Americans made approval of even this weakened text contingent on U.S. acceptance of companion wording, aimed directly at Washington, reaffirming "the principle of non-intervention by an American state in the internal or external affairs of the other American states" and reiterating "that each state has the right to develop its cultural, political, and economic life freely." Moreover, the Declaration of San José was approved only after the delegates of eight countries had given speeches supporting both Cuba's right to self-determination and the revolution's economic reforms. Although the vote in favor of the declaration was unanimous, 19–0, it was marred by Mexico's abstention and by the decision of Peru's foreign minister to appoint another member of his delegation to sign a resolution he considered offensive. Venezuela's foreign minister also refused to sign and declined to appoint a replacement; from Caracas, President Betancourt had to order him to turn the delegation over to another diplomat. Ambassador Bonsal privately evaluated the resolution as "a serious disappointment," and the State Department admitted that it "falls considerably short of what we would like to have had adopted." When called and asked for his approval, a resigned President Eisenhower told an aide that "if this is the best that the Secretary can achieve, he felt he had no choice but to accept it."[70]

Back in Washington a week later, Herter tried to explain: "Latin Americans were extremely sensitive to what they call intervention," he told the NSC, and "Cuba, in its presentation to the OAS, had gone into a lengthy description of past U.S. intervention in Latin America." The secretary of state's words prompted the president to ask "whether the Cubans had indicated that they were delighted with U.S. intervention in 1898." Herter replied that "they had given no indication that the U.S. had been of any help."[71]

At the same time, Democratic presidential candidate John F. Kennedy complained that "our prestige has fallen so low that . . . we were unable to persuade our former Good Neighbors to pass a resolution even criticizing Cuba by name." Back in Cuba, Foreign Minister Raúl Roa summed up his view of the San José meeting by telling a television audience that Secretary of State Herter was "nothing more than a sausage full of air without even a skin of ideas," that Brazil had acted as Washington's "pimp," and, most memorably, that another U.S. ally, Argentine president Arturo Frondizi, was "the sticky concentration of all human excrement." Roa was especially offended by the decision of an unidentified OAS official to turn off the Cuban delegation's microphone, leaving Roa unable to reply to Herter's accusation that Roa's words had "a Soviet imprint." The Cuban foreign minister consequently had walked over to Herter and told him face to face that "his methods reminded me of Hitler." Herter told the NSC that "Roa was completely and utterly irrational."[72]

AS RELATIONS WITH CUBA continued to deteriorate, the State Department's moderates slowly lost their influence and in some cases their jobs. First to go was Assistant Secretary of State Rubottom, who was gently pushed out in late July and named ambassador to Argentina. He yielded the assistant secretaryship to Thomas Mann, a career official who had frequently advocated a tougher stance while serving as assistant secretary of state for economic affairs. Undersecretary Dillon soon was telling Eisenhower that "the State Department has become much more aggressive."[73] Rubottom served in Buenos Aires for a year before being forced into retirement when the new Kennedy administration did not offer him another post. He was forty-nine years old.

Others were less fortunate, and the specific case that quieted any remaining moderate career officers was that of William Wieland, who had been named director of State's Office of Caribbean and Mexican Affairs four months before Castro marched into Havana. An experienced professional, Wieland's first experience in Latin America had come in 1933–34 as a newspaper correspondent in Havana, and he subsequently spent the war years in the U.S. embassy in Rio de Janeiro. In 1946 he entered the Foreign Service, working his way up the State Department ladder while serving in several Latin American capitals. In 1956 he returned to Washington, where one of his assignments was to determine whether the Batista government had violated the terms of the U.S.-Cuban mutual security agreement. Since the answer was obvious, Wieland had participated in drafting the proposal to initiate the required aid cutoff, an action for which he was never forgiven by Ambassador Earl Smith, who pointed a finger in Wieland's direction when the Senate Judiciary Subcommittee to Investigate the Administration of the Internal Security Act began to seek out the individuals responsible for the Cuban debacle. Smith's predecessor, Arthur Gardner, also told Senator Eastland's subcommittee that Wieland was "leaning much too far to the left."[74]

Nothing more was needed to trigger Wieland's loyalty investigation, and Adolf Berle, a Latin Americanist advising John F. Kennedy, soon wrote in his diary that "the F.B.I. came to see me. They are investigating Roy Rubottom and Bill Wieland for the State Department, the charge being that they turned over Cuba to Castro."[75] The testimony against Wieland was embarrassingly weak, and much of the investigation focused on his personal life, with the subcommittee's staff director inquiring whether he had any contact with former undersecretary of state Sumner Welles, whose homosexuality had obliged him to resign in 1943:

MR. SOURWINE: Did you have any knowledge of anyone referring to you as Sumner Welles' fair-haired boy in Havana?

MR. WIELAND: No, sir.

MR. SOURWINE: It has been testified that you were so known. . . . As a Government administrator, are you aware that sexual deviation, and especially homosexuality among employees, presents a very special security problem?

MR. WIELAND: Yes, sir. . . .

MR. SOURWINE: Have you ever had to deal with this problem in any way?

MR. WIELAND: No, sir.[76]

By that time Wieland's career was over, torpedoed by innuendo, with no one bothering to look at what exactly he had said or done. Had investigators taken the time to do so, they would have discovered that Wieland was never pro-Castro. The diplomat had made his first enemy when he took seriously his oath to uphold the law stipulating that military aid not be used to repress internal dissent, but this position did not mean that he supported the revolution; indeed, Wieland wrote his first warning message five weeks after the rebels marched into Havana: "We should be extremely cautious about giving any impression that we are so anxious to help Castro in the face of his anti-American statements."[77]

Wieland persistently argued against a cut in Cuba's sugar quota but did so only because he believed it would benefit the revolutionary government by inflaming Cuban nationalism.[78] The Eastland subcommittee interpreted this perfectly reasonable argument as evidence of disloyalty. In actuality, the subcommittee discovered that Wieland, like Rubottom, was a middle-of-the-road, plain-vanilla professional, perhaps not the brightest star in the firmament but completely competent and clearly committed to doing his best to protect U.S. interests. Wieland was not, however, a fortune-teller, so, like many of his colleagues, he watched and waited, growing increasingly uneasy but doing so more slowly than some others, including Mann, whose impatience was more in tune with the times. This patience was Wieland's downfall. When he finally had the opportunity to defend himself—"I was never an admirer of Castro," he told Eastland's subcommittee in 1961—his reputation had already been smeared, and he was forced into retirement.

Washington's Cuba policy probably would have evolved as it did with or without Rubottom being fired and Wieland being pilloried, but there is no way to know for certain. Looking at these two cases, State Department moderates either learned to keep their mouths shut or, more commonly, quietly moved on to other posts as part of normal rotations. That freed Thomas Mann and his successors to appoint hard-liners.

AS WASHINGTON WAS PURGING its ranks of moderates, Havana had its eye on the September U.N. General Assembly, which Castro planned to attend. The tone was set just before the Cuban delegation departed for New York, when the State Department restricted Castro's travel to the island of Manhattan. Cuba promptly evened the score by restricting the travel of Ambassador Bonsal and then, the day before Castro's arrival in New York, moved ahead in the tally by announcing the nationalization of the Cuban branches of three major U.S. banks: "It is not possible for a considerable portion of national banking to remain in the hands of imperialistic interests that inspired the reduction of our sugar quota by an act of cowardly and criminal economic aggression."[79]

Then the scoring accelerated. Fifteen minutes after his plane landed, Castro had his first formal complaint for U.N. secretary-general Dag Hammarskjöld: an "uncivil and violent" plainclothes security officer had roughly pushed Castro's arm back into his car when he waved to an airport crowd of several hundred supporters. After one night in the midtown Hotel Shelburne, the Cubans accused the hotel management of "extortion" for demanding a ten-thousand-dollar security deposit, and Castro's initial inclination was to pitch a tent in Central Park, telling reporters, "We are used to sleeping in the open air." [80] It is sometimes alleged that the Cubans were evicted for grilling chickens in their rooms, but that canard was the fabrication of the Republican Congressional Committee, which in 1963 produced an error-laced chronology of U.S.-Cuban relations with an entry for 18 September 1960: "Cuban delegation kills and plucks chickens in hotel suite, generally conduct selves in barbaric manner." [81]

Rather than pay the security deposit, the Cuban delegation transferred to Harlem's Hotel Theresa, a move U.S. officials dismissed as grandstanding—something Castro could use "as proof of the fact that he and his revolution belonged to the humble and oppressed peoples and cared nothing for luxurious hotels in the so-called 'aristocratic' area of New York." Arriving in Harlem at the head of a lily-white seventy-seven-person delegation, Castro instructed one of the principal Afro-Cuban rebel leaders, Major Juan Almeida, to fly up to New York and meet with community leaders. Almeida's plane was promptly seized by U.S. claimants seeking compensation for their expropriated Cuban property, but Nikita Khrushchev seized the major asset—the visiting Soviet premier drove up to Harlem for talks and a front-page picture of himself hugging Castro. [82] At the same time, the Cuban exile community was engaged in a "Journey of Mourning"—a pilgrimage from Miami by sixty-two anti-Castro Cuban women to pray in St. Patrick's Cathedral for an end to the revolution. Unknown to the reporters covering the story, the pilgrimage had been organized and funded by the CIA—the agency called it a "Caravan of Sorrow," part of the agency's "special operation in New York" during the meeting of the General Assembly, which also included CIA-engineered demonstrations to fuel the curbside acrimony between pro- and antirevolutionary demonstrators. One such confrontation led to the death of a nine-year-old Venezuelan girl, killed by a stray bullet while dining with her vacationing parents. [83]

Then came the main event, what remains to this day the longest speech in General Assembly history—4.5 hours—in which Fidel Castro basically expressed his wish that the United States drop off the face of the earth. This central theme was woven through remarks that focused on the colonial and the continuing postcolonial exploitation of Third World countries by international capitalists, drawing special attention to Washington's continuing effort to subjugate the Cuban people. Among his milder comments was a reference to the Democrats' presidential candidate as "an illiterate and ignorant millionaire"; nodding to bipartisanism, he quickly added that Republican Richard Nixon was not a bit better—"both lack political brains."[84] The Cuban leader then returned to Havana in a Soviet aircraft to avoid the seizure of another plane.

The day after Castro's speech, the State Department warned U.S. citizens not to travel to Cuba and again instructed Ambassador Bonsal to cease seeking compensation for expropriated property—"Our best bet is to wait for a successor regime." State also scheduled a meeting with senior Pentagon officials to determine how to react to one of Cuba's central complaints, the continuing U.S. occupation of Guantánamo. At the meeting, Admiral Arleigh Burke voiced the hope that Cuba would do something rash so that "we could defend the base and then we ought to go and take Santiago again." Another participant suggested that "it was time to turn Cuba back to Spain."[85]

The State Department was preparing a detailed response to Castro's "unfounded accusations, half-truths, malicious innuendoes and distortions of history," a response that made little effort to discriminate between fact and fiction; for example, to counter Cuba's charge that the United States was using the Swan Islands to "promote subversion in our country, violating all international treaties, including those related to radio frequency," the State Department simply lied: "There is a private broadcasting station on the islands, operated by the Gibraltar Steamship Company. The United States Government understands that this station carries programs in Spanish which are heard in Cuba, and that some of its broadcast time has been purchased by Cuban political refugees." The Gibraltar Steamship Company was a front, owned and operated by the CIA.[86]

As the Joint Chiefs were preparing to defend Guantánamo and as the State Department was preparing its public response, CIA director Allen Dulles began the first NSC meeting after Castro's New York speech by observing that Cuba had become "virtually a member of the Communist bloc," an assessment seemingly confirmed by Cuba's votes during the 1960 General Assembly: of the 102 ballots, the Cuban government sided with the Soviet Union 89 times, compared to only 20 times with the United States; on most of those 20 issues, the United States and the Soviet Union were in agreement.[87] After Dulles had spoken, Undersecretary of State Douglas Dillon handed other NSC members a list of the steps that had been or were about to be taken in retaliation. The most important was closure of Cuba's largest industrial plant, the Nicaro nickel plant, which had been built by the U.S. General Services Administration during World War II and remained

U.S. government-owned but operated by a private contractor, Freeport Sulphur Company, which had also been developing its own nickel and cobalt mine at Moa Bay, forty miles to the east.

In 1953, seeking to ensure that Nicaro would not be mothballed after the end of the Korean War, as it had been after the end of World War II, the Batista government had granted Nicaro an exemption from taxes, but that arrangement ended in October 1959 when the new revolutionary government issued Law 617, imposing an export tax on all metals and minerals. Claiming that the tax made continued operation uneconomical, the United States first sought to sell Nicaro to the Cuban government, which offered $5.4 million for a facility the U.S. government had built at a cost of $110 million, with the offer contingent on a U.S. commitment to purchase Nicaro's output for five years. This deal, the State Department complained, "would amount to our *paying* the [Cuban government] to take Nicaro off our hands." Instead, the United States closed the facility.[88]

Meanwhile, the Cubans were holding their own meetings in Havana. Soon after Castro's New York trip, the government issued its sweeping Urban Reform Law, which was not aimed at the United States but nonetheless affected a substantial number of U.S. property owners. The measure nationalized all commercial property and converted residential tenants into purchasers, who would make payments to the government, while the government would pay the former owners up to six hundred dollars per month. The next shoe to drop—Law 890 of 14 October—was clearly punitive: it nationalized a new group of U.S. properties ranging from Colgate's soap factory to Pan American's airport equipment to Swift's meatpacking plant; even *Reader's Digest* lost its printing facility. A few days later, Cuba also lodged a formal complaint with the U.N. General Assembly, charging the United States with "continuing intimidation, harassments, reprisals and acts of aggression and intervention." The complaint cited two concrete incidents—a late September airdrop of weapons to counterrevolutionaries in the Escambray Mountains and an early October landing of counterrevolutionaries in Oriente Province. These acts, Cuba complained, were examples of "the machinery of invasion set in motion by the State Department, the Pentagon and the imperialist rulers of the United States." U.S. Ambassador to the United Nations James Wadsworth assured the General Assembly that "there is no threat from the United States of aggression against Cuba."[89]

WHILE NEITHER SIDE could prove its point, Cuba's complaint included an irrefutable charge of "repeated statements by both candidates for the Presidency of the United States cynically advocating aggression, intervention and subversion." In August, Richard Nixon had told the Veterans of Foreign Wars that "the United States has the power—and Mr. Castro knows this—to throw him out of office," and in September the Republican candidate added that "we could give it to Mr. Castro in 24 hours." John Kennedy had responded with a major speech "about the most glaring failure of American foreign policy today—about a disaster that threatens the security of the whole Western Hemisphere—about a Communist menace that has been permitted to arise under our very noses, only 90 miles from our shores. I am talking about the on[c]e friendly island that our own shortsighted policies helped make communism's first Caribbean base: the island of Cuba."[90]

Although Kennedy's criticism of Cuba was harsh, Nixon was the Democratic hopeful's principal target, and he was assisted the next night by the moderator of the second presidential debate, whose first sentence was, "Mr. Vice-president, Senator Kennedy said last night that the Administration must take responsibility for the loss of Cuba." Placed immediately on the defensive, an irritated Nixon shot back, "Cuba is not lost, and I don't think this kind of defeatist talk by Senator Kennedy helps the situation one bit." During the debate, Kennedy needled Nixon for his 1955 visit to Cuba, where he "praised the competence and stability of the Batista dictatorship. That dictatorship had killed over 20,000 Cubans in 7 years."[91]

All this rhetoric only amplified the letters constituents were sending to President Eisenhower. "I demand that our proud nation take immediate action to avenge the barbaric thievery practiced by Fidel Castro," wrote one irate Texan. "Our dignity has been invaded by a gangster, and you must not rest until he is punished." Another Texan offered to administer the punishment: "I am confined to a wheelchair but I can still shoot a rifle. Like every other American I hate war but if that is what it takes to destroy that Communist animal at our front door then I say, 'So be it.' Authorize the Army to issue me a rifle and let me be the first to enter Havana. If you will I can guarantee that Communist Castro will never kill any more Americans." Similar messages followed: "I voted and supported you in 1952 and 1956 but I am very sorry now that I did so," and worse yet, "I am at present heading the Nixon-Lodge workers in my community, I feel however that I cannot continue to do so unless you as the Republican Party leader show enough strength and conviction to dispose of this malignant enemy."[92]

In this electoral context, Richard Nixon asked the president to ban U.S. exports to Cuba. "We must also think how this action will affect the American people," Eisenhower replied, suggesting that an embargo might backfire—"It tends to look as though we are acting not against Castro, but against the Cuban people." Nonetheless, he passed along Nixon's request to senior presidential advisers, saying that Nixon wanted "to take some action with respect to Cuba at an early date."[93] Pouring on the criticism, Kennedy spent the same day telling one immigration-sensitive Florida audience that "Cuba has been lost to the Communists," a second group that "in Cuba the Communists have gained a satellite," and a third gathering that "I wasn't the Vice President who presided over the Communization of Cuba." Also campaigning in hotly contested Florida, Nixon responded by calling the Castro government "an intolerable cancer" and arguing that "there comes a time when patience which we have been displaying is no longer a virtue and that time is at hand." He promised the American Legion that the administration would "very promptly take the strongest possible economic measures." The next day President Eisenhower issued an executive order prohibiting all exports to Cuba except food and medicine. The legionnaires passed a resolution urging an invasion if the ban on exports did not work.[94]

Neither the Democrats nor the Cubans let Eisenhower's ball land in their court before firing it back. Cuba's response was to nationalize what was left of U.S. property—166 separate businesses that had somehow escaped earlier expropriation. The Kennedy campaign criticized Eisenhower's move as "too little, too late" and demanded more pressure: "We must attempt to strengthen the non-Batista democratic anti-Castro forces in exile, and in Cuba itself, who offer eventual hope of overthrowing Castro. Thus far these fighters for freedom have had virtually no support from our Government."[95]

The fourth and final presidential debate occurred the night after this statement, and now it was Nixon's turn to go on the attack, calling Kennedy's proposals "the most dangerously irresponsible recommendations that he's made during the course of this campaign." From that point forward, Nixon repeatedly emphasized that he was not in favor of the "little 'pipsqueak' dictator, Castro, down in Cuba. The question is not who is against Castro. The question is how you handle him." Calling that the campaign's central question, Nixon challenged Kennedy to a fifth debate to focus exclusively on Cuba.[96]

Secretary Herter was probably referring to this last-minute campaign rhetoric, to the trade embargo, and to Cuba's final round of expropriations when he concluded that the situation was "hopeless from the point of view of diplomatic negotiations."[97] At the moment, Che Guevara was leading a three-month tour of communist countries, signing one trade agreement after another, and President Eisenhower was receiving ever-increasing pressure from the U.S. private sector, including a letter from the president of the U.S. Chamber of Commerce demanding "quick and positive action." At this point, the president wondered aloud "whether the situation did not have the appearance of beginning to get out of hand," and as his penultimate presidential expression of displeasure he recalled Ambassador Bonsal once again. This time the envoy and his wife sailed out of Havana's harbor with their car and the family dog. Arriving in the United States, Bonsal told reporters that he had returned "for what would apparently be a long stay," and for emphasis Secretary Herter took the highly unusual step of naming Bonsal to another post. Bonsal would serve as the interim U.S. ambassador to the OAS concurrently with his now-pointless position as ambassador to Cuba in absentia.[98]

Deprived of the unflappable Bonsal, the embassy gave up completely, reporting that "the United States faces in Soviet-supported Castro's Cuba an intolerable threat to its prestige and its security which has to be eliminated." Clearly unaware that the CIA was already hard at work on an exile invasion, the embassy suggested that "the United States might have to consider intensive economic warfare including para-military measures against Cuba," and the next day embassy staffers recommended not simply severing diplomatic relations but also "an active program of sabotage." A formal break might even be helpful, opening "the way for more vigorous economic and propaganda measures inconsistent with the maintenance of diplomatic relations." President Eisenhower then canceled Cuba's sugar quota for the first quarter of 1961 and recalled the embassy's chargé to Washington. When he arrived, he agreed with Herter: the situation was "entirely hopeless." A few days later, the president instructed the State Department to explore with other Latin American countries a simultaneous termination of diplomatic relations and to try to arrange the break before Kennedy's inauguration on 20 January.[99] Peru quickly agreed to go along, and Uruguay announced that it was considering a break, while the U.S. embassy in Caracas predicted that Venezuela would also follow suit.

U.S. diplomats "have been pressuring the Latin American governments to break relations with us," Fidel Castro complained to a mass audience celebrating the second anniversary of Batista's ouster. Since most U.S. embassy officials were spies and saboteurs, he continued, the embassy staff should be reduced to eleven, the number of Cuban diplomats in the United States.

The State Department's Bureau of Intelligence and Research had noted earlier "that new policies are formulated during these lengthy public appearances, [Castro's] fertile mind grasping a new idea and translating it into an official pronouncement without prior consultation with his advisors." Such appears to have been the case in this instance, where the Cuban leader's initial remark about reducing the embassy staff prompted what the U.S. Information Agency transcriber described as "wild applause." The strong crowd reaction clearly surprised Castro, whose next words suggested that his proposal was impromptu: "Permit me to finish the thought. The fact that we have established an order while speaking has served in this case to discover a desire of the people. We are not going to say all officials, but not a single official more than the number we have in the United States, which is eleven; and these gentlemen have more than 300 officials here, of which 80 percent are spies. If they all want to go, well then, let them go." The audience replied with a chant, "¡Que se vayan!" which in this context best translates as "Good riddance!"[100]

Castro had barely left the podium when Cuban officials awoke the senior U.S. official remaining in Havana at 1:20 A.M. to hand him a note demanding that the embassy staff be reduced to eleven within forty-eight hours. President Eisenhower decided instead to close the embassy. Having put up with "a long series of harassments, baseless accusations, and vilification," he said, "there is a limit to what the United States in self-respect can endure. That limit has now been reached."[101]

We cannot let the present government there go on.
—President Eisenhower to President-Elect
Kennedy, 19 January 1961

THE BAY OF PIGS

"Before dawn Cuban patriots in the cities and in the hills began the battle to liberate our homeland"—so read the press bulletin issued by the Cuban Revolutionary Council but written by CIA officer David Atlee Phillips.[1] The landing had begun in the predawn hours of 17 April 1961, two days after eight Cuban-piloted B-26 bombers had set out from Nicaragua to destroy Cuba's air force. The damage had been incomplete, and now, at dawn, the Cuban air force began its counterattack, disabling two of the brigade's ships before they could unload their cargo, and the assault began to disintegrate. Early the next morning, national security adviser McGeorge Bundy warned President John F. Kennedy, "I think you will find at noon that the situation in Cuba is not a bit good."[2]

That was an understatement. "They are in a real bad hole," reported the chief of naval operations, Arleigh Burke, after rushing to the White House for the noon meeting. "We got over there in the Cabinet Room. The President was talking with CIA people, State Department people and Rostow and a lot of other people. They were talking about Cuba. Real big mess." The Joint Chiefs of Staff may have approved the invasion, but Admiral Burke's immediate reaction was to make certain that the Department of Defense not take the blame, dictating a memorandum for the record during the ride back to the Pentagon: "Nobody knew what to do nor did the CIA who were running the operation and who were wholly responsible for the operation know what to do or what was happening. A lot of things have happened and they have caused to happen and [that] we the JCS don't know anything whatever about. We have been kept pretty ignorant of this and have just been told partial truths." Admiral Burke failed to mention that his navy was involved up to its scuppers and that he had been among the first senior officials to propose the adventure: more than a year earlier, on 26 February 1960, he had sent the State Department a "paper indicative of current Navy thinking" that included a discussion of how "the U.S. could assist rebel groups covertly to overthrow the present government."[3] A navy task group under the command of Admiral John Clark had escorted the CIA's brigade to the battle site and had turned over the landing craft to the invaders, and on the morning of 19 April, Clark's carrier, the *Essex*, had launched navy fighters to protect rebel planes from Castro's air force. Below the flight deck, two thousand U.S. Marines had been issued live ammunition and were ready to fight should JFK permit U.S. troops to enter the battle.[4]

But the nation's new president, John Kennedy, would not allow the marines to be deployed, and the navy fighters came too late to be useful, so Admiral Clark's principal role was to receive and forward reports on the debacle. Sitting offshore at 11:18 A.M. on 19 April, he received a message from the beach: "Please send help. We cannot hold." Thirteen minutes later, he received another: "Out of ammunition. Men fighting in water." A half hour after that, Clark reported that the area held by the brigade "appears to be one quarter to one half mile along the beach to a depth of about one quarter [mile] under artillery fire with tanks and vehicles to both east and west. Believe evacuation impossible without active [U.S.] engagement with Castro forces." Then the brigade's radio operator sent his final message: "Am destroying all equipment and communications. Tanks are in sight. I have nothing left to fight with. Am taking to the woods. I cannot wait for you." A few minutes later Clark radioed the Pentagon, "Castro is waiting on beach."[5]

That evening CIA director Allen Dulles told Richard Nixon, "This is the worst day of my life"; Attorney General Robert Kennedy thought that Dulles "looked like living death." Dean Rusk complained that the Bay of Pigs was "one hell of a way to close out my first hundred days as secretary of state."[6]

"Castro is far better organized and more formidable than we had supposed," presidential adviser Arthur Schlesinger Jr. wrote in his diary on Day 2 of the three-day debacle. Cubans clearly had not been sitting idly while U.S. voters passed the torch to the Kennedy generation. As JFK was receiving his party's nomination, Fidel Castro was telling Cubans that "our enemies are used to threatening countries, they are used to trampling on the sovereignty of nations and issuing orders. But there are no Yankee soldiers commanding our armies anymore, and there are no workers without weapons to defend themselves." During the preceding year, Cuba had established diplomatic relations with every communist government except that of East Germany and had signed cooperative accords with all but Albania, in the process doubling Cuba's credit lines and disposing of 70 percent of the 1961 sugar harvest. Then, two days before Kennedy's inauguration, Banco Nacional president Che Guevara had returned from a three-month tour of communist countries, his briefcase bulging with trade agreements. The U.S. press had occasionally noted Guevara's travels, including his Beijing speech characterizing the United States as an imperialist power and his Shanghai address announcing that communism "has defeated capitalism in all fields."[7]

But this was to be expected from the Argentine adventurer, always considered a dyed-in-the-wool communist; Fidel Castro was the person watched most closely, and his problem was perceived not so much as communist leanings as mental imbalance: the CIA's first JFK-era report began with the premise that "no sane man undertaking to govern and reform Cuba would have chosen to pick a fight with the US," especially since Washington had done nothing provocative—the breakdown in relations "is not a function of US policy and action, but of Castro's psychotic personality. It is evident, on the testimony of his supporters at the time, that Castro arrived in Havana in a high state of elation amounting to mental illness." From there, things went downhill, as Castro "became convinced that the US would never understand and accept his revolution, that he could expect only implacable hostility from Washington. This was the conclusion of his own disordered mind, unrelated to any fact of US policy or action."[8]

The principal concrete problem in early 1961 was that Cubans were exporting their revolution to the rest of Latin America—"Cuba becoming a center for Latin American Communist activities" is how the CIA had begun its National Security Council briefing a year earlier. According to the U.S. embassy, no sooner had Castro reached power than he announced that "Nicaraguans should take to the mountains and fight for the freedom as Cubans had done, and could count beforehand on complete support of Cuban people." Within months, Cuba had supported *Granma*-like invasions not simply of Nicaragua but also of Panama, the Dominican Republic, and Haiti, and at 1960's 26th of July celebration, Castro had promised "to continue making the nation the example that can convert the Cordillera of the Andes into the Sierra Maestra of the hemisphere." Three weeks later he told another audience, "Our slogan is: 'Today our country is free forever, and someday all the Americas will be free forever.'"[9]

In mid-1960 President Eisenhower had told the British prime minister, Harold Macmillan, that "this kind of change, when it brings Communism in its wake, is intolerable from the standpoint of our national interests and that of the liberal democratic Christian tradition which we all share."[10] So when the president discussed Cuba with the president-elect on 19 January 1961, a day before the transition, Eisenhower told JFK directly, "We cannot let the present government there go on," and Treasury Secretary Robert Anderson added that "in the final analysis the United States may have to run Castro out of office."[11] The Joint Chiefs of Staff told the new secretary of defense the same thing a week later—"The primary objective of the United States in Cuba should be the speedy overthrow of the Castro Government, followed by the establishment of a pro-U.S. Government." Then the chiefs handed Secretary of Defense Robert McNamara their view of the options, an elaborate table with escalating steps, from Step 1, economic pressure, to Step 7, a U.S. invasion. Step 3 was to "train and equip small vol[unteer] force Cuban exiles to invade, establish a center of resistance for anti-Castro Cubans to rally to establish pro-U.S. Govt."[12]

After this meeting McNamara drove across the Potomac to the White House, where JFK and his other senior advisers were waiting to be briefed by CIA director Allen Dulles. Bundy's notes indicate that "the judgment expressed without dissent was that Cuba is now for practical purposes a Communist-controlled state," so the discussion focused on how to over-throw its government. Restraining voices came from the State Department's Rusk and Thomas Mann, who warned that a U.S. invasion would have "grave political dangers to our position throughout the Western hemisphere," which prompted President Kennedy to ask the chair of the Joint Chiefs what he thought of Step 3, the proposal to use the exiles being trained by the CIA in Guatemala. General Lyman Lemnitzer responded that any such exile invasion "would have very little chance of success," while the minutes indicate that Dulles and aide Tracy Barnes "took a very opti-mistic view of the force's ability to land and hold a beach head." The presi-dent asked the two sides to see if they could produce a single conclusion, then ended the meeting with his first directive about Cuba: "A continuation and accentuation of current activities of the Central Intelligence Agency, including increased propaganda, increased political action and increased sabotage." Clearly anxious to do something, JFK asked Bundy a few days later, "Have we determined what we are going to do about Cuba?"[13]

At the same time, the CIA had set out to convince the Joint Chiefs to endorse the agency's plan. Painting the rosiest possible picture, a CIA briefer "emphasized that the proposed strike could be conducted with no overt U.S. military support other than the provision of one LSD, and that the force once committed would not have to be evacuated in the event of inability to hold the initial objective area, as it could, if required, disperse and continue to survive." The CIA emphasized that "the likelihood of success was very high in terms of staying in the initial objective area long enough and in sufficient control to permit the introduction of a 'Provisional Government' and provide a rationale for the subsequent employment of overt military force, if desired."[14]

One flaw marred this rosy picture: Step 3, a "surprise" attack, had recently been featured on the front page of the *New York Times*. The first specific information had come from the *Hispanic American Report*, a news digest published by Stanford University's Latin American studies program, whose director, Ronald Hilton, had learned about the CIA's facility: "Reliable observers in Guatemala say that without doubt there is in Retalhuleu a large and well-fortified base where Cuban exiles are being trained to invade Castro's fortress. . . . It is generally believed among responsible Guatemalans that there is only one possible source for the funds necessary for such a major project, namely the U.S. Government acting through the C.I.A." Hilton's scoop had been picked up by *The Nation*, although it, too, had a limited readership, and the cover was blown off the invasion preparations only when the *New York Times* ran its story on 10 January 1961: "U.S. Helps Train an Anti-Castro Force at Secret Guatemalan Air-Ground Base." There, on the front page, was a map pinpointing the U.S. facility.[15]

As the Joint Chiefs had warned Secretary McNamara, the operation was a security nightmare—any journalist could have uncovered the story simply by talking with Guatemalans living near the training base: "Firing, explosions, aircraft orbiting over an objective area, parachute drops, and an abnormal number of unfamiliar aircraft in the area are a dead giveaway." Indeed, the reporter would not have needed to visit the area, since "leaflets have been circulated in Guatemala City by the Communist Party giving many of the details of the activity. Although there are some inaccuracies in this material, much of it is accurate." In fact, the reporter would not have needed to leave the United States, for leaks were also coming out of Miami—newspapers in March quoted both Cuban opposition leader Tony de Varona's promise that an invasion would come "very soon" and another exile leader's declaration that "today we stand on the threshold of an adventure far greater than has yet been written in Cuban history." Ten days before the invasion, the *New York Times* reported that in Miami "the preparations against Dr. Castro are an open secret. They are discussed in the streets, Cuban cafes and restaurants and almost everywhere that two or more Cubans congregate." After giving an interview to yet another reporter whose questions indicated an exceptionally clear picture of the entire operation, Schlesinger warned President Kennedy that "if an enterprising magazine writer could pick all this up in Miami in a couple of weeks, Habana must be well posted on developments."[16]

Several participants blamed the invasion's failure on these security breaches and especially on the Miami chatter—what the CIA's inspector general called "the gregariousness of Cuban exiles." This was not a new charge; at the first meeting of what was to become the agency's Bay of Pigs task force, Colonel J. C. King had warned that "he knew of no Latin American country whose people were less secure operationally than Cubans." General David Gray agreed ("Cubans cannot keep quiet"), as did Grayston Lynch, one of the two CIA officials most directly responsible for the brigade, who wrote that "the average Cuban is a highly emotional, vocal, and thoroughly likable individual. Consequently, as an intelligence operative, he is his own worst enemy. When entrusted with a most secret matter, he will solemnly agree never to tell a living soul, even under the pain of death, and he truly means it. But all too soon, he discovers, he will have to tell someone or he will explode from the effort of holding the secret in." And the Cubans were not the only talkative participants. The British picked up on the plan before any Cuban (or even President Eisenhower) had seen it; in late November 1959, Great Britain's Foreign Office informed the country's Washington embassy about "various pieces [of] information that have reached us" and asked the ambassador to snoop around: "The US authorities may be contemplating trying to stimulate or support an anti-Castro movement along the lines of the action they took in Guatemala some years ago. . . . Can you find out?"[17]

Now, seventeen months later, JFK was worried by what he read in the newspapers, and he asked his principal aides, including McNamara, "whether there had been any statements by Castro indicating knowledge of the plan." Two weeks earlier, the Joint Chiefs had warned the defense secretary that "it can . . . be presumed that Castro knows practically all about the operation *except* when, where, and in what strength." McNamara had apparently not heard the warning, however, for his response to JFK's question "was in the negative."[18]

But of course Castro knew; everyone knew. As early as August 1960, Cuban intelligence knew that 45 military advisers, many of them U.S. citizens, had begun training as many as 185 "old Batistianos and simple mercenaries" in Guatemala, and the Guatemalan communist party soon was providing Cuba with regular reports on the training camp via the Soviet embassy in Mexico City. By the time of JFK's inauguration, Cuban intelligence had produced an exceptionally detailed report on the CIA's training facilities. A month earlier, on 31 December 1960, Cuba had requested an urgent meeting of the U.N. Security Council to discuss a "sinister plan" to invade Cuba by "war criminals who have sought refuge in the United States." The meeting had begun on 4 January, barely two weeks before Kennedy's inauguration, with Foreign Minister Raúl Roa laying out Cuba's detailed charges that the United States was training "mercenaries" in Guatemala; Roa specifically named the Retalhuheu airfield. U.S. ambassador to the United Nations James Wadsworth had replied that Roa's charges "are empty, are groundless, are false, are fraudulent." Cuba's leaders, he continued, "have been crying 'wolf' for the past six months over an alleged 'imminent invasion' of their country, and thereby are fast making themselves ridiculous in the eyes of the rest of the world." The Security Council adjourned without taking action.[19]

Meanwhile, preparations continued. After the November election, a lame-duck President Eisenhower had told his senior advisers that he wanted "all done that could be done on the Project with all possible urgency." By this time, CIA officials had set up the Retalhuheu base and were training Cuban exiles, and the senior trainer, marine colonel Jack Hawkins, a respected World War II veteran of guerrilla warfare in the Philippines, was telling officials in Washington about "the superior characteristics of the individuals" who had been selected, insisting that they "would have no difficulty inflicting heavy casualties on a much larger force."[20] But in January, just days before JFK's inauguration, a representative from the Joint Chiefs warned CIA officials that Cuba's "200,000 militia each with a sub-machine gun is, in itself, a pretty strong force if they do nothing more than stand and pull the triggers," to which the agency responded that "less than 30 percent of the population is still with Fidel," and "in this 30 percent are included the negroes, who have always followed the strong men in Cuba, but will not fight." At the same time, an interdepartmental group concluded that there was no longer "any hope of overthrowing the Castro regime with economic warfare measures alone, even if they include an effective blockade."[21] A week later, President Eisenhower dropped a year's worth of preparation into the lap of his successor.

THESE PREPARATIONS WERE BEING OVERSEEN by the CIA's deputy director for plans, Richard Bissell, the heir apparent to Allen Dulles as director of central intelligence. Bissell operated through a special Caribbean unit—Branch 4 of the Western Hemisphere Division (WH/4), led by J. D. "Jake" Esterline, an Office of Strategic Services veteran with experience behind enemy lines in Burma who had been the army's chief instructor in guerrilla warfare before entering the CIA, where his first responsibility had been to help overthrow the Arbenz government in Guatemala. As a branch chief, Esterline should have reported to division chief J. C. King, but as Esterline later explained, "J. C. was sort of gently eased out of things. . . . Our orders came directly from Bissell."[22]

Bissell, in turn, dominated every detail. "His mind was swift and penetrating, and he had an unsurpassed talent for lucid analysis and fluent exposition," recalled Arthur Schlesinger. "He had extraordinary gifts of exposition. We all listened transfixed . . . fascinated by the workings of this superbly clear, organized and articulate intelligence, while Bissell, pointer in hand, would explain how the invasion would work." Richard Goodwin characterized Bissell as "a cultivated man with impeccable credentials— good school, good family, good war—a social acquaintance of many Kennedy intimates, including the president's own family." But it was not simply that he could talk comfortably and confidently to the Kennedy elite; his successful management of the U-2 project had also given him a reputation for getting things done, and in early 1961 McGeorge Bundy had suggested that Kennedy name Bissell undersecretary of state for political affairs. "The man who fills this job will have to be an active and decisive person, quite different from the ordinary foreign service type," Bundy wrote. Kennedy demurred, perhaps because Bundy added that "if Dick has a fault it is that he does not look at all sides of the question."[23]

Bissell unquestionably had the leading role in convincing JFK to go ahead with the exile invasion—White House logs indicate thirteen informal Oval Office meetings between the two men in the three months before the invasion; as Bissell's secretary told Seymour Hersh, "He was there all the time." One of Bissell's senior CIA colleagues, Robert Amory, noted that "Kennedy was extremely fond of Dick Bissell, had a very high regard for him. I think he regarded Dick as probably one of the four or five brightest guys in the whole Administration." "Kennedy was seduced," added Arthur Schlesinger. "All of us — Kennedy and Bundy and the rest — were hypnotized by Dick Bissell to some degree, and assumed that he knew what he was doing."[24]

And Bissell's vision was easy to endorse. The CIA had run up a string of covert successes in the postwar era — in Greece, the Philippines, Iran, and of course Guatemala, all balanced by only one failure, the 1958 effort to unseat Indonesia's Sukarno. As the agency had grown accustomed to quiet, inexpensive victories, the executive branch had grown accustomed to action unfettered by public debate and congressional consultation. A few lies might be needed to deflect inquiries from the press, but no one worried about getting caught — seven years had passed since the Guatemala coup, and nothing had yet been published to challenge the State Department's denial of any complicity.[25]

U.S. officials were therefore free to focus on the planned invasion, where one key question had always been how the Cuban population would react to the landing of a paramilitary force. The plan the CIA outlined in its pre-inaugural briefing of Secretary of State Dean Rusk called for the U.S.-trained exiles "to seize and defend a small area."

> It is expected that these operations will precipitate a general uprising throughout Cuba and cause the revolt of large segments of the Cuban Army and Militia. The lodgements, it is hoped, will serve as a rallying point for the thousands who are estimated to be ready for overt resistance to Castro but who hesitate to act until they can feel some assurance of success. A general revolt in Cuba, if one is successfully triggered by our operations, could serve to topple the Castro regime within a period of weeks. If matters do not eventuate as predicted above, the lodgement established by our force can be used as the site for establishment of a provisional government which can be recognized by the US, and hopefully by other American states, and given overt military assistance. The way will then be paved for United States military intervention aimed at pacification of Cuba, and this will result in the prompt overthrow of the Castro government.[26]

Rusk was probably alerted by the CIA's string of caveats ("it is expected . . . ," "it is hoped . . . ," "if matters do not eventuate as predicted . . ."), but the agency's briefing also contained a counterbalancing string of optimistic revelations, including news that its effort to create a civilian Democratic Revolutionary Front (Frente Revolucionario Democrático [FRD]) had yielded "excellent results," but that assessment was not simply optimistic; it was dead wrong. The CIA had assigned the job of creating this unified exile political organization to Howard Hunt, later made famous by Watergate, and he held FRD leaders in contempt: "I considered them shallow thinkers and opportunists," he wrote. "For Latin American males their caliber was about average; they displayed most Latin faults and few Latin virtues." This evaluation probably helps explain why, as the CIA's inspector general subsequently concluded, "as the project grew, the Agency reduced the exile leaders to the status of puppets."[27]

The CIA also told Rusk that the U.S. propaganda offensive (nine hours of daily broadcasting via Radio Swan) had fueled Cubans' disaffection, adding that more than words were being sent: "We have delivered, via twelve maritime missions, over 15,000 pounds of arms ammunition and demolition materials to resistance elements in Cuba. As of 13 January, we had dropped over 36,000 pounds of arms, leaflets and food on thirteen overflights"; most important, 560 Cuban personnel were now training in Guatemala. Additional recruits would soon be available, the CIA added, and "with the recent acquisition of 37 U.S. Army Special forces instructors, training should be completed by our target date." On the single occasion when CIA briefers were more candid (in mid-February they admitted that they had only "a good chance of overthrowing Castro"), they followed this cautious evaluation with a definite, "or at the very least causing a damaging civil war."[28]

The Joint Chiefs continued to oppose the project, but no one in the Pentagon seemed willing to lie down in front of the CIA's truck, and Defense officials eventually accepted Bissell's rosy scenarios, which were buttressed by a series of optimistic reports: "The opposition forces in the Escambray are enjoying great popularity with the Cuban people," the agency asserted confidently on 10 March, and a few days later it estimated "that Castro had the support of fewer than 20 per cent of the people and that fewer than 10 per cent of these supporters were true *fidelistas*." Then came the information that "disenchantment of the masses has spread through all the provinces. Spokesmen of opposition groups say that Santiago de Cuba and all of Oriente Province is seething with hate."[29] By early February, the chiefs were softening, telling Secretary McNamara that "timely execution of this plan has a fair chance of ultimate success"; at an interdepartmental meeting four days later, the representative of the Joint Chiefs of Staff "indicated he was confident that the strike force would be able to hold the beachhead at least six days." Even without an uprising, "the main body of the landing party could retreat to the mountains and maintain themselves there indefinitely." By mid-March, the chiefs were advising McNamara "that a decision to proceed with the operation be made at the earliest practicable date."[30]

Plan opponents were at an overwhelming disadvantage after the Pentagon conceded. "Here we were," Schlesinger noted years later, "a bunch of ex-college professors sitting around faced by this panoply of the Joint Chiefs of Staff, Allen Dulles, a legendary figure, and Dick Bissell, the man who invented and promoted the U-2. It was rather difficult even to open one's mouth sometimes, in the face of these guys." And at a meeting held the day before the inauguration, one of the few five-star generals in the nation's history had told a lieutenant (junior grade), "We cannot let the present government there go on"; Kennedy, Arthur Schlesinger wrote, would have had a difficult time explaining why he had canceled a military expedition "advocated, sanctioned, and supported by the general who commanded the largest successful amphibious landing in history." And, Schlesinger continued, CIA director Allen Dulles "kept emphasizing what he called the 'disposal problem.' . . . What Dulles did not add, but what Kennedy fully understood, was that the domestic political implications of Kennedy's cancellation of this expedition would be very considerable." Bissell ended one mid-March memo with the vague threat that if the invasion were to be scrapped, "the alternative would appear to be the demobilization of the paramilitary forces and the return of its members to the United States. It is, of course, well understood that this course of action too involves certain risks."[31]

But at this point the administration was not especially concerned about domestic politics, nor was it merely a victim of Eisenhower-era momentum, and the upcoming failure was not simply the result of misleading reports from Bissell's CIA.[32] The documents suggest that President Kennedy and most of his key advisers exuded the same can-do attitude as Bissell. They were the people who had defeated Hitler and Tojo, and Thucydides was right: Cubans would be no problem.

Although the Kennedy inner circle was poised to act, some senior officials nonetheless tried to stop the train after it had left the station. Schlesinger told Kennedy that he would back a "swift, surgical stroke," but the agency's plan "seems to me to involve many hazards; and on balance . . . I am against it." U.S. allies would interpret the invasion as unprovoked bullying, he warned, and the United States would find itself on the same moral plane as Moscow; in the end, "Cuba will become our Hungary." This message must have come through, for a week later JFK told Richard Goodwin that he adamantly opposed the use of U.S. troops: "I'm not going to risk an American Hungary. And that's what it could be, a fucking slaughter."[33] Assistant Secretary Thomas Mann was also opposed: the plan would not work, he said, primarily because a popular uprising against Castro was unlikely, so "we would, I believe, be far better off to do whatever has to be done in an open way and in accordance with the American tradition."[34] Only Senator J. William Fulbright and Undersecretary of State Chester Bowles consistently opposed the operation on principle. "The Castro regime is a thorn in the flesh; but it is not a dagger in the heart," Fulbright told Kennedy. "To give this activity even covert support is of a piece with the hypocrisy and cynicism for which the United States is constantly denouncing the Soviet Union in the United Nations and elsewhere. This point will not be lost on the rest of the world—nor on our own consciences for that matter." Bowles said the same thing.[35]

With these two exceptions, the argument made by the plan's opponents was not that overthrowing Castro's government was wrong but either that it would fail or that it would damage U.S. relations with the rest of the world, especially Latin America—as Rusk worried, "We might be confronted by serious uprisings all over Latin America if U.S. forces were to go in," and Mann added that "the effect on our position of hemispheric leadership would be catastrophic." So, McGeorge Bundy warned the president,

> when you have your meeting this afternoon on Cuba, I think you will find that there is a divergence of view between State on the one hand and CIA and Defense on the other. Defense and CIA now feel quite enthusiastic about the invasion from Guatemala—at the worst they think the invaders would get into the mountains, and at the best they think they might get a full-fledged civil war in which we could then back the anti-Castro forces openly. State Department takes a much cooler view, primarily because of its belief that the political consequences would be very grave both in the United Nations and in Latin America.

Writing just before leaving for his post as ambassador to India, John Kenneth Galbraith weighed in on State's side, reminding Kennedy that "Dulles got Guatemala at the price of losing all South America."[36]

But this argument was undermined by reports that many Latin American leaders were every bit as enthusiastic as the CIA. At their 19 January meeting, President Eisenhower had told Kennedy that "we are constantly getting the private opinions of the heads of Latin American governments that we should do something," and in February, Guatemala's Miguel Ydígo-

ras Fuentes urged JFK to unleash the Cubans being trained in his country—when a new Cuban government is installed, he wrote, "the people of
Latin America will recover their morale and will have the United States
and yourself as their saving leader who fulfills its undertakings." The CIA's
Office of National Estimates agreed that *overt* intervention "would remind
many people of the Soviet intervention in Hungary," but "most Latin American governments would at least privately approve of *unobtrusive* US support for an opposition move against Castro." Schlesinger heard the same
thing when he sounded out elite opinion during a three-week trip to South
America in February: Peru's Víctor Raúl Haya de la Torre had "an exceedingly sharp condemnation of Castro," Argentina's Arturo Frondizi believed
that "Castro was a threat to the hemisphere," and the attitude of Bolivia's
Víctor Paz Estensorro "may be described as including a strong private condemnation of Castro, a fervent hope that the US might rid the hemisphere
of him, and a profound disinclination to identify himself publicly, except in
the most marginal way, with anti-Castro action." For leaders such as Paz, a
covert invasion by Cuban paramilitary forces would be an ideal alternative
to either a continuation of the Cuban revolution or a U.S. invasion.[37]

A day after receiving Schlesinger's report, President Kennedy gathered
with his senior foreign policy advisers to hear Bissell present the CIA's plan.
Aware of the undercurrent of opposition, Bissell's deputy, Tracy Barnes,
had warned his boss that "our only chance is to be very firm in our position
and be very strong in urging the need for the proposed action." Rising to the
challenge, Bissell was at his reassuring best, telling JFK that "the assault
force was to consist of an amphibious/airborne assault with concurrent
(but no prior) tactical air support, to seize a beachhead contiguous to ter-
rain suitable for guerrilla operations. The provisional government would
land as soon as the beachhead had been secured. If initial military operations were successful and especially if there were evidence of spreading
disaffection against the Castro regime, the provisional government could
be recognized and a legal basis provided for at least non-governmental [i.e.,
covert CIA] logistic support."[38]

Worried that an amphibious landing with air support would tie the
operation too obviously to the United States, Kennedy requested a plan
where the U.S. hand would be less obvious, and Bissell went back to his
office to tinker with the details, making the landing in darkness and having
the ships away from the area by dawn. He also switched the invasion's location from Trinidad to the more isolated Bay of Pigs. These changes secured
McGeorge Bundy's endorsement; the CIA, he told Kennedy, had "done a

remarkable job of reframing the landing plan so as to make it unspectacu-lar and quiet, and plausibly Cuban in its essentials. . . . I have been a skep-tic about Bissell's operation, but now I think we are on the edge of a good answer. I also think that Bissell and Hawkins have done an honorable job of meeting the proper criticisms of the Department of State."[39]

When JFK went around the table at one final meeting with his advisers on 4 April, only Senator Fulbright and Secretary Rusk were opposed, and Rusk's negative vote was not strongly asserted—"I have always had a deep regret that I did not oppose the Bay of Pigs more forcefully," he lamented years later. "Rusk had plenty of private misgivings," wrote Schlesinger in his diary, "but he never, to my knowledge, opposed the operation, never argued against it, never told the President to call it off." Two days after the invasion's collapse, JFK commented, "There is only one person in the clear—that's Bill Fulbright. And he probably would have been converted if he had attended more of the meetings." With varying levels of enthusiasm, all the others advised the president to go ahead—"Let 'er rip" was the vote of the most experienced person at the table, Adolf Berle.[40] The next day, Schlesinger handed JFK his memo indicating that "on balance . . . I am against it," but on 11 April, Robert Kennedy took Schlesinger aside and told him that "the president has decided to go ahead and there is no point in up-setting him further by continuing to raise questions." That left Schlesinger with little choice but to concede: "From that point on, my negative memos would only be irritating."[41]

PRESIDENT KENNEDY IMMEDIATELY ACCEPTED responsibility for the failure, but he also appointed a commission chaired by General Maxwell Taylor to determine who *really* was to blame. In addition to its chair, the Taylor Commission (or Committee) was composed of Attorney General Ken-nedy, CIA director Dulles, and Admiral Burke. Meeting secretly, it heard tes-timony from more than fifty witnesses at twenty hearings over the course of the next month.[42] CIA inspector general Lyman Kirkpatrick also launched an internal agency investigation, which was far more critical—so critical of the CIA, in fact, that deputy director C. P. Cabell advised Dulles to destroy the inspector general's report: "This is not a useful report for anyone inside or outside the Agency." Instead, Dulles added a long rebuttal drafted by Bis-sell's deputy, Tracy Barnes, calling it "Part 2 of 2 Parts" to ensure that the inspector general's report would not stand alone in the historical record.[43] (The single surviving copy did not see the light of day until declassified at the request of the National Security Archive in early 1998, thirty-six years after it was written.) Barnes and other CIA officials who participated in the failed project generally criticized any assessment that faulted their preparation or execution. Howard Hunt, for example, wrote that the purpose of the Taylor Commission was "to whitewash the New Frontier by heaping guilt on CIA" and that all of the critical comments in the memoirs of Kennedy-era authors combined to create "an unparalleled campaign of vilification and obloquy that must have made the Kremlin mad with joy."[44]

But what exactly *had* gone wrong? The CIA had told Kennedy officials before the battle that the rebels were "the best-trained men in Latin America," and just before the attack, Colonel Hawkins, a much-decorated combat hero, had reported that

> these officers are young, vigorous, intelligent and motivated with a fanatical urge to begin battle for which most of them have been preparing in the rugged conditions of training camps for almost a year. I have talked to many of them in their language. Without exception, they have utmost confidence in their ability to win. They say they know their own people and believe after they have inflicted one serious defeat upon opposing forces, the latter will melt away from Castro, who they have no wish to support. They say it is Cuban tradition to join a winner and they have supreme confidence they will win all engagements against the best Castro has to offer.

"I share their confidence," Hawkins added. "The Brigade is well organized and is more heavily armed and better equipped in some respects than U.S. infantry units. The men have received intensive training in the use of their weapons, including more firing experience than U.S. troops would normally receive."[45]

The brigade's fighters clearly possessed much bravery, but some had been braver than others. When the battle had obviously been lost early on 19 April, a Cuban patrol boat had approached one of the brigade's disabled ships, the *Houston*, grounded one hundred yards from the beach. Firing from the shore, brigade members killed four of the six Cuban militiamen in the patrol boat, and a CIA observer reported that the remaining two Cubans, taken prisoner, "were executed because of the logistical problems they made for the survivors." Then the *Houston*'s captain saw his escape route: he grabbed the captured patrol boat and, joined by the commander of the brigade's Fifth Battalion, the chaplain, and three doctors—all officers—fled to the open sea after "bidding their men to scatter and make out for themselves." The CIA observer hypothesized that this type of leadership "might indicate a reason why the 5th Battalion seemed reluctant to go ashore." At the same time, Admiral Clark was trying to convince the undamaged ships to return to the battle and unload their supplies. Two of them did so, but two others continued southward, with one captain radioing that "he would have trouble with his crew if he attempted to turn north." He eventually turned the boat around, but the fourth boat was 218 miles south of the Bay of Pigs by noon on the second day of the three-day battle.[46]

The story was the same when it came time to evaluate the performance of the Cuban pilots: before the battle, Colonel Hawkins reported they were "motivated, strong, well trained, armed to the teeth, and ready." He considered the crews "equal to the best U.S. Air Force squadron." But a U.S. contract pilot told a different story in a postbattle debriefing:

MR. [ROBERT] KENNEDY: You say then that you did not find the Cuban pilots to be very good?

MR. HAYDEN: No. When the chips were down and the going was tough, they found excuses NOT to do the job.

MR. KENNEDY: What percentage would you say did do their job?

MR. HAYDEN: I'd say that not over 35 per cent of them did.

Stanley Beerli, an air force colonel on loan to the CIA as chief of air operations, interrupted to point out that "in our early missions, we had some Cuban crews making as many as three passes over heavily defended targets," to which Hayden replied, "That was in the early days when they smelled victory. When the going got tough, we had trouble even getting them into the aircraft. On D+2, it took us several hours to get some of their crews in the aircraft, and then they aborted the mission." Beerli eventually admitted that his gung-ho Cuban pilots "were good until things started going wrong," and by the morning of 19 April, "he had to beg them to go."[47] The CIA's independent assessment included the information that "on D plus 1 it became necessary to utilize American civilian pilots to protect the beachhead area due to the fact the Cubans were either too tired or refused to fly" and that "on the morning of D plus 2 American pilots again were pressed into service for protection of the beachhead area for two reasons (1) the reluctance of the Cuban pilots to fly more combat sorties without air to air cover and (2) the Americans were attempting to build morale and develop a will to win."[48]

Ignoring these efforts to shift the blame to the brigade's fighters, both the CIA's inspector general and the Taylor Commission instead pointed to a basic conceptual flaw, and here the inspector general pulled no punches:

> The fundamental cause of the disaster was the Agency's failure to give the project, notwithstanding its importance and its immense potentiality for damage to the United States, the top-flight handling which it required—appropriate organization, staffing throughout by highly qualified personnel, and full-time direction and control of the highest quality. . . . Insufficiencies in these vital areas resulted in pressures and distortions, which in turn produced numerous serious operational mistakes and omissions, and in lack of awareness of developing dangers, in failure to take action to counter them, and in grave mistakes of judgment. There was failure at high levels to concentrate informed, unwavering scrutiny on the project and to apply experienced, unbiased judgment to the menacing situations that developed.

Kirkpatrick argued that this problem had arisen with the radical shift away from a "long, slow clandestine build-up of guerrilla forces" to what actually happened thirteen months later. Because the operation was a special project, few were privy to this evolution; the plan evolved within the confines of a "complex and bizarre organizational situation" where no one had the knowledge, the opportunity, and the nerve to stand up and tell Bissell that he was creating "an overt military enterprise that was too large for the Agency's capabilities."[49]

After making this central point—Bissell had mismanaged the overall effort—the inspector general added a frank criticism of lower-level CIA personnel: "In many cases, the reason for assigning a given person to the project was merely that he had just returned from abroad and was still without an assignment"; worse yet, the CIA units asked to supply personnel "had in some instances given the project their disposal cases." Of the forty-two officers who held the principal operational jobs in WH/4, seventeen were ranked in the lowest third of their respective grade, nine were in the lowest tenth, and "some of the people who served the project on contract turned out to be incompetent." Almost none of the hundreds of agency personnel working directly with Cubans spoke Spanish or had any knowledge of Latin America, and some openly sneered at the people they were training. "They considered the Cubans untrustworthy and difficult to work with. Members of the Revolutionary Council have been described to the inspectors as 'idiots' and members of the brigade as 'yellow-bellied,' [while] some of the contract employees, such as ships' officers, treated the Cubans like dirt." The inspector general concluded that "the Agency, and for that matter, the American nation is not likely to win many people away from Communism if the Americans treat other nationals with condescension or contempt, ignore the contributions and the knowledge which they can bring to bear, and generally treat them as incompetent children whom the Americans are going to rescue for reasons of their own."[50]

Both the inspector general and the Taylor Commission also placed some blame on President Kennedy for dictating crucial details, beginning with his veto of a landing at the populated region around Trinidad, directly adjacent to the Escambray Mountains where guerrilla operations might have been possible, and insistence on a less favorable but nearly deserted site where U.S. assistance would be less obvious. CIA officials did not complain at the time JFK made his decision, but when subsequently asked why the more remote site had been selected, Jake Esterline shot back, "There was no other goddam place." JFK's 11 March veto of Trinidad came at the insistence of Dean Rusk and Thomas Mann, both of whom expressed concern that deniability would be impossible as long as the air strikes were coming from outside Cuba: Mann "hammered at the point repeatedly and wanted to know if there wasn't some area where they could land on a ready made area." The Bay of Pigs had a landing strip marginally adequate for use by the rebels, while Trinidad did not. At one earlier meeting, Rusk had asked if perhaps the CIA could drop a bulldozer near Trinidad and quickly construct a runway, prompting Esterline to reply sarcastically that "if I ever make a suggestion like that to Mr. Dulles, I should be summarily fired." That, Esterline noted "is the last time I ever went to a meeting with Mr. Rusk."[51]

More important than the site selection was Kennedy's decision to whittle away at the plan, constantly reducing the scope of U.S. involvement. The Taylor Commission concluded that "the leaders of the operation were obliged to fit their plan inside changing ground rules laid down for non-military considerations, which often had serious operational disadvantages." Writing in retirement, the CIA's Dulles concluded that "among the Pres[idential] advisers there were enough Doubting Thomas to dull the attack, but not enough to bring about its cancellation."[52] The ostensible goal was to maintain plausible deniability, and administration officials continually rejected CIA requests for more obvious U.S. involvement, beginning in January, when the secretary-designate, Rusk, turned down Bissell's request to use the Opa Locka airfield in southern Florida for support flights, and ending three days before the assault, when the State Department rejected the CIA proposal to use sonic booms to scare the Cubans because such booms could come only from U.S. aircraft.[53]

At the same time, everyone directly involved in the operation considered plausible deniability an impossible condition. A senior CIA official remarked, "You can't say that fifteen hundred Cubans got together in a sort of Michael Mullins Marching and Chowder Society and acquired aircraft and ships and ammunition and radios and so on and so forth all by their little selves. The American hand would clearly show in it." This was also the view of the admiral who loaned the brigade its landing craft after dutifully painting out any identifying marks: "There was nothing on them that said U.S., but I don't know who would have thought they belonged to anybody else." Those who took this position included former president Eisenhower, who accepted JFK's invitation to talk immediately after the invasion: "I was astounded, I said, 'Mr. President, how could you expect the world to believe that we had nothing to do with it? Where did these people get the ships to go from Central America to Cuba? Where did they get the weapons? Where did they get all the communications and all the other things that they would need? How could you possibly have kept from the world any knowledge that the United States had been assisting the invasion?" But all of these comments came after the fiasco. No one warned President Kennedy before the invasion that denial would be impossible. Clearly grasping at straws, Arthur Schlesinger was typical when he suggested to JFK that it would be possible "to show that the alleged CIA personnel were errant idealists or soldiers of fortune working on their own."[54]

The crucial change dictated by the quest for deniability was a series of decisions limiting air support. "By holding back air support," Richard Nixon wrote, "Kennedy had doomed the operation," but Nixon failed to note that the first limitation was imposed by the Eisenhower administration, when Undersecretary of State Livingston Merchant told the Special Group "that it would be impossible politically to carry out three days of pre-invasion bombing."[55] Bissell accordingly revised the plan to include bombing only one day before the invasion, although this reduced the probability that all of Castro's air force would be destroyed before the invasion and although everyone directly involved in the project continued to insist that wiping out all of Castro's planes was essential. A few days after Bissell's revision, the CIA's briefing notes for secretary-designate Rusk included the flat assertion that "control of air and sea in the objective area is absolutely required. The Cuban Air Force and naval vessels capable of opposing our landing must be knocked out or neutralized before our amphibious shipping makes its final run into the beach. If this is not done, we will be courting disaster." At a 1996 conference, Esterline seemed surprised that his message was not passed to the president: "It never occurred to me before that Dick Bissell might not be relaying what we were saying to Kennedy—what was so desperately vital to the success of this thing. And we—believe me—we didn't spell it out just once, we spelled it out every day as we went along."[56]

Had Eisenhower and Kennedy not reduced the prelanding bombing, it is unclear whether a sufficient number of Cuban exiles could have been recruited to fly the aircraft. To train Cubans to operate a thirty-plane air force, the CIA brought more than 150 U.S. personnel to an airfield at Nicaragua's Puerto Cabezas, but the agency, worried that the Cuban pilots "may lack the motivation to take the stern measures required against targets in their own country," soon requested permission to use U.S. pilots.[57] Deniability dictated that U.S. personnel not be authorized to fly the planes in combat.

Then President Kennedy decided to cancel air support by U.S. Navy pilots on the morning of the invasion, thereby signing what Esterline saw as the brigade's death warrant: "It was totally predictable. If we didn't have air superiority for a couple of days, until things could happen inside Cuba, we were dead." Calling JFK's decision a "devastating blow," Dulles wrote, "Had I known that there might be no second air strike at the Bay of Pigs and that no air cover would be provided, my judgment would have been very similar to the estimate I gave at the time of Guatemala—some chance of success with the air cover, none without it."[58] Hunt also viewed the destruction of Castro's air force as "basic to the success of the entire invasion," and Barnes agreed: "The plan that was appraised was modified by elimination of the D-Day airstrike. Had the Cuban Air Force been eliminated, all these estimates might have been accurate instead of underestimated." Grayston Lynch described hearing that JFK had canceled the air support as "like learning that Superman is a fairy."[59]

In the end, the few air attacks that were permitted proved inadequate. The first came on 15 April, two days before the invasion, and U.S. officials subsequently could not even agree on their purpose: the CIA's Esterline believed that they had sought to destroy Castro's air force on the ground, but the Joint Chiefs' Lemnitzer insisted that "they were never intended to accomplish the destruction of the Castro air force. They were to lend plausibility to the story that the strikes had been launched from within Cuba."[60] The 15 April attack failed to meet either objective. Twelve of Castro's eighteen planes were knocked out of combat, leaving him with two T-33 jet trainers, two British propeller-driven Sea Furies, and two or three B-26s, while what little air cover Kennedy permitted was plagued by snafus—a last-ditch attack by rebel bombers on 19 April was to have had protection from U.S. fighters from the *Essex*, but, depending on whose story one selects, they were either flying too high to be of help or were over the beach at the wrong time. "Inexplicably sloppy performance on the part of the Navy," concluded CIA historian Jack Pfeiffer.[61]

One fact is indisputable, however: since the pre-invasion strikes on 15 April met with only partial success, without air cover the rebels were at a dramatic disadvantage in their slow-moving ships and their exposed positions on the beach. As Esterline had argued, "We've got to have control of the air, or these ships which are deck-loaded with gasoline can't operate, because they could go all of 5 to 6 knots per hour, 5 to 6 knots." But even if these problems had not existed, a team of three officers who conducted an evaluation of the volunteer force in early March had warned that "the odds are about 85 to 15 against surprise being achieved in the attack against Castro's Cuba. If surprise is not achieved, it is most likely that the air mission will fail. As a consequence, one or more of Castro's combat aircraft will likely be available for use against the invasion force, and an aircraft armed with 50 caliber machine guns could sink all or most of the invasion force." He was right. Castro's two T-33s, each with two .50-caliber machine guns, inflicted the heaviest damage on the brigade.[62]

PERHAPS THE MOST intriguing explanation for the invasion's failure, this one not mentioned by either the inspector general or the Taylor Commission, was that it was never intended to succeed—that at some point in the plan's evolution, the invasion became little more than bait, designed to lure Kennedy to commit to battle; then, when standing at the edge of failure, he would have no choice but to authorize the use of U.S. troops and thereby to end the Cuban Revolution. Arthur Schlesinger took this view: "Dickie Bissell was prepared to accept any reductions, any changes, in the plan so long as it went forward. He was convinced, I believe, that if it failed, military intervention would follow."[63] Although Schlesinger publicly stated this belief at an academic conference held decades after the invasion's failure, he twice warned the president before the invasion: on 31 March that "the real belief [of Miami's exiles] is that the logic of the situation will require the US to send in Marines to make sure that the invasion is a success," and on 5 April that "if the landing fails to trigger uprisings and defections in the Militia (and the evidence that it would do so is inconclusive), the logic of the situation could well lead us, step by step, to the point where the last step would be to dispatch the Marines."[64]

Bissell denied that he had been involved in any such bait-and-switch subterfuge, but few mortals writing for the historical record would volunteer that they had engineered a military debacle while simultaneously deceiving their commander in chief. Bissell also varied his story: in his 1975 oral history, he downplayed the need for the local support that he had previously considered crucial ("We didn't look for any help from the locals in that [initial] phase"), and he outlined a scenario that had never before been mentioned: if "you had a beachhead that couldn't be dislodged, then that might have been the time to press, through diplomatic channels, for a cease fire and a supervised election." In the end, Bissell may not have known exactly what he had expected to occur. "After he was fired, Bissell spent much of his time contriving ingenious justifications," White House aide Richard Goodwin later wrote. "As obsessively as the Ancient Mariner, he recounted his sad tale of promises broken, decisions not taken, fatal hesitations—all fabricated to divert attention from his own fabulous staggering miscalculation."[65]

Since even Bissell seemed so uncertain, Schlesinger's bait-and-switch hypothesis would be little more than speculation had not Dulles left behind some supporting evidence—handwritten notes in the Allen Dulles Papers uncovered by Lucien Vandenbroucke. There the CIA director admitted to having failed to be completely candid with the president about "the realities of the situation" and conceded that the CIA's plan had some holes in it:

> We did not want to raise these issues . . . which might only harden the decision against the type of action we required. I have seen a good many operations which started out like the B of P—most under complete secrecy—non-involvement of the US [and] initial reluctance to authorize supporting actions. This limitation tends to disappear as the needs of the operation become clarified. [We] felt that when the chips were down—when the crisis arose in reality, any action required for success would be authorized, rather than permit the enterprise to fail.[66]

Was this the thinking as the CIA prepared its invasion? All the major participants are now dead, and barring the discovery of some new documents, the truth will never be known for certain. The fact that there was no plan for the next steps—for how to proceed after the beach had been secured—

may have indicated nothing more that the belief that Cubans would rise up and join the invaders. But securing the beach may have been when Dulles, Bissell, and others expected JFK to send in the marines waiting offshore on the *Essex*. "The whole plan of the CIA . . . was Phase 2, the U.S. invasion," argued both Philip Brenner and Piero Gleijeses at a 1996 conference, and theirs is a convincing argument.[67]

SOME COWARDICE, much inadequate staffing, many White House demands for deniability (which changed the site and limited the air cover), and JFK's refusal to be led into a commitment of U.S. forces—all of these factors help to explain the invasion's failure. But their explanatory power pales in comparison to the one crucial miscalculation: Cubans, the CIA believed, would welcome the invaders. Eleven days before the invasion, the agency reported,

> It is generally believed that the Cuban Army has been successfully penetrated by opposition groups and that it will not fight in the event of a showdown. It is also certain that the police, who despise the militia, will not fight. The morale of the militia is falling. They have shown little wish to fight. . . . It is generally believed [redacted] that approximately 55 to 80 percent of the militia units will defect when it becomes evident that the real fight against Castro has begun.

And this was not the first such prediction. Since mid-1960, the CIA had been reporting on "mounting evidence of internal dissatisfaction and mounting opposition to the Castro regime," on "an encouraging upswing . . . noticeable in the number of prominent defectors," and on the Catholic Church becoming "increasingly outspoken against Communism in Cuba." By the time Kennedy's staff was preparing to move into the White House, Bissell's deputy, Barnes, was explaining that "basic to the plan is the expectation that . . . the landing in force will encourage and produce active internal opposition to Castro." But in describing one planning meeting, the CIA's Hunt asserted that "neither during this nor other meetings was it asserted that the underground or the populace was to play a decisive role in the campaign. The contrary has been alleged by many writers who did not take part in our councils."[68]

Two separate reports suggest that Barnes was correct and Hunt was mistaken. One came from information provided by five Bay of Pigs participants who managed to escape capture, work their way to Havana, and sneak into the Brazilian embassy. After debriefing the men, the embassy reported to Itamaraty that an uprising had been promised: "It was constantly said that as soon as their landing took place, numerous supporters, among the troops of the revolutionary Government, and the great number of uprisings in the Cuban interior, would make the work of the invaders significantly easier." A Canadian embassy report was identical: "Captured prisoners stated that a fundamental postulate of the operation was the expectation of anti-Castro uprisings throughout Cuba and the defection without a fight of a large proportion of the Cuban armed forces."[69]

Back in Washington, Secretary Rusk told the Taylor Commission that an internal uprising had been considered "utterly essential," and McGeorge Bundy filled in the plan's details: the invaders simply needed to win the first battle, thereby demonstrating that they "were better fighters, with better equipment," just as Colonel Hawkins had assured everyone. Then, after that initial showing, "defections would begin; uprisings would occur in other parts of the island, and so on." Obviously, commented Marine Corps Commandant David Shoup, Admiral Clark "wouldn't be taking 30,000 additional rifles if we didn't think there was going to be somebody to use them." He never expected the small paramilitary force to "overthrow Castro without support. They could never expect anything but annihilation."[70] In his memoir, the CIA's inspector general, Kirkpatrick, concluded that the expectation of local support had been a simple error of judgment, which led to "a complete miscalculation by the CIA operators of what was required to do the job."[71]

Many factors no doubt contributed to the defeat, but the fundamental flaw—the bedrock error—was the failure to understand that the Cubans would fight back. "What could they have thought of us Cubans?" asked Fidel Castro. "Who would believe that a people would be so stupid to receive them with open arms?"

We are going to give them all a medal and say thanks to [Nicaragua's Luis] Somoza [for allowing the use of Puerto Cabezas], the State Department, Mr. Kennedy, and Mr. Dulles for being so noble and so democratic and respectful of international laws and human rights, for preparing this group to liberate us from agrarian reform and urban reform and from all these teachers and literacy workers. Come again to bring the Yankee administrators; come again to close the beaches, to form aristocratic clubs, to give us unemployment, to bring back the soldiers for the barracks which have been transformed into schools, to bring lower wages and higher prices. Come again to exploit and rape.[72]

In the end, the United States was left with nothing but lies, a policy captured best by Arthur Schlesinger, who on 10 April wrote to JFK that "if some of our representatives cannot evade in debate the question whether the CIA has actually helped the Cuban rebels, they will presumably be obliged, in the traditional pre–U-2 manner, to deny any such CIA activity." He encouraged JFK to prepare an evasive answer for Cuba's inevitable claim that the invasion was U.S.-assisted, and "when lies must be told, they should be told by subordinate officials."[73]

Thus, in response to a request from an Alabama newspaper, the Department of Defense "categorically denied that any elements of the Alabama National Guard, units or individuals, had participated as such in any training program for anti-Castro rebels." The "as such" was crucial: the Pentagon knew that the CIA had hired independent specialists to train the Cuban pilots, that all of them happened to be members of the Alabama Air National Guard, and that four guard members had been killed during bombing runs in Cuba.[74] Others were clearly unwitting participants in the denial. Famously, U.N. ambassador Adlai Stevenson was misled into the most mortifying moment of his public career. A week before the first air strike, Schlesinger had flown to New York to brief Stevenson, arriving late, during the middle of Tracy Barnes's explanation that, yes, a group of Cubans was about to invade their homeland, and, yes, the U.S. had assisted with funds and training, but, no, the United States was not going to be involved. Neither Barnes nor Schlesinger made any effort to tell Stevenson the truth: that the entire effort was a CIA operation. Schlesinger's diary characterized this incomplete briefing as "an unfortunate misunderstanding," noting that Stevenson opposed the operation but "is prepared to try and make the best possible U.S. case."[75]

A week later, on Saturday, 15 April, a Cuban pilot climbed into a B-26 with Cuban air force markings and took off for Miami from the Puerto Cabezas air base, the existence of which Barnes had failed to mention to Ambassador Stevenson. Before landing, the pilot, Mario Zúñiga, opened his canopy and fired a few rounds from his pistol into one of the two engines, then landed his crippled aircraft, told U.S. immigration officials that he had defected from Castro's air force, and requested asylum. At that moment, eight exile-piloted B-26s were bombing three different Cuban airfields, seeking to knock out Castro's air capability.[76]

By 10:30 A.M., Cuban foreign minister Raúl Roa was standing before the U.N. General Assembly, pleading for help. A meeting of the General Assembly's First (Political) Committee was quickly scheduled for later in the day, and at that meeting, Roa charged the United States with bombing Cuba from bases in Guatemala and the United States. Stevenson insisted that the bombing had been done by defecting Cuban pilots. Holding up a picture of Zúñiga's aircraft, he pointed to "the markings of Castro air force on the tail, which everyone can see for himself. The Cuban star and the initials F.A.R. (for Fuerza Aérea Revolucionaria) are clearly visible." "Entirely false" was how Guatemala's U.N. envoy characterized Roa's claim that the invading forces had been trained in his country.[77]

Within hours, the cover had been blown (the eight machine guns on Zúñiga's B-26 were mounted in the nose cone; the six machine guns on Cuba's B-26s were mounted on the wings), and on Sunday evening Stevenson fired off a telegram to Secretary Rusk, the first two words of which were "Greatly Disturbed." Stevenson went on to say that he "had definite impression from Barnes when he was here that no action would be taken which could give us political difficulty." Now, Stevenson continued, "no one will believe that bombing attacks on Cuba from outside could have been organized without our complicity." Still unaware that the United States had engineered the entire episode, Stevenson added, "nor can I understand if we could not prevent such an outside attack from taking place at this time why I could not have been warned and provided pre-prepared material with which to defend us." Early the next morning, 17 April, a few hours after the brigade had landed, McGeorge Bundy flew up to New York to apologize and tell Stevenson the truth. With his mission accomplished, Bundy telephoned Rusk to report that the ambassador had agreed "to pick up the pieces and to see where he can go," but, Bundy noted, "there is a morale problem."[78]

If such a problem indeed existed, Stevenson initially hid it well. Later that day, when Foreign Minister Roa told the General Assembly that Cuba was being invaded "by a mercenary force organized, financed and armed by the Government of the United States and coming from Guatemala and Florida," Stevenson replied that Roa's charges were "totally false," a reply seconded once again by the Guatemalan representative, who added that his country "had never allowed and would never allow its territory to be used for the organization of acts of aggression against its American sister republics." Two days later, Stevenson cabled Rusk to say that he, too, was now ready to lie: "Having started this operation and having already paid heavy political price for it, I hope we will use covert means to maximum, to make it succeed and succeed fast. . . . Overt aid, if decided upon, must be based on sound legal position even if it is fiction."[79] A few hours later the invasion collapsed, making Stevenson the final senior official to climb aboard a sinking ship.

Cuba, in contrast, now claimed a solid triumph, as Richard Goodwin reported after a meeting with Che Guevara several months later: "He wanted to thank us very much for the invasion—that it had been a great political victory for them—enabled them to consolidate—and transformed them from an aggrieved little country to an equal." The day after the defeat, JFK told a gathering of newspaper editors that his patience was "not inexhaustible," adding emphatically that his government "will not hesitate in meeting its primary obligations which are the security of our Nation." But the administration clearly wanted the topic off the front pages: the minutes of a National Security Council meeting two days later "noted the President's view that there should be no further discussion outside the Government of the meaning of recent landings in Cuba, since the object now is to move forward."[80]

But what about the 1,179 prisoners? Cuba offered to exchange them for five hundred bulldozers, an idea that appeared to emerge unrehearsed from one of Fidel Castro's speeches: "Thousands and thousands of tractors have been distributed," he told the audience of peasant farmers, focusing on Cuba's agrarian reform, but "there are still not enough tractors to break all the ground." The prisoners' labor could help: "The least they can do is earn the bread they eat [and] if imperialism does not want its worms to work, let it exchange tractors and machinery for them." More specifically, he suggested, "let them send 500 bulldozers and we will return" the prisoners. Castro then asked for a vote: "If the peasants here are in agreement with this proposal, let them raise their hands. Good."[81]

Confusion immediately arose over the type of implement demanded. Castro had first used the Spanish word "*tractores*," then had switched to the English "bulldozers," and then had used "*tractores*" again but described bulldozer-like equipment: "The tractors must be of the tread-type, not with rubber tires, and the good ones that are used for building roads." Whatever the model, a "Tractors for Freedom" fund-raising committee was quickly assembled, cochaired by Eleanor Roosevelt, Milton Eisenhower, labor leader Walter Reuther, and banker Joseph Dodge, who informed the Cuban government that they would solicit private donations for the tractors.

The Cubans immediately sent ten of the prisoners to the United States to negotiate with the committee, but the talks hit snag after snag. The first occurred just an hour after the men arrived in Miami, when they were refused rooms at the Dupont Hotel because one of the ten was insufficiently Caucasian. The negotiations dragged on while Republicans objected to what they considered blackmail and while the fund-raising committee, claiming a heretofore unrecognized expertise in tropical farming, discussed the type of tractors that would be most appropriate for Cuba. In June, the committee telegraphed the Cuban government, "We are willing to make available 500 agricultural tractors with plowing accessories, disks, and harrows of the types needed the most to increase Cuba's agricultural production and raise the standard of living of the Cuban people."[82] Meanwhile, all of the captives were sentenced to thirty years in prison.

The committee then sent a group of agricultural experts to Havana, and by that time the central question was not the type of equipment Cubans should or should not want but whether the payment would be an "indemnity" for harming Cuba, as the Cubans insisted, or a "ransom" for the prisoners, as Washington preferred. Unable to reach an agreement, the experts returned to the United States, and in late June, the committee disbanded, returning unopened envelopes containing donations from more than seventy thousand citizens. Only in December 1962, after the missile crisis, were the prisoners exchanged for about sixty million dollars in food and medicine.[83]

IN THE MEANTIME, Cuba's revolutionary government had a solid victory. Arthur Schlesinger had warned JFK that the operation "would fix a malevolent image of the new Administration in the minds of millions," and as Schlesinger soon discovered while traveling in Europe, the invasion had done just that. It also tapped into the deepest well of Cuban nationalism, creating what probably stands as the most enthusiastic May Day audience in any country's history. "Rights do not come from size," Fidel Castro told the crowd. "Right does not come from one country being bigger than another. That does not matter. We have only a limited territory, a small nation, but our right is as respectable as that of any country, regardless of its size."[84]

There can be no long-term living with Castro as a neighbor.
— Taylor Commission, June 1961

7

STATE-SPONSORED TERRORISM

It was not the best time to reside in Camelot. "Everyone appeared to be jumping on everyone else," reported Undersecretary of State Chester Bowles following a cabinet meeting the day after the Bay of Pigs surrender. "It was about as grim as any meeting I can remember in all my experience in government, which is saying a good deal. The President was really quite shattered."[1] President John F. Kennedy had made the mistake of putting his eggs in a flimsy basket, out of which the bottom had fallen, and now he had to decide what to do next. Asked for advice, former president Dwight D. Eisenhower could offer no specific help beyond an admonition that "the U.S. would have to get rid of Castro." Former vice president Richard Nixon told JFK the same thing, and so did many others, from Florida senator George Smathers to Nicaraguan general Anastasio Somoza, leading Bowles to estimate that "if you had taken a vote at those first few meetings on what to do next after the Bay of Pigs, you would have had a three-to-one vote to invade Cuba." Perhaps the most imaginative advice came from McGeorge Bundy's principal assistant, Walt Rostow, who suggested trying elsewhere: "We have, initially, not done terribly well," he admitted, and now "there is building up a sense of frustration and a perception that we are up against a game we can't handle"; fortunately, Rostow continued, "there is one area where success against Communist techniques is conceivable and where success is desperately required in the Free World interest. That area is Viet-Nam."[2]

But most eyes, including those of the methodical Robert McNamara, remained fixed on Cuba. The defense secretary returned to the Pentagon after the 20 April cabinet meeting and ordered the Joint Chiefs to develop a plan for the military overthrow of the Cuban government. Two weeks later, he was handed a sobering answer from an interagency committee chaired by Assistant Secretary of Defense Paul Nitze: overthrowing Fidel Castro would be too expensive. An invasion would involve many civilian casualties and imperil the U.S. position of leadership in the Free World.[3]

Almost everyone who cooled down a bit before offering advice said the same thing. "If we react in frustrated anger we are likely to intensify the mistake," warned Senate majority leader Mike Mansfield. Returning from a three-week fence-mending trip to all ten South American capitals, Adlai Stevenson agreed, as did Arthur M. Schlesinger Jr. after a quick trip to Europe.[4] Bowles, whose Yale education had clearly not included instruction in spelling, summarized, "We have emerged as the antagonist of a petty Latin American Communist dictator and with all our power and influence unable to quite persuade others to see the world as we see it. The net result will be to pump some air back into Castro's deflated prestige and to renew in many people's minds the memory of the USA as the clumsey, insensitive, interfering 'collasus of the north.'" Norman Mailer assessed the invasion as "one of the blunders of the century." Recalling his campaign endorsement, Mailer now wrote to the president, "I may have made the error of sailing against the stereotype that you were a calculating untried over-ambitious and probably undeserving young stud who came from a very wealthy and much un-loved family." Speaking for much of the East Coast intelligentsia that had crowded around the stylish Kennedys, Mailer accused JFK of driving Cuba into Moscow's arms "as deliberately and insanely as a man setting out to cuckold himself." Meanwhile, Schlesinger was assuring Herbert Matthews that there would never be another Bay of Pigs.[5]

But something had to be done. Both the State Department and the CIA were especially concerned that the continued existence of Cuba's revolutionary government would destroy the new administration's reformist policy toward the rest of Latin America—reactionary leaders might refuse to institute essential reforms, leaving those affected by the Revolution of Rising Expectations with no alternative to a Castro-type rebellion; at the same time, genuine reformers at the other end of the political spectrum might insist that Washington underwrite their too-radical reforms with the tacit threat that failure to help would provoke a turn toward the Cuban model. But there was hope: "If Castro were eliminated, the US would be in a much stronger position to insist upon adoption of a program of moderate, evolutionary change by the ruling groups in Latin America." Two days after this assessment came the Nitze report, which advised against an invasion but nonetheless warned that "as long as Castro thrives, his major threat— the example and stimulus of a working communist revolution—will persist," and Secretary of State Dean Rusk emphasized the same point at the following day's National Security Council (NSC) meeting: "The U.S. must take all measures to precipitate his downfall or face the possibility that all South America will come under Communist influence."[6] Castro had to go.

But engineering his exit had now become more difficult. The Bay of Pigs had provoked the roundup of Cuba's remaining dissidents, and the nucleus of an opposition movement—tens of thousands of Cubans—had already left the island; as a result, the State-CIA joint report noted, "every key national figure in Cuban society, with the notable exception of the Catholic hierarchy, is by now either a dedicated supporter of communism and the Castro regime or a non-Communist so deeply committed to the regime as to be unlikely to turn against it."[7] To make matters even worse, the Soviet Union was increasing its support, symbolized by a goodwill visit by Soviet cosmonaut Yuri Gagarin, the first human in space. As Cuban pilots buzzed the welcoming crowd in their newly unveiled MiGs, Castro pinned a recently minted medal, the Order of Playa Girón, on Gagarin's uniform.

Castro had immediately capitalized on the U.S. attack. The day after the preemptive air strikes, he announced that the revolution had turned to socialism, and within a few days he was using the failed attack to build Cubans' pride: "They should have been ashamed to be engaged in this battle of Goliath against David," he told an elated audience after the brigade's defeat, "and to lose it besides." But now, he warned his 26th of July audience, the gloves were off and Cubans had to be ready to "fight to the last man against whoever sets foot on our land." Summing up the situation from his Havana vantage point, the Canadian ambassador wrote that the invasion "substantiated the Government's warnings against imperialist aggression from the United States; the ardent patriotism which it excited enabled the Castro regime to suppress all internal opposition, to step up the pace of its 'socialist' revolution and to sanctify as sacrifices the exigencies of the economic crisis which Cuba is experiencing."[8]

And Cuba was not the only country with a domestic political audience. In a speech delivered the day the brigade landed at the Bay of Pigs (but before the news reached Washington), Senator Barry Goldwater, the rising star of the Republican Party, used Cuba as an example of the new administration's "astounding timidity and indecision," telling the Daughters of the American Revolution, "We should make it absolutely clear, in the most explicit terms, that Communist governments will not be tolerated in the Western Hemisphere—and that the Castro regime, being such a government, will be eliminated." As Goldwater stood up to talk, the Cuban "failure" was still considered a Republican legacy; by the time he sat down, it was becoming the new administration's first major foreign policy initiative. After the Bay of Pigs, Schlesinger recalled, "concern for the domestic political implications of Castro and Cuba was driving both Kennedys."[9]

The new administration thus had little choice but to pick itself up, dust itself off, and start all over again, driven not simply by the imperatives of domestic politics or by the personal sting of defeat but also by the pervasive Cold War fear of a tilt in the ever-fragile balance of power. Together, these conditions produced what came next: the Kennedy administration's multifaceted attack on the Cuban government: diplomatic isolation, sabotage and assassination, and economic pressure.[10]

THE FIRST STEP was to isolate Cuba diplomatically from other Latin American countries. Doing so could be achieved only within the constraints of the inter-American legal system, so the State Department waited only four days after the Bay of Pigs to instruct U.S. embassies to inquire not simply whether Latin Americans would agree to an Organization of American States (OAS) meeting of consultation but also whether the meeting could be called under Article 6 of the Rio Treaty; unlike the 1960 San José meeting, called under the OAS charter, Rio Treaty sanctions would be mandatory. The State Department justified using the more demanding Rio Treaty because the Castro government's ties with the Soviet Union had become a menace to regional security.[11]

A welcome early reply came from the Colombian government of Alberto Lleras Camargo, which agreed to help with a meeting's organization—but only after "very bad impression caused by frustrated invasion [has] dissipated." Other major Latin American leaders were far less enthusiastic. Despite several months of coaxing the new government of João Goulart, Secretary Rusk reported that pivotal Brazil "felt that the attitude that should be taken toward Cuba was to try to bring it back as a full member of the American system rather than to put it outside." Worse yet, as the U.S. ambassador to the OAS soon discovered, this opposition was not passive: "Brazil has gone to work energetically doing missionary work to achieve a negative vote" on any proposal to hold a meeting, reported Delesseps Morrison, and Itamaraty had picked up an important ally: "The Mexican Ambassador has stated to me that they will not make a campaign and will be 'fatalistic' about having this meeting that they do not want," but Mexico, too, was "going to press hard to defeat the Colombian proposal."[12]

In late 1961, however, just when U.S. officials had resigned themselves to the idea that no meeting would take place, Fidel Castro announced, "I am a Marxist-Leninist and will be a Marxist-Leninist until the last day of my life." Striking while the iron was hot, Lleras Camargo within hours converted what had been Washington's diplomatic probe into Colombia's formal request for a meeting of consultation under Article 6 of the Rio Treaty, and the OAS Council, obliged by its rules to vote yes or no, immediately scheduled a meeting of consultation for 22 January at Punta del Este, Uruguay. A few days later the United States picked up an important ally when President Rómulo Betancourt told JFK that Venezuela would support collective sanctions; that backing would help balance the opposition of Mexico, but the administration was stymied when it sought Argentina's help to balance Brazil.[13]

The Rio Treaty required fourteen votes—two-thirds of the treaty's twenty-one signatories—for the imposition of mandatory sanctions, and on the eve of the conference, the United States had only twelve: an odd-bedfellow coalition of moderate anticommunist democrats such as Colombia's Lleras Camargo and Venezuela's Betancourt on the one hand and the region's traditional strongmen such as Paraguay's Alfredo Stroessner and Nicaragua's Somoza on the other.[14] Of the remaining nine countries, Cuba would obviously oppose any resolution, as would what came to be known as the Soft Six (Argentina, Bolivia, Brazil, Chile, Ecuador, and Mexico). That left two undeclared participants, Uruguay and Haiti.

Geographically wedged between two of the Soft Six and far removed from the United States, Uruguayans had balked even at serving as the conference host, but Rusk was determined to obtain their vote, and he was assisted by General Edward Lansdale, who reported that "the OAS meeting is to be supported by public demonstrations in Latin America, generated by CIA, and a psychological campaign assisted by the USIA."[15] Some combination of Lansdale's chanting demonstrators and Rusk's arm-twisting eventually succeeded.

The fourteenth vote, Haiti, proved the most elusive, with Rusk reporting from Punta del Este that a "full day and night of most intensive negotiations has failed to produce a formula on which there can be more than 13 votes."[16] Then Morrison, the U.S. ambassador to the OAS, took Haitian foreign minister René Chalmers into a side room for a heart-to-heart discussion of development projects the United States might fund under the new Alliance for Progress, a significant change in U.S. policy since Haiti, delinquent in its debt payments, had been suspended from the U.S. aid program. After inspecting Morrison's dangling bait for about an hour, the Haitian envoy found himself especially attracted to the idea of expanding Haiti's airport to accommodate jet aircraft, and that offer cinched the deal.

François "Papa Doc" Duvalier's government may have emerged as the clearest winner at Punta del Este (the Port-au-Prince runway soon was being lengthened with a $2.8 million grant from the U.S. Agency for International Development), but Washington won, too: the OAS approved a resolution that "the present Government of Cuba, which has officially identified itself as a Marxist-Leninist government, is incompatible with the principles and objectives of the inter-American system, [and] this incompatibility excludes the present Government of Cuba from participation in the inter-American system." Cuba's suspension continues to this day.[17]

Although a significant step had been taken to isolate Cuba, U.S. officials were disappointed by the six abstentions, especially regional leaders Mexico, Brazil, Chile, and Argentina. "They let us down," Rusk reported, but he also told JFK that "we should not exaggerate the character of the differences recorded at Punta del Este," a point Fidel Castro confirmed years later when he told East Germany's Erich Honecker that in the early 1960s in Latin America, "not a single country had a friendly attitude toward us."[18]

WHAT MORE COULD BE DONE? How about a program of sabotage focused upon blowing up "such targets as refineries, power plants, micro wave stations, radio and TV installations, strategic highway bridges and railroad facilities, military and naval installations and equipment, certain industrial plants and sugar refineries."[19] The CIA proposed just that approach a month after the Bay of Pigs, and the State Department endorsed the proposal, as did Attorney General Robert Kennedy; indeed, the president's brother liked the idea so much that he claimed to have invented it: "My idea is to stir things up on [the] island with espionage, sabotage, general disorder, run & operated by Cubans themselves," all of which might not overthrow Castro, "but we have nothing to lose in my estimate." Aide Richard Goodwin agreed: "If the best happens we will unseat Castro. If not, then at least we will emerge with a stronger underground." Former Brazilian President Juscelino Kubitschek reinforced this message by warning Kennedy that "any direct military action against Cuba would rouse vast areas of public opinion against the U.S. [Kubitschek] would favor some form of indirect action."[20]

In early November, six months after the Bay of Pigs, JFK authorized the CIA's "Program of Covert Action," now dubbed Operation Mongoose, and named Lansdale its chief of operations. A few days later, President Kennedy told a Seattle audience, "We cannot, as a free nation, compete with our adversaries in tactics of terror, assassination, false promises, counterfeit mobs and crises."[21] Perhaps—but the Mongoose decision indicated that he was willing to try.

General Lansdale appeared to be a good choice. He had risen through the military ranks as an expert on guerrilla warfare, beginning in 1943 in the Pacific, and after the war he had been assigned to help the Philippine government defeat the Huk rebellion. In 1953 he was transferred to Saigon to advise the French forces and later the South Vietnamese government on counterinsurgency. Now promoted to the position of assistant secretary of defense for special operations, Lansdale was something of a duck out of water in Washington—"completely uninhibited in dealing with politicians and civilians," recalled Roswell Gilpatric, an urbane Kennedy appointee. Worse yet, the CIA's Tom Parrott found Lansdale "totally incompetent," and the agency's Richard Helms saw that "those who worked side by side with him didn't believe that he was the miracle worker that other people made him out to be." One such coworker was the CIA's Sam Halpern, who characterized Lansdale as "a good Madison Avenue man in a gray flannel suit who could sell refrigerators to Eskimos, and that's about what he did in this case." "Overrated" was the term used by Chester Bowles, who emphasized, however, that Operation Mongoose was a higher-level failure: "The liberals were looking for a cheap way out."[22]

Helping Lansdale with the day-to-day planning and execution would be an interagency Caribbean Survey Group, but policy decisions would be made by what came to be known as the Special Group (Augmented)—the Eisenhower era's old Special Group, now augmented by Robert Kennedy and, as chair, General Maxwell Taylor, the president's military adviser. RFK was the dominant figure, always insisting on more—more ideas, more action, more quickly. "The final chapter on Cuba has not been written," he announced at one of the group's early meetings; overthrowing the Castro government was now "the top priority of the United States Government—all else is secondary—no time, money, effort, or manpower is to be spared."[23]

With behavior that bordered on bullying, the younger Kennedy soon alienated the State Department's coordinator of Cuban affairs, John Crimmins, who found RFK "abrasive, unpleasant, arbitrary." So did a significant number of CIA officials, including Thomas Parrott, who considered RFK "an unprincipled sinister little bastard," while Sam Halpern dismissed him as "this boy, really, this hot-tempered boy." Even a friendly critic such as Bowles noted that RFK "was all over the lot—as were lots of liberals, I might add—so absorbed with domestic affairs that they knew very little about world politics or other affairs. Yet they carried over into world affairs the same sort of confidence they had in talking about domestic affairs, the same assurance, which they weren't entitled to." Another friendly critic, Pentagon attorney Joseph Califano, watched with dismay: "As Robert Kennedy pressed for tougher actions, I thought: he is obsessed with Castro; he is pursuing a total war with Castro. The intensity I had admired in his dealing with Mississippi governor Ross Barnett and Alabama governor George Wallace now struck me as vengeful."[24]

For his part, General Lansdale enthusiastically accepted RFK's marching orders and quickly settled on both a broad strategy ("the regime is to be overthrown by a popular movement of Cubans from within Cuba") and some initial steps, "centered around the selection and eventual introduction into Cuba of a nucleus of anti-Castro Cubans; once they are in the country and in a position to operate, then a number of collateral supporting actions would be taken." The details of these supporting actions were vague—a month after receiving presidential approval, Lansdale reported only that his "special project team is working on bold new actions," which ranged from heaven ("enlisting the cooperation of the Church to bring the women of Cuba into action") to hell ("exploiting the potential of the underworld in Cuban cities to harass and bleed the Communist control apparatus").[25]

Badly burned by the Bay of Pigs, the CIA now warned that overthrowing the Cuban government would not be easy. "Of the 27 or 28 agents CIA now has in Cuba, only 12 are in communication and these communications are infrequent. A team of 7 that were infiltrated December 19th were captured and two of them were on TV in a 'confession show' last Saturday night." Undeterred, Lansdale and his associates spent the holidays fleshing out their plan, which they presented to the Special Group (Augmented) in early 1962. The general idea was to generate within Cuba something called a "climactic moment," which would trigger a rebellion. Such a moment will come from an angry reaction of the people to a government action (sparked by an incident), or from a fracturing of the leadership cadre within the regime, or both. (A major goal of the Project is to bring this about.) The popular movement will capitalize on this climactic moment by initiating an open revolt. Areas will be taken and held. If necessary, the popular movement will appeal for help to the free nations of the Western Hemisphere. The United States, if possible in concert with other Western Hemisphere nations, will then give open support to the Cuban people's revolt. Such support will include military force, as necessary.

Unlike the Bay of Pigs operation, which assumed that disaffected Cubans were poised to join the invaders and capable of overthrowing the Castro government, Operation Mongoose explicitly envisioned that "final success will require decisive U.S. military intervention."[26]

BUT THE UNITED STATES first had to create a climatic moment by making life miserable for everyday Cubans. There were two distinct parts to this effort. One—the Economic Denial Program—was administratively separate from Operation Mongoose, but the two were peas in the same conceptual pod: both were aimed at generating discontent, one through sabotage and the other through economic deprivation.

Of the two, Mongoose at first was by far the more important, probably because Lansdale's January 1962 plan sketched out such a breathtaking panorama—thirty-two specific activities, each assigned to a part of the U.S. government. The CIA received the lion's share of the responsibility, including Task 21 ("inducing failures in food crops") and Task 30 ("sabotage actions"). Lansdale gave the agency three weeks to produce a concrete schedule for "the sabotage of

(1) shipping in Cuban waters and harbors,
(2) Cuban transport facilities,
(3) communications facilities,
(4) equipment for the refining of petroleum,
(5) facilities for producing and distributing power,
(6) industry,
(7) food supplies,
(8) key military and police installations."

The Department of Defense was assigned the supporting role of supplying the saboteurs with transportation—Lansdale's eye-popping wish list included "two submarines, PT boats, Coast Guard type cutters, Special Forces trainers, C-54 aircraft, F-86 aircraft [for intimidating sonic booms], helio-couriers, Army leaflet battalion, and Guantanamo as a base for submarine operations." If all the participants did their jobs, Cuban living conditions would deteriorate, disaffection would grow, and a climactic moment would occur. Lansdale pinpointed the first two weeks of October 1962 as the date of the government's downfall.[27]

After attending enough Special Group (Augmented) meetings to get a feeling for how Mongoose was unfolding, Robert Kennedy asked the CIA's new director, John McCone, for his opinion of General Lansdale and the Cuban effort. Skeptical from the beginning, McCone clearly did not want to annoy the younger Kennedy by throwing cold water on the approach RFK so vigorously endorsed, but the CIA chief gently warned that "(a) an opera-tion of this type, as presently planned, has never been attempted before, (b) it will be extremely difficult to accomplish, (c) the CIA and the U.S. Gov-ernment are short on assets to carry out the proposed program." At the same time, Richard Bissell's replacement as deputy director of operations, Richard Helms, worried that the number of available Cuban saboteurs was "not as great as we were led to believe," and within a week of receiving Lans-dale's original plan, the CIA had begun to argue that "it is not likely that we can make the resistance groups self-sustaining as is envisioned in Gen-eral Lansdale's 'Concept of Operation.'"[28] The State Department's Bureau of Intelligence and Research was even more concerned: "I am afraid we may be heading for a fiasco," warned the bureau's director, Roger Hilsman. "The concept appears to depend in large measure on building up an inter-nal political action organization *in Cuba* which would enjoy the support of the majority of the Cuban people. Presumably, it would be primarily CIA's job to build such an organization. I have seen no hard intelligence which would lead me to support that there exists, or that the Agency has assets for bringing into existence in the near future, an internal political action organization which would assure the support of the majority of the Cuban people against the Castro regime." If an internal uprising failed to occur, Hilsman worried that General Lansdale might become a Dr. Strangelove, engineering his own climactic moment to force the United States into an invasion.[29]

Dismissing these naysayers, the Department of Defense lined up solidly behind Lansdale. Within two weeks it had cobbled together a cluster of thirteen exotic schemes, each with its own name: Operation Dirty Trick would "provide irrevocable proof that, should the Mercury manned orbit flight fail, the fault lies with the Communists et al. in Cuba"; Operation Good Times was to "prepare a desired photograph, such as an obese Castro with two beauties in any situation desired, ostensibly within a room in the Castro residence, lavishly furnished, and a table brim[m]ing over with the most delectable Cuban food with an underlying caption (appropriately Cuban) such as 'My ration is different.' Make as many prints as desired on sterile paper and then distribute over the countryside by air drops or agents." A month later, the Joint Chiefs of Staff sent Secretary McNamara an even more imaginative set of proposals—eight different scenarios that could be used as pretexts to invade. The suggestions included eleven ways to fake an attack on Guantánamo—"lob mortar shells from outside of base," "sink a boatload of Cubans enroute to Florida," "demonstrate convincingly that a Cuban aircraft has attacked and shot down a chartered civil airliner." Wisely selecting an expendable subspecies, the Pentagon suggested that "the passengers could be a group of college students."[30]

In mid-March Lansdale told JFK that "the chance of fracturing the regime and creating a valid revolution is becoming more feasible," adding that "CIA professionals were now agreeing." That was news to McCone, who was sitting in on the meeting, and the agency countered five days later with a discouraging national intelligence estimate (NIE) describing Cuba's internal opposition as "limited, uncoordinated, unsupported, and desperate." The Joint Chiefs of Staff then warned that Lansdale's targeted date for Castro's overthrow, the first two weeks of October, would be too late; Castro had to be stopped now, not six months from now, and the Joint Chiefs "see no prospect of early success in overthrowing the present communist regime either as a result of internal uprisings or external political or psychological pressures." Instead, the chiefs urged McNamara to obtain a green light for a return to basics: "a national policy of early military intervention in Cuba [should] be adopted by the United States."[31]

In what may have been a coordinated effort, on the same day the CIA's principal Mongoose official, William Harvey, reminded McCone that Lansdale's plan rested on the buildup of frustration among the Cuban people, and now, after three months of all preparation and no action, it was becoming obvious that Mongoose would take too much time. Why not think instead of directly triggering the climactic moment or, if that was not possible, of creating a provocation and then "interven[ing] immediately with sufficient military strength to eliminate organized military opposition"?[32]

Never forgetting why his predecessor now lived in unwelcome retirement, McCone was reluctant to jump off the high dive without first seeing if there was any water in the pool, especially since the NIE had warned that an invasion would be only the beginning: "A prolonged US military occupation of Cuba would probably be necessary."[33] Clearly upset by the CIA's inaction, Lansdale told Harvey in early August that it was time to put up or shut up: either to focus on producing an invasion-justifying provocation or to "give careful consideration as to whether, in the face of other heavy demands and commitments, the Clandestine Service can long continue to afford the present level of effort against Cuba." Not authorized to make such a decision, Harvey gave McCone a memo laying out four options, from the cancellation of Mongoose to a straight-up U.S. invasion. In between were two options that constituted a "soft" and a "hard" form of Mongoose, and McCone was urged to continue supporting the hard version, "triggering of a planned revolt in Cuba to be supported immediately by US military forces." Harvey said that the operation still "has an excellent chance of succeeding," but he acknowledged that the light at the end of General Lansdale's tunnel had receded; instead of the original target of October 1962, Castro's overthrow was now promised by late 1963.[34]

As McCone digested these memoranda, he continued to worry about Lansdale's sophomoric, gung ho attitude, and he was not alone—at a Special Group (Augmented) meeting a few days later, all the participants seemed to be backing away from the end of the diving board, with McGeorge Bundy opposed to the use of navy submarines, Alexis Johnson opposed to any violent form of sabotage, and Maxwell Taylor worried that unseasoned junior officers had seized too much control. Back in his office, McCone wrote out his thoughts: "The meeting was unsatisfactory . . . and left me with a feeling that very considerable reservation exists as to just where we are going with Operation Mongoose."[35]

But the Pentagon remained fired up. On 21 August, Robert McNamara told a meeting of high-level officials, "We should take every possible aggressive action in the fields of intelligence, sabotage and guerrilla warfare, utilizing Cubans." With RFK seated at the table, McCone clearly felt obliged to agree that these things could be done but observed that the results to date had been disappointing, and Bundy reminded everyone that the Joint Chiefs' alternative, an invasion, could have a major cost—serious negative repercussions on U.S. interests elsewhere. McCone's minutes indicate that this meeting, too, "was inconclusive with respect to any particular course of action," but by this time, placating the president's hotheaded brother had become part of the game, so two days later the CIA director sought out RFK to reassure him that the agency was in full agreement not only that "Cuba was our most serious problem" but also that ousting Castro "was the key to all of Latin America; if Cuba succeeds, we can expect most of Latin America to fall."[36]

With McNamara recommending an infusion of new energy and with the Joint Chiefs recommending an invasion, but with senior State Department and CIA officials reluctant to go along, it fell to the chair of the Special Group (Augmented), General Taylor, to find some common ground. He agreed with the Joint Chiefs that there was "no likelihood of an overthrow of the government by internal means and without the direct use of U.S. military force" but was vague with his recommendation that President Kennedy approve "a somewhat more aggressive program." The president, in turn, ordered that Mongoose activity should be increased "with all possible speed."[37]

This obscure directive required yet another plan, which Lansdale produced in a week. It contained not thirty-two but fifty-six action items, although most of the additions reflected Taylor's recommendation that the focus be expanded to protecting the rest of Latin America from Cuban-style insurgents. The Cuba-focused items reiterated existing plans (Item 27 was "major sabotage operations") and added a few new projects with little chance of affecting Castro's government. Item 20, for example, involved developing a means of delivering propaganda via hot-air balloons, which was approved on the understanding that it would give Cuban exiles something to do—"keep them busy on projects like this, which are less dangerous than projects in which they might otherwise engage."[38]

A few days later, the CIA's deputy director for intelligence, Ray Cline, threw cold water on Lansdale's new plan: "All available evidence indicates that the prospects for a spontaneous internal uprising against Castro without outside help are extremely small and that, if one should occur, its chances of success would be nil." The Pentagon concluded three weeks later that a climactic moment was never going to trigger Castro's ouster unless it was a part of a military revolt, which seemed highly unlikely. But an impatient Robert Kennedy insisted on accelerated action, prompting Lansdale to promise "a series of proposals in the near future (with sabotage given priority attention)." Now becoming desperate, he asked the navy to prepare a fireworks display—to "fire star-shells from a submarine to illuminate the Havana area at night." With the heavens exploding, Lansdale's idea was "to generate a rumor inside Cuba about portents signifying the downfall of the regime."[39]

Meeting with Mongoose officials a day after U-2 overflights had revealed the existence of Soviet missiles in Cuba but before the administration had decided what to do about them, the attorney general again complained that "the Operation had been under way for a year, that the results were discouraging, that there had been no acts of sabotage, and that even the one which had been attempted had failed twice." The CIA had a response at hand: yet another set of nine sabotage proposals—"a demolition attack by a hit-and-run raider team on the Matanzas power plant," for example—but the minutes indicate that RFK was not placated: "The Attorney General then stated that in view of this lack of progress, he was going to give Operation Mongoose more personal attention. In order to do this, he will hold a meeting every morning at 0930 with the Mongoose operational representatives."[40]

THEN CAME THE MISSILE CRISIS. In mid-1962, an NIE concluded that "on balance, Castro is in a stronger position now than appeared likely a few months ago." Militarily, the Cuban armed forces were better prepared to suppress an insurrection and could easily repel another Bay of Pigs–style invasion, largely because the Soviet Union was pouring weapons into Cuba, including a completely new air force featuring forty-five MiG jet fighters flown by sixty bloc-trained Cuban pilots. Finally, an anti-Castro military revolt was now out of the question. Cuba, in short, was not going to be another Guatemala, and unless the United States was willing to send in the marines—lots of marines—physical force was not going to solve Washington's problem.[41]

With the discouraging NIE in their hands, both senior and midlevel officials gathered in Secretary Rusk's office a week later to consider Washington's options. Ominously, an aide preparing Rusk for the meeting noted that "General Lansdale called this morning to inquire whether we had done a paper on policy toward the establishment of a Soviet Base in Cuba. I told him not yet. He may bring this up. You will recall that it was decided that the possibility was too remote to waste time on."[42]

But the possibility was not considered remote either at CIA headquarters, where the agency's principal Mongoose official was warning that Moscow might use Cuba as a military base, or at the Pentagon, where the Navy was distributing several reports about extensive military construction at eight separate sites, including a description of some newly arrived missiles ("20ft–21ft in length and 18 inch in diameter, red in color with yellow nose cones") and the behavior of Russian troops ("can be seen frequently swimming in the nude"). Looking over these reports, State's Bureau of Intelligence and Research acknowledged "unusually heavy Soviet shipments" but concluded that "the most likely explanation of Moscow's stepped up military assistance is that it is designed to enhance the Cuban regime's defense capabilities." In mid-September, a special NIE concluded that an offensive base "would be incompatible with Soviet practice to date and with Soviet policy as we presently estimate it."[43]

But the intelligence community was not the only group drawing conclusions; the mainstream media also knew of the Soviet arms shipments, and rising coverage culminated in a mid-September issue of *Time* magazine featuring James Monroe on its cover with the caption: "The Monroe Doctrine and Communist Cuba." Placed on the defensive less than two months before the off-year election, JFK promised that "if at any time the Communist buildup in Cuba were to endanger or interfere with our security in any way . . . or become an offensive military base of significant capacity for the Soviet Union, then this country will do whatever must be done to protect its own security and that of its allies." Standing before the U.N. General Assembly a few days later, Soviet foreign minister Andrei Gromyko warned that an attack on Cuba would mean war, but that only served to provoke Congress, which promptly passed a joint resolution asserting that "the United States is determined . . . to prevent in Cuba the creation or use of an externally supported military capability endangering the security of the United States." Hyperpartisan to the end, former president Harry Truman blamed everything on the Republicans: "The reason we're in trouble in Cuba is that Ike didn't have the guts to enforce the Monroe Doctrine."[44] Cuba had once again become an election issue.

And once again the debate was about the possibility of a shift in the global balance of power. The two weapons that would soon become the bone of contention were SS-4 medium-range missiles capable of hitting any target south of an arc traced between Dallas and Washington, D.C., and SS-5 intermediate-range missiles capable of reaching anywhere in the contiguous forty-eight states except the Pacific Northwest. Since the Kremlin's arsenal contained only about seventy-five relatively inaccurate long-range intercontinental missiles, the Cuba-based SS-4s and SS-5s would increase significantly the damage the Soviet Union could inflict with a first strike and, as State Department analysts soon reported, represented "a serious dilution of US strategic deterrent capability." Even the shorter-range SS-4s could destroy about 40 percent of the nation's strategic bombers before crews could get the engines running.[45]

In September and early October, Ambassador Anatoly Dobrynin repeatedly looked senior U.S. officials in the eye and denied that the Soviet Union was placing offensive missiles in Cuba, and on 18 October, Gromyko personally assured President Kennedy that Soviet aid was exclusively for "the purpose of contributing to the defense capabilities of Cuba and the development of its peaceful economy."[46] This assurance came four days after a U-2 overflight had confirmed the missiles' presence and four days before JFK went before the public to announce his response—the imposition of a naval quarantine and a demand that the Soviet Union remove all its offensive weapons.

The crisis ended when Khrushchev agreed to withdraw "the arms Kennedy says are worrying him." Referring to the bargaining that had occurred during the intervening days, Khrushchev explained that "the imperialists have stood by their positions of strength, stubborn as they are, knowing that humanity is fighting to avoid a thermonuclear war." JFK could afford to be belligerent, he continued, because the wealthy Kennedys had private bomb shelters that were "not within the reach of the humble people of the United States."[47]

The adjective "Cuban" is placed in front of the term "missile crisis" because that is where the missiles were located, not because Cuba had anything to do with its resolution. The editor of the newspaper *Revolución* apparently learned of the Kennedy-Khrushchev agreement while listening to the radio and broke the news to Castro, who responded by cursing the Soviet leader: "Son of a bitch! Bastard! Asshole!" "Fidel went on in that vein for quite some time," Carlos Franqui recalled; "the Russians had abandoned us, made a deal with the Americans, and never even bothered to inform us." Years later, Castro rationalized that "it was not possible [for the Soviets] to consult us, due to lack of time, with regard to the final solution," but few would have envied Anastas Mikoyan when he arrived in Cuba for a fence-mending visit just days after the crisis ended. "We were profoundly incensed," Castro recalled in 1968, and he used the word "bitter" to characterize his discussions with Mikoyan: "endless arguing and counter-arguing . . . characterized by total and complete disagreement."[48]

But Mikoyan managed to begin the reconciliation process, which continued during Castro's monthlong visit to the Soviet Union in the spring of 1963; returning home, he gave the appearance of having been mollified, telling Cubans about "the affection shown toward the Cuban revolution, the affection shown toward Cuba, the sympathy, the interest. It was an incredible thing."[49] But much more tangible was Moscow's agreement to boost economic aid; in early 1964 the Soviets pledged to increase trade by 22 percent, to pay substantially more than the world price for Cuban sugar, and to provide almost half of their exports on credit, with repayment terms left to future discussions. In addition to this increased aid, Cuba's consolation was that the capitulation came from Moscow, not Havana: "We did not give a single inch," Castro recalled in 1990. "If those missiles had been ours, they would still be there."[50]

As for the logic behind the missiles, Castro repeatedly justified his decision to accept their placement as a defensive move—a deterrent—telling journalist Bill Moyers that Cuba feared an invasion: "That danger, in our opinion, existed in a real manner. This was behind the decision to set the strategic missiles in Cuba."[51] Robert McNamara admitted that "if I had been a Cuban leader, I think I might have expected a U.S. invasion," and a State Department memo written only days before the crisis listed seventeen hostile acts that had already been taken against Cuba, and the list did not include the menacing Caribbean military maneuvers such as the recent "Quick Kick," which involved seventy-nine ships and forty thousand U.S. troops. Most of the seventeen were secret operations, but Cubans almost certainly knew much of what Arthur Schlesinger did—that the CIA's Task Force W had mushroomed to four hundred U.S. employees overseeing the sabotage and guerrilla operations of "over fifty proprietary fronts, its own navy of fast boats, a rudimentary air force and two thousand Cuban agents."[52] By 1962, the largest CIA station in the world was located in Miami, and its only job was to overthrow the Cuban government.

But now the missiles were on their way back to the Soviet Union, leaving Cuba with nothing more than Khrushchev's claim that the United States had promised not to invade. On 27 October, JFK had in fact written to Khrushchev that if the Soviet Union would withdraw its offensive weapons under U.N. supervision, then the United States would "give assurances against an invasion of Cuba."[53] No initial misunderstanding existed on this point, but the Pentagon soon prepared an elaborate document concluding that the president had promised to forgo only an "armed seizure by U.S. forces," while other actions such as a "Bay of Pigs–type operation" had not been ruled out.[54] The State Department's Bureau of Intelligence and Research simultaneously recommended against any attempt to tie up all the loose ends of the crisis into a single written document, since by avoiding being explicit "the US would preserve its freedom for future action to force the downfall of Castro." Nonetheless, three days later, JFK told reporters that he stood by his no-invasion pledge: "We will not, of course, abandon the political, economic, and other efforts of this hemisphere to halt subversion from Cuba nor our purpose and hope that the Cuban people shall some day be truly free. But these policies are very different from any intent to launch a military invasion of the island."[55]

Such statements were for public consumption; behind closed doors the next day, the president told his closest advisers that "our objective is to preserve our right to invade Cuba."[56] One way around the pledge was to point out that it was contingent on on-site inspection of the Soviet withdrawal, and Cubans had refused to allow that: "Our country will never be inspected by anyone," Castro said; "within our frontiers, we are the ones who rule, and we are the ones who do the inspecting. That is all there is to it."[57] Since Cuba would not permit an inspection, Rusk told the Senate in early 1963, Washington's pledge was no longer binding, and by late April JFK was talking as if the pledge had never been made, asking McNamara, "Are we keeping our Cuban contingency invasion plans up to date?" Early in the Johnson administration, McGeorge Bundy commented that "this pledge was always subject to Cuba's good behavior," and a Nixon-era memorandum concluded that "Castro's refusal to permit UN verification meant the agreement did not become operative and the U.S. is not bound."[58]

As JFK told the NSC, "The time will probably come when we will have to act again on Cuba," but at least for now the crisis was over, as the United States and the Soviet Union jointly informed U.N. secretary-general U Thant during the first week of 1963. The CIA then reported that "the Soviets have withdrawn 42 strategic missiles and 42 jet bombers and their related equipment, and about four or five thousand personnel probably associated with the maintenance and operation of this equipment." This "represents all the strategic weapons placed in Cuba by the Soviets."[59]

NOW WHAT? The United States had prevailed in the missile crisis, but the victory had been sobering, and almost everyone was having second thoughts about reckless behavior. With RFK's I-want-to-meet-every-morning criticism ringing in his ears, Lansdale had gone into overdrive: in the midst of the missile crisis, he gave the Special Group (Augmented) a memo indicating that three well-armed sabotage teams were en route to Cuba and that ten more were ready to depart, all with the goal of "major acts of sabotage." As the world teetered on the brink of war, the Special Group told Lansdale that "no major sets of sabotage should be undertaken at this time," but "this decision will be reviewed in about a week."[60]

As it turned out, the October crisis served as a cold shower for Operation Mongoose. After a year during which the United States had held almost-daily meetings, had infiltrated agents and arms, and had attempted to sabotage shipping and occasionally taken potshots at waterfront targets, Cuba's revolution showed no sign of weakening. One of the officers on the State Department's Cuba desk captured the mood perfectly: "The entire operation was pathetic, and I ruefully longed for a way to turn it off."[61] In early November a CIA memo concluded that "hindsight must now reveal to others, as well as it has to us, that a Chief of Operations (i.e. Lansdale) was never actually needed," and now it was time to kill the operation—but, as a CIA officer advised, it should be done gently:

> Absolutely no attempt on our part should be made to unseat Lansdale. Remember that the Attorney General was fighting Lansdale's battle as recently as two weeks ago. Secondly, McNamara and Gilpatric still look upon Lansdale as something of a mystic and are on the defensive by virtue of his relationship with the Attorney General. Practically everyone at the operating level agrees that Lansdale has lost his value. Bundy and Taylor are not impressed with him. [The Defense Intelligence Agency's] Bill Quinn and company obviously have his number as do we. With a political solution to the Cuban problem [the missile crisis] in hand reflecting great credit on the part of the President, the A.G. will drop Lansdale like a hot brick.

And so it was: two months later, Bundy told President Kennedy that "there is well nigh universal agreement that Mongoose is at a dead end, [and] we think the Mongoose office should be disbanded."[62] General Lansdale was tactfully relieved of his responsibilities, Operation Mongoose was quietly mothballed, and a lower-level interdepartmental committee chaired by the State Department—not by the Pentagon or the CIA—was created to coordinate U.S. policy toward Cuba.[63]

But the sabotage did not stop. Lansdale could easily be packed off into retirement, but what about the dozens of Cuban exile groups that had blossomed under CIA patronage? In late March 1963, the administration publicly announced not only that exile attacks "are neither supported nor condoned by this Government" but also that "we intend to take every step necessary to insure that such raids are not launched, manned, or equipped from U.S. territory."[64]

That statement was only partially true. The administration intended to halt the attacks on shipping—the March statement came after two exile strikes on Soviet freighters off Cuba and after officials learned of the imminent publication of a *Life* magazine article featuring several pages of pictures of a raiding party in action. A worried Secretary Rusk warned JFK that the raids might precipitate a major international incident but added that he had "no objection to raiding if people were actually put ashore." Putting raiders on Cuban soil was fine in theory, replied McCone, but "the raiders will not go ashore because they know they will be caught."[65] Robert Mc-Namara suggested a compromise that appealed to JFK: "making it difficult for the raiders to attack targets not of our choosing." The president basically instructed the CIA to "tell the raiders that they must not attack Soviet ships—but could attack purely Cuban targets." The CIA's Richard Helms was not in the room, but if he had been present he might have said what he would say three days later: "Although these groups may start out to get a non-Soviet target, once you let them go, you can never really be sure what they will do."[66]

In practice, JFK's decision meant that the administration tried with varying degrees of enthusiasm to stop unauthorized sabotage—typically potshots at civilian shipping—by freelance Cuban exiles; at the same time, raids by CIA-controlled exile groups had resumed almost immediately after the missile crisis.[67] On 3 April 1963, a week after JFK's decision on unauthorized raiders, the president and his advisers sat down to discuss what more might be done. "I like an active covert program," wrote Gordon Chase, a young foreign service officer lacking knowledge of the island but nonetheless detailed to the NSC as Bundy's "Cuba" aide. In preparing Bundy for the meeting, Chase advised that "a good sabotage program is one of the few tools we can use to really hurt Castro economically"—and, Chase continued, the new State Department–chaired Coordinating Committee had endorsed an expanded effort to harass shipping by using "incendiaries which would be timed to go off in international waters," by placing abrasives in ships' machinery, and by attacking Soviet ships entering and leaving Cuba. "The risks are not as great as they seem," he said.[68]

Chase's memorandum clearly reflected the continuing influence both of the Pentagon, which proposed a major escalation that would include the chemical and bacterial contamination of Cuba's food supply, and of the CIA, which now had a new chief to run its Cuba program, Desmond FitzGerald; he told McCone, "I intend to submit to you in the near future a request for policy approval to mount sabotage operations against Cuban-owned ships and cargoes as the first stage of a broader sabotage program."[69]

All of this meant that one of John Crimmins's jobs as director of the State Department's Miami branch was to stop the unauthorized raiders while turning a blind eye to CIA-sponsored attacks. It was no small assignment. When asked how he knew which operatives were freelance and which were not, he replied, "Just personal relationships with [CIA Miami station chief Theodore] Shackley and with some of his people. I knew the elements of the exile community . . . that were, let's say, close to the agency, and others who were not." But, he added, "the agency had responsibility of its own, and I did not get very much involved with them," and he never trusted Shackley to tell the truth. Crimmins's successor in Miami, Harvey Summ, told a similar story: "My main function there was to prevent Cuban exiles on their own from trying to mount operations"—that is, "to prevent non-US related Cubans from doing things we did not want them to do."[70]

To avoid interference by law enforcement personnel, one agency-approved exile leader recalled that "we were in advance given 30 or 31 different words, [one] for every day . . . in a sealed envelope, and you opened that envelope the date that corresponded to the one that you were running; and if anyone would stop you, you'd just say, 'Alpha!', 'Omega!', 'Kennedy!'"—whatever the code word was for that day—and the authorities would turn a blind eye. For the unauthorized freelancers, in contrast, Summ developed a fairly elaborate routine: "Our informants would play along with them until the moment when a raid was about to be launched, either by air or by sea, and then the appropriate authorities of the US enforcement agency would jump them. And they knew them all—it was kind of a friendly thing. Many of the US enforcement people knew Spanish. They would call the Cubans by their first names, and suddenly somebody would materialize in the Everglades or at an airstrip or what-have-you, and 'Sorry, boys!,' they'd say, and take them in. But according to our guidelines, we would not prosecute. They would be released the next day. Sometimes, the boat or the plane would be impounded, but sometimes even they would be released. And then the whole process would start all over again."[71]

All the while, new sabotage plans were continually being created, with the NSC's Walt Rostow advocating blowing up Cuba's electrical grid to create "a sense of hopelessness" and with the Special Group (Augmented) considering the distribution of counterfeit pesos that would force the government to replace all the currency in circulation—"a most expensive and troublesome procedure." In early October 1963, the CIA asked the Special Group to approve a package of nine new sabotage operations, and in late October the agency requested permission to attack thirteen more targets, including an electric power plant, an oil refinery, and a sugar mill.[72] Not to be outdone, the coordinator for Cuban affairs sent the Special Group a Mongoose-like "Proposal for Air Strikes against Cuban Targets." Now back in Washington, Crimmins had a broad range of activities in mind, but his immediate focus was on Texaco's former refinery in Santiago: "We propose to attack the refinery in December with a commando group firing 4.2 mortars." If the commandos were to fail, then Crimmins wanted approval for a bombing run by Cuban exiles operating out of a Nicaraguan airfield, using "a U.S. sterile combat type aircraft, with foreign commercial markings."[73]

Menacing as all this may sound, it amounted to a lot of bun but very little burger. As Bundy told JFK, "The leaders generally shoot at whatever is the biggest object within reach," then rush back to Miami and hold a press conference. Years later, John Crimmins referred to the attacks as "all minor league stuff"; Ted Shackley recalled that "they could take people in and out of Cuba and make caches, but once they tried to go inland, even a quarter of a mile, the trouble would start"; and Sam Halpern recollected that "once in a while, we had to try some sabotage operations but they were few and far between, and as you can see from the record none of the big ones really succeeded." But most of that was said years later; the consensus in the autumn of 1963 was captured by Gordon Chase: "Pretty soon, as they become more expert, they may start to hit something worthwhile."[74]

When November began, there were so many sabotage plans being implemented that the Special Group held a meeting simply to update senior officials who had been unable to attend all the recent gatherings. Rusk, McNamara, and RFK listened as the CIA's FitzGerald reported on four successful recent strikes ("against a power plant, oil storage facilities, a sawmill, and . . . a floating crane in one of Cuba's harbors") and passed out a list of targets awaiting attention. When FitzGerald had finished, one unidentified participant, eager to raise the ante, inquired "whether an air strike would be effective on some of these principal targets." A discussion ensued, and "the consensus was that CIA should proceed with its planning for this type of activity looking toward January."[75]

Ten days later, President Kennedy was killed in Dallas.

THE OAS MEETING at Punta del Este, the missile crisis, and Operation Mongoose had all occurred as Indochina was rapidly emerging as Washington's foreign policy focus, but the overthrow of Cuba's revolutionary government remained a major goal of U.S. policy.[76] The less adventuresome State Department now had much more to say about how that goal might be achieved, however, and after a thorough review, Secretary Rusk reported that economic and diplomatic isolation was the preferred focus, telling the cabinet that he intended "to tighten the noose around the Cuban economy and to increase the isolation of the Castro regime from the political life of the hemisphere until that regime becomes a complete pariah." For its part, the CIA downgraded Task Force W into a new Special Affairs Staff whose highest priority was "to exacerbate and stimulate disaffection in the Cuban armed forces." Specifically, U.S. officials sought to "convince them that their future lies only in disposing of Castro."[77]

What exactly the memo's author, Desmond FitzGerald, meant by "disposing" is not known, but he was part of a small group trying to assassinate Fidel Castro. CIA officials had begun to talk about murdering Cuba's revolutionary leaders on 11 December 1959, when J. C. King, chief of the agency's Western Hemisphere Division, sent Allen Dulles a memorandum recommending that "thorough consideration be given to the elimination of Fidel Castro." Dulles initialed his approval.[78]

Here again, what Colonel King meant by the Cuban leader's "elimination" is uncertain. A month later, Dulles told the Special Group that "we do not have in mind a quick elimination of Castro, but rather actions designed to enable responsible opposition leaders to get a foothold." He probably was referring to the upcoming Bay of Pigs invasion, but the CIA had simultaneously begun to hatch a variety of murder plots, and they began to involve senior officials outside the agency on 10 March 1960, when Admiral Arleigh Burke suggested to the NSC that "any plan for the removal of Cuban leaders should be a package deal, since many of the leaders around Castro were even worse than Castro." Burke subsequently argued that his comment referred to the general task of overthrowing Cuba's government, not to assassination, but the ball had clearly started rolling, and the minutes of a Special Group meeting four days later reveal that the participants held "a general discussion as to what would be the effect on the Cuban scene if Fidel and Raul Castro and Che Guevará should disappear simultaneously."[79]

The first assassination attempt occurred in July 1960, after a CIA agent in Havana identified a Cuban with access to Raúl Castro who was willing to gather intelligence. Colonel King and Richard Bissell's deputy, Tracy Barnes, instructed the agent to forget about intelligence gathering and instead to encourage the Cuban to murder the younger Castro by promising ten thousand dollars "after successful completion." A few hours later, for reasons never explained, Allen Dulles told Barnes to rescind the instructions, but the agency's Havana station replied that the wave-off message had arrived too late—the Cuban had already left to accomplish the deed. When he returned and said "that he had not had an opportunity to arrange the matter," he was told to desist.[80]

A carefully scripted assassination effort began a month later when Bissell asked the director of the CIA's Office of Security, Colonel Sheffield Edwards, to locate someone who could murder Fidel Castro. Edwards assigned the job to James O'Connell, chief of the Operational Support Division in Edwards's Office of Security, who suggested working through an intermediary, Robert Maheu, a private investigator O'Connell had used in the past.[81] After agreeing to participate, Maheu approached John Rosselli, aptly described as "an underworld figure" by a subsequent Senate investigating committee, and told him that high government officials had authorized the payment of $150,000 for Castro's assassination. Unwilling to take the word of an intermediary, Rosselli asked to talk directly to a CIA official, and so Maheu arranged for Rosselli to meet with O'Connell at New York's Plaza Hotel in mid-September. Reassured, Rosselli then took Maheu to Florida to meet Salvatore "Sam" Giancana ("a Chicago-based gangster," according to the Senate committee) and Santo Trafficante ("the Cosa Nostra chieftain in Cuba").[82]

As O'Connell was establishing these contacts, the CIA's Technical Services Division was preparing the murder weapon—a set of poison pills. The first batch would not dissolve in water, but the second batch was tested on monkeys and "did the job expected of them." By that time, Giancana and Trafficante had contacted Tony de Varona, a Batista-era political leader now living in Miami who claimed to have access to a worker in a restaurant frequented by Castro. Either de Varona or the restaurant worker demanded some money in advance, so Colonel King withdrew an undetermined amount of cash from the CIA's vault and gave it to O'Connell, who in turn passed both the money and the pills to Maheu. He, in turn, flew to Miami and met with Rosselli, Trafficante, and de Varona. Rosselli later testified that Maheu "opened his briefcase and dumped a whole lot of money on his lap," then handed over the pills, warning that they "couldn't be used in boiling soups and things like that, but they could be used in water."[83]

This attempt on Castro's life never occurred, and both the cash and the pills were returned. That was not the end of the Mafia-CIA collaboration, however; in late 1961, a new player, the CIA's William Harvey, entered the game. Unlike O'Connell, Harvey actually knew how to commit murder: he had spent all of 1961 directing the CIA's notorious ZR/RIFLE project, which, according to the delicate wording of the Senate investigating committee, created "a general capability within the CIA for disabling foreign leaders." Just before he left the CIA, Bissell asked Harvey to take over supervision of the agency's relationship with the mafia, specifically requesting that he explore "application of ZR/RIFLE program to Cuba." Harvey agreed, and his first move was to ask Colonel Edwards to put him in touch with Rosselli. The three met in Miami, where they cut Maheu and Giancana out of the project. Then, at a second meeting in New York, Harvey handed Rosselli four new poison pills "that would work anywhere and at any time with anything." Rosselli gave the new pills to Tony de Varona, who this time asked for weapons as payment for his role in getting the pills into Castro's food. Rosselli passed the request to Harvey, who went to the CIA's sabotage cupboard in Miami and withdrew explosives, detonators, rifles, handguns, radios, and a boat radar, all of which he loaded into a U-Haul truck and handed over to Rosselli in a parking lot.[84]

Then he sat back and waited. In May, Rosselli reported that the pills and weapons had reached Cuba, but nothing happened, and in early autumn a now-impatient Harvey flew to Miami, prodding first Rosselli, who had to admit that he could not deliver, and then de Varona, who had to admit that he could not recover the pills. (Their location remains a mystery to this day.)[85] Harvey shut down this part of the assassination operation in February 1963, and Rosselli ended up the assassination victim: in 1976, a few months after he testified to Senate investigators, Miami police found his body stuffed into a fifty-five-gallon drum. Unknown assassins killed Sam Giancana a few days before he was to talk with the same investigators.

As this Mafia-CIA linkage was being developed in early 1961, the CIA independently recruited its own assassin, a highly placed Cuban official, army major Rolando Cubela, code-named AM/LASH. He originally wanted simply to defect, but the CIA instead urged him to remain in Cuba and, since he had access to Cuban leaders, to help with Fidel Castro's murder. After much nurturing, Cubela agreed to carry out the task, asking for a high-powered rifle and some hand grenades. Meeting with Cubela in Paris on 22 November 1963, the day JFK was shot, CIA case officer Nestor Sánchez promised that the weapons would be air-dropped into Cuba, but the agency wanted Cubela to employ a more subtle ball-point pen with a hypodermic needle so fine that Castro would not notice its insertion. Sánchez recalled that "AM/LASH did not think much of the device and complained that the agency surely could come up with something more sophisticated than that." Like the poison pills, the whereabouts of the poison pen remain a mystery to this day.[86]

As the Mafia and the Cubela plots were thickening, the CIA began exploring additional opportunities. One was handled by the CIA's Office of Medical Services, which impregnated a box of Castro's favorite cigars with a botulinum toxin "so potent that a person would die after putting one in his mouth." While the agency searched for a way to get the cigars to Castro (they were never used), Harvey's CIA task force also explored two other weapons. One was an attempt "to determine whether an exotic seashell, rigged to explode, could be deposited in an area where Castro commonly went skin diving." CIA's Technical Services Division discarded the scheme as impractical, but it liked a related idea: attorney James Donovan, who was negotiating with Castro for the release of U.S. citizens in Cuban jails, would give the Cuban leader a contaminated skin diving suit. Technical Services swabbed a snorkel with a tuberculosis bacillus and dusted the suit with a debilitating fungus (madura foot, which sometimes requires amputation), but Donovan, who was to be an unwitting participant, gave Castro a different suit.[87] The contaminated suit never left the agency's laboratory.

WHEN THE PARTIAL DISCLOSURE of Cubela's activities surfaced in 1966, Rusk requested an explanation from Richard Helms, who had now become the CIA's director. Helms replied that "the Agency was not involved with [AM/LASH] in a plot to assassinate Fidel Castro . . . nor did it ever encourage him to attempt such an act."[88] Helms made no mention of the poison pen or the air-dropped weapons, but a few months later columnist Jack Anderson published an article about the Mafia-assisted plotting to kill Castro, and this time President Lyndon Johnson asked for an explanation. Helms instructed the CIA's inspector general, J. S. Earman, to conduct an investigation, and his 1967 report was the key document guiding a Senate investigation led by Frank Church in 1975. "Can we plausibly deny that we plotted with gangster elements to assassinate Castro?," asked Earman rhetorically. "No, we cannot," he answered, for "there are plenty of non-gangster witnesses who could lend confirmation" to Anderson's story. Testifying under oath before the Church Committee, Helms admitted that his 1966 report to Rusk had been "inaccurate." But, he continued, AM/LASH must have been a rogue project ("simply low level fellows scheming and so forth"); if not, then Helms had no idea what could have been happening: "I honestly cannot help you. I don't recall these things going on at the time."[89]

Dean Rusk also claimed ignorance ("a complete mystery to me"), and Senator Church's committee obtained a long list of similar denials—from Robert McNamara, Roswell Gilpatric, Maxwell Taylor, McGeorge Bundy, Walt Rostow, Theodore Sorensen, John McCone, and finally Richard Goodwin, who, like the others, told investigators that "I never heard of such a thing." While continuing to deny knowledge of any specific activity, Goodwin in 1975 fingered McNamara as the instigator but then backtracked before the Church Committee; thirteen years later, Goodwin again named McNamara, writing in 1988 that at a May 1961 meeting, the secretary of defense, "having sat through an hour of inconclusive discussion, rose to leave for another appointment and, firmly grasping my shoulder with his right hand, announced, 'The only thing to do is eliminate Castro.' I listened, puzzled, thinking, Isn't that just what we have been talking about for a month? when the CIA representative looked toward McNamara and said, 'You mean Executive Action.' McNamara nodded, then, looking toward me: 'I mean it, Dick, it's the only way.' I had never heard the phrase 'Executive Action' before. But its meaning was instantly apparent. Assassination."[90]

The two Kennedy brothers did not live to testify before the Senate committee, but they clearly had at least a general awareness of the plotting. In late 1961 President Kennedy broached the topic with journalist Tad Szulc, whose notes indicate that "JFK said he raised [the] question because he was under terrific pressure from advisers (think he said intelligence people, but not positive) to okay a Castro murder. Sed [*sic*] he was resisting pressures." The CIA's inspector general also reported that "Attorney General Robert Kennedy was fully briefed by Houston and Edwards on 7 May 1962. A memorandum confirming the oral briefing was forwarded to Kennedy on 14 May 1962. The memorandum does not use the word 'assassinate,' but there is little room for misinterpretation of what was meant." Perhaps the word was not needed, for, as Bissell later told Bill Moyers, "a President typically says that he wants to get rid of someone. And obviously, he and everybody else involved would much rather get rid of someone in a rather nice way. But if the emphasis is on getting rid of him whatever—by whatever means have to be used, this I would have taken as an authorization."[91]

How high up did knowledge go within the CIA? The same man who swore under oath, "I don't recall these things going on at the time," former agency director Richard Helms, also swore that his predecessor, John McCone, "was involved in this up to his scuppers just the way everybody else was," but the closest approximation to a smoking gun is the paperwork that came from a 10 August 1962 meeting attended by all the Special Group members, including three cabinet members, McCone, Rusk, and McNamara. The meeting's minutes do not contain the word "assassination," but Goodwin, McCone, and Harvey all recalled that assassination was treated at the meeting as part of a general discussion of what Operation Mongoose ought to be doing in its next phase. McCone said that he and Edward R. Murrow, the famed journalist who was now directing the U.S. Information Agency, took strong exception to assassinating anyone, and after that "the subject was just dropped."[92]

But was it? Three days later, Lansdale wrote a memo to four midlevel officials, including the CIA's Harvey, assigning them tasks "in compliance with the desires and guidance expressed in the August 10 policy meeting"; among Harvey's tasks was listed "liquidation of leaders." Harvey called Lansdale's office the second he received this memo "and, in his absence, pointed out to Frank Hand the inadmissibility and stupidity of putting this type of comment in writing," adding, "We would write no document pertaining to this and would participate in no open meeting discussing it."[93]

Then he alerted deputy director Helms to Lansdale's gaffe, and in this warning memo he admitted that "the question of assassination, particularly of Fidel Castro, was brought up by Secretary McNamara at the meeting of the Special Group (Augmented) in Secretary Rusk's office on 10 August. It was the obvious consensus at that meeting, in answer to a comment by Mr. Ed Murrow, that this is not a subject which had been made a matter of official record. I took careful notes on the comments at this meeting on this point, and the Special Group (Augmented) is not expecting any written comments or study on this point."[94] This statement can be interpreted in two ways: either the Special Group's members did not want to assassinate anyone, or they did not want the record to indicate that they were discussing the subject. About Harvey there is absolutely no doubt—he had recently given Rosselli the poison pills, and he would soon try to pass along both a poison pen and a U-Haul filled with weapons. As for the others, Hamlet's mother was probably correct: sometimes people protest too much.

Assassination was indisputably in the air, and just as a visitor from outer space could watch a basketball game for ten minutes and recognize that the idea is for one team to toss the ball through the hoop and the other to prevent it, so even the most naive U.S. official probably understood that assassination was not ruled out when Robert Kennedy announced that ending the Castro government was "the top priority of the United States Government—all else is secondary—no time, money, effort, or manpower is to be spared." He did not make such statements only once; as Helms later noted, he and RFK "were constantly in touch with each other on these matters. The Attorney General was on the phone to me, he was on the phone to Mr. Harvey, to Mr. Fitzgerald, his successor. He was on the phone even to people on Harvey's staff." One CIA staffer remarked that the Kennedys "were just absolutely obsessed with getting rid of Castro"; they "were on our back constantly to do more damage to Cuba, to cause an uprising, to get rid of Castro." As Earman's report begins, "We cannot overemphasize the extent to which responsible Agency officers felt themselves subject to the Kennedy administration's severe pressures to do something about Castro and his regime."[95]

With the president's brother breathing down his neck, it is not surprising that Richard Bissell instructed William Harvey to explore the "application of ZR/RIFLE program to Cuba," that the CIA tested exploding seashells and a snorkel dusted with tuberculosis, or that an unidentified CIA official circulated a memorandum, "What Would Happen If Castro Died?," in which the author worried that killing only Castro would not be sufficient — "an assassination program," he added, "would have to be targeted against Fidel *and* Raúl Castro, Ernesto 'Che' Guevara, and several other key communists to have any chance of creating enough chaos."[96]

Thus while it is no doubt true, as Richard Helms testified, that Robert Kennedy never told him to kill Castro — "not in those words, no" — it is also probably true, as Helms continued, that RFK "would not have been unhappy if [Castro] had disappeared off the scene by whatever means." Did Helms ever inquire? Not if his testimony to the Church Committee is to be believed: "To go up to a Cabinet officer and say, am I right in assuming that you want me to assassinate Castro or try to assassinate Castro, is a question it wouldn't have occurred to me to ask." But everyone in the Kennedy administration simply took it for granted, as General Taylor's Bay of Pigs investigating commission had asserted, that "we are in a life and death struggle which we may be losing, and will lose unless we change our ways and marshall our resources with an intensity associated in the past only with times of war." Specifically, in the case of Cuba, "there can be no long-term living with Castro as a neighbor."[97]

With this type of talk constantly in the air, the best and the brightest of the Kennedy generation made a number of immoral decisions, and it is remarkable how many of them involved Cuba. Helms told talk-show host David Frost that asking the Mafia to help kill Castro was "one of the great regrets of my life [and] a case of poor judgment." Bissell agreed, telling Bill Moyers, "We were a little too free and easy then in our whole attitude toward the possibility of assassination."[98]

These second thoughts came years after the fact. The assassination attempts ended not because everyone realized they were wrong but because they showed little chance of success. "Cuban males are not suicidal," wrote the head of the CIA's Miami office.

They love life, particularly the good life of women, food, and alcohol. As a result, if they ever were to attempt an assassination operation, one of their main objectives would have been to survive the event that was to make them a national hero. Thus, while brave and dedicated to the cause of defeating Castro, Cubans did not see themselves as being prepared to pay the ultimate price—their own lives—in order to kill Castro. Built into all their assassination outlines was action at a distance, an element that inevitably reduced any prospects of success.

Or, as the CIA's inspector general concluded, "What Cubela really wanted was a high-powered, silenced rifle with an effective range of hundreds or thousands of yards. . . . He was quite sure that we could devise some technical means of doing the job that would not automatically cause him to lose his own life."[99]

So ended the U.S. government's attempts on Castro's life, primarily because no one could be found to do the job. Among the highest levels of the administration, only Chester Bowles consistently voiced his disapproval of the sneaky invasions by proxy forces and the hit-and-run sabotage raids, and he certainly would have opposed assassination had he not been shunted off to the U.S. embassy in India. But he kept his most trenchant criticism to himself: "The Cuban fiasco demonstrates how far astray a man can go who lacks a basic moral reference point," he wrote in his diary. "The question which concerns me most about the new Administration, particularly the President, is that basically it lacks a sense of integrity or conviction on what is right and wrong."[100]

With everyone turning to the new focus on Indochina, perhaps the same end could be achieved without murder. In mid-1963, the State Department's Bureau of Intelligence and Research produced a memo suggesting how flimsy were the reeds for which Kennedy administration officials were now grasping: since "personal dignity is the touchstone of the Latin American personality," why not "take advantage of Castro's vanity, accuse him of sporting a beard simply because he has no chin. His proprietor Khrushchev needs no beard, dare his vassal to be man enough to shave." With taunts like this, the United States could "destroy his self-esteem, sabotage his revolution, force him to conclude that his situation is hopeless and, as in the case of his political idol Eduardo Chibás, in 1951, drive him to suicide or to acts of complete irrationality."[101]

When, precisely, did the assassination efforts end? In 1971, former president Johnson told journalist Leo Janis that during the JFK era, "We had been operating a damned Murder, Inc., in the Caribbean." LBJ's comment has always been taken to mean that he ended the practice, and some documents suggest that such was the case, but only in 1972–73, under President Richard M. Nixon, did CIA directors Richard Helms and then William Colby issue internal memoranda banning assassination. Prompted by the Church Committee's damning report, in 1976 President Gerald R. Ford issued an executive order that "no employee of the United States Government shall engage in, or conspire to engage in, political assassination," and in 1981 President Ronald Reagan added to the prohibition: "No person employed by *or acting on behalf of* the United States Government shall engage in, or conspire to engage in, assassination."[102]

AS THE KENNEDY ADMINISTRATION was preparing the Bay of Pigs invasion, launching Operation Mongoose, and plotting assassination, it was simultaneously setting up what was known at the time as the Economic Denial Program—an attempt to cut Cuba off from the noncommunist world. Washington soon would come to call the effort an embargo; Havana dubbed it a blockade. By whatever name, this attempt to cripple Cuba's economy began to take shape in 1960, when the Eisenhower administration suspended Cuba's sugar quota and prohibited U.S. exports other than food and medicine. On the surface, the sugar cutoff represented a simple tit-for-tat retaliation following Cuba's takeover of the petroleum refineries, and the prohibition on exports to Cuba was, at least in its timing, a transparent effort to help Richard Nixon win the presidency. In retrospect, however, the moves shared the three-step logic of Operation Mongoose: damage the island's economy, generate discontent, and thereby undermine Cuba's revolutionary government.

The first step was an easy one; it took almost no effort at all to throw Cuba's economy into a tailspin by terminating an intimate trading relationship with the United States. When President Eisenhower entered office in 1953, Cuba ranked sixth in the world as an importer of U.S. goods; when he left office in 1961, Cuba's U.S. imports were down 97 percent from Batista's final year in office, and the elimination of Cuba's sugar quota was responsible for most of a similar drop in Cuban exports to the United States, from $490 million in 1958 to $35 million in 1961. (More than half of what continued was in difficult-to-replace cigar tobacco.) A similar decline occurred in tourism, the second-largest source of hard currency in Batista's final years.[103]

Along with these numbers came 1,001 inconveniences in Cubans' every-day lives, since almost everything they touched was tied in one way or another to U.S. standards: the island's farms and factories worked almost exclusively with U.S. machinery, for which replacement parts now had to be purchased indirectly (and clandestinely) through third countries; the island's measurements were taken in U.S.-standard inches and feet, its plumbing used U.S.-standard threaded pipe (to screw a metric-standard fitting onto a U.S.-standard pipe is to ruin both), and its electrical system was based on the U.S. standard 110 volts, not the European 220. Even the simplest electrical devices generally were of the type used by the United States but not by the world's other principal suppliers—Cubans needed lightbulbs that screwed into their sockets, for example, not the smooth European type with notches, and Cubans now also needed not only voltage transformers but adapters to plug the round prongs on the cords of European appliances into U.S.-style wall receptacles. Even in those cases where replacement merchandise was identical in type and quality, geography almost always dictated higher shipping costs—three times higher in the case of rice, for example—and there simply was no readily available replacement for essential additives required by the expropriated U.S. oil refineries, additives that "Cuba has been trying desperately to obtain from the West," the CIA reported.[104] Food was an especially gnawing problem. "The Cuban public possibly would rebel if essential food items were not available," wrote FBI director J. Edgar Hoover, noting that Polish lard was not up to U.S. standards, and by mid-1961 the U.S. press was publishing stories with titles such as "Cubans Grumble over Shortages" and "Shortages Deepen Austerity in Cuba."[105] The embargo was having its intended effect.

As Cubans struggled to adjust to life without the U.S. sugar market and U.S. suppliers, the Kennedy administration set out to tighten the screws. Aside from the sugar quota, President Eisenhower had left untouched Cuban exports to the United States because, as the minutes of one late 1960 meeting indicate, "any restriction on imports from Cuba would have to be taken under the 'trading with the enemy' act, and we are not ready to take the step of designating Cuba as an enemy." Eisenhower officials had wrestled with this question for months, never quite reaching a consensus, but not because they were divided over the desirability of tightening the embargo; rather, use of the 1917 Trading with the Enemy Act would have to be based on a declaration that Cuba constituted a threat to hemispheric security, and as Secretary of State Christian Herter had told the president,

"This is an area which the Rio Treaty contemplates would be treated in a multilateral way." Herter's final recommendation was that "given the extent to which this step would commit the new Administration, this decision be left to them."[106]

The new Kennedy officials had solved the multilateral problem by engineering the meeting at Punta del Este—the one where Haiti provided the decisive vote. As with the Eisenhower-era cut in Cuba's sugar quota, Florida's growers of other crops were especially eager to dispose of their Cuban competition, and they nudged the process along. Florida Senator George Smathers had dropped by the White House even before JFK unpacked to urge his friend and former Senate colleague to end the import of Cuban products that competed with Florida's winter crops. The president turned to McGeorge Bundy for advice, and Bundy in turn wrote to Secretary Rusk to call "attention to the letter which Senator George A. Smathers wrote to you suggesting urgent consideration of placing an embargo on Cuban fruits, vegetables and other commodities." The Trading with the Enemy Act was "the most effective measure available," Rusk replied, and State was preparing to take the plunge, needing only to work out the details with Treasury officials. He promised a final recommendation "early next week."[107]

The new administration's officials were still finding their way through the bureaucratic maze, however, and "early next week" came and went; then so did the Bay of Pigs, and in its frenzied aftermath JFK again asked for "prompt recommendations with regard to trading with Cuba." This request triggered the next day's telegram to all U.S. embassies in Latin America (the cable that eventually led to Punta del Este), but at this low point the United States could not have it both ways: a unilateral move would be fatal to multilateral cooperation, so the NSC decided not to impose an immediate trade embargo.[108]

Florida's citrus producers continued to lobby, and congressional pressure continued to intensify, soon zeroing in on the important foreign aid bill intended to transform the stodgy Mutual Security Agency into a new Agency for International Development. In August, Florida representative Dante Fascell stood up during the bill's final consideration in the House and proposed an amendment permitting the president to establish a total embargo on trade with Cuba, which the floor manager accepted without dissent; indeed, the only discussion of Fascell's proposal was whether it should be expanded to permit the president to halt aid to third countries assisting Cuba. The language finally adopted simply authorized but did not require the president to establish and maintain "a total embargo upon all trade between the United States and Cuba."[109] But this initiative also came at the time when the United States was still seeking approval for an OAS meeting of consultation, and Venezuelan president Rómulo Betancourt told a visiting President Kennedy exactly what his State Department advisers had been saying—that "any unilateral action on the part of the United States would be extremely harmful." That is why the administration waited until three days after the U.S. delegation's return from Punta del Este to place a total embargo on trade, an embargo that in time became the longest-running economic sanction in U.S. history, continuing for the balance of the twentieth century and into the twenty-first.[110]

The next-easiest way to damage the Cuban economy would be to strangle Cuba's tourist trade, a target that became especially attractive after the gamblers and beach lovers stopped visiting the island and nearly all remaining U.S. travelers were left-leaning critics of the administration's Cuba policy. The effort had begun during Eisenhower's final week in office, when the State Department announced that all existing U.S. passports were invalid for travel to Cuba. This announcement had come in reaction to a "Christmas in Cuba" trip by 326 U.S. citizens, a trip sponsored by the Fair Play for Cuba Committee and underwritten by the Cuban government. Individuals wanting to visit the island would now have to seek specific permission, which would be granted only in unusual circumstances, generally for reporting the news, conducting research, or representing an international humanitarian organization such as the Red Cross. This was nothing new: during the 1950s, all U.S. passports had carried a printed message: "This passport is not valid for travel to or in Communist controlled portions of China, Korea, Viet-Nam or to or in Albania." Now, in 1961, the State Department's Passport Office simply began stamping "Cuba" after Albania, along with the warning that "a person who travels to or in the listed countries or areas may be liable for prosecution."[111]

This restriction was of questionable legality. The secretary of state's power to control travel had been exercised only occasionally in the years since it had been granted by the 1926 Passport Act, and the president's authority to require a passport for foreign travel, granted by the 1952 Immigration and Nationality Act, had never been exercised for travel anywhere in the Western Hemisphere.[112] Moreover, in 1958 the Supreme Court had sharply limited the discretionary authority granted by these two laws when in *Kent v. Dulles* it overruled the State Department's refusal to issue two passports because the applicants were unwilling to provide affidavits that they were not communists. Asserting that freedom of movement was "basic in our scheme of values," the Court ruled that the State Department had assumed an administrative power that the law had never intended—the 1926 Passport Act had given the secretary of state the job of issuing passports, not the power to establish litmus tests governing their issuance. Until that power had been granted, "the right to travel is a part of the 'liberty' of which the citizen cannot be deprived without due process of law under the Fifth Amendment."[113]

Kent v. Dulles involved the fundamental right of citizens to travel freely, and both Rockwell Kent and his fellow traveler received their passports. But the Court's narrow 5–4 decision suggested that a reversal was possible, and in any event, the Eisenhower ban quickly reduced travel to a trickle. The little that continued nonetheless stuck in the craw of the new Kennedy administration, and the annoyance became especially acute in mid-1963 when a group of sixty U.S. students announced their plan to fly to Havana via Prague. The Special Group was informed that some of the leaders might be communists ("the FBI is doing a check"), but even if they were not, "when the group returns, their passports will be picked up."[114] "Other steps may be considered," warned the president, and in fact his brother was lying in wait: "A week to ten days after the return of the students, Justice Department will send to the White House, for clearance, its recommendations for action against these students. Justice estimates that it would be able to start Grand Jury proceedings about three days after its recommendations are approved." This single trip generated enough memoranda (including the president's personal decision about how many of the students to prosecute) to fill five large folders in the Kennedy archives.[115]

The administration preferred to avoid these highly publicized confrontations, however, for they especially rankled the nation's intellectual community, which considered the travel ban an attack on the freedom of expression. A less confrontational approach would involve making travel as difficult as possible. By this time all scheduled U.S. flights to Cuba had been discontinued, and at the time of the missile crisis, only twenty nonbloc flights by five airlines landed in Cuba each week; after October, Cuba's only air links with the noncommunist world were via Madrid and Mexico City.[116]

That did not keep Secretary of the Army Cyrus Vance from producing a list of no fewer than twenty-five steps that could be taken to break those two remaining links. Step 7, for example, would "persuade Mexico to fingerprint, in addition to photographing, all persons leaving for or arriving from Cuba, and to provide data to parent country of the nationals involved." Step 15 would "encourage Latin American governments to institute administrative procedures, such as exhaustive examination of manifests, air-worthiness checks of aircraft, baggage inspection and inspection of health and other documents, all designed deliberately to delay and otherwise make difficult to carrying of passengers to Cuba." That step, in turn, was linked both to Step 18 ("persuade Mexico to refuse the introduction of Soviet-made aircraft in the Havana–Mexico City route on technical grounds. This will create an obstacle to Cubana, since the Britannia aircraft now used are falling into disrepair.") and to Step 19 ("cut off the supply of spare parts for Cuba's Britannia aircraft").[117]

As a result, a year after the missile crisis, the CIA estimated that only about twenty-five hundred "Free World" travelers would arrive in Cuba in 1963, compared with about five thousand in 1962.[118] The dramatic drop in travel by *non*-U.S. nationals could not be sustained, but with many ups and downs and with the notable exception of the Carter years, the Eisenhower-initiated effort to restrict travel by U.S. citizens to Cuba continued into the twenty-first century.

The Economic Denial Program also included an effort to cut Cuba's maritime links to the rest of the world. Doing so was obviously crucial — Cuba is an island, after all, and Moscow's merchant fleet was so small that most Soviet-bloc trade had to be carried in ships chartered from Western owners. Aware of this vulnerability, in 1960 the Eisenhower administration had explored an effort to halt the charter of oil tankers but eventually decided that this plan was impractical — "There was no way to keep Cuba from getting surplus tankers," John McCone had argued. The new Kennedy administration decided that preventing Cuba from getting oil tankers was worth the effort, however.[119] Officials at first submitted a formal proposal to the NATO Council that member governments prohibit ships flying their flags from carrying cargo to Cuba, and when the council refused to do so, the State Department began to badger individual NATO members. Five (Belgium, Canada, France, Germany, and Turkey) agreed to stop permitting their ships to be chartered by the Soviet bloc for trade with Cuba, but five others (Denmark, Greece, the Netherlands, Norway, and the United Kingdom) replied that they lacked the legal authority to dictate routes to their private shippers, and vessels from Norway and the United Kingdom carried half of all the cargo entering Cuba.[120]

Then the missile crisis assisted the U.S. effort by raising insurance rates, and the State Department soon could report that the number of nonbloc ships entering Cuba had declined from 128 in January 1962 to 12 in January 1963.[121] Still dissatisfied, the NSC's Gordon Chase spotted a one-month increase in nonbloc shipping and asked the State Department to warn the governments whose citizens owned the offending ships that the United States was "contemplating further action." State replied that little more was possible: "No sharpening of the existing orders would reduce the amount of free world shipping to Cuba. The ships now in the trade are beyond our control."[122] But the Special Group (Augmented), like Chase, was determined to reduce the number to zero, and in October the group instructed the Department of Commerce to "look into the feasibility of initiating additional pressures designed to prohibit free world shipping to Cuba." At this point the State Department's Harvey Summ recalled that he participated "in countless meetings where we were pushing an unwilling [Department of State Bureau of European Affairs] to try to get rough with its clients. They would say, 'Is it worth disturbing our European relationships just for this useless attempt to make life difficult for Cuba?'"[123]

The Special Group (Augmented) and the President apparently thought so, and JFK did his best to convince Britain's visiting foreign secretary to ban ships flying the Union Jack from Cuban ports. Lord Home agreed to do what he could but noted that the United States was being hoisted on its own petard: to the extent that U.S. pressure had reduced the number of ships willing to enter Cuba, those that continued could now demand higher rates, making the trade more attractive. There must be some way the British could help, Kennedy interrupted, but at that point the British envoy shifted the topic from shipping to trade and basically ruined the meeting: "In passing, Lord Home mentioned that the UK was negotiating with Cuba for the sale of some busses."[124]

Meanwhile, the Economic Denial Program was registering some success in halting Cuba's access to U.S.-manufactured goods through third countries, in blocking some Cuban purchases of non-U.S. products, and in reducing Cuba's sugar sales. As one senior CIA official recalled, at staff meetings McCone would say, "Have you reminded the station chiefs everywhere in the world that if they know that some transaction involving trade to Cuba is taking place, try to do something about it. Try to make it unsuccessful."[125] Although most of the island's sugar crop had been committed to the Soviet Union and other bloc countries, in 1962 a sharp drop in European sugar beet production more than doubled the value of what Cuba could sell on the world market, leading the CIA to propose that "the United States should break the sugar market," which could easily be manipulated. The NSC considered the idea but concluded that it would cost too much:

"It would be difficult to disguise the fact that the proposal is economic war-fare waged by the U.S. against a small country," and a sugar price decline would also harm other producers: "For the U.S. to sponsor a program delib-erately designed to reduce the world price of sugar to 4 cents per pound, a level below the cost of production in a number of friendly countries, would . . . be damaging to our relations with the less developed countries." In the end, the Kennedy administration decided not to act. European sugar production recovered, world sugar prices soon dropped by a third, and the Department of Agriculture concluded that any U.S. attempt to lower prices further "would cause more problems than it would be worth."[126]

Such an effort might not even be needed, since the Economic Denial Program seemed to be having its desired effect. In April 1963, the Special Group (Augmented) was told that Cuba's per capita gross national product had dropped by an astounding 30 percent, in large measure as a conse-quence of the decline in trade with the West.[127] Nonetheless, Gordon Chase concluded that "our present policy of isolating Cuba from the Free World is not going to bust Castro," and by mid-1963 the question was what more could be done. In July, the administration found something—the frosting on the embargo cake: invoking the Trading with the Enemy Act, the White House issued a blocking order that froze all Cuban assets in the United States, including thirty-three million dollars in Cuban government de-posits in U.S. banks; much more important, the United States prohibited anyone subject to its jurisdiction from engaging in unlicensed financial transactions with Cuba. "Where serious hardship can be proven, remit-tances by persons residing in the US to members of their immediate family residing in Cuba will be authorized by special license," but this and a gen-eral license to export food and medicine represented the only exceptions.[128] No other transactions, period.

The Trading with the Enemy Act became the embargo's legal back-bone. It required an "enemy"—either a declaration of war or a national emergency—and in 1963 such a designation was already available: Presi-dent Truman's never-revoked Executive Proclamation 2814 from Decem-ber 1950, which declared a national emergency when North Korea invaded South Korea. The act also required implementing rules and procedures— the Cuban Assets Control Regulations, which with exceptionally careful wording provided that "no person subject to the jurisdiction of the United States may purchase, transport, import, or otherwise deal in or engage in any transaction with respect to any merchandise outside the United States if such merchandise: (1) Is of Cuban origin; or (2) Is or has been located in or transported from or through Cuba; or (3) Is made or derived in whole or in part of any article which is the growth, produce, or manufacture of Cuba."[129]

The embargo was now complete. "We are not going to crush Castro with this one," wrote Chase, but "it will show the U.S. public and our Allies that we are still after Castro."[130]

AT ABOUT THIS TIME, Cuba offered to talk about the two nations' differences. Writing four decades later, Goodwin recalled that "the withdrawal of Soviet missiles from Cuba changed the atmosphere, and Kennedy dispatched an emissary to talk with the Cuban delegate to the United Nations, in hopes of laying the groundwork for some rapprochement. Then the president died, and the embargo was frozen in place."

Both the central thrust and the title of Goodwin's article ("President Kennedy's Plan for Peace with Cuba") were misleading. JFK had no plan, and Cuba made all of the initiatives to establish a modus vivendi.[131] Havana's first probe had come just after Kennedy's election, while Dwight Eisenhower was still president, when the U.S. embassy reported on Castro's public expressions of a willingness "to negotiate with the United States on an open agenda and on the basis of equality and mutual respect." The embassy recommended against pursuing Castro's initiative, arguing that "any indication of readiness on the part of the United States to negotiate outstanding differences with Cuba in the absence of fundamental changes in the attitude of the Revolutionary Government would be interpreted by friends and enemies of the United States alike as weakness and would discourage the spirit of resistance among the Cuban opposition," some members of which were, of course, being readied for the Bay of Pigs.[132] Rather than talk, the United States severed diplomatic relations.

Impressed by what he considered Castro's mild reaction to the Bay of Pigs invasion, Senate majority leader Mike Mansfield encouraged JFK "to explore this reaction rather than merely to dismiss it curtly," and a few weeks later, *New York Times* correspondent Tad Szulc returned from Havana to tell Arthur Schlesinger that "Castro indicated that he would be interested in the resumption of some form of relationship with us, provided that we agree to quit trying to 'destroy' his revolution." The Cuban leader specifically indicated a willingness to discuss the issue of compensation for expropriated property, and, Szulc continued, "he made a point of speaking with utmost respect about the President." The White House offered no response, but Szulc soon received another feeler, this one from Cuba's ambassador to the OAS, Carlos Lechuga. This time, the journalist took it to a midlevel State Department officer, Robert Hurwitch, who passed it along to senior officials with a note of skepticism: Lechuga was "conducting a campaign for easing tensions in order that Cuba might remain a member in good standing within the inter-American community and at the same time maintain its political-military ties with the Bloc."[133] Rather than respond, the Kennedy administration launched Operation Mongoose.

The next Cuban feeler came in April 1962, when Brazilian foreign minister Francisco San Tiago Dantas, visiting Washington, informed Rusk that Brazil's ambassador to Cuba had reported that "a serious struggle for power was going on between the Castroites and the old line Communists." Dantas offered to explore further this split, and Rusk agreed that the Brazilian ambassador in Havana should make an appointment to see Castro and "inquire whether Brazil could be of any assistance in freeing Castro from the pressure of the old line Communists." Two weeks later, Dantas informed U.S. ambassador Lincoln Gordon that "Fidel's response was a statement of cordial appreciation" and that he would like to talk with U.S. officials. This time Goodwin threw cold water on the initiative. Although he could barely find Brazil on a map, Goodwin told Assistant Secretary of State Edwin Martin that it would be better to work through a European power or perhaps directly with the Cuban mission to the United Nations, since "Latin American sincerity and concepts of security are notoriously poor. I believe we would be really asking for trouble, in the form of future exposure, were we to rely on Latins for this project; especially the Brazilians."[134] The Dantas initiative died quietly.

But after the missile crisis, when the deteriorating situation in Indochina was rapidly replacing Cuba as the principal focus of U.S. foreign policy, McGeorge Bundy seemed especially eager to clear Cuba from the agenda, perhaps with a negotiated settlement. In early 1963, he sent JFK a long memo recommending that Operation Mongoose be disbanded, that day-to-day Cuba work be handed over to the State Department, and—surprisingly— that "we should intensify our investigation of ways and means of communicating with possibly dissident members of the Castro regime, perhaps including even Fidel himself. [New York attorney James B.] Donovan, for example, has an invitation to be Castro's guest at the beach." Having helped work out the release of the Bay of Pigs captives, Donovan was now negotiating the freedom of other U.S. citizens held in Cuban prisons, but nothing came of his beach visit with Castro—the same one where the CIA had planned for Donovan to give the Cuban leader an infected wet suit.[135]

A few months later the CIA's deputy director, Richard Helms, informed his boss, McCone, that yet another outsider, ABC news reporter Lisa Howard, had recently returned from interviewing the Cuban leader, and "it appears that Fidel Castro is looking for a way to reach a rapprochement with the United States Government, probably because he is aware that Cuba is in a state of economic chaos." In a follow-up memo, Helms reminded McCone that Castro's initiative via Howard was only one of a half dozen similar efforts, and McCone, Bundy, and others apparently were inclined to take seriously these attempts: on 3 June, the Special Group (Augmented) agreed that it would be useful to explore "establishing channels of communication with Castro."[136]

But the State Department's Bureau of Inter-American Affairs was opposed. It considered Castro's gesture a post-missile-crisis effort to reduce Cuba's dependence on the Soviet Union and a tacit admission by Castro that the "economy is not doing well, and he needs trade with the United States." A positive U.S. response would therefore run counter to U.S. interests—if the Cuban economy improved, "support for the regime from within Cuba might well become wider"; worse yet, "a precedent would be established for other communist regimes in the hemisphere, and the U.S. effort to keep them out of this area and to establish its special status would fall to the ground. It could mean the death of the Inter-American System." And if that were not bad enough, Latin America's economic development was hanging in the balance: "Acceptance of a communist regime will completely dry up investment there as well as encourage capital flight. The success of the Alliance for Progress will become clearly impossible."[137]

The bureau's memo climbed the bureaucratic ladder, arriving on Rusk's desk two days before a meeting the CIA had requested to discuss renewed hit-and-run raids by Florida-based exiles. Aware that Rusk was worried that the raids could be tied to the United States, agency officials promised "that every trace of U.S. involvement in the program possible would be concealed." Rusk reluctantly conceded, but having yielded to the CIA on this issue, he then "asked for views concerning the prospects of Castro's reconciliation with the United States," noting that the Cuban leader had moderated his anti-U.S. rhetoric after returning from his trip to Moscow. Ignoring the position of his own Latin American bureau, Rusk argued that exploring closer relations might be a good idea. But despite his 3 June agreement to explore communications with the Castro government, McCone now took the position espoused by the Bureau of Inter-American Affairs, emphasizing that an agreement "would make Castro respectable in the eyes of Latin

America." He understood that he could not simply dismiss Rusk's initiative, however, especially since the secretary had just conceded on hit-and-run raids, so the CIA director agreed rather vaguely "to probe wherever possible to find out what Castro really has on his mind." Then he went back to his office and placed a memo in the files: "I made it abundantly clear during the meeting, and privately to Secretary Rusk afterwards, that I felt a rapprochement out of the question."[138]

Little more was said or done during the summer, but in mid-September, the Cubans sent another feeler, this time through William Attwood, a journalist and magazine editor who had recently completed a two-year stint as JFK's ambassador to Guinea and who was now serving as an adviser to Adlai Stevenson at the U.S. mission to the United Nations. Attwood reported that "according to neutral diplomats and others I have talked to at the U.N. and in Guinea, there is reason to believe that Castro is unhappy about his present dependence on the Soviet bloc . . . and that he would like to establish some official contact with the U.S. and go to some length to obtain normalization of relations with us."[139]

A few days later, after obtaining White House permission to explore this feeler, Attwood was in a quiet corner of Lisa Howard's New York apartment, talking with Cuba's Carlos Lechuga while her other guests, invited to make the meeting seem accidental, sipped their cocktails. Although Lechuga complained about the continuing exile raids and the July blocking order that had frozen Cuban assets in U.S. banks, the discussion was generally cordial, and the two men agreed to seek their respective governments' permission to hold further meetings.

Both Washington and Havana were willing to continue, but they had difficulty agreeing on where a second meeting should be held: worried about the domestic political fallout in the event that the talks became public knowledge, the administration rejected Havana's suggestion that Attwood visit Cuba, while the Cubans rejected Washington's suggestion that Castro adviser René Vallejo come to New York. To keep the ball rolling, Cuba proposed that Lechuga and Attwood discuss an agenda for future talks, and, according to Chase, "Bill agreed that this might be a good way for the Cubans to convey what was on their mind. . . . As soon as Lechuga calls Bill to set up an appointment for the discussion of an agenda, Bill will get in touch with us."[140]

Three days later, President Kennedy was dead.

It will never be known whether accommodation might have been possible. The CIA opposed accommodation and was joined in its opposition by the State Department's Bureau of Inter-American Affairs. Would JFK have overridden this opposition? As David Halberstam has noted, President Kennedy frequently told his liberal advisers that he agreed with what they suggested but asked them to be patient if, for political reasons, at that time he could not move in the direction they favored; perhaps something could be done during a second term. Richard Goodwin may thus have acquired his confidence in Kennedy's willingness to negotiate a settlement, but those who saw only the public president knew nothing but intransigence. When asked by a reporter about rumors that Cuba was interested in negotiation, JFK had responded in March, "I don't see any evidence that there is in prospect a normalization of relations between Cuba and the United States." Four months later he was asked again: No, he replied, "I don't see that any progress is going to be made along these lines as long as Cuba is a Soviet satellite."[141] That stands as President Kennedy's final public statement about accommodation with Cuba.

There would be no popular uprising, no pretext
American invasion of Cuba, no coup, and no
assassination of Castro. The bearded devil had won.
— CIA *Miami Station Chief Theodore Shackley*

8

HE'S GOING TO BE THERE
UNTIL HE DIES THE JOHNSON
ADMINISTRATION

Lyndon Johnson's first recorded presidential comment about Cuba came six days after John Kennedy's assassination, when the new president asked CIA director John McCone "how we planned to dispose of Castro." According to McCone's memorandum of the conversation, LBJ "said he did not wish any repetition of any fiasco of 1961, but he felt that the Cuban situation was one that we could not live with and we had to evolve more aggressive policies." Two days later McCone came back to the Oval Office for another meeting, and his notes indicate that LBJ was persistent: "The President again raised the question of what we were going to do in Cuba." He was promised a presentation of policy options in forty-eight hours.[1]

The record of that 2 December presentation is lost to history. "I have never attended a Presidential meeting," wrote NSC staffer Gordon Chase, asking to participate, and at first Bundy agreed that Chase could sit in as the note taker. But then someone remembered that LBJ did not like large meetings, Chase was uninvited, and no minutes were taken.[2] But the participants' briefing notes indicate that all of them went into the meeting prepared to advocate the same thing. Chase readied Bundy with a memo advocating "a vigorous, tough, and nasty policy . . . in order to make life as difficult for Castro and as expensive and unpleasant for the USSR as possible." Assistant Secretary of State Edwin Martin primed his boss, Dean Rusk, to recommend employing "all means available to the U.S. Government, short of military force, to bring about a degree of disorganization, uncertainty and discontent in Cuba"; Martin specifically advocated both "sabotage of Cuban ships outside Cuban territorial waters" and "hit-an[d]-run strikes against appropriate selected targets." A CIA briefer advised McCone to recommend "a continuation of present policy with certain intensification . . . designed to create and maintain a high state of anxiety within the Castro regime regarding US intentions."[3]

Although all of this pointed to increased sabotage, LBJ responded by asking the NSC Standing Group to expand the range of options. Then he went back to his office and called the chair of the Senate Committee on Foreign Relations, J. William Fulbright, who warned against doing anything dramatic. "I'm not getting into any Bay of Pigs deal," Johnson interrupted to agree. "No, I'm just asking you what we ought to do to pinch their nuts more than we're doing."[4]

As LBJ was talking with Fulbright, the Standing Group was instructing John Crimmins, the State Department's coordinator of Cuban affairs, to produce a paper listing the pluses and minuses of every possible option, from doing nothing to a full-scale U.S. invasion; at the same time, the CIA prepared a fresh analysis of the situation inside Cuba. The agency concluded that "Castro's position within Cuba appears to be eroding gradually" but that he was improving both his ability to stifle internal dissent and his capacity to counter exile raids, so that only a U.S. invasion or a blockade would guarantee the elimination of his government, and "both of these actions would result in a major crisis between the US and the USSR (in Cuba and/or Berlin) and would produce substantial strains in the fabric of US relations with other countries—allied as well as neutral." Since no one wanted to trigger a major international crisis only days after JFK had been buried, the CIA simply recommended more of what was already being done—"expanding and intensifying the category of sabotage and harassment."[5]

Doing so required reopening the question of raids by freelance (or "autonomous") Cuban exiles, which the CIA had continued to fund while keeping them somewhat leashed. Now it asked the Standing Group to recommend removing the tether—the "relaxation of our present policy banning all independent (non-CIA controlled or sponsored) Cuban exile maritime raids and air strikes." The bland pluses-and-minuses document prepared by Crimmins neither specifically agreed nor disagreed. As instructed, Crimmins simply laid out the advantages and disadvantages of specific sabotage operations, including "selective covert relaxation of U.S. controls against Cuban exile groups in Florida wishing to undertake sabotage and infiltration activities" and "air attacks against carefully selected, important economic installations by autonomous Cuban exile group(s) operating from bases outside the United States."[6]

With both the CIA and State Department documents before them, on 13 December the NSC Standing Group decided to advise against resuming the freelance exile operations but recommended the intensification of the ongoing program of CIA-controlled sabotage.[7] Two days later, Bundy gave the president a twenty-two-page briefing paper laying out his options, and on 19 December LBJ met with his senior advisers. This time Gordon Chase and his notepad were present.[8]

The CIA's Desmond FitzGerald began by reporting on four recent sabotage operations, then segued into a detailed discussion of a new initiative by CIA-controlled exiles to blow up a power plant in Matanzas province. The target's principal advantage was its exposed location, directly accessible to maritime raiders. Both Army Secretary Cyrus Vance and Army Chief of Staff Earle Wheeler favored the attack and suggested breaking the Kennedy ban by using freelance pilots to bomb the facility. Although McGeorge Bundy did not voice disapproval of the general concept of sabotage, on the specific power-plant case he suggested "that we might want to lie low for now" while the United States was launching a diplomatic effort to condemn the Castro government for sneaking arms into Venezuela. He was supported by Rusk, who worried that the Soviets might slow or even reverse their post–missile crisis troop withdrawal, and by Deputy Undersecretary of State U. Alexis Johnson, who worried that Cuba might retaliate by shooting down another U-2 spy plane.

With his advisers evenly divided, all eyes turned to the new president, who was going to make his first formal decision on Cuba. He gave each side half a loaf, nixing the Matanzas raid but agreeing that "low-risk sabotage efforts could go forward along with the planning necessary to develop an air strike capability."[9]

But the meeting was not over, and Johnson would have to make more decisions. Continuing in his role as briefer, FitzGerald reopened the issue of supporting sabotage by freelance Cuban exiles. LBJ had been prepared by Bundy's 15 December briefing paper—two of the twenty-two pages gave the pros and cons of "unleashing the exiles," but Bundy found more cons than pros: "the disadvantages were believed to be over-riding." "Since March 30, 1963 we have taken the public position that we will not tolerate the violation of U.S. neutrality laws," and "we would prefer that these completely autonomous, amateur exile raiders operate from non-U.S. territory. However, we may not have this option. Generally speaking, such amateurs have their homes in Florida and don't want to move."[10]

As vice president, one of LBJ's few recorded views on Cuba had been to oppose freelance attacks; now, as president, LBJ merely asked how much the U.S. government was spending to subsidize these "autonomous" groups.[11] After FitzGerald replied that the CIA was spending five million dollars a year, a skeptical Bundy argued that "we cannot expect too much effect from their raids," and the discussion simply petered out. No formal decision was made, which meant that a confusing status quo continued: the freelance groups would not be unleashed, but the CIA was allowed to keep them on the payroll.[12]

WHAT OCCURRED ON 19 DECEMBER would happen again and again during the Johnson years, frustrating aides such as Harry McPherson, who complained that in LBJ's White House, "very frequently, you can't tell when something is happening. You have a meeting; it's called for the purpose of developing a policy; you finish the meeting and you're really not sure whether the policy is any different from what it was when you walked in the room."[13] Then senior officials would move on to the next issue on the White House agenda, leaving officials in the policy-implementing trenches to live with this ambiguity. In the case of Cuba, the result was to make sabotage a gray area of U.S. policy.

Bundy did not like gray areas. He had been living with Operation Mongoose for more than two years and was clearly uncomfortable with the vague sabotage license that LBJ had now extended. After letting the matter rest over the holidays, Bundy asked LBJ in early January to devote one more hour of his time to a cabinet-level review of the Cuban sabotage operation, telling the president "that Rusk has never liked it and that McNamara thinks it does very little good. McCone and the CIA are for it, and so are most of the middle-level officers dealing with the Castro problem. I myself consider the matter extremely evenly balanced, but before hearing full argument, my guess is that in your position I would stop sabotage attacks on the ground that they are illegal, ineffective, and damaging to our broader policy."[14]

Although LBJ agreed to the review, in early 1964 he was focused on domestic issues. A day before Bundy's request, he had gone before a joint session of Congress not only to declare the War on Poverty but also to launch an intensive effort to gain congressional approval of what would become the Civil Rights Act of 1964, a landmark proposal to ban discrimination in public accommodations, to create the Equal Employment Opportunity Commission, and to authorize the Justice Department to force school integration in federal courts—all major attacks on segregation.

Thus occupied, LBJ had little time for Cuba. Nevertheless, he had to make time in early February, when the Coast Guard apprehended four Cuban fishing boats in U.S. waters about two miles off the Dry Tortugas. The boats and their crews were taken to Key West, then turned over to Florida officials for prosecution—basically, for fishing without a license. The Cuban government responded by announcing that it was turning off the water supply at Guantánamo until the Cubans were released.

Concerned about the domestic political consequences of the dispute, an uncertain LBJ picked up the telephone to ask an old friend and mentor, "What do you think the attitude of the country is, the Senate? Are they indignant about cutting this water off?" Georgia senator Richard Russell cut Johnson off: "They're just tired of Castro urinating on us and getting away with it." He agreed that LBJ should downplay the incident, but, he continued,

> I think there's a latent feeling there, and it may not explode right now, but one of these days, they are going to say, "Well, we've just been a bunch of asses in this country to continually back down and give away and say excuse me every time we come in collision with one of these little countries, because they're small—and particularly these Communist countries." And when that there blows, now, somebody is going to get hurt, and nobody will know just when the boiler is ready to give on it. But there's a slowly increasing feeling in this country that we're not being as positive and as firm in our foreign relations as we should be.

LBJ took the position that "we ought to have told them to get on back home and not make a big incident of it."[15]

But it now was a big incident: the Cuban fishermen were sitting in a Florida jail and Guantánamo was without water. LBJ's response was nonconfrontational. He ordered the navy to make the base self-sufficient in water and, for security reasons, to fire most of the Cuban workers.[16] The president then instructed Bundy to work with Florida officials to dispose of the legal issues, and Bundy in turn gave the job to Chase, who quickly discovered that officials in Florida were equally eager to send the Cubans home; in the interim, "they are receiving first-class treatment in jail." The charges soon were dismissed against all but the four captains, who received six-month suspended sentences and five-hundred-dollar fines. The Czech embassy paid the fines, and the Cubans departed with their ships. The fish were confiscated.

The fishing incident foreshadowed LBJ's general approach to Cuba. Unlike the Kennedy brothers, "he didn't act like a president whose mettle was being tested and felt that he had to be very macho about this," recalled Crimmins. "LBJ was very, very cautious about this. He was not at all interested in posturing or taking a dramatic stand on this issue. I was very impressed by his restraint."[17]

Perhaps he would do the same with Bundy's pending request for a review of sabotage operations, although the initial signal was not promising: in the wake of the fishing episode, Johnson asked the Joint Chiefs the same question he had asked the CIA's McCone on 28 November: How could Castro be overthrown? The chiefs considered the matter for two weeks, then gave LBJ their advice: sabotage. But, they quickly added, he should not count on it working; indeed, they continued, sabotage was not something they would have advocated without LBJ's request for more options—in preparing their report, they had experienced "difficulty identifying promising actions against Castro which have not been previously considered, and in some cases tried. It is a hard fact that little remains which offers promise of real effectiveness in removing Castro short of a blockade or an ascending scale of military action up to or including invasion."[18]

The chiefs' message was followed the next day by an equally cautious memo from Gordon Chase that would have captured the attention of any politician preparing to face the voters in seven months. It began by advising "a variety of unilateral, bilateral, and multilateral actions and pressures, both defensive and offensive, which stop short of military intervention/blockade." But then Chase paused, drew a deep breath, and recommended that this advice "be tempered slightly by the domestic political situation." The question involved walking down a narrow political path: "While we do not want to appear as 'coexisting with the Soviet satellite,' insofar as possible, we will apply pressures against Cuba in such a way that, in the absence of unusual occurrences, we will 'keep the lid on' Cuba" during the upcoming electoral campaign. That meant little or no sabotage.[19]

The CIA's counterargument came in a lengthy report promoting intensified sabotage "designed to supplement and support the overall economic denial program by damaging economically important installations and to add to Castro's economic problems by forcing him to divert money, manpower and resources from economic to internal security activities." Specifically, the CIA wanted permission to unleash the freelance exile groups. To gain this permission, the agency promised that "every item of financial and logistical support has been handled in a manner as to provide maximum protection against proof of CIA or U.S. participation."[20]

These memos constituted the background preparation for Bundy's requested review of sabotage operations. It occurred on 7 April, and once again the agenda was based on the prior deliberations of the NSC Special Group, which had considered three types of sabotage. First, every member of the Special Group had endorsed "indirect economic sabotage with a low level of visibility and detection. Programs of this sort involve possible overseas sabotage of Cuban ships and possible addition of contaminating elements to sensitive Cuban imports (not food)." Second, the Special Group was divided about whether to resume the CIA-controlled "sabotage raiding"; third, it was also divided about whether to continue funding the freelance groups, which, the CIA warned, "will begin operations soon unless action is taken to try to stop them."[21]

Getting in one last lick, Chase emphasized the domestic electoral calendar in a memo preparing Bundy for the meeting. Whatever kind of attack had been or might be "tolerable in 1963 or 1965, is intolerable in the spring and summer of 1964," Chase wrote. With the election only seven months away, "I do not favor using the raiding apparatus in Florida, at least at this time."[22] Opposition also came from the new hard-line assistant secretary of state for Latin America, Thomas Mann, but not for reasons of electoral politics; he simply thought that none of the proposed options would work, and the two most powerful cabinet members, McNamara and Rusk, agreed. As McNamara told LBJ, "The covert program has no present chance of success." The opinion was not quite unanimous, however; after listening in silence to the naysayers, General Maxwell Taylor reported that the Joint Chiefs favored the CIA's proposed program in its entirety. "They believe the program has never been given a fair test and that we should move forward with it in the interests of making Castro's life as hard as possible."[23]

The outcome? In 1975 a Senate Committee reported that "on April 7, 1964, President Johnson decided to discontinue the use of *CIA-controlled* sabotage raids against Cuba." That finding is probably accurate, since the Senate investigators had access to the uncensored minutes of the meeting. Three decades later, one crucial fragment of the minutes remains classified and unavailable to researchers: "Secretary Rusk recommended to the President that [redacted] the question be discussed again following the resolution of OAS events and the Cuban use of the [surface-to-air-missile] sites. The President accepted this recommendation."[24]

Although LBJ may have intended to close the door on sabotage, no one controlled the freelance groups, and no one told the CIA to stop bankrolling them. And they, of course, had no intention of stopping their hit-and-run raids. Exile leader Manuel "Artime is expected to strike again sometime this week," Chase warned Bundy two months after LBJ's 7 April decision; "there appears to be little to do except to hold onto your hat along with the rest of us."[25]

The Cuban government could do little more than complain, as it did in June with an especially biting protest note: "Today, June 19, at 11:45 A.M., an armed plane launched a criminal bombing attack on the Marcelo Salado sugar mill in the town of Caiberien, Las Villas Province, and one of the bombs exploded in the settlement where women and children, relatives of the workers at the sugar mill are living. The airplane took off from United States territory." In reply, Secretary Rusk argued that "the Government of Cuba undoubtedly knows the difficulties of preventing determined persons from evading surveillance," and that statement was at least partially true: three months later, an exile group shelled a Spanish ship in Cuban waters, killing three seamen and wounding six others, and the attackers were so autonomous that the Pentagon could not identify them beyond "some anti-Castro group, name unknown."[26]

This distinction between "freelance" or "autonomous" and "CIA-controlled" exile attacks was no doubt lost on the Cubans, but Washington continued to make it throughout LBJ's tenure. Shortly after LBJ's 1964 electoral victory, the CIA sought permission to fund a new coalition of freelance exiles, Representación Cubana del Exilio (RECE), whose leadership included Jorge Mas Canosa. The State Department was adamantly opposed: "Our support of exile organizations has probably produced more problems than results. Our experience in supporting clandestine and commando activities by autonomous exile groups has been especially negative, and such activities are at the heart of the RECE proposals." But by this time, eleven months after the 7 April meeting, State opposed only freelancers; in the same memo, the department argued that "the use of disciplined, directly controlled Agency resources would be more effective and, on balance, less risky than resort to autonomous or semi-autonomous exile groups."[27]

Thus encouraged, the CIA again prepared to swing into action, and within a few weeks, Bundy was warning LBJ that the new CIA director, Admiral William Raborn, "has recommended reactivation of a paramilitary effort against Cuba."[28] Raborn found it "one of the most comforting things to me as an American citizen to see a democracy which is a true democracy, which we have in this country, able to support an agency such as the Central Intelligence Agency, that can do the many things which our Government could not do openly and get in the back alley at times and fight the Communists on their own terms." Bundy told LBJ that Raborn was recommending

> "(1) maritime raids by commando teams against coastal targets,
>
> (2) use of underwater demolition teams to blow up ships in Cuban ports,
>
> (3) night attacks on major Cuban merchant vessels while in Cuban territorial waters,
>
> (4) air bombing of selected targets in Cuba,
>
> (5) deception operations designed to give the impression of imminent invasion by U.S. forces."[29]

The most negative response came from the State Department, which reminded everyone that "the paramilitary program [redacted] was abandoned after a reasonable trial, because of the decision that the damage to our broad interests, especially our relations with the USSR and the Vietnamese situation, would be disproportionate to the benefits which we might obtain in terms of our Cuban policy." And, the memo continued, "there were, in practice, very limited benefits."[30]

Admiral Raborn's sabotage proposal was quietly shelved, and some holdover Kennedy-era officials believed that the fizz had gone out of the water. When he had opened the State Department's Cuba office in Miami in January 1963, Crimmins had found the largest CIA station in the world and "a whole series of freelance operations directed against Cuba by exiled groups"; his replacement, Harvey Summ, reported that during LBJ's presidency, "the intensity of efforts to overthrow Castro declined markedly."[31] But only in 1977, during the Carter administration, did a presidential directive definitively end the toleration of freelance sabotage raids, and despite the flawed memory of some CIA officials, the most that could be said about sabotage during the LBJ era was said by Chase, who wrote that "there was substantial movement towards reducing the noise-level capacity of *autonomous* exile groups." "I think this is all to the good," Chase added. For every Chase, however, there was a Senator Tom Dodd, who told the American

Legion that "we must put an end to the folly of restraining and handicapping those patriotic Cubans who seek to bring aid to the freedom fighters in their homeland."[32]

So the sabotage efforts never stopped during LBJ's presidency. "The agency sent out lots of operational instructions," recalled the CIA's Ray Cline, "and they were still going out years later when I was station chief in Germany, which wasn't till 1966. We continued to get messages occasionally saying go do something to interfere with or damage a shipment of economic supplies of some kind to Cuba in Western Europe. . . . There were lots of little gimmicks like spoiling the bearings in certain kinds of machinery, putting flat bearings in instead of ball bearings, trying to adulterate petrol supplies with sugar and various contaminants."[33] None of these efforts was as spectacular as burning down a Havana department store or bombing a sugar mill, and such attempts were what Desmond FitzGerald probably meant in 1964 when he confided to a colleague that "unfortunately, the new President isn't as gung-ho on fighting Castro as Kennedy was" or what Ray Cline meant when he recalled, "I don't think there was a big change in policy, but after Jack's death the spirit was just a little different." The official who saw this most clearly was State's Crimmins, who later recalled that "during the Kennedy period, I used to get a call from McGeorge Bundy or one of his assistants every day about something, about some problem that they saw or didn't understand or something like that." But then, he continued, "under Johnson, the calls dropped down to probably once a week, and then maybe once every two weeks or once a month by '65, when I got out."[34]

BUT WHAT ABOUT THE POSSIBILITY of reaching an accommodation? JFK had been murdered before deciding how to respond to Fidel Castro's signals that he wanted to resolve the two nations' differences. Most of those signals had been filtered through the U.S. mission to the United Nations via ABC correspondent Lisa Howard, whose early 1963 interview with Castro had made him appear receptive to a reduction in tensions, and a few weeks before Kennedy's death she published an article reporting that "in recent months, Fidel Castro has stated and restated his desire for more amicable relations with the United States."[35] Bundy had given Chase the task of coordinating the Attwood-Lechuga diplomatic minuet that began in Howard's New York apartment, and in the process Chase became a partisan of rapprochement. A few days before JFK's assassination, when Chase sensed that the opponents of negotiation were gaining the upper hand, he produced a three-page memorandum listing the "numerous advantages which accrue from a discreet approach to Castro."[36]

The context was entirely different ten days later, when Chase wrote to Bundy that "the events of Nov 22 would appear to make accommodation with Castro an even more doubtful issue than it was." The problem was domestic politics: Kennedy could have gotten away with reconciliation, but now "a new President who has no background of being successfully nasty to Castro and the Communists (e.g. President Kennedy in October, 1962) would probably run a greater risk of being accused, by the American people, of 'going soft.'" Lechuga waited only a few days after Kennedy's death before approaching Howard once again to say that Castro wanted to continue talking with the new administration. She went to Attwood, Attwood went to Chase, and Chase went to Bundy: "The ball is in our court; Bill owes Lechuga a call. What to do?"[37] When Bundy did not respond immediately, Chase offered his advice:

> The mood should be roughly as follows: Fidel, we are content to let events continue on their present course. We intend to maintain, and whenever possible, to increase our pressure against you until you fall; we are pretty certain that we will be successful. Moreover, you can forget about getting "another Cuba" in the Hemisphere. We have learned our lesson and "another Cuba" is simply not going to happen. However, we are reasonable men. We are not intent on having your head per se; neither do we relish the suffering of the Cuban people. You know our central concerns — the Soviet connection and subversion. If you feel you are in a position to allay these concerns, we can probably work out a way to live amicably together and to build a prosperous Cuba. If you don't feel you can meet our concerns, then just forget the whole thing; we are quite content to continue on our present basis.

Bundy waited two weeks, until the 19 December meeting about sabotage, and then told the president, "We are essentially faced with a decision as to whether or not we are prepared to listen to what Castro has to say."[38]

The minutes do not record LBJ's reaction, but note taker Gordon Chase remarked the next day that "from the tenor of the President's Thursday meeting, I would surmise that it was somewhere between lukewarm and cool." It was closer to frigid. LBJ's initial instinct had been to "dispose" of Castro, not to negotiate, and confidants such as Bill Moyers advocated a hard line — "Mr. President," Moyers wrote at the time of the Guantánamo water crisis, "I would like to suggest that you really keep pressure on Bundy and Rusk and McCone and others to press forward on what we can do about Cuba—about subversion, espionage, and intelligence."[39]

Fidel Castro had no way of knowing the situation, of course, and four days later he personally asked Howard to "tell the President (and I cannot stress this too strongly) that I seriously hope that Cuba and the United States can eventually sit down in an atmosphere of good will and of mutual respect and negotiate our differences." He even did something that seems absolutely extraordinary: he volunteered his country as a whipping boy during the upcoming electoral campaign. "If the President feels it necessary during the campaign to make bellicose statements about Cuba or even to take some hostile action—if he will inform me, unofficially, that a specific action is required because of domestic political considerations, I shall understand and not take any serious retaliatory action."[40]

By then it was too late, as Chase told another senior NSC staffer: any hint of a willingness to talk "is the kind of signal that we want to give when Castro is relatively down and out, and not when he is riding at a relatively high level. My own estimate is that this is a relatively high point for Castro." With Bundy's approval, Chase instructed Bill Attwood to back away— "While the door was not closed on further contact with Lechuga, the timing was not now considered right."[41] Apparently relieved by the evidence that "domestic political considerations reinforce our national security decision to keep a reasonable amount of pressure on Cuba," an unidentified State Department official summarized U.S. policy in mid-March: "We will spin the negotiations out; this will not be hard in view of the communication difficulties. At the same time, however, we will stay loose. If, per chance, it appears that we can eject the Soviets and, at the same time, believe it will benefit rather than hinder the Administration in November, we may want to speed up the time-table rather than wait to collect the dividend after November."[42]

At this point in early 1964 the Democrats were not certain that the Republicans were going to commit suicide by nominating Barry Goldwater; all that the Democrats understood was that Johnson had been elected vice president, not president, and that he had no national following. And since Democratic strategists also knew that the electorate was not going to see Cuba as a shining example of their party's achievement, they had already begun girding for the election by preparing a 38-page list of favorable statements that Republican leaders had made about the Cuban Revolution prior to 1961; looking over the list, Chase told Theodore Sorensen "that a good case can be made that our troubles with Communist Cuba began with the Republicans." Thirty-eight pages would not be enough for LBJ, however, so Chase and a State Department colleague more than doubled the page count, creating a 107-page chronology that tied Republicans to a host of Cuba-related ills, and Chase could now report that he had "plenty of good ammunition with which to retaliate if the Republicans get rough."[43]

Then, out of the blue, Democratic senator William Fulbright issued a call for accommodation: "We have become transfixed with Cuba, making it far more important in both our foreign relations and in our domestic life than its size and influence warrant." He argued that the United States should instead accept "the continued existence of the Castro regime as a distasteful nuisance but not an intolerable danger."[44] Fulbright's voice was amplified when the *New York Times* appeared in the role originated by Lisa Howard: in July the paper quoted Castro as proposing "extensive discussion of all issues" and promising to halt aid to Latin American subversives, to release all political prisoners, and to negotiate payment for expropriated property. LBJ's political advisers could not imagine nibbling at this bait on the eve of the nominating conventions: "After November 3, we will be able to focus harder on some of the 'unthinkable thoughts' such as the possibilities for accommodation with Castro," Chase told Bundy. In the meantime, officials should be aware that Cuba's offer to talk was probably insincere, or so State's Bureau of Intelligence and Research hypothesized: "Castro wants to appear conciliatory in the face of the upcoming OAS Foreign Ministers Conference which will consider Venezuela's complaints against Cuban subversion." The bureau further warned that any softening of the U.S. position would doom the OAS meeting scheduled to convene in a few days.[45]

But within days of LBJ's landslide election, when his advisers no longer had a worry in the world, they began to reconsider: "With November 3 behind us, we can usefully do some basic review work on Cuba," Chase wrote, informing Bundy that the State Department's Coordinator of Cuban Affairs had been asked to "outline the major problems and the possible options, including accommodation."[46]

Mandate in hand, Lyndon Johnson had turned his attention elsewhere, and the Kennedy era's near-obsession with Cuba was gone forever. In early 1964 national security adviser McGeorge Bundy had begun encouraging everyone to face reality: "The chances are very good that we will still be living with Castro some time from now," he had told President Johnson; "we might just as well get used to the idea." A few months later Thomas Mann told LBJ that Castro was "going to be there until he dies," and in 1966 the CIA even acknowledged that the Cuban government enjoyed "substantial popular support and acquiescence," concluding that "the present regime will maintain an unassailable hold on Cuba indefinitely." Meanwhile, the administration's other problems had multiplied, and a few months after the 1964 election, Secretary Rusk wrote to Bundy to oppose a CIA proposal to resume a Mongoose-like sabotage program: there was no time for Cuba given "the current situation in the Dominican Republic and the status of the conflict in Viet-Nam, not to mention other problems around the world." The CIA's Ted Shackley could see the handwriting on the wall: "There would be no popular uprising," he wrote, "no pretext American invasion of Cuba, no coup, and no assassination of Castro. The bearded devil had won."[47]

SO WHAT DID LBJ FAVOR? The note takers at the 19 December meeting had seen the answer immediately: "Promote greater economic blockade," wrote one; a second noted that LBJ "appeared particularly interested in the subject of economic denial and returned to it several times"; according to a third, "The President was most interested in economic denial actions."[48] Implementing such a policy would not be easy, since it would require the cooperation of other governments, all of which were strongly predisposed to sell Cuba (or any other country) whatever it wanted to purchase. Economic isolation would therefore require a seasoned diplomat who could convince both reluctant allies and Congress to support the administration's effort. That seasoned diplomat was Thomas Mann.

His efforts could not begin for a few weeks, however: as Mann was settling into his office, the new assistant secretary received an opportunity— the discovery of a Cuban arms shipment on the beaches of Venezuela that fit perfectly with what had become the principal post-missile-crisis fear about Cuba: that it would subvert its neighbors. Augmenting this fear was the ingrained Cold War vision of Latin America's vulnerability, a vision captured by the CIA's Raborn when he wrote, "The great danger in Latin America is the weakness of governments, which invites unrest, dissidence, and potentially the collapse of law and order, leading to chaos." This assessment was based on the belief that Latin Americans were prone to be swept up into mob action; as Senator Bourke Hickenlooper explained the 1965 breakdown of order in the Dominican Republic, "You can drive a bunch of sheep with one dog and do a pretty good job of it, without comparing these people to dogs, I don't mean that." What he meant, Hickenlooper continued, was that "we have a mob of 500 people or 1,000 people, and five or ten . . . are Communists, who are trained in subversion and revolution and things like that. They can get in there and immediately spring into the leadership because they know what to do, and the mob follows them."[49]

Such an analysis was rendered plausible by Cuba's early attempts to subvert Latin American governments. Cuba-based rebels had struck out for Panama, Haiti, Nicaragua, and the Dominican Republic shortly after Batista's fall, but the smoking gun of government sponsorship had been absent until just before Kennedy's death, when Venezuela announced the discovery of three tons of arms on the beaches of the Paraguaná Peninsula, not far from the nation's principal oilfields. On 28 November, with LBJ now in the White House, Venezuela announced that it had traced the weapons to Cuba through the serial numbers of the Belgian rifles (which had been sold to the Cuban army) and through the boat captured along with the arms (the outboard motor of which had recently been shipped from Montreal to Cuba's agrarian reform institute). Venezuela's response had been to request an OAS meeting of consultation, and the State Department had seconded the request with its first LBJ-era statement about Cuba, which condemned the Castro government for "fomenting violence in other American Republics."[50]

Mann was not enthusiastic about turning the matter over to the OAS. In 1960 he had warned that Latin Americans "all belong to the same family, and they are not going to be anxious to pick our chestnuts out of the fire." The Eisenhower administration had nonetheless taken its concern to the OAS and, as Mann had predicted, had come away with the toothless Declaration of San José. Two years later, at Punta del Este, the organization's foreign ministers had suspended Cuba's membership in the OAS, and the Kennedy administration had continued to look for additional opportunities. In early 1963, the Pentagon had suggested that "the OAS should vote, under the Rio Pact, to punish Castro's aggression. This action could take the form of a resolution for all members to take such action including the use of force as individually considered appropriate." This suggestion had not been acted on, but the arms discovery might lead to a consensus to do more to truly isolate Cuba from the rest of Latin America, even if such consensus stopped short of a green light to invade. Would the votes be there? "These nations ain't as silly as we attribute them to be," Senator Richard Russell told a worried LBJ. "They're not nearly as bad as everybody makes out like they are." Hickenlooper was less sure; at difficult moments, he said, "the OAS drags its feet and drags and orates and yells, 'Viva Bolivar,' and then goes off to a siesta."[51] Now, in early 1964, it was time to see who was correct.

With Venezuela's request and the Johnson administration's blessing, the OAS Permanent Council quickly appointed a five-nation team (including the United States) to investigate the arms shipment. Cuba received an opportunity to respond, but Foreign Minister Raúl Roa replied that his government did not recognize the OAS's jurisdiction, not simply because Cuba had been suspended from the organization at Punta del Este but also "because it is a colonial ministry of the State Department."[52] The investigating team went ahead anyway and in early 1964 issued its verdict: guilty as charged.

This finding would have led to an immediate meeting of consultation had not Panama severed diplomatic relations with the United States in mid-January after twenty-four Panamanian students were killed and several hundred more wounded in disturbances over the issue of flying Panama's flag in the Canal Zone. The flag riots had inflamed nationalist passions throughout the region, especially in Mexico, and when the OAS investigating team's Venezuela verdict was released in late February, the State Department was still hammering out an agreement with Panama to review every issue related to the canal — the first step in what would become the 1977 Carter-Torrijos Treaty returning the Canal Zone to Panama. Only after U.S.-Panamanian diplomatic relations had been reestablished could a meeting of consultation be scheduled.

That process took several months, and only in mid-1964 did the hemisphere's foreign ministers finally convene in Washington. Secretary of State Rusk sat through the opening formalities and then rose to remind his Latin American colleagues that "by its very nature international communism is aggressive and expansive" and to warn that "deceit is a standard element in their tactics." He next turned to an assessment of Fidel Castro, focusing on "his temperament and ambition" but adding that "the dynamics of his internal situation, the counsel of those whom he serves and those who serve him — all compel him to promote subversion."[53]

After three days of similar speeches, the foreign ministers voted 15–4 "to condemn emphatically the present Government of Cuba for its acts of aggression and of intervention against the territorial inviolability, the sovereignty, and the political independence of Venezuela." Two years after the 1962 suspension of Cuba's OAS membership, the new penalty was suspension of all bilateral diplomatic and consular relations, of all trade (except food and medicine), and of all sea transportation. Bolivia, Chile, Mexico, and Uruguay voted against the resolution (Venezuela, the complainant, was ineligible to vote), but because the meeting of consultation had been called under Article 6 of the Rio Treaty, making mandatory any resolution passed by a two-thirds majority, Bolivia and Chile soon severed relations, and in early September Uruguay announced that it too would comply with the resolution. In Latin America, that left only Mexico with formal diplomatic and economic ties to Cuba, whose isolation from the rest of Latin America was now as complete as it ever would be. "The meeting was a success," reported Secretary Rusk.[54]

WITH THAT ACCOMPLISHED, the administration then turned to focus on halting Cuba's trade with the rest of the noncommunist world. This effort had already required an extraordinary amount of time and energy—"The most outstanding characteristic of our isolation measures is that they are exceedingly difficult to implement," Gordon Chase had noted in late 1963. The State Department concurred: convincing Washington's allies to stop trading with Cuba had required "intense US diplomatic pressure applied virtually on a day-to-day basis in capitals throughout the world."[55]

Perhaps the easiest step was to cut Cuba off from the International Monetary Fund (IMF), from which the Batista government had borrowed twenty-five million dollars in September 1958. Cuba's revolutionary government inherited this debt and at first agreed to repay it. However, the Cubans later not only failed to do so but also refused to comply with an IMF demand that they eliminate exchange restrictions; instead, in April 1964 Cuba withdrew from the fund, a move that automatically made it ineligible for World Bank development loans. The Johnson administration had held the door open wide, but "the Cubans have saved us the trouble of kicking them out," wrote Chase. "They withdrew when it became clear that the IMF was about to act."[56]

Cuba's exclusion from the OAS and the IMF left the Johnson administration free to focus on two more ambitious activities: shipping and trade. Of the two, the reduction of shipping was the easier to implement. Despite the major challenges posed by attempting to track all 17,426 nonbloc ships in the world's merchant fleet, U.S. officials did so, reporting, for example, that exactly 433 merchant ships flying flags of twenty-two noncommunist countries had made 572 trips to Cuba in the first eight months of 1962.[57] Then in early 1963 President Kennedy had prohibited ships calling on Cuba from carrying U.S. government-financed cargoes, which meant that someone had to create and maintain two lists—one list of government-financed exports, and a second list of all ships entering Cuban ports—and then ensure that nothing on the first list was loaded onto a ship on the second.[58] In practice, Washington shifted much of this burden to the private sector: every two weeks the U.S. Maritime Administration simply published in the *Federal Register* a list of noncommunist ships that had carried goods to or from Cuba since the first day of 1963. Shippers then bore responsibility for obtaining copies of the *Federal Register* every two weeks (no easy task in pre-Internet days), for knowing whether the cargo waiting to be loaded was government-financed, and then, of course, for refusing to load the cargo if the ship had been listed. Government officials did not escape all the work, however, since the first list had to be updated continuously, which meant that every Cuban port had to be monitored night and day, and the CIA soon complained that the effort was taxing its resources—"Several hundred people, both here and abroad, have been devoting a good bit of their time to simply keeping track." If the White House wanted to do more, the CIA "would need, first and foremost, funds and people."[59]

Just after Kennedy's assassination, officials told LBJ that "there is plenty of room for improvement. There are still roughly 30 Free World ships per month in the Cuban trade. Free World countries still send many commodities to Cuba which Cuba needs desperately."[60] As vice president, Johnson already knew that JFK's shipping ban had been less than successful: in 1962, characterizing allies' behavior as "disappointing," an aide had reported that "the UK and Norway, whose ships have carried the majority of the cargoes to Cuba, have taken the position that the imposition of government controls would violate their cherished principles of free shipping."

Fearing for the safety of their ships, the regularly scheduled cargo companies suspended their services during the missile crisis and to date had not resumed them. The CIA reported that U.S. pressure had "effectively removed Free World cargo lines from the Cuban trade."[61] That accomplishment left the Johnson administration with the more difficult task of halting the chartered vessels still carrying goods to Cuba. Most of these ships—410 in 1964—flew the flags of noncommunist countries but sailed under charter to the Soviet Union and its Eastern European allies. Kennedy-era officials had made no progress in this arena, and the State Department concluded that they never would: "Even if the free world charterers were to deny use of their ships in the Cuba trade, the USSR could shift these ships to other runs and use their own in sending goods to Cuba. In view of the present surplus of shipping, it is out of the question from a practical point of view to try to persuade other countries to deny all shipping to the USSR."[62]

Congress nonetheless tried its hand immediately after JFK's assassination by stipulating that aid be terminated to any government that failed to prevent ships registered under its flag from transporting goods to or from Cuba, and at LBJ's 19 December meeting, the State Department's coordinator of Cuban affairs suggested that the president consider how this amendment "can be used to reinforce our economic denial program." The problem, as the Defense Intelligence Agency had recently reported, was that any effort to halt the charters would soon be irrelevant, since Soviet bloc ships were now becoming available, and at the 19 December meeting, Bundy warned that "we should not deceive ourselves. We should recognize that the Soviets are capable of handling all Cuba's shipping needs even if we are able to eliminate Free World shipping to Cuba."[63]

The State Department nevertheless decided to focus on halting the remaining noncommunist charters entering Cuban ports, and some progress was made: "Following repeated strong diplomatic approaches by the United States," State reported in mid-1964 that five countries (Honduras, Liberia, Panama, West Germany, and Turkey) had agreed to halt shipping, that the Lebanese were preparing to cooperate (although they reneged almost immediately), and that Greece had prohibited new commitments. But no progress had been made with other major shippers, including the United Kingdom, whose "ships constituted about half of the nonbloc vessels entering Cuba. Canada also refused to cooperate, as did Guyana, which was selling rice to Cuba, but those were the only two countries in the Western Hemisphere with significant maritime traffic to Cuba during LBJ's tenure. After three years of intense U.S. pressure, the number of nonbloc ships entering Cuban ports dropped from 410 in 1964 to 227 in 1967.[64]

This effort to halt shipping paled when compared to the attempt to stop Cuba's trade with noncommunist countries. As vice president, Johnson had urged JFK to increase the pressure on allies refusing to cooperate with Washington's embargo—the minutes of one 1962 NSC meeting show LBJ arguing, "We have got to be tough. He wants to drag our feet on help to those countries that help Castro, and those countries that opposed Castro, we should help quickly. We should do all we can to hurt Castro and we can't ignore or reward those who play with the enemy." The CIA had agreed, with Desmond FitzGerald proposing the creation of an "economic warfare group"; now, a few days after JFK's assassination, the agency noted that "there is still considerable opportunity for tightening the economic noose around Castro." FitzGerald led off LBJ's 19 December briefing by noting "that equipment vitally needed in Cuba, some of U.S. origin, reaches the island via Canada and Great Britain." Stopping those shipments was exactly the type of nut-pinching LBJ had in mind, and the minutes indicate that "the President directed that the agencies prepare a detailed memorandum (including the names of companies and commodities involved in Free World trade with Cuba) which, inter alia, will be useful in his forthcoming talks with Prime Ministers [Lord] Home [of Great Britain] and [Lester] Pearson [of Canada]."[65]

The British became the first to experience LBJ's patented brand of arm-twisting. The specific issue was a sale of four hundred buses by the Leyland Motors Corporation, with credit guaranteed by Her Majesty's government. "The President made clear the depth of American concern on trade with Cuba," wrote the note taker at a mid-February meeting between LBJ and British prime minister Alec Douglas-Home, but Lord Home responded "that the British had a firm national policy in favor of peaceful trade with any country—a policy he could not reverse." "You didn't get any commitment from Home at all?," inquired an aide. "None whatever," LBJ replied. Two weeks later, LBJ gave the same message to a visiting Harold Wilson, leader of the British Labour Party and shadow prime minister. As unsympathetic as Home, Wilson replied that "it was British policy to encourage trade across the board."[66]

U.S. officials then proceeded to construct a mountain out of a molehill. Undersecretary of State George Ball told a Roanoke, Virginia, audience that without the buses, "the level of Cuban morale would be further impaired," and Secretary Rusk told Congress that "400 additional buses would almost double the public transport of Habana. Without this replacement of existing transport in Cuba's capital city, the efficiency of the Cuban economy would be further impaired." In a less public forum, the Joint Chiefs encouraged LBJ to persevere despite the British rebuff—to continue "what we have been doing all along, with steady pressure on our 'friends,' like the British, not to give us the knife."[67] LBJ was clearly upset when a third British official walked into the Oval Office in late April: "We just, by god, don't want to be open to this charge that our friends are selling anything to Cuba," he told British foreign secretary Rab Butler. "Nixon is running around all over the country raising hell and you just find some way to avoid it."[68]

The next friend with a knife was France, which in mid-1964 announced the sale of twenty locomotives to Cuba. Aware of LBJ's ongoing effort to strong-arm the British (and of his anger about France's recent decision to recognize the People's Republic of China), senior French leaders sensibly avoided visits to the White House, so U.S. officials instead took their complaint about the locomotives to the Quai d'Orsay. They reported that the French "were apologetic but said that the firm needed the business," and a U.S. envoy received the same reply after a second try several months later, with the receiving French diplomat twisting the knife by noting that U.S. wheat sales to the Soviet Union "had made the task of isolating Cuba very difficult." Ball reconciled what the French and others considered Washington's contradictory policy by telling his Roanoke audience that denying wheat to Soviet Union "would in the long run make little sense, since the Soviet Union imports from the free world only about one-half of 1 percent of its gross national product. But Cuba presents a wholly different situation. It is a small island with meager natural resources and a low level of industrial development."[69]

The French no doubt considered their response surprisingly civil in light of the Johnson administration's recent halt in military aid, triggered because France had refused to stop its ships from trading with Cuba. The aid amounted to less than one hundred thousand dollars, and the cutoff had been evenhanded—"U.S. Curtails Aid to Five Countries That Sell to Cuba," read the front-page *New York Times* headline; "the Johnson Administration has apparently chosen to risk good relations with its allies and two key nonaligned countries rather than permit them to go on defying the United States policy." It was simply a matter of enforcing the law—specifically, a 1963 law stipulating that aid be cut to nations whose ships and aircraft continued to travel to Cuba. The law had given such countries sixty days to change their ways, and fourteen offenders had agreed to do so; five had not, however, and their aid was stopped. Britain and Yugoslavia also lost one hundred thousand dollars, but the big losers were Morocco, which lost twenty million dollars in economic aid, and Spain, which lost thirty million dollars in military aid.[70]

"Spain should be a high priority target," Bundy had advised two months earlier, shortly after Madrid had signed a three-year trade agreement to purchase Cuban sugar at substantially above the world price; in return, Cuba would purchase a broad variety of Spanish goods.[71] But when the United States announced its aid cut, the Spanish government reminded Washington that it was not "aid" at all but a treaty obligation, promised in exchange for naval and air bases that the Pentagon considered vital to controlling the western Mediterranean and for which leases had recently been extended for five years in return for "support for the Spanish defense effort at a suitable level through the granting of military aid to the Spanish armed forces." The United States awkwardly reversed its decision, and Spain continued to trade with Cuba while receiving U.S. aid. "This especially bugs us," Chase told Bundy.[72]

LBJ's first-year disputes with Britain, France, and Spain set the stage for additional sanctions, as the Johnson administration continued to focus on pressuring allied governments, one on one. U.S. embassies around the globe were instructed to help, with their performance evaluated by NSC staffer William Bowdler. In 1966 he zeroed in on Italy, complaining to Bundy's replacement, Walt Rostow, that U.S. officials in Rome were not doing enough to stop an Italian firm's proposed sale of a fertilizer plant. Bowdler asked Rostow to "remind Secretary Rusk of the importance which the President attaches to our Cuban isolation program and ask him to look into the Italian case."[73]

Attention shifted to London a few weeks later, when Bowdler reported on "two more potential leaks in our Cuban isolation policy"—another Cuban purchase from Britain and an effort by the Soviets to obtain overflight rights for their Moscow-Havana run. Fortunately, he told Rostow, "State is working hard on both." Then the British, intent on supplying the fertilizer plant that Italy had agreed to forgo, stuck in another knife. "We are making strong efforts at high levels to persuade British not to guarantee credit for Cuban purchase of fertilizer plant," the embassy cabled from Paris, which had been informed of the deal because the French, knife in hand, were also refusing to cooperate with the United States on another sale. If both the French and the British made deals with Cuba, the United States would find it "very difficult to hold other governments in line." U.S. envoys in Paris received three pages of detailed instructions about how to explain the importance Washington attached to its isolation policy, while the British received a visit from Treasury Secretary Henry Fowler, who indelicately pointed out that the deal "might be especially criticized in US in light of recent announcement that US will increase defense expenditures by $35 million in UK next year." Ambassador-at-Large Averell Harriman and Secretary of State Rusk were more diplomatic in their personal messages to Foreign Secretary George Brown, but they could not stop the forty-five-million-dollar sale, which went through with an accompanying government guarantee.[74]

Such setbacks occurred, but success was more frequent. After the OAS ban, Cuba's already modest trade with Latin American countries slowed to a trickle, and European trade declined almost as much, in part because Cuba was now trading primarily with the Soviet bloc. U.S. diplomats nonetheless remained intent on ending even the most trivial trading relationship, including one with nonaligned Austria that had traditionally amounted to cash purchases of a handful of cigars. A modest blip occurred in early 1965, however, when an Austrian firm sold Cuba some ball bearings that had been manufactured in the United States. The State Department requested the cooperation of the U.S. suppliers, and the CIA soon reported that the Austrian company "has agreed to end all shipments to Cuba by the end of this month."[75] State employed a different tactic after learning that a French company had begun importing nickel from Cuba: the Treasury Department simply announced a ban on the import of French products containing nickel, primarily stainless steel, and the French stopped their purchases from Cuba. Treasury took the same tack when Italy began buying Cuban nickel, and the State Department reported that "the apparent result of these efforts on our part has been to force the Cubans to ship through third parties through the free port of Rotterdam. The United States as of late 1968 had not discovered the final destination of these shipments, but was working on the problem. In the meantime, we estimated that transshipment and handling costs in Rotterdam were adding to Cuba's foreign exchange problems."[76]

The net result clearly disadvantaged Cuba. "The United States has been unable to stifle completely Cuba's foreign trade," admitted the State Department at the end of LBJ's presidency, and "when Cuba has something to sell there is usually someone to buy it, although often only at heavily discounted prices or through expensive middlemen. When Cuba has hard cash there is always someone to sell to her, though usually at high unit prices. We have, therefore, been unable to cause the collapse of the Cuban economy, nor did we think we would be able to do so. As a result of US efforts, however, as well as the Cuban regime's own economic mismanagement, the Cuban economy has remained stagnant since Castro came to power and the per capita national income has actually declined." And, as the British ambassador added from Havana, "the need to maintain enormous armed forces ... in a perpetual state of readiness involves a tremendous drain on Cuba's resources—notably in men with technical skills, as well as huge expense. Another major drain on the competent manpower and energy available to the regime is the vast apparatus of the security services and the police."[77]

All this was nut-pinching at its very best, and LBJ's Democrats patted themselves on the back in their 1964 platform—"The Cuban economy is deteriorating." But U.S. actions clearly were not leading to the collapse of Cuba's revolutionary government, aided by Soviet subsidies, and the CIA reported late in LBJ's tenure that "Castro and his supporters are in full control."[78] If the contest, then, was to see which side could expend sufficient time, money, and energy to achieve its goals, then the United States had lost. But given the costs Cuba incurred, it can hardly be said to have won.

IN THEIR 1964 PLATFORM, LBJ's opponents had promised to increase Cuba's costs: "We Republicans will recognize a Cuban government in exile; we will support its efforts to regain the independence of its homeland; we will assist Cuban freedom fighters in carrying on guerrilla warfare against the Communist regime; we will work for an economic boycott by all nations of the free world in trade with Cuba; and we will encourage free elections in Cuba after liberty and stability are restored." Goldwater's Republicans made a number of additional promises, including a worrisome one to "move decisively to assure victory in South Vietnam"; in contrast, throughout the campaign, LBJ resisted his advisers' pleas to escalate that war.[79]

Looking at this choice, voters gave Lyndon Johnson more than 61 percent of the popular vote — at the time the most lopsided presidential victory in the nation's history. Mandate in hand, LBJ said nothing about Cuba in his State of the Union address two months later; instead, he focused on a plan to construct what he called the Great Society, and his blueprint was breathtaking in scope — from something he called Medicare for the elderly to Head Start for the young. Johnson's ability to convince the public to pay for these initiatives stands as his most remarkable political achievement.

It was all the more remarkable because his cajoling took place in an atmosphere of rising unrest over the war in Vietnam, which President Johnson, for all his political gifts, simply misunderstood in the same way he underestimated the determination of Cuba's revolutionaries. "LBJ is a bully," concluded Arthur M. Schlesinger Jr. "Through all his life he has discovered that, if you leaned on people hard enough, you pounded them hard enough, their breaking point eventually came. . . . He transferred this notion to international relations and assumed there must be a breaking point therefore: just pound the bastards long enough." And then, Schlesinger continued, LBJ's natural inclination was reinforced when his electoral landslide "made him feel that he could do what he wished in Indochina."[80] Barely a month after his inauguration, LBJ took the decisive step that rival Republicans had proposed during the campaign, authorizing the first deployment of regular U.S. troops in Vietnam. A few weeks later, he further escalated the conflict by launching Operation Rolling Thunder, a sustained bombing campaign against North Vietnam. To protest this escalation, an eighty-two-year-old Detroit pacifist, Alice Herz, did what Buddhist monks were doing in Saigon—as an act of both protest and solidarity, she publicly killed herself by self-immolation.

In this context State Department officials sat down to hammer out the U.S. position on upcoming talks about Cuba with Canada and Britain. Not surprisingly, State proposed "the maintenance of the present low-cost, low-risk policy," but two weeks later, the dishes again started to rattle in the Caribbean cupboard. This time, a rebellion had erupted in the Dominican Republic. U.S. Ambassador Tapley Bennett warned Thomas Mann of a communist takeover; Mann tucked Bennett's dispatches into his briefcase, drove to the White House, and convinced LBJ to send in more than twenty thousand U.S. Marines, the first such U.S. action in Latin America since the 1920s. Echoing Bennett, Mann vigorously defended the invasion by characterizing the rebellion as "an episode in the Communist war of liberation technique," and CIA Director William Raborn asserted without a shred of evidence that "the [Communist] party leaders saw to it that all the right people had guns."[81]

A few weeks later, newly elected New York senator Robert Kennedy returned from an unpleasant trip to Latin America. In Chile, reported the *New York Times*, students "threw eggs, rocks and money" at RFK, and when he tried to engage them in dialogue, "some tried to kick him, others spat at him and still others burned a U.S. flag." That same day, the *Times*'s front page featured a picture of a Uruguayan spitting in the face of visiting Secretary of State Dean Rusk.[82] Returning to Washington, RFK told his Senate colleagues how he interpreted this animosity: "In the years following World War II, we were content to accept, and even support, whatever governments were in power, asking only that they not disturb the surface calm of the hemisphere. We gave medals to dictators; praised backward regimes; and became steadily identified with institutions and men who held their lands in poverty and fear." The governments backed by the United States included "the bloody and corrupt tyranny of Batista which we supported to the moment of its collapse." And the result? "What brought about Mr. Castro and communism in Cuba was our support of Batista."[83]

LBJ reacted by withdrawing even further from Latin America, and the only significant attention he gave Cuba came in late 1965 when Fidel Castro accused the U.S. press of "an incessant propaganda campaign against the Revolution" that included the charge that Cubans were not free to leave the island. That idea was nonsense, Castro said:

> It is not we who are opposed to letting those who want to leave to go, but the imperialists. And since that's the case, we are even ready to open a small port in some place so that anyone who has a relative here doesn't have to run any risk and doesn't have to expose their relatives to any risk. We can open up, let's say for an example, the port of Camarioca in Matanzas, which is one of the closest ports, where anyone with a relative in Cuba can come . . . and once there we will advise the family members that someone has come to pick them up and take them away safely.

"Now the imperialists have the floor," he added. "Let's see what they do and what they say."[84]

Standing at the base of the Statue of Liberty five days later, President Johnson replied that "the dedication of America to our traditions as an asylum for the oppressed is going to be upheld." All Cubans, he said, were welcome.[85]

So began the Camarioca boatlift—the departure of several thousand Cubans, most of them in small boats, many operated by inexperienced crews. With the situation rife with the potential for accidents and with the prospect of a continuous flow for the indefinite future, the two sides reached an agreement in early November to make the trip safer and more orderly: Cuba would close Camarioca, and both sides would open up an air bridge between Varadero and Miami. For its part, the United States agreed to provide sufficient air transportation to permit three to four thousand Cubans to leave each month, while Cuba agreed to implement a complex process of selecting and processing the emigrants. The air bridge opened on 1 December 1965—two "Freedom Flights" a day, five days a week—and continued until April 1973, when the last of 260,500 Cubans arrived.[86]

The new flow of Cuban immigrants had an unexpected repercussion— it enlarged significantly the number of Cubans living in legal limbo. The initial wave of Cubans had been admitted as temporary visitors, as if they were tourists or on business, but after the Bay of Pigs the NSC decided that Cuban nationals currently holding U.S. visitors' visas would receive refugee status, as would all additional Cuban arrivals.[87] At the time, complex U.S. refugee laws allowed the attorney general to grant humanitarian "parole" to anyone fleeing a crisis who could reach U.S. shores, with the understanding that parolees would leave after normal conditions were restored in their homeland. But what if normalcy never returned? Here the Cubans were unlike the Hungarians or the Poles, who could then apply to become permanent residents, because the quirky law allowing for adjustment of status from parolee to resident did not apply to citizens of the Western Hemisphere. They had to go home to apply for a visa at a U.S. consulate. Cubans could not do so, of course; even if the Cuban government had been willing to approve such a procedure, the United States no longer operated a consulate in Cuba. Cuban parolees' only recourse was to go to a third country, apply for a U.S. visa, and then return to the United States. Recognizing the impracticality of such a procedure, Congress passed the 1966 Cuban Adjustment Act, creating a procedure for Cubans—and only Cubans—to become permanent residents after one year in the United States as parolees.[88] The Cuban Adjustment Act subsequently underlay all U.S. policy toward Cuban immigration.

Cuba then disappeared from Washington's consciousness. In early 1965, Gordon Chase had informed McGeorge Bundy that the State Department had decided to focus its attention elsewhere: Rusk "recently told John Crimmins that he wants no new initiatives on Cuba policy for the time being. Apparently, he wants to keep the temperature low while we are sorting out our Vietnam problem."[89] The CIA received the same message and began mothballing its Miami station, shutting down Radio Americas on Swan Island, and shelving its regular Cuban reporting after informing in-house readers that "the workload imposed by developments elsewhere has forced a standdown of the *Cuban Weekly Summary*. This will be the last issue for an indefinite period."[90]

"Developments elsewhere" referred to Southeast Asia, of course. Lower-level U.S. diplomats continued to march in and out of foreign chancelleries, lodging their pro forma requests that Country X end its Cuba trade or that Country Y stop its Cuba shipping, and U.S. officials continued to condemn Cuban internationalism, with efforts including a September 1967 OAS meeting of consultation to condemn Cuba "for its repeated acts of aggression and intervention against Venezuela and for its persistent policy of intervention in the internal affairs of Bolivia and of other American states."[91] But that meeting occurred long after Cuba had dropped off the agenda of senior U.S. officials, many of whom had turned their attention to getting off a fast-sinking ship. McGeorge Bundy, for example, jumped to the Ford Foundation, and Thomas Mann left for the Automobile Manufacturers Association. Those who remained had their hands full convincing the increasingly skeptical public that the light was shining ever brighter at the end of the Vietnamese tunnel. When that light was snuffed out by the Tet Offensive in early 1968, a beaten president announced that he would not be a candidate for reelection. Then came a year of war and a national election, and no one was surprised when LBJ did not mention Cuba in his final State of the Union address.

MUTUAL HOSTILITY AS A FACT
OF LIFE THE NIXON-FORD YEARS

The war in Vietnam dominated the 1968 election. With half a
million U.S. troops already in Indochina, the year began with LBJ's call for
three hundred thousand more soldiers and, to suggest how close the Pentagon had come to scraping the bottom of the barrel, with the suspension of
draft deferments for graduate students. When the deeply divided Democrats
convened their disastrous convention in Chicago, Mayor Richard Daley's
police surrounded the hall with barbed wire and used tear gas and attack
dogs in an unsuccessful attempt to clear the streets of antiwar protesters.
The supporters of Senator George McGovern and the other peace candidate, Senator Eugene McCarthy, asked for a two-week recess so that some
semblance of order and civility could be restored, but their request was refused and the party instead nominated Vice President Hubert Humphrey,
who faced an exceptionally steep uphill battle: not only did many people
dislike the war, but others disliked paying for it. LBJ's record fiscal year
1969 budget proposal included a 10 percent income-tax surcharge, which a
Democratic Congress enacted just before the campaign began.

Republican conventioneers at Miami, in contrast, were on their best behavior, nominating Richard Nixon to run on a platform promising both
fiscal restraint and "a progressive de-Americanization of the war." "Not
every international conflict is susceptible of solution by American ground

forces," they said. Neither major party said much about Cuba. The Republicans simply promised not to forget "the Cuban people who still cruelly suffer under Communist tyranny," while the Democrats admitted that "Castro's Cuba is still a source of subversion" but congratulated themselves because "the other Latin American states are moving ahead under the Alliance for Progress."[1] With these vague references as the only hints, no one knew what the next administration's policy would be—the best bet was a continued neglect of Latin America, including Cuba.

So no one was surprised when President Nixon failed to mention the region in his 1969 inaugural address, and many attributed the appointment of Nelson Rockefeller to lead a study mission to the region—one of the new president's first official acts—as an effort to find a useful but peripheral role for a leader of the eastern Republican establishment. Grandson of the founder of Standard Oil, Rockefeller's first government job had been as director of FDR's Office for the Coordination of Commercial and Cultural Relations between the American Republics, and over the ensuing years his interest in the region had been fueled less by his family's substantial investments than by a commitment to market-based development strategies and by an intense fascination with both pre-Columbian and modern Latin American art. By 1969, Rockefeller was the most prominent Republican with experience in Latin American affairs and the logical choice to help set the tenor of the new administration's policy.

But he was also the governor of New York and unable to devote much time to Nixon's assignment, and the report he delivered in late August ranked low on specifics and high on banalities: "We went to visit neighbors and found brothers," it began. "We went to listen to the spokesmen of our sister republics and heard the voices of a hemisphere. We went to annotate, to document, and to record. We did so; and we also learned, grew, and changed." They did not learn anything about Cuba, which was not simply left off the itinerary but completely absent from the document's twenty pages of graphs and charts; the country's name was even left off the maps. But Cuba was mentioned occasionally in the text, where its principal role was to serve as a sword of Damocles hanging over the hemisphere: "There is only one Castro among the twenty-six nations of the hemisphere; there can well be more in the future. And a Castro on the mainland, supported militarily and economically by the communist world, would present the gravest kind of threat to the security of the Western Hemisphere."[2]

This statement led directly to one of the report's central recommendations: more military aid. "Many of our neighbors . . . have been puzzled by the reduction in U.S. military assistance grants in view of the growing intensity of the subversive activities they face. They were concerned that their young people were being drawn to Cuba in never-diminishing numbers, for indoctrination and for instruction in the arts of propaganda, the skills of subversion, and the tactics of terror." To those who worried that the military might employ U.S.-supplied weapons to repress human rights, Rockefeller responded that "a new type of military man is coming to the fore and often becoming a major force for constructive social change in the American republics." Richard Nixon had written almost exactly those words seven years earlier, in 1962: "The military in Latin America is a great stabilizing force and includes some of the ablest and most dedicated leaders in the hemisphere." The Pentagon agreed: "We definitely are looking at a new breed of cat," argued the head of the U.S. Southern Command in 1970. "They are proud, of course, being of Spanish origin, and they are impatient with the lack of progress. They see their nations being misled or mishandled and I think in many cases this leads to their stepping in and taking over." And what about the military's record of human rights abuses? "We should be prepared to, somehow or other, live with the excesses of which many of them are accused."[3]

No one in Washington wanted to encourage these excesses, of course, but some strong force was needed to stand up to Cuban subversion, and in Latin America the choice was not perceived as abuse versus no abuse, since these were people of Spanish origin—or, as the Nixon administration's fourth and final assistant secretary of state for Latin America explained, democracy and its accompanying respect for human rights and its emphasis on negotiation and compromise were difficult to practice in societies that had emerged from Spanish colonial control. The real-world choice in Latin America, then, was Cuban-supported communist abuse versus noncommunist abuse, and the former threatened U.S. security, while the latter did not. With Cuba clearly on his mind, the commanding general of the U.S. Southern Command noted that "our record of recovery of countries that have gone down the drain is practically nil. We haven't gotten any of them back once they have gone. This is what we have got to stop."[4]

After the Rockefeller report had been delivered, President Nixon chose Halloween night to make his initial statement of Latin American policy. He formally dropped any lingering U.S. interest in promoting democracy ("We must deal realistically with governments in the inter-American system as they are"), proposed trade and private foreign investment as a substitute for foreign aid (within a year State Department officials were referring to the Alliance for Progress in the past tense), and promised a new hands-off attitude: "Often we in the United States have been charged with an overweening confidence in the rightness of our own prescriptions, and occasionally we have been guilty of the charge. I intend to change that."[5]

Events in Chile would soon demonstrate that the Nixon administration had no intention of implementing this hands-off policy, but this approach appealed to the new deputy assistant secretary of state responsible for Cuba, Robert Hurwitch, who recalled, "We wanted to encourage in every appropriate way that our friends to the south learn to stand on their own two feet—*to become mature*. . . . We would not let their problems become our responsibility. Slowly over time, just as with a young adult leaving home for the first time, we felt confident that the initial pain and the feeling that 'you don't love me anymore' would eventually be replaced by the gratifying sense of independence, freedom, and the respect and dignity one achieved as a mature person."[6] The Johnson administration had already scaled back the U.S. level of responsibility for "developing" Latin America, and under Richard Nixon, Washington completely dropped that responsibility.

Two months after his inauguration, the president requested a fresh look at U.S. policy toward Cuba, setting in motion an elaborate interagency process that led to a national security study memorandum outlining four policy options:

"(A) seek to negotiate with the U.S.S.R. limitations upon Cuban conduct

(B) accept U.S.S.R. interest in Cuba for its utility as a Soviet vulnerability open to U.S. retaliatory action and thus restraining Soviet action against U.S. interests elsewhere

(C) support overt or covert harassing and spoiling operations in Cuba

(D) offer to dismantle restrictive policy and re-establish normal relations without Cuban concessions."[7]

Meeting with his senior Latin American advisers, President Nixon ruled out Option D by instructing everyone "to follow a very tough line on Cuba. This was very important in terms of other things he was doing. Perhaps in hijacking matters we might do something, but generally he wanted a tough line, and he did not want to hear press speculation that we were considering a new policy."[8] This private statement of the new administration's policy was accompanied by a clarifying cable to all U.S. diplomatic posts in Latin America: "In recent months there has been continuing reference by some public and official circles of the Hemisphere to the question of Cuba, including the possibility of a re-integration of the present Cuban government into the inter-American system." One feature of this talk "has been rumor-mongering about [U.S. government] interest in altering its policy in favor of some sort of accommodation." U.S. envoys were instructed to inform their host governments that "there is no basis in fact for such speculation about a change in policy toward Cuba. That policy remains unaltered."[9]

Throughout his presidency, Nixon held firm against even the slightest relaxation of the embargo. In early 1970, for example, when the new chair of the Inter-American Economic and Social Council wanted to raise the question of reestablishing relations with Cuba, national security adviser Henry Kissinger correctly predicted that "the President is absolutely firm on this and his answer will be no." A year later, the State Department received the same response after Senator Jacob Javits pressured the department to allow Cuban physicians to attend the Inter-American Congress of Cardiology in San Francisco. "I'm pretty sure he opposes it," Kissinger said, "but I'm willing to try it on him [although] my instinct is the President will oppose it." He did.[10]

The new president's only public use of the word "Cuba" in 1969 had come during his Halloween speech, and it had presaged a continued emphasis on isolation: "The 'export' of revolution is an intervention which our system cannot condone, and a nation like Cuba which seeks to practice it can hardly expect to share in the benefits of this community." Nor was Cuba mentioned in his February 1970 foreign policy message to Congress, despite the fact that the president called it "the most comprehensive statement on foreign and defense policy ever made in this country"; indeed, in 1970 President Nixon did not say "Cuba" once in public, although in December he was obliged to refer to the island when a reporter asked, "Mr. President, do you think that United States security is threatened at all by Soviet military activity in the Caribbean, including the submarine base in Cuba?" Nixon's full reply: "No, I do not." After those four monosyllables, he moved on to a question about the Middle East. In 1971 "Cuba" passed the president's lips a couple of times, but with no substance and suggesting intransigence: "Until Cuba changes its policy toward us we are not going to change our policy toward Cuba. . . . As long as Castro is adopting an anti-American line, we are certainly not going to normalize our relations with Castro. As soon as he changes his line toward us, we might consider it. But it is his move."[11]

By this time, Nixon was fully focused on other matters. Indeed, after his first full year in the White House, the president ordered his three principal White House aides (H. R. "Bob" Haldeman, John Ehrlichman, and Henry Kissinger) to stop bothering him with insignificant places such as Latin America. "I have decided that our greatest weakness was in spreading my time too thin—not emphasizing priorities enough"; so, he told Kissinger, on foreign policy, "all I want brought to my attention are the following items.

1. East-West relations.
2. Policy toward the Soviet Union.
3. Policy toward Communist China.
4. Policy toward Eastern Europe, provided it really affects East-West relations at the highest level.
5. Policy toward Western Europe, but only where NATO is affected and where major countries (Britain, Germany and France) are affected."

The president acknowledged that "great pressures will build up to see this and that minor official from the low priority countries. All of this is to be farmed out to [Vice President Spiro] Agnew," but, Nixon told Kissinger, do not let anyone "think that I do 'not care' about the under-developed world. I do care, but what happens in those parts of the world is not, in the final analysis, going to have any significant effect on the success of our foreign policy." The conclusion: aside from the topics listed, "I do not want to see any papers on any of the other countries," including "all of Latin America and all of the countries of the Western Hemisphere with the exception of Cuba."[12]

President Nixon died before anyone could ask him why he exempted Cuba from his "Do Not Disturb" order, but he was apparently consulted on almost everything to do with that country. Perhaps Cuba was linked to East-West issues and to relations with the Soviet Union, or perhaps he considered Castro "an implacable and dangerous enemy," as he wrote in his post-presidential memoir. Indeed, he accused Cuba's revolutionaries of almost every imaginable sin—from assisting violent U.S. radicals ("Cuban military officers instructed them") to corrupting Lee Harvey Oswald: "Certainly one of the major factors which warped his mind and drove him to this terrible deed was his contact with communism generally, and with Castro's fanatical brand of communism in particular." Cuba, Nixon had written in 1964, "is a dangerous threat to our peace and security. . . . We cannot tolerate the presence of a communist regime 90 miles from our shores."[13]

And many observers would have added, as Kissinger did, that Nixon's decision not to dismiss Cuba entirely was influenced by his close friendship with Cuban-born Charles (Bebe) Rebozo, "who hated Castro with a fierce Latin passion." This animosity, Kissinger continued, guaranteed that Nixon "would be constantly exposed to arguments to take a hard line; he would never want to appear weak before his old friend." Others, including special assistant Alexander Butterfield, pointed out that Nixon in general "hated with a passion," a characteristic Attorney General Richard Kleindienst also noticed: "One of the problems he had—and it might have been his great, limiting factor—was that he carried around within him grudges; it was the small, dark side of his character." And after his 1960 loss to JFK, he may well have carried an enormous grudge against the Cuban Revolution. Whatever the cause, Kissinger noted, Nixon "disliked Castro intensely."[14]

Not enough of the Nixon papers have been declassified to explain Kissinger's role in the administration's Cuba policy, but almost everyone close to the president eventually noted, as Interior Secretary Walter Hinkle did, that "there were two sides to Richard Nixon—the dark and the light side. I always played to his light side; if you did, he would just light up. If you played to his dark side, he would turn inward. Kissinger played to his dark side; he did it more than anyone else."[15] While it is therefore not difficult to imagine the tone of any discussion these two might have had about Cuba, it is not certain they even had one. Kissinger, too, had little interest in Latin America—in his memoir, he characterized the region as "the backwaters of policy."[16] Publicly, he mouthed whatever words his aides handed him, but he could not possibly have believed what he told the House Committee on Foreign Affairs—that "the United States and Latin America share precious common bonds" and that these "shared aspirations and values of human respect and dignity make it possible for us to cooperate for the common good"—fine words, to be sure, but the proof of Kissinger's Latin American pudding came in his private words of encouragement when he visited Chilean dictator Augusto Pinochet: "You did a great service to the West in overthrowing Allende," he told this usurper, adding, "We are sympathetic with what you are trying to do here," and "We want to help, not undermine you."[17]

The weak impression from today's incomplete documentation is that Kissinger helped check any inclination President Nixon might have had to even the score with Cuba. A revealing example came late one evening in mid-1970, when Kissinger telephoned Nixon to report that "a heavily armed boat has left Miami manned by Cubans to sink a Soviet tanker." A

Coast Guard ship had been escorting the tanker, Kissinger continued, and "I think we should let that Coast Guard ship shepherd that Soviet tanker out of harm's way." Nixon agreed. Kissinger also appears to have had his own policy on exile activities. A memo about sabotage that Kissinger received from aide Alexander Haig began, "Sometime ago the President, with a marginal note, suggested that we should not inhibit Cuban exile activity against their homeland." Haig continued, "We have, of course, under existing policy continued to do so and are thus in conflict with the President's handwritten directive." Rather than sending Nixon a memo, Haig suggested a quiet talk "so that the President does not have to treat this as a test of his manhood." Alternatively, Haig continued, Kissinger might want to continue existing efforts to stop the exile raids and simply accept "that the bureaucracy is operating on one policy and the President another."[18]

In the State Department, meanwhile, a Sears-Roebuck vice president was brought in as assistant secretary of state for Latin America, and one of his two deputies, Hurwitch, bore primary responsibility for Cuba. A career officer, Hurwitch had been a Cuba desk officer during the Kennedy administration, and after the Bay of Pigs he had become State's first special assistant for Cuban affairs. In this role, Hurwitch served as the department's representative at General Edward Lansdale's Mongoose meetings whenever senior officials were unavailable, and when State was assigned a task, he would do it. Just before he was quietly shoved aside, Lansdale singled out Hurwitch for special praise.[19]

During the Nixon administration, one of Hurwitch's principal tasks was to explain the administration's Cuba policy to Congress, then dominated by Democrats, and he especially irritated Senator J. William Fulbright, whose 1971 proposal to review U.S. policy toward Cuba had the clear goal of normalizing relations. Assigned to kill the initiative, Hurwitch argued that nothing should be changed until Cuba stopped supporting Latin American subversives. Unwilling to concede the smallest point, Hurwitch later recalled, "I enjoyed these public and congressional appearances, especially the open give and take during question periods. No matter how partisan these meetings might become, as long as one remained calm and objective, the sessions usually terminated on a respectful note." Senator Fulbright eventually threw up his hands in exasperation. "Mr. Hurwitch," he said at the end of one 1971 hearing, "your self-righteousness and moralism gets awfully boring."[20]

He was simply doing his job, of course, voicing the administration's policy and serving as its lightning rod. On those few occasions during the Nixon years when the political atmosphere became too heavily charged over Cuba policy, Hurwitch was sent up to Capitol Hill to give Senator Fulbright and his colleagues an opportunity to voice their displeasure; then Hurwitch would go back to his office and await instructions. The Nixon-Kissinger disinterest explains why these instructions were few.

But while no sense of urgency existed, the threat of "losing" Latin America was growing when Nixon entered the White House. For several years, the Soviet Union had been successfully normalizing relations, beginning (after Cuba) with Brazil in 1961, Chile in 1964, Colombia and Peru in 1968, and then Bolivia, Venezuela, and Ecuador in 1970—a total of eleven when added to the World War II–era relationships with Mexico (1942), Uruguay (1943), and Argentina (1946). Moreover, the group included all the region's larger countries. As Moscow was establishing diplomatic relations, Havana was openly encouraging Latin American insurgents—"Cuba has never nor will it ever deny support to a revolutionary movement," Castro promised a Havana audience celebrating the centennial of Lenin's birth in April 1970. "As long as there is imperialism, as long as there are people struggling, willing to fight for their people's liberation from imperialism, the Cuban revolution will support them. Let this be quite clear."[21]

How much of Castro's speech was just talk? Following the breakdown of Che Guevara's Bolivian *foco* in 1967, Cuba's strategy appeared to move away from the support of rural insurgents and toward the backing of urban guerrillas, but unlike the solid evidence of Che's body stretched out on a table in rural Bolivia, much less proof demonstrated Cuban support for these urban groups, and Cuba, like the Soviet Union, was also in the process of normalizing relations with all but the most reactionary Latin American governments.[22] Perhaps Castro's words were intended simply to nourish the revolutionary fervor of his home audience.

This hypothesis seemed especially plausible in light of Cuba's economic problems. In May, a month after his Lenin centennial speech, Castro had announced the failure of the ten-million-ton sugar harvest, which had been invested with enormous significance. The goal had been announced seven years earlier, in 1963, when Castro bragged that the island's "bourgeois competitors will realize that they cannot compete with us [because] we have the 'sugar atomic bomb' in our hands. What does that mean? It means that in 1970 we will be ready to exceed the figure of ten million tons of sugar, we will be able to export ten million tons of sugar."[23] The ten-million-ton harvest subsequently became a slowly developing obsession, and vast resources were mobilized to ensure its success. Then in 1970, when every stalk had been cut and Cuba had come up short, Castro offered to resign during his 26th of July speech.

The audience refused to consider his resignation, but Moscow was concerned. For nearly a decade, the Soviets had been paying premium prices for sugar and providing petroleum at less than half the world price, and in years when these subsidies were not enough, the Soviet Union had supplied credits to cover the red ink; Cuba essentially did not have to worry about running out of money until the failure of the ten-million-ton harvest triggered a reassessment of these arrangements. The two governments set up the Joint Commission for Economic, Scientific, and Technological Cooperation, which soon led to Cuba's incorporation into the communist bloc's Council for Mutual Economic Assistance, a move designed to encourage more effective economic planning as well as to facilitate trade and provide additional aid. Each of five separate bilateral agreements in 1972 represented a Soviet subsidy: Cuba's debt was rescheduled on the most generous terms imaginable (amounts already owed became due in installments beginning fourteen years later, in 1986, with no interest), a line of credit was opened for 1973–75 with similarly generous terms, a low-interest $360-million loan was provided for the construction of new factories and the improvement of electrical power facilities and the sugar industry, and new prices were struck for Soviet purchases of both sugar and nickel— twelve cents per pound for sugar (when the world price was seven cents) and $5,450 per ton of nickel (when the world price was $3,500). As these arrangements took effect, the Defense Intelligence Agency reported that "the military, economic, and political ties between Cuba and the U.S.S.R. are closer than ever."[24]

Cuba did what it could to reciprocate, and one such payback had occurred just before President Nixon's election, in August 1968, three days after the Soviet invasion of Czechoslovakia, when Fidel Castro had vaguely lamented "the truly traumatic situation of foreign occupation" but justified the invasion as the only alternative to Prague's realignment "with pro-Yankee spies and agents, and with other enemies of socialism."[25] Two years later, he used his Lenin centennial speech to offer an unequivocal endorsement: "There are some who do not want to pardon this country because of the position it adopted in the Czechoslovakia case," he began, waving away this criticism by explaining that "what was important for us was the counterrevolutionary process occurring there, this process of betraying Marxism."

> We cannot forget the Czechoslovak news agency, which wrote about Che in terms worse than the UPI and AP. There were numberless cases like this, slandering other countries including Cuba, for that was liberalism, yes indeed, liberalism. And I believe that was the moment, under those circumstances, when one must know how to evaluate, how to react in the revolutionary fashion. Only the imperialists would have benefitted if that had not been nipped in the bud, if that had not been cut at the root.

Years later, one member of the audience, filmmaker Saul Landau, recalled that the Cuban leader left immediately after he finished speaking, "looking like he was going to vomit."[26]

Cuba also served the Soviet Union as a thorn in the side of the United States. Early in the Nixon administration, one such annoyance was the Venceremos Brigades—groups of left-leaning U.S. citizens, most of them college students, who began traveling to Cuba to help with the ten-million-ton sugar harvest. The first contingent of 216 arrived via Mexico in December 1969, a second group of 687 left from Canada three months later, and a third group of 409 went in mid-1970. "Venceremos is the Spanish translation of Benito Mussolini's slogan which the Italian dictator employed to exhort his legions to kill American soldiers," an outraged Senator James O. Eastland told his colleagues, capturing perfectly the era's supercharged emotions. "The organizers of the brigade are dedicated enemies of the United States and of free men everywhere." Fortunately, he continued, his Committee on the Judiciary was preparing to expose this subversion: "We intend to light the shadows that surround this vicious operation—to drive from those shadows the missiles—in human form—which have been fashioned on the Communist island and fired at America."[27]

Eastland would have had a more serious issue to address if he had waited a few months, when the Soviet Union seemed poised to violate the agreement that had ended the 1962 missile crisis, this time with submarines. Until 1969, no Soviet naval ship had ever entered the Caribbean, but then a small flotilla spent six weeks visiting Cuban ports. The visits may have been nothing more than Moscow's tit-for-tat—the deployment occurred a month after two U.S. warships had conducted exercises in the Black Sea— but a few months later Soviet defense minister Andrei Grechko had visited

Havana, and a second deployment followed in May 1970; ominously, this deployment included a nuclear-powered attack submarine. In late August, a photo-reconnaissance flight detected a new construction project on Alcatraz Island in the middle of Cienfuegos Bay on Cuba's southern coast, followed by a third deployment in September that included a large landing craft carrying two barges of the type used by the Soviets to handle radioactive waste.[28]

The CIA had been worrying about this specific problem since early 1963, for such a development would unquestionably tilt the existing military balance: unlike the United States, which maintained forward strategic submarine bases in Scotland, Spain, and Guam, the Soviets had never previously possessed a forward navy base, deploying their Northern Fleet submarines from bases along the Kola Peninsula east of Norway and their Pacific Fleet submarines from the western coast of Siberia, along the Sea of Okhotsk. The lack of a forward base seriously reduced the Soviet submarines' "on-station" time—as defense analyst Herbert Scoville noted, "it would take Russian submarines a minimum of six days in the Atlantic and eight days in the Pacific to reach the nearest launch stations, so that the transit time to and from home ports, in many cases a quarter to a third of the duration of the patrol, seriously degrades the operations readiness of the Russian fleet."[29] And a submarine base in Cuba not only would dramatically increase fleet efficiency, especially if it included replacement crews, but also would significantly complicate the Pentagon's task of tracking both the Soviet attack submarines that often tailed U.S. carrier battle groups and, much more important, the Soviet Union's strategic submarines—the ones whose missiles would level U.S. cities in the event of war. To further compound this problem, in the event of successful strategic arms limitation talks, acquisition of a forward base in Cuba would allow the Soviets to reduce their number of submarine-launched ballistic missiles with no loss of capability.

A Soviet submarine base in Cuba also would clearly violate the Kennedy-Khrushchev agreement that had ended the missile crisis, the central part of which was contained in JFK's response to a conciliatory message from Khrushchev:

> 1. You would agree to remove these weapons systems from Cuba under appropriate United Nations observation and supervision; and undertake, with suitable safeguards, to halt the further introduction of such weapons systems into Cuba.

2. We, on our part, would agree—upon the establishment of adequate arrangements through the United Nations to ensure the carrying out and continuation of these commitments—(a) to remove promptly the quarantine measures now in effect and (b) to give assurances against an invasion of Cuba.

This agreement between Washington and Moscow had a sticking point, of course: Fidel Castro had refused to admit U.N. inspectors, and as JFK told the press several weeks after the crisis, "until that is done, difficult problems remain." Eight years later, Kissinger told Nixon that "the agreement was never explicitly completed because the Soviets did not agree to an acceptable verification system (because of Castro's opposition) and we never made a formal non-invasion pledge." But, Kissinger continued, "whatever the phraseology of the 1962 understanding, its intent could not have been to replace land-based with sea-based missiles."[30]

The issue ultimately was fairly easy to resolve and, as in the missile crisis, without involving Cuba. The negotiations began with several conversations between Kissinger and Soviet ambassador to the United States Anatoly Dobrynin. "If we had let the thing go, we might have gotten into a real confrontation two months from now," Kissinger explained weeks later. "We felt it was important that the Soviets realize that they were getting to the edge of what might lead to a reassessment of policy for us." Then Kissinger flew off to Europe with the president, and during their absence Kissinger aide Alexander Haig claimed to have solved the problem with a hard-nosed conversation with Dobrynin: "I told him that the Soviets would either remove the base at Cienfuegos or the United States would do it for them. . . . Presently, the Soviets started to withdraw their naval forces from the vicinity." Both Nixon and Kissinger also took full credit for resolving the issue, but three decades later, Haig insisted the credit was his: "I did it just like it says in my book."[31]

The central point is that Moscow conceded. Ambassador Dobrynin immediately replied to the White House that "the Soviet side strictly adheres to its part of the understanding on the Cuban question and will continue to adhere to it in the future on the assumption that the American side, as President Nixon has reaffirmed, will also strictly observe its part of the understanding." A few days later Kissinger hand delivered Nixon's response nailing down the details, and on 13 October the official Soviet news agency, TASS, issued a statement that there had never been a submarine base at Cienfuegos. Kissinger informed President Nixon that "we appear to have resolved, without a public confrontation, the potentially explosive issue of a Soviet base in Cuba," and with that, Nixon concluded, "the crisis was over. After some face-saving delays, the Soviets abandoned Cienfuegos."[32]

Although much of the documentation from this period remains classified, the brief submarine base issue apparently constituted the only time President Nixon had anything significant to do with Cuba, and the settlement was negotiated between Moscow and Washington, with no participation by Havana. Kissinger commented that after the Cienfuegos flap, "Cuban-American relations relapsed into the familiar torpor" as the administration focused on other matters.[33]

One of those matters was Indochina. On the morning of his first full day in the White House, Nixon had opened the private wall safe that LBJ had shown him during a pre-inaugural courtesy visit, and inside the new president found a single page—the Pentagon's Vietnam situation report for 19 January 1969, giving the previous week's death toll and the count for LBJ's final year in office: almost 15,000 U.S. soldiers killed and more than 95,000 wounded, thousands of them disabled permanently. Nixon put the report back in the safe and later wrote that he "left it there until the war was over, a constant reminder of its tragic cost."[34] He soon announced the details of his policy of "Vietnamization"—increased aid to the South Vietnamese army matched by the phased withdrawal of all 537,000 U.S. soldiers. At the same time, Kissinger began secret negotiations with North Vietnamese officials in Paris.

An entirely different set of negotiations had also begun with the Chinese communist government, whose existence the United States had refused to recognize since 1949. The first talks occurred in Warsaw, and by mid-1970, sufficient progress had been made to encourage a partial lifting of the ban on U.S. citizens' travel to China. Then came the ping-pong diplomacy: after playing in a Japanese tournament in April 1971, the U.S. ping-pong team was invited to continue on to China, and the Nixon administration responded to this invitation by slightly relaxing the economic embargo that had been initiated by President Truman. A few months later Henry Kissinger flew secretly to Beijing, and in July President Nixon announced that he, too, would visit China. In October, only a few days before the United States stopped using its veto to keep the People's Republic of China out of the United Nations, the president revealed that yet another set of negotiations had been occurring, this time with the Soviet Union, and had progressed to the point that he would also visit Moscow. Nixon's critics were astounded.

The president's announcement of his visit to China coincided with Senator Fulbright's introduction of a resolution expressing the sense of a Democratic Congress that the president should "take steps to review United States policy toward Cuba with the objective of beginning a process which would lead to the reestablishment of normal relations."[35] In mid-September, Fulbright's Foreign Relations Committee had held a hearing on the resolution, where the senator asked Deputy Assistant Secretary Hurwitch, "Granted, they are not nice people and . . . you wouldn't want to have them to dinner, but what really can they do of any consequence? Doesn't it seem a little ridiculous that the United States with 200 million people is so frightened by this poor little bedraggled country with 8 million peasants who are dependent almost for their daily bread upon a subsidy from Russia? You build Cuba up as if it is a tremendous behemoth that is about to devour all Latin America. It seems to me that you have no sense of proportion." The administration's sense of proportion was just right, Hurwitch replied, and then danced around the ring with Fulbright for a couple of hours, bobbing and weaving as the Arkansas senator became increasingly sarcastic ("Of course, in view of the outstanding success of our national policies for the last 10 years, I suppose there is no reason for you to review it") and increasingly accusatory: "Without Cuba there it would be more difficult to squeeze more money out of the Congress for your military assistance, wouldn't it?"[36] When they were weary, the two men retired to their respective corners.

But then Nixon made his announcement about traveling to Moscow, and a curious reporter asked if this emerging détente might be expanded. Nixon replied that any approach to additional countries "would depend upon the situation at that time. For example, Cuba is one possibility." That statement, however, was as far as things went, and after Fulbright's resolution garnered only one additional cosponsor (Edward Kennedy), Nixon told CBS's Dan Rather that "there has been no indication whatever that Castro will recede one inch from his determination of exporting Castro-type revolution all over the hemisphere. As long as he is engaged in that kind of operation, our policy isn't going to change." The journalist followed up by asking what might happen if Castro were to give such an indication; Nixon replied that "he couldn't possibly survive, in my opinion, unless he had this policy of 'foreign devils.'"[37]

THAT EXCHANGE OCCURRED in early 1972, the year antiwar liberals seized control of the Democratic Party, offering voters a genuine choice in November. The Republican platform asserted that Cuba's support of Latin American insurgents made the country "ineligible for readmission to the community of American states," while the Democrats argued that "the time has come to re-examine our relations with Cuba and to seek a way to resolve this cold war confrontation." The ensuing campaign focused primarily on the war in Vietnam, with the Democrats promising to "end that war by a simple plan that need not be kept secret: the immediate total withdrawal of all Americans from Southeast Asia," but Henry Kissinger deprived Nixon's opponents of this issue a week before Election Day when he announced a negotiating breakthrough: "Peace is at hand," he said. On the nation's other issues, the Republicans pledged to "safeguard the right of responsible citizens to collect, own and use firearms" and reaffirmed their view that prayer "should be freely permitted in public places—particularly by school children while attending public schools." In contrast, the Democrats decided to champion a constitutional amendment granting women the same rights as men—"a priority effort," read their platform, which also advocated school busing to achieve racial integration, an amnesty for draft dodgers, and a ban on the sale of inexpensive handguns known as Saturday night specials.[38] On 7 November, George McGovern carried Massachusetts and the District of Columbia, garnering 17 electoral votes to Richard Nixon's 520. Five weeks later, Kissinger gathered reporters to announce that he had spoken too soon—the peace negotiations had reached an impasse and the bombing might have to resume because the North Vietnamese were raising "one frivolous issue after another."[39]

As strange as it may seem, at this moment the United States and Cuba put their heads together to address a common problem: aircraft hijacking. Something had to be done. On 11 November, four days after Nixon's landslide, three armed men hijacked a Southern Airways DC-9 in the skies over Alabama, beginning a twenty-nine-hour, four-thousand-mile odyssey that took the aircraft first to Jackson, Mississippi, and then to Detroit, where the plane circled as the airline scrambled to put together the ten-million-dollar ransom the hijackers had demanded. With the money not yet ready, the DC-9 landed for fuel in Cleveland, and the hijackers warned FBI snipers that they were prepared to detonate their hand grenades at the slightest provocation. The next stop was Toronto, where the plane circled the field for three hours, still waiting for the ransom; when it arrived, the hijackers landed, only to discover that it amounted to less than they had requested; they then ordered the plane back into the air, this time heading for Knoxville. There they circled the airport at thirty-three-thousand feet while airline executives searched for more cash and tried to comply with a new demand—that the money be accompanied by a letter on White House stationery indicating that the cash was a "grant" from the federal government. With the aircraft's fuel gauge approaching empty, the hijackers first threatened to end the whole affair by crashing into the nearby Oak Ridge atomic energy facility; then they reconsidered, flew to Lexington, Kentucky, for more fuel, returned to circle over Knoxville for another three hours, and, with fuel running low once more, landed at Chattanooga, where they accepted what cash the airline had managed to acquire—two million dollars—and then headed for Havana.

After failing to negotiate surrender terms with Cuban authorities, the hijackers ordered the pilot to fly back to Key West, where he asked for charts and clearance to fly to Switzerland. First, however, the plane stopped for fuel at Orlando, where the hijackers shot the copilot in the shoulder. The FBI, having decided that enough was enough, shot out the plane's tires just as it was gathering sufficient speed to take off. The craft somehow got into the air and headed back to Havana, where the plane circled José Martí Airport while an anxious ground crew lay down a carpet of fire-retardant foam. The pilot then landed in a shower of sparks, and the hijackers surrendered to Cuban authorities. "The only moment we felt we were going to die was when they shot the co-pilot," commented one passenger, but another admitted that the entire episode "scared hell out of me." The wife of a third passenger told reporters that her husband probably needed a stiff drink.[40]

The incident offered a sad commentary on modern life. Until 1959, neither Cuban nor U.S. airports had what are known today as "security procedures"—passengers simply checked their bags, received their boarding passes, and walked out to the aircraft. Pilots regularly invited young passengers to visit the cockpit, the door of which often remained open during flight. The Federal Aviation Administration did not order that all passengers be screened until 1972 and even then allowed each airline to define the word "screened"; not until later that year did two U.S. airlines, American and TWA, announce that they would begin inspecting all hand luggage. Only in late 1973, after 159 U.S. aircraft had been hijacked in a dozen years—with 85 of them going to Cuba—did President Nixon order the federal government to take on the task of screening all passengers.[41]

Cuba's participation in the world of aircraft hijacking had begun in October 1958, just before Batista's fall, when rebels commandeered a domestic flight. A few days later, several rebel sympathizers took over an international flight from Miami to Varadero and forced the pilot to attempt a nighttime landing on a beach in Oriente, killing seventeen passengers. The 26th of July Movement disavowed any connection with the attempt, and there the matter rested for two months until Batista's fall, when many of his abandoned associates began hijacking planes to flee to the United States. The first takeover occurred a few hours after Batista fled, when armed Batistianos diverted a domestic flight to the United States. Other northbound hijackings followed, and in each case the United States granted political asylum to the arriving Cubans but returned the aircraft.

A new twist was added when Cuba's revolutionary government began refusing to honor its predecessor's debts to U.S. citizens, so creditors began waiting for a hijacking; when one occurred, they would rush to the local courthouse, wave their default judgment in front of a magistrate, and obtain an order to seize the hijacked airplane. Twelve such seizures had occurred by mid-1961 when the tables began to turn: on 1 May, a small commercial plane was diverted to Cuba from its flight between Marathon and Key West. In mid-July hijackers targeted a larger aircraft, and this time the Cuban government refused to return the plane until the United States handed over twenty-four previously hijacked Cuban planes and ships.

Cuban authorities clearly considered the hijackings a nuisance, however, and they soon agreed to exchange the aircraft for a single hijacked Cuban navy ship; thereafter, a modus vivendi was reached, allowing Kissinger to report in 1970 that "Cuba has now become one of the best behaved of the hijacking states, since it immediately allows the planes and passengers to return and often jails the hijackers. It recently returned its first hijacker, and offered to return all hijackers provided we would do the same (a commitment we cannot make because of the political asylum aspect)." A few months later, Robert Hurwitch told Congress that "the arrangements that exist result in very good treatment of American hijacked aircraft and their passengers."[42]

However accommodating Cuban authorities may have been, these episodes were never a laughing matter to the airlines or to their terrified passengers, and the November 1972 murder of a Houston gate attendant and the Southern Airways extravaganza the same month convinced the Nixon administration to start talking. Cuba had indicated its willingness to negotiate in late 1969, and, Hurwitch recalled, "we pursued that very actively. But it petered out by the spring of 1971. There were not so many hijackings. Peoples' attention shifted elsewhere and it only renewed [after] these two, one right after the other, very dramatic hijackings." The indirect negotiations began in mid-November, with Hurwitch serving as the principal U.S.

adviser to the Swiss negotiators. He recalled that they "proceeded at a brisk pace, and it did not take long to hammer out the details: in early December the two countries reached agreement on a five-year pact committing both sides to punish hijackers or return them."[43] The agreement could not be called a treaty because the United States did not recognize the government of Cuba, and to negotiate and ratify a treaty with a government is, ipso facto, to recognize its existence.* The hijacking accord was therefore called a "memorandum of understanding," and while it was signed by the foreign ministers of both countries—Secretary of State William P. Rogers in the case of the United States—it was formally exchanged by the diplomats of Czechoslovakia representing Cuba and Switzerland representing the United States.[44]

"We took an important bilateral action on February 15, 1973," reported President Nixon, and, with increasingly rare exceptions, the hijacking stopped. Calling the agreement "an important step forward," in late 1975 Assistant Secretary of State William D. Rogers told Congress that "Cuba has carried [the agreement] out scrupulously," but it had a downside, Hurwitch recalled: "The signing of this accord immediately spurred into action those elements in our country who advocated closer relations with Cuba," and administration officials went out of their way to emphasize that the agreement had no broader purposes—within a hour of the memorandum's signing, Secretary of State Rogers told reporters that the agreement "does not foreshadow a change of policies as far as the United States is concerned."[45]

Hijacking was not the only example of U.S.-Cuban cooperation during the Nixon years. The two countries continued to share data on tropical storms—after commercial telecommunications ended in the early 1960s, one Telex line was kept open between the Cuban weather service and the Miami office of the U.S. National Weather Service—and U.S. hurricane-

---

*In a formal sense, the United States had never withdrawn the recognition it granted the revolutionary government in January 1959; rather, in January 1961, the United States simply withdrew its diplomatic and consular personnel without ever saying that it was withdrawing its recognition of the Castro government. This formal recognition was just that, however—a formality; in everyday life, the United States did not recognize the Castro government, but as Secretary of State Dean Rusk explained in the mid-1960s, "We don't deny that there is a state of Cuba and that this particular government is the government of that country. We don't have relations with it . . . but the fact that we asked the Swiss Government to represent our interests there means that we contemplated there would be matters which we wish to discuss" (Rusk Press Conference, 5 November 1965, *DOSB*, 29 November 1965, 862).

tracking aircraft continued to operate over Cuba several times a year, with flight clearance obtained from Cuba via Switzerland.[46] But Secretary Rogers was correct: after the hijacking agreement, no further significant discussions took place between Washington and Havana, perhaps because the two sides did not share another equally pressing concern, perhaps because neither side had the desire to improve relations, or perhaps because the Nixon administration's attention was focused elsewhere: at precisely the moment when the hijacking agreement was being negotiated, a Washington jury was listening to evidence that would eventually convict G. Gordon Liddy and James McCord of conspiracy, wiretapping, and burglary for their role in the Watergate break-in. (Rather than go through the trial, E. Howard Hunt and four other defendants, three of them Cuban veterans of Operation Mongoose, had already entered guilty pleas.) Out on bail, McCord accused one of President Nixon's closest friends, former attorney general John Mitchell, of ordering the Watergate burglary, forcing the president to make a nationwide telecast lamenting that some of his now-tainted subordinates "may have done wrong in a cause they deeply believed to be right" and to fire his two principal aides, H. R. Haldeman and John Ehrlichman, and his counsel John Dean.

With a full investigation now inevitable, President Nixon also accepted the resignation of Attorney General Richard Kleindienst, replacing him with Elliot Richardson, who promptly named Harvard law professor Archibald Cox as a special Watergate prosecutor. Then came the main event: Senator Sam Ervin's Watergate hearings, which began in May 1973, three months after the hijacking agreement, and continued into August. Each day provided a fascinating new glimpse into the darkest reaches of the Nixon White House, prompting huge audiences to curtail their summer plans to watch the unusual live TV coverage, especially when Dean testified that Nixon had been involved in the burglary's cover-up. On another day, an obscure White House aide revealed that the president had a system to record his conversations, triggering a yearlong struggle for possession of the tapes. And if all of these developments were not exciting enough, in October Vice President Spiro Agnew was caught with his hand in the till and forced to resign, pleading no contest to the reduced charge of failing to pay income tax on the bribes he had received years earlier.

Ten days later Attorney General Richardson resigned rather than execute President Nixon's order to fire the increasingly menacing special Watergate prosecutor (an acting attorney general carried out the order), and the circling buzzards began landing to inspect the carcass. It was not quite ready to be picked: a feisty president flew off to Disney World, where he told an audience that "the people have got to know whether or not the President is a crook—well, I'm not a crook." The year ended with House minority leader Gerald Ford being sworn in as Agnew's replacement, the first such appointment under the Twenty-fifth Amendment. Nixon was soon named an unindicted coconspirator when federal perjury charges were brought against Haldeman, Ehrlichman, Mitchell, and four other White House aides. Still hoping to avoid full disclosure, Nixon responded by releasing heavily edited transcripts of some of the sought-after tape recordings, whose crude language and gratuitous ethnic slurs shocked almost everyone, including Senate Republican leader Hugh Scott, who called the president's vocabulary "disgusting." Unsatisfied by the partial disclosure and unpersuaded ·by the administration's claim to executive privilege, the Supreme Court then ruled unanimously that the president had to produce the unedited tapes. Released on 5 August 1974, they revealed that Nixon had obstructed the Watergate investigation from the very beginning. Three days later, he gave his televised resignation speech, and on 9 August, Ford was sworn in as the nation's first unelected president. Looking back at five and a half years of otherwise-dramatic change in U.S. foreign policy, Kissinger simply noted that "the Nixon Administration spent little time on Cuba, treating mutual hostility as a fact of life."[47]

SIX DAYS AFTER Gerald Ford assumed the presidency, Kissinger walked into the Oval Office for what had already become the new president's standard 9:00 A.M. foreign policy briefing. "We need to talk about Cuba," he said. "Nixon had strong personal views," refusing to budge despite the fact that many Latin American governments now opposed Cuba's continued isolation. Five years earlier, in mid-1969, the Nixon administration had predicted that "no OAS country seems likely to resume diplomatic relations or trade with Cuba," but Mexico had never broken trade or diplomatic relations, and in early 1970 Eduardo Frei's Christian Democratic government had announced that Chile was also resuming trade relations; diplomatic relations were reestablished a few months later, immediately after the inauguration of Salvador Allende. Two years later the Peruvian government formally proposed rescinding the 1964 OAS ban on economic and diplomatic relations, and when its proposal was rejected (by a vote of seven to thirteen, with three abstentions), Peru reopened its Havana embassy anyway.[48] Cuba established relations with four of Britain's former Caribbean colonies (Barbados, Guyana, Jamaica, and Trinidad and Tobago) later in

1972, with Argentina's new Peronist government in 1973, with Panama and Venezuela in 1974, and with Colombia in early 1975. Cuba was also welcomed back into the Latin American caucus at the United Nations, from which it had been excluded since 1964, and in 1975 the Castro government was elected to a Latin American slot on the U.N.'s Economic and Social Council. By the time Ford had learned his way around the White House, then, the 1964 sanctions were being ignored by almost half the OAS members (in 1973, Chile's Pinochet had again severed relations) and by three other nonmember Western Hemisphere countries—Canada, the Bahamas, and Guyana.

The same held true elsewhere. Along with Canada, nearly all of Washington's other NATO allies had always rejected Washington's requests that they break relations with Cuba, and in early 1975 they were joined by West Germany, which resumed diplomatic relations after a twelve-year hiatus. At the same time, Cuba was signing new trade agreements with four major NATO allies—Spain, France, Canada, and Great Britain.[49]

Seeing what had already occurred and what more was in the offing, Kissinger told Ford in August 1974, "We have to loosen up or we isolate ourselves," and the transition briefing book handed to the new president the same day noted that the United States needed a new approach since "Cuba's isolation in the Hemisphere is rapidly coming to an end." Focusing on an upcoming OAS meeting in Quito, where several Latin American governments were certain to propose lifting the organization's 1964 ban on trade with Cuba, Kissinger advised the president, "We should keep the initiative and not look like we were forced grudgingly." Ford agreed, but when asked about Cuba at his first news conference a few days later, he responded as Nixon always had: "If Cuba changes its policy toward us and toward its Latin neighbors, we, of course, would exercise the option, depending on what the changes were, to change our policy."[50]

But Cuba was clearly not a high or even a middling priority for a president whose immediate task was to revitalize a deeply demoralized administration, nor was it a salient issue to many Latin American governments, and some flatly opposed normalization. When it became apparent that the countries supporting repeal lacked the necessary votes, the new U.S. administration backed away: meeting with President Luis Echeverría on the U.S.-Mexican border in late October, President Ford told reporters that "it was not expected that our attitude would change toward Cuba," and at Quito a few weeks later the United States abstained on the resolution to permit trade and diplomatic relations that fell two votes short of the required two-thirds majority. That outcome was probably fine with Fidel Castro, who a few years earlier had characterized the OAS as an "indecent garbage heap," vowing that "Cuba will return to the OAS on the day when it throws the United States out."[51]

The issue briefly went into remission after the November Quito meeting, only to return to the agenda in the spring of 1975. With another OAS meeting scheduled for July in Costa Rica, Deputy Assistant Secretary of State Harry Shlaudeman wrote up the consensus within the department's Latin American bureau, underscoring a warning that "the OAS sanctions are clearly no longer enforceable" and concluding that the overall policy of isolating Cuba "is now no more than marginally effective at best." Two major questions could no longer be put off: whether to allow the foreign subsidiaries of U.S. firms to trade with Cuba, and whether to try to stop the repeal of the 1964 sanctions at the Costa Rica meeting. Requesting Secretary Kissinger's prompt decision on both questions, Shlaudeman added the especially important datum that Cuba "has gradually abandoned the export of revolution to Latin America."[52]

Obviously aware that he had a tenuous claim on the White House and especially concerned about the electoral challenge being mounted by former California governor Ronald Reagan, President Ford seemed reluctant to pursue détente with Cuba—when asked again about the possibility of change in early 1975, he told a Florida audience, "We think it is in our best interest to continue the policies that are in effect at the present time."[53]

But Secretary of State Kissinger unleashed a storm of protest by striking an entirely different chord three days later, telling a Houston audience, "We see no virtue in perpetual antagonism between the United States and Cuba."[54] The response: "We have a substantial Cuban population in the Miami area who in recent years has become naturalized," wrote the sheriff of Palm Beach County, a lifelong Republican; "the Republican Party and its candidates might lose this enviable voting block if the United States government, under your leadership, were to resume relations with Cuba." Miami mayor Maurice Ferré wrote to the president to ask who had control of foreign policy; inquiring about the apparent difference between the president's statement in Florida and Kissinger's speech in Houston, Ferré said that "the natural conclusions can only be: 1. That you were aware of Kissinger's statement to be pronounced a few days later and deliberately misguided the American people, [or] 2. That Secretary Kissinger did not inform you of his declaration. . . . Mr. President, it is obviously either his credibility or yours." Then came a telegram from the chair of Florida's Republican National Hispanic Assembly, who was "appalled at Sec of State Kissinger's statement about moving toward establishing relations with Communist Cuba" and promised that his organization would soon launch a campaign "informing the nation of the threat presented by the prevailing course of affairs with regards to recognizing Cuba."[55]

Complaints came from all over the country, almost always from solid Republicans, among them William Pawley, an Eisenhower-era adviser on Cuba who wrote to Senator Edward Kennedy: "I notice by the press that you are to join the other two extremely stupid Senators, [Jacob] Javits and [Claiborne] Pell, for a trip to Cuba to further contribute to the terrible tragedy for America that your brother the President and your brother the Attorney General made in turning Cuba over to the Russians for the rest of time." Apparently concerned that he had not made his point with sufficient clarity, a month later Pawley again wrote to Kennedy: "I often wonder whether you, as a comparatively young Senator, and other members of the Senate and House who appear to hold similar views, have made up your minds that you are willing for yourselves, your children and grandchildren to live in a communist-controlled United States, which really means communist-controlled world, because when our country is lost, we have no place else to go."[56] Arguing for a military invasion, Pawley also told President Ford that "at least 50,000 Cubans could be recruited in a matter of days, and if we found it necessary to take a leaf out of Russia's book, we can use 50,000 South Koreans, plus our Navy and Air Force." Five days later, he wrote yet again, suggesting that "the Russians should be notified to assemble all of their citizens in Havana within from 24 to 36 hours and our Air Force and Navy could proceed to destroy the airports and all other military installations, including a submarine base reportedly established at Cienfuegos. The José Martí airport, which I built in 1929 and opened in 1930, should also be made inactive."[57]

Pawley could cause trouble in the conservative circles Reagan was courting, but even more worrisome were letters from grassroots opinion leaders such as Raúl Comesañas, a Cuban American living in New Jersey, who told President Ford that "since this week-end when Henry Kissinger made his remarks on Cuba, my phone has not stopped ringing and the concern for such remarks is running at an all time peak. I must warn you in all honesty that this is not good for you or the country. . . . I don't know who is advising you now but it doesn't look like they're doing a good job of it, [and] pressure is building up for me and other Cuban leaders to come out against you over this issue." The Delaware Veterans of Foreign Wars agreed, as did the Rancho Bernardo, California, Republican Women's Club. "We are gravely concerned," the club's letter began, wondering what was to be gained by talking with Castro: "To establish relationships with him now is just another step toward the complete and total undermining of the principles for which this country stands. No wonder we have lost so much stature in the eyes of the world when decisions of this nature are allowed to be made." The same message came from the Deep South, with the Adams County, Mississippi, Republican Party expressing "concern and grief over the prospect of our government recognizing the Communist government of Castro's Cuba."[58]

Every presidential library has at least a folder or two of correspondence from citizens upset by some aspect of U.S. policy toward Cuba, but Ford's library has perhaps the most, and he served as president for only twenty-nine months. Some of this correspondence would have arrived regardless of the administration's policy, including a regular flow of letters from Cuban Americans such as Alejandro Fidel Valdes, president of the Pro-Cuban Government in Exile, who wrote Ford to complain that his earlier letters had been answered by a lower-level official. To entice the president to read this missive, Valdes outlined "part of my solution to the Cuban problem," which centered on turning over the U.S. base at Guantánamo to Valdes and his six-member executive committee. Other letters described tragic cases such as that of Juana M. Gómez, who had come to the United States in the late 1960s and by 1975 was widowed, unemployed, and unhappy—and wondering if someone such as Vice President Rockefeller would be willing to provide her and her mother with financial assistance to return to Cuba. But most of this correspondence was from irate voters, many moved to write by Secretary Kissinger's Houston speech, and their letters reflected not simply a dislike of the Cuban government but also a general dismay over détente with the Soviet Union and Communist China. Every one of these letter writers seemed prepared to move into the political ranks led by Reagan, and the situation was already worrying the president.[59]

And so Cuba was tucked back in the closet, but the OAS was meeting in July and the issue could not be avoided forever, so on 9 June 1975, Assistant Secretary of State Rogers sat down with Kissinger. A registered Democrat who had declined an earlier offer of the position, preferring not to be associated with the Nixon administration, Rogers had been called again on the day Nixon resigned and was now clearly determined to move the reconciliation process along.[60] Kissinger was impatient and irascible, interrupting to dismiss Rogers's suggestion of a more conciliatory policy: "Cuba is not important," he said. "Cuba can do nothing for us but embarrass us in Latin America." Rogers replied that U.S. intransigence was creating friction with other, more important third countries; specifically, a Canadian subsidiary of a U.S. firm had just signed a contract to sell steam boilers to Cuba, and Ottawa was strongly pressuring the United States to address the question of trade by other U.S. subsidiaries. Kissinger brushed off the pressure as posturing—"The Canadians want to show that they can make the Secretary back-up."[61]

Rogers responded by switching to a different dimension of the problem: "Our position is being continually chiselled away by Congress." Here Kissinger was less dismissive. The balance of power between the two branches of government had shifted significantly since the 1974 off-year election, held eight months before this discussion. The Republicans had been punished for Watergate with a stunning fifty-two-seat shift in the House, characterized by Kissinger as a "McGovernite landslide," adding that the new group of liberals was "violently opposed to intervention abroad, especially in the developing world, ever suspicious of the CIA, deeply hostile to covert operations, and distrustful of the veracity of the executive branch."[62]

Senator William Fulbright had lost his seat in the Arkansas primary to fellow Democrat Dale Bumpers, but Fulbright had been replaced by an entire platoon of extremely energetic liberals—the Democrats had an overwhelming 291–144 advantage in the House—and before departing from the Senate, Fulbright had energized majority leader Mike Mansfield, primarily by convincing him to serve on the U.S. delegation to a conference at Tlatelolco in early 1974. Mansfield had returned to tell his colleagues about "increasing support in the hemisphere for re-inclusion of Cuba in the over-all affairs of the Americas" and to argue that "this nation would be well advised to consider its present non-policies on Cuba." At Mansfield's prodding, the State Department finally agreed to validate the passport of the Foreign Relations Committee's widely respected staff director, Pat Holt, who traveled to the island in mid-1974, talked with Castro, and returned to say that "Cubans would welcome better relations with the United States," adding what more and more members of Congress were coming to believe: "The U.S. policy of isolating Cuba has been a failure."[63] Then, just after Nixon's resignation, Democratic senator Javits and Republican senator Pell had become the first elected U.S. officials to visit Cuba since 1960. They, too, returned with a positive assessment of the Cuban government.

Washington's previous prevailing view of revolutionary Cuba had been captured by the CIA analysts who wrote in 1967 that "Castro has a deep and abiding animosity toward the US." As a result, "his underlying fear of, and hostility toward, the US—as well as his interest in fostering revolutions abroad—would remain strong obstacles to any major betterment of US-Cuban relations." Former ambassador Philip Bonsal had recently said much the same thing to the Committee on Foreign Relations: pushing for détente with Cuba would be a waste of time, he insisted, since Castro's anti-U.S. attitude was "a major bulwark of his personal power" and therefore was not something he could negotiate away. Perhaps, but who knew for sure? Javits and Pell had encountered a more moderate Castro who seemed reasonable and willing to negotiate, so they argued that "the time is ripe for beginning the process of normalization." A few months later, Ohio's Charles Whalen, a Republican, became the first member of the House to visit Cuba since 1961; upon his return, he emphasized a second reason to negotiate a new relationship: "Our Cuban policy is increasingly out of step with the rest of the world."[64]

Other members of Congress voiced the economic concerns of their constituents. Appearing as a witness before a Senate agricultural subcommittee in November 1975, Louisiana's ultraconservative representative John Breaux began by seeking common ground with the subcommittee chair: "You and I differ philosophically on a number of issues," he observed, but both men could surely agree that "our embargo policy is not working in our best interests." Absolutely, replied George McGovern, also from a farm state; "it doesn't make very much sense to forego a market a few miles off our shores." Breaux was thinking exactly the same thing, and "at the top of the agricultural list happens to be rice which we have a heck of a surplus of," while Cuba had a large demand. In the mid-1950s, the United States had sold Cubans about 187,000 tons of rice per year. As a result of the embargo, however, the Cubans "are buying it from Russia now. Some of our producers have been successful in recently selling rice to Russia, which I applaud. This is to our best interest [but] Russia is now selling it to Cuba. Why don't we sell it directly?"[65] A few months later, the elder statesman of U.S. agriculture, Orville Freeman, secretary of agriculture under both JFK and LBJ and now president of Business International Corporation, told a House committee that "since it is clear the embargo has not worked, and the Castro government seems certain to continue for the foreseeable future, U.S. business asks the obvious question of whether it makes sense to be excluded from a market that is virtually on their doorstep."[66]

So why not sit down and talk? Vietnam was history, détente was in full bloom, Nixon was gone, and now several members of a newly rambunctious Congress, reporting that Cubans were ready to negotiate, seemed poised to take matters into their own hands. Senator Edward Kennedy soon sent two staffers to Havana, perhaps as a prelude to his own visit, and in early 1975 he introduced a bill to end the embargo. Representative Jonathan Bingham introduced a House companion to Kennedy's bill, and others joined in. Appearing on NBC's *Today* show after a May visit to Havana, Senator McGovern advocated a unilateral lifting of the embargo on food and medicine and a U.S.-Cuban version of ping-pong diplomacy—an exchange of baseball and basketball teams. He had taken with him one request from Massachusetts senator Edward Brooke that Cuba allow Luis Tiant's parents to visit the United States to see their son pitch for the Boston Red Sox and another from Senator John Sparkman that Cuba return the two-million-dollar ransom from the 1972 Southern Airways hijacking.[67]

The Cubans offered no immediate response, but they had been especially conciliatory to the reporters accompanying McGovern, with Fidel Castro insisting, "We owe it to ourselves to live in peace." Returning from a late-summer visit to Havana, Representative Stephen Solarz said much the same thing. He reported that "the Cuban people are better fed, better housed, better clothed, better educated, and are healthier than before the revolution or the imposition of the blockade. There is no unemployment, very little crime, and no drug problem." In this context, Solarz argued, "the continuation of the trade embargo and political isolation of the Castro regime serves no useful purpose."[68]

But not every member of Congress agreed that détente should be extended to Cuba, with the Florida delegation appearing especially determined to hold the line. Miami representative Claude Pepper's district had become between 30 and 40 percent Cuban, and many of them were now citizens, eligible to vote. (When Pepper died in 1989, he was replaced by Ileana Ros-Lehtinen, the first Cuban émigré and the first Hispanic woman elected to Congress.) Pepper told his colleagues, "I would never have our country take in friendship the bloody hand of Fidel Castro," while another Florida representative, Bill Chappell Jr., also voiced his opposition to restoring relations with a government that had "trained guerrillas, including American citizens, to subvert and infiltrate governments including the United States." Chappell was especially upset by "the terrorist Venceremos brigade and the distribution of the publication *Granma* among Americans urging them to kill and steal." It followed, then, that "any efforts to enter into friendly and normal relations with the Castro regime would, in fact, be detrimental to the best interests and the security of the United States." Even otherwise liberal Florida Democrat Dante Fascell opposed the normalization of U.S.-Cuban relations. But administration officials recognized that most of this congressional opposition was little more than playing to the home audience—obligatory but perfunctory, and barely heard in the State Department. "All of the political pressure was in the direction of dropping the embargo," recalled deputy assistant secretary Harry Shlaudeman, "even from Republicans. We were hearing almost daily from these people on the Hill."[69]

IN THIS CONGRESSIONAL CONTEXT and with the Costa Rica OAS meeting on the near horizon, Assistant Secretary Rogers had sat down to convince Henry Kissinger to talk with the Cubans. Rogers argued on that June day that the handful of Claude Peppers were no match for the Mike Mansfields in new Ninety-fourth Congress, especially if the new group of antiembargo liberals could forge an alliance with conservatives such as Breaux who saw Cuba as an opportunity to expand trade. "Congress will get ahead of us on Cuba policy," Rogers warned. "So what!" Kissinger interrupted. "Cuba is not a popular issue." Rogers persisted; Kissinger dug in his heels: "I will not cater to the propensity of the Democrats to make unilateral concessions." Rogers shifted back to the Canadians, who were pushing to permit their subsidiaries of U.S. firms to trade with Cuba. OK, Kissinger paused, but if Washington offered to talk, "what would you say if the Cubans said, 'screw you.' Suppose they don't answer?" Then he reminded Rogers that the United States had been down this road before: "I favored a probe with Cuba last year but there was no answer; what new now can be said?"[70]

This reference was to the process that had begun in June 1974, when a liberal Democrat, Frank Mankiewicz, who was about to film an interview with Fidel Castro, inquired whether Kissinger would like to send a message to the Cuban leader. A few months earlier, Kissinger had told a visiting Argentine foreign minister, "Cuba is not an overwhelming issue for us. If we can coexist with the Peoples [*sic*] Republic of China, we can coexist with Cuba," so he had given Mankiewicz an unsigned note indicating his interest in exploring the differences that separated the two countries. Mankiewicz had returned from Havana with Castro's assurance that Cuba was prepared to discuss the issues dividing the two countries, and just prior to Nixon's resignation, the United States had taken a small but symbolic step by easing the embargo to allow scholars and journalists to travel to Cuba and to permit Cuban books and other educational materials to be imported. The next step was to push a bit harder, recalled Cuban negotiator Ramón Sánchez-Parodi: "As a way of testing the sincerity of Kissinger's proposals, we stated that a precondition for beginning the talks was for me to be given a one-year, multiple-entry visa to the U.S. This had never been done before. . . . To our surprise, the request was granted."[71]

Nothing more had occurred during the few remaining days of the Nixon administration, but soon after Ford became president, a member of Cuba's U.N. mission had met with one of Secretary Kissinger's key aides, Lawrence Eagleburger, with the principal topic of discussion the travel restrictions on Cuba's U.N. diplomats. As Kissinger later commented, the Eagleburger contact "wasn't an initiative. It was just an attempt to feel out the situation."[72] Nevertheless, on 11 January 1975, Eagleburger had met secretly with Sánchez-Parodi at a LaGuardia Airport coffee shop. "It was really weird," Sánchez-Parodi recalled. "Eagleburger and Mankiewicz arrived and were in a terrible hurry. We tried one regular restaurant but the wait was too long, so we ended up at the fast food place. At one point during our meeting a blind guy came up, trying to sell us ballpoint pens."[73] In his 1999 memoir, Kissinger recalled that the meeting had not gone well—Sánchez-Parodi had asserted that lifting the embargo had to precede the discussion of any other issues; Eagleburger had rejected that idea, and the two sides had simply agreed that "when they had something more to say to each other, they would be in touch."[74]

Now, six months later, in June 1975, Rogers was attempting to convince Kissinger to get back in touch. Cuba's attitude had been offensive from the start, Kissinger replied, when "Castro told Mankiewicz that the mere fact that Cuba had survived was a victory for them and a defeat for us. They treat us with contempt." Then Kissinger abruptly changed course: "But since all of these things are going to happen, we might as well start a dialogue." Kissinger did not explain what he meant by "all of these things" (probably a combination of the pressure to permit subsidiary trade, the Latin American initiative to remove OAS sanctions, and the congressional prodding to ease the embargo), but change seemed more likely now, on 9 June 1975, than at any time in the preceding fifteen years. Kissinger issued quick instructions: "It is better to deal straight with Castro. Behave chivalrously; do it like a big guy, not like a shyster. Let him know we are moving in a new direction; we'd like to synchronize; New York City under the UN mantle would be the place; steps will be unilateral; reciprocity is necessary; we shall stop until we get some reciprocity."[75]

Rogers had won his point, so he did not take time to mention that the

Cubans had already reciprocated both in word and in deed: referring to Kissinger's Houston speech three months earlier, Fidel Castro had told a group of Canadian journalists, "We consider Dr. Kissinger's recent statements on Cuba as positive." Furthermore, a week before the Kissinger-Rogers discussion, Castro had returned three hijackers to the United States. Much more important than these small gestures was the perception that Cuba was ending its support of Latin American revolutionary movements. In 1973 the State Department's John Crimmins had told Congress that "the Cuban support in its policy of the export of revolution continues in various areas," and in early 1974, Kissinger had identified Cuba's subversion of Latin American governments as the core reason for continued U.S. animosity.[76] But in his March 1975 Houston speech, the secretary of state had noted that "nations that in the early sixties felt most threatened by Cuban revolutionary violence no longer feel the menace so acutely." Later that year, the Defense Intelligence Agency reported that "Cuba is virtually inactive in subversive support in Latin America at this time," and the State Department agreed, telling Congress that both Cuba and the Soviet Union "have in recent years pursued policies and programs aimed at improving relations with established Latin American governments. As a parallel to this approach, they have tended to channel their active support to legal and 'legitimate' local Communist parties, and have largely broken off support for guerrilla and terrorist groups."[77]

The result of all this? At the San José OAS meeting held a month after the Kissinger-Rogers conversation, the United States voted with the majority on a freedom-of-action resolution: each OAS member was now free to conduct relations with Cuba "at the level and in the form that each State deems desirable."[78]

THIS CONCESSION LEFT the Ford administration with a second problem: trade by foreign-based subsidiaries of U.S. corporations. While generally wholly owned by their U.S.-based parents, these subsidiaries were not simply branch offices; rather, they were legally separate firms, incorporated in and subject to the laws of their host countries, none of which had an embargo on trade with Cuba. But the parent companies were subject to the laws of the United States, which prohibited trade with Cuba by any U.S. corporation or its overseas subsidiaries. The question, then, was simple: Whose laws would prevail?[79]

U.S. law had been the answer until 1973, when Argentina's new Peronist government extended a two-hundred-million-dollar credit to Cuba for the purchase of Argentine goods and announced its intention to extend an additional one billion dollars in credits over the next five years. A Cuban purchasing delegation soon arrived in Buenos Aires and began contacting several Argentine subsidiaries of U.S. firms about prices and delivery schedules. The problem, as Secretary Kissinger had warned President Nixon at year end, was not simply that sales by these subsidiaries would be illegal under U.S. law; in addition, the Cuban-Argentine agreement stipulated that Argentine ships would transport half the goods purchased, and the United States had permanently banned any ship entering a Cuban port from refueling or resupplying (bunkering) in U.S. ports or from carrying cargoes subsidized by the U.S. government. U.S. law also denied foreign aid to the government of an offending ship's country of registry, and in the Argentine case that would halt five hundred thousand dollars per year in military training.[80]

By the mid–twentieth century, for reasons related primarily to their country's history of dependent development, Argentines had become especially sensitive to foreign economic pressure. Not coincidentally, therefore, Juan Perón had made economic nationalism a central feature of his government from 1947 to 1955, when he had positioned Argentina to occupy what he called a Third Position between the two postwar blocs. Eager to trade with any willing purchaser, post-Perón governments had reluctantly yielded to U.S. pressure to isolate Cuba, but in 1973 the Peronists had returned to power, and the aging Perón's advisers insisted that Argentine law would govern the Argentine subsidiaries of U.S. corporations. So Kissinger had warned Nixon that "a confrontation over our Cuban denial policy is most likely to undo our efforts to develop a closer working relationship with Argentina and place the substantial U.S. investment in Argentina ($1.3 billion) in a precarious condition." Kissinger recommended that Nixon authorize the Argentine-based subsidiaries of U.S. corporations to trade with Cuba "if they can demonstrate that they face serious Argentine retaliation or possibly closure," and from the Tlatelolco meeting of foreign ministers, the secretary cabled that "Argentina is moving in our direction of every issue but Cuba; on that one we will continue to have trouble."[81] In the midst of the recriminations over the fall of Chile's democratic Allende government, neither Nixon nor Kissinger was eager for a fight with another of Latin America's major countries, so in April 1974, four months before Nixon's resignation, he gave the Argentine subsidiaries of three U.S. corporations—Ford, General Motors, and Chrysler—special permission to sell vehicles to Cuba.

This was not the first exception to the ban on subsidiary trade, but the dozen or so earlier cases had involved humanitarian considerations, and the size of the Argentine exception—for 11,500 vehicles worth about $150 million—was far larger than any previous exception. The Nixon administration went out of its way to emphasize that the exception did not constitute a change in policy: when asked if his emphasis on the word "exception" in his announcement implied that no policy shift had occurred, State Department spokesperson John King replied, "I am not 'implying' that there has been no change. I am asserting it." Nonetheless, the new Ford administration found itself a prisoner of the Argentine decision as other important countries began to follow—Spain granted Cuba $900 million in credits in late 1974, France $350 million in early 1975, and by mid-1975 Canada had added $155 million and the British $850 million.[82] Some of the products Cuba wanted to purchase with these credits would probably be manufactured by U.S. subsidiaries, and blocking the sales would open the Ford administration to charges that it was violating the General Agreement on Tariffs and Trade's rules prohibiting extraterritorial jurisdiction—a dispute subject to adjudication that the United States was almost certain to lose.

At the same time, powerful U.S. corporations were beginning to grumble that the prohibition on subsidiary trade imperiled relations with their host governments. In this context, the U.S. ambassador to Mexico cabled Kissinger that "American automobile companies were told flatly last week to obtain permission from the Dept. of State to export to Cuba." Moreover, the ambassador continued, "all manufacturing firms with an export capability, which include U.S. subsidiaries and Mexican firms using U.S. components, have been asked by the IMCE (Mexican Institute of Foreign Trade) to participate in Mexican trade show to be held in Cuba in March. If we do not act promptly and favorably on applications for exemptions from the Foreign Assets Control regulations and [for] permission to export to Cuba U.S. origin components, I am certain that our bilateral relations with Mexico will suffer markedly and the position of U.S. investment in Mexico will be damaged."[83]

The ambassador's cable arrived from Mexico just as U.S. officials were wrestling with an application by U.S.-based Litton Industries to permit its Canadian subsidiary to sell office equipment to Cuba. The case was the second involving a Canadian subsidiary: at almost exactly the same time as U.S. officials had granted the Argentine exception, Cuba had signed a contract to purchase thirty locomotives from MLW-Worthington of Canada, 52 percent of which was owned by U.S.-based Studebaker-Worthington. The

U.S. government eventually granted a license after the Canadian government had sent a formal note reminding the Ford administration that the United States had promised "to be as accommodating as possible with respect to such cases to avoid a jurisdictional conflict between the laws and policies of the two governments."[84]

After the Mexican and Canadian decisions, Deputy Secretary of State Robert Ingersoll prepared a memo for President Ford on behalf of the NSC Undersecretaries Committee, which had bureaucratic responsibility for processing the applications for exceptions: since Cuba's trade with noncommunist countries was growing rapidly, Ingersoll warned, the United States "increasingly risks confrontation with friendly governments and threatens the stability of US investment abroad." Argentina had hinted that U.S.-owned subsidiaries would be expropriated if they refused to sell to the Cubans, and Canada and Mexico had insisted that the extraterritorial application of U.S. law violated their sovereignty. But these disputes merely constituted the tip of the iceberg: "Conflicts with Spain, Belgium, Venezuela and other countries may be in the offing if we continue to enforce these regulations. The future political cost of such enforcement can be expected to exceed any lingering benefit to US policy." Ingersoll asked permission to rewrite U.S. regulations to permit the subsidiaries of U.S. firms to conform to the policies of their host countries.[85]

President Ford agreed, formally eliminating all the restrictions and host-country penalties on U.S. subsidiaries trading with Cuba, but the administration did not concede entirely—subsidiaries would still have to apply for licenses, but now the administration would presume a favorable response if the foreign-made products contained "an insubstantial proportion of United States–origin materials, parts, or components," with the term "insubstantial" defined as 20 percent or less of a product's total value.[86] To Congress, Assistant Secretary Rogers explained the move as "a measure to remove a recurrent source of friction between the United States and friendly countries," and he explained the U.S. vote to end the OAS ban on trade as an effort to remove "the anomaly of mandatory sanctions which were no longer acceptable to the majority of OAS members." But, he admitted, both changes were also intended to signal Cuba "that we have put a policy of permanent hostility behind us. We are ready to begin a dialogue."[87]

BUT WAS CUBA READY? Fidel Castro had told several members of the U.S. Congress that he was, and he had already sent special envoy Ramón Sánchez-Parodi to the LaGuardia meeting. At that time, Kissinger's aide,

Lawrence Eagleburger, had given the Cuban an aide-mémoire suggesting that both sides "identify and define the issues which may be discussed, and in what order we might best discuss them."[88] Sánchez-Parodi had responded that nothing could be discussed until Washington had lifted the embargo, a stance that appeared to close the matter.

The question of why the Cubans did not respond remains unanswered. Perhaps Fidel Castro should be taken at his word: he told a Cuban audience in April 1976 that "nothing can be negotiated while a knife is being held against our chest," and he wanted the embargo removed while the two nations talked about their differences. The delay may also have reflected Cuban domestic politics—just as Washington was divided between the Claude Peppers and Mike Mansfields, no doubt Cuban officials had differing views about the wisdom of détente. Or Ambassador Bonsal's view may have been correct: perhaps Cuba's revolutionary government needed a threatening United States to maintain domestic support. Another reasonable guess is that the Cuban position simply reflected the belief that time was on Cuba's side, since the Ford administration was the weakest since Herbert Hoover and an overwhelmingly Democratic Congress was pushing for unilateral U.S. concessions. Those same Democrats might win the White House in 1976. For whatever reasons, the aide-mémoire Eagleburger gave Sánchez-Parodi at LaGuardia on 11 January elicited no response from Cuba, and Rogers cooled his heels for six months. Then, on 11 June, two days after convincing Kissinger to negotiate, the assistant secretary went public, complaining to Congress that "the United States has made several gestures on its part toward Cuba recently [and] Cuba has not reciprocated."[89]

The Cubans immediately consented to another secret meeting, this one held ten days later at Washington's National Airport and intended to be brief. The participants (Eagleburger, Rogers, and Cuba's Nestor García) simply arranged to hold a meeting on substance, which occurred two weeks later, on 9 July, at a private dining room at New York's Hotel Pierre. Sánchez-Parodi again flew up from Havana, and the U.S. side again came away from the meeting believing that Cuba was demanding that the embargo be lifted before negotiations could begin. Years later, however, Sánchez-Parodi told Peter Kornbluh and James Blight, "I had come from Havana with a long list of issues to discuss." For some reason, however, Eagleburger and Rogers did not give Sánchez-Parodi an opportunity to raise those matters: "Eagleburger was obviously in a hurry. It seemed to me that he was more interested in not missing his shuttle flight than in discussing issues standing in the way of normalization of US-Cuban relations."[90]

A quarter century later, Kissinger recalled that he interpreted the Cuban position as an unacceptable bargaining ploy: "Castro was demanding a major unilateral American concession as an entrance price for further negotiations"; if the United States agreed, Cubans would have no incentive to negotiate further. For his part, Sánchez-Parodi, also recalling the meeting two decades later, said that after the Hotel Pierre encounter, "it seemed to us that Ford was running for re-election and didn't want [rapprochement with Cuba] to be an issue that his opponents, especially Ronald Reagan, could use against him."[91]

With Washington convinced of Cuban intransigence and with Havana convinced that the Ford administration was no longer interested in negotiating, at least until after November, the face-to-face dialogue was suspended. But the process of conciliation nevertheless continued. Three weeks after the Hotel Pierre meeting, the United States had supported the OAS freedom-of-action resolution, and Cuba had responded almost immediately by returning the two-million-dollar ransom from the 1972 Southern Airways hijacking. A senator with close ties to the airline (and Fulbright's successor as chair of the Foreign Relations Committee), Alabama's John Sparkman, told reporters that the gesture was appreciated as "very solid evidence that the Cuban Government is genuinely interested in improved relations with the United States"; now, he continued, "it is our turn to act," urging the Ford administration to lift restrictions on the sale of food and medicine.[92] The president was not willing to go that far, but he agreed to permit the foreign subsidiaries of U.S. firms to trade with Cuba; two days later, Luis Tiant's parents arrived in Boston to watch their son pitch for the Red Sox, a significant concession by the Cuban government, which in its struggle to keep athletes from defecting had always made it clear that immigration meant abandoning one's family. In a minor but equally symbolic move, the U.S. Coast Guard announced that it would not press charges against a Cuban boat caught taking lobsters illegally off Cape Cod.

Then the abrasive issue of Puerto Rican independence ground down the wheels of accommodation. In August, the U.S. ambassador to the United Nations, Daniel Patrick Moynihan, complained to President Ford that "Cuba tried to clobber us on Puerto Rico in the UN," and in September, Assistant Secretary Rogers publicly criticized Cuba's effort to convince the United Nations to address the status of Puerto Rico as an "unwarranted interference in the internal affairs of the United States and Puerto Rico." Cuba did not desist, however, and in early October it took the issue to the

General Assembly, where Ambassador Ricardo Alarcón called Puerto Rico "a Latin American territory at the very center of the Caribbean oppressed by colonialism" and lamented that Washington was using parliamentary procedure "to gain time while it tries to carry out a maneuver designed, once again and in vain, to conceal the colonial nature of its domination over that territory." Years later, Alarcón commented that in the mid-1970s, the United States "did not understand what was going on in the United Nations. Everyone else knew Puerto Rico was an old issue, not something newly manufactured by Cuba. We were not giving new emphasis to the issue; it was just that the United States for some reason began hearing our concerns. We had been saying the same thing for more than a decade."[93]

It is uncertain why the Cuban government raised this issue at such a delicate moment in the reconciliation process and despite evidence from a secret ballot showing that only about 4 percent of Puerto Ricans favored independence. Castro was always unimpressed by these electoral data, telling Barbara Walters in 1977 that "some North Americans say that the problem is that the majority of Puerto Ricans do not want independence. Well, 20 or 30 years before U.S. independence, many North Americans did not want the independence of the United States." Referring to Rogers's September 1975 statement, Castro told a Cuban audience that the Ford administration had recently

> made strong statements against us, simply because we expressed our solidarity with the Puerto Rican people. Cuban solidarity with Puerto Rico dates back to the last century—since the time we were two Spanish colonies, the last two colonies on this continent, since the time when we fought together for our independence, since the time when Martí founded his revolutionary party to fight for the independence of Cuba and contribute to the independence of Puerto Rico. It comes from our history, from Martí, and from our internationalist principles and the feeling that Puerto Rico is a Latin American nation, a nation that has resisted for more than 75 years the attempts to dissolve it and absorb it, to destroy it.

Having wrapped Puerto Rican independence in the mantle of Cuban history, Castro promised in late 1975, "We will never renounce our solidarity with Puerto Rico." U.S. officials had a different view: "It's American territory," Secretary Kissinger subsequently said. "I don't see how the Cubans could believe we wouldn't be upset about Puerto Rico."[94]

Increasingly vulnerable to attacks from the Republican Right, Gerald

Ford probably felt that he had no alternative but to harden his stance, especially after Ronald Reagan told a Florida audience that the United States had its own principles and that one of them was that Puerto Rico was a part of the United States. The president responded, "I was very upset with the Cuban action where they led the fight, so to speak, in trying to indicate that Puerto Rico should be independent of the United States." But he again did not close the door to further discussions; like Rogers, Ford followed the negative comment with a positive one: "I repeat that there is no reason why in the long run there shouldn't be a resumption of good rapport between the Cuban people on the one hand and the American people on the other." [95]

A NEW AND DEFINING INGREDIENT was then added to the stew: three days after the president's comment, Secretary Kissinger announced that Cuba had become involved in the rapidly snowballing civil war in Angola, warning that "a policy of conciliation will not survive Cuban meddling in Puerto Rico or Cuban armed intervention in the affairs of other nations struggling to decide their own fate." Castro responded quickly that if accommodation with the United States required Cuba to stop supporting revolutionaries in Angola and separatists in Puerto Rico, then "at that price there will never be any relations with the United States." [96]

Cuba's genetic roots are as deep in Africa as they are in Europe, a fact that may help explain why Cuba's sympathies lay with African political movements seeking to end both European colonial control and sub-Saharan Africa's remaining white-supremacist governments. "The blood of many African peoples flows through our veins," commented Raúl Castro during a 1977 visit to Angola. "Thousands of Africans uprooted from their lands shed their blood for our independence during the last century, many of them were among the great patriots and outstanding military leaders who fought against Spanish colonialism for 30 years. Only the reactionaries and the imperialists are surprised by the fact that the descendants of those slaves who gave their lives for the freedom of our country have shed their blood for the freedom of their ancestors' homeland." Fidel Castro had already said that "those who once sent enslaved Africans to America perhaps never imagined that one of those places that received the slaves would send soldiers to fight for the liberation of black Africa." [97]

But ethnic and racial solidarity does not completely explain Cuba's presence in Africa, since many of Cuba's early activities there focused not on the sub-Saharan region of Cuban ancestry but on the predominantly Arabic Mediterranean states. In late 1961, for example, a Cuban ship carried weapons to the National Liberation Front of Algeria and returned with seventy-six wounded Algerian rebels and twenty children, most of them war orphans. In early 1965, Cuba moved into sub-Saharan Africa when Che Guevara led four hundred Cuban troops in support of Zairean and Angolan rebels, but the commitment was brief. Che left after seven months, and by 1967 the only Cuban military personnel in sub-Saharan Africa were helping rebels in Guinea-Bissau to oust the Portuguese; the Cubans remained until the war's end in 1974. Overall, the best estimate is that fewer than two thousand Cuban troops were in Africa between 1961 and 1974.[98]

However modest, Cuba's presence in both north and sub-Saharan Africa probably reflected a substantial dose of revolutionary idealism as well as a determination to play a wider role in world affairs, a role symbolized best by Cuba's active participation in the nonaligned movement, one of whose fundamental goals was African decolonization and majority rule. Cuban president Osvaldo Dorticós had represented Cuba at the first nonaligned summit, held in 1961 in Belgrade, Yugoslavia, and for more than a decade the movement had served the Castro government as a major diplomatic platform, compensating for Cuba's ouster from both the OAS and the Latin American caucus at the United Nations. In 1972 Castro visited five African countries as part of a two-month trip that included the Soviet Union and Eastern Europe, and the following year he led Cuba's delegation to the movement's fourth summit, held in Algiers. At the same time, Cuba was sending a small number of military advisers and medical personnel to Sierra Leone, Equatorial Guinea, Somalia, and Algeria.[99]

During this period Washington was focused on accommodation with China and détente with the Soviet Union, and it noticed the nonaligned movement primarily when it ventured into Middle Eastern politics, where it invariably clashed with U.S. policy. Fidel Castro openly participated in this clash with his September 1973 speech to the nonaligned conference in Algeria, in which he strongly criticized Israel's treatment of the Palestinians. A few days later Cuba and Israel broke relations, and during the October War, Cuba sent several hundred specialists in armored warfare to Syria. Cuba welcomed PLO chair Yasir Arafat in 1974, and a year later supported the U.N. General Assembly resolution condemning Zionism as a form of racism.

But lingering colonialism and white minority governments in sub-Saharan Africa rivaled the Palestinian problem as the principal symbol of this North-South conflict, and in the mid-1970s Angola had the misfortune to become the specific bone of contention. Facing a divided but determined independence movement in Angola and a chaotic post-Salazar political scene at home, the Portuguese announced in early 1975 that they would grant Angolans their independence, setting 11 November as the day of departure. Meeting in Alvor, Portugal, the Portuguese and the three rebel factions fighting for independence agreed that during the eleven-month interregnum they would form a transitional coalition government to supervise elections.

The absence of a unified independence movement reflected the fact that what the world called "Angola" was not a nation but a Portuguese-ruled amalgam, deeply divided along ethnic, racial, regional, class, and ideological lines, and in the mid-1970s these sociocultural divisions found their political expression in the three contending independence movements. The Alvor agreement therefore broke down within days, as all of the sides turned to international backers for help. Agostinho Neto's Popular Movement for the Liberation of Angola (MPLA), already supported by Yugoslavia and less consistently by the Soviet Union, had recently turned to Cuba. Holden Roberto's National Front for the Liberation of Angola (FNLA) sought support from the United States, from the People's Republic of China, and from the government of Roberto's brother-in-law, President Joseph Mobutu of neighboring Zaire. The third side of the rebel triangle, Jonas Savimbi's National Union for the Total Independence of Angola (UNITA), found aid from apartheid South Africa, the People's Republic of China, and eventually the United States.[100]

Although Havana had begun to support Neto's MPLA in the 1960s, the first Cubans to set foot in Angola since 1965 were an army officer and a Central Committee policy analyst who arrived on 3 January 1975, a week before the Alvor agreement was reached.[101] The United States had also remained apart from Angola's lengthy liberation struggle, in part because U.S. officials were focused on Indochina but primarily because of confidence in Portugal, a NATO ally. U.S. activity had been limited to the CIA's annual subsidy to Holden Roberto's Zaire-based FNLA — a modest six thousand dollars but enough to permit the Kissinger aide who chaired the interagency task force on Angola to characterize the FNLA leader as "a longtime client of the United States."[102]

Roberto, who had not set foot in Angola for thirteen years, was an unfortunate choice as an ally. John Stockwell, the most intimately involved CIA official, reported that "it is virtually impossible to find an American official, scholar or journalist, who is familiar with [the FNLA], who will testify positively about its organization and leadership." When he signed on to the Angola task force, Stockwell had asked a senior State Department official why the United States supported Roberto and had been told, "I'll be damned if I know; I have never seen a single report or memo which suggests that the FNLA has any organization, solid leaders, or an ideology which we could count on." Piero Gleijeses reached the same conclusions after conducting numerous interviews with those involved: The CIA station chief in Luanda, for example, claimed that "this organization was led by corrupt, unprincipled men who represented the very worst of radical black African racism," and the U.S. consul general remarked that the FNLA was "totally disorganized."

But Roberto was anti-Soviet, and twelve days after the Alvor agreement was reached, Roberto's subsidy billowed from six thousand dollars to three hundred thousand dollars per year; four days later, his FNLA attacked a radio station and captured an MPLA activist, which in the context of the Alvor agreement was a move equivalent to the South's firing on Fort Sumter. Neto's MPLA retaliated, and the Angolan civil war was under way. A month later the CIA opened a station in Luanda, and the Soviet Union resumed its arms shipments to the MPLA, which had been suspended since 1972. Then, as the State Department's assistant secretary for Africa later wrote in his candid memoir, "after March–April of 1975, the difficulty of establishing causality becomes more complicated."[103]

Only Gleijeses has invested the time to figure it out. The story he tells is that on 17 July, Secretary Kissinger, acting against the advice of his own African bureau, led by Assistant Secretary Nathaniel Davis, convinced President Ford to authorize $6 million in arms for Roberto's FNLA, laundered through Zaire's Mobutu. "We'll send [former U.S. ambassador to Zaire Sheldon] Vance to Mobutu with $1 million, and take a CIA guy with him. We'll tell him we have $6 million, and more if needed, and ask him to come up with a program. It may be too late because Luanda is lost. Unless we can seize it back, it is pretty hopeless." Aware that the State Department's Africanists adamantly opposed supporting Roberto's FNLA, Kissinger added, "We'll have a resignation from Davis, then I'll clean out the AF bureau."[104]

Davis resigned the next day, and the State Department's African specialists were cut out of the process by moving Angola policy to the secretary's seventh-floor suite under William Hyland. A week later, Kissinger came back to Ford for an additional $8 million, and on 29 July, the first planeload of arms, plucked from the CIA's Texas stockpile of sanitized foreign-made weapons, was flown to Kinshasa; an additional $10.7 million was authorized in August, and a final $7 million followed on 27 November, bringing the total to $31.7 million for fiscal 1975 and exhausting the CIA's reserve fund.[105]

The Soviet Union also increased its assistance, and Fidel Castro sent military advisers to train MPLA fighters, seeming to confirm Washington's principal explanation for Cuban activity in Africa—that multiracial Cuba was acting on behalf of lily-white Moscow. South Africa also increased its support of the third warring faction, Savimbi's UNITA, and in August Pretoria sent its regular army to take possession of hydroelectric facilities in southern Angola.* In September, with all sides reinforced and with the mid-November independence day approaching, Zaire's Mobutu sent two of his own army battalions to fight alongside the FNLA in the north; by October, they were only thirteen miles from the capital. On 23 October the South African army launched a major military offensive from the south, also heading for Luanda.

At this point the Cubans swept in to save Neto's MPLA. Requested in May, a 480-member Cuban military advisory mission had begun arriving in late July, but the pace was exceedingly slow, and by late September, Angola still had only about fifty Cubans. The South African move to control the hydroelectric facilities spurred Cuban action, however, and three ships carrying weapons and 300 advisers/instructors left Havana in mid-September. But only on 4 November—twelve days after South Africa launched its northward offensive toward Luanda—did Cuba send the initial planeload of what would become a major combat force of perhaps 30,000 troops.[106]

The issue of timing is obviously crucial to fixing responsibility—were the Cuban troops sent as an aggressive move by Havana (or Moscow) or in reaction to aggression by South Africa? Most direct observers have fudged their answers, following the lead of Davis, who wrote that "smaller-scale South African involvement in Angola preceded the dispatch of large numbers of Cuban troops from the Caribbean; but small-scale Cuban intervention preceded South African involvement." But, Davis continued, "the Soviets and Cubans were no doubt aware of both the U.S. covert interven-

---

*Germans ruled Angola's southern neighbor, Namibia (South West Africa), until World War I, when South Africa seized the territory. After the war, South Africa assumed administration under Article 22 of the Covenant of the League of Nations and a mandate agreement by the League council. In 1946, the United Nations assumed supervisory authority; in 1966, the General Assembly revoked South Africa's mandate; and in 1971, the International Court of Justice ordered South Africa to withdraw.

tion of July–August 1975 and the open incursions by Zaire before the final decision was made to dispatch large numbers of Cuban troops."[107]

Most observers agree that Cuba's military involvement was incremental, governed more by unfolding events than by an overarching strategy, but until Gleijeses conducted his research, no one outside the Cuban government seemed certain about what kind of Cubans arrived and when, with the primary confusion arising over the distinction between advisers or instructors on the one hand and regular combat forces on the other. Fidel Castro claimed from the beginning that "the first *Cuban instructors* arrived in Angola at the beginning of October," but the U.S. consul in Luanda cabled Washington that "[redacted] told me on October 9 that he had received information from a reliable source on October 8 that *Cuban troops* and arms had landed in Angola." Such a cable that could easily have led Hyland to believe—erroneously—that Cuba had sent regular military units to Angola "well before the first South African started fighting" on 23 October.[108]

Using interviews and documents from Cuban, Angolan, and CIA sources, Gleijeses determined the precise temporal sequence, down to the minute (6:45 P.M. on 4 November, twelve days after the South Africans launched their offensive) that the first plane left Havana for Brazzaville with one hundred Cuban heavy weapons specialists. Kissinger told a completely different story in his 1999 memoir, but he used careful wording buttressed by cavalier scholarship to rewrite history, and Gleijeses caught the former secretary of state in the act: "In his memoirs, Kissinger cites one of my articles to support his claim that the Cuban intervention 'began in May, accelerated in July, and turned massive in September and October,' which is precisely the opposite of what my article said."[109]

"We sent our first military unit at a time when the South African regular troops invaded Angola on October 23, 1975," Castro told Barbara Walters. "They sent their regular army. So we had to make a decision. Either we would sit idle, and South Africa would take over Angola, or we would make an effort to help. That was the moment. On November 5 we made the decision to send the first military unit to Angola to fight against the south African troops."[110]

That same day, Kissinger warned Congress about Cuba's growing presence in Angola, but he failed to mention South Africa's participation in the war. This oversight was leaked to the press by the State Department's disgruntled Africanists; on 22 November, the *Washington Post* reported that South African combat forces were heavily involved, and as the CIA's Stockwell later wrote, "the propaganda and political war was lost in that stroke.

There was nothing the [CIA's] Lusaka station could invent that would be as damaging to the other side as our alliance with the hated South Africans was to our cause." The obituary was written by Hyland: "In the end we were allied with South Africa—the kiss of death."[111]

On 11 November the Portuguese had left as promised, and the MPLA, holding Luanda with Cuba's help, announced the establishment of the People's Republic of Angola. With Cuban forces continuing to arrive, the MPLA then went on the offensive, and on 1 December Secretary Kissinger wired an update to all U.S. diplomatic posts: "The large influx of Soviet arms, and Cuban troops to man them, continues," he began. From the south, UNITA had reached to within two hundred miles of Luanda, but that was the edge of its ethnic area, and more progress would be difficult; to the north, FNLA forces had been repulsed.[112] South Africa soon began withdrawing, and in mid-February the Organization of African Unity (OAU) recognized Neto's MPLA as the government of Angola.

That decision did not mean the end of the Angolan civil war, however, for Zaire and South Africa continued to support Roberto's FNLA and Savimbi's UNITA. The Ford administration wanted to do so as well, but Congress, reflecting the public's post-Vietnam caution, would have none of it: only eight months after evacuating the Saigon embassy, the Senate voted overwhelmingly (54–22) to prohibit any U.S. aid for military activity in Angola. Informed of the vote, President Ford called an impromptu news conference: "How can the United States, the greatest power in the world, take the position that the Soviet Union can operate with impunity many thousands of miles away with Cuban troops?" Characterizing the aid cutoff as "an act of total irresponsibility," State's William Hyland wrote that it "virtually guaranteed a Communist victory."[113]

The CIA continued sending the FNLA and UNITA five million dollars that had been authorized prior to the cutoff, while the White House fought unsuccessfully to have the ban rescinded. When that effort failed, in early 1976 the Ford administration turned its attention directly to Cuba. "I think sooner or later we have to crack the Cubans," Kissinger told Ford on 15 March. "I think we have to humiliate them. If they move into Namibia or Rhodesia, I would be in favor of clobbering them. That would create a furor and we might have to come out for black rule. But I think we might have to demand they get out of Africa." "What if they don't?," asked the president. "I think we could blockade," Kissinger replied.[114]

The public saber-rattling began a week later, with Kissinger telling a Dallas audience that "the United States cannot acquiesce indefinitely in the presence of Cuban expeditionary forces in distant lands" and warning that further Cuban moves in Africa would provoke "forthright and decisive action." In what appeared to be a coordinated effort, the Pentagon announced a few days later that it was engaged in a "review of possible action which might be taken with regard to Cuba." The review produced a list of military measures resembling Operation Mongoose — "blockade; port mining, strikes and invasion" — but by this time it was clear that the escalation of pressure against Cuba would have the effect of "aligning ourselves, *de facto*, against Black African interests." That is, to attack Cuba because it was assisting black Africa would be interpreted everywhere as Washington assigning "great importance to the survival of white racist regimes."[115]

Caution became the order of the day. Two weeks earlier, President Ford had defeated Ronald Reagan in the Florida primary by a narrow 53–47 percent margin; Ford would have to do better if he hoped to carry the state in November. Then Reagan began using Cuba as he turned up the heat leading up to the next crucial primary in Illinois — asked on *Meet the Press* what he would do, Reagan advocated rescinding the OAS freedom-of-action resolution and tightening the embargo. Ford was equally tough, sending a warning that Cuba's "introduction of 12,000 combat troops in Angola is simply unacceptable" and ending any possibility of détente. But with his hands tied by Congress, the president had no answer when asked how he would respond if Cuba were to intervene against the white government of Rhodesia. He replied vaguely, "We have diplomatic, we have economic, and we have military options."[116]

In the end, nothing much happened. The State Department forced the cancellation of a set of exhibition baseball games arranged by Major League commissioner Bowie Kuhn, and the Commerce Department began stricter enforcement of the regulations limiting the proportion of U.S.-made components included in any product sold to Cuba by foreign subsidiaries of U.S. firms. Campaigning for the Democratic nomination, Jimmy Carter could see what had become obvious: President Ford, he said, had issued an ultimatum to the Cubans about Angola, but "the world knows that we were speaking with a hollow voice."[117]

The administration's only major step was to shoot itself in the foot: the United States vetoed Angola's application for membership in the United Nations, explaining that "the continuing presence and apparent influence of Cuban troops, massive in number in the Angolan context, is the basis of our view."[118] Most observers saw the vote and not the explanation, and it effectively boxed Ford into the exceptionally awkward position of ostracizing Africa's newest black government, which had now been recognized by forty-one of the forty-six OAU members. Carter was already telling campaign audiences that U.S. foreign policy should promote greater respect for human rights, and he now had the perfect example: the Ford administration's apparent hostility toward majority rule in southern Africa.

Republicans could easily say that they were not prejudiced against black Angolans, but this statement did not necessarily reflect Kissinger's thinking. "I have a basic sympathy with the white Rhodesians," he told the NSC after returning from a fence-mending trip to Africa, "but black Africa is absolutely united on this issue, and if we don't grab the initiative we will be faced with the Soviets, and Cuban troops." Kissinger hoped the black-on-black Angolan civil war would drag on, because if peace came, Rhodesia would be next in the line of fire, and "such a development would put us in the position of either acquiescing to another Cuban move in that area and thus destroying governments on our side or resisting in the name of white supremacy, and the latter would be impossible to do."[119]

Before leaving on his trip, Kissinger had told the NSC, "I will identify with African aspirations," which obviously meant "we can't say Rhodesia is a danger because it is a bad case." But "if the Cubans are involved there, Namibia is next and after that South Africa, itself. We must make the Soviets pay a heavy price. If the Cubans move, I recommend we act vigorously. We can't permit another move without suffering a great loss. We must separate the African issue from Cuba. Otherwise, it will be seen as Soviet strength and US weakness. We need to impress others with our will." Secretary of Defense Donald Rumsfeld agreed, as did President Ford. To avoid having U.S. policy seen as an effort to slow the progress of majority rule, both Rumsfeld and Ford wanted to market southern Africa as a Cold War battlefield: "We must tie in the Soviets and Cubans."[120]

Doing so was not at all difficult. The Cubans were obviously in Africa and just as obviously using Soviet weapons, and the U.S. public had become accustomed to thinking of Cuba as an aggravating pea in the Soviet pod. But was it? In 1975–76, both Ford and Kissinger repeatedly said so, and Ford later wrote that "there was no doubt in my mind that the Cuban troops, with Russian weapons, were acting as proxies for the Soviets."[121] But with access to Soviet documents released following the end of the Cold War, Kissinger eventually reached a different conclusion: "We could not imagine that [Castro] would act so provocatively so far from home unless he was pressured by Moscow to repay the Soviet Union for its military and economic support. Evidence now available suggests that the opposite was the case." Fidel Castro had said the same thing twenty years earlier: "The Soviet Union never requested that a single Cuban soldier be sent to Angola."[122]

What Secretary Kissinger never modified was his view that Cuba was too big for its britches. "We must demonstrate the limits of Cuban strength," he told Argentine foreign minister César Guzzetti. "It is absurd that a country of 8 million that has no resources should send expeditionary forces halfway around the globe." Kissinger also never modified his deep chagrin over the congressional decision to tie his hands: "We were in a good position in Angola," he lamented in a 1976 conversation with Chilean dictator Augusto Pinochet. "We thought Angola could become the Viet-Nam of Cuba. This would have occurred if Cuba had begun to sustain 20 casualties a week. Cuba could not have stood that for long. We had the forces for that. Congress stopped us."[123]

AND WHAT ABOUT RECONCILIATION? A few hours after the February 1976 OAU vote recognizing Neto's MPLA as the government of Angola, a reporter asked President Ford whether any possibility remained of détente with Cuba. His answer: "Right now there isn't a possibility—it's zero."[124] Two months earlier the president had first announced that Cuba's involvement in Angola "ends, as far as I am concerned, any efforts at all to have friendlier relations," and Castro had responded, "We are not going to sit back with folded arms when we see an African country, our sister, that is suddenly being devoured by the imperialists and brutally attacked by South Africa." In an especially hard-hitting speech, Castro now complained that "the Yankee imperialists have hundreds of thousands of soldiers overseas. . . . What moral and legal right do they have to complain that Cuba is sending military instructors and aid to countries in Africa and other underdeveloped parts of the world?" This back-and-forth was accompanied by name-calling: campaigning in Florida, Ford referred to Castro as "an international outlaw"; Castro responded by calling the U.S. president "a vulgar liar."[125]

So although Assistant Secretary Rogers later commented that "the Cuban initiative essentially had played itself out before Angola," the dispute over Africa clearly bore responsibility for ending a promising moment of accommodation between Washington and Havana.[126] A final effort had occurred just as the Cuban deployment was beginning, when Frank Mankiewicz's partner, Kirby Jones, returned from Havana in November 1975 with a message: Cuba was ready to discuss the specific issue of family visits, a topic the United States had proposed at the Hotel Pierre meeting in July.

This development therefore represented a concession to the United

States. Cubans apparently had seen that the U.S. negotiating approach differed from that of the Cubans; as Eagleburger had explained, the U.S. preferred "small steps, 1 to 26 and then ambassadors. [The Cubans] didn't act that way, they wanted it all at once"—that is, an end to the embargo. After the Hotel Pierre meeting, when the Cuban demand that the embargo be lifted immediately was rebuffed, Kissinger noted that "the Cubans didn't understand the idea of reciprocity—how to take small steps"; now, after a few months of thinking it over, however, they were indicating a willingness to accept the step-by-step U.S. approach by agreeing via Jones to meet on the narrow topic of family visits. There consequently is no small irony in the fact that after Cuba had turned its negotiating strategy on its head, the U.S. side adopted the original Cuban approach because the United States now had a big-ticket item to discuss, Cuban adventurism in Africa, on which, Rogers and Eagleburger assured Kissinger, "we will not move piecemeal."[127]

There the situation stood on 12 January 1976, two months after Angola's independence and Jones's message, when Cuba's García met Assistant Secretary Rogers at Washington's National Airport to discuss family visits. Reading from talking points, Rogers used the meeting to insist that Cuba's dispatch of troops to Angola had poisoned the atmosphere; García replied that he had come to talk about family visits and could add nothing to what Castro had already said publicly about Angola—that Cuba opposed colonialism and white-supremacist governments and was determined to support Africa's liberation movements. The meeting lasted forty-five minutes, and Rogers reported to Kissinger that "there was nothing in [García's] manner or in his words which betrayed a sensitivity to the recent developments in Angola." The assistant secretary added that Cuba may have decided "that there is little possibility of doing anything fundamental with the United States until after November. By then, it may reckon, the Angolan game will have been played out." Eagleburger and García held a follow-up meeting three weeks later in New York, this time focusing on family visits. As Eagleburger recorded the Cuban position, however, "Conditions are not favorable to starting a continued flow of visits to Cuba, much less the establishment of a regular airlift."[128]

By this time hope had evaporated, with Rogers recalling that although meetings continued in January and February 1976 "we had no sense that those discussions could lead to the kind of changes we had envisioned a year earlier." Characterizing Havana's position as "insolent," Kissinger wrote that "the curtain fell on meetings between the Cuban and American officials for the remainder of the Ford Administration." Years later, he blamed the failure of these secret meetings entirely on Castro, who, Kissinger asserted, "needed the United States as an enemy to justify his totalitarian grip on the country and to maintain military support from the Soviet Union."[129]

The secretary of state may have failed to notice that by 1976, Cuba had a new grievance—the renewal of armed attacks, with exiles shelling a Soviet freighter near Cuba in February and attacking two Cuban fishing boats in April. Havana responded by accusing the United States of harboring the assailants and reminding U.S. officials that the 1973 antihijacking agreement specifically required both countries to punish anyone engaged in terrorist attacks. Cuba's protest note indicated that the attacks "bear the unmistakable stamp of similar acts perpetrated from United States territory by bands of ex-Cubans" and "that in the past this type of attacks [*sic*] was inspired, organized, and protected by the CIA."[130]

Three days later, two Cuban diplomats were killed in Lisbon when a bomb exploded in the Cuban embassy, and on 30 April a Cuban American radio personality in Miami who had criticized the exile attacks lost both legs when a bomb destroyed his car. In mid-1976 an especially violent Cuban exile, Orlando Bosch, working under the aegis of a new Coordinating Committee of United Revolutionary Organizations (Coordinación de Organizaciones Revolucionarias Unidas [CORU]), launched a wave of terrorist bombings aimed at Cuba's overseas airline facilities—Jamaica on 9 July, Barbados on 10 July, and Panama on 18 August. Barbados was hit again on 6 October and this time, a bomb destroyed a Cubana airliner six minutes after takeoff, killing all seventy-three people aboard.

It was one of the saddest moments in Cuban history. Fifty-seven Cubans had been killed, including every member of the country's Olympic fencing team, along with eleven young Guyanese, six of whom were flying to Cuba to begin their medical studies. "Who, if not the CIA . . . is capable of such deeds?," asked a subdued President Castro at the Havana memorial service, tying the attacks to Angola: "Resentful of Cuba's contribution to the defeat the imperialists and racists suffered in Africa, in recent months the government of the United States has unleashed a series of terrorist actions against Cuba."[131]

Kissinger denied U.S. responsibility—"The charge by Fidel Castro that the United States or its government or any agency of the government had anything to do with the explosion of that airliner is totally false." But to accept or to dismiss this denial depends on an interpretation of Kissinger's phrase "anything to do with the explosion."[132] Did the United States plant the bomb? No. Did it support CORU, nominally based in Pinochet's Chile? Not in 1976—as CORU's Armando López Estrada told CBS's Bill Moyers, "Right now, we don't have the support of the United States government." But, López Estrada added, "we learned from them. We use the tactics that we learned from the CIA, because we—we were trained to do everything. We are trained to set off a bomb; we were trained to kill." And, he continued, if the United States now wanted to step aside, then "we have to do it for ourselves."[133]

As Castro had threatened, Cuba's response to the Barbados bombing was to abrogate the 1973 antihijacking accord, "and we will not again sign any such agreement with the United States until the terrorist campaign unleashed against Cuba is definitely ended."[134] On 7 November, five days after Jimmy Carter's election, another bomb destroyed the Cubana de Aviación office in Madrid.

Who has told the United States that the people of
Latin America cannot choose socialism? Who has
granted them the role of gendarme and tutor of our
destiny? Why do we have to accept as a model a
capitalist society that exploits the sweat of others, that
discriminates against blacks, exterminates Indians,
and denigrates Chicanos, Puerto Ricans, and other
Latins, that prostitutes women and sexually exploits
children—a society of violence, vice, alienation and
crime? Who can oblige us to live forever under an
egoistic, pitiless system condemned by history?
  —*Fidel Castro, January 1979*

There really is no way to bridge the gap between our
positions.
  —*Robert Pastor, December 1978*

10

RECONCILIATION
AND ESTRANGEMENT
THE CARTER YEARS

Cuba was not an issue in the 1976 campaign. There was nothing to argue about: both party platforms took similar swings at the Castro
government, both candidates opposed normalizing relations, and both
ignored Cuba in the three presidential debates.[1] And as with Cuba, so with
most other policy issues. Pollsters reported that the contest involved "character"—that the always crucial moderates who had voted for Lyndon Johnson in 1964 and then switched to Richard Nixon in 1968 were looking for
a president who knew the difference between right and wrong and whose
administration would be based on simple honesty. Democratic challenger
Jimmy Carter succeeded in focusing the campaign on just that issue, attacking arrogant, cynical manipulators—out-of-touch politicians who
earned praise for adding the word "détente" to the everyday vocabulary but
then threw it away by adding a second unfamiliar word, "Watergate."

It was clearly not a good time to be either a Republican or a Washington
insider, and Gerald Ford was both. A member of Congress since 1948, he
was as moderate as Carter at a time when his party was moving to the right
under the prodding of California governor Ronald Reagan, who had picked

up the conservative banner dropped by Barry Goldwater in 1964. In 1976, Reagan was demonstrating that a Hollywood actor could claim the White House, but his victory did not come until 1980; now, voters had to choose between President Ford and challenger Jimmy Carter, both of whom appeared decent if wooden. In addition, Carter sometimes seemed a bit too pious, but no one questioned his intelligence—a problem for Ford—and when Carter confessed to a *Playboy* interviewer that he occasionally experienced lust in his heart, polls showed that voters applauded his honesty, probably because they could bet the farm he would never do anything more than think about it.[2]

During the campaign Carter criticized the realpolitik that for the past eight years had been guiding U.S. policy to support Latin America's most brutal dictators, promising that "we will once again be a beacon light for human rights throughout the world," although he then added, "I do not wish to see us swing from one extreme of cynical manipulation to the other extreme of moralistic zeal."[3] With little said about Cuba during the campaign, the best indicator of the new administration's policy appeared in the two reports issued by the private Commission on U.S.-Latin American Relations, chaired by the corporate attorney who had been LBJ's ambassador to the Organization of American States (OAS), Sol Linowitz. The commission's 1974 report, issued just after Nixon's resignation, had argued that isolating Cuba had failed to advance U.S. interests, and an update issued immediately after Carter's election urged the incoming administration to "take the initiative in launching a sequence of reciprocal actions" leading to a normalization of relations. Suggested steps included a White House condemnation of terrorist attacks by Cuban exiles and a partial lifting of the embargo to permit sales of food and medicine in the hope that Cuba would reciprocate by withdrawing its troops from Angola, by ceasing to carp on the issue of Puerto Rican independence, and by releasing U.S. citizens held in Cuban jails.[4] The Linowitz Commission's staff director, Robert Pastor, became the NSC's principal Latin Americanist.

Pastor aroused the suspicion of traditional cold warriors such as General William Odom, on loan to the NSC from the Pentagon, who considered him excessively liberal ("He was left—way, way left"), which may have been true at the time on some issues, such as the all-consuming Panama Canal treaties. A young political scientist, Pastor aged toward the center, and on Cuba he kept moving rightward after he had reached the ideological midpoint. By 1980, even Fidel Castro chided the visiting NSC staffer: "We keep hearing that Pastor is the real hardliner in the Administration," to which

Pastor replied, "Perhaps you hear that because . . . my own views on Cuba have changed, and I have been disappointed and disillusioned."[5]

WHAT HAPPENED? A good place to begin is with the administration's internal ideological disputes, which were most clearly reflected in bureaucratic politics. The new secretary of state, Cyrus Vance, had far more Washington experience than anyone in the White House. In the late 1950s, he had taken leave from Wall Street to serve as counsel to the Senate Armed Services preparedness subcommittee, and when JFK was elected, Vance had moved to Robert McNamara's Pentagon, becoming a champion of Operation Mongoose: at one point, Vance proposed a sabotage attack on a Matanzas power plant; on another occasion, he developed a twenty-five-step plan to harass U.S. citizens who traveled to Cuba. But Vietnam, not Cuba, became the defining issue for Vance's generation, and in 1968 he had been one of the "Wise Men" who went public with their advice to end the bombing and begin negotiating with Hanoi. Years later, when a reporter asked how he would like to be remembered, Vance replied, "For being a reasonably decent, honest person."[6] That he was.

And so undoubtedly was national security adviser Zbigniew Brzezinski, who shared Vance's long history of opposing the Cuban Revolution—in 1962, the future national security adviser had referred to Fidel Castro as "a reckless Cuban Fuehrer" and called the continuation of his communist government "a humiliation." But as President Carter soon discovered, Vance and Brzezinski deadlocked almost immediately over the central question of how to handle Cuba's involvement in Africa. Seeking the "sequence of reciprocal actions" mentioned by the Linowitz Commission, Brzezinski's National Security Council (NSC) staff insisted on a linkage between normalization and Cuba's withdrawal, while Vance's State Department preferred to treat Africa as just one of many issues to be negotiated.[7]

Historian Nancy Mitchell, the most thorough student of the Vance-Brzezinski relationship, was undoubtedly correct to conclude that the differences between the two men were greatly overstated; that said, the bumping occasionally became unusually rough during the Carter years, and it seemed to reflect a fundamental difference in worldviews.[8] A political science professor cut from the same bolt of cloth as Henry Kissinger, Brzezinski brought an exceptionally narrow Cold War perspective to nearly every policy dispute, and in the case of Cuba this approach invariably meant interpreting moves by the Castro government as evidence of Soviet intentions: "Castro is a puppet of the Soviet Union," he told reporters, "and we view him as such."[9] In sharp contrast, Vance viewed Castro's motivation as a question to be explored rather than assumed. The secretary of state tended to take up each new issue as a lawyer would, by establishing the facts, by seeking to determine how those facts might affect his client's interests, and by identifying a strategy to protect them, while Brzezinski simply dropped a Cold War template atop whatever the issue of the day might be, at the same time criticizing Vance for not having such a template: Vance, Brzezinski wrote in his diary, "doesn't like to think in broader conceptual terms." Brzezinski's mind, in contrast, was welded shut by one broad concept—Wayne Smith, the State Department's principal Cuba specialist, noted that "whatever the Soviets or Cubans did, Brzezinski believed that they were 'testing' us."[10]

Over his four-year tenure, President Carter grew ever closer to the hardline Cold War views of his national security adviser, and Smith correctly noted that on Cuba policy, "the NSC was always a large part of the problem, constantly putting logs in the road."[11] In expanding his influence, Brzezinski was assisted by the nation's domestic political winds, which filled his Cold War sails—from mid-1977 onward, a hard-line approach to international relations clearly went over better with the U.S. public than did Secretary Vance's emphasis on negotiation and compromise, and by mid-1979 Brzezinski was not alone in warning the president that his responses to Cuba's policies in Africa and elsewhere "are almost certain to be an important foreign policy campaign issue in 1980." The Cubans did not miss this state of affairs: "There are two policy lines in the U.S. leadership now," a high-ranking Cuban official told a Soviet diplomat late in 1979. "In the last several months the Brzezinski line took over."[12]

Brzezinski was also aided by the Cuban Americans who were emerging as a significant political force in a rapidly growing Florida, which now had seventeen electoral votes, up from eight in Harry Truman's day. Alfredo Durán, a Bay of Pigs veteran, had been elected chair of the state's Democratic Party, and from the beginning he and other exiles had buttressed Brzezinski's hard-line views by taking issue with the second Linowitz Report, telling reporters that détente with Cuba "would be a tremendous mistake." In early 1977 Durán was one of seven Cuban Americans who flew to Washington to oppose normalizing relations. Puerto Rico–born Miami mayor Maurice Ferré, the first Hispanic to serve as chief executive of a major U.S. city, wrote to President Carter to say the same thing, as did Fidel Castro's sister: "I have chosen liberty, Christianity and patriotism over slavery, atheism and treason. You, Mr. President, must now choose how your name will go down in history." Eisenhower-era ambassador Earl E. T. Smith also weighed in with an apocalyptic warning, insisting to the new president that "it is our duty and obligation to prevent the entire Caribbean from becoming a red lake. To coddle Castro means further surrender to Communist imperialism." At the same time, Florida's ever-alert citrus growers voiced their opposition to any change that might lead to competition from Cuba, and several of the holders of certified claims wrote to insist that a fair financial settlement had to precede normalization of relations.[13]

It is difficult to determine precisely how much this opposition—and especially the rising Cuban American political clout—affected the Carter administration's policy toward Cuba, but at a minimum it slowed those who were supporting normalization. At one of his first strategy sessions with Brzezinski and Vance, the newly inaugurated president instructed the secretary of state to consult with Durán, and from that point forward, the Carter archives are dotted with discussions about how to use U.S. policy toward Cuba to bolster the administration's standing among Florida's Cuban American community.[14]

Vance remained in the State Department saddle for more than three years, resigning only when the president rejected Vance's advice and went ahead with the ill-fated effort to rescue the U.S. embassy personnel being held hostage in Iran. On Cuba, however, the secretary lost a key argument almost immediately when Carter sided with Brzezinski on the crucial question of whether Fidel Castro was Moscow's puppet: four months into his presidency, Carter publicly referred to Cuba as "a client state" of the Soviet Union.[15] Fidel Castro took the first opportunity (a visit by Senator Frank Church) to reply that "Cuba was in no way acting as a proxy for the Russians," and U.S. policy documents occasionally reflected this view: a mid-1978 presidential review memorandum concluded, for example, that "Cuba is not involved in Africa solely or even primarily because of its relationship with the USSR. Rather, Havana's African policy reflects its activist revolutionary ethos and its determination to expand its own political influence in the Third World at the expense of the West." The NSC's Pastor also tried to alter the administration's thinking: "Let me suggest that we try to use a different term to refer to the Cubans other than 'Soviet puppet,'" he wrote, trying to convince Brzezinski. "The word 'puppet' suggests that the Cubans are engaging in revolutionary activities because the Soviets have instructed them to do so. That, of course, is not the case." The one U.S.-based scholar who knew best took the same view: "Never in my thirteen years of research

on Cuban foreign policy," wrote Piero Gleijeses, "have I encountered one instance in which the Cubans allowed the Soviets to push them around."[16]

Gleijeses was not asked for his opinion, however, and Pastor's suggestion
was ignored. Trying to identify the balance of opinion about Africa during
the Carter years, CIA/NSC staffer Paul Henze recalled that "Cubans were
seen entirely as Soviet proxies. . . . The Cubans in many ways from the Washington point of view looked like ideal mercenaries, the men the Soviets
could use for any purpose they chose." President Carter's Special Coordination Committee, chaired by Brzezinski, reached the same rough consensus:
Havana and Moscow "have developed a potent combination: Cuban troops
(whose introduction into trouble spots implies fewer risks and who swim
better in a Third-World sea) backed by Soviet wherewithal." After President
Carter had accepted this position, he kept it: "It is obvious that Castro is a
puppet of the Soviet Union," he wrote in 1979, at the same time the White
House prepared a statement that "Cuba has become increasingly dependent on the Soviet Union and, at the same time, increasingly an instrument
of Soviet foreign policy, directed and controlled from Moscow."[17]

Other disagreements soon surfaced, but the new administration at first
had no firm Cuba policy. Vance failed to mention the country in the statement prepared for his confirmation hearing, and when asked his view, he
replied with a line from the Linowitz Commission: "If Cuba is willing to live
within the international system, then we ought to seek ways to find whether
we can eliminate the impediments which exist between us and try to move
toward normalization." Did "living within the international system" mean
removing troops from Africa? That issue was joined five days after Carter's
inauguration, when U.S. ambassador to the United Nations Andrew Young
told CBS News that "there's a sense in which the Cubans bring a certain
stability and order to Angola." Young's comment may have been accurate:
asked about the remark while appearing before a House committee, one
of the nation's few experts on Angola replied, "I do not even think it is a
question of agreeing. It is such an obvious fact that for anybody to deny it
indicates that the person does not appreciate the realities of Angola." Accurate or not, it was not U.S. policy, and the State Department quickly took
exception, pointing out that "neither Ambassador Young nor the Secretary
of State condones the presence of Cuban troops in Angola."[18]

No one wanted to start off the first week with a fight, however, and Secretary Vance deftly threaded a verbal needle at his first major press conference, indicating that Cuba's troop deployment in Angola was "not helpful"
but specifically rejecting the Ford administration's position that Cuba's

withdrawal from Angola was a precondition to negotiations. "I don't want to set any pre-conditions," he said. But a few days later President Carter made a get-acquainted visit to the Department of Agriculture, where someone in his audience asked about Cuba and the president responded by ticking off an entire list of preconditions: "I would very much like to see the Cubans remove their soldiers from Angola," he began, and "if I can be convinced that Cuba wants to remove their aggravating influence from other countries in this hemisphere, will not participate in violence in nations across the oceans, will recommit [to] the former relationship that existed in Cuba toward human rights, then I would be willing to move toward normalizing relationships."[19]

Vance tried to smooth over Carter's statement, telling reporters that "there was some misunderstanding with respect to some remarks which he made at the Agriculture Department as to whether or not they were preconditions to talks." The president, Vance continued, had simply been indicating "that those were important subjects that would have to be discussed in any meeting which we might have with the Cubans." Thus reminded of the need to be careful, Carter was ready the next day when the question arose a second time:

> I would like to do what I can to ease tensions with Cuba. It's only 90 miles, as you know, from the Florida coast. And I don't know yet what we will do. Before any full normalization of relationships can take place, though, Cuba would have to make some fairly substantial changes in their attitude. I would like to insist, for instance, that they not interfere in the internal affairs of countries in this hemisphere, and that they decrease their military involvement in Africa, and that they reinforce a commitment to human rights by releasing political prisoners that have been in jail now for 17 or 18 years, things of that kind.

But, he quickly added, "the preconditions that I describe would be prior to full normalization," not prior to preliminary talks. "You couldn't possibly arrive at a solution to some of those questions without discussions."[20]

However qualified it may have been, President Carter's Department of Agriculture comment clearly indicated that the initial balance within the administration favored the thinking of the Linowitz Commission, and in mid-March the president made it official: "I have concluded that we should attempt to achieve normalization of our relations with Cuba," began a secret presidential directive. "To this end, we should begin direct and confidential talks in a measured and careful fashion with representatives of the Government of Cuba. Our objective is to set in motion a process which will lead to the reestablishment of diplomatic relations." The next day Secretary Vance informed Congress that the administration had already halted aerial reconnaissance overflights of Cuba. "That pleases us," Castro told ABC News reporter Barbara Walters. "We appreciate that gesture."[21]

A real bombshell had come six days earlier, when the president surprised everyone by ending the prohibition on travel to Cuba. This prohibition had existed in one form or another since the final days of the Eisenhower administration, when the president had issued Public Notice 179 declaring U.S. passports invalid for travel to Cuba unless specifically validated by the Department of State.[22] At the time, it was unclear whether the government had the authority to issue such a notice, and the State Department soon triggered a test case by refusing to validate Louis Zemel's passport so that he could use it "to satisfy my curiosity about the state of affairs in Cuba and to make me a better informed citizen." After the case wound its way through the lower courts, the Supreme Court decided in 1965 that Zemel had not provided a sufficiently good reason. Unlike its 1958 ruling in *Kent v. Dulles*, where the Court found that the executive branch had exceeded its statutory power by denying Rockwell Kent a passport because of his political beliefs (he was a communist), Zemel had been denied permission "not because of any characteristic peculiar to appellant, but rather because of foreign policy considerations affecting all citizens." Absent any discrimination against Zemel, the Court ruled that his constitutional right to freedom of movement was not absolute, just as the right to free speech did not permit citizens to shout "Fire!" in a crowded theater; specifically, the Court upheld the ban on travel to Cuba as "supported by the weightiest considerations of national security."[23]

The matter did not end there, however. In 1963, two years before the *Zemel* ruling, the Department of Justice had triggered another test case by confiscating the passports of a group of fifty-eight students as they returned from a visit to Cuba and by filing a criminal indictment against the trip's organizers, including Lee Levi Laub, a twenty-four-year-old black political activist, and others whom McGeorge Bundy's aide, Gordon Chase, described as "the real culprits in this whole travel-to-Cuba operation . . . a pretty unsavory bunch." That they may have been, but unlike Zemel, who had sued the federal government because he had been denied permission to travel to Cuba, the students had already made the trip without permission, so the government had to take the initiative, charging the trip's organizers with failing to have their passports validated for travel to Cuba.

Laub's attorney argued that Congress had never written a law authorizing the government to validate passports, and a lower court agreed, dismissing Laub's indictment. In 1967 the Supreme Court denied the government's appeal.[24]

In his policy-defining December 1963 meeting on Cuba, President Johnson had decided on "a policy of selective prosecution." This approach did not deter everyone, however, and a few months later Bundy wrote to LBJ that "every time holiday season rolls around, we face the problem of dealing with American students who want to go to Cuba in violation of our travel controls." Attorney General Robert Kennedy apparently agreed, asking Arthur Schlesinger Jr., "What's wrong with that? If I were 22 years old, that is certainly the place I would want to visit. I don't see how we can prosecute every student who wants to see Cuba." Noting that there were two schools of thought about what to do, with RFK's Department of Justice favoring relaxation and others favoring continued controls, Bundy asked LBJ to select an option. Johnson checked the box next to "I do not want a relaxation of controls," and then wrote in longhand: "I am of the *second* school, and so was JFK."[25]

Unwilling, therefore, to give up even in the wake of the 1967 *Laub* defeat, the Johnson administration replaced Eisenhower's Public Notice 179 (which had simply declared U.S. passports invalid for travel to Cuba) with an elaborate effort to place the travel ban under the *Zemel v. Rusk* "national security" umbrella. Johnson officials did so by rewriting the appropriate section of the Code of Federal Regulations to permit the secretary of state to require a specifically endorsed passport in any case where travel "would seriously impair the conduct of U.S. foreign affairs." To make this new regulation operative for Cuba, the administration then issued Public Notice 257, which stated that "unrestricted travel to or through Cuba would seriously impair the conduct of U.S. foreign affairs."[26]

But that approach also failed. In late 1967, the U.S. Court of Appeals for the District of Columbia ruled that the new regulations were valid but applied only to travel involving the use of a U.S. passport—that is, U.S. citizens could go to Cuba but could not present their passports to Cuban authorities.[27] When Jimmy Carter launched his drive for the presidency in the mid-1970s, "The Secretary of State is without power to impose any criminal sanctions against an American citizen who travels to Cuba without a special validation of his passport," wrote the head of the U.S. Passport Office. "Where the U.S. passport is not used . . . there would be no violation of U.S. law."[28]

The Carter administration therefore did not inherit a ban on travel to Cuba—the courts had ruled in *Zemel v. Rusk* that the government could restrict travel when "supported by the weightiest considerations of national security" but that freedom of movement could not be denied without due process of law and that Congress had never passed a law on which to base that due process.* Rather than attempt to have such a law passed, the Kennedy, Johnson, Nixon, and Ford administrations had turned instead to the obscure Trading with the Enemy Act, which allows the president, after first declaring a national emergency, to prohibit U.S. citizens from spending money in any specifically designated country. Passed in 1917 when the United States entered World War I, the law was intended to prohibit transfers by U.S. nationals to German nationals—everything from stopping German Americans from mailing sausages to hungry relatives to stopping U.S. firms from sending royalty payments to German firms for their manufacturing patents. When the war ended, a congressional joint resolution repealed nearly all the laws associated with the conflict, but not the Trading with the Enemy Act, which succeeding administrations continued to use for a variety of purposes.

The most notable use came with the very first law passed by the Congress elected in 1932 along with FDR, which expanded the president's ability to use the act not simply in time of war but also "during any other period of national emergency declared by the President," an amendment that enabled the new administration to regulate international financial flows during the 1933 Banking Holiday and throughout the depression.[29] Another national emergency was declared in December 1941, immediately after Pearl Harbor, and yet another when China entered the Korean War in 1950. That conflict had ended with a truce in 1953, but unlike World Wars I and II, the end of the shooting in Korea did not signal an end to the Cold War, so President Truman's national emergency was never terminated. In mid-1963, then, the Kennedy administration merely had to cite the Trading with the Enemy Act as its authority to issue Regulation 201(b) as part of the Cuban Assets Control Regulations, which forbid all unlicensed financial transactions between Cuba and U.S. nationals.[30]

---

* In *Kent et al. v. Dulles* (357 U.S. 116, June 1958), the Court had ruled that "freedom of movement is basic to our scheme of values" and that the laws governing the issuance of passports "do not delegate to the Secretary [of State] authority to withhold passports to citizens because of their beliefs or associations, and any Act of Congress purporting to do so would raise grave constitutional questions."

Because it was designed to control financial flows, the Trading with the Enemy Act was administered by the Department of the Treasury, and in 1976, just before Jimmy Carter's election, a department official told Congress that "we have no jurisdiction in Treasury over travel per se. We do not attempt to control travel itself; we only attempt to control the financial side of travel, the payment to Cuba. If a businessman goes without making any payment to a Cuban national there's nothing we can do about it."[31] But travelers could not pay for a Cuban visa, a Cuban taxi ride from the airport, a Cuban hotel, a Cuban meal, a Cuban telephone call, a Cuban anything. Everyone understood that this was simple legal legerdemain—the use of an antiquated law to achieve an end (a travel ban) that the courts would otherwise not permit under the Constitution—but it worked: for the dozen years prior to President Carter's election, only those few U.S. nationals whose trips were fully funded by the Cuban government could legally set foot on the island.[32]

But this strategy worked imperfectly. In the Ford administration's final days, the secretary of the treasury was informed about a Canadian firm's ads in major U.S. newspapers offering all-inclusive tours of Cuba prepaid to the firm, not Cuba. The firm was clearly seeking "to induce Americans to visit Cuba in violation of United States laws," and the memo's author suggested ordering U.S. banks to refuse to deal with the offending firm. Treasury Secretary William Simon had thirteen days left in office, however, and nothing was done.[33]

Then came the Carter administration. It decided to place its reassessment of the Cuba travel ban in the broader context of the 1975 Helsinki accords, which had called for greater respect for human rights and specifically mentioned the goal of increased travel and communications between East and West. Most U.S. citizens thought of this as a Western attempt to nudge the Soviet Union and its allies toward greater freedom for their "captive people" and toward generally greater contact with the noncommunist world, but at an early March press conference, President Carter surprised everyone by announcing that he was also "assessing our own nation's policies that violate human rights as defined by the Helsinki agreement. . . . I want to be sure that we don't violate those rights." In fact, he had already concluded the assessment and, he continued, the one place where the United States was clearly open to criticism was in the Trading with the Enemy Act's restrictions on citizens' freedom of movement. He therefore instructed the secretary of the treasury to end the ban on travel not only to Cuba but also to Vietnam, Cambodia, and North Korea. For Cuba, the

Cuban Assets Control Regulations were revised to permit "persons who visit Cuba to pay for their transportation and maintenance expenditures."[34]

U.S. citizens were now free to visit Cuba for the first time in sixteen years, and within a month, a delegation of fifty-two Minnesota business leaders, including executives of General Mills, Pillsbury, Control Data, and Honeywell, were knocking on doors in Havana, looking for new customers. Within a year, more than four hundred U.S. companies had sent sales representatives to Cuba, a shipping line had begun testing the market for weeklong cruises between New Orleans and Havana, and, since the floodgates appeared to be about to open, the Treasury Department had revised its regulations to permit travel agents to arrange transportation and to permit travelers to use personal checks, travelers checks, and credit cards in Cuba. "We have no problems or complaints with respect to any of that?," asked an incredulous Miami representative Dante Fascell. "No, we do not," replied the Carter administration's assistant secretary of state.[35]

AS TRAVELERS (especially Cuban Americans) began making their reservations, President Carter publicly announced that he was exploring "whether relations with Cuba can be improved on a measured and a reciprocal basis." This statement did not go unnoticed in Cuba, and in addition to expressing his appreciation for Carter's decision to end surveillance overflights, Fidel Castro now commended the new president as a man with "a sense of morals," and he assured a visiting Senator George McGovern that Cuba would continue to cooperate with the United States to end aircraft hijacking.[36] Two months later, the State Department informed Cubans of an impending terrorist attack, and Cuba responded with a thank-you note. Robert Pastor also argued for a public statement against terrorism "to dispel the pervasive feeling that the [U.S. government] is not taking action against the Cuban exiles." The Cubans clearly had difficulty believing that the new U.S. administration represented a decisive break from the past. After all, Castro told Barbara Walters, the CIA was probably still up to its old tricks, a remark that prompted her chiding reply: "I sometimes think that you feel everything, everything comes back to the CIA." "I am not the only one," Castro shot back. "Everybody here thinks about the CIA. . . . The CIA has made plans to assassinate the leaders of the revolution for more than 10 years, and you don't want me to think about the CIA?"[37]

But skeptical Cubans probably saw the fundamental question not as whether the CIA was still plotting assassination but whether Jimmy Carter or any other president had the political capital (and a willingness to invest it) to accommodate the Cuban Revolution. The central indicator was clearly the embargo. During the 1974–75 Ford-Kissinger rapprochement, Castro had insisted that the reconciliation process had to begin with a unilateral U.S. decision to end the trade embargo—"the blockade is, for us, a knife in the throat, which creates a negotiating situation which we will never accept." He reiterated that position in early 1977: just days after Carter lifted the travel ban, Castro commented that "the United States maintains a blockade against Cuba. We don't have a blockade against the United States. The United States has a naval base on our soil by force; we don't have any naval base in U.S. territory. The United States promoted attacks and subversion against our country—the mercenary invasions. We haven't organized subversion against or sent mercenary invaders to the United States. They are the ones who must stop this kind of operation; they must lift the blockade and this kind of activity against Cuba." President Carter responded that Castro's insistence on an immediate end to the embargo "is something that he is not likely to achieve."[38]

But Castro continued to insist. When asked in late 1978 about "the minimum necessary for there to be a dialogue," he replied, "An end to the economic blockade." Privately, however, the Cuban leadership had apparently decided to live with the embargo while discussing other issues of mutual concern, one of which was a new U.S. law, the Fishery Conservation and Management Act of 1976, that had unilaterally created a U.S. fishery conservation zone extending two hundred miles from shore.[39] As Congress had been considering this law to protect the U.S. fishing industry and to conserve offshore fishing resources, Cuba had been investing heavily in its fishing industry, and by the mid-1970s Cuban boats were regularly fishing just outside the twelve-mile U.S. limit. "We have historical rights to fish in those seas," Castro insisted, but without a formal bilateral agreement, the new U.S. law conflicted with that right—if it existed. Further complicating the matter, Cuba had initially responded by claiming its own two-hundred-mile limit. Since only ninety miles of water separate the two countries, a maritime boundary was now needed.

On 12 January 1977, the outgoing Ford administration informed the Cuban government that in six weeks the United States would require a permit to fish within the newly extended zone, and the Cubans waited only a few days after Carter's inauguration to approach the United States (via the Swiss) on both the fishing and boundary issues. The State Department responded by sending its director of Cuban affairs, Culver Gleysteen, to meet with the first secretary of the Cuban mission to the United Nations, Nestor

García. After the two men hammered out the procedures to be followed, their governments began six days of intensive negotiations in late March in New York. The talks then recessed so that the negotiators could consult with senior officials, and in late April they resumed in Havana, where agreement was quickly reached on two formal documents.

The agreement on fishing began by stating what the 1976 law required: Each year, the U.S. government would determine both the total sustainable catch off U.S. shores and the "harvesting capacity" of U.S. fishing vessels; officials would then allocate the excess among the various nations of the world. The new agreement then stipulated that in making this allocation, the U.S. government would take into consideration "the need to minimize economic dislocation in cases where vessels of the Republic of Cuba have habitually fished." The agreement on a maritime boundary was more precise: reached by splitting the ocean between the United States and Cuba, it was a list of seventeen coordinates tracking the midpoint between the two nations' coasts, beginning immediately south of Florida's Marathon Key and running westward into the Gulf of Mexico; the boundary became a line connecting the coordinates.[40]

In announcing the two agreements, Assistant Secretary of State Terence Todman promised further progress—a hint of additional discussions that led to a June agreement to open "interests sections" in one another's capitals. In strictly formal terms, this third agreement stipulated that the government of Switzerland would open a "U.S. Interests Section" within the Swiss embassy in Havana, while the government of Czechoslovakia would open a "Cuban Interests Section" within the Czech embassy in Washington; the human beings operating these interests sections would not be Swiss and Czech, however, but U.S. and Cuban, and they would work in the modern U.S. embassy on Havana's Malecón and the stately Cuban embassy on Washington's Sixteenth Street, a few blocks from the White House. Both buildings had been consigned to Swiss and Czech caretakers since early 1961.[41]

BY THIS TIME Carter's honeymoon with Cuba was nearly over. The problem was Africa. The Carter campaign had characterized Cuba's decision to send combat forces to Angola as "regrettable" but had argued that it "need not constitute a threat to U.S. interests," and U.N. ambassador Andrew Young had gone a step further with his assertion that Cuba was a stabilizing factor in that strife-torn country. But the Pentagon was worried that "Castro is establishing an infrastructure in Angola that could sup-

Angola and Zaire

port further military operations elsewhere in southern Africa," and a few weeks after Carter's inauguration, a group of Angola-based Zairean rebels launched a drive into Zaire's Katanga province, now renamed Shaba. That action caused President Carter to begin to retract what he had said during the campaign.[42]

As with many such disputes, the Shaba conflict had its genesis in the land swaps common among late-nineteenth-century European imperialists—exchanges so casual that they became the object of after-dinner jesting by a British prime minister, Lord Salisbury, who told a London banquet audience in 1890, "We have been giving away mountains and rivers and lakes to each other, but we have only been hindered by the small impediment that we never knew exactly where those mountains and rivers and lakes were."[43] In the case of Shaba, the pre-independence borders drawn by European colonizers had split the Lunda people among three countries—Angola, Zambia, and the Katanga/Shaba region of Zaire, a country three times the size of Texas.

In 1960, only weeks after the multiethnic Zaire (today's Democratic Republic of the Congo) had secured its independence from Belgium, Katangans led by Moise Tshombe announced their succession, which the central government of President Joseph Kasavubu and Prime Minister Patrice Lumumba resisted. Although the fighting did not stop completely when Tshombe's forces capitulated in 1963, it did subside dramatically a year later, when he became the Congo's prime minister. His tenure was brief, however—in 1965, Tshombe was overthrown by General Joseph Mobutu, who dissolved the civilian government, assumed all legislative and executive powers, and triggered the flight of about 250,000 Katangans across the border into Angola. That number included roughly 20,000 to 30,000 soldiers identified by Western journalists as "Kantangan gendarmes," and these fighters sought to retake Shaba in early March 1977, just as President Carter was ordering an effort to normalize relations with Cuba.[44]

The dispute involved substantially more than ethnic considerations, for mineral-rich Shaba was the heart of the Zairean economy, producing two-thirds of the world's cobalt, a third of the world's industrial diamonds, and 7 percent of the world's copper. As Undersecretary of State George Ball had told JFK years earlier, the United States consumed three-fourths of this cobalt, plus the lion's share of Zaire's diamonds and copper. The situation remained much the same during Jimmy Carter's time, when Representative Don Bonker, a liberal Democrat with a special interest in Africa, explained to his colleagues why the United States needed to back Zaire's dictator: "There are important minerals at stake." President Carter's CIA director recalled being similarly worried because "Cuban mercenaries in Angola stirred up tribal warfare in the copper- and cobalt-producing region of Zaire."[45]

The Cold War concern over access to strategic minerals thus became entwined, willy-nilly, with a long-standing ethnic dispute in an unfamiliar corner of Africa *and* with the budding U.S.-Cuban détente. The Cubans went out of their way to deny involvement. Cornering a visiting French journalist, Fidel Castro insisted that "Cuba is not in any way involved in the events in Zaire. . . . There is not a single Cuban instructor in Zaire. There is not a single Cuban soldier in Zaire. There is no Cuban presence in Zaire. . . . We did not participate in either the training, equipping or formation of the revolutionary forces that began the struggle in Shaba." He said the same thing a few days later to ABC's Barbara Walters, and he sent vice president Carlos Rafael Rodríguez to New York to reiterate his message in person to a skeptical secretary of state. Cyrus Vance told Rodríguez that the United States had good information to the contrary, but, as Vance later admitted, the evidence was "ambiguous and, as it turned out, not very good."[46]

In fact, it was wrong, as Piero Gleijeses has demonstrated. In addition, according to a declassified German document containing the verbatim minutes of a 1977 meeting between Fidel Castro and East German premier Erich Honecker, Castro reported that the Katangans "went off in four different directions with four battalions. We didn't know about this, and we think that the Angolans didn't either."[47]

U.S. officials were not privy to that conversation, but after a week of looking at the evidence, they began distancing themselves from the charge of Cuban involvement. Secretary Vance took the lead, admitting that "we have no hard information that there are others than the Kantangan gendarmes with the group. There have been rumors of Cubans being with them. We have no hard evidence." President Carter told reporters the same thing a few days later, but he did so after announcing two million dollars in emergency military aid to Mobutu's mineral-rich dictatorship; a few days later, Carter told reporters that the U.S. was also supporting the French and Moroccan troops fighting alongside Mobutu's forces.[48] The United States then offered Mobutu an additional $15 million in "nonlethal" military assistance, which Secretary Vance made a valiant effort to justify to Congress, some of whose members wondered whether this was simply an attempt to circumvent the prohibition on aid to the warring factions in next-door Angola. A suspicious boost had already occurred in U.S. military aid to Mobutu (from $3.5 million in fiscal 1975, when Congress stopped aid to Angola, to $32.5 million in fiscal 1978), and some of that increase almost certainly had found its way into the coffers of Holden Roberto's FNLA. A suspicious Representative Bonker noted, "I have always felt that we were compensating President Joseph Mobutu for his material support of Holden Roberto," and in his 1995 memoir, General Colin Powell wrote, "We had our uses for Mobutu, in this case, to funnel arms to anticommunist rebels in Angola."[49]

To this $32.5 million, President Carter now proposed adding the new $15 million package of "nonlethal" military aid. Characterizing the increase as "very modest," the president struggled to explain away Mobutu's brutality: "I know that there are some problems in Zaire with human rights as there are here and in many other countries. But our friendship and aid historically for Zaire has not been predicated on their perfection in dealing with human rights." It was one of Carter's least-convincing performances and, to human rights activists, one of his most disappointing, and it gave Fidel Castro the opportunity to comment that the United States was "talking with amazing hypocrisy about human rights."[50]

After three hard-fought months, the Shaba conflict ended with the dispersal of the Katangan rebels, but that closed only the first chapter in the saga of Cuban activities in Africa during the Carter years. As the conflict was ending, Castro told Walters that Western aid to Zaire was "why we have stopped the program of evacuation of Cuban military personnel from Angola, because we have more than justified reasons to believe that behind all this could be an ulterior plan of aggression against Angola." That country, of course, was a source of Cuban pride—in 1976, Castro had told cheering Cubans that "when, on the 27th of March, the last South African soldiers, after a retreat of 700 kilometers, crossed the border back into Namibia, one of the most brilliant pages had been written in the liberation of black Africa."[51] Candidate Carter's Africa position paper had taken a different view—it had accused both Cuba and the Soviet Union of "cynical racism and violence" in Angola, but during the campaign he repeatedly argued that Africa was something more than a Cold War battleground, criticizing the Ford-Kissinger policy for allowing Cuba to seize the racial high ground: "We clung to the Portuguese until the last minute, and had no working relationship with the Angolan people. We let the Soviet Union and Cuba preempt us in the minds of the natives."[52]

Cuba was not relaxing on a bed of Angolan roses, however. Although direct U.S. involvement had ended in 1975 at Congress's insistence, Agostinho Neto's government had continued to face a daunting array of challenges from internal opponents (a May 1977 coup attempt led by Interior Minister Nito Alves), from South Africa, from U.S.-assisted Zaire, from Holden Roberto's Zaire-assisted FNLA, from Jonas Savimbi's UNITA (supported by both South Africa and Zaire), and from a small but worrisome group of separatists in Angola's oil-rich Cabinda province. Neto's MPLA government probably could not have survived this multifront challenge without the help of thirty-six thousand Cuban troops and military instructors, and it certainly could not simultaneously have opened military training camps, as it did, for national liberation movements from Rhodesia, South Africa, and Namibia.[53]

Nonetheless, Cubans optimistically planned that MPLA forces would take over all battlefield operations, assisted by a much smaller number of Cuban advisers and a strong cadre of military instructors. In April 1976, Raúl Castro traveled to Luanda to discuss the timing of Cuba's withdrawal, and a year later Fidel Castro told East Germany's Erich Honecker, "We are reducing our troop strength continuously. This year we plan to leave 15,000 men stationed there. By the end of 1978 there should be only 7,000," most of them instructors. But, a worried Castro continued, his Angolan allies were not doing well on the battlefield: "The Defense Ministry is doing hardly anything to fight bandits in the north and south of the country. . . . An army general staff does not really exist. The country may have 70,000 men under arms but the army is practically not organized."[54]

Cuba's withdrawal stopped soon thereafter, probably because, as the NSC's Pastor wrote, "the whole situation changed with the invasion of Shaba province in March. The consequent introduction of Moroccan troops and the threat of counter-invasion caused Neto to ask the Cubans to reverse the flow and start sending Cuban troops back to Africa. This they did." Then in May came the unsuccessful but deadly Alves coup—seven MPLA Central Committee members were killed—an event, Pastor continued, that "doubtless helped accelerate Cuban troops [*sic*] movements back to Angola." By mid-1978 more than five thousand Cubans had returned. At the same time, Fidel Castro made it clear that Cuba was determined both to preserve the Neto government and to use Angola as the hub of its support of Africa's other liberation movements, even at the cost of halting rapprochement with the Carter administration. "The United States is reportedly willing to improve relations with Cuba," Castro told reporters during his March 1977 visit to Tanzania, which occurred two weeks after the Shaba crisis began. "Sometimes they mention conditions. To cite just one example, they say we must stop giving our solidarity to the revolutionary movements in Africa. We feel that these issues are not matters for negotiation."[55]

Castro then flew to East Germany, where he told Honecker not only that "the liberation struggle in Africa has a great future" but also that it "is the most moral thing in existence. If the socialist states take the right positions, they could gain a lot of influence. Here is where we can strike heavy blows against the imperialists." A few months later, President Carter complained that "the Cubans have, in effect, taken on the colonial aspect that the Portuguese gave up," and he expressed his hope "that there will be some inclination on the part of the Cubans to withdraw their forces from Angola." Raúl Castro replied that "the ruling circles in the United States are wasting their time by obstinately making an improvement in state relations with our country dependent on the withdrawal of the internationalist Cuban troops in Angola"; Fidel Castro said the same thing: "We're now helping and we'll go on helping Angola. We're now helping and we'll go on helping Mozambique. We're now helping and we'll go on helping the Ethiopian Revolution. If that is why the United States is blockading us, let them go on blockading us." If Carter thought that Cuba would abandon its friends in Africa, "then in the same manner that in the past we fought against five presidents of the United States, we will now fight against the sixth."[56]

Castro used the same speech to clarify Cuba's position on a variety of additional issues, all of them annoying to Washington: to promise that Cuba would continue backing Puerto Rican independence and building its ties with progressive Third World movements, to accuse the Carter administration of hypocrisy ("Can any government that maintains a criminal blockade, that attempts to starve millions of human beings to death, speak of human rights?"), to denounce the continued U.S. occupation of Guantánamo and U.S. troop deployments abroad (mentioning Panama, the Philippines, Turkey, Greece, Okinawa, and South Korea), and to criticize the treatment of U.S. minorities—"a society where millions and millions of persons of Mexican descent are discriminated against, where Puerto Ricans . . . are held in contempt, where Latin people are scorned, where the Indians were exterminated, where millions and millions of blacks are discriminated against."[57] The honeymoon was over.

By this time the focus of U.S. concern had shifted across the continent from Angola to the Horn of Africa, where the Red Sea joins the Gulf of Aden and where U.S. interests were far more substantial: as a worried Brzezinski confided to his diary, "If Ethiopia and South Yemen become Soviet associates, not only will access to Suez be threatened, and this involves the oil pipeline from Saudi Arabia and Iran, but there will be a serious and direct political threat to Saudi Arabia. This is something we simply cannot ignore." And, he told the president, "Soviet success in Ethiopia, even if limited to the defeat of the Somalis but not involving the penetration of Somalia as such, will have a significant demonstration effect elsewhere in Africa."[58]

The Horn of Africa

The problem was centered in Ethiopia, where the CIA reported that the Soviet Union had been sending weapons and Cuba had been sending advisers and where Moscow and Havana were planning to use Cuban troops in a combat role.[59] For decades, Ethiopia had been Washington's most reliable African ally. During World War II, it had allowed the Allies to construct a communications base at Asmara, and in 1953 the United States had stepped in to replace a British military mission, subsequently providing hundreds of millions of dollars in economic aid and military hardware plus training for more than thirty-five hundred Ethiopian military personnel in the United States. In return, Ethiopian emperor Haile Selassie had faithfully supported the United States in international forums and had permitted four thousand U.S. military personnel to operate Kagnew Station in Asmara, the largest U.S. military base in Africa and one of the largest electronic intelligence-gathering and communications-relay facilities in the world. As a code interceptor for the Army Security Agency reminisced, "Asmara was a city with many Churches and Mosques, divergent in religion as it was with its people. Asmara was also a city with many Bars and Night-clubs. After enjoying all the culture that Asmara had to offer, it was great to just kick back and enjoy the nightlife. The stories on this page (Spook's Alley Section) deal with real life situations and are therefore unsuitable for children of any age. These are stories of young men growing up into adult-hood in a land far from home. We worked hard and some of us played hard. It's a time of my life that I'll never forget." Some Ethiopians would probably not forget, either, and in 1975, a year after Haile Selassie's fall, the Ford ad-ministration had to address the Ethiopian government's request that the base be closed.[60]

The stories about these young servicemen coming of age were set in one of the world's poorest countries, where, as Tom Farer, an international legal expert focusing on human rights, wrote in 1979, "the depth of Ethiopian misery is pretty much invulnerable to exaggeration," where "the average peasant must walk eight hours in order to reach a road on which wheeled vehicles of any kind can move," and "where tens of thousands can die of starvation while their government exports grain." Fidel Castro agreed: "Look at what your friend Haile Selassie did," he told Barbara Walters. "When he died there were only 125 doctors in . . . a country with over 30 million inhabitants."[61]

Listening to this 1977 comment, an alert intelligence analyst would have suspected that Cuba was in the process of developing its ties with the mili-tary government that had overthrown Haile Selassie in 1974. That process had begun almost by accident, in early 1976, when a high-level delegation led by Ricardo Alarcón, Cuba's ambassador to the United Nations, arrived in the Ethiopian capital, Addis Ababa, to lobby at the special meeting called by the Organization of African Unity (OAU) to discuss recognition of An-gola's new MPLA government. A second Cuban delegation arrived the next day, this one led by a key member of the Communist Party Central Commit-tee, Osmani Cienfuegos.

While both delegations focused on the OAU meeting, the Cubans also established contact with Ethiopia's new leaders, launching an exception-ally delicate balancing act between Ethiopians and neighboring Somalis, who were sparring over the impoverished Ogaden Desert, formally a part of Ethiopia but populated primarily by about three-quarters of a million ethnic Somalis. This conflict in part involved the possession of territory, but it also represented the continuation of a five-hundred-year-old clash between Islamic Somalis and the dominant Coptic Christians living in the Ethiopian highlands, and it is not clear that anyone in Havana understood the dispute—only naïveté can explain the Cubans' belief that they could befriend Ethiopia's new leaders without jeopardizing Cuba's existing relations with left-leaning Somalia, where a small contingent of Cuban doctors, military trainers, and sugar experts had been stationed since the early 1970s.

Nothing more than talk occurred during the 1976 OAU meeting in Addis Ababa, but in December, Ethiopia signed a military aid agreement with the Soviet Union. Early the following year, Ethiopia turned sharply to the left when Lieutenant Colonel Mengistu Haile Mariam emerged as the leader of the Derg, the military junta controlling the government. Cuba reacted by sending a military mission. In contrast, the spanking-new Carter administration announced that Ethiopia would have its military aid reduced for human rights violations, about which there was no question: it had tortured and killed thousands of its opponents, including Haile Selassie, who had been strangled in his palace basement in 1975. Three weeks after the U.S. aid reduction, another Cuban aircraft touched down in Addis Ababa, this one carrying Fidel Castro, and he and the Derg issued a joint communiqué calling for unity among the region's progressive forces—wishful thinking about the Ogaden dispute between Ethiopia and Somalia.

U.S.-Ethiopian relations subsequently cooled dramatically. In April, the Mengistu government retaliated for the aid reduction by closing the Kagnew Station and by expelling the forty-six-member U.S. military advisory mission that had been in the country continuously since 1954; tit for tat, Washington announced a halt in previously approved arms deliveries and the cancellation of all remaining credits. Colonel Mengistu responded by traveling to Moscow, where he signed another aid agreement, and within days the State Department's Hodding Carter noted the arrival in Ethiopia of "50 or so Cuban military technicians." In mid-June, President Carter twice expressed his interest in establishing relations with Ethiopia's archrival, Somalia, but the United States had not settled on a policy when Somali troops invaded the Ogaden a few days later. Only in late August did the new administration's Policy Review Committee (PRC) decide against supplying arms. Instead, the PRC minutes indicate that "we should keep up dialogue with the Somalis, even though we do not want to supply arms, and that we should reciprocate the Ethiopians' desire to talk to us about their present predicament." The Kremlin was more decisive: it announced an end of its aid to Somalia and stepped up arms deliveries to Ethiopia, where Cuba now had about 400 military and 150 civilian personnel.[62]

Somali forces quickly pushed to the northern edges of the Ogaden, and the ability of Ethiopia's army to recover the territory was reduced by the soldiers' unfamiliarity with new Soviet weapons. To solve this problem of plenty of equipment but no one able to use it, the Cuban cavalry once again rode to the rescue: Cuban troops arrived in late 1977 and early 1978, and this time, unlike Angola, there was no question about close Cuban-Soviet collaboration—they arrived in a Soviet airlift. The Cubans provided Piero Gleijeses with a letter from Leonid Brezhnev to Fidel Castro, dated 27 November 1977, indicating the confluence of interests: "We are pleased that our assessment of events in Ethiopia coincides with yours, and we sincerely thank you for your timely decision to extend internationalist assistance to Socialist Ethiopia."[63]

As the Cubans assumed responsibility for operating the Soviet equipment, including tanks and jet fighters, Somalia severed its relations with Havana and expelled all Cuban personnel, then turned to face the Ethiopian-Cuban counteroffensive. Unsuccessful on the battlefield, the Somalis soon retreated behind their border, worrying Washington that Ethiopia would not simply reclaim the Ogaden but take over Somalia as well, and CIA director Stansfield Turner warned that the Somalis "will be no match for the Ethiopians if the latter are accompanied by Cubans." Fearful that Congress would tie the administration's hands in the Horn as it had Kissinger's in Angola, Brzezinski's NSC staff devised a plan that encouraged regional governments to provide military assistance: Saudi Arabia, Iran, Egypt, and Pakistan, all heavily armed with U.S. weapons, were informed that Washington would not object if they delivered military equipment to Somalia.[64]

The Ethiopians did not yield to the temptation to continue into Somali territory, however; instead, they celebrated with the Cubans. In April, Mengistu visited Havana, where he was awarded the Order of Playa Girón; in September, Ethiopia reciprocated with a decoration when Fidel Castro visited Addis Ababa.

The Carter administration seemed helpless. As the NSC's specialist on the Horn of Africa noted, to this point, "the Soviets and Cubans have legality and African sentiment on their side in Ethiopia—they are helping an African country defend its territorial integrity and countering aggression." He therefore suggested taking action elsewhere: "The way to bring home to the

Soviets and Cubans the high cost of further consolidation of their position in the Horn is to cool relations in other areas," wrote Paul Henze. Robert Pastor agreed ("I think the only course for us to pursue is by trying to raise the cost of Cuba's involvement") but did not want to end the normalization process: "It would only underscore our impotence. I think we should stay where we are."[65]

Pastor's advice was unlikely to be accepted by senior administration officials, who were now clearly worried. Turner reminded the president that "there are now 10,000 Cubans in Ethiopia and a billion dollars worth of Soviet equipment that was not there a year ago." Brzezinski asked his closest colleagues, "Where do they go next?" One possible answer was Zimbabwe/Rhodesia, where Cuba was open about its policy: in early 1976, Vice President Carlos Rafael Rodríguez had told a former State Department official that Cuba was training the Patriotic Front guerrillas battling Ian Smith's white minority government in Rhodesia, and "if and when they decide, we would support them in policy and in practice."[66]

That would severely stretch Cuba's abilities, since it now had become involved in a second Ethiopian conflict, this one involving its northern territory of Eritrea, and it would not be resolved quickly. Seized by the Italians in 1885 and then handed over to the British at the end of World War II, Eritrea's postwar fate had been determined by a 1952 U.N. decision to "federate" the region with Ethiopia, allowing for only modest regional autonomy, and that arrangement had ended entirely in 1962 when Haile Selassie disbanded the local legislature and formally annexed the country, a move that triggered a surge in the strength of an independence movement, the Eritrean People's Liberation Front. Ironically, Cuba had trained that group during the Haile Selassie era, apparently doing a good job: the People's Liberation Front had been poised for victory at the time of Jimmy Carter's inauguration. But once the Cuban-supported Ethiopian army had defeated the Somalis in the south, it redeployed to face the Eritreans in the north, and the result was a prolonged stalemate featuring bloody campaigns between Eritrean and Ethiopian forces. The Carter administration encouraged regional allies to support anti-Soviet and anti-Cuban forces but decided that "it would not be desirable to become involved in supporting the rebellion ourselves." Instead, Brzezinski's deputy, David Aaron, met with Ethiopia's Mengistu: "I told him we didn't oppose his revolution at all," Aaron recalled. "The only thing we were concerned about was what he was doing with the Soviet Union, and [I] said, 'As long as you have the Soviets here and the Cubans here, you will be an enemy.'"[67]

While the dust never settled in the Horn of Africa during the Carter administration, in mid-1978 Washington's attention was drawn back to Shaba, where Katangan rebels had launched a second effort to separate their province from General Mobutu's central government. Fidel Castro had not had anything more than an exchange of pleasantries with the chief of the new U.S. Interests Section since his arrival nine months earlier, but Castro now took advantage of this diplomatic link to inform Washington that Cuba was not involved, directly or indirectly, in what came to be known as Shaba II: "I was called to President Castro's office," cabled Lyle Lane, and the Cuban leader "ticked off following points carefully and deliberately: A. That there is not even one Cuban with the Katangan forces in Shaba; B. Cuba has had no [repeat] no participation either directly or indirectly in the Shaba affair; C. Cuba has provided no [repeat] no weapons or other material to the Katangan forces; D. Cuba has not [repeat] not trained the Katangan forces; E. Cuba has not in fact had any contact either military or civil with the Katangans since the end of war in Angola at least two years ago." Lane noted that "since this is the first substantive conversation I have had with Castro since the opening" of the U.S. Interests Section, "it is obvious that he attached great importance to getting the above message about the Shaba crisis promptly and accurately to the highest levels of the" U.S. government.[68]

Secretary Vance responded immediately, cabling Lane, "We have noted President Castro's assurances that Cuba is in no way involved with the Katangan forces in Shaba. We trust that this is the case." But Shaba II came only weeks after the unfavorable end to the Ogaden war, and President Carter, clearly influenced by Brzezinski, decided to ignore Castro's assurances; instead, the president called the Cuban leader a liar, telling reporters, "We believe that Cuba had known of the Katangan plans to invade and obviously did nothing to restrain them from crossing the border. We also know that the Cubans have played a key role in training and equipping the Katangans who attacked." Three weeks later, Carter charged that "Castro could have done much more, had he genuinely wanted to stop the invasion. He could have interceded with the Katangans themselves. He could certainly have imposed Cuban troops near the border, because they are spread throughout Angola, to impede the invasion. He could have notified the Zambian Government of this fact. He could have notified the Organization of African Unity. He could have notified the world at large that an invasion designed to cross and to disturb an international border was in prospect. And he did not do any of these things." State Department spokesperson

Tom Reston also questioned Castro's assurances, prompting the Cuban foreign ministry to call in Lane again to say, "We consider the declarations of Reston absolutely dishonest and an act of bad faith. We cannot understand why a constructive gesture on our part should be met in this way." Then the interests section chief added his comment: "What is obviosly [*sic*] bugging the Cubans is the renewed allegation by the spokesman despite Castro's denial to me."[69]

The State Department's Wayne Smith later wrote that "this definitely had not been Jimmy Carter's finest, or most truthful, hour," and the Cuban documents declassified for Gleijeses suggest why. While they do not prove Cuba's noninvolvement beyond a reasonable doubt, they include Fidel Castro's fourteen-page message to Angolan leader Agostinho Neto in February 1978, hand carried to Luanda by Central Committee member Jorge Risquet, urging Neto to restrain the Katangans because a second offensive could have dire consequences: "The imperialists seek a pretext, a political 'justification' to launch an open attack on Angola. The renewal of the Shaba war could provide the context." The day before returning to Havana, Risquet received Neto's handwritten response: "I am in full agreement with the views expressed by the Cuban leadership."[70]

But absolute proof of what Cuba did or did not do must await the opening of archives to future generations, since the Cubans may have provided Gleijeses with only those documents that demonstrate Cuba's noninvolvement; indeed, Cuban officials may have fabricated these documents. Aware of these possibilities, Gleijeses was convinced of only one thing: "The United States had no evidence of its own that Cubans had joined the Katangans in Zaire or supported them in Angola."[71] Once out of office, Zbigniew Brzezinski also employed conditional adverbs, writing that the unrest in Zaire was "*apparently* fomented with some Angolan and *probably* Cuban assistance." Such qualifications differed substantially from the rock-solid position he took at the height of the crisis in late May 1978, when he announced that the matter involved more than just negligence—Castro's failure to do something—but also active Cuban involvement: "We have sufficient evidence to be *quite confident* in our conclusion that Cuba shares the political and moral responsibility for the invasion."[72]

By mid-1978, events in Africa clearly were taking a severe toll on the budding U.S.-Cuban rapprochement. Meeting with Representative Stephen Solarz, an indignant Castro expressed "a sense of personal hurt that his efforts to remain uninvolved and even to head off [the Shaba] attack had been received so poorly in [the] US."[73] Six months later, he told the NSC's

Pastor and the State Department's Peter Tarnoff, "I was happy when Carter was elected." At first "there were gestures, gestures on both sides," but "then later a very serious thing happened; the events related to Shaba. At this time we made a gesture, we talked to Mr. Lane of the U.S. Interests Section. This was a friendly gesture by us especially considering that we had already made statements before that Cuba had had nothing to do with Shaba. It was a confidential communication. Twenty-four hours later, we received a reply which was positive and thirty-six hours later it was leaked out. Forty-eight hours later came the brutal denial in the form of an accusation against Cuba. This hurt us very much. We have never used lies as a way of conducting policy."

Returning to Washington, Tarnoff and Pastor told President Carter that Castro's ire went far beyond Africa: "We were viewing a man who had bottled up 20 years of rage and was releasing it in a controlled but extremely impassioned manner." The Cuban leader complained that "the U.S. has thousands of troops all over the world. But you raised the problem of our presence in Africa saying that we are trying to 'shift the balance.' I do not understand. For thirty years the U.S. has been shifting the balance in favor of its allies." Tarnoff and Pastor added that "his presentation seemed almost like a catharsis, something he needed to get out of his system. His principal message was that Cuba wanted to be treated with respect."

As for substance, the two U.S. envoys concluded that "positions are clear, and neither side looks like it will budge. We therefore do not see the need for any more meetings." In a major speech on Latin American policy given two weeks later, Assistant Secretary of State Pete Vaky did not mention Cuba.[74]

In the meantime, Shaba II ended like Shaba I: within weeks, the Katangans had been driven back into Angola by Mobutu's army, assisted by French, Belgian, Moroccan, and Senegalese troops, most of them flown to Zaire by the U.S. Air Force.[75] The Neto government subsequently disarmed the Katangan gendarmes and moved them away from the border, the Mobutu government forced FNLA leader Holden Roberto into a Parisian exile and eventually made its peace with the MPLA. In 1979, the MPLA's Neto died of cancer in a Moscow hospital, but his policies continued under his successor, Eduardo dos Santos, who faced a continuous low-level insurgency from Jonas Savimbi's UNITA.

Some remarkable steps had been taken in 1977—ending the travel ban, negotiating the boundary and fishing agreements, and opening the interests sections. Minor steps continued. In January 1978, the Treasury Department began allowing U.S. residents to send close relatives in Cuba up to five hundred dollars every three months, and the Coast Guard held talks in Havana with the Cuban Border Guard, with the two sides agreeing to improve communications, to cooperate in search and rescue operations, and to work together to curb drug trafficking.

But Africa blocked further progress. President Carter had inherited a policy that favored continued white-supremacist governments in southern Africa, and both domestic politics and Carter's beliefs required the United States to realign with many of the African forces that Cuba had been supporting for years. The administration clearly had hoped to participate in negotiating a peaceful transition to majority rule in Africa, but doing so might not be possible, with or without Cuba's help. This hope had dimmed considerably by early 1978, just after the Ogaden war, when the president sharply criticized "an ominous inclination on the part of the Soviet Union to use its military power—to intervene in local conflicts, with advisers, with equipment, and with full logistical support and encouragement for mercenaries from other Communist countries, as we can observe today in Africa." Cuba now had about thirty-two thousand military and civilian advisers in Africa, including eleven thousand in Ethiopia, where a year earlier they had none. "Is there a point beyond which we are not going to go?" asked Representative Dante Fascell. "Can we, without protest, allow Cuba's military to make mischief around the world?" Like every other Cold War president before him, Carter promised that "we will match, together with our allies and friends, any threatening power."[76]

A few weeks later, President Carter publicly declared an end to the reconciliation he had so enthusiastically endorsed a year earlier, telling reporters, "There is no possibility that we would see any substantial, further improvement in our relationship with Cuba as long as [Castro is] committed to this military intrusion into the internal affairs of African people." A few weeks later, fifty-three senators supported (and only twenty-nine opposed) a resolution calling for the closure of the Havana interests section and for an end to any further effort to normalize relations until Cuba had completely withdrawn from Africa.[77]

Only a few months earlier, Fidel Castro had asked Senator Frank Church to tell the president that "he understands that the process of normalizing relations between Cuba and the United States has to be slow and . . . he is pleased at what the President has done so far." The Cuban leader also asked Church to explain to Carter Castro's "difficulty in responding to gestures from the United States," since Cuba had no surveillance flights to stop or embargo to lift. But Castro surely knew that he could have reciprocated in Africa, where Cuba was expanding its role. It is difficult to overemphasize how much this strategy annoyed almost everyone in Washington, even Wayne Smith, now director of the State Department's Office of Cuban Affairs and among the most enthusiastic advocates of rapprochement. In mid-1978 he captured the consensus: "They value the normalization process with us, but they value what they perceive to be important political gains in Africa even more." Similarly, a *Washington Post* headline from the same period captured the discouraging mood: "U.S. Seen Powerless to Contain Cuba in 3rd World." "We are stuck on Africa," Brzezinski reported to the president. "We should have no illusions about their intentions in Africa. They will not be helpful."[78]

ENTER THE CUBAN AMERICAN COMMUNITY. "The opportunity to solve the Cuban problem is *now*," wrote Bernardo Benes to Zbigniew Brzezinski in March 1978, just after returning from three days of talks in Mexico with one of Castro's closest confidants, José Luis Padrón—and just after Ethiopia's Cuban-supported army had evicted Somalia from the Ogaden. At the time, Benes was something of a rarity—a moderate Cuban exile living in Miami, where he had built a new life as a banker and an active participant in Democratic Party politics. Now, Benes informed Brzezinski, Padrón had been assigned responsibility for overseeing the release of Cuba's political prisoners—a thousand in 1978 and the rest by the end of 1979—and he had met with Benes to discuss "the possibility for President Carter and Dr. Z.B. to take a public position which will enhance their human rights policy as it related to the freedom of Cuban political prisoners." No one was certain exactly what that meant, and so Brzezinski, rushing out of town, asked his principal aide, David Aaron, to review Benes's memo and "give me some recommendations when I come back. In the meantime, have someone . . . phone Benes and simply tell him that we thank him for the information and that the matter will be taken on from here by us, or something to that effect."[79]

Would that it were so simple. The Cuban government had first approached Benes in mid-1977, and by early 1978 either he or someone close to him (the name of the individual remains classified) had met with the NSC's Pastor, who, in turn, had told Brzezinski that "Castro and the other members of the revolution have been so hostile to the Cuban-American community in the past and so disinterested in a dialogue for any reason, that this new initiative must have been taken for clear political reasons."

Pastor hypothesized that Cuban officials had recognized the political clout of ethnic interest groups and wanted the Cuban American community on their side as bargaining continued with the Carter administration. He ended his memo by asking for permission to encourage Benes—"I believe that it is very much in our interest."[80]

But Brzezinski checked the "Disapprove" box, and there the matter rested for two months until Frank Carlucci, the acting CIA director, informed Brzezinski that Benes was not sitting on his hands; he had twice contacted the CIA's chief of station in Mexico City, and at their second meeting, he had reported that José Luis Padrón had a message for Brzezinski: "Castro's reply to you was that he is prepared to initiate immediate secret talks on all issues without the knowledge of the Soviets."[81]

This was a reference to a recent exchange of notes carried by one of the president's close advisers, Coca-Cola board chair Paul Austin, whom Carter had entrusted with a cordial letter to Fidel Castro. "I had hoped it would be possible for you and me to move towards full normalization of relations," the president had written, clearly referring to Africa, "and I would like to see progress made in removing the obstacles that impede forward movement." Castro had replied with an equally cordial letter. "I thank you very much for your gesture," he began, "and I highly prize the form in which you have decided, unlike previous leaders of your country, to use this type of constructive communication with us." Now, a month after Castro's response and two days after Carlucci's memo to Brzezinski, came Benes's handwritten message that "the opportunity to solve the Cuban problem is *now*," to which he added in imperfect English that Padrón "is a new breed of technocrat that recognise the need for change. Headed by Padron fully backed by Castro that has tremendous power of decision that want to take a different approach starting immedtly probably to slowly evolve into a Yugoslavia. . . . However if this faction losses present momentum radical will take over again. . . . There are very firm impression taken from side conversations with both Jose Luis Padron and Fidel Castro." Benes ended by noting, "We can establish direct telephone comunication from your office right now with Castro himself."[82]

The impatient Benes, thinking that he was being brushed off by the White House, had gone to Dante Fascell, Benes's representative in Congress and the powerful chair of the Committee on International Relations, who convinced Secretary Vance to hear Benes's story. After listening to what Benes had to say, Vance asked his executive secretary, Peter Tarnoff, to step into his office, and the ball started rolling: within days, two State Department officials (Tarnoff and Undersecretary of State David Newsom) and two NSC officials (Aaron and Pastor) had been designated to pursue the Benes initiative. Of the four, Newsom was by far the most senior—"quiet and no world beater," in Henry Kissinger's words, but those who had followed Newsom's career knew that this assessment missed the mark; broadly recognized as a consummate diplomat, he had recently been named undersecretary of state for political affairs, the highest rank traditionally reserved for a career officer.[83] Given his position, Newsom should have taken the lead, but Padrón had told Benes that Cuba wanted to deal with Brzezinski or President Carter, not the State Department, so the first U.S. envoy to meet with Padrón in New York was a compromise—Aaron, a former foreign service officer now serving as Brzezinski's deputy.

Preparing for the meeting, Aaron planned to say that Cuban military intervention in Africa was the principal obstacle to improved relations and in particular that "the United States draws the line in Southern Africa. The intervention of Cuban combat forces into the struggle in Rhodesia and Namibia will have the most serious adverse consequences."[84] But when Aaron zeroed in on Cuba's foreign policy, Padrón simply confirmed what had now become obvious—the Cubans were not about to leave Africa—and then turned to what he considered the meeting's principal question: Would the United States be willing to admit several thousand released political prisoners?

While this issue was not what the U.S. side wanted to discuss, it nonetheless had the hallmark of that elusive "reciprocal gesture" Washington had been seeking since Vance had suggested at his confirmation hearing that a prisoner release would be "one indication that Cuba is seriously interested in starting a dialogue." President Carter had repeatedly voiced his hope that these prisoners would be freed, but until now Fidel Castro had simply toyed with a response: "They like to tell us that we must release Cuban counterrevolutionary prisoners," he had told a Havana audience a few months before the Aaron-Padrón meeting; fine, he continued, shifting to address Washington, but first "you free an equal number of U.S. blacks who had to go to jail because of the regime of exploitation, the hunger, the poverty, the discrimination and the unemployment that the United States reserves for a large part of the black population, and we'll release all the counterrevolutionary prisoners who are left in Cuba."[85]

Now Castro had apparently changed his mind. Lacking instructions on how to answer Padrón's question, Aaron returned to Washington, and Newsom personally took charge. At a first meeting at the St. Regis Hotel in New

York and then at a second in Newsom's suburban Washington home, the senior U.S. envoy went out of his way to be respectful: "I speak as someone who recognizes and respects the sovereignty of Cuba," he said; "I realize that Cuban policy is separate from Soviet policy." This acknowledgment made all the difference in the world to Padrón, who told State's Wayne Smith that "when, during our meeting at his home, Ambassador Newsom himself served our drinks and his wife served dinner, our preconceived ideas about the arrogance of all American officials went out the window." But however diplomatic the Newsoms' actions, this feather smoothing simply constituted a prelude to an effort to engage the Cuban envoy on the issue of Africa, and here Newsom failed. Padrón responded politely but without making any commitment: "We believe that as the climate of trust develops, as Angola and Ethiopia are given believable guarantees that there will be no intervention by regular troops from foreign countries, there will be no further need for, and they will not object to, the withdrawal of any troops now supporting them."[86]

Other issues were also raised. Selecting a perennial bone of contention, Padrón acknowledged that U.S. expropriation claims were legitimate, but while "the United States was fully justified to defend the principle of compensation [and] Cuba was willing to discuss the modalities of such compensation," the U.S. note taker included Padrón's comment that "Cuba also had a bill to present to us for economic harm suffered as a result of acts of aggression and the blockade." Turning to an issue Padrón had raised earlier, Newsom said that Puerto Rico "is self-governing and can become independent if it wishes," but he added that President Carter had decided not to grant clemency to the Puerto Rican separatists who had attempted to assassinate President Truman in 1950 and who had opened fire from the gallery of the House of Representatives in 1954. Cuba had offered to swap them for U.S. citizens held in Cuban jails, and Newsom indicated that "the United States would still be interested in the idea of an exchange if other persons could be found."[87]

The possibility of such a prisoner exchange had been explored a year earlier, when simply reaching an agreement on the number of such prisoners had not been easy, primarily because the two sides had different definitions of dual nationality; in early 1977, the U.S. counted 751 U.S. citizens residing in Cuba, both free and imprisoned, but Cuba recognized only 84 of them as U.S. citizens. The two governments also differed over the definition of "political prisoner." (The United States defined Everett D. Jackson as a political prisoner, for example, while the Cubans judged him a common criminal: arrested in early 1969 during a failed attempt to fly a small airplane secretly into Cuba, at his trial Jackson told a Cuban court that his camera equipment was for photographing Cuban concentration camps and that his guns were for survival hunting.) As a result, the exact number of prisoners who were U.S. citizens was never determined precisely. When briefed by the State Department prior to his mid-1977 visit to Cuba, Senator Frank Church had been told that there were 23 U.S. citizens in Cuban jails and that 7 of them could be classified as political prisoners.[88] After the senator's visit, the Cubans released the only woman among the 7—María del Carmen y Ruiz, a naturalized U.S. citizen who had been convicted of espionage in 1969—an action that should have left 6 U.S. citizens imprisoned, but the Cuban government now considered 2 of the 6 to be exclusively Cuban, and the State Department apparently agreed, because in 1978 it reported that only 4 U.S. citizens were being held for political crimes.[89]

Fidel Castro refused to take no for an answer to Cuba's request for the release of the four Puerto Rican nationalists, and on this matter he was nothing if not persistent. The Cuban leader had first made the exchange offer to the Ford administration in January 1975, and now, months after the end of the Newsom-Padrón meetings, he told Tarnoff and Pastor, "I do not understand why you are so tough on the Puerto Ricans. The US could make a gesture and release them, then we would make another gesture—without any linkage—just a unilateral humanitarian gesture."[90] Pastor fully agreed, at least on the three who had terrorized the House of Representatives; he had already written to Brzezinski, "I am struck at how pathetic these three cases are, and how compassionate the decision would be to release these three individuals." It took Pastor the better part of a year to convince his colleagues, but in 1979 the Carter administration agreed to the deal, and the Cubans lived up to their part of the bargain, waiting ten days after President Carter granted the four Puerto Ricans executive clemency, then freeing what they considered the final four U.S. citizens held in Cuban jails for political crimes, including Jackson and another prisoner with a similar résumé, Lawrence Lunt, who subsequently wrote about the CIA-directed sabotage that had landed him in jail: "I'd done quite a lot in five years to destabilize Castro's communist regime."[91]

Meanwhile, the Newsom-Padrón meetings in New York and Washington had a life of their own. After the St. Regis meeting, Vance had told President Carter that it would be worthwhile to continue the talks, while Brzezinski said the opposite.[92] But how could Jimmy Carter, of all people, decline to pursue the release of several thousand political prisoners? He sided with Vance, and so the negotiators sat down to discuss the prisoners' disposal; here Padrón had already made it clear that "we don't want to free a large number of prisoners if they stay here to present us with the problem of unemployment, of their inability to adapt while they are receiving siren calls from the United States to join their relatives and begin a new life." Plus, of course, "these people are not in jail for the fun of it—they have committed serious crimes."[93]

The Carter administration did not want to accept anyone without a careful background check, so the negotiations required careful attention to detail: Would the term "political prisoner" apply to previously released but still-disaffected individuals or simply to those incarcerated at the moment? Or at what moment? Would all political prisoners be allowed to depart? Would they be forced to depart? How many family members would be allowed to accompany each of them? Could the prisoners' release and departure be phased so that their arrival in the United States would not be disruptive? The exchanges were civil and professional, the concessions were mutual, and at an August meeting in Atlanta, the two sides reached an informal agreement. Cuba handed over documentation for forty-eight prisoners so that the United States could begin processing their visas and said that another five hundred would be ready to depart by the end of 1978.[94]

THE OGADEN WAR, Eritrea, and Shaba II were all fresh news, and President Carter was concerned that a public announcement might suggest he was willing to turn a blind eye to Cuba's behavior in Africa. He therefore accepted Brzezinski's advice that the administration implement the agreement as quietly as possible, without comment by any senior official. At the same time, attitudes were hardening within the administration. The NSC staff was especially upset, with a young Robert Gates, on loan from the CIA, complaining to David Aaron that "it is quintessentially State Department thinking to want to continue talks when we are getting nothing. . . . We look over-eager and are losing any credibility. They believe we are hooked on this dialogue of the deaf and that such high-level talks can be continued at no cost. Why should we go ahead?"[95] At the same time, Vance's deputy secretary of state, Warren Christopher, had apparently been convinced of Brzezinski's darker interpretation of Cuban intentions, and the two men coauthored an update for the president that emphasized how little had been accomplished and at so much effort.

Puerto Rico was a perfect example—not a major problem like Africa, but a telling one. In May 1977, just as the fishing and maritime boundary agreements were being initialed and as negotiations to open the interests sections were moving ahead, Castro had told Barbara Walters that "as long as there is one Puerto Rican—just one—who aspires to his country's independence, we have the moral and political duty to support him." The following August, the Cubans raised the issue in the U.N. Committee of Twenty-four, the body that handled questions of decolonization, and State's Wayne Smith recalled that the Cuban effort was deeply resented in Washington. A year later, just after the Atlanta meeting and just after Shaba II, the State Department concluded that Cuba was putting on a show at Washington's expense: "Castro undoubtedly has no illusions about the strength of the independence movement within Puerto Rico. But, from both an ideological and tactical standpoint, this lack of internal appeal is irrelevant [sic]. What is important to Castro is the wide support that Cuba can attract in the UN and the Non-Aligned Movement for resolutions critical of the US on an issue involving colonialism. The repeated raising of this issue cast[s] the US in an unflattering role. We suspect that Castro derives considerable satisfaction from US discomfort over Puerto Rico."[96]

So when Christopher and Brzezinski updated the president a month later, they wrote, "We were disappointed by Cuba's recent attitude . . . despite several messages from us to Cuban authorities stressing that the Puerto Rican issue was of special importance to the U.S. Government." A few days later, during preparations for another round of talks to be held in Mexico City, Brzezinski wrote to the president that "over the past year the Cubans have been marginally forthcoming to your concerns on human rights and Cuban prisoners (albeit for their own reasons) but have been completely unresponsive on Puerto Rico and Africa."[97]

The Mexico City meeting occurred on 28 October. It was supposed to focus on Cuba's policy in Africa, but U.S. negotiators again hit a stone wall, as Aaron reported to the President: "The private meeting with the Cubans resulted in a complete impasse. The Cubans were on a very tight leash and spoke largely for the record. . . . Because of the impasse on Africa, no further meeting was scheduled." In the margin, Carter wrote, "Do not plan another."[98]

By the autumn of 1978, then, the balance of opinion had shifted dramatically in Washington, where Cuba was now seen as nothing but trouble. But as the government-to-government negotiations sputtered, the Cubans accelerated the talks they had opened with the exile community more than a year earlier. Although never enthusiastic about this private diplomacy, administration officials had nonetheless cooperated with Benes and his business partner, Carlos Dascal. At the conclusion of the St. Regis meeting, Newsom suggested to Padrón that "we could continue to communicate through Benes who is known to us and thus avoid any questions which would be raised by a direct call from you to the Department of State."[99]

As the two governments began the tedious processing of political prisoners, the Cubans decided to make the agreement an occasion for improving relations with the exile community in Florida: speaking to visiting Cuban American journalists on 6 September—their very presence in Havana something of a breakthrough—Castro said that the prisoner release was a gesture of good faith aimed at Cubans living abroad. It apparently had its desired effect: the State Department informed President Carter that "many who have opposed normalization are now urging us to lift the embargo on medicines and to take other steps that would encourage Castro to move forward with family reunification and release more prisoners."[100]

Meanwhile, Benes and other moderate leaders were putting together a group of seventy-five Cuban Americans to discuss in Havana the implementation of the agreement that had been reached in Atlanta. At a first meeting in late November, Castro told the group that the Cuban government had agreed to release approximately four thousand prisoners in batches of four hundred per month but that Washington was dragging its feet—"several months ago we gave them the first lists [of released prisoners], and the only group that has been processed is the first group, this in a period of—well, we are at the end of November, almost three months. In a period of almost three months they have processed a small group, nothing more, and we have given them a large number of lists." Taking the lead for like-minded Cuban Americans, Benes complained to the White House that "there are 5,000 ex-political prisoners in Cuba with exit permit[s] waiting to leave Cuba and no place to go. Very sad!!!"[101]

Secretary Vance had already promised Cuban Americans that he would speed up the processing, but there was little he could do because the Immigration and Naturalization Service had to approve every visa, and the service was part of the Department of Justice, which was in no hurry. An exasperated Robert Pastor told Brzezinski that "the only way [Attorney General Griffin] Bell will get his act together is for the President to call him or send a personal message." Two months later, Wayne Smith, now chief of the U.S. Interests Section, cabled from Havana that the delay in issuing visas had become "an embarrassment which we should not continue to accept." At this point, Brzezinski complained to the president, who soon sent a hand-written note to his old friend Bell: "You & Ben[jamin Civiletti] should expedite processing of released Cuban prisoners." OK, replied a still-reluctant Civiletti, noting that doing so would mean waiving security screening, and anyone found to be ineligible after entering the United States could not be returned to Cuba. But if the president believed that "a crash program is imperative for foreign policy reasons, it can be accomplished with the risks and costs as indicated above."[102]

Wayne Smith noted that processing eventually did speed up, "and although it never actually reached the 400-per-month figure, it came close several times." Prior to the May 1980 onset of the Mariel boatlift, after which an accurate count became impossible, the United States had admitted about fifteen thousand released prisoners and their families.[103] Among them was Rolando Cubela, the CIA's AM/LASH who had tried to assassinate Castro during the Mongoose years, and Huber Matos, who had been arrested in 1959 for opposing the leftward tilt of the new revolutionary government. He was released twenty years to the day after his arrest.

TWO WEEKS AFTER President Carter had discontinued the Padrón-Newsom talks, conservative columnists Rowland Evans and Robert Novak threw an additional bucket of water on the normalization embers by charging that "the Soviet Union is surreptitiously arming Cuba with Mig23 aircraft of the type now deployed in Europe for nuclear attack against NATO." The MiG-23s, Evans and Novak asserted, were "an attack, not an air-defense aircraft," and the "model now in Cuba has never before been delivered to a Soviet ally."[104]

This disclosure reopened the issue of what types of weapons Moscow had agreed not to install in Cuba as its concession to end the 1962 missile crisis. President Kennedy's initial address to the nation had focused on missiles, but he had also warned that "jet bombers, capable of carrying nuclear weapons, are now being uncrated and assembled in Cuba," and his quarantine order had included both missiles and "bomber aircraft." At issue in 1962 were forty-two Ilyushin IL-28 light bombers with a six-hundred-mile flight radius that were not specifically mentioned in the crisis-ending exchange of messages between Kennedy and Nikita Khrushchev: JFK had demanded the removal of "all weapons systems in Cuba capable of offensive use"; Khrushchev, in turn, had agreed vaguely to the removal of "the weapons you describe as offensive." The NSC's Samuel P. Huntington, on loan from Harvard, now told Brzezinski that "the heart of the agreement, the Kennedy-Khrushchev letters of October 27–28, are very general and vague as to what weapons are covered." Nonetheless, in late 1962 the Russians had removed the Ilyushins. At that time, no mention was made of the MiG-21 fighters that the Soviets were delivering to Cuba, and now in 1978 these aircraft were being replaced by new-generation MiG-23s.[105]

Although Evans and Novak sounded confident that these new jets violated the 1962 Kennedy-Khrushchev agreement, no one in Washington was certain. The central question—Were the MiG-23s offensive weapons?—could not be answered without looking inside the aircraft, because the Soviet Union produced both defensive fighter-interceptor and offensive fighter-bomber versions of the MiG-23. The latter, called the MiG-23D, was deployed only in the Soviet Union and had the capacity to deliver nuclear weapons; the former, called the MiG-23F, had been sold abroad to governments such as Egypt and was not configured to carry nuclear weapons. "If the MiG-23s exported to Cuba in 1978 were the F model, they were clearly replacements for the MiG-21s," reported one expert, "but only the internal wiring for the bomb bays, invisible to the eye of electronic surveillance, prevents a MiG-23 from being loaded with nuclear weapons."[106]

With the question of which version had been exported to Cuba still undecided, President Carter told reporters, "We would consider it to be a very serious development if the Soviet Union violated the 1962 agreement." Fortunately, he continued, "they have assured us that no shipments of weapons to the Cubans have or will violate the terms of the 1962 agreement." Fidel Castro gave the same assurance: "They are tactical aircraft, absolutely defensive." With no one rising to carry the Evans and Novak protest further, the discussion at home ended, but the president had clearly not understood the damage he would do to U.S.-Cuban relations when he promised that he would not simply take the Soviets at their word: "We will monitor their compliance with the [1962] agreement very carefully."[107] To do so the United States would resume SR-71 reconnaissance flights over Cuba. "They invented this phony Mig23 crisis and used it as a pretext to violate Cuban airspace," Castro complained. "One of Carter's gestures that we most appreciated was the fact that he suspended those flights. And one of the things that most irritates us today is the fact that without any type of justification . . . the flights have resumed."[108]

In the months after the missile crisis, the overflights had been considered essential—"We could not go without continuing aerial surveillance," the CIA's John McCone had said—but by the late 1970s, satellite reconnaissance had replaced aircraft, whose principal military purpose was now to improve U.S. readiness by making the Cubans reveal their air defense radar, and that intelligence was already in hand and could be updated quickly.[109] Historically, however, the flights had also sought to intimidate and infuriate. "Occasional low altitude surveillance of 'suspicious' areas should be undertaken in such fashion as to be clearly visible to the Cuban people," wrote a Pentagon analyst in early 1963, a few months after the missile crisis. "Still later, suitably timed, the United States/OAS should initiate very frequent low altitude surveillance . . . to deflate Castro's image." Such flights would be timed to coincide with "frequent leaks of planned US invasion and appropriate denials to frustrate the suspicious Castro."[110]

In full agreement with what Gordon Chase had told McGeorge Bundy a decade earlier—"It is always tough to justify overflights over someone else's airspace when that someone else doesn't like them"—the Carter State Department now opposed resuming the flights, but one of the NSC's most hawkish staffers argued that U.S. domestic politics trumped the increasingly remote hope for improved bilateral relations. "Unless we have occasional flights just to see what they can find, we put ourselves in the position of appearing to be too trusting of the Soviets and Cubans. Once the alarm is sounded, it is too late to defend ourselves against the accusation of negligence. . . . If the position State now requests be formally confirmed, it will almost inevitably be leaked by Vance or [Vance adviser Marshall] Shulman at some point in order to show the Soviets how much 'confidence' we have in them—and all hell could break loose in the press again."[111]

The president sided with the hawks. A month after the overflights resumed, Tarnoff and Pastor traveled to Havana to talk about Africa. They met with Vice President Carlos Rafael Rodríguez, who complained that "the plane is not only offensive and illegal, but it also broke many windows and eardrums across Cuba." The next day Castro cornered the U.S. representatives and let go with both barrels: "One thing we had taken into account in the past was the gesture by the U.S. in suspending the flights. I spoke with appreciation and publicly several times on this matter. However, on November 12th after 10:30 A.M. explosions from the plane began to be heard all over Cuba. We saw with great surprise this brutal violation of our sovereignty and the resumption of a policy of espionage on Cuban territory which we thought was one thing President Carter had stopped." Tarnoff tried to explain that the surveillance flights were necessary to give President Carter's MiG-23 assurance domestic credibility, but Castro was not appeased; he also raised a second grievance: "We have also seen a resumption of past practices and provocations at the naval base at Guantanamo. . . . Sometimes the provocations were words, shots or pointed guns and even — although it is not very decorous to mention it, your sailors taking down their pants and showing their behinds." After asking for photographs of the mooning, Tarnoff promised Castro, "We will study them carefully."[112]

The resumption of surveillance flights severely impaired bilateral relations—"We felt we were back in a completely different era," complained Rodríguez—but by 1978 administration officials wanted to focus on Africa and only Africa. Cuba's Africa policy had dominated Undersecretary Newsom's 18-page, single-spaced memorandum of his conversation with Padrón at the St. Regis Hotel in June, and in August a 173-page policy review had estimated that Cuba had between forty and fifty thousand troops in Africa, the lion's share in Angola and Ethiopia. The report concluded, "Our diplomatic warnings that continued Cuban military presence there will make progress toward normalization impossible do not appear to have had any appreciable effect." At his New York meeting in June, Newsom heard exactly what Tarnoff and Pastor would hear six months later in Havana: "We reiterated our position that the embargo was related to their military activities in Africa, and they completely and unequivocally rejected that." As Castro commented several years later, "When there were no troops in Angola, relations with the United States were bad. Whether there are troops in Angola does not make any difference. . . . The United States could invent something else."[113]

Brzezinski informed Carter that "they said they don't negotiate our troops abroad, and we shouldn't negotiate there's [*sic*]." At the same time, U.S. envoys in Havana reported not simply on Castro's comment that relations were "going badly" but also on the Cuban leader's "most sarcastic comments we have ever seen here regarding President Carter." And those comments were simply a prelude to the Cuban leader's New Year's Day speech five weeks later. Celebrating the twentieth anniversary of his rebel victory, he gloated that "imperialism not only suffered a defeat at the Bay of Pigs. It suffered another Bay of Pigs in Angola and another in Ethiopia. Three Bay of Pigs defeats in 20 years!" By this point the chief of the U.S. Interests Section, an invited guest, had already walked out of the auditorium, and he therefore did not hear Castro's response to the U.S. demand that Cuba remove its troops from Africa: "Cuba cannot be pressured, not intimidated," he said. "Neither in this hemisphere nor in any part of Africa are we thinking of bowing our heads in submission."[114]

Here, on New Year's Day 1979, was the same Cuban leader who only a few months earlier had graciously thanked President Carter for his "constructive communication" through a Coca-Cola executive. Now Castro did more than point with pride to Cuba's successes; he also bragged that when the revolution had triumphed twenty years earlier, "Yankee imperialists considered themselves the absolute owner of this hemisphere, and that no Latin American or Caribbean country had the right to choose an economic, political or social system other than the unmerciful neocolonial, underdeveloped capitalism granted to us Latin Americans, the rotten and hypocritical pseudo-democracy or feudal oligarchies, the satraps in the style of Somoza, Duvalier, Stroessner, or the fascist recipe applied to Chile, Uruguay and other unfortunate peoples of this hemisphere." Cuba would soon host the sixth summit of the nonaligned movement, the Cuban leader would become the movement's spokesperson until the next summit, and Cuba seemed assured of being elected to one of the two seats traditionally reserved for Latin America on the U.N. Security Council. These developments apparently reduced Cuba's incentive to bargain. "Cuba is not opposed to trade and even diplomatic relations with the United States," Castro said, but first "the United States must unconditionally suspend its economic blockade of Cuba because it is an uncivilized, arbitrary, discriminatory, hostile and aggressive act." Until then, the Carter administration's continuation of the embargo constituted "full proof of the infinite hypocrisy of its human rights rhetoric."[115]

"There really is no way to bridge the gap between our positions," Pastor had already concluded. "I'm left with a feeling that our policies have gotten away from us, and we need to re-think where we've come, and what are our objectives."[116]

JIMMY CARTER HAD NO TIME for rethinking; he had his hands full with a faltering U.S. economy. Perhaps no president could have prevented the 9 percent OPEC oil price increase in March 1979, which was accompanied by the decision of five OPEC members to tack on an additional surcharge that made the increase closer to 30 percent, but Carter seemed especially impotent when skyrocketing fuel prices cascaded through the economy to produce double-digit inflation. Seeking to break these price increases, the Federal Reserve provided a strong dose of old-time religion—tightening credit, pushing home mortgage rates up to 12 percent (more than double the postwar norm), halting home construction, reducing consumer demand, and increasing unemployment. "Gas Shortage Spurs Carter Decline in Poll," headlined the *New York Times* story reporting that the president's approval rating had dropped to 26 percent, below that of Richard Nixon in the days immediately prior to his resignation.[117]

With his popularity plummeting, Carter retreated to Camp David, where he reassessed his presidency for two weeks before returning to Washington to address the nation in prime time. He said that he, too, was upset by "the long lines which have made millions of you spend aggravating hours waiting for gasoline," but he offered no solution other than belt-tightening: "I am asking for you for your own good and for your Nation's security to take no unnecessary trips, to use carpools or public transportation whenever you can, to park your car one extra day per week, to obey the speed limit, and to set your thermostats to save fuel." These practical steps were not welcomed by a public accustomed to ample supplies of everything, but listeners were especially upset by what seemed to be the president's central message: the situation was their fault. He called it "the crisis of the American spirit," and while clearly intending to speak as a caring Dutch uncle, the president sounded instead like a Calvinist minister: "Too many of us now tend to worship self-indulgence and consumption. Human identity is no longer defined by what one does, but by what one owns," leading to "growing doubt about the meaning of our own lives and . . . threatening to destroy the social and the political fabric of America."[118]

The next week's polls reported that the public disliked what immediately became known as Carter's "malaise speech." Instead of a lecture, voters wanted to know when there would be an adequate supply of inexpensive gasoline, when the price of food would stop rising, and when jobs would again become plentiful—that is, when the economy would get back on track and their lives would return to normal. President Carter offered no answer to these questions.

Then there was the problem of foreign policy vision, supplemented inside the Beltway by talk of a growing estrangement between Brzezinski's NSC and Vance's State Department. In late 1978, just prior to a meeting with major allies, Brzezinski had told Carter that "one of the major concerns of the other leaders present at Guadeloupe will be to obtain from you a sense of your strategic direction. In part, this is due to some anxiety that this Administration does not have any overall scheme, and that the United States is no longer prepared to use its power to protect its interests or to impose its will on the flow of history." Accustomed to Henry Kissinger's powerful presence, the press was already suggesting that the lack of an "overall scheme" reflected the president's unwillingness to grant full responsibility for foreign policy to any single individual. Brzezinski had already been obliged to produce a telling memorandum instructing cabinet members how they might "infuse greater clarity into public understanding of our foreign policy," and the president had already found it necessary to defend his administration when a reporter observed that "Mr. Brzezinski and Secretary of State Vance seem to have differing views" on many issues. "I'm President, and I make the final decisions," snapped an uncharacteristically testy Carter; "I'm the one who shapes the policy." The rumors about bickering were nonsense, President Carter insisted—among his foreign policy team "there is an overwhelming compatibility."[119]

In this context Cuba reappeared on the president's desk in the form of a memo from Brzezinski a few days after the "malaise" speech. The document warned that "Cuba's military/subversive successes (and our actual or perceived responses) are almost certain to be an important foreign policy campaign issue in 1980." Brzezinski suggested several steps to retake the initiative, one of which was to "increase the cost to Cuba itself of its revolutionary activity," but, he added in the next sentence, "Cy Vance is reluctant."[120]

So now, on Cuba, an already overwhelmed president had to mediate between his two key foreign policy advisers, and he seemed increasingly to favor Brzezinski's harder line, which pollsters identified as the position also favored by public opinion. Only a few years earlier, at the height of the Vietnam debacle, the nation's sobered voters had seemed increasingly willing to accept a complex global environment devoid of either clear victories or easy answers—not simply to accept but to embrace détente, symbolized by the 1972 Strategic Arms Limitation Treaty (SALT) with the Soviet Union. But now, in mid-1979, with a second SALT agreement awaiting ratification by the Senate, the public was reconsidering. While waiting for a leader to voice renewed confidence in the special nobility of U.S. foreign policy—while waiting for Ronald Reagan to characterize the Cold War as a struggle against what he called an "evil empire"—both the voters and Jimmy Carter were moving away from Vance's complex interdependence and toward Brzezinski's traditional postwar realpolitik.

In late summer, a reporter dared to ask Vance the question on everyone's mind: "Have you considered resigning?" Clearly upset, the secretary of state responded with atypical muscle: "I have the responsibility under the President for the development and implementation of the foreign policy of the United States, and that includes all aspects of that policy. I will do just that." A few days later, Brzezinski recommended that Carter pursue a more aggressive foreign policy: "that we be less hesitant in explicitly condemning Soviet-Cuban exploitation of instability in the Third World and that we ostracize Cuba."[121]

President Carter was not the only incumbent able to feel the shifting public mood; so, too, did congressional Democrats, among the most worried of them Senator Richard Stone, a Florida Democrat up for reelection in 1980 and already in political trouble for his vote to ratify the Panama Canal treaties. Stone served on the Senate Committee on Foreign Relations, which in mid-1979 had begun consideration of the SALT II agreement that Carter and Soviet premier Leonid Brezhnev had recently signed in Vienna. On 17 July, the committee was hearing opinions about SALT and the U.S.-Soviet military balance from two retired admirals, Elmo Zumwalt, a former chief of naval operations, and Thomas Moorer, a former chair of the Joint Chiefs of Staff, both of whom believed that the Carter administration had been underfunding the military. Taking advantage of the platform offered by the Senate committee, Zumwalt argued that the Soviets, aware of the Pentagon's inadequate budget, "have become increasingly contemptuous of our lack of will and power"; Moorer agreed, adding that money was not the only issue: the Carter administration had also foolishly given away the strategically important Panama Canal to a government led by a politically unreliable leader, Omar Torrijos. "I called attention to the fact that there was a Torrijos-Castro-Moscow axis, in my opinion, and that before very long you would see this in operation along Central America, and I think that is exactly what is happening in Nicaragua," where on that very day Sandinista rebels were chasing Washington's most complaisant ally out of their country.[122]

The State Department's Wayne Smith had arrived at Senator Stone's office an hour before the committee hearing, the diplomat's last courtesy call before departing for Havana and his new position as chief of the U.S. Interests Section. As he walked in, two army officers from the Defense Intelligence Agency (DIA) were walking out after informing the senator that the Soviet Union had increased its troop strength in Cuba. Stone chatted briefly with Smith, then walked over to the hearing, where he listened quietly to Zumwalt and Moorer. When Stone's turn to question the admirals arrived, he asked "whether you think a direct or indirect effort to establish a military base would be established by the introduction of a large number of combat troops of the Soviet Union into Cuba." Both witnesses immediately understood the senator's awkwardly worded question: "There is no question in my mind," replied Zumwalt, and Moorer added, "Absolutely. Yes, sir." Stone reminded everyone that he had been concerned about Cuba's receipt of the MiG-23s a few months earlier, and "if, in addition to that, there were a major introduction of Soviet combat troops into Cuba, could there be any further doubt that we just do not care about protecting our hemisphere against Soviet military bases?" "None whatever," Admiral Moorer answered. "It would be the height of folly for the United States to permit that to happen."[123]

Although Secretary Vance quickly reassured Senator Stone that "there is no evidence of any substantial increase of the Soviet military presence in Cuba," the DIA officers who had briefed the senator had been correct: there *was* some new evidence indicating a growing Soviet presence in Cuba—a mid-July intelligence report from the National Security Agency (NSA) that, according to one NSC staff member, contained intercepted "chatter indicating tank crews running combat exercises."[124] The report had been triggered in March 1979, a few months after the MiG-23 flap and just as U.S. and Soviet negotiators were finishing work on SALT II, when Brzezinski had asked the NSA to review its information on the Soviet presence in Cuba, much of which had not been fully processed because the agency had been focusing every available electronic eye on Iran after the fall of the shah in January. ("We had totally dropped our coverage of the Caribbean," recalled Brzezinski's principal military aide.) Responding to Brzezinski's request, the NSA analyzed its data and concluded that a change had occurred in Cuba, and the two DIA officers had reported this conclusion to Senator Stone. Brzezinski received the news a few days later: "In late July, I saw the first report that the Soviets might have a unit in Cuba," he wrote, "and I alerted the President to this on July 24, pointing out that it could have serious repercussions for SALT." If the Soviets were violating the 1962 agreement barring offensive weapons in Cuba, why would anyone trust them to comply with a treaty calling for a reduction in strategic weapons?[125]

At exactly this moment, the CIA learned from sources within Cuba that the Soviet unit had scheduled a training exercise for 17 August, and a spy satellite was positioned to record the event. After the NSA had analyzed the photographs, it inserted its conclusion into the government's highly classified daily intelligence digest: "A Soviet combat brigade" was in Cuba. It consisted of about twenty-six hundred soldiers, forty tanks, and sixty armored personnel carriers, and it had no clear advisory or training connection to Cuban forces.[126]

Although it has never been established why the NSA used the word "combat" to describe the brigade, CIA director Stansfield Turner offered the most plausible explanation: bureaucratic self-promotion. Turner noted that the NSA possessed one clear fact—"This unit was doing field training on its own, not simply training Cubans"—but, he added, "the NSA's decision to use the term 'combat' was not based on hard factual evidence." Indeed, the NSA was not equipped to reach *any* conclusion, since it was primarily an intelligence-gathering agency; according to Turner, it should have sought the CIA's help with analysis and interpretation. But, Turner continued, since the NSA was "a proud, highly competent organization that does not like to keep its light under a bushel," it had no intention of sharing its hot news: "The name of the game was getting credit for the scoop. The NSA had, in its view, an important report and couldn't resist being the first to get it on the street." Turner was convinced that "the NSA's excursion into interpretation and its subsequent wide distribution of its conclusion were the genesis of this crisis."[127]

Whatever the explanation, within two days the NSA's report had been leaked to Clarence Robinson, a writer for *Aviation Week and Space Technology*, who telephoned Undersecretary Newsom for a prepublication comment. Thus alerted to the pending publicity, Newsom and Vance decided to inform eight senior members of Congress, including the chair of the Senate Committee on Foreign Relations, Frank Church, whose Idaho constituents were among those who had been moving to the right while Church appeared to be going in the other direction—he had already been criticized for serving as floor manager of the unpopular Panama Canal treaties, and his 1977 trip to Cuba had also proven costly, with a mocking Ronald Reagan telling radio listeners that Church "spent four days with Fidel Castro and departed for home saying, 'I leave with the impression I have found a friend.'"[128] Although the 1980 election was more than a year away, Idaho Republicans were already running television ads showing Church and Castro smiling at one another.

Campaigning in Idaho during the Labor Day recess, Church received Newsom's call and then telephoned Vance to urge that the news of the brigade be made public before *Aviation Week* hit the newsstands, only to learn that the administration had decided to wait to see if the story would be picked up by the major media. Church disagreed, and after being denied telephone access to President Carter, he called a news conference in his Boise living room to demand "the immediate withdrawal of all Russian combat troops from Cuba." Back in Washington four days later, Church canceled his committee's scheduled SALT hearing so that it could receive a secret briefing on the combat brigade; when the briefing ended, he stepped into the hallway to tell reporters that "there is no likelihood whatever that the Senate would ratify the SALT II Treaty as long as Russian combat troops remain stationed in Cuba."[129]

Subsequent evaluations of Senator Church have been harsh, and he did not defend himself by preparing a memoir before his death in 1984, but the administration had only itself to blame. It had dreadfully mismanaged its relations with the Democratic Congress, and nowhere was this failure more obvious than in the administration's refusal to exploit the political advantage to be gained by joining ranks with the group of legislators who were also pressing for normalization with Cuba. The group was led by Senator Church, who, while not bowled over by Castro's warm reception, as Reagan claimed, had returned from his mid-1977 visit to report that U.S. policy "has failed, monumentally. Instead of isolating Cuba from the world at large, we have managed only to isolate ourselves from Cuba. . . . It is high time for us to discard a policy which the world community views, at best, as unworthy of a great nation and, at worst, as petulant and self-defeating."[130] The Linowitz Commission had also taken this position, and many administration officials agreed. But no one in the White House paid Church the least attention.

A similar fate had awaited Senator George McGovern's early 1977 initiative to permit two-way trade with Cuba, which he attached to the State Department's fiscal 1978 authorization bill. While agreeing with the "basic thrust" of McGovern's proposal, Secretary Vance reminded President Carter that "so far all the steps . . . have been on our side." The president wrote "True" in the memo's margin and added "I agree" in the margin where Vance said he opposed admitting Cuban sugar. At the end of the memo, Carter penned, "Don't forget Cuban troops all over Africa." Here Brzezinski shared Vance's view, advising the president that "any lifting of the embargo on Cuban goods sold to the United States should await negotiations," and in the margin of this memo Carter added another "I agree."[131]

With no help from the White House, McGovern had to limit his proposal to food and medicine and to trade in one direction only, and even then conservative senator Jesse Helms promised a floor fight. A month later, Republican senator Robert Dole joined Helms, speaking out against any easing of the embargo, and the voice of these pro-embargo forces was amplified significantly by the weekly radio broadcasts of the Republicans' up-

and-coming star, who took to the airwaves to criticize the visit to Cuba of a South Dakota basketball team (which had been defeated by a team of Cuban all-stars) and to lambaste what he called the "Soviet-Cuban assault on Africa. Now we've removed all obstacles to American travel to Cuba and we are negotiating, or at least discussing, re-opening of trade and political relations with the Cuban government. And, oh yes! We've ordered a halt to buying chrome from Rhodesia. It looks like we're going to lose more than a basketball game before the foolishness ends. This is Ronald Reagan. Thanks for listening."[132]

If Senator McGovern had counted on White House support to balance this conservative opposition, he was sadly disappointed. "I am not persuaded that the Cuban people need access to U.S. food and medicine," Brzezinski told Carter, encouraged by advice from a hardening Robert Pastor to "be careful not to give away easy and friendly gestures . . . until we can be assured that there will be appropriate and reciprocal gestures by Cuba." Brzezinski also warned Carter that "so far we seem to be taking more initiatives towards Castro than he is towards us," and here Carter once again penciled "I agree" into the margin. Then Brzezinski came to the legislative punch line: "You promised McGovern that you will maintain a position of neutrality on this bill, and I would recommend that this posture be not that of benevolent neutrality but rather of skeptical neutrality," agreeing with Pastor that "any lifting of the embargo on Cuban goods sold to the United States should await negotiations with the Cubans on normalization. Otherwise, Cy Vance will have little or no leverage to achieve some of the concessions that will be necessary to make normalization politically palatable to the US — e.g., release of Americans from jail, etc." Pastor — the NSC staff member whom at least one colleague considered "left — way, way left" — recommended that "we simply hang back and wait to see what happens."[133]

So the administration did not exactly oppose McGovern's initiative but also did not support it. Seeing the handwriting on the wall, Senator McGovern withdrew his proposal, lamenting that it "has been watered down to the point of being nearly meaningless, if not meaningless." All that Church, McGovern, and their like-minded congressional colleagues could accomplish during the Carter years was to repeal the JFK-era prohibitions on economic assistance to third countries that furnished aid to Cuba or that permitted their ships and aircraft to transport goods to or from Cuba.[134]

After Church's Boise press conference, the issue was not the Carter administration's mismanaged relations with congressional Democrats but a possible violation of the 1962 Kennedy-Khrushchev agreement. The day after the bomb from Boise, a State Department spokesperson admitted, "We have recently confirmed the presence in Cuba of what appears to be a Soviet combat unit," but he could not say whether the brigade violated the Kennedy-Khrushchev agreement since "I have no way to determine at this point the brigade's mission."[135] In 1962, the only mention of ground forces had come in a letter from Khrushchev on 20 November 1962: prodded by JFK, the Soviet leader had agreed to "ship out of Cuba those groups of our military personnel which although not directly involved in servicing the rocket weapons now removed still had something to do with guarding those installations."[136]

Although the State Department wanted to downplay the issue, Brzezinski and White House domestic political advisers convinced President Carter that the brigade could be turned into an example of strong leadership. Accepting the president's decision, Vance became appropriately bellicose, telling reporters, "We regard this as a very serious matter affecting our relations with the Soviet Union. The presence of this unit runs counter to long-held American policies." Then he drew what would become the administration's line in the sand: "I will not be satisfied with maintenance of the status quo." Two days later, Carter said the same thing: "This status quo is not acceptable."[137]

So began a month of tough talk, with Brzezinski telling reporters that the combat brigade "is not an acceptable arrangement for us" and with Carter reminding journalists, "I said this was a matter of great concern to us, that the status quo was not acceptable." A few days later, however, he appeared to back off a bit: "The present brigade of Soviet troops in Cuba is not a threat to the security of our country." When a confused member of the audience reminded the president that "you said that the status quo is unacceptable," he answered, "That's right." The questioner continued, "And you'll take appropriate measures to alter it?" "That's correct," Carter responded.[138]

"These are Brzezinski's ideas," complained Fidel Castro three days later, characterizing the national security adviser as "one of the most erratic and most stupid people among the U.S. government advisers [and] a dangerous man for peace." Then Castro added his understanding of how the winds were blowing in Washington: "Among Carter's advisors, those who have been struggling against the improvement of relations have won"—and, he continued, indicating how far relations had deteriorated, "unless I believe, and I do not, that Carter is a fool, a simpleton or an idiot who lets himself be deceived so stupidly by anyone, then I must stop thinking that Carter is a man of ethical principles." For seventeen years, the Soviet troops had been operating a training center in Cuba, he said, and "all successive U.S. presidents knew about this fact, this installation. The CIA knew about the installation. President Kennedy knew about it; Johnson knew about it; Nixon knew about it." So "I ask myself, why have they now raised this problem about an installation that is 17 years old? Why now?"[139]

Castro had two answers to his own question. One was that the United States wanted to harass the Cuban government on the eve of the nonaligned summit, which got under way in Havana on 3 September, four days after Senator Church's Boise press conference: "Perhaps they thought that . . . this could be used to make demands on Cuba and the Soviet Union and humiliate Cuba, hinder Cuba's work as a leader of the nonaligned movement." The Cuban leader placed greater emphasis on a second reason, however: "The fact that Carter's reelection is in a crisis." Nevertheless, Castro said, the U.S. president did not have "the right to threaten peace." In sum, "Carter's action regarding this problem has been dishonest, insincere and immoral, and he is deceiving world and U.S. public opinion by making people believe that the Cubans and the Soviets have taken a new step, an irresponsible step, that we have created a problem and that we have changed the status quo existing since the October 1962 crisis. I emphatically and categorically state that this is a lie, that this is dishonest, and that this is insincere and immoral."[140]

During this period, Vance met six times in Washington with Soviet ambassador Anatoly Dobrynin and twice in New York with Soviet foreign minister Andrei Gromyko, who complained to the U.N. General Assembly that "all sorts of falsehoods are being piled up concerning the policies of Cuba and the Soviet Union." While both Soviet diplomats were more tactful than Castro, their position resembled that of the Cuban leader: the number of Soviet troops had not increased since they arrived nearly two decades earlier, and they were training the Cuban armed forces, not acting as an independent combat unit. "The Soviets have essentially made what they consider to be a concession and offered a way out of the impasse by reiterating both publicly and privately that the unit is attached to a 17-year old training center," wrote the NSC official responsible for tracking the issue. "Having said that 'all contentions about the arrival in Cuba of organized combat units are totally groundless,' there is no possibility of them retreating substantially from that position."[141]

Whatever their mission, some Soviet troops had been in Cuba continuously since at least the missile crisis, when U.S. reconnaissance photos first revealed the existence of "four organized, mobile, and powerful armored Soviet units" totaling perhaps 17,500 personnel. Unlike the highly visible missiles and bombers, the withdrawal of these Soviet ground personnel had been difficult to verify—eight months after the crisis ended, a special Senate Preparedness Subcommittee had reported "no evidence that any of the combat troops associated with the four mobile armored groups have been withdrawn," but it also emphasized that "no one in official United States circles can tell, with any real degree of confidence, how many Russians are now in Cuba." President Kennedy had said the same thing when asked for his count: "We can't call the roll."[142]

The brigade discovered by the NSA in 1979 was probably one of the four units from 1962. It consisted of between twenty-six hundred and three thousand personnel, organized into three motorized rifle battalions, one tank battalion, and one artillery battalion and support units. The brigade's purpose was never explained: it may have served as a trip wire; more likely it symbolized Moscow's commitment to Cuba after the 1962 capitulation. Fidel Castro offered that explanation, telling U.S. envoys in early 1980, "We wanted them here as a symbol of solidarity." A few months earlier, the U.S. intelligence community had also concluded that the brigade's "most likely mission is to provide a small but concrete Soviet commitment to Castro, implying a readiness to defend Cuba and his regime."[143]

Such nuances were lost in Washington's file cabinets. What remained in retrievable memory was the fact that over the course of 1963, the Soviet Union had withdrawn all of its offensive weapons, including all combat units. The year ended with a CIA-DIA report that "no organized Soviet ground combat units remain in Cuba" and with CIA director McCone telling LBJ that "the Soviet activities were entirely of a training nature."[144] Six years later, in 1969, the Nixon administration concluded that roughly a brigade—"an estimated 2,000 to 3,000 Soviets"—remained as technical advisers, and McGeorge Bundy, who left Washington in 1966, recalled that the White House had known all along that some troops had remained: "We did not think small numbers of Soviet ground forces in Cuba were a serious matter," he commented. "We did not see how they could threaten our country or any other in the hemisphere."[145]

For whatever purpose, two or three thousand Soviet military personnel clearly had remained as a ticking bomb waiting to be detonated in 1979 by election-sensitive Democrats. The Republicans pounced immediately, beginning with Ronald Reagan, who argued that SALT II should not be ratified "till the Russian troops clear out of Cuba." "The Soviets obviously are testing the water," insisted New Hampshire's Republican senator, Gordon Humphrey. "If left unchallenged, the Soviets will surely increase their overt military presence in Cuba and, inevitably, prepare to move Soviet forces into other countries in this hemisphere." Faced with that prospect, Humphrey concluded that "there is no room for compromise on this issue," as he and four equally conservative colleagues introduced a resolution insisting "on the expeditious removal of Soviet combat troops and their support units from Cuba."[146]

The senators said nothing about how to achieve this removal. Much had changed since 1962 — the Soviets had grown significantly stronger, and this time they might not blink. Then what? Most of a panel of experts assembled by Zbigniew Brzezinski concluded that arguing that there was no room for compromise would be reckless; indeed, there was room for nothing else — no reasonable way to make Soviet leaders withdraw a force that they insisted did not exist.[147] Denied the photographs of missile sites that Adlai Stevenson had displayed so effectively to the Security Council in 1962, the Carter administration had no evidence to support its claim that a combat brigade so much as existed, and, according to a poll of U.S. embassies, the same allies who had rallied behind Washington in 1962 now accepted Moscow's denials. Gromyko's advice was simple: "It is high time you honestly admit this whole affair is artificial and is proclaimed to be closed."[148]

Seeking to save the SALT II treaty, President Carter made one last effort, writing to Soviet general secretary Leonid Brezhnev in late September, "The presence of a brigade of Soviet troops in Cuba which we consider to have a combat capability is of genuine and deep concern," he began. "You and I have long labored — you much longer than I — to achieve SALT II. It would be a tragedy for our nations if this labor of peace was now jeopardized because our two governments were not able to resolve a problem which one side considered to be of grave concern to itself." An unmoved Brezhnev replied immediately by repeating what Gromyko had said: "My advice to you: discard this story. We have a military training center in Cuba which has existed there for more than seventeen years. It fulfills its training function according to an agreement with the Cuban government. It does nothing more and can do nothing more. You can be completely at rest in this regard."[149]

With no reasonable alternative, President Carter accepted Brezhnev's advice. Addressing the nation on 1 October, he said that "this unit appears to be a brigade of two or three thousand men," and "it's been organized as a combat unit. Its training exercises have been those of a combat unit." The problem, he continued, is that "the Soviet Union does not admit that the unit in question is a combat unit"; rather, Moscow classified it as a training center and promised only "that they will not change its function or status as a training center." Anticipating his critics, the president acknowledged that "a confrontation might be emotionally satisfying for a few days or weeks for some people, but it would be destructive to the national interest and to the security of the United States." And, he added, "this is not a large force, nor an assault force. It presents no direct threat to us. It has no airborne or seaborne capability." Most important, "the brigade issue is certainly no reason for a return to the cold war"—that is, for the Senate to refuse to ratify SALT II.[150]

Brzezinski consoled the president by observing that JFK had also said the Berlin Wall was unacceptable, but at the time "we had no choice but to live with it. Kennedy was not prepared to knock it down. Neither are we prepared to create a military confrontation in order to get the Soviets to remove their troops from Cuba. But," he continued, "Kennedy did something else," and that was to adopt a very tough public posture. Brzezinski suggested that Carter do the same, justifying it as a way to attack another Kennedy, Senator Edward Kennedy, Carter's increasingly popular rival for the Democratic presidential nomination: "It will put Kennedy on the spot. By toughening up our posture vis-a-vis the Soviets, you will either force Kennedy to back you, or to oppose you. It will be difficult for him to remain silent. If he backs you, he is backing an assertive and tough President; if he opposes you, he can easily be stamped as a latter-day McGovernite."[151]

The administration's restraint was completely lost on Senate Republicans, many of whom were waiting to be heard as soon as the chaplain finished his prayer the morning after Carter's speech. First off was Jesse Helms, who called the address "a reaffirmation of America's weakness [and] under such conditions, SALT II is impossible." Next up was Senate minority leader Howard Baker, who told his colleagues, "We stood toe to toe with the Russians and, unlike 1962, we blinked"; incidentally, he added, SALT II is "a treaty which I believe is inherently unequal." Mocking the president as "a little like Macbeth: full of sound, but lacking the fury, and signifying nothing," Utah's Orrin Hatch declared that "the Monroe Doctrine which protected the Western hemisphere from foreign aggressions for 150 years is a dead letter. Jimmy Carter's timid, weak leadership within America, is little more than a hollow shell of its former greatness."

After searching for a full day, the Democrats finally found someone willing to come to the president's defense—Senator Claiborne Pell, the Foreign Relations Committee's ranking Democrat after Frank Church—but Pell's heart was clearly not in the task: "It would be nice if we could push them all out," he almost sighed, "but that does not seem in the cards for the moment." No sooner had he finished than Texas Republican John Tower picked up the mocking tone: "President Carter once said the status quo is unacceptable, but changed his mind and decided Tuesday night that it is acceptable." And then there was Senator Kennedy, who suggested a few months later that "the false draw in Cuba may have invited the Soviet invasion of Afghanistan."[152]

Delighted by this Democratic backbiting, Senate minority leader Howard Baker had already reminded his colleagues that "it was not this Senator or any other member on this side of the aisle who made the announcement that there were combat troops in Cuba. It was not a Republican Senator, who declared that the status quo was unacceptable, or that the Russian troops had to be moved or else the SALT treaty would be defeated." The most trenchant criticism came privately from George Kennan, who told Arthur Schlesinger Jr. that the administration's handling of the dispute "violates every elementary diplomatic rule. We got our facts wrong; we overreacted wildly; we pushed the Russians against a closed door; we preferred domestic politics to foreign policy; and now we have painted ourselves into the corner and don't know how to get out." The press was every bit as critical. "Jimmy Carter's Cuban fiasco," wrote *New York Times* columnist Tom Wicker, "ranks right up there with the Dewey campaign of 1948 for snatching defeat from the jaws of victory," while the *Baltimore Sun* called the administration's handling of the brigade "a major national embarrassment that reflects poorly on President Carter." The *Washington Post* reported that "nearly all those familiar with the details of this latest Cuban crisis agree that it was badly mishandled."[153]

In his presidential memoir, Carter brushed this criticism off as a tempest in a teapot—"Eventually, after some difficult weeks, we weathered the storm over the troops in Cuba." When the storm had subsided, "I began my laborious series of private meetings with individual senators to explain the advantages of SALT II, and continued to pick up votes." But Secretary Vance disagreed, noting in his memoir that "the administration had been seriously hurt by the episode"; similarly, the State Department's William Attwood believed that the brigade flap "all but wrecked any chance of Senate ratification of the SALT II Treaty." The most accurate assessment probably came from Senate majority leader Robert Byrd, who commented that SALT II would have been ratified before the brigade issue arose but that its approval subsequently became "problematical."[154] In early November, the Committee on Foreign Relations approved the treaty by a vote of nine to six, one vote shy of the two-thirds majority that would be required in the full Senate, and the committee mustered its nine votes only after adding an "Understanding Concerning Soviet Military Forces in Cuba," which required the president to "affirm that the United States will assure that Soviet military forces in Cuba (1) are not engaged in a combat role, and (2) will not become a threat to any country in the Caribbean or elsewhere in the Western Hemisphere."[155]

In late December, the Soviet Union invaded Afghanistan, and President Carter reacted by asking the Senate to table SALT II. "In the end, everyone lost," concluded Newsom. Clearly determined that Vance be saddled with the blame, Brzezinski told the president that "the management of the Cuban issue was left almost entirely to State, with Cy chairing the PRC and Newsom the mini-PRC. The [Special Coordination Committee], which I chair and which is responsible for crisis management (PD-2), was not convened because Cy wanted to retain control."[156] That single memo spoke volumes both about Brzezinski and about foreign policy making during the Carter years. Other casualties included Democratic senators Stone and Church, who failed in their bids for reelection, and if President Carter was correct to write that concern over the combat brigade slowly petered out, it did so only because the public's attention was drawn to a more explosive story in early November, when supporters of Iran's revolutionary government stormed the U.S. embassy in Teheran, seizing sixty hostages. Within days, ABC News had assigned a young journalist to provide daily updates on the hostage crisis, and nothing happening in Cuba could compete with the fiery mullahs. By year's end, Carter's assessment seemed correct: no one cared whether the Soviet brigade stayed or went.

IF ANY LATIN AMERICAN ISSUE could compete with Iran for the attention of senior U.S. officials, it was the turbulence in Nicaragua, where a suspiciously named rebel group had ended the Somoza dynasty in July 1979.* Although the Cuban government had openly encouraged the Sandinistas throughout their two-decade struggle, Washington was nonetheless surprised when Nicaragua's new leaders waited only one week after their victory before flying to Havana to participate in Cuba's traditional 26th of July celebration.[157]

Was Cuba getting back in the business of promoting revolution in Latin America? In early 1979 the CIA had been alerted by the comment of a senior Cuban official that "during the 1980s at least five Latin American governments will fall because of revolutionary efforts led by Communist-leftist opposition forces." Two weeks later, Maurice Bishop had overthrown the government of the tiny island nation of Grenada and promptly established diplomatic relations with Havana. The two governments soon signed an agreement providing for Cuban aid in developing Grenada's public health infrastructure and its fishing and tropical agricultural industries, prompting the DIA to characterize the Bishop coup as "a major gain for Cuban influence in the area" and to warn about Cuba's ties with Jamaica and Guyana, whose left-leaning government was already "inculcating the students with the teachings of Marxism-Lenninism [sic]." The DIA added that the situation was potentially worse in the "Latin" part of the region, given the "deeply rooted cultural and psychological conditions stemming from the ethnic composition and sociological and religious perceptions of the Latin American societies," whatever that meant.[158] In the meantime, a worried Robert Pastor focused on Grenada, warning Brzezinski that the island "could become a training camp for young radicals from the other islands." He suggested gunboat diplomacy—"sending a number of naval vessels to the region—perhaps using the [recent] volcanic eruption at St. Vincent as a cover. We should ask permission from Grenada to use their port at Georgetown [sic] as a way to help the people on St. Vincent. They would be in a difficult position to refuse; its presence couldn't help but have an impact, however, on the new revolutionary government."[159]

Only a year earlier, the director of the State Department's Office of Cuban Affairs, Wayne Smith, had assured Congress that Havana had finally outgrown its revolutionary stage. "The Cubans are prepared to accept more normal standards of international behavior," he had said, and, as for the

---

*Nicaragua's Frente Sandinista de Liberación Nacional took its name from Augusto César Sandino, a nationalist who had fought U.S. Marines occupying the country in the 1920s and early 1930s.

Soviet Union, the DIA had reported that Moscow was no longer giving much attention to Latin America: "The direct transfer of sizable amounts of financial and material aid to South American guerrilla or urban terrorist groups appears to have ceased." Pastor agreed, telling Brzezinski that "Cuba has quite deliberately eschewed any form of military involvement in Latin America or the Caribbean since 1967."[160] At this point—1978—the "Cuba" problem was Africa, not Latin America.

In mid-1979, at the height of concern over the Soviet combat brigade, Fidel Castro acknowledged that Cuba was providing Grenada's revolutionary government with military assistance.[161] A month later he announced that Cuba would also supply this tiny southeastern Caribbean nation with heavy construction equipment and 250 workers to build a new international airport—supposedly to accommodate tourists but also a convenient refueling stop for Cuban aircraft ferrying troops to Africa. In early 1980, just after Grenada had voted against a U.S.-sponsored U.N. resolution condemning Moscow's invasion of Afghanistan, the DIA told Congress that "Grenada may be considered to be a member of the Soviet-Cuban camp."[162]

Nicaragua's delegation chose to be absent on the day the General Assembly voted, an absence that never would have occurred during the Somoza era. Castro had warned the Sandinistas not to provoke the United States, but he had also agreed to send Nicaragua hundreds of Cuban teachers and medical personnel, a move interpreted by Washington as a bid for influence and perhaps as a prelude to the establishment of a Cuban military presence in Central America. Determined not to surrender Washington's overwhelming influence in Nicaragua, President Carter invited the Sandinista leaders to visit the White House, where he did his best to distance himself from the long history of U.S. support for the Somoza dictatorship— Robert Pastor recalled that Carter told Sandinista leaders that "if you don't hold me responsible for everything that happened under my predecessors, I will not hold you responsible for everything that occurred under your predecessors."[163]

The Carter administration also sought congressional approval of an aid package to help with Nicaragua's postwar reconstruction, with Deputy Secretary of State Warren Christopher warning that "the situation is still fluid. The moderate outcome we seek will not come about if we and other likeminded nations walk away now." But many members of Congress had already concluded that the administration was seeking to lock the door of an already empty barn: at the same time Christopher was making his appeal,

Sandinista leaders were again in Havana, this time as honored guests at the nonaligned summit, and in Washington, conservative representative Robert Bauman was charging that Nicaragua had become "a new beachhead for communism in the Americas."[164]

With Grenada and Nicaragua as their evidence, the U.S. intelligence community reversed its position that Cuba had ceased promoting revolution in Latin America, and in early 1980 Tarnoff and Pastor traveled again to Havana, this time to tell Fidel Castro that the United States was "deeply concerned about Cuban efforts to assist groups dedicated to the overthrow of constituted governments by force and to undermine democratic institutions." Castro gave a noncommittal reply, apparently preferring to wait six weeks until he was speaking to a more receptive audience; then he warned that proletarian rebellion was again sweeping the region, and "if they try to stop it, they will create a colossal Vietnam in Central America, or one even bigger, in the hemisphere, because the struggle of the people cannot be stopped."[165] The CIA also warned that "El Salvador would probably be the next one to fall" and that Guatemala "probably ranks, in Cuba's perception, as the number two target behind El Salvador."[166] Two months later, both Grenada's Maurice Bishop and Nicaragua's Daniel Ortega spoke at Havana's May Day rally, and in July Fidel Castro reciprocated, traveling to Managua to help the Sandinistas celebrate the first anniversary of their revolution. Joining them were the PLO's Yasir Arafat and representatives of the Soviet Union, East Germany, Bulgaria, and Romania.

AS THE U.S. INTELLIGENCE reassessment was occurring, other events continued to undermine the Carter administration. First came the botched attempt to rescue the hostages in Iran in April 1980, a failure that appeared to confirm the public's growing perception of Jimmy Carter as inept. But even if the attempt had succeeded, it would have been difficult for any president to be reelected while inflation was running at 1 percent a month and while commuters were waiting in long lines for gasoline priced at an outrageous eighty cents per gallon.

Although it probably was not needed, Cuba then hammered a final nail into the administration's coffin. In early 1978, the first U.S. Department of Commerce official to visit Cuba in seventeen years had reported that sugar still dominated the island's economy, accounting for 80 to 90 percent of export earnings, and he noted that sugar prices had plummeted from an astronomical sixty-four cents per pound in 1974 to less than eight cents in

1978.[167] The Soviet Union was continuing to purchase Cuba's sugar, but in the boom years of the mid-1970s, Cuba had diverted much of its crop to capitalist markets, earning valuable foreign exchange but also exposing the island's economy to the fickle forces of supply and demand.[168] Falling sugar prices then led Cuba both to borrow from obliging Western bankers, who were awash in petrodollars, and to reduce imports, which had already declined significantly by the beginning of the Carter administration, and in late 1977 Castro warned that further belt-tightening was on the horizon: "We shouldn't speak of . . . improving living conditions. We believe that our revolutionary people should be told very frankly that our present living conditions must be continued." And, he continued, "if the price of sugar were to go up we should not let ourselves be lured into trying to improve the level of consumption." Instead, Cuba would use any increased income to invest in development projects, avoiding any increase in consumption "for a period of seven or eight years." Repeating this dreary news to the National Assembly in mid-1978, he lengthened his discouraging estimate to another twenty years of economic problems, with or without the U.S. embargo. "Other generations will live better," he told labor leaders a few months later. "We have to think more about development than consumption."[169]

As Castro had predicted, the Cuban economy continued to deteriorate during the balance of 1978 before worsening significantly in 1979, when Cuba was struck by a string of natural calamities—a rust disease that reduced the sugar crop by about a quarter, a mold disease that destroyed most of the tobacco crop, and an outbreak of African swine fever that severely reduced the availability of pork, which is in Cuba what beef is in the United States.

In mid-1980, Castro hinted that he held the United States responsible for some of this misfortune, but he found plenty of blame to spread around, including some for the Soviet Union, which had fallen behind in its shipment of lumber, slowing housing construction, which Castro called "one of the country's supercritical issues." Cubans themselves were not blameless; Raúl Castro criticized Cuban workers for their "irresponsibility, self-serving behavior, negligence, and a buddy-system [*socialismo*] which, in addition to making many problems more serious, prevent the solution of others." But most of the blame went to international economic forces that locked Cuba into unfavorable terms of trade, especially in sugar. "We are in a terrible global picture!," Castro said. "We are sailing in a sea of difficulties [and] the shore is far away." He could only urge Cubans to hold tight: "Of course, we wish we had more," he continued, but "our goals have to be very realistic and they have to be relatively modest."[170]

Cuba also was not doing well in the international political arena. The DIA characterized Castro's ties to the Soviet Union as "closer than ever," but in early 1980 the cost of this closeness proved significant when Cuba was called on to oppose a U.S.-sponsored U.N. resolution condemning the Soviet invasion of Afghanistan. Speaking briefly to the General Assembly, foreign minister Raúl Roa did not endorse the Soviet action and said only that "we shall not vote against socialism," but the Soviet invasion killed Cuba's chances for a seat on the Security Council, which it had expected to win by virtue of its leadership of the nonaligned movement.[171] Cuba's lobbying for the seat included Castro's first appearance at the General Assembly since 1960: in October 1979, two months before the Soviet invasion, he gave a moderate speech on behalf of the nonaligned nations.[172] But Cuba could not overcome U.S. lobbying against the Security Council bid, and after a record number of ballots, the General Assembly adjourned without selecting a full complement of Security Council members for the next session.

The Soviet Union had invaded Afghanistan by the time the General Assembly reconvened in early January, and Cuban diplomats, seeing the handwriting on the wall, withdrew in favor of Mexico. Having suffered a major diplomatic defeat, Castro publicly blamed Washington, but he privately commented that Moscow's invasion "is embarrassing for [a] revolutionary movement." The United States had sponsored the U.N. resolution condemning the invasion, however, and Castro insisted that "we could not possibly align with the United States against the Soviet Union." The Cuban leader did not endorse the Soviet invasion until a year after it occurred, and his lukewarm approval was followed immediately by an expression of "hope that the situation in the area will continue to be normalized, on the basis of full sovereignty, noninterference in internal affairs, peace and good relations among all the states in the region."[173]

Castro was correct to emphasize that Moscow had been Cuba's only steadfast benefactor—capitalist markets could come and go and capitalist prices could rise and fall, but for nearly two decades, the Soviet Union had been paying above-market prices for sugar and nickel and charging below-market prices for petroleum, and during the booming mid-1970s, the USSR had even kept the oil flowing while permitting Cuba to sell much of its sugar for Western hard currencies. When the price of sugar dropped and the price of petroleum rose, the Soviets boosted their subsidy payments from $150 million in 1970 to more than $1.8 billion in 1978 and to more than $3 billion when the sugar and tobacco blights hit in 1979. That year, the Soviet Union paid forty-four cents per pound for Cuba's sugar, more than four times the average world market price.[174] Castro reciprocated where he could—his unenthusiastic endorsement of the invasion of Afghanistan was an exception; more typical was his wholehearted support of Moscow's side of the Sino-Soviet split: "Others can bite the hand that feeds them; Cuba, its children of today and tomorrow, will recognize and eternally appreciate what the Soviet Union means to our country." Asked if he considered Russia "a free country," in 1977 Castro replied, "I think it is the freest of all countries."[175]

The Soviet Union never underwrote the entire Cuban economy, however, and Havana was continuously looking for new sources of income, especially in the late 1970s, when sugar prices had collapsed and Cubans were being urged to tighten their belts. "We do not like tourism," Castro told a Havana audience in late 1978, "but we have to be realistic." At this time, Bernardo Benes and other members of Florida's Cuban community obtained permission for a special type of tourism—for exiles to visit their families. "I don't know how Castro thinks he will be able to deal with the inevitable onslaught of Yanqui consumerism," commented the NSC's Pastor. Some Cubans may have felt threatened by the prospect, but not Fidel Castro, at least initially: "Are tourists going to influence us?," he asked. "It could be the other way around."[176]

But it clearly was not. The visitors brought a glimpse of how Cubans had prospered in the United States—lining up at the Miami check-in counter for their charter flights, they struggled with dishwasher-sized boxes and suitcases bulging with everything from disposable diapers to microwave ovens, and the recipients of these gifts soon could be seen on Havana's streets wearing Grateful Dead T-shirts and strange new running shoes emblazoned with distinctive swooshes. The exiles also brought stories of how their hard work had led to an affluence that relatives left behind in Cuba could only dream of achieving.

After more than a year of family visits by perhaps 120,000 exiles, in early 1980 the DIA noted "an increasing number of reports of discontent in Cuba. This appears to be caused by Cuba's lagging economy. Shortages are reported to have reached such a level that a black market of almost all consumer goods is flourishing." Pointing out what he called "the problem of delinquency," Castro warned in late 1979, "We will build however many jails are needed . . . to put an end to this criminal offensive," with a broad definition of "criminal" that included "the lumpen, the antisocial, the slacker, the scoundrel, the unreliable."[177]

AS THE VISITING EXILES kept arriving with their largesse, as the economy continued to deteriorate, and as most Cubans discovered that black-market goods were priced beyond their means, many began to consider moving to Miami. One way to do so was to claim political asylum under the standard established by the 1952 U.N. refugee convention and its 1967 protocol: like most nations, Cuba had agreed that asylum could be sought by "any person who is *outside of any country of such person's nationality* . . . and who is unable or unwilling to return . . . because of persecution or a well-founded fear of persecution on account of race, religion, nationality, membership in a particular social group, or political opinion."[178] For island-bound Cubans, the first task was to reach foreign soil, and the only avenue to asylum open to most Cubans was to enter a foreign embassy in Havana. Both by customary international law and by a resolution of the 1928 Inter-American Conference, embassies are respected as "foreign" sovereign territory, immune from the jurisdiction of the host state. Few governments are eager for their embassies to become known as havens for asylum seekers, however, in part because such a reputation causes friction with the host state and in part because it is often impossible to determine whether an individual has "a well-founded fear of persecution" or simply wants to leave for personal reasons, including economic deprivation. In the meantime, the host embassy has to feed and house the asylum seeker, and if asylum is granted, the host country must then negotiate safe passage out of the country.

Such a situation arose in Havana in May 1979, when twelve Cubans sought asylum in the Venezuelan embassy by crashing a bus through the embassy gates. Thus alerted, the Cuban police were ready a few weeks later when several more Cubans tried to force their way into the same compound; after the dust had settled, one Cuban had been wounded and the asylum seekers had been arrested. Two more Cubans were arrested when they made a similar attempt in July, and the first fatality occurred in early 1980, when Cuban guards opened fire on a truck attempting to crash into the grounds of the Venezuelan ambassador's residence. On the same day, twenty-five thousand workers were furloughed from Havana's cigar factories because the blue mold had destroyed the tobacco crop.

One obvious result of the shooting was to encourage disaffected Cubans to look for an embassy other than that of Venezuela. One alternative, Peru's, was perfectly situated on about ten acres of land on busy Fifth Avenue, the Millionaires' Row of 1920s-era mansions stretching westward from the Almendares River into the Havana suburb of Miramar. On 16 January, the same day as the shooting at the Venezuelan embassy, twelve Cubans drove a station wagon onto the Peruvian embassy grounds and requested asylum. Refusing to consider the request, embassy officials turned the twelve over to Cuban police, but then, in an uncommon twist, the Peruvian government in Lima condemned its own embassy's refoulement, and the Cuban government, seeking to maintain good relations, promptly marched the twelve back onto the embassy grounds. At the same time, Cuba reinforced its guard at the embassy gates and issued a public warning that safe-conduct exit permits would never be given to individuals who forced their way into embassies; all those who received asylum from a foreign embassy would have to remain inside the embassy until they died or decided to return to Cuban soil, whichever came first.

Cuban authorities also focused on another avenue of departure, the hijacking of Cuban boats. One such incident had occurred in October 1978, when several disaffected Cubans forced the crew of a barge to take them to Florida, where they were immediately paroled into the United States. On 1 February 1980, sixty-five Cubans seized another barge at gunpoint and forced the captain to take them from Cárdenas to the Florida keys. Admitted immediately, all sixty-five were walking the streets of Miami's Little Havana by that evening.

No one in Washington appears to have understood how much Cuban officials were annoyed by the U.S. insistence that Cuba prosecute aircraft hijackers while the United States rolled out a red carpet for ship hijackers. Washington at least recognized the incongruity, however, and in April, Brzezinski told President Carter that the new attorney general, Benjamin Civiletti, was working on a paper that would address the issue of Cuban hijackers. He was laboring at a leisurely pace, however, and in June, when Civiletti's Justice Department finally completed its report, it concluded that nothing could be done: the hijackers were "technically subject to federal prosecution under the kidnapping or inter-state transportation of stolen property statutes," but "there is a very minimal likelihood of conviction." The basic problem was that "these cases must be prosecuted in the Southern District of Florida, where we would face juries sympathetic to the defendant refugees."[179]

Determined to stop the hijackings, the Cuban government hinted at another approach, with Fidel Castro broaching the topic obliquely in early March at the end of a long speech to the Federation of Cuban Women. The United States "encourages illegal departures from Cuba, the hijacking of boats, and it receives the hijackers almost as if they were heroes," he began.

We hope that they will take steps to discourage illegal departures from Cuba; if not, we will have to take our own steps. We already did this once, [and] we're not going to be taking steps against those who try to leave the country illegally while the United States encourages their illegal departure. Once before we found ourselves obliged to take steps in this area; . . . on one occasion we had to open the port of Camarioca. And it seems to us an indicator of the immaturity of the U.S. government that it is once again creating similar circumstances, because, for sure, we have always followed the principle that this revolution is a voluntary association. Voluntary![180]

Listening to this speech and remembering their government's 1965 decision to open the port of Camarioca to anyone wishing to leave, disaffected Cubans could have reasonably interpreted Castro's words as an invitation to pack their bags.

Three weeks later, six Cubans crashed a bus through the gates of the Peruvian embassy, killing a Cuban guard. At that point, said an upset Fidel Castro, "we could not take any more." He announced that the remaining guards were being withdrawn—anyone who wanted to leave by that route was welcome to do so, and within two days about *ten thousand* Cubans had crowded onto the Peruvian embassy grounds. Commenting on "the hunger of many people on that island to escape political deprivation of freedom and also economic adversity," President Carter said that "our hearts go out to the almost 10,000 freedom-loving Cubans who entered a temporarily opened gate at the Peruvian Embassy."[181]

With chaos on their lawn, the beleaguered Peruvian diplomats saw no alternative but to begin processing the asylum requests; the Cuban government agreed to permit the asylum seekers to leave, and nearby Costa Rica agreed to serve as an intermediate stop. On 16 April, the first flight carrying 153 Cubans arrived in San José, where they were greeted by Costa Rican president Rodrigo Carazo, whose welcoming remarks focused on Cuba's denial of human rights. Finding Carazo's remarks offensive and aware that the Costa Rican leader would have the opportunity to repeat this performance when he greeted each planeload, the Cuban government closed the air bridge, opened the port of Mariel, and announced that anyone in Florida who wanted to pick up a friend or relative could do so. "We have ended our protection of the peninsula of Florida," read a front-page *Granma* editorial; "now they will begin to harvest the fruit of their policy of encouraging illegal departures from Cuba, including the hijacking of boats." "From Florida comes the announcement of the departure of private boats to pick up anti-social elements," read yet another front-page *Granma* editorial. "We are not opposed to their being carried off."[182] So began the Mariel boatlift.

A special task force chaired by Vice President Walter Mondale estimated that the Castro government might permit anywhere from 100,000 to 1.2 million Cubans to leave, and the president was cautioned that "the situation is likely to get much worse before it gets better." When asked what he intended to do about it, a hapless President Carter replied, "I don't know how else to answer your question except to say we're doing the best we can."[183] It is a felony to transport a nonresident without a visa into the United States, and the State Department warned that "many more vessels with Cuban refugees on board are sure to follow if Cuban exiles believe nothing will happen if they violate U.S. law." Mondale's task force added its warning that "once they arrive in the US, they apply for asylum as political refugees, and it will prove virtually impossible to do anything but permit these Cubans to remain." Asked to explain why, a key aide informed President Carter that the laws governing refugees were "filled with contradictions, implausibilities, unrealistic assumptions and impractical answers." Basically, "our laws never contemplated and do not adequately provide for people coming to our shores directly for asylum." U.S. law conceived of refugees as sitting in camps overseas, waiting for the United States to accept a fair share.[184]

The Immigration and Naturalization Service (INS) did the best that could be done under the circumstances, announcing that if the boat owners reported to INS officials in Key West and unloaded their passengers into INS custody, the fine would be one thousand for each person, and the boat carrying the passengers would be held only until the owner had paid the fine. But in the chaotic conditions at Key West, most boat owners unloaded and departed without being fined, and many who were fined were allowed simply to accept the summons to appear in court and then sailed straight back to Cuba to pick up another load. "Clearly, our strategy is not working," reported the vice president's task force, and President Carter exacerbated the enforcement problem by responding to a reporter's question with his promise to "continue to provide an open heart and open arms to refugees seeking freedom from Communist domination and from economic deprivation, brought about primarily by Fidel Castro and his government." "The whole situation was not helped by the President's answer," admitted cabinet secretary Jack Watson.[185]

Carter's promise was influenced by an episode that had occurred three days earlier in front of the U.S. Interests Section, when Cuban security forces and bused-in thugs had attacked a group of about 800 Cubans who had approached the building to request visas. In the melee, half the Cubans rushed into the building, which, while large, was not equipped to house 383 guests. "We had no experience as innkeepers prior to May 2, but are acquiring it and getting better at job as we go along," cabled an unflappable Wayne Smith, chief of the Interests Section. While searching for cots and food (and for cooks to prepare it), Smith told Washington, "We are relaxed and prepared to live with [the] situation," but, he continued, conditions were anything but calm beyond the Interests Section compound: "Cuba is going through its most convulsive moment in 20 years. Tens of thousands of people are leaving [the] country through Mariel, hundreds of thousands of others are thinking about it and still other hundreds of thousands are spending most of their waking hours hunting down and savaging those who are leaving."[186]

Back in Washington "we were really on overload," recalled a White House domestic policy adviser, Stuart Eizenstat: "I mean just unbelievable overload even for the White House which is always on overload. We were on extra circuits. We had the primary election campaign [with Senator Edward Kennedy emerging as a serious challenger]. We had the hostage crisis. We had a deteriorating economy. . . . We had gas lines and a new energy policy. It was an almost unbelievable time."[187] In addition, 827 boats carried 40,000 Cubans to Florida during the first two weeks of May. The administration announced that it would beef up enforcement at the same time it was attempting to arrange a meeting with the Cubans. Clearly not yet ready to defuse the crisis, Havana delayed the meeting until 17 June, when Pastor and Tarnoff arrived in Havana again. This time Castro refused to receive them, shunting them off to José Luis Padrón and Ricardo Alarcón, who recalled the discussion as especially intense — "like four guys talking to one another very frankly."[188]

Frank it was. "We have two immediate issues to raise," Tarnoff started off, "the immigration question in general and the disposition of the persons in the U.S. Interests Section." "Once again, the U.S. side deals with only those matters which are in its own interest," Padrón replied, "ignoring those issues which are the essence of the problems between us. . . . No progress will be possible if your desire is to deal exclusively with the points you raise, sidestepping all the other issues which have been affecting our relations since the Revolution. . . . We are not prepared to discuss partial aspects, no matter how pressing and urgent the U.S. may think they are." The conversation went downhill from there, with Alarcón blaming everything on the United States: "Before the Revolution, the U.S. had a single Latin American immigration policy which covered all these cases, including Cuba. However, starting with the Revolution, the U.S. Government instituted a special policy for Cuba alone, the intent of which was to subvert and destabilize our country. From that time, Cuban emigration to the U.S. became part and parcel of the U.S. policy of aggression." "Just imagine how many Latin Americans would have immigrated to the U.S. if they had had the incentive which certain sectors of Cuban society have had," Padrón added, washing Cuba's hands of the entire matter: since international law considered the Interests Section to be U.S. soil, "it is up to the U.S. to solve this aspect of our problems." Pastor responded by complaining, "You have behaved in a belligerent and provocative manner toward the U.S." Moreover, he asserted, "The U.S. is not a hostile nation, and when we behave in a manner which might be interpreted as hostile, it is usually with just cause."[189]

The meeting continued for more than seven hours, producing forty-five single-spaced pages of near-verbatim notes before Pastor and Tarnoff flew back to Washington, where they reported that Cubans would not discuss either Mariel or the asylum seekers at the Interests Section "unless we expressed a readiness to negotiate a removal of the embargo, abandoning our base at Guantanamo, and ceasing the overflights. In addition, the Cuban side was unusually polemical, retracing 20 years of alleged American hostility to Cuba and raising trivial complaints." Their conclusion: "We clearly have reached a dead-end."[190]

That left Wayne Smith with the task of negotiating his guests' departure from the Interests Section, and his job was complicated considerably when it became evident that the right hand of the U.S. government did not know what the left was doing: in early July, only hours before Smith was scheduled to meet with Cuban vice president Carlos Rafael Rodríguez to negotiate an end to the occupation, the NSA sent an intimidating SR-71 reconnaissance flight over Havana, resulting, according to an upset Smith, "in loud sonic boom almost knocking members of [the U.S. Interests Section] from their chairs and almost certainly resulting in material damage in Havana area." During his May Day speech a few weeks earlier, an angry Fidel Castro had complained about "the explosions which you hear every so often all over the country, because the breaking of the speed of sound creates these noises. Walls shake, glass windows shake each time the SR-71 goes by." Now, Smith wondered, "Would it not have been advisable to hold off on overflight at least until we heard what Carlos Rafael Rodríguez had to say on [the] subject? If any progress was made in meeting with him this afternoon it may well have been counteracted by this morning's flight."[191]

With the Interests Section crowded by several hundred asylum seekers and with the flow of Cubans from Mariel reaching its peak, the situation was further complicated by the continuing arrival in South Florida of uncounted thousands of Haitians. Haitians had for years been taking advantage of prevailing ocean currents to drift in rafts toward U.S. waters, usually landing first in the Bahamas, where smugglers helped the migrants complete the voyage. "There are approximately 40,000 Haitian 'boat people' in Florida and more are arriving daily," reported the vice president's task force in late April, and of this number "approximately 10,000 have filed for asylum status which has almost uniformly been denied"; indeed, despite universal awareness of the repressive behavior of Haiti's government, only about 250 Haitians received asylum between 1970 and 1980.[192]

Mariel thus prompted complaints from the black community. Why, they asked, were tens of thousands of Cubans accepted with no questions asked while almost all Haitians were sent back? When a black reporter inquired about this discrepancy, President Carter replied that the two groups were being handled equally "and strictly in accordance with the American law." The president failed to mention that two different laws applied—one for Cubans and one for everyone else. The 1966 Cuban Adjustment Act simply allowed any Cuban who reached U.S. shores to remain; the new 1980 Refugee Act, in contrast, set up extremely restrictive procedures for everyone else. President Carter was not oblivious to the double standard, and later that day he announced not only that the United States would begin admitting those Haitians who qualified after they had been screened at the U.S. Navy base at Guantánamo, but also that the United States would cease admitting the Cubans fleeing from Mariel.[193]

A few hours earlier, Carter's aides had informed him that "the fines (none have been collected) and occasional seizures (nine) have only marginally reduced the number of boats leaving for Mariel," emphasizing that "we cannot continue indefinitely to cope with arrivals at the present rate of 13,000 per week." According to his advisers, "The time has come to take firm measures both to restrict the boat traffic and to regularize the flow of refugees." The president agreed, but when he ordered the Coast Guard to stop the flow, he was criticized not only by Cuban Americans but also by his principal political rival, Ronald Reagan: "For us to threaten the boat people and shut off this rescue mission that's been going on, I can't agree with that. . . . I just can't understand the lack of humanitarianism in shutting that off."[194]

"The handling of the refugees was not the highlight of the Carter Administration," confessed Eizenstat. "The situation was totally mishandled." Only the fleeing Haitians and their U.S. supporters were pleased, and their pleasure was short-lived, for in September the hastily constructed refugee processing center at Guantánamo was being closed: "Current policy at the base is to permit the transit of Haitian migrants to the United States. We will work to see that these people are returned to Haiti instead."[195]

Notwithstanding the words chiseled into the base of the Statue of Liberty, a substantial majority of the U.S. public has traditionally told pollsters that it strongly opposes immigration from anywhere, and in the case of the Mariel boatlift, this general anti-immigration predisposition was exacerbated by the evidence that some of the arrivals were criminals and that others appeared to have mental problems, rendering them "excludable" under the regulations governing the admission of immigrants. "We detained the ones who other refugees pointed out as having been in jail," explained an INS employee several years later. "Otherwise, there wasn't much we could've done. We were dealing with a government that refused to cooperate, with an influx of people who brought no records and whose names we could not even verify." Still other arrivals were not prepared for the reception they received during their preliminary screening in Key West: incarceration for those hapless enough to admit to having been convicted of serious nonpolitical crimes or to volunteer some piece of evidence that they might endanger the community.[196] The rest were divided into two categories: those with relatives willing to take them in were released; those without relatives were sent to one of four "processing centers"—in actuality, minimum-security prisons.

The first of these centers was located at Eglin Air Force Base in Northwest Florida, but that facility quickly reached capacity; other centers were then hastily opened at Fort Chaffee, Arkansas; Fort Indiantown Gap, Pennsylvania; and Fort McCoy, Wisconsin. Few of the arriving Cubans were pleased by relocation to these remote locales, and in June about three hundred of the eighteen thousand at Fort Chaffee registered their displeasure by storming the gate and setting out for greener pastures. Five were shot before the others were convinced to return to the base. The mayor of Fort Smith had seen this coming: "I went out there and saw that a lot of them were covered with tattoos. I knew they couldn't be productive. There might be a Desi Arnaz or two out there, but mostly they were going to be killing one another."[197]

Some of these internees were truly dangerous, and in a formal note the United States protested "in the strongest possible terms the cynical actions of the Government of Cuba in sending to the United States hardened criminals who constitute a danger to any society. These actions, which contravene basic decency as well as international law and practice, cannot be accepted by any civilized society." By September, 1,774 Cubans known to have committed violent crimes in Cuba were being held in U.S. penitentiaries, and another 400 were undergoing psychiatric evaluations that in some cases would lead to permanent institutional care.[198]

By that time Cuba had stopped the exodus. Several years later, Fidel Castro explained, "We solved the Mariel problem before the elections. We were the ones who stopped it because we didn't want to harm Carter. This is the truth." If it was the truth, it only indicated how badly the Cuban leader misjudged the situation, for the damage to the president's approval rating on the eve of an election had already been done—a full summer of Cuba thumbing its nose at U.S. immigration law and President Carter's seeming impotence. The U.S. government estimated the total number of *marielitos* at 129,000, but there will never be a tally of the cost—financial, human, or political—of the Mariel crisis. After looking over the documents left behind by his predecessors, the director of the Reagan administration's Office of Cuban Affairs commented that Mariel was "the event which destroyed any prospect of improved bilateral relations under President Carter."[199]

"YOU START WITH NO FILES, no records, all new staff," commented General Odom, Brzezinski's military aide; "it takes five or six months just to get your feet on the ground." That has always been true, especially when a change in leadership involves a change in party control, but some administrations find their footing more quickly than others. On Cuba, the Carter appointees never found theirs. In the end, six weeks before President Carter's defeat by Ronald Reagan, Robert Pastor flew down to inspect the U.S. Navy base at Guantánamo, then wrote to Brzezinski that if Castro dared touch the U.S. installation, "I would personally recommend that we respond by erasing Holguin Air Base in Cuba." No one took him seriously—"This is a nutty idea," Pastor's immediate supervisor penciled in the margin, with Brzezinski adding, "I agree." But it was a final melancholy confirmation of the conclusion Cyrus Vance reached in his memoir: "We seemed unable to maintain a sense of perspective about Cuba."[200]

We don't have any dealings with Cuba. If they'd ever like to rejoin the civilized world, we'd be very happy to help them. But not under the present circumstances.
—President Ronald Reagan, April 1982

11

BACK TO SQUARE ONE
THE REAGAN YEARS

"My opinion of the Russians has changed most drastically," President Jimmy Carter told reporters on the final day of 1979. "It's only now dawning upon the world the magnitude of the action that the Soviets undertook in invading Afghanistan." Any clear thinker should have expected Moscow to do something like that, replied Carter's principal rival, Ronald Reagan, who believed that "the Soviet Union underlies all the unrest that is going on. If they weren't engaged in this game of dominoes, there wouldn't be any hot spots in the world." To counter the invasion of Afghanistan, he suggested increased pressure on Cuba. A surprised interviewer followed up: "You're not suggesting that we consider putting the heat on Cuba in retaliation for Afghanistan?" Absolutely, Reagan replied: "I'm suggesting we might blockade Cuba."[1]

So began the election year. The administration's handling of foreign policy was certain to be a central campaign issue as long as fifty-two U.S. embassy personnel remained hostages in Iran, but President Carter had a second Achilles heel, the domestic economy. In announcing that he would mount a challenge for the Democratic nomination, Senator Edward Kennedy asked the party faithful why anyone would support the reelection of a Democrat who had brought the nation "three more years of Republican inflation, three more years of Republican interest rates, and three more years of Republican economics."[2] Over the next six months, the Massachusetts senator captured much of Carter's base, scooping up a third of the party's delegates in the primaries and, at the very end of his challenge, flatly ignoring the nominee, an incumbent president, standing inches away on the podium at their convention's closing ceremony.

Then the deeply divided Democrats set out to stop Ronald Reagan's resurgent Republicans. Calling Carter's Cuba policy "dangerous and incomprehensible," the Republican platform promised to "stand firm with countries seeking to develop their societies while combating the subversion and violence exported by Cuba and Moscow," a not-so-oblique reference to the turmoil in Central America, where "the Carter Administration stands by while Castro's totalitarian Cuba, financed, directed, and supplied by the Soviet Union, aggressively trains, arms and supports forces of warfare and revolution." Only in the 1960 Kennedy-Nixon contest had Cuba received more attention; now it was featured in Ronald Reagan's everyday stump speech:

> How has Fidel Castro reciprocated the friendship offered by President Carter? Since 1976, Russian pilots have begun flying air cover over the island. Soviet submarines have been sent to Castro's navy. Nuclear-capable fighter bombers have appeared at Cuban air bases, and a Soviet combat force is discovered holding military maneuvers there. Apparently, to Mr. Carter, this was the last straw. The status quo—that's Latin for "the mess we're in"—he said was unacceptable, a few weeks later, it seems, was acceptable.

All this, Reagan said, is a perfect example of what happens when an indecisive leader comes face to face with an adversary bent on expansion: "a foreign policy bordering on appeasement."[3]

This get-tough view attracted not only conservative Republicans who opposed the Nixon-Kissinger policy of détente but also traditional blue-collar Democrats and especially those Democratic elites who had come to feel homeless in a party dominated by leaders they considered dangerously liberal (Senator Kennedy) or hopelessly inept (President Carter). At the time of Carter's 1976 election, these elites did not yet have the name by which they would become known—neoconservatives—but that was the year they joined with Reagan Republicans to re-create the McCarthy era's Committee on the Present Danger, whose purpose was "to alert American policy makers and opinion leaders and the public at large to the ominous Soviet military buildup." The 150-member committee had one simple explanation for almost every foreign policy problem, an explanation voiced best by Eugene Rostow, who went on to direct the Reagan administration's Arms Control and Disarmament Agency: the Soviet Union, he said, is "seeking not to preserve but to destroy the state system that was organized under the Charter of the United Nations in 1945, and to replace it with an imperial system dominated by its will." Both Nixon-Kissinger Republicans and Democrats of all stripes had been duped into thinking that détente was possible, while Moscow "continues, with notable persistence, to take advantage of every opportunity to expand its political and military influence throughout the world"—witness the invasion of Afghanistan.[4]

And then, alongside this superpower aggression, voters had the Iranian hostage crisis to provide daily evidence of the Carter administration's inability to cope with even a second-rate power; couple that foreign policy debacle to the dismal economy, and the result was preordained: 489 to 49 in the Electoral College, with the Democrats also losing control of both the Senate and enough House seats (thirty-two) to give conservatives ideological control. Many members of the Committee on the Present Danger soon would be moving to Washington, and one of them, Jeane Kirkpatrick, would craft the new administration's policy toward Latin America.

Characterizing the Republican triumph as "a victory of the extreme right wing in U.S. politics," Fidel Castro reminded Cubans that "the United States has always been the sworn enemy of our nation"; now, with Reagan in the White House, "there is a danger he might throw all caution to the winds." That possibility seemed quite plausible at first, when the rhetoric of the nation's new leaders suggested an anticommunist holy war. At his initial presidential news conference, Reagan slammed shut the door to détente by saying that the Kremlin could not be trusted—that Soviet leaders "reserve unto themselves the right to commit any crime, to lie, to cheat," and a month later he attributed this to a fundamental immorality, asserting that the Soviet "ideology is without God, without our idea of morality in the religious sense—their statement about morality is that nothing is immoral if it furthers their cause, which means they can resort to lying or stealing or cheating or even murder if it furthers their cause."[5]

This type of talk reached its extreme fairly early, however; its apogee came in 1983, when the president told a group of Christian evangelicals that "there is sin and evil in the world, and we're enjoined by Scripture and the Lord Jesus to oppose it with all our might," then characterized the Kremlin as "the focus of evil in the modern world." These words triggered a recoil within a worried foreign policy establishment, with an aging George

Kennan picking up his pen to warn that "at the end of our present path . . . lies no visible destination but failure and horror." Chastened, perhaps, and then certainly overtaken by events within the Soviet Union, where Mikhail Gorbachev became premier in 1985, a certain moderation soon came to characterize the administration's approach to East-West relations.[6]

The Reagan policy toward Latin America also experienced a similar early burst of extremist talk, but it was not followed by moderation. In the 1980 campaign, the Republicans lacked a high-level "Latin America" voice similar to that of the Democrats' 1976 Linowitz Commission; instead, the Republicans had the self-styled Committee of Santa Fe, composed of five little-known conservatives who gave a Latin American focus to the ideas of the Committee on the Present Danger. "The Americas are under attack," their manifesto began; "the Caribbean rim and basin are spotted with Soviet surrogates and ringed with socialist states." The committee suggested radio broadcasts to undermine the Cuban government—an idea whose time would soon come—but "if propaganda fails, a war of national liberation against Castro must be launched."[7]

Fidel Castro characterized the committee's report as "ignorant, delirious, and irresponsible" and the committee itself as "a reactionary clique of the extreme right with an openly warmongering and fascist foreign policy."[8] But four of the five committee members assumed positions in the new administration, including Roger Fontaine, who replaced Robert Pastor as the Latin Americanist on the NSC staff but never wielded Pastor's influence. Overall, commented General William Odom, a conservative Carter appointee who was held over on Reagan's National Security Council staff, "the average IQ on the NSC dropped twenty points. They let children take charge, people like Oliver North and Bud McFarlane," supervised by national security adviser Richard Allen, "the lightest of lightweights."[9]

Georgetown University professor Jeane Kirkpatrick, the new ambassador to the United Nations, was no lightweight. Earlier, while writing her doctoral dissertation on Argentine politics, she had come to see Latin America as a Hobbesian nightmare. Now she turned to address the administration's most vexing Latin American problem, the rebellion in El Salvador. Without ever having set foot in the country, she wrote that the uprising had its origin in that country's political culture, which "emphasizes strength and *machismo* and all that implies about the nature of the world and the human traits necessary for survival and success. Competition, courage, honor, shrewdness, assertiveness, a capacity for risk and recklessness, and a certain 'manly' disregard for safety are valued." This assessment was but the country-specific consequence of Kirkpatrick's general theory of Latin American politics: "Violence or the threat of violence is an integral part of these political systems—a fact which is obscured by our way of describing military 'interventions' in Latin political systems as if the system were normably [*sic*] peaceable. Coups, demonstrations, political strikes, plots, and counterplots are, in fact, the norm."[10] Since Latin Americans were inclined toward dictatorship, Kirkpatrick advised President Reagan to accept the inevitable and support the friendly dictators, a choice made palatable by the argument that these friends were fairly benign authoritarians who left most citizens alone, while the alternative was unfriendly communist totalitarians who controlled citizens' every waking moment. This authoritarian/totalitarian dichotomy quickly became one of the administration's defining intellectual perspectives.[11]

SO WHERE DID CUBA fit into this worldview? The Reagan administration initially focused on what Kirkpatrick called the Castro government's efforts "to succor, bolster, train, equip, and advise revolutionaries." Convinced that Cuba could not do so without assistance, Reagan-era officials shared none of the Carter administration's ambivalence; they agreed unanimously that the tail in Havana was being wagged by the dog in Moscow. "They have a colony 90 miles off our shore," Reagan told a campaign audience, "and anyone who thinks it isn't owned lock, stock and barrel by the Soviet Union is naive." After his election, President Reagan referred to Cuba as "a stooge for the Soviet Union," as "little more than a surrogate for a faraway totalitarian power," and as a country that "sells its young men as Soviet cannon fodder."[12]

Secretary of state-designate Alexander Haig said the same thing during his confirmation hearing and, consistent to the end, two decades later recalled that "the problem with Nicaragua was Castro, and the problem with Castro was Moscow—he was a proxy for the Soviet Union."[13] Kirkpatrick also took the position that Cuba is "doing for the Soviet Union what the Gurkha mercenaries did for nineteenth-century England." Cuba, she said, was "a colony of the Soviet Union," a view also held by one of her closest State Department allies, Assistant Secretary Elliott Abrams, who commented that in return for economic subsidies, "Cuba sends combat and backup troops to countries where the Soviets seek to establish a sphere of influence." The State Department told Congress, "We must be clear about Cuba. It is a Soviet surrogate."[14]

Talking directly with the Castro government, as the Carter administration had done, therefore made no sense; moreover, this view suggested a potential new role for Cuba—as a site to demonstrate the Reagan administration's commitment to rolling back the borders of communism. Defense Secretary Caspar Weinberger recalled that Haig announced his intention a few days before the inauguration when the president-elect gathered his new foreign policy team at Blair House: "Al Haig, with perhaps more passionate intensity than usual, was telling the President that Poland [the Solidarity challenge] was one thing, but that the real problem we were facing, and would have to confront, was the increasing Communist inroads into and attempts to dominate our Caribbean and Central American neighbors. . . . The principal target of his emotion was clearly Cuba." Uneasy with the direction Haig was taking, Weinberger continued, "after some time, I broke in to inquire quietly where all of this was leading and what it was we should be doing. Al, who has never liked to be interrupted, stopped in mid-flight, turning one of his withering command glares in my direction and said that it was quite clear we would have to invade Cuba."[15]

Invade? Haig had opposed normalizing relations with Cuba at his confirmation hearing a few days earlier, but he had proposed nothing dramatic. Nor had he ever suggested anything as drastic as an invasion when he had worked on Cuba during Lyndon Johnson's presidency—referring to Haig as "sort of a note-taker," the State Department's John Crimmins recalled that in the mid-1960s, Haig "wasn't so hard-nosed with respect to Cuba as he turned out later to be," and in those early days Conservative Caucus leader Howard Phillips had dismissed Haig as "a personable, attractive, fanny-kisser." But now he was the secretary of state, and as he was leaving the Blair House meeting, he handed aide Robert McFarlane his first assignment: "I want to go after Cuba, Bud. I want you to get everyone together and give me a plan for doing it." "It wasn't what any of us had expected to hear," McFarlane remembered. "It was as though Haig had come into office thinking, 'Where can we make a quick win?' and judged that place to be Cuba."[16]

As instructed, McFarlane set to work with the help of two new assistant secretaries of state, Paul Wolfowitz and Richard Burt, while Haig "badgered me for the results weekly." At the same time, Haig told a secret briefing of NATO allies that his initial foreign policy focus would be Central America: "We have not yet decided on the precise steps we will take to deal with the situation; we will, however, in some way have to deal with the immediate source of the problem—and that is Cuba." When Haig's remark was leaked to the press, presidential counselor Edwin Meese poured fuel on the fire:

"The President has said many times he would like potential or real adversaries to go to bed every night wondering what we will do the next day. I don't think we would rule out anything."[17]

So here was Cuba once again, a month after the inauguration, splashed across the front page of every major U.S. newspaper, while the president's domestic advisers wanted everyone's focus on the tax cuts and government-shrinking initiatives known as the Reagan Revolution. In early March, President Reagan sought to defuse the issue by telling CBS's Walter Cronkite that Haig had been misunderstood—"I don't think in any way that he was suggesting an assault on Cuba"—while McFarlane, Wolfowitz, and Burt tried to calm Haig down:

> The long-term interests of the United States and the West would be best served by using a Soviet intervention in Poland to forge new attitudes at home and abroad about defense spending and countering Soviet advances, to launch a few new initiatives in this direction. Action against Cuba should therefore be delayed until this new anti-Soviet attitude is consolidated and until we begin to benefit from some of the initiatives engendered by it. We would then be in a much improved position not only to cut Cuba down to size but to cope with Cuban and Soviet responses in other locales.

Haig was clearly annoyed. "What you've given me is bureaucratic pap," he complained. "I want you to go back to the boards, get [U.S. Southern Command chief] General Paul Gorman, the CIA, and anybody else you need, but give me something I can take to the President so that he can show substantial gain during his first year in office."[18]

Years later, Haig downplayed this early episode: "It wasn't a big deal. We needed to get a bracket around Fidel Castro; it was that simple. We just needed to get him out of Central America." None of Haig's associates at the time agreed, however—they were convinced that Haig was determined to bring Castro down.[19]

This extreme thinking was shelved in short order, in part because it was distracting, in part because it seemed to be leading to an invasion, which no one in Washington really wanted, but mostly because it was identified with Alexander Haig, who proved unable to meld into a team where most senior officials had been working together for years. Badly misjudging this social situation, Haig failed to realize that he had been invited to join a small club and, once inside, was supposed to treat his fellow members as friendly colleagues, not bureaucratic rivals. "It took me only forty-eight hours to realize there was a palace guard," Haig recalled. "When I would tell the president I needed to say something to him privately, he would say—'OK, boys, give us some time,' but one of them, usually [Michael] Deaver, would be back in two minutes, pointing to his watch and pushing me out."[20]

In addition to restricting Haig's access and presumably his influence, senior White House aides quickly discovered the secretary's thin skin, and they soon began to taunt him with little slights such as assigning him an undesirable seat on Air Force One and placing him far down a receiving line—the type of slights that would grate on the rank conscious. And, as Haig recalled a quarter century later, still with obvious anger, "there wasn't a day when they didn't have the press in to say I was a wild man." Perhaps that fact explains why gossipy Washington soon began commenting on the decline of Haig's influence within the administration; his reputation certainly was not strengthened when President Reagan was shot two months into his tenure and Haig rushed to the White House press room, where, visibly shaking at the podium, he made his signature "I am in control here" remark. "Even after the vice-president was back in Washington," Reagan later wrote, "I was told he maintained that he, not [Vice President] George [H. W. Bush], should be in charge. I didn't know about this when it was going on. But I heard later that the rest of the cabinet was furious. They said he acted as if he thought he had the right to sit in the Oval Office and believed it was his constitutional right to take over."[21]

A few days after the assassination attempt, well-connected journalist Tad Szulc reported that "a senior White House official privately commented that Secretary Haig's verbosity on the issues of El Salvador and Cuba was becoming something of a problem, that he was a 'loose cannon.'" Nancy Reagan agreed: "Once, talking about Cuba in a meeting of the National Security Council, he turned to Ronnie and said, 'You just give me the word and I'll turn that f—— island into a parking lot.'" What Haig missed while in office he saw while preparing his memoir: on Cuba "I was virtually alone."[22] And the reason he was alone is that senior administration officials had better things to do with their time than become engaged in a controversy, let alone a confrontation, with Cuba. Central America and other Cuba-related problems could be handled without engaging Havana.

CUBA'S LEADERS PROBABLY LACKED a full appreciation of this Washington infighting, but they were clearly concerned about the new administration's strident anticommunism. When Secretary Haig warned that if Cuba continued to supply arms to Central American rebels, the United States would "deal with it at its source," Fidel Castro replied as expected: "We will never be like the Christians of ancient Rome who meekly gave up their lives to their enemies. We are capable of fighting and we will fight with indomitable ferocity to defend our rights."[23] But the Cuban leader had several additional problems to confront, the most immediate of which was renewed exile attacks. Just before Reagan's electoral victory, Miami-based Omega 7 had assassinated a member of the Cuban mission to the United Nations. (President Carter had cabled Castro his "deepest regret over this cowardly and reprehensible deed" and promised to identify and prosecute the murderers.) Three sabotage raids on Cuba occurred immediately after the 1980 election, accompanied by a press statement in which another exile group, Alpha 66, announced that it intended to "create as much havoc as we can" and dared the Justice Department to prosecute: "If the Neutrality Act includes anyone conspiring against Fidel Castro, they'd better start building a few jails. We'd love a political trial. We really would." A few months later, just after Cuban authorities arrested five exiles who had landed in Cuba on a mission to assassinate Castro, Alpha 66 leader Umberto Alvarado promised to infiltrate more saboteurs to "destroy Cuban industry, transportation and communication."[24]

These events led the exasperated Cuban leader to ask, "How is it that in the United States news conferences are held in public offices announcing the landing of mercenary commando groups to carry out attacks on leaders of the revolution, and yet the U.S. government does not say a word? It does absolutely nothing." Turning to the issue of the day, the Cuban leader then accused the Reagan administration of responsibility for an outbreak of dengue fever. After reviewing the history of U.S. biological attacks, he asked, "Why should it be surprising that imperialism has once again fallen to the temptation of treacherously using biological weapons against Cuba? What can be expected of a government whose policy is characterized by its cynicism, lies and a total lack of scruples?"[25]

The Cuban leader probably did not realize at the time that sabotage would not be his principal problem with Cuban exiles, for a new group had appeared in Miami: the Cuban American National Foundation (CANF). Formed soon after Ronald Reagan's election by a group of Cuban American leaders, several of them veterans of the Bay of Pigs, CANF had the encouragement of the president-elect's initial national security adviser, Richard Allen, but it probably would have been created anyway—it was an idea whose time had come: tens of thousands of Cuban Americans had become citizens and voters, many had acquired significant fortunes, and now they were beginning the time-honored process of elbowing their way into the political arena.[26] The foundation began by vigorously supporting the administration's policies in Central America; in turn, a grateful President Reagan soon began going out of his way to be encouraging. "I'm especially pleased to have the opportunity to say a few words in support of the much needed work of the Foundation," the president told a 1983 CANF banquet. "It fills a great service to the American people and the people of other countries with information about life in Cuba and conditions in that brutally repressive society"—"an organization which plays a vital and unique role."[27] During the Reagan years, CANF would take an ever-expanding part in the formulation of Cuba policy, and during the ensuing Bush and Clinton administrations, the foundation basically seized control.

During Reagan's tenure, however, Cuba's most pressing concern alongside the traditional Cuban American terrorism was the island's deteriorating relations with the rest of Latin America. During a May 1980 meeting with East German premier Erich Honecker, Castro had spoken too soon in recalling Cuba's isolation in the early days of the revolution and noting that "this situation has changed a lot." Only a few months later, relations with Venezuela turned sour when its courts acquitted four men accused of bombing the 1976 Cubana flight from Barbados, an exceptionally sensitive issue in Cuba, and matters were exacerbated by Cuba's refusal to grant safe passage out of the country to a group of Cubans who had claimed asylum in the Venezuelan embassy, thereby saddling Venezuela's two diplomats in Havana with sixteen long-term guests. Relations with nearby Jamaica subsequently deteriorated even more dramatically—in late 1980, only five days before Ronald Reagan's election, Jamaican prime minister Michael Manley was defeated by conservative Edward Seaga, who used his victory speech to call for the expulsion of Cuba's ambassador. President Reagan hailed Seaga's victory as "a great reverse in the Caribbean situation."[28]

During 1980–81, Cuba's relations had also deteriorated with Peru (over the embassy invasion that triggered the Mariel boatlift), with the Bahamas (over the sinking of a Bahamian patrol boat by Cuban jets), and with Colombia (after captured M-19 guerrillas confessed that they had been trained in Cuba).[29] Castro reacted to Colombia's decision to suspend diplomatic relations by characterizing President Julio César Turbay as "a toy of the Colombian oligarchy, the Colombian army, and imperialism"—harsh words that probably reflected how little Castro had to lose: Havana's relations with Bogotá had been frosty since 1979, when Colombia had led the effort to block Cuba's bid for a seat on the U.N. Security Council. Then the blocking role had been assumed by Costa Rica, where Cuba's ties had been strained by President Rodrigo Carazo's criticism of Cuba's human rights violations during the evacuation of Cuban asylum seekers from the Peruvian embassy. Now, in late 1980, only weeks after Ronald Reagan's election, Costa Rica threw another log on the fire by sending U.N. secretary-general Kurt Waldheim a letter from a recently released Cuban prisoner, Huber Matos, who had been granted asylum in Costa Rica. The letter accused the Cuban government of holding political prisoners, and its circulation at U.N. headquarters prompted Castro to charge that Costa Rica had joined "a counter-revolutionary campaign against Cuba organized by the imperialist Government of the United States." The Carazo government responded by severing what Castro dismissed as "the tenuous, almost ridiculous ties Costa Rica maintains with us." [30]

A few days later, Mexico landed a completely unexpected blow when it announced that President Reagan had agreed to attend a summit meeting of aid donors and recipients in Cancún, but only on the condition that Fidel Castro be excluded. The Cuban leader should have been an automatic participant as chair of the nonaligned movement, but as a State Department memo indicated, "Faced with the prospect of losing the US if Cuba were invited, the organizers opted for a US presence." Seeking an invitation, Castro met at Cozumel with Mexican president José López Portillo but returned to Havana with only a joint statement indicating that Cuba was being excluded because of "the well-known position of the United States." Obviously frustrated, the Cuban leader could do little more than criticize Reagan as "the almighty and indispensable gentleman [who] has arrogantly prohibited that Cuba's voice be heard." [31]

As Miami exiles were launching their new wave of sabotage attacks and as much of Latin America was distancing itself from Cuba, the government found itself facing a third pressing problem: the economy. It had recovered a bit since the late 1970s, helped by rising sugar prices that allowed Castro to be upbeat at the twentieth anniversary celebration of the Bay of Pigs victory in April 1981, but then the recovery had stopped and the Cuban leader had a different story to tell fifteen months later: "We have difficulties and will continue to have difficulties in the next few years. . . . In the near future our overall economy will grow little or not at all." [32]

It was the same old problem: the economy still rested on sugar, and while the 1979 harvest had been the second-largest in Cuban history—eight million tons—the world price had plummeted from twenty-eight cents a pound in 1980 to nine cents in mid-1982. Fortunately, Castro continued,

Cuba was largely insulated from this decline, since "80 percent of our trade is with the socialist countries and 20 percent with the Western countries, [but] this 20 percent is very important. It has a specific weight greater than 20. We use hard currency to import medicines, food, raw materials for feed, raw materials for industry and in construction." The situation was so bad, he warned, that layoffs were possible.[33]

Cubans had heard this story both before and after 1959, but in the 1970s the gyrations in world sugar prices had been accompanied by something new and, at first blush, positive—the recycling of petrodollars that had begun after the first OPEC price increase in 1973. During the Nixon-Ford years, this increased liquidity had coincided with the renewal of Cuba's relations with the West, and many Western nations had added government-guaranteed loans to the packages containing diplomatic recognition. Using the credit being offered seemed prudent, for this period was also characterized by a spectacular rise in the price of sugar from four cents a pound in 1970 to an astronomical sixty-four cents a pound at one point in 1974. Cuba had cut back on imports when sugar prices fell later in the 1970s, but the retrenchment never matched the drop in export earnings, and the gap had been filled by borrowing more and more petrodollars.[34]

At the very end of the 1970s, lenders began tucking their wallets back in their pockets, worried initially by the prospect that Poland's large debt could not be serviced and, with their eyes sensitized, by the growing evidence that few Third World borrowers were earning enough money to repay their loans. The chickens came home to roost in 1982 when Mexico announced that it could no longer service its debt. That calamity to an oil exporter highlighted the risks of lending to a sugar exporter at a time when world prices were headed for the basement, eventually bottoming out at 3.6 cents per pound.

The most basic rule of U.S. politics is that an economic downturn is bad news for incumbents, and this rule governed the CIA's thinking in late 1981 when it concluded that the Cuban government "is facing its most serious domestic problems since it came to power." Fidel Castro was on the ropes—"dwelling inordinately on the past" and "brooding about the incredible problems of Cuba's underdevelopment"; his speeches were now lapsing into "uncontrolled monologue"; and "over the past two years he has fumbled, lost his place in the reams of notes and papers that he now usually brings to the podium." Most important, he has "seemed to lose contact with his audiences," and as a result of both the sagging economy and declining charisma, "his unfulfilled promises of a better future have already begun to undermine his legitimacy." The report then turned to the period immediately ahead: "It is possible for the first time in 20 years to contemplate scenarios in which Cuban figures might try to topple the Castros." Should a coup occur—or should Castro think that a coup was about to occur—"under pressure and great psychological strain," he might "throw caution to the winds and try to provoke a military conflict with the United States." Only such an action might save him: "He would then once again be at the center of a major international crisis out of which he could emerge again triumphant."[35]

This analysis came at the same time that Secretary Haig was talking about turning Cuba into a parking lot, and it gave cooler heads an alternative: tighten the economic screws. A tightening had begun just days after the 1980 election, when newly empowered hard-liners within the Carter administration had resumed strict enforcement of the secondary boycott on Cuban nickel, returning to the policy of the mid-1960s, when President Johnson had banned the import of European stainless steel containing Cuban nickel. The Nixon administration had relented in early 1971 because the ban had annoyed major U.S. allies, and Cuba again began selling about 70 percent of its nickel production to Western buyers. Some of the metal was undoubtedly being used to make products imported by the United States, so two weeks after the Reagan triumph, the Department of the Treasury once again banned French stainless steel products containing Cuban nickel. After the inauguration, the United States began what one administration official referred to as a "quantum tightening of economic embargo by stronger restrictions on Cuban content from third countries," and, wrote State's senior official on Cuba, "third countries henceforth found it more practical to acquire their nickel elsewhere than from Cuba."[36]

Equally hostile noneconomic moves soon followed. Three months after President Reagan's inauguration, the United States expelled two diplomats at Cuba's U.N. mission, accusing them of spying and of seeking to purchase prohibited electronic equipment. The United States also reinstated the twenty-five-mile limit on travel of Cubans attached to the U.N. mission, which President Carter had dropped; moved some Cuban personnel from the blue list (total immunity) to the white list (with less immunity); tightened housing, employment, and travel restrictions on Cuban diplomats in Washington; and began seizing books and periodicals imported from Cuba.[37]

The intended recipients went to federal court to challenge the seizure of these printed materials, and when a Who's Who of civil liberties groups

·joined the case of *Nation v. Haig*, it threatened to become a landmark dispute over First Amendment freedoms. Clearly aware that it would lose in court, Treasury lifted the publication ban in early 1982, but the policy reversal covered only single copies, and even then the Treasury dragged its feet: not until February 1985 did the department clarify its position to allow anyone to import single copies.[38] Still annoyed, civil libertarians sought relief from Congress, which took its time but eventually specified that the Trading with the Enemy Act "does not include the authority to regulate or prohibit, directly or indirectly, the importation from any country, or the exportation to any country, whether commercial or otherwise, of publications, films, posters, phonograph records, photographs, microfilms, microfiche, tapes, or other informational materials." Even then, the Office of Foreign Assets Control narrowly interpreted this definition in its implementing regulations, and only in 1991, when faced with a lawsuit, did the office lift its ban on importing Cuban artwork.[39]

These actions—resuming the nickel ban, restricting Cuba's diplomats, banning the entry of publications—constituted but a prelude. In April 1982, the administration made its first major move, ordering a halt in the Miami-Havana charter flights that had become the most convenient route to Cuba after 1977, when President Carter had lifted the travel ban. U.S. travelers quickly adjusted by flying through third countries, but the administration subsequently announced that the Kennedy-era travel ban was being reinstated: as of 15 May 1982, only journalists, researchers, government officials, and Cuban exiles visiting close relatives would be allowed to spend money in Cuba.[40]

About forty thousand U.S. residents had traveled to Cuba in 1981, and most of them would not have been affected by the new regulations because they were visiting relatives, but the ban's reinstatement touched a civil-liberties nerve among the set of citizens predisposed to contest most Reagan foreign policy initiatives, and with the help of the American Civil Liberties Union, they filed suit (*Regan v. Wald*) to block implementation of the new travel restrictions.[41] The case spent two years filtering through the lower courts before the Supreme Court finally heard oral arguments in April 1984. Lawyers there focused not on the right to travel and not on the right to spend money (the basis of previous legal challenges) but on the technical question of what, precisely, President Carter had done in light of subsequent legislation restraining the president's right to impose peacetime embargoes.

In 1977, he had issued Regulation 560, granting U.S. residents a general license to spend money while in Cuba. Two months later, Congress had amended the Trading with the Enemy Act by restricting to *wartime* the president's regulatory powers under the act, but it grandfathered any presidential authority in effect on 1 July 1977, regardless of whether the authority had originally been exercised during a time of war or peace.[42] The fate of *Regan v. Wald* hinged on whether President Carter was "exercising authority" over travel to Cuba when he lifted the travel ban in April 1977. By a 5–4 vote, the Supreme Court ruled in June 1984 that he was indeed "exercising authority," as evidenced by Regulation 560, which granted a general license to travelers. The new peacetime/wartime distinction was therefore irrelevant, and the president retained the grandfathered power to regulate transactions with Cuba. President Reagan's actions in 1982, therefore, were legal: using his grandfathered authority, he had simply amended Carter's Regulation 560 to narrow dramatically the scope of permissible transactions.[43] With modifications that variously reduced or enlarged the list of eligible travelers, the 1982 Reagan restrictions continued into the twenty-first century.

So, in the early Reagan years, Cuba's recently gushing well of petrodollars had dried up, sugar prices had declined, and the United States was doing what it could to reduce the island's foreign exchange earnings. As a result, in mid-1982 Cuba was using 65 percent of its meager convertible currency earnings simply to service its debt, and in August the Banco Nacional notified Western creditors that Cuba could no longer meet its scheduled repayments.[44]

ALL THIS WAS A SIDESHOW; the center ring featured the battle over Central America—in particular, the mushrooming conflict in El Salvador, which the State Department characterized as a "textbook case of indirect armed aggression by communist powers through Cuba." Issued a month after President Reagan's inauguration, State's white paper claimed to present "definitive evidence" of Havana's support of the guerrillas, and a few days later Secretary Haig accused Cuba of being "the platform, the instigator, and the operative leadership behind the situation in El Salvador."[45]

"Lies, lies and more lies," responded Fidel Castro. "It is not true—and I repeat it here with absolute moral authority—that there are Cuban military advisers in El Salvador. It is a lie that some of the arms supplied by the USSR for our defense are being redistributed in Central America. It is a lie that Cuba is supplying arms and military equipment to the Salvadoran patriots." Then an exasperated Castro sat down for an interview with the editors of a Mexican magazine, *Proceso*. "We have been held hostage since 1959," he complained, and during that time "we haven't had twenty-four peaceful hours." Now "Reagan has declared himself the world's police officer. He prohibits change. In Central America, in Africa, in Asia. Not a leaf can move on a tree without his OK, because behind every unauthorized movement is a Soviet conspiracy or a Soviet-Cuban conspiracy." Clearly convinced that no hope existed for improved relations, Castro characterized the new administration's appointees as fascists and accused President Reagan of "walking in Hitler's footsteps." He conceded that "the U.S. system is not fascist, but it is my deepest conviction that the group that constitutes the main nucleus of the current U.S. administration is fascist; its thinking is fascist."[46]

The Cuban leader had good reason to worry—the early threatening rhetoric had been merely a signal that the new administration's anti-Castro pitchers were warming up in the bullpen. When they were ready, it was time for some hardball, with Haig explaining what came next as a signal to the Soviet Union: "a plain warning that their time of unresisted adventuring in the Third World was over, and that America's capacity to tolerate the mischief of Moscow's proxies, Cuba and Libya, had been exceeded." This warning required a show of military force—"A credible willingness to apply it to the degree necessary simply could not be disregarded," Haig wrote, so in late October 1981, the U.S. Navy launched a month of maneuvers off Cuba's shores.[47]

Cuba, of course, went on full military alert, and the question of U.S. bellicosity again became a front-page story—the first question at President Reagan's November 1981 press conference began with the accusation that "a high state of belligerency seems to personify your foreign policy." A defensive president replied, "We have no plans for putting Americans in combat in any place in the world," but by this time the fact that a plan to attack Cuba was being prepared had become common knowledge: "Reagan's Goal: Cutting Castro Down to Size" had been the cover story of an April edition of *U.S. News and World Report*. "A still guarded and highly controversial plan to achieve that objective has been drafted," the article began. "The 'Haig plan' catalogs a broad range of measures calculated to bring the Cuban ruler into line—including a possible blockade and other military action." Now, a few months later, dozens of U.S. warships were maneuvering just outside Cuban waters, and newspapers were reporting that the Pentagon had been asked "to study a show of airpower, large naval exercises, a quarantine on the shipment of arms to the island, a general blockade as part of an act of war, and an invasion by American and possibly Latin American forces."

Seeking direct confirmation, reporters were ushered into Secretary Haig's office, where he acknowledged that the Department of Defense had been asked to produce a study of "a quarantine or even stronger action."[48]

Cuba had already begun beefing up its defenses. Visiting Moscow when Secretary Haig first began threatening to go to the source of Central American instability, Castro promised, "We will fight to the death for each piece of our territory in case imperialism attacks us," and the Soviet press reported that Leonid Brezhnev had reassured Castro of the Kremlin's continuing support.[49] When the U.S. maneuvers began, Cuba supplemented its military alert by creating a civilian militia—1.2 million members of the new Milicias de Tropas Territoriales, who trained initially after work and on weekends and then once a month on "Sunday Defense Days." When PBS journalist Robert MacNeil questioned the need for this effort, an incredulous Castro shot back, "Do we really have to explain that? Look, . . . we are not going to wait until the government of the United States decides to attack the country to start to prepare." Castro also took the unusual step of writing letters to the editors of both the *New York Times* and the *Washington Post* to accuse the Reagan administration of setting the stage for an invasion with "a campaign of falsehood and lies," including the "absolutely false" assertion that Cuba had sent up to five hundred troops to El Salvador.[50]

Castro's words probably influenced no one, but with critics now referring to Central America as another Vietnam, did the administration really want to provoke a military confrontation with Cuba and quite possibly the Soviet Union? The *U.S. News and World Report* article had noted that Reagan's domestic political advisers "are loath to court an international crisis that would further divert attention from the administration's economic program" and that they had begun an effort "to rein in Haig," but it was no easy task to control a secretary of state who had recently walked up to Nicaragua's ambassador in Washington, "stuck a finger in her face, and said, 'You better tell the boys down south, you know, your government, that they better behave themselves, otherwise they're really going to be in for it.'" "Haig was like that," continued the U.S. ambassador to Managua, who recalled the episode. "You never knew what he was going to say." After a few such episodes and less than a year into the new administration, the press began quoting unnamed White House officials about Haig's petulant, overbearing manner, especially "his spectacular blowups at morning staff meetings." At White House meetings, "he pounded the table and seemed ready to explode," President Reagan recalled. "The intensity of his attitude surprised and worried me."[51]

Those who wanted to tone down the talk about Cuba were supported from Havana by Wayne Smith, still the chief of the U.S. Interests Section, who sent cable after cable urging less tough talk and more diplomatic engagement, never receiving a response.[52] In late October 1981, both the Mexican ambassador to Cuba and the Cuban vice minister of foreign relations, Ricardo Alarcón, informed Smith that Cuba wanted to negotiate an end to the conflict over El Salvador. The envoy reported this offer to Washington and again received no reply; Smith, a moderate liberal in a State Department that had turned sharply conservative, was being cut out of the action. Meanwhile, as Peter Kornbluh later discovered, Mexico was directly pressuring the administration: driving President Reagan to the airport after the close of the October 1981 Cancún summit, Mexican president López Portillo pointed out that he had endured intense domestic criticism by excluding Fidel Castro; would Reagan now return the favor?[53] Specifically, at López Portillo's July meeting with Castro in Cozumel, the Cuban leader had expressed a willingness to talk with the United States. Would Reagan agree to do so?

Haig later dismissed Mexico's involvement ("López Portillo had nothing to do with it; we had decided ourselves to see if Cuba wanted to talk"), but the Mexicans surely were involved at some level, because on 23 November Haig found himself in the Mexico City home of Foreign Minister Jorge Castañeda, being introduced to Cuban vice president Carlos Rafael Rodríguez. According to Haig, "It was not my intention to threaten or intimidate Rodríguez. He knew well enough what the relative strengths of our two countries were. At this moment, two nuclear carrier groups were off the coast of Cuba, and the timing of their arrival greatly influenced my decision to attend this meeting. The uncompromising rhetoric of a new American President whose election filled Cubans with anxiety had already reached their ears." But Haig worried that Rodríguez might not take the Reagan hostility seriously: "Based on the experience of the last twenty years, the Cubans must have believed that the United States was weak," he wrote.[54] Perhaps that fear explains why he began by warning that "the mood of the people of the United States is definitely militating toward a change in our relations with Cuba, a change that is not positive for Cuba." But then, seemingly starting over, his tone abruptly softened: "We are thoroughly familiar with the reality of Cuba," he said, "We have analyzed with great care the needs of Cuba, in the sense of its hopes for the future. It seems to us that the Cuban people have suffered a great deal from sacrifices imposed from abroad. We believe that the possibility still exists for a normalization of its relations not only with the United States, but with all of this hemisphere." An offer followed: "I know that President Reagan considers trade with Cuba a possibility."[55]

Refusing to touch this bait, Rodríguez replied with a simple "Thank you very much," then turned to the core issue, Central America, which became the principal focus for the rest of the meeting, with Haig telling Rodríguez that "nobody gave Cuba the divine right to interfere in the internal affairs of the countries of this hemisphere." The Cuban vice president had already explained that "the information you are spreading about Nicaragua is a complete falsification," but he acknowledged helping overthrow the Somoza dictatorship and continuing to support the Sandinista government with a small number of military advisers but primarily with doctors and teachers — in Nicaragua, he said, "we have there 2,759 people, of which 2,045 are teachers." Haig replied that Rodríguez misunderstood: "I'm not saying that you don't have a significant number of teachers there, but they are teaching your philosophy to Nicaraguan children." The Cuban replied that "it would be very difficult for our 2,700 teachers to teach Marxist-Leninism to little Indians"; moreover, "I do not believe that the United States has any right to interfere in matters related to the presence of Cuban teachers in Nicaragua. This, and what they are teaching, is a question for the Nicaraguan government to decide. I can assure you, that these are elementary school teachers who can hardly teach Marxist-Leninism." As for El Salvador, Rodríguez added that Cuba had sent neither troops nor advisers, and he went out of his way to underline that Moscow was not the force behind Cuban involvement in Central America.

Two decades later, Haig's principal recollection of the meeting was that he had been offended by Rodríguez's attitude, remembering the Cuban vice president as "arrogant," but at the time the secretary of state appeared to take no offense: when the two sides had laid out their positions and it was clear that no progress was going to be made, Haig simply offered to send ambassador-at-large Vernon Walters to Havana or New York for further talks, and the meeting ended. Nothing more was heard from Havana, and in his State of the Union address two months later, President Reagan warned that "toward those who would export terrorism and subversion in the Caribbean and elsewhere, especially Cuba and Libya, we will act with firmness."[56]

This warning came at a time when firmness was becoming difficult: a year into the Reagan era, the attentive U.S. public had become deeply divided over what exactly was occurring in El Salvador, the focus of Washington's Latin American policy. Many observers agreed with the administration that El Salvador represented a case of communist aggression, but an equal number considered the rebellion an indigenous uprising against a tyrannical regime. With this increasingly acrimonious debate dominating the news, President Reagan summoned Walters to the Oval Office.

A retired lieutenant general and a gifted linguist, as he liked to inform anyone who would listen, Walters had spent ten of his childhood years in Europe, and "by the time I was 10, I was quadralingual. And I don't mean I spoke four languages. I mean you couldn't tell me from a native." In World War II he added Portuguese to his repertoire while serving as liaison with the Brazilian expeditionary force — "I was the only American in the middle of 19,000 Brazilians in Italy for a year and a half. That was about as total immersion as you can get." As a Cold War military attaché, Walters had helped engineer or at least encourage the 1964 military coup against Brazil's left-leaning Goulart government and had drawn the authoritarian/totalitarian distinction years earlier than Jeane Kirkpatrick in response to the release of documents demonstrating his role in the coup: "I am convinced that if the [1964] revolution had not occurred, Brazil would have gone the way of Cuba. Perhaps there have been some excessive shows of zeal under the regime. They are very small alongside of what would have happened if Brazil had gone Communist. We would not have isolated cases of police brutality such as occur in many countries. We would have had another Gulag archipelago. Authoritarian rightist regimes always disappear eventually. They have never been able to perpetuate themselves. Communist regimes, once they seize power, never let go." [57]

That thinking was not in vogue when it was published during the Carter era, so Walters had spent those years on the sidelines before Haig brought him back to the State Department, initially as a special emissary to reassure South America's military governments of the new administration's friendship, and then as ambassador-at-large. Now, on 1 March 1982, Walters was in the Oval Office receiving instructions from the president and secretary of state: Walters was to travel to Havana and determine what would be required to convince the Cubans to leave Central America. Walters asked if he was authorized to offer anything as an incentive, but, he recalled, an impatient Haig interrupted to insist simply "that we had to find out definitely whether Castro was irrevocably committed to supporting all of these Marxist so-called 'liberation movements,' or whether we could strike some sort of deal with him. If not, then the sooner we found out the better." The envoy later wrote that he thought Haig was aware that no deal was possible, "but for the record he wanted it known that he had tried." Haig himself recalled, "I did not believe that the time had come for talks with the Cubans," but President Reagan wanted to try.[58]

Flying to Havana three days later, Walters worried that "there was nothing to prevent Castro, if he so wished, from giving me some slow-working poison," but for a still-unexplained reason the Cubans decided not to murder him; instead, he was immediately ushered into a meeting with Fidel Castro and Carlos Rafael Rodríguez. Walters began by telling the two Cubans, "'I have not come here to threaten you, but I must tell you a truth which is as old as history. When a great country like mine feels threatened in what it regards as its vital interests, as for example in Central America, then we are prepared to consider all options, without exceptions.' I paused for effect and then repeated, 'Without exceptions.'"[59]

It was a poor opening gambit. Say what you will about Fidel Castro, up to this moment he had never been known to be bullied; indeed, his bedrock position had always been that Cubans would never again kneel in submission (*doblegar*) to Washington's demands and that he personally would fight to the death rather than yield—he had ended his most recent 26th of July speech with the promise that "this country may be erased from the face of earth, but it will never be intimidated or humbled." He had recently vowed before a second audience that "the one thing we will never do is fall on our knees at the feet of imperialism and beg for peace" and told a third that "this country cannot be threatened, it cannot be made to bow and scrape" and a fourth that "Cuba will not be brought to its knees."[60]

Apparently oblivious to the possibility that he had touched the most sensitive nerve in Fidel Castro's body (or that Cubans might have been upset by yet another military exercise just getting under way off Cuba's coast), Walters was unable to explain why it seemed as if "the Cuban leader worked throughout the meeting to control an inner agitation." In addition to the threat, another part of this agitation might have reflected the fact that the famously loquacious Walters would not let the equally loquacious Castro say much but kept interrupting. Walters was "full of anecdotes of a life which was rich in anecdotes, but which we knew," recalled Rodríguez; "It was not a complete waste of time . . . but we went nowhere."[61] On the topic of Central America, Walters reported that Castro made it clear "that it was his 'revolutionary duty' to help 'liberation movements' like his own

to overthrow the tyrants put in power by the 'Wall Street imperialists'";
nonetheless, "the last thing he repeated to me before we left the conference
room was, 'Everything is negotiable.'" This information somehow failed to
sink in, for the envoy concluded that "nothing Castro had said during my
visit gave me the impression that he was really prepared to negotiate seriously with us." In saying their good-byes, Walters noted, the Cubans used
"Hasta luego," while he was careful to respond with the somewhat more
final "Adios."[62]

No one in Cuba read Walters's report, of course; instead, the Cuban
government heard President Reagan's public statement six weeks later:
"We don't have any dealings with Cuba. If they'd ever like to rejoin the civilized world, we'd be very happy to help them. But not under the present
circumstances." On the heels of this statement came the largest military
maneuvers the United States had ever conducted in the Caribbean, the purpose of which was to train for an attack on "Brown," a hostile Caribbean
country that was aiding "Yellow," a Central American ally. The maneuvers,
Ocean Venture '82, involved forty-five thousand troops, including marine
amphibious landing units and sixty ships arranged in two carrier battle
groups. At one point during the five-week exercise, Air Force B-52s simu-
lated Vietnam-style carpet bombing of Brown's ports and airfields.[63]

During these maneuvers, the Cubans made another offer to negotiate:
at a diplomatic reception in late May 1982, Raúl Castro approached Interests Section chief Wayne Smith and, according to the CIA, asked him "to
inform Secretary Haig directly of the seriousness of Cuba's intentions regarding talks." Moreover, the CIA continued, "Raúl apparently sensed that
his comments in such an informal atmosphere might not be considered
official, and he therefore stressed that he was speaking in an official capacity." The CIA appropriately concluded that "Havana wants Washington
to know that the numerous Cuban offers to negotiate enjoy the backing of
the full leadership," but the agency cast this assessment in the most negative possible light, interspersed with statements that "Havana will persevere in the promotion of violent revolution as long as the guerrilla elite
continues to rule Cuba"; that "Castro has no real commitment to the peace
process"; that "Cuba's repeated offers to negotiate on Central America are
an effort to buy time and gain a propaganda advantage"; and that "Castro
needs a major diversion to refocus popular attention away from the seemingly insurmountable economic problems." Concluding that there was "no
credible evidence that Havana is ready to offer any significant concessions,"
the agency advised against further talks, which would merely "buy time

in which the US media could be exploited to pressure Washington to halt military assistance to the Salvadoran Government."[64]

The Reagan administration thus never explored Cuba's repeated offers to negotiate. Instead, it took the public position that Cuba was intransigent. A month after the CIA's assessment of Raúl Castro's offer, the State Department's coordinator of Cuban affairs wrote in *Foreign Affairs* that "the Castro government chose support for 'wars of national liberation' over the benefits of normalization with the United States," and testifying before Congress a few months later, Assistant Secretary of State Thomas Enders acknowledged that Haig and Walters had met with Cuban officials, but "in each case we were told that what could be talked about was the bilateral agenda—migration, tourism, intelligence overflights, the embargo, diplomatic relations, Guantanamo. Puerto Rico and the Third Country agenda—Cuba's aggressive actions in Central America and Africa—were not negotiable."[65]

That statement was not true, and Wayne Smith was outraged. "The administration simply lied," he said of Enders's testimony. "All administrations construe things in ways most favorable to them and stretch the truth a bit in the process. This one, however, went beyond any limits of decency. It had no qualms at all about misrepresenting the facts altogether." By this time Smith was a private citizen: after the administration failed to consult with him about Haig's Mexico City meeting with Rodríguez, Smith concluded that he had lost officials' confidence. When the Walters meeting occurred right under Smith's nose in Havana, Smith was not even informed that Walters was coming. And in mid-1982, when no one in Washington responded to his cables about Raúl Castro's initiative, Smith resigned his commission, ending at age fifty a brilliant career in the Foreign Service. "Wayne Smith won't be thanked by Mr. Reagan for speaking plainly," read a *New York Times* editorial, "but the rest of us are in his debt."[66]

WHY DID THE Reagan administration refuse to negotiate? Many of the documents needed for a confident answer are still classified, but those currently available suggest that the CIA's view was dominant—that Cuba's offer to negotiate was a ploy, an attempt merely to buy time for El Salvador's leftist rebels, who, along with Nicaragua's Sandinistas, would "distract American attention and resources from areas of more vital Soviet security concern." No one embraced this view more completely than agency director William Casey, one of Ronald Reagan's closest confidants. Casey argued that Moscow was not so reckless as to provoke a direct confrontation; instead, it "takes maximum advantage of third world surrogates like Cuba."[67] If there were to be talks, then, they should be with Moscow, not Havana.

Perhaps another reason for the refusal to negotiate was the firm conviction that a leopard cannot change its spots. In late 1982, the CIA had argued that "the very nature of the Castro regime precludes anything but an adversary relationship," and by that time President Reagan had already said that the spots had to go before the relations could be normalized: "What it would take is Fidel Castro recognizing that he made the wrong choice quite a while ago, and that he sincerely and honestly wants to rejoin the family of American nations." While Cuban documents will have to be declassified before it is possible to know whether Cuba's offer to negotiate over Central America was sincere, no one ever doubted Castro's promise that the spots were going to stay: "When the imperialists say that we want to live in peace we must break our ties with the socialist community, we say that those ties will never be broken, never."[68]

A complete explanation for the failure to negotiate also requires some reference to the bureaucratic turmoil in Washington. Raúl Castro made his offer to Wayne Smith in late May 1982, just before the conflict between Secretary Haig and senior White House officials came to a head during President Reagan's nine-day trip to meet with European leaders. By all accounts, Reagan's close contact with Haig over these days exacerbated the personal uneasiness that had been developing during the preceding eighteen months. During the trip Haig received his unfavorable seat assignment on Air Force One, and he recalled being "treated as if I wasn't even a member of the government; the prime minister of Italy even apologized to me because he felt bad that I was excluded from Reagan's meeting with him." (But here, at least, Haig felt he had the last laugh: "As I was cooling my heels in the outer office, the door suddenly opened and they asked me to come in. President Reagan had fallen asleep and they didn't know what to do. He did it again that afternoon when we met with the Pope—just fell asleep.")[69]

During the trip a conflict also arose over substance: the Israeli army crossed the border into Lebanon to attack Palestinian fighters who had been shelling Israel's northern settlements. Haig "went to the President and told him I had to see [Israeli prime minister Menachem] Begin, but Meese told Reagan not to let me go." A frustrated Haig tagged along for the rest of the trip, but Saudi King Khalid died just after the return to Washington, and the President asked Vice President Bush and Defense Secretary Weinberger to represent the United States at his funeral. "Obviously I should have gone with Bush; I'm the Secretary of State," Haig recalled, but the game was already over. Haig was not in Riyadh when Bush and Weinberger met with the new Saudi authorities, "but I had a man in the room who told me what they said: 'We want you to know that Alexander Haig no longer speaks for the United States.'"[70]

The secretary of state apparently failed to perceive a subtle shift in the balance between the State Department and the White House caused by the departure of William Clark, a longtime Reagan confidant, from his position as Haig's deputy secretary of state to become the president's national security adviser, replacing the ineffectual Richard Allen, whom Haig considered "a non-player with a big mouth tied to Jesse Helms." Now, with the secretary continuing to complain that the White House staff was undercutting his authority, a series of stormy sessions led Haig again to threaten to resign; as usual, he made his threat indirectly, during the heat of a discussion with others. But Clark took it to the president, who called Haig aside the next day to say that his resignation had been accepted. Stunned, he blamed the president's decision on Clark ("the Number One snake in the world"), on Nancy Reagan ("a mean bitch when she gets going"), on Michael Deaver ("a known faggot who controlled Momma — he did her hair"), and on White House chief of staff James A. Baker III (for whom Haig had scant affection but no pithy comment). Together, they "had participated in the brilliantly orchestrated symphony of character assassination against me in the news media."[71]

U.S.-CUBAN RELATIONS did not improve after George Shultz became secretary of state in mid-1982. A longtime Reagan supporter and reliable team player who had been serving as chair of Reagan's Economic Policy Advisory Board, Shultz had been a perfectly respectable professor until a tragic moment of moral impairment led him to accept a deanship. Once on that slippery slope, he soon accepted President Nixon's offer to become secretary of labor, then director of the Office of Management and Budget, and finally secretary of the treasury, resigning three months before Nixon to become president of Bechtel Corporation. While Shultz's colorless public persona may have been the opposite of Haig's, the new secretary was one of the most prominent members of the Committee on the Present Danger, and he shared Haig's demonic view of the Soviet Union as "the greatest military power of any tyranny in history." In Shultz's analysis, "The fundamental difference between East and West is not in economic or social policy, but in the moral principles on which they are based. It is the difference between tyranny and freedom."[72]

On Cuba "Shultz was 100 percent better," recalled State's coordinator of Cuban affairs; "he had a pretty balanced view of foreign relations, and unlike Haig he never spoke without thinking." Asked at his confirmation hearing about the possibility of negotiations, the nominee replied that Cuba would first have to change its "aggressive and unsettling activity," mentioning Africa but emphasizing Central America, where arms "come via Cuba from the Soviet Union, apparently to Nicaragua and thereby into various guerrilla hands and become quite a destabilizing force." But overthrowing the Castro government was not one of Shultz's priorities. To the extent that Cuba was fueling unrest in Central America, he sought to solve the problem in Central America, not by going to the alleged source. And while the new secretary of state did not absolutely rule out better relations, he insisted that "there's nothing to talk about in the pattern of behavior that we see with Cuba right now." For the moment, Shultz told an interviewer soon after his appointment, "I think the best strategy—and I'm sure the President does—with respect to Cuba is right where we are."[73]

The escalating violence in Central America had come home to Washington in the form of the administration's requests to Congress for military assistance, which fueled the seemingly interminable debate over what exactly was occurring in the region, with a focus inherited from President Carter's lame-duck period, when the CIA had warned that the Salvadoran government would probably fall without substantial U.S. aid. Like both Haig and Shultz, the agency argued that the Salvadoran insurgents' arms were coming from Cuba via Nicaragua, whose government was thought by many to be the product of Cuban assistance. As candidate Reagan had said on the campaign trail when the Sandinistas were still trying to overthrow the Somoza dynasty, "There is no question but that most of the rebels are Cuban-trained, Cuban-armed, and dedicated to creating another Communist country in this hemisphere."[74]

President Reagan's new assistant secretary of state for Latin America, Thomas Enders, was convinced that Cuba (and therefore the Soviet Union) had already seized control in Nicaragua—Enders called it "the preserve of a small Cuban-advised elite of Marxist-Leninists," and Ambassador Lawrence Pezzullo recalled that Enders, visiting Managua, told the Sandinista leadership that "we're coming to a crossroads with you guys. And if we don't reach an accommodation, it's going to be a problem for you. Because we're a big country, and I'm just telling you. I don't want to threaten you, but the fact of the matter is, we can hurt you." Pezzullo's recall of Enders's words was probably not exact but almost certainly captured his tone and demeanor, because Enders took this approach with anyone he considered his subordinate, and no one who ever worked under him considered the assignment a career highlight. "He was so cold," recalled State's principal Cuba officer, "that you'd go into his office and he wouldn't raise his eyes." A key congressional staffer added that "Enders is one of those rare people who can be offensive just by the way he walks into a room."[75]

With Enders handling U.S. diplomacy and the CIA reporting that "the Cuban influence in the Nicaragua military has been pervasive," President Reagan signed his administration's basic policy document on Nicaragua—a presidential finding that it was necessary to "support and conduct [one word redacted] paramilitary operations against the Cuban presence in Nicaragua and the Cuban-Sandinista support infrastructure in Nicaragua." With that the administration began to create its own guerrilla war, training and arming a variegated array of anti-Sandinista groups that were soon identified by a collective noun, the contras (counterrevolutionaries).[76] Meanwhile, the administration was also launching a crash program to halt what it perceived as a Cuban-instigated rebellion in nearby El Salvador, with the CIA charging that Cubans were providing Salvadoran guerrillas with basic training "in tactics, weapons, communications, and explosives at temporary training schools and on military bases scattered around Nicaragua" and that some then "travel to Cuba through Nicaragua for more specialized training in sabotage and demolition." By early 1982 President Reagan was telling the OAS that "guerrillas, armed and supported by and through Cuba, are attempting to impose a Marxist-Leninist dictatorship on the people of El Salvador as part of a larger imperialistic plan."[77]

Most qualified observers considered the problem more complicated, with prominent centrists such as William D. Rogers, the Ford administration's principal Latin Americanist, characterizing the Reagan analysis as "arrant nonsense." On the crucial issue of what was causing the war in El Salvador, almost every U.S. observer with firsthand experience in the country believed that the Salvadoran conflict was fundamentally a civil war pitting a ruthless military (recently covered with the fig leaf of a civilian president, El Salvador's first since 1932) against a broad array of social forces, from the Catholic Church to Marxist guerrillas. One of the principal interpreters of this conflict was Robert White, a widely respected former U.S. ambassador to El Salvador, who, like Rogers, characterized as "towering nonsense" the administration's effort to blame everything on Cuba—"it is tactically and factually wrong." He argued instead that "the guerrilla groups, the revolutionary groups, almost without exception began as associations of teachers, associations of labor unions, campesino unions, or parish organizations which were organized for the definite purpose of getting a schoolhouse up." On the other side, White continued, "the Salvadorans on whom the success of the Reagan formula depends are rotten to the core. Nothing we can do can instill morale into a Salvadoran military officer corps which has earned the contempt of the civilized world by its routine practice of torture and assassination. Nothing we can do can prevent the economic collapse of the country as the rich and powerful systematically export the wealth of El Salvador into their foreign bank accounts." In distinct contrast, ultraconservative Senator Jesse Helms praised El Salvador's "enlightened and astute entrepreneurial class" and warned that "if we sit back and do nothing, or if we do the wrong thing, El Salvador will fall within 30 to 60 days. Here we are saying 'We can't do anything with that government, they're not perfect.' Well, my friends, neither is our government. But at least it's anti-communist."[78]

Siding with Senator Helms, the administration asserted that the imperfections in El Salvador's authoritarian institutions were minor when compared to the totalitarian alternative, which would allow the Soviet Union, using its Cuban puppet, to expand into a region long considered part of the U.S. sphere of influence. "Many of our citizens don't fully understand the seriousness of the situation," warned President Reagan, "so let me put it bluntly: There is a war in Central America that is being fueled by the Soviets and Cubans. They are arming, training, supplying and encouraging a war to subjugate another nation to communism, and that nation is El Salvador. The Soviets and the Cubans are operating from a base called Nicaragua. And this is the first real Communist aggression on the American mainland."[79]

Digging in their heels, the administration's Senate critics narrowly defeated an April 1982 "get-tough-with-Cuba" resolution restating the pledge from the days of the 1962 Missile Crisis—that the United States would use force to halt Cuban subversion in Latin America.[80] The razor-thin margin resolved nothing, however, nor did a year of further debate that lasted until mid-1983, when hawkish Democrat Henry Jackson and dovish Republican Charles Mathias proposed creating a commission to examine the problem and recommend a policy that could command broad support. The president jumped at the opportunity, appointing Henry Kissinger to chair the

National Bipartisan Commission on Central America, a group comprising thirteen members, none of whom claimed any knowledge of Central America. Eleven were confirmed cold warriors, and one—Kissinger—had already endorsed the administration's view of Central America as a symbol of U.S. resolve, arguing that "if we cannot manage Central America, it will be impossible to convince threatened nations in the Persian Gulf and in other places that we know how to manage the global equilibrium."[81] One of the two non–cold warriors was San Antonio mayor Henry Cisneros, a nod to the proposition that the views of a Hispanic American might be useful; the other was Yale economic historian Carlos Díaz-Alejandro, a Cuban American who had been one of the Committee of Seventy-five negotiating with the Castro government during the Carter years. To some observers, his participation suggested that Díaz-Alejandro might be a traitor—claiming to speak for Florida's Cuban American population, exile leader Jorge Mas Canosa of the new Cuban American National Foundation told a reporter, "We really question his background to be on a commission that will have access to classified information." But, as William LeoGrande observed, it would have been unseemly to dismiss one of the Commission's two Hispanic members and the only one of the thirteen who could claim to be an expert on some aspect of Latin America, so "Díaz-Alejandro got to stay, and Henry Cisneros had someone to talk to."[82]

IN OCTOBER, as the Kissinger Commission was preparing its report, Washington's focus shifted to the southeastern Caribbean island of Grenada, where a coup had overthrown the government of Maurice Bishop, forcing a climax to the drama that had begun in 1979 when Bishop had seized power in his own coup and quickly moved to develop close ties with Cuba: just six months after Bishop's takeover, the DIA had concluded that Grenada was part of the Soviet-Cuban bloc.[83] Plenty of evidence pointed in that direction by the time of Ronald Reagan's election: in late 1980 speech, Bishop had told a cheering Havana audience, "At the Bay of Pigs, Cubans gave the world the example of how a small nation with a small number of people can defeat imperialism." Next up to the podium that day was Sandinista defense minister Humberto Ortega, who warned the newly elected U.S. leaders that "now it won't be so easy to strangle us as it once was, because in the first place Cuba, Grenada and Nicaragua are not alone in relations with other revolutionary movements of the world and especially with progressive, revolutionary governments and with the socialist camp."[84]

What was anyone in Washington to make of Grenada, an impoverished

Caribbean ministate of eighty thousand souls subsisting on the export of bananas and nutmeg? The Reagan administration focused on the national security implications of the island's new airport, due for completion in mid-1984 with the help of six hundred Cuban construction workers under the supervision of a British contractor. "Grenada doesn't even have an air force," worried President Reagan. "Who is [the airport] intended for?"[85] "Tourism," the Bishop government answered, and the first step to increased tourist traffic was to replace the existing airport at Pearls on the northeastern coast, where the runway was perilously short and unable to accommodate jets, forcing arriving tourists to fly first to nearby Barbados and connect with smaller propeller-driven aircraft. But why bother? Grenada was nothing special as a Caribbean vacation site, so many potential visitors simply told their travel agents to book them rooms on jet-accessible islands, especially since praying for a safe touchdown at Pearls was only the most exciting part of the trip; the capital of St. George's and the principal tourist beach at Grande Anse were an hour away by taxi. Apparently unfamiliar with this geography, no one in either the Carter or the Reagan administration understood why the Bishop government would consider it desirable to have a modern airport at Point Salines, immediately adjacent to Grande Anse and five minutes from St. George's.

The U.S. Agency for International Development considered the new airport a waste of money, while U.S. security officials saw it as a convenient refueling stop for Cubans shuttling to and from Africa or as a base for the subversion of nearby Caribbean ministates or even Venezuela. The CIA added speculation that a new barracks for construction workers "will probably be used as a Cuban military training area for neighboring islands' radicals," and the agency's general concern was that "Havana is getting a free hand to use the island for its own purposes." The view that Cuba was the Kremlin's puppet converted Grenada's new airport into "a serious challenge from Moscow," which, in turn, converted Grenada into a perfect opportunity to do what the president had in mind in early 1983 when he signed National Security Decision Directive 75: "The U.S. must rebuild the credibility of its commitment to resist Soviet encroachment on U.S. interests and . . . use U.S. military forces where necessary."[86]

And so the Reagan administration suspended diplomatic relations by excluding Grenada from the responsibilities of the new U.S. ambassador to the Eastern Caribbean, based in Barbados, and refused to accredit Grenada's new ambassador, Dessima Williams. She came to Washington anyway as ambassador to the OAS, where she conveyed the message that

Grenada wanted to patch up its relationship with the United States, telling Congress in June 1982 that "in March and again in August, 1981, our Prime Minister wrote President Reagan, expressing a desire for better relations between our two countries. To this date, no reply from President Reagan has been received."[87]

The administration had no inclination to talk; instead, it did what it could to isolate Grenada from the West, opposing multilateral development bank loans and unsuccessfully lobbying European Economic Community countries not to provide credits for completing the airport. Then came the saber rattling: from August through mid-October 1981, the United States conducted its Ocean Venture '81 maneuvers off the Puerto Rican island of Vieques, focusing on a mythical island, "Amber and the Amberdines," a name that made the target seem suspiciously like Grenada, since the Grenadines lie just to the north. Called before a House subcommittee to explain these exercises, the State Department denied any attempt to intimidate.[88]

During this period President Reagan visited Barbados to warn members of the Organization of Eastern Caribbean States that Grenada "bears the Soviet and Cuban trademark, which means that it will attempt to spread the virus among its neighbors." Reporting a few months later on Maurice Bishop's trip to Moscow, the CIA added a similar warning, but Bishop then traveled to Washington, where he told two senior administration officials of his desire "that we move toward better relations." Deputy Secretary of State Kenneth Dam and national security adviser William Clark replied that the United States would be willing to do so, but "the first step would be that he should stop what was quite a campaign of attacks on the United States, and that would indicate that he had a desire for better relations, and that is where the matter was left." Bishop subsequently made a second trip Moscow, where Soviet Foreign Minister Andrei Gromyko congratulated him for the clever way he was using a series of "seminars" to develop relations with opposition leaders from nearby Caribbean islands: the seminars have "a very scientific and scholarly form," Gromyko commented, so "the imperialists will be hard-pressed to accuse you of being conspirators who need to be crushed by armed force."[89]

In October 1983, however, rivals imprisoned and then murdered Bishop. The conspirators' motives remain obscure to this day, but in that supercharged situation no one could guarantee the safety of the U.S. students studying at a for-profit medical school on the island, and the invasion to protect them began six days after Bishop's murder. It was over almost immediately: eight thousand U.S. troops confronted only minor opposition as they seized control of the island. "We did a real nice job on that place," reported a navy aviator. "That's the kind of real training we need."[90]

Fidel Castro had ordered the 784 Cubans on the island to resist only if directly attacked, but 24 of them were killed and 57 were wounded during the invasion. No one knows who fired first.[91] What is known is that on 26 October, the day of the invasion, U.S. Interests Section chief John Ferch awoke in the middle of the night to a telephone call from Ken Skoug, the State Department's coordinator of Cuban affairs: "We needed to tell the Cubans that we didn't want to harm their personnel," Skoug recalled, who dictated a note demanding an immediate halt to any Cuban resistance. Ferch dressed and raced to the Interests Section, translated the note into Spanish, put it on Interests Section letterhead, and at 7:00 A.M. set out for the Ministry of Foreign Relations and his designated formal contact, vice minister Ricardo Alarcón. After handing the note to an angry Alarcón, Ferch recalled what his predecessor, Wayne Smith, had said: "When Castro has a message, it will come via José Luis Padrón." Ferch therefore took a second copy of the note to Cuba's Ministry of Tourism, where Padrón was waiting. "After reading the note Padron left the room to call Castro," Ferch reported. "When he returned he said that Castro had already received the note [via Alarcón] and had only one question—quote: What is the United States going to do with the Cuban dead and wounded?"[92]

The answer was up in the air. The next day the Senate considered keeping the prisoners until Cuba accepted the return of the Mariel excludables, but the administration dragged its feet only briefly; after informing Cuba of its intention to grant asylum to any Cuban desiring to defect, the United States returned the wounded Cubans to Havana on a Red Cross aircraft on 2 November. Every senior Cuban leader was waiting to honor the injured at the airport. A final group of Cubans was repatriated on 9 November, and three days later the United States sent back the bodies of the twenty-four dead.[93]

When it occurred, the invasion was justified not simply as an effort to protect the lives of the U.S. medical students but also as a response to a request from the Organization of Eastern Caribbean States. It was, President Reagan said, a preemptive attack on "a Soviet-Cuban colony, being readied as a major military bastion to export terror and undermine democracy. We got there just in time." An angry but subdued Fidel Castro denied this charge, but faced with the reality of the U.S. takeover, his only retaliatory step was to pay the *New York Times* to print his funeral eulogy. The matter nearly ended there—all that was needed for closure was for Secretary Shultz to land on the almost-finished Point Salines runway a few months after the invasion and announce that "it's certainly a facility that is needed here in one way or another and I'm sure it will be completed."[94] After an infusion of nineteen million dollars from the U.S. Agency for International Development, the airport opened a year after the invasion.

THE GRENADA INVASION also marked the end of any significant interest in Cuba during Ronald Reagan's years in the White House. The last reference to Cuba in Shultz's State Department memoir comes on page 344, about a third of the way into the volume; more than five years remained before the end of his tenure, but the secretary of state recalled nothing more worth mentioning about Cuba. President Reagan's memoir is similar—Cuba disappears about halfway through—and both books seem to reflect events: Cuba simply faded into the background, as senior officials moved on to other challenges. "There was no special briefing when I was appointed," recalled John Ferch, the Foreign Service officer who replaced Wayne Smith as chief of the U.S. Interests Section. "Obviously, this was not going to be a high-priority assignment. Just before leaving for Havana [Undersecretary of State] Larry Eagleburger called me up and said, 'I can't send you down there without anything. Go and tell them that if they give MiGs to the Sandinistas there's going to be hell to pay.' That was the sum of my instructions." Ferch promptly communicated this message to Alarcón, "but he told me to talk to the Nicaraguans—basically, that was their way of telling us to stick it in our ear." Cuba's response was reported to Washington, but Ferch could not recall receiving an acknowledgment, let alone instructions on how or whether to proceed.[95]

Cuba received some attention only because Central America remained the nation's principal foreign policy challenge. Issued three months after the Grenada invasion, the report of the Kissinger Commission resolved nothing, primarily because it began by dismissing as unimportant the crucial question of what was causing the turmoil ("Whatever its roots in the past, the crisis in Central America exists urgently in the present"); the pages that followed were laced with admonitions about "the advance of Soviet and Cuban power on the American mainland," which suggested that the problem, if not the cause, was communist adventurism. Accompanying the commission's recommendation of a major boost in economic and military aid was President Reagan's warning that "like a roving wolf, Castro's Cuba looks to its peace-loving neighbors with hungry eyes and sharp teeth."[96]

The left side of the U.S. political spectrum challenged the proposal to increase military aid, while conservative senator Jesse Helms criticized the proposal for more economic assistance as "a mandate for socialism, financed by the U.S. taxpayer." But the modal response was that of conservative representative Robert Lagomarsino, who paused briefly to thank the "fine Americans who spent 6 months settling the problems of Central America," and then plunged back into the ongoing struggle for the votes of the dwindling number of congressional moderates stuck in the middle, a struggle that now focused on President Reagan's request for an $8.9 billion economic and military aid package. On this issue Reagan's memoir is anything but silent: "My battles with Congress over Central America went on for almost the entire eight years I was in the White House."[97]

The Kissinger Commission had issued its report a few weeks before the New Hampshire primary, just as the United States began preparing for the 1984 election. After several months of standing in a circle and shooting at one another, the Democrats nominated the least wounded, former vice president Walter Mondale, who, mirabile dictu, selected a woman, Geraldine Ferraro, as his running mate. They ran on a platform that was tough on Cuba but soft on the day's principal litmus tests, calling for ratification of the Equal Rights Amendment, advocating almost equal rights for homosexuals, proposing tough regulations on the handguns known as Saturday night specials, and insisting on an end to U.S. support for anti-Sandinista paramilitary forces in Nicaragua. The Republicans were tougher on Cuba and just about everything else, saying nothing about the rights of homosexuals and refusing to endorse the Equal Rights Amendment but pledging to support an antiabortion amendment to the Constitution. Far from criticizing Saturday night specials, the Republicans instead promised "to continue to defend the constitutional right to keep and bear arms," and on Central America they promised "continued assistance to the democratic freedom fighters in Nicaragua."[98] When the dust settled in November, Minnesota and the District of Columbia had gone to Mondale and Ferraro. Every other state went to Ronald Reagan and George Bush—a 525–13 margin in the Electoral College.

Cuba had made a cameo appearance during the primaries when candidate Jesse Jackson proposed that the United States start talking to the Castro government and then did just that: in the middle of a fact-finding trip to Central America, Jackson flew from El Salvador to Havana, where he asked Fidel Castro to release not only a number of U.S. citizens held in Cuban prisons, primarily for illegal entry while transporting drugs from

Colombia, but also a number of long-term Cuban prisoners who had been convicted of a broad variety of crimes against state security that ranged from sabotage to vocal opposition to the government. Jackson then resumed his Central American trip, but on his return flight to the United States he stopped in Havana to pick up twenty-two jailed U.S. citizens, twenty-six Cuban political prisoners, an unidentified female relative, and a Cuban accused of being a U.S. intelligence agent who had been released from prison in 1982.

Jackson also brought back a message from Fidel Castro: if the United States would resume normal visa processing in Havana (the processing President Carter had suspended in 1980 at the height of the Mariel crisis, immediately after the melee in front of the Interests Section), Cuba would accept the return of several thousand Mariel arrivals who were excludable under U.S. immigration laws, some because of a history of mental illness but most because of their criminal records, but had managed to enter undetected during the confused crisis.[99]

Fidel Castro had characterized all the departing *marielitos* as "the dregs of our society" but denied having sent anyone he considered excludable. The most the Cuban leader would admit was that "there may be an individual who a long time ago committed a crime of violence and did his time. And now that he is completely free, he wanted to go to the Yankee paradise. Well, good luck to him." Castro took the position that "after an individual has served his sentence, well that's it. He has canceled his debt to justice and the law. He should have the same right as any other citizen: of traveling to the United States." As for those considered excludable for mental problems, Castro insisted that "if any mental patient left here, it was because their relatives claimed them and nobody was aware of their illness."[100]

During their June 1980 trip to Havana, State's Peter Tarnoff and the NSC's Robert Pastor had been unable to persuade Cuba to accept the excludables, and the new Reagan administration's coördinator of Cuban affairs, Kenneth Skoug, recalled that the fate of the excludables rested alongside Central America as the principal issue of U.S.-Cuban relations; he certainly considered negotiating their return one of his primary responsibilities, commenting that "the pressure to get the excludables home" was "enormous."[101] On its side, Cuba clearly wanted to resume normal immigration processing—in early 1983, the chief of the Cuban Interests Section in Washington formally requested resumption of the visa processing that President Carter had ended in 1980. The State Department responded by handing the envoy a note indicating that Cuba would first have to accept the return of 789 especially undesirable *marielitos* held in Atlanta's maximum-security federal penitentiary, adding that others would be presented for repatriation after the 789 were back in Cuba. Following those steps, the United States would be willing to consider a resumption of normal visa processing. Cuba called this proposal "unacceptable" because it "intended to impose upon Cuba unilateral solutions to a problem which originates in the aggressive policies practiced by the U.S. government against Cuba." Havana added, however, that it was willing to talk about the matter. Washington replied by inquiring why Cuba had not mentioned the 789 and by reiterating its willingness to talk after they had been returned to Cuba.[102]

At this point a hopeful sign emerged from an exchange over the unrelated and potentially explosive issue of airplane hijacking—a spate of United States–to–Cuba hijackings, most by homesick *marielitos*, began in 1982 and intensified through mid-1983, when the State Department publicly shifted some of the blame to Cuba for its failure to return or punish hijackers. Cuban authorities quickly handed U.S. officials their response: a list of all hijackers and the prison terms that they had received. The prompt Cuban response (and the data indicating twelve- to twenty-year sentences) suggested that Cuba was willing to cooperate on an issue of concern to both governments.[103]

Several minor and unrelated incidents then slowed progress—the United States expelled two more diplomats attached to Cuba's U.N. mission, alleging that they had been spying, and restricted those who remained to within a twenty-five-mile radius of Manhattan. The Reagan administration also launched another round of Caribbean military maneuvers (Operation Solid Shield '83), including two overflights by SR-71 spy planes, prompting the head of the Cuban Interests Section in Washington to invite State's coordinator of Cuban affairs to lunch. "It was the only lunch he ever bought me," recalled Skoug; "he wanted to find out why we had sent the planes. 'Did you mean to humiliate us,' he asked? I said of course not, and that was it." But that was "it" on the U.S. side only; Cuba responded with four days of civil defense exercises. In September, the U.S. Senate approved a new anti-Castro initiative, Radio Martí, and House approval seemed a certainty. José Luis Padrón warned John Ferch, "You're making a big mistake doing this," and a month later the United States invaded Grenada.[104] Relations hit rock bottom.

But the United States still wanted to repatriate the excludables, so in mid-1984 the State Department inquired about Cuba's interest in negotiation. The Cuban government replied that immigration talks would be inappropriate before the upcoming U.S. presidential election, but a few weeks later Jesse Jackson returned from Havana with the message that Cuba would take the excludables. First, however, Havana wanted to talk not only about the repatriation process but also about resuming visa processing as it had existed prior to the 1980 riot in front of the U.S. Interests Section.[105] Jackson's message helped break the logjam. On 12 July, two weeks after Jackson's return, the two governments began talks in New York. State Department negotiator Michael Kozak, a knowledgeable but low-ranking deputy legal adviser, began by telling Ricardo Alarcón, the much higher ranking vice minister of foreign relations, that Cuba had to break the ice by agreeing to accept not 789 but 2,746 excludables. Then Kozak quickly added, "We are prepared, in the context of a resolution of the problem of the excludables, to deal with Cuban migration to the United States in a normal manner."[106]

Alarcón heard Kozak out, then accepted the list of excludables and requested a recess to consult with his government, which "spent tons of hours discussing this issue. We went through the 2,746 name by name."[107] While Alarcón was in Havana, Fidel Castro gave a conciliatory 26th of July speech singling out Jesse Jackson for special praise as "a man of convictions, an honest and brave man" who wanted to open lines of communication; specifically, the Kozak-Alarcón meeting in New York, until this point a secret, was the "result of Jackson's visit to our country."[108]

Ferch watched Castro's televised speech and thought, "He's trying to explain why he was negotiating with the devil, and he was probably trying to convince himself." Ferch then hurried over to a diplomatic reception, where the Cuban leader called aside the U.S. envoy: "I want you to carry a message to the American people," he recalled Castro saying. "I want you to tell them I'm very serious about this. I consider it a moral commitment." Ferch later typed up his notes:

[Castro] continued with the same themes for the next 15 to 25 minutes. . . . At one point, he seemed to pause for breath, I tried to ask a question about next steps, problems he might see with implementation, I forget what else. I needn't have tried. Once his lungs were refilled, he returned to the theme, overriding my words with a hand wave of dismissal. Since I obviously had not been invited into the Presence to converse, I sat back and let questions fill my mind: "Who does this guy think he is? What is this obsession with the American people? Does he really think I can tell 220-plus million people anything? Ok, I'll tell my brother-in-law in Toledo, Ohio. But first I'll have to remind him who Fidel Castro is."

Then, Ferch continued, when Castro "finally got it clear that I understood, he gave me a couple of cigars and said goodbye." Later that night, Ferch reported to Washington, "Fidel is a man who has strode the world stage for so long that he conceives of himself as a world actor. He 'knows' that the American people are puzzled by his agreement, and he wants to tell them."[109]

A few days later, Alarcón returned to New York with Cuba's pledge to accept all 2,746 excludables if the United States would agree to return them in small batches of 100 per month. With that, the two other issues on the agenda were easily resolved: the United States agreed first to grant immigration visas to up to three thousand former prisoners and their immediate families and second to resume normal immigration processing at the U.S. Interests Section, which simply meant applying the criteria and procedures applicable to every other country: up to twenty thousand visas per year under established preference categories, plus an unlimited number of immigrant visas for parents, spouses, and unmarried minor children of U.S. citizens.[110]

THE AGREEMENT LASTED only five months, until 20 May 1985, when Radio Martí went on the air. In response, Cuba ended the repatriation of excludables and added that it would no longer permit Cuban Americans to visit relatives, that it also might cancel the 1973 antihijacking agreement, and that it was considering retaliation with its own broadcasts to the United States.[111]

Radio Martí had a long family history. Its most distant relative was Radio Free Europe, the Cold War propaganda effort established in 1949 to undermine Soviet control of Eastern Europe. Its closest cousin was Radio Americas, the clandestine shortwave Swan Island radio station authorized by President Eisenhower's 1960 Bay of Pigs directive, when the idea of weakening the Castro government with radio broadcasts enjoyed wide bipartisan support—while Eisenhower was issuing his secret directive, Karl Mundt was publicly asking his Senate colleagues to appropriate one hundred thousand dollars for a public effort "to cultivate friendship with the people of Cuba" by purchasing airtime on commercial stations whose broadcasts reached Cuba. Both the American Legion and the White House liked Senator Mundt's idea, with the president directing that "efforts should be expedited to reach the Cuban people by radio, in order to explain U.S. actions and attitudes and to make clear the friendliness of the U.S. people."[112]

So was born another close cousin, *Cita Con Cuba*, a one-hour shortwave program broadcast every evening by the Voice of America (VOA). The officials directing Operation Mongoose repeatedly cloned this modest effort, and by late 1961 the CIA was supporting anti-Castro radio programs on no fewer than sixty Latin American and three Florida AM radio stations, plus Radio Americas from Swan Island, and in these broadcasts the agency went significantly beyond Senator Mundt's idea of cultivating friendship: "Radio programs and other propaganda media, directed at Cuba, will continue to encourage low risk, simple sabotage, and other forms of active and passive resistance." By mid-1962 the CIA had added funding of a powerful Boston-based commercial station, WRUL, whose major purpose, reported the U.S. Information Agency (USIA), "is to encourage resistance against Castro and to warn other Latin American countries of the dangers of Communism." The CIA's Radio Americas expanded from shortwave to the standard AM dial, with programs "written and taped by Cuban exiles working under Agency supervision and control," plus three commercial AM stations carrying programs purchased by the Cuban Freedom Committee, which was controlled directly by the agency. Some of these programs were meant to appear "as broadcasts by Cuban guerrillas inside Cuba."[113]

All of the broadcasts on the standard AM dial violated the 1949 Geneva Telecommunications Convention and especially the 1937 North American Regional Broadcasting Agreement, both of which had been negotiated with the full support of the United States; indeed, a major reason for the 1937 negotiations had been to eliminate interference from "border blasters," the English-language radio stations that evaded regulation by locating beyond U.S. borders, usually in northern Mexico, but another strong reason was to minimize natural interference between stations on the narrow AM broadcasting band. USIA Director George Allen was therefore understandably reluctant to violate these agreements, telling the National Security Council "that the International Telecommunications Conventions contained the principle that nations wishing to broadcast internationally should do so by short-wave and that standard wave or television broadcasts should use only enough power to cover the territory of the broadcasting state."[114] Allen's argument did not carry the day.

After Washington had taken the liberty of ignoring these agreements by broadcasting to Cuba, the Cuban government felt no compunction about retaliating, first with its own broadcasts (*Radio Free Dixie*, *La Voz de INRA*, *The Friendly Voice of Cuba*) and then with jamming to blot out the broadcasts that were being beamed to Cuba from dozens of spots across the AM dial. That tactic greatly annoyed the many completely uninvolved U.S. radio broadcasters who happened to share frequencies with targeted stations. When Cubans jammed the CIA-funded WGBS broadcasts from Miami, for example, they also scrambled signals from stations operating on the same wavelength (710 kHz) as far away as New York and Louisiana. Facing financial losses, the affected station owners booked the first available flights to Washington, where their impressive political clout came from their numbers (thousands of stations spread out across the country in every congressional district), from their ownership of a powerful medium of communications, and from their symbiotic relationship with farmers, the nation's single-most-powerful lobbying group, who relied heavily on radio to provide timely information about market and weather conditions.[115]

By mid-1962 the CIA had concluded that radio would not encourage Cubans to rebel and was therefore willing to end the broadcasts that were prompting the Cuban jamming, but the State Department, which considered the broadcasts "essential," successfully opposed the move.[116] As the 1960s rolled on and attention turned to Vietnam, it became clear that only a handful of powerless Cuban exiles seemed to care one way or the other, and the result was a slow but steady reduction in the broadcasts. Radio Americas was finally shut down in May 1968, while the last survivor, *Cita Con Cuba*, continued into the mid-1970s only because of the fear that President Nixon's best friend, Cuban American Bebe Rebozo, would insist that bureaucratic heads roll if anyone tampered with this Miami-based program.

In 1973, as the Watergate scandal sucked the Nixon administration into its death spiral, the hour-long *Cita Con Cuba* was trimmed to a half hour, but with a rebroadcast of the evening original added the next morning, so that the program had the same amount of airtime but half the content. The experiment worked: in mid-1974, the USIA reported that "reaction to this change, either in the Cuban Government, the Cuban public, or the Cuban exile community in the United States, has been nil." The time was nearly ripe for the final cut; all that was missing was for both State and the parent USIA to acknowledge that the program's strident anti-Castro tone had become an embarrassment. They did so a month before President Nixon's resignation, when the USIA conceded that the broadcasts were "hamhanded," with content "increasingly irrelevant to Cuban realities and to this administration's policies."[117] *Cita con Cuba* quietly left the airwaves a few weeks after Nixon resigned, and Cuba was temporarily free of propaganda broadcasts from the United States.

Signs of a revival appeared during the Carter years. Referring to the battle deaths of Cubans in Africa, in 1978 Miami representative Dante Fascell told his House colleagues that "the Cuban people really don't know the extent of their damage" and suggested using radio to inform them. The hawkish wing of the Carter administration quickly picked up Fascell's idea: "VOA has no special programming for Cuba," lamented NSC staffer Paul Henze. "It simply broadcasts on medium-wave [AM] from the Florida Keys the same Spanish-language program it beams to all of Latin America." Such an approach threw away a powerful resource, Henze argued; radio broadcasts "have an enormous potential for exercising influence."[118] Six weeks later, in mid-1980, Cuban vice president Carlos Rafael Rodríguez asked Interests Section chief Wayne Smith for clarification of a broadcasting bill that Senator Jesse Helms had just introduced in Congress—a proposal to rename whatever the VOA was broadcasting in Cuba's direction as Radio Free Cuba. "The time is long past due for us to stop trying to paper over the existence of a Communist regime in our own Hemisphere but start doing something about it," Senator Helms had said.[119]

Helms was acting on behalf of Miami's Cuban exile community, and while the Helms proposal did not become law during the final months of the Carter administration, the measure soon became recognized as the first major skirmish in a campaign that would eventually lead to Cuban Americans' capture of United States policy toward Cuba. Shortly after President Reagan's election, a group of Miamians created the Cuban American National Foundation, and only a few months later the administration notified Congress that it was considering creating what came to be known as Radio Martí. By September the president had signed an executive order establishing the Presidential Commission on Broadcasting to Cuba, including CANF chair Jorge Mas Canosa as one of its members, and had asked Congress to approve radio service "to provide for the broadcasting of accurate information to the people of Cuba."[120]

This proposal was submitted late in the 1981 session, however, and it died after clearing only the House Committee on Government Operations. Coming back for a second try in 1982, the proposal was defeated by a coalition of groups opposing the administration's hostile Cuba policy and of broadcasters fearing Cuba's retaliatory jamming. One trade journal warned that "Cuba is proposing dozens of high-power stations—two of them 500 kw—that could create havoc with the signal patterns of stations across the

U.S." In August 1982, Cuba demonstrated these jamming capabilities with four hours of interference by a new and extremely powerful *Voice of Cuba*, transmitting from Havana on six AM frequencies, including the one that had tentatively been selected for Radio Martí, 1040 kHz. That happened to be the frequency of WHO, a politically powerful Des Moines radio station and one of only eleven clear channel stations in the country, broadcasting to farmers from Louisiana to the Canadian border.* "You better believe we're troubled by what happened last evening," replied the station's general manager when asked about Castro's August broadcast. "But technically there's nothing we can do about it except try to prevent Radio Martí from becoming a fact of life on 1040 [kHz]. Otherwise, it literally puts us out of business at night. It would be devastating."[121]

WHO responded by hiring a Washington lobbying firm and enlisting the support of the Iowa Farm Bureau and the Iowa Dairy Industry Commission. Professor William LeoGrande, one of the most articulate critics of the administration's overall Cuba policy, thus came to share the congressional witness table with the president of the National Association of Broadcasters, who had no apparent interest in U.S. foreign policy but warned that "the problem of Cuban interference is real and quickly worsening." If the United States were to begin broadcasting to Cuba, Castro would probably go ahead with his threat to create no fewer than 187 border blasters, and then "all across the nation, broadcasters and the public can expect substantial radio interference."[122]

Facing this opposition, the 1982 proposal to create Radio Martí died as it had in 1981, but only after the House voted approval by a wide margin (250–134); the Senate Foreign Relations Committee also approved (11–5), but the full Senate never considered the bill. The administration then moved to divide its opposing coalition by writing into the authorizing legislation a five-million-dollar fund to compensate stations for losses incurred by Cuban interference. Along with an agreement to broadcast on 1180 kHz (far from WHO's 1040 kHz and on a frequency that VOA had already been using to broadcast into the Caribbean from Marathon Key), the compensation fund guaranteed passage. With the broadcasters mollified, LeoGrande and his fellow opponents of a hostile Cuba policy now stood alone: "Surely,"

---

*The concept of clear channels refers to high-powered radio stations that from 1928 to the 1980s operated to provide evening service to rural areas that were not served by low-power ground-wave local radio signals and therefore depended on evening sky-wave transmissions from distant high-powered stations.

one such opponent said, "the Congress cannot justify the cruel denial of moneys for such domestic programs as school lunches, health care for the elderly, and student loans and, simultaneously, authorize moneys for a propaganda contest." Surely Congress can, replied Representative Claude Pepper, another powerful Miami legislator recently befriended by CANF: "I can imagine a tearstained mother sitting in a little cottage, somewhere in Cuba, with her face close to the photograph of a dear son who lost his life in Angola or in Ethiopia, sent there by Castro to further the imperial interests of the Soviet Union. And that tearstained mother wondering why her son had to be used by Castro as a servant of Soviet imperialism. We, through this instrumentality, can tell the people of Cuba about the aggression of Castro as an instrument of the Soviet Union."[123]

The proposal to create Radio Martí passed the House by a three-to-one margin; the Senate did not even bother with a roll-call vote. President Reagan promptly signed the Radio Broadcasting to Cuba Act, and Radio Martí began broadcasting on Cuba's independence day, 20 May 1985.[124] Once on the air, the station quickly became a prized possession of Florida's Cuban American community and therefore a symbol of the willingness of both major political parties to cater to the demands of Cuban Americans, whose voting strength in Florida was growing by the hour. In 1996, the Clinton administration sided with CANF and allowed the Office of Cuban Broadcasting to move from Washington to Miami, and by the early twenty-first century Radio Martí was broadcasting twenty-four hours a day, seven days a week, on thirteen shortwave frequencies and at 1180 on the standard AM dial.

RADIO MARTÍ AND Cuba's retaliatory cancellation of the five-month-old migration agreement poisoned the bilateral atmosphere. Six weeks after the broadcasts began and just days after the kidnapping of thirty-nine U.S. citizens in Lebanon, President Reagan included Cuba in his warning that "the American people are not—I repeat—not going to tolerate intimidation, terror, and outright acts of war against this nation and its peoples. And we're especially not going to tolerate these attacks from outlaw states run by the strangest collection of misfits, loony tunes, and squalid criminals since the advent of the Third Reich." The Cuban government replied in kind: "Reagan cannot be taken seriously," Fidel Castro told reporters two days later. "He is one of the most lying politicians that ever existed in the world. In addition, he is one of the most unscrupulous. He is a big liar, the biggest liar that has ever occupied the United States presidency.

. . . He does not even tell the truth by chance. Everything he says is a lie." Seizing on President Reagan's reference to the Third Reich, Castro added that "Reagan's method is that of Goebbels, yes, it is Hitler's method." Asked about the charge of Cuban terrorism, Castro responded that "Reagan is the biggest terrorist in history." Asked how the president's words would affect Cuba, he simply shrugged: "We have been ostracized for a long time; and we have learned to live with it."[125]

But the Cuban leader clearly preferred not to live with it. He had recently welcomed a visit by two farm-state representatives, Jim Leach, a Republican from Iowa, and Bill Alexander, a Democrat from Arkansas, accompanied by a delegation of Arkansas business leaders, some of whom recalled the days when Cuba had been a major consumer of Arkansas rice, and all of whom would have welcomed an opportunity to reopen that market. One recent study had concluded that the embargo had cost Arkansans 1,418 jobs. Upon his return, Alexander published an op-ed piece in the *New York Times* under the title "Let's Talk with Castro": "If we can negotiate with the Russians," he wrote, "surely we can talk with the Cubans. What do we have to lose?"[126]

While the Cuban government always found time to welcome members of Congress who might challenge the administration's hostile policy, Castro and other leaders spent the mid-1980s focused on the country's second international debt crisis in four years, a continuation of the 1982 crisis but now much more serious. In 1982 Cuba had been seeking its creditors' forbearance for the first time, and its $3 billion debt paled alongside such major debtors as Mexico, which was teetering on the edge of an $83 billion default. At that time, therefore, a group of thirteen creditor governments had quickly agreed to reschedule its share of Cuba's debt, about $1.3 billion, and private Western banks had rescheduled the balance, giving Cuba some medium-term breathing room—the debt was to be repaid in installments beginning in December 1985. But almost no new Western financing (public or private) occurred after the rescheduling agreement, and insufficient export earnings prevented Cuba from servicing its debt coming due in 1983, 1984, and 1985, despite two more reschedulings. Another was needed in 1986, and Cuba's central bankers complained that the rescheduling terms were "far from what in a more recent period have been granted to other countries of the region."[127]

In the simplest sense, the problem was the same one Cuba had encountered four years earlier: as Fidel Castro told Cubans in early 1986, "The country's essential economic problem in the five-year period from 1981 to

1985 was that while we had a more-than-acceptable growth rate, the growth was insufficient where most needed: in the export of goods and services and in import substitution."[128] The Soviet Union had continued to help, primarily by purchasing Cuban sugar at high prices (in 1986 for eight times the world price, or fifty cents a pound when the world price averaged six), but in time this commodity became less important than petroleum, which the Soviet Union had been selling Cuba at bargain prices since Anastas Mikoyan first bartered Soviet oil for Cuban sugar in 1960. Subsidized petroleum slowly emerged as one of the central mechanisms of Soviet aid, and by 1977 (a typical year in the six-year period between the first and second OPEC price increases) Moscow was charging Cuba $7.40 a barrel when the world price was $12.50, and Cuba paid that bargain price in overvalued sugar.[129]

In 1979, however, the value of petroleum more than doubled after the second OPEC price increase, and Cuban officials saw an opportunity: Moscow had committed to providing a certain amount of oil at a certain price, and the Kremlin did not care how Cuba used that oil. Cuba began to conserve every drop it could and reexport what it managed to save, selling its Soviet oil at world-market prices. In 1981 Cuba pocketed $151 million in hard currency, or about 11 percent of total convertible currency earnings. Conservation subsequently increased significantly and world oil prices rose slightly, allowing Cuba to boost its reexport earnings to $262 million in 1982. World prices fell in 1983 and 1984, but Cuba continued to boost its conservation and to resell even more of its low-cost Soviet oil, with reexport earnings in those two years coming in at a shade less than $500 million, or 42 percent of the country's total convertible currency earnings, twice the proportion earned by sugar.[130]

But then the bottom fell out of the petroleum market. "We have lost hundreds of millions of dollars," Castro complained as prices plummeted from twenty-six dollars a barrel in late 1985 to thirteen dollars a barrel in March 1986. "We are losing more than $300 million this year." Coupled with low prices for the sugar Cuba sold on Western markets (hovering at about four cents a pound, which, as Cuba's Banco Nacional reported, does "not even cover the costs of the most efficient producers"), the decline in the value of oil reexports forced Cuba to declare a debt moratorium and to begin yet another round of negotiations to reschedule the $3.5 billion debt owed to Western creditors.[131] When no agreement could be reached, Cuba announced an indefinite suspension of repayments on all medium- and long-term commercial debt, and several weeks later it suspended payment on even short-term debts to commercial lenders. "We have never experienced as we do today such a small supply of convertible currency," Fidel Castro told Communist Party leaders in late 1986.[132]

With trade in convertible currency now about half what it had been a few years earlier, Cuba again sat down with Western creditor governments in 1988 to request that already overdue debts for 1987 and 1988 be rescheduled over fifteen years with a five-year grace period. The creditors surely understood that they could not extract blood from this stone (repayments scheduled for 1988 amounted to about four times what Cuba expected to earn in hard currency), but an agreement still could not be reached, and the Cuban government had nothing to show for seven months of bargaining as the thirty-fifth anniversary of the attack on the Moncada Barracks approached. On that day Fidel Castro told a Santiago audience, "We have to pay cash for everything we buy."[133] When Ronald Reagan left office six months later, Cuba had still not been able to restructure its debt.

Meanwhile, Cubans learned to tighten their belts. "These are difficult times," Castro told a 1986 audience, "but when weren't the times difficult for revolutionaries?" Later that year he warned Cubans to "be ready to face the difficulties that will unfortunately come, because sometimes one cannot buy something until one has the money in hand."[134] With that the country embarked on its own version of structural adjustment, involving an austerity program, a change in economic norms that came to be known as "rectification," and a search for new sources of hard currency.

The austerity program announced in late 1986 was basically the same medicine that citizens of other debt-afflicted Third World countries were being forced to swallow: twenty-seven belt-tightening measures, including significant hikes in electricity rates and bus fares, plus a reduction in consumption via the diversion of production to export markets. "It is a pity we cannot consume all our lobster production," Fidel Castro said, but "we have to sell our production to the rich Japanese, French, Spaniards, Canadians, and others so they may eat lobster. We do not have any lobsters left for ourselves."[135]

Rectification—formally, "el proceso de rectificación de errores y tendencias negativas"—was another matter entirely, a complex mélange of policies encouraging Cubans to work harder, to combat inefficiency, and especially to end the recent resurgence of market-oriented individualism. Castro had for years been nagging Cubans to do more work, warning that the revolution would fail if discipline continued to flag and productivity to decline: "Our worst enemies could not have done us more damage," he had told one audience in 1980.[136] Now, six years later, Castro admitted that Cuba had failed to meet the goals of its 1981–85 five-year plan for several reasons, including the traditional bugaboo of low sugar prices, but he emphasized that Cubans simply were not working hard enough. Then he turned to his second central theme, mismanagement: "The supply of consumer goods—and especially clothing, shoes, home furnishings, sheets and towels—has been inadequate and unstable. There are problems of variety, of choice, of inappropriate sizes, of poor quality construction, of obsolete and repetitive design, aggravated by distribution problems that at times border on the irrational." These matters were treated in such detail that *Granma* required three days to publish the entire report.[137]

At that point the party congress to which Castro had been speaking began a long recess, from February until November, and during this interregnum the two central problems Castro had identified—sloth and mismanagement—were supplemented by a third: resurgent capitalist values. This, too, was nothing new: "The deeper I think and meditate, the less capitalistic I feel," Castro had said in early 1985. "I am becoming more and more distant from capitalism, mentally, spiritually, philosophically. Each day I am more convinced about the advantages of the socialist system over the capitalist system, more convinced that capitalism has no future." A year later he told Cubans that "we have some indecent people, negligent people, . . . irresponsible people," reserving particular criticism for the free peasant markets that had been established in 1980 in an effort to increase the supply of eggs, vegetables, and other staples that state-controlled agriculture seemed unable to produce in sufficient quantity. But in these markets, "some individuals sell a head of garlic for a peso and put it in their own pocket," with no regard for the impact of high prices on the rest of society. The culprits were not the small farmers, "working honestly by the sweat of their brow and receiving in return the education of their children, their medical care, all the opportunities that everyone now enjoys, but outside middlemen who, far from working the land honestly, have enriched themselves by trading, stealing, and selling at high prices, exceptionally high prices." By 1985 garlic had virtually disappeared from Cuba's state grocery stores, as had pork, cheese, many vegetables, and even tropical fruit.[138]

Such abuses had to stop. "We don't want to have a cultural revolution here," Castro warned, referring to China in a way that could easily have been interpreted as a thinly veiled threat; "we don't want to resolve these problems with extremist methods, unleashing the masses against those responsible for such irritating activities." Instead, the farmers' markets were closed.[139]

The Cuban leader then took his complaints about capitalistic tendencies to the Central Committee of the Communist Party, blaming it (and himself) for seeking to boost production by resorting to material incentives. "We began to be infected by a commercial spirit, liberalism, and other vices. Voluntary work practically ended [and] we began to corrupt the workers by trying to resolve everything with money." He continued this line of criticism when the Third Party Congress reassembled at year end: "The peasants were beginning to show signs of corruption," he said, using the farmers' markets to underscore a much broader problem. "We started playing at capitalism," but "socialism is not built with capitalist mechanisms"; instead, "we have to show capitalists [that] socialists and communists are not one but ten times more capable of solving the problems resulting from a country's development." Two years later, as the Soviet Union began experimenting with market mechanisms—perestroika—Castro continued to insist that Cuba "must never play nor flirt with capitalist things."[140]

As the austerity program was reducing consumption and as the rectification process was reducing the most obvious forms of private-sector activity, Cuban leaders also embarked on a search for new sources of hard currency; they soon rediscovered tourism. In the 1950s, more than a quarter of a million tourists had visited each year, with a peak of 300,000 just before Batista's ouster. Those numbers had plummeted in the early 1960s and remained low until President Carter ended the travel ban. "We do not like tourism," Castro had commented at the time, but "one of our natural resources is the sea, the weather, the sun, the moon, the palm trees, and so forth. These are the natural resources of our country and we have to take advantage of them, even if we do not like tourism." The next year the number of Western tourists climbed to 179,000, declining by only a little after President Reagan reinstated the U.S. travel restrictions in 1982, as Canadians and others filled the gap. In 1984, 166,000 Western tourists visited, every one of them bringing hard currency—about sixty-seven million dollars in 1984, compared to only eight million dollars in 1978.[141]

Cubans needed to build further on those numbers. In its 1985 rescheduling request, Cuba's Banco Nacional noted that a European firm had been hired to help manage four existing hotels at the beach resort of Varadero; that Argentine hoteliers had signed contracts to build eight new hotels, also at Varadero; and that Cuba was considering the development of five other tourist sites. In late 1986 Castro formally announced that tourism would again be encouraged: "This is a gold mine," he said; "tourism can be the source of employment for tens of thousands of our countrymen." In his foreign travels, the Cuban leader began touting Cuba as a tourist destination—visiting Caracas in 1989, he spoke in glowing terms about the island's pristine beaches, inviting Venezuelans to visit so that "tourism can be for us what oil is for you." A year later, the tourist industry was one of the few positive things he could mention when he announced the beginning of the Special Period: tourism, he said, "is going to be a source of jobs for thousands of people. These jobs will pay well and they will not be as hard as growing sweet potatoes." Western tourists were still not his cup of tea ("Their incomes have largely been the result of pillaging the Third World," he had said two years earlier), but he now had to overlook their shortcomings; regardless of how they had earned their money, tourists "can produce hundreds of millions of dollars for the country." [142]

Tourists thus again became a prominent feature of the Cuban landscape and the nation's economy. Their numbers swelled to 340,000 in 1990, exploded to 1,774,000 in 2000, and passed the 2,000,000 mark in 2004, spending more than two billion dollars and generating more than 40 percent of Cuba's convertible foreign exchange. [143]

THE DEBT CRISIS, the austerity program, the process of rectification, and the resurgence of tourism were occurring in Cuba at exactly the time the Reagan administration was provoking a constitutional crisis in the United States: unwilling to accept a congressional ban on funding Nicaragua's anti-Sandinista contras, the administration was secretly arming them anyway by soliciting money from third countries and by diverting the profits from a second, completely independent subterfuge, a complex arms-for-hostages exchange with the government of Iran. As these efforts became public, the president appointed an investigative commission chaired by former senator John Tower, while Congress appointed its own special committees led by Senator Daniel Inouye and Representative Lee Hamilton, and the U.S. Court of Appeals appointed a special independent counsel, retired judge Lawrence Walsh. These Iran-contra investigations and subsequent trials continued throughout President Reagan's remaining two years in office, greatly weakening his administration. NSC aide Oliver North vacillated between the Fifth Amendment and in-your-face bravado, but only a presidential pardon saved him: he was convicted of three felony counts of destroying documents, accepting an illegal gratuity, and obstructing Congress. National security adviser John Poindexter was convicted of five felony charges; Robert McFarlane, his predecessor, was allowed to plead guilty to four misdemeanor charges after a hapless attempt to commit suicide with Valium. Defense Secretary Caspar Weinberger was indicted on six felony counts of perjury and obstructing the Iran-contra investigators. Assistant Secretary of State Elliott Abrams pleaded guilty to two misdemeanor counts of withholding information from Congress, bargained down from felony charges of perjury. And nine minor officials were either convicted or entered guilty pleas in response to indictments ranging from tax evasion to theft of government property. No smoking gun was found in the Oval Office, but senior administration officials completely stopped thinking about relatively insignificant problems such as Cuba.

Dozens of midlevel and junior officials were assigned to implement U.S. policy toward the island, however, and they were being visited continually by the Washington representative of the Cuban American National Foundation, Frank Calzon, whose principal goal at this time was restoration of the migration agreement that Cuba had suspended when Radio Martí went on the air in mid-1985. Since then, the doors to the U.S. consulate in Havana had been closed, but no one had revoked Cubans' right to apply to immigrate to the United States, so Cuban Americans had opened up a new route for their relatives via third countries, primarily Panama. By paying substantial fees, Cuban Americans could obtain exit visas for their relatives in Cuba and entry visas into Panama; these relatives could then apply for visas at the U.S. consulate in Panama City. But this route to the United States was time-consuming and expensive—one journalist with close ties to Miami's Cuban Americans reported that Cuba charged Panamanian travel agents fifteen hundred dollars per exit visa, which the travel agents sold to U.S.-based relatives for twenty-five hundred dollars each, and that was only the first item on a long list of expenses. Worst of all, the exit visa was no guarantee of success. Would-be immigrants in Panama needed U.S. visas, and numerical caps and a worldwide backlog left many Cubans stranded indefinitely in Panama.[144]

On the U.S. side, this third-country processing did nothing to address Washington's continuing desire to return the Mariel excludables. In mid-1986, when an aide to Senator Edward Kennedy was traveling to Havana and when Fidel Castro had recently commented favorably about the 1984 migration agreement (an example of "reasonable compromises for both sides"), the State Department's coordinator of Cuban affairs, Kenneth Skoug, asked Kennedy's aide to inquire about restoration of the migration agreement. The aide returned from Havana with a concrete proposal: Cuba would resume implementing the 1984 migration agreement if the United States would grant Cuba access to frequencies for broadcasting to the United States—a quid pro quo for the Radio Martí broadcasts.[145]

A meeting was arranged almost immediately at the U.S. embassy in Mexico City, where the Cuban side, represented again by Ricardo Alarcón and José Antonio Arbesú, requested so many broadcasting frequencies— four clear channels—that the U.S. negotiators (Skoug and assistant legal adviser Michael Kozak) immediately dismissed the proposal as unrealistic. The Cuban envoys responded by beginning what Skoug considered a "grossly offensive" presentation of other Cuban grievances, and "when it was Kozak's turn to respond, Alarcón and Arbesú found something amusing to discuss between themselves, obliging Kozak to ask for their attention so the session could continue. By 10:00 P.M. it was clear that there was no point in extending the talks. The unrealism of the Cuban proposal and rudeness with which it was presented led Kozak to tell Alarcón that he disagreed with much that the latter had said but was in full concurrence that further conversation would be a waste of time. On this note, the Mexico City talks ended in failure."[146] Skoug and Kozak nonetheless remained convinced that the Cuban government valued emigration as a safety valve and as a mechanism to rid the island of dissenters, so they recommended increasing the pressure on Havana by turning off the immigration safety valve—a presidential proclamation prohibiting the entry of Cubans through third countries.[147]

But closing the Panama route dismayed Cuban Americans who could pay the hefty costs for their relatives, and CANF's Calzon tugged at congressional sympathies by emphasizing the special obligation to admit former political prisoners who had been on the verge of gaining visas when the 1980 Mariel crisis had ended their processing. No one could oppose entry of a handful of former political prisoners, and less than a month after President Reagan closed the Panama route, a House subcommittee was holding hearings to criticize the presidential proclamation. Subcommittee chair Gus Yatron began by indicating that the script had been written by CANF: "Before I call our first witness, I also want to commend the Cuban American National Foundation, and in particular, Mr. Frank Calzon, . . . in assisting with today's hearing."[148]

Elliott Abrams explained that the administration would like nothing better than to grant visas to the former political prisoners and to resume normal visa processing, but visa denial was the only weapon the United

States retained to force the Castro government to accept the Mariel excludables. And denying visas was not simply policy; it was the law. The Immigration and Nationality Act of 1952 required a suspension of normal visa processing when any country refused to take back excludables. CANF responded by rolling out its heavy weapon, Armando Valladares, a high-visibility political prisoner freed in 1982. Asked to evaluate the argument that the United States should refuse to accept political prisoners until Cuba accepted the return of the Mariel excludables, Valladares answered, "You cannot punish Castro by punishing people who have worked against Castro." Painted into something of a humanitarian corner, the administration did not put up much of a defense; indeed, Abrams gave the impression of agreeing with those who argued for resuming visa processing. But "the INS just lay down in the middle of the road and said, 'The law's the law,'" Skoug recalled, "while the Cuban Americans, who hated the approach we had taken, threatened to take their concerns to their friends in the White House. This is when Abrams began fidgeting." Nonetheless, he stuck to his argument: Cuba had to take back the excludables, and a unilateral U.S. concession would eliminate any incentive for Cuba to do so.[149]

U.S. officials apparently were correct to believe that the promise of renewed visa processing was an important incentive, for several months later, in mid-1987, the chief of the Cuban Interests Section in Washington, Ramón Sánchez-Parodi, called on Skoug to suggest a meeting to discuss restoring the migration agreement. "This news kept me euphoric for several hours," Skoug recollected, although nothing occurred immediately because the dust needed to settle after an exposé of U.S. spying broadcast on Cuban television complete with footage from hidden cameras. A few months later, Alarcón reminded the chief of the U.S. Interests Section that Sánchez-Parodi's offer remained on the table, and in early November the two sides finally met in Montreal and hammered out an agreement—or, more accurately, the United States accepted Cuba's concession: Alarcón opened the talks by announcing that Cuba was willing to restore the 1984 migration agreement and accept the excludables if the United States would agree simply to continue to negotiate the issue of radio frequencies. A few more issues were discussed—troops in Angola, the return of a hijacked aircraft—but the mood was completely different from the mid-1986 meeting in Mexico City. "At the conclusion of the second day, there was a good-humored round of drinks," Skoug recalled, and the Cubans "gave no impression that they thought they had surrendered." Subsequent discussions of Cuban access to U.S. radio frequencies were unproductive, Skoug reported, "other than to help the Cubans cover their retreat on the Migration Agreement."[150]

Two weeks later, the United States and Cuba formally announced that visa processing would resume in Havana and that Cuba would accept the Mariel excludables. U.S. regulations were also rewritten to resume third-country visa processing, and by this time CANF's influence within the Reagan administration had reached the point that the Immigration and Naturalization Service (INS) agreed to an extraordinary arrangement whereby each year the foundation would select, transport, and arrange for the settlement in the United States of up to four thousand Cuban refugees living in third countries. "There was special concern about the Cubans in Peru," Skoug remembered, "the ones who left first and were now trapped in Peru with no jobs and no future. We thought, 'What the hell? What's a few more Cubans?'"[151]

While the INS retained the final word on each proposed entrant, the arrangement made CANF an immigration gatekeeper, increasing the group's political weight within the Cuban community. CANF's Operation Exodus began in September 1988, when 671 Cubans arrived from Costa Rica and Panama, with CANF bearing the costs through its Cuban Exodus Relief Fund (CERF), which in addition to transportation provided grants for rent, school tuition, and meals to individuals and families coming from Peru, Spain, Panama, and Costa Rica. Taxpayers soon began picking up the tab when CERF was certified by the INS as a voluntary agency similar to the Red Cross, making it eligible to receive government funding for the resettlement process. In 1991 CANF also received a separate $1.7 million grant from the Office of Refugee Resettlement of the U.S. Department of Health and Human Services.[152]

No sooner had the agreement been announced than more than a thousand incarcerated excludables set fire to the Oakdale, Louisiana, INS detention center. Two days later, nearly fourteen hundred excludables rioted at Atlanta's maximum-security federal penitentiary, seizing ninety-four hostages, burning three cell blocks, and killing one inmate. Attorney General Edwin Meese quickly agreed to a moratorium on returning the excludables while the Department of Justice conducted reviews of about four thousand cases. More than two thousand were eventually freed; of those who remained in custody, few were repatriated during the Reagan years: only 201 of the original 2,746 Cuban excludables had been returned in the five months the migration agreement was in effect before Radio Martí went on the air, and the deportations after the agreement's restoration were even fewer—14 in May and 5 more in December 1988. All of those deported were violent criminals.[153]

Two decades later, U.S. Interests Section chief James Cason said, "We're still working on the 2,746. Every week a flight comes in with two or three more of these guys—a plane chartered by U.S. marshals from Oakdale, who turn them over to the Cubans and fly home." In 2005 the Supreme Court ruled that the excludables could not be detained indefinitely when their removal was not reasonably foreseeable, and during oral arguments for the case, the Bush administration stated that "it is no longer even involved in repatriation negotiations with Cuba." By that year, "no one is looking for excludables to send back," Cason continued, "but if one of the 2,746 gets into trouble, he's taken to Oakdale and then put on the plane." In 2008 the numbers had dropped to one flight every two weeks or so, each with a few excludables.[154]

AFTER THEY HAD NEGOTIATED the migration agreement, midlevel officials turned to focus on an international effort to condemn Cuba's human rights violations, another tactic that reflected the increased influence of CANF, which created an offshoot, the International Coalition for Human Rights in Cuba, funded by a stream of grants from the federally funded National Endowment for Democracy.[155] Here CANF worked primarily through Elliott Abrams, the administration's first assistant secretary of state for human rights, who shifted jobs in mid-1985 to become assistant secretary for Latin America. In his earlier post, Abrams had called Fidel Castro "one of the most vicious tyrants of our time," but only in 1985 did the State Department begin to ratchet up its statements of concern. In December, the president's annual Human Rights Day message asserted that "Cuba stands out as the country where institutionalized totalitarianism has consistently violated the rights of the citizens." Lower-level officials then produced a bill of particulars that the United States introduced in November 1986 as a U.N. General Assembly resolution condemning Cuba. "Much of this was due to the work of the Cuban-American National Foundation," reported Kenneth Skoug.[156]

A few months later Abrams excoriated Fidel Castro as "a latter day version of Stalin or Hitler," and in his 1986 human rights message the president referred to "Castro's gulag" as "an outrage against civilization, [a] grotesque brutality." In 1987, the administration downplayed Human Rights Day entirely because Soviet general secretary Mikhail Gorbachev was visiting Washington, but in 1988 Reagan returned to 1986 levels, criticizing "totalitarian dungeons like Cuba." As the indictment grew increasingly strident, two major human rights groups warned that exaggeration was damaging the administration's credibility: "By placing unsupportable allegations at the forefront of its human rights campaign, the State Department hinders efforts to improve the human rights situation in Cuba [and] the State Department would do well to substitute accuracy for ideology as the guiding principle of its human rights reporting."[157]

The administration continually focused on the central charge that Cuba held and mistreated political prisoners—about a thousand, Abrams had estimated in 1983. When asked about that number, Fidel Castro admitted to "a few hundred" but then modified his answer by adding that "there is no one in jail for political or religious beliefs"; rather, the few hundred had been convicted of criminal acts, and most were terrorists, not political prisoners: "I would like to see what the United States would do if a group of U.S. citizens came to Cuba and we trained them to set off explosive devices in the United States, to perpetrate sabotage in the United States, to land on the beaches of the United States. I ask: What would you do with them?" As for the charge of torture, Castro always maintained that "our consciousness was formed by the struggle against torture. In more than 20 years, the revolution has not physically mistreated one single prisoner."[158]

The Reagan administration also took its charges to the U.N. Commission on Human Rights, where Ambassador Vernon Walters accused Cuba of "compiling a record of brutality and oppression which ranks proportionately among the great tragedies of this century." With former prisoner Armando Valladares serving as a member of the U.S. delegation, in 1987 the administration came within one vote of gaining approval of a resolution censuring Cuba; thus encouraged, it came back to Geneva the following year, this time with Valladares serving as chief of the U.S. delegation. Since the 1987 effort had failed primarily because it was unable to gain the support of Latin America's representatives on the commission, this time President Reagan joined in the lobbying, but the U.S. initiative again failed to pass. Skoug interpreted the outcome as evidence that "sympathy for Cuba and antipathy to the United States still were in vogue" in the United Nations: "Allegiance to race and culture . . . enabled Latin American leaders to overlook inconvenient facts."[159]

Few of these Latin American leaders attempted to defend Cuba's human rights record; rather, the sentiment seemed to be that the U.S. effort involved gross exaggeration and was tainted by a double standard: at about the same time President Reagan was condemning Cuba as "the country where institutionalized totalitarianism has consistently violated the rights of the citizens," his assistant secretary of state was telling reporters, "I have confidence that Chile is in good hands"—the hands of Augusto Pinochet. Castro noted the hypocrisy: "You told me the United States is concerned over human rights," he replied to PBS's Robert MacNeil in early 1985. "This is amazing. When we see the excellent relations it has with the military government of Argentina, where thousands of people disappeared; the excellent relations with Pinochet who murdered and caused so many people to disappear; the excellent relations with South Africa, which oppresses 20 million blacks—I am really amazed."[160]

Others actors quietly worked to gain the release of political prisoners, with an especially important role played by the Catholic Church and in particular by a delegation from the U.S. Catholic Conference, which represents the nation's bishops. Castro welcomed the group to Havana in 1985, six weeks after the United States and Cuba had signed the original migration agreement, which provided for the emigration of up to 3,000 already released political prisoners. The bishops sought to augment that number by requesting the release of 147 current prisoners; Castro offered to free 75, most of them not on the bishops' list, but no prisoners had been released before the migration agreement was suspended in May. The bishops kept trying, however, and 67 former political prisoners and 37 family members finally arrived in Miami in September 1986. Assistant Secretary of State Abrams downplayed the significance of their release, characterizing the negotiations as Castro's "crude attempts to take advantage of the Church."[161]

In mid-1987 an additional 348 current and former prisoners were freed and allowed to leave, but it was no longer possible to isolate the influence of the church (especially New York's tenacious archbishop, John Cardinal O'Connor, who in 1988 became the first Catholic cardinal to visit Cuba since 1959) from the influence of others working for the release of political prisoners at the same time, including Senator Edward Kennedy, French president François Mitterand, Spanish prime minister Felipe González, and even French naturalist Jacques Cousteau, who had struck up a friendship with Fidel Castro while filming in Cuban waters. Although the Reagan administration was not directly involved in any of these negotiations, its effort to spotlight Cuban human rights abuses may have contributed to Cuba's decision to release the prisoners. The full story will not be known until the Cuban archives are opened.

AND SO THE REAGAN YEARS came to an end. U.S.-Cuban relations started off bad and stayed bad, but much had changed since 1980, when candidate Ronald Reagan had proposed a blockade of Cuba, or even since the mid-1980s, when a deputy assistant secretary of state had warned that "the Soviet Union has moved from having a marginal presence and little influence to being a major actor with multifaceted activities throughout Latin America and the Caribbean."[162] By the end of Reagan's second term, no one was concerned about Moscow's Latin America policy, and the Cuban American community was now generating most of Washington's interest in Cuba. But aside from Radio Martí, a victory achieved in 1983, nearly all of CANF's efforts consisted of minor nibbling around the edges of established policy.[163]

Career officers such as Kenneth Skoug began preparing for new assignments. After six years of single-minded implementation of the Reagan administration's Cuba policy, Skoug was promoted to the position of chargé d'affaires in Nicaragua, but the assignment turned out to be empty: since the Reagan administration would not allow Nicaragua's ambassador into the United States, the Sandinistas retaliated by refusing to allow Skoug to take up his post in Managua. After a brief stint as deputy chief of mission in Venezuela, the disappointed diplomat, obliged to retire, returned to his suburban Washington home and began writing his memoir just as the Cold War was coming to an end. He noted that "when Reagan left office, Cuba was a less influential force in regional politics, well on its way to becoming a nuisance and an anachronism rather than a threat to U.S. security."[164]

There will be no improvement of relations with Cuba.
It simply cannot be.
—George H. W. Bush, 1989

Often, the less there is to justify a traditional custom,
the harder it is to get rid of it.
—Mark Twain, 1876

12

UNWAVERING HOSTILITY
THE GEORGE H. W. BUSH
ADMINISTRATION

"Fidel Castro's recent attempts to rejoin the mainstream of the Latin American community should be viewed with skepticism." So began the tutorial prepared for the new Bush administration's assistant secretary of state for Latin America, Bernard Aronson. Characterized by Secretary of State James Baker as "a rare breed—a bona fide Democrat who supported aid to the contras," Aronson was an obscure neoconservative with no knowledge of Spanish, no experience in Latin America, and no readily apparent grasp of the issues confronting the region. What he brought to the table was an ability to work with moderate opposition leaders in Congress to end the deeply divisive dispute over U.S. policy in Central America. "I had no desire to further the debilitating ideological warfare of that period," wrote Baker. "It was critical to our overall foreign policy to remove this issue from the domestic political arena." "We don't need this," agreed the former ambassador to Nicaragua, Lawrence Pezzullo; "we've become a Banana Republic." The question was how to break out of Washington's Central American stalemate, which had created an exceptionally sour mood. "I was up at the Council [on Foreign Relations in New York] last night," Pezzullo commented a few weeks after Bush's inauguration, "with a bunch of people, including Elliott Abrams. There's no way to begin this discussion anymore.

And I went home just feeling, you know, where the hell do we go as a country anymore? . . . It turns your stomach. I mean, I found last night I haven't
been that depressed in a long time. . . . I wouldn't even hazard an honest
comment to those people."[1] Aronson's job was to close the chasm between
moderates such as Pezzullo and radical conservatives such as Abrams.

The perennial problem of Cuba remained. Aronson's briefing tutorial
summarized the level of Cuban subversion in each of the region's countries, from Mexico ("little evidence of Cuban subversion") and Venezuela
("no known Cuban operations") to Colombia at the other extreme, with
Cuba "heavily involved in helping radical groups." Although the conclusion
of State's professionals was nothing new—"Cuba is compounding existing problems by encouraging destabilization and armed insurrection"—
the overall tone of the document was light-years away from the thinking
that had greeted Reagan administration officials eight years earlier: revolutionary Cuba still posed problems, but they were nothing to get excited
about.[2]

So while Aronson focused on Central America, he handed initial responsibility for Cuba to his principal deputy, Michael Kozak, a pugnacious career
officer who gave House members a paraphrase of what Secretary Baker had
said at his Senate confirmation hearing: "As long as the Castro regime refuses to make concessions in areas of concern to us, relations cannot and
should not improve." Harvard's Jorge Domínguez agreed ("relations are bad
and in my judgment, they should be"), as did Columbia's Pamela Falk, but
a contrary view came from California representative George Crockett, who
chaired the House Foreign Affairs Subcommittee on Western Hemisphere
Affairs. "I am an opponent of our policy toward Cuba," Crockett had begun,
arguing that it would be preferable to negotiate an end to nearly three decades of hostility. Kozak replied that the United States had already tried
that approach, citing a long series of sterile exchanges: "If that is as far as it
is going to go, you don't need to have constant meetings." He reserved particular criticism for the way Cubans were exploiting visits by members of
Congress, including Crockett: "They are always sending messages through
intermediaries. We have told them again and again: You want to give us a
message, say it directly. We are always here to talk."[3]

Kozak downplayed the fact that Washington and Havana had recently
been engaged in intense face-to-face talks about Angola and Namibia and
that these discussions had been successful: six weeks after George Bush's
election, Cuba, Angola, and South Africa had signed agreements provid-

ing for Namibia's independence and the withdrawal of Cuban troops from Angola. The agreements had been reached only after the warring sides— including the United States—realized they were mired in an interminable conflict, the U.S. negotiator reported. The Reagan administration had launched its Africa policy by warmly receiving the foreign minister of apartheid South Africa, Pik Botha, but by early 1983 virtually everyone had come to appreciate the damage being done to U.S. interests by supporting a white supremacist regime. At that point President Reagan ordered that "the U.S. will seek to reduce the Cuban presence and influence in southern Africa by energetic leadership of the diplomatic effort to achieve a Cuban withdrawal."[4]

Although the military pressure on Cuba and on Angola's MPLA had continued—in 1986 Washington resumed aid to UNITA rebels after a ten-year hiatus—the administration placed its central emphasis on energetic diplomacy, which revealed, as Secretary of State George Shultz told his Mexican counterpart, "that South Africa will not give up Namibia as a buffer as long as Cuban and Soviet presence persists in Angola. That is a fact, he said, that we have to deal with."[5] And so they did, dealing with the situation through intense negotiations that were now leading to Namibian independence and Cuban withdrawal from Angola. The first detachment of Cuban soldiers left Angola ten days before Bush's inauguration, and the final Cuban troops arrived home as promised in mid-1991.[6]

Why, then, did State's Kozak fail to point out that Havana and Washington had been engaged in successful negotiations, choosing instead to emphasize the sterile exchanges? Part of the explanation probably lies in the bureaucratic division of labor (State's Africanists had handled the Angola/Namibia negotiations, while Kozak's Latin Americanists had seen no progress in their area of responsibility, Central America), but a better explanation is the administration's view that on Africa it had been negotiating not with Cuba but with the Soviet Union. President Bush had been referring to Cuba as "a pawn of the Soviets" since the 1970s. Fidel Castro, he said, "gets his sugar subsidy and in return he sends young Cubans to Angola, Ethiopia, and Nicaragua to fight and die for his Soviet bosses. It's a sad truth but under Castro today Cuba has only two big exports—sugar and death." Secretary of State Baker agreed, denying any significant role to Cuba or to the warring factions in Africa, writing in his memoir that it was purely a Great Power struggle and that by the late 1980s, "neither of the superpowers had overriding reasons for being embroiled in this conflict.

It was time to move on to more critical issues—and the Angolan civil war seemed ripe for resolution."[7]

And so Cuba was on its way out of southern Africa, courtesy of several years of patient diplomatic work by the Reagan State Department; the Bush administration could now move on to those more critical issues, by far the most of important of which was the collapse of the Soviet Union. The Gorbachev era had begun in early 1985, just after the beginning of Ronald Reagan's second term, and the CIA soon reported that the Soviet leader "knows, as did his two predecessors, that the USSR cannot underwrite the economic and social development of any but a very few Third World countries." For the moment, Cuba could count on being one of the chosen few, but the disintegration of the communist world was visible by the time of George Bush's election in late 1988; a month later, Castro warned Cubans that "you cannot only expect difficulties from the enemy, but also from our own friends."[8]

But he did not appear too concerned when he traveled to Venezuela a few weeks later for the inauguration of Carlos Andrés Pérez: when asked about Gorbachev's reforms, Castro diplomatically replied that the Soviet leader "is seeking his formulas for the development of the Soviet people," while "we are the Caribbean and perhaps perestroika would not have the same effects here." As for Gorbachev himself, Castro exclaimed, "What an open-minded man. What a fresh imagination he has. My conversations with him have always been excellent." Unlike some Soviet officials, "Gorbachev treats me as an equal, with a lot of consideration, without any type of paternalism, and with a lot of frankness." Castro's overall impression: "I like him a lot."[9]

Castro still held to this view in early April 1989, three months after Bush's inauguration, when the Cubans welcomed Gorbachev, the first Soviet premier to visit Havana since Leonid Brezhnev in 1974. Thinking that perestroika might be crossing the Atlantic, all three major U.S. networks sent their news anchors to Havana, but they had little to report. Gorbachev's colorless fifty-two-minute speech to the National Assembly was upstaged by Castro's forty-six-minute introduction, which became remarkably moderate after a few warm-up remarks about imperialism that prompted Interests Section chief John Taylor to walk out. The Cuban leader conceded that "if a socialist country wants to build capitalism, we have to respect its right to build capitalism." This uncharacteristic live-and-let-live blandness continued at a joint press conference, with Gorbachev responding to a question about perestroika by suggesting diplomatically that "each country solves the problems of its socialist transformation according to its own conditions." Gorbachev added that "Soviet-Cuban relations are continuing to expand and grow stronger," and Castro dismissed a question about Cuba's debt to the Soviet Union by observing, "We have never had any financial problems with the USSR, never."[10]

Then a Spanish reporter asked about Central America: "What role will the USSR, together with the United States, play? Will it play the role of an ambassador? Will it speak on behalf of Cuba and help solve the problem?" Stop right there, Castro interrupted: "Do you think this is a colony?" Cubans could speak for themselves. "It was never my intention to offend you or Cuba," the reporter began to apologize, but Castro cut him short, directing the reporters' attention to what he considered the major story of the day, Gorbachev's innocuous speech to the National Assembly. "Have you sent out reports on today's events? Then what kind of reporters are you? Have you sent out reports? But it was the most important event. This [press conference] is just the dessert." Speaking briefly to reporters after Gorbachev's departure the next day, Castro characterized the visit "as historical, excellent, excellent. . . . He was truly very happy. He was very happy, very joyful, very satisfied."[11]

Perhaps Gorbachev was happy because Cuba presented none of the problems found on the Soviet Union's western border, where Poland's Solidarity was about to win a stunning electoral victory, basically overthrowing the communist regime that had held power since 1945, and where Hungarians were about to provide anyone living in the East with an avenue to the West by opening their border with Austria. "What phenomenon are we facing?" asked Fidel Castro in mid-1989. "At times I even wonder if it would not be better for those new generations that were born under socialism in Poland and Hungary to take a little trip to capitalism so that they can find out how egoistic, brutal, and dehumanizing a capitalist society is." If the socialist community were to disappear, he warned, "the imperialist powers would throw themselves like beasts over the Third World. They would once again distribute the world among themselves, as in the worst of times, before the first proletariat revolution."[12]

Four months later the East Germans opened the Berlin Wall, and a few weeks thereafter the Czechs overthrew their communist leaders simply by standing in the freezing rain in Wenceslas Square—a Velvet Revolution, they called it. At the same time, the Soviet Union was disintegrating, and Fidel Castro was reconsidering his live-and-let-live attitude: at the end of 1989, he was complaining,

It is disgusting that many in the USSR are dedicating themselves to denying and destroying the historic feat and the extraordinary merits of that heroic people. That is not the way to rectify and overcome the unquestionable mistakes made in a revolution that was born in czarist authoritarianism, in a huge, backward, and poor country. . . . It is said that socialism should be improved. Nobody can oppose this principle that is inherent to and applies constantly to every human work. But can socialism be improved by abandoning the most elementary Marxist-Leninist principles? Why do the so-called reforms have to have a capitalist direction?

"Communism is on the wane," gloated President Bush a few months later. "In our hemisphere, there's only one left, and that's Castro. And I don't know what he believed, but he darn sure can't be excited about the way things are going for good old Communists—going down the drain."[13]

The drain was opened wider at the early 1990 meeting of the Council for Mutual Economic Assistance (CMEA), where Moscow demanded that CMEA members begin trading with hard currency at market prices. "CMEA countries continue to exist," a dismayed Castro reported, but "the declared purpose of some of these countries is to construct capitalism."[14] In late 1990 a reunited Germany announced that it would end development aid to Cuba, while Czechoslovakia indicated that it would no longer furnish Cuba with diplomatic and consular representation in the United States. These jabs paled in comparison to the jolt delivered on 1 January 1991, when the U.S. dollar replaced the ruble as the CMEA's accounting unit. A month later, the CMEA disbanded, ending forever the complex web of agreements that had underwritten so much of the Cuban Revolution.

NEITHER HAVANA NOR WASHINGTON seemed the least bit interested in a bilateral adjustment to fit this new global reality. President Bush made it clear that he was not budging ("What's the point of my talking to him?"), and an equally intransigent Fidel Castro told Cubans that "it is a great illusion, a false illusion, to believe that revolutionary processes can live or survive by granting concessions." The Soviet bloc countries "began by making small concessions, then more and newer concessions; they gave the end of the little finger, then they were asked for another bit, then came the finger, followed by the hand, afterward the arms; later, their heads were snapped off." That was not going to occur in Cuba.[15]

The trajectory of post–Cold War U.S.-Cuban relations was forecast with those words. Earlier, when it was still difficult to foresee the complete collapse of the Soviet bloc, Castro had claimed that "men who are left alone and persevere are the ones who triumph," and he soon came to repeat this theme over and over as Cuba found itself ever more alone: "If we were to wake up and learn that the USSR had disintegrated—something that we hope never happens—even under those circumstances, Cuba and the Cuban revolution would resist." Then, when the Soviet Union collapsed, Castro told a 1992 audience, "it is during difficult times that men and women are truly put to the test. It is during difficult times that you find out who is really worth something."[16]

Of all the peculiar behavior that accompanied the unraveling of the Soviet bloc, nothing was more curious than the extraordinary emphasis the Bush administration placed on breaking Moscow's ties with Cuba. The arm-twisting officially began at the first Bush-Gorbachev summit, held in Malta in early December 1989, but the groundwork had been laid a year earlier, at Secretary Baker's confirmation hearing, when Florida senator Connie Mack voiced the view that Gorbachev's objective was to obtain Western credits, "and it would seem to me that before we, as a nation, were to get into a position where we would be encouraging credits from the West, that we should, in fact, make a statement, a strong statement, about the importance of eliminating that $4 to $6 billion that is going to Cuba." "That would be an excellent way to start," Baker had replied, but then he took no immediate steps to pressure Moscow, so members of Congress provided the initial encouragement, submitting a number of bills designed to force the Soviet Union to end aid and trade with Cuba.[17]

Only in late 1989 did the administration pick up the challenge. Just before departing for Malta, President Bush declared that "the Soviet Union should stop feeding Fidel Castro," and in Malta he pressured Gorbachev to make Cuba withdraw from Central America. The Soviet leader replied that doing so was not within his power ("No one can really give orders to Castro, absolutely no one") and suggested instead that the United States talk directly with the Cubans, who, Gorbachev privately told Bush, were eager to talk: during Gorbachev's April visit to Havana, Castro "asked me, in effect, to help normalize US-Cuban relations. . . . I say this for the first time in the most private way." In his memoir, the president wrote that he brushed this offer aside without comment, and at two press conferences immediately after Malta, he reiterated his demand that Moscow stop aiding Cuba.[18]

There the question rested for the first half of 1990, only to surface once again when Gorbachev visited Washington in May, just as he was coming under additional pressure from rival Boris Yeltsin, who advocated accelerated political and economic reforms. In March 1989 Yeltsin had scored a major electoral victory by winning the right to represent Moscow in the Soviet Union's new Congress of Deputies. A year later, "Gorbachev was unquestionably in danger," recalled Brent Scowcroft; President Bush added, "I certainly wanted to give [Gorbachev] a boost if I could." The two sides first talked in Washington, then flew to Camp David, where, Bush later wrote, "after supper, Gorbachev again took me aside, this time to ask whether Baker had talked to me about his discussions with [Soviet foreign minister Eduard] Shevardnadze on financial questions. He explained that he did not want to raise the question of needing money from the United States in front of his own team. I told him Jim had mentioned it, but that there were still difficult political problems to overcome, problems he was aware of, such as aid to Cuba." [19] After Gorbachev's departure, President Bush used his next *five* news conferences to emphasize the need for Moscow to end its aid to Cuba. "We are trying to help them," he said, "but we have some problems [and] certain things have to happen before I, as President, will make recommendations for direct financial aid." Specifically, "I find it a little contradictory to think that they will continue to spend $5 billion a year for Cuba." "It is a real irritant," added Secretary Baker. "We have great difficulty with the concept of economic assistance . . . at a time when the Soviet Union continues to pour billions of dollars into Cuba." [20]

"What shamelessness!," Fidel Castro told his 1990 26th of July audience. "That is how far Mr. Bush's sickening obsessiveness goes. . . . Now that the enemy is no longer the socialist bloc, now that the enemy is no longer the USSR, we are the imperialists' enemy." [21]

A year passed, and Bush and Gorbachev met again in London, where the president told reporters that the Soviet leader was moving in the right direction ("He points out that there's much, much less aid going into Cuba"). Ten days later, Bush flew to Moscow for a formal summit and a speech to the Soviet people, going out of his way to emphasize that "the United States poses no threat to Cuba. Therefore there is no need for the Soviet Union to funnel millions of dollars in military aid to Cuba." When asked a few days later about Gorbachev's reaction, the president replied that events were moving in a satisfactory direction—the Soviets, he said, "have significantly reduced their contribution to Cuba. But look, I'd love to see them eliminated." His summary of the trip for a U.S. audience: "I had an opportunity to tell him that one way the Soviet Union would have vastly improved receptivity here would be to do exactly that."[22]

Then he began his summer vacation in Kennebunkport, Maine, while Gorbachev required the aid of the new president of the Russian Federation, Boris Yeltsin, to overcome a coup attempt. Adjusting to the rapidly changing power configuration in Moscow, President Bush began to focus on Yeltsin instead of Gorbachev but still emphasized Cuba: "We heard Boris Yeltsin, I think, properly, say, 'Look, there's not going to be any aid from Russia, from the Russian Republic, to Castro.' That's good." Now, he added, acknowledging the Soviet collapse, "as these other Republics come front and center, we then must determine what their role will be and how they can help with peace, or what they're going to do about distancing themselves from the last remaining Communist dictator in this hemisphere. I'm talking about Fidel Castro."[23]

A few days later Baker met with both Yeltsin and Gorbachev in Moscow, and the secretary of state focused once again on Cuba: "I pushed both of them hard on several issues from our old agenda, in particular military supplies to Afghanistan and financial subsidies for Cuba, and the Soviet military presence on the island. I said that the West would be far more willing to support them and to help them with their debt if it was clear they were no longer subsidizing Communist regimes around the world." Baker was surprised when both Yeltsin and Gorbachev "jumped at my offer, and indeed were almost competitive in trying to be cooperative." With the Russians desperate for Western aid, "I was stunned by how swiftly we could make progress. Gorbachev agreed in my meeting with him to begin withdrawing the Soviet brigade in Cuba. Without expecting him to say yes, I asked as we were walking to our press conference in St. George's Hall if he could mention this. He said he could, and did. This announcement dominated the press coverage of our meeting and created considerable angst and hard feelings in Cuba, which learned about it for the first time from those press accounts. Later, Yeltsin told me that all military and economic assistance to Cuba would be cut off by January 1, 1992, and that all Soviet military personnel in Cuba would be out of Cuba by the same date."[24]

Angst and hard feelings hardly captured the reaction of the Cuban government. A front-page *Granma* editorial lambasted Soviet authorities for capitulating to Washington's demands "without saying one single word to our country" and promised that "Cuba will never agree to being betrayed or sold out to the United States, and to keep from being returned to slavery we are ready to fight to the death." A few weeks earlier, Castro had reminded his 1991 26th of July audience of John Quincy Adams's "ripe apple" prediction that Cuba would eventually become part of the United States, vowing that "we will never resign ourselves to return to the past. We will never again resign ourselves to be again a neo-colony and a Yankee possession. Never. Let us see which of the two is more persevering and which of the two is stronger."[25]

By this time East Germany had been absorbed into West Germany, the Warsaw Pact had disbanded, and the president of the Russian Republic, Boris Yeltsin, had laid claim to the Kremlin's corner office. Facing the fact that he literally had no desk at which to sit, Mikhail Gorbachev announced his resignation as the premier of a country that no longer existed, and in a blink, it seemed, an era was over. Six months later, Yeltsin was in Washington, promising a joint session of Congress that communism "has collapsed, never to rise again." Now, he continued, "I am inviting the private sector of the United States to invest in the unique and untapped Russian market. And I am saying, do not be late." In response to the Bush administration's insistence that Moscow cut off what little was left of its aid to Cuba, Yeltsin added, "We have corrected the well-known imbalances in relations with Cuba," and "our commerce with Cuba is based on universally accepted principles and world prices."[26]

WHAT EXACTLY HAD CUBA LOST? In the late 1980s, the State Department had placed the Soviet subsidy at $5.5 billion per year—$4.0 billion in economic aid and trade subsidies and $1.5 billion in military assistance—a sum representing about a quarter of Cuba's gross national product.[27] For 1991, the CIA estimated that economic aid still reached $2.5 billion, but that figure represented the amount on which Russia and Cuba had agreed, not actual deliveries, and in mid-1991 the CIA reported that "Cuba has received only oil and grain since January and is pressing for scheduled shipments of consumer goods such as butter, canned meat, and milk." In October, Castro told Cubans what they already knew from the empty shelves: in the first nine months of the year, Cuba had received none of the promised rice and only 7 percent of the promised lard, 11 percent of the condensed milk, 16 percent of the cooking oil, 18 percent of the canned meat, and 22 percent of the powdered milk.[28]

Some military aid continued. A full year passed before Cuba and Russia negotiated a timetable for the withdrawal of the combat brigade in September 1992, and another decade passed before Russia announced in October 2001 that it was closing its electronic intelligence-gathering station at Lourdes, a facility whose value had steadily declined as communications technology had moved ahead and as costs had escalated. In addition to the expense of operating the facility, the rent had gone from zero during the Soviet years (1964 to 1991) to $90 million in 1992, $160 million in 1993, and $200 million in 1996. Cuba was still charging that amount in late 2000 when President Vladimir Putin visited Cuba and asked that the lease be renegotiated and take into account the country's debt that Russia had inherited from the Soviet Union.[29] A year later Putin announced that Russia was closing Lourdes, a move that President George W. Bush hailed as "another indication that the cold war is over." The Cuban reaction was contained in a statement consuming *Granma*'s entire front page: "The agreement on the Lourdes Electronic Radar Station has not been canceled, since Cuba has not given its approval." The Russians nevertheless closed the base.[30]

A full assessment of what Cuba had lost with the demise of the Soviet bloc must begin by recalling that Cubans had been tightening their belts since their austerity/rectification program began in late 1986, several years before the Soviet collapse. In mid-1988 Castro had warned that "1987, 1988, and perhaps the next two or three years will be the most difficult years for the revolution concerning convertible foreign exchange," but only late in 1989 did the full magnitude of the problems posed by the Soviet-bloc turmoil become apparent. In his 1989 26th of July speech, Castro had simply warned Cubans, "We live in a time of great economic problems," but each subsequent 26th of July speech reported even bleaker news: he referred in 1990 to the "catastrophe in the socialist bloc" and in 1991 to "the disasters in Eastern Europe." In 1992, all doubt was gone: Cuba had suffered "a terrible blow."[31]

It was not simply that Cuba's economic and military aid was gone. From the 1960s to the late 1980s, about 70 percent of Cuba's trade had been with the Soviet Union, plus an additional 15 to 18 percent with the CMEA countries of Eastern Europe. Most of this trade simply evaporated between 1989 and 1992. Petroleum imports fell by 86 percent, fertilizer by 81 percent, and animal feed by 71 percent, all of which crippled domestic production. Then, as luck would have it, Cuba's terms of trade took a significant turn for the worse: between 1989 and 1992, world prices for major Cuban imports (wheat, chicken, milk, and petroleum) all rose dramatically, while the value of Cuba's exports dropped precipitously—sugar by 20 percent and nickel by 28 percent.[32]

As a CIA analyst had noted years earlier, "a major reduction in Soviet aid would force Cuba to

(a) reduce substantially economic activity and the already austere standard of living,

(b) default on its hard currency debt to the West, and

(c) forgo any hope of economic growth over the next several years."

Item (b) had already occurred; now it was time for (a) and (c). There simply was no way to adjust quickly: Cubans had the lowest possible credit rating, making cash-and-carry or barter their only trading options, and they would need time to develop an ability to market in the Western world—"They do not have a banking system," commented one U.S. official in mid-1989; "I mean that is a very primitive country."[33]

The Bush administration intended to do what it could to keep Cuba as "primitive" as possible, and Cuba's adjustment was made even more difficult by the obvious fact that Fidel Castro did not want to change. In late 1988 he told Cubans that "socialism is, and will be, the hope, the only hope," and a month later he added, "Socialism or Death!" to the end of one of his speeches.[34] Then in late 1989, a month after the fall of the Berlin Wall, the Cuban leader warned that "if capitalism returned some day to Cuba, our independence and sovereignty would disappear forever. We would be an extension of Miami, a simple appendix of the Yankee empire."

It is understandable why a Cuban born in the 1920s would reason that capitalism implied U.S. domination, but Castro's dislike of market economics went far beyond the history of U.S.-Cuban relations; with or without the United States, he continued, capitalism means

exaltation of individual selfishness and national chauvinism, the empire of irrationality and anarchy in investment and production, the ruthless sacrifice of the peoples to blind economic laws. It is the empire of the strongest, the exploitation of man by man, every man for himself. In the social order, capitalism implies many other things: prostitution, drugs, gambling, begging, unemployment, abysmal inequality among citizens, depletion of natural resources, poisoning of the atmosphere, seas, rivers, forests, and especially the looting of underdeveloped countries by industrialized capitalist countries. In the past, it meant colonialism, and, in the present it means the neocolonization of billions of human beings through more sophisticated economic and political methods that are also less costly, more effective, and ruthless.

For those reasons, Castro explained, the Cuban Revolution "had to sweep the capitalist system away" in the early 1960s, and "it will never come back." "Socialism will not crumble in Cuba!," he told another audience a few weeks later. "Here we are not ashamed to speak of Lenin and to praise Lenin while others are taking Lenin's name off streets and parks and tearing down statues of Lenin, Marx, and Engels."[35]

If he was worried about the monumental odds stacked against the now-isolated island, Castro did not say so; instead, he told Cubans in early 1990 that "an honor that none of us ever imagined has befallen our current population—we are confronting the empire, fiercely defending our independence, the flag of the revolution, and the flag of socialism. This is an exceptional hour of struggle." He had told an earlier gathering of Cuban women that "it's an enormous privilege to be a witness to this epoch, to be a protagonist in this moment of history of our country. I assure you that this moment is more important than any other that our country has lived through in any prior epoch. Whether or not there is war, whether or not there is a special period, this moment is the most important in the history of our country." A few months later, he again emphasized that Cubans were privileged to face this new challenge: "No time has been more worthy than this one. No other time has been more heroic or glorious than this time. No other time has given us such an opportunity to make ourselves greater. . . . Let's hear it loud and clear. Let's hear it loud and clear: Socialismo o muerte! Patria o muerte! Venceremos!"[36]

Cubans began to comprehend the full implications of that challenge on 29 August 1990, when *Granma*'s front page carried a formal notice, "Information for the Population," focusing on depleted petroleum supplies, which "force us to adopt a series of special measures." First, gasoline supplies would be cut by 30 percent, while electricity use would be reduced by 10 percent. Failure to conserve would lead to one day a week without electricity at peak hours for everyone and a thirty-day cutoff for households that did not reduce their energy usage. If the supply of Soviet oil kept dropping, these initial cutbacks would be followed by the economy's transformation "from a normal situation to a special period in peacetime." A month later, Castro told a Havana audience that "the concept of the special period in peacetime has emerged [and] we will have to undergo this trial." The term had been introduced nine months earlier, when Castro, perhaps trying to add a ray of sunshine to an otherwise bleak picture, distinguished between a "special period during wartime," when a blockade would make all exports and imports impossible, a situation worse than "a special period in peacetime," when trade would still be possible.[37]

From that point forward the word "austerity" took on a meaning far beyond the dictionary definition of simple living conditions; for Cubans, the Special Period signified severe deprivation, including hunger, as average daily caloric consumption dropped by more than 30 percent, from 2,908 calories in the 1980s to 1,863 calories in 1993, when the U.S. Department of Agriculture was recommending a minimum daily caloric intake of between 2,100 and 2,300 calories. Some economic indicators fell like rocks (export earnings by as much as 80 percent), while others soared (unemployment from less than 8 percent to 34 percent), but all of them went in the wrong direction.[38]

The petroleum shortages were especially damaging, halting 50 percent of industrial activity and 70 percent of public transportation, including most of the Soviet-bloc trucks and buses, which, a candid Castro now confessed, had been junk from the beginning: The Bulgarian trucks "are such garbage and they had so many problems that no one else would buy them," while "the Hungarian buses get six kilometers to the gallon, fill the city with smoke, poisoning everyone. Those buses would ruin any country, I tell you, ruin it." Into the urban transportation gap came the Chinese, who agreed to exchange Cuban sugar for Chinese rice and bicycles—thousands of bicycles crowding Havana's streets, now almost completely free of private automobiles, provided the only alternative to walking, underscoring what was obvious to any visitor: Cuba's economy had shrunk by between a third and a half.[39]

"Castro will not survive this," gloated President George H. W. Bush in late 1991, while Assistant Secretary Aronson assured Congress that "time is not on the side of the last Stalinist regime in this hemisphere." The administration grew only more confident in 1992, with Bush commenting that "Castro is showing signs of desperation," that "we are closer than ever to our goal of returning freedom to Cuba," that "the Castro dictatorship cannot and will not survive," and that "the guy's trying to keep his snorkel out of the water." As the State Department told Congress that "Castro's communism is a dinosaur approaching extinction," books began appearing with titles such as *Fidel Castro: The End of the Road* and *Castro's Final Hour*, both best sellers in Miami.[40]

BEYOND THE PLEASURE OF GLOATING, why would anyone in Washington continue to care about Cuba? After U.S. investors had accepted their losses and moved on in the early 1960s, U.S. officials had continued to lavish attention on this small island because its alliance with the Soviet Union made it a threat to U.S. security. But now, a generation later, the Soviets had packed their bags and left, and as they departed, a dramatic change occurred in the participants in the Washington policy-making process: since Cuba no longer posed even a modest threat, the national security bureaucracy redeployed its resources, reducing the number and especially the quality of the individuals responsible for the now-inconsequential job of watching Cuba go down the drain. A generation earlier, Robert McNamara would never have considered handing over the Pentagon's responsibility for Cuba to Nancy Dorn, age thirty-one, completely untested and lacking training or experience in Latin America. Nonetheless, in 1989, Richard Cheney tapped Dorn to become the principal civilian Latin Americanist in the Pentagon— deputy assistant secretary of defense for inter-American affairs—simply because no one higher on the patronage pecking order asked for the job. And now, since the best and the brightest had been pulled away to more important work, she was supported by a bureaucracy that could produce nothing better than this 1989 report:

> Conclusion: the indigenous production of small arms is further evidence of Cuba's determined effort to possibly enter the international arms export market, in an effort to continue to support Castro's obsession as a revolutionary in keeping regional and Third World guerrilla movements supplied especially in El Salvador, as well as to obtain/bring-in much needed hard currency to help prop-up Cuba's fledging [*sic*] economy.[41]

What in the world did "Cuba's determined effort to possibly enter" mean? What did the author intend to communicate with that phrase? And what did the supervisor's handwritten evaluation of the document, "Good Work," mean? It meant that competent national security analysts, always in short supply, had been reassigned to tasks that mattered. Cuba was no longer one of them.

Why, then, did President Bush and national security adviser Scowcroft write in their memoir that they rarely contacted Gorbachev without bringing up Cuba?[42] Of all the topics that Washington might reasonably have placed on the U.S.-Soviet agenda, why was so much emphasis given to convincing Moscow to halt its aid to Cuba? Or, to take one specific issue, why would withdrawal of the Soviet brigade from Cuba be the centerpiece of the Gorbachev-Baker news conference when the U.S. secretary of state visited Moscow in September 1991?

The answer is that politics, like nature, abhors a vacuum, and as the national security community turned its attention elsewhere, the Cuban American community spread into the vacant territory: Jorge Mas Canosa, founder and chair of the Cuban American National Foundation, was also visiting Moscow that September, each evening calling home reports to CANF's Miami radio program, *La Voz de la Fundación*, and he told listeners that Secretary Baker had simply wrapped up the agreement that he, Mas Canosa, had negotiated. Arriving in Moscow on 4 September with U.S. representative Larry Smith, Mas Canosa had immediately begun talks with Soviet authorities. "On the fourth or fifth day these efforts had advanced considerably, and we knew that it was at the point of being resolved." The Gorbachev-Baker press conference took place on 11 September.[43]

Cuban Americans had used the Reagan years to organize themselves for battle, and now, with the end of the Cold War, they were perfectly positioned to make their move. Philip Brenner had been among the first to capture this change, writing in 1990 that the Bush administration "has delegated Cuba policy to an active congressional group, inspired by domestic lobbies." Indeed, Congress now included its first Cuban American: in 1989 Miami representative Claude Pepper died, and a special election was needed to fill the seat of this Democrat who had focused a long career on protecting Social Security for South Florida's retirees. It passed to Ileana Ros-Lehtinen, a Republican who would build her career on catering to the intransigent wing of Miami's Cuban American community, the part that remained intent on undermining the Cuban government. Ros-Lehtinen's campaign had been managed by the president's son, Jeb, who knew what it would take to fire up her natural constituency: his father needed to attend a Ros-Lehtinen fund-raiser and promise that "there will be no improvement of relations with Cuba. It simply cannot be."[44]

But winning this commitment from the Republicans represented only half the battle for the territory abandoned by national security officials; what cemented the Cuban American community's control over post–Cold War U.S. policy toward Cuba was its capture of the other half—the Democrats. As the 1990s unfolded, the Democrat most eager to win the Cuban American vote was New Jersey's Robert Torricelli, but during the Bush administration he was challenged for that title by several Democratic office seekers, including powerful Miami representative Dante Fascell, who, when asked why the United States should treat Cuba harshly while helping Russia, replied as any vote-maximizing politician would: "We do not have

2 million Soviets living in Miami, Florida, or in New Jersey. . . . That makes a big difference, I want to tell you."[45]

No one knows the precise voting strength of the Cuban American community during the Bush years. In 1990 census takers counted 1,053,197 Cuban Americans, of whom 298,481 were native-born (that is, born in the United States but with at least one parent born in Cuba) and 379,864 were naturalized citizens. Many of the native-born were too young to vote, of course, and some of the naturalized Cubans undoubtedly failed to do so, but the numbers were of great significance because they were concentrated in two large swing states, light-pink Florida and baby-blue New Jersey, and because politicians on both sides of the aisle had learned by the mid-1980s that the first step to winning the Cuban American vote was to promise exactly what President Bush did at the Ros-Lehtinen fund-raiser: uncompromising hostility toward the Cuban government.

But by the time George H. W. Bush entered office, the Cuban American community wanted more than pledges of continued hostility from smooth-talking Anglo politicians; they wanted access to power so that they could hasten Castro's downfall. Cuban Americans could gain this access by electing their own such as Ros-Lehtinen, but that would take time; meanwhile, when the Cold War ended, the only well-organized representative of their interests was the Cuban American National Foundation. As a result, September 1991 found CANF's Mas Canosa in Moscow at the same time as Baker. Mas Canosa was speaking, he said, on behalf of the hundreds of thousands of Cuban Americans who would troop to the polls in 1992. Anyone who wanted to win Florida's electoral votes would be eager to curry Mas Canosa's favor, and Secretary Baker would soon resign to direct the president's reelection campaign.

CANF had earned its voice in Republican Party discussions by vigorously supporting the Reagan administration's policies in Central America, by delivering the Cuban American vote, and by offering generous financial support to Republican (and some Democratic) candidates. Although himself a generous personal contributor, Mas Canosa's genius was to convince wealthy Cuban Americans to allow him to vacuum their pockets and to deploy their money through a CANF satellite, the Free Cuba Political Action Committee.[46] Appreciating this support, leaders of both political parties eagerly sang CANF's praises, none more frequently or effusively than President Bush. "Right from my heart I want to congratulate the Foundation," he told its members during the 1988 campaign, and the praise continued throughout his presidency, almost always accompanied by a public accolade for CANF's leader: "All I would like to say to you, Jorge, is keep up your battle," or "Hey, Jorge is the only guy that can take on that '60 Minutes' crowd and come out ahead. He did. He did just great."[47]

Secretary Baker ensured that State Department officials consulted regularly with the Cuban American leadership—so regularly that Representative Ros-Lehtinen joked at one 1993 committee hearing that the deputy assistant secretary responsible for Cuba, Robert Gelbard, "is practically an honorary Miami resident. I tell him I see him in Miami almost as much as I see my Chairman"—that is, Torricelli. John Ferch, a career officer who served as chief of the U.S. Interests Section from 1982 to 1985, recalled that "when he heard of my appointment, the [CIA] station chief in Mexico City arranged for me to meet Jorge Mas Canosa." Ferch continued, "I tried to stay in regular contact with [Mas Canosa], calling on him every time I went through Miami."[48]

Lacking control of the executive branch, Democrats such as Torricelli could not provide this level of attention, but they could invite Mas Canosa to participate in congressional hearings, where the Democrats vied with the Republicans to shower him with praise.[49] The CANF leader clearly reveled in this recognition, as would most mortals, but it did much more than stroke his ego: it cemented his position as the Cuban American godfather, not simply one representative but the personification of the Cuban American community.

Cuban Americans probably could have made a wiser choice. Obviously intelligent, Mas Canosa was also a bully—a man who, wrote journalist Ann Louise Bardach, "adopted a scorched-earth policy toward those who opposed him." Ferch agreed: "If you're looking for a dictionary definition of 'fanatic,' there's Jorge Mas Canosa. I wouldn't want to meet him in a dark alley." "He was a zealot," recalled Kenneth Skoug, the director of State's Office of Cuban Affairs during much of the Reagan era. "Frank Calzon [the CANF representative in Washington] was more emotional; he wore his heart on his sleeve. Mas Canosa was smoother. He would hint. You know he knows that you're talking to the Cubans, and he wants to be part of the discussion, to be sure nothing happens, important or unimportant, without his knowledge. 'You wouldn't talk with the PLO without talking with the Israelis,' he would say. Then he would add, just very casually, 'I wouldn't want relations between your office and the Cuban American community to get any worse.' You got the message." Skoug had seen firsthand what happened to career officers who failed to gain CANF's seal of approval: his predecessor as office director, Myles Frechette, "wanted to go to Havana as chief of the Interests Section, but the Cuban Americans said no. Eventually, he got his embassy, but it was the embassy in Cameroon, a real disappointment." Ferch almost met a similar fate: "When I was up for the embassy in Honduras, [Florida senator] Paula Hawkins asked Senator [Jesse] Helms to put a hold on me, saying I was too soft on communism. Where did Hawkins get it in her head to think that? It had to be the Cubans in Miami. Only after I was appropriately hawkish at my confirmation hearing—primarily about Cuba's involvement in drug trafficking—only then did Hawkins say it was OK to lift the hold."[50] And those events occurred during the Reagan years; Mas Canosa wielded even more power in the Bush administration, when national security officials were not vying for control of U.S. policy.

Mas Canosa's bullying style may have worked well among Cuban Americans in Miami, whose intolerance was criticized by Americas Watch in a special 1992 report, but an abusive style wears poorly in Washington, where it is one thing to win a battle and quite another to humiliate your opponents. Such humiliation often seemed to give Mas Canosa great satisfaction. Had he not died of cancer in 1997, this style probably would have led to his downfall, especially since he combined it with a tendency to wildly exaggerate the facts or at times to completely invent reality. Indeed, one of Mas Canosa's defining characteristics was his scant regard for precision. For example, his résumé read: "served as a member of the invasion forces *at the Bay of Pigs*," which would seem to suggest that the CANF leader was, in fact, "at the Bay of Pigs." Instead, however, he was nowhere near the site but was floating on a ship four hundred miles away, off eastern Cuba, part of a diversionary force that never went ashore. The incident perfectly illustrates Mas Canosa's lifelong ability to stay far out of harm's way, an ability first evidenced when he expressed his opposition to the Batista government in the late 1950s but then promptly enrolled in a North Carolina junior college, returning to Cuba a week after Batista fled.[51]

In time Washington would have caught on to him, but in the early 1990s Mas was hitting full stride after a decade of careful preparation, and he did so just as the Soviet bloc was collapsing and as George Bush was beginning the second year of his presidency, when newspapers were running headlines about how "Rising Hopes for Castro's Fall Have Cubans in Miami Abuzz." This particular article noted that Governor Bob Martínez, a Democrat, had recently announced the creation of an eighteen-member Florida Commission on a Free Cuba to assess how Castro's downfall would affect Florida. The governor had asked Mas Canosa to chair the commission, in part because he was the obvious choice and in part because CANF had already created a more ambitious Commission for the Economic Reconstruction of Cuba. The Florida Commission's report noted that "the opening of a new market of 11 million people directly off the Florida coast could be the signal for an era of unprecedented prosperity in South Florida, and the Commission welcomes and endorses on-going private sector efforts to prepare for this development."[52]

Planning a postrevolutionary Cuba was a minor activity; CANF focused on overthrowing the Cuban government, primarily by encouraging sufficient disaffection to trigger a rebellion. This strategy was nothing new, of course—it had been U.S. policy since Operation Mongoose (the Carter years excepted), but now, with Cuba standing alone and its economy collapsing, almost everyone reasoned that this time it would work. CANF's principal tactic was to insist on launching anti-Castro television broadcasts to encourage disaffection. Radio Martí was already working to achieve that goal—with characteristic hyperbole, Mas Canosa told members of Congress that "eighty-six percent of the Cuban people are tuned into Radio Martí at any given time"—and Florida representative Larry Smith, a major recipient of CANF funds, argued that television would be even more effective: "Imagine the impact in Cuba of seeing Cuban-Americans shopping in fully stocked American food stores."[53]

Like Radio Martí, TV Martí was also an old idea, dating from March 1960, when President Dwight D. Eisenhower authorized "a powerful propaganda offensive" as part of the Bay of Pigs package. The clandestine Radio Swan was up and operating within two months, but hiding the source of television signals proved more difficult, since the rudimentary 1960s technology would have required broadcasting from airplanes, and the only possible source of airborne television programs was the U.S. government. Many Cubans, therefore, would perceive TV broadcasts as a form of U.S. intervention, allowing Castro to tap into the deep strain of Cuban nationalism—as U.S. Information Agency director George Allen told the National Security Council a month after President Eisenhower's authorization, "If Mexico or Canada beamed programs to one of our cities from aircraft, we would be furious." Agreeing that TV broadcasts would be counterproductive, both Vice President Richard Nixon and acting secretary of state C. Douglas Dillon recommended that the proposal be shelved.[54]

The State Department again objected when the idea resurfaced during the Kennedy years: "These broadcasts would probably be construed as violating United States treaty commitments, could be easily jammed, and would expose United States TV and radio stations to retaliatory measures." As a compromise, the air force refitted DC-6s to serve as flying transmitters for emergency situations ("including that of actual invasion") but not for regularly scheduled propaganda purposes.[55]

The idea rested for more than two decades, until late in the Reagan administration, when CANF began to push for the creation of the television equivalent of Radio Martí. In late 1987 Mas Canosa and CANF's Washington lobbyist, Calzon, convinced one of the principal recipients of the foundation's campaign contributions, Florida senator Lawton Chiles, to crack open the door with a feasibility study, burying a one-hundred-thousand-dollar earmark in a mammoth government-wide appropriations bill. Since only a handful of Cubans owned satellite dishes, the feasibility question centered on whether Cubans' rooftop antennas could receive television signals beamed from a blimp tethered to Florida's Cudjoe Key, 120 miles to the north, a distance that stretched the physical limits of the medium.[56]

In 1988, as the feasibility study was being conducted by the Advisory Board for Radio Broadcasting to Cuba, chaired by Jorge Mas Canosa, another recipient of CANF campaign contributions, conservative Democratic senator Ernest Hollings, slipped a $7.5 million earmark for start-up costs into another complex appropriations bill. Only at the very last moment did opponents realize what was occurring, and the two House subcommittees that should have handled an authorization rushed to hold a hearing. It opened with one of the two subcommittee chairs, Democratic representative George Crockett, complaining that "there is no legislation pending before us. That is what is so unusual about this whole thing. Someone simply got the brilliant idea that they could by working with the conferees in Conference Committee, in opposition to the chairman of the Subcommittee, slip through an appropriation." Now, he continued, the conference committee could meet later that afternoon, and "this hearing may well be the only discussion in the House of this controversial and unprecedented proposal."

Mas Canosa was on hand to respond: the proposed bill was a logical step following the previous year's feasibility appropriation, which, he said, had been used to hire "four top U.S. engineering firms to investigate technical issues, one of Washington's best international law firms to evaluate legal questions; and Price Waterhouse to generate accurate financial estimates. These six studies concluded that a TV Martí program is technically possible, legally sound, and financially reasonable."[57] Two academic specialists presented an opposing view, but their criticism was brushed aside by well-prepared Florida legislators: "Quite honestly, your testimony leaves me absolutely flabbergasted," Representative Larry Smith told American University professor Philip Brenner. "Do you have any studies, any statistics?" Before Brenner could reply, Smith added a welter of additional questions, all of them hostile, leading Crockett to intercede: "Mr. Smith. In fairness to the witness I think we ought to ask one question at a time and give him a chance to respond." Brenner was allowed to utter two words before Smith interrupted: "Mr. Mas, let me ask you a question. . . . Has anyone ever told you that Radio Martí was a stupid exercise or a waste of money?" "No one," Mas Canosa replied. Then the colored lights began blinking in the hearing room, calling members to a floor vote, and by that time the imbalance had become so obvious that the other subcommittee chair, Florida representative Dan Mica, clearly felt guilty: "We will not be able to come back," he said as the session ended, but "we have to run a fair committee here. Dr. Brenner, you have five seconds to respond."[58]

The start-up appropriation was approved a month before the 1988 election, and the immediate future was predictable—president-elect Bush had always been an enthusiastic supporter of Radio Martí, the 1988 Republican platform had included a plank supporting television broadcasting, and the nominee for secretary of state, James Baker, endorsed the idea during his confirmation hearing. "We will push forward our proposal on TV Marti," the newly inaugurated president promised a Cuban American audience. "It is important that the people of Cuba know the truth."[59] As the start-up appropriation was being used to hire personnel and purchase equipment, a bill to put TV Martí on the air permanently began wending its way through Congress, not as a sub rosa earmark but as a transparent thirty-two-million-dollar authorization.

As with the radio legislation of the early 1980s, domestic broadcasters opposed the television bill, fearing that the new station would interfere with existing signals. TV Martí would have to broadcast at very high power to reach Cuba, and because the signals were to be beamed from a tethered, unpowered blimp, their direction could swing as the wind dictated. Liberal Democrats also criticized TV Martí, believing it an unnecessary provocation, and they were joined by a number of Cuban Americans who recalled that the Castro government had reacted to Radio Martí by suspending the 1984 immigration agreement: "The Cuban community in the U.S. will suffer," wrote Manuel Gómez, president of the little-known Cuban American Committee Fund. "And for what? To increase the political fortunes of the bunch of self-appointed liberators in Miami who are backing the project?"

Gómez was no match for CANF, which was spending unprecedented sums to influence the legislation, and the Democrats offered only perfunctory opposition; indeed, one new Democratic senator, Joseph Lieberman, elected with significant CANF contributions, responded directly to Gómez: "TV Martí would help to maintain the spirit of a free Cuba."[60]

In early 1990, a bit later than proponents had hoped, President Bush signed the Television Broadcasting to Cuba Act.[61] The first test broadcasts came six weeks later, on channel 13, which, like all of Cuba's VHF channels (2 through 13), was already registered as a Cuban station with the International Frequency Registration Board. But the Bush administration pointed out that the Cubans were not broadcasting continuously on channel 13 and that the predawn hours from 3:45 to 6:45 A.M. had been selected for the U.S. broadcasts to avoid interfering with Cuban programming. An angry Fidel Castro nonetheless accused the Bush administration of "using a frequency that is ours and that no one has a right use but us," and the Cuban government filed a complaint with the International Telecommunications Union, whose Frequency Registration Board informed the State Department that high-powered broadcasts from the U.S. blimp would violate international broadcasting agreements by causing "harmful interference" to an existing Cuban station.[62] But the board had no enforcement power, and the Bush administration chose to ignore the admonition.

A few days before TV Martí went on the air, six U.S. clear-channel radio stations were disrupted when Cuba broadcast one of Castro's marathon speeches—a 3.5-hour monologue that an official of the National Association of Broadcasting called a "possible shot across the bow preceding an all-out radio war."[63] Cuba also announced that for the next several months, no further visas would be processed for family visits by Cuban Americans, but the principal Cuban counter was to jam the broadcasts, an effort that apparently succeeded. In 1993, officials of the U.S. Interests Section spent two months driving around predawn Havana with a battery-powered Sony Watchman, stopping frequently to check for reception. While no signal was picked up in Havana or its suburbs, the U.S. officials found an occasional break in the jamming far to the west, beyond Mariel, but, they reported, "the region is very sparsely populated and the reception that is possible along the coast fades out before reaching the central highway about six to eight kilometers further inland." On this particular day, "the TV Martí signal was completely overshadowed by Channel 13, TVT, the CBS affiliate station in Tampa, Florida."[64]

Other data also demonstrated that very few Cubans were watching the station. Supporters had feared that such would be the case from the beginning of the effort, and TV Martí's 1988 authorizing legislation had included a required test of audience acceptance. It consisted of two U.S. Information Agency surveys of Cubans arriving in Miami between 28 March and 12 May 1990. Twenty-six percent of respondents had tried to view TV Martí. But U.S. Government Accountability Office analysts noted that 21 percent of the respondents claimed to have watched TV Martí on days when there was no broadcast and that the statistical projections on the reception of TV Martí were based on a sample of respondents who did not resemble the general population of Cuba. Thus "the survey results differ widely from information reported by the U.S. Interest[s] Section in Havana[, which] reported that less than one percent of persons interviewed in Cuba had been able to view TV Marti." This assessment did not differ significantly from the view of the director of audience research of the Office of Cuban Broadcasting, who conducted two audience surveys in December 1991 and April 1992: "TV Martí had virtually no viewership," she later reported in a sworn affidavit, adding that the office "has taken steps to conceal the results of the surveys." For her whistle-blowing, she added, "I was removed as Director of Audience Research."[65]

In 1992 the Advisory Commission on Public Diplomacy recommended shutting down the station (it was "simply not cost-effective," noted the commission chair), and in 1993 an attempt was made to do so. Instead, Congress created a special panel to study "the purpose, policies, and practices of radio and television broadcasting to Cuba." The panel concluded that both Radio and TV Martí should be continued but noted fourteen shortcomings, including the two stations' weak and highly politicized leadership, a swipe at the Advisory Board of Cuban Broadcasting, which had been chaired by Mas Canosa since its establishment in 1984.[66]

Mas Canosa held this post until the day he died in 1997, for the political cost of meddling with TV Martí clearly outweighed the dollar cost of continuing to operate it. Instead, the following years were spent trying to improve reception. Afternoon broadcasts were added in 1992, and UHF broadcasts commenced in 1997, even though the Broadcasting Board of Governors reported to Congress that "the Cuban government is able to block the UHF transmissions just as effectively as it had the VHF transmissions" and even though all estimates of viewership remained extremely low.[67] Citing an obligation in its lease, the Department of Defense refused to allow broadcasting from its base at Guantánamo, but satellite broadcasting opened new avenues, and in late 2003 TV Martí began beaming signals via a Spanish commercial satellite (Hispasat) to the limited number of Cubans who had access to satellite dishes. At the same time, the station also began streaming its signal to Internet users and broadcasting to rooftop antennas from aircraft. In a 2005 interview, the chief of the U.S. Interests Section was unwilling to estimate the station's viewership, but he did observe that the cost—$189 million from 1989 through 2005—was high when calculated on a per-viewer basis.[68]

Would Cubans watch if they could? It is difficult to imagine anyone with a satellite dish opting for TV Martí over the hundreds of alternative stations, but for Cubans limited to traditional antenna reception and able to avoid the government's jamming, the answer would depend on the attraction of competing Cuban television broadcasts when compared to the offerings on TV Martí. One thing working against a growing viewership in the early twenty-first century was the polemical tone of the programming, which increased dramatically after 1996 when Congress required the Office of Cuba Broadcasting to relocate to South Florida. "TV Marti has atrophied," commented Dan Fisk, the principal compiler of the Helms-Burton Act and no friend of the Cuban government. "Moving the facilities to Miami sacrificed its effectiveness, making it simply another Miami radio station [and] a mouthpiece for the Miami Cuban American Community."[69]

The broadcasts' tone would tend to limit the Cuban audience to those viewers who shared the station's assessment of the Cuban government. A short vignette in late 2006, for example, began with East Germans toppling a statue of Lenin, then Iraqis pulling over a statue of Saddam Hussein, and finally Fidel Castro tripping and falling in 2004 as he walked off the podium following a graduation ceremony. The point, of course, was that dictators fall, but it might have been lost on many Cubans, who merely watched an elderly man's painful mishap. In the early twenty-first century, a typical schedule was as follows:

6:00 to 6:30 P.M.	*The Week in Review*, a review of the preceding week's top news stories
6:30 to 7:00	*The Boss's Office*, a satirical situation comedy centered around El Jefe, the tyrannical leader of the oppressed citizens of the Republic of Siguaraya
7:00 to 7:30	*The Wasp Network*, a nonfiction miniseries about five Cubans convicted of spying in the United States
7:30 to 8:00	*Cuba: The Hour of Change—Socialism to Democracy*, a roundtable discussion featuring guests such as the

	University of Miami's Jaime Suchlicki, an outspoken critic of the Cuban government
8:00 to 8:30	*The Failure of the Revolution*, a discussion of the government's multiple shortcomings
8:30 to 9:00	*The Artistic World*, featuring the latest news from Hollywood
9:00 to 9:30	*Panorama*, a talk show featuring Suchlicki
9:30 to 10:30	Repeat of 6:00 to 7:00 programs[70]

As this effort to create and then operate TV Martí got under way in the late 1980s, Washington simultaneously turned its attention to tightening the embargo. "Economic sanctions are of limited effectiveness," secretary-designate Baker had argued at his early 1989 confirmation hearing, and "they hurt U.S. . . . businesses almost as much as they hurt the sanctioned country." But Cuba would be an exception, and later in 1989 the Bush administration announced that it would support "anything that can be done to tighten up loopholes in the embargo," always with the understanding that "you also have to be sure in doing that you don't do something that backfires."[71] Specifically, the new administration would not support a proposal by Florida senator Connie Mack to prohibit the overseas subsidiaries of U.S. firms from trading with Cuba.

Mack's proposal was yet another effort to interfere with Cuba's third-country trade, an effort almost as old as the Cuban Revolution but one that had peaked early, during Lyndon Johnson's administration. Subsequent initiatives had rarely left the drawing board, largely because third countries had made it clear that they would not cooperate, but Mack now proposed a narrowly focused ban on trade involving U.S.-owned subsidiaries in third countries.

These subsidiaries had been exempted when the Trading with the Enemy Act was first invoked in 1963, primarily because including them would have caused friction with U.S. allies who considered the subsidiaries subject to their laws, not Washington's. In practice, however, nearly all of these subsidiaries had refused to trade with Cuba.[72] In the mid-1970s the Ford administration had acceded to the demands of several close allies that U.S. subsidiaries operating in their countries be allowed to trade with Cuba. Whether buying or selling, in every case the U.S. parent had to apply for a license from the Office of Foreign Assets Control (OFAC), but approval had been almost automatic after 1975, even during the Reagan years, when the value of U.S. subsidiary trade generally hovered around $300 million per

year, about 80 percent of which came from subsidiaries based in Switzerland (the foreign home of U.S. grain giant Cargill), the United Kingdom,
Canada, and Argentina. Cuban imports from U.S. subsidiaries more than
doubled when Cuba lost its Soviet-bloc suppliers, rising from $332 million
in 1989 to $705 million in 1990, and the alert Cuban American lobby took
notice. The result was Senator Mack's proposal to reverse President Ford's
1975 decision. Unsuccessful in 1989, Mack resubmitted the proposal twice
in 1990, but one bill to which it was attached failed to gain congressional
approval, while the other passed Congress but was vetoed because President Bush opposed an unrelated section of the bill.[73]

In 1991, CANF's Mas Canosa took over the task of ensuring passage of
what had come to be known as the Mack Amendment, beginning with
another appearance before the House Subcommittee on Western Hemisphere Affairs, which now had a new chair: Representative George Crockett
had retired, and his place had been taken by Robert Torricelli, whose aide,
Richard Nuccio, had already been working with CANF representatives to
craft what Mas Canosa now unveiled prematurely as the Cuban Democracy
Act. At this point, he said, it was only "a series of recommendations," the
first of which was the centerpiece: "the United States should close the loop-
hole in the U.S. economic embargo of Cuba that allows foreign subsidiaries
of U.S. businesses to trade with Havana." The administration was opposed:
the initiative "would create a foreign policy problem with a lot of allies who
rightly believe that would be an assertion of U.S. law into their territory and
who would be prepared to retaliate in direct ways. Our analysis is that the
benefits that we could gain in terms of embargo enforcement are relatively
minimal."[74]

Relative to what? $705 million in trade was not relatively minimal to
Mas Canosa, who was willing to annoy any ally if doing so would hasten
the collapse of Cuba's government; indeed, Mas Canosa considered such
actions his duty: "Some type of solution has to be induced, promoted, to
make certain that a transition to democracy can happen. Our role—and our
responsibility—is to do what we can to bring about that day."[75]

Mas Canosa's "series of recommendations" soon became a formal bill:
in early 1992 identical measures were submitted in the House by Torricelli
and in the Senate by Florida's Bob Graham, who was up for reelection. The
heart of the proposed Cuban Democracy Act was Mack's prohibition on
subsidiary trade, and that provision was the focus of the initial hearings by
the full House Committee on Foreign Affairs, chaired by Florida representative Dante Fascell, who turned the microphone over to the first witness.

But Fascell had neglected to provide the type of introduction that Torricelli felt appropriate, so he almost immediately interrupted the witness: "Mr. Mas Canosa, before you proceed, you should be introduced in broader terms."

> I only hope that if the freedom of the United States is ever imperiled that I would have both the courage and the commitment to make the sacrifices that you have made for the Cuban people. When Cuba is again free, your name and your efforts are going to be written across the pages of Cuban history. Your contribution has been incalculable. And for that the American people, who share your desire for a free Cuba, owe you a great debt of gratitude.

Thrown off balance by Torricelli's fawning, Mas Canosa seemed embarrassed ("Thank you. Thank you. Thank you, Mr. Chairman. I deeply appreciate your words. Thank you.") but quickly recovered his composure and cut to the chase: "I am grateful that we have moved beyond the sterile debate over whether to dialogue with Fidel Castro to a more promising discussion of options for accelerating Castro's departure from power." In that regard, "it is truly distressing that at a time when the new Russian leadership has radically reduced trade relations and eliminated subsidies to Castro, U.S. companies are extending a trade lifeline to Fidel Castro through their foreign subsidiaries."[76]

Two weeks later, a State Department representative was seated at the same witness table, trying to convince Fascell's committee to reject Mas Canosa's initiative. "The United States has followed a policy of isolating Cuba diplomatically and economically for three decades," began Robert Gelbard, a career officer, and "we continue that policy today." But just as the U.S.-based subsidiaries of Japanese or Italian firms had to conform to U.S. law, so the overseas subsidiaries of U.S. companies had to operate under the laws of their hosts, not one of which had an embargo on trade with Cuba. "We commend the Cuban Democracy Act for its goal of bringing about peaceful democratic change in Cuba," Gelbard continued; "where we differ is not in the goal but in aspects of the strategy. Where the Cuban Democracy Act would demand adherence by our allies to a policy similar to ours, we would respect their sovereignty."[77]

The discussion that followed rehashed the conversation that had occurred seventeen years earlier within President Ford's State Department, when William Rogers had convinced Henry Kissinger to permit subsidiary trade; now, however, it was a public discussion involving Congress, and it was occurring in 1992, an election year. Ten days after Gelbard's testimony, with White House advisers aware of the awkward corner into which the administration was being painted, the president announced that he would use his existing authority to implement two of the minor proposals contained in the Cuban Democracy Act—and, he continued, while some other provisions of the bill were objectionable "as currently written," he promised to sign the measure "with the appropriate changes."[78]

Five days later, Democratic presidential candidate Bill Clinton told a group of wealthy Cuban Americans in Miami that the Bush administration "has missed a big opportunity to put the hammer down on Fidel Castro and Cuba." In contrast, he continued, "I have read the Torricelli-Graham bill and I like it."[79]

President Bush promptly sunk to the challenge: when the House Committee on Foreign Affairs met a few weeks later, it had before it a concession letter from the president ("I support the action your committee is taking") and conciliatory words from State's Gelbard ("We consider the Torricelli amendment a significant improvement"). It was not quite a blanket endorsement, however: the president still believed that the committee needed to "refine" certain provisions, but not a word was said about subsidiary trade. During June and July, the two sides negotiated minor refinements, and then, on the eve of the presidential nominating conventions, the administration formally threw in the towel: "Today," Gelbard told Congress, "I am pleased to be able to tell you that the administration supports the new House and Senate versions of the bill."[80]

Representatives Fascell and Torricelli had ensured that not a single contrary witness appeared at any of the seven sessions the House Committee on Foreign Affairs devoted to the Cuban Democracy Act, but the Senate had invited former U.S. Interests Section chief Wayne Smith, who could not resist commenting on the about-face: "With all due respect to Ambassador Gelbard, who is a professional doing his job, I would suggest that the fact that he has completely reversed his testimony of April of this year, suggests that this really had to do with election year politicking, and posturing, and nothing to do with the merits of the case."[81]

Smith was simply saying aloud what everyone knew to be true—the Democrats were focused on winning Florida, and the Republicans absolutely could not let that happen. After his Miami fund-raising speech, Clinton told reporters, "It has pained me to watch for 30 years as Cuban Americans always voted Republican when I thought most of them should be Democrats." The Democrats kept up the pressure, with Representative

Stephen Solarz taking the lead: "This is the moment, it seems to me, for us to step up the pressure, not relax it."[82] By this time, Clinton had seized leadership of the Democratic Party, and he clearly intended to be more hostile toward Cuba than President Bush.

The Democrats therefore brushed aside Wayne Smith and the handful of liberal activists he represented (What were they going to do—vote Republican?), but dismissing the opposition of the U.S. business community was another matter entirely. Cuba's new move into tourism meant that new hotels would need elevators, to take an example that was highly salient to Otis Elevator Corporation, which told Congress that if its Mexican subsidiary "is forced by this legislation to give up its business relationship with Cuba, then companies such as Hitachi, Schindler, and others will gladly fill the void." Similarly, Cuba's loss of Soviet-bloc trade meant new opportunities for Western food suppliers, and the vice chair of U.S.-based Cargill also warned Congress that the proposed legislation would force subsidiaries of U.S. companies "to surrender to Japanese, European and other foreign companies their market share in entire segments of international commodities trade." And, he added, pointing to another major problem, the proposed act "would also place U.S.-related businesses in the untenable position of having to choose between complying with the laws of their host country and those of the United States." Summing up, the U.S. Chamber of Commerce told Congress that "the United States can no longer afford to formulate policy that is principally symbolic, without regard to the real-world consequences for U.S. companies."[83]

Perhaps. But there are many "real" worlds, and in 1992 the one in which President Bush lived was the real world of electoral politics. He knew that few business leaders would turn against the Republicans because he supported a ban on subsidiary trade—the Cuban market was not terribly large—but Florida was another story: it was the home of hundreds of thousands of Cuban American voters, and President Bush, facing a formidable Democratic rival, knew that he could not hope to retain the White House without carrying the nation's fourth-largest state. And so, with the Cold War over, both major political parties gave Cuban Americans what they wanted—lots of tough talk and a low-cost policy designed to accelerate Castro's final hour, currying favor with an important bloc of voters who asked only for control of what had now become a minor foreign policy sideshow.

As the campaign entered its final month, both candidates sent letters to Congress endorsing the Cuban Democracy Act, and when the measure breezed through Congress, the president tucked the unsigned legislation into his briefcase and flew to Miami, where he singled out Jorge Mas Canosa as "one of the very key forces behind this Cuban Democracy Act" and where he told a cheering audience, "I am certain in my heart that I will be the first American President to set foot on the soil of a free and independent Cuba. Thank you. Thank you all, and God bless you. Now I will sign the Defense Authorization Act, giving the force of law to the Cuban Democracy Act of 1992." President Bush carried Florida eleven days later, and subsidiary license applications, which had risen to an all-time high of $728 million in 1992, dropped to $1.6 million in 1993. By 1994, the number of licensed transactions by U.S.-owned subsidiaries had fallen to zero.[84]

WHILE THE CUBAN DEMOCRACY ACT sought primarily to halt subsidiary trade, the measure contained additional provisions designed to hasten Castro's downfall. Some involved third countries: to cut off Cuba's shipping, for example, the law prohibited third-country ships from entering U.S. ports for 180 days after leaving a Cuban port, a stipulation that ended visits to Cuba by third-country cruise companies using ports in South Florida.[85] Another provision authorized the president to cut aid (including debt relief) to any country providing assistance to Cuba.

The new law was especially tough on U.S. nationals accused of violating the Trading with the Enemy Act, authorizing OFAC to levy civil penalties of up to fifty thousand dollars. OFAC had previously been required to ask the Department of Justice to pursue alleged violators with criminal charges, which are based on a presumption of innocence until proven guilty beyond reasonable doubt. But "given the realities of case load and the many competing priorities within a local U.S. attorney's office," OFAC complained, "prosecutorial discretion often dictates that minor violations of the embargo go unprosecuted." Moreover, winning a conviction had become difficult in the relatively few cases that had been prosecuted: even "well-documented violations of the Cuban assets control regulations may be difficult to prove in court, given the strict standards required to be met in demonstrating criminal culpability. As a result, scores of embargo violators have gone unpunished." OFAC suggested a way around this difficulty: just as the Internal Revenue Service proceeds when underpayment of taxes is suspected but fraud (a criminal act) is not charged, "civil penalties would provide us with the means of deterring wrongdoers without wrestling with this nearly impossible criminal standard." If conservatives were concerned by this encroachment on the Sixth Amendment, they did not say so, and three very lonely liberal members of the House were the only ones to warn, unsuccessfully, about "the possibilities of mistaken or arbitrary administrative decisions."[86]

The Cuban Democracy Act therefore allowed OFAC to create a powerful new set of enforcement procedures. Typically, a violation was uncovered by U.S. Customs when an individual returned to the United States with Cuban goods or when a U.S. immigration officer asked, "What countries have you visited?" Anyone with an ounce of common sense would not lie to a federal officer (to do so is a felony), and if the answer was "Cuba," Customs or Immigration notified OFAC's enforcement branch, which then sent the alleged violator a request for information. If OFAC did not consider the response exculpatory or if no response was received (as was often the case), OFAC sent a second letter. This "pre-penalty" notice stated how much the violator was being fined. Then came the moment of truth: the accused violator had to decide whether (a) to ignore the letter, (b) to pay the fine, or (c) to ask for a hearing, in which case an administrative judge would decide the case in a civil hearing that offered none of the guarantees provided those accused of a crime, the most important of which was the right to be considered innocent until proven guilty; instead, the accused had to present evidence that s/he had *not* been trading with the enemy. Should the judge rule against the alleged violator, payment was due at that time. If the alleged violator had selected option (a) and ignored the pre-penalty notice, OFAC would send a third letter, a "default penalty notice" that gave a deadline for paying the fine and indicated the steps that would be taken should payment not be forthcoming. Included in the list of steps was seizure of the violator's property, including garnishment of wages.[87]

In addition to halting subsidiary trade and to increasing enforcement of the embargo, the Cuban Democracy Act also included a lengthy section, "Support for the Cuban People," that permitted the donation of food to individuals and nongovernmental organizations, the export of medicine and medical supplies, and, to increase communications, the resumption of direct mail service and payment to the government of Cuba for telecommunications services. This part of the new law was "built on the experience of the collapse of communism in Eastern Europe," commented Representative Torricelli. "Our experience has been that those regimes, no matter how tightly controlled, no matter how strong their military ultimately fell from the power of ideas. So we are opening communications of mail and telephone so that people will know the truth."[88]

Taken together, these provisions came to be known as Track 2, a term going back to 1962, when the Kennedy administration's Walt Rostow had proposed "a Two-Track covert operation. Track One would consist of a heightened effort to move along the present Mongoose lines [while] Track Two would consist of an effort to engage Cubans more deeply, both within Cuba and abroad, in efforts of their own liberation." The House Committee on Foreign Affairs explained the 1992 version of Track 2 as "creating openings to democratic opposition groups that will shape Cuba's future," but there were additional purposes, including the desire of Cuban Americans to ease suffering during the Special Period and to reduce the barriers to contact across the Straits of Florida. Mas Canosa had unsuccessfully resisted these carrots, but as a consolation he could point to the sticks that he and other hard-liners had lobbied into law.[89]

The Cuban Democracy Act allowed the president to waive its sanctions if the Cuban government held free elections supervised by international observers, if it permitted opposition parties to organize and campaign with full access to all media, and if it showed respect for civil liberties and human rights. A year earlier, Assistant Secretary Aronson had promised that "the United States has no blueprint for Cuba," but the law now stipulated what constituted a free and fair election, and Cuba's acceptance of that blueprint represented a nonnegotiable demand: the president was authorized to lift or waive the new sanctions when—and only when—Cuba capitulated. And then, for good measure, the Cuban Democracy Act added the requirement that Cuba accept the prevailing U.S. blueprint of how an economy should be organized, stipulating that sanctions could not be waived unless Cuba "is moving toward establishing a free market economic system."[90]

"We have nothing to learn from the U.S. system of government," replied a *Granma* editorial published four days after Aronson's speech. If Washington wanted to dictate what kind of elections Cuba should have, then "Cuba could demand that the United States put an end to the farce of its moronic electoral squabbles [*trifulcas electoreras*] and to its pointless presidential contests where the lucky one can be chosen by barely thirty percent of the electorate." And how about discussing democratic policy *outputs* instead of the U.S. emphasis on democratic *procedures*? "Cuba could also demand that the United States end the social inequality and the discrimination that causes infant mortality in the black population to be two times higher than in the white, or that causes fifty percent of the homes of Native Americans to be without toilets." As for a return to a market economy, Castro had already declared that "the only thing capitalism has brought to four billion human beings is hunger and misery," so in Cuba "there will be no market economy, or whatever they call that mess that has nothing to do with social-ism. Our economy will be a programmed economy, a planned economy. We do not believe in that craziness."[91]

The Cuban leader's intransigence failed to discourage President Bush, whose garbled syntax did not obscure his point: "The beautiful thing about Cuba is because of the industry of those people and because of the affection that a lot of Americans have for the people of Cuba, Cuba, once free and once under democracy, will have a real shot at forward movement in terms of helping their people through at a reinvigorated economy. There's no question about that. It could be the success story of the nineties." Accept-ing his party's presidential nomination, he told cheering Republicans, "I look forward to being the first President to visit a free, democratic Cuba."[92] Even if Calvin Coolidge had not already claimed that distinction in 1928, voters would not give Bush the opportunity; in early November, Cubans learned that they would have to deal with a new U.S. leader, one who had criticized George H. W. Bush for being too soft on Cuba.

As President Bush packed his bags, he did so with the satisfaction that truly extraordinary changes had occurred during his presidency—he and national security adviser Brent Scowcroft titled their memoir *A World Trans-formed* and did so for good reason. But President Bush left U.S. policy toward Cuba just as he had found it in 1989, in a state of unwavering hostility. As Congress was putting the finishing touches on the Cuban Democracy Act, Fidel Castro had warned Cubans that "all the resources that the empire directed against the socialist countries and the international communist movement, they now devote to a single purpose: to fight Cuba, to weaken Cuba, to defeat Cuba, to crush Cuba." At least he had the satisfaction of pointing out that "those who have called us lackeys so many times, who have called us a satellite country so many times, cannot admit that we are the most independent people of the world."[93] He was incorrect; everyone in Washington was now willing to give up the old Soviet-surrogate charge, and both presidential candidates were pleased to see that Cuba was now alone in the world.

The United States has done more than any other
country to try to bring an end to the Castro government
. . . and we will continue to do that by whatever
reasonable means are available to us.
—*Bill Clinton, August 1994*

13

BLESSINGS OF LIBERTY
THE CLINTON ADMINISTRATION

The 1992 election was about the faltering U.S. economy, not
Cuba. Both party platforms took pro forma swipes at the Castro government, as did both candidates in their nomination acceptance speeches,
with President George H. W. Bush reiterating his desire to become the first
president to visit a democratic Cuba and Bill Clinton specifying Cuba as
one of his targets as a champion of democracy.[1] But the focus was on an
economy in recession, and Bush found it impossible to defend against attacks by both Clinton and third-party populist Ross Perot; on Election Day,
the president barely managed a one-hundred-thousand-vote win in Florida,
a state Republicans had taken by a million votes in 1988. In addition to
handing Democrats the White House, voters also added two more Cuban
Americans to the House of Representatives. Democrat Robert Menéndez,
a former mayor of Union City, New Jersey, won in a new district drawn to
maximize Hispanic voting strength, outspending his opponent fifteen to
one. Among his most generous campaign contributors was CANF's Jorge
Mas Canosa, who also supported the other Cuban American newcomer,
Miami republican Lincoln Díaz-Balart, whose aunt had once been married
to Fidel Castro. A staunch Batista supporter and member of the Cuban
Congress, Díaz-Balart's father had opposed the 1955 amnesty granted to

his former brother-in-law, and the family had the good luck to be in Europe when the dictator fell. They never returned to Cuba.[2]

With the election over and the transition under way, Senator Jesse Helms used the confirmation hearing for the prospective secretary of state, Warren Christopher, to inquire about the new administration's Cuba policy. The nominee's prepared statement had included a promise to maintain the embargo, which was enough for everyone except the skeptical North Carolina senator, who dredged up a sentence from one of Christopher's 1977 speeches when he was serving as the Carter administration's deputy secretary of state and had it projected onto a large screen for everyone at the confirmation hearing to see: "We hope to reestablish normal relations with Cuba." Senator Helms acknowledged that sixteen years had elapsed since that sentence had been uttered, and he observed that the president-elect had said the opposite to Florida audiences during the just-completed campaign, but for the record he wanted to know: "Who is going to prevail in this, Mr. Clinton or you?" "The President always prevails," Christopher replied. Unsatisfied, Helms continued:

> MR. HELMS: Do you think that any normalization should take place?
> MR. CHRISTOPHER: It's very hard to envisage it taking place with Castro still in place.
> MR. HELMS: Maybe we ought to use force to support the people who yearn for freedom in Cuba?
> MR. CHRISTOPHER: We ought to keep all our options open.
> MR. HELMS: Does the administration intend to modify or weaken the Cuban Democracy Act?
> MR. CHRISTOPHER: I have no such present intention.

When Helms pressed further, asking whether Christopher supported the Mack Amendment, which prohibited trade by U.S. subsidiaries located in third countries, Christopher had no answer, unaware of the amendment's details. Senator Paul Sarbanes stepped in to guide the secretary-designate to the proper response: "My understanding of President Clinton's position and yours is that you support the Cuban Democracy Act of which the Mack Amendment is a part. . . . Is that not correct?" Christopher took the lifeline: "That's correct, Senator."[3]

Everything Christopher said suggested he would have no conflict with either Senator Helms or the new president's national security adviser, Anthony Lake, who placed Cuba on his short list of five "outlaw states that not only choose to remain outside the family [of nations] but also assault its basic values."[4] But neither of President Clinton's two principal foreign policy appointees seemed to have any genuine interest in Cuba. The one person who might have given the island some attention was Mario Baeza, the first Cuban American to be selected as assistant secretary of state for inter-American affairs, but Baeza, a Wall Street lawyer specializing in mergers and acquisitions, had recently participated in a two-day privatization seminar in Havana, an action the conservative wing of the Cuban American community considered evidence of his willingness to engage in a dialogue with the Castro government. "Most of his opinions on Cuba are antithetical to the Cuban community," complained CANF's José Cárdenas, and a few angry telephone calls from Florida torpedoed Baeza's nomination. Faced with the task of finding a new nominee, the Clinton administration waited several months before settling on a career officer, Alexander Watson, an able administrator and an effective public speaker who could be counted on to advance whatever policy his superiors selected.

Watson had barely been confirmed when the Senate Select Committee on Intelligence held the new Congress's first hearing on Cuba, and so his principal deputy, Robert Gelbard, presented the administration's initial policy statement: "We believe we can best foster an environment for peaceful change in Cuba by continuing to isolate the Cuban government diplomatically, politically and economically." Watson repeated that position to Congress a few months later, and both statements faithfully reflected the thinking of President Clinton, whose first presidential comment about Cuba came during a March press conference at which he reiterated his support for the Cuban Democracy Act. Asked ten days later whether he would be willing to meet with Fidel Castro, the president said that doing so was out of the question, and for the rest of his first year in office, Clinton answered with the same three words—"freedom and democracy"—when asked what would be required to change U.S. policy.[5]

Virginia Republican John Warner used the same phrase as he called the Senate intelligence committee to order so that it could hear Deputy Assistant Secretary Gelbard: "We seek simply to instill freedom and democracy to hopefully improve the constantly degrading lifestyle of the people of that sad nation." When moderate Republican John Chafee noted that "we've tried the embargo for 34½ years and it doesn't seem to have worked too well," Florida's Bob Graham jumped in with what would also become the administration's response: "Castro stands isolated, a political dinosaur in an evolving world. This is not the time to throw Castro a lifeline." Arizona's Dennis DeConcini agreed, calling Cuba "the socialist version of 'Jurassic

Park,'" while Nebraska's Bob Kerrey voiced the near-perfect Senate consensus: "Castro is a goner."[6]

But a handful of House members agreed with Senator Chafee that it was time to reconsider U.S. policy. This group coalesced around New York's Democratic representative Charles Rangel, a leader of the Congressional Black Caucus, who in May unveiled a sweeping proposal to repeal the trade embargo, the travel ban, and the entire Cuban Democracy Act, including the Mack Amendment. Rangel was no friend of Fidel Castro ("We are all concerned about the removal of a dictator," the New Yorker said), but he preferred a foreign policy that emphasized carrots rather than sticks.[7] So did California representative Howard Berman, who launched a more focused effort to weaken the ban on travel by U.S. citizens to a number of countries, including Cuba; his proposed Free Trade in Ideas Act would allow unrestricted travel by individuals seeking to import informational materials or to participate in educational programs. The measure was based on a 1969 Supreme Court ruling that citizens had a constitutional right to obtain information from any source: "It is the purpose of the First Amendment to preserve an uninhibited marketplace of ideas in which truth will ultimately prevail," the Court had ruled. "It is the right of the public to receive suitable access to social, political, esthetic, moral and other ideas and experiences which is crucial here. That right may not be constitutionally abridged."[8] Twenty-four years later, restrictions on travel to a half dozen countries still kept citizens from fully participating in this marketplace of ideas.

Initially ignored when introduced during the 1992 election year, Berman's proposal captured the administration's attention a year later when a House subcommittee attached it to the State Department's authorization bill. Reluctant to have State's hands tied by legislation, as a compromise Secretary Christopher agreed to write a formal letter asking Berman to withdraw the measure in exchange for an immediate relaxation of the regulations to permit a limited amount of travel for "informational" purposes, plus a full review "of our existing sanctions programs, policies, and legislation to ensure they properly reflect our mutual commitment to the dissemination of information and ideas." The relaxed regulations allowed individuals to obtain licenses to travel to purchase and import educational materials, and they authorized licenses for individuals seeking to participate in "educational or religious activities," broadly defined to include performing artists.[9]

Berman's early success served as a wake-up call for the dominant conservative wing of the Cuban American community, and three House Foreign Affairs subcommittees soon had scheduled a joint hearing on travel to Cuba. The tone was set by one of the subcommittee chairs, liberal Democrat Sam Gejdenson, whose opening remarks included the now-obligatory nod at regime change ("This Congress, and I think the American people, want desperately to see a democratic government in Cuba") but focused on the omission of one important group—Cuban Americans—from Berman's initiative: "There are many of us in Congress who think the policies that preclude many Americans from traveling to see relatives is counterproductive." Florida's Ileana Ros-Lehtinen disagreed; in her view, Congress needed "to help stimulate the fall of an evil dictator who has enslaved the Cuban people," not open any more doors to travel. Like the Berman initiative, she continued, Gejdenson's comments were part of a broader campaign to undo the embargo, engineered by "folks with a political, not a humanitarian agenda who would rather serve Castro's propaganda interests than help the people of Cuba free themselves." First-term representative Lincoln Díaz-Balart agreed and then offered a preview of his future role as the least-subtle member of Congress, departing from the hearing's topic to focus with conspicuous passion on the sins of Fidel Castro ("a cold-blooded murderer") and to lament the decision of other Latin American presidents to include Castro at an Ibero-American summit in Brazil ("disgusting"). Then came testimony from a CANF representative, who argued that the "lifting of the embargo would amount to a betrayal of the Cuban people's hopes for freedom and democracy, a moral Bay of Pigs."[10]

Similarly sweeping warnings dotted the two-hour hearing, which focused on travel by Cuban Americans to visit their relatives. Although burdened with substantial restrictions by both Washington and Havana, this travel had been allowed to continue in 1982 when President Reagan reinstituted the general travel ban that President Carter had relaxed. A decade later, family visits had become a substantial business for several charter companies, one of which was selling out two flights a day. The cost of a ticket was high—several hundred dollars for a short flight—but charter operators insisted that theirs was not an easy way to earn a living. One complained that "a gentleman named Carlos Doltz, claiming to work for Congressman Lincoln Díaz-Balart, gave numerous interviews stating that the Airline Brokers flights were totally illegal [and] a Miami-based paramilitary unit also publicly stated that it will attack all persons traveling to Cuba. Moreover, a Spanish-speaking radio station has reported that all persons who travel to Cuba will lose their medicaid, medicare and social security benefits." A few days later, Alpha 66 spokesman Humberto Pérez held a press conference to repeat an earlier announcement that his organization would begin attacking visitors inside Cuba: "We will use force, including the possibility of kidnaping tourists for ransom." In mid-1996 the Miami office of Marazul Charters was firebombed, a repeat of a 1989 bombing.[11]

AS CONGRESS WAS SETTING the tone of U.S. policy for the Clinton era, nearly every other government in the world was taking a different approach. In June 1993, Canada announced that it would resume the economic aid program halted in 1978 to protest Cuba's activities in Africa; the twenty-three participants at the July Ibero-American Summit in Brazil gently but pointedly criticized the U.S. embargo; and in October the U.N. General Assembly voted for a second time (and by a margin of 88–4, with 57 abstentions) to urge an end to the U.S. embargo. President Clinton repeatedly acknowledged this allied opposition ("Nobody in the world agrees with our policy on Cuba"), but which of the eighty-eight really cared? "Every time I see President Mitterand, he tells me how wrong I am about Cuba," Clinton commented, but neither France nor any other U.S. ally would jeopardize its relations with Washington over relatively unimportant Cuba, so the president always added that U.S. policy would not be affected: "I think we're right about Cuba and they're wrong"; the embargo, he said, "is hastening the day when the outdated communist system will collapse."[12]

As for the contest with Congress over the control of U.S. policy, why bother? The president had at least a million other ways to spend his time, and Cuba itself was becoming less menacing every day. Just before the 1992 election, Fidel Castro had announced that Cuba was unable to continue construction of its Juraguá nuclear power facility, a plant that Senator Helms worried might be used to fabricate nuclear weapons and that, regardless of its purpose, was "kind of like Chernobyl." Now it had been mothballed. Even more reassuring was the State Department's first Clinton-era terrorism report, released in April 1993, which indicated that Cuba was no longer training Latin American insurgents. Also in April, President Clinton traveled to Vancouver for his first meeting with Russia's Boris Yeltsin, and at their joint news conference the president reported that "the day of massive subsidies between Russia and the Government of Cuba is over." Yeltsin also pointed out that the irritating Soviet military brigade was being withdrawn, and by midyear the CIA reported that Cuba was receiving "no Russian military subsidy whatsoever." Concurrently, Cuba's flagging economy mandated drastic cuts in its military budget: the army and navy were reduced by two-thirds and the air force by half, prompting U.S. Navy intelligence to report that the Cuban military "no longer poses a credible offensive threat."[13] By 1998 the Defense Intelligence Agency (DIA) reported that Cuba's military had been transformed "from one of the most active militaries in the Third World into a stay-at-home force that has minimal conventional fighting ability." The army had continued to cut back its training exercises, the navy had mothballed most of its fleet, and the air force had grounded nearly all of its aging aircraft. "Conclusion: At present, Cuba does not pose a significant military threat to the U.S. or to other countries in the region."[14]

The DIA warned, however, that Cuba's "intelligence and counterintelligence systems directed at the United States appear to have suffered little degradation," but a full appreciation of that sentence became evident only after the Clinton years, in late 2001, when the FBI discovered that the principal author of this 1998 DIA report, Ana Belén Montes, was a Cuban spy. "Montes did enormous damage," wrote her CIA counterpart, Brian Latell. "Unfortunately, it never occurred to me during the entire time I knew her that she was diligently working for Fidel." Montes pled guilty and began a twenty-five-year prison sentence after telling the judge, "I did what I thought was right to counter a grave injustice. I engaged in the activity that brought me before you because I obeyed my conscience rather than the law. I believe our government's policy towards Cuba is cruel and unfair, profoundly unneighborly, and I felt morally obligated to help the island defend itself."[15]

But Montes's professional assessment was scrupulously accurate—whatever military challenge Cuba once might have mounted in faraway Africa or nearby Latin America had clearly become a thing of the past. So ended a concern of every president since Dwight Eisenhower.

Even more interesting was a cooperative spirit that appeared to characterize Cuba's approach to the United States. In mid-1993 Cuban leaders sent the crew of a Cuban airliner to Miami to testify before a grand jury in a hijacking case, and a month later Cuba handed over two drug traffickers whom U.S. authorities had chased into Cuban airspace. Nor, apparently, was Cuba participating in drug trafficking, a clandestine business about which there will probably never be a consensus regarding the Cuban government's role. In 1989 the State Department had reported that "there is no doubt that Cuba is a major transit point in the illegal drug flow," while three weeks later the CIA had concluded that "Cuba has played only a minor role in the drug trafficking between South America and the US."[16] Some reports continued to surface about drug traffickers' use of Cuban waters and airspace, but President Clinton noted just after his 1996 reelection that "it has not been confirmed that this traffic carries significant quantities of cocaine or heroin to the United States," and the director of the Office of National Drug Control Policy, General Barry McCaffrey, told a 1999 Washington audience, "I do not see any serious evidence, current or in the last decade, of Cuban government overt complicity with drug crime." Representative Díaz-Balart complained that McCaffrey "continues to cover up the well-known, established, reiterated, longstanding participation by the Castro dictatorship in drug trafficking," but he simply blurted out this statement, as was his custom, offering no evidence to support his charges.[17] At exactly the same time he was making them, U.S. Coast Guard and Drug Enforcement Administration officials were meeting with Cuban authorities to discuss antitrafficking cooperation, leading to an upgrade in the U.S. telex link with Cuba's Border Guard and to the assignment of a Coast Guard officer to the U.S. Interests Section to coordinate antidrug operations. Fidel Castro devoted his 1999 26th of July speech to outlining Cuba's effort to stop the use of its territory for drug trafficking, and a few months later the State Department reported that U.S. and Cuban officials "have exchanged dozens of telexes this year in an attempt to identify suspect smuggling operations and make seizures."[18]

Cuba's drug cooperation was arguably in the country's own interest, but in September 1993 the Castro government also agreed to do something it would have preferred not to do: accept the return of about fifteen hundred more jailed Cubans who had committed crimes in the United States since the 1984 post-Mariel repatriation agreement. This move took place in the context of several conciliatory statements by senior Cuban officials, including a December comment by Fidel Castro: "I do not consider Clinton to be a warmonger of a president, but a man of peace." Six months later, the president of the government's Committee on Economic Cooperation declared Cuba's willingness to negotiate a settlement of outstanding claims from 1959 and the early 1960s; two weeks after that, Cuban foreign minister Roberto Robaina was quoted as saying, "We are pleased to see that [the new Clinton administration] is not using a language as aggressive as that of the previous Government."[19]

President Clinton declined to comment when asked about the offer to negotiate a claims settlement, but State's Gelbard had a response for Robaina: "By saying nice things about President Clinton, they hope there will be a warmer climate," and "by saying there is a changed policy, they hope there will be a changed policy. There is no changed policy." What Cuba may have perceived as change was either wishful thinking or misperception, he continued, since the change in travel regulations reflected nothing more than Representative Berman's demand that the administration comply with a Supreme Court ruling, and the only other significant change early in the Clinton era—a decision to expand telephone service to Cuba—simply constituted the implementation of a Track 2 provision of the Cuban Democracy Act, mandated by Congress.[20]

The new administration's decision to brush off any suggestion of accommodation reflected the widely shared belief that the Castro government was about to collapse of its own accord. In late 1991 Jorge Mas Canosa had promised that "we are going to see a Free Cuba very soon," while conservative commentator Susan Kaufman Purcell had advised readers of *Foreign Affairs* that "it is only a matter of time before Cuban communism collapses," vaguely estimating that the demise would occur "sooner rather than later." In early 1993, Cuban-born journalist Carlos Alberto Montaner added yet another volume to the The-Revolution-Is-Doomed bookshelf, *On the Brink of Collapse*.[21] With almost everyone predicting the government's impending downfall, why not wait? Since 1989 the island's economy had contracted by at least a third, and just before Clinton's inauguration, the government had again cut monthly food rations. Electricity blackouts had been increased to a minimum of eight hours per day (residents of Havana soon would have electricity for only four to eight hours a day), and in mid-1993 Cuba appealed to the United Nations for help with two nutrition-related nerve diseases—optic neuropathy, characterized by blurring and progressive loss of vision, and peripheral neuropathy, a painful tingling, weakness, and loss of coordination of arms and legs. The outbreak had begun in 1991, and by mid-1993 Cuba was reporting more than forty-five thousand cases.[22]

As the economy continued to contract, even the tightly controlled Cuban press began to lament the deterioration of social norms, especially "the black market that is spreading across the island [where] anything can be obtained at exorbitant prices in dollars or local currency [even if] it is known that most of those goods were stolen." In mid-1993, *Juventud Rebelde* published an especially pessimistic column that lamented seeing "children begging for chewing gum or some other sweet from tourists; worse yet is seeing our pretty girls serving as canes for aging foreign men." In September, *Granma* ran articles about a gang of young men who stole foreign-made clothing off the backs of bus passengers for resale on the black market; on one occasion, a disrobed passenger was killed when gang members threw him off a moving bus.[23]

These infractions by "delinquent elements" did not surprise anyone who had read the CIA's mid-1993 national intelligence estimate, which had predicted that an incident "could provoke regime-threatening instability at any time." The situation would only worsen as the economy continued to contract, and "the impact on the population has already been devastating." Summing up the view from Washington, Assistant Secretary of State Watson told Congress in late 1993 that "Cuba is a country at a dead end,"[24] while the State Department's new director of Cuban affairs, Dennis Hays, showed visitors to his office a chart of Cuba's dwindling oil supplies to explain why it was only a matter of months until the economy would grind to a complete halt. And Hays was correct: petroleum had become Cuba's gravest problem. Just before President Clinton's inauguration, the government had suspended the ten-gallon monthly gas ration because foreign suppliers were providing only short-term credit at exceptionally high interest rates, reflecting the risk that such loans might not be repaid: after Cuba had defaulted on its international debt in 1986 and then defaulted on three subsequent reschedulings, it now owed Western public and private bankers about nine billion dollars. With no prospect of improvement, in 1992 the Paris Club refused a fourth rescheduling, and the bond markets reacted by knocking down the value of Cuba's existing debt to about twenty cents on the dollar.[25]

Cuba now had to pay cash for almost everything—"to the very last cent," Fidel Castro told his subdued 26th of July audience in 1993, seated indoors in a Santiago theater instead of standing outdoors in the traditional mass rally. "All our problems would be over if we had a machine to print dollar bills, but those little machines are in Washington and apparently they are very difficult to copy." The U.S.-based Cuban American community had plenty of dollars, however, and to attract them Castro announced the repeal of the law prohibiting the possession and use of foreign currency: "The idea behind this is to acquire foreign exchange," he explained, and Cubans able to obtain dollars, primarily through family remittances, would be allowed to shop at the dollar stores—*diplotiendas*—that until now had been reserved for diplomats and tourists. The step was controversial (Castro considered it such a major departure that he had to tell his audience that what he had said "was not a slip of the tongue"), and, as time would soon tell, it was a step taken at the top of an especially slippery slope. Only a few months later, Vice President Carlos Lage admitted that legalization was creating new inequalities, favoring Cubans with expatriate relatives, and Castro subsequently commented that "it pained us to have to install a system of two valid currencies, with only a part of the people having access to one of them."[26]

The next steps must have been equally painful to anyone committed to a command economy: to create jobs and to redistribute remitted currency, the government then authorized individual private enterprise in 117 service occupations such as shoe repair and hairdressing, and to increase food production leaders created a new form of agricultural organization, a hybrid producer cooperative—Unidades Básicas de Producción Cooperativa (UBPC)—in which the state retained landownership but allowed agricultural workers, until now state employees, to form cooperatives, to purchase inputs (seeds, fertilizer, and so forth) from the government on credit, and then to dispose of as they saw fit any output beyond specified sales to the government.[27] When combined with the reopening of the farmers' markets that had existed prior to rectification in the mid-1980s, the UBPCs met with almost immediate success in terms of increasing the supply of food. Prices were high, but now Cubans with dollars could afford to pay, and by the end of President Clinton's first term the UBPCs were producing two-thirds of Cuba's domestic food supply.[28]

At the same time, the government redoubled its investment in tourism. Here, Castro said, the problem was that "we do not have enough capital to develop tourism at the pace we want," so the government had no choice but to pursue joint ventures with foreign investors: "We can accept partnerships of this kind, with common sense," Castro had announced in 1991. Carefully targeted foreign investment had been permitted since 1982, but only ten years later, as Cuba approached the darkest moment of the Special Period, was the constitution revised to authorize private partnerships with the government, and Castro was still adjusting to the change in mid-1993: "Who would have thought that we, so doctrinaire, we who fought foreign investment, would one day view foreign investment as an urgent need?"[29]

These market-oriented measures could not immediately help pull Cuba out of its economic free fall, and in early 1994 the prevailing view in Washington was that a collapse still loomed just over the near horizon—Representative Robert Torricelli used the word "imminent" in March as he opened a hearing on a bill requiring the State Department to prepare a plan for the inevitable Cuban transition. "The bill strikes an important, forward-looking note," conceded Assistant Secretary Watson, speaking for the administration, but "we would prefer not to tie ourselves to a specific plan now."[30]

This yes-and-no response set the tone for a subdued hearing that differed dramatically from one held a week earlier, when Representative Rangel's subcommittee had conducted a marathon eleven-hour session on his proposed Free Trade with Cuba Act. Virtually everyone with an interest in Cuba had asked to be heard, including New York's liberal representative José Serrano, who drew attention to a recent comment by President Clinton that Cuba policy would remain unchanged but that China was so big that the United States had no choice but to engage it. He asked, "What does that mean, Cuba is too little, we have to step on it?" Exactly, said South Florida Republican Clay Shaw: "I learned long ago that when you have your foot on the neck of a snake, you do not let it up."[31] No one could come close to matching Representative Díaz-Balart, however, who focused on the third-country investors expressing an interest in Cuba's new program of joint ventures. "Some in the business community are clearly tempted by the slave labor available in Cuba," he began, visibly upset; then the words came pouring out:

> To collaborate with the Cuban dictatorship is not only a brittle and risky investment, it manifests a racist attitude toward the Cuban people. It is a racist attitude because the tyrant that oppresses Cuba is the son of a Spanish soldier of the army of colonial occupation at the end of the last century, that army that oppressed the Cuban people. At that time, the United States helped that people achieve its freedom. The most ruthless of the colonial rulers was Valeriano Weyler, known to the Cubans as the butcher of the reconcentration of the peasantry. The father of the Cuban tyrant of today was a soldier of the butcher Weyler, and his son, who profoundly hates the Cuban people, has become the butcher of the Cubans in the 20th century. It is a historical embarrassment that today there are still collaborationists in the brutality being committed against the Cubans, just as they existed yesterday, and just as they existed when Hitler massacred the Jews in the crematoriums.

"I've heard a lot of things," replied a mystified Rangel, "but this is something new to me."[32]

A mood-changing response came from a panel of potential U.S. investors, supplemented by a brief research report from Washington's respected Institute for International Economics indicating that U.S. exports to Cuba might approach two billion dollars if the embargo were lifted. Next came presentations from exporters who complained that the embargo "benefits only our foreign competitors" and from travel industry executives who estimated that absent the embargo, five million people would fly each year between Cuba and the United States. Especially well represented was the telecommunications industry, which estimated that the market for Cuba's international communications was worth more than a half billion dollars over the next five years, while additional opportunities existed for the modernization of Cuba's domestic telecommunications infrastructure.[33]

Rangel's committee also listened as two midlevel administration officials reiterated President Clinton's opposition to any change in U.S. policy, and they were followed by a remarkably diverse set of public witnesses with no obvious economic axe to grind, ranging from Jorge Mas Canosa, who wanted the embargo tightened because Fidel Castro, operating "the worst repressive system that humankind has ever known, . . . is the worst killer that any people living in the Western Hemisphere has ever suffered," to Jesse Jackson, who wanted the embargo lifted because it was hurting the Cuban people.[34]

On balance, the hearing on Rangel's bill ended in a draw, which in Congress always favors the status quo, especially when it is defended by the White House. Four days later, President Clinton promised a Miami audience that his administration would not relax the embargo.[35]

AS THESE DISCUSSIONS CONTINUED in Washington, Cubans were returning to a time-honored way of coping with economic adversity. In 1991 the CIA had predicted that "illegal emigration is likely to continue growing rapidly as economic conditions deteriorate," and even if economy-spurring reforms were instituted, as they were in 1993, "popular confidence is so low that thousands of Cubans will still try to leave the island."[36]

There were two ways to depart: legally and illegally. The legal way required two pieces of paper: an entry visa from a foreign country and an exit visa from the Cuban government. (Cuba's Penal Code prohibited leaving "without complying with the legal formalities.") One foreign country, the United States, had agreed in 1984 to issue up to 20,000 *immigrant* visas per year, but only about 2,000 had been issued annually in the years since 1984 because the standards applying to Cubans seeking to immigrate were the same as those for any other foreign national, and not many Cubans met those standards. Specifically, the United States had a worldwide cap of 675,000 immigrant visas. To allocate those 675,000 visas among the much larger number of applicants, the United States had established preference categories, some based on job skills but most based on family relationship to a U.S. citizen or permanent resident, and each category had a separate subcap.

Extremely few Cubans had the special job skills required for an immigrant visa, and those who did (mostly sports figures) rarely applied because they knew they could not obtain the Cuban government's permission to leave; thus, nearly all would-be legal immigrants needed U.S.-based relatives, and Cubans had difficulty obtaining these family-reunification visas because too few Cubans qualified: the worldwide allocation of visas for relatives of *permanent U.S. residents* was low, while the allocation for relatives of U.S. *citizens* was much higher— and, as the State Department explained, "there is an exceptionally low rate of naturalization among the Cuban American community." As a result, only 2,003 Cubans obtained visas to immigrate to the United States in 1993.[37]

The issuance of nonimmigrant visas to Cubans — primarily to visit family members but also for a variety of other purposes such as attendance at professional conferences — was guided by a completely different set of regulations; most important was the requirement that a visa officer in the U.S. Interests Section make a specific judgment that the recipient would leave the United States before the visa expired. Until the Special Period, this problem had not arisen, largely because the Cuban government had restricted nonimmigrant exit visas for family visits to women over sixty and men over sixty-five. But in 1990, as the economy deteriorated and unemployment soared, the government first lowered the limit to thirty for women and thirty-five for men and then lowered it again to twenty for both men and women. These actions led to a major spike in applications — whereas only 3,681 Cubans had applied for nonimmigrant visas to visit the United States in 1988, more than 34,000 applied in 1990 and more than 32,000 applied during the first six months of 1991, when the Interests Section stopped accepting nonimmigrant visa applications until it had cleared its backlog.[38]

The illegal ways to leave were limited only by human imagination and the fact that Cuba is surrounded by water. A few people swam across Guantánamo Bay onto the U.S. Navy base; another handful tried to leave by air, including a Cuban air force pilot who had already flown his MiG to the United States but in late 1992 flew a small plane back, landed on a coastal highway, picked up his waiting wife and two children, and returned to Florida. A week later, a Cuban commercial pilot flew his airliner to Miami; almost everyone aboard appears to have been part of the plot, because 48 of the 53 passengers requested asylum. Yet another illegal route was the one that had triggered the 1980 Mariel boatlift — through the doors of foreign embassies. In 1990 about 50 Cubans requested asylum in five European embassies. None was allowed to leave, but their failure was only a temporary deterrent:

114 asylum seekers broke into the Belgian ambassador's residence in mid-1994, and two weeks later 21 Cubans drove a truck through the gates of the German embassy. Castro pledged that "whoever enters an embassy by force will never receive permission to leave the country."[39]

The sea therefore became the principal illegal route to the United States. One Cuban windsurfed the 110 miles from Varadero to Marathon Key, but most who chose the water route either hijacked boats or built makeshift vessels; many simply lashed some scrap lumber to inner tubes and pushed off into the Florida Current with the hope of being picked up by the U.S. Coast Guard or of floating toward the keys or the Bahamas. Until the Special Period, only 40 or 50 Cubans were setting off by raft each year, but the number reaching the United States began to pick up, rising from 59 in 1988 to 391 in 1989 to 467 in 1990. Except for the few who could be identified as having criminal records, all were classified as illegal entrants but granted what the Immigration and Naturalization Service had come to call "humanitarian parole." Under the 1966 Cuban Adjustment Act, after one year all such Cuban parolees were allowed to become permanent legal residents. Cuba viewed the Cuban Adjustment Act as "migration aggression," comparing it to dangling candy in front of a child.[40]

The number of rafters kept rising as the Cuban economy kept sinking. The Coast Guard rescued 2,565 Cubans in 1992 and a record 3,656 during President Clinton's first year in office; by mid-1994 the CIA reported that "economic desperation and Havana's faltering interception capabilities will drive greater numbers of Cubans to attempt to leave the country." But, the agency continued, "the chances for another mass migration along the lines of the 1980 exodus remain slim."[41]

Words spoken too soon. Six weeks later, about forty Cubans were killed when a hijacked tugboat sank while it was attempting to flee across the Straits of Florida, and the unprecedented death toll was only a harbinger of what would soon be known as the rafter crisis. The cause of the tugboat tragedy is still debated, but members of the U.S. House of Representatives had no doubts, passing a resolution condemning the Cuban government for deliberately sinking the vessel. Representative Dan Burton told his colleagues that "Fidel Castro's thugs" were responsible: "The thought of a Cuban boat pulling up alongside a tugboat when women are holding children over their head to show that there are innocent women and children on board, and then washing them overboard with power hoses. When the women took the children down into the hold, Castro's thugs pulled up alongside and deliberately directed the hoses into the hold so they would sink that tugboat and kill those people. It just boggles the imagination." The State Department was less certain of the details, claiming that Cuban patrol boats had rammed the tugboat, an explanation that came close to the one offered by Cuba. According to Castro, a second tugboat had taken off in hot pursuit, and this second boat was trying to stop the hijacking "on a dark night and with a rough sea. Given these conditions, they were trying to stop the tugboat until the border guard boats arrived. This is how the accident took place: the boat trailing behind rammed into the tugboat's stern." Accusing U.S. officials of "an evil, cynical smear campaign," the Cuban leader asserted, "Our authorities had nothing to do with the incident."[42]

Oscar Wilde had this type of situation in mind when he observed that the truth is rarely pure and never simple, and the recriminations would have continued indefinitely had not everyone's attention shifted to a new spate of hijackings: first came the commandeering of a fishing boat on 25 July, which was not a major event, but on the 26 July national holiday, an audacious group of disaffected club-wielding citizens seized one of the ferries that runs across the bay from Havana to the suburb of Regla, and a week later a second ferry was hijacked. Both sailed out of the harbor and onto the high seas, where a U.S. Coast Guard cutter came to their rescue, taking aboard those who indicated they wished to leave Cuba and allowing those who did not to take the ferries back to Havana. The Cuban government called in the chief of the U.S. Interests Section to complain, but the Coast Guard continued its rescue patrols.

On 4 August Cuban authorities foiled the takeover of a third ferry, but in the melee a police officer was killed. By this time the hijackings had become both a nuisance to commuters (the ferries were temporarily halted after the officer's death) and a major public phenomenon, drawing crowds to the Old Havana docks, where on 5 August the first large-scale disturbances in the revolution's thirty-five-year history broke out and quickly spread westward along the Malecón. Touring the affected areas in the early evening, Fidel Castro complained to a trailing television crew, "We are not the ones opposed to the departure of those who want to leave. The United States is opposed. They deny visas to these people"; yet when they hijack a boat, "they are welcomed as heroes." Obviously still upset by the accusation that his government had sunk the first tugboat, Castro argued, "We are truly guarding the U.S. coasts, and in exchange, when there is an incident, any accident, they accuse us of cruelty, murder, and all that." Fine, Castro warned, Cuba was ready to wash its hands of the problem: if the United

States continued to welcome hijackers, "we will remove the obstacles to any vessel that wants to leave."

An hour later he said the same thing at a hastily scheduled news conference, focusing this time on Washington's failure to follow through on the 1984 agreement to admit up to twenty thousand Cubans a year. Castro had been coy when first asked if another Mariel boatlift was in the offing—"We are not opposed to anything," he had replied—but now, at the news conference, he explicitly warned that if the United States did not stop encouraging the illegal departures, Cuba would not only allow any boat to leave but also welcome U.S. boats seeking to pick up friends or relatives. The next day he added that the police would be "much more flexible" about enforcing the law against illegal departures, and for those who found this wording too oblique, he spelled it out: "Becoming more flexible allows more people to leave." Two days later a group of Cubans hijacked a navy utility boat, killed one of its officers, forced three others to swim for their lives, and then headed out to sea, where, as had now become commonplace, they hailed a U.S. Coast Guard cutter, which took everyone to Key West. "They have done all in their power to provoke us," complained an incensed Castro, throwing open the door: "The problem is no longer ours but theirs," passing to Washington the matter of preventing another Mariel boatlift. "Let them handle that unpleasant task."[43]

With the number of rafters growing by the hour, Florida governor Lawton Chiles sought assistance from President Clinton, who had lost the only election of his life in the 1980 race for Arkansas governor after his opponent ran TV ads showing rioting Mariel Cubans at Fort Chaffee in northwestern Arkansas. Clinton recalled that the ads told viewers "that the governors of Pennsylvania and Wisconsin cared about their people and they got rid of the Cubans, but I cared more about Jimmy Carter than the people of Arkansas." Fourteen years later, President Clinton was vacationing on Martha's Vineyard and entertaining Castro confidant Gabriel García Márquez when Governor Chiles issued his plea for help. "Castro has already cost me one election," the president told García Márquez, "he can't have two." Clinton asked the Colombian novelist "to tell Castro that if the influx of Cubans continued, he would get a very different response from the United States than he had received in 1980 from President Carter."[44] Clinton directed the Coast Guard to detain any U.S. boat heading toward Cuba, a strategy that would have stemmed the 1980 flow from Mariel but would not work now, when about two thousand Cubans a day were coming on flimsy rafts.

With the situation deteriorating rapidly, the president's senior aides gathered in Washington to devise a response. Like the president, Secretary Christopher was on vacation, but most other senior policymakers were there, some with vivid memories of the Mariel fiasco, including Undersecretary of State Peter Tarnoff and national security adviser Anthony Lake, both Carter-era officials, and Attorney General Janet Reno, who had been Dade County prosecutor in 1980. They recommended a policy of "demagnetizing" the United States: the Coast Guard would continue to pick up the rafters, but they would no longer be taken to the United States and granted humanitarian parole; instead, Reno announced, everyone picked up would be detained "at appropriate facilities."[45] President Clinton was more explicit the next day, explaining that Cubans rescued at sea would be taken to the U.S. Navy base at Guantánamo "while we explore the possibility of other safe havens within the region." Asked if this policy meant that the administration was abandoning the Cuban Adjustment Act, the president hinted at what would become his "wet foot/dry foot" policy: those apprehended at sea would be held at Guantánamo until some solution other than admission to the United States could be found, while anyone who managed to reach U.S. soil would be detained but not taken to Guantánamo. Speaking vaguely, the president said that the latter group of Cubans "will be now treated like others who come here."[46]

But doing so was not possible—the 1966 Cuban Adjustment Act allowed any Cuban reaching U.S. soil to stay, and therein lay the race-laden problem for President Clinton, as it had for his predecessor in 1991 when a military coup against the government of Jean-Bertrand Aristide had sparked a dramatic spike in the number of Haitian rafters, and President George H. W. Bush had ordered a tent city constructed at Guantánamo. "I don't want to have a policy that acts as a magnet," Bush had explained. "Let me assure you it is not based on some race or double standard. If the Cubans started out, a new Mariel boatlift started out, the same thing would happen. It is a consistent policy."[47]

But the inconsistency was obvious: any Cuban picked up at sea was brought to Florida, while any Haitian was taken to Guantánamo, and during the 1992 campaign Bill Clinton had criticized the double standard, implicitly charging the Bush administration with racism. A few days after the Democrat's victory, however, the Coast Guard informed the president-elect that two hundred thousand now-hopeful Haitians who had heard his criticism were preparing to depart for the United States, a situation that obliged Clinton to announce that he would continue the Bush policy. But Haitian rafters kept coming throughout 1993 and into 1994 (two thousand were being picked up *daily* in April 1994), and the number taken to Guantánamo grew so large that immigration officials began holding asylum hearings aboard Coast Guard ships. Those unable to demonstrate a well-founded fear of persecution were returned directly to Port-au-Prince.[48]

Leaving undecided the ultimate fate of dry-foot Cuban rafters (nearly all would eventually be admitted), the new 1994 policy meant that the wet-foot Cubans intercepted at sea were to join the fifteen thousand Haitians already at Guantánamo. Polls indicated overwhelming support for this evenhanded policy, and President Clinton did not think it would be a problem in Miami: "I've talked to Cuban-Americans, of course, exhaustively for years now, and we've been in touch with them and the Florida congressional delegation—I believe this policy will have broad support. I will be surprised if it does not have broad support."[49]

Surprised he was; later in the evening the president left his own birthday party for an hour-long meeting with Florida governor Chiles and CANF chair Mas Canosa, who had flown up to express their dismay. "All of us would have preferred that the Cubans not be taken to Guantánamo," Mas Canosa commented the next day, "but that was the decision of the U.S. government and the U.S. president and it is irreversible." In return for this concession, Mas Canosa had demanded a blockade; the president rejected that idea but agreed to tighten the embargo. First, travel would be greatly curtailed, with all general licenses canceled and specific licenses limited to Cuban Americans "for humanitarian reasons involving extreme hardship" and to a handful of others for narrowly limited purposes. Second, gift parcels would be limited and cash remittances prohibited entirely except on a case-by-case basis—again, only for extreme humanitarian reasons such as terminal illness or severe medical emergency.[50]

With that accomplished, Mas Canosa returned to Florida, leaving the president to his immigration crisis. The number of rafters picked up by the Coast Guard reached a record 3,253 on 23 August, five days after the announcement that they would be taken to Guantánamo. With vivid footage of high-sea interdictions now a lead story on the nightly news, on 25 August a reporter took advantage of an opportunity to shout out the question on everyone's mind: "Fidel Castro says there's a simple way to stop the exodus of Cuban refugees, and that is to open up a high-level dialog between Washington and Havana. What's so bad about that?" President Clinton replied with something new: "We have offered a resumption of talks on the whole issue of immigration." Fidel Castro told reporters the same thing a few hours later: "I do not want to be indiscreet, but the possibility of talks on migration topics is advancing."[51] The next day, Cubans willing to take their chances at Guantánamo hijacked another ferry.

The talks began on 1 September and quickly led to an agreement. The United States would take three steps: first, Cubans rescued at sea would continue to be taken to unspecified "safe haven facilities outside the United States"; second, the United States would "discontinue granting parole to all Cuban migrants who reach U.S. territory in irregular ways"; and, third, as an alternative to illegal entry, the United States would accept not *up to* twenty thousand Cuban immigrants a year, as it had agreed in 1984, but *a minimum* of twenty thousand Cubans each year. For its part, Cuba agreed to stop the exodus.[52]

Left unanswered was the question of how exactly the twenty thousand immigrant visas were going to be allocated, since so few Cubans qualified under the existing preference categories. The solution was a lottery, with *Granma* publishing an article describing how it would be conducted: any Cuban could mail an empty envelope to the U.S. Interests Section between 15 November and 31 December, with the name, address, marital status, number of minor children, and Cuban ID card number printed in the upper-left-hand corner. Five thousand of the envelopes would be drawn at random and the senders notified so that they could begin the immigration paperwork. In addition to lottery winners, Cubans with petitioning relatives in the United States could continue to apply, and expedited treatment would be given to former political prisoners and those already on preference-category waiting lists.[53]

U.S. officials still had to figure out how to dispose of the twenty-three thousand internees already at Guantánamo and another eighty-five hundred who had been taken to a U.S. military base in Panama — "We're working on that" was all President Clinton could tell reporters. Most of the children, the ill, and the elderly were in the process of being granted humanitarian parole, while others had voluntarily returned to Cuba, but those who remained quickly found themselves in a situation that was desperate: as the Pentagon explained to Congress, officials were "stuck with 15,000 young males [and] very few women," summer temperatures at Guantánamo were reaching an oppressive 120 degrees, and as a result "there are Cubans who are mutilating themselves. They are injecting diesel fuel into their veins in order to get into the hospitals in hopes that they can come to the United States for medical treatment." But as President Clinton reiterated, "To admit those remaining in Guantánamo without doing something to deter new rafters risked unleashing a new, massive exodus of Cubans."[54]

The administration sought to return the remaining fifteen thousand to Cuba, while the Castro government was not eager to accept them, especially after early October talks in Havana about implementing the lottery, which the State Department had entrusted to its Cuba desk officer, Dennis Hays. The Cuban negotiator, Ricardo Alarcón, wanted nothing to do with him. "Trying to endure Hays was a major problem for me," he recalled. "Our discussions were boring because they were so predictable and so repetitive: Hays would give us his sermon not once but as many times as we indicated we were willing to stay in the room." In thirty years, no U.S. official had annoyed him more — "and you can quote me on that. Hays was rigid and arrogant, the worst kind of diplomat." The veteran Alarcón much preferred to deal with Undersecretary of State Peter Tarnoff, with whom Alarcón had negotiated during the Carter years. During the Reagan-Bush era, Tarnoff had served as president of New York's Council on Foreign Relations, and Alarcón, then vice minister of foreign relations, had traveled regularly to the United Nations. The two men would meet in Manhattan for "a couple of martinis, and talk and talk" — "Petey," Alarcón continued, switching to fluent English, "was a good guy."[55]

After Hays's animosity-creating October visit to Havana, Alarcón decided to negotiate through Tarnoff, beginning with a 23 January meeting in New York, where Tarnoff stressed the administration's desire to dispose of the Guantánamo internees. Hays was kept in the dark, but in mid-April he and Alarcón were scheduled for a six-month follow-up to their October meeting, and Alarcón, aware that Guantánamo would be the principal issue, again contacted Tarnoff, whom President Clinton authorized to hammer out a solution. Without telling Hays, Tarnoff met with Alarcón in New York on 17 April. The two men made some progress and agreed to meet again after checking with their governments. The next day an unsuspecting Hays found Alarcón unwilling to discuss the Guantánamo internees. On 29 April Tarnoff and Alarcón held a third meeting, this time in Toronto, where they closed the deal: the United States would grant humanitarian parole to the Cubans already at Guantánamo, and any subsequent Cuban migrant intercepted at sea would be returned directly to Cuba.[56]

Return rafters to Cuba? When Jesse Helms heard Attorney General Janet Reno announce the agreement, he marched straight to the Senate floor, accused the administration of being "an accomplice in Castro's repression of the Cuban people," and demanded that the United States "strangle his brutal dictatorship once and for all."[57] CANF's Mas Canosa echoed those sentiments before a House subcommittee two weeks later — the agreement was an "announcement that the United States will now be co-wardens of Castro police state," and the negotiations were a "bumbling keystone cop exercise conducted by amateur diplomats." Tarnoff was a career foreign service officer and no amateur, so Mas was probably referring to Morton Halperin, the senior director for democracy on the National Security Council staff, who had been the NSC liaison with the State Department during Tarnoff's negotiations with Alarcón. Two decades earlier, in 1970, Halperin had resigned from the Nixon NSC staff to protest the U.S. bombing of Cambodia, and his reputation as a liberal had made him a natural target for Helms and Mas Canosa even before the agreement to repatriate Cubans. Halperin had joined the Clinton NSC only after the Senate had refused to confirm him as assistant secretary of defense for democracy and peacekeeping.

At the subcommittee hearing, Representative Burton charged, "We have people in the administration who have publicly stated that they support some of the views of the leftist groups around the world, and have said that they saw nothing wrong with the Communist aggression in Angola, and elsewhere, sponsored by Fidel Castro. In particular, I am talking about Morton Halperin." Mas Canosa also complained about "counterculture, unreconstructed leftist political appointees at the National Security Council still pursuing their anachronistic pipe dreams and attempting to salvage their last remaining icon, Fidel Castro," while Ros-Lehtinen asked Tarnoff, "Did Morton Halperin initiate the idea of holding secret talks?" Tarnoff replied that Halperin had been a logical participant, given his responsibility for promoting democracy, but that he was not responsible for the agreement.[58] "No wonder the true career professionals at the State Department in charge of Cuban affairs asked for reassignment," Mas Canosa observed, referring to the understandably offended Hays, who had been completely unaware of the negotiations until Tarnoff met with him after the agreement had been reached, just hours before it was announced. "I was not surprised by his request for reassignment," Tarnoff commented. (Hays soon resigned from the foreign service to become CANF's Washington representative.)[59]

Despite Florida representative Peter Deutsch's complaint that "we are sending people back into that hell hole," on 8 May 1995, a U.S. Coast Guard cutter docked at Cuba's Puerto Cabañas navy base carrying thirteen interdicted rafters. Officers from the U.S. Interests Section went aboard to explain how to apply for one of the twenty thousand visas, and then the thirteen Cubans were handed over to Cuban authorities, who had promised to take no action against the returnees. It was the first time Cubans had been repatriated, and President Clinton faced the formidable challenge of explaining this dramatic change in U.S. policy: "There is no realistic alternative," he told the Cuban American community. "We simply cannot admit all Cubans who seek to come here."[60]

THE PRESIDENT'S OWN PARTY had deserted him after the embargo-tightening capitulation to Mas Canosa — "The Embargo Must Go" had been the title of a *Washington Post* opinion article coauthored by the chairs of the Senate Committee on Foreign Relations, Claiborne Pell, and the House Committee on Foreign Affairs, Lee Hamilton, both widely respected moderate Democrats.[61] Even those with memories stretching back to Vietnam could not recall a similar joint critique by Congress's two principal foreign policy leaders, and that action was only the prelude to President Clinton's autumn woes: two months later, both Pell and Hamilton lost their positions as committee chairs as Republicans scored major victories in the 1994 off-year elections. Fifty-four seats shifted in the House of Representatives, giving Republicans control of the lower chamber for the first time since 1954, while eight seats shifted in the Senate, handing Republicans control of that body as well.

In the House, Torricelli lost his leadership of the foreign affairs subcommittee on Western Hemisphere affairs to Burton, a hyperpartisan Indiana conservative who announced at his first hearing, "We intend to make the democratization of Cuba a high priority." Of course, it had already been a high priority of Representative Torricelli, but he tended to turn on and off like a lightbulb, depending on his audience, and never matched Burton's pit-bull approach to politics. "We have the opportunity to deal a lethal blow to the Castro regime," the new chair said, seizing the Cuban pant leg: "No matter how hard Castro works, no matter what price he is willing to have the Cuban people pay in the loss of their freedom, we will work just as hard, and we will do just as much, and we will never, ever stop fighting to ensure that this dictatorship is brought to an end."

That said, Burton recognized Ileana Ros-Lehtinen, now the subcommittee's second-ranking member, who argued that new legislation was needed to curtail foreign investment in Cuba — "Foreign investors are now bailing out Castro," she complained, and Representative Lincoln Díaz-Balart agreed: "The fundamental reason that Castro has been able to remain in power is because of the assistance and the cooperation that he has received from other nations and their investors." Burton then offered the floor to "my good friend, Jorge Mas," who replied in kind: "The Cuban-American community could not have expected a dearer friend or someone more devoted to securing Cuba's freedom to assume the chairmanship of this subcommittee." Mas then denounced the *Washington Post* for its "propaganda effort to rescue Fidel Castro" (the op-ed article by Pell and Hamilton) and condemned Cuba as "'The Bangkok of the Caribbean' for its promotion of sex and virgin Cuban women." But Mas reserved his strongest criticism for "international profiteers who have invested in Cuba." The hearing's highlight was his unveiling of CANF's Hall of Shame, a three-page list of third-country investors accompanied by Mas Canosa's pledge "that as long as I live and as long as the Cuban American National Foundation exists, we will work to see and to ensure that when the dawn of democracy finally arrives in Cuba, each one of these deals will be rendered null and void by a new democratic Cuban leadership." When that day arrives, he promised, "those profiteers will be run out of town."[62]

Senator Jesse Helms had beaten Burton's House subcommittee to the punch. The day after the 1994 election Helms told reporters that "high on my list of priorities [is] to do everything possible as chairman to help bring freedom and democracy to Cuba," and five days before Burton, the North Carolinian took to the Senate floor to unveil his first major legislative proposal as chair of the Committee on Foreign Relations, the Cuban Liberty and Democratic Solidarity (Libertad) Act of 1995, soon known as the Helms-Burton Act. "It's time to tighten the screws," he said, and at this point the best way to do so was to deter foreigners from investing in Cuba.[63]

Unlike Representative Burton, who could be counted on to oppose any sentence uttered by a Democrat and to endorse anything said by a Republican, Senator Helms, nicknamed "Senator No," had a reputation for opposing almost everything proposed by anyone. Few proposals from either side of the aisle escaped his criticism, especially anything that might restrict God-given individual liberties such as the right to smoke on airliners. In the 1970s and early 1980s, most observers had dismissed Helms as a quaint unreconstructed southerner, but they had been forced to take him seriously after the Republicans regained control of the Senate in 1986 and Helms became the second-ranking member of the Committee on Foreign Relations just as Mikhail Gorbachev was launching glasnost and perestroika. The Reagan administration encouraged Gorbachev's reforms, of course, but Helms worried that Moscow might be offering Washington a Trojan horse: "We must consider whether or not this detente is a means to promote cultural change in the United States in order to so alter our traditional way of life that a convergence or merging of the American and Soviet systems can occur."[64]

Like Senator Joseph McCarthy a generation earlier, Helms complained that the Soviets had willing accomplices within the U.S. foreign policy bureaucracy—after six years of watching Reagan-era policy toward Central America, which included promoting such distasteful palliatives as distributing land to peasants, the senator had concluded that "the State Department and the CIA have bent every effort to install leftist regimes throughout the hemisphere. For them, socialism is the wave of the future." And that was not the worst of it, Helms insisted, expanding his indictment to eye-popping dimensions:

> Anyone familiar with American history, and particularly American economic history, cannot fail to notice the control over the Department of State and the Central Intelligence Agency which Wall Street seems to exercise. This campaign against the American people—against traditional American culture and values—is systematic psychological warfare. It is orchestrated by a vast array of interests comprising not only the Eastern establishment but also the radical left. Among this group we find the Department of State, the Department of Commerce, the money center banks and multinational corporations, the media, the educational establishment, the entertainment industry, and the large tax exempt foundations. Mr. President, a careful examination of what is happening behind the scenes reveals that all of these interests are working in concert with the masters of the Kremlin in order to create what some refer to as a new world order.

Now the man with these thoughts had become chair of the Senate Committee on Foreign Relations and had set his sights on Cuba. "It used to be that Americans stood united about this Communist threat 90 miles off our shore," he told his Senate colleagues in 1995, complaining about the Tarnoff-Alarcón immigration agreement. "But now we are changing, a la Neville Chamberlain, who went over to Munich and consulted with Adolf Hitler and came back and said, 'We can have peace in our time. We can do business with Adolf Hitler.' But nobody could do business with Adolf Hitler, and we should not be doing business with Fidel Castro."[65]

With that the Helms-Burton proposal began to wind its way through Congress. First came hearings before both men's committees, where the complexity of the proposal became evident: the plan comprised an extended list of actions to be continued, initiated, or intensified against the Cuban government, cobbled together by Senator Helms's committee staffer Dan Fisk from drafts by multiple authors, including Ignacio Sánchez, a Miami attorney representing Bacardí, and Nicolás Gutiérrez, another Miami attorney representing the National Association of [former] Sugar Mill Owners of Cuba.[66] Not surprisingly, therefore, the Helms-Burton proposal focused on property the Castro government had nationalized three decades earlier and was now marketing to foreign investors. The centerpiece was Title III, whose purpose was to deter these investors by exposing them to litigation in U.S. courts if they "trafficked" in property that the Castro government had expropriated without compensation in 1959 and the early 1960s. A second part of Title III, later separated into its own Title IV, denied U.S. visas to third-country nationals who invested in Cuban property formerly owned by U.S. nationals.

The most controversial section of Title III initially was the one that allowed U.S. nationals to use federal courts to seek monetary damages from these third-country investors "whether or not the United States national qualified as a United States national at the time of the Cuban government action." While Title III would not convert Cuban Americans into claimants (it would simply give them standing to use U.S. courts to sue foreign investors), the congressional hearings clearly indicated that Cuban Americans were, in fact, seeking to become certified claimants who would share in any settlement negotiated with a post-Castro government.[67] Such ambitions understandably alarmed the original 5,911 claimants from the 1960s, all U.S. nationals at the time, who vigorously opposed the dilution of their claims by newcomers. Speaking for thirty U.S. corporations holding more than half of the original $1.8 billion in certified claims, the president of the Joint Corporate Committee on Cuban Claims told Congress, "We can reasonably expect that tens if not hundreds of thousands of Cuban-Americans will file Title III lawsuits. . . . The harm U.S. certified claimants will suffer as a result of the enactment of Title III is indisputable. The U.S. State Department has estimated the total value of Cuban-American claims at $94 billion. U.S. certified claims, by contrast, total [with interest] $6 billion. Faced with the prospect of tens of billions of dollars in federal court judgments, the Cuban Government will have neither the means nor the incentive to negotiate a settlement of the U.S. certified claims." These certified claimants took the position that "individuals who were Cuban nationals at the time their property was confiscated must seek resolution of their claims in Cuban courts." The State Department agreed—"Universally accepted principles of international law bar the United States from espousing claims of individuals who were not U.S. citizens at the time of loss."[68]

But both voices were drowned out by a Cuban American chorus, including the president of the Association of Cuban Banks, who insisted that "distinctions by nationality should have no place in a rule of law environment." A somewhat different position was taken by Gutiérrez, representing the former owners of Cuba's sugar mills, four of which had belonged to his family: to deny Cuban Americans access to U.S. courts would violate the Equal Protection Clause of the Fourteenth Amendment, Gutiérrez argued, but he was willing to compromise by creating a second tier of claims that would give priority to the original claimants. In the end, a different compromise was reached: the Foreign Claims Settlement Commission was authorized to determine the losses of all U.S. nationals, whether or not they qualified as nationals of the United States at the time their property was expropriated, but only if the loss exceeded fifty thousand dollars (a threshold that would eliminate all but the largest Cuban claimants) and only for the purpose of suing third-country investors, not for sharing in a negotiated claims settlement with the Cuban government.[69]

All this provided a sideshow of interest to relatively few; also of scant interest were the Title II provisions stipulating U.S. policy toward a post-Castro Cuban government, although Representative Rangel criticized the Title II effort to define in great detail the nature of a Cuban government that would be acceptable to Washington—first a "transition government" and then a "democratically elected government," neither of which could include Fidel or Raúl Castro, even if the Cuban electorate chose one of them in a fair contest.* No one paid Rangel much attention—the 1994 election had sapped liberals' political strength—and the State Department urged critics to focus instead on what would become the principal bone of contention: the Title III provisions that might trigger "complex international litigation and bitter disputes with major trading partners."[70]

The Republicans now running Congress brushed aside these concerns. "I understand the administration has found many reasons to oppose strengthening the embargo," wrote Senate majority leader Robert Dole, eager to claim co-ownership of what he called "the Helms-Dole 'Libertad' legislation" but unable to attend a committee hearing because he was busy

---

* In the draft legislation, a "democratically elected" government was defined as one that had accepted thirteen separate measures, including taking steps to return nationalized property to U.S. citizens or providing compensation. The version signed into law broadened this definition substantially, adding, for example, the stipulation that a democratic government would be defined by the absence of interference with the broadcasts of Radio and TV Martí.

campaigning for the 1996 Republican presidential nomination. Dole's principal Republican rival, Texas senator Phil Gramm, attended, however, and he argued that the solution "is to get rid of Fidel Castro, and that is what I want to see us do."[71]

The Burton version cleared the House Committee on International Relations in July, and Speaker Newt Gingrich scheduled floor debate after the summer recess. With sentiment running heavily in favor of passage, Secretary Christopher warned Gingrich that he would recommend a presidential veto: the stipulation denying U.S. visas to third-country investors "will create enormous frictions with our allies," he charged, also objecting "to the overly rigid list of more than a dozen 'requirements' for determining when a transition or a democratic government is in power," which were too inflexible to permit creative diplomacy during a transition.[72] Dismissing this warning, the House passed the bill in September by an overwhelming 294–130 margin, and all eyes then shifted to the Senate, where Helms had delayed his committee's markup because Republican senator Nancy Kassebaum had made it clear that she agreed with Secretary Christopher's position, and if she were to vote with the Democrats, united in their opposition, the Committee on Foreign Relations would be deadlocked.

In early October, President Clinton gave a broad-ranging speech about democracy and human rights that contained a brief paragraph announcing a relaxation of the embargo: news organizations such as CNN would be allowed to open bureaus in Cuba, restrictions would be eased to permit more travel for educational and religious purposes, and Cuban Americans, while still limited to traveling once every twelve months and only for extreme humanitarian need, would simply have to sign an affidavit provided by an airline charter company, not obtain a specific license from the Department of the Treasury. In addition, the president announced a new program to fund nongovernmental organizations (NGOs) "to promote peaceful change and protect human rights," with the first NGO, Freedom House, paid to disseminate informational materials to Cubans, to sponsor trips by democratic activists to Cuba, and to publish materials written by Cuban dissidents. The president explained these changes as an effort to encourage a "peaceful transition to a free and open society," and in fact, all fell within the scope of Track 2 activities envisioned by the 1992 Cuban Democracy Act; nonetheless, the speech represented a clear departure from the more hostile U.S. policy adopted at the time of the rafter crisis, and conservatives interpreted it as an effort by Democratic soft-liners—the handful of Morton Halperins—to adopt a less hostile approach to Cuba.[73]

Criticizing the president's announcement, Dole used it to justify the unusual step of placing the Helms-Burton proposal on the Senate calendar before it had been approved by the Committee on Foreign Relations, thereby skirting Senator Kassebaum's opposition. The Democrats responded with a filibuster, and the bill would have died after a failed cloture vote had not Senator Helms agreed to delete the provision that the administration opposed most strenuously—the Title III stipulation that U.S. nationals could sue third-country investors in federal courts for trafficking in confiscated property. (The other major White House objection, the provision denying visas to third-country investors, had already been removed from the Senate version of the bill.) The Senate then approved the gutted measure, and Helms prepared to fight in conference committee.

The House appointed its conferees almost immediately, but the divided Senate waited until mid-December, just before the holidays, so no action could be taken until January. In this case, time was on the proponents' side, for it allowed an additional ingredient to be added to the legislative stew: a group of Cuban American pilots called Brothers to the Rescue. The group itself was not new; Cuban American aircraft owners had been patrolling the Straits of Florida since 1991, searching for rafters and notifying the Coast Guard when a pilot identified small craft needing rescue. Cuban authorities at first scrambled their MiGs as the flights approached, not knowing whether the aircraft intended to overfly their country, perhaps to drop incendiaries on sugar fields or leaflets on Havana, as in the early years of the revolution, or perhaps to land on a highway and pick up family members, as had occurred in 1992.

Three international flight corridors cross Cuba, linking North and Central and South America, and in the mid-1990s these corridors were being used every day by about 350 civil aircraft, half of them scheduled U.S.-flag carriers. Since neither Cuba nor the United States wanted to engage in risky, ad hoc behavior in this area, the two governments quickly adopted a protocol that allowed the Cuban American search-and-rescue flights to continue while providing a measure of security to Cuba and safety to travelers: the Federal Aviation Administration (FAA) notified Cuban air traffic controllers in advance of each flight, detailing the flight plan and giving each of the Brothers' planes a unique transponder code to clearly identify the aircraft, and the Brothers agreed to notify Cuban controllers by radio prior to crossing south of the twenty-fourth parallel, roughly halfway between Cuba and mainland Florida. The Brothers' flights soon had become routine—by 1992, they were flying several sorties a day, and at the peak of the rafter crisis in mid-1994 the CIA reported that "many who attempt illegal departure by sea do so because they think that this volunteer group's efforts have increased their chances for survival."[74]

Fewer flights continued after the crisis ended, but the Brothers then began making passes over Havana. The first such overflight occurred on 13 July 1995, during a remembrance of those killed in the tugboat incident, when Brothers' leader José Basulto broke away from the flotilla of Cuban American boats below and, with a Miami television cameraman filming from the copilot's seat, overflew Havana and dropped several thousand flyers reading "Not Comrades, Brothers." Basulto repeated this feat on 9 and 13 January 1996, this time dropping leaflets reading "Fight for Your Rights," "Your Neighbors Feel the Same Way You Do—Change Things Now," and "The People Own the Streets."

The Cuban government protested to Washington. "We warned them," Fidel Castro would recall. "We let them know in calm words, really, in reasonable words, that, please, do what you can to avoid those flights." Undersecretary of State Tarnoff confirmed the receipt of Cuba's protests and said that since mid-1995 "not only representatives of the FAA but State Department officials have been meeting with Mr. Basulto and the Brothers to make sure that they understood the kinds of reactions that we were detecting in Havana."[75] The FAA did nothing to stop the overflights, however, even though each had occurred after the Brothers had filed a false flight plan. On 15 January, two days after his most recent overflight and just as the Helms-Burton conferees were sitting down to negotiate, Basulto told a Radio Martí interviewer that the Brothers were again preparing to leaflet Havana. A month elapsed, but on 24 February three Brothers' aircraft approaching Cuban territory were intercepted by Cuban air force jets. Two were shot down, killing four crew members. The strategy of provocation had provoked.

There is no justification for shooting down unarmed civilian aircraft, as the International Civil Aviation Organization, the Inter-American Commission on Human Rights, and the U.N. Security Council declared. But Fidel Castro tried to explain: "Those airplanes came constantly, each time with more daring: they violated our territorial waters, they flew over our capital and threw out their pamphlets. I wonder if there is any country that would permit that." While condemning the shoot down, the four-member investigating team from the International Civil Aviation Organization also criticized "a pattern of flights near and over Cuban airspace," noted that Cuban authorities had complained to the United States on seven different occasions between 15 May 1994 and 4 April 1995, and pointed out that Cuba had issued public warnings beginning on 14 July 1995 and that those warnings were broadly publicized in the Florida press. To gain near-unanimous approval of a U.S.-sponsored resolution condemning the shoot down (the vote was 13–2, with Russia and China opposed), the Security Council also reaffirmed "the principle that each State shall take appropriate measures to prohibit the deliberate use of any civil aircraft" for the type of activities in which the Brothers were engaged.[76]

President Clinton denounced the shoot down "in the strongest possible terms" and two days later promised to "move promptly to reach agreement with the Congress on the pending Helms-Burton Cuba legislation." He also closed the barn door, directing the secretary of transportation "to make and issue such rules and regulations that the Secretary may find appropriate to prevent unauthorized U.S. vessels from entering Cuban territorial waters." The FAA revoked Basulto's pilot's license for six months.[77] Meanwhile, House and Senate conferees quickly reached an agreement with the White House, whose principal negotiator, Richard Nuccio, had helped write the 1992 Cuban Democracy Act. The president called the agreement "a strong, bipartisan response" and urged Congress to adopt it.[78]

The compromise Nuccio brokered restored the Title III right of U.S. nationals to sue foreign investors for trafficking in confiscated property. The administration only insisted on a presidential waiver authority, and in return, it yielded on every other point and accepted an entirely new provision codifying the embargo—hitherto a presidential proclamation and therefore subject to the president's rescission, the embargo would now become a part of U.S. law. "I have been remiss in not thanking Richard Nuccio also for his help," said Representative Burton, casting a smiling eye toward the White House aide during a hearing held the day after negotiations concluded. "We really appreciate all the help he gave us yesterday. You worked long and hard and you are one of those unsung heroes that nobody knows about, but we appreciate very much what you did." Ros-Lehtinen agreed: "We like and respect and admire Mr. Nuccio."[79]

A complex thirty-nine pages, each crafted with lapidary attention to detail, the final version of the Helms-Burton Act was divided into an introduction and four titles. Dominating the introduction was a list of twenty-eight "Findings" that served as the indictment of the Castro government and the justification for the punishment that followed—"The Cuban Government engages in the illegal international narcotics trade," for example, and "Fidel Castro has defined democratic pluralism as 'pluralistic garbage.'"

No similar list appears anywhere else in the history of U.S. legislation. The closest historical parallel is the Declaration of Independence list of grievances against King George III, and his indictment was limited to only eighteen transgressions.

Title I, "Strengthening International Sanctions," contained the section codifying the embargo plus a host of additional provisions. Most were minor, such as reducing U.S. aid to any country assisting Cuba to complete its Juraguá nuclear facility, but one prohibited the entry of third-country products made with goods of Cuban origin—Swiss chocolate made with Cuban sugar, for example, or Chinese stainless steel made with Cuban nickel.

Title II, "Assistance to a Free and Independent Cuba," defined in elaborate detail the nature of a transitional Cuban government and then a democratically elected government. Fidel Castro called this section the most surprising part of Helms-Burton: "It's the first time in history, and for the first time in the life of our country, that we see another nation, another government, taking the trouble to develop a program for 'a period of transition in Cuba.'" Among its two dozen provisions—also unique in the history of U.S. legislation—Title II stipulated that Cuba had to be "moving toward a market-oriented economic system" and that its government not include either Fidel or Raúl Castro, despite the fact that President Clinton had gone on record saying that "the United States does not pick leaders or delete leaders for other countries. We let people make their own decisions."[80]

Title III, "Protection of Property Rights of United States Nationals," authorized the use of U.S. courts to sue third-country citizens who invest or otherwise "traffic" in property that previously belonged to a U.S. national, including Cubans who were not U.S. nationals at the time they lost their property.

Title IV, "Exclusion of Certain Aliens," denied entry into the United States of foreigners (and their spouses, minor children, and agents) who invest in Cuban property confiscated from U.S. nationals. Law professor Andreas Lowenfeld found it "hard to believe that Ms. Jones, the daughter of a corporate executive from Toronto, might be stopped at the border when she returns from her summer vacation for her junior year at Vassar, but that is what the statute says."[81]

The Senate approved the conference report the day after Richard Nuccio threw in the administration's towel; the House followed a few days later; and in mid-March President Clinton signed the Cuban Liberty and Democratic Solidarity (Libertad) Act of 1996. "The Cuban people must receive the blessings of liberty," he said at the signing ceremony, surrounded by a dozen members of Congress and a Who's Who of Cuban American leaders. "This day is another important step toward that ultimate goal that so many of you in this audience have worked so hard for, for so very, very long. Thank you very much." The president then shook a few hands before walking back to the Oval Office, while aides handed out a statement explaining exactly what the president understood he had just signed. Citing seven of the law's provisions that might be construed to undermine the president's constitutional authority, Clinton wrote, "I will construe these provisions to be precatory"—as simply an expression of Congress's wishes. But there was no wiggle room in the section codifying the embargo, and so here the president could only trace out the foundation for a successor's constitutional challenge: "Section 102(h), concerning the codification of the economic embargo, and the requirements for determining that a transitional or democratically elected government is in power, could be read to impose overly rigid constraints on the implementation of our foreign policy."[82]

"That a president would knowingly surrender so completely his ability to make foreign policy is astonishing," wrote Professor William LeoGrande; Nuccio later explained that "those who recommended signature to [Clinton] did not understand the full implications of Helms-Burton." Nuccio recalled attending a meeting where the attorney general, secretary of defense, and chair of the Joint Chiefs of Staff were all "shocked" to learn that the still-unsigned law codified the embargo. But adviser George Stephanopoulos said, "'The President has to sign the bill' [and] I realized this was not a meeting to review the President's options. The President's decision had already been made for him." No evidence indicates that President Clinton worried about any of these problems at the time—"I signed it regretfully but not reluctantly," he said—and only in his memoir did he acknowledge how "supporting the bill was good election-year politics in Florida, but it undermined whatever chance I might have if I won a second term to lift the embargo." This observation came in hindsight, however; in 1996 proponents of the bill clearly hoped that tightening the embargo would quickly lead to regime change in Cuba. "It is difficult to see how Castro can sensibly continue to hope that his dictatorship can survive the rough provisions of this legislation," commented Senator Helms. "Castro's days are indeed numbered."[83]

THE NATIONAL ASSOCIATION OF MANUFACTURERS warned that the Helms-Burton Act was likely to become "a perpetual irritant," repeating in 1997 what the State Department had been saying all along: the United States could not assert jurisdiction over the behavior of non-U.S. nationals abroad. Senator Helms had argued in response that his law constituted a perfectly legitimate effort to stop third-country investors from acquiring property confiscated from U.S. citizens, but then he weakened his argument by admitting that the protection of property rights was only incidental to the law's central purpose: "to deny Fidel Castro what he needs most to survive: hard cash." One of the measure's coauthors agreed: "We're not doing this to win lawsuits," said Gutiérrez, the Miami attorney representing Cuba's former sugar mill owners; "the main objective is to drive foreigners out of Cuba." [84]

The principal question raised by Helms-Burton, then, was whether it was appropriate for Washington to threaten foreigners with legal action in order to hasten the collapse of the Cuban government. Senator Helms obviously believed that the answer was yes, while third-country investors and their governments thought otherwise. Now caught somewhere in the middle, President Clinton tapped Undersecretary of Commerce Stuart Eizenstat to replace Nuccio as the special representative for the promotion of democracy in Cuba and assigned Eizenstat the task of negotiating a modus vivendi with upset third countries.

Eizenstat spent nearly two years cobbling together an agreement that would satisfy foreign investors and their governments without provoking Senator Helms, but his appointment placed the issue on the back burner while President Clinton focused on his reelection. It was not much of a contest. "The defense of freedom in Cuba is not a Republican issue," the president insisted, and in accepting the Democratic nomination he demanded that Cuba "finally join the community of democracies." [85] The 1996 Republican platform accused the president of "extending the duration of Communist tyranny" in Cuba, a reference to Clinton's modest relaxation of the embargo in October 1995, while the party's nominee, Kansas senator Robert Dole, promised that "the appeasement policy of the Clinton administration will be replaced with an iron resolve to bring Fidel Castro down." At one of the presidential debates, Dole criticized the administration's decision to waive Title III of the Helms-Burton Act ("If you want to send a signal you've got to send a signal, Mr. President"), but with Clinton's four-year record, it was simply not possible to accuse him of being soft on Cuba. The Democrats also had an almost unbeatable ally in the U.S. economy, which was as strong as anyone could remember, and President Clinton coasted to an easy win, becoming the first Democrat in two decades to carry

Florida. In New Jersey, Robert Torricelli rode the president's coattails into the Senate.[86]

The very modest controversy over implementing Helms-Burton then shifted to the Senate Committee on Foreign Relations, where Madeleine Albright, about to become the new secretary of state, used her confirmation hearing to criticize the Cuban government as "an embarrassment to the hemisphere." As the U.S. permanent representative to United Nations, she had spearheaded the effort to condemn Cuba's shoot down of the Brothers to the Rescue planes, and her zeal had clearly impressed committee chair Jesse Helms, but he was not happy about the administration's Title III waiver and what he considered its halfhearted implementation of the law's other provisions. Albright's simple reply—"I want to work with you on this subject"—brought the senator aboard: "I'm not going to push you on it," he responded.[87] The difference between Albright's reception and the hostile grilling of Warren Christopher four years earlier could not have been greater, underscoring the extent to which the administration's Cuba policy had come to reflect Helms's wishes.

But his influence would not go unchallenged during Clinton's second term, nor would the power of the Cuban American community go untested, especially after CANF's Jorge Mas Canosa died of cancer in late 1997. The Castro government was no longer doing anything significant to challenge concrete U.S. interests—the early 1990s had seen the end of Cuba's overseas military activities, the end of Cuba's support of what the U.S. government considered terrorism, the end of Cuba's alleged drug trafficking, and the end of Cuba's illegal immigration.

The immigration solution had been especially instructive. After the 1994–95 agreements terminating the rafter crisis, the U.S. bureaucracy took charge of managing the legal immigration of 20,000 Cubans per year: 3,000 family reunification visas, between 2,000 and 3,000 refugee visas, and initially between 14,000 and 15,000 lottery visas. Sign-ups for the lottery occurred in 1994, 1996, and 1998, when 541,000 Cubans applied (on top of the 190,000 who had applied in 1994 and 435,000 in 1996); thereafter, the Cuban government refused to permit another round of applications, and the Interests Section simply chipped away at the backlog.[88] The U.S. Coast Guard vigorously enforced the wet foot/dry foot policy created in 1995, taking rafters intercepted at sea back to Cuba unless they claimed a fear of persecution, in which case they were taken to Guantánamo for a formal asylum hearing. Included in one repatriation were six hijackers of a Border Guard ship, which Fidel Castro characterized as "a constructive act. . . . By doing so they're sending a message to potential hijackers that this type of action will not go unpunished."[89] This 1997 repatriation won the administration no friends in the Cuban American community, nor did a mid-1999 incident when the Coast Guard used pepper spray and a water cannon to keep six struggling Cubans from reaching dry land. But with no further hijackings and with fewer Cubans setting out in flimsy rafts, the problem was reduced to a low-volume flow featuring handsomely paid professional smugglers making nighttime pickups in high-speed boats to elude Cuban and U.S. authorities.

A John Kennedy or especially a Jimmy Carter would have been delighted to inherit this "neutralized" Cuba, but President Clinton reacted to these dramatic changes by announcing that one more step was needed: Cuba had to become democratic, and "until I see some indication of willingness to change, it's going to be very difficult to persuade me to change our policy."[90] Coming in the early days of his second term, this comment positioned the administration to ignore the island. "No one in Washington believes Clinton wants to change," wrote Professor Philip Brenner, adding that several important domestic and international interests were negatively affected by Washington's Cuba policy, and they were demanding attention.[91]

Cuba's trading partners had begun to demand Washington's attention in 1992, just days before Bill Clinton was first elected, with a U.N. General Assembly vote condemning the embargo. Cuba had requested a debate on the embargo a year earlier, but the United States had insisted that it was not an appropriate topic for the General Assembly to address, and Cuba had pulled the request when it saw that the vote would not go in its favor. But State Department officials had warned at the time that Cuba's hand would be strengthened if the proposed Torricelli ban on subsidiary trade were enacted, and they were correct: in 1993, the General Assembly voted 59–3 (with 71 abstentions) to approve a resolution on "The Need to Terminate the U.S. Economic, Trade and Financial Blockade against Cuba."[92] The General Assembly's approval of similar resolutions subsequently became an annual affair, with approval always coming by a lopsided margin; most early abstainers, including all fifteen members of the European Union, moved to oppose the United States after President Clinton signed the Helms-Burton Act: the 1996 vote was 137–3, with 25 abstentions.

Enter the Pope. For a decade, the Cuban government had slowly worked toward an accommodation with the Catholic Church, no small achievement given Cuban leaders' early antipathy toward the conservative church. In 1961 relations had hit bottom when three Spanish priests were among

the captured invaders at the Bay of Pigs. Two weeks later the Cuban government canceled all foreign priests' residence permits and closed Cuba's
parochial schools.[93] Relations remained frosty until the Cuban government
took note of the changes triggered by Vatican II—no revolutionary could
ignore what came to be known as liberation theology, especially with the
church's active involvement in Central America's struggles in the 1970s,
and in 1980 Fidel Castro told visiting East German premier Erich Honecker that he attached great significance to the fact that "there are many
priests with a revolutionary attitude in Latin America."[94] The revolution's
announcement of its willingness to coexist with progressive Catholicism
came in 1985–86, when the Cuban Council of State published *Fidel and
Religion*, a book-length transcript of Fidel Castro's conversations with a
Brazilian priest-theologian. In early 1987 this volume was the only book
on display in the windows of Old Havana's principal bookstore, La Nueva
Poesía.

As a signal of improved relations, the government created a new Office
of Religious Affairs, and by 1989 Fidel Castro was telling reporters, "I feel
great respect for religion," making earlier disagreements seem like ancient
history: "There may have been conflicts with the church, but weren't there
conflicts during the French Revolution, the Spanish civil war, and in the
life of Simón Bolívar? . . . We teach not to kill, not to steal, not to desire
the women of one's fellow men. Those are Christian principles." Two years
later the Cuban Communist Party opened its membership to believers, and
in 1992 the Cuban Constitution was amended to designate the government
as "secular" rather than "atheist."[95] In 1997 Christmas was restored as a
holiday—it had been canceled since 1969, ostensibly because Cuba needed
the day's labor to harvest ten million tons of sugar.

While striving to be accommodating, the church had occasionally used
a critical voice, as in September 1993, at the depth of the Special Period,
when a pastoral letter from Cuba's bishops both applauded the government's market-oriented economic reforms and criticized "the exclusive
and ubiquitous presence of the official ideology [which] generates a feeling of fatigue caused by constant repetition of guidance and instructions."
The bishops also criticized the "excessive control by State Security agencies
which at times reaches even into the strictly private lives of individuals"
but balanced this statement with a pointed attack on the U.S. embargo:
"We bishops of Cuba reject any kind of measure that in order to punish the
Cuban government serves to aggravate the problems of our people," a message Pope John Paul II repeated from Rome in his 1994 "state of the world"

address delivered four months later.[96] In late 1996 Fidel Castro traveled to the Vatican and personally invited John Paul II to visit.

All the major U.S. news anchors were on hand a year later when the Pope landed in Havana. Pulling no punches during his four-day visit, he strongly criticized any infringement on religious freedom and emphasized that human liberation "cannot be reduced to its social and political aspects"; it also had to include "the exercise of freedom of conscience—the basis and foundation of all other human rights." Then came words that the Cuban government would have found more welcome—criticism of "the resurgence of a certain capitalist neo-liberalism which subordinates the human person to blind market forces."

> From its centers of power, such neo-liberalism often places unbearable burdens upon less-favored countries. Hence, at times, unsustainable economic programs are imposed on nations as a condition for further assistance. In the international community we thus see a small number of countries growing exceedingly rich at the cost of the increasing impoverishment of a great number of other countries; as a result the wealthy grow ever wealthier, while the poor grow even poorer.

At his departure ceremony a few hours later, the Pope openly criticized the U.S. embargo: "No nation can live in isolation," he began; "the Cuban people, therefore, cannot be denied the contact with other peoples necessary for economic, social and cultural development, especially when the imposed isolation strikes the population indiscriminately, making it ever more difficult for the weakest to enjoy the bare essentials of decent living." If this statement was not sufficiently direct, John Paul's final words included a plea to end "oppressive economic measures, unjust and ethically unacceptable, imposed from outside the country."[97]

President Clinton had granted PBS's Jim Lehrer an interview on the day the Pope arrived in Havana—as luck would have it, the same day that special prosecutor Kenneth Starr issued headline-grabbing subpoenas in his investigation of the president's alleged obstruction of justice to cover up a sexual affair with a White House intern. Much of the interview focused on the president's defense, but Lehrer and Clinton engaged in some discussion of Cuba, with Lehrer noting that the Pope had urged an end to the U.S. embargo. "His Holiness is a very great man," replied the president, but "his position on this is identical to that, as far as I know, of every other European leader. And only time will tell whether they were right or we were." Lehrer persisted, asking why Cuba was being treated differently from China,

North Korea, and especially Vietnam. The president replied, "We can have a greater influence through economic sanctions in Cuba than we can in other places."[98]

The Pope's visit clearly strengthened the hand of those pushing for a less hostile policy, however, and two months later the president cited John Paul's visit as the reason for a slight easing of the embargo. Ros-Lehtinen had predicted such a relaxation—"The Clinton Administration is always looking for any excuse that will do to try to lift some of the economic sanctions," she complained three weeks before the announcement, and the Pope's visit "is as good an excuse as any."[99] The new changes were modest: streamlined licensing for exports of medicine and medical supplies, resumption of direct charter flights, and increased remittances of up to twelve hundred dollars a year to relatives in Cuba. The remittance policy was thus restored to its status prior to August 1994, when Jorge Mas Canosa had interrupted President Clinton's birthday party to insist on a tightened embargo in exchange for not condemning the administration's new wet foot/dry foot immigration policy. The changes also returned U.S. policy on charter flights to its status before the February 1996 shoot down of the Brothers to the Rescue aircraft.

President Clinton correctly stated that the changes "will make it easier for Cuban Americans to visit loved ones on the island and for humanitarian organizations to provide needed assistance." After the shoot down, the Treasury Department's Office of Foreign Assets Control (OFAC) had continued to allow U.S.-based charter companies to arrange *indirect* flights through third countries for licensed travelers (researchers, journalists, and Cuban Americans for humanitarian reasons involving extreme hardship), but that approach typically meant a short hop to Nassau and often a long wait for a flight to Havana. Six months later, OFAC authorized a somewhat easier arrangement that was, by general agreement, just plain silly: it allowed passengers to stay aboard aircraft that flew from Miami, landed in the Bahamas, and then immediately continued on to Cuba—provided that the flight number was changed. After the March 1998 relaxation, authorized charter companies could skip Nassau and again fly directly between Miami and Havana.[100]

INTERNATIONAL OPPOSITION TO Helms-Burton turned out to be a genuine problem. Given the tectonic shifts they had recently applauded on their eastern borders, Europeans were having difficulty understanding Washington's continuing effort to isolate Cuba. Europe's diplomats in Washington undoubtedly cabled explanations about the growing strength of Cuban Americans and the imperatives of Florida politics, and European leaders had little desire to fight with Washington over faraway Cuba, but avoiding conflict became difficult after passage of the Torricelli Act, with its ban on subsidiary trade, and virtually impossible after Helms-Burton, with its claims to extraterritorial jurisdiction not simply over third-country investors but also over any financial institution that loaned money to make an investment.

Canada complained first, perhaps because Canadian firms had the most to lose—they had been among the principal beneficiaries of President Ford's 1975 decision to allow the foreign subsidiaries of U.S. companies to trade with Cuba. Occasional disputes were inevitable, but prior to Helms-Burton they had been handled by the normal give-and-take that characterizes close friendships. In 1978, for example, a Canadian subsidiary of Pickers Corporation was initially denied permission to sell X-ray equipment to Cuba because the U.S. content exceeded the established 20 percent limit, but the sale was authorized after the State Department argued that otherwise "the US Cuban embargo will again become a serious irritant in US-Canadian relations."[101] Accustomed to this flexible policy, Canadians were understandably concerned in 1989 when Senator Connie Mack introduced his proposal to reestablish the ban on subsidiary trade, and Canada's minister of justice issued a preemptive order prohibiting Canadian-based U.S. subsidiaries from complying with Mack's proposal should it become law.

President Bush vetoed the measure, avoiding a dispute, but Representative Torricelli reintroduced the ban on subsidiary trade as part of the 1992 Cuban Democracy Act, and again the Canadian government took preemptive action, this time with an unusual public warning to the U.S. Congress that "passage of the Mack Amendment would have extremely unfortunate consequences for companies that would be forced to make an invidious choice between complying with U.S. law or that of Canada." When the measure became law three months later, Canada's Foreign Extraterritorial Measures Act was amended to prohibit Canadian subsidiaries of foreign firms from complying, and the government announced that "Canadian companies will carry out business under the laws and regulations of Canada, not those of a foreign country."[102] After the huffing and puffing ended, however, all Canadian-based subsidiaries of U.S. firms quietly stopped trading with Cuba.

The stakes rose considerably with passage of the Helms-Burton Act, when purely Canadian firms became subject to legal action in U.S. courts.

"Helms-Burton has transformed a United States–Cuba problem into a much broader trade and investment issue," commented former Canadian prime minister Kim Campbell. "The United States is free to not have economic ties with Cuba. It is equally free to try to persuade others to adopt similar policies. What Canada or any other self-respecting sovereign state will not accept—and will never accept—is the unilateral imposition on it of another country's policy." More than just pride was involved: In 1995, Canada's exports to Cuba amounted to $108 million, while imports totaled $194 million. Those numbers accounted for less than 1 percent of Canada's trade, but more significant was the prospect immediately ahead. By 1996, thirty-seven Canadian firms had opened offices in Cuba, where they were involved in thirty joint ventures with the Cuban government, including the construction of more than 4,000 hotel rooms in eleven different locations, many to be used by Canadians vacationing in Cuba—120,000 in 1995, 600,000 in 2006. Some of these hotels and other investments would almost inevitably infringe on property that the Cuban government had seized from U.S. claimants.[103]

Threatened by Helms-Burton, these Canadian investors naturally sought help from their members of Parliament, one of whom noted that Helms-Burton "says volumes about the arrogance of the people who would advance that kind of legislation." Another called it "totally reprehensible," while a third dubbed it "an example of the inability of the United States to accept the fact that smaller countries also have rights." A fourth stood up to say that "as a proud, certified western Canadian or, as the Liberals like to call us, redneck, I do not appreciate another country's telling Canada how to run our foreign policies. I do not agree with Canadian foreign policy, but that is for us . . . to decide." The handful of legislators seeking to downplay the dispute tried to explain that Helms-Burton was an exercise in domestic politics—"After the election in the U.S. this annoyance will disappear," one said—but the majority was unwilling to wait: Parliament again amended its Foreign Extraterritorial Measures Act to read that any Helms-Burton judgment "shall not be recognized or enforceable in any manner in Canada."[104]

Senator Helms complained that Canada's position "is precisely what Neville Chamberlain advocated about dealing with Hitler," but his was an atypical reaction; both sides seemed anxious to avoid a situation where push might come to shove. "We just have a different approach here, and we'll try to find a way to manage our differences," explained President Clinton when he welcomed Canadian prime minister Jean Chrétien to Washington in 1997. For its part, the United States waived Title III, and Canada did not take any retaliatory step when twenty-four executives and their family members from one company—but only one, Sherritt International—were denied U.S. visas under Title IV.[105]

Washington's southern neighbor was equally upset, with a Mexican diplomat probably capturing public sentiment when he complained about Senator Helms's effort "to pressure the residents of its *patio trasero*," the rear courtyard where servants wash the laundry. The Mexican government noted "the notorious incompatibility of the Helms-Burton Act with international law" and promised to "continue to firmly defend the right of its citizens to conduct business activities anywhere in the world." But President Ernesto Zedillo sidestepped the issue during a visit to Washington a few days after the House passed its version of Helms-Burton—grateful for the Clinton administration's 1994 bailout of Mexico's collapsing peso, he responded with a terse "We did not discuss that" when asked if he and Clinton had talked about Cuba. The Mexican Congress was unwilling to overlook what many considered an attack on the nation's sovereignty, however, and it followed the Canadian example by passing legislation imposing substantial fines on any Mexican national who complied with Helms-Burton. A month later Zedillo joined twenty-two other heads of state at an Ibero-American summit in approving a resolution expressing "firm rejection" of Helms-Burton. The eleven-member Inter-American Juridical Committee had already expressed the unanimous opinion that "the domestic courts of a claimant State are not the appropriate forum for the resolution of State-to-State claims."[106]

The United States ignored the Ibero-American summit, but the Europeans could not be brushed off so easily. Like the Canadians, the European Parliament had vigorously condemned the 1992 Torricelli Act, approving one resolution calling it "a flagrant violation of international law on free trade" and a second asserting that "although the international legal order allows individual states to take restrictive trade measures to defend their own national interests, it does not legitimize the imposition of such measures on third countries."[107] Now, four years later, the European Union (EU) protested Helms-Burton even before President Clinton had signed the measure, noting that its "provisions, if enacted and implemented, risk leading to legal chaos." After Helms-Burton became law, the EU initiated a complaint under the elaborate dispute settlement mechanism of the World Trade Organization (WTO), the first step of which was to request formal discussions with the United States. The complaint asserted that Helms-

Burton violated wTo rules by restricting the entry into the United States of European products made with Cuban raw materials and by threatening to deny visas to Europeans alleged to be trafficking in property claimed by U.S. nationals.[108]

"As you know, we've been severely criticized by our European allies," the president commented one day before a decision was required on whether to waive Title III, the Helms-Burton provision allowing U.S. claimants to sue third-country nationals for "trafficking" in confiscated property. The criticism had been especially severe a few weeks earlier at a White House meeting with EU leaders, where the president of the European Commission told reporters that "the extraterritorial elements of this law have received worldwide condemnation." The meeting had been cordial, he added, but "we did raise our concerns about the legislation in no uncertain terms." Clinton responded by promising to review the issue, and he soon announced a suspension of Title III, the first of a still-unbroken string of semiannual waivers—but, he warned, if third-country investors continue to invest in property claimed by U.S. nationals, "they can face the risk of full implementation of Title III."[109]

At this point the president appointed Eizenstat to negotiate a modus vivendi with the nation's trading partners. Eizenstat was a good choice— as the administration's ambassador to the EU in 1993–94, he had helped resolve complex property restitution issues in postcommunist Eastern Europe, but he had sailed into those negotiations with the wind to his back, since everyone wanted to reach a quick agreement. No one wanted a fight over Helms-Burton, either, but after three rounds of unfruitful discussions, the EU moved to Step 2, asking the wTo to create a panel to adjudicate the dispute, and the clock started ticking on a rigid process of fact-finding, argumentation, decision, appeal, and implementation. The EU Council of Ministers also issued both a regulation prohibiting any EU citizen from complying with a Helms-Burton judgment and a resolution allowing any European affected by a Helms-Burton judgment to recover damages in EU courts.[110]

These events occurred during the weeks immediately before and after the 1996 U.S. election, as did the EU's consideration of a "Common Position" on relations with Cuba. Adopted in early December, the Common Position emphasized constructive engagement to encourage a peaceful transition to pluralist democracy, respect for human rights, and improved living conditions. While the part of the Common Position that called for greater economic cooperation with Cuba could not have been welcome in Washington, President Clinton looked on the bright side, hailing the document's support for democracy. "We have helped clear the air on Cuba," agreed visiting Irish prime minister John Bruton, also president of the European Council, but he warned that "Europe will remain firmly opposed to all extraterritorial legislation, whatever its source, and will continue to defend its interests."[111]

At her confirmation hearing three weeks later, Madeleine Albright congratulated Eizenstat for nudging the Europeans to adopt their Common Position, but the WTO clock was still ticking, and a panel of judges soon would have to be appointed to hear the dispute. When the panel was appointed in February, U.S. officials used off-the-record press briefings to hint that they intended to invoke a national-security escape clause to deprive the WTO of its right to proceed. Doing so would seriously undermine the fledgling institution that the United States had been instrumental in creating only two years earlier; if the United States could simply say "national security" and thereby remove itself from WTO jurisdiction, others would surely follow suit on issues they considered important.[112] Recognizing the damage that could be done, Eizenstat and European negotiators hammered out a provisional understanding by April: the Clinton administration would continue to suspend Title III and seek waiver authority for Title IV (the title denying visas to corporate executives who invested in confiscated property), while the Europeans would develop a set of norms—"disciplines"—for dealing with property confiscated without compensation.[113]

A full year later, in May 1998, a permanent agreement was reached just before a G-8 summit in London, where President Clinton introduced it as "a pathbreaking common approach to deter investment in illegally expropriated property." Then he handed the microphone to Secretary Albright, who filled in the details about the disciplines to which EU governments had agreed. Their citizens could continue to invest in property confiscated without compensation, but they would have no government assistance: "no government loans, no government grants, no subsidies, no fiscal advantages, no government participation, and no government commercial advocacy in support of investments in illegally expropriated property." In turn, the Clinton administration agreed to continue waiving Title III and to obtain authority to waive Title IV. Tony Blair, the host prime minister, captured the spirit of the moment: "We've avoided a showdown."[114]

Instead, the showdown came between the administration and Congress, to whom Eizenstat trumpeted the agreement as his generation's equivalent of the Treaty of Westphalia: "The understanding we reached with the EU on

May 18 represents a historic breakthrough," he told one House committee; "for the first time we have established multilateral disciplines among major capital exporting countries." It was, he argued immodestly, "an extraordinary achievement." True, he admitted, European investors were still free to invest in property confiscated from U.S. claimants, but they "can expect absolutely no help or assistance from their governments, and will stand naked in an insecure and dangerous environment."[115] David Wallace, the chief executive officer of Lone Star Industries and chair of the Joint Corporate Committee on Cuban Claims, presented a contrary view, complaining that the agreement was "without teeth and will, as a practical matter, do little to 'inhibit and deter' future foreign investment." It had been reached "at great and unfair cost to U.S. certified claim holders," and "the unkindest cut of all is that the accord does not affect *existing* investments in unlawfully confiscated properties." (The Cuban government had already sold part of Lone Star's former cement factory at Mariel.)[116]

Many members of Congress were upset by the administration's promise to continue waiving Title III, but at least they were not surprised because President Clinton had already done so four times. What *was* new? The agreement's stipulation that "application of the disciplines and the exercise of a Title IV waiver will be simultaneous." In her London press conference, Albright had glossed over this commitment to obtain legislation authorizing a Title IV waiver, and no one had asked whether she expected Senator Helms and like-minded legislators to pass such a measure. Back in Washington, everyone knew the answer, but the ranking Democrat on the House Committee on International Relations, Lee Hamilton, wanted Eizenstat to acknowledge the implications: "In order to be clear, if the Congress refuses to enact the waiver on Title IV in the Helms-Burton Act, the U.S.-EU agreement falls apart."

> MR. EIZENSTAT: The happiest person in the world if that happens will be Fidel Castro.
> MR. HAMILTON: But it falls apart.
> MR. EIZENSTAT: It falls apart.[117]

In a world where corporate executives spend much of their time commuting among major business capitals, Title IV could be more than a minor annoyance, as the White House had recognized from the beginning: in the clarifying statement issued when he signed Helms-Burton, President Clinton wrote that he would implement Title IV "in a way that does not interfere with my constitutional prerogatives and responsibilities" to conduct foreign policy.[118] No one knew what that statement meant until the April 1997 provisional understanding with the EU, when the administration promised to "apply rigorous standards to all evidence submitted to the Department of State for use in enforcing Title IV. The U.S. is committed to a thorough, deliberate process in order to ensure careful implementation of Title IV. This will involve discussion with all affected parties in order to consider all relevant information prior to Title IV actions." In other words, the administration would drag its feet on enforcement.[119]

And there the matter rested. The State Department created a special unit within its Office of Cuban Affairs to enforce Title IV, and President Clinton claimed to be vigorously implementing it, but his administration excluded from the United States only a few executives, none of them Europeans.[120] Although an assistant secretary of state said that the State Department was seeking to obtain permission to waive Title IV, the Clinton administration never formally asked Congress to provide waiver authority. Nor did Clinton's successor: Although it claimed to be investigating twenty-eight possible third-country traffickers in confiscated U.S. property, the George W. Bush administration took until April 2004 to make its first and only trafficking determination, and that was the first such action since 1997. The EU took the position that until "a waiver is granted to the EU under Title IV of the Helms-Burton Act, we will continue to abide by the Understanding of 11 April 1997. Thereafter, the EU will implement the disciplines."[121]

While the United States took a verbal and diplomatic beating from its allies over Helms-Burton, it probably achieved at least some of its goal, which was to hamper Cuba's economic recovery by deterring third-country investment. "Several companies have withdrawn from commitments or altered their plans in Cuba in order to avoid determinations of trafficking," reported Assistant Secretary of State Alan Larson in 1998, and the number of potential investors who quietly backed away after their lawyers explained Helms-Burton may have been larger than anyone imagined.[122]

AS THE POPE WAS URGING the United States to end its embargo and as major U.S. allies were challenging Helms-Burton, domestic opposition to the administration's Cuba policy was also growing. This opposition included the usual suspects, particularly members of the academic community and Washington's left-of-center policy institutes, but it attracted additional adherents as Cubans' Special Period suffering tugged at even hardened hearts. "This national grudge against Cuba is out of step with the changes occurring the world," concluded a fact-finding delegation from the

American Public Health Association during President Clinton's first year in office. "Surely in this day, with the Cold War behind us, the most powerful nation in the world can devise a policy that does not cause suffering among an entire population." A few months later economist Carmen Diana Deere, a past president of the Latin American Studies Association who had spent much of the Special Period conducting research in rural Cuba, told Congress that "in the post–Cold War era, the embargo can only be viewed as an inhumane and punitive policy." Such a position might be expected from Deere, whose personal library included a complete run of the *Monthly Review*, but surprising support for her position came from Roger Fontaine, a neoconservative from the Reagan era's Committee of Santa Fe, who concluded that the Cuban people "have surely suffered enough. I don't think it is morally possible to make matters worse in the hope somehow, some day it will all get better. It's simply not acceptable to follow a strategy designed to make the lives of most Cubans so desperate that they will rise in bloody revolt."[123]

"That surprises me," remarked Raymond Molina, president of the Broad Front for the Freedom of Cuba, who had been invited to participate in a mid-1995 congressional hearing. Fontaine, Molina said, "has always been a conservative," and people like him "know their way around town and they could do substantial harm." Representative Díaz-Balart nodded his agreement, criticizing the "coalition of folks who are now trying to save Castro. It is not only the ideologues to the left. You have people who want to make a buck now."[124]

Díaz-Balart was correct, but he misunderstood the diversity of the opposition: some opponents sought an opportunity to invest and trade; others, like Deere, who had always decried the embargo as inhumane, were now joined by some who found the embargo indefensible in a post–Cold War environment; but Díaz-Balart missed a third group that stretched across the political spectrum and held a view expressed well by Arthur Schlesinger Jr., who believed that ending the embargo would be the best way to promote change. "Lift the embargo," he wrote to the *New York Times* in early 1997, "and drown the regime in American tourists, investments and consumer goods." A similar antiembargo argument came from Elizardo Sánchez, then Cuba's most visible human rights activist, who used the same newspaper to say the same thing: "American policy impedes the transformation we seek," he wrote from Havana. "How can one sincerely argue that the cause of a more open Cuba would not be advanced by having as many Americans as possible in the streets of Havana?"[125]

These three groups had different goals—pecuniary, humanitarian, and political—but all would be advanced by an end to the embargo. The largest by far was the segment arguing that contact with U.S. citizens would bring political change, but it was also the least cohesive, a shortcoming New York's Council on Foreign Relations tried to correct soon after Pope John Paul II's visit when it created a Task Force on U.S.-Cuban Relations in the 21st Century, composed of twenty moderates and conservatives and led by two moderate former assistant secretaries of state for inter-American affairs, William D. Rogers and Bernard Aronson. Unveiled in early 1999, the task force report advocated a modest relaxation of the embargo in the same spirit as Schlesinger and Track 2 of the Cuban Democracy Act—as a strategy to undermine the Castro government: "Every aspect of U.S. foreign and economic policy toward Cuba should be judged by a very pragmatic standard: whether it contributes to rapid, peaceful, democratic change in Cuba."[126]

Such thinking also seemed to lie behind an October 1998 proposal from Senators John Warner, a Republican, and Christopher Dodd, a Democrat, who convinced twelve other senators to join them in asking President Clinton to create a bipartisan commission modeled after the 1983 Kissinger Commission on Central America. "More and more Americans from all sectors of our nation are becoming concerned about the far-reaching effects of our present U.S.-Cuba policy on United States interests and the Cuban people," they wrote; it was time for "a thoughtful, rational, and objective analysis of our current U.S. policy." They included with their request an endorsement by seven foreign policy luminaries, including former secretary of state Henry Kissinger, former secretary of defense Frank Carlucci, former Senate majority leader Howard Baker, and, linking this group to the Council on Foreign Relations task force, William D. Rogers.[127]

"Castro has done nothing to merit any wholesale reassessment of U.S. policy," complained Jorge Mas Santos, who had replaced his deceased father as CANF's president. "The Commission proposal is only the latest ploy of an anti-sanctions business lobby." That was also the view of the three Cuban Americans in Congress: "Some people in the business community care nothing at all about the absolute lack of political freedom, human rights, or independent organized labor in Cuba," they wrote to President Clinton. "We believe that those commercial interests seek to take advantage of the enslaved Cuban people for their personal financial gain."[128] The administration did not share the three's reasoning but reached a conclusion of which they approved: "We do not support establishing such a commission at this time," replied Secretary Albright. Her response took more than two months to prepare because the administration would not consider handing policy-making initiative to a commission it could not control but also could not simply dismiss the senators' request, so similar to the Pope's, that the United States rethink its policy.

But in its classic try-to-please-everyone style, the Clinton White House decided in early 1999 to link its refusal to appoint a commission with a significant relaxation of the embargo, which the president announced on the same day Albright replied to the senators. These changes focused on greater people-to-people contact: travel licenses would be easier to obtain, remittances would be liberalized to allow any U.S. resident to send money to almost anyone in Cuba, cultural exchanges would be expanded under streamlined procedures, charter flights would be authorized between cities other than Miami and Havana, food and agricultural inputs could be donated or sold to NGOs and to Cuba's small private sector (principally family-operated restaurants), and direct mail service would be reestablished. The State Department cited the Warner-Dodd initiative and the Council on Foreign Relations task force as indicators of "a growing consensus that there is a transition coming and that we should be pro-active in finding ways of supporting that transition." The Clinton administration sought "to promote a very nascent, non-governmental sector in Cuba."[129]

The Cuban government's response came from Ricardo Alarcón, now president of Cuba's national assembly, who called the relaxation "deceptive" because the embargo's core—the ban on trade—was staying in place while the subversive Track 2 elements were being expanded. Someday the United States would have to stop tinkering, he said, but in the meantime Cuba would not oppose relaxing the embargo: "If they want to revise it, let them revise it."[130]

The three Cuban Americans in Congress focused their indignation on the first visible effect of the relaxation—a baseball game in Havana between the Baltimore Orioles and the Cuban national team. The fact that Cuba lost (3–2 in eleven innings) offered no consolation for Representative Ileana Ros-Lehtinen; at a hearing four days before the game, she argued that "with every pitch, the belief of the Cuban people that the United States would never engage their oppressor will be eroded slowly. With every swing, the hopes of political prisoners and dissidents for solidarity from the superpower just 90 miles away will gradually be shattered." Nodding in agreement, CANF's Mas Santos called the game "a disastrous step in foreign policy" and predicted that the stands would be full only because Castro "is going to force people to go there and sit there." Even more unfavorable was Otto Reich, chair of the U.S.-Cuba Business Council, who pulled out all the stops: "We can equate this game with the 1936 Berlin Olympics," he said. "It didn't deter Hitler from militarizing the Rhineland, or annexing the Sudetenland, or invading my own grandparents' native land of Austria, just two years after that; then killing them."[131]

The relaxation created travel opportunities unseen since Jimmy Carter's presidency. U.S. academic institutions could now become OFAC subcontractors—they could obtain specific licenses to conduct travel-related transactions and then use those institutional licenses to authorize travel by students and faculty. Even high schools could obtain licenses (with the added stipulation that teachers must accompany the students, of course), and general licenses—licenses that did not require OFAC's specific authorization—were granted to almost any nonprofit organization with letterhead. This category included such diverse groups as religious organizations and amateur athletic teams, and individuals without an organizational affiliation could obtain a specific license for almost any type of educational, cultural, or humanitarian purpose—to study Santería for personal growth or to write an article evaluating Cuban rums for the local newspaper. Only formal tourism remained strictly prohibited, but travel providers quickly overcame that obstacle by arranging "educational" travel packages for alumni clubs, fraternal groups, horticultural societies, Art Deco preservation clubs, and the local Friends of the Zoo. In December 1999, the first direct flight from New York City in four decades landed in Havana, where arriving passengers found that the week's entertainment options included a concert series by the Milwaukee Symphony. The Yanquis were back.

But not all of them. Left out was the business community and in particular the powerful, well-organized U.S. agriculture industry—agribusiness. The president's relaxation authorized the export of food and agricultural inputs such as seeds and fertilizer, but only to independent nongovernmental organizations, and the few NGOs in Cuba, primarily churches, were expecting to receive donations, not to make purchases. The 1999 relaxation nonetheless rekindled an interest that had been ignited in the early 1990s when the Soviet bloc disappeared and Cuba began increasing its food purchases from the West. At that point, U.S. producers started complaining about being deprived of a market they had dominated before 1959, when they provided perhaps a quarter of all Cuba's food. In mid-1994, representatives of the National Oilseed Processors Association had told a House agricultural subcommittee that Cuba was importing three hundred million tons of soybeans and sunflower oil a year, and U.S. producers could capture the market if the United States were to lift the embargo. The president of the Rice Millers' Association outlined a similar scenario: in the early 1950s, Cuba had purchased about half of all U.S. rice exports, and the millers wanted that market back. So did the National Pork Producers Council, whose representative told the same subcommittee that Cuba, now at the depths of the Special Period, was nevertheless importing about twenty-five thousand tons of pork and other prepared meat a year—eleven million people importing more pork than Mexico's hundred million, he sighed, and "we exported none of this total." Without the embargo, "Cuba could likely become one of the top 10 export destinations for United States pork."[132]

This testimony represented a dramatic turnaround from the late 1970s, when the Carter administration had argued that "Cuba does not represent a substantial incremental market for any specific U.S. industries"; U.S. policy now made no sense to the nation's business media, and the *Wall Street Journal* ran a mid-1994 editorial under the title "Lift the Embargo." But the embargo made good sense to Florida farmers, who had heard Fidel Castro loud and clear in 1977 when he told Barbara Walters that if Cubans could only buy but not sell to the United States, they would buy nothing—"not even an aspirin for headaches, and we have a lot of headaches." Now, in 1994, the worried president of Florida's Farm Bureau Federation told Congress that "our climate is very much the same as Cuba. They grow the same commodities we grow . . . and they have some definite advantages in plentiful, cheap labor, they do not have the regulatory restrictions that we have, and our cost of production just continues to go up." Executives of the Florida Citrus Mutual and the Indian River Citrus League agreed; their producers were "gravely concerned" by the talk about opening up agricultural trade, noting that Cuba was already invading U.S. citrus markets in third countries.[133]

This 1994 House hearing was therefore a draw, with a slight advantage going to pro-embargo and protectionist forces. Then came President Clinton's birthday tightening of the embargo in mid-1995, the Brothers to the Rescue shoot down and passage of Helms-Burton in early to mid-1996, and finally the autumn U.S. presidential campaign, when nothing would be done to rile the Cuban American community.

Two months after President Clinton's second inauguration, however, the "humanitarians" began to develop an unplanned but natural coalition with agribusiness. The American Association for World Health published a three-hundred-page study arguing that "the U.S. embargo of Cuba has dramatically harmed the health and nutrition of large numbers of ordinary Cuban citizens."[134] The primary author, psychiatrist Peter Bourne, President Carter's former envoy on world health and hunger, had been concerned about the embargo since a 1977 visit to Cuba, when he received a list of twenty-two drugs made only in the United States. Although medicine and medical supplies had always been eligible for specific licenses, the burdensome procedures for obtaining them had meant a de facto prohibition, so Bourne had asked the NSC's Robert Pastor for help, and during that optimistic moment Pastor had little difficulty obtaining a license for the sale of eighty million dollars in medicine.[135] Cuba rejected the offer because it was tendered as a special favor, and there the matter rested during the Reagan-Bush years, only to resurface in 1993 when the American Public Health Association, presaging the 1997 report of its sister organizations, criticized the embargo as inhumane.[136] At that time, secretary of state–designate Warren Christopher had no good answer when asked why it was U.S. policy to send food and medicine to Iraq and not to Cuba, but a few months later Assistant Secretary of State Alexander Watson told Congress that humanitarian sales were licensed "when there is adequate on-site inspection and other appropriate means to verify that the export is not misused," with the term "misused" left undefined. Commentator Mark Falcoff gave the conservative explanation: "The purpose of this restriction is to prevent Castro from reexporting the drugs to gain dollars for other purposes; from using them in the mistreatment of political prisoners, particularly in psychiatric hospitals; and from diverting medicines from the United States into dollar-only stores or from using them for the benefit of foreigners who come to Cuba for medical treatment." And so someone in Cuba had to monitor end use, and the Department of Commerce had a short list of persons would qualify: a representative of the license applicant, a representative of a religious or charitable group, a third-country diplomat, or an international NGO.[137]

Four years later, the American Association for World Health complained that this end-use monitoring and other licensing provisions "actively discourage any medical commerce." Also complaining were the authors of a report published in the principal journal of the Canadian Medical Association agreed, vigorously criticizing "insuperable bureaucratic restrictions" leading to "inordinate delays, cost increases and limited access to some of the most important medical products. These obstacles amount to a de facto embargo on medical supplies." Cuban human rights activist Elizardo

Sánchez also pointed out that "denying medicine to innocent citizens is an odd way of demonstrating support for human rights," insisting that "America should lift its embargo on sales of food and medicine." The U.S. Catholic Conference seconded this position and suggested after the Pope's visit that ending restrictions on the sale of food and medicine would be "a noble and needed humanitarian gesture."[138]

Agribusiness leaders could see the coalition that was ready to be mobilized, and in early 1998 they created a new organization, Americans for Humanitarian Trade, linking more than 600 businesses and trade associations with 140 religious and human rights groups, all dedicated to repealing the embargo on food and medicine. An initial effort occurred in the Senate, where Dodd and Warner proposed to exempt food and medicine from all existing or future economic sanctions. The measure survived its first vote, 60–38, but not its second, when Robert Torricelli successfully proposed an amendment to exclude any country accused of being a state sponsor of terrorism. The votes occurred soon after the National Association of Manufacturers had released its report criticizing sanctions that "have now been in effect against Cuba under nine Presidents, and to little or no avail," and not long after the National Foreign Trade Council had midwifed another new organization, USA Engage, to push for an end to all unilateral trade sanctions. Its roster included many of the nation's largest corporations, including agribusiness giant Archer Daniels Midland, whose chair and chief executive officer, Dwayne Andreas, understood exactly what was driving U.S. policy: "Nixon opened up trade with China, Bush went much further with Russia, Reagan outdid both of them, but this little island, why? Because every presidential candidate is invited to Miami to make a speech to a handful of rich Cubans, and the candidate says, 'I will never speak to Castro.' The result is that we look to the rest of the world like idiots. Beautiful little island, and we're the only people who won't trade with them." Like other USA Engage members, Andreas also knew what the Department of Agriculture would report a few days before the 1998 off-year elections—that U.S. agricultural exports to Cuba would amount to about $1 billion a year without the embargo.[139]

With the backing of the nation's farmers and agribusiness leaders, the new Congress that assembled in 1999 soon had two dozen different antisanction bills to consider—"Stoked by Farm Interests, Anti-Sanctions Movement Builds in Both Chambers," read a *Congressional Quarterly* headline, capturing the moment. The principal bill to lift all embargoes on food and medicine came from Missouri senator John Ashcroft, long a reliable embargo supporter but now focused on what he knew would be a difficult 2000 reelection campaign. "More than one-fourth of Missouri's farm marketing came from sales overseas," he told his colleagues, and additional customers were desperately needed. "There is a crisis in rural America," agreed Nebraska senator Robert Kerrey; "export markets have shrunk, commodity prices have plummeted, and rural incomes have decreased at an alarming rate. Yet while this is occurring, both Congress and the President have continued to pursue a foreign policy that places restrictions on our agricultural producers."[140] Long the strongest lobbying force in Washington, the nation's farmers were on the march.

Wondering where this march would end, a House subcommittee promptly scheduled a hearing at which Representative Ros-Lehtinen warned, "We are at a critical juncture where the wrong step, such as weakening U.S. policy, could have devastating effects." A State Department representative assured her that nothing more was planned beyond January's relaxation—which, he added, was fully consistent with the Track 2 policy she had helped write into law in 1992. Ros-Lehtinen also listened quietly as a representative of the U.S. Catholic Church recommended what the Pope had advocated: dialogue and reconciliation. Next came testimony from a group of conservative hard-liners, beginning with sociologist Irving Louis Horowitz, who lamented "a strange alliance between conservative business forces and radical intellectual elements." The intellectuals could be dismissed as impotent, Horowitz argued, but the business community was both powerful and selfishly single-minded, with "only an allegiance to the bottom line and to trade." The traditional "Castro is the devil" messages followed, presented this time by Otto Reich ("Fidel Castro's legacy is simple and indelible: death, destruction and despair") and by CANF's Mas Santos: the sale of food and medicine would only strengthen the government in Havana, he insisted, and "as we speak, the Cuban dictator is unleashing what can only be described as his final offensive against the Cuban people."[141]

But no one offered a strategy to head off the farmers, now building up an impressive head of steam. Representatives of the American Farm Bureau Federation told the House Committee on Agriculture what everyone could see: after nearly four decades, "U.S. sanctions on this tiny island nation have not had an impact in ending Castro's influence." The Farm Bureau emphasized, however, that President Clinton's January relaxation would be no help at all. Specific cases could not be cited because the new regulations for shipments of food and medicine had been published only days earlier, but "we understand that the new policy will require exporters to obtain an exporting license, covering a specific already-negotiated sale. Each export request will be reviewed on a case-by-case basis," and might or might not be approved. Well, continued the Farm Bureau's spokesman, a no-nonsense Arkansas farmer, "I liken it to a town that has two stores. Both of them have the same products for sale at relatively the same prices; [at] one of them you have to stand in line to get checked out, and then when you get there, they will decide whether they are going to sell it to you or not. The other one doesn't have a line. You go up there and . . . buy it. Now which one would you buy that product from?"

The president of the National Corn Growers Association agreed ("Potential sales are seriously limited by licensing rules and expensive shipping constraints"), but he focused on the general wisdom of any embargo, as did the president of Farmland Industries, the nation's largest farmer-owned cooperative, who criticized Washington's half dozen existing embargoes for having "damaged both our producers' livelihoods and thousands of people employed in exporting agricultural products." The president of the North American Export Grain Association also emphasized that "it is the American farmers who have been the losers," and the Corn Growers Association estimated that Cuba might purchase up to three million tons of corn a year without the embargo. Worst of all, the president of Farmland Industries argued, the embargo had had the opposite effect of what was intended—it was "just exactly what Castro has wanted in Cuba [and] had we changed our policy long ago, that regime would be totally different than it is today." The rice growers agreed: "We lost our largest commercial market, and Fidel Castro still rules in Cuba." Himself a Texas farmer, Representative Charles Stenholm agreed: "This failed policy has allowed Thailand and China to take the rice market."[142]

As one conservative farm-state representative after another crossed over to the antiembargo ranks, the thirty-seven-year ban on exports of most food and medicine seemed doomed, particularly in the Senate, where the nation's less-populated agricultural states enjoy disproportionate power. The House was a different matter—in late July, the Committee on Appropriations rejected by a 29–23 vote a proposal to lift the embargo on food and medicine. The Senate, however, took up Ashcroft's proposal to end all embargoes on food and medicine as an amendment to the fiscal 2000 agriculture appropriations bill. The opposition consisted primarily of Senator Torricelli and Florida's two senators, with Connie Mack providing the fireworks: "Freedom is not free," he said, his voice rising in an accusatory tone. "Today we hear from our colleagues that the farmers of our Nation are undergoing a difficult time. So today, they have put before us a fundamental question: Does this great Nation, the United States of America, support freedom, or do we support terror?" The few senators in attendance were unimpressed, and a roll-call vote on a motion to table Ashcroft's amendment failed by a surprising margin, 70–28.[143]

With so many senators voting to end all embargoes on food and medicine, proponents of the measure felt confident of overcoming House reluctance, so a few days after the vote, one senator from each of the Dakotas flew to Havana with a group of farmers to tout the special virtues of their durum wheat, the grain of choice for making pasta and, of course, couscous. In October, Illinois governor George Ryan led a similar delegation, becoming the first governor to visit Cuba in four decades. By that time observers were predicting a quick end to the embargo on food and medicine, but they had underestimated the hard-driving opposition of Representatives Díaz-Balart and Ros-Lehtinen, who relied on Republican whip Tom DeLay to remove Ashcroft's measure during the House-Senate conference. Antiembargo legislators were furious, but few members of either chamber were willing to send the mammoth agriculture appropriations bill back to conference. The antiembargo forces would have to start over.

THEN THE CLINTON CUBA POLICY acquired a new complication on Thanksgiving Day 1999, when a seventeen-foot boat that had left the Cuban port of Matanzas two days earlier capsized off the Florida coast, drowning eleven of the fourteen passengers, including the mother of one of the three survivors, a five-year-old boy named Elián González, who was found clinging to an inner tube off of Fort Lauderdale. Released into the custody of his great-uncle, Lázaro González, a battle royal promptly began when his father, Juan Miguel González, asked that the boy be returned to him in Cuba, while Lázaro, who had come to the United States in the mid-1980s, requested that Elián be granted asylum. Forced to decide, the Immigration and Naturalization Service concluded in early January that the great-uncle had no legal basis to act on behalf of Elián, that the boy's father had the legal authority to speak on behalf of the child in immigration matters, and that contrary to the claim of Florida's Cuban American community, "there is no objective basis to believe that Elián is at risk of persecution or torture." INS Commissioner Doris Meissner set a 14 January deadline for the boy to be returned to his father's custody in Cuba.[144]

The day after the INS issued its ruling, demonstrators who opposed

Elián's return to Cuba shut down much of Miami, and Representative Dan Burton subpoenaed the boy to testify before the Committee on International Relations. With the political stakes running high at the beginning of this election year, Vice President (and Democratic presidential hopeful) Al Gore broke with the administration, endorsing congressional proposals to grant Elián permanent residency and, to keep the family intact, to offer the same to his father, stepmother, half-brother, and grandparents, none of whom had expressed a wish to emigrate. In hotly contested New York, where he was campaigning for the Senate against Hillary Clinton, Rudolph Giuliani suggested not just permanent residence but citizenship. Mentioning one of the era's most prominent conservatives, President Clinton joked, "We have finally found the one immigrant Pat Buchanan wants to keep in America."

But the president understood that the situation was no laughing matter: "Maybe it's just because I'm not running for anything, but I just somehow wish that whatever is best for this child could be done. The poor kid has already lost his mother, and whatever happens, I'm sure he's going to carry certain burdens into his early adolescence that most of us did not carry. . . . Plainly he would have more economic opportunity in this country. But all the evidence indicates that his father genuinely loved him and spent a great deal of time with him back in Cuba."[145] Such a statement contrasted sharply with Uncle Lázaro's police record—four drunk driving arrests—and with the oral pyrotechnics of his hyperkinetic daughter, Marisleysis, who quickly became a media personality with her fiery front-porch pledges to keep Elián in Miami even if doing so meant defying the law.

In March a federal judge ruled that there was no compelling reason why Elián should be granted an asylum hearing, emphasizing that Attorney General Reno had the sole authority to determine the boy's custody. After exhaustive negotiations proved unfruitful, Reno set a mid-April deadline for the family to turn the child over to federal authorities, who would transfer him to his father's custody. When the deadline passed, federal agents stormed the González home, with one eyewitness reporting that Elián "cried and seemed terrified as all around him people screamed, cursed and fought against a line of federal agents who formed a wall with shields and automatic weapons as a cloud of tear gas and pepper spray wafted down the street." The operation took three minutes, but the lasting media impression was a photograph of a helmeted federal marshal in body armor pointing an automatic rifle at a man holding a bewildered Elián, who was being pulled from the closet where he had been hiding. The boy was flown immediately to Washington and reunited with his waiting father, but they could not return to Cuba before the legal wrangling was over—only in late June did the Supreme Court decline to hear the case, allowing Elián to go home to a hero's welcome.[146]

In the history of U.S.-Cuban relations, 2000 will always be the year of Elián, but 2000 was also the year the United States granted permanent normal trade relations to China, which was not a democracy and, like Cuba, stood accused of the repression of dissidents. Supporters of trade with China nonetheless argued that change was more likely to occur with engagement than with isolation, and no one made this point more eloquently than the House majority leader, Richard Armey, a Texas Republican: "Free and open trade is not only the best way to make China a free and open nation, but it may be the only way." He continued, addressing the speaker of the House, "A market is simply an arena in which there is a sharing of information about market transactions, informations about desires, wants, hopes and dreams, and economic conditions. But, Mr. Speaker, one cannot share that information about economics without also sharing information about culture, politics, religion, and values. Information, Mr. Speaker, is the life blood of a market. It is also poison to dictators, because dictators know that it is the truth that will set one free."[147] Coming soon after the Warner-Dodd call for a commission to rethink U.S. policy toward Cuba, Armey's remarks highlighted a severe intellectual schism within the Republican Party, which some members of Congress attempted to close by arguing that Cuba was special—the embargo "has not worked the way it should have worked because we have not been turning the screws on him and screwing him down and putting pressure on him, so that his people will rise up and throw him out." After all, continued Republican whip Tom DeLay, Cuba "is not Eastern Europe, this is not the Soviet Union, this is a tiny island."

"It finally happened," replied New York Representative José Serrano, born on an even-smaller Caribbean island, Puerto Rico. "The last speaker let the cat out of the bag. Cuba is a small island, not a large European country. That is the problem. If it was a large European country or an Asian country, he would be lobbying, as he did, for free trade with Cuba, because he was the chief sponsor of lobbying on behalf of President Clinton for free trade with China. But he said it. Cuba is a small island, and for 41 years, we have been saying, you are a small island, you are insignificant, you speak another language, we are going to step all over you." "It was never about what was right," Serrano concluded, "it was about Cuba being a small little island, and China being a big country."[148]

But Cuba was not the only country whose embargo legislators were targeting, and Cuba's purchasing power was hardly insignificant when combined with that of Iran, Libya, North Korea, and Syria, with whom trade in food and medicine would also have been authorized under Senator Ashcroft's proposed Food and Medicine for the World Act. A conciliatory Senator Helms served as a bellwether when his Committee on Foreign Relations reconsidered the measure in March 2000, conceding that Ashcroft's bill "represents the will of the Senate, and indeed of this committee's membership. Last summer 70 Senators opposed tabling it." Helms stipulated only that sales be for cash, and the Senate voted its approval.[149]

The House struggled to reach a similar agreement. In an appropriations subcommittee, a Republican representing eastern Washington's grain producers, George Nethercutt Jr., added a provision lifting the embargo on food and medicine, and he even overcame Republican whip Tom DeLay's staunch opposition in the full committee markup, when DeLay's attempt to strip the measure was defeated, 35–24. Then the Republican whip began behind-the-scenes maneuvering to remove Nethercutt's proposal without a vote, while antiembargo House members turned their attention to a second bill, this one making appropriations for the Department of the Treasury, whose Office of Foreign Assets Control had primary responsibility for administering the Trading with the Enemy Act. Three separate amendments were proposed during the July floor debate—one by Representative Rangel stipulating that no money could be used to enforce any part of the embargo; a second by Representative Mark Sanford, a libertarian-conservative South Carolina Republican, stipulating that no funds could be used to enforce the travel ban; and a third by Representative Jerry Moran, a conservative Kansas Republican, stipulating that no funds could be used to enforce the embargo on sales of food and medicine.

The fascinating floor debate pitted this unlikely trio against the three Cuban American representatives in the House, Díaz-Balart, Menéndez, and Ros-Lehtinen. Sanford reminded his listeners that he had voted for the Helms-Burton Act, but now, four years later, he said aloud what a clear majority had come to believe: "What we need to get away from in our current national policy is having three congressional districts drive our policy toward Cuba." Next up was Menéndez, whose assignment was to counter Moran's food and medicine proposal: Menéndez argued that it would allow

U.S. producers to sell "chemicals that can be used for weaponry, including bombs, biological and chemical weaponry." Moran replied that his proposal did nothing of the kind. Then Ros-Lehtinen jumped in with a completely different assertion: the Cuban government would buy the food and medicine and sell it to third countries "so that it can further increase its war chest, a war chest which it uses to torture, to harass, to intimidate and to oppress the Cuban people." She failed to explain why a third country would not buy directly from the United States to avoid a Cuban markup, returning instead to the argument she often used to criticize any weakening of the embargo: Moran's proposal "sends the signal that the United States will no longer serve as a moral compass." Moran did not respond; instead, he pointed out that "not one step of progress has been made toward sanction relief and reform that we have been promising our farmers in Kansas." Opening new markets, he insisted, had great importance "to farmers and ranchers who are trying to eke out a living."

The House then voted on all three measures. Rangel's proposal to forbid enforcement of any part of the embargo was defeated, 241–174, but Sanford's travel proposal was approved by a surprisingly wide margin, 232–186, and Moran's food and medicine amendment garnered even greater support, passing 301–116.[150] While these votes made a major statement about House sentiment, they would clearly constitute bad policy: the Sanford and Moran amendments simply stated that no money could be used to enforce the ban on travel and on sales of food and medicine during the upcoming fiscal year—that is, travel and sales of food and medicine would continue to be illegal, but the law would not be enforced during the 2001 fiscal year. Such provisions opened a Pandora's box that few wanted to face, and with no comparable proposal in the Senate's version of the Treasury appropriations bill, the Moran and Sanford amendments were dropped in conference.

These three House votes on the Treasury bill occurred on the same day that the Senate approved the Agriculture appropriations bill containing Ashcroft's amendment lifting the embargo on sales of food and medicine, and Representatives DeLay and Nethercutt soon thereafter reached an agreement on the House version. The Trade Sanctions Reform and Export Enhancement Act of 2000 that emerged from conference committee allowed exports of food and medicine to any embargoed country, but in the single case of Cuba it prohibited U.S. public or private financing.[151]

On balance, the opponents of trade embargos walked away with a bit more than half a loaf: the new law required the president to terminate all unilateral bans on food and medical exports, prohibited new embargos without congressional agreement, and, unlike other appropriations measures, did not expire at the end of the fiscal year, since it was passed as a separate law embedded in an appropriation measure. But embargo opponents were disappointed by the constraints on sales to Cuba; in addition to the ban on private or public financing, the new law required exporters to apply for a general license that would be valid for one year only and to notify the Department of Commerce of each sale, giving the department eleven days to deny permission for the shipment. "The cash only or third-country financing basis will unnecessarily restrict the sales of food and medicine to Cuba," argued Illinois senator Richard Durbin, who did not realize that the law would be interpreted to mean that only food could be exported under the new regulations; specific licenses and end-use monitoring would still be required for each shipment of medicine or medical equipment. Senator Dodd promised that "next year I will be back in this Chamber seeking to put our relations with the Cuban people on the same footing as those of other peoples around the world," but his threat rang hollow.[152] Three weeks later, a Republican would win the White House, and with the nation's farmers now partially placated, Dodd undoubtedly understood that the moment for change had passed.

OVERALL, THE MOST STRIKING FEATURE of President Clinton's second-term policy was how thoroughly Cuba was ignored. Normal exchanges certainly occurred between the two governments, and the shadowy interlocutor's role played by New Mexico's Bill Richardson remains unexplored, but Cuba's presence was clearly negligible. That was understandable—why bother to engage Cuba? It had been nothing but trouble for the previous eight administrations, it was now doing little to attract U.S. attention, and a White House move in any direction would trigger the vociferous opposition of some powerful group. The administration's "Cuba" policy thus became a function of negotiations with third parties—with the Europeans over Helms-Burton, with the Cuban American community over Elián, with agribusiness over exports, and with U.S. liberals over travel and medical exports. Those who pushed hard enough got a bit of what they wanted—except for those who wanted Elián to stay in the United States, of course, but only because he could not be divided into two parts. In all this, Cuba was a bystander.

Bill Clinton never stopped voicing his hope for a better U.S.-Cuban relationship, however. Early in his first term, he had expressed a desire for

Cubans to "go into the 21st century a free people in partnership with us," and at the time of the Pope's visit, the president had commented that "nobody in the world would be happier than me to see a change in Cuba and a change in our policy before I leave office." The opening of his presidential archives will provide insight into how (and whether) this wishful thinking fit into the debates over policy; for now, the only evidence is the president's regular statements of disappointment and his equally frequent assertions that the fault was Cuba's: "They have blown every conceivable opportunity to get closer to the United States," he said a few days into the twenty-first century, repeating his belief that Cuba's principal leader simply did not want friendly relations. "Every time we do something, Castro shoots planes down and kills people illegally, or puts people in jail because they say something he doesn't like. And I almost think he doesn't want us to lift the embargo, because it provides him with an excuse for the failures, the economic failures of his administration."[153]

And so President Clinton ended his eight-year tenure with one final expression of what appeared to be genuine disappointment: "I wish we could have done better," but Fidel Castro apparently was not going to retire, as Helms-Burton mandated, nor was he going to let Cuba become a convert to liberal democracy, let alone to free-market economics, as Helms-Burton also required. So that was that. The president held out only one hope: Castro, he said, "can't last forever. Nobody lives forever."[154]

We're the only hope in Cuba.
—*James Cason, Chief of Mission, Havana, 2005*

14

MORE BLESSINGS OF LIBERTY THE GEORGE W. BUSH ADMINISTRATION

Sending Elián González back to Cuba with his father had been the right thing to do, Bill Clinton wrote in his memoir, but "I was still concerned that it could cost Al Gore Florida in November." It probably did. Anyone who had followed Elián's prolonged ordeal could reasonably conclude that his return had aroused an intense sense of betrayal in Little Havana, and when the dust settled in 2000, the Democrats had lost the state by 537 votes, handing all of Florida's twenty-five electoral votes to the Republicans and giving George W. Bush the presidency with a five-vote electoral college margin. Fidel Castro attributed the narrow Republican victory to the "decisive role played by the Cuban-American terrorist mafia," and—wording aside—everyone agreed. If only a handful of Florida's 800,000 Cuban Americans had chosen Gore rather than Bush, the Democrat would have been moving into the White House.[1]

Less certain is whether a few hundred more votes for the Democrats would have led to a different policy toward Cuba, since nothing in the vice president's record indicated an interest in doing anything different from what George W. Bush was now preparing to do. "The chickens are coming home to roost," Gore had told Floridians in 1993, just as Cuba's economy was hitting rock bottom. "There are tremendous opportunities in Cuba if they can just get rid of this dictator." He repeated himself on the campaign trail seven years later: "I'm a hardliner on Castro," he assured an October audience; "I do not favor any opening to the Castro government."[2] Bush took an identical position, and his party's platform adopted what his father and then President Clinton had already turned into a bipartisan Cuba policy: "a continued effort to promote freedom and democracy."[3]

President-elect Bush clearly owed a debt to Cuban Americans, and Fidel Castro warned that the island could become the target of "the hatred of the most extremist and reactionary sectors, now euphoric over the ascent to power of a new government to which they maintain such strong ties."[4] Strong they were. One immediate payoff was the appointment of several Cuban Americans to Cuba-related posts, with Washington lobbyist Otto Reich nominated to be assistant secretary of state for Western Hemisphere affairs, career diplomat Lino Gutiérrez named Reich's deputy assistant secretary, army colonel Emilio González given the Caribbean/Central America portfolio on the National Security Council staff, Adolfo Franco named administrator for Latin America of the U.S. Agency for International Development (AID), and Mauricio Tamargo appointed chair of the Foreign Claims Settlement Commission. All had migrated to the United States as children or adolescents, as had Mel Martínez, a Pedro Pan who became secretary of housing and urban development, the first Cuban American to hold a cabinet post. All of these men had deep ties to the anti-Castro world—Colonel González spoke for most if not all the appointees when he remarked, "I'm about as involved in South Florida and the Cuban-American community as you can get."[5]

Reich was the only appointee to provoke a controversy. "I hope that the administration of George W. Bush can find another candidate for this job," wrote Nobel prize winner Oscar Arias, the former president of Costa Rica. Arias complained that Reich had worked to undermine Central American peace efforts during the Reagan years, when, as director of the State Department's scandal-plagued Office of Public Diplomacy, he was repeatedly accused of fabricating administration-friendly news. A subsequent investigation by the comptroller general confirmed that Reich's office "engaged in prohibited, covert propaganda activities designed to influence the media," but these were minor peccadilloes when compared to the concurrent Iran-contra investigation, and Reich had escaped prosecution.[6]

Saddled with this baggage, Reich now sought Senate confirmation as the new administration's principal Latin Americanist. The election had left the upper chamber deadlocked, fifty to fifty, with Vice President Richard

Cheney slated to play the role of tiebreaker, but Vermont Republican James Jeffords announced that he would become an independent and vote with the Democrats, and with that Joseph Biden replaced Jesse Helms as chair of the Senate Committee on Foreign Relations, while Christopher Dodd, one of Reich's strongest critics from the Reagan years, took over the subcommittee that would have first crack at Reich's nomination. Firmly convinced that the nominee was a dishonest conniver, Senate Democrats refused to grant Reich a hearing, let alone a vote, so he had to settle for a recess appointment when the Senate took its 2001 winter break. That appointment automatically expired when Congress adjourned in late 2002, and the administration subsequently created a new position that did not require Senate confirmation—special envoy for Western Hemisphere initiatives—which Reich occupied until mid-2004.

During his three years on the federal payroll, Reich focused almost exclusively on Cuba, with one central message: "We have made—and will stand by—a moral, political, and legal commitment to promote a rapid, peaceful transition to democracy." His replacement as assistant secretary of state, Roger Noriega, a Kansas-born Mexican American who had served as a staff member on Jesse Helms's Committee on Foreign Relations, emphasized that this policy would not be passive: "We intend to help create the conditions that will bring to an end the hemisphere's only totalitarian government."[7]

The task of overseeing these midlevel officials was handed to Colin Powell, a retired four-star general and onetime presidential hopeful whose nomination as secretary of state was broadly praised as a sign of moderation. Powell had had almost no exposure to Latin America, however, and his only comment about the region during his confirmation hearing was a throwaway line avowing an interest in the "500 million people who live in this wonderful hemisphere of ours." But he had already revealed his view about Cuba: on a page of predictions jotted down a decade earlier, just as the Cold War was ending, he had written, "Cuba isolated, irrelevant." Now, at his confirmation hearing, Powell took repeated jabs at Fidel Castro as "an aging starlet" and "that relic in Cuba" while assuring Senator Helms that "it is President Bush's intention to keep the sanctions in place." Castro, Powell said, was "living in a time warp, and we should do nothing that encourages him or gives him the wherewithal to stay any longer."[8] But there was no hint that the new secretary of state wanted to spend either time or political capital on the island.

The senior officials joining Powell on the State Department's seventh floor may have dismissed Cuba as irrelevant, especially after the attention-riveting terrorist attacks on 11 September, but the president's domestic political advisers took a different view. While winning in the Electoral College, George Bush had lost the popular vote, the Republicans had suffered a net loss of four seats in the Senate and two in the House, and Florida's fickle voters seemed to be turning from vivid red to light pink.[9] The 2000 census indicated that two-thirds (833,120) of the nation's 1,254,439 Cuban Americans lived in Florida. That state's elections board did not collect voter registration about country of origin (anyone with a Latin American background was classified as "Hispanic"), but the best estimates held that roughly 425,000 Cuban Americans were registered to vote, making them 4 percent of Florida's 10.8 million registered voters. Of these Cuban American voters, specialists in South Florida politics estimated that perhaps 80 percent had voted Republican in 2000, and Bush would probably need to capture the same proportion to win reelection in 2004.[10]

The result of these calculations was obvious: after the 2000 election, Cuban Americans were handed U.S. policy toward Cuba in the same way that agricultural interests have traditionally received U.S. farm policy—not unchecked, of course, but allowed to go one step beyond the high-level lobbying access that Cuban immigrants had earned after two decades of generous campaign contributions and solid bloc voting. Cuban Americans were now permitted to place their hands directly on the levers of power, and while the political beliefs of the Cuban American community were becoming increasingly diverse, such was not the case for the conservatives appointed by President Bush. They had always dreamed of overthrowing Cuba's revolutionary government, and they were now positioned to attack relentlessly.

Standing between them and the Castro government were the domestic political groups pursuing the opposite goal of ending the embargo. This meant that the new Bush appointees would have to wage a two-front campaign, one offensive to make life as difficult as possible for the Cuban government, and the other defensive and to thwart any effort to weaken the embargo. The second front was located on Capitol Hill, where the congressional staffer who had cobbled together the Helms-Burton Act warned fellow conservatives that "Congress led the effort to strengthen the embargo and is now, slowly but surely, undoing it." Buoyed by their recent victory opening the door to sales of food and medicine, in 2001 the same anti-embargo groups once again swung into action, and Congress had barely assembled before the legislative hopper was filled with no fewer than eleven proposals, all with embargo-relaxing titles such as the Free Trade with Cuba Act.[11] Liberals were responsible for most of these proposals, but the same agribusiness organizations that had championed sales of food and medicine in 2000 were also gearing up for further attacks on barriers to trade, and especially ominous was the evidence of support from conservative groups, including the Texas state legislature, which waited only four months after its favorite son's inauguration to pass a resolution asking Congress to remove restrictions on trade and travel, noting that sanctions "hinder Texas' export of agricultural and food products."[12] President Bush did not agree, but he did argue in his first State of the Union address that "selling into new markets creates new jobs," and other conservatives were now advancing the familiar Track 2 argument. In the view of the right-leaning Cato Institute, for example, "the best way of achieving reform in Cuba is through engagement," including "the revocation of all legislation currently constituting the economic embargo." Calling the embargo's legislative centerpiece "one of the most ill-advised policies of the United States," a second Cato report argued that the Helms-Burton Act had "isolated ordinary Cubans from the influence of American ideas, and strengthened the hand of the very government the policy was supposed to undermine."[13]

In 2000 the Trade Sanctions Reform and Export Enhancement Act (TSRA) had nudged open the door to several markets previously closed to U.S. farmers, but pro-embargo legislators had made Cuban purchases unlikely by obliging Cuba and only Cuba to pay in cash.[14] Thus, while the TSRA granted Cuba access to U.S. food at a huge potential savings in shipping costs, the cash-only restriction plus licensing paperwork made sales difficult, and the Cuban government had indicated that it had no intention of buying U.S. food as long as the TSRA contained a restriction on financing.[15]

In late 2001, therefore, a group of farm-state senators inserted into the 2002 farm bill a measure to repeal the prohibition on credit sales.[16] Realizing that the provision would pass in an up-or-down vote, the administration asked New Hampshire's conservative senator Robert Smith to propose one amendment allowing repeal only after the president had certified that Cuba was not involved in acts of international terrorism, and New Jersey's Robert Torricelli proposed a second amendment allowing repeal only after the Cuban government had returned all convicted U.S. felons living in Cuba. Rejecting both proposed amendments by an overwhelming margin, 61–33, senators then approved repeal of the prohibition on private financing by voice vote, but the House version of the farm bill contained no such provision, and Republican leaders stripped the Senate measure from the bill.[17]

As this was occurring in Washington, Cuba was backing away from its early refusal to purchase U.S. food: declining an offer of aid after an uncommonly destructive hurricane in late 2001, the Castro government instead asked to purchase food under expedited procedures. Having offered to help, the Bush administration could hardly refuse this request, and negotiations were soon under way between Cuba and several major U.S. exporters. The year ended with a boatload of poultry and corn sailing into Havana's harbor, the first significant trade with Cuba since 1963.

Now the camel's nose was inside the tent, and it clearly liked what it smelled—"It's past time to lift the embargo," read a *Wall Street Journal* editorial, published just as Congress began considering the 2002 farm bill, and a few days later the foreign trade subcommittee of the Senate Committee on Commerce held its first-ever hearing on U.S. policy toward Cuba. "Our government is standing in the way of a vast new market for Missouri farmers," complained Democratic senator Jean Carnahan, focusing again on the prohibition of private financing. North Dakota Democrat Byron Dorgan echoed those sentiments: "We have a good many American farmers who need to find a foreign home for their product," and more was at stake than profits: "I think poor, sick, and hungry people in Cuba are the victims of these policies, and I personally believe that it is immoral to use food as a weapon."[18]

Dorgan's reference to the sick came from the TSRA's linkage of food and medicine, and in 2002 this linkage again helped forge a coalition between agribusiness and health-focused humanitarian groups such as the Americans for Humanitarian Trade with Cuba, formed in 1998 in response to reports about deteriorating medical conditions in Cuban hospitals. The group united twenty-three state affiliates and a heavy-hitting advisory council that included banker/philanthropist David Rockefeller, former U.S. trade representative Carla Hills, former secretary of defense Frank Carlucci, former Federal Reserve chair Paul Volker, and former surgeon general Julius Richmond.

And so, just as the commerce committee was holding its food hearing in May, a foreign relations subcommittee was preparing a medicine hearing for June, where one witness after another condemned the administration's efforts to deter trade in medicine and medical knowledge. One research psychiatrist spoke of his experience with Cuban doctors, with whom "I have spent many hours at psychiatric hospitals viewing patients who were suffering from side effects of older-generation antidepressant and antipsychotic drugs, because they didn't have access to the newer drugs with a more benign side-effect profile." Like Senator Dorgan, the physician considered this state of affairs immoral, but he also saw it as pigheaded: "We are told that we just 'need to keep the pressure on a little longer.' As a scientist, I would never do the same experiment for forty years if it didn't work."[19] Other witnesses emphasized that medicine was a two-way street, and the United States might benefit from Cuban advances in fighting sickle cell disease and meningitis and in developing drugs for lowering cholesterol and inhibiting clotting; another witness noted that Cuba would also be an ideal site for cooperative clinical trials with U.S. pharmaceutical companies, since it had one of the world's most comprehensive data sets from which to select participant pools.

Had this hearing been held a few years earlier, these antiembargo witnesses would have been followed by a vigorous rebuttal from Jorge Mas Canosa or another senior representative of the Cuban American National Foundation, but the light from CANF's candle was now flickering dimly. The most obvious problem was that Mas Canosa's son had taken over as CANF's chair, and the young Jorge Mas Santos clearly lacked his father's dominating personality. Some hard-liners also felt that the foundation seemed to be turning soft under Mas Santos's leadership. CANF spokeswoman and board member Ninoska Pérez Castellón offered this principal complaint when she resigned in mid-2001, and twenty more board members followed her out the door.

The foundation's public image had also been severely damaged in 1998, the year after Mas Canosa's death, when acknowledged terrorist Luis Posada Carriles claimed that CANF had funded his activities, a charge that arose again in 2006 when another former board member, José Llama, one of several Cuban Americans arrested in Puerto Rico in 1997 for plotting to murder Fidel Castro, began publicly demanding that CANF repay the $1.4 million it had borrowed from him in the mid-1990s to help finance the purchase of a fast boat and related supplies to attack Cuban targets. Sandwiched in between the resignations and this terrorism accusation was the mid-2003 resignation of CANF's executive vice president and Washington representative, Dennis Hays, who was said to be upset by the foundation's attack on the Bush administration's decision to return a group of twelve Cuban rafters but may have been at least equally dismayed by a dramatically reduced budget. CANF's principal asset was the common stock of MasTec, the company created by Jorge Mas Canosa, and the value of its shares had plummeted from fifty-two dollars at the time of his death to eight dollars at the time of Hays's resignation, when the foundation's Washington office — a handsome Jefferson Place townhouse across Lafayette Square from the White House — was up for sale.

CANF's problems were also exacerbated significantly by a growing diversification among Cuban Americans, as illustrated by an unexpected query during a question-and-answer session President Bush held in Southern California in 2006: A middle-aged Cuban American began with the comment that "coming to this great land is the best thing that has ever happened to me," but then asked, "I would like to go to Cuba . . . and I don't understand, how can we trade with Vietnam — we lost over 50,000 Americans there — how can we trade with Communist China [and] we can't even go to Cuba?"[20] This question was posed in California, not Miami, where a 2003 poll indicted that only 34 percent of Cuban Americans would vote for a candidate who proposed easing the embargo. But even that minority was significantly larger than it would have been a few years earlier, and the growing diversification of Cuban American opinion was indicated by the 62 percent of Miami's Cuban Americans who thought it was more important to spend money on improving the quality of their lives in the United States than on overthrowing the Castro government. That number rose to 72 percent among Cuban Americans below the age of forty-five.[21]

With CANF weakening and Cuban Americans showing signs of spreading out across the political spectrum, the hard-line anti-Castro position would now have to be defended primarily by Cuban Americans holding appointments in the executive branch and by the three Cuban American members of Congress. They had their hands full in 2002, which was proving to be a banner year for Cuba travel by their colleagues, nearly all of whom returned with a conciliatory attitude. The first to go were Republican senators Arlen Specter and Lincoln Chafee, and Specter's report to the Senate argued that U.S. policy "has tended to make, if not quite a martyr, at least a sympathetic person of President Castro." (And, he added, Castro's authoritarian rule was unexceptional; in Latin America, dictatorship "is just a way of life.") After Specter came six House Democrats, including moderate Vic Snyder from rice- and pork-growing Arkansas, who returned with a photo of his group alongside Cubans at a Matanzas church. Holding up the photo on the House floor, he asked, "Is their opportunity for freedom increased by having Americans never see them, by having Americans never come to their church and visit with them and talk about America?" In April, twenty-four Californians arrived in a delegation led by Senator Barbara Boxer, who now seemed more determined than ever to promote food exports. When the administration claimed that none of the food reached everyday Cubans, she responded with a testy, "Castro can't eat all the food. OK?"[22]

Then came former President Jimmy Carter, whose six-day visit in May 2002 was highlighted by a speech criticizing the embargo because it "freezes the existing impasse, induces anger and resentment, restricts the freedoms of U.S. citizens, and makes it difficult for us to exchange ideas and respect." At a press conference just before leaving for Havana, the former president remarked that "an American company should have the right to visit any place on earth and the right to trade with any other purchaser and supplier on earth." The administration's response came six days later, when President Bush flew to Miami to celebrate the one hundredth anniversary of Cuban independence. Calling Fidel Castro "a relic from another era," he promised to continue the embargo "until Cuba's government shows real reform."[23]

Bush's wet blanket did nothing to stop the parade of visits by U.S. agribusiness, including a delegation led by North Dakota's Republican governor, John Hoeven, that left Havana only hours before two more members of Congress arrived with a delegation featuring a former secretary of agriculture and another set of U.S. food exporters and overlapped with a visit by Tampa mayor Richard Greco, who was shepherding fifteen local business leaders intent on convincing Cubans to use the city's port for food shipments. All of these visits constituted but a prelude to the main event: a privately organized food exhibition in Havana in September featuring 933 representatives of 288 U.S. vendors from thirty-three states, Puerto Rico, and the District of Columbia, plus the agricultural commissioners from ten states, all eager to tap into the Cuban market. To attract would-be customers to their booths, egg marketer Radlo Foods brought along the world's fastest omelet maker (thirty seconds), the California Raisin Marketing Board brought along its Dancing Raisins, and Minnesota agroexporters brought along the state's governor, former professional wrestler Jesse "The Body" Ventura. Fidel Castro was among the crowd of Cuban visitors, who were especially deep around the booths handing out samples of Skippy peanut butter, Spam, Jell-O, and Philadelphia cream cheese—a lamentable commentary on revolutionary taste. In the end, more than 70 U.S. firms signed more than ninety-two million dollars in sales contracts. On her flight home with vendors who had sold 190 tons of apples and a million pounds of turkey, North Carolina's agriculture commissioner drafted a never-published op-ed article for the state's newspapers: "With our economy on the skids, state budgets in shambles and our farmers going bankrupt, does it make any sense to continue a 40-year-old embargo with Cuba when there is so much to be gained by both countries? I don't think so."[24]

All of this activity led to a ramping-up of the debate heard a year earlier, but the 2002 effort to end the restrictions on agricultural sales differed in its indirect approach: instead of proposing an outright repeal of the TSRA prohibition of credit sales, Kansas representative Jerry Moran, a conservative Republican who had helped pass the original law, tried to achieve the same end by returning to the Clinton-era tactic of amending the Treasury appropriations bill to forbid the use of funds to enforce the ban on credit sales. Ignoring President Bush's promise to veto any such measure, the House approved Moran's amendment by voice vote, but there the ball stopped rolling; final consideration was delayed by a variety of unrelated election-year disputes, and Congress, eager to hit the campaign trail, adjourned after passing a stopgap continuing resolution.[25] Two of the strongest advocates of the embargo were heading out the door permanently (Jesse Helms retired; Robert Torricelli withdrew from his reelection campaign because of an influence-peddling scandal), but the November off-year election gave Republicans a noticeable boost—two additional seats in the Senate and with them control of the upper chamber, and eight additional seats in the House, where the GOP now had a comfortable twenty-four-seat advantage.[*] In February 2003, Moran's initiative was quietly removed from that year's omnibus spending bill.

The battle immediately resumed, with Senator Max Baucus from wheat-growing Montana seeking to repeal the prohibition on financing agricultural exports.[26] His proposal was only the most ambitious of several, but hope for passage had been dampened not only by the election results but also, five months later, by Cuba's arrest of seventy-five dissidents. In the end, the only relaxation proposal to gain full Senate approval in 2003 was a narrowly focused bill granting a general license for travel to sell U.S. agricultural and medical products, and even that modest measure was quietly dropped in conference. In 2004, two similar measures met similar fates.[27]

---

[*]Congress's Cuban American ranks grew from three to four with the election of Mario Diáz-Balart, brother of Lincoln, who captured one of the two additional House seats allotted to Florida after the 2000 census. In 2004, Florida's Mel Martínez won election to the Senate, where he was joined in 2006 by New Jersey's Robert Menéndez. Martínez yielded his House seat to another Cuban American, Albio Sires.

ALONGSIDE FOOD, a parallel struggle was occurring over travel, which President Clinton had dramatically liberalized in January 1999. "For a country that is supposed to be suffering a near-total quarantine, Cuba fairly hums with American voices," reported the conservative Cato Institute in 2001. It was easy to retighten what Clinton had relaxed, however, and stricter enforcement began immediately after Bush took office, with Treasury's Office of Foreign Assets Control (OFAC) issuing 766 pre-penalty notices in 2001, a sharp increase from the 188 issued during President Clinton's final year in office. By this time, however, most of those involved knew that these notices could safely be ignored: for a decade, OFAC had been mailing them and then following up a few months later with default penalty notices informing travelers of their fines. At that point, targeted travelers merely had to demand hearings, and then they could forget about the entire matter— the case would be suspended indefinitely since OFAC had no administrative judges to hold hearings. The Bush administration promptly hired three judges and announced that suspended cases were being reactivated. The Customs Service began stationing special inspectors at Canadian airports to identify travelers with U.S. passports arriving from Cuba, and Treasury began dragging its feet on licensing qualified travel, with the Center for Constitutional Rights complaining about OFAC's "deliberate strategy of discouraging the filing of license applications [by] incessantly demanding detailed information concerning travel itineraries and the bona fides of the organizations sponsoring trips and their travelers, and for sitting on this information once it is provided."[28]

With this foot-dragging, with stepped-up enforcement, and with legal travel already something of an ordeal—charter flights with 5:00 A.M. check-ins, for example—would-be travelers turned to Congress for relief. The House had already attempted to relax enforcement in 2001, prodded by an unlikely new member, first-term Arizona Republican Jeff Flake, a Goldwater conservative who combined libertarian sentiments with an internationalist outlook gained by serving as a Mormon missionary in southern Africa. Like many conservatives, he enthusiastically endorsed free trade, and like all libertarians he agreed with the Supreme Court's 1964 view that "freedom of movement is the very essence of our free society. . . . Once the right to travel is curtailed, all other rights suffer." With this Court decision in hand, Flake argued that "it is a fundamental right of every American to travel. Every one of us ought to have the right to go to Cuba to see what a mess Fidel Castro has made of that island," and in early 2001 he proposed to end enforcement of the travel ban. His proposal passed by a substantial margin, 240–186, but immediately after the 11 September attacks, Senator Byron Dorgan, the champion of agricultural sales, announced that he would withdraw a Senate companion to Flake's proposal.[29]

At about this time a Washington consulting firm released a study estimating the economic impact of lifting travel restrictions on the U.S. economy: an increase in gross domestic product by as much as $1.6 billion and between sixteen thousand and twenty-three thousand new jobs—plus, of course, the profits that come from such growth. Citing these economic incentives and helped by former president Jimmy Carter, who criticized the travel ban as "an imposition on the human rights of American citizens," Flake tried again in 2002.[30]

President Bush responded by pledging to veto any attempt to lift the ban, but Congress was not deterred. Flake's proposal passed by an impressive margin (ninety-five votes compared to fifty-four a year earlier), and this time the Senate also took up the issue with a hearing, where witness after witness characterized OFAC as the bureaucracy from hell. One told of being fined seventy-five hundred dollars for a one-day trip to bury his parents' ashes on the grounds of the Pentecostal church where they had been missionaries in the 1950s. Another, a seventy-five-year-old retired Wisconsin schoolteacher, told of joining a Canadian cycling group: "They assured me that it was perfectly legal for Americans to travel" but not to spend money in Cuba. She therefore paid the Canadian group, and "it would not have occurred to me to tell anything other than the truth," answering "Cuba" when a U.S. Customs officer asked where she had been.

> To my surprise, this answer set the Customs agent into a rage. She yelled as she searched my luggage and was unable to find any purchases. . . . Then she went into a full-scale tirade. She demanded that I remove my fanny pack and show its contents all over the counter. She snatched my passport from a pile of my belongings strewn on the counter, shouted at me to pick up my belongings, and left to make a photocopy. When she returned, she handed me my passport and warned me with a touch of glee, "You'll be hearing from the Treasury Department."

Her seventy-five-hundred-dollar default penalty notice arrived in the mail a year later.[31]

Such stories boiled the blood of libertarians such as Jeff Flake, and it did not help that OFAC's petulant director huffed back with a Washington-bureaucrat response: "Well, I'm certainly sorry that someone is dissatisfied." The travel restrictions also bothered liberals, of course, and displeased farm-state moderates such as Senator Dorgan, whose constituents needed to make sales calls, and he now added the post-9/11 complaint that "at a time when we are worried about terrorism, we have people down at the Treasury Department who are chasing retired school teachers."[32] The Senate Appropriations Committee promptly reported a Treasury bill that included a provision similar but not identical to Flake's House amendment, but there the effort ended. In 2002, the Senate never passed a Treasury appropriation for the upcoming fiscal year; instead, it recessed to wage the off-year election campaign, and just as it had deleted Representative Moran's amendment repealing the prohibition on private financing of agricultural sales, the new Congress stripped Flake's travel amendment from the omnibus fiscal 2003 measure it approved in February.

In early 2003 the White House seized the initiative, easing restrictions for Cuban Americans while tightening them for others. Specifically, the definition of a "close relative" who could be visited once a year was expanded to include all relatives, whether by blood, marriage, or adoption, within three degrees of relationship with the traveler.[33] At the same time, licenses would no longer be issued for people-to-people educational exchanges, the most common form of travel by non–Cuban Americans, ending the popular travel tours sponsored by hundreds of nonprofits such as the Metropolitan Museum of Art and the National Trust for Historic Preservation and especially by college alumni associations.

Capitol Hill immediately responded. Senator Baucus had already introduced a repeal of the travel ban as part of his United States–Cuba Trade Act, and Wyoming Republican senator Michael Enzi, a libertarian-conservative cut from the same bolt of cloth as Flake, submitted his Freedom to Travel to Cuba Act, which would prohibit the president from regulating travel to Cuba. The House entered the debate a few days later, when Flake submitted a bill whose purpose was clear from its title—the Export Freedom to Cuba Act contained travel language identical to Enzi's.[34]

Enzi's proposal received a hearing from the Committee on Foreign Relations, where Assistant Secretary of State Roger Noriega promised a presidential veto. The committee nonetheless gave its approval by an unexpectedly large margin, 13–5, but the chamber's Republican leaders made it clear that they would refuse to schedule a vote on this or any other standalone embargo-relaxing measure, so the bill's proponents turned to their fallback option—another amendment to the Treasury appropriations bill, which had to be voted on to keep the department operating: the House voted 227–188 to accept an amendment prohibiting enforcement of the travel ban, this time by a reduced thirty-nine-vote margin, reflecting dismay over Cuba's recent arrest of the seventy-five dissidents. Lamenting the arrests, Flake agreed that "it's time to get tough with Cuba. And there's no better way to get tough than to have Americans export their freedom and values there." His was a predictable Track 2 argument; the surprise came from the Senate, which had avoided a vote during the administration's first two years. Indeed, the full Senate had not voted on travel to Cuba since mid-1999, when it had voted 55–43 to table Christopher Dodd's proposal to end the travel ban. Now, in 2003, the Senate did an about-face, defeating a motion to table the travel relaxation by a 59–36 vote.[35]

All again came to naught, as Senator Baucus complained in late 2003. "When the Senate and House have approved the same amendment, there ought to be nothing for conferees to reconcile." But, he continued, "here we are with an omnibus bill that does not include our amendment." Stripping the amendment was "a blatantly political move calculated to improve [the administration's] standing with a small number of constituents in Florida."[36]

AS BAUCUS'S CHARGE SUGGESTED, the 2004 election campaign had already begun, and the Cuban American community was feeling neglected. The president had personally overseen the last two 20 May Independence Day celebrations, one on the White House lawn and the other in Miami, but Bush's 2003 Independence Day message had been nothing but a forty-second prerecorded restatement of what Bill Clinton had said a decade earlier: "My hope is for the Cuban people to soon enjoy the same freedoms and rights as we do." A few weeks later the Coast Guard had intercepted a hijacked boat in the Straits of Florida and returned the hijackers to Cuba. Enough was enough, wrote ninety-eight prominent Cuban Americans associated with the Cuban American National Foundation, complaining in an open letter to the president not simply about the hijackers' return but also about the administration's failure to upgrade Radio and TV Martí and its refusal to indict Fidel Castro for murder in the shoot down of the Brothers to the Rescue: "Current policy toward Cuba has not varied significantly from that of the previous administration."[37] The president responded by announcing the creation of the Commission for Assistance to a Free Cuba, charged with the task of drawing up a plan to hasten the end of the Castro government and then with assisting with the island's political and economic reconstruction.[38]

So began the quest for Cuban American votes in 2004. The Republi-

can platform asserted that the restrictions on trade and travel "must remain in place as long as the Cuban government refuses to hold free and
fair elections, ease its stranglehold on private enterprise, and allow the
Cuban people to organize, assemble, and speak freely." The Democrats'
much milder platform supported a Track 2 approach: "effective and
peaceful strategies to end the Castro regime as soon as possible," including "a policy of principled travel to Cuba that promotes family unity and
people-to-people contacts through educational and cultural exchanges."
The Democrats' candidate, Massachusetts senator John Kerry, had called
for an end to the travel ban years earlier but said little about Cuba during
the 2004 campaign.[39] Clearly intent on winning Florida by more than 537
votes, the president visited frequently, always promising something like
"Over the next four years I will continue to work to ensure that gift of freedom reaches the men and women of Cuba." He occasionally added a bit
more—in Tampa, for example, he said that "Fidel Castro has turned Cuba
into a major destination for sex tourism" and that his administration had
"put a strategy in place to hasten the day when no Cuban child is exploited
to finance a failed revolution." Castro used much of his 2004 26th of July
speech to refute the charge, and during his response he joined Bush in the
gutter with a discussion of the president's earlier problems with alcohol.[40]

A few months later President Bush carried Florida by 381,000 votes, winning 51 percent of the national vote to Kerry's 48 percent, while Republicans gained four seats in the Senate (giving them a 55–44 edge, with one independent) and three in the House (now 232–202, with one independent).
The outcome increased even further the difficulty of mounting an effective
challenge to the administration's trade and travel policies, although the
inconclusive Capitol Hill battle over relaxing or tightening the embargo
seemed poised to continue indefinitely. For now, four years of effort by the
forces pushing for a relaxation had yielded nothing beyond agricultural
sales, and a few days after the election, a newly confident OFAC threatened
those sales by announcing that the term "payment of cash in advance" was
being redefined from payment before delivery of the goods to payment
"prior to shipment of the goods from the port at which they are loaded."

It was a wily stratagem. "We are about to screw up a market," warned
Minnesota representative Colin Peterson at a hastily called House hearing. Peterson happened to be a Democrat, but the concern was bipartisan:
the Republican committee chair labeled the new definition "disturbing."[41]
Why get upset over a rule that simply advances payment by a few days? The
president of the Missouri Farm Bureau explained: "If Cuba purchases U.S.

agriculture goods in the manner defined within the regulation, Cuba would risk possible seizure of the product because at the time of payment, ownership is transferred to Cuba while the product is still in U.S. ports." As soon as the food belonged to Cuba, anyone with a legal claim against the Cuban government could ask a judge to seize a shipment before it left port, sell it at government auction, and hand the proceeds to the claimant. Such actions had triggered Cuba's original rationing in mid-1961, when a prepaid shipment of lard was seized to satisfy a claim, and claimants had followed the same tack twice in 2003, when two hijacked Cubana aircraft had been placed on the auction block. Understandably reluctant to expose its food to a similar risk, the head of Cuba's purchasing agency announced that he intended to cancel U.S. food purchases.[42]

The House and Senate soon added identical provisions to the Transportation-Treasury appropriations bill prohibiting the use of funds to enforce OFAC's new definition, while Senator Baucus placed a hold on the confirmation of six senior Treasury nominees until the dispute could be settled. In July, forced to weigh its priorities, the administration opted to fill the vacant positions, releasing U.S. exporters to ship their goods as soon as they had been advised by a third-country bank that payment had been received from Cuba but allowing the bank to delay passing payment to the exporter until the food arrived in Cuba.[43]

That strategy did not satisfy exporters, however, and after Democrats regained a congressional majority in 2006, several bills were introduced to ease the restrictions on agricultural exports. At the end of George W. Bush's tenure, both sides could claim that the glass was half full: for eight years, the administration had turned back every effort to ease U.S. agricultural producers' business transactions with Cuba, while U.S. farmers nonetheless used the TSRA, passed at the end of the Clinton years, to open a significant new market, as evidenced by the growth of U.S. food exports to Cuba after that date:

2000	$ 0
2001	4.6 million
2002	139.8 million
2003	248.4 million
2004	388.7 million
2005	351.4 million
2006	328.2 million
2007	440.2 million

Almost overnight, the United States had become a major source of Cuba's imported food, and everyone seemed to want a piece of the market: Louisiana governor Kathleen Blanco's delegation of farmers came home with $15 million in orders; Nebraska governor David Heineman's delegation sold $17 million in beans, wheat, and soybean meal, an amount upped to $27 million a few months later when the Nebraskans returned for a trade fair at which 171 U.S. firms signed $260 million in contracts for food and agricultural products. Governor John Balducci led one of two Maine trade delegations, the first of which pumped $10 million into the state's economy. One successful vendor commented that "this contract will help to put increased production into our newly retrofitted and automated sardine plant in Prospect Harbor, keeping much needed sardine canning jobs in Maine."[44] Nothing was more indicative of this grassroots interest than the growing number of smaller exporters who needed help finding their way through the maze of restrictions to make sales without breaking the law. Seeing this need and wanting to fill it, a Washington law firm specializing in global finance recruited a new attorney, Steven Pinter, snatching him away from a seventeen-year career at OFAC, where he had been the senior sanctions adviser.

WHILE THE SEEMINGLY interminable fights over food sales and travel were occurring in Washington, the Bush administration was spending eight full years attempting to undermine the Cuban government. Little beyond planning (and trying to get Otto Reich confirmed) had occurred during 2001, and not until a minor but telling incident in early 2002 did the public catch a glimpse of what was to come. In March 2002, the United Nations held a development summit in Monterrey, Mexico, and President Bush refused to attend if Fidel Castro was present. Hoping for a successful meeting (and himself no friend of the Cuban Revolution), Mexico's Vicente Fox telephoned to ask Castro to come early and depart quickly—"You could come on Thursday, . . . attend that lunch, even sit by me, and after this event— you have already made your speech—you go back." Castro grudgingly accepted the plan: he gave his speech, ate his lunch, and then announced, "I will not be able to stay with you any longer. A special situation created by my participation in this summit forces me to return immediately to my country." When asked about Castro's hasty departure, Bush said, "I know of no pressure placed on anybody." Fox could not imagine what the fuss was about: "He was here, he participated in the conference, and he returned to Cuba—nothing more."[45]

The matter probably would have rested there had not Mexico decided to support a resolution criticizing Cuba at the next month's meeting of the U.N. Commission on Human Rights. After the resolution passed by a narrow margin, 23–21 with 9 abstentions, a furious Castro called a press conference to lash out at the president of Uruguay, whose government had introduced the resolution, calling him an "abject Judas" for agreeing to present a resolution "conceived and hatched with Washington's help by [Mexican] Foreign Minister [Jorge] Castañeda." Clearly intent on informing Mexicans that their president had caved in to U.S. pressure, the Cuban leader then reached over and turned on a tape recorder, and there was Fox's voice on one end of the telephone line, asking Castro to behave at Monterrey and to make his visit as brief as possible.[46] No doubt Fox was embarrassed, but Castro was excluded from the discussions at Monterrey and Cuba lost in the Commission on Human Rights—just what the Bush administration wanted.

Out of the blue two weeks later came a U.S. claim that Cuba was developing biological weapons. Speaking on "Additional Threats from Weapons of Mass Destruction" only eight months after the 9/11 terrorist attacks, outspoken Undersecretary of State John Bolton announced that "the United States believes that Cuba has at least a limited offensive biological warfare research-and-development program." With that sentence he slipped Cuba into the debate stream that was leading to the U.S. invasion of Iraq.[47]

Questioned by reporters, other administration officials contradicted Bolton's assertion, with the assistant secretary of state for intelligence and research explaining that a difference existed between an "effort" and a "program" and that within the intelligence community, "all of us agree that it's not a program. . . . To have a program, you need to be able to have a factory that tests the weapon, that puts the weapon in a bomb or a shell and/or does research and development on that sort of weapons program, and has a unit within the military specifically designated for a weapons capability. That whole process of [biological weapons] warfare is called a program [and] we don't see that in Cuba." As one medical doctor explained to Congress, "We could also say that many American drug companies have the capability of bioterrorism because they are growing large amounts of bacteria or viruses, which is what the chemists are doing in order to make vaccines. To make vaccines, you need to grow bugs. . . . Just growing a lot of bugs does not make one a purveyor of bioweapons."[48]

Fidel Castro immediately denied the charge, and the Bush administration's formal statement of U.S. national security strategy, issued four months after Bolton's assertion, contained a discussion of bioweapons and bioterrorism but no mention of Cuba. (The general view within the State Department was captured by Secretary Powell's chief of staff, Lawrence Wilkerson, who later commented, "I knew John Bolton when he was Undersecretary of State. I know I cannot trust his views.") Otto Reich had already repeated the charge, however, as did his successor in 2003 and Bolton again in 2004, and each time Cuba's denials became more vigorous, moving from Castro's calm statement that "Cuba had never undertaken research or development of a single biological weapon" to an abrupt dismissal of "insane lies about biological weapons." In the end, the Bush administration announced that "it was unclear whether Cuba has an active offensive biological warfare effort now, or even had one in the past," while the less ambivalent Castro dismissed Bolton as a "super-liar" and washed his hands of the entire matter: "May they all go to hell or wherever they want to go. They're idiots."[49]

Bolton's original charge may have been designed to cast a shadow over the Cuban visit of former president Jimmy Carter, who flew into Havana a week after the accusatory speech. "I did not come here to interfere in Cuba's internal affairs," he told his University of Havana audience in a speech broadcast live on Cuban radio and television, "but to extend a hand of friendship." Speaking in Spanish, he acknowledged that "my nation is hardly perfect in human rights" but also noted that civil liberties provide U.S. citizens with the opportunity to confront their shortcomings, and he added pointedly, "That fundamental right is also guaranteed to Cubans. It is gratifying to note that Articles 63 and 88 of your constitution allow citizens to petition the National Assembly to permit a referendum to change laws if 10,000 or more citizens sign it. I am informed that such an effort, called the Varela Project, has gathered sufficient signatures and has presented such a petition to the National Assembly."[50]

Named for a progressive nineteenth-century priest, the Varela Project was an outgrowth of the Christian Liberation Movement, formed in 1988 by Catholics belonging to the Havana parish of Cerro and led by Oswaldo Payá. Despite these roots, the project was a secular movement attempting to exercise the right granted by Article 88 of Cuba's constitution, which, as Carter noted, allowed everyday citizens to petition for new laws. Two days before Carter's arrival, Payá and his colleagues had presented a petition signed by 11,020 Cubans to the National Assembly, asking for freedom to operate private businesses and freedom for political prisoners, plus a revision of existing laws to permit freedom of expression and association, including a new pluralist electoral law that, if accepted, would trigger competitive elections within a year.

The government's immediate reaction was to gather a credibility-challenging eight million signatures on its own petition asking the National Assembly to declare untouchable the central principles of Cuba's revolutionary system. One of the world's most docile assemblies promptly obliged, adding to the constitution a provision stipulating that socialism and Cuba's existing political, social, and economic institutions are "irrevocable, and Cuba will never return to capitalism."* Then it dismissed the Varela petition.

The exclusion from the Monterrey summit, the criticism by the U.N. Commission on Human Rights, the thinly veiled threat about bioterrorism, and President Carter's support of the Varela Project occurred in the context of Washington's "regime-change" rhetoric that had already led to the invasion of Afghanistan and would soon lead to the invasion of Iraq. Would Cuba be next? Havana's initial reaction to the 11 September attacks had been to volunteer emergency medical assistance and to offer U.S.-bound airliners the use of Cuban airfields as a safe haven. "The government of our country strongly repudiates and condemns the attacks," Castro said within minutes, "and hereby expresses its most heartfelt sympathies to the American people for the painful, unjustifiable loss of human lives."[51]

But on 20 September President Bush told a joint session of Congress that "every nation, in every region, now has a decision to make: either you are with us, or you are with the terrorists." Cuba had not been "with" the United States for the past four decades, of course, and Castro's response two days later indicated no willingness to change that fact. "Terrorism today is a dangerous and ethically indefensible phenomenon," he insisted, but Bush's speech was "the blueprint for the idea of a global military dictatorship imposed through brute force"; U.S. foreign policy, Castro said, had been captured by "extremist ideologues and the most belligerent hawks."[52]

Dismissing Castro's statement that terrorism was indefensible, the State Department a few months later accused Cuba of continuing "to view terror

---

*"Socialism and the revolutionary political and social system established by this Constitution, having been tested by years of heroic resistance to aggression of all types and to the economic war of the most powerful imperialist government that has ever existed, and having demonstrated its capacity to transform the country and create a completely new and just society, is irrevocable, and Cuba will never return to capitalism."

as a legitimate revolutionary tactic" and thereafter charged that Cuba has "actively continued to oppose the U.S.-led Coalition prosecuting the global war on terror and has publicly condemned various U.S. policies and action." Cuba, in turn, accused the Bush administration of using the 9/11 attacks "as a pretext to impose on the planet a policy of terror and force," and while it initially had not objected strenuously to the use of the U.S. base at Guantánamo as a prison for alleged terrorists, by 2005 Havana's forbearance had disappeared completely:

> More than a century has gone by and this piece of our territory is still forcibly occupied today, bringing shame and horror to the world when it is known to have been turned into a torture center, where hundreds of people pulled in from different parts of the world are kept in detention. They do not take them to their own country because there may be laws that would make things difficult for them to illegally hold these people by force, kidnapped for years, overriding any legal procedure, and to the amazement of the entire world, these people are being subjected to sadistic and brutal torture.[53]

On balance, then, the terrorist attacks made bad U.S.-Cuban relations worse, although those inclined to search for silver linings could argue that the wars in Afghanistan and Iraq may have benefited Cuba by distracting administration officials. Lower-level functionaries continued to implement the hostile policy laid out before 9/11, however, especially after September 2002, when the chief of the U.S. mission at the Interests Section, Vicki Huddleston, was replaced by another veteran career diplomat, James Cason, in what initially appeared to be a normal three-year rotation of two career officers. But Huddleston had received her instructions from the Clinton administration, while Cason received his from acting assistant secretary of state Otto Reich, who told him, "You don't have a mission; you're *on* a mission, and it's to bring liberty back to Cuba."[54]

Cason needed no encouragement—"We're the only hope in Cuba," he said, explaining how he had converted Huddleston's relatively modest effort to support Cuban dissidents into a full-scale onslaught. Less than a week after his arrival, he hosted the first of many meetings of dissidents in his home, where he promised U.S. aid, beginning with a booklet, *Martí Secreto*, containing reflections about democracy by Cuba's principal national hero, which he handed to each of the seventeen guests. Eighteen more dissidents visited the next day, and each also received a pledge of U.S. assistance, the booklet, and copies of reports on human rights in Cuba. Cason then took to the road, first to Cienfuegos in October, meeting with two dissidents and handing out more books and twenty shortwave radios, and he had soon logged more than six thousand miles, moving from one end of the island to the other to assure dissidents of U.S. support.

The Cuban government responded by restricting Cason and all other Interests Section personnel and their families to Havana province—"Our kids can't even go to the beach at Varadero," Cason complained—but the more important reaction came in March 2003, when the government moved against the citizens whom Cason had been encouraging, arresting seventy-five prominent dissidents. Other such sweeps had previously occurred, but as the director of Americas Watch told Congress, the 2003 crackdown "is the worst we've seen in a decade or more."[55] The government had arrested nearly every major dissident except Oswaldo Payá, who was saved, perhaps, by his international prominence. Three months before the crackdown he had received the European Community's Andrei Sakharov Award for Freedom of Thought. Others who were not so lucky included Marta Beatriz Roque, one of the so-called Group of Four who had been imprisoned in 1997 for releasing a remarkable document, "The Country Belongs to Us All [La Patria Es de Todos]," that broke new ground by accusing Cuba's Communist Party leaders of being "in the unenviable company of Stalin, Mussolini, Hitler, Franco, Trujillo, Pol Pot and Saddam Hussein." The political punch line: "It is impossible to continue leading the nation to its ruin without expecting an uncontrolled awakening of the populace in search of a rightful space within a civil society with democratic institutions. . . . It is better to discuss solutions now than to plunge our homeland into mourning tomorrow." The document's criticism of the government's economic policies was equally severe, with comments on "the proverbial inefficiency of the productive system" and "severe rationing that has lasted now 35 years—a world record!" Criticizing "a regime anchored in the past and which lives in the past," the authors called for internationally supervised competitive free elections.[56]

This statement had earned the members of the Group of Four several years in jail, and now, in 2003, Roque was sentenced to twenty more years. Another of the seventy-five was Oscar Biscet, who was already in jail when the others were arrested. Released in October 2002 after serving a three-year sentence for a variety of offenses, including "insult to the symbols of the homeland," Biscet had been rearrested six weeks later and was tried and sentenced along with the others: he received a sentence of twenty-five years in prison. A third of the seventy-five was Héctor Palacios Ruiz, a three-time Amnesty International prisoner of conscience after his imprisonments in 1994, in 1997 (as another of the Group of Four), and in 1999. A leading member of two dissident federations, Concilio Cubano and Todos Unidos, Palacios was accused of using his home to distribute books and magazines provided by the U.S. government.[57]

The seventy-five were charged under various laws including the Law for the Protection of Cuban National Independence and the Economy, or Law 88, which had been Cuba's reaction to Track 2 of the Cuban Democracy Act and to the Helms-Burton Act. Law 88 prohibited providing information to the U.S. government or its agents that could be used to strengthen the embargo or destabilize Cuban society. First had come Law 80, the 1996 Law of Reaffirmation of Cuban Dignity and Sovereignty, in which the Cuban National Assembly specifically "repudiates the Helms-Burton Law and declares its irrevocable decision to adopt the measures in its power as a response." Law 88 was one such measure, with Foreign Minister Felipe Pérez Roque arguing that "those who put themselves at the service of the power that is attacking our people must be aware that there are laws to prosecute and to punish this conduct." Article 4 of Law 88 prohibited electronic publishing via Web sites such as Miami-based CubaNet, which used U.S. government funds to pay dissident journalists to send stories from Cuba; Article 6 prohibited the distribution of any "subversive materials" provided by the U.S. government; and Article 7 prohibited working with any medium, including radio and television, that assisted U.S. policy.[58]

Law 88 was used for the first time in the trials of the seventy-five dissidents, where evidence included testimony by twelve security agents who had infiltrated several dissident organizations, supplemented by documents indicating the dissidents' ties to the U.S. government or to U.S. government-funded NGOs. One undercover agent accused Alfonso Valdes, a board member of the Varela Project, of meeting at the Interests Section with a U.S. government auditor to verify that Valdes was receiving the money and equipment that AID was paying a U.S.-based NGO to deliver.

Some of this evidence was credible, and some of it would never have stood up in an impartial courtroom, but the principal issue was not the evidence but the law itself. Law 88 clearly represented a draconian infringement on freedom of association and expression, but just as taking money from al-Qaeda was illegal in the United States,* so the Cuban government,

---

*Sec. 321 of the Antiterrorism and Effective Death Penalty Act of 1996 (PL 104-132, 110 *Stat.* 1214, 3 June 1996).

openly and repeatedly threatened, had made it illegal to accept Washington's money. And just as the Bush administration used national security to justify the denial of due process to suspected terrorists held in secret overseas prisons and at Guantánamo, so did Felipe Pérez Roque: Cuba had to protect itself following "the decision of Mr. Cason to convert the North American interests section in Havana and his residence into practically a headquarters for the subversion of Cuba. . . . These judicial proceedings have to be understood as Cuba's action when left with no other alternative on the path of confrontation and provocation that the U.S. government has chosen for its relations with Cuba."[59] The average sentence of the seventy-five dissidents was nineteen years in prison.

The official note informing Cuban citizens of the arrests cited "the shameless and repeated provocation of the head of the United States interests section in Cuba" and asserted that "no country, as powerful as it may be, has the right to convert its diplomatic representation into the organizer, funder, chief and general headquarters of activities to destabilize, subvert the constitutional order, break the laws, conspire against the social development, sabotage the economic relations, threaten the security and destroy the independence of another country." Fidel Castro used harsher language in his May Day speech. Referring to the dissidents as "mercenaries on the payroll of Bush's Hitler-like government," he promised that Cuba would defend itself "in the face of sinister plans against our country on the part of the neo-fascist extreme right and its allies in the Miami terrorist mob."[60]

Can the Bush administration, then, be fairly accused of provoking the arrests? Washington's embrace of the dissidents could have prompted their arrests, but Assistant Secretary of State Roger Noriega considered that idea nonsense: "Castro has been slapping his people around since Jim Cason was in junior high school and he needs no pretext for throwing people in jail."[61] A reasonable argument could be made for both positions, but at the time almost everyone in Washington agreed with Noriega: Secretary of State Powell called the arrests "despicable repression," Senator Baucus labeled them "appalling acts of repression," the House of Representatives condemned the crackdown by a vote of 414–0, and the entire board of directors of the Cuba Policy Foundation, created in 2001 with the goal of ending the embargo, simply gave up: "We organized, funded and supported the Foundation because we hoped, and had reason to believe, that its energetic efforts to modify the ban on Cuba trade, travel and investment might succeed over time. We can only conclude, however, that in spite of its claims to the contrary, Cuba does not share our enthusiasm for a more open relationship. For this reason we have tendered our resignations. Daily operations of the Foundation will cease as of this date."[62]

Human rights NGOs were equally critical: Amnesty International characterized the arrests as "an alarming step backwards," and the executive director of Americas Watch criticized Washington's provocative behavior but added that "no one should have any illusions about the character of the Cuban Government. No one should romanticize any aspect of this cruel system, or make any excuses for Fidel Castro's abuses."[63]

The arrests also upset Cuba's relations with the European Union, which had opened its first mission in Havana only days before the roundup, at a moment when the EU was considering Cuba's application for membership in the new Cotonou trade agreement providing preferential tariffs and other forms of economic assistance to African, Caribbean, and Pacific countries. Reacting to the arrests, the EU announced that it would freeze Cuba's application and that member states would reduce high-level government visits, would begin inviting dissidents to their national day celebrations, and would conduct an early reevaluation of the EU's Common Position. Completed in July, the evaluation stipulated that any aid to Cuba "should be channeled through governmental institutions only if a direct benefit for the population or meaningful contribution toward economic opening and reform in Cuba is ensured."[64]

Castro unloaded with both barrels at his 26th of July speech five days later, using the fiftieth anniversary of the Moncada attack to blast the person he considered most responsible for Europe's reaction, Spanish prime minister José María Aznar, as "an individual of markedly fascist lineage and ideology." Cuba, Castro said, would no longer accept European aid: "The sovereignty and dignity of this people are not open to discussion with anyone, much less with a group of former colonial powers historically responsible for the slave trade, the plunder and even extermination of entire peoples, and the underdevelopment and poverty suffered today by billions of human beings whom they continue to plunder."[65]

Much of the international reaction reflected not only the arrests but also the Cuban government's handling of a separate incident that occurred just as the seventy-five trials were getting under way: on 2 April, three Cubans seized a ferry and set off toward Key West, only to run out of gas and be taken into custody by the Cuban navy. In nine days, the three were tried, convicted, sentenced to death, and executed.

This hijacking had occurred in the immediate wake of two airplane hijackings, one on 19 March and the other on 1 April. As with Law 88, Foreign

Minister Pérez Roque explained that the death penalty "is not consistent with our philosophy of life, but we have been a country under attack. We are a country facing an ongoing effort to destabilize us, and we have to use all the resources in our reach." A few days later Fidel Castro offered a more elaborate explanation of why a hijacking by Cubans would be interpreted as destabilization by the United States: by failing to discourage hijackers (it was not yet clear whether the hijackers of the two aircraft would be tried in U.S. courts), the Bush administration was seeking to ignite an immigration crisis that would provide an excuse to invade Cuba. In this sense, Castro argued, the hijackers could be lumped together with the seventy-five imprisoned dissidents: "We cannot ever hesitate when it is a question of protecting the lives of the sons and daughters of a people determined to fight until the end, arresting the mercenaries who serve the aggressors and applying the most severe sanctions, no matter how unpleasant it is for us, against terrorists who hijack passenger boats or planes or commit similarly serious acts."[66]

BY MID-2003 the United States had Cuba on the defensive and isolated, and there it stayed through the 2004 election. The election's wake saw several significant changes in foreign policy personnel, including Powell's replacement by national security adviser Condoleezza Rice—a not unexpected shift, since anonymous White House insiders had long been pulling reporters aside to criticize Powell's failure to fall in lockstep behind the administration's hawkish ideologues. (Lawrence Wilkerson, Powell's long-time aide, who was often thought to voice Powell's views, had characterized the administration's approach to Cuba as the "dumbest policy on the face of the earth.")[67] For Latin America, many of the administration's right-wing political appointees were replaced by career officials, all of whom appeared ready to implement whatever policy came from higher authority. But those higher authorities had their hands full with Iraq and other more pressing problems, and the leitmotif of Bush's second-term Cuba policy had already been set by the report of his Commission for Assistance to a Free Cuba, unveiled in May 2004, just before the campaign began. The accompanying press release had trumpeted the report as a major new departure, but it was unique only in its length—423 pages; otherwise, it was simply the latest in a series of U.S. transition plans for Cuba that stretched back to 1901 or, in the case of Cuba's revolution, to the days before the Bay of Pigs, when the State Department, contemplating "the happy day when some friendlier government may come to power," informed President Eisenhower, "We are now updating some draft contingency plans looking toward the attitudes, policies, and programs of assistance and rehabilitation which we might then find appropriate."[68]

A first-things-first policy had concentrated on getting rid of the revolutionary government, however, and formal planning for the regime's aftermath began only late in the Cold War, only in response to lobbying by the Cuban American National Foundation, and only locally—in the state of Florida, where Republican governor Bob Martínez created the Governor's Commission on a Free Cuba, which Democratic governor Lawton Chiles reactivated in 1991. On both occasions, the commissioners were supposed to assess how a post-Castro Cuba would affect Florida, but both were chaired by CANF's Jorge Mas Canosa, and he added a discussion of how to help the Cuban people engineer a transition to liberal democracy and neoliberal markets.

Federal-level planning began when the Soviet bloc collapsed, spurred by a recommendation of the 1992 Cuban Democracy Act that the United States "initiate immediately the development of a comprehensive United States policy toward Cuba in a post-Castro government."[69] The Clinton administration did not lunge at this congressional bait, but it also did not fail to nibble. In early 1994 AID's administrator for Latin America, Mark Schneider, told Congress that the agency itself had not yet begun to develop a plan for postrevolutionary Cuba but had commissioned a group of academics to prepare a "pre-planning" document—"a snapshot of current economic and social conditions and the general political environment." The result was a 674-page study prepared by some of the nation's most respected Cuba specialists, and after it had been completed, an ever-cautious AID was finally ready to begin to get ready—and not a moment too soon, Schneider warned: "After 35 years we may finally be approaching the transition to freedom in Cuba[, and] the U.S. must be prepared to accompany them on that journey."[70]

Cuban Americans were already hard at work. By 1993 CANF had produced a transition program consisting of fifty steps ranging from wishful thinking ("Put an end to hatred and revenge") to concrete actions ("Privatize most assets").[71] Two years later, the International Republican Institute, one of the core grantees of the government-funded National Endowment for Democracy (NED), was supporting a Florida-based "Cuban Transition Committee" chaired by Jeb Bush to produce step-by-step instructions on how exactly to establish democracy in Cuba. The 1996 Helms-Burton Act made planning mandatory, and AID set immediately to work; ten months later, the White House released the required report, "Support for a Democratic Transition in Cuba," which specified how the United States would help the Cuban people meet the challenges of democratic governance. The report included the assumption that a transition was imminent, the assurance that between four and eight billion dollars in U.S. aid would be quickly provided, and President Clinton's promise "to support the Cuban people when they embark upon that process of change." The State Department claimed to have distributed more than ten thousand copies of AID's report inside Cuba.[72]

Cuban officials were not pleased by any of this planning, with National Assembly leader Ricardo Alarcón among the first to complain that "the United States does not have the right to decide, directly or through its agents in Miami, how Cuba's society should be organized." Then Fidel Castro jumped in, asking a Havana audience, "Who has given the U.S. government the divine right to make plans for the government of another country? Who has given it the right to establish a transition government? Who has given it the right to trample in this way on the dignity, the honor and the sovereignty of another people, to tell them what social regime they have to have?"[73]

Paying no heed, AID continued to fine-tune its design, reporting to Congress in 1999 that it had completed work on its plan to assist the island's residents in holding free elections and now needed three million dollars to plan for providing food and water. Since the agency had no idea how to accomplish this task, it subcontracted the planning to universities, think tanks, consultants, and conservative advocacy groups such as the U.S.-Cuba Business Council, which was paid to produce a report on how the private sector would assist Cuba's economic transition. It was money well spent, council president Otto Reich assured Congress: "When a free democratic and market-oriented Cuba opens the door to genuine economic development and commercial opportunity, U.S. companies will be second to none in gaining access to the Cuban market."[74]

These efforts served as a foundation for the work of the Commission for Assistance to a Free Cuba, which in mid-2004 unveiled its plan with an explicit statement of Washington's goal ("To bring about an expeditious end to the Castro dictatorship") and with Secretary Powell's pledge "to help the Cuban people put Castro and Castroism behind them forever." Released at the same moment when Iraqis were converting Washington's chipper "mission accomplished" mood into a sobering recognition that the nation had embarked on yet another dreary slog, the commission's report asserted that any U.S. action must be taken in consultation with the Cuban people but left no doubt about who would backstop almost everything: for example, "The U.S. Government, if requested by the transition government, should be prepared . . . to keep all schools open during an emergency phase of the transition in order to keep children and teenagers off the streets."[75]

The commission's plan consisted of individual chapters devoted to the U.S. role in "Meeting Basic Human Needs," "Establishing Democratic Institutions," "Establishing the Core Institutions of a Free Economy," "Modernizing Infrastructure," and "Addressing Environmental Degradation"— AID contracts for one and all—but what little attention the report received resulted from its first-things-first chapter specifying how to undermine the Castro government: "Hastening Cuba's Transition" contained sixty-two recommendations, and at the document's unveiling ceremony President Bush promised, "We're not waiting for the day of Cuban freedom; we are working for the day."[76]

While the commission's plan produced only a slight ripple in Iraq-focused Washington (the *Post* buried the story on page 28), it captured the attention of Cuba's government, which responded with a protest march in front of the U.S. Interests Section, where Fidel Castro read an open letter to President Bush: "You have no right whatsoever, except for that of brute force, to intervene in Cuba's affairs and, whenever the fancy takes you, to proclaim the transition from one system to another and to take measures to make this happen." Cubans knew their history, he later warned: "Once the United States owned everything in Cuba: the mines, hundreds of thousands of the best hectares of land; the ports and its facilities; the electrical system, transportation, banking, commercial activities, etcetera, and the idiots believe that they will return here and that we will call on them on bended knees: 'Come and save us again, Oh Saviors of the World! Come and we shall give you everything we have.'"[77]

The sixty-two recommendations fell into two categories—those that tightened the embargo and those that encouraged the development of a dissident movement on the island. Tightening the embargo involved new restrictions on travel, gift parcels, and remittances. Since people-to-people exchanges had already been curtailed, the revised travel regulations primarily affected Cuban American family visits and academic programs. The commission estimated that between 160,000 and 200,000 U.S. residents were still visiting Cuba each year and cast the 125,000 "claiming to visit family" in a surprisingly negative light: Assistant Secretary Noriega explained that most of these alleged family visits were by recent émigrés who in many cases "did not have any particular problem with the regime, so they were not leaving for political reasons. They were essentially being sent out as cash cows to shovel money back [and] on the first day that they get a green card, and they can travel freely, the practice was to bundle up a bunch of clothing and other articles and cart them back to Cuba to sell them."[78]

Not any longer. The new regulations limited family visits to once every three years (instead of once a year) and to a much-reduced range of immediate family members. Moreover, the trips would now be limited to fourteen days (no time limit had previously existed), to expenses of $50 a day (down from $167, which was the federal government's per diem for Cuba), and to only forty-four pounds of baggage (down from whatever the aircraft could carry and the traveler could afford).

The changes governing educational travel were equally significant. No fewer than 760 two-year licenses had been issued to U.S. colleges since the 1999 Clinton relaxation, and the commission reported that some academic institutions "regularly abuse this license category and engage in a form of disguised tourism." The new regulations reduced the 760 dramatically by requiring each license applicant to be an accredited college or university, to operate a structured academic program no shorter than ten weeks, and to exclude any but its own students. Programs operated by academic organizations that were not accredited colleges—Vermont's widely respected School for International Training, for example—were no longer eligible to apply for licenses, and smaller colleges that relied on sister institutions to fill their classes now found it impossible to generate enough students to make their programs feasible. California Democratic representative Barbara Lee proposed legislation to prohibit enforcement of this part of the new regulations, but Lincoln Díaz-Balart condemned her initiative as "another 'reward Castro' amendment. Reward the firing squads, reward the imprisonment of the opponents. That is what this amendment is all about." Like other embargo-relaxing proposals, Lee's was accepted by the House but deleted in conference.[79]

As with travel, so with gift parcels. The United States had previously permitted *paquetes* valued at up to two hundred dollars to be sent each month to any Cuban, and the commission complained that 50,650 such parcels worth $243 million had been sent in 2003; in addition, the Cuban government was earning another $18 million a year in delivery charges. The new regulations kept the value limit at two hundred dollars but reduced the number of gift parcels from once per month to an individual to once per month to a household. The modified rules also restricted recipients to immediate family members and significantly reduced the list of eligible commodities by prohibiting, for example, clothing and personal hygiene items.[80]

And as with *paquetes*, so with remittances, which were already restricted to three hundred dollars per household in any three-month period; however, travelers had been allowed to carry up to three thousand dollars for up to ten different households, a form of currency transfer that added up to a substantial amount of money. With more than a hundred thousand legal travelers and an untold number of for-hire "mules" traveling through third countries, the commission estimated remittances at perhaps one billion dollars a year, with the government capturing three-quarters of that money through its dollar stores. The new regulations restricted remittances to the remitter's narrowly defined immediate family and reduced the amount that any traveler could carry from three thousand dollars to three hundred dollars.

Fidel Castro characterized these measures as "brutal, pitiless and cruel," but they were only the first type of noose-tightening activity.[81] The second way to hasten Cuba's transition was to undermine the government from within by supporting the dissidents who might jell into a movement similar to Poland's Solidarity or Czechoslovakia's Charter 77. The commission recommended spending an initial thirty-six million dollars for this support and another five million dollars to promote disaffection by publicizing the government's shortcomings, plus unspecified amounts to increase the effectiveness of Radio and TV Martí, to launch an international solidarity campaign, and to prepare for future criminal trials by creating a list of Cuban government officials "credibly alleged to have participated in torture or other serious human rights abuses."[82]

A few of these activities could be implemented with relative ease—it was expensive but not difficult to arrange for the U.S. Air Force's Special Operations Wing to beam TV Martí's programs into Cuba from international airspace, and within three months President Bush was telling a Miami campaign audience, "We launched the first of what will be regular airborne broadcasts into Cuba."[83] But nurturing another country's dissidents is more of an art than a science. The first step obviously is to prepare the ground—a significant number of Cubans must become disaffected, but almost everyone in Washington believed such already to be the case, in part because AID claimed to have empirical evidence: in 1998–99, the agency paid University of Florida researchers to hit a new scholarly low for survey research—an opinion poll, mistitled "Measuring Cuban Public Opinion," which, since it could not be conducted in Cuba, involved polling a "sample of Cuban emigres who had been in the United States three months or less." These 1,023 individuals "were overwhelmingly convinced that political and economic changes were necessary." Equally unsurprising was the discovery that "the perception of regime leaders and institutions is highly negative." These data were reinforced by such leading dissidents as René Gómez Manzano, who told Congress (via a telephone hookup) that 90 percent of the Cuban population opposed the Castro government.[84]

With Step 1 accomplished, it was now time to nurture this alleged disaffection into active opposition. The Bush administration also contracted much of that job to third parties, most of them U.S.-based NGOs operated by Cuban Americans, which, after deducting their administrative expenses, would sprinkle taxpayers' money on the Cuban landscape; the U.S. Interests Section would then nourish whatever sprouts might appear. This process had begun years earlier with President Clinton's October 1995 announcement of a $500,000 AID grant to Freedom House to disseminate information about democracy inside Cuba, to sponsor trips by democratic activists to Cuba, and to publish materials written by Cuban dissidents. The Helms-Burton Act had listed a number of similar activities it wished to encourage, and by 1998 Freedom House had been joined by twelve additional NGOs; a year later, the thirteen had grown to nineteen, with a commensurate increase in funding, such as AID's support of Reich's U.S.-Cuba Business Council, whose original grant of $267,000 ballooned to $567,000 and then topped out at $852,000.[85]

In the final full year of the Clinton administration, AID had requested a 50 percent budget increase to strengthen Cuba's civil society, an amount the new Bush officials further augmented. By late 2005, the agency had funded thirty-nine U.S.-based organizations, including Creighton University's law school, in Omaha, Nebraska, where AID assistant administrator Adolfo Franco had received his legal training. (For $750,000, Creighton agreed to prepare a report on how other transitions had handled property restitution as a way "to develop lessons learned for the Cuba transition.") It was Hogs at the Trough Day for what the Agency now called its "program partners," and AID was not the administration's only delivery vehicle; a significant increase also occurred in the Cuba programs of the government-funded NED, from $765,000 in President Clinton's final year to $3 million in 2005.[86]

Most of these expenditures seemed to have the additional purpose of supporting Cuban Americans. During the first five years of the George W. Bush administration, the NED poured $202,000 into Washington lobbyist Frank Calzon's Center for a Free Cuba, for example, and the single-largest Cuba-related NED recipient, the International Republican Institute, basically served as a conduit to pass along almost all of NED's $1.8 million (through 2004) to the Miami-based Cuban Democratic Directorate, most of it used to meet its Cuban American payroll. In 2005, the NED began direct funding of the directorate with a $664,000 grant, primarily to operate a shortwave radio station.

The extent to which this "Cuba democracy" aid had become a mechanism to support Cuban Americans became apparent in 2006, when the U.S. Government Accountability Office released a highly critical report concluding that "USAID's internal controls over the awarding of Cuba program grants and the oversight of grantees do not provide adequate assurance that the grant funds are being used properly." Specifically, in one grant to a Miami-based Cuban American group, the accountability office found "significant commingling of funds between the Executive Director's personal bank account, the USAID account, and the private donations account"; another grant had "time charges that do not appear to be logical or correct"; a third featured "questionable travel expenses"; and a fourth had "questionable expenses paid to family member of grantee manager." Other grantees "could not justify some purchases made with USAID funds, including a gas chainsaw, computer gaming equipment and software (including Nintendo Gameboys and Sony Playstations), a mountain bike, leather coats, cashmere sweaters, crab meat, and Godiva chocolates." "That's part of our job," replied Frank Hernández Trujillo of the Grupo de Apoyo de la Democracia, which had purchased the Nintendo games, "to show the people in Cuba what they could attain if they were not under that system." Shaking his libertarian head, Representative Jeff Flake commented, "If this doesn't call for change in direction or personnel, I don't know what will."[87]

Many of these AID contracts and NED grants were closely coordinated with the U.S. Interests Section in Havana. Paying the Miami-based Cuban Democratic Directorate to launch a new shortwave radio station might nurture Cuban disaffection, for example, but only if Cubans could receive its broadcasts, and making sure that they could do so was a high priority for AID's Adolfo Franco, who told Congress, "We won't be satisfied until every Cuban household has a short-wave radio."[88]

The responsibility for purchasing these radios fell to U.S. taxpayers, but via a circuitous route: in the final months of the Clinton administration,

AID signed a $320,000 contract with the University of Miami "to provide support for a Program to develop Cuban civil society through training seminars." The idea was for the university's Institute for Cuban and Cuban American Studies to conduct "a series of six seminars for Cuban citizens on issues related to civil society and free enterprise." Since the project director, ultraconservative Jaime Suchlicki, was certainly not going to be allowed to enter Cuba, and since the Cubans selected by the University of Miami to attend the seminars would almost certainly not receive exit visas to travel to the United States, the seminars were to be held in Panama. By early 2002, Professor Suchlicki, having spent more than half of the $320,000 ($168,869.72—nearly all of it on salaries and overhead costs for the University of Miami), informed AID that "the Cuban government will not allow citizens to travel [redacted—probably "to Panama"] to participate in the democratization seminars that we had planned. We have therefore cancelled all seminars."

Rather than returning the remaining $151,130.28, Suchlicki suggested that the contract be revised to focus on providing "short-wave radios and literature to groups in Cuba." AID promptly extended all but $4,753 of the grant, and the University of Miami began sending the shortwave radios to the Interests Section in the diplomatic pouch.[89] After the radios arrived in Cuba, the Interests Section assumed responsibility for getting them into Cubans' hands—so explained the section's public affairs officer as she unwrapped a small black leatherette case to show a researcher its contents: a palm-size Chinese-made radio with rechargeable batteries and a recharger, plus copies of the Universal Declaration of Human Rights and *Martí Secreto*, the booklet of Martí's sayings about democracy. The Interests Section developed various ways to distribute the packages—one was offered to every Cuban leaving an Interests Section function, for example—and after eight years, AID had handed out more than twenty-three thousand radios.[90]

Interests Section personnel also set up outside loudspeakers to stream Radio Martí to passers-by and to visitors waiting in line to enter the consulate and placed a replica of a solitary confinement jail cell at the consulate entrance. They replaced the Interest Section's traditional outdoor Christmas tree with a large lighted "75" to commemorate the group of incarcerated dissidents, and they celebrated the Fourth of July in the garden of James Cason's residence with a three-story Statue of Liberty featuring a "75" instead of Liberty's torch. The Interests Section also opened a public Internet facility with a direct uplink via its rooftop satellite dish that bypassed Cuba's Internet and featured a service unavailable elsewhere in

Cuba: free high-speed printers with an unlimited supply of paper and toner. In early 2008 the Interests Section Internet computers were being used by more than fifty Cubans a day, nearly all of them college age or slightly older and each pushing the print button every minute or so while latecomers awaited their turn alongside stacks of publications such as *Did You Know?*, a fourteen-page document subtitled *75 Facts the Castro Regimes [sic] Hides from Cubans and Visitors.*

Fidel Castro complained that "never, perhaps, has any government so abused and offended its diplomatic status and immunity as the United States government by writing signs and exhibiting offensive placards attacking our country." The Cuban government struck back with a formal protest note and introduced a series of five brief television spots depicting Interests Section chief James Cason dressed in a wizard's outfit, flying about Havana and waving a magic neoliberal wand to shut down Cuba's social welfare system—schools, medical clinics, pensions—and to restore racial discrimination.[91]

"They need a 'Darth Vader' to personify as evil," Cason commented, noting that the diplomatic breakdown was all but complete: "We have been invited to nothing, not even to other embassies' national day celebrations, because the Cubans have made it clear that they will not attend any diplomatic function where Interests Section personnel might be present." The only Cuban government official to whom Cason was allowed to speak was the director of North American affairs at the Ministry of Foreign Relations. "I can't even talk with someone like the historian of the city of Havana," Cason lamented; "every time we ask, [the Ministry of Foreign Relations] sends our request back with a three-word note: 'No se concede'"—permission denied.[92]

In 2004, fourteen of the seventy-five arrested dissidents, including Marta Beatriz Roque, received parole (*licencia extrapenal*) for health reasons, and by early 2005, she and two of the other members of the Group of Four testified before a House subcommittee via telephone from the U.S. Interests Section. None of the three was bashful about expressing approval of the commission's recommendations: Félix Bonne said, "I am completely in agreement with current United States policy toward Cuba," while Roque characterized Cason as "a very, very great man," adding that the Cuban government might want "to promote to the people that Cason is gay, but we are sure he is not." She also argued against lifting the travel ban: "It is not good for us that tourists come to Cuba. Some people say, 'You are going to have the Cubans in touch with democracy.' No. We will have a little more prostitution because the tourists come to Cuba, and the prostitution is increasing all the time. We have a little more drugs." Prostitution and drugs, she said, were "things that we did not have before 1959."[93]

But other dissidents went out of their way to distance themselves from U.S. policy. Elizardo Sánchez criticized the commission's report as "totally counterproductive," while Oswaldo Payá added that "it is not right, nor do we accept, any external element, whether from the United States of America, Europe or anywhere else, trying to design the Cuban transition process." Eloy Gutiérrez-Menoyo labeled the commission "a total interference that does not benefit the building of democracy in Cuba," and Manuel Cuesta Morúa claimed that "the United States has absolutely no right to define the how, what or when, or the pace and timing of the democratic transition in Cuba." After meeting with dissidents in 2002, former president Jimmy Carter reported that "they were unanimous in expressing . . . opposition . . . to any funding of their efforts from the U.S. government. Any knowledge or report of such financial support would just give credibility to the long-standing claims of President Castro that they were 'paid lackeys' of Washington."[94]

Relations again hit rock bottom in 2005, shortly after another career diplomat, Michael Parmly, replaced Cason. On Human Rights Day, 10 December, Parmly gave a scorching speech to dissidents invited to his residence: "The Cuban regime does not represent the people, nor does it have any interest in bettering their lives. Rather, the regime is obsessed with self-preservation. It maintains itself by isolating Cubans from the rest of the world, keeping Cubans artificially poor and dependent on a State that demands unquestioned compliance, and instilling fear among those who question the regime's lies."[95]

Diplomats rarely utter such hostile words about the government to which they are accredited, but Parmly's outburst was only a prelude to what came five weeks later, when he flipped a switch and a streaming electronic ticker similar to the type seen in New York's Times Square burst into life. This one ran across the Interests Section's broad eastern face and featured Spanish-language quotations by individuals ranging from the Reverend Martin Luther King Jr. ("I have a dream that one day this nation will rise up") to rocker Frank Zappa ("Communism doesn't work because people like to own stuff"), plus reassuring messages such as "Don't worry that you will lose your home after the transition; that's not certain" and a heavy dose of straight political commentary: "In a free country they don't harass those who intend to emigrate [and] they don't have tourist apartheid. Is Cuba a free country?"[96]

The ticker was three years in the making, delayed by the State Department's legal office, which claimed that it would violate Article 41 of the 1961 Vienna Convention on Diplomatic Relations.* When that objection had been overruled, the device had to be designed and built—electronic panels fitted inside each sixth-story east-facing window that completely destroyed a stunning view of the Malecón and the distant Morro from the office of the chief of the Interests Section. "Obviously, it had to be up high," commented a wistful Michael Parmly, who inherited the project, "but it would have been just as effective on the fifth floor."[97]

Six days after the ticker was turned on, the Cuban government claimed that the Bush administration was "intent on breaking the minimal diplomatic links which exist between Cuba and the United States." In a speech that could have been given in 1961, Fidel Castro added that "no government on earth can tolerate such an affront to its dignity and sovereignty," promising that Cuba "will strike back with all the strength of our moral fortitude and we shall persist in our determination to fight to the death against any act of belligerence by the restless and brutal empire that threatens us."[98] In 2005 the Cuban government had responded to the Interests Section's "75" sign by installing a series of billboards across the street, the most vivid of which featured a vampire-like President Bush with blood dripping from his fangs as he presided over torture at Iraq's Abu Ghraib prison. The ticker called for a more elaborate reply—a mass of 138 flagpoles erected immediately in front of the Interests Section, each sixty-six feet tall and each flying a black mourning flag with a single white star, one flag for each year since Cuba had begun its struggle for independence in 1868. First raised on a breezy February day, the flags completely blocked a new message streaming across the ticker: "The resources could have been better used for general repairs."

FOUR MONTHS LATER, Fidel Castro was in the hospital. "It will not be much longer," predicted John Negroponte, the U.S. director of national intelligence; "months, not years." Forty-six years earlier, U.S. ambassador Philip Bonsal had offered exactly the same forecast: the Castro government

---

*"The premises of the [diplomatic] mission must not be used in any manner incompatible with the functions of the mission."

would last "months rather than years." Negroponte's comment came a few weeks after President Bush's Republicans suffered significant losses in the 2006 off-year elections, losing control of both houses of Congress, and a dozen or so candidates soon took to the campaign trail, seeking the presidency by outlining their positions on health care and a host of other problems. When not campaigning in Florida, none of these hopefuls said much about Cuba, and President Bush failed to mention Cuba in his lengthy review of U.S. global policies before a mid-2007 audience at the Naval War College. When one questioner finally asked him for his "assessment of the situation in South America," Bush replied, "I've got good relations with a lot of the leaders in the neighborhood," citing Cuba as a remaining problem but one that would eventually be resolved: "One day, the good Lord will take Fidel Castro away." The audience interrupted with a cheer.[99] A few days later, the Interests Section ticker carried a message from Secretary of State Condoleezza Rice: "All of you must know that you have no greater friend than the United States of America." Not long thereafter, President Bush reminded a Washington audience "about how much work the United States has to do to help the people of Cuba realize the blessings of liberty."[100]

I am doing my best to persuade the Cubans that if only they will be good they will be happy; I am seeking the very minimum of interference necessary to make them good.

—President Theodore Roosevelt, 1907

CONCLUSION

BENEVOLENT DOMINATION

Had the United States been allowed to select its neighbors, it never would have chosen Cuba. No doubt Cubans would reply that living alongside the United States has been no picnic, either, even if it is true, as the United States has invariably insisted, that it has only had Cuba's best interests at heart. As William Howard Taft declared at the start of the twentieth century,

> The record of the nine years since the beginning of the Spanish War, looked at from an impartial standpoint, is on the whole an unblemished record of generous, earnest effort to uplift these people.

And as George H. W. Bush explained at the end of the century,

> What's the point of my talking to [Castro]? All I'd tell him is what I'm telling you, to give the people the freedom that they want. And then you'll see the United States do exactly what we should: Go down and lift those people up.[1]

The problem, of course, is that most people do not want a neighboring power to lift them up, regardless of how well intentioned the effort might be, and Cuba's revolutionary generation grew up in a society that left it particularly opposed to uplifting by the United States. Instead, Cubans repeatedly insisted on being treated as anyone would like to be treated by their neighbors—that is, as equals and with respect. They said so publicly:

The Cuban Government and the Cuban people are anxious to live in peace and harmony with the Government and the people of the United States; and they are also desirous of intensifying their diplomatic and economic relations, but on the basis of mutual respect.

And they said so privately:

Tell the President (and I cannot stress this too strongly) that I seriously hope that Cuba and the United States can eventually sit down in an atmosphere of good will and of mutual respect and negotiate our differences.

And the message occasionally was heard, as in late 1978, when Peter Tarnoff and Robert Pastor met with Fidel Castro and then reported to President Carter,

His principal message was that Cuba wanted to be treated with respect.[2]

WHAT DID WASHINGTON not understand about "respect"? The two envoys had been visiting Havana just after the United States had resumed its spy plane overflights, which, as Castro pointed out, violated Cuba's sovereignty. Tarnoff and Pastor could hardly disagree, but the archives offer no evidence that anyone paused to consider how U.S. officials would react—would *have* to react—if another country's warplanes were making supersonic passes over Washington, D.C. Any U.S. president would be crucified for failing to order the Pentagon to blow the next such intruder out of the sky, but when it comes to Cuba, U.S. officials have always seemed to assume that they can do more or less what global opinion will tolerate, and sometimes a bit more, especially if they insist, as Teddy Roosevelt did in 1907, that he was only trying to make Cubans good, or, as President George W. Bush did in 2008, that the United States sought only to help Cubans enjoy "the blessings of liberty." Fidel Castro put his finger on what has always been the central problem for Cuban nationalists, telling Tarnoff and Pastor that "it is difficult to talk to you, a powerful, rich and highly developed country with a mentality of arrogance."[3]

The overflights may have cracked a window or two in Havana, but unlike the interminable economic embargo, far and away the longest in U.S. history, they did no serious physical damage. They were offensive because they made a disrespectful statement—a statement that on the hierarchy of peoples, Cuba ranked beneath the United States. U.S. officials had been making similar statements to this particular generation of Cubans since 1960, when Vice President Richard Nixon reminded voters that "the United States has the power—and Mr. Castro knows this—to throw him out of office." Coming eighteen years later, the Carter-era overflights were simply one more lesson in Realpolitik 101, the goal of which was to teach a group of slow learners what Thucydides said twenty-five hundred years ago: the strong can do what they want and the weak will accept what they must.

It is difficult to imagine a worse aphorism on which to build a healthy relationship. Of course Cuba's revolutionaries understood that they had been dealt a weak geostrategic hand, inheriting a modest patch of real estate near a superpower with a population thirty times larger and an economy several hundred times bigger. Nonetheless, after 1959 Cuban officials' consistent response to the Thucydides lecture was to give Washington the finger, as Fidel Castro did more politely than usual in 1961, two weeks after the Bay of Pigs: "We have only limited territory, a small nation, but our right is as respectable as that of any country, regardless of size." In your dreams, Nixon had bragged to a campaign audience: "We could give it to Mr. Castro in 24 hours."[4]

What did Havana not understand about power? Not much, as the Reagan administration's Jeane Kirkpatrick noted at the height of the Central American imbroglio in 1984: "Once we give them a line they cannot cross, they won't cross it."[5] Fully aware of their northern neighbor's power, all Cuban governments have faced the central question of Washington's determination to use it. That determination varies with the time and the situation. After one major miscalculation (the missile crisis), Cubans became exceptionally astute at determining the line they could not cross without triggering a revolution-ending reaction, while the United States has been equally adept at feeling out the costs of its options. Thucydides and Richard Nixon and Alexander Haig were all correct—the United States could turn Cuba into a parking lot, but doing so might have led to a reprisal against a vulnerable U.S. outpost during the Soviet era, and after about 1990 it simply would have been a distraction from other, more important, problems. And, of course, no one knows how much it might cost to subdue today's Cubans.

So both sides learned to live without crossing the line. The United States basically did nothing too bold or aggressive after the early 1960s, limiting itself to an economic embargo and then, after the Cold War, to the tutelary approach adopted by turn-of-the-century Progressives, among them Secretary of War William Howard Taft, who explained to the readers of *National*

Geographic exactly what the Roosevelt administration was attempting to accomplish in Cuba: "To teach them a higher and better civilization." That was in 1907; ten months earlier, Taft had said the same thing directly to Cubans: "We are here only to help you on. With our arm under your arm, lifting you again on the path of wonderful progress."[6]

Consistently oblivious to how most people would react to this condescending attitude, Taft then went home to campaign for the presidency, leaving his successors to set Cubans on the proper path—not once, but often. For more than a century, these successors have continued producing what now amounts to an entire bookcase of plans for a new and improved Cuba. The most recent plan, unveiled in 2004 by a suitably named Commission for Assistance to a Free Cuba, first defines what Washington means by "a Free Cuba" and then explains in some detail how Cubans can (and must) reach that goal, beginning with regime change. That requirement, too, is nothing new; today's plan simply updates an early-twentieth-century blueprint produced by Taft's contemporary, Governor-General Leonard Wood, who was first to identify what Washington has always considered Cuba's central problem: "No one wants more than I a good and stable government, of and by the people here, but we must see that the right class are in office."[7]

Global opinion in today's world makes it impossible to do what Wood did—force Cubans to amend their constitution to authorize U.S. intervention—but the plan produced by today's Commission for Assistance to a Free Cuba is equally intent on seeing the right kind of people govern Cuba. In this the commission reflects the lead of Congress, which has laid out its own plans for improving Cuba, each more detailed than the last until 1996 and the culminating Helms-Burton Act, which today specifies the type of economic system Cubans must operate, the type of political system they must establish, and even the names of specific individuals whom Cubans are not allowed to select as their leaders.

Like the island's residents in Taft's day, Cuba's revolutionary generation clearly got the message but reacted differently: it flatly rejected Washington's plans. "When they talk about reforms in Cuba, it is a precondition that we cannot accept," Fidel Castro explained, "because it has to do with independence and the sovereignty of our nation. It would be like if we were to give a precondition to the United States that it must change something in the Constitution in order for us to open up relations again. That's absurd." Thank you, then, but no thanks. "We do not want to be something else. We do not want to be Yankees. We want to be what we are. Cuban, and

Latin American, and internationalists. We want to speak Spanish. We want to keep our culture." José Martí said the same thing a century earlier: "El vino, de plátano; y si sale agrio, ¡es nuestro vino!"[8]

Nobody in Washington listened. Just do it our way, President George W. Bush insisted, and you Cubans will be on your way to enjoying "the blessings of liberty."[9] And what if Cubans nevertheless continued to balk at accepting Washington's plan for their uplifting? Then the United States had a plan for that, too: "Hastening Cuba's Transition" was the title of chapter 1 of the report of the Commission for Assistance to a Free Cuba, forty-eight pages listing sixty-two steps the United States intended to take to trigger regime change. Unveiling this comprehensive catalog, President Bush promised, "We're not waiting for the day of Cuban freedom; we are working for the day."[10]

On close inspection, chapter 1 of the report contained no new departure, perhaps because its authors had difficulty thinking of anything that had not already been tried. They wrote a lot about support for Cuban dissidents, but that meant funneling nine-tenths of the budget to subsidize Cuban Americans, most based in electorally critical Florida. The support of this powerfully placed minority was twinned with a few tightening twists of the half-century-old embargo, but that, too, was old hat. From its beginnings in 1962, the embargo sought to make life on the island so miserable that Cubans would force a change in their government. Then we could all move on to the uplifting, chapters 2–6 of the report.

A HOSTILE POLICY toward any particular Cuban government has always been only a symptom of the underlying problem: Washington's uplifting mentality. Clearly delusional, for more than a century this mentality has led otherwise sensible people to believe that these Caribbean neighbors will welcome the opportunity to be guided toward a higher and better civilization by the United States of America, even if these same sensible people would be outraged should some foreign government create a Commission to Improve the United States, especially if this imagined commission were to begin its report by listing sixty-two steps it intended to take to overthrow the current government in Washington.

Every once in a while, one of these sensible people suggests that the mere announcement of a U.S. plan for Cuba's improvement might have the counterproductive effect of stiffening the resolve of Cuban nationalists, but for nearly half a century the response has always been to stay the course, for success is just around the corner. At first that seemed reasonable; who would have dreamed that it would be so difficult to make Cuba's revolutionaries behave as Washington wished? Not Thucydides, and certainly not Senator Allen Ellender, back from an on-site investigation a few days before Batista's fall. "The Cubans are a good people," he wrote in his diary; "they are very sensitive and easily aroused, but I have a feeling that they would listen to reason. The Cubans look upon us as big brothers." The U.S. embassy agreed, sending Washington a reassuring assessment just as Cuba's revolutionaries were launching their final push to power: "It is improbable that a Government actively unfriendly to the United States could exist for any length of time." The Pentagon repeated this shibboleth the day after Batista fled: "Any new Government will probably have to face realities and seek closer relations with the United States."[11]

All of these assessments were made plausible by the fact that earlier generations of Cubans may have contested and finessed the reality of U.S. power but basically had been forced to accept it. Cuba's revolutionary generation was determined to confront it. No one is sure why — Hunter Thompson probably came closest to a good answer when he noted that "every now and then the energy of a whole generation comes to a head in a long fine flash" and that this flash occurs "for reasons that nobody really understands at the time — and which never explain, in retrospect, what actually happened."[12] In Cuba, the revolution began as an amorphous but wildly popular quest for social, political, and economic reform. Unable to interpret this long fine flash but clearly aware that it threatened to alter what Washington considered a satisfactory relationship, the dark suits in the Eisenhower administration concluded that the revolution was not a popular grassroots movement but the machinations of a bearded misfit. They personalized the revolution. In less than a year, Secretary of State Christian Herter was telling his British counterpart, "We do not think that the Cuban people will tolerate Castro indefinitely. Opposition within the country is mounting and his downfall is probably only a question of time." The embassy calculated that it would be "months rather than years," and the CIA agreed: "I had to see Allen Dulles this morning on another matter," the British ambassador reported in late 1959, "and took the opportunity to discuss Cuba on a strictly personal basis. In reply to my question of how long he thought Castro was likely to last, Mr. Dulles said that, if he had to guess, he would say something in the range of eight months."[13]

The revolution was always easily conceived as the work of one alpha male. "Fidel is the leader of the Cuban Revolution," Herbert Matthews told his boss after the *New York Times* sent him to Havana in mid-1960; "he made it, he runs it, and it is his Revolution."[14] In one sense, that was indisputable: Fidel Castro was central to almost everything—or at least everything important—that occurred in Cuba for half a century. But no island is a man. While Castro's talents were indeed extraordinary, his political base was wide and deep, resting on a population fed up with economic deprivation or social injustice or political corruption—and often a combination of all three. And many of these fed-up Cubans were already convinced that the United States, constantly intervening to place the right class in office, was at least partially responsible for their country's condition. While few Cubans bargained for the rigid command economy or for the stifling political intolerance that befell their island, the Cuban Revolution—that long fine flash—clearly constituted a deep-seated expression of Cuban volition.

But given Fidel Castro's larger-than-life figure and Washington's inability to recognize how the past influenced Cubans' perceptions of the present, U.S. eyes found it easy to see the revolution as little more than one man's excesses. Concluding that the Cuban people were sobering up—"Castro is obviously in very great difficulty"—Eisenhower- and Kennedy-era officials thought Cuba could be brought back to normal by the Bay of Pigs invasion, which the CIA was certain most Cubans would welcome. "Less than 30 percent of the population is still with Fidel," the agency reported three months before the attack."[15] That initial miscalculation was followed by Operation Mongoose, the effort to create disaffection with sabotage—blow up enough power lines and burn enough of the sugar crop, the logic went, and Cubans will throw the rascal out. In early 1962, Mongoose chieftain Edward Lansdale predicted Castro's ouster by October. If not, then CIA-hired assassins would kill the man and end the Cuban Revolution.

But the Cubans fought back, and Washington, for its part, could not sustain its early intensity when most eyes began to refocus on Indochina. For several years, fewer predictions held that the end was near, and the CIA even acknowledged that the Cuban government enjoyed "substantial popular support and acquiescence," concluding that "the present regime will maintain an unassailable hold on Cuba indefinitely."[16] After Vietnam, the effort to effect a reconciliation failed when Havana and Washington came to loggerheads over Africa. Ronald Reagan's offensive against the Soviet Union's evil empire followed, and the CIA, still focusing on the revolution as the work a single mortal, returned to its view that the end was near. After two decades in power, at fifty-five a graying Fidel Castro had recently "fumbled, and lost his place in the reams of notes and papers that he now usually brings to the podium when he speaks"; worse yet, he "seemed to lose contact with his audiences." As for substance, the Cuban leader's speeches had become frightfully dark — "despairing" and "brooding about the incredible problems of Cuba's underdevelopment." With his charismatic faculties reduced, his confidence gone and his dreams unrealized, the Fidel Castro of 1981 was no longer an unassailable leader: "Disagreement among key leaders and interest groups is probably higher than in many years, and it is likely to get worse," agency analyst Brian Latell predicted, and "it is possible for the first time in 20 years to contemplate scenarios in which Cuban figures might try to topple the Castros."[17]

Anything can be contemplated, of course, but a coup did not occur. When asked to explain why, the CIA's answer was always "Moscow's subsidies" — Castro could never stand alone, and the Soviet Union's demise therefore triggered a raft of ever-more-confident glimpses of the bright light at the end of the tunnel. Clearly optimistic, in 1993 the CIA said that there was "a better than even chance that Fidel Castro's government will fall within the next few years," but the most confident voice came from the White House, where the first President Bush repeatedly predicted, "Castro will not survive this."[18] The rest of Washington agreed, with the State Department, the Pentagon, and Congress saying much the same thing: "Castro's communism is a dinosaur approaching extinction."[19]

When the Cuban government did not collapse as predicted in the early 1990s, U.S. officials went against the advice offered by every Las Vegas professional: they doubled down with a second round of identical predictions, now more than ever predicated on the conviction that the Cuban Revolution was only one man: "No matter what the dictator intends or plans, *Cuba será libre pronto.*" That view, expressed by the second President Bush in 2003, was shared by the Commission for Assistance to a Free Cuba ("Soon the Cuban people will be freed from Fidel Castro's repressive rule"), by the Department of State ("Castro's rickety system cannot last much longer"), by the Agency for International Development ("The Castro regime is entering its final phase"), by Congress ("The 77-year old Cold War dinosaur's days are surely numbered"), by the Office of the Director of National Intelligence ("It will not be much longer . . . months, not years"), and by the record holder for guessing wrong about Cuba, the CIA's longtime Cuba analyst, now retired (Castro "is near death").[20]

Celebrating the twentieth anniversary of the Bay of Pigs, Fidel Castro had made his own prediction in 1981: "We will still be here in another 20 years." Sure enough, he was. But by 2001 time was no longer on the side of Cuba's revolutionary generation. That year, Bill Clinton ended his eight-year effort to strangle the island's economy with the observation that Fidel Castro "can't last forever. Nobody lives forever." True enough, but the Cuban leader had run through ten U.S. presidents by 2007, when George W. Bush, now nearing the end of his presidency, could only add a religious twist to Clinton's lament: "One day the good Lord will take Fidel Castro away."[21]

WHEN THAT DAY COMES, we might turn at last to the single-most-interesting question about U.S.-Cuban relations—not when the Cuban leader will go, but how Washington's unproductive policy managed to keep going. No other policy can compare. The U.S. refusal to recognize the Soviet Union lasted only sixteen years, the People's Republic of China only twenty-two. The United States has not simply declined to have normal diplomatic and economic relations with Havana for half a century; it has also spent most of these past five decades openly and actively trying to overthrow the island's government—or, in the euphemism-cloaked circumlocutions of today's Commission for Assistance to a Free Cuba, trying to "hasten Cuba's transition."

Why did Washington doggedly pursue such a policy? The belief that the Cuban Revolution was little more than the work of one man who could not last forever has never explained U.S. policy. Concrete interests have fueled the animosity. From the beginning, early in the nineteenth century, the island has regularly posed a threat to two important and entirely legitimate U.S. interests. At that time, Cuban-based pirates were preying on U.S. shipping, and the United States was also concerned that a potent European power might acquire Cuba from Spain and use it as a base to threaten U.S. security. Fast-forward to the mid–twentieth century, and it is easy to see how both economic and security interests again suffered—and suffered gravely—from the Cuban Revolution, with economic interests the first to be attacked: U.S. investors lost a lot of money in the years immediately after Batista's fall, and some had enough political clout to walk into the Oval Office and demand help.

Perhaps the traditional influence of economic elites in almost every society explains the ease with which the protection of these parochial interests became public policy, but in the Cuban case, the transfer of private woes onto public shoulders was aided by the perception of a threat to U.S. security. Historians will argue forever about how this concern for the nation's security came to govern Washington's policy toward revolutionary Cuba, but there is no doubt that U.S. officials were poised to pounce without the prodding of disgruntled investors. CIA director Allen Dulles conceived of communism as a cancer, and when he had seen Guatemala fall ill, he had moved quickly and decisively to snip out the tumor. Now it had metastasized to Cuba.

But the Cuban Revolution occurred at a moment of much confusion about the appropriate treatment. Analysts were struggling to understand the rising generation of Latin Americans who had spit on Vice President Nixon only a few months earlier, and U.S. officials were almost ready to acknowledge the need to break up large landholdings and distribute small plots to peasants, even if some of that land belonged to influential U.S. investors. Sensing Washington's mental struggle, one major investor deftly shifted gears and sought the help of Senate majority leader Lyndon Johnson, *not* because Cuba's agrarian reform institute had seized his land but because "Cuba is being dominated and run by agents of Soviet Communism." The agrarian reform was not what Cuban revolutionaries claimed it to be—an effort to change the island's unjust landowning structure and to minimize foreign domination of an agroexport economy; rather, it was simply an indicator of "a deliberate Communist effort to block the flow of American capital to all Latin-America, create eventual chaos and soften the hemisphere for Communism."[22]

This explanation of U.S. policy—an easily constructed condominium of interests between economic elites and national security officials—probably comes close to reflecting what actually happened, even if it begs the question that has mesmerized so many students of the revolution: were the leaders of Cuba's 26th of July Movement communists from the beginning, or did U.S. hostility in a rigid bipolar world force them into Moscow's arms? Some observers insist that Cuba's tilt toward the Soviet Union came in response to U.S. actions; others point out that most of Washington's actions came in response to hostile Cuban behavior; still others remind us that Cuban behavior was conditioned by the republic's unfortunate history, the leitmotif of which was injustice, corruption, and domination by the United States. In the end, Allen Dulles was probably wise to declare this chicken-egg question unanswerable: "Futile to argue when he became a communist."[23]

Dulles jotted that down in the 1960s; were he afforded the perspective we have today, he would probably argue that the revolutionaries of 1959 were determined, first and foremost, to renegotiate many of their society's political and economic relationships, among them the intimate but grossly subservient relationship Cuba had developed with its northern neighbor. When a future generation gains access to the Cuban archives, it may uncover the hand of hard-core communists guiding what occurred, but it is a far safer bet they will discover that the Cuban Revolution's *international* dimension reflected a nonideological decision to attack the *domestic* structures that allowed a nearby superpower to dominate Cubans' economy, their politics, and their lives. Everything else was consequence, not cause.

The one indisputable fact is that by 1960 Washington saw Cuba as a security threat. The protection of economic interests subsequently became relatively insignificant, while the rollback of communism became the overarching interest underlying U.S. policy.

Then why did the United States not change its policy after the end of the Cold War, when Cuba no longer threatened U.S. security? Part of the answer is a third interest, one that often trumps all others: politicians' interest in winning elections. "Ninety-eight percent of U.S. voters never think of Cuba," insisted John Ferch, a former chief of the U.S. Interests Section; "the only people who think Cuba is important are the Cubans in Miami." No one responsible for U.S. foreign policy would have paid these immigrant asylum seekers much attention if they had settled in Wyoming, which has two senators and one representative and therefore three votes in the Electoral College. But the Cuban refugees chose instead to settle primarily in booming Florida, whose two senators and twenty-five representatives make it the fourth-largest prize in the quadrennial winner-take-all Electoral College sweepstakes. And so, complained the frustrated chief executive officer of agribusiness heavyweight Archer Daniels Midland, "every presidential candidate is invited to Miami to make a speech to a handful of rich Cubans, and the candidate says, 'I will never speak to Castro.' The result is that we look to the rest of the world like idiots."[24]

Nowhere is the world's opposition more obvious than in the annual U.N. General Assembly vote urging the United States to scrap its embargo; the 2008 tally against U.S. policy was 185–3. But who really cares? Washington has found it easy to ignore this annual exercise because none of the 185 countries has done anything more than vote. With the possible exception of the international challenge to the Helms-Burton Act (and this only because the law violated a legal principle by asserting extraterritorial jurisdiction), no post–Cold War government has ever cared enough about Cuba to irritate Washington. When the world's deference is coupled with the Pentagon's disinterest and with the fact that those who suffered property losses a half century ago are either dead or quickly heading in that direction, it is easy to see why twenty-first-century Cuba is simply another tropical island to everyone — to everyone, that is, except Cuban Americans, many of whom react with acute dismay whenever Washington seems to forget how important the island is to them.

Given this fact of political life, how is it possible to bring this harsh half-century quarrel to a sensible conclusion and arrive at The End? A prior question, still unanswered, is when will the Cuban American community cast its ballots and make its campaign contributions on some basis other than which party's candidates promise to be more vigorous in their hostility toward Cuba's revolutionary government? Some dispersion is already occurring, but no one knows how long it will take for Cuban Americans to spread out and behave like Irish Americans or Italian Americans; the safe hypothesis is that today's aging generation of hard-core revolutionaries and diehard counterrevolutionaries will first have to fade away. Then, as the next generation makes changes in Cuba, Cuban Americans' assessments of those changes will slowly diversify until at some point the pollsters will announce that it is safe to declare victory without risking the loss of Florida's electoral votes.

The mortality tables suggest that this point will come sooner rather than later. When it does, then the easy part will be over; the difficult-to-answer question will be whether the United States can abandon its ideology of benevolent domination. In the uplifting vision etched into today's report of the Commission for Assistance to a Free Cuba, an army of AID contractors and NED grantees will soon be standing shoulder to shoulder with Cuba's postrevolutionary generation, helping construct a new and improved country. Perhaps the uplifting will work this time, but no one should be surprised if this latest generation of U.S. officials discovers what the Roosevelt-Taft generation of equally optimistic Progressives found a century ago, when Governor-General Wood complained that "it is next to impossible to make them believe that we have only their own interests at heart."[25] What lesson of the past hundred years could be more obvious—and more obviously unlearned—than that Cubans simply do not want to be uplifted by the United States of America?

Thucydides would answer that it does not matter what they want. And if past experience is a guide to predict the future, then the best wager would be that the United States will use some combination of carrots and sticks to convince Cubans to install leaders willing to accept a little uplifting. But as Wood's generation discovered, it is one thing to make a people acquiesce and another to make them good. That seems particularly true about post–Cold War Cuba policy, which has invariably equated "good" with "democratic," for it is based on the simplistic belief that democracy is about ousting tyrants and installing democrats—or, as Woodrow Wilson once phrased it, about teaching Latin Americans to elect good men.[26] The problem, and the inescapable conclusion to be drawn from the hundred-year history of U.S.-Cuban relations, is that there are no democrats waiting on the Cuban sidelines for an opportunity to govern after the island's undemocratic leaders have died or been forced out. Ignoring this history, each new Washington generation vows to help make Cuba democratic, even if that means, as Senator Henry Cabot Lodge phrased it in 1906, shaking Cubans by their necks until they behave.

But democracy is not about replacing bad leaders with good leaders; rather, it is a method of governance, simply one good way people have developed to get along without shaking one another by the neck. Democracy is therefore best conceived as a never-ending process of nonviolent contestation and accommodation, a process that requires the slow, ceaseless perfection of rules and procedures in a crowded environment where everyone has a right to help determine who gets what, when, and how. For this reason, successful democracies are invariably characterized by leaders who have honed their abilities to negotiate and compromise. Democracies require people who know how to bargain.

This is an acquired skill; nobody is born a democrat. People become democrats by sharpening their negotiating skills slowly, through debates with others who disagree, often in fundamental ways and often over truly important issues. Washington's view has always been clear: Cubans failed to develop these skills during their first century of independence, even though the United States was helping almost continuously. But only one senior U.S. official has ever recognized that this assistance might have contributed to the problem. This epiphany came in 1908, when yet another imposed governor-general, Charles Magoon, noticed that the Platt Amendment had encouraged Cubans to opt out of politics; whatever the problem to be solved, he told President Roosevelt, the amendment had created the belief that "the United States should and will attend to the matter."[27]

Here, then, is the fatal flaw undermining the century-long U.S. effort to uplift Cuba, seen in today's bipartisan statements that the United States remains committed to having Cubans enjoy the blessings of liberty: these statements retard any effort by Cubans to negotiate among themselves the thousands of issues, large and small, that continuously arise out of human interaction. These announcements of benevolent domination encourage the Cuban exile community to continue doing what most of it has done since 1959—stand on the sidelines in Miami, wearing its intransigence as a badge of honor while pushing the United States to attend to the matter. And, logic suggests, these statements encourage an equal intransigence among Cubans living on the island. No rational Cuban on either side of the Straits of Florida would go through the arduous process of negotiation and compromise while the president stands on the White House lawn and waves a 423-page plan to solve everything.

Of course, Cubans may not want to create a democracy, with or without U.S. assistance. Like the United States for much of its history, they might prefer some form of oligarchy or a type of democracy that would seem strange to U.S. citizens—perhaps one where the popular vote determines who becomes president, or one where the playing field is leveled by public campaign funding. Those things are not for the United States to determine for Cubans, as investment banker Dwight Morrow tried to tell Ambassador Enoch Crowder during a 1922 business trip to Havana: "Of course, the Government in Cuba has been and is very bad. It is possible, yes, it is probable, that the United States might run Cuba much better. As I get older, however, I think I become more and more convinced that good government is not a substitute for self-government. The kind of mistakes that America would make in running Cuba would be different from those that the Cubans themselves make, but they would probably cause a new kind of trouble and a new kind of suffering."[28]

Both a committed democrat and an exceptionally accomplished negotiator, Morrow would no doubt be disappointed by the continued absence of liberal democracy in Cuba. But since today's circumstances are so similar to 1922 (Crowder was overseeing Washington's "Moralization Program," a direct ancestor of today's Commission for Assistance to a Free Cuba), Morrow would probably write much the same letter today. And since what he wrote in 1922 had no impact whatever on U.S. policy, today he might bolster his argument by including a copy of Thomas Jefferson's enduring contribution to democratic practice, a simple declaration he and his fellow oligarchs tacked up on walls throughout the thirteen British colonies in 1776: it said that all people, including presumably the Cubans, have the right to institute their own government, laying its foundation on such principles and organizing its powers in such forms as to them shall seem most likely to effect their safety and happiness.

That has always been the central message from Cuba's revolutionaries. "We have a different tradition, a different culture, our own way of thinking," Fidel Castro repeated continually for five decades, while Jefferson's children somehow failed to understand why this revolutionary generation steadfastly refused Washington's uplifting.[29] This failure is surprising, since Jefferson's revolutionary thinking is now our conventional wisdom. But the mere existence of a Commission for Assistance to a Free Cuba is proof that the United States still cannot concede to Cubans the right of self-determination, while Cubans apparently consider this concession the essential first step toward accommodation.

José Martí offered this advice to his compatriots: "One must not attribute, through a provincial antipathy, a fatal and inbred wickedness to the continent's fair-skinned nation simply because it does not speak our language, or see the world as we see it, or resemble us in its political defects, so different from our own." We do not know whether today's Cubans have taken Martí's advice to heart, but we know of at least one Cuban leader who was never reluctant to discuss the multiple defects of his fair-skinned neighbor, but who nonetheless considered accommodation inevitable. "We cannot move, nor can the United States," Fidel Castro pointed out. "Speaking realistically, someday some sort of ties will be established." Perhaps if Washington were to concentrate on controlling its compulsion to uplift, which to Cubans is clearly an especially annoying defect, then the citizens of that infernal little republic might be a little less irritating, a little more willing to accommodate legitimate U.S. interests. The only alternative is another half century of hostility, and in the end there still will be no escape. After all, Castro concluded, one fact can never change: "We are neighbors."[30]

NOTES

Unless otherwise identified, all Fidel Castro speeches are from the Cuban government's Web site, http://www.cuba.cu/gobierno/discursos/.

Abbreviations

In addition to abbreviations used in the text, the following source abbreviations are used in the notes.

AFP	*American Foreign Policy, Current Documents*
AID	U.S. Agency for International Development
ARA	Bureau of American Republics Affairs, Department of State
AWF	Ann Whitman File, Dwight David Eisenhower Library, Abilene, Kansas
CF	Country File
CFR	*U.S. Code of Federal Regulations*
CIA	Central Intelligence Agency
CRS	Congressional Research Service
DDE	Dwight David Eisenhower
DDEL	Dwight David Eisenhower Library, Abilene, Kansas
DDRS	Declassified Documents Reference System
DIA	Defense Intelligence Agency
DOS	Department of State
DOSB	*Department of State Bulletin*
FDR	Franklin Delano Roosevelt
FDRL	Franklin Delano Roosevelt Library, Hyde Park, New York
FOIA	Documents obtained via Freedom of Information Act, in possession of author
FR	*Federal Register*
FRUS	*Foreign Relations of the United States*
GAO	U.S. Government Accountability Office (formerly General Accounting Office)
GRFL	Gerald R. Ford Library, Ann Arbor, Michigan
ILM	*International Legal Materials*
INR	Bureau of Intelligence and Research, Department of State
INS	Immigration and Naturalization Service
JCL	Jimmy Carter Library, Atlanta, Georgia
JFK	John F. Kennedy
JFKL	John F. Kennedy Library, Boston, Massachusetts
LANIC	Latin American Network Information Center, University of Texas, Austin

LBJ	Lyndon Baines Johnson
LBJL	Lyndon Baines Johnson Library, Austin, Texas
LC	Manuscript Division, Library of Congress, Washington, D.C.
Memcon	Memorandum of Conversation, Department of State
NIE	National Intelligence Estimate
NSA	National Security Archive, Washington, D.C.
NSAM	National Security Action Memorandum
NSC	National Security Council
NSDM	National Security Decision Memorandum
NSFJ	National Security Files, Lyndon Baines Johnson Library, Austin, Texas
NSFK	National Security Files, John F. Kennedy Library, Boston, Massachusetts
NSSM	National Security Study Memorandum
NYT	*New York Times*
PC	*The United States and Castro's Cuba, 1950–1970: The Paterson Collection* [microform] (Wilmington, Del.: Scholarly Resources, 1998)
PL	Public Law
POF	President's Office Files, John F. Kennedy Library, Boston, Massachusetts
PPP	*Public Papers of the Presidents of the United States*
PRO	Public Records Office (now the National Archives), London, England
RG59	Record Group 59, General Records of the Department of State, National Archives and Records Administration, Washington, D.C.
RNSA	National Security Affairs, Records of the Office of the National Security Adviser, Country File, Jimmy Carter Library, Atlanta
SSC	Special Coordination Committee (Carter administration)
Stat.	*U.S. Statutes at Large*
TIAS	*Treaties and Other International Acts Series*
USINT	U.S. Interests Section, Havana, Cuba
UST	*U.S. Treaties and Other International Agreements*
WCPD	*Weekly Compilation of Presidential Documents*
WHCF	White House Central Files
WHOF	White House Office Files, Dwight David Eisenhower Library, Abilene, Kansas
ZBC	Zbigniew Brzezinski Collection, Jimmy Carter Library, Atlanta, Georgia

Introduction

1. Louis A. Pérez Jr., *Essays on Cuban History: Historiography and Research* (Gainesville: University Press of Florida, 1994), 116; Fernando Ortíz, "Las relaciones económicas entre los Estados Unidos y Cuba," *Revista Bimestre Cubana* 22 (July–August 1929): 583.

2. Huntington Wilson, "The Relation of Government to Foreign Investment," *Annals of the American Academy of Political and Social Science* 68 (November 1916): 301.

3. Herter Telephone Log, 11 July 1960, Folder CAH Telephone Calls, 7/1/60 to 8/31/60 (3), Box 13, Christian Herter Papers, DDEL; President's Statement on Closing the Embassy, 3 January 1961, *PPP*, 388; "Transfer: January 19, 1961, Meeting of the President and Senator

Kennedy," 19 January 1961, Folder "Kennedy, John F. 1960–61 (2)," Box 2, Augusta–Walter Reed Series, Post-Presidential Papers, DDEL. These are the minutes taken by Eisenhower aide Wilton Peters. See also *FRUS* 1961–63, 10:44; "Account of My December 6th, 1960 Meeting with President-Elect Kennedy," December 1960, Folder "ACW Diary—December 1960," Box 11, Ann Whitman Diary Series, AWF.

4. Castro Speech, Havana, 16 April 1981; Robert C. McFarlane with Zofia Smardz, *Special Trust* (New York: Cadell and Davies, 1994), 177–78. For the blockade proposal, see *60 Minutes* (CBS) interview with Dan Rather, recorded 26 January 1980, audio CD, Ronald Reagan Presidential Library, Simi Valley, California.

5. Remarks at a Debate Watch Party, Coral Gables, Florida, 30 September 2004, *WCPD*, 2196; Remarks at Newport, Rhode Island, 28 June 2007, *WCPD*, 2 July 2007, 882.

6. Nixon Speech to Veterans of Foreign Wars, Detroit, 24 August 1960, in U.S. Congress, Senate, *Freedom of Communications: Final Report of the Committee on Commerce, United States Senate*, pt. 2, *The Speeches, Remarks, Press Conferences, and Study Papers of Vice President Richard M. Nixon, August 1 through November 7, 1960*, 87th Cong., 1st sess., 1961, 30; see also 219; Alexander Haig quoted in Nancy Reagan with William Novak, *My Turn: The Memoirs of Nancy Reagan* (New York: Random House, 1989), 242.

7. Arthur M. Schlesinger Jr., *Journals, 1952–2000*, ed. Andrew Schlesinger and Stephen Schlesinger (New York: Penguin, 2007), 596.

8. John Crimmins Oral History, 10 May 1989, U.S. Foreign Affairs Oral History Collection, Association for Diplomatic Studies and Training, Arlington, Virginia; LBJ Telephone Conversation, 2 December 1963, Folder "December 1963 [1 of 3] Chrono File," Box 1, Recordings and Transcripts of Telephone Conversations and Meetings, JFK Series, LBJL.

9. Bundy, Memorandum of Conversation with the President, 19 February 1964, *FRUS* 1964–68, 31:11.

10. Norweb to Secretary of State, 14 January 1946, 837.00/1-1466, RG59.

11. 2 March 1901, 31 *Stat.* 897.

12. Press Conference with Foreign Correspondents, 19 December 1991, *PPP*, 1647.

13. Wood to Senator Foraker, 11 January 1901, Box 30, Leonard Wood Papers, LC.

14. *Report to the President* (Washington, D.C.: U.S. Commission for Assistance to a Free Cuba, May 2004), xxi.

15. Khrushchev's Comment to Western Diplomats in Moscow, 18 November 1956, reported in *The Times* (London), 19 November 1956, 8.

16. Allen Dulles, "My Answer to the Bay of Pigs," n.d., Allen Dulles Papers, Princeton University. On 15 July 1983, this document was photocopied for Lucien Vandenbroucke; in 1999, however, the manuscript could no longer be found in the Dulles Papers. Vandenbroucke kindly provided a copy, along with the title, although neither this nor any other title appears on the sixty-six-page document. A quite different 1965 typescript, also titled "My Answer to the Bay of Pigs," is in Folder 17, Box 62, of the Dulles Papers at Princeton University.

17. *In Defense of National Sovereignty: Cuba Replies to the U.S.A. Note* (Havana: Public Relations Department, Ministry of State, Republic of Cuba, 1959); McGeorge Bundy, "Memorandum of Discussion on Cuba," 28 January 1961, *FRUS* 1961–63, 10:61.

18. Castro Interview, 1974, published as Frank Mankiewicz and Kirby Jones, "Conversation with Fidel Castro," *Oui*, January 1975, 114.

Chapter 1

1. Instructions, J. Q. Adams to Hugh Nelson, U.S. Minister to Spain, 28 April 1823, in *Writings of John Quincy Adams*, ed. Worthington Chauncy Ford (New York: Macmillan, 1913–17), 7:413.

The first use of U.S. forces came in 1822, when the navy landed on Cuba's northwest coast to burn a pirate station; five landings for the same purpose followed in 1823: 8 April at Escondido, 16 April at Cayo Blanco, 11 July at Siquapa, 21 July at Cabo Cruz, and 23 October at Camarioca. In October 1824, the seventh landing occurred near Matanzas, but Cuba's monopoly on U.S. attention was broken the following month when the navy landed in Puerto Rico. The ninth landing occurred in Sagüa La Grande in March 1825.

2. *Congressional Globe*, 9 April 1869, appendix 18–30. See also Eric T. L. Love, *Race over Empire: Racism and U.S. Imperialism, 1865–1900* (Chapel Hill: University of North Carolina Press, 2004).

3. López Roberts to Fish, 18 September 1869, Fish to López Roberts, 13 October 1869 (Fish's acknowledgment "with regret"), both in U.S. Congress, House, Exec. Doc. 160, 41st Cong., 2nd sess., 1870, 133, 138.

4. Fish to Robert Schenck, 15 January 1876, letterbook, p. 325, Container 216, Fish Papers, LC. The first State Department message about the *Virginius* was sent to Congress on 13 June 1870; the second followed on 5 January 1874. For a Cuban perspective on U.S. policy during this era, see Emilio Roig de Leuchsenring, *Cuba y los Estados Unidos, 1805–1898* (Havana: Sociedad Cubana de Estudios Históricos e Internacionales, 1949), esp. chap. 14 ("Hamilton Fish, the worst enemy in the United States of the revolutionaries of '68") and chap. 20 ("How in 1869 the United States denied Cubans were capable, insulted their virtue, and denigrated their character"). For a useful recent overview, see Jay Sexton, "The United States, the Cuban Rebellion, and the Multilateral Initiative of 1875," *Diplomatic History* 30 (June 2006): 335–65.

5. Adam Badeau, Confidential Memorandum, 23 October 1883, Consular Despatches from Havana, RG59.

6. Olney to Cleveland, 25 September 1895, Grover Cleveland Papers, LC.

7. Olney to Dupuy de Lôme, 4 April 1896, Dupuy de Lôme to Olney, 4 June 1896, both in *FRUS* 1897, 540–48.

8. Annual Message, 7 December 1896, *FRUS* 1896, xxxiii, xxxv.

9. Kirk H. Porter and Donald Bruce Johnson, comps., *National Party Platforms, 1840–1964* (Urbana: University of Illinois Press, 1966), 108.

10. Annual Message, 6 December 1897, *FRUS* 1897, xx.

11. Theodore Roosevelt, *Life of Thomas Hart Benton* (Boston: Houghton Mifflin, 1887), 175–76; Theodore Roosevelt, "American Ideals," *Forum* 18 (February 1895): 749; *Address of Hon. Theodore Roosevelt before the Naval War College, Newport, R.I., Wednesday, June 2, 1897* (Washington, D.C.: Navy Branch, U.S. Government Printing Office, 1897), 5–6.

12. Taft to Philander C. Knox, 9 September 1911, William Howard Taft Papers, LC.

13. Henry Cabot Lodge, "Our Blundering Foreign Policy," *Forum* 19 (March 1895): 16–17.

14. Annual Message, 6 December 1897, *FRUS* 1897, xv; John W. Foster, recounting a conversation with McKinley, in *Diplomatic Memoirs* (Boston: Houghton Mifflin, 1909), 2:256.

15. Statement to the Associated Press, 24 January 1898, in *Letters of Grover Cleveland, 1850–1908*, ed. Allan Nevins (Boston: Houghton Mifflin, 1933), 492.

16. *New York Journal*, 9 February 1898, 1; for documents covering the episode, see *FRUS* 1898, 1007–22.

17. *Congressional Record*, 19 December 1927, 808.

18. *New York Journal*, 12, 15 February 1897.

19. Platt to Isaac H. Bromley, 18 December 1895, in Louis A. Coolidge, *An Old-Fashioned Senator: Orville H. Platt of Connecticut; the Story of a Life Unselfishly Devoted to the Public Service* (1910; reprint, Port Washington, N.Y.: Kennikat, 1971), 1:266; Cleveland to Olney, 26 April 1898, Richard Olney Papers, LC. Neither Platt to Isaac H. Bromley, 18 December 1895, nor Platt to H. Wales Lines, 25 March 1898 (see chap. 1, n. 32) can be found in the Platt Papers at the Connecticut State Library, whose curator observed that the great bulk of the senator's papers "were destroyed by a misguided clerk." For the argument that the explosion of the *Maine* was an accident, see H. G. Rickover, *How the Battleship Maine Was Destroyed* (Washington, D.C.: Naval History Division, Department of the Navy, 1976), 91, 104.

20. Louis A. Pérez Jr., *Cuba between Empires, 1878–1902* (Pittsburgh: University of Pittsburgh Press, 1983), 178; U.S. Congress, House, *Commercial Relations of the United States with Foreign Countries during the Years 1898 and 1897*, House Document 483, 55th Cong., 2nd sess., 1898, 1:135; Annual Message to Congress, 7 December 1896, *FRUS* 1896, xxxi.

21. Adams to Hugh Nelson, 28 April 1823, in *Writings of John Quincy Adams*, ed. Ford, 7:372–73.

22. Jefferson to Monroe, 23 June, 24 October 1823, in *The Writings of Thomas Jefferson*, ed. Albert Ellery Bergh (Washington, D.C.: Thomas Jefferson Memorial Association, 1903–7), 15:454, 478–79.

23. *Congressional Globe*, 5, 15 May 1848, 599, 632.

24. Lodge, "Our Blundering Foreign Policy," 16–17.

25. U.S. Congress, House, *Commercial Relations*, 1:134–35.

26. Campbell to Buchanan, 18 May 1848, Consular Despatches from Havana, RG59; Joseph J. Dimock, *Impressions of Cuba in the Nineteenth Century: The Travel Diary of Joseph J. Dimock*, ed. Louis A. Pérez Jr. (Wilmington, Del.: Scholarly Resources, 1998), 85, 140, 13.

27. *Message from the President of the United States to the Two Houses of Congress at the Commencement of the Second Session of the Thirty-second Congress*, House Ex. Doc. 1, 32nd Cong., 2nd sess., 6 December 1852, 5.

28. *Congressional Globe*, 16 February 1859, 1062, 15 February 1859, 160, 26 February 1859, 1344–45, 1848, 1851; Adam Badeau, Confidential Memorandum, 23 October 1883, Consular Despatches from Havana, RG59.

29. Henry Cabot Lodge, "Our Duty to Cuba," *Forum* 21 (May 1896): 282, 287; Atkins to Olney, 5 May 1896, in Edwin F. Atkins, *Sixty Years in Cuba: Reminiscences of Edwin F. Atkins* (Cambridge, Mass.: Riverside, 1926), 235–36.

30. Lee to Judge [William R. Day, Assistant Secretary of State], 12 January 1898, Lee to Assistant Secretary of State, 13 January 1898, both in Consular Despatches from Havana, RG59. For Lee's strong annexationist preferences, see Lee to William R. Day, 18 January 1898, Consular Despatches from Havana, RG59.

31. *New York Journal*, 18, 23 February 1898; *New York World*, 20, 21 February 1898; Platt to

H. Wales Lines, 25 March 1898, reprinted in Coolidge, *Old-Fashioned Senator*, 1:271; *Congressional Record*, 23 May 1900, 5893; Shelby M. Cullom, *Fifty Years of Public Service* (Chicago: McClurg, 1911), 283–84; Bryan quoted in *NYT*, 1 April 1898, 1. Pulitzer's paper headlined, "War Fever Rising from *World*'s Evidence."

32. The ratified treaty is 30 *Stat.* 1754, 11 April 1899. For the Cuban concern about being excluded from these deliberations, see Emilio Roig de Leuchsenring, *Cuba no debe su independencia a los Estados Unidos*, 2nd ed. (Havana: Sociedad Cubana de Estudios Históricos e Internacionales, 1950); Herminio Portell Vilá, *Historia de Cuba en sus relaciones con los Estados Unidos y España* (Havana: Montero, 1938–41), esp. vol. 3, chaps. 2–3; Roig de Leuchsenring, *Cuba y los Estados Unidos*.

33. Major General S. B. M. Young in *Brooklyn Eagle*, 6 August 1898, 3.

34. Woodford to McKinley, 17 March 1898, *FRUS* 1898, 687; Annual Message of the President, December 1898, *FRUS* 1898, xlvi. Senator Henry Teller's motivation probably included a desire to protect his Colorado constituents' sugar beet market from competition with low-cost Cuban cane. See Horatio S. Rubens, *Liberty: The Story of Cuba* (New York: Brewer, Warren, and Putnam, 1932), 341; George W. Auxier, "The Propaganda Activities of the Cuban *Junta* in Precipitating the Spanish-American War, 1895–1898," *Hispanic American Historical Review* 19 (August 1939): 304; Nathaniel Wright Stephenson, *Nelson W. Aldrich: A Leader in American Politics* (New York: Scribner's, 1930), 157; Leon Burr Richardson, *William E. Chandler, Republican* (New York: Dodd, Mead, 1940), 580; David F. Healy, *The United States in Cuba, 1898–1902: Generals, Politicians, and the Search for Policy* (Madison: University of Wisconsin Press, 1963), 24–27.

35. Wood to Roosevelt, 18 August 1899, Theodore Roosevelt Papers, LC; Roosevelt to Lodge, 21 July 1899, in *Selections from the Correspondence of Theodore Roosevelt and Henry Cabot Lodge, 1884–1918*, ed. Henry Cabot Lodge (New York: Scribner's, 1925), 1:413–14.

36. Wood to McKinley, 12 April 1900, Leonard Wood Papers, LC; José Martí, "Nuestra América," 30 January 1891, in *Obras Completas* (Havana: Editorial Nacional de Cuba, 1963), 6:20.

37. Root to Wood, 14 April 1900, General Classified Files, 1898–1945, Record Group 350, Records of the Bureau of Insular Affairs, National Archives and Records Administration, Washington, D.C.; Wood to Roosevelt, 8 February 1901, Wood Papers; Root to Wood, 20 June 1900, Elihu Root Papers, LC. For the most helpful guide to these machinations and the underlying fear that Cubans, left to themselves, would elect inappropriate leaders, see Pérez, *Cuba between Empires, 1878–1902*, 304–12.

38. Kirk H. Porter and Donald Bruce Johnson, comps., *National Party Platforms 1840–1964* (Urbana: University of Illinois Press, 1966), 113 (Democrats), 124 (Republicans).

39. Wood to Platt, 6 December 1900, Wood to Root, 8 February, 30 May 1901, all in Wood Papers; Wood to Root, 19 January 1901, Root Papers; Wood to Root, 16 June 1901, General Classified Files, 1898–1945, Record Group 350, Records of the Bureau of Insular Affairs. The Platt Amendment is 31 *Stat.* 897, 2 March 1901.

40. Wood to Roosevelt, 12 April 1901, Roosevelt Papers; Root to Wood, 2 March 1901, Root Papers.

41. Wood to Roosevelt, 28 October 1901, Wood Papers; Platt to Edwin F. Atkins, 11 June 1901, Orville H. Platt Papers, Connecticut State Library, Hartford. "Dejaron en Cuba un país mediatizado, se apoderon de todo, lo comparon todo y convirtieron el país en una neo-

colonia" (Speech, Havana, 7 February 1997, in *Granma*, 11 February 1997, 5). For the views of the Constituent Assembly, see Emilio Roig de Leuchsenring, *Historia de la Enmienda Platt* (Havana: Cultural, 1935), 1:125–52. On the use of Platt Amendment in the first decades of the century, see Louis A. Pérez Jr., *Cuba under the Platt Amendment, 1902–1934* (Pittsburgh: University of Pittsburgh Press, 1986); Cosme de la Torriente, "The Platt Amendment," *Foreign Affairs* 8 (April 1930): 364–78.

42. Roosevelt Annual Message, 6 December 1904, *FRUS* 1904, xli; Steinhart to Secretary of State, 8 September 1906, in "Appendix E: Cuban Pacification," *Annual Reports of the War Department for the Fiscal Year Ended June 30, 1906* (Washington, D.C.: U.S. Government Printing Office, 1906), 444–45. A naturalized U.S. citizen who had lived in the United States for the three decades prior to independence, Estrada Palma won an uncontested election in late 1901 without leaving his home in upstate New York.

43. Roosevelt to Henry L. White, 13 September 1906, Roosevelt Papers; Lodge to Roosevelt, 16 September 1906, in *Selections*, ed. Lodge, 2:232–33. Roosevelt's message was communicated via acting secretary Bacon to Steinhart, 10 September 1906, Steinhart to Secretary of State, 14 September 1906, and Roosevelt to Taft, 28 September 1906, all in *Annual Reports of the War Department*, 445, 446–47, 481.

44. Taft to Roosevelt, 20 September 1906, in *Annual Reports of the War Department*, 469; Taft to Charles Taft, 17 May 1901, 4 October 1906, Taft to Beekman Winthrop, 16 September 1904, Taft to Helen Taft, 20, 22 September 1906, all in Taft Papers; *Annual Reports of the War Department*, 456.

45. *Annual Reports of the War Department*, 463, 478, 482, 519, 543; Roosevelt to Lodge, 27 September 1906, in *Selections*, ed. Lodge, 2:234; Roosevelt to Taft, 26 September 1906, Roosevelt to Kermit Roosevelt, 23 October 1906, both in *The Letters of Theodore Roosevelt*, ed. Elting E. Morison (Cambridge: Harvard University Press, 1951–54), 5:425, 465; Roosevelt Speech to the Harvard Union, 23 February 1907, in Theodore Roosevelt, *Presidential Addresses and State Papers* (New York: Review of Reviews, 1910), 6:1178–79.

46. William H. Taft, "Some Recent Instances of National Altruism," *National Geographic* 18 (July 1907): 438; Speech of Provisional Governor William Howard Taft, Opening Day Exercises of the National University of Havana, 1 October 1906, reprinted in *Annual Reports of the War Department*, 541–42.

47. Roosevelt to Taft, 22 January 1907, in *Letters of Theodore Roosevelt*, ed. Morison, 5:560; William Franklin Sands, *Our Jungle Diplomacy* (Chapel Hill: University of North Carolina Press, 1944), 62; Magoon to Root, 16 April 1908, Root Papers.

48. Lieutenant Colonel R. L. Bullard, "How Cubans Differ from Us," *North American Review* 186 (November 1907): 421; Magoon to Roosevelt, 16 April 1908, Roosevelt Papers.

49. Magoon to Roosevelt, 16 April 1908, Taft to Roosevelt, 22 September 1906, both in Roosevelt Papers; Wood to Root, 8 February 1901, Wood Papers; Taft to Charles Taft, 9 October 1906, Taft Papers. On the creation of Cuba's army, see Louis A. Pérez Jr., *Army Politics in Cuba, 1898–1958* (Pittsburgh: University of Pittsburgh Press, 1976), chap. 2. On the Magoon years generally, see David A. Lockmiller, *Magoon in Cuba: A History of the Second Intervention, 1906–1909* (Chapel Hill: University of North Carolina Press, 1938); Allan Reed Millett, *The Politics of Intervention: The Military Occupation of Cuba, 1906–1909* (Columbus: Ohio State University Press, 1968).

50. Zimmermann to von Eckhardt, 16 January 1917, in *Official German Documents Relating*

to the World War (New York: Oxford University Press, 1923), 2:1337. On the 1917 intervention, see Leo J. Meyer, "The United States and the Cuban Revolution of 1917," *Hispanic American Historical Review* 10 (February 1930): 138–66; Louis A. Pérez Jr., *Intervention, Revolution, and Politics in Cuba, 1913–1921* (Pittsburgh: University of Pittsburgh Press, 1978); James Brown Scott, "The Attitude of the United States toward Political Disturbances in Cuba," *American Journal of International Law* 11 (April 1917): 419–23; Robert F. Smith, *The United States and Cuba: Business and Diplomacy, 1917–1960* (New Haven: Yale University Press, 1960).

51. Dulles to Lansing, 14 February 1917, 337.11/162, RG59.

52. Burton J. Hendrick, *The Life and Letters of Walter H. Page* (Garden City, N.Y.: Doubleday, Page, 1923–25), 1:204; for a direct letter expressing the same idea in different words, see Wilson to Tyrrell, 22 November 1913, Woodrow Wilson Papers, LC.

53. John Bassett Moore, Untitled Memorandum, 21 October 1913, John Bassett Moore Papers, LC; Long to Lansing, 15 February 1918, 711.13/55, RG59.

54. Davis to Long, 4 January 1921, 837.00/1949, RG59.

55. Division of Latin-American Affairs, "Synopsis of General Crowder's 13 Memoranda," 14 November 1923, 123 C 8812/51, RG59.

56. Stokely W. Morgan, "American Policy and Problems in Central America," Lecture to the Foreign Service School, Department of State, 29 January 1926, Entry 623, RG59. Senator Bruce added (*Congressional Record*, 20 January 1928, 1787), "We have never gone into one of these harassed countries in the Caribbean Sea, or in Central America, except to confer benefits of incalculable value upon them."

57. Welles to Roosevelt, 18 May 1933, in *Franklin D. Roosevelt and Foreign Affairs*, ed. Edgar B. Nixon (Cambridge: Harvard University Press, 1969), 1:141.

58. U.S. Department of State, *Report of the Delegates of the United States of America to the Sixth International Conference of American States, Held in Habana, Cuba, January 16 to February 20, 1928* (Washington, D.C.: U.S. Government Printing Office, 1928), 61.

59. Judah to White, 30 April 1929, Francis White Papers, Herbert Hoover Library, West Branch, Iowa; Stimson Diary, 25 November 1930, Henry Stimson Papers, Yale University, New Haven, Connecticut; see also Judah to White, 31 May 1928, White to Judah, 4, 9 June 1928, White Papers. For a detailed catalog of predepression investments, see Max Winkler, *Investments of United States Capital in Latin America* (New York: World Peace Foundation, 1928), esp. 180–92.

60. Duggan to Wilson, 17 January 1933, 710.11/1776½, RG59; Welles to FDR, undated but with a filing date of inauguration day ("3-4-33"), Folder "Cuba 1933–35, 42–44," Box 28, President's Secretary's File, FDRL.

61. *The Nation*, 19 April 1933, 433; for the evaluation of Machado's popularity, see Welles to Roosevelt, 18 May 1933, in *Franklin D. Roosevelt and Foreign Affairs*, ed. Nixon, 1:141; for the advice to withdraw recognition, see Welles to Hull, 8 August 1933, 837.00/3616, RG59; Welles to Hull, 9 August 1933, *FRUS* 1933, 5:344.

62. Sumner Welles, "Memorandum," 1 March 1921, 837.00/2216, RG59; Crowder, "Recent Cabinet Crisis," 21 April 1923, enclosed with Crowder to Hughes, 23 April 1923, 837.00/85, RG59.

63. Memorandum of Telephone Conversation between Hull and Welles, 5 September 1933, Memorandum of Telephone Conversation between Caffery and Welles, 5 September 1933, Welles to Hull, 7, 8 September 1933, all in *FRUS* 1933, 5:380–404.

64. Adolf Berle Diary, 1 February 1942, Adolf Berle Papers, FDRL.

65. For two differing views of the 1933–34 intervention, see Sumner Welles, *Relations between the United States and Cuba: Address by the Honorable Sumner Welles, Assistant Secretary of State, before the Young Democratic Club of America, District of Columbia Division, Washington, March 29, 1934*, Department of State Publication 577 (Washington, D.C.: U.S. Department of State, 1934); Jorge Renato Ibarra Guitart, *La mediación del 33: ocaso del machadato* (Havana: Editorial Política, 1999). Also useful are Luis E. Aguilar, *Cuba 1933* (Ithaca: Cornell University Press, 1972); Irwin F. Gellman, *Roosevelt and Batista: Good Neighbor Diplomacy in Cuba, 1933–1945* (Albuquerque: University of New Mexico Press, 1973); Jules R. Benjamin, *The United States and Cuba: Hegemony and Dependent Development, 1880–1934* (Pittsburgh: University of Pittsburgh Press, 1977).

66. Braden to Gerald Keith, 24 August 1942, Folder "Correspondence Diplomatic 1942 I–L," Box 8, Spruille Braden Papers, Columbia University, New York; Welles to Roosevelt, 7 December 1942, 837.001/Batista, Fulgencio/80, RG59; *Congressional Record*, 8 December 1942, 9229. On the abrogation, see Harry J. Guggenheim, "Amending the Platt Amendment," *Foreign Affairs* 12 (April 1934): 445–57.

67. Fidel Castro, Interview, June 1978, in Wayne S. Smith, *The Closest of Enemies: A Personal and Diplomatic Account of U.S.-Cuban Relations since 1957* (New York: Norton, 1987), 144.

Chapter 2

1. Norweb to Secretary of State, 14 January 1946, 837.00/1-1446, RG59.

2. Braden to James H. Wright, Department of State, 20 July 1942, Folder "Correspondence Diplomatic 1942 Wr–Z," Box 9, Spruille Braden Papers, Columbia University, New York.

3. Dean Acheson, *Present at the Creation: My Years in the State Department* (New York: Norton, 1969), 160; Philip W. Bonsal, *Cuba, Castro, and the United States* (Pittsburgh: University of Pittsburgh Press, 1971), 66; Arthur M. Schlesinger Jr., "Good Fences Make Good Neighbors," *Fortune*, August 1946, 163. Some observers found Braden's features attractive, and one career officer serving on his staff recalled him as "the kind of chief that you can bleed and die for" (Merwin L. Bohan Oral History, 15 June 1974, 47, Harry S. Truman Library, Independence, Missouri).

4. George S. Messersmith to Braden, 15 January 1942, Folder "Correspondence Diplomatic 1942 M–R," Box 8, Braden Papers.

5. U.S. Department of Justice, Federal Bureau of Investigation, Special Intelligence Service, *Annual Report 1944–1945*, undated typescript, 40, 81, in possession of the author.

6. U.S. Department of State, Bureau of Public Affairs, Historical Office, *United States–Cuban Relations, 1935–1945*, Research Project 463, June 1963, Folder "Cuba General 'United States–Cuban Relations 1935–1945,' 6/63," Box 38A, NSFK. The exception was Axis spy Heinz August Lüning—"The Canary"—who was captured in Havana in 1942 and promptly executed ("History of Latin American Military Cooperation in the War Effort," 3 September 1944, Record Group 165, Records of the War Department General and Special Staffs, National Archives and Records Administration, Washington, D.C.). For Cubans' World War II service in the U.S. armed forces, see Topping to Rubottom, "Summary Statement of Relations between the United States and Cuba," 26 September 1952, 611.37/9-2652, RG59.

7. Ellis O. Briggs, *Proud Servant: The Memoirs of a Career Ambassador* (Kent, Ohio: Kent State University Press, 1998), 176, 183. The war also prompted smaller but significant booms in Cuban exports of henequen, manganese, and chromium. The 1942 contract for the purchase of all Cuba's sugar at 2.65 cents per pound (not the higher figures quoted in the text) was between the U.S. Defense Supplies Corporation and the Instituto Cubano de Estabilización de Azúcar; a copy of the 28 January 1942 contract is in Folder "Correspondence Diplomatic 1942 S–We," Box 9, Braden Papers. For U.S.-Cuban cooperation in the war effort, see U.S. Tariff Commission, *Economic Controls and Commercial Policy in Cuba* (Washington, D.C.: U.S. Tariff Commission, 1946), esp. 40–43.

8. Braden to Secretary, "Comments Concerning the Cuban Political Situation . . . ," 29 May 1943, 837.00/9298, RG59; Messersmith to Welles, 12 July 1940, 711.37/342, RG59.

9. Braden to Secretary, "Comments Concerning the Cuban Political Situation . . . ," 29 May 1943, 837.00/9298, RG59; Braden to Secretary, "Fundamental Conditions in Cuba and Their Effect on our Relations," 22 November 1943, attached to "Cuban Governmental Corruption and United States Aid," 30 November 1943, 837.00/9398, RG59.

10. Laurence Duggan to Secretary, 4 June 1943, 123 Braden, Spruille/325, RG59. For Braden's numerous reports on corruption in 1943, see Folder "Correspondence Diplomatic 1943 B(misc)–C," Box 10, Braden Papers, which includes a twenty-page memo, "Fundamental Problems of Corruption in Cuba," [1942]. For Braden's anticorruption instructions to embassy personnel, see Braden to Briggs and Nufer, 27 December 1943, Folder "Correspondence Diplomatic 1943 M–N," Box 11, Braden Papers.

11. The informal request was an inflammatory editorial in the pro-Batista *Prensa Libre*, 4 June 1943, that alleged "grave antagonisms" between the ambassador and the Cuban president. For Braden's side of the story, see the series of communications, beginning with Braden to Secretary, 4 June 1943, in 123 Braden, Spruille/318–319, RG59, and esp. the twenty-four-page letter, "Personal and Very Confidential," Braden to Secretary, 14 December 1943, Folder 164, Box 53, Cordell Hull Papers, LC.

12. Secretary of State Hull and the Ambassador of Cuba, Senor Dr. Aurelio F. Concheso, Memcon, Subject: Ambassador Braden, 5 January 1944, Hull Papers. The best source of documents on the 1943 flap is the correspondence filed under "Briggs, Ellis O." in Folder "Correspondence Diplomatic 1943 Briggs," Box 10, Braden Papers.

13. Steven J. Schwartzberg, *Democracy and U.S. Policy in Latin America during the Truman Years* (Gainesville: University Press of Florida, 2003).

14. Braden to Secretary of State, "Recent Political Developments," 19 December 1944, 837.00/12-1044, RG59; Braden to Roberto MacEachen, 11 January 1945, Folder "Correspondence Diplomatic 1945 (Cuba) L–NA," Box 16, Braden Papers; Braden, "Agenda for Washington," 20 January 1945, 837.00/1-2045, RG59.

15. Spruille Braden, "Agenda for Washington," 20 January 1945, 837.00/1-2045, RG59 ("volatile"); "More from the Cuban Ambassador . . . ," Memcon, Guillermo Belt, Ambassador of Cuba, and Briggs, ARA, 25 June 1947, 837.61351/6-2547, RG59 ("low boiling point"); Briggs, *Proud Servant*, 144.

16. "Gradual Relapse of Cuban Politics into Conventional Pattern," 27 March 1946, 837.00/3-2746, RG59; Norweb to Secretary of State, 14 January 1946, 837.00/1-1446, RG59.

17. "Gradual Relapse of Cuban Politics into Conventional Pattern," 27 March 1946,

837.00/3-2746, RG59; Norweb to Secretary of State, 14 January 1946, 837.00/1-1446, RG59; Wilson to Duran, Barber, and Briggs, 31 January 1946, 837.00/1-3146, RG59.

18. Harry S. Truman, *Dear Bess: The Letters from Harry to Bess Truman, 1910–1959*, ed. Robert H. Ferrell (New York: Norton, 1983), 39, 34; Truman to Ernie Roberts, 18 August 1948, President's Secretary's Files: Personal File: C., Harry S. Truman Library, Independence, Missouri.

19. John Gunther, "Batista: The Stenographer Who Became Dictator," *Reader's Digest*, August 1941, 62.

20. John Paton Davies, *Foreign and Other Affairs* (New York: Norton, 1964), 57.

21. Harley A. Notter to Laurence Duggan, 12 September 1939, 710.11/2417½, RG59; Braden, "Agenda for Washington," 20 January 1945, 837.00/1-2045, RG59.

22. Speech to the Pan American Union, Washington, D.C., 15 April 1946, *PPP*, 200–202.

23. On this period, see Charles D. Ameringer, *The Cuban Democratic Experience: The Auténtico Years, 1944–1952* (Gainesville: University Press of Florida, 2000), esp. 28.

24. Schlesinger, "Good Fences," 167–68.

25. Memcon with Mexican Foreign Minister Ezequiel Padilla, by Merwin L. Bohan, Technical Officer of the U.S. Delegation, Mexico City, 29 January 1945, *FRUS* 1945, 9:72–73; *FRUS* 1945, 1:731.

26. For the proposal by Uruguayan foreign minister Eduardo Rodríguez Larreta, see *DOSB*, 25 November 1945, 864–66; the U.S. reaction is *DOSB*, 2 December 1945, 892; see *Consulta del gobierno del Uruguay y contestaciones de los gobiernos* (Washington, D.C.: Unión Panamericana, 1946) for the Mexican position (52) and a similar response from Brazil (10).

27. Address in Mexico City, 3 March 1947, *PPP*, 166; 4, 6 March 1947, Diaries, Box 232, President's Secretary's Files, Harry S. Truman Library, Independence, Missouri.

28. Roger R. Trask, "The Impact of the Cold War on United States–Latin American Relations, 1945–1949," *Diplomatic History* 1 (Summer 1977): 278. For the Mexican position, see *FRUS* 1947, 8:35.

29. *PPP*, 2 September 1947, 431.

30. Inter-American Treaty of Reciprocal Assistance, 62 *Stat.* 1681, 2 September 1947.

31. Special Message to the Congress on Greece and Turkey, 12 March 1947, *PPP*, 180.

32. "X" [pseud., George F. Kennan], "The Sources of Soviet Conduct," *Foreign Affairs* 25 (July 1947): 566–82; Edward Miller, Speech to the Pan American Society of New England, Boston, 26 April 1950, in *DOSB*, 15 May 1950, 770.

33. Diary, 1 November 1946: "So far as we are concerned I feel we're very shortsighted in South America" (*The Eisenhower Diaries*, ed. Robert H. Ferrell [New York: Norton, 1981], 137); Chester J. Pach Jr., "The Containment of U.S. Military Aid to Latin America, 1944–49," *Diplomatic History* 6 (Summer 1982): 225–43.

34. "U.S. Policy toward Inter-American Collaboration," NSC56/2, 18 May 1950, *FRUS* 1950, 1:630. For the early resistance, see Saltzman to Diplomatic Representatives in the American Republics, 30 July 1948, *FRUS* 1948, 9:218–20; Joint Strategic Survey Committee, "United States Assistance to Other Countries . . . ," 29 April 1947, *FRUS* 1947, 1:736–50; for Kennedy, see *Congressional Record*, 17 August 1951, 10290; on the aid issue, see Stephen G. Rabe, "Eisenhower and Latin America: Arms and Dictators," *Peace and Change* 11 (Spring 1985): 50.

35. 3 *UST* 2901; *TIAS* 2467; Memcon, DOS and Ambassador Machado, 17 December 1951, 737.5-MSP/12-1751, RG59; Embassy to DOS, 27 December 1951, 737.5-MSP/12-2751 RG59; Embassy to DOS, 7 January 1952, 737.5-MSP/1-752, RG59; Milton Eisenhower Oral History, 6 March 1965, 119–20, John Foster Dulles Oral History Project, Princeton University, Princeton, New Jersey. Agreements creating U.S. military missions in Cuba had already been signed with the air force (1 *UST* 887; *TIAS* 2166), the army (2 *UST* 1677; *TIAS* 2309), and the navy (2 *UST* 1689; *TIAS* 2310). During Batista's ensuing six-year dictatorship, Cuba received fifteen million dollars in U.S. military assistance.

36. H. Bartlett Wells, "A Study in Cuban American Relations," 8 September 1947, 711.37/9-847, RG59.

37. James N. Cortada, "Component Elements of Cuban Temperament," 4 February 1948, 837.50/2-948, RG59.

38. Walker to Woodson, Daniels, and Armor, "Three Principal Candidates in Cuban Elections," 1 June 1948, 837.00/6-148, RG59; for an analysis of the election ("remarkable for the few incidents of violence"), see Butler to Secretary of State, "Comments on Cuba's General Elections, June 1, 1948," 10 June 1948, 837.00/6-1048, RG59; Mallory to Secretary of State, "Some Questions and Answers Regarding Cuba's General Elections on June 1, 1948," 24 May 1948, 837.00/5-2448, RG59; Mallory to Secretary of State, "Compilation of Election Returns, Cuban General Elections, June 1, 1948," 28 July 1948, 837.00/7-2848, RG59.

39. Butler to Secretary of State, "Comments on Cuba's General Elections, June 1, 1948," 10 June 1948, 837.00/6-1048, RG59.

40. Collins to Secretary of State, "Political Situation in Cuba," 21 September 1948, 837.00/9-2148, RG59; Embassy to DOS, 28 September 1948, 837.002/9-2448, RG59; Beaulac to DOS, 11 March 1952, 737.00/3-1152, RG59.

41. A typical warning is Norweb to Secretary of State, 14 January 1946, 837.00/1-1446, RG59. As minister of labor, Prío had ended the legal Popular Socialist (Communist) Party's grip on the Cuban labor movement. See "Political Notes, Cuba, October 5–11, 1947," 21 October 1947, 837.00/10-2147, RG59; "Political Notes, Cuba, November 2–8, 1947," 12 November 1947, 837.00/11-1247, RG58; Walker to Woodson, Daniels, and Armor, Office Memorandum: "Three Principal Candidates in Cuban Elections," 1 June 1948, 837.00/6-148, RG59.

42. Weeka [*sic*] 16 to State, Army, Navy, Air Departments from Embassy in Havana, 20 March 1949, 837.00 (W)/3-1849, RG59; Weeka [*sic*] 17 to State, Army, Navy, Air Departments from Embassy in Havana, 25 March 1949, 837.00 (W)/3-2549, RG59.

43. Embassy to DOS, 31 August 1950, 737.001/8-3150, RG59; Memcon, ARA with Ambassador Luis Machado, 6 September 1950, 737.001/9-650, RG59.

44. Robert Butler to Edward G. Miller Jr., 27 December 1950, 611.37/12-2750, RG59. See also "Political Development in Cuba," 19 April 1951, 737.00/4-1951, RG59; Beaulac to Secretary of State, 24 September 1951, 737.00/9-2451, RG59.

45. DOS, "Policy Statement: Cuba," 11 January 1951, 611.37/1-1151, RG59; Beaulac to DOS, "Conversation with President Prío," 16 November 1951, 611.37/11-1615, RG59. See also two memoranda of conversation, both titled "Matters Involved in U.S. Relations with Cuba," 3, 5 October 1951, 611.37/10-351 and 10-551, RG59; Beaulac to Secretary of State, 24 September 1951, 737.00/9-2451, RG59.

46. Norweb to Secretary of State, "Cuba—Political Review for 1947—Possible Trends in 1948," 13 January 1948, 837.00/1-1348, RG59.

47. DOS, "Policy Statement: Cuba," 11 January 1951, 611.37/1-1151, RG59.

48. Mallory to Secretary of State, "Compilation of Election Returns, Cuban General Elections, June 1, 1948," 28 July 1948, 837.00/7-2848, RG59; V. Lansing Collins Jr. to Secretary of State, "Recent Remarks of Batista Appearing in the Habana Press," 13 September 1948, 837.00/8-1348, RG59; Butler to Secretary of State, 22 November 1948, 837.001 Batista, Fulgencio/11-2248, RG59; "Political Development in Cuba," 19 April 1951, 737.00/4-1951, RG59.

49. For the poll, see *Bohemia*, 16 December 1951, 127, 146; for the embassy report, see Embassy to DOS, 19 December 1951, 737.00/12-1951, RG59; for the embassy's analysis prior to Chibás's suicide, see Embassy to DOS, "Havana Herald Article on the Political Situation and Presidential Aspirants for 1952; Embassy Comment," 8 January 1951, 737.00/1-851, RG59. Ambassador Braden considered Chibás "a wealthy, erratic young man with considerable shrewdness" (Braden to George Messersmith, 1 May 1943, Folder "Correspondence Diplomatic 1943 M–N," Box 11, Braden Papers).

50. *Gaceta Oficial*, 10 March 1952, 4609.

51. Embassy to DOS, 11 March 1952, 737.00/3-1152, RG59; Batista speech reprinted in *Diario de la Marina*, 11 March 1952, 1; Embassy to DOS, 11 March 1952, 737.00/3-1152, RG59.

52. Miguel Angel Campa to Ambassador Beaulac, 11 March 1952, enclosed with Despatch 1472, 11 March 1952, 737.00/3-1152, RG59; briefing memo for meeting between Cuban chargé and Edward Miller Jr., Bureau of American Republics Affairs, 18 March 1952, 737.00/3-1852, RG59.

53. *Gaceta Oficial*, edición extraordinaria, 4 April 1952, 30. In the interim, Congress would be suspended and Batista would rule with the army's backing and with the advice of the eighty-member Consultative Council. Memo, 24 February 1953, 737.00/2-2453, RG59; Memcon by the Ambassador in Cuba, 22 March 1952, *FRUS* 1952–54, 4:869; for the embassy's analysis, see Embassy to DOS, 8 April 1952, 737.03/4-852, RG59.

54. Embassy Weekly Report to the DOS, 14 March 1952, 737.00(w)/3-1452, RG59; Memcon, 22 March 1952, *FRUS* 1952–54, 4:869.

55. U.S. Department of Justice, Federal Bureau of Investigation, Special Intelligence Service, *Annual Report 1944–1945*, 40, 49–50, 80, 82.

56. Memcon, Beaulac and Miguel Angel Campa, Minister of State, 22 March 1952, enclosed with Beaulac to DOS, 24 March 1952, Embassy to DOS, 24 March 1954, both in *FRUS* 1952–54, 4:868n, 869. On the circumstances leading to the break in relations, see R. Hart Phillips, *Cuba: Island of Paradox* (New York: McDowell, Oblensky, 1959), 262–63.

57. Beaulac to Secretary of State, 17 March 1952, 737.00/3-1752, RG59; Beaulac to Secretary of State, 22 March 1952, 737.00/3-2252, RG59; Beaulac to Secretary of State, 24 March 1952, 737.02/3-2452, RG59; Adrian Holman to Foreign Office, 11, 14 March 1952, AK1015/8, Folder 97516, Foreign Office 371, PRO. Acheson added that "the Department of State naturally deplores" Batista's coup (Acheson to Truman, "Memorandum for the President," 24 March 1952, *FRUS* 1952–54, 4:871). See also Edward G. Miller Jr. to Ambassador to Chile Claude Bowers, 27 March 1952, Assistant Secretary Lot Files, Lot 53D26, Box 4, RG59.

58. *Diario de la Marina*, 28 March 1952, p. 1 of photo supplement. For the U.S. message of recognition, see Beaulac to Minister of State, 27 March 1952, enclosed with Beaulac to Secretary of State, 27 March 1952, 737.02/3-1752, RG59. Batista's 27 March 1952 press statement is enclosed with Beaulac to Secretary of State, 28 March 1952, 737.02/3-2852, RG59;

the chronological list is Embassy to DOS, 1 April 1952, 737.02/4-152, RG59. Matthews Notes, "Havana, April 6th," Box 2, Herbert Matthews Papers, Columbia University, New York.

59. Harry A. Scott, Canadian Ambassador, to Secretary of State for External Affairs, 2 April 1953, PC.

60. Edward G. Miller Jr. to Fulgencio Batista, 15 December 1952, 737.11/12-1552, RG59; Weekly Report to the Department of State, 14 March 1952, 737.00(w)/3-145, RG59. Visiting Havana a few weeks later, *New York Times* journalist Herbert Matthews wrote in his notes, "It looks as if B. is in for a long time" (Matthews notes, "Havana, April 6th," Box 2, Matthews Papers). On the impact of the coup, see Louis A. Pérez Jr., *On Becoming Cuban: Identity, Nationality, and Culture* (Chapel Hill: University of North Carolina Press, 1999), 447.

Chapter 3

1. Grupo Cubano de Investigaciones Económicas de University of Miami, *Un estudio sobre Cuba* (Miami: University of Miami, 1963), 843 (income), 833, 835 (health), 837 (literacy), 841 (newspapers); Eugene Desvernine Oral History, "Cuba: 1956–61. Castro the Rebel and Castro in the Early Years of His Rule," 13 May 1985, PC; N. R. Guiteras to Fernando de Baca, Special Assistant to President, 19 December 1974, Folder "CO39 Cuba, 11/1/74–12/31/74," Box 15, WHCF, Subject File, GRFL.

On Cuba's prerevolutionary economy, see also Julián Alienes y Urosa, *Características fundamentales de la economía cubana* (Havana: Biblioteca de Economía Cubana, Banco Nacional de Cuba, 1950); Gustavo Gutiérrez, *El desarrollo económico de Cuba* (Havana: Junta Nacional de Economía, 1952), esp. 9; U.S. Tariff Commission, *The Effects of the Cuban Reciprocity Treaty of 1902* (Washington, D.C.: U.S. Government Printing Office, 1929), 166, 373n.

2. International Bank for Reconstruction and Development, *Report on Cuba* (Baltimore: Johns Hopkins University Press, 1951), 39–40, 42, 57, 65; see also Harry T. Oshima, "A New Estimate of the National Income and Product of Cuba in 1953," *Food Research Institute Studies* 2 (November 1961): 214; Juan Felipe Leal, "Las clases sociales en Cuba en vísperas de la revolución," *Revista Mexicana de Ciencia Política* 19 (October–December 1973): 99–109.

3. Melchor W. Gastón, Oscar A. Echeverría, and René F. de la Huerta, "Por que reforma agraria," unpublished study, [1957?], for the Agrupación Católica Universitaria, Havana, 6, in possession of the author. This study represents the findings of a sample survey of one thousand households conducted over a ten-month period beginning in November 1956; see also Vladimir Akulai and Domingo Rodríguez Fragoso, "La situación socio-económica del campesinado cubano antes de la Revolución," *Islas* 54 (May–August 1976): 56–80; Lowry Nelson, *Rural Cuba* (Minneapolis: University of Minnesota Press, 1950), esp. chap. 11.

Cuba, Tribunal Superior Electoral, Oficina Nacional de los Censos Demográfico y Electoral, *Censos de población, viviendas y electoral: informe general* (Havana: Fernández, 1955), 209, 213; U.S. Department of Commerce, Bureau of Foreign Commerce, *Investment in Cuba: Basic Information for United States Businessmen* (Washington, D.C.: U.S. Government Printing Office, 1956), 187; International Bank for Reconstruction and Development, *Report on Cuba*, 441.

4. Cuba, Tribunal Superior Electoral, Oficina Nacional de los Censos Demográfico y Electoral, *Censos*, 99, 143; International Bank for Reconstruction and Development, *Report on Cuba*, 404, 18, 434.

5. U.S. Department of Labor, Bureau of Labor Statistics, *Foreign Labor Information: Labor in Cuba* (Washington, D.C.: Department of Labor, 1957), 16, 21; Gastón, Echeverría, and de la Huerta, "Por que reforma agraria," 33; U.S. Department of Commerce, Bureau of Foreign Commerce, *Investment in Cuba*, 5; International Bank for Reconstruction and Development, *Report on Cuba*, 47.

6. R. M. Connell to Secretary of State, 26 November 1948, 837.52/11-2648, RG59; Francisco López Segrera, "Psicoanálisis de una generación (1940–1959)," *Revista de la Biblioteca Nacional* 10 (September–December 1969): 99–120.

7. Embassy to DOS, 13 April 1950, 737.001/4-1350, RG59.

8. "Cuba—A Summary of Situations, Interests and Policies Affecting the United States," Memorandum Attached to Wellman to Rubottom and Neal, 24 February 1953, 737.00/2-2453, RG59; Philip W. Bonsal, *Cuba, Castro, and the United States* (Pittsburgh: University of Pittsburgh Press, 1971), 281; Matthews notes, "Havana, April 6th," 1952, Box 2, Herbert Matthews Papers, Columbia University, New York.

The five coups were 5 September 1933 against Carlos Manuel de Céspedes; 15 January 1934 against Ramón Grau San Martín; 17 January 1934 against Carlos Hevia; 23 December 1936 against Miguel Mariano Gómez; and 10 March 1952 against Carlos Prío. Four of these ousters were more or less gunpoint evictions, but Gómez was impeached by the Batista-controlled Senate.

9. Edmund A. Chester, *A Sergeant Named Batista* (New York: Holt, 1954), 256 ("nice fellow"); Bureau of Intelligence to MID, 19 November 1953, 737.521/11-1953, RG59; Harry A. Scott to Secretary of State for External Affairs, 2 April 1953, PC. For a critical Cuban commentary on these ties, see Francisco A. Pardeiro, "Penetración de la oligarquía financiero Yanque en la economía de la Cuba capitalista," *Universidad de la Habana* 183 (July–December 1967): 193–259; Wellman, "Cuba—A Summary of Situations, Interests and Policies Affecting the United States," 20 February 1953, 737.00/2-2453, RG59; Ambassador Arthur Gardner in U.S. Congress, Senate, Committee on the Judiciary, Subcommittee to Investigate the Administration of the Internal Security Act and Other Internal Security Laws, *Communist Threat to the United States through the Caribbean*, 86th Cong., 1st sess., pt. 9, 665. Cooperation with the United States was a hallmark of Batista's recollections from exile: see, for example, *Cuba Betrayed* (New York: Vantage, 1962), 37 (a translation of *Respuesta* [Mexico City: Sánchez, 1960]).

10. On Batista's unpopularity, see Topping to Rubottom, "Summary Statement of Relations between the United States and Cuba," 26 September 1952, 611.37/9-2652, RG59; Memorandum, 16 August 1953, Enclosed with Topping to Cabot, 26 August 1953, 837.00/8-2653, RG59 ("his regime is unpopular"); Woodward to Secretary of State, 1 September 1953, 737.00/9-153, RG59 ("his regime is unpopular"); Cabot to Acting Secretary of State, 1 February 1954, 737.00/1-1454, RG59 (Batista "is probably unpopular with a majority of voters"), repeated in Wellman to Cabot, "Monthly Summary for Caribbean Affairs, February 1954," 23 February 1954, 737.00/2-2354, RG59. For the embassy's reports on the November 1954 election, see "Joint Weekly Report," 3, 10 November, 22 December 1954, 737.00(w)/11-354, 11-1054, 12-2254, RG59.

11. NSC Meeting, 21 December 1954, *FRUS* 1952–54, 2:838.

12. "Cuba," [1955], Richard M. Nixon Pre-Presidential Papers, Series 361, Vice President Central American Trip, 1955, Box 1, File Unit "Briefing Folder Notes from Oral Briefing," National Archives and Records Administration Pacific Region, Laguna Niguel, California.

13. "Toast by the Vice President to the President of Cuba, Havana (National Palace)," [8 February 1955], Richard M. Nixon Pre-Presidential Papers, Series 361, Box 2; Holland to Patterson, 20 August 1954, 737.11/8-1554, RG59; Embassy to DOS, "Joint Weeka [*sic*] 6 for State, Army, Navy and Air Departments from SANA," 10 February 1955, 737.00(W)/2-1055, RG59; Nixon to Batista, 23 February 1955, Richard Nixon Papers, Series 362, Box 1, National Archives and Records Administration Pacific Region, Laguna Niguel, California. Most of the documents for Nixon's monthlong 1955 trip are in Department of State Central File 033.1100-NI, RG59. Nixon used the term "president-elect" because Batista had taken an "electoral leave" from the presidency on 14 August 1954, and Andrés Domingo y Morales del Castillo served as acting president for the next six months. Batista was inaugurated for a four-year term on 24 February 1955.

14. Harry A. Scott to Secretary of State for External Affairs, 2 April 1953, PC; Embassy to DOS, quoting Batista, 12 July 1950, 737.001/7-1250, RG59.

15. Memcon, John Topping and Aurelio Concheso, 1 September 1953, *FRUS* 1952–54, 4:900; Embassy to DOS, "Political Aspects—Briefing Book on Cuba," 1 April 1957, 737.00/ 4-157, RG59; Embassy to DOS, 10 June 1954, 737.001/6-1054, RG59; U.S. Department of Labor, Bureau of Labor Statistics, *Foreign Labor Information*, 3; Thruston Morton to Senator Hubert Humphrey, 24 June 1953, 737.00/5-2853, RG59; State Department Draft of a Response to a Question from Senator Bourke Hickenlooper, 16 June 1953, 737.00/6-1653, RG59; Cabot to Acting Secretary of State, 1 February 1954, 737.00/1-1454, RG59; Embassy to DOS, 18 February 1958, 611.37/2-1858, RG59; Embassy to DOS, 1 April 1957, 737.00/4-157, RG59. Ambassador Henry Cabot Lodge: Minutes of NSC Meeting, 10 March 1955, *FRUS* 1955–57, 6:615.

16. James Hagerty quoting Nixon, 11 March 1955, Folder "Hagerty Diary, March 1955," Box 1a, Diary Entries, James C. Hagerty Papers, 1953–61, DDEL; "Political Development in Cuba," 19 April 1951, 737.00/4-1951, RG59; Eisenhower to Macmillan, 8 August 1960, *FRUS* 1958–60, 6: 1051; Memorandum of Telephone Conversation, 26 February 1953, John Foster Dulles Papers, Seeley Mudd Library, Princeton University, Princeton, New Jersey. See also Diary, 26 February 1954, Box 16, DDE Diary Series, AWF; Hagerty quoting Eisenhower, 1 March 1954, in James C. Hagerty, *The Diary of James C. Hagerty: Eisenhower in Mid-Course, 1954–1955*, ed. Robert H. Ferrell (Bloomington: Indiana University Press, 1983), 23.

17. John Foster Dulles, "Thoughts on Soviet Foreign Policy and What to Do about It," *Life*, 3 June 1946, 112–26, 10 June 1946, 118–30 (quotations from 3 June, 114, 118); Dwight D. Eisenhower Oral History, 28 July 1964, John Foster Dulles Oral History Project, Princeton University, Princeton, New Jersey; U.S. Congress, Senate, Committee on Foreign Relations, *Study Mission in the Caribbean Area, December 1957, Report of Senator George D. Aiken*, 85th Cong., 2nd sess., 20 January 1958, 1.

18. Thomas Mann Oral History, 3, Dulles Oral History Project. See also the similar evaluations by two foreign service officers who worked with Dulles, Merwin Bohan (Oral History, 15 June 1974, 84, Harry S. Truman Library, Independence, Missouri) and Richard Rubottom (Oral History, 12 June 1966, esp. 5, 7, 18 and 45, Dulles Oral History Project).

19. NSC meeting, 19 June 1958, *FRUS* 1958–60, 5:29.

20. Staff Study, 6 March 1953, for "United States Objectives and Courses of Action with Respect to Latin America," 11, NSC Report 144/1, 18 March 1953, S/S-NSC files, Lot 63D351, National Archives and Records Administration, Washington, D.C.; an edited version of NSC 144/1 is reprinted in *FRUS* 1952–54, 4:6–10.

21. U.S. Special Study Group, J. H. Doolittle, Chair, "Report on the Covert Activities of the Central Intelligence Agency," 30 September 1954, CIA FOIA.

22. Embassy to DOS, 19 October 1953, 737.00/10-1953, RG59; Gardner to DOS, 20 October 1953, 611.37/10-2053, RG59.

23. NSC 144/1, 18 March 1953, *FRUS* 1952–54, 4:9; Discussion of NSC 5613/1, 6 September 1956, *FRUS* 1955–57, 6:106–12; Leonard S. Dysinger to Assistant Chief of Staff, Department of the Army, "Development of Force Bases for a Time-Phased FY 57 Mutual Defense Assistance Program in the Middle East and Latin America," 27 May 1955, PC. See also Robert O. Kirkland, *Observing Our Hermanos de Armas* (New York: Routledge, 2003), esp. chap. 4; Michael J. Francis, "Military Aid to Latin America in the U.S. Congress," *Journal of Inter-American Studies* 6 (July 1964): 389–404; Carl John Regan, "The Armed Forces of Cuba: 1933–1959" (master's thesis, University of Florida, 1970), 124.

24. Beaulac to Secretary of State, 9 January, 15 July 1953, *FRUS* 1952–54, 4:882, 895; Embassy to DOS, 19 February 1953, 737.5-MSP/2-1953, RG59; Embassy to DOS, 5 February 1953, 737.5-MSP/2-553, RG59; *FRUS* 1952–54, 4:876–77, 920. The military assistance advisory group was not sent; instead, the existing U.S. armed forces missions in Cuba began performing those functions. See Embassy to DOS, 14 July 1952, 737.5-MSP/7-1452, with copy of agreement attached, RG59. At the end of World War II, the United States had sixty-three military personnel attached to the U.S. embassy in Havana; see J. J. Muccio to Spruille Braden, 19 January 1945, Folder "Correspondence Diplomatic 1945 (Cuba) L–NA," Box 16, Spruille Braden Papers, Columbia University, New York.

25. "Joint Weeka [*sic*] 35 for State, Army, Navy and All Departments from SANA," 28 August 1953, 737.00(w)/8-2853, RG59.

26. Jacob D. Esterline Oral History, 10–11 November 1975, 69, NSA; Merwin L. Bohan to C. O. Cobb, 22 September 1971, PC; Bonsal, *Cuba, Castro, and the United States*, 31; Manuel Antonio ("Tony") de Varona to Senator Hickenlooper, 3 May 1958, PC.

27. On Gardner's preference for Europe, see John Foster Dulles to Eisenhower, 27 February 1953, folder "Cuba (3)," Box 8, International Series, AWF; for the list of weapons, see Memorandum, Office of the Army Attaché, American Embassy, Havana, 18 August 1953, 737.5-MSP/8-1853, RG59.

28. Connett to Hoyt, "Cuban Requests for Military Equipment," 25 October 1954, *FRUS* 1952–54, 4:914–16; Memorandum of Discussion of the DOS–Joint Chiefs of Staff Meeting, 30 January 1959, *FRUS* 1958–60, 6:388–89.

29. U.S. Air Force Mission to Cuba to Assistant Chief of Staff, G-3, Department of the Army, "Development of Force Bases for a Time-Phased FY57 Mutual Defense Assistance Program in the Middle East and Latin America," 27 May 1955, PC; Embassy to DOS, "Military Assistance Program Development," 27 July 1956, 737.5-MSP/7-2756, RG59.

30. Allen Dulles to Fulgencio Batista, 15 July 1956, PC; John Dorschner and Roberto Fabricio, *The Winds of December* (New York: Coward, McCann, and Geoghegan, 1980), 147; G. Gregg Webb, "New Insights into J. Edgar Hoover's Role," *Studies in Intelligence* 48, no. 1 (2004): 45–58; Lyman B. Kirkpatrick Jr., *The Real CIA* (New York: Macmillan, 1968), 162; Memcon, Deputy Secretary of State Murphy, Ambassador Gardner, and Cuban Minister of Interior Santiago Rey, 7 January 1957, 737.00/1-757, RG59.

31. Embassy to DOS, 18 February 1958, 611.37/2-1858, RG59. A year earlier, the embassy had reported that BRAC was not fully effective, but "there were indications that it would

shortly become so" (Embassy to DOS, 1 April 1957, 737.00/4-157, RG59); Kirkpatrick, *Real CIA*, 156, 162, 164, 166, 174; Earl E. T. Smith, *The Fourth Floor: An Account of the Castro Communist Revolution* (New York: Random House, 1962), 124.

32. Memo, Ralph A. Dungan to President Kennedy, "Covert Operations in Cuba Prior to 1958," 15 October 1962, Folder "Ralph Dungan 7/62–12/62," Box 62A, POF; Kirkpatrick, *Real CIA*, 164; Allen Dulles, *The Craft of Intelligence* (New York: Harper and Row, 1963), 232. In 1957 Kirkpatrick even allowed his picture to be taken with a smiling President Batista, a picture Batista immediately had published in the *Diario de la Marina* (14 May 1957, unnumbered first page of photo supplement, immediately following 20B).

33. Gardner to DOS, 20 October 1953, 611.37/10-2053, RG59; Embassy to Department, "Cow for President Batista," 23 June 1954, attached to 737.11/6-2154, RG59; Embassy to Department, 21 June 1954, 737.11/6-2154, 25 June 1954, 737.11/6-2554, RG59; Eliseo Riera-Gómez to John M. Cabot, 20 March 1954, including a newspaper clipping from *El Mundo* with a photo of Mrs. Gardner on Batista's arm with a smiling ambassador alongside, filed with Warren Olney (Department of Justice) to Acting Secretary of State, 14 May 1954, 737.00/5-1454, RG59; Gardner to Undersecretary of State, 7 January 1954, 737.00/1-754, RG59; Gardner to Secretary of State, 21 July 1954, 737.00/7-2154, RG59; Memcon, Ambassador Gardner and ARA, 26 October 1954, *FRUS* 1952–1954, 4:916; Gardner to Rubottom, 20 April 1957, PC.

34. R. D. Muir to Mrs. McCaffree, 16 October 1953, 737.11/10-1653, RG59; Memcon, "Proposed Newspaper Story on Batista and Communism," 19 May 1954, 737.11/5-1954, RG59.

35. Memcon, Rubottom and Ambassador de la Campa, 20 March 1957, PC; Memorandum of Telephone Conversation, Gardner to Rubottom, 20 April 1957, PC.

36. Eisenhower to Gardner, 11 January 1957, Folder "Cuba (2)," Box 8, International Series, AWF. "Dulles said they had the worst time trying to force Ambassador Gardner out. He wanted desperately to stay" (Matthews to the Publisher et al., 20 May 1957, Folder "H. Matthews Cuba Memoranda," Box 2, Matthews Papers).

37. U.S. Congress, Senate, Committee on the Judiciary, Subcommittee to Investigate the Administration of the Internal Security Act and Other Internal Security Laws, *Communist Threat*, pt. 9, 664–65.

38. Confidential embassy files, included with a memo from the State Department's Richard Cushing to Herbert Matthews, [1957], Folder "Notes, Clippings, Letters for Chapter 4 of His Book," Box 3, Matthews Papers. The U.S. embassy sent Washington two dispatches about the attack on 26 July (both 737.00/7-2653), a third on 28 July (737.00/7-2853), and a fourth on 31 July (737.00/7-2853), RG59. The last of these contains a 30 July memorandum of a conversation with ambassador Aurelio Fernández Concheso, who made the accusation against Castro.

39. *Tampa La Gaceta*, 2 December 1955, 12. Cubans could follow Castro's U.S. fund-raising in *Bohemia*, 6 November 1955, 60, 82–83, and 20 November 1955, 59, 81–83. See also Embassy to DOS, 23 November 1955, 737.00/11-2355, RG59; Embassy to DOS, 14 December 1955, 737.00/12-1455, RG59.

40. Castro had been admitted to the United States in October by the San Antonio regional office of the Immigration and Naturalization Service (INS), which at the time merged entry data for several border stations in southeastern Texas. The State Department clearly wanted him out of the United States when his thirty-day tourist visa expired; a midlevel official hand

carried a memorandum to the INS, asking (1) that Castro be warned that his political activities were not appropriate for a visitor, and (2) that the INS limit any extension of his visa to thirty additional days. The State Department later asked INS officials "not to permit further extension of Fidel Castro's stay." For the hand-carried letter, Welch to del Guercio, 22 November 1955, see 737.00/11-2255, filed with Embassy to DOS, 10 November 1955, 737.00/11-1055, RG59; for the later request, see Newbegin to Lyon, 1 December 1955, 737.00/12-155, RG59; Leonhardy to Newbegin, 23 November 1955, 737.00/11-2355, RG59. See also Richard Cushing to Herbert Matthews, [1957], Folder "Notes, Clippings, Letters for Chapter 4 of His Book," Box 3, Matthews Papers.

41. "The group was wiped out in a combined air-land operation." Embassy to DOS, 3 December 1956, 737.00/12-0356, RG59; on the Santiago uprising and smaller disturbances in Holguín and the Cuban city of Guantánamo, see Embassy to DOS, 3 December 1956, 737.00/12-356, RG59; Memcon, "Visit of Cuban Ambassador," 6 December 1956, 737.00/12-656, RG59. The exact numbers are disputed: see Thomas G. Paterson, *Contesting Castro: The United States and the Triumph of the Cuban Revolution* (New York: Oxford University Press, 1994), 70; Tad Szulc, *Fidel: A Critical Portrait* (New York: Morrow, 1986), 20; Regan, "Armed Forces of Cuba," 131; Rufo López-Fresquet, *My Fourteen Months with Castro* (Cleveland: World, 1966), 122.

42. *NYT*, 24 February 1957, 1, 34, 25 February 1957, 1, 11, 26 February 1957, 13.

43. R. Hart Phillips to Herbert Matthews, 5 March 1961, Folder "H. Matthews Correspondence 1961," Box 1, Matthews Papers. To clarify this episode for his memoir and to refute Ambassador Gardner's claim that the embassy had arranged the meeting, Matthews asked various participants to recount how the trip to the Sierra had unfolded. The responses, including helpful letters from Ted Scott and Ruby Phillips, are in Folder "H. Matthews Correspondence 1961," Box 2, Matthews Papers; see also Matthews's correspondence with Jerry W. Knudson, Folder "Matthews, H. L. Cuba–Knudson, J. W. Correspondence," Box 36, Matthews Papers. On the entire episode, see Richard E. Welch Jr., "Herbert L. Matthews and the Cuban Revolution," *The Historian* 47 (November 1984): 1–18; Herbert L. Matthews, *The Cuban Story* (New York: Braziller, 1961); Jerry W. Knudson, *Herbert L. Matthews and the Cuban Story* (Lexington, Ky.: Association for Education in Journalism, 1978); Anthony DePalma, *The Man Who Invented Fidel: Cuba, Castro, and Herbert L. Matthews of the New York Times* (New York: Public Affairs Press, 2006).

44. *NYT*, 24 February 1957, 34.

45. Embassy to DOS, 28 February 1957, 737.00/2-2857, RG59.

46. Memorandum of Telephone Conversation, Matthews and Rubottom, 28 February 1957, 737.00/2-2857, RG59; Canadian Ambassador, Havana, to Secretary of State for External Affairs, Ottawa, "Annual Review of Events in Cuba—1957," 14 January 1958, PC.

47. Frank Lausche in U.S. Congress, Senate, Committee on Foreign Relations, *Executive Sessions of the Senate Foreign Relations Committee, Together with Joint Sessions with the Senate Armed Services Committee (Historical Series)*, vol. 17, 89th Cong., 1st sess., 1965, made public September 1990, 588. Former ambassador Arthur Gardner shared this view that his articles biased the administration against Batista: U.S. Congress, Senate, Committee on the Judiciary, Subcommittee to Investigate the Administration of the Internal Security Act and Other Internal Security Laws, *Communist Threat*, pt. 9, 666, 675. For a highly critical analysis

of Matthews's impact on U.S. policy, see William E. Ratliff, ed., *The Selling of Fidel Castro: The Media and the Cuban Revolution* (New Brunswick, N.J.: Transaction, 1987); slightly less critical is DePalma, *Man Who Invented Fidel*.

48. *NYT*, 25 February 1957, 11; *NYT*, 26 February 1957, 13.

49. *NYT*, 9 June 1957, 1, 13; Rubottom to Secretary of State, "Cuban Political Situation," 12 June 1957, 737.00/6-1257, RG59.

50. Smith to Secretary of State, 4 August 1957, 737.00/8-557, RG59; Memorandum of Telephone Conversation, Chapin (Cuba) and Leonhardy (ARA), 2 August 1957, 737.00/8-257, RG59.

51. Smith to Secretary of State, 4 August 1957, 737.00/8-557, RG59; Stewart to Wieland, 5 August 1957, 737.00/8-557, RG59.

52. Herter to Sinclair Weeks (Secretary of Commerce), 9 October 1957, Folder "Chronological File—October 1957 (4)," Box 3, Christian A. Herter Files, DDEL.

53. Stewart to Wieland, 5 August 1957, 737.00/8-557, RG59. A few days later, the *Times* published another long Matthews article criticizing the Batista government: see "The Shadow Falls on Cuba's Batista," *NYT Sunday Magazine*, 11 August 1957, 14, 38, 40, 43.

54. NSC, "Reported Decline of U.S. Prestige Abroad," 11 September 1953, Folder "Miscellaneous (3) (Sept 1953)," Box 5, NSC Series, Subject Subseries, Office of the Special Assistant for National Security Affairs: Records 1952–61, WHOF. Milton Eisenhower's interest in Latin America had begun when he served as a delegate to a 1946 conference in Mexico. Subsequently, he recalled, "from 1946 to '52 I had read essentially every book and article that had been written, just to satisfy my own curiosity" (Milton S. Eisenhower Oral History, 6 March 1965, 2, Dulles Oral History Project).

55. For President Eisenhower's comment about his brother, Milton, in mid-1953, see *The Eisenhower Diaries*, ed. Robert H. Ferrell (New York: Norton, 1981), 238.

56. *NYT*, 24 February 1957, 1.

57. "Memorandum for the Record," 17 September 1954, Folder "Latin America, U.S. Policy toward (3) 1954–60," Box 12, NSC Series, Briefing Notes Subseries, Office of the Special Assistant for National Security Affairs: Records, 1952–61, WHOF; President Eisenhower to George Humphrey, 27 March 1957, Folder "George M. Humphrey (4)," Box 21, Administration Series, AWF.

58. Dulles, 5 November 1957, in *DOSB*, 25 November 1957, 826; Armistead I. Selden Jr., Oral History, John Foster Dulles Papers, Mudd Library, Princeton University.

59. Department of State Circular, 26 March 1958, 033.100-NI/3-2658, RG59.

60. Richard Nixon, *Six Crises* (1962; New York: Simon and Schuster, 1990), 202, 204; Hubert Herring, *A History of Latin America from the Beginnings to the Present*, 2nd ed. (New York: Knopf, 1964), 491. See also the memoir of the vice president's translator, Vernon Walters, *The Mighty and the Meek: Dispatches from the Front Line of Diplomacy* (London: St. Ermin's, 2001), 30–31.

61. For the cables from Caracas, see Folder "Vice President's South American Tour—April 27–May 15," Box 23, Lot File 61D332, Office Files of Maurice M. Bernbaum, 1954–59, Bureau of Inter-American Affairs, RG59; Nixon, *Six Crises*, 215; Memorandum of Telephone Conversation, Burrows (Venezuela) and Rubottom and Sanders, 13 May 1958, *FRUS* 1958–60, 5:226–27.

62. Memorandum of Discussion at the 366th Meeting of the NSC, 22 May 1958, *FRUS* 1958–60, 5:240.

63. Nixon, *Six Crises*, 219, 231n; William Snow to Secretary of State, 15 May 1958, *FRUS* 1958–60, 5:237; see also *DOSB*, 9 June 1958, 952–58.

64. U.S. Congress, House, Committee on Foreign Affairs, Subcommittee on Inter-American Affairs, *A Review of the Relations of the United States and Other American Republics*, 85th Cong., 2nd sess., June–July 1958, 12, 70, 76–77. For Estrada's side of the story, see the book-length interview by Agustín Blanco Muñoz, *Pedro Estrada Habló* (Caracas: Editorial José Martí, 1983); Judith Ewell, *The Indictment of a Dictator: The Extradition and Trial of Marcos Pérez Jiménez* (College Station: Texas A&M University Press, 1981).

65. *DOSB*, 30 June 1958, 1090–91 (Kubitschek); *Congressional Record*, 21 January 1959, 996–98 (Frondizi); *DOSB*, 19 January 1959, 89–105 (Milton Eisenhower); U.S. Congress, Senate, Committee on Foreign Relations, *Mutual Security Act of 1959*, 86th Cong., 1st sess., pt. 1, 14 May 1959, 551 (Church).

66. Embassy to DOS, 10 February 1958, in *FRUS* 1958–60, 6:21; DOS to Embassy, 26 March 1958, *FRUS* 1958–60, 6:77; Draft Memo Prepared in the Office of Middle American Affairs, 25 July 1958, *FRUS* 1958–60, 6:170; Embassy to DOS, 16 September 1957, 737.00/9-1657, RG59.

67. 3 *UST* 2901; *TIAS* 2467.

68. Embassy to DOS, 16 June 1958, *FRUS* 1958–60, 6:108. Military aid for Batista's final year, FY1959, totaled $576,000.

69. Memorandum of Telephone Conversation with DOS, 29 May 1957, 737.00/5-2957, RG59; Embassy to DOS, 7 February 1958, *FRUS* 1958–60, 6:18–19.

70. DOS to Embassy, "Military Equipment for Cuba," 3 October 1957, 737.00/9-2557, RG59; Embassy to DOS, 13 September 1957, 737.00/9-1357, RG59; Embassy to DOS, 3 October 1957, 737.00/9-2557, RG59; Smith to DOS, 7 February 1958, *FRUS* 1958–60, 6:19, 108.

71. Leonhardy to Rubottom, "Disapproval Cuban Purchase Incendiary Bombs," 4 April 1957, 737.5-MSP/4-357, RG59.

72. DOS to Representative Marguerite Stitt Church, 8 July 1957, 737.00/6-1957, RG59; U.S. Congress, Senate, Committee on Foreign Relations, *Study Mission*, 4, 50; Embassy to DOS, 28 February 1958, *FRUS* 1958–60, 6:40; *NYT*, 6 February 1958, 3.

73. Memcon, "Arms to Cuba," Ambassador de la Campa, William Snow, and William Wieland, 3 March 1958, 737.56/3-358, RG59; Wieland to Snow, 7 March 1958, 737.00/3-759, RG59.

74. ARA to Acting Secretary, "Order to Stop Shipment of Rifles to Cuban Army," 14 March 1958, 737./3-1458, RG59.

75. Prío was indicted twice, in 1954 and 1958. For details, see U.S. Senate, Committee on Foreign Relations, *Review of Foreign Policy, 1958*, 85th Cong., 2nd sess., February–March 1958, 358–59; Acting Secretary of State to President, 23 December 1958, Folder "Cuba, May 1959–September 1960 (1)," Box 4, NSC Series, Subject Subseries, Office of the Special Assistant for National Security Affairs: Records, 1952–61, WHOF; Wieland to Rubottom, 17 January 1958, *FRUS* 1958–60, 6:11; Wellman to Miller, 19 November 1952, 737.11/11-952, RG59; Memcon, Snow and General Joseph Swing, Director of INS, 3 July 1957, 737.00/7-357, RG59; ARA (Snow) to Acting Secretary of State, 25 July 1957, 737.00/6-2557, RG59.

76. U.S. Senate, Committee on Foreign Relations, *Review*, 359–60, 363.

77. ARA to Acting Secretary, "Order to Stop Shipment of Rifles to Cuban Army," 14 March 1958, 737./3-1458, RG59; *Congressional Record*, 20 March 1958, 4948–49 (Powell). Paterson (*Contesting Castro*, chap. 11) provides unexcelled coverage of decision making on the arms cutoff.

78. Snow to Secretary of State, 24 March 1958, *FRUS* 1958–60, 6:66–67, 305n; Acting Secretary of State to President, 23 December 1958, Folder "Cuba, May 1959–September 1960 (1)," Box 4, NSC Series, Subject Subseries, Office of the Special Assistant for National Security Affairs: Records, 1952–61, WHOF.

79. Embassy to DOS, 16 March, 1 April 1958, *FRUS* 1958–60, 6:61, 76. At the time, Güell was both minister of state (foreign minister) and prime minister. For examples of Ambassador Smith's reversal effort, see Embassy to DOS, 18 March, 13 April 1958, *FRUS* 1958–60, 6:65, 83–84.

80. Memoranda of Discussions at the Department of State–Joint Chiefs of Staff Meetings, 2 May, 27 June 1958, *FRUS* 1958–60, 6:90, 118.

81. Embassy to DOS, 16 June (2 cables), 3 July 1958, *FRUS* 1958–60, 6:108, 110, 127–28; on sending the jet trainers, see Rubottom to Murphy, 26 June 1958, Wieland to Stroh, 3 July 1958, *FRUS* 1958–60, 6:116, 123.

82. Embassy to DOS, 20 July 1958, Stewart to Snow, 24 July 1958, Rubottom to Secretary of State, 11 August 1958, *FRUS* 1958–60, 6:158–59, 167, 193. Ambassador Smith had urged reconsideration on 16 July (a negative decision was made on 29 August [737.00/8-2958, RG59]), and he made one last unsuccessful request for the trainers on 11 September (*FRUS* 1958–60, 6:154, 203, 207). On the Guantánamo water supply, see Snow to Herter, 31 July 1958, Steward to Anderson, 5 August 1958, *FRUS* 1958–60, 6:177–79, 183–85.

83. A. S. Fordham to Selwyn Lloyd, 18 November 1958, AK1015/63, FO371/132165, PRO; A. S. Fordham to Selwyn Lloyd, 3 February 1959, AK1011/1, FO371/139398, PRO; Embassy to Secretary of State, 16 July 1958, 737.00/7-1658, RG59; Embassy to DOS, 22 October 1958, 611.37/10-2258, RG59; Memcon, ARA and Ambassador Smith, 22 November 1958, 737.00/11-2248, RG59.

84. Embassy to Secretary of State, 2 July 1958, 737.00/7-258, RG59; Memcon, "Cuba," Frank Shupp and William A. Wieland, 28 May 1958, 737.00/5-2858, RG59; *DOSB*, 28 July 1958, 153.

85. For coverage of U.S. honors to the Tabernilla family, see Paterson, *Contesting Castro*, 103, 138; Jules Dubois, *Fidel Castro: Rebel-Liberator or Dictator?* (Indianapolis: Bobbs-Merrill, 1959), 180, 243. General Francisco Tabernilla y Dolz had three sons in the military: Colonel Francisco Tabernilla y Palmero was the commander of the army's tank regiment, Lieutenant Colonel Carlos Tabernilla y Palmero was commander of the army air force, and Lieutenant Colonel Marcelo Tabernilla y Palmero was commander of the army air force's light bomber squadron.

86. DOS to Charles Porter, 11 June 1958, with Porter's letter to Department of State, June 14, 1958, attached, Tony de Varona to Bourke Hickenlooper, 3 May 1958, all in PC; Santiago Consul to DOS, 21 February 1958, *FRUS* 1958–60, 6:34–35.

87. Earl Smith to Secretary of State, 14 March 1958, 737.00/3-1458, RG59; Speech by Earl Smith in New York, 20 November 1958, PC; Memcon, Smith and Güell, 15 August 1958, Embassy to DOS, 22 October 1958, Memcon, Smith and Rivero Agüero, 15 November 1958, *FRUS* 1958–60, 6:195, 241, 253.

88. Senator Ellender's Press Conference in Havana, 12 December 1958, 033.1100-E/ 12-1658, RG59; Embassy to DOS, 16 December 1958, *FRUS* 1958–60, 6:285n; Diary Entry, 14 December 1958, *FRUS* 1958–60, 6:285–89.

89. Wayne S. Smith, *The Closest of Enemies: A Personal and Diplomatic Account of U.S.-Cuban Relations since 1957* (New York: Norton, 1987), 18–19, 29; Stewart to Snow, 24 July 1958, Draft Memorandum Prepared in the Office of Middle American Affairs, 25 July 1958, *FRUS* 1958–60, 6:164, 170.

90. For the most complete English-language discussion of the complex web of organizations and individuals opposing Batista, see Julia E. Sweig, *Inside the Cuban Revolution: Fidel Castro and the Urban Underground* (Cambridge: Harvard University Press, 2002); on the urban fronts, see Gladys Marel García-Pérez, *Insurrection and Revolution: Armed Struggle in Cuba, 1952–1959* (Boulder, Colo.: Rienner, 1998); Paterson, *Contesting Castro*. The CIA's assessment of the attack on the presidential palace is included in Folder "316th Meeting of the National Security Council, March 14, 1957," Box 8, NSC Series, AWF. Morgan told his own story in correspondence with Herbert Matthews: see two folders titled, "H. Matthews Cuba Statements, Releases, etc. 1958," Box 2, Matthews Papers.

91. INR, "The 26th of July Movement since the Abortive General Strike of April 9, 1958," 15 August 1958, Wardlaw to Hill, 25 September 1958, *FRUS* 1958–60, 6:197, 216; NSC Briefing, "Cuba," 29 October 1958, FOIA (CIA).

92. Information memorandum, Orville Anderson (ARA), 3 November 1958, *FRUS* 1958–60, 6:249; see also CIA, Special NIE, "The Situation in Cuba," 24 November 1958, DDRS; Acting Secretary of State to President, 23 December 1958, Folder "Cuba, May 1959–September 1960 (1)," Box 4, NSC Series, Subject Subseries, Office of the Special Assistant for National Security Affairs: Records, 1952–61, WHOF. See also INR, "Biographic Report: Andres Rivero Aguero, President-Elect of Cuba, BR No. 264," 5 November 1958, FO371/139399, PRO; A. S. Fordham to Selwyn Lloyd, 3 February 1959, AK1011/1, FO371/139398, PRO.

93. Paterson, *Contesting Castro*, 219, 221; Draft Memorandum Prepared in the Office of Middle American Affairs, 25 July 1958, *FRUS* 1958–60, 6:172; U.S. Congress, Senate, Committee on the Judiciary, Subcommittee to Investigate the Administration of the Internal Security Act and Other Internal Security Laws, *Communist Threat*, pt. 9, 739; Earl E. T. Smith, *Fourth Floor*, 166–68; Louis A. Pérez Jr., *Army Politics in Cuba, 1898–1958* (Pittsburgh: University of Pittsburgh Press, 1976), 164; Max Holland, "Private Sources of U.S. Foreign Policy: William Pawley and the 1954 Coup d'Etat in Guatemala," *Journal of Cold War Studies* 7 (Fall 2005): 36–73; Memorandum for the Record, J. C. King, "First Meeting of General Maxwell Taylor's Board of Inquiry on Cuban Operations Conducted by CIA," 23 April 1961, Folder "Cuba-Subjects Para-Military Study Group Taylor Report Part II Meetings I and II," Box 61A, NSFK. Pawley's curriculum vitae is attached to a letter detailing his anticommunist activities, including his claim to having helped overthrow Guatemala's Arbenz government in 1954 (Pawley to Scowcroft, 25 March 1976, Folder "Cuba—Correspondence on (7)," Box 2, NSC Latin American Affairs Staff: Files, 1974–77, GRFL).

94. Earl E. T. Smith, *Fourth Floor*, 170–71; editorial note, *FRUS* 1958–60, 6:298–99; "Cuba: Summary of the Present Position and Likely Developments in Cuba," 23 December 1958, FO371/139398, PRO.

95. Folder "392nd Meeting of the National Security Council, December 23, 1958," Box 10, NSC Series, AWF; Acting Secretary of State to President, 23 December 1958, Folder "Cuba,

May 1959–September 1960 (1)," Box 4, NSC Series, Subject Subseries, Office of the Special Assistant for National Security Affairs: Records, 1952–61, WHOF; Gordon Gray, "Memorandum of Conversation with the President, Wednesday, 26 December 1958," 30 December 1958, Folder "Meeting with the President—1958 (1)," Box 3, Special Assistant Series, Presidential Subseries, Office of the Special Assistant for National Security Affairs: Records, 1952–61, WHOF. For the four NSC minutes, see the folders of the 380th, 384th, 389th, and 391st meetings of the NSC, Box 10, NSC Series, AWF, and the CIA's Special NIE, "The Situation in Cuba," 24 November 1958, DDRS.

96. "Havana Gay, but Alertness in Air," *Miami Herald*, 30 December 1958, 6A; DOS to Embassy, 31 December 1958, *FRUS* 1958–60, 6:330–31; U.S. Congress, Senate, Committee on Foreign Relations, *Executive Sessions of the Senate Foreign Relations Committee, Together with Joint Sessions with the Senate Armed Services Committee (Historical Series)*, vol. 10, 85th Cong., 2nd sess., 1958, made public November 1980, 774. Smith told Tabernilla that he would pass along the request for U.S. support only if Batista had granted his approval (U.S. Congress, Senate, Committee on the Judiciary, Subcommittee to Investigate the Administration of the Internal Security Act and Other Internal Security Laws, *Communist Threat*, pt. 9, 709–10).

Chapter 4

1. *Revolución*, 3 January 1959, 4. There are several slightly different versions of this speech in Spanish, but in each the gist is unmistakable. Ricardo Martínez Victores, *7RR: La historia de Radio Rebelde* (Havana: Editorial de Ciencias Sociales, 1978), 477–78.

2. R. Richard Rubottom Jr. Oral History, 12 June 1966, 81, 48–49, 85, John Foster Dulles Oral History Project, Princeton University, Princeton, New Jersey.

3. U.S. Congress, Senate, Committee on Foreign Relations, *Executive Sessions of the Senate Foreign Relations Committee (Historical Series)*, vol. 11, 86th Cong., 1st sess., 1959, 49.

4. J. F. Dulles to President, "Recognition of the New Government of Cuba," 7 January 1959, Folder "Cuba (1) 1959," Box 4, WHOF, International Series, Office of the Staff Secretary: Records, 1952–61; "Telephone Call from the President," 7 January 1959, Folder "Memoranda of Telephone Conversations, White House January 4, 1959 to April 15, 1959," Box 13, Telephone Call Series, Papers of John Foster Dulles, DDEL; Allen Dulles in U.S. Congress, Senate, Committee on Foreign Relations, *Executive Sessions*, 11:125–26.

5. Phyllis D. Bernau to Mr. Secretary, 9 January 1959, Folder "Memoranda of Telephone Conversations, White House, January 4, 1959 to April 15, 1959," Box 13, Telephone Calls Series, Dulles Papers; Herter, "Memorandum of Telephone Conversation with the President," January 6, 1959, Box 6, Christian A. Herter Papers, DDEL. On Eisenhower's reluctance, see Memorandum, "Telephone Calls January 10," Folder "Telephone Calls—January 1959," Box 38, DDE Diary Series, AWF; Telegram, Smith to DOS, 10 January 1959, attached with untitled memorandum, John A. Calhoun to General Goodpaster, 12 January 1959, Folder "Dulles, January 1959 (2)," Box 11, Dulles-Herter Series, AWF. For the president's same-day letter accepting the resignation and expressing appreciation for "distinguished performance," see Folder "Cuba (1) 1959," Box 4, WHOF, International Series, Office of the Staff Secretary: Records, 1952–61. For Eisenhower's unsuccessful effort to find Smith another embassy, see "Telephone Calls, January 7, 1959," Memorandum, n.d., both in Folder "ACW Diary—January 1959 (2)," Box 10, Ann Whitman Diary Series, AWF.

6. Wayne S. Smith, *The Closest of Enemies: A Personal and Diplomatic Account of U.S.-Cuban Relations since 1957* (New York: Norton, 1987), 42; Matthews to Castro, 2 February 1959, Folder "Notes, Clippings, Letters for Chapter 4 of His Book," Box 3, Herbert Matthews Papers, Columbia University, New York. See also Richard E. Welch Jr., *Response to Revolution: The United States and the Cuban Revolution, 1959–1961* (Chapel Hill: University of North Carolina Press, 1985), esp. 33; on Bonsal's appointment, see D. E. Boster to Mr. Henderson, 14 January 1959, Folder "Greene-Boster Chronological January 1959 (3)," Box 14, Special Assistants Chronological Series, Dulles Papers.

7. Speech, 13 January 1959, reprinted in *Revolución*, 14 January 1959, 2 (emphasis added); Speech, Havana, 20 January 1959. Castro had made a similar comment at a rally a few days earlier (*Revolución*, 17 January 1959, 4).

8. Embassy to DOS, 15 January 1959, in *FRUS* 1958–60, 6:364; *Revolución*, 14 January 1959, 2.

9. "The charge that the United States supplied arms for Batista's operations against the rebels or that the missions assisted these operations in any way is completely false" (Press Release, 15 January 1959, *DOSB*, 2 February 1959, 162–64).

10. Claudio M. Medel Fuentes to JEMC Local, "Cooperación ofrecida por la Mis Ejto EUA en Cuba," 19 December 1958, PC. On the number of advisers, see Embassy to DOS, 17 February 1953, 737.5-MSP/2-1953, RG59. U.S. officials had understood from the beginning that this aid could cause political problems; see, for example, Embassy to DOS, 5 February 1953, 737.5-MSP/2-553, RG59.

11. "Draft White Paper on Cuba," 113, probably 12 May 1959 but filed as 611.37/1-159, RG59; U.S. Congress, House, Committee on Foreign Affairs, *Cuba and the United States: Thirty Years of Hostility and Beyond*, 101st Cong., 1st sess., 1, 2 August and 20, 21, 27 September 1989, 174 (Shifter).

12. Dwight D. Eisenhower, *Waging Peace, 1956–1961* (Garden City, N.Y.: Doubleday, 1965), 520; "Memo of the President's Briefing before His Press Conference, July 22, 1959," *FRUS* 1958–60, 6:567 ("nice guy").

13. "Synopsis of State and Intelligence Material Reported to President," 24 and 16 January 1959, DDE Diary Series, AWF; White House Staff Notes 500, 14 February 1959, PC. The withdrawal offer was made on 27 January and was accepted the same day by the Cuban minister of state, Roberto Agramonte.

14. Southcom Intelligence Summary, 2 January 1959, PC.

15. U.S. Congress, Senate, Committee on Foreign Relations, *Study Mission in the Caribbean Area, December 1957, Report of Senator George D. Aiken*, 85th Cong., 2nd sess., 20 January 1958, 5; on the Sears and Woolworth stores, see American Chamber of Commerce of Cuba, *Cuba: Facts and Figures* (Havana: American Chamber of Commerce of Cuba, 1957), 18.

16. Embassy to DOS, 22 October 1958, 611.37/10-2258, RG59; Consul to DOS, 19 January 1959, Embassy to DOS, 3 February 1959, both in *FRUS* 1958–60, 6:373, 395.

17. Untitled Memorandum from [Redacted] to the Director, 4 February 1959, Folder "Dulles, February 1959," Dulles-Herter Series, AWF; John S. D. Eisenhower, "Synopsis of State and Intelligence Material Reported to the President," 21 January 1959, DDE Diary Series, AWF; Matthews quoting Powell, 13 March 1959, Box 3, Matthews Papers; Notes "Havana, Feb. 15 to 19, 1959," Box 2, Matthews Papers; Embassy to DOS, 18 February 1959, *FRUS* 1958–60, 6:401. Matthews had written that "the reports of Benzedrine are not true."

18. *Time*, 26 January 1959, 41; Dulles: U.S. Congress, Senate, Committee on Foreign Relations, *Executive Sessions*, 11:125. This was a repetition of what Dulles had told the NSC a few days earlier: Minutes, Folder "394th Meeting of the National Security Council, January 22, 1959," Box 11, NSC Series, AWF. Alexandr Fursenko and Timothy Naftali place the number of executions at 521 in the first three months of 1959 (*One Hell of a Gamble: Khrushchev, Castro, and Kennedy, 1958–1964* [New York: Norton, 1997], 8).

19. D. E. Boster to S/S, 19 January 1959, Folder "Greene-Boster Chronological File January 1959 (2)," Box 14, Special Assistants Chronological Series, Dulles Papers; *Congressional Record*, 26 January 1959, 1154–55.

20. *FRUS* 1958–60, 6:403. "Behind me are others more radical than I," Fidel Castro added in his 21 January speech announcing his brother's promotion.

21. Adam Clayton Powell Jr., *Adam by Adam: The Autobiography of Adam Clayton Powell Jr.* (New York: Dial, 1971), 190. On 17 February, Powell wrote to President Eisenhower to suggest that he invite Castro to visit Washington as soon as possible; the president politely declined to do so (Folder "171(2) Cuba," Box 857, WHCF, Official File OF 169, DDEL).

22. Folder "403rd Meeting of the National Security Council, April 23, 1959," Box 11, NSC Series, AWF; Embassy to DOS, 18 February 1959, Hall (INR) to Cumming, 18 November 1959, both in *FRUS* 1958–60, 6:403, 672; Matthews to Dryfoos, Merz, Catledge, Markel, Freedman, 15 March 1960, Box 2, Matthews Papers. On 26 January, Dulles had worried about Raúl to the Senate Committee on Foreign Relations: "We do not think that Castro himself has any Communist leanings. His brother is more irresponsible" (U.S. Congress, Senate, Committee on Foreign Relations, *Executive Sessions*, 11:125).

23. *Revolución*, 10 April 1959, 2. Castro's Sierra Maestra Manifesto of 12 July 1957, issued jointly with Ortodoxo leaders Raúl Chibás and Felipe Pazos, had placed significant emphasis on prompt elections, as had the article he wrote for *Coronet* magazine: "The provisional government's chief task will be to prepare and conduct truly honest general elections within twelve months" ("Why We Fight," *Coronet*, February 1958, 81–82). The Sierra Maestra Manifesto is reprinted in *Bohemia*, 28 July 1957, 69, 96–97.

24. *NYT*, 26 January 1959, 3; "Why We Fight," *Coronet*, February 1958, 82.

25. Snow to Dillon, 20 February 1959, *FRUS* 1958–60, 6:407–8; Herter to J. W. Fulbright, 19 March 1959, Folder "March 1959 (2)," Box 6, Chronological File, Christian A. Herter Files, DDEL.

26. Snow to Dillon, 20 February 1959, Wieland to Rubottom, 19 February 1959, both in *FRUS* 1958–60, 6:407, 404–6.

27. Notes "Havana, Feb. 15 to 19, 1959," Box 2, Matthews Papers.

28. U.S. Congress, Senate, Committee on Foreign Relations, *Executive Sessions*, 11:126; British Ambassador, Washington, D.C., to Foreign Office, 2455, 24 November 1959, PRO. Dulles acknowledged, however, that Castro "apparently has very wide popular backing throughout the island."

29. Embassy to DOS, 18 February 1959, *FRUS* 1958–60, 6:402.

30. Embassy to DOS, 13 March 1959, 737.00/3-1359, RG59; Embassy Report on Fidel Castro TV Appearance, 13 March 1959, 737.00/3-1358, RG59. "I am not anti-American or anti–United States," Castro told Herbert Matthews at about the same time; "I am anti-American policies" (Notes from a Meeting with Fidel Castro, 17 February, in Notes, "Havana, Feb. 15 to 19, 1959," Box 2, Matthews Papers).

31. U.S. Congress, Senate, Committee on Foreign Relations, *Events in United States–Cuban Relations: A Chronology 1957–1963 Prepared by the Department of State*, 88th Cong., 1st sess., 29 January 1963, 3; "Responsibility of Cuban Government for Increased International Tensions in the Hemisphere," *DOSB*, 29 August 1960, 342.

32. Mann to Undersecretary, 24 March 1959, Philip Bonsal Papers, LC.

33. Herter to J. W. Fulbright, 19 March 1959, Folder "March 1959 (2)," Box 6, Chronological File, Herter Files, DDEL; CIA, "Political and Economic Situation in Cuba," 12 March 1959, PC; Memorandum of Discussion at the 400th Meeting of the NSC, 26 March 1959, Embassy to DOS, "Growth of Communism in Cuba," 14 April 1959, both in *FRUS* 1958–60, 6:440–41, 458.

34. Minutes, Folder "400th Meeting of the National Security Council, March 26, 1959," Box 11, NSC Series, AWF; Max V. Krebs to Roy R. Rubottom Jr., 31 March 1959, Folder "March 1959 (1)," Box 6, Chronological File, Herter Files. For State's suggestion that Eisenhower leave town, see Calhoun to Acting Secretary of State, 13 March 1959, *FRUS* 1958–60, 6:430. In his memoir, the president indicated, "I was more than irritated by the news of the invitation and of Castro's acceptance" (Dwight D. Eisenhower, *Waging Peace*, 523). For good coverage of the trip, see Alan McPherson, "The Limits of Populist Diplomacy: Fidel Castro's April 1959 Trip to North America," *Diplomacy and Statecraft* 18 (March 2007): 237–68.

35. Rufo López-Fresquet, *My Fourteen Months with Castro* (Cleveland: World, 1966), 27; Robert A. Stevenson Oral History, 19 September 1989, Foreign Affairs Oral History Project, Association for Diplomatic Studies and Training, Arlington, Virginia; *NYT*, 18 April 1959, 10.

Castro's assigned interpreter, U.S. Army colonel Vernon Walters, later wrote that "on the *Meet the people* [*sic*] program he did not do well largely because he insisted on speaking in English, which he did quite badly. As we left the studio, he told me this and said that he would not make the same mistake again. From then on I would translate for him on all his calls." Nonetheless, in Castro's next scheduled meeting, this one with Vice President Nixon, the two men spoke alone and in English for more than two hours before Walters and Cuba desk officer Robert Stevenson joined the conversation (Vernon Walters, *The Mighty and the Meek: Dispatches from the Front Line of Diplomacy* [London: St. Ermin's, 2001], 149; see also Vernon Walters, *Silent Missions* [Garden City, N.Y.: Doubleday, 1978], 625; Stevenson to Bonsal, 22 April 1959, Bonsal Papers).

36. *NYT*, 18 April 1959, 10; Memorandum of Conference between President and Acting Secretary of State, 18 April 1959, *FRUS* 1958–60, 6:475.

37. Nixon's memorandum of this meeting with Castro is reprinted in Jeffrey J. Safford, "The Nixon-Castro Meeting of 19 April 1959," *Diplomatic History* 4 (Fall 1980): 426–31. Castro apparently did not enjoy the encounter: he told López-Fresquet, who was waiting outside Nixon's vice presidential suite in the Senate, "This man has spent the whole time scolding me" (*My Fourteen Months*, 169). This seems congruent with the view of the Cuba desk officer, who was also waiting outside: Nixon "has said that he had talked to Dr. Castro 'just as a father'" (Robert Stevenson to Bonsal, 22 April 1959, Bonsal Papers).

38. Memorandum, "Evaluation of the Unofficial Visit to Washington by Prime Minister Fidel Castro of Cuba," 23 April 1959, Folder "Christian A. Herter April 1959 (2)," Box 11, Dulles-Herter Series, AWF.

39. Fidel Castro, "Why We Fight," *Coronet*, February 1958, 84–85. The agrarian reform

mentioned in the March 1957 Sierra Maestra Manifesto had promised redistribution of unused land and state land and the conversion of tenant farmers into proprietors (*Bohemia*, 28 July 1957, 96).

40. Embassy to DOS, 6 January 1959, Consulate Santiago to DOS, 14 January 1959, both in *FRUS* 1958–60, 6:345–46, 361; *Wall Street Journal*, 8 January 1959, 1, 3; see also Dwight D. Eisenhower, *Waging Peace*, 552. "This has been a real popular movement, of that there is no doubt at all," a visiting U.S. professor wrote in his diary in mid-January. "I haven't yet met anyone who is really unhappy about the revolution" (Robert Alexander Diary, 11 January 1959, Robert Alexander Papers, Rutgers University, New Brunswick, New Jersey).

41. Decree-Law 135, 10 March 1959, lowered rents of less than one hundred pesos by 50 percent, those of one hundred to two hundred pesos by 40 percent, and those of more than two hundred pesos by 30 percent. The 1957 telephone rate increase was especially sensitive because the contract authorizing it had been signed at a public ceremony attended by the U.S. ambassador only hours after a disastrous urban underground attack on the presidential palace. See Jules Dubois, *Fidel Castro: Rebel—Liberator or Dictator?* (Indianapolis: Bobbs-Merrill, 1959), 155–56.

42. Safford, "Nixon-Castro Meeting," 428.

43. The government promulgated the agrarian reform law on 17 May and published it as an eleven-page "edición extraordinaria especial" of the *Gaceta Oficial*, 3 June 1959. Article 275 of the 1940 Constitution had vaguely provided for the separation of the production of cane and its grinding into sugar, specifying that a future law would regulate the two processes "sobre la base de la división de los dos grandes factores que concurren a su desarrollo; industriales o productores de azúcar y agricultores o colonos, productores de caña."

44. Johnson to Kleberg, 20 June 1959, Folder "Foreign Relations Cuba," Box 68, Subject File, LBJA, LBJL.

45. Kleberg to Johnson, 25 June 1959, Folder "Foreign Relations Cuba," Box 68, Subject File, LBJA, LBJL. The chief executive of King Ranch Inc. from 1935 until his death in 1974, Kleberg had inherited the family business from his parents, Robert Kleberg Sr. and Alice Gertrudis King. For similar pleas to Senator Johnson, see Box 68, LBJA, Subject File Foreign Relations, Cuba, LBJL; Box 674, 1959 Subject Files, Foreign Relations, Senate Papers, LBJL; and Boxes 80, 135, and 136 of Johnson's Vice Presidential Papers, 1961 and 1962 Subject Files, LBJL.

46. Memcon, DOS, 24 June 1959, Unsigned White House Staff Note, 25 June 1959, *FRUS* 1958–60, 6:539–41, 552n; Kleberg to Johnson, 25 June 1959, Folder "Foreign Relations Cuba," Box 68, Subject File, LBJA, LBJL ("ancient and absurd levels").

47. Herter to President, 7 July 1959, *FRUS* 1958–60, 6:552; DOS to Embassy, 22 May 1959, *FRUS* 1958–60, 6:510.

48. Memcon, "Meeting with American Sugar Interests Regarding the Situation of Their Properties in Cuba," 24 September 1959, *FRUS* 1958–60, 6:605–11.

49. Nichols's firm owned 365,000 acres of sugar property in Cuba (Robert A. Stevenson to Bonsal, 4 August 1959, Bonsal Papers). Most of the materials from investors are filed in Boxes 804, 805, 834, General File GF 122, WHCF, DDEL, and in Boxes 857, 858, Official File OF171, WHCF, DDEL.

50. Memcon, "Protection of American interests in Cuba," 22 December 1959, *FRUS* 1958–60, 6:708.

51. Embassy to DOS, 11 May 1959, *FRUS* 1958–60, 6:510.

52. Stevenson to Bonsal, 29 June 1959, Bonsal to Stevenson, 4 July 1959, both in Bonsal Papers.

53. Herter to Eisenhower, 7 July 1959, Box 9, Dulles-Herter Series, DDE Papers, AWF; Minutes, Folder "411th Meeting of the National Security Council, 25 June 1959," Box 11, NSC Series, AWF. This was the third time the NSC had discussed Cuba's agrarian reform: earlier discussions had occurred on 21 May and 18 June; a fourth discussion occurred on 9 July; see Box 11, NSC Series, AWF.

54. On the inevitability of clashes, see Jules R. Benjamin, "Interpreting the U.S. Reaction to the Cuban Revolution, 1959–1960," *Cuban Studies* 19 (1989): 145–65.

55. Rice to Smith, 25 February 1960, *FRUS* 1958–60, 6:812.

56. Embassy to DOS, 6 December 1960, *FRUS* 1958–60, 6:1151. Six weeks later, Rubottom told his colleagues that communism was "a much better basis on which to place our cause than U.S. economic interests in Cuba" (27 June 1960, *FRUS* 1958–19, 6:964).

57. Embassy to DOS, 9 March 1959, *FRUS* 1958–60, 6:422.

58. Memcon, Bonsal, Braddock, and López-Fresquet, 2 June 1959, enclosed with Braddock to DOS, 3 June 1959, 837.16/6-358, RG59. The U.S. note, 11 June 1959, is reprinted in *DOSB*, 29 June 1959, 958–59.

59. Rubottom to DOS, 23 June 1959, 838.16/6-2259, RG59; for other U.S. investments, see U.S. Congress, House, Committee on Foreign Affairs, Subcommittee on Inter-American Affairs, *Claims of U.S. Nationals against the Government of Cuba*, 88th Cong., 2nd sess., July–August 1964, 40–44; Stephen G. Rabe, *Eisenhower and Latin America: The Foreign Policy of Anticommunism* (Chapel Hill: University of North Carolina Press, 1988), 120. The exact number of acres to be nationalized was 1.864 million.

60. Embassy to DOS, 12 June 1959, *FRUS* 1958–60, 6:529.

61. Roa to Bonsal, 15 June 1959, *FRUS* 1958–60, 6:533; for the U.S. note of 11 June, the Cuban reply of 15 June, and a 12 October U.S. response, see Folder "Cuba," Box 4, White House Council on Foreign Economic Policy, Randall Series, Subject Subseries, DDEL.

62. John L. Loeb, "To the Stockholders," 23 August 1960, PC; Philip Rosenberg, "Letter to the Stockholders," 26 October 1960, Joshua Bernhardt Papers, American Heritage Center, University of Wyoming, Laramie. Leroy Denman to Robert Kleberg, 24 August 1970, PC; U.S. Foreign Claims Settlement Commission, *Annual Report to the Congress for the Period January 1–December 31, 1970* (Washington, D.C., 1973), 59–61. I am indebted to Louis A. Pérez Jr. for sharing the Loeb and Rosenberg documents. On these lingering claims into the twenty-first century, see Matías F. Travieso-Díaz, "Expropriation Claims Involving the Cuban Sugar Industry," in *Reinventing the Cuban Sugar Agroindustry*, ed. Jorge F. Pérez-López and José Alvarez (Lanham, Md.: Lexington Books, 2005), 198–205.

63. Burke: Memorandum of Discussion at the 435th Meeting of the NSC, 18 February 1960, *FRUS* 1958–60, 6:792. See also Louis A. Pérez Jr., "Incurring a Debt of Gratitude: 1898 and the Moral Sources of United States Hegemony in Cuba," *American Historical Review* 104 (April 1999): 356–98. On Castro's plummeting popularity among U.S. citizens, see David Robert Jenkins, "Initial American Responses to Fidel Castro, 1957–1959" (Ph.D. diss., University of Texas, 1992), 225–26.

64. Truman's 28 April 1959 speech and informal remarks are reprinted in *Truman Speaks* (New York: Columbia University Press, 1960), 92; "Truman Bids U.S. Be Firm to Soviet," *NYT,*

31 July 1959, 1, 3; Lippmann: *New York Herald Tribune*, 23 July 1959, 12. Truman changed his view after the October 1962 missile crisis, calling Castro "a modern-day Quisling" and arguing that "somehow we must seek a way of helping the Cuban people to liberate themselves" (*Washington Post*, 24 February 1963, 1).

65. U.S. Congress, Senate, Committee on the Judiciary, Subcommittee to Investigate the Administration of the Internal Security Act and Other Internal Security Laws, *Communist Threat to the United States through the Caribbean*, 86th Cong., 1st sess., pt. 1, 14 July 1959; *Congressional Record*, 13 July 1959, 13221–22, 13236; Special NIE for Latin America, 30 June 1959, *FRUS* 1958–60, 5:395.

66. Embassy to DOS, 7 July 1959, DOS to Embassy, 18 July 1959, both in *FRUS* 1958–60, 6:554, 565; see also Allen Dulles's comment a few days later ("certainly the Communists had been helped by the removal of President Urrutia") in Minutes, Folder "414th Meeting of the National Security Council, July 23, 1959," Box 11, NSC Series, AWF.

67. Embassy to DOS, 2 August 1959, *FRUS* 1958–60, 6:580–82; Rubottom Oral History, 51.

68. Embassy to DOS, 7 July 1959, Hill to Rubottom, 6 August 1959, *FRUS* 1958–60, 6:554, 585; Stevenson Oral History. A career officer from 1947 to 1973, Hill was considered "a most effective operator" by State's John Crimmins, and a good indicator of Hill's professional reputation came when he was sent the Dominican Republic as chargé six days after Trujillo was assassinated. His career subsequently went sideways, and he died of cancer in December 1973 at the age of fifty-two (Obituary, *NYT*, 28 December 1973, 32; John Crimmins Oral History, 23 May 1964, JFKL).

69. Willauer to Rubottom, 30 April 1959, *FRUS* 1958–60, 6:493–94.

70. U.S. Congress, Senate, Committee on the Judiciary, Subcommittee to Investigate the Administration of the Internal Security Act and Other Internal Security Laws, *Communist Threat*, pt. 5, 17 July 1959, 245, 257, 274, 297, 299. Braden also worried that Castro was permitting the Soviet Union to store bombers in Cuba's many natural caves.

71. Embassy to DOS, 14 September 1959, *FRUS* 1958–60, 6:599.

72. Embassy to DOS, 17 October 1959, *FRUS* 1958–60, 6:627–28; Philip W. Bonsal, *Cuba, Castro, and the United States* (Pittsburgh: University of Pittsburgh Press, 1971), 108; Minutes, Folder "422nd Meeting of the National Security Council, October 19, 1959," Box 11, NSC Series, AWF; Pedro L. Díaz Lanz to President, 31 October 1959 (with a copy of the leaflet attached), Folder "171 (2) Cuba," Box 857, Official File OF 169, WHCF, DDEL. A 9 November State Department press release attributed the casualties to "stray rounds of 20 and 40 mm shell fragments from anti-aircraft fire of the Cuban armed forces or from grenades or bombs thrown from automobiles by terrorists."

73. Speech, Havana, 26 October 1959. For the embassy's analysis, see *FRUS* 1958–60, 6:642–43. Arrested immediately after his protest resignation, Matos was imprisoned for twenty years, then sent into exile.

74. Press Release 760, 27 October 1959, *DOSB*, 16 November 1959, 715–18; "Ambassador Bonsal's Call on the President of Cuba," 27 October 1959, and Cuba's response, "Raúl Roa to Mr. Ambassador," 13 November 1959, both in Folder "Cuba," Box 4, White House Council on Foreign Economic Policy, Randall Series, Subject Subseries, DDEL. Roa's "bitter experience" was a reference to the two federal indictments of Carlos Prío for aiding anti-Batista rebels.

75. Matthews to Dryfoos, Merz, Catledge, Markel, Freedman, 15 March 1960, Box 2, Matthews Papers; "Telephone Calls, Monday, October 26, 1959" and "Telephone Calls, Tuesday, October 27, 1959," Telephone Calls Series, Herter Papers; *DOSB*, 23 November 1959, 757–58.

76. Eisenhower Press Conference, 28 October 1959, *PPP*, 751; "Raúl Roa to Mr. Ambassador," 13 November 1959, Folder "Cuba," Box 4, White House Council on Foreign Economic Policy, Randall Series, Subject Subseries, DDEL.

77. Bonsal to DOS, 18 October 1960, Folder "Cuba [Background material on Cuba Used in Compiling Plank/Chase Report]," Box 5, NSFJ, Files of Gordon Chase; "Conversation with Mr. Rufo Lopez Fresquet, Minister of Finance," 9 November 1959, Bonsal Papers; Memcon, "Our Future Relations with Cuba," 18 September 1959, Embassy to DOS, 30 October 1959, Memo, Carlos Hall, "Random Observations While on Leave in Cuba October 18–November 8," all in *FRUS* 1958–60, 6:603–5, 648–49, 672.

78. Christian Herter, "Memorandum for the President. Subject: Current Basic United States Policy toward Cuba," 5 November 1959, Folder "Cuba (1) 1959," Box 4, International Series, WHOF, Office of the Staff Secretary: Records: 1952–61; Sir H. Caccia to Secretary of State, Telegram 2455, 24 November 1959, PRO.

79. John Topping to Richard B. Owen, 6 November 1959, 737.00/11-659, RG59; Embassy to DOS, 6 November 1959, *FRUS* 1958–60, 6:658–59.

80. Embassy to DOS, "Suggested Operations Plan for Cuba," 27 November 1959, 611.37/11-2759, RG59; see also Department of State Staff Summary Supplement, 30 November 1959, Box 19, Records of the Staff Research Group, WHOF. Although titled "Suggested Operations Plan for Cuba," it was not a plan but rather the embassy's interpretation of what was occurring in Cuba (Rubottom Oral History, 69–70).

81. "Estimate of Economic Outlook for Cuba," 14 December 1959, *FRUS* 1958–60, 6:701–2; Meeting, 30 December 1959, *FRUS* 1958–60, 6:716–17, 722; Embassy to DOS, "Suggested Operations Plan for Cuba," 27 November 1959, 611.37/11-2759, RG59.

82. Embassy to DOS, "Suggested Operations Plan for Cuba," 27 November 1959, 611.37/11-2759, RG59.

83. NSC 5902/1, 16 February 1959, *FRUS* 1958–60, 5:92.

84. U.S. Congress, House, Committee on Foreign Affairs, Subcommittee on Inter-American Affairs, *Report on United States Relations with Latin America*, 86th Cong., 1st sess., 12 May 1959, 6; Roa's 24 September address to the U.N. General Assembly is reported in Bonsal to Rubottom, [late September 1959], *FRUS* 1958–60, 6:612. On the U.N. votes, see James Martin Keagle, "Toward an Understanding of U.S. Latin American Policy" (Ph.D. diss., Princeton University, 1982), 180.

85. Embassy to DOS, "Suggested Operations Plan for Cuba," 27 November 1959, 611.37/11-2759, RG59; Hill to Rubottom, 4 December 1959, *FRUS* 1958–60, 6:689.

86. Bonsal to Rubottom, 23 February 1959, Bonsal, "Notes on Cuba," [late 1959], both in Bonsal Papers; Herter to Selwyn Lloyd, 5 November 1959, *FRUS* 1958–60, 6:654.

87. NSC meeting, 10 December 1959, *FRUS* 1958–60, 6:699–700; Office of Naval Intelligence, *Bulletin*, 16 December 1959, PC; Rubottom to Dillon, 28 December 1959, *FRUS* 1958–60, 6:716; NIE, 29 December 1959, *FRUS* 1958–60, 5:417. Bissell's one remaining noncommunist was probably López-Fresquet.

Chapter 5

1. Khrushchev's Comment to Western Diplomats in Moscow, 18 November 1956, reported in *The Times* (London), 19 November 1956, 8; Batista to Eisenhower, 1 February 1958, Folder "Cuba(2)," Box 8, International Series, AWF; James Gavin, *War and Peace in the Space Age* (New York: Harper, 1958), 3, whose view was shared by Allen Dulles (see Allen Dulles to President, 19 August 1959, Folder "CIA Vol. II (7)," Box 8, WHOF, Office of the Staff Secretary: Records, 1952–61, Subject Series, Alphabetical Subseries); Eisenhower Press Conference, 26 January 1960, *PPP*, 127.

2. Speeches, Dallas, Texas, 13 September 1960, Oklahoma City, 3 November 1960, both in U.S. Congress, Senate, *Freedom of Communications: Final Report of the Committee on Commerce, United States Senate*, pt. 1, *The Speeches, Remarks, Press Conferences, and Study Papers of Senator John F. Kennedy, August 1 through November 7, 1960*, 87th Cong., 1st sess., 1961, 224, 881–82.

3. Castro's 18 January comments came during an appearance on a radio program to receive public donations to purchase weapons to defend the country's airspace; Eisenhower press conference, 26 January 1960, *PPP*, 125. For United Fruit's ties to the Eisenhower administration, see Piero Gleijeses, *Shattered Hope: The Guatemalan Revolution and the United States, 1944–1954* (Princeton: Princeton University Press, 1991), 361–66.

4. Press Conference, 28 October 1959, *PPP*, 751, 753; NSC Meeting, 14 January 1960, *FRUS* 1958–60, 6:746; Samuel E. Belk to Gray, "Background for the Cuba and Dominican Republic Items . . . ," 13 January 1960, Folder "Cuban Situation (2) 1959–60," Box 6, WHOF, Office of the Special Assistant for National Security Affairs: Records, 1952–61, NSC Series, Briefing Notes Subseries; Rubottom to Secretary of State, "Removal of Certain Cuban Exiles from the Florida Area," 30 December 1959, 737.00/12-3059, RG59. For evidence that virtually every senior foreign policy official was aware of the problem, see *FRUS* 1958–60, 6:633–35, 643–46.

5. For the requests for stepped-up enforcement, see Embassy to Secretary of State, 29 January, 1 February 1960, Folder "Cuba (2) January–April 1960," Box 4, WHOF, Office of the Staff Secretary: Records, 1952–61, International Series (the 1 February cable is also *FRUS* 1958–60, 6:779); Press Release, 26 January 1960, Folder "171 (2) Cuba," Box 857, WHCF, Official File OF167, DDEL. Most of the records regarding the effort to halt the bombings, including Executive Order 10863, are in Folder "Cuba," Box 2, WHOF, Cabinet Secretariat: Records, 1953–61, but see also Folder "Cabinet Meeting of March 25, 1960," Box 15, Cabinet Series, AWF; Folder "CI 69," Box 22, WHOF, Cabinet Secretariat: Records, 1953–61; Fabián Escalante, *The Secret War: CIA Covert Operations against Cuba 1959–62*, trans. Maxine Shaw (Melbourne, Australia: Ocean, 1994), 159–61.

6. For the Cuban government's list of bombings, see Escalante, *Secret War*, 159–61.

7. Rubottom to Secretary of State, "Removal of Certain Cuban Exiles from the Florida Area," 30 December 1959, 737.00/12-3059, RG59; "Cuban Refugees in Florida," 8 November 1960, Folder "Cabinet Meeting of November 9, 1960," Box 16, Cabinet Series, AWF.

8. Rubottom to Secretary, "Recall of Ambassador Philip W. Bonsal from Cuba for Consultation," January 1960, Philip Bonsal Papers, LC. For the embassy characterization of Castro's 18 January speech, see *FRUS* 1958–60, 6:747; Embassy to DOS, 26 January 1960, 737.00(W)/

1-2660, RG59; for Bonsal's return after two months in Washington, see Embassy to DOS, 22 March 1960, 737.00(W)/3-2260, RG59.

9. Ambassador Allan Anderson, Havana, to Secretary of State for External Affairs, Ottawa, "Annual Review of Events in Cuba—1959," 13 January 1960, PC.

10. Embassy to DOS, 6 December 1960, *FRUS* 1958–60, 6:1152; Matthews Radio Interview, "Yale Reports," 15 January 1961, Folder "Latin America Correspondence and Miscellaneous Items," Box 3, Herbert Matthews Papers, Columbia University, New York; NSC Meeting, 17 March 1960, *FRUS* 1958–60, 6:857–58; Memcon, "Cuban Situation: Meeting with Representatives of the National Foreign Trade Council," 7 June 1960, *FRUS* 1958–60, 6:942.

11. Embassy to DOS, 21 January 1960, *FRUS* 1958–60, 6:755–56.

12. INR Biographic Report, "Fidel Castro: The First Year," Report BR 312, 17 March 1960, 3, 5, in possession of the author; Bonsal, "Memorandum of Conference with the President, January 25, 1960," *FRUS* 1958–60, 6:763–65; see also 760; Desk Diary Entry, 6 July 1960, DDE Diary Series, AWF; Eisenhower Press Conference, 26 January 1960, *PPP*, 129–30, and Press Statement, 134–36; Herter to President, "Latin American Reaction to January 26, 1960 Statement on United States–Cuban Relations," n.d., Folder "Christian Herter February 1960," Box 12, Dulles-Herter Series, AWF.

13. Foreign Minister Raúl Roa's proposal was cabled to Washington: Braddock to Secretary of State, 23 February 1960; for the U.S. response, see Secretary of State to Embassy Havana, 23 February 1960, both in Folder "Cuba (2) January–April 1960," Box 4, WHOF, Office of the Staff Secretary: Records, 1952–61, International Series.

14. For this agreement and a credit agreement mentioned in the following paragraph, see *Gaceta Oficial*, 8 March 1960, 5737–41. For details, see "No. 250 the Soviet-Cuban Commercial Agreement," 18 February 1960, Folder "Cuba January–June 1960," Box 3, Records of the Special Assistant on Communism, 1956–61, Bureau of American Republics Affairs, Lot 62D24, RG59; see also Chancery, Mexico City, to Department, 9 December 1959, AK1223/132, FO371/139475, PRO; Alexandr Fursenko and Timothy Naftali, *One Hell of a Gamble: Khrushchev, Castro, and Kennedy, 1958–1964* (New York: Norton, 1997), 11–15, 25–31; Alexandr Alexéev, "Cuba depués del triunfo de la revolución," *América Latina* 9 (September 1984): 56–67, 11 (November 1984): 54–61.

15. Intelligence Briefing Notes, 13–20 February 1960, PC; NSC meeting, 18 February 1960, *FRUS* 1958–60, 6:792.

16. Meeting of DOS and Joint Chiefs of Staff, 8 January 1960, *FRUS* 1958–60, 6:732; NSC Meeting, 14 January 1960, *FRUS* 1958–60, 6:742.

17. "Possibilities for Salvaging Cuba," 18 February 1960, *FRUS* 1958–60, 6:794–800. The term "ARA" refers to the State Department's Office of American Republic Affairs, which was renamed the Bureau of Inter-American Affairs in October 1949 but kept ARA as its cable address and informal title.

18. Burke, "Recommendations for U.S. Action in Cuba," 26 February 1960, *FRUS* 1958–60, 6:814–19; but see also 873; Joint Chiefs to Secretary of Defense, 2 March 1960, *FRUS* 1958–60, 6:822.

19. Speech, 5 March 1960, *Revolución*, 7 March 1960, 3, 5–7.

20. Herter to Selwyn Lloyd, 5 November 1959, Cable 2335, AK1223/88, FO371/139474, PRO; British Ambassador, Washington, D.C., to Foreign Office, Cable 2455, 24 November 1959,

PRO. Although an informal arms cutoff had begun earlier, the United States formally halted all arms shipments to Cuba and the Dominican Republic in early October 1959 (*DOSB*, 16 November 1959, 717).

21. Much of the cable traffic from Washington to London is reprinted in *FRUS* 1958–60, 6:653–65. For the British side, see the documents in FO371/13470–75, PRO, especially Fordham to Hankey, 29 May 1959, AK1223/14, 8 July 1959, AK1223/20. See also "Ambassador Bonsal's Call on the President of Cuba," 27 October 1959, Raúl Roa to Mr. Ambassador, 13 November 1959, both in Folder "Cuba," Box 4, White House Office on Foreign Economic Policy, Randall Series, Subject Subseries, DDEL. For a similar effort to halt Cuba's purchase of patrol boats from Italy, see "Progress Report on Cuba," 27 April 1960, Folder "Cuba, May 1959–September 1960 (2)," Box 4, WHOF, Office of the Special Assistant for National Security Affairs: Records, 1952–61, NSC Series, Subject Subseries.

22. The United States rejected Castro's charge in an aide-mémoire, 4 June 1960, reprinted in *DOSB*, 20 June 1960, 994–95. The initial embassy reports on the explosion and drafts of the U.S. note are in Folder "Cuba (2) January–April 1960," Box 4, WHOF, Office of the Staff Secretary: Records, 1952–61, International Series; Embassy to DOS, 8 March 1960, *FRUS* 1958–60, 6:824–25; Rubottom to Bonsal, 23 March 1960, Bonsal Papers; Robert A. Stevenson Oral History, 19 September 1989, Foreign Affairs Oral History Project, Association for Diplomatic Studies and Training, Arlington, Virginia; NSC Meeting, 10 March 1960, *FRUS* 1958–60, 6:832–33.

23. A heavily redacted copy of the plan is reprinted in *FRUS* 1958–60, 6:850–54; the full original is in Folder "CIA Policy re Cuba (17 March 1960)," Box 4, WHOF, Office of the Staff Secretary, International Series; a copy is reprinted in the *Newsletter of the Society for Historians of American Foreign Relations*, September 2002, 4–10. For the King and Dulles statements, see U.S. Congress, Senate, Select Committee to Study Governmental Operations with Respect to Intelligence Activities, *Alleged Assassination Plots Involving Foreign Leaders: An Interim Report*, 94th Cong., 1st sess., 20 November 1975, 92–93; see also Stephen G. Rabe, *Eisenhower and Latin America: The Foreign Policy of Anticommunism* (Chapel Hill: University of North Carolina Press, 1988), 128. On the bureaucratic organization of covert action, including the 5412 Committee, see *FRUS* 1964–68, 12:xxxiii–xxxvii.

24. "Memorandum of a Conference with the President," 17 March 1960, "Memorandum of a Telephone Conversation . . . ," 19 March 1960, both in *FRUS* 1958–60, 6:861–63, 866.

25. "Progress Report on Cuba," 24 May 1960, Folder "Cuba, May 1959–September 1960 (2)," Box 4, WHOF, Office of the Special Assistant for National Security Affairs: Records, 1952–61, NSC Series, Subject Subseries.

26. Herter, "Memorandum of a Conference with the President," 17 March 1960, *FRUS* 1958–60, 6:861; Castro's 27 March 1960 statement occurred during a television appearance; the U.S. reaction was a State Department press release, 30 March 1960, *AFP* 1960, 202.

27. U.S. Congress, House, Committee on Foreign Affairs, Subcommittee on Inter-American Affairs, *Claims of U.S. Nationals against the Government of Cuba*, 88th Cong., 2nd sess., July–August 1964, 34–35.

28. Ibid., 115–19, 124.

29. Irving H. Miller to President Eisenhower, 11 August 1960, Folder "171 (2) Cuba," Box 857, WHCF, Official File 169, DDEL; U.S. Congress, House, Committee on Foreign Affairs,

Subcommittee on Inter-American Affairs, *Claims of U.S. Nationals*, 116, 123, 124; Philip W. Bonsal, *Cuba, Castro, and the United States* (Pittsburgh: University of Pittsburgh Press, 1971), 4; "Memorandum of Telephone Conversation . . . ," 1 April 1960, *FRUS 1958–19*, 6:878.

30. Rubottom to Bonsal, 26 May 1960, *FRUS 1958–60*, 6:929. On the U.S. government's effort to discourage companies from accepting Cuba's offer to negotiate compensation, see Memcon, "Cuban Offer to Compensate Shell," 27 March 1964, Folder "Cuba Country Volume II, 3/64–5/64," Box 17, NSFJ, CF, Cuba.

31. "Memorandum of a Conversation," 30 June 1960, Meeting, 7 June 1960, "Memorandum of a Conference," 27 June 1960, all in *FRUS 1958–60*, 6:940, 959–61, 974.

32. Samuel E. Belk to Gordon Gray, 31 March 1960, Folder "Cuban Situation (1) 1959–60," Box 6, WHOF, Office of the Special Assistant for National Security Affairs: Records, 1952–61, NSC Series, Subject Subseries; *DOSB*, 2 May 1960, 704–8; *DOSB*, 13 June 1960, 962; *DOSB*, 20 June 1960, 994–95.

33. "Memorandum of a Conversation, Washington, May 2, 1960," *FRUS 1958–60*, 6:907.

34. Gordon Gray to Douglas Dillon, 29 April 1960, "Memorandum of a Conference with the President," 17 March 1960, both in *FRUS 1958–60*, 6:903, 862. After the 17 March meeting, see *FRUS 1958–60*, 6:934, 936, 946, and esp. 959–68. The capacity of a fourth Cuban-owned refinery, Refinería Cabaiguán in Las Villas, was dwarfed by that of the three foreign-owned facilities: two thousand versus eighty-two thousand barrels per day. The first Soviet crude, a small shipment, had arrived in April 1960 and had been processed at the Cabaiguán refinery (Jorge F. Pérez-López, "Cuban Hard-Currency Trade and Oil Reexports," in *Socialist Cuba: Past Interpretations and Future Challenges*, ed. Sergio G. Roca [Boulder, Colo.: Westview, 1988], 130).

35. On 17 May, the Cuban government asked Texaco to purchase three hundred thousand tons of Russian crude from the Banco Nacional. The subsequent chronology is outlined in "What Happened in Cuba," *Texaco Topics*, August 1960, 7–8.

36. Bonsal to Rubottom, 6 June 1960, *FRUS 1958–60*, 6:935–38; A. S. Fordham to Selwyn Lloyd, 3 February 1959, AK1011/1, FO371/139398, PRO; Guevara speeches reported in *NYT*, 6 February, 1960, 1, 21 March 1960, 1; Leland L. Johnson, "U.S. Business Interests in Cuba and the Rise of Castro," *World Politics* 17 (April 1965): 445; see also Castro Speech, Havana, 24 February 1960: "One cannot consider a country free if its economy is in the hands of foreigners."

37. Rubottom to Secretary of State, 2 June 1960, *FRUS 1958–60*, 6:934–36. Castro's comment is mentioned in "Progress Report on Cuba," 16 June 1960, Folder "Cuba, May 1959–September 1960 (3)," Box 4, WHOF, Office of the Special Assistant for National Security Affairs: Records, 1952–61, NSC Series, Subject Subseries; "Notes on the Discussion at the Special Meeting of the NSC," 22 June 1960, *FRUS 1958–60*, 6:951; Anderson and Dillon suggested that the airlines could claim that the Soviet oil was "of improper grade or not adequate in terms of octane" ("Questions Concerning a Program of Economic Pressures against Castro," 27 June 1960, *FRUS 1958–60*, 6:958–66).

38. Bonsal to Rubottom, 28 June 1960, *FRUS 1958–60*, 6:969. As elsewhere in Latin America, Cuban law permitted the state to "intervene" a company—that is, to assume management without assuming ownership. For an oil company perspective, see "What Happened in Cuba," *Texaco Topics*, August 1960, 7–8.

39. Gordon Chase, "Memorandum for Mr. Plank. Subject: 1960 Cuban Intervention of American Oil Companies—Post Mortem," 4 November 1963, Folder "Cuba [Background Material on Cuba Used in Compiling Plank/Chase Report]," Box 5, NSFJ, Gordon Chase Files.

40. *DOSB*, 25 July 1960, 141–42 (U.S. protest); *FRUS* 1958–60, 6:984, 987 (NSC meeting); Embassy to DOS, 29 June 1960, 737.00(W)/6-2960, RG59; Memo of a Telephone Conversation, Herter and Anderson, 14 July 1960, *FRUS* 1958–60, 6:1013–14. On the spare parts, see "Progress Report on Cuba," 11 August 1960, Folder "Cuba, May 1959–September 1960 (6)," Box 4, WHOF, Office of the Special Assistant for National Security Affairs: Records, 1952–61, NSC Series, Subject Subseries; Minutes of NSC meeting, 21 July 1960, *FRUS* 1958–60, 6:1023–24.

The immediate losers were the oil companies. Texaco placed its losses (for the refinery, ocean terminals, and 375 service stations) at fifty million dollars, making it the tenth-largest certified claimant. Much of what Esso lost was Cuban government money, for the recently completed refinery expansion had been largely underwritten by Batista's Financiera Nacional. Texaco's claim still totaled seventy-one million dollars, making it the eighth-largest claimant (U.S. Foreign Claims Settlement Commission, *Annual Report to the Congress for the Period January 1–December 31, 1972* [Washington, D.C.], 414).

41. The original treaty (33 *Stat.* 2136) was signed in December 1902 and ratified by the United States in March 1903. The Sugar Act is better known as the Jones-Costigan Act (PL 73-213, 9 May 1934, 48 *Stat.* 670); it assigned Cuba a large quota but did not eliminate the sugar tariff, although a new bilateral agreement concluded at the same time lowered the tariff on Cuban sugar.

42. Canadian Ambassador to Secretary of State for External Affairs, 2 April 1953, PC; NSC Minutes, 26 March 1959, Memcon, 24 June 1959, both in *FRUS* 1958–60, 6:518–19, 541.

43. "Cuban Economic Prospects, 1959 and Proposed U.S. Action," 1 July 1959, *FRUS* 1958–60, 6:551.

44. Bonsal to Rubottom, late September 1959, Wieland to Rubottom, 9 December 1959, Mann to Rubottom, 23 December 1959 [erroneously dated 1958], Turkel to Robottom, [December 1959], all in *FRUS* 1958–60, 6:615, 693, 712, 696n.

45. NSC meeting, 1 December 1959, *FRUS* 1958–60, 6:684; "Legislative Leadership Meeting, 15 March 1960," "Notes on Legislative Leadership Meeting, 9 June 1960," both in Folder "Legislative Leaders—1960 March–April (2)," Box 2, Legislative Meetings Series, AWF; "Memorandum for Mrs. Whitman," 8 June 1959, Folder "Staff Notes June 1–15, 1959 (2)," Box 42, DDE Diary Series, AWF.

46. HR 9313 (Budge, R-Idaho) and HR 9376 (St. George, R-New York) in *Congressional Record*, 6 January 1960, 735. The latter proposal would have prohibited Cuban imports above the world market price (*Congressional Record*, 30 June 1960, 15244).

47. *Congressional Record*, 30 June 1960, 15245, 15228, 15243. Of the thirty-one representatives who participated in the debate, only Democrat Barratt O'Hara (p. 15231) uttered a word of opposition, primarily in reaction to Rivers's suggested military occupation: "Good neighbors do not invade the neighbors' homes." For the entire debate, see 15227–48.

48. Desk Diary Entry, 6 July 1960, DDE Diary Series, AWF; PL 86-592, 74 *Stat.* 330, 6 July 1960; Presidential Proclamation 3355 is 25 *FR* 6414; it and the accompanying statement are reprinted in *DOSB*, 25 July 1960, 140–41; *NYT*, 8 July 1960, 20; Eisenhower to Arthur Hays Sulzberger, 8 July 1960, Folder "DDE Dictation, July 1960," Box 51, DDE Diary Series, AWF. The

proclamation cut the 1960 quota by 700,000 tons—about 2.3 million of Cuba's 3.2-million-ton 1960 quota had already been shipped. Subsequent proclamations by the Eisenhower and Kennedy administrations suspended Cuba's quota, and in 1962 the Foreign Assistance Act was amended [Sec. 620(a)] to eliminate the quota until Cuba had paid for confiscated U.S. property. In 1974, the Sugar Act was allowed to expire, and with it any Cuban claim to a quota.

49. Castro Speeches, 23–24 June 1960 (began at 10:00 P.M.), 24 June 1960, 6 July 1960; Bonsal to Secretary of State, 7 July 1960, Folder "Cuba (3) May–July 1960," Box 4, WHOF, Office of the Staff Secretary: Records, 1952–61, International Series.

50. For Law 851, which denied any right of appeal, see *Gaceta Oficial*, 7 July 1960, 16367–68. For the U.S. sugar program and purchases from Cuba during the 1950s and earlier, see the tables in *Congressional Record*, 30 June 1960, 15236–41; U.S. Congress, House, Committee on Agriculture, *History and Operations of the U.S. Sugar Program*, 87th Cong., 2nd sess., 14 May 1962; Jorge F. Pérez-López, *The Economics of Cuban Sugar* (Pittsburgh: University of Pittsburgh Press, 1991), esp. 128–35.

51. Castro Press Conference, Havana, 10 July 1960. For a list of companies whose assets were nationalized, see U.S. Congress, House, Committee on Foreign Affairs, Subcommittee on Inter-American Affairs, *Claims of U.S. Nationals*, 41–44, 129; Embassy to DOS, 11 August 1960, 737.00(W)/8-1160, RG59. Sinclair operated service stations and owned a storage facility but no refinery.

52. A. J. Goodpaster, "Memorandum of Conference with the President, July 11, 1960, 9 A.M., Newport," 13 July 1960, Folder "Staff Notes July 1960," Box 51, DDE Diary Series, AWF; Herter Telephone Log, 11 July 1960, Folder CAH Telephone Calls, 7/1/60 to 8/31/60 (3), Box 13, Christian Herter Papers, DDEL.

53. Statement to U.N. Security Council, 18 July 1960, Herter press conference, 21 July 1960, both in *DOSB*, 8 August 1960, 199, 207–8; Karl E. Mundt, "How Cuban Freedom Really Was Won," *Reader's Digest*, August 1960, 168.

54. Statement by the President Concerning Premier Khrushchev's Announcement of Support for the Castro Regime in Cuba, 9 July 1960, *PPP*, 568; "Responsibility of Cuban Government for Increased International Tensions in the Hemisphere," *DOSB*, 29 August 1960, 318; for Khrushchev's comments, see *AFP* 1960, 207, 208, 210; for the U.S. response, see *AFP* 1960, 211.

55. Castro Radio Interview, 19 July 1960.

56. Gates to Secretary of State, 26 July 1960, Don Paarlberg to the Staff Secretary (Goodpaster), "Meeting with the President on Cuban Sugar, 11:00 A.M., Wednesday, July 6, 1960," both in *FRUS* 1958–60, 6:1034–35, 979–80. See also Gates to Herter, 16 July 1960, Folder "Cuba, May 1959–September 1960 (6)," Box 4, WHOF, Office of the Special Assistant for National Security Affairs: Records, 1952–61, NSC Series, Subject Subseries.

57. Joseph Blau to President, 10 July 1960, J. Lester Albertson to President, 9 July 1960, both in Folder "122 Cuba (6)," Box 805, WHCF, General File GF 122, DDEL.

58. James M. Lambie Jr., "Notes on Legislative Leadership Meeting August 16, 1960," Folder "Legislative Leaders 1960 (4)," Box 3, Legislative Meetings Minutes, AWF; Anderson: Memorandum of a Conference, "Questions Concerning the Program of Economic Pressures against Castro," 27 June 1960, *FRUS* 1958–60, 6:959; "Possible U.S. Economic Courses of Action Regarding Cuba," 26 July 1960, *FRUS* 1958–60, 6:1035–37, and State Department re-

sponse, 4 August 1960, 1049. In January, the president suggested to Herter, "We could quarantine Cuba. If they (the Cuban people) are hungry, they will throw Castro out" (Memcon, 25 January 1960, *FRUS* 1958–60, 6:764; see also 731, 741, 760).

59. Macmillan to Eisenhower, 22, 26 July 1960, *FRUS* 1958–60, 6:1005n, 1033; see also 2 July 1960, 1000n.

60. NSC meeting, 7 July 1960, *FRUS* 1958–60, 6:980–81, 985–86 (Dulles); see also Memorandum of Discussion, 8 July 1960, 993, and NSC Meeting, 15 July 1960, 1015; NSC Meeting, 7 July 1960, *FRUS* 1958–60, 6:985–86 (Anderson); 15 July 1960, *FRUS* 1958–60, 6:1018 (emissary report); see also Rubottom to Secretary of State, 25 July 1960, *FRUS* 1958–60, 6:1027; for one victory, see 1096. Anderson also favored cutting Cuba's two underwater communications cables, which would "eliminate all communications by Cuba with the outside world except by radio."

61. Rubottom to Secretary of State, 25 July 1960, *FRUS* 1958–60, 6:1027; Don Paarlberg to Staff Secretary (Goodpaster), "Meeting with the President on Cuban Sugar, 11:00 A.M., Wednesday, July 6, 1960," 7 July 1960, *FRUS* 1958–60, 6:979–80.

62. Memorandum of Conference with President, 15 February 1960, *FRUS* 1958–60, 6:788; Herter to President, "Possible Action to Prevent Castroist Takeover of Dominican Republic," 14 April 1960, Folder "Christian Herter April 1960 (1)," Box 12, Dulles-Herter Series, AWF; Memorandum of Conference with President, 16 May 1960, PC; "The Problem of Cuba in the OAS," 30 June 1960, *FRUS* 1958–60, 6:971–73.

63. DOS, "Responsibility of the Cuban Government for Increased International Tensions in the Hemisphere," *DOSB*, 29 August 1960, 317–46; Castro Speech, Pinar del Río, 21 August 1960.

64. Press Conference, 24 August 1960, *PPP*, 654–55; the updating on the Bay of Pigs preparations had occurred on 18 August (*FRUS* 1958–60, 6:1057–60).

65. Moon Sool Kwon, "The Organization of American States and the Cuban Challenge" (Ph.D. diss., Claremont Graduate School and University, 1970), 143–47; A. J. Thomas Jr. and Ann Van Wynen Thomas, "Democracy and the Organization of American States," *Minnesota Law Review* 46 (December 1961): 370–71; J. Fred Rippy and Alfred Tischendorf, "The San Jose Conference of American Foreign Ministers," *Inter-American Economic Affairs* 14 (Winter 1960): 59–72; Rabe, *Eisenhower and Latin America*, 159.

66. Herter, Memorandum of Telephone Conversation with Nelson Rockefeller, 3 August 1960, Folder "CAH Telephone Calls, 7/1/60 to 8/31/60 (3)," Box 13, Herter Papers; Herter's speech is reprinted in *DOSB*, 12 September 1960, 395–400.

67. Speech, Havana, 23 August 1960.

68. *Congressional Record*, 25 August 1960, 17657–58.

69. "Telephone Calls August 25, 1960," Folder "Christian Herter August 1960 (2)," Box 13, Dulles-Herter Series, AWF.

70. Eisenhower to Goodpaster, 28 August 1960, *FRUS* 1958–60, 6: 1062; the Declaration of San José is *AFP* 1960, 219–20; Bonsal, *Cuba, Castro, and the United States*, 162–63; DOS, "Progress Report on Cuba," 8 September 1960, Folder "Cuba, May 1959–September 1960 (6)," Box 4, WHOF, Office of the Special Assistant for National Security Affairs: Records, 1952–61, NSC Series, Subject Subseries.

71. Folder "Discussion of the 458th Meeting of the National Security Council, Wednesday, September 7, 1960," Box 13, NSC Series, AWF.

72. JFK Statement, 20 October 1960, in U.S. Congress, Senate, *Freedom of Communications*, pt. 1, 680; Marchant (Havana) to Foreign Office, "Extracts from Foreign Minister's T.V. Speech on the O.A.S. Meeting," 3 September 1960, Foreign Office 371/148196, PRO (Roa); Folder "Discussion of the 458th Meeting of the National Security Council, Wednesday, September 7, 1960," Box 13, NSC Series, AWF (Herter).

73. Memo of Meeting with President, 29 November 1960, *FRUS* 1958–60, 6:1131.

74. U.S. Congress, Senate, Committee on the Judiciary, Subcommittee to Investigate the Administration of the Internal Security Act and Other Internal Security Laws, *Communist Threat to the United States through the Caribbean*, pt. 9, 86th Cong., 2nd sess., August 1960, 697 (Smith), 671 (Gardner).

75. Diary, 15 September 1960, in Adolf A. Berle, *Navigating the Rapids, 1918–1971*, ed. Beatrice Bishop Berle and Travis Beal Jacobs (New York: Harcourt Brace Jovanovich, 1973), 716.

76. U.S. Congress, Senate, Committee on the Judiciary, Subcommittee to Investigate the Administration of the Internal Security Act and Other Internal Security Laws, *State Department Security: Testimony of William Wieland*, 87th Cong., 1st and 2nd sess., 1961–62, 656, 609; see also U.S. Congress, Senate, Committee on the Judiciary, Subcommittee to Investigate the Administration of the Internal Security Act and Other Internal Security Laws, *State Department Security: The William Wieland Case*, 87th Cong., 1st and 2nd sess., 1961–62, 31. For the homophobia gripping Washington at the time, see Truxton Decatur, "We Accuse . . . Sumner Welles," *Confidential*, November 1956, 12–15, 62–64; Eric Paul Roorda, "McCarthyite in Camelot: The 'Loss' of Cuba, Homophobia, and the Otto Otepka Scandal in the Kennedy State Department," *Diplomatic History* 31 (September 2007): 723–54.

77. Wieland to Rubottom, 19 February 1959, *FRUS* 1958–60, 6:406.

78. Ibid., 9 December 1959, 693.

79. Cuban Government Statement, reprinted in *DOSB*, 17 October 1960, 603–4.

80. *NYT*, 19 September 1960, 18, 18 September 1960, 16; for the comment about sleeping in the park, see *NYT*, 20 September 1960, 1. The arm-shoving apparently occurred when Castro's wave prompted several dozen greeters to attempt to scale a ten-foot wire fence for a closer look.

81. Republican Congressional Committee, "The Cuban Issue: A Chronology," 16 May (?) 1963, John Sherman Cooper Papers, University of Kentucky, Lexington; also in PC. In his memoir, CIA inspector general Lyman B. Kirkpatrick Jr. wrote of "the bearded Cubans in their rumpled uniforms carrying live chickens into their hotel lobby" (*The Real CIA* [New York: Macmillan, 1968], 181).

82. Embassy to DOS, 24 September 1960, 737.00(W)/9-2460, RG59; Ralph L. Crowder, "Fidel Castro and Harlem: Political, Diplomatic, and Social Influences of the 1960 Visit to the Hotel Theresa," *Afro-Americans in New York Life and History* 24 (January 2000): 79–92; Embassy to DOS, 3 October 1960, 737.00(W)/10-360, RG59 (aircraft seizures); *NYT*, 21 September 1960, 1 (Castro-Khrushchev photo).

83. CIA, "Briefing Papers Used by Mr. Dulles and Mr. Bissell—President-Elect Kennedy," 18 November 1960, *FRUS* 1961–63, vols. 10–12, microfiche supplement, document 232.

84. Castro's Speech, 26 September 1960, is U.N. Document A/PV.872, 117–36. The official translation of Castro's speech, 26 September 1960, is U.N. General Assembly, Fifteenth Ses-

sion, Official Records, 872nd Plenary Meeting, Document A/PV.872, 117–36. The speech is also available from LANIC.

85. Mann to Bonsal, 27 September 1960, Memorandum of Discussion at the Department of State—Joint Chiefs of Staff Meeting, 30 September 1960, both in *FRUS* 1958–60, 6:1073, 1079.

86. Response, 12 October 1960, in *AFP* 1960, 222–38; "Brief History of Radio Swan," Folder "Cuba, Subjects, Paramilitary Study Group, Taylor Report, Part III, Annex 2," Box 61A, NSFK. The Gibraltar Steamship Company owned no steamships. Its president was Thomas Dudley Cabot, the former director of the State Department's Office of International Security Affairs, and the CIA's David Atlee Phillips operated the Swan Island station. After a 1961 interagency task force determined that Radio Swan was "compromised," it was renamed Radio Americas and the Gibraltar Steamship Company "sold" the station to another CIA-owned company, the Vanguard Service Corporation (Howard H. Frederick, *Cuban-American Radio Wars: Ideology in International Communications* [Norwood, N.J.: Ablex, 1986], 5–7, 41; Lawrence C. Soley and John S. Nichols, *Clandestine Radio Broadcasting: A Study of Revolutionary and Counterrevolutionary Electronic Communication* [New York: Praeger, 1987]).

87. On the votes, see James Martin Keagle, "Toward an Understanding of U.S. Latin American Policy" (Ph.D. diss., Princeton University, 1982), 180; for Dulles's comment at the NSC Meeting, 29 September 1960, see *FRUS* 1958–60, 6:1074.

88. "Progress Report on Cuba," 4 August 1960, Folder "Cuba, May 1959–September 1960 (5)," Box 4, WHOF, Office of the Special Assistant for National Security Affairs: Records, 1952–61, NSC Series, Subject Subseries; *DOSB*, 17 October 1960, 604–5. For the details of the taxation issue, see "Staff Note," 18 November 1959, Folder "Staff Notes—Nov. 1959 (2)," Box 45, DDE Diary Series, AWF; Robert E. Marriam, "Memorandum for the Record," 28 April 1960, Folder "Staff Notes—April 1960 (1)," Box 49, DDE Diary Series, AWF.

89. Embassy to DOS, 21 October 1960, 737.00(W)/10-2160, RG59; Wadsworth Speech, 18 October 1960, U.N. Doc. A/4543; Michael W. Gordon, *The Cuban Nationalizations: The Demise of Property Rights in Cuba* (Buffalo: Hein, 1976); Peter J. Grilli, Howard B. Klein, and James M. Michener, "Legal Impediments to Normalization of Trade with Cuba," *Law and Policy in International Business* 8 (1976): 1037.

90. JFK Speech, Cincinnati, 6 October 1960, in U.S. Congress, Senate, *Freedom of Communications*, pt. 1, 510–11; Nixon Speech to Veterans of Foreign Wars, Detroit, 24 August 1960, and Press Conference, Springfield, Missouri, 21 September 1960, U.S. Congress, Senate, *Freedom of Communications*, pt. 2, *The Speeches, Remarks, Press Conferences, and Study Papers of Vice President Richard M. Nixon, August 1 through November 7, 1960*, 30, 219. In both cases, Nixon qualified his remarks, telling a reporter after his Veterans of Foreign Wars speech that an invasion "is simply out of the question."

91. U.S. Congress, Senate, *Final Report of the Committee on Commerce, United States Senate*, pt. 3, *The Joint Appearances of Senator John F. Kennedy and Vice President Richard M. Nixon and Other 1960 Campaign Presentations*, 87th Cong., 1st sess., 1961, 147–48.

92. Brooks Hamilton to James Hagerty, 30 June 1960, Folder "122 Cuba (5)," Box 805, WHCF, General File GF 122, DDEL; Thomas O. Wilson to President Eisenhower, 17 October 1960, Folder "122 Cuba (6)," Box 805, WHCF, General File GF 122, DDEL; Felix H. Savoie Jr. to President, 17 October 1960, Folder "122 Cuba (7)," Box 805, WHCF, General File GF 122, DDEL.

93. "Memorandum of Conference with the President, October 13, 1960," "Memorandum of Conference with the President, October 17, 1960," both in *FRUS* 1958–60, 6:1084–87, 1089.

94. U.S. Congress, Senate, *Freedom of Communications*, pt. 1, 1148, 1157, 1160, 1168; *Proceedings of the Forty-second National Convention of the American Legion*, Miami Beach, Florida, 18–20 October 1960, reprinted in U.S. Congressional Serial Set 12370; for Nixon's comments, see 29; for Resolution 361, see 80.

95. U.S. Congress, Senate, *Freedom of Communications*, pt. 1, 681. Nixon later complained (*The Memoirs of Richard Nixon* [New York: Grosset and Dunlap, 1978], 220–21) that JFK took unfair advantage by advocating what he knew from CIA briefings the Republicans were already planning but Nixon could not disclose. The extent of Kennedy's knowledge remains unclear. A senior CIA official subsequently wrote that "a search of CIA records has failed to confirm that Dulles briefed Kennedy on the status of Cuban covert action planning in either of their two sessions held before the election" (John L. Helgerson, *Getting to Know the President: CIA Briefings of Presidential Candidates, 1952–1992* [Washington, D.C.: Center for the Study of Intelligence, Central Intelligence Agency, n.d.], 54; McGeorge Bundy, "Nixon's Comments on Your Briefing on Cuba before the Election," 14 March 1962, Folder "Cuba General 1/62–8/62," Box 26, NSFK).

96. U.S. Congress, Senate, *Freedom of Communications*, pt. 2, 757, 715.

97. NSC Meeting, 20 October 1960, *FRUS* 1958–60, 6:1099.

98. Arthur Motley to President, 15 November 1960, Folder "OF 171 (3)," Box 858, WHCF, Official File 171 (3), DDEL; INR, "Cuban Economic Mission to the Sino-Soviet Bloc," Intelligence Report 8430, 23 March 1961 (Guevara trip); 29 November 1960, *FRUS* 1958–60, 6:1127 (Eisenhower comment); Herter to President, 16 October 1960, *FRUS* 1958–60, 6:1088; *NYT*, 4 January 1961, 3. Bonsal left Cuba on 28 October, a week before the U.S. election, never to return.

99. Embassy to DOS, 5 December 1960, Embassy to DOS, 6 December 1960 (proposed steps), NIE, 8 December 1960, Embassy to DOS, 16 December 1960, all in *FRUS* 1958–60, 6:1142, 1148, 1162–63, 1168, 1183–85. For the text of the quota cancellation, see *DOSB*, 2 January 1961, 18; 22 December 1960, *FRUS* 1958–60, 6:1185 ("hopeless" comment by chargé Daniel Braddock); "Memorandum of Conference with the President, 29 December 1960" (instructions), Stevenson to Coerr, 30 December 1960, both in *FRUS* 1958–60, 6:1188–89. Haiti, the Dominican Republic, Guatemala, and Nicaragua had already severed relations.

100. Speech, Havana, 2 January 1961; Bureau of Intelligence and Research Biographic Report, "Fidel Castro: The First Year," 17 March 1960, 4. At the time of the speech, there had been no Cuban ambassador in Washington for a year, and only thirteen of Cuba's twenty-eight consular offices in seventeen states remained open, but the total number of Cuban diplomats in the United States, including consuls, still numbered 101, and 10 of them were stationed in Havana's Washington embassy. In his speech, Castro claimed that 300 U.S. officials were in Cuba under diplomatic immunity, but the State Department's *Diplomatic List* for January 1961 put the number at 80, and when preparing for the departure of U.S. personnel the embassy requested a charter airplane for 50 passengers. For the embassy cables regarding Castro's speech, one of which recommended that the United States "break relations immediately," see Folder "Cuba (7) January 1961," Box 4, WHOF, Office of the Staff Secretary: Records, 1952–61, International Series. For memos regarding White House deliberations

over Castro's speech, see Folder "Cuba (1)," Box 8, International Series, AWF. On U.S. espionage in Cuba at the time, see J. Edgar Hoover to Herter, 16 June 1960, "Progress Report on Cuba," 17–20 June 1960, both in Folder "Cuba, May 1959–September 1960 (3)," Box 4, WHOF, Office of the Special Assistant for National Security Affairs: Records, 1952–61, NSC Series, Subject Subseries.

101. The notes terminating relations are reprinted in *DOSB*, 23 January 1961, 103–4; for the president's statement, 3 January 1961, see *PPP*, 388.

Chapter 6

1. Joseph Burkholder Smith, *Portrait of a Cold Warrior* (New York: Putnam's, 1976), 346. The CRC's six bulletins are reprinted in Jon Elliston, *Psywar on Cuba: The Declassified History of U.S. Anti-Castro Propaganda* (Melbourne, Australia: Ocean, 1999), 49–51; on Phillips, see Jacob D. Esterline Oral History, 10–11 November 1975, St. Croix, U.S. Virgin Islands, 95, NSA.

2. Bundy, "Memorandum for the President," 18 April 1961, Folder "Cuba General 4/1/61–4/21/61," Box 114A, POF.

3. "Admiral Burke's Conversation with CDR Wilhide," 18 April 1961, *FRUS* 1961–63, 10:274; "Recommendations for U.S. Action in Cuba," 26 February 1960, *FRUS* 1958–60, 6:814, 818.

4. James G. Blight and Peter Kornbluh, eds., *Politics of Illusion: The Bay of Pigs Invasion Reexamined* (Boulder, Colo.: Rienner, 1998), 105 n. 28. After all the dust settled, CIA historian Jack B. Pfeiffer also concluded that "there is reason to suggest that the Navy deliberately destroyed records which reflected on their poor performance" ("Bitter Recriminations: The Navy CAP [Combat Air Patrol] at the Bay of Pigs, 19 April 1961," 26 December 1984, DDRS).

5. *FRUS* 1961–63, 10:294n, 298, 362, 300.

6. Richard Nixon, "Cuba, Castro and John F. Kennedy," *Reader's Digest*, November 1964, 289; Richard Nixon, *The Memoirs of Richard Nixon* (New York: Grosset and Dunlap, 1978), 233; Dean Rusk as told to Richard Rusk, *As I Saw It* (New York: Norton, 1990), 216–17; Robert Kennedy, Memorandum, 1 June 1961, quoted in Arthur M. Schlesinger Jr., *Robert Kennedy and His Times* (Boston: Houghton Mifflin, 1978), 446. Schlesinger had privileged access to the Robert Kennedy Papers, and this memorandum is among many documents that are not yet available to general researchers at the Kennedy Library.

7. Arthur M. Schlesinger Jr., *Journals, 1952–2000*, ed. Andrew Schlesinger and Stephen Schlesinger (New York: Penguin, 2007); Castro Speech, San Julián, Pinar del Río, 21 August 1960; "Cuban Economic Mission to the Sino-Soviet Bloc," INR, Intelligence Report 8430, 23 March 1961, DDRS; *NYT*, 21 November 1960, 8, 28 November 1960, 63.

8. CIA, Board of National Estimates, "Memorandum for the Director," 21 February 1961, CIA, FOIA. For similar evaluations, see Dean Rusk's 1962 comment ("emotional, irresponsible") and a cable from the U.S. embassy in Moscow ("unstable"), *FRUS* 1961–63, 10:970, 974.

9. NSC Briefing, "Cuba," 15 March 1960, CIA, FOIA; Embassy Report of 22 January 1959 Press Conference, *FRUS* 1958–60, 6:383; U.S. Department of State, "Responsibility of Cuban Government for Increased International Tensions in the Hemisphere," *DOSB*, 29 August 1960, 341; Castro Speech, 21 August, 1960. Comments of this type by Cuban leaders regularly

circulated among U.S. officials. See, for example, the speech summaries in Folder "Cuba General 1/63," Box 37A, NSFK.

10. Eisenhower to Macmillan, 8 August 1960, *FRUS* 1958–60, 6:1050.

11. "Transfer: January 19, 1961, Meeting of the President and Senator Kennedy," 19 January 1961, Folder "Kennedy, John F. 1960–61 (2)," Box 2, Augusta–Walter Reed Series, Post-Presidential Papers, DDEL. These are the minutes taken by Eisenhower aide Wilton Peters. See also *FRUS* 1961–63, 10:44, and "Account of My December 6th, 1960 Meeting with President-Elect Kennedy," December 1960, Folder "ACW Diary—December 1960," Box 11, Ann Whitman Diary Series, AWF.

12. Joint Chiefs of Staff to McNamara, "U.S. Plan of Action in Cuba," *FRUS* 1961–63, 10:57–59.

13. McGeorge Bundy, "Memorandum of Discussion on Cuba," 28 January 1961, *FRUS* 1961–63, 10:61–62, 62n; NSAM 10, 6 February 1961, JFKL.

14. CIA WH/4, "Memorandum for the Record," 30 January 1961, *FRUS* 1961–63, vols. 10–12, microfiche supplement, document 241. The landing ship dock (LSD) was the *San Marcos*. It carried smaller landing craft to the general area; they were then unloaded and turned over to the Cuban rebels.

15. *Hispanic American Report* 13 (November 1960): 583; *The Nation*, 12 November 1960, 360; *NYT*, 10 January 1961, 1; additional photographic evidence was provided by *Time*, 27 January 1961, 26. For an account of how Hilton obtained this information, see his "Commentary," *World Affairs Report* 12 ([April?] 1982): n.p. See also Victor Bernstein and Jesse Gordon, "The Press and the Bay of Pigs," *Columbia University Forum* 10 (Fall 1967): 5–13; Joseph Burkholder Smith, *Portrait of a Cold Warrior* (New York: Putnam's, 1976), 345; Arthur M. Schlesinger Jr., *A Thousand Days: John F. Kennedy in the White House* (Boston: Houghton Mifflin, 1965), 261; Gilbert Harrison Oral History, 6 October 1967, 10–11, JFKL.

16. Joint Chiefs of Staff to Secretary of Defense McNamara, 10 March 1961, *FRUS* 1961–63, 10:131; *Hispanic American Report* 14 (May 1961): 214; *NYT*, 7 April 1961, 2; Schlesinger to President, "Howard Handleman on Cuba," 31 March 1961, Folder "Cuba General 1/61–3/61," Box 114A, POF.

17. CIA, Inspector General, "Inspector General's Survey of the Cuban Operation and Associated Documents," [15 February 1962], 86, NSA; Michael Warner, "Lessons Unlearned: The CIA's Internal Probe of the Bay of Pigs Affair," *Studies in Intelligence* (Winter 1998–99): 93–101; Memorandum for the Record, "First Meeting of Branch 4 Task Force, 9 March 1960," Folder "178-10002-10158," Ford Library Project File, "President Kennedy's Assassination: Photocopies of Collected Documents, 1959–1992," GRFL; "Memorandum for Record of the Taylor Committee . . . 24 April 1961," Folder "Cuba—Subjects Para-Military Study Group Taylor report Part II Meetings 1 and 2," Box 61A, NSFK; Foreign Office to British Ambassador in Washington, 23 November 1959, NSA. With some minor excisions, the twenty-six-page "Memorandum for the Record" is also in Luis Aguilar, ed., *Operation Zapata: The "Ultrasensitive" Report and Testimony of the Board of Inquiry on the Bay of Pigs* (Frederick, Md.: University Publications of America, 1981), 81–93. See also Grayston L. Lynch, *Decision for Disaster: Betrayal at the Bay of Pigs* (Washington, D.C.: Brassey's, 1998), 15, 44, which was written decades later, with some loss of accuracy. The Inspector General's report is reprinted in Peter Kornbluh, ed., *Bay of Pigs Declassified* (New York: New Press, 1998), 23–102.

18. Joints Chiefs of Staff to Secretary of Defense McNamara, 10 March 1961, Memcon, 29 March 1961, *FRUS* 1961–63, 10:131, 177.

19. "Informe sobre los campamentos y bases de mercenarios en Guatemala, Nicaragua y la Florida," 12 January 1961, NSA; see also Aleksandr Fursenko and Timothy Naftali, *One Hell of a Gamble: Khrushchev, Castro, and Kennedy, 1958–1964* (New York: Norton, 1997), 57, 90; *AFP* 1960, 254–56 (Wadsworth).

20. Entry for 29 November 1960 in the CIA's chronology of the Bay of Pigs operation, dated 23 April 1961, *FRUS* 1961–63, vols. 10–12, microfiche supplement, document 259; 5412 Committee Meeting, 8 December 1960, *FRUS* 1958–60, 6:1175.

21. Tracy Barnes quoting General David Gray, *FRUS* 1961–63, 10:43; CIA, "Increasing Opposition to Castro/Shortage of Consumer Goods/Lack of Currency," Report 00-A3177796, [late January] 1961, PC. As the source of its data on Castro's support, the CIA cited "a private survey made recently in Cuba" (Memcon, 13 January 1961, *FRUS* 1961–63, 10:28).

22. Esterline Oral History, 90.

23. Blight and Kornbluh, *Politics of Illusion*, 43; Schlesinger, *Thousand Days*, 241; Richard N. Goodwin, *Remembering America: A Voice from the Sixties* (Boston: Little, Brown, 1988), 174; Bundy, "Memorandum for the President," 25 February 1961, Folder "Bundy, McGeorge 2/61–4/61," Box 62, Staff Memoranda, POF.

24. Seymour M. Hersh, *The Dark Side of Camelot* (Boston: Little, Brown, 1997), 186; Robert Amory Jr. Oral History, 9 February 1966, 19–20, JFKL; Blight and Kornbluh, *Politics of Illusion*, 64–65.

25. "Charges of Intervention in Guatemala Denied," *DOSB*, 15 February 1954, 251–52. On the influence of the Guatemala case on the thinking about Cuba, see Alex Roberto Hybel, *How Leaders Reason: U.S. Intervention in the Caribbean Basin and Latin America* (London: Blackwell, 1990), 70–106; Lucien S. Vandenbroucke, "The 'Confessions' of Allen Dulles: New Evidence on the Bay of Pigs," *Diplomatic History* 8 (Fall 1984): 372; Lawrence Freedman, *Kennedy's Wars: Berlin, Cuba, Laos, and Vietnam* (New York: Oxford University Press, 2000), 125.

26. "Briefing of Secretary of State Designate Rusk," January 1961, 13–14, *FRUS* 1961–63, vols. 10–12, microfiche supplement, document 236. For a similar briefing of president-elect Kennedy, see "Briefing Papers Used by Mr. Dulles and Mr. Bissell—President-Elect Kennedy," 18 November 1960, *FRUS* 1961–63, vols. 10–12, microfiche supplement, document 232.

27. Howard Hunt, *Give Us This Day* (New Rochelle, N.Y.: Arlington House, 1973), 81; E. Howard Hunt with Greg Aunapu, *American Spy: My Secret History in the CIA, Watergate, and Beyond* (New York: Wiley, 2007), 118. Formed by the CIA in the spring of 1960, the FRD was different from the Cuban Revolutionary Front (Frente Revolucionario Cubano), which was also formed by the CIA, but on 22 March 1961. See Joseph Burkholder Smith, *Portrait*, 344–45; CIA, Inspector General, "Inspector General's Survey of the Cuban Operation and Associated Documents," [15 February 1962], NSA, 85–92. For first-person evaluations of working with the exile leaders, see *FRUS* 1961–63, 10:32 (Willauer), 202 (Schlesinger), 95–107, 358. In their rebuttal, Bissell and Tracy Barnes wrote that this criticism "has little if any basis in fact." See Kornbluh, *Bay of Pigs Declassified*, 215.

28. Inspector General, "Inspector General's Survey of the Cuban Operation and Associated Documents," [15 February 1962], NSA, 143; CIA, "Cuba," 17 February 1961, *FRUS* 1961–63, 10:104, where a handwritten note on the cover sheet indicates "Bissell's View."

29. CIA Information Reports, "Indications in Camaguey of Increasing Dissatisfaction

with Castro Government," 10 March 1961, "Diminishing Popular Support of the Castro Government," 16 March 1961, "Signs of Discontent among the Cuban Populace," 6 April 1961, all in NSA.

30. JCS to McNamara, 3 February 1961, *FRUS* 1961–63, 10:69. At this point, the invasion plan was for a landing at Trinidad, near the Escambray Mountains (*FRUS* 1961–63, 10:83, 128).

31. CIA, "Revised Cuban Operation," 15 March 1961, *FRUS* 1961–63, 10:148; Blight and Kornbluh, *Politics of Illusion*, 64, 43–44.

32. See Richard E. Welch Jr., *Response to Revolution: The United States and the Cuban Revolution, 1959–1961* (Chapel Hill: University of North Carolina Press, 1985), 85.

33. Schlesinger to President, "Cuba," 5 April 1961, Folder "Cuba Security, 1961," Box 115, POF; Goodwin, *Remembering America*, 174.

34. Mann to Rusk, 15 February 1961, *FRUS* 1961–63, 10:97.

35. Fulbright had no brief for Castro, referring to the Cuban leader as "an unshaven megalomaniac" in a memo, "Cuba Policy," 29 March 1961, Folder 1, Box 38, Fulbright Papers, Special Collections Division, University of Arkansas Libraries, Fayetteville. Fulbright handed this memo, written by his senior staff Latin Americanist, Pat Holt, to JFK during a flight to Florida on 30 March (Pat Holt Interview by Author, Bethesda, Maryland, 1 May 1978). See also Karl E. Mayer ed., *Fulbright of Arkansas: The Public Positions of a Private Thinker* (Washington, D.C.: Luce, 1963), 200–205. Bowles to Rusk, 31 March 1961, *FRUS* 1961–63, 10:178; see also Chester Bowles, *Promises to Keep: My Years in Public Life, 1941–1969* (New York: Harper and Row, 1971), 327–28, 444.

36. Memcon, 22 January 1961, *FRUS* 1961–63, 10:50 (Rusk); Mann to Secretary, "The March 1960 Plan," 15 February 1961, Folder "Cuba, General, 1/61–4/61," Box 35A, NSFK; Bundy, "Memorandum for the President," 8 February 1961, Folder "Cuba Security, 1961," Box 115, POF; Galbraith to Kennedy, 3 April 1961, Folder "Galbraith, John Kenneth 3/61–10/61," Box 28A, Special Correspondence, POF.

37. "Transfer: January 19, 1961, Meeting of the President and Senator Kennedy," 19 January 1961, Folder "Kennedy, John F. 1960–61 (2)," Box 2, Augusta-Walter Reed Series, Post-Presidential Papers, DDEL; Miguel Ydígoras Fuentes to President Kennedy, 28 February 1961, enclosed with Memcon, "Letter from President Ydigoras of Guatemala," 7 March 1961, Folder "Guatemala General 2/61–3/62 and undated," Box 101, NSFK; CIA, Office of National Estimates, "Memorandum for the United States Intelligence Board: Subject: Probable International Reactions to Certain Possible US Courses of Action against the Castro Regime," 11 February 1961, *FRUS* 1961–63, vols. 10–12, microfiche supplement, document 242 (emphasis added); Arthur Schlesinger Jr., "Memo to the President: Latin American Trip, 12 February–3 March [1961]," 10 March 1961, Box WH40, White House Files, Classified Subject Files, Latin America, General, 1960–61, Arthur M. Schlesinger Jr. Papers, JFKL.

38. Barnes to Bissell, 1 March 1961, *FRUS* 1961–63, vols. 10–12, microfiche supplement, document 244.

39. Minutes of Meeting with President, 11 March 1961, *FRUS* 1961–63, 10:143; Bundy to JFK, 15 March 1961, *FRUS* 1961–63, 10:158. Colonel Jack Hawkins was chief of WH/4's Paramilitary Staff Section; see also Bundy, "Memorandum of Meeting with the President on Cuba—February 8, 1961," 9 February 1961, Folder "Cuba Security, 1961," Box 115, POF.

40. Memcon, 22 January 1961, *FRUS* 1961–63, 10:50; Dean Rusk Oral History, pt. 3, 19

February 1970, 90–91, JFKL; General David Gray, "Memorandum for the Record: Summary of White House Meetings," 9 May 1961, Folder "Cuba, Subjects, Paramilitary Study Group, Taylor Report, Part III, Annex 16," Box 61A, NSFK; Schlesinger, *Journals*, 118–19. Berle's comment is not in the 4 April meeting record prepared significantly after the fact, on 9 May (see *FRUS* 1961–63, 10:185); the comment first appears in Charles J. V. Murphy, "Cuba: The Record Set Straight," *Fortune*, September 1961, 224. For Berle's strong and early support of the Bay of Pigs invasion, see *FRUS* 1961–63, 10:84. It is not clear whether Bowles attended the meeting.

41. Schlesinger, 31 May 1996, in Blight and Kornbluh, *Politics of Illusion*, 80; Schlesinger, *Thousand Days*, 243; Schlesinger, *Journals*, 109. When Walter Lippmann wrote that Schlesinger had been a proponent of the invasion, McGeorge Bundy asked the columnist to issue a correction: "Schlesinger persistently opposed the operation," Bundy said, "and assisted in staff work related to it only after making the argument against it as strongly as he knew how" (Bundy to Lippmann, 2 May 1961, PC). For the paper trail on Schlesinger's opposition, see Welch, *Response to Revolution*, 203 n. 22.

42. The commission's report consists of four memoranda: (1) "Narrative of the Anti-Castro Cuban Operation Zapata," (2) "Immediate Causes of Failure of Operation Zapata—Summary," (3) "Conclusions of the Cuban Study Group," and (4) "Recommendations of the Cuban Study Group." Taken together, these four memoranda are labeled "Part I" in the Kennedy Library, Box 61A, NSFK. Box 61A also contains the verbatim transcripts of the Taylor Commission private hearings, which are referred to as "Part II." (Boxes 62, 63 and 64 contain additional testimony and documents.) A lightly sanitized version of both parts is available from DDRS and as a useful book, Luis Aguilar, ed., *Operation Zapata: The "Ultrasensitive" Report and Testimony of the Board of Inquiry on the Bay of Pigs* (Frederick, Md.: University Publications of America, 1981).

43. *"An Analysis of the Cuban Operation* by the Deputy Director (Plans) Central Intelligence Agency," 18 January 1962, NSA, reprinted in Kornbluh, *Bay of Pigs Declassified*, 133–234. Cabell's letter is included at the end of this document.

44. Hunt, *Give Us This Day*, 213–14; for Grayston Lynch's similar attack, see Lynch, *Decision for Disaster*, 153–68. Two additional reports are exceptionally useful: the report of a major participant, marine colonel Jack Hawkins ("Record of Paramilitary Action against the Castro Government of Cuba, 17 March 1960–May 1961," 5 May 1961, CIA FOIA), and the place to begin, CIA historian Jack Pfeiffer's "The Bay of Pigs Operation, Volume III, Evolution of CIA's Anti-Castro Policies, 1950–January 1961," [late 1970s], in Box 1, "CIA Miscellaneous," JFK Assassination Records Collection, National Archives and Records Administration, Washington, D.C. This mysterious 295-page document was discovered by Professor David M. Barrett of Villanova University, whose generosity is deeply appreciated. The official Cuban government analysis of the Bay of Pigs is *Playa Girón: derrota del imperialismo* (Havana: Ediciones R., 1962), in four volumes: vol. 1, *La invasión y los héroes*, vol. 2, *Reacción internacional*, vol. 3, *La batalla de la ONU*, and vol. 4, *Los mercenarios*. All of these documents are easier to understand after reading the valuable introduction by Kornbluh, *Bay of Pigs Declassified*, which reproduces Kirkpatrick's report and the Barnes rebuttal; see also Blight and Kornbluh, *Politics of Illusion*.

45. CIA to General Taylor, 26 April 1961, *FRUS* 1961–63, 10:221. Secretary McNamara later remarked (*FRUS* 1961–63, 10:441) that Hawkins's "presentations were so onesided that

he made little influence on my judgment," but Bissell (Richard M. Bissell Jr. Oral History, 17 October 1975, NSA, 32) subsequently attributed his positive evaluation of the brigade's chances to Hawkins's briefings.

46. "Mr. Robertson's Report of Activities on Barbara J," 4 May 1961; Grayston Lynch, "After Action Report on Operation," 4 May 1961, *FRUS* 1961–63, 10:253–54, 249; Lynch, *Decision for Disaster*, 92. There are two conflicting reports on the number killed and the number taken prisoner and murdered. Cf. *FRUS* 1961–63, 10:249 and 253–54; on Captain Clark, see 263. The Fifth Battalion commander was Ricardo Montero Duque, a former officer in Batista's army.

47. "Memorandum for Record of the Taylor Committee at the Conference Room (Room 214) Director of Central Intelligence Agency at 1350 Hours 24 April 1961," Folder "Cuba, Subjects Para-Military Study Group Taylor Report Part II," Box 61A, NSFK (this verbatim transcript varies somewhat from the published minutes [*FRUS* 1961–63, 10:356]); for Hawkins's early evaluation, sec *FRUS* 1961–63, 10:22; Colonel Stanley Beerli, "Memorandum for the Record: Second Meeting of the Green Study Group," 24 April 1961, *FRUS* 1961–63, 10:356. A contract pilot who helped train the Cuban pilots complained that his students were always "talking excitedly, gesturing wildly, and contributing greatly to the atmosphere of tension and intrigue" (Albert C. Persons, *Bay of Pigs: A Firsthand Account of the Mission by a U.S. Pilot in Support of the Cuban Invasion Force in 1961* [Jefferson, N.C.: McFarland, 1990], 23, 56).

48. CIA, "Narrative of Air Activity," 26 April 1961, *FRUS* 1961–63, 10:387–89; for a quite different first-person account by a Cuban exile pilot, see Eduardo Ferrer, *Operación Puma* (Miami: International Aviation Consultants, 1975).

49. Inspector General, "Inspector General's Survey of the Cuban Operation and Associated Documents," [15 February 1962], NSA, 34–35, 40, 45–46.

50. Ibid., 41–44, 95–97.

51. *FRUS* 1961–63, 10:143, 144; Esterline Oral History, 51; see also Richard M. Bissell Jr., "Reflections of the Bay of Pigs," *Strategic Review* 12 (Winter 1984): 69–70; Lynch, *Decision for Disaster*, 31.

52. "Conclusions of the Cuban Study Group," Box 61A, NSFK; Allen Dulles, "My Answer to the Bay of Pigs," n.d., Allen Dulles Papers, Princeton University. See introduction, n. 16, for an explanation of this undated handwritten manuscript.

53. CIA, "Briefing of Secretary of State Designate Rusk," January 1961, entry for 14 April 1961 from untitled CIA chronology, 23 April 1961, both in *FRUS* 1961–63, vols. 10–12, microfiche supplement, documents 236, 259.

54. Robert Amory Jr. Interview by CIA historian Jack Pfeiffer, JFKL, 127–28; Robert Lee Dennison, *The Reminiscences of Admiral Robert Lee Dennison, U.S. Navy (Retired)* (Annapolis: U.S. Naval Institute, 1975), 336; Malcolm Moos, "Interview with President Dwight D. Eisenhower, Gettysburg, Pa., Nov. 8, 1966," Folder "Kennedy, John F. 1962–67 (1)," Box 2, Augusta-Walter Reed Series, Post-Presidential Papers, DDEL; Schlesinger to JFK, 10 April 1961, *FRUS* 1961–63, 10:199. See also Richard Helms, *A Look over My Shoulder: A Life in the Central Intelligence Agency* (New York: Random House, 2003), 176.

55. Nixon, *Memoirs*, 233; "Special Group Meeting—Cuba," 29 December 1960, *FRUS* 1961–63, vols. 10–12, microfiche supplement, document 234.

56. "Briefing of Secretary of State Designate Rusk," January 1961, *FRUS* 1961–63, vols. 10–12, microfiche supplement, document 236; Blight and Kornbluh, *Politics of Illusion*, 67–68.

57. CIA, "Briefing of Secretary of State Designate Rusk," January 1961, *FRUS* 1961–63,

vols. 10–12, microfiche supplement, document 236; "Memorandum for Record of the Taylor Committee at the Conference Room (Room 214) Director of Central Intelligence Agency at 1350 Hours 24 April 1961," Folder "Cuba, Subjects Para-Military Study Group Taylor Report Part II," Box 61A, NSFK. Puerto Cabezas was selected because it is 250 miles closer than Guatemala.

58. Esterline Oral History, 82; Allen Dulles, "My Answer," 28–31. In a handwritten draft of this typewritten manuscript, Dulles wrote, "There came a time when in order for the Brigade to act, you had to have a show of USA power. It might have been a relative [sic] limited one— air cover to compensate for the loss of air strikes. You had to pay some price for victory—but wasn't that better than defeat?"

59. Hunt, *Give Us This Day*, 165; Barnes quoted in Warner, "Lessons Unlearned," 97; Lynch quoted in the still-valuable volume by Peter Wyden, *Bay of Pigs: The Untold Story* (New York: Simon and Schuster, 1979), 302.

60. Esterline Oral History, 76; "Seventeenth Meeting of the Para-Military Study Group," 18 May 1961, Box 61A, NSFK (Lemnitzer).

61. Jack B. Pfeiffer, "Bitter Recriminations: The Navy CAP [Combat Air Patrol] at the Bay of Pigs, 19 April 1961," 26 December 1984, DDRS. See also Admiral Dennison's memoir, *Reminiscences*, 356–57; Esterline Oral History, 52; Blight and Kornbluh, *Politics of Illusion*, 169.

62. *FRUS* 1961–63, 25 April 1961, vol. 10, esp. 363; see also 24 April 1961, 10:334–56; Esterline Oral History, 52; the three officers' report, 10 March 1961, *FRUS* 1961–63, 10:120–34 (quotation 125) and 343 (inspection).

63. Wayne Smith, a career foreign service officer who was working on the State Department's Cuba desk at the time, agreed that "Bissell went ahead with the plan, cancellation of the air strike and all, because he thought that if he could just put the guys ashore, no matter what else happened, the president will not let it fail—he will order in U.S. forces." Blight and Kornbluh, *Politics of Illusion*, 69 (Schlesinger), 101 (Wayne Smith); see also Thomas Powers, *The Man Who Kept the Secrets: Richard Helms and the CIA* (New York: Knopf, 1979), 116–17.

64. Schlesinger to President, "Howard Handleman in Cuba," 31 March 1961, Folder "Cuba General 1/61–3/61," Box 114A, POF; Schlesinger to President, "Cuba," 5 April 1961, Folder "Cuba Security, 1961," Box 115, POF.

65. Bissell Oral History, 32–33; for Bissell's denial, see "Response to Lucien S. Vandenbroucke, 'The "Confessions" of Allen Dulles: New Evidence on the Bay of Pigs,'" *Diplomatic History* 8 (Fall 1984): 377–80, published before the comments by Schlesinger and Smith but, as the title suggests, in direct response to the same charge by Vandenbroucke, "'Confessions'"; Goodwin, *Remembering America*, 175.

66. Dulles indicates that he was writing to correct the errors of fact and especially interpretation in the recently published memoirs by Schlesinger and Theodore Sorensen: "Never had a man's friends done their hero a greater disservice than have Schlesinger and Sorensen in their apologia for the B of P."

67. Blight and Kornbluh, *Politics of Illusion*, 89–91. For a contrary view, see Lyman B. Kirkpatrick Jr., *The Real CIA* (New York: Macmillan, 1968), 196.

68. CIA Information Report, "Diminishing Popular Support of the Castro Government," 16 March 1961, NSA; "Progress Report on Cuba," 11 August 1960, 24 August 1960, Folder "Cuba (May 1959–September 1960)(6)," Box 4, White House Office Files, Office of the Special Assistant for National Security Affairs: Records, 1952–61, NSC Series, Subject Subseries,

DDEL; Barnes to Bissell, "Material for Policy Meeting on Cuba, 3 January 1961," 2 January 1961, *FRUS* 1961–63, vols. 10–12, microfiche supplement, document 237; Hunt, *Give Us This Day*, 77. Today's CIA asserts that all of this and the assessments cited in nn. 21 and 29 came from the agency's operations officers, not from the agency's intelligence arm. CIA historian Nicholas Dujmovic notes that "the analysts were completely cut out of deliberations before the Bay of Pigs, and they could have told the operators that there was no potential for an anti-Castro uprising" ("Elegy of Slashes," *Studies in Intelligence* 51 [September 2007]: 38); Nicholas Dujmovic, Telephone Interview by author, 4 December 2007).

69. Brazilian Embassy in Havana to Brazilian Secretary of State, 9 May 1961, Canadian Embassy in Havana to Undersecretary of State for External Affairs, Ottawa, 27 April 1961, both NSA.

70. *FRUS* 1961–63, 10:500–501 (Shoup), 43 (Gray), 451 (Rusk), 456–57 (Bundy). For Bissell's view, see Freedman, *Kennedy's Wars*, 379.

71. Kirkpatrick, *Real CIA*, 184–85, 202.

72. Speech, Havana, 17 May 1961.

73. Schlesinger to Kennedy, 10 April 1961, *FRUS* 1961–63, 10:200.

74. *Birmingham News*, 23 April 1961, 1. On 18 April, two of the six B-26 flights were flown by the Alabamans; on 19 April, two of the three B-26 flights were flown by the Alabamans, and both were shot down. See Inspector General, "Inspector General's Survey of the Cuban Operation and Associated Documents," [15 February 1962], NSA, 32; Lynch, *Decision for Disaster*, 59. For coverage of the Alabamans' participation, see Wyden, *Bay of Pigs*, esp. 156; Warren Trest and Don Dodd, *Wings of Denial: The Alabama Air National Guard's Covert Role at the Bay of Pigs* (Montgomery: NewSouth, 2001).

75. Schlesinger, *Journals*, 110–11.

76. Wyden, *Bay of Pigs*, 174–76.

77. U.N. General Assembly, Fifteenth Session, First Committee, 1149th Meeting, 15 April 1961, U.N. document A/C.1/SR.1150.

78. Stevenson to Rusk, 16 April 1961, *FRUS* 1961–63, 10:230; Memorandum of Telephone Conversation, Bundy and Rusk, 17 April 1961, *FRUS* 1961–63, 10:259–60. Secretary Rusk also recalled, "I was taken by surprise when I learned that these were not genuine defections but were feigned" (Rusk Oral History, 95).

79. Stevenson to Rusk, 19 April 1961, *FRUS* 1961–63, 10:297. "We must have legal position at least as firm as USSR has in Laos," Stevenson continued.

80. Goodwin, "Memorandum for the President: Subject: Conversation with Comman-dante Ernesto Guevara of Cuba," 22 August 1961, *FRUS* 1961–63, 10:642–45; Speech to American Society of Newspaper Editors, 20 April 1961, *PPP*, 304; "Record of Actions by the National Security Council . . . April 22, 1961," 24 April 1961, Folder "National Security Council Meetings 1961 478—4/22/61," Box 313, NSFK.

81. Speech, Havana, 17 May 1961, in *Revolución*, 18 May 1961, 5.

82. For the Cuban position, see Ministerio de Relaciones Exteriores, *Cuba demandó indemnización; el imperialismo dijo ino!* (Havana: Ministerio de Relaciones Exteriores, 1961). For the Tractors for Freedom Committee, see Welch, *Response to Revolution*, 90–91; Haynes Johnson, *The Bay of Pigs: The Leaders' Story of Brigade 2506* (New York: Norton, 1964), 231–46.

83. Nine prisoners accused of crimes during the Batista era were not released, and the

last of the nine remained in jail until 1986. Many individuals helped secure the prisoners' release, and State's Cuba desk officer, Robert Hurwitch, received the State Department's Distinguished Service Award for his part in the effort. Robert A. Hurwitch, *Most of Myself: An Autobiography in the Form of Letters to His Daughters* (Santo Domingo, D.R.: Editora Corripio, 1990), chap. 8, is largely about the effort. For the treatment of the prisoners, see Lawrence R. Houston, CIA, to Theodore C. Sorensen, "Conditions and Life for the Brigade Prisoners in Cuban Prisons," 9 October 1962, NSA.

84. Schlesinger to President, 11 February 1961, *FRUS* 1961–63, 10:92–93; Castro Speech, Havana, 1 May 1961.

Chapter 7

1. Notes on Cabinet Meeting, 20 April 1961, *FRUS* 1961–63, 10:305. Bowles's alleged softness toward the Cuban revolution dated from early 1959, when he published a letter urging patience with Cuba's revolutionaries (*NYT*, 25 January 1959, E10).

2. Memorandum for the Record, "Meeting with General Eisenhower at Gettysburg, June 23, 1961," *FRUS* 1961–63, 10:614n; Richard Nixon, *The Memoirs of Richard Nixon* (New York: Grosset and Dunlap, 1978), 234; *Congressional Record*, 20 July 1961, 13062 (Smathers); Memorandum for the Record, "Meeting with the President and the Taylor Group at 1700, 13 June 1961," *FRUS* 1961–63, 10:574 (Somoza); Chester Bowles Oral History Fragments, Folder "Cuba: Bay of Pigs," Box W-57, Arthur M. Schlesinger Jr. Papers, JFKL; Rostow to McNamara, "Notes on Cuba Policy," 24 April 1961, Folder "Cuba Security 1961," Box 115, POF.

3. McNamara to Lemnitzer, 20 April 1961, *FRUS* 1961–63, 10:306–7; Interagency Task Force on Cuba, "Cuba and Communism in the Hemisphere," 4 May 1961, *FRUS* 1961–63, 10:466.

4. Mansfield to President, "The Cuban Aftermath," 1 May 1961, "Background Memo on Senator Pell's Thoughts Regarding Cuba," 13 May 1961, both in Folder "Cuba General 5/1/61–5/15/61," Box 114A, POF; Adlai Stevenson, *The Papers of Adlai Stevenson*, ed. Walter Johnson (Boston: Little, Brown, 1979), 8:81; Schlesinger to President, 3 May 1961, *FRUS* 1961–63, 10:424–25.

5. Bowles Diary, 27 January 1962, Folder 155, Box 392, Chester Bowles Papers, Yale University; Norman Mailer, "An Open Letter to John Fitzgerald Kennedy and Fidel Castro," in Norman Mailer, *The Presidential Papers* (New York: Putnam's, 1963), 64–66; Matthews Notes on Lunch with Arthur Schlesinger, 30 June 1961, Box 27, Herbert Matthews Papers, Columbia University.

6. INR and Office of National Estimates, "Facts, Estimates, and Projections," 2 May 1961, Interagency Task Force, "Cuba and Communism in the Hemisphere," 4 May 1961, NSC Meeting, 5 May 1961, all in *FRUS* 1961–63, 10:422, 463, 480.

7. INR and Office of National Estimates, "Facts, Estimates, and Projections," 2 May 1961, *FRUS* 1961–63, 10:418.

8. Speech, Colón Cemetery, 16 April 1959, *Revolución*, 17 April 1961, 6–7, 12–13; Radio Address, 23 April 1961; Speech, Havana, 1–2 May 1961; Speech, Havana, 26 July 1961, in *Revolución*, 28 July 1961, 1; Canadian Chargé d'Affaires to the Secretary of State for External Affairs, 15 June 1961, NSA. In Castro's words, "We are here right under their nose and we have made a socialist revolution."

9. Barry Goldwater, "Tragic Situation in Cuba: Evil Is Caused by Good Men Who Do Noth-

ing," 17 April 1961, reprinted in *Vital Speeches* 27 (1 May 1961): 419–23; James G. Blight and Peter Kornbluh, eds., *Politics of Illusion: The Bay of Pigs Reexamined* (Boulder: Rienner, 1998), 125 (Schlesinger [1996]); for additional Republican criticism, see *Congressional Record*, 29 March 1961, 5191–92.

10. For excellent coverage of this policy, see Richard E. Welch Jr., *Response to Revolution: The United States and the Cuban Revolution, 1959–1961* (Chapel Hill: University of North Carolina Press, 1985), esp. 99.

11. Circular Telegram, 23 April 1961, *FRUS* 1961–63, 10:325–26.

12. Embassy, Bogotá, to DOS, 6 May 1961, *FRUS* 1961–63, 12:251–52; Goodwin, "Memorandum for the President," 22 August 1961, Folder "Cuba Security, 1961," Box 115, POF; Memcon, "Situation in Brazil and Brazilian Attitude toward Cuban Problem," 25 September 1961, Morrison to Woodward, 15 November 1961, both in *FRUS* 1961–63, 12:260, 265.

13. Castro Speech, Havana, 2 December 1961; Memcon, "Conference between President Kennedy and Venezuelan President Betancourt," 16 December 1961, *FRUS* 1961–63, 12:273; DOS to Embassy, Argentina, 26 December 1961, Goodwin to Woodward, 4 January 1962, Memcon, "Redrafts of Argentine Resolutions for 8th MFM," 18 January 1962, all in *FRUS* 1961–63, 12:278, 282–83, 293. For Schlesinger's evaluation of Frondizi, see "Memo to the President: Latin American Trip, 12 February–3 March," 10 March 1961, Folder "Latin America, Latin American Report, 3/10/61," Box WH-40, Schlesinger Papers.

14. Rusk (Punta del Este) to DOS, 23 January 1962, *FRUS* 1961–63, 12:297.

15. Lansdale, "The Cuba Project," 18 January 1962, *FRUS* 1961–63, 10:713.

16. Rusk to DOS, 30 January 1962, *FRUS* 1961–63, 12:304.

17. Commenting on his own press coverage, Morrison wrote that the Uruguayan newspaper *El Dia* carried a story that he "turned turned in his expense account for the day: Breakfast, $1.50; Taxi in the morning, $2; Lunch, $2.50; Afternoon taxis, $3; Dinner with the foreign minister of Haiti, $5,000,000." The story in *El Dia* cannot be found (a brief allusion to bribery appears in the 29 January edition, 9), but the Haitian delegate was clearly sensitive to the rumors, and he did not want to leave town without responding to reports that he had accepted a bribe. He inserted his explanation in the conference record: the difference in philosophy between communism and democracy "is the sole reason for the change in the position and attitude of my country." U.S. Congress, Senate Committee on Foreign Relations and House Committee on Foreign Affairs, *Inter-American Relations: A Collection of Documents . . .* , Joint Committee Print 100-168, 100th Cong., 2nd sess., December 1988, 282; Delesseps S. Morrison, *Latin American Mission: An Adventure in Hemisphere Diplomacy* (New York: Simon and Schuster, 1965), 192; Arthur M. Schlesinger Jr., *A Thousand Days: John F. Kennedy in the White House* (Boston: Houghton Mifflin, 1965), 783.

18. Rusk (Punta del Este) to DOS, 31 January 1962, *FRUS* 1961–63, 12:307; Rusk, "Post Mortem on Punta del Este," 6 April 1962, in *The Cuban Missile Crisis, 1962: A National Security Archive Document Set*, ed. Laurence Chang (Alexandria, Va.: Chadwyck-Healey, 1990), document 198; Transcript of Meeting between Fidel Castro and East German Premier Erich Honecker, Havana, 25 May 1980, *Cold War International History Project Bulletin* 8–9 (Winter 1996): 203. Castro added that "Mexico only entertained formal relations with us, but no relations of a friendly nature."

19. CIA, "Program of Covert Action Aimed at Weakening the Castro Regime," 19 May 1961, *FRUS* 1961–63, 10:556, 559–60.

20. Handwritten Notes, 7 November 1961, quoted in *FRUS* 1961–63, 10:666 (not yet available to researchers at the Kennedy Library); Goodwin to President, 22 August 1961, Folder "Cuba Security, 1961," Box 115, POF; Memcon, President Kennedy and Ex-President Kubitschek, 15 September 1961, in *FRUS* 1961–63, 10:655.

21. JFK Speech, University of Washington, 16 November 1961, *PPP*, 725. For JFK's authorization, see *FRUS* 1961–63, 10:666, which summarizes the 3 November discussion and JFK's decision, but the official minutes of the meeting, if they were taken, are lost. For JFK's summary, see his "Memorandum to the Secretary of State, . . . ," 30 November 1961, in *FRUS* 1961–63, 10:688–89.

22. Roswell Gilpatric Oral History, 5 May 1970, 8–9, JFKL; Parrott quoted in Don Bohning, *The Castro Obsession: U.S. Covert Operations against Cuba, 1959–1965* (Washington, D.C.: Potomac, 2005), 85; Richard Helms Oral History, 16 September 1981, LBJL; Chester Bowles Oral History, 1 July 1970, JFKL; Chester Bowles Oral History Fragments, Folder "Cuba: Bay of Pigs," Box W-57, Schlesinger Papers. On JFK's early respect for Lansdale, see NSAM 9, 6 February 1961.

23. Helms to McCone, 19 January 1962, McCone, "Memorandum for the Record," 22 November 1961, both in *FRUS* 1961–63, 10:720, 685. The Caribbean Survey Group consisted of representatives from the Departments of Defense and State, the USIA, and the CIA. The Special Group, an Eisenhower holdover, was a renamed 5412 Committee, which until the Missile Crisis met every Thursday afternoon to oversee covert action.

24. John Crimmins Oral History, 10 May 1989, U.S. Foreign Affairs Oral History Collection, Association for Diplomatic Studies and Training, Arlington, Virginia; Parrott quoted in Seymour M. Hersh, *The Dark Side of Camelot* (Boston: Little, Brown, 1997), 278; Halpern in Blight and Kornbluh, *Politics of Illusion*, 117; Bowles Oral Histories, 1 July 1970, 2 February 1965, JFKL; Joseph A. Califano Jr., *Inside: A Public and Private Life* (New York: Public Affairs, 2004), 121; Benjamin C. Bradlee, *Conversations with Kennedy* (New York: Norton, 1975), 143.

25. Lansdale to Members of the Caribbean Survey Group, 20 January 1962, "Memorandum from the Chief of Operations, Subject: Cuba," 7 December 1961, Memcon, Special Group Meeting, 8 December 1961, all in *FRUS* 1961–63, 10:691–95, 721.

26. McCone, Memo, 27 December 1961, "The Cuba Project," 18 January 1962, both in *FRUS* 1961–63, 10:701, 710–18; "Guidelines for Operation Mongoose," 14 March 1962, NSA.

27. CIA to Special Group, "Cuba," 24 January 1962, *FRUS* 1961–63, 10:727; Lansdale, "The Cuba Project," 18 January, 20 February 1962, both in *FRUS* 1961–63, 10:710–18, 745–47.

28. J. E. Earman, "Memorandum for the Record," 12 January 1962, McCone, "Memorandum for the Record," 25 January 1962, Helms to McCone, 19 January 1962, "The Cuba Project," 24 January 1962, all in *FRUS* 1961–63, 10:703, 728–30, 719–20, 723.

29. Hilsman to U. Alexis Johnson, 20 February 1962, *FRUS* 1961–63, 10:748.

30. William H. Craig to Lansdale, "Possible Actions to Provoke, Harrass [*sic*], or Disrupt Cuba," 2 February 1962, NSA; Report by the Department of Defense and Joint Chiefs of Staff Representative on the Caribbean Survey Group, "Justification for U.S. Military Intervention in Cuba," 9 March 1962, NSA.

31. Lansdale, "Meeting with President," 16 March 1962, NSA; CIA, NIE for Cuba, 21 March 1962, *FRUS* 1961–63, 10:774; Lyman Lemnitzer to McNamara, 10 April 1962, in *The Kennedys and Cuba: The Declassified Documentary History*, ed. Mark J. White (Chicago: Dee, 1999), 118–19.

32. Harvey to McCone, 10 April 1962, *FRUS* 1961–63, 10:788. In January 1962, Operation Mongoose had been taken out of WH/4 and organized as a one-country program, Task Force W [named for pre–Civil War filibuster William Walker]. See Bohning, *Castro Obsession*, 89; Ted Shackley with Richard A. Finney, *Spymaster: My Life in the CIA* (Dulles, Va.: Potomac, 2005), 50.

33. Kent to McCone, 10 April 1962, *FRUS* 1961–63, 10:783–84. The duration of U.S. forces' stay had also worried the regional commander of U.S. Navy forces during the Bay of Pigs invasion: "We would have been in there for years" (Robert Lee Dennison, *The Reminiscences of Admiral Robert Lee Dennison, U.S. Navy (Retired)* [Annapolis: U.S. Naval Institute, 1975], 416).

34. Lansdale to Harvey, "CIA Draft Operational Plan B+," 6 August 1962, Folder "Special Group (Augmented) General 8/62," Box 319, NSFK; William Harvey to Director of Central Intelligence, "Operation Mongoose—Future Course of Action," 8 August 1962, *FRUS* 1961–63, vols. 10–12, microfiche supplement, document 289.

35. McCone, "Memorandum on Meeting of the Special Group," 16 August 1962, *FRUS* 1961–63, 10:940–41. The next day Lansdale sent Bundy a handwritten note apologizing for the meeting: "It's no easy thing to make the big organizations come up with practical answers, although I'll keep trying" (Lansdale to Bundy, 17 August 1962, Folder "Special Group (Augmented) General 8/62," Box 319, NSFK).

36. McCone, "Discussion in Secretary Rusk's Office . . . ," 21 August 1961, McCone, Memcon, "Cuba," 23 August 1962, both in *FRUS* 1961–63, 10:949, 955.

37. Taylor to President, 17 August 1962, *FRUS* 1961–63, 10:944–45; NSAM 181, 23 August 1962, NSFK.

38. The new plan is Lansdale to Special Group (Augmented), 31 August 1962, *FRUS* 1961–63, 10:974–1000. See also CIA, "Memorandum: Notes of the Special Group (Augmented) Meeting, 27 September 1962 (as told by the Deputy Director of Central Intelligence to Knoche)," 28 September 1962, *FRUS* 1961–63, vols. 10–12, microfiche supplement, document 307; Harvey to Director of Central Intelligence, "Operation Mongoose—Future Course of Action," 8 August 1962, *FRUS* 1961–63, vols. 10–12, microfiche supplement, document 289; "Operation Mongoose: Main Points to Consider," 26 October 1962, and Thomas A. Parrott, "Minutes of Meeting of the Special Group (Augmented) on Operation Mongoose," 26 October 1962, which directs the CIA to continue developing the balloon project, both in Folder "Special Group (Augmented), General 10/62–12/62," Box 319A, NSFK; Chase to Bundy, "Cuba Coordinating Committee—Covert Operations in Cuba," 3 April 1963, Folder "Chron. File 10/62–4/63 (Folder 1 of 3)," Box 1, Gordon Chase Papers, JFKL.

39. Ray S. Cline to Acting Director of Central Intelligence, "Prospects for Spontaneous Uprising in Cuba without Outside Assistance," 6 September 1962, Folder "Special Group (Augmented) General 9/62," Box 319, NSFK; Cyrus R. Vance, Secretary of the Army, Memorandum for the Chair, Joint Chiefs of Staff, enclosing "Draft State-Defense Contingency Plan for a Coup in Cuba," 26 September 1963, Folder 5, Box 6, Joseph Califano Papers, National Archives and Records Administration, Washington, D.C.; Lansdale to Special Group (Augmented), "Action Proposals, Mongoose," 11 October 1962, NSA; Lansdale to General Johnson, "Illumination by Submarine," 15 October 1962, both Folder "Special Group (Augmented) General 10/62–12/62," Box 319A, NSFK.

40. Helms, "Memorandum for the Record," 16 October 1962, *FRUS* 1961–63, 11:46. The CIA's Richard Helms later recalled that few if any such meetings took place. U.S. Senate,

Select Committee to Study Governmental Operations with Respect to Intelligence Activities, *Alleged Assassination Plots Involving Foreign Leaders. An Interim Report*, 94th Cong., 1st sess., 20 November 1975, 147n; for the Matanzas power plant comment, see CIA to Special Group (Augmented), "Operation Mongoose/Sabotage Proposals," 16 October 1962, *FRUS* 1961–63, vols. 10–12, microfiche supplement, document 321.

41. "The Situation and Prospects in Cuba," NIE 85-2-62, 1 August 1962, *FRUS* 1961–63, vols. 10–12, microfiche supplement, document 288. This document replaced the NIE of 21 March 1962.

42. Unidentified Author (probably Hurwitch), "Thoughts for 2:30 Meeting," 10 August 1962, *FRUS* 1961–63, 10:921–23.

43. Harvey to Lansdale, 17 August 1962, Chief of Naval Operations Anderson to DOS, 24 August 1962, both in *FRUS* 1961–63, 10:942, 962; the INR memo is Roger Hilsman to Acting Secretary, "Soviet Military Shipments to Cuba," 25 August 1962, Folder "Cuba Security, 1962," Box 115, POF; "The Military Buildup in Cuba," Special NIE 85-3-62, 19 September 1962, NSA. On the data analysis underlying the NIEs, see John T. Hughes with A. Denis Clift, "The San Cristobal Trapezoid," *Studies in Intelligence* 36 (Winter 1992): 41–56; Michael Douglas Smith, "Revisiting Sherman Kent's Defense of SNIE 85-3-62," unclassified extracts from *Studies in Intelligence* 51 (September 2007): 29–33.

44. *Time*, 21 September 1962 (released to newsstands 15 September); JFK Press Conference, 13 September 1962, *PPP*, 674; Gromyko's 21 September 1962 warning is reprinted in *Kennedy and the Press: The News Conferences*, ed. Harold W. Chase and Allen H. Lerman (New York: Crowell, 1965), 324. For a useful summary of these exchanges, see Gaddis Smith, *The Last Years of the Monroe Doctrine, 1945–1993* (New York: Hill and Wang, 1994), 105–8; S. J. Res. 230; 76 *Stat.* 697, 3 October 1962; Truman's Speech to Hartford Democrats as reported in *NYT*, 9 September 1962, 49.

45. Raymond L. Garthoff, Office of Politico-Military Affairs, Department of State, "The Military Significance of the Soviet Missile Bases in Cuba," 27 October 1962, *FRUS* 1961–63, vols. 10–12, microfiche supplement, document 434.

46. Ambassador Dobrynin's denials were on 4 September to Robert Kennedy, on 6 and 7 September to Theodore Sorensen, and on 13 October to Chester Bowles. Gromyko had met with JFK in Washington after his U.N. speech. James H. Hansen, "Soviet Deception in the Cuban Missile Crisis," *Studies in Intelligence* 46, no. 1 (2002): 49–58.

47. Foreign Broadcast Information Service, *Daily Report: Foreign Radio Broadcasts*, 29 October 1962, HHHH 11.

48. Carlos Franqui, *Family Portrait with Fidel: A Memoir* (New York: Random House, 1984), 194. Castro's 25–26 January 1968 speech is reprinted in James G. Blight and Philip Brenner, eds., *Sad and Luminous Days: Cuba's Struggle with the Superpowers after the Missile Crisis* (Lanham, Md.: Rowman and Littlefield, 2002), 35–71, quotations 57–58. For the Soviet version of the Castro-Mikoyan conversations, see "Mikoyan's Mission to Havana: Cuban-Soviet Negotiations, November 1962," *Cold War International History Project Bulletin* 5 (Spring 1995): 58–115, 159–60.

49. Mikoyan's visit was 2–26 November 1962; his conciliatory "Farewell Statement to the Cuban People," 26 November 1962, is in Folder "Cuba General 11/21/62–11/30/62," Box 37, NSFK; CIA Intelligence Memorandum, "Castro and Communism: The Cuban Revolution in Perspective," 9 May 1966, DDRS; CIA, "Review of Current Program of Covert Action against

Cuba," [February 1964], Folder "Intelligence Covert Program 1/64–6/65," Box 24, NSFJ, CF, Cuba. The indispensable treatment of Cuban-Soviet relations in the wake of the missile crisis is Blight and Brenner, *Sad and Luminous Days*. Castro's televised news conference is reprinted in *Revolución*, 5 June 1963, 1–6, with an exceptionally favorable comment about Khrushchev on 6.

50. Speech to the Confederation of Cuban Workers, Havana, 29 January 1990; James G. Blight, Bruce J. Allyn, and David A. Welch, *Cuba on the Brink*, rev. ed. (Lanham, Md.: Rowman and Littlefield, 2002), 225; for the Cuban perspective, see Carlos Lechuga, *Cuba and the Missile Crisis*, trans. Mary Todd (Melbourne, Australia: Ocean, 2001).

51. Transcript, CBS Reports, "The CIA's Secret Army," 10 June 1977, PC. Castro had said the same thing in a November 1962 letter to U.N. secretary-general U Thant (reprinted in Blight and Brenner, *Sad and Luminous Days*, 210–13) and on a second occasion in 1975 (Frank Mankiewicz and Kirby Jones, "Conversation with Fidel Castro," *Oui*, January 1975, 158).

52. Bruce J. Allyn, James G. Blight, and David A. Welch, eds., *Back to the Brink: Proceedings of the Moscow Conference on the Cuban Missile Crisis, January 27–28, 1989* (Cambridge: Center for Science and International Affairs, Harvard University, 1992), 7; James G. Blight and David A. Welch, *On the Brink: Americans and Soviets Reexamine the Cuban Missile Crisis* (New York: Farrar, Straus, and Giroux, 1989), 238; James G. Hershberg, "Before 'The Missiles of October': Did Kennedy Plan a Military Strike against Cuba?" in *The Cuban Missile Crisis Revisited*, ed. James A. Nathan (New York: St. Martin's, 1992), 237–80; for the Soviet-Cuban perspective, based on declassified Soviet documents, see Aleksandr Fursenko and Timothy Naftali, *One Hell of a Gamble: Khrushchev, Castro, and Kennedy, 1958–1964* (New York: Norton, 1997); Philip Brenner, "Thirteen Months: Cuba's Perspective on the Missile Crisis," in *The Cuban Missile Crisis Revisited*, ed. Nathan, 187–217; Arthur M. Schlesinger Jr., *Robert Kennedy and His Times* (Boston: Houghton Mifflin, 1978), 478; "Actions Taken by the United States against the Castro Regime," enclosed with Department of State, "Memorandum for Mr. Bromley Smith the White House," 19 October 1962, Folder "Cuba General, 10/1/62–10/14/62," Box 36, NSFK.

53. JFK's 27 October letter to Khrushchev and Khrushchev's 28 October letter to Castro ("the United States will not invade Cuba with its own forces, nor will it permit its allies to carry out an invasion") are reprinted in *DOSB*, 19 November 1973, 635–55, and in *The Cuban Missile Crisis, 1962: The 40th Anniversary*, 2nd ed., ed. Laurence Chang and Peter Kornbluh (New York: New Press, 1998), 234, 249. The letters are also among the several thousand documents in the National Security Archive's invaluable collection, *The Cuban Missile Crisis, 1962*, ed. Laurence Chang (Alexandria, Va.: Chadwyck-Healey, 1990).

54. McNaughton to Nitze, "The U.S. 'Anti-Invasion' Guarantee in the Cuban Settlement," 5 November 1962, *FRUS* 1961–63, vols. 10–12, microfiche supplement, document 496. On the early understanding that the United States had pledged not to invade, see entry for 29 October 1962, Dwight D. Eisenhower, *The Eisenhower Diaries*, ed. Robert H. Ferrell (New York: Norton, 1981), 391; Schlesinger to President, 29 October 1962, Martin to Rusk, 30 October 1962, and McManus, "Demise of Operation Mongoose," 5 November 1962, all in *FRUS* 1961–63, vols. 10–12, microfiche supplement, documents 457, 463, 493. For the documents regarding the no-invasion guarantee, see Jim Hershberg, "Anatomy of a Controversy: Anatoly F. Dobrynin's Meeting with Robert Kennedy, Saturday, 27 October 1962," *Cold War International History Project Bulletin* 5 (Spring 1995): 75–80.

55. JFK Press Conference, 20 November 1962, *PPP*, 830–38; Roger Hilsman, INR, to Secretary, "Negotiations on Cuba: The Advantages of Stalemate," 17 November 1962, *FRUS 1961–63*, vols. 10–12, microfiche supplement, document 543.

56. Executive Committee Meeting, 21 November 1962, *FRUS 1961–63*, 11:509–10.

57. Radio/TV Speech to the Cuban People, 23 October 1962, LANIC. See also Castro to Khrushchev, 28 October 1962, NSA, and esp. Castro to U. Thant, 15 November 1962, reprinted in Blight and Brenner, *Sad and Luminous Days*, 210–13. In his 27 October letter to JFK (reprinted in *DOSB*, 19 November 1973, 646), Khrushchev had noted that Cuba's permission would be required.

58. U.S. Congress, Senate, Committee on Foreign Relations, *Executive Sessions of the Senate Foreign Relations Committee, Together with Joint Sessions with the Senate Armed Services Committee (Historical Series)*, vol. 15, 88th Cong., 1st sess., 11 January 1963, 23; JFK to McNamara, 29 April 1963, McNamara to JFK ("I wish to assure you that our contingency plans for invasion of Cuba have been and are being maintained and up to date"), 7 May 1963, both in *FRUS 1961–63*, 11:712, 791, 802; *FRUS 1964–68*, 31:27 n. 7; Nixon: NSSM 23, "Cuba," 2 July 1969, 17n, NSA.

59. JFK Notes for NSC Meeting, 22 January 1963, *FRUS 1961–63*, 11:669; Adlai Stevenson and Vasily Kuznetsov to U Thant, 7 January 1963, *FRUS 1961–63*, 11:655; McCone, "Memorandum for the Record," 9 January 1963, *FRUS 1961–63*, vols. 10–12, microfiche supplement, document 592.

Among the most useful studies of the missile crisis are the volumes that emerged from a series of conferences among the surviving participants organized by James G. Blight and associates between 1987 and 1992. See James G. Blight and David A. Welch, *On the Brink: Americans and Soviets Reexamine the Cuban Missile Crisis* (New York: Farrar, Straus, and Giroux, 1989); James G. Blight, *The Shattered Crystal Ball: Fear and Learning in the Cuban Missile Crisis* (Savage, Md.: Rowman and Littlefield, 1990); Bruce J. Allyn, James G. Blight, and David A. Welch, eds., *Back to the Brink: Proceedings of the Moscow Conference on the Cuban Missile Crisis, January 27–28, 1989* (Cambridge: Center for Science and International Affairs, Harvard University, 1992); James G. Blight, Bruce J. Allyn, and David A. Welch, *Cuba on the Brink*, rev. ed. (Lanham, Md.: Rowman and Littlefield, 2002). See also Sheldon M. Stern, *Averting "The Final Failure": John F. Kennedy and the Secret Cuban Missile Crisis Meetings* (Stanford, Calif.: Stanford University Press, 2003); Fursenko and Naftali, *One Hell of a Gamble*; Raymond L. Garthoff, *Reflections on the Cuban Missile Crisis*, rev. ed. (Washington, D.C.: Brookings, 1989); and the classic Graham Allison, *Essence of Decision: Explaining the Cuban Missile Crisis* (Boston: Little Brown, 1971) and Graham Allison and Philip Zelikow, *Essence of Decision: Explaining the Cuban Missile Crisis*, 2nd ed. (New York: Longman, 1999).

60. [Lansdale?], "Operation Mongoose: Main Points to Consider," 26 October 1962, Thomas A. Parrott, "Minutes of Meeting of the Special Group (Augmented) on Operation Mongoose," 26 October 1962, both in Folder "Special Group (Augmented) General 10/62–12/62," Box 319A, NSFK. On the continuing supplies to two existing sabotage/intelligence-gathering teams, see Helms to Director of Central Intelligence, "Operation Mongoose—Support of Assets inside Cuba," 7 December 1962, Folder "Special Group (Augmented) General 10/62–12/62," Box 319A, NSFK.

61. Robert A. Hurwitch, *Most of Myself: An Autobiography in the Form of Letters to His Daughters* (Santo Domingo, D.R.: Editora Corripio, 1990), 2:131; see also Hilsman to Rusk,

"Prospects for Overthrowing Castro from Within," 17 November 1962, *FRUS* 1961–63, vols. 10–12, microfiche supplement, document 543.

62. George B. McManus, "Demise of Operation Mongoose," 5 November 1962, *FRUS* 1961–63, vols. 10–12, microfiche supplement, document 493; Bundy to President, "Further Organization of the Government for Dealing with Cuba," 4 January 1963, Folder "Cuba Security 1963," Box 115, POF. In May 1963 Lansdale unwillingly retired and the position of assistant secretary of defense for special operations was abolished. On Lansdale, see Cecil B. Currey, *Edward Lansdale: The Unquiet American* (Boston: Houghton Mifflin, 1988), esp. 255; Jonathan Nashel, *Edward Lansdale's Cold War* (Amherst: University of Massachusetts Press, 2005); Edward Lansdale, *In the Midst of Wars: An American's Mission to Southeast Asia* (New York: Harper and Row, 1972).

63. The replacement interdepartmental committee was chaired by a coordinator of Cuban affairs, initially Deputy Assistant Secretary of State Sterling J. Cottrell, who held both positions for a few months until he could find a full-time coordinator. That was John Crimmins, a career officer who had been stationed in Miami as the State Department's coordinator of relations with Cuban exile groups. On the State Department's grant of primacy, see Bundy to President, "Further Organization of the Government for Dealing with Cuba," 4 January 1963, Folder "Cuba Security 1963," Box 115, POF; NSAM 213, 8 January 1963, NSFK; Bundy to Members of the NSC Standing Group, "Committee Responsibilities in Cuban Affairs," 22 May 1963, Folder "Cuba General, 5/16/63," Box 38A, NSFK.

64. Department of State and Department of Justice Press Release, 30 March 1963, Folder "Cuba, General, Standing Committee 4/63," Box 38, NSFK.

65. Rusk to President, 28 March 1963, Folder "Cuba Security 1963," Box 115, POF; for Rusk's opposition and McCone's reply, see *FRUS* 1961–63, 11:742; Andrew St. George, "Vamos! The Buccaneers Attack the Soviet Prey," *Life*, 12 April 1963, 19–25.

66. NSC Executive Committee Meeting, 29 March 1963, *FRUS* 1961–63, 11:739–43. The minutes of a Special Group meeting two weeks later, on 11 April, quote McCone expressing "great skepticism about the desirability of proceeding with sabotage operations" (*FRUS* 1961–63, 11:758). Helms is quoted in Chase to Bundy, "Cuba Coordinating Committee — Covert Operations in Cuba," 3 April 1963, Folder "Chron. File 10/62–4/63 (Folder 1 of 3)," Box 1, Chase Papers.

67. For a list of the seven sabotage attacks in late 1962 and early 1963 ("machinegunned a Cuban vessel," "shelled hotel on Havana waterfront," etc.), see Untitled and Undated Memorandum, Folder "Cuba General 4/63–11/63," Box 115, POF. On the sabotage operations, see U.S. Senate, Select Committee, *Alleged Assassination Plots*, 125, 148, 173; *FRUS* 1961–63, 11:739–58; Roswell Gilpatric Oral History, 5 May 1970, JFKL; Blight and Brenner, *Sad and Luminous Days*, 264 n. 146; Bradley Earl Ayers, *The War That Never Was: An Insider's Account of CIA Covert Operations against Cuba* (Indianapolis: Bobbs-Merrill, 1976).

68. Chase to Bundy, "Cuba Coordinating Committee — Covert Operations in Cuba," 3 April 1963, Chase to Bundy ("these groups are relatively ineffective and inactive"), 27 March 1963, both in Folder "Chron. File 10/62–4/63," Box 1, Chase Papers.

69. Califano, *Inside*, 120; FitzGerald to Director of Central Intelligence, "Outline of a Program to Exacerbate and Stimulate Disaffection in the Cuban Armed Forces," 19 March 1963, NSA.

70. Crimmins Oral History; Harvey Summ Interview, 25 March 1982, PC. On stopping the

unauthorized raids, see *FRUS* 1961–63, 11:739–43. For a brief memoir by the employee who in January 1959 opened the CIA's Miami station (code-named JMWAVE), see Justin F. Gleichauf, "A Listening Post in Miami: Keeping Up on Cuba," *Studies in Intelligence* 10 (Winter-Spring 2001): 49–53; the autobiography of the CIA chief of station from January 1962 to June 1965 is Shackley with Finney, *Spymaster*. The State Department opened its Miami office in February 1963 with Crimmins as the officer in charge, but in May he moved back to Washington as the coordinator of Cuban affairs. For State's attempt to place the CIA's Miami station under its control, see Brubeck to Bundy, 7 February 1963, Folder "Cuba General, 2/63," Box 37A, NSFK.

71. *CBS Reports with Bill Moyers*, "The CIA's Secret Army," 10 June 1977, PC; Harvey Summ Oral History, 5 March 1993, Association for Diplomatic Studies and Training, U.S. Foreign Affairs Oral History Collection, Arlington, Virginia.

72. Rostow to Desmond FitzGerald, 4 June 1963, Folder "Cuba Security 1963," Box 115, POF; "Covert Actions against Cuba," [July 1963], Folder "Cuba General 7/63," Box 39, NSFK. On the counterfeit currency plan, which was never implemented, see Alexander Haig, "Memo for Mr. Vance: Meeting of the National Security Council Standing Group," 2 October 1963, *FRUS* 1961–63, vols. 10–12, microfiche supplement, document 711. On the October requests, see U.S. Senate, Select Committee, *Alleged Assassination Plots*, 173.

73. Coordinator of Cuban Affairs to Special Group, "Proposal for Air Strikes against Cuban Targets," 21 October 1963, *FRUS* 1961–63, vols. 10–12, microfiche supplement, document 715 (accompanying catalog misidentifies author as Cottrell).

74. Bundy to President, April 3, 1963, Gordon Chase to McGeorge Bundy, 27 March 1963, both in *FRUS* 1961–63, vols. 10–12, microfiche supplement, documents 645, 637; Ayers, *War That Never Was*, 90; Crimmins Oral History; Shackley with Finney, *Spymaster*, 72; Halpern quoted in Blight and Kornbluh, *Politics of Illusion*, 117; Halpern Oral History, Cold War History Project, NSA; Chase to Bundy, 12 September 1963, *FRUS* 1961–63, 11:864.

75. Memorandum for the Record, 12 November 1963, FitzGerald to Bundy, 9 August 1963, both in *FRUS* 1961–63, 11:887, 854; Califano, *Inside*, 124.

76. NSC Meeting, 22 January 1963, *FRUS* 1961–63, 11:669.

77. Rusk, "Review of the Cuban Situation and Policy," Talking Points for Discussion with Cabinet, 28 February 1963, FitzGerald to McCone, "Outline of a Program to Exacerbate and Stimulate Disaffection in the Cuban Armed Forces," 19 March 1963, both in *FRUS* 1961–63, vols. 10–12, microfiche supplement, documents 629, 634.

78. U.S. Senate, Select Committee, *Alleged Assassination Plots*, 92. The CIA eventually acknowledged eight separate attempts to assassinate Castro (U.S. Senate, Select Committee, *Alleged Assassination Plots*, 71); in 1977, Fidel Castro claimed that twenty-four attempts had occurred (Transcript, *CBS Reports with Bill Moyers*, "The CIA's Secret Army," 10 June 1977, PC). Other Cubans had a higher number: Fabián Escalante, *Executive Action: 634 Ways to Kill Fidel Castro* (Melbourne, Australia: Ocean, 2006).

79. Meetings, 13 January, 10 March, 14 January 1960, all in U.S. Senate, Select Committee, *Alleged Assassination Plots*, 93, 110, 115. At a meeting on 9 March, King had remarked that Mongoose would be a long, drawn-out affair "unless Fidel and Raul Castro and Che Guevara could be eliminated in one package." Burke asserted that King was not referring to assassination.

80. Cable dated 21 July 1960, in U.S. Senate, Select Committee, *Alleged Assassination Plots*,

73; for Bissell's speculation about why the murder was called off, see U.S. Senate, Select Committee, *Alleged Assassination Plots*, 94.

81. U.S. Senate, Select Committee, *Alleged Assassination Plots*, 74; on Maheu, see Howard J. Osborn to Deputy Director of Central Intelligence, "Maheu, Robert A.," 24 June 1966, NSA; for Edwards's and O'Connell's affidavits, see David W. Belin, "Interview with Colonel Sheffield Edwards," 9 April 1975, "Interview with James O'Connell," 17 May 1975, both in Commission on CIA Activities within the United States, DDRS.

82. On the role of John "Handsome Johnny" Rosselli (sometimes spelled "Roselli"), see Howard J. Osborn, Director of Security, to Director of Central Intelligence, "Roselli, Johnny," 19 November 1970, CIA FOIA. .

83. J. S. Earman, Inspector General, CIA, "Report on Plots to Assassinate Fidel Castro," 23 May 1967, 30–32, PC; U.S. Senate, Select Committee, *Alleged Assassination Plots*, 81–82, which contains a slightly different version of the Miami meeting. Testimony about the amount of money varied from ten thousand dollars to fifty thousand dollars. A lightly redacted version of the Earman report has been published as *CIA Targets Fidel: Secret 1967 CIA Inspector General's Report on Plots to Assassinate Fidel Castro* (Melbourne, Australia: Ocean, 1996). A useful chronology of the Mafia episode is Sheffield Edwards, "Memorandum for the Record," 14 May 1962, *FRUS* 1961–63, 10:807–9.

84. J. S. Earman, Inspector General, CIA, "Report on Plots to Assassinate Fidel Castro," 23 May 1967, 39, 50, 84–85, PC; for evaluations of Harvey, see Thomas Powers, *The Man Who Kept the Secrets: Richard Helms and the CIA* (New York: Knopf, 1979), 149–50; Bohning, *Castro Obsession*, 94–95; E. Howard Hunt with Greg Aunapu, *American Spy: My Secret History in the CIA, Watergate, and Beyond* (New York: Wiley, 2007), 125.

85. U.S. Senate, Select Committee, *Alleged Assassination Plots*, 84–85; for Harvey's affidavit, see David W. Belin, "Interview with Mr. William K. Harvey," 10 April 1975, Commission on CIA Activities within the United States, DDRS.

86. U.S. Senate, Select Committee, *Alleged Assassination Plots*, 88–89, quoting J. S. Earman, Inspector General, CIA, "Report on Plots to Assassinate Fidel Castro," 23 May 1967, 93a, PC; see also 106. In mid-1965 the CIA ended its relationship with Cubela; he was arrested in Havana a few months later and spent the next fourteen years in jail.

87. J. S. Earman, Inspector General, CIA, "Report on Plots to Assassinate Fidel Castro," 23 May 1967, 21–22, PC; U.S. Senate, Select Committee, *Alleged Assassination Plots*, 73, 85–86.

88. U.S. Senate, Select Committee, *Alleged Assassination Plots*, 178.

89. Ibid., 178–79; J. S. Earman, Inspector General, CIA, "Report on Plots to Assassinate Fidel Castro," 23 May 1967, 131–32, PC; Jack Anderson, "Did Plot By CIA to Kill Castro Backfire on US?" *Miami Herald*, 3 March 1967, 7A; Drew Pearson and Jack Anderson, "Castro Counterplot," *Washington Post*, 7 March 1967, C13. Anderson was apparently tipped off by Rosselli.

90. Dean Rusk as told to Richard Rusk, *As I Saw It* (New York: Norton, 1990), 216; U.S. Senate, Select Committee, *Alleged Assassination Plots*, 119–20, 165n (McNamara), 154 (McCone). For Goodwin's initial fingering of McNamara, see Branch and Crile, "The Kennedy Vendetta," *Harpers*, July 1975, 61; for his backtracking, see U.S. Senate, Select Committee, *Alleged Assassination Plots*, 165n; for Goodwin's later accusations, see Richard N. Goodwin, *Remembering America: A Voice from the Sixties* (Boston: Little, Brown, 1988), 189.

91. Notes on Conversation, 9 November 1961, *FRUS* 1961–63, vols. 10–12, microfiche sup-

plement, document 278; J. S. Earman, Inspector General, CIA, "Report on Plots to Assassinate Fidel Castro," 23 May 1967, 130, PC; Transcript, *CBS Reports with Bill Moyers*, "The CIA's Secret Army," 10 June 1977, PC.

92. U.S. Senate, Select Committee, *Alleged Assassination Plots*, 99–100, 164–65; J. S. Earman, Inspector General, CIA, "Report on Plots to Assassinate Fidel Castro," 23 May 1967, 112, PC. Murrow favored nonviolent sabotage: "putting glass and nails on the highways, leaving water running in public buildings, putting sand in machinery, wasting electricity, taking sick leave from work, damaging sugar stalks during the harvest" (Murrow to McCone, 10 December 1962, NSA).

93. U.S. Senate, Select Committee, *Alleged Assassination Plots*, 162; Harvey to Helms, "Operation Mongoose," 14 August 1962, *FRUS* 1961–63, vols. 10–12, microfiche supplement, document 290; see also *FRUS* 1961–62, 10:923.

94. Harvey to Helms, "Operation Mongoose," 14 August 1962, *FRUS* 1961–63, vols. 10–12, microfiche supplement, document 290; for Lansdale's denial of involvement in or knowledge of any assassination plot, see David W. Belin for the Commission on CIA Activities, "Deposition of Edward G. Lansdale," 16 May 1975, esp. 16, DDRS.

95. U.S. Senate, Select Committee, *Alleged Assassination Plots*, 150; J. S. Earman, Inspector General, CIA, "Report on Plots to Assassinate Fidel Castro," 23 May 1967, 4, PC; CIA staffer Samuel Halpern quoted in Hersh, *Dark Side of Camelot*, 268; for a review of Hersh's book that questions whether the Kennedy brothers were obsessed with Castro, see Ernest R. May and Philip D. Zelikow, "Camelot Confidential," *Diplomatic History* 22 (Fall 1998): 642–53.

96. CIA to Park F. Wollam, "What Would Happen If Castro Died?," 6 October 1961, *FRUS* 1961–63, vols. 10–12, microfiche supplement, document 275.

97. "Recommendations of the Cuban Study Group," 134, Box 61A, NSFK; U.S. Senate, Select Committee, *Alleged Assassination Plots*, 151–52; Califano, *Inside*, 125.

98. David Frost, "An Interview with Richard Helms" (1978), in *Studies in Intelligence*, Special Unclassified Edition, Fall 2000, 130; Transcript of Bissell Interview, *CBS Reports with Bill Moyers*, "The CIA's Secret Army," 10 June 1977, PC.

99. Shackley with Finney, *Spymaster*, 57; J. S. Earman, Inspector General, CIA, "Report on Plots to Assassinate Fidel Castro," 23 May 1967, 92, PC.

100. Bowles Diary, "Thoughts on the New Administration," 3 June 1961, Folder 154, Box 392, Bowles Papers.

101. George C. Denny Jr. to Mr. Crimmins, "Cuba: Possible Courses of Action," 25 July 1963, Folder "Cuba, Subjects, Policy, 5/63–8/63," Box 55, NSFK.

102. Leo Janis, "The Last Days of the President," *Atlantic Monthly*, July 1973, 35, 39; Bowdler to Bundy, "Plots to Assassinate Castro," 21 January 1966, Folder "Cuba Country [W. G. Bowdler File] [1 of 2], Volume I, 4/64–1/66," Box 18 [2 of 2], NSFJ, CF, Cuba; Califano, *Inside*, 127; U.S. Senate, Select Committee, *Alleged Assassination Plots*, 282; Executive Order 11905, 18 February 1976; Executive Order 12333, 4 December 1981 (emphasis added).

103. Cuba continued to purchase some food and medicine, but most of these sales stopped when U.S. claimants began asking courts to seize shipments after they had been legally transferred to Cuban hands but before they had physically left the United States. For the trade data, see Susan Schroeder, *Cuba: Handbook of Historical Statistics* (Boston: Hall, 1982), 433; U.S. Congress, House, Committee on Interstate and Foreign Commerce, *Trade with Cuba*, 87th Cong., 1st sess., 1961, 56; Dean Rusk to President, "Questions Arising from

Senator Smather's [*sic*] Recommendation That Remaining Exports from Cuba to the United States be Embargoed," 24 February 1961, Folder "Cuba Security, 1961," Box 115, POF. In 1957 and 1958 U.S. tourists added perhaps $120 million to the Cuban economy, but that amount was more than balanced by imports necessary to sustain the tourist industry and by the expenditures of Cuban tourists visiting the United States (Cuban Economic Research Project, *A Study on Cuba: The Colonial and Republican Periods, the Socialist Experiment* [Coral Gables, Fla.: University of Miami Press, 1965], 570).

104. CIA, "Cuban Supply and Demand of Crude Oil and Refined Petroleum Products," 6 May 1963, *FRUS* 1961–63, vols. 10–12, microfiche supplement, document 674. The cost of shipping a ton of rice was $3.50 from New Orleans, $12.00 from China (Donald L. Losman, "The Embargo of Cuba: An Economic Appraisal," *Caribbean Studies* 14 [October 1974]: 103–4).

105. J. Edgar Hoover to Attorney General, "Foreign Economic Matters—Cuba," 18 April 1961, Folder "Cuba General 4/1/61–4/21/61," Box 114A, POF; *NYT*, 15 July 1961, 1, 30 August 1961, 1.

106. "Memorandum of Conference with the President, October 13, 1960," 15 October 1960, Folder "Staff Notes October 1960 (1)," Box 53, DDE Diary Series, AWF; Herter to President, 5 January 1961, *FRUS* 1961–63, 10:19–20; for the early wrestling, see NSC meeting, 22 June 1960, "Questions Concerning the Program of Economic Pressures against Cuba," 27 June 1960, both in *FRUS* 1958–60, 6:949–52, 963–64; James S. Lay Jr. to NSC, "U.S. Policy toward Cuba and the Dominican Republic," 12 July 1960, Folder "Cuba (May 1959–September 1960)(3)," Box 4, WHOF, Office of the Special Assistant for National Security Affairs: Records, 1952–61, NSC Series, Subject Subseries.

107. NSAM 19, 15 February 1961, 23, 21 February 1961, both in Box 328, NSFK; Rusk to President, "Questions Arising from Senator Smather's [*sic*] Recommendation That Remaining Exports from Cuba to the United States be Embargoed," 24 February 1961, Folder "Cuba Security, 1961," Box 115, POF.

108. "Record of Actions by the National Security Council . . . April 22, 1961," Folder "National Security Council Meetings 1961 No. 478—4/22/61," Box 313, NSFK; "Record of Actions by the National Security Council . . . May 5, 1961," Folder "National Security Council Meetings 1961 No. 483—5/5/61," Box 313, NSFK.

109. *Congressional Record*, 18 August 1961, 16292; PL 87-195, Section 620(a), 4 September 1961. Section 401(m) of the Mutual Security Act of 1960 (PL 86-472, 74 *Stat.* 140) had already stipulated that "no assistance shall be furnished under this Act to Cuba."

110. Memcon, JFK and Betancourt, 16 December 1961, *FRUS* 1961–63, 12:273; Proclamation 3447, 3 February 1962, 27 *FR* 1085 (reprinted in *DOSB*, 7 November 1960, 715–16), banned exports, imports, and imports from third countries of any goods of Cuban origin. The president's authority to proclaim an embargo was both Fascell's amendment (Sec. 620[a]) and the Export Control Act of 1949. To implement JFK's proclamation, on 7 February the administration published its initial Cuban Import Regulations (27 *FR* 6974); they were amended on 24 March to prohibit imports from third countries of goods with Cuban components. Food, medicine, and medical supplies continued to be exempted from the embargo until May 1964, when new regulations (29 *FR* 6381, 14 May 1964) revoked a general license for these goods.

111. *DOSB*, 6 February 1961, 178. Section 1185(b), Title 8, U.S. Code made it "unlawful for

any citizen of the United States to depart from or enter, or attempt to depart from or enter, the United States unless he bears a valid United States passport" or unless the president has specifically authorized an exception. Section 1544 of Title 8 provided for the punishment of anyone who "willfully and knowingly uses or attempts to use any passport in violation of the conditions or restrictions therein contained, or of the rules prescribed pursuant to the laws regulating the issuance of passports." On the "Christmas in Cuba" trip, see Van Gosse, *Where the Boys Are: Cuba, Cold War America, and the Making of the New Left* (London: Verso, 1995), 161.

112. The Passport Act is 44 *Stat.* 887. In 1918 and again in 1941, Congress also enacted related legislation making it unlawful to enter or leave the United States without a valid passport if a war or a national emergency had been declared (see 40 *Stat.* 559, 22 May 1918, 55 *Stat.* 252, 21 June 1941). Section 215(B) of the 1952 Immigration and Nationality Act, passed at the height of McCarthyism, allowed the president to proclaim a ban on travel, after which it would "be unlawful for any citizen of the United States to depart from or enter, or attempt to depart from or enter, the United States unless he bears a valid passport."

113. *Kent et al. v. Dulles*, 16 June 1958, 357 U.S. 116.

114. CIA, "Memorandum for Special Group Meeting: Additional Actions against Cuba," 28 May 1963, *FRUS* 1961–63, vols. 10–12, microfiche supplement, document 675. Fifty-nine U.S. students arrived in Havana on 1 July 1963 and returned to Prague on 29 August 1963.

115. Press Conference, 1 August 1963, *PPP*, 616; Gordon Chase to Bundy, 9 August 1963, *FRUS* 1961–63, vols. 10–12, microfiche supplement, document 705; for JFK's decision, see Chase to Bundy, 27 September 1963, Folder "Chron. File 8/63–12/63," Box 1, Chase Papers. The five folders are in Box 45, NSFK.

116. Chase to Bundy, "Isolation of Cuba," 14 February 1963, Folder "Cuba General, 2/63," Box 37A, NSFK; "Travel of Latin American Students to Cuba for Subversive Training," [October 1963], Folder "Cuba General 10/63," Box 39, NSFK; H. Jon Rosenbaum, "Brazil's Foreign Policy and Cuba," *Inter-American Economic Affairs* 23 (Winter 1969): 39.

117. Vance to McNamara, 15 March 1963, *FRUS* 1961–63, 12:245–46.

118. "Memorandum for the NSC's Standing Group," [for NSC meeting, 23 April 1963], *FRUS* 1961–63, vols. 10–12, microfiche supplement, document 660; "Travel of Latin American Students to Cuba for Subversive Training," [October 1963], Folder "Cuba General 10/63," Box 39, NSFK; Gordon Chase, "Memorandum for the President, Meeting on Cuba—December 19, 1963," 15 December 1963, Folder "Chron. File 8/63–12/63," Box 1, Chase Papers.

119. NSC Meeting, 21 July 1960, *FRUS* 1958–60, 5:449.

120. Burris to Vice President, "U.S. Proposals on Cuba to NATO," 28 June 1962, Folder "Memos to the Vice President from Colonel Burris, Jan. 1961–June 1962 [1 of 2]," Box 5, Vice Presidential Security File, LBJL; Burris to Vice President, "Appeal to NATO Allies on Cuba," 3 October 1962, Folder "Memos to the Vice President from Col. Burris, July 1962–April 1965 [2 of 2]," Box 6, Vice Presidential Security File, LBJL; Department of State, "Response of NATO Members to U.S. Demarches on Cuban Shipping," 24 September 1962, PC; Carl Kaysen to President, 30 September 1962, Folder "Kaysen, Carl," Box 64, POF.

121. Rusk, "Review of the Cuban Situation and Policy: Talking Points for Discussion with Cabinet," 29 February 1963, ARA to all ARA Diplomatic Posts, 4 February 1963, Vance to McNamara, "Cuba Shipping Restrictions," 5 February 1963, U. Alexis Johnson to Bundy, 30

January 1963, all in *FRUS* 1961–63, vols. 10–12, microfiche supplement, documents 629, 610, 611, 608.

122. Gordon Chase to Bundy, 17 April 1963, Department of State (?), "Memorandum for the NSC's Standing Group," [prepared for Standing Group meeting, 23 April 1963], both in *FRUS* 1961–63, vols. 10–12, microfiche supplement, documents 654, 660.

123. Alexander Haig, "Memo for Mr. Vance: Meeting of the National Security Council Standing Group," 2 October 1963, *FRUS* 1961–63, vols. 10–12, microfiche supplement, document 711; Harvey Summ Oral History.

124. Memcon, "Cuban Shipping," 4 October 1963, *FRUS* 1961–63, 11:873; Morris H. Morley, "The United States and the Global Economic Blockade of Cuba: A Study in Political Pressures on America's Allies," *Canadian Journal of Political Science* 17 (March 1984): 25–48.

125. Ray Cline Oral History, 31 May 1983, in *The Cuban Missile Crisis, 1962: A National Security Archive Document Set*, ed. Chang, document 3309; Rusk to Embassy in London, 30 August 1962, *FRUS* 1961–63, 10:970; McCone, "Memorandum on Cuban Policy," 25 April 1963, "Memorandum for the NSC's Standing Group," [prepared for meeting, 23 April 1963], both in *FRUS* 1961–63, vols. 10–12, microfiche supplement, documents 670, 660.

126. McCone, "Memorandum on Cuban Policy," 25 April 1963, *FRUS* 1961–63, vols. 10–12, microfiche supplement, document 670; Bromley Smith, "A Contingent Plan for Increasing World Production of Sugar," 5 July 1963, enclosed with Bromley Smith, "Memorandum for National Security Council Standing Group," 9 July 1963, Thomas L. Hughes to Secretary Rusk, "Effects of Loss of Cuban Sugar on Free World Sugar Market," 19 April 1963, all in *FRUS* 1961–63, vols. 10–12, microfiche supplement, documents 670, 697, 663; Standing Group Meeting, 16 July 1963, *FRUS* 1961–63, 11:852.

127. "Memorandum for the NSC's Standing Group, Annex 6," [prepared for Standing Group meeting, 23 April 1963], *FRUS* 1961–63, vols. 10–12, microfiche supplement, document 660.

128. 28 *FR* 6974, 9 July 1963; DOS Circular Telegram 40, 6 July 1963, Folder "Cuba Subjects Blocking Documents 6/1/63–8/15/63," Box 45, NSFK; Chase to Bundy, "Cuba Coordinating Committee—Covert Operations in Cuba," 3 April 1963, Folder "Chron. File 10/62–4/63 (Folder 1 of 3)," Box 1, Chase Papers; Chase to Bundy, "Cuba—Pending Items," 9 August 1963, *FRUS* 1961–63, vols. 10–12, microfiche supplement, document 705.

129. The Trading with the Enemy Act is PL 65-91, 6 October 1917, 40 *Stat.* 411; similar legislation was passed for the War of 1812 (2 *Stat.* 778, 6 July 1812) and the Civil War (37 *Stat.* 257, 13 July 1861); for Executive Proclamation 2814, see 3 *CFR* 99. The Trading with the Enemy Act's original implementing regulations are the Cuban Assets Control Regulations (31 *CFR* 515, consolidating earlier regulations), 28 *FR* 6974, 9 July 1963, and were administered by the Office of Foreign Assets Control (OFAC) of the Department of the Treasury, the successor to the Office of Foreign Funds Control, established when Germany invaded Norway in 1940 but officially created in December 1950 following China's entry into the Korean War. The ban on U.S. exports to Cuba was administered by the Bureau of Export Administration of the Department of Commerce (15 *CFR* 770, 785, 799); it assigned Cuba to Country Group Z, which required a specific license for all exports.

See U.S. International Trade Commission, *The Economic Impact of U.S. Sanctions with Respect to Cuba*, Investigation 332-413, Publication 3398 (Washington, D.C.: U.S. International

Trade Commission, 2001); U.S. Congress, House, Committee on International Relations, Subcommittees on International Trade and Commerce and on International Organizations, *U.S. Trade Embargo of Cuba*, 94th Cong., 1st sess., 1975; Peter J. Grilli, Howard B. Klein, and James M. Michener, "Legal Impediments to Normalization of Trade with Cuba," *Law and Policy in International Business* 8, no. 4 (1976): 1007–54; Diane E. Rennack and Mark Sullivan, *Cuba: U.S. Economic Sanctions* (Washington, D.C.: CRS, 1995); Paul A. Shneyer and Virginia Barta, "The Legality of the U.S. Economic Blockade of Cuba under International Law," *Case Western Reserve Journal of International Law* 13 (Summer 1981): 451–82.

130. Chase to Bundy, "Imposition of Blocking Controls on Cuba," 11 June 1963, Folder "Cuba Subjects Blocking Documents 6/1/63–8/15/63," Box 45, NSFK.

131. Richard Goodwin, "President Kennedy's Plan for Peace with Cuba," *NYT*, 5 July 2000, A17.

132. Embassy to DOS, 5 December 1960, *FRUS* 1958–60, 6:1145.

133. Mansfield to John F. Kennedy, "The Cuban Aftermath," 1 May 1961, Folder "Cuba General 5/1/61–5/15/61," Box 114A, POF; Szulc to Schlesinger, 23 June 1961, Folder "Schlesinger, Arthur M. 5/61–6/61," Box 65, POF; Memcon, Szulc and Hurwitch, 13 July 1961, *FRUS* 1961–63, 10:624–25.

134. Rusk to Gordon, 14 April 1962, Gordon to DOS, 3 May 1962, Goodwin to Martin, 24 May 1962, all in *FRUS* 1961–63, 10:792–93, 805, 822.

135. Bundy to President, "Further Organization of the Government for Dealing with Cuba," 4 January 1963, Folder "Cuba Security 1963," Box 115, POF; Chase, "Mr. Donovan's Trip to Cuba," 4 March 1963, NSA; McCone to President, 10 April 1963, *FRUS* 1961–63, 11:755–56. A few months later, Bundy appeared willing to accept a "Titoist" version of Castro: "A Sketch of the Cuban Alternatives," 21 April 1963, Folder "Cuba General Standing Committee [*sic*] 4/63," Box 38, NSFK; see also Gordon Chase, "Cuba—Policy," 11 April 1963, NSA; Chase, "Some Arguments against Accommodation—A Rebuttal," 12 November 1963, Folder "Cuba General 11/10/63–11/12/63," Box 39A, NSFK.

136. Helms to McCone, 1 May 1963, *FRUS* 1961–63, vols. 10–12, microfiche supplement, document 671. The State Department's Sterling Cottrell received the same message (Cottrell to Edwin Martin, 2 May 1963, *FRUS* 1961–63, vols. 10–12, microfiche supplement, document 672). Howard's ten-hour interview with Castro occurred on 22 April 1963. For the list of other efforts, see Helms to McCone, 5 June 1963, *FRUS* 1961–63, vols. 10–12, microfiche supplement, document 685; see also U.S. Senate, Select Committee, *Alleged Assassination Plots*, 173–74.

137. "Future Relations with Castro," 20 June 1963, *FRUS* 1961–63, 11:838–42.

138. Desmond FitzGerald, "Meeting in the Office of the Secretary of State re. Discussion of Proposed Covert Policy and Integrated Program of Action towards Cuba," 22 June 1963, McCone, "Meeting with Secretary Rusk—21 June 1963—re Cuba," 24 June 1963, both in *FRUS* 1961–63, 11:842–44, 844–45.

139. Attwood, "Memorandum on Cuba," 18 September 1963, Folder "Cuba Subjects William Atwood [*sic*] 9/63–11/63," Box 45, NSFK.

140. Chase, Memorandum for Mr. Bundy, "Approach to Castro," 19 November 1963, Folder "Chron. File 8/63–12/63 (Folder 2 of 4)," Box 1, Chase Papers. For the most complete recounting of Attwood's effort to negotiate with Cuba, see Attwood to Gordon Chase, 8 November

1963, Folder "Cuba Subjects William Atwood [*sic*] 9/63–11/63," Box 45, NSFK. For a useful collection of documents with a valuable introduction, see "Kennedy and Castro: The Secret Quest for Accommodation," NSA Electronic Briefing Book 17, 16 August 1999, which contains Attwood's 1975 testimony to a Senate committee. For a key Cuban perspective on the Attwood/Lechuga/Howard talks, which places much of the initiative on the U.S. side and downplays the role of Lisa Howard, see Carlos Lechuga, *In the Eye of the Storm: Castro, Khrushchev, Kennedy, and the Missile Crisis* (Melbourne, Australia: Ocean, 1995), chap. 10, 195–211.

141. David Halberstam, *The Best and the Brightest* (New York: Penguin, 1983), 20; JFK Press Conferences, 6 March, 17 July 1963, *PPP*, 243, 571. JFK's final public use of the word "Cuba" occurred on 18 November, when he warned a Miami audience, "We in this hemisphere must also use every resource in our command to prevent the establishment of another Cuba in this hemisphere" (*PPP*, 872–77). For Kennedy's discomfort with his party's liberals, see esp. Chester Bowles's telling vignette about the 1960 campaign: "On almost every occasion he was uneasy and occasionally contentious, as though uncomfortable with the demand put upon him to demonstrate his liberal credentials by a show of emotional commitment to liberalism, a commitment he did not possess" (Chester Bowles, *Promises to Keep: My Years in Public Life, 1941–1969* [New York: Harper and Row, 1971], 444).

Chapter 8

1. McCone, Memoranda of Conversations, 28, 30 November 1963, *FRUS* 1961–63, 11:896.

2. Chase, "Memorandum for Mr. Bundy," 2 December 1963, Folder "Chron. File 8/63–12/63," Box 1, Gordon Chase Papers, JFKL. LBJ's schedule for 2 December 1963 shows, "6:00 P.M. Cuba—Cabinet Room (Mr. Bundy)" (Folder "Appointment File [Diary Backup] December 2, 1963," Box 2, President's Appointment File [Diary Backup] 12/1/63–12/30/63, LBJL). Neither the *FRUS* editors nor the LBJ Library's archivists have uncovered the minutes of this meeting. See *FRUS* 1961–63, 11:898.

3. Chase, "U.S. Policy towards Cuba," 2 December 1963, Folder "Chron. File 8/63–12/63," Box 1, Chase Papers; Edwin Martin to Rusk, "Your Meeting with the President on Cuba," with attached "Talking Points on Cuba," 2 December 1963, *FRUS* 1961–63, vols. 10–12, microfiche supplement, document 721; Chester Cooper to John McCone, "Considerations for U.S. Policy toward Cuba and Latin America," 1 December 1963, Folder "Intelligence Volume I, 11/63–11/64," Box 24, NSFJ, CF, Cuba.

Martin's briefing notes were upbeat: "Our present program has had success in creating new, or aggravating existing, vulnerabilities in Castro's domestic and international situation . . . although covert program has not had sufficient time to demonstrate the capability to exploit latent internal opposition." The CIA recommendation also included continual offshore U.S. military maneuvers to "cause frequent Cuban military alerts and constant movement of Cuban forces throughout the island." To deny Castro a natural ally, the CIA also recommended a continuation of "the current policy of collaborating with the United Kingdom to bring about the downfall of the Cheddi Jagan government in British Guinea [*sic*]."

4. Telephone Conversation, 2 December 1963, Folder "December 1963 [1 of 3] Chrono File," Box 1, Recordings and Transcripts of Telephone Conversations and Meetings, JFK

Series, LBJL. The library's typescript of this conversation is edited, but the voice copy is complete, as is the transcript in *Taking Charge: The Johnson White House Tapes, 1963–1964*, ed. Michael R. Beschloss (New York: Simon and Schuster, 1997), 87.

5. CIA, "Cuba—A Status Report," 12 December 1963, *FRUS* 1961–63, vols. 10–12, microfiche supplement, document 725.

The Standing Group of the National Security Council was a successor to the executive committee established during the missile crisis, and its members included Attorney General Robert Kennedy, Secretary of Defense Robert McNamara, CIA Director John McCone, national security adviser McGeorge Bundy, and presidential counselor Theodore Sorensen.

6. Johnson administration officials regularly cited the March 1963 Justice and State statements of a cutoff as if it had been complete. In response to one critic in 1967, for example, the State Department said that "since March 1963 we have made a concerted effort to prevent hit-and-run raids against Cuba from US territory by Cuban exile groups" (DOS, "The Facts Pertaining to Paul Bethel's Charges Concerning Cuba," 8 March 1967, DDRS). Crimmins's expanded list is "Possible Further Unilateral and Bilateral Actions to Increase Pressure on Cuba (Short of Use of Force)," [before 12 December 1963], *FRUS* 1961–63, vols. 10–12, microfiche supplement, document 727.

7. *FRUS* 1961–63, 11:901–2.

8. The options memorandum is "Meeting on Cuba—December 19, 1963," 15 December 1963, Folder "Chron. File 8/63–12/63," Box 1, Chase Papers; see also Gordon Chase, "Memorandum for Mr. Bundy," 18 December 1963, Folder "Chron. File 8/63–12/63," Box 1, Chase Papers. In addition to Chase's detailed notes (*FRUS* 1961–63, 11:904–9), one page of minutes was taken by acting CIA director Marshall Carter and a more detailed set was taken by Desmond FitzGerald, who was chief of the CIA's Special Affairs staff, which had responsibility for the CIA's sabotage operations ("Memorandum for the Record: Meeting with the President on Cuba at 1100 on 19 December 1963," "Meeting at the White House 19 December 1963," both in *FRUS* 1961–63, vols. 10–12, microfiche supplement, document 733; see also Earle G. Wheeler, "Meeting with President on Cuba, 1100 hrs. 19 Dec 1963," Folder 27, Box 6, Joseph Califano Papers, National Archives and Records Administration, Washington, D.C.).

9. Chase, "Memorandum of Meeting with President Johnson. Subject: Cuba," 19 December 1963, *FRUS* 1961–63, 11:904–9.

10. "Meeting on Cuba—December 19, 1963," 15 December 1963, Folder "Chron. File 8/63–12/63," Box 1, Chase Papers.

11. As vice president, Johnson had argued, "We would be irresponsible if we did not act against the raiders who were carrying out irresponsible actions that could result in getting us involved in a war"; however, he did not oppose the CIA-controlled sabotage that was occurring at the same time ("Summary Record of the 42d Meeting of the Executive Committee of the National Security Council," 29 March 1963, *FRUS* 1961–63, 11:742).

12. On the CIA's financial support of exile leaders, which ended only in 1978, see CIA general counsel Anthony A. Lapham to Robert J. Lipshutz, Counsel to the President, 30 September 1978, Folder "Cubans, 3/77–10/78," Box 12, Staff Office Files, Counsel—Lipshutz, JCL, which also contains documents describing the extent and methods of CIA payments. On the estimated four hundred exile groups, see "Memorandum for the National Security Council

Standing Group, Annex 7, Exile Problems," [April 1963], Folder "Cuba General, Standing Committee [*sic*] 4/63," Box 38, NSFK; Peter Kornbluh, ed., *Bay of Pigs Declassified: The Secret CIA Report on the Invasion of Cuba* (New York: New Press, 1998), 216.

13. Harry McPherson Oral History, 24 March 1969, interview 4, tape 1, 1, LBJL.

14. Bundy to President, "Sabotage against Cuba," 9 January 1964, *FRUS* 1964–68, 32:547–48.

15. Telephone Conversation, LBJ and Sen. Richard Russell, 11 February 1964, *FRUS* 1964–68, 32:580–83; Telephone Conversation, LBJ and Richard Russell, 7 February 1964, Recordings of Telephone Conversations, White House Series, WH6402.09, PNO 1932, LBJL.

16. One desalinization plant was in operation by August, and two more were on line by the end of the year. There had been 3,244 Cubans employed on the U.S. base in late 1962; that number had dropped slowly in 1963, reaching 2,257 at the beginning of the fishing boat incident in February 1964. Six months later, the number had dropped to 753; by October 1965 it had dropped to 550, with most of the replacements coming from nearby Jamaica. See McNamara to President, "Guantanamo Base," 28 August 1964, Folder "Guantanamo Volume I General 2/64–2/64," Box 23, NSFJ, CF, Cuba; G. H. Decker, Memorandum for President, "Cuban Work Force Employed at Naval Base, Guantanamo," 6 September 1962, in *The Cuban Missile Crisis, 1962: A National Security Archive Document Set*, ed. Laurence Chang (Alexandria, Va.: Chadwyck-Healey, 1990), document 364; "Guantanamo Water Crisis," n.d., Folder "Notes on Foreign Policy Issues," Box 105, Office Files of Bill Moyers, LBJL; Bromley Smith to President, "Memorandum of Conference with the President, February 7, 1964, 9:00 A.M.—Subject Cuba," Bromley Smith to President, "Memorandum of Conference with the President, February 7, 1964, 4:45 P.M.—Subject Cuba," Folder "Meetings with the President on Cuba," Box 1, NSFJ, Files of Bromley K. Smith; Chase to Bundy, "Cuban Fishermen," 15, 19 February 1964, Folder "Guantanamo Water Crisis/Cuban Fishing Boats 2/64 [2 of 3]," Box 23, NSFJ, CF, Cuba. Most of the documents on this incident are in five folders in Box 3, NSC Histories, Guantanamo Water Crisis, February 1964, LBJL.

17. John Crimmins Oral History, 10 May 1989, Foreign Affairs Oral History Project, Association for Diplomatic Studies and Training, Arlington, Virginia.

18. Maxwell Taylor, Chair, Joint Chiefs of Staff, to President, "Possible Actions against the Castro Government," 21 March 1964, *FRUS* 1964–88, 32:618–19.

19. "Disband, as discreetly as possible, [redacted] sabotage raiding apparatus in Florida [redacted] keep on the shelf [redacted] capacity to sabotage Cuban merchant ships calling at foreign ports." Chase, "U.S. Policy towards Cuba April to November 1964," 22 March 1964, attached to Chase, "Cuban Policy—April to November, 1964," 23 March 1964, both in Folder "Cuba U.S. Policy Volume II, 12/63–7/65," Box 29, NSFJ, CF, Cuba.

20. "Review of Current Program of Covert Action against Cuba," [January–February 1964], *FRUS* 1964–68, 32:550–61; on the authorship, see 550n.

21. [Gordon Chase?], "Memorandum for Discussion of Covert Program against Cuba," 7 April 1964, Folder "Intelligence Covert Program 1/64–6/65," Box 24, NSFJ, CF, Cuba. See also Desmond FitzGerald, "Meeting at the White House 7 April 1964, Subject—Review of Covert Program Directed against Cuba," 7 April 1974, *FRUS* 1964–68, 32:626–29.

22. Chase to Bundy, "Cuban Covert Program," 7 April 1964, Folder "Intelligence Covert Program 1/64–6/65," Box 24, NSFJ, CF, Cuba. Chase wanted to maintain the exile sabotage capability, but "if we cannot keep it on the shelf, then I favor its elimination."

23. CIA, "Meeting at the White House 7 April 1964: Subject—Review of Covert Program Directed against Cuba," 7 April 1964, *FRUS* 1964–68, 32:626–29.

24. U.S. Senate, Select Committee to Study Governmental Operations with Respect to Intelligence Activities, *Alleged Assassination Plots Involving Foreign Leaders: An Interim Report*, 94th Cong., 1st sess., 20 November 1975, 137 (emphasis added); CIA, "Meeting at the White House 7 April 1964: Subject—Review of Covert Program Directed against Cuba," 7 April 1964, *FRUS* 1964–68, 32:626–29.

25. Chase to Bundy, "Cuba," 8 June 1964, Folder "Cuba Overflights Volume I 1/64–1-65," Box 29, NSFJ, CF, Cuba.

26. CINCLANT to Ruekda, Joint Chiefs of Staff, 15 September 1964, Embassy of Czechoslovakia to Secretary of State Dean Rusk, 20 June 1964, Rusk to Ambassador of Czechoslovakia, June 1964, all in Folder "Cuba Exile Activities [1 of 2], Volume III, 1964–1965," Box 22, NSFJ, Cuba.

27. DOS, "Memorandum to Members of the 303 Committee," 1 March 1965, DDRS. On RECE, see María Cristina García, *Havana USA: Cuban Exiles and Cuban Americans in South Florida, 1959–1994* (Berkeley: University of California Press, 1996), 136–37.

28. Bundy to President, "Covert Action against Cuba," 26 June 1965, *FRUS* 1964–65, 32:718–19.

29. Raborn, 19 July 1965, in U.S. Congress, Senate, Committee on Foreign Relations, *Executive Sessions of the Senate Foreign Relations Committee, Together with Joint Sessions with the Senate Armed Services Committee (Historical Series)*, vol. 17, 89th Cong., 1st sess., 1965, 932; Bundy to President, "Covert Action against Cuba," 26 June 1965, *FRUS* 1964–68, 32:718.

30. Coordinator of Cuban Affairs [John Crimmins], "Summary Statement of U.S. Policy toward Cuba," [June 1965], Folder "Cuba U.S. Policy Volume II, 12/63–7/65," Box 29, NSFJ, CF, Cuba. For Bundy's opposition to Raborn's proposal, see Bundy to President, "Covert Action against Cuba," 26 June 1965, *FRUS* 1964–68, 32:718–19.

31. Crimmins Oral History; Harvey Summ Interview, 25 March 1982, PC. Summ led the State Department's Miami office from February 1963 to April 1965.

32. Presidential Directive/NSC-6, 15 March 1977, JCL; Chase, "Memorandum for Mr. Bundy," 19 June 1964, Folder "Chron. File 4/1/64–6/19/64," Box 2, Chase Papers (emphasis added). For the flawed memories, see the CIA's Samuel Halpern's comment that "we finally got sabotage stopped completely in April of 1964," and the CIA's Theodore Shackley's comment that "in April 1964, President Johnson put a stop to boom-and-bang operations against Cuba." James G. Blight and Peter Kornbluh, *Politics of Illusion: The Bay of Pigs Invasion Reexamined* (Boulder, Colo.: Rienner, 1998), 117; Ted Shackley with Richard A. Finney, *Spymaster: My Life in the CIA* (Dulles, Va.: Potomac, 2005), 76; Senator Thomas J. Dodd, "Vietnam and Latin America: The Danger of a Hemispheric Vietnam," Speech to the National Convention of the American Legion, 25 August 1965, reprinted in *Vital Speeches* 31 (15 September 1965): 706–9.

33. Ray Cline Oral History, 31 May 1983, in *Cuban Missile Crisis, 1962: A National Security Archive Document Set*, ed. Chang, document 3309.

34. Desmond FitzGerald to Joseph Burkholder Smith, in Smith, *Portrait of a Cold Warrior* (New York: Putnam's, 1976), 384; Cline Oral History. Summ agreed: "After Kennedy's assassination, late 1963 on, the whole Cuban issue was off front and center as Johnson increasingly

became involved in Vietnam" (Harvey Summ Oral History, 5 March 1993, Foreign Affairs Oral History Project, Association for Diplomatic Studies and Training, Arlington, Virginia).

35. Lisa Howard, "Castro's Overture," *War and Peace Report*, September 1963, 3. State Department officials worried about the impact of Howard's reporting and tried to convince the White House to ask ABC not to air her program: "This interview would strengthen the arguments of 'peace' groups, 'liberal' thinkers, Commies, fellow travelers, and opportunist political opponents" (William Brubeck to McGeorge Bundy, "Memorandum: Lisa Howard's Interview with Fidel Castro," 8 May 1963, Folder "Contacts with Cuban Leaders [2 of 2] 5/63–4/65," Box 21, NSFJ, CF, Cuba).

36. Chase, "Some Arguments against Accommodation—A Rebuttal," attached to "Memorandum for Mr. Bundy. Subject: Cuba," 12 November 1963, Folder "Cuba General 11/10/63–11/12/63," Box 39A, National Security Files, JFKL.

37. Chase to Bundy, 25 November, 2 December 1963, *FRUS* 1961–63, 11:890, 897. A week later, Chase was still trying to obtain an answer on whether to call (Chase to Bundy, "Cuba-Standing Group Meeting," 9 December 1963, Folder "Meetings 12/63–3/65," Box 24, NSFJ, CF, Cuba).

38. Chase to Bundy, 3 December 1963, *FRUS* 1961–63, 11:899. NSC executive secretary Bromley Smith had tried to nix negotiations in a mid-December meeting with LBJ and aide Bill Moyers: "I recommended that . . . any contact between Attwood and Castro representative should be avoided" (Bromley Smith, "Memorandum for the Record," [after 13 December 1963], Chase, "Memorandum of Meeting with President Johnson. Subject: Cuba," 19 December 1963, both in *FRUS* 1961–63, 11:902, 907–8).

39. Chase to Bundy, 20 December 1963, *FRUS* 1961–63, 11:908n; Moyers and Walter Jenkins, Telephone Conversation with President, 8 February 1964, in *Taking Charge*, ed. Beschloss, 234. Moyers's message indicates that his hard-line position reflected the influence of Attorney General Robert Kennedy.

40. Lisa Howard, undated summary of message from Fidel Castro, 12 February 1964, *FRUS* 1964–68, 32:592–93.

41. Chase to Bromley Smith, "Memorandum for BKS. Subject: Attwood Activities," 22 January 1964, Chase, "Memorandum for the Record, Subject: Bill Attwood Activities," 24 January 1964, both in Folder "Cuba Contacts with Cuban Leaders [1 of 2] 5/63–4/65," Box 21, NSFJ, CF, Cuba.

42. Chase, "U.S. Policy towards Cuba April to November 1964," 22 March 1964, attached to Chase, "Cuban Policy—April to November, 1964," 23 March 1964, Folder "Cuba U.S. Policy Volume II, 12/63–7/65," Box 29, NSFJ, CF, Cuba.

43. Chase to Sorensen, "Cuba and the Republicans," 26 April 1963, "Analysis of a Series of Public Statements on Cuba, 1959–1960," both in Folder "Cuba—General, Review of Eisenhower Administration Statements on Cuba, March 1963–April 1963," Box 38, NSFK, Cuba; Chase to Bundy, "Plank/Chase Cuban Project," 22 January 1964, enclosing "U.S./Cuban Relations—January 2, 1959 to January 3, 1961," Folder "Plank/Chase Report on U.S.-Cuban Relations, 1959–60," Box 4, NSFJ, Files of Gordon Chase. Part 4 of the report is titled "Republican Performance: A Political Annex."

44. *Congressional Record*, 25 March 1964, 6231. Asked about Fulbright's comments at his next press conference, Secretary Rusk said, "I would not agree. I think that Castro is more

than a nuisance. He is a threat to this hemisphere." Rusk was vague when a reporter followed up by inquiring, "Are we as a government still committed to bringing down Castro?" (*DOSB*, 13 April 1964, 570, 574). On the complications posed by Fulbright's speech, see Chase to Bundy, 25 March 1964, Folder "Contacts with Cuban Leaders [2 of 2] 5/63–4/65," Box 21, NSFJ, CF, Cuba.

45. *NYT*, 6 July 1964, 1; Chase to Bundy, "After November 3—Cuba," 7 October 1964, Folder "Chase, G.," Name File, NSFJ; INR to Acting Secretary, "Castro Proposes U.S.-Cuban Rapprochement," 6 July 1964, DDRS.

46. Chase to Bundy, "Cuba—Miscellaneous," 10 November 1964, *FRUS* 1964-68, 32:289–92.

47. Bundy Memorandum of Conversation with President, 19 February 1964, *FRUS* 1964–68, 31:11; Mann Telephone Conversation with President, 11 June 1964, Rusk to Bundy, 30 August 1965, both in *FRUS* 1964-68, 32:659, 727; CIA, Directorate of Intelligence, "Castro's Cuba Today," 30 September 1966, FOIA; Shackley with Finney, *Spymaster*, 76. Hints of Castro's interest in accommodation continued to arise from time to time during the Johnson administration; all received a cool U.S. response. See, for example, Rostow to President, "U.S.-Cuban Relations," 22 December 1967, *FRUS* 1964-68, 32:748–49.

48. Acting CIA Director Marshall Carter, "Memorandum for the Record: Meeting with the President on Cuba at 1100 on 19 December 1963," Desmond FitzGerald, "Meeting at the White House 19 December 1963," both in *FRUS* 1961-63, vols. 10–12, microfiche supplement, document 733; Earle G. Wheeler, "Meeting with President on Cuba, 1100 hrs. 19 Dec 1963," Folder 27, Box 6, Califano Papers. The next day's NSAM instructed the State Department to produce a study of trade between the West and Cuba, detailing the commodities and the principal firms involved, the steps that had been taken so far to stop the trade, and recommendations for further action (NSAM 274, "Cuba-Economic Denial Program," 20 December 1963, Folder "Cuba-Economic Denial Program," Box 2, NSFJ, National Security Action Memorandums).

49. U.S. Congress, Senate, Committee on Foreign Relations, *Executive Sessions*, 17:512, 803, 808, 894–95, 968.

50. *DOSB*, 16 December 1963, 913; for Venezuela's charges, see *FRUS* 1961-63, 12:352–54; on this early Caribbean filibustering, see *FRUS* 1958–60, 5:324–26, 346, 418, 453–54; Jorge I. Domínguez, *To Make a World Safe for Revolution: Cuba's Foreign Policy* (Cambridge: Harvard University Press, 1989), 117.

51. Mann, 18 February 1960, in U.S. Congress, Senate, Committee on Foreign Relations, *Executive Sessions*, vol. 12., 86th Cong., 2nd sess., 1960, 154; Department of Defense, "General Pressures to Create a Contingency," 11 March 1963, Folder 9, Box 6, Califano Papers; Telephone Conversation, LBJ and Richard Russell, 7 February 1964, Recordings of Telephone Conversations, White House Series, WH6402.09, PNO 1932, LBJL; U.S. Congress, Senate, Committee on Foreign Relations, *Executive Sessions*, 17:967, 1052 (Hickenlooper).

52. Roa to OAS, 3 February 1964, in *The Blockade: A Documentary History*, ed. Paul Hoeffel and Sandra Levinson (New York: Center for Cuban Studies, 1979), 29.

53. Rusk Speech, 22 July 1964, *DOSB*, 10 August 1964, 174–79.

54. "Summary Record on National Security Council Meeting No. 536, July 28, 1964," Folder "NSC Meetings, Vol. 2, Tab 9, 7/28/64," NSFJ, NSC Meetings File. See also INR to Sec-

retary of State, "The Significance of the July 1964 OAS Foreign Ministers Meeting," 14 September 1964, DDRS. The text of the resolutions, the votes, and the explanatory statements by Chile and Mexico are reprinted in *DOSB*, 10 August 1964, 179–84. Many OAS governments had already severed relations with Cuba—the first had been Trujillo's Dominican Republic (June 1959), followed almost immediately by Duvalier's Haiti (August 1959). In 1960, Guatemala, Nicaragua, Paraguay, and Peru broke relations. On Mexico, see Kate Doyle, *Double-Dealing: Mexico's Foreign Policy toward Cuba*, National Security Archive Electronic Briefing Book (Washington, D.C.: NSA, 2003).

55. Chase to Bundy, "U.S. Policy towards Cuba," 2 December 1963, Folder "Chron. File 8/63–12/63," Box 1, Chase Papers; DOS, "The Department of State during the Administration of President Lyndon B. Johnson, November 1963–January 1969," vol. 1, Administrative History, chap. 6, Western Hemisphere Security, n.d., 15–16, Folder "Chapter 6 (Inter-American Relations): Section A," Administrative History of the Department of State, LBJL.

56. Chase to Bundy, "Caribbean—Miscellaneous," 6 April 1964, Folder "Cuba Memos re. 'Cuba Miscellaneous' 11/63–6/6," Box 20, NSFJ, CF, Cuba. For the U.S. brief against Cuba's behavior in the IMF, see Rusk to U.S. Embassy, Paris, 3 March 1964, Folder "Cuba Cables Volume II 3/64–5/64," Box 16, NSFJ, CF, Cuba; Robert V. Roosa to President, 3 April 1964, Folder "IT24 International Monetary Fund," Box 5, WHCF, International Organizations (IT), LBJL, which indicates that Cuba withdrew 2 April, just before a 5 April meeting of the IMF board that would have declared Cuba ineligible to use the fund.

57. For this pre-missile-crisis effort, see U.S. Department of Commerce, Maritime Administration, "Free World Shipping in the Cuban Trade (January 1 through August 31, 1962)," 2 October 1962, in *The Cuban Missile Crisis, 1962: A National Security Archive Document Set*, ed. Chang, document 484.

58. NSAM 220, "U.S. Government Shipments by Foreign Flag Vessels in the Cuban Trade," 5 February 1963, Box 1, NSFJ, National Security Action Memorandums.

59. CIA, "Additional Actions against Cuba," 28 May 1963, *FRUS* 1961–63, vols. 10–12, microfiche supplement, document 675. The CIA assumed an additional task of preparing monthly reports, "Shipping to Cuba during [month and year]." For a sampling, see Folder "Cuba (Codeword) Shipping 1964," Box 35, NSFJ, CF, Cuba. For a hint of the exceptional effort to track Cuban shipping, see Franklin D. Roosevelt Jr. to President, 12 July 1963, enclosing "List of Free World and Polish Flag Vessels Arriving in Cuba since January 1, 1963," Folder "Cuba General 4/63–11/63," Box 115, POF.

60. Chase, "Memorandum for the President: Meeting on Cuba—December 19, 1963," 15 December 1963, Folder "Chron. File 8/63–12/63," Box 1, Chase Papers.

61. Colonel Burris to Vice President, "Appeal to NATO Allies on Cuba," 3 October 1962, Folder "Memos to the Vice President from Col. Burris, July 1962–April 1965 [2 of 2]," Box 6, Vice Presidential Security File, LBJL; CIA Intelligence Brief, "Shipping to Cuba during December 1964," DDRS. Colonel Howard Burris was the vice president's military aide.

62. Memcon, Dean Rusk, Edwin M. Martin, et al., "Cuban Developments; Possible Informal Meeting of Foreign Ministers," 5 September 1962, in *Cuban Missile Crisis, 1962: A National Security Archive Document Set*, ed. Chang, document 349.

63. Chase, "Memorandum of Meeting with President Johnson, Subject: Cuba," 19 December 1963, *FRUS* 1961–63, 11:908 (Bundy), 905 (Crimmins); DIA to McNamara, 8 October 1963,

FRUS 1961–63, 11:874. Section 301(e)(1)(B) of the Foreign Assistance Act of 1963 (PL 88-205, 77 *Stat.* 379, 16 December 1963) added the ban to Section 620 of the Foreign Assistance Act of 1961.

64. DOS, "Background Paper: Shipping Services to Cuba," 17 July 1964, DDRS; DOS, "The Department of State during the Administration of President Lyndon B. Johnson, November 1963–January 1969, Volume I, Administrative History, Chapter 6, Western Hemisphere Security," n.d., 22–23, Folder "Chapter 6 (Inter-American Relations): Section A," Administrative History of the Department of State, LBJL. On the Lebanese backsliding, see CIA Intelligence Report, "Weekly Cuban Summary," 17 February 1965, Folder "Cuba CIA Daily and Weekly Summaries, Volume II, 2/65–5/65," Box 36, NSFJ, CF, Cuba.

65. NSC Meeting, 5 May 1962, *FRUS* 1961–63, 10:488; Colonel Burris to Vice President, "U.S. Proposals on Cuba to NATO," 28 June 1962, Folder "Memos to the Vice President from Colonel Burris, Jan. 1961–June 1962 [1 of 2]," Box 5, Vice Presidential Security File, LBJL; Standing Group Meeting, 1 October 1963, *FRUS* 1961–63, 11:872; CIA, "Cuba—A Status Report," 12 December 1963, *FRUS* 1961–63, vols. 10–12, microfiche supplement, document 725; CIA, "Memorandum for the Record: Meeting with the President on Cuba at 1100 on 19 December 1963," *FRUS* 1961–63, vols. 10–12, microfiche supplement, document 733; Chase, "Memorandum of Meeting with President Johnson. Subject: Cuba," 19 January 1963, *FRUS* 1961–63, 11:904–9.

66. "Memorandum for the Record," 13 February 1964, Folder "United Kingdom Meetings with Wilson 3/2/64," Box 213, NSFJ, CF, Europe and USSR, United Kingdom; DOS, "Tour d'Horizon with Harold Wilson, Leader of British Labor Policy," 2 March 1964, Folder "United Kingdom Meetings with Wilson 3/2/64," Box 213, NSFJ, CF, Europe and USSR, United Kingdom. For Cuba's long relationship with Leyland, see George Lambie, "Anglo-Cuban Commercial Relations in the 1960s: A Case Study of the Leyland Motor Company Contracts with Cuba," in *The Fractured Blockade: West European–Cuban Relations during the Revolution*, ed. Alistair Hennessy and George Lambie (London: Macmillan, 1993), 163–96.

67. George Ball, "Principles of Our Policy toward Cuba," Speech, 23 April 1964, in *DOSB*, 11 May 1964, 742–43; Bundy to President, "JCS Views on Cuba," 17 April 1964, Folder "Cuba U.S. Policy Volume II, 12/63–7/65," Box 29, NSFJ, CF, Cuba; Rusk, Statement to the Senate Committee on Foreign Relations, 13 March 1964, *DOSB*, 30 March 1964, 30.

68. LBJ recounted this version of what he had told Butler in a telephone conversation with J. William Fulbright, 29 April 1964, Folder "April 1964 [3 of 3] Chrono File," Box 4, Recordings and Transcripts of Telephone Conversations and Meetings, WH Series, LBJL.

69. DOS, "The Department of State during the Administration of President Lyndon B. Johnson, November 1963–January 1969, Volume I, Administrative History, Chapter 6, Western Hemisphere Security," n.d., 12, Folder "Chapter 6 (Inter-American Relations): Section A," Administrative History of the Department of State, LBJL; U.S. Embassy Paris to DOS, "French Credits for Cuba," 5 August 1964, Folder "Cuba Cables Volume III, 6/64–8/64," Box 16, NSFJ, CF, Cuba; George Ball, "Principles of Our Policy toward Cuba," Speech, 23 April 1964, in *DOSB*, 11 May 1964, 741. The October 1963 wheat deal had gone through over LBJ's opposition: "The Vice President thinks that this is the worst foreign policy mistake we have made in this administration" (Arthur M. Schlesinger Jr., *Robert Kennedy and His Times* [Boston: Houghton Mifflin, 1978], 597).

70. *NYT*, 19 February 1964, 1, 2. Section 301(e)(1)(B) of the Foreign Assistance Act of 1963

added Section 620(a)(3) to the Foreign Assistance Act of 1961 and did not allow a presidential waiver. Senator Fulbright noted that "what we terminated with respect to Britain and France, in fact, can hardly be called aid; it was more of a sale promotion program under which British and French military leaders were brought to the United States to see—and to buy—advanced American weapons" (*Congressional Record*, 25 March 1964, 6230).

71. Chase, "Memorandum of Meeting with President Johnson. Subject: Cuba," 19 January 1963, *FRUS* 1961–63, 11:904–9; Domínguez, *To Make a World*, 188–89.

72. Chase to Bundy, "Caribbean and Other," 2 March 1965, Folder "Cuba Memos re. 'Cuba Miscellaneous' 11/63–6/65," Box 20, NSFJ, CF, Cuba; DOS, "The Department of State during the Administration of President Lyndon B. Johnson, November 1963–January 1969, Volume I, Administrative History, Chapter 6, Western Hemisphere Security," n.d., 18, Folder "Chapter 6 (Inter-American Relations): Section A," Administrative History of the Department of State, LBJL. For a summary of Spanish-Cuban relations at the time, see George Lambie, *The Blockade on Cuba: West European–Cuban Relations during the Revolution*, Working Paper of the Caribbean Institute and Study Center for Latin America (Río Piedras: Inter-American University of Puerto Rico, 1995), 11–16.

73. Bowdler to Rostow, "European Trade with Cuba," 26 September 1966, Folder "Cuba [W. G. Bowdler File] Vol. II [2 of 2]," NSFJ, CF, Cuba.

74. Bowdler to Rostow, "Memo for Walt Rostow," 17 November 1966, Folder "Cuba [W. G. Bowdler File] Vol. II [1 of 2]," NSFJ, CF, Cuba; DOS to U.S. Embassy Paris, "ECONAD Agenda Nov. 17," 16 November 1966, Folder "Cuba [W.G. Bowdler File] Vol. II [1 of 2]," NSFJ, CF, Cuba; U.S. Embassy Paris to DOS, "British Fertilizer Plant for Cuba," 15 December 1966, Folder "France Cables Vol. X, 10/66–1/67," Box 173, NSFJ, CF, France; DOS, "The Department of State during the Administration of President Lyndon B. Johnson, November 1963–January 1969, Volume I, Administrative History, Chapter 6, Western Hemisphere Security," n.d., 26, Folder "Chapter 6 (Inter-American Relations): Section A," Administrative History of the Department of State, LBJL.

75. CIA Intelligence Report, "Weekly Cuban Summary," 24 February 1965, Folder "Cuba CIA Daily and Weekly Summaries volume II 2/65–5/65," Box 36, NSFJ, CF, Cuba.

76. DOS, "The Department of State during the Administration of President Lyndon B. Johnson, November 1963–January 1969, Volume I, Administrative History, Chapter 6, Western Hemisphere Security," n.d., 19–20, Folder "Chapter 6 (Inter-American Relations): Section A," Administrative History of the Department of State, LBJL. The Italian cutoff came in June 1968; a similar prohibition on Czech imports containing Cuban nickel occurred in November 1969.

77. J. H. A. Watson, British Embassy in Cuba, to Michael Stewart, Foreign Office, 17 May 1966, Folder "Cuba [W. G. Bowdler File] Vol. II [2 of 2]," NSFJ, CF, Cuba.

78. DOS, "The Department of State during the Administration of President Lyndon B. Johnson, November 1963–January 1969, Volume I, Administrative History, Chapter 6, Western Hemisphere Security," n.d., 24–25, Folder "Chapter 6 (Inter-American Relations): Section A," Administrative History of the Department of State, LBJL; CIA Current Intelligence Weekly Special Report, "Castro's Cuba Today," 30 September 1966, Folder "Cuba [W. G. Bowdler File] Vol. II [1 of 2]," NSFJ, CF, Cuba; see also CIA, "Key Issues and Prospects for Castro's Cuba," NIE 85-67, 2 March 1967, Folder "85, Cuba," Box 9, NSFJ, National Intelligence Estimates. An edited version appears in *FRUS* 1964–68, 32:736–37.

79. Kirk H. Porter and Donald Bruce Johnson, comps., *National Party Platforms 1840–1964* (Urbana: University of Illinois Press, 1966), 688–89.

80. Arthur M. Schlesinger Jr. Oral History, 4 November 1971, LBJL.

81. Crimmins to Mann, "US-UK-Canadian Talks on Cuba," 15 March 1965, *FRUS* 1964–68, 32:709–10; U.S. Congress, Senate, Committee on Foreign Relations, *Executive Sessions*, 17:835, 893.

82. *NYT*, 17 November 1965, 1, 14, 15. Rusk was in South America to attend an OAS foreign ministers' meeting in Rio and had taken advantage of the trip to visit Argentina and Uruguay.

83. *Congressional Record*, 9 May 1966, 10090–107.

84. Speech, Havana, 28 September 1965. At the time, about eight hundred Cubans were leaving each month—three hundred through Mexico, three hundred through Spain, and two hundred in small boats. See Gordon Chase to Redmon, "Cuban Refugees in the United States," 9 April 1965, Folder "Cuba Refugees 10/63–1/65," Box 30, NSFJ, CF, Cuba.

85. 3 October 1965, *PPP*, 1039–40.

86. The 6 November 1965 agreement, a memorandum of understanding between the Embassy of Switzerland in Havana and the Foreign Ministry of Cuba, is 17 *UST* 1046, *TIAS* 6063, reprinted in *DOSB*, 29 November 1965, 850–53. For a description of the implementation procedures, see U.S. Congress, House, Committee on Foreign Affairs, Subcommittee on Inter-American Affairs, *Cuba and the Caribbean*, 91st Cong., 2nd sess., July–August 1970, 46–56; U.S. Congress, Senate, Committee on the Judiciary, Subcommittee to Investigate Problems Connected with Refugees and Escapees, *Cuban Refugee Problem*, 89th Cong., 2nd sess., March–April 1966, pt. 1, 4. For the Camarioca exodus, see Félix Roberto Masud-Piloto, *With Open Arms: Cuban Migration to the United States* (Totowa, N.J.: Rowman and Littlefield, 1988), 57–70.

87. NSC Action 2413, "U.S. Policy toward Cuba," 4 May 1961, *FRUS* 1961–63, 10:482–83. For a helpful analysis of this early immigration, see Research Institute for Cuba and the Caribbean, Center for Advanced International Studies, University of Miami, *The Cuban Immigration 1959–1966 and Its Impact on Miami–Dade County Florida*, Study for the Department of Health, Education and Welfare, Contract HEW WA-66-05 (Miami: University of Miami, 1967).

88. PL 89-732, 80 *Stat.* 1161, 2 November 1966, stipulated that any Cuban parolee who "has been physically present in the United States for at least one year, may be adjusted by the Attorney General, in his discretion and under such regulations as he may prescribe, to that of an alien lawfully admitted for permanent residence." For an especially clear explanation of the complex situation prior to the 1966 legislation, see Larry M. Eig, *Cuban Adjustment Act of 1966*, CRS Report 93-253A (Washington, D.C.: CRS, 1993).

89. Chase to Bundy, "Caribbean and Other," 2 March 1965, Folder "Cuba Memos re. 'Cuba Miscellaneous' 11/63–6-65," Box 20, NFS, CF, Cuba, LBJL.

90. Bowdler to Rostow, "Cuba," 18 December 1967, *FRUS* 1964–68, 32:747–48, slightly redacted to omit "Radio Americas on the Swan Islands"; for the more abridged original that nonetheless does not redact these six words, see Folder "Cuba [W. G. Bowdler File] Vol. II [2 of 2]," NSFJ, CF, Cuba; CIA, "Weekly Cuban Summary," 5 May 1965, DDRS; see also Harvey Summ Interview, 25 March 1982, PC. The Miami station was not completely closed until the early 1970s.

91. *DOSB*, 16 October 1967, 490–99; CIA Intelligence Information Cable, "Proof of Cuban Government Involvement in Landing of Guerrillas in Venezuela," 21 October 1966, Folder "Bowdler Memos [1 of 2]," Box 1, NSFJ, Name File; CIA, "Status of Insurgency in Venezuela," 5 April 1967, Folder "Guerilla [*sic*] Problem in Latin America," Box 2, NSFJ, Intelligence File; DOS to U.S. Embassies, "Cuba Policy," 5 January 1968, Folder "Cuba [W. G. Bowdler File] Vol. II [1 of 2]," NSFJ, CF, Cuba; *DOSB*, 7 March 1966, 383–85; U.S. Congress, Senate, Committee on the Judiciary, *The Tricontinental Conference of African, Asian and Latin American Peoples: A Staff Study*, 89th Cong., 2nd sess., 7 June 1966; DOS, "The Department of State during the Administration of President Lyndon B. Johnson, November 1963–January 1969, Volume I, Administrative History, Chapter 6, Western Hemisphere Security," n.d., 35–36, 53–57, Folder "Chapter 6 (Inter-American Relations): Section A," Administrative History of the Department of State, LBJL.

Chapter 9

1. Kirk H. Porter and Donald Bruce Johnson, comps., *National Party Platforms 1840–1972* (Urbana: University of Illinois Press, 1973), 723 (Democrats), 761–62 (Republicans).

2. Nelson A. Rockefeller, *The Rockefeller Report on the Americas: The Official Report of a United States Presidential Mission for the Western Hemisphere* (Chicago: Quadrangle, 1969), 15, 17, 34, 38. On Rockefeller and Latin America, see Darlene Rivas, *Missionary Capitalist: Nelson Rockefeller in Venezuela* (Chapel Hill: University of North Carolina Press, 2002); Gerard Colby with Charlotte Dennett, *Thy Will Be Done: The Conquest of the Amazon: Nelson Rockefeller and Evangelism in the Age of Oil* (New York: HarperCollins, 1976).

3. Rockefeller, *Rockefeller Report*, 60, 32; Richard Nixon, *Six Crises* (1962; New York: Simon and Schuster, 1990), 208–9; U.S. Congress, House, Committee on Foreign Affairs, Subcommittee on Inter-American Affairs, *Cuba and the Caribbean*, 91st Cong., 2nd sess., July–August 1970, 98–90.

4. U.S. Congress, Senate, Committee on Foreign Relations, *Shlaudeman Nomination*, 94th Cong., 2nd sess., May–June, 1976, 87; U.S. Congress, House, Committee on Foreign Affairs, Subcommittee on Inter-American Affairs, *Cuba and the Caribbean*, 99.

5. "Action for Progress in the Americas," Address before the Inter-American Press Association, Washington, D.C., 31 October 1969, *DOSB*, 17 November 1969, 409–14; on the use of the past tense to describe the alliance, see U.S. Congress, House, Committee on Foreign Affairs, Subcommittee on Inter-American Affairs, *Cuba and the Caribbean*, 26.

6. Robert A. Hurwitch, *Most of Myself: An Autobiography in the Form of Letters to His Daughters* (Santo Domingo, D.R.: Editora Corripio, 1990), 2:264–65.

7. NSSM 32, "Cuba," 2 July 1969, 16n, NSA. For the president's request for the study by the Departments of State and Defense and the CIA, see NSSM 32, 21 March 1969, NSA.

8. Memcon, "Latin America, Part III: Cuba," 27 September 1969, NSA. Parts I and II dealt with the report by Governor Nelson Rockefeller and a discussion of Panama treaty negotiations.

9. Secretary of State to All American Republic Diplomatic Posts, "U.S. Policy toward Cuba," 17 February 1970, NSA.

10. William Watts, "Wednesday Morning Operations Staff Meeting," 4 February 1970,

DDRS; Telephone Conversation, Undersecretary of State John Irwin and National Security Adviser Kissinger, 20 April 1971, DDRS.

11. Address to the Inter-American Press Association, 31 October 1969, *PPP*, 900. In 1969, Nixon referred twice to the missile crisis, but both were references to arms imbalances between the superpowers and had nothing to do with Cuba (*PPP* 1969, 248, 303). The "most comprehensive" remark to reporters, 18 February 1970, is *FRUS* 1969–76, 1:114, with the foreign policy report's introduction on 195–203 and the full report in *PPP* 1970, 116–90. For Nixon's 1970 comments, see Press Conference, 10 December 1970, *PPP* 1970, 1108, and references to the missile crisis, but in statements about East-West relations, not about Cuba (*PPP*, 409, 556). For comments in 1971, see *PPP*, 25 February 1971, 247, and a principal statement on Cuba in 1971 in response to a question from the American Society of Newspaper Editors (*PPP*, 16 April 1971, 544–45; see also 25 February 1971, 247).

12. Nixon to Haldeman, Ehrlichman, and Kissinger, 2 March 1970, *FRUS* 1969–76, 1:204–6.

13. Richard Nixon, *The Memoirs of Richard Nixon* (New York: Grosset and Dunlap, 1978), 203, 471; Richard Nixon, "Cuba, Castro and John F. Kennedy," *Reader's Digest*, November 1964, 283, 298.

14. Henry Kissinger, *Years of Renewal* (New York: Simon and Schuster, 1999), 771; for Rebozo, see Henry Kissinger, *White House Years* (Boston: Little, Brown, 1979), 641; Nixon, *Memoirs*, 220–21; Gerald S. Strober and Deborah H. Strober, *Nixon: An Oral History of His Presidency* (New York: HarperCollins, 1994), 45 (Butterfield), 39 (Kleindienst).

15. Strober and Strober, *Nixon*, 40.

16. Kissinger, *Years of Renewal*, 799.

17. U.S. Congress, House, Committee on International Relations, *Report of Secretary of State Kissinger on His Trip to Latin America*, 94th Cong., 2nd sess., 4 March 1976; see also U.S. Congress, House, Committee on International Relations, *Report of Secretary of State Kissinger on His Visits to Latin America, Western Europe, and Africa*, 94th Cong., 2nd sess., 17 June 1976, 3; DOS, Memcon, June 8, 1976, Santiago, Chile, DDRS. For the materials regarding Kissinger's meetings in Santiago, see Folder "Kissinger—Appointments, Talkers," Box 10, National Security Adviser, NSC Latin American Affairs Staff: Files, 1974–77, GRFL.

18. Nixon-Kissinger Telephone Conversation, 5 August 1970, DDRS; Haig to Kissinger, "Cuba, Items to Discuss with the President," 3 October 1971, Box 128, Henry A. Kissinger Series File, NSC Files, White House Special Files, Nixon Presidential Materials, National Archives and Records Administration, Washington, D.C.

19. Lansdale to Deputy Undersecretary of State for Political Affairs, "Cuba, Operation Mongoose," 28 January 1963, NSA. Hurwitch became special assistant for Cuban affairs in June 1962, but after the October missile crisis he was demoted to deputy coordinator of Cuban affairs at the same time Sterling Cottrell was named to the new position of coordinator of Cuban affairs. McGeorge Bundy told JFK that "Hurwitch has done a very able job within the Department, but he is a little junior for a major job of interdepartmental coordination" (Bundy to JFK, 4 January 1963, *FRUS* 1961–63, 11:649).

20. U.S. Congress, Senate, Committee on Foreign Relations, *United States Policy toward Cuba*, 92nd Cong., 1st sess., 16 September 1971, 18–19; Hurwitch, *Most of Myself*, 2:293.

21. Castro added, "The day will come when all nations will join in this homage to Lenin; the day will come when all states will join in this tribute to Lenin; the day will come when

the whole of humanity will join in praising Lenin. We do not have the smallest doubt of this" (Speech, Havana, 23 April 1970).

22. On the perception of Cuba's move toward support of urban insurgents, see U.S. Congress, House, Committee on Foreign Affairs, Subcommittee on Inter-American Affairs, *Cuba and the Caribbean*, 60, 66.

23. Speech, Havana, 27 November 1963; on the dislocations caused by the ten-million-ton quest, see CIA, Directorate of Intelligence, "Castro's Cuba Today," 30 September 1966, FOIA.

24. U.S. Congress, House, Committee on International Relations, Subcommittee on International Political and Military Affairs, *Soviet Activities in Cuba*, pts. 6 and 7, *Communist Influence in the Western Hemisphere*, 94th Cong., 2nd sess., 1976, 7 (October 1975), 103 (September 1976) (Defense Intelligence Agency). The five agreements were published in *Granma*, weekly English ed., 14 January 1973. The Soviet Union continued this aid through the Nixon-Ford years: see U.S. Congress, House, Committee on International Relations, Subcommittees on International Trade and Commerce and on International Organizations, *U.S. Trade Embargo of Cuba*, 94th Cong., 1st sess., 1975, 166; U.S. Congress, House, Committee on International Relations, Subcommittee on International Trade and Commerce, *United States–Cuba Trade Promotion*, 94th Cong., 2nd sess., 22 July 1976, 33.

25. Speech, Havana, 23 August 1968, reprinted in James G. Blight and Philip Brenner, *Sad and Luminous Days: Cuba's Struggle with the Superpowers after the Missile Crisis* (Lanham, Md.: Rowman and Littlefield, 2002), 215–45.

26. Castro Speech, Havana, 23 April 1970; Saul Landau Interview by Author, Chapel Hill, North Carolina, 6 November 2006.

27. "The Venceremos Brigade—Agrarians or Anarchists?" *Congressional Record*, 16 March 1970, 7462–67.

28. White House Situation Room to Kissinger, "Evening Notes," 16 December 1971, DDRS; U.S. Congress, House, Committee on Foreign Affairs, Subcommittee on Inter-American Affairs, *Cuba and the Caribbean*, 137; U.S. Congress, House, Committee on International Relations, Subcommittee on Inter-American Affairs, *Impact of Cuban-Soviet Ties in the Western Hemisphere*, 95th Cong., 2nd sess., March–April 1978, 119. For a chronology of the Cienfuegos dispute, see "U.S.-Soviet Understanding on Submarine Base in Cuba," Box 128, Henry A. Kissinger Series File, NSC Files, White House Special Files, Nixon Presidential Materials; Kissinger meeting with *Time* Magazine Correspondents, Washington, D.C., 9 December 1970, *FRUS* 1969–76, 1:289.

29. Sherman Kent, Office of National Estimates, to Director of Central Intelligence, "Memorandum: Cuba a Year Hence," 22 April 1963, *FRUS* 1961–63, vols. 10–12, microfiche supplement, document 665; Herbert Scoville Jr., "Missile Submarines and National Security," *Scientific American* 226 (June 1972): 24; Admiral Robinson to Kissinger, "Soviet Naval Activity in Cuba," 8 January 1971, in Folder "Cuba 2," Box 128, Henry A. Kissinger Series File, NSC Files, Nixon Presidential Materials; NSSM 144, "Soviet Naval Deployments in the Caribbean," 13 March 1972, Senior Review Group Meeting, "Cuba/USSR—Military Activity in Cienfuegos," 19 September 1970, both in NSA. For the navy, see U.S. Congress, House, Committee on International Relations, Subcommittee on Inter-American Affairs, *Arms Trade in the Western Hemisphere*, 95th Cong., 2nd sess., June–August 1978, 308, 531.

30. Kennedy to Khrushchev, 27 October 1962, *PPP*, 814, *DOSB*, 12 November 1962, 743;

Press Conference, 20 November 1962, *PPP*, 831; Kissinger, *White House Years*, 633, 647. For President Nixon's understanding of the Kennedy-Khrushchev agreement, see his interview response, 4 January 1971, *PPP*, 17–18.

31. Kissinger Telephone Conversation with Chuck Bailey, *Chicago Sun-Times*, 16 October 1970, DDRS; Alexander M. Haig Jr., *Caveat: Realism, Reagan, and Foreign Policy* (New York: Macmillan, 1984), 100; Alexander M. Haig Jr. with Charles McCarry, *Inner Circles: How America Changed the World* (New York: Warner, 1992), 254–55; Alexander M. Haig Jr. Interview by Author, Arlington, Virginia, 16 December 2004. Secretary Haig's files in the Nixon Presidential Papers at the National Archives (Boxes 955 to 1022 of the NSC Series Files) contain no evidence to corroborate his version; see in particular the Folder "Cuba," Box 1000.

32. Kissinger to President, "My Recent Conversations with Ambassador Dobrynin," 14 October 1970, NSA; Kissinger-Helms Telephone Conversation, 28 May 1971, DDRS; Nixon, *Memoirs*, 486, 489; Television Interview, 4 January 1971, *PPP*, 18; Press Conference, 17 February 1971, *PPP*, 163; Kissinger, *White House Years*, 632–52, esp. 647.

33. Kissinger, *Years of Renewal*, 771.

34. Nixon, *Memoirs*, 369.

35. S. Res. 160, *Senate Journal*, 30 July 1971, 577.

36. U.S. Congress, Senate, Committee on Foreign Relations, *United States Policy toward Cuba*, 10–11, 19.

37. Press Conference, 12 October 1971, *PPP*, 1032; Interview, 2 January 1972, *PPP*, 11; for similar comments during 1972, see 264, 405; *DOSB*, 4 December 1972, 653.

38. Porter and Johnson, *National Party Platforms*, 816 (Democrats), 853 (Republicans).

39. Kissinger Press Conference, Washington, D.C., 16 December 1972, in *NYT*, 17 December 1972, 2.

40. This account of the hijacking has been constructed from contemporary periodical coverage of the incident. See esp. *NYT*, 13 November 1972, 1, 55.

41. U.S. Congress, House, Committee on Foreign Affairs, *Aircraft Hijacking*, 91st Cong., 2nd sess., September 1970, 161–80; U.S. Congress, Senate, Committee on Commerce, Science, and Transportation, *Administration's Emergency Anti-Hijacking Regulations*, 93rd Cong., 1st sess., 9–10 January 1973, esp. 20–33. For concern over hijackings during the Johnson administration, see Folder "Cuban Hijacked Airliners," Box 21, NSFJ, CF, Cuba.

42. Kissinger to Peter Flanigan, "Possible Actions against Countries Which Are Uncooperative on Hijacking," 31 October 1970, NSA; Hurwitch: U.S. Congress, Senate, Committee on Foreign Relations, *Aircraft Hijacking Convention*, 92nd Cong., 1st sess., June–July 1971, 67.

43. U.S. Congress, Senate, Committee on Foreign Relations, Subcommittee on Inter-American Affairs, *Hijacking Accord between the United States and Cuba*, 93rd Cong., 1st sess., 20 February 1973, 9; Hurwitch, *Most of Myself*, 2:269, 272.

44. "Memorandum of Understanding on the Hijacking of Aircraft and Vessels," Exchange of Notes at Washington and Havana, 15 February 1973, 24 *UST* 737; *TIAS* 7597; 12 *ILM* 370; U.S. Congress, Committee on International Relations, *Toward Improved United States–Cuba Relations*, 95th Cong., 1st sess., 23 May 1977, 30–31.

45. Hurwitch, *Most of Myself*, 2:272; *PPP*, 3 May 1973, 511; *DOSB*, 20 October 1975, 599; William J. Jorden to Henry A. Kissinger, "Status of Cuban Hijackers Case," 28 March 1973, NSA; for Secretary Rogers's comment, see *NYT*, 16 February 1973, 1, 5.

46. U.S. Congress, House, Committee on International Relations, Subcommittees on International Trade and Commerce and on International Organizations, *U.S. Trade Embargo*, 170–71.

47. Kissinger, *Years of Renewal*, 772–73.

48. NSSM 32, "Cuba," 2 July 1969, NSA, annex 130; on Chile, see Second Annual Report to the Congress on United States Foreign Policy, 25 February 1971, *PPP*, 246; OAS Permanent Council, "Acta de la sesión extraordinaria celebrada el 13 de junio de 1972," OEA/Ser.G/CP/ACTA 75/72, esp. 4–5, 43.

49. *Intelligence Handbook: Cuba: Foreign Trade*, Report A9ER 75-69 (Washington, D.C.: CIA, 1975), 16.

50. "Cuba Policy," 15 August 1974, Folder "Issues and Accomplishments in Latin America (1)," Box 10, National Security Adviser: NSC Latin American Affairs Staff: Files, 1974–77, GRFL; Memcon, Kissinger and William D. Rogers, 15 August 1974, Folder "August 15, 1974 — Ford, Kissinger," Box 5, National Security Adviser: Memoranda of Conversations, 1973–1974, GRFL; Ford Press Conference, 28 August 1974, *PPP*, 65. Kissinger was also concerned about a proposed gathering of Latin American foreign ministers in Buenos Aires to which Cuba's foreign minister was almost certain to be invited (Stephen Low to General Brent Scowcroft, "The Cuba Problem," 14 September 1974, Folder "Cuba (1)," Box 3, National Security Adviser: Presidential Country Files for Latin America, 1974–77, GRFL).

51. Ford Press Conference, 21 October 1974, *PPP*, 419–20; Castro Speech, Havana, 22 April 1970. For Latin American opposition to normalization, see Brent Scowcroft, Memorandum for the President's File, 29 September 1974, Folder "President Ford — Memcon — September 29, 1974 — Antonio Azeredo da Silveira, Foreign Minister, Brazil," Box 12, National Security Adviser: NSC Latin American Affairs Staff: Files, 1974–77, GRFL.

52. [Harry Shlaudeman], Bureau of Inter-American Affairs, "Latin America: Cuba Policy," n.d., referred to as an "Issues Paper" and attached to "Memorandum for Lieutenant General Brent Scowcroft from George S. Springsteen," 7 February 1975, Folder "Cuba (3)," Box 3, National Security Adviser: Presidential Country File for Latin America, 1974–77, GRFL.

53. Press Conference, Hollywood, Florida, 26 February 1975, *PPP*, 294.

54. In his memoirs, Kissinger explained the difference between his and Ford's comments as part of a bad cop/good cop arrangement he had made with the president, but the archives contain no document indicating such an arrangement. For Kissinger speech, see "The United States and Latin America: The New Opportunity," 1 March 1975, *DOSB*, 24 March 1975, 364; Kissinger, *Years of Renewal*, 776–77. The one recorded Ford-Kissinger meeting prior to the Houston speech occurred on 28 February, during which there was no discussion of the tactic Kissinger mentioned in his memoir (Memcon, 28 February 1975, 3, Folder "February 28, 1975 — Ford, Kissinger," Box 9, National Security Adviser: Memoranda of Conversations, 1973–77, GRFL).

55. William R. Heidtman to President, 17 September 1974, Folder "CO 39 Cuba, 8/9/74–10/31/74," Box 15, White House Central File, GRFL; Maurice A. Ferré to President, 3 March 1975, Folder "Cuba — Correspondence on (1)," Box 2, National Security Adviser: NSC Latin American Affairs Staff: Files, 1974–77, GRFL; José Manuel Casanova to President, 17 March 1975, Folder "Cuba — Correspondence on (2)," Juan E. Pérez Franco to President, 28 February 1976, Folder "Cuba — Political, Military (2)," both in Box 2, National Security Adviser: NSC Latin American Affairs Staff: Files, 1974–77, GRFL.

56. Pawley to Kennedy, 23 January 1975, "Cuba—Correspondence on (4)," Box 2, National Security Adviser: Latin American Affairs Staff: Files, 1974–77, GRFL; Pawley to Kennedy, 27 February 1975, "CO39 Cuba, 4/1/74–5/31/75," Box 5, WHCF, GRFL.

57. Pawley to President Ford, 5 September 1974, "CO39 Cuba, 11/1/74–12/31/74," Box 5, Subject File, WHCF, GRFL; Pawley to President Ford, 2 April 1975, "CO39 Cuba, 4/1/74–5/31/75," Box 5, Subject File, WHCF, GRFL; Pawley to President Ford, 6 June 1975, "Cuba—Correspondence on (4)," Box 2, National Security Adviser: Latin American Affairs Staff: Files, 1974–77, GRFL; Pawley to General Scowcroft, 25, 30 March 1976, both in "Cuba—Correspondence on (7)," Box 2, National Security Adviser: Latin American Affairs Staff: Files: 1974–77, GRFL.

58. Raúl E. L. Comesañas to President, March 4, 1975, Folder "CO 39 Cuba, 10/1/75–1/20/77," Box 15, Subject File, WHCF, GRFL; Clarence Hungerford to President, 27 March 1975, Mrs. Samuel Skier to President, 21 March 1975, both in Folder "Cuba—Correspondence on (2)," Box 2, National Security Adviser: NSC Latin American Affairs Staff: Files, 1974–77, GRFL; E. B. Ogden Jr. to President, 12 June 1975, Folder "Cuba—Correspondence on (5)," Box 2, National Security Adviser: NSC Latin American Affairs Staff: Files, 1974–77, GRFL.

59. Alejandro Fidel Valdes to President, 17 June 1975, Folder "Cuba—Correspondence on (5)," Box 2, Subject File, WHCF, GRFL; Valdes to President, 14 October 1975, Folder "CO 39 Cuba, 10/1/75–1/20/77," Box 15, Subject File, WHCF, GRFL; Jeanne W. Davis to Jon Howe, "Response to Mrs. Gomez Who Requests Assistance in Returning to Cuba," 31 July 1975, Folder "CO 39 Cuba, 6/1/75–12/31/75," Box 15, Subject File, WHCF, GRFL. For similar correspondence, see Folders "CO39," Boxes 14 and 15, Subject File, WHCF, GRFL. For documents indicating Ford's concern with Reagan's challenge, see Folder "Countries—Cuba," Box 6, Presidential Handwriting File, GRFL.

60. William D. Rogers Interview by Author, Washington, D.C., 20 June 2003.

61. Memcon, "Cuba Policy: Tactics before and after San Jose," 9 June 1975, NSA. Other participants in the Kissinger-Rogers discussion included Deputy Undersecretary of State Lawrence Eagleburger and the director of policy planning, Winston Lord, both of whom supported Rogers. Two decades later, Kissinger recalled that normalizing relations with Cuba "wasn't a big deal for us. It wasn't China, Egypt or the Middle East. . . . I didn't focus on Cuba." Typescript notes of Philip Brenner, meeting with Kissinger and others, Pocantico Hills, New York, 23 August 1993, 4. Also useful is James Blight et al., "United States–Cuban Détente: The 1974–76 Initiative and the Angolan Interventions," Unedited Transcript of a Briefing Held in Pocantico Hills, New York, 23 August 1993, 32, in possession of the author. I am indebted to Brenner and Blight for sharing these notes.

62. Kissinger, *Years of Renewal*, 826.

63. U.S. Congress, Senate, Committee on Foreign Relations, *The Inter-American Conference of Tlatelolco in Mexico City: Report of Senator Mike Mansfield*, 93rd Cong., 2nd sess., March 1974, 4–5; U.S. Congress, Senate, Committee on Foreign Relations, *Cuba: A Staff Report*, 93rd Cong., 2nd sess., 2 August 1974, 10–11.

Holt's visit was arranged through Cuba's mission to the United Nations, whose chief at the time recalled, "We were happy to see anyone from the Congress, and we knew that Holt was speaking for a man we respected, Senator Fulbright" (Ricardo Alarcón Interview by Author, Havana, 11 March 2005). For Fulbright's frustration over earlier efforts to obtain State Department clearance for Holt, see Fulbright to Kissinger, 16 November 1973,

Folder "Trips—U.S. Officials," Box 13, National Security Adviser: NSC Latin American Affairs Staff: Files, 1974–77, GRFL. The Foreign Relations Committee's ranking Republican, George Aiken, had nonetheless telephoned the White House to say, "I'm not sure that this is a very good idea. . . . If you want, Fulbright and I can turn this off quickly so let me know" (Tom Korologos to General Scowcroft, "Cuba Trip," 12 August 1974, Folder "Cuba (1)," Box 3, National Security Adviser: Presidential Country Files for Latin America, 1974–77, GRFL).

64. CIA, "Key Issues and Prospects for Castro's Cuba," NIE 85-67, 2 March 1967, DDRS; Bonsal in U.S. Congress, Senate, Committee on Foreign Relations, Subcommittee on Western Hemisphere Affairs, *U.S. Policy toward Cuba*, 93rd Cong., 1st sess., April 1973, 40; for the Javits and Pell report, see U.S. Congress, Senate, Committee on Foreign Relations, *The United States and Cuba: A Propitious Moment*, 93rd Cong., 2nd sess., October 1974. In March 1975, the two senators introduced a resolution (S. Res. 96) "expressing the sense of the Senate that the United States should seek a normalization of relations with the Government of Cuba." For Whalen, see U.S. Congress, House, Committee on International Relations, *Cuba Study Mission: A Fact-Finding Survey, June 26–July 2, 1975*, 94th Cong., 1st sess., 15 July 1975, 9. Shortly after Whalen returned, the CRS's respected Latin America specialist, Barry Sklar, also visited Cuba, and his report generally supported Whalen's observations (U.S. Congress, House, Committee on International Relations, *United States–Cuban Perspectives—1975, Conversations on Major Issues with Cuban Officials, Report of a Study Visit to Cuba*, 94th Cong., 2nd sess., 4 May 1976).

65. U.S. Department of Commerce, Domestic and International Business Administration, Bureau of East-West Trade, *United States Commercial Relations with Cuba: A Survey*, August 1975, 29; U.S. Congress, Senate, Committee on Agriculture and Forestry, Subcommittee on Agricultural Production, Marketing, and Stabilization of Prices, *Rice Programs*, 94th Cong., 1st sess., 14 November 1975.

66. U.S. Congress, House, Committee on International Relations, Subcommittee on International Trade and Commerce, *United States–Cuba Trade Promotion*, 94th Cong., 2nd sess., 22 July 1976, 4–5. Freeman made the same point to the Carter administration in a letter to National Security Adviser Zbigniew Brzezinski, 13 December 1977, Folder "CO38 1/1/78–3/31/78," Box CO-21, Subject File, WHCF, JCL. During 1975–76, Kissinger's State Department opposed all congressional resolutions seeking either to discourage or encourage closer relations. See the letters from Robert J. McCloskey, Assistant Secretary of State for Congressional Relations, Folder "CO 39 Cuba, 4/1/74–5/31/75," Box 5, Subject File, WHCF, GRFL; Folder "CO 39 Cuba 6/1/75–12/31/75," Box 15, Subject File, WHCF, GRFL; and Folder "ND 18-3, War Prisoners," Box 70, Subject File, WHCF, GRFL.

67. The Kennedy bill was S. 935, 4 March 1975, *Senate Journal 1975*, 154. On the same day, Senators Javits and Pell introduced their resolution (S. Res. 96) expressing the sense of the Senate that the United States should seek the normalization of relations with Cuba. *Senate Journal 1975*, 154–55; the Bingham proposal was H.R. 6382, 24 April 1975. Bingham stopped encouraging reconciliation after Cuba supported the November 1975 U.N. General Assembly resolution equating Zionism with racism. For McGovern, see U.S. Congress, Senate, Committee on Foreign Relations, *Cuban Realities, May 1975: A Report by Senator George S. McGovern*, 94th Cong., 1st sess., August 1975; George McGovern, "A Talk with Castro," *New York Times Magazine*, 13 March 1977, 20, 76–79.

68. U.S. Congress, House, Committee on International Relations, *Cuba Study Mission*, v

(Whalen); U.S. Congress, House, Committee on International Relations, *United States Relations with Cuba: Report of a Special Study Mission to Cuba, August 30–September 3, 1975*, 94th Cong., 1st sess., 31 October 1975, 6, 11–12 (Solarz).

69. U.S. Congress, House, Committee on International Relations, Subcommittee on International Political and Military Affairs, *Soviet Activities in Cuba*, pts. 6 and 7, 33; U.S. Congress, House, Committee on International Relations, Subcommittees on International Trade and Commerce and on International Organizations, *U.S. Trade Embargo*, 141, 146–47; U.S. Congress, House, Committee on Foreign Affairs, Subcommittee on Inter-American Affairs, *Cuba and the Caribbean*, 22; Typescript notes of Philip Brenner, meeting with Kissinger and others, Pocantico Hills, New York, 23 August 1993 (Shlaudeman).

70. Memcon, "Cuba Policy: Tactics before and after San Jose," 9 June 1975, NSA.

71. Frank Mankiewicz Interview by Author, Washington, D.C., 18 June 2003; Memcon, Foreign Minister Alberto Vignes of Argentina and Secretary Kissinger, 5 October 1973, NSA; James Blight et al., "United States–Cuban Détente: The 1974–76 Initiative and the Angolan Interventions," Typescript of Conversations in Havana, 14–15 December 1992, 6–7, in possession of the author.

72. Typescript notes of Philip Brenner, meeting with Kissinger and others, Pocantico Hills, New York, 23 August 1993. The 1974 meeting at New York's LaGuardia Airport was the first of at least seven; it was followed by a second on 11 January 1975, also at LaGuardia; a third on 21 June 1975 at Washington's National Airport; a fourth on 30 June 1975 at Eagleburger's Washington home; a fifth on 9 July 1976 at New York's Pierre Hotel; a sixth on 12 January 1976 at National Airport; and a seventh on 7 February 1976 in New York.

In February 1975, the Ford administration expanded the travel range of Cubans from 25 to 250 miles beyond U.N. headquarters, thereby enabling Cuban diplomats to come to Washington. A second unilateral U.S. move came the following April, when the United States granted visas to a Cuban law professor and three students to participate in a moot court competition (Kissinger, *Years of Renewal*, 776).

73. Blight et al., "United States–Cuban Détente," 11. Also participating was Nestor García of the Cuban U.N. mission.

74. Kissinger, *Years of Renewal*, 776; for Eagleburger's minutes of the meeting, see Memorandum for the Secretary, "Meeting in New York with Cuban Representatives," 11 January 1975, DDRS.

75. Memcon, "Cuba Policy: Tactics before and after San Jose," 9 June 1975, NSA.

76. Castro quoted in *NYT*, 30 March 1975, 17; U.S. Congress, Senate, Committee on Foreign Relations, *Department of State Appropriations Authorization, Fiscal Year 1974*, 93rd Cong., 1st sess., April 1973, 177–78 (Crimmins, who noted that "there has been clear evidence of a much more selective and much more carefully targeted effort"); Kissinger Press Conference, 10 January 1974, *DOSB*, 4 February 1974, 122.

77. U.S. Congress, House, Committee on International Relations, Subcommittee on International Political and Military Affairs, *Soviet Activities in Cuba*, pt. 3, 8–9 (DIA), 67 (State Department).

78. The vote on 29 July 1975 was 16–3 (Chile, Paraguay, and Uruguay opposed), with Brazil and Nicaragua abstaining (OEA/Ser.F/II. Doc. 9175, Rev. 2 [1975]). This vote permitted bilateral relations; it did not end Cuba's suspension from the OAS.

79. The Cuban Assets Control Regulations defined a person subject to the jurisdiction of the United States to include any U.S.-based corporation and "any partnership, association, corporation, organization *wheresoever organized or doing business* which is owned or controlled by" a U.S.-based corporation (emphasis added). A subparagraph of the regulations (Section 515.541) provided an exemption for "any non-banking association, corporation, or other organization, which is organized and doing business under the laws of any foreign country," but this did apply to any product with a U.S.-made component and to "any person subject to the jurisdiction of the United States." On the legal issues involved, see Peter J. Grilli, Howard B. Klein, and James M. Michener, "Legal Impediments to Normalization of Trade with Cuba," *Law and Policy in International Business* 8, no. 4 (1976): esp. 1015–16. On the original trade ban, which exempted most foreign subsidiaries, see Gordon Chase to Bundy, "Imposition of Blocking Controls on Cuba," 1 June 1963, Department of State, Circular Telegram 40, 6 July 1963, both in Folder "Cuba Subjects Blocking Documents 6/1/63–8/15/63," Box 45, NSFK.

80. Kissinger to Nixon, "Argentina and Our Cuban Denial Policy," 30 December 1973, Folder "Cuba—Economic, Social—Sanctions (1)," Box 2, National Security Adviser: NSC Latin American Affairs Staff: Files, 1974–77, GRFL.

81. Kissinger to Nixon, "Argentina and Our Cuban Denial Policy," 30 December 1973, Folder "Cuba—Economic, Social—Sanctions (1)," Box 2, National Security Adviser: NSC Latin American Affairs Staff: Files, 1974–77, GRFL; Jack B. Kubisch to Secretary, "Argentina and Our Cuban Denial Policy," 21 December 1973, Box 2, National Security Adviser: NSC Latin American Affairs Staff: Files, 1974–77, GRFL; Brent Scowcroft to President, 21 February 1974, Folder "HAK Trip Mexico," Box 48, Henry A. Kissinger Series File, NSC Files, Nixon Presidential Materials.

82. *Washington Post*, 20 April 1974, A1 (King); U.S. Congress, House, Committee on International Relations, Subcommittee on Inter-American Affairs, *Impact of Cuban-Soviet Ties in the Western Hemisphere*, 95th Cong., 2nd sess., March–April 1978, 157.

83. Joseph John Jova to Secretary of State, 28 January 1975, Folder "Cuba—Economic, Social—Sanctions (2)," Box 2, National Security Adviser: NSC Latin American Affairs Staff: Files, 1974–77, GRFL. For the grumbling by corporate giants such as Union Carbide and Du-Pont, see *Journal of Commerce*, 6 May 1975, 1, 19; *Wall Street Journal*, 17 July 1975, 1, 22 August 1975, 4.

84. Grilli, Klein, and Michener, "Legal Impediments," 1017n; *Washington Post*, 24 February 1974, A10; *Journal of Commerce*, 19 March 1974, 47.

85. Robert Ingersoll, "Cuba Policy—Our Constraints on U.S. Subsidiaries," 25 February 1975, Folder "Cuba—Economic, Social—Sanctions (2)," Box 2, National Security Adviser: NSC Latin American Affairs Staff: Files, 1974–77, GRFL. See also the prodding by Secretary Kissinger: Kissinger to President, "Lifting Third Country Constraints on Trade with Cuba," 12 August 1975, Kissinger to President, "Third Country Sanctions against Cuba," 19 August 1975, both in Folder "Cuba (3)," Box 3, National Security Adviser: Presidential Country Files for Latin America, 1974–77, GRFL; Kissinger to President, "Third Country Sanctions against Cuba," 5 August 1975, Folder "Cuba-Economic, Social-Sanctions (2)," Box 2, National Security Adviser: Presidential Country Files for Latin America, 1974–77, GRFL.

86. NSDM 305, 15 September 1975, folder "NSDM 305," Box 1, National Security Adviser:

National Security Decision Memoranda and National Security Study Memoranda, GRFL. NSDM 305 required several regulatory changes (40 *FR* 55314–15, 28 November 1975). First, the Department of the Treasury amended the Cuban Assets Control Regulations by revoking the old prohibition (Part 515.412 and 515.541) and adding a new Part 515.559 authorizing the Department of Commerce to license the foreign-based subsidiaries of U.S. firms to export to Cuba. The Department of Commerce also had to revoke the regulation denying bunker fuel to ships that had called at a Cuban port after 1 January 1963, and the Department of State had to waive the part of Section 620(a) of the Foreign Assistance Act of 1961 that prohibited aid to countries that allowed their ships to trade with Cuba. Only in 1977 did Congress repeal the shipping blacklist (Section 123, PL 95-88, 3 August 1977). The 1992 Cuban Democracy (Torricelli) Act would reimpose the embargo on subsidiary trade with Cuba but not the blacklist.

87. The Rogers statement, 23 September 1975, is reprinted in *DOSB*, 20 October 1975, 597, 599. For details of license applications, see John Marsh to Senator Henry Jackson, 24 March 1976, Folder "Cuba—Trade Liberalization," Box 5, John Marsh Files, 1974–77, GRFL; Legislative Referral Memorandum, 20 July 1976, Folder "CO 39 Cuba, 6/1/76–1/20/77," Box 15, Subject File, WHCF, GRFL. Kissinger remarked years later that "lifting the sanctions in the OAS served our interests, it wasn't for the Cubans. We did it for Argentina" (Typescript notes of Philip Brenner, meeting with Kissinger and others, Pocantico Hills, New York, 23 August 1993).

88. DOS Aide-Mémoire, 11 January 1975, NSA.

89. Castro Speech, Havana, 19 April 1976, in *Granma*, 20 April 1976, 2; U.S. Congress, House, Committee on International Relations, Subcommittees on International Trade and Commerce and on International Organizations, *U.S. Trade Embargo*, 154 (Rogers).

90. Kissinger quoting Sánchez-Parodi ("We cannot negotiate under the blockade") in Kissinger, *Years of Renewal*, 780; Sánchez-Parodi in Blight et al., "United States–Cuban Détente." On 30 June, an agenda-setting meeting had occurred at Eagleburger's Washington home, sandwiched between the 21 June meeting at National Airport and the 9 July meeting at the Hotel Pierre. The near-verbatim Hotel Pierre memcon is Folder "Cuba 2/78–4/78," Box 10, Geographic File, Zbigniew Brzezinski Collection, JCL; also available through DDRS.

91. Kissinger, *Years of Renewal*, 776; Sánchez-Parodi in Blight et al., "United States–Cuban Détente." This was also the view of José Antonio Arbesú, then a member of the Americas Department of the Central Committee of the Communist Party of Cuba, who told Philip Brenner, "From the Cuban perspective, elections were the decisive factor on the U.S. side" (Notes, Arbesú Interview with Phillip Brenner, 18 April 1995).

92. Sparkman Press Conference, 11 August 1975, in *NYT*, 12 August 1975, 4.

93. Memcon, 27 August 1975, Folder "August 27, 1975—Ford, Ambassador Daniel Patrick Moynihan (UN)," Box 14, National Security Adviser: Memoranda of Conversations, 1973–77, GRFL; United Nations, Official Records of the General Assembly, 30th Session, Plenary Meetings, vol. 2, 25 November 1975, 1007; Alarcón Interview.

94. Barbara Walters, "An Interview with Fidel Castro," *Foreign Policy* 28 (Fall 1977): 42; Castro Speech, Havana, 22 December 1975, in *Granma*, 24 December 1975, 2–3; see also Speech, Havana, 29 September 1975; Typescript notes of Philip Brenner, meeting with Kissinger and others, Pocantico Hills, New York, 23 August 1993 (Kissinger).

Given their common colonial experience and their physical proximity, it is no surprise that Cubans have championed Puerto Rican independence since the nineteenth century, including that sister island in one of Cuba's most important historical documents, José Martí's "Las bases del Partido Revolucionario Cubano," 10 April 1892, Article I, "El Partido Revolucionario Cubano se constituye para lograr con los esfuerzos reunidos de todos los hombres de buena voluntad, la independencia absoluta de la Isla de Cuba, y fomentar y auxiliar la de Puerto Rico."

95. Television Interview, 3 November 1975, *PPP*, 1787.

96. Kissinger quoted in Barry A. Sklar, "Cuba: Normalization of Relations," CRS Issue Brief IB75030, updated 17 May 1977, 41–42; Castro Speech, Havana, 22 December 1975, in *Granma*, 24 December 1975, 3.

97. Castro Speech, Havana, 19 April 1976, in *Granma*, 20 April 1976, 2; Raúl Castro Speech to the First Congress of the MPLA, Angola, December 1977, in *Granma*, weekly English ed., 18 December 1977, 2.

Although Cuba's 1981 census registered the proportion of Cubans with black skin at 12 percent (*Censo de población y viviendas*, 1981, 16:cvii), that number would seem low to visitors using a U.S. definition of "black skin." For a discussion of data on race in Cuba prior to 1959, see Carlos Moore, *Castro, the Blacks, and Africa* (Los Angeles: Center for Afro-American Studies, University of California, Los Angeles, 1988), appendix 2, 357–65.

98. On Algeria, see the comments by Ahmed Ben Bella during a 1962 visit to Cuba in *Revolución*, 17 October 1962, 7; for the U.S. reaction, see *DOSB*, 23 August 1965, 319; Piero Gleijeses, "Cuba's First Venture in Africa: Algeria, 1961–1965," *Journal of Latin American Studies* 28 (February 1996): 159–95.

On early Cuban activity in sub-Saharan Africa, see Piero Gleijeses, *Conflicting Missions: Havana, Washington, and Africa, 1959–1976* (Chapel Hill: University of North Carolina Press, 2002); William J. Durch, *The Cuban Military in Africa and the Middle East: From Algeria to Angola*, Professional Paper 201 (Alexandria, Va.: Center for Naval Analyses, 1977), 17–20. For background, see two important works by William M. LeoGrande, "Cuban-Soviet Relations and Cuban Policy in Africa," *Cuban Studies* 10 (January 1980): 2–37, and *Cuba's Policy in Africa, 1959–1980* (Berkeley: Institute of International Studies, University of California, 1980). Also useful are two publications by principals: Ernesto Guevara, *Pasajes de la guerra revolucionaria: Congo*, ed. Aleyda March (Barcelona: Mondadori, 1999), and Jorge Risquet, *El segundo frente del Che en el Congo: Historia del Batallón Patricio Lumumba* (Havana: Casa Editora Abril, 2000).

99. U.S. Congress, House, Committee on International Relations, Subcommittee on Inter-American Affairs, *Impact of Cuban-Soviet Ties*, 157; for the CIA's estimate of the Cuban forces in Africa in early 1976, see George Bush to President, "The Cuban Presence in Africa," 9 April 1976, Folder "Africa—General (3)," Box 1, National Security Adviser: Presidential Country Files for Africa, 1974–77, GRFL.

100. For the international forces behind the three factions, see Gerald J. Bender, "Kissinger in Angola: Anatomy of a Failure," in *American Policy in Southern Africa: The Stakes and the Stance*, ed. René Lemarchand (Washington, D.C.: University Press of America, 1978), 65–143; Gleijeses, *Conflicting Missions*, 235–42; LeoGrande, *Cuba's Policy in Africa*, 13–15. For the background, see Gerald J. Bender, *Angola under the Portuguese* (Berkeley: University of

California Press, 1978); Raymond Garthoff, *Détente and Confrontation: American-Soviet Relations from Nixon to Reagan*, rev. ed. (Washington, D.C.: Brookings Institution, 1994), chap. 15, 556–93, esp. the studies cited in 557 n. 1.

101. For the U.S. understanding of early Cuban activities in Angola, see "National Security Study Memorandum 32—Cuba," 2 July 1969, NSA, annex 114–15.

102. Gleijeses, *Conflicting Missions*, 246, 279–80, notes that in 1970, the CIA was paying Roberto about one thousand dollars per month; Richard C. Thornton, *The Nixon-Kissinger Years: Reshaping America's Foreign Policy* (New York: Paragon House, 1989), 328; William G. Hyland, *Mortal Rivals: Superpower Relations from Nixon to Reagan* (New York: Random House, 1987), 135–36, 141.

103. U.S. Congress, House, Committee on International Relations, Subcommittee on Africa, *United States–Angolan Relations*, 95th Cong., 2nd sess., 15 May 1978, 7 (consul-general); Gleijeses, *Conflicting Missions*, 237–38; Nathaniel Davis, "The Angola Decision of 1975: A Personal Memoir," *Foreign Affairs* 56 (Fall 1978): 120–21. In his memoir (*Years of Renewal*, 791), Kissinger dates U.S. involvement from 19 April 1975.

104. Kissinger, *Years of Renewal*, 808.

105. John Stockwell, *In Search of Enemies: A CIA Story* (New York: Norton, 1978), 206–7.

106. Using CIA estimates, Stockwell (U.S. Congress, House, Committee on International Relations, Subcommittee on Africa, *United States–Angolan Relations*, 12–13) places the number of Cubans in the initial advisory mission at about 260, but Gleijeses's much smaller number of about 50, based on Cuban documents, is probably correct. It is corroborated by Gabriel García Márquez's fascinating *Operación Carlota*, first published as a pamphlet (Lima: Mosca Azul, 1977) and obviously written with the very close collaboration of Cuban officials. It is translated and reprinted in David Deutschmann, ed., *Changing the History of Africa: Angola and Namibia* (New York: Ocean, 1989), 41–60. See also Gleijeses, *Conflicting Missions*, 254, 259–61, 265–72.

107. Davis, "Angola Decision of 1975," 122–23.

108. Castro Speech, Havana, 19 April 1976, in *Granma*, 20 April 1976, 2; U.S. Consul, Luanda, to Secretary of State, "Cuban Troops in Angola," 10 October 1975, DDRS; Hyland, *Mortal Rivals*, 143.

109. Gleijeses, *Conflicting Missions*, 307, 271n. Kissinger's memoir also displays a tendency to overlook or omit crucial information on Angola; for example, he correctly noted (Kissinger, *Years of Renewal*, 832) that the Organization of African Unity deadlocked in its vote to recognize the Neto government at its Addis Ababa meeting on 11–12 January 1976 but failed to mention that the vote was twenty-two to recognize the MPLA government and twenty-two to continue working for a government of national unity, with not one African government advocating recognition of the U.S.-supported FNLA or UNITA. More revealing is Kissinger's failure to mention his efforts to ensure the stalemate, which are covered in CIA agent John Stockwell's *In Search of Enemies*, 193, 233, and DOS Telegram, 3 January 1976, Folder "Angola—Presidential Message," Box 2, National Security Adviser: Presidential Country Files for Africa, 1974–77, GRFL.

110. Walters, "Interview with Fidel Castro," 39. Castro said the same thing to the Cuban people on 19 April 1976; see *Granma*, 20 April 1976, 2.

111. Stockwell, *In Search of Enemies*, 202; Hyland, *Mortal Rivals*, 146.

112. Secretary of State to All Diplomatic Posts, "Angolan Situation and U.S. Initiatives," 1 December 1975, DDRS.

113. The 19 December vote was on an amendment by Senator John Tunney to the Department of Defense appropriations bill for fiscal 1976 (HR 9861), which had the CIA's funding buried within it; despite the president's direct plea to House speaker Carl Albert, on 27 January 1976 the House vote on the Tunney amendment was equally lopsided, 323-99, leaving Ford no option but to sign the bill. Amendments to appropriations bills last only for the fiscal year of the appropriation, however, but a permanent prohibition was added in mid-1976 by Senator Dick Clark's amendment to the International Security Assistance and Arms Export Control Act of 1976 (PL 94-329), an authorization bill that prohibited "assistance of any kind" to "any nation, group, organization, movement or individual to conduct military or paramilitary operations in Angola." For the president's 27 January 1976 letter to Albert, see *PPP*, 93–94; for the Senate vote and floor debate on the Tunney amendment, see *Congressional Record*, 19 February 1976, 42209-10; for President Ford's remarks to reporters, 19 December 1975, see *PPP*, 1981; Hyland, *Mortal Rivals*, 145–46; see also Kissinger's statement, 29 January 1976, *DOSB*, 16 February 1976, 174–82.

114. Memcon, March 15, 1976, Folder "March 15, 1976—Ford, Kissinger," Box 18, National Security Adviser: Memoranda of Conversations, 1973–77, GRFL. On the continued spending, see U.S. Congress, House, Committee on International Relations, Subcommittee on Africa, *United States–Angolan Relations*, 14, 27; on the recision attempt, see, among other memos in the same folder, Clinton A. Granger and Les Janka to Brent Scowcroft, "Overt Funding for Angola," 16 January 1976, Folder "Angola (3)," Box 1, National Security Adviser: Presidential Country Files for Latin America, GRFL.

115. Kissinger's Dallas speech was 22 March 1976; it and the Joint Chiefs statement were reported in *Washington Post*, 26 March 1976, A22, and *NYT*, 24 March 1976, 6; Harry E. Bergold, Acting Assistant Secretary of State for International Security Affairs, to Secretary of Defense, and attached policy paper, "U.S. Policies with Respect to Possible Cuban Military Intervention in Rhodesia and Namibia," 23 March 1976, Folder "Cuba—Military Intervention in Africa, 3/23/76," Box 3, Richard Cheney Files, 1974–77, GRFL.

116. Jim Conner to Jim Shuman, 12 March 1976, Folder "Countries—Cuba," Box 6, Presidential Handwriting File, GRFL; "Talking Paper for Meeting with Senator McClure," 24 March 1976, Folder "President Ford—Appointments (8)," Box 11, National Security Adviser: NSC Latin American Affairs Staff: Files, 1974–77, GRFL; Ford Press Conference, 2 May 1976, *PPP*, 1413.

117. "While some margin of flexibility over 20 percent was permitted when the regulations were issued, because of Cuban involvement in Angola such flexibility is no longer possible" (Department of Commerce, July 1976 in U.S. Congress, House, Committee on International Relations, Subcommittee on International Trade and Commerce, *United States–Cuba Trade Promotion*, 30–31). The documents regarding Kuhn's baseball diplomacy are available from the National Security Archive; for Carter's comment to reporters, 22 July 1976, see U.S. Congress, House, Committee on House Administration, *The Presidential Campaign 1976*, 95th Cong., 2nd sess., 1978, 1:444.

118. For the statement justifying the U.S. vote, see *DOSB*, 19 July 1976, 100. A second U.N. vote came on 22 November 1976, when the lame-duck administration abstained on the vote

admitting Angola to the United Nations. For the background, see Folder "Angola (5)," Box 2, National Security Adviser: Presidential Country Files for Africa, GRFL.

119. Minutes, NSC Meeting, 11 May 1976, Folder "NSC Meeting, May 11, 1976," Box 2, National Security Adviser: NSC Meetings File, GRFL.

120. Kissinger: Minutes, NSC Meeting, 7 April 1976, Folder "NSC Meeting, April 7, 1976," Box 2, National Security Adviser: NSC Meetings File, GRFL; for Rumsfeld and Ford, see "U.S. Policies with Respect to Possible Cuban Military Intervention in Rhodesia and Namibia," 23 March 1976, Folder "Cuba—Military Intervention in Africa, 3/23/76," Box 3, Richard Cheney Files, 1974–77, GRFL; Minutes, NSC Meeting, 7 April 1976, Folder "NSC Meeting, April 7, 1976," Box 2, National Security Adviser: NSC Meetings File, GRFL.

121. Gerald R. Ford, *A Time to Heal: The Autobiography of Gerald R. Ford* (New York: Harper and Row, 1979), 358; Ford to House Speaker Carl Albert, 27 January 1976, *PPP*, 93–94; *DOSB*, 16 February 1976, 174–82; Hyland, *Mortal Rivals*, 142.

122. Kissinger, *Years of Renewal*, 816; Castro: Speech, Havana, 19 April 1976, in *Granma*, 20 April 1976, 2. See also Garthoff ("There is no evidence that the Soviet leaders applied any pressure on Cuba"), *Détente and Confrontation*, 568–69; Piero Gleijeses, "Moscow's Proxy?: Cuba and Africa, 1975–1988," *Journal of Cold War Studies* 8 (Fall 2006): 98–146. Anatoly Dobrynin insisted that the Cubans went "on their own initiative and without consulting us" (*In Confidence: Moscow's Ambassador to America's Six Cold War Presidents* [New York: Random House, 1995], 362); Carlos Rafael Rodríguez ("When the decision to dispatch Cuban forces into Angola was made, we communicated nothing about it to the Soviet Union"), transcript of meeting with Alexander Haig, Mexico City, 23 November 1981, in *Cold War International History Project Bulletin* 8–9 (Winter 1996): 210.

123. Memcon, Kissinger and Foreign Minister César Augusto Guzzetti and Aides, Santiago, Chile, 6 [*sic*] June 1976, NSA; Memcon, Kissinger and President Augusto Pinochet, Santiago, Chile, 8 June 1976, DDRS; Kissinger, *Years of Renewal*, 825–33.

124. *Washington Post*, 11 February 1976, 2 (not in *PPP*), 8 February 1976 (*PPP*, 225), 25 February 1976 (*PPP*, 444); "Cuba," Question and Answer Sheet in President's Briefing Book, 26 February 1976, Box 46, Ron Nessen Papers, GRFL; Ford, *Time to Heal*, 345–46, 358–59.

125. Press Conference, 20 December 1975, *PPP*, 1988; Speech, Havana, 22 December 1975, in *Granma*, 24 December 1975, 2–3; Naturalization Ceremony, Miami, 28 February 1976, *PPP*, 465; Speech, Havana, 19 April 1976, in *Granma*, 20 April 1976, 2.

126. "The Cubans did nothing after the July [1975] meeting." In a subsequent interview, Rogers agreed that the Angola dispute hardened all positions. Typescript notes of Philip Brenner, meeting with Kissinger and others, Pocantico Hills, New York, 23 August 1993; Rogers Interview.

127. Typescript notes of Philip Brenner, meeting with Kissinger and others, Pocantico Hills, New York, 23 August 1993; Rogers Interview; Eagleburger and Rogers to Secretary, "A Meeting with the Cubans," 24 December 1975, NSA.

128. Eagleburger and Rogers to Secretary, "Cuban Family Visits," 12 January 1976, DDRS and NSA.

129. Memcon, 7 February 1976, Folder "Cuba 2/78–4/78," Box 10, Geographic File, Zbigniew Brzezinski Collection, JCL (Eagleburger); Typescript notes of Philip Brenner, meeting with Kissinger and others, Pocantico Hills, New York, 23 August 1993 (Rogers); Kissinger, *Years of Renewal*, 784–86, 779.

130. Speech, Havana, 19 April 1976, in *Granma*, 20 April 1976, 2; for the protest note, see folder "Cuba—Political, Military (2)," Box 2, National Security Adviser: NSC Latin American Affairs Staff: Files, 1974–77, GRFL.

131. Castro's 15 October 1976 funeral speech is reprinted in U.S. Congress, House, Committee on International Relations, *Toward Improved United States–Cuba Relations*, 95th Cong., 1st sess., 23 May 1977, 23–9. For Luis Posada Carriles's memoir of the bombing, see his autobiography, *Los caminos del guerrero* (n.p., 1994), 212–22; for CORU's responsibility, see Brzezinski to President, "Cuban Exile Terrorist Activities," 20 July 1977, Folder "Cuba, 5–10/77," Box 13, RNSA.

132. *DOSB*, 8 November 1976, 573–74; David Lazar to Brent Scowcroft, "Castro's Charges and Termination of Hijacking Agreement," 29 October 1976, Brent Scowcroft to Phil Buchen, "Castro's Charges and Termination of Hijacking Agreement—Your Memorandum of October 19," 2 November 1976, both in Folder "Cuba (8)," Box 4, National Security Adviser: Presidential Country Files for Latin America, 1974–77, GRFL. Also useful in assessing U.S. involvement are the documents in Folder "Cuba—Cubana Airlines Crash," Box 2, National Security Adviser: NSC Latin American Affairs Staff Files, GRFL.

133. Transcript, *CBS Reports with Bill Moyers*, "The CIA's Secret Army," 10 June 1977, PC.

134. The accord was due to expire or be extended in February 1978. With Castro's required six-month notification, the pact expired on 15 April 1977. Kissinger warned (*DOSB*, 8 November 1976, 573–74) that "we will hold the Cuban Government accountable for any actions that result from their decision," a warning repeated in the formal U.S. note denying the accusations in Castro's funeral speech and protesting the cancellation ("Message to the Swiss Embassy—Havana," 11 November 1976, Folder "Cuba—Hijacking," Box 2, National Security Adviser: NSC Latin American Affairs Staff: Files, 1974–77, GRFL).

Chapter 10

1. The Republican platform condemned Cuba's intervention in the affairs of other nations and endorsed "the aspirations of the Cuban people to regain their liberty" but promised nothing concrete, while Democrats promised to normalize relations if Cuba "abandons its provocative international actions and policies," ends its support of Puerto Rican independence, and releases U.S. citizens held in Cuban prisons for political reasons. For the candidates' few comments about Cuba during the campaign, see U.S. Congress, House, Committee on House Administration, *The Presidential Campaign 1976*, 95th Cong., 2nd sess., 1978, 1:894–95, 1023, 3:110.

2. *Playboy*, November 1976, 63–86. The interview was on newsstands three weeks before the election.

3. U.S. Congress, House, Committee on House Administration, *Presidential Campaign 1976*, 1:1043; Carter's principal campaign speech on human rights was to B'nai Brith on 9 September 1976, 1:710–12. The new president's first major statement on Latin America policy came on 14 April 1977, *PPP*, 611–16.

4. *The Americas in a Changing World* (New York: Center for Inter-American Relations, 1974); and *The United States and Latin America: Next Steps* (New York: Center for Inter-American Relations, 1976); Stephen Low to General Scowcroft, "Presentation to President of Report by Commission on U.S.-Latin American Relations—Tuesday, October 29," 23 October 1974,

Folder "CO 1–9 South and Central America, 8/9/74–4/30/75," Box 6, WHCF, Subject File, GRFL.

5. William E. Odom Interview by Author, Washington, D.C., 7 April 2005; Memcon, Peter Tarnoff, Robert Pastor, and Wayne Smith with Fidel Castro, Carlos Rafael Rodríguez, and José Luis Padrón, Havana, 16 January 1980, in "Cuba: President Carter's Trip, May 12–17, 2002," Vertical File, JCL. Of the U.S. negotiators, Cuba's Ricardo Alarcón clearly preferred Tarnoff and Smith; Pastor, he said, "sometimes gives the impression of arrogance" (Ricardo Alarcón Interview by Author, Havana, 11 March 2005).

6. *NYT*, 14 January 2002, 14.

7. Zbigniew Brzezinski, "Cuba in Soviet Strategy," *New Republic* 147 (3 November 1962): 7–8. The State Department position is best summarized in an untitled memorandum from the Department's executive secretary, C. Arthur Borg, to Brzezinski, 28 March 1977, Folder "1/20/77–3/30/77," Box CO-20, WHCF, Subject File, Executive, JCL. State's position contrasts with that of the NSC, expressed in Brzezinski to President, "PRC Meeting on Cuba—August 3, 1977," 5 August 1977, Brzezinski to Vice President, "United States Policy to Cuba," 18 August 1977, both in Folder "Meetings—PRC 29: 8/3/77," Box 24, Subject File, ZBC. The ZBC is several thousand pages of Brzezinski's personal papers, donated to the JCL; they are archived separately from the Records of the Office of the National Security Adviser.

8. Nancy Mitchell, "Tropes of the Cold War: Jimmy Carter and Rhodesia," *Cold War History* 7 (May 2007): 263–83.

9. *Washington Post*, 8 September 1979, A8; see also *NYT*, 23 September 1979, 1, 4; Zbigniew Brzezinski, *Power and Principle: Memoirs of the National Security Adviser, 1977–1981* (New York: Farrar, Straus, Giroux, 1983), 146, 183, 187, 455.

10. Brzezinski Diary, 28 December 1978, in Brzezinski, *Power and Principle*, 520; Wayne S. Smith, *The Closest of Enemies: A Personal and Diplomatic Account of U.S.-Cuban Relations since 1957* (New York: Norton, 1987), 129.

11. Wayne Smith Interview by Author, Washington, D.C., 22 July 2004.

12. Brzezinski to President, "NSC Weekly Report #104," 27 July 1979, Folder "Weekly Reports to the President, 102–120: 7/79–12/79," Box 42, Subject File, ZBC; Record of Conversation, A. Seletskii, Soviet Embassy, Havana, and José Antonio Arbesú, 27 December 1979, Folder "USSR-US Conference, 3/95: Briefing Book II," Box 117, Vertical File, JCL.

13. Durán quoted in *Miami News*, 21 December 1976, 3; *NYT* 26 February 1977, 3; Maurice A. Ferré to Carter, 14 February 1977, Folder "CO38 1/20/77–3/31/77," WHCF, Subject File, JCL; Juanita Castro to Carter, 12 May 1977, Folder "CO38 6/1-77–6/30/77," Box CO-20, Subject File, JCL; Earl E. T. Smith to Carter, 7 March 1977, Folder "CO38 4/1/77–5/31/77," Box CO-20, WHCF, Subject File, JCL; for the citrus producers and claimants, see U.S. Congress, House, Committee on International Relations, Subcommittees on International Trade and Commerce and on International Organizations, *U.S. Trade Embargo of Cuba*, 94th Cong., 1st sess., 1975, 488–89; Brzezinski to Charles J. Pilliod Jr., Chairman of the Board, Goodyear Tire and Rubber Company, 1 July 1977, Folder "CO38 1/20/77–1/20/81," Box CO-21, WHCF, Subject File, JCL. Also participating in the meeting with Secretary Vance were former Cuban president Carlos Prío and Cuba's never-inaugurated president-elect (in 1958), Andrés Rivero Agüero, plus two other Bay of Pigs participants: Manolo Reboso, a Miami city commissioner, and Erneido Oliva, the brigade's military commander.

14. Brzezinski, Memorandum for Record, 29 January 1977, DDRS; Vance to President,

1 September 1978, Folder "State Department Evening Reports, 9/78," Box 39, Plains File, JCL; Brzezinski to Hamilton Jordan, "A Presidential Meeting with Cuban Political Prisoners," 18 September 1979, Folder "Cuban Political Prisoners, 12/8/78–1/15/80," Box 17, Hispanic Affairs—Torres, JCL; David Aaron to Phil Wise, "Cuban Political Prisoners," 6, 8 November 1979, Folder "Cuba 11/79–3/80," Box 14, RNSA.

15. Speech, Notre Dame University, 22 May 1977, *PPP*, 959.

16. Pastor to Brzezinski, "Cuba as a Soviet Puppet," 21 September 1979, Folder "CO38 7/1/79–1/20/81," Box CO-21, WHCF, Subject File, JCL; Frank Church to President, "Visit to Cuba," 12 August 1977, Folder "CO38 1/20/77–1/20/81," Box CO-20, WHCF, Subject File, JCL; Pastor to Brzezinski, "Your Lunch with Senator Church: Cuba," Folder "Meetings— PRC29: 8/3/77," Box 24, Subject File, ZBC; Response to Presidential Review Memorandum 36, "Soviet/Cuban Presence in Africa," 18 August 1978, 15–16, Folder "Presidential Review Memoranda 36–47," Box 105, Vertical File, JCL; Piero Gleijeses in *Diplomatic History* 31 (September 2007): 796.

17. Paul Henze Oral History, 9 May [?], NSA; "SCC Meeting—March 23, 1978, Cuba's Role in Africa: U.S. Responses," n.d., DDRS; Carter Handwritten Notes and "Statement," [September–October 1979], Folder "Cuba: Soviet Brigade (Miscellaneous), 9–10/79," Box 16, RNSA.

On Henze, see Edward G. Shirley, "Can't Anybody Here Play This Game?," *Atlantic Monthly*, February 1998, 48. A CIA officer on loan to Brzezinski's NSC staff who had served undercover in Ethiopia during the Nixon years, 1969–72, Henze later wrote *Horn of Africa: From War to Peace* (New York: Macmillan, 1991), and *Layers of Time: A History of Ethiopia* (New York: St. Martin's, 2000).

As president, Carter never ceased referring to Cuba as a Soviet surrogate: *PPP*, 1978, 904–5, 974, 977; *PPP*, 1979, 1602, 1754–57, 1802–6. Early drafts of his final statement on the subject were even more accusatory: Draft 3, for example, asserted that "Mr. Castro has sold the independence of his country to the Soviet Union" and referred to the Soviet combat brigade as "the latest manifestation of Moscow's dominance of Mr. Castro. It raises the level of that dominance" ("Draft Three, Proposed Report to the Nation on Soviet Troops in Cuba," 28 September 1979, DDRS). See also Jimmy Carter, *Keeping Faith: Memoirs of a President* (New York: Bantam, 1982), 235; Brzezinski, *Power and Principle*, 342.

18. U.S. Congress, Senate, Committee on Foreign Relations, *Vance Nomination*, 95th Cong., 1st sess., 11 January 1977, 17. Ambassador Young made his comment during a 25 January 1977 interview with CBS newsman Dan Rather; the State Department issued its response on 2 February during the normal daily press briefing; for Angola expert Gerald Bender, see U.S. Congress, House, Committee on International Relations, Subcommittee on Africa, *United States–Angolan Relations*, 95th Cong., 2nd sess., 25 May 1978, 25.

19. Vance Press Conference, 31 January 1977, *DOSB*, 21 February 1977, 142; Carter Comment, 16 February 1977, *PPP*, 173; Brzezinski to President, "Weekly National Security Report," 19 February 1977, DDRS.

20. Vance Press Conference, 4 March 1977, *DOSB*, 29 March 1977, 282; Carter Remarks during Telephone Call-In Program, 5 March 1977, *PPP*, 294.

21. Presidential Directive/NSC-6, 15 March 1977, Folder "Presidential Directives 1–20," Box 100, Vertical File, JCL; U.S. Congress, House, Committee on International Relations, *Foreign Assistance Legislation for Fiscal Year 1978*, pt. 1, 95th Cong., 1st sess., 16 March 1977, 14, 20 (Vance). The English-language transcript of the televised portion of Walters's 19 May 1977

interview is in Folder "CO38 7/1/77–8/31/77," Box CO-20, WHCF, Subject File, Countries, JCL; for the Spanish version, see *Bohemia*, 1 July 1977, 44–67. A second document containing material not used in the telecast is Barbara Walters, "An Interview with Fidel Castro," *Foreign Policy* 28 (Fall 1977): 22–51.

22. 26 *FR* 492, 16 January 1961.

23. *Zemel v. Rusk*, 381 U.S. 1 (1965).

24. Chase to Bundy, "Travel to Cuba," 17 September 1964, Folder "Cuba—Travel to Cuba by Americans Volume I, 12/63–9/64," Box 32, NSFJ, CF, Cuba; *United States v. Laub et al.*, 385 U.S. 475 (1967).

25. Memcon, Meeting with President Johnson, 19 December 1963, *FRUS* 1961–63, 11:909; *DOSB*, 6 January 1964, 10–11; Bundy to President, "Student Travel to Cuba," 21 May 1964, Folder "Cuba—Travel to Cuba by Americans Volume I, 12/63–9/64," Box 32, NSFJ, CF, Cuba. On the attorney general's brief attempt to terminate the travel ban, see Robert Kennedy to Dean Rusk, "Travel to Cuba," 12 December 1963, Abba Schwartz and Abram Chayes to Acting Secretary, "Travel Regulations," 13 December 1963, Chase to Bundy, "Travel Controls—Cuba," 18 December 1963, all in Folder "Cuba—Travel to Cuba by Americans Volume II [1 of 2], 12/63–7/65," Box 32, NSFJ, CF, Cuba; Arthur M. Schlesinger Jr. Diary, 13 December 1963, in *Journals, 1952–2000* (New York: Penguin, 2007), 214.

26. Public Notice 179, 16 January 1961, is 26 *FR* 492; Public Notice 257, 14 March 1967, is 32 *FR* 4140.

27. 32 *FR* 4122, 4140, both 16 March 1967; *Lynd v. Rusk*, 389 F.2d 940, 20 December 1967.

28. The 1 August 1975 Passport Office opinion is reprinted in U.S. Congress, House, Committee on International Relations, Subcommittee on International Trade and Commerce, *United States–Cuba Trade Promotion*, 94th Cong., 2nd sess., 22 July 1976, 9–10.

29. At this time, the Trading with the Enemy Act (PL 65-91, 65 *Stat*. 411) stated, "During the time of war or during any other period of national emergency declared by the President, the President may . . . investigate, regulate, direct and compel, nullify, void, prevent or prohibit, any . . . transactions involving, any property in which any foreign country or national thereof has any interest, by any person, or with respect to any property, subject to the jurisdiction of the United States." The best indication of congressional intent can be found in the *Congressional Record*, 9 July 1917, esp. 4842–43; Joint Resolution 3, 3 March 1921, 41 *Stat*. 1359.

30. President Truman's 17 December 1950 declaration is Executive Proclamation 2814, 3 *CFR* 99. JFK's prohibition began on 8 July 1963, when the Treasury Department replaced the Cuban Import Regulations with today's Cuban Assets Control Regulations (31 *CFR* 515). The most reliable published source of information on these issues is Michael Krinsky and David Golove, *United States Economic Measures against Cuba* (Northampton, Mass.: Aletheia, 1993), esp. 113.

31. U.S. Congress, House, Committee on International Relations, Subcommittee on International Trade and Commerce, *United States–Cuba Trade Promotion*, 44.

32. Brzezinski to President, "Cuba: Travel Restrictions, Visitation Rights, and Sugar Smut Disease," [February–early March 1977], Folder "Cuba, 1–4/77," Box 13, RNSA. Minor exceptions were made for members of Congress and their staff, for journalists and academics pursuing research projects, and for a small number of Cuban Americans—about one thousand

in 1976—to visit relatives in Cuba, usually as a humanitarian gesture involving terminal illnesses.

33. John H. Harper to Secretary Simon and Undersecretary Thomas, "Illegal American Tourism to Cuba via Canada," 7 January 1977, William Simon Papers, Lafayette College, Easton, Pennsylvania.

34. Press Conference, 9 March 1977, *PPP*, 340–41; Brzezinski to President, "Cuba: Travel Restrictions, Visitation Rights, and Sugar Smut Disease," [February–early March 1977], Folder "Cuba, 1–4/77," Box 13, RNSA.

35. U.S. Congress, House, Committee on International Relations, Subcommittee on Inter-American Affairs, *United States Policy toward the Caribbean*, 95th Cong., 1st sess., June 1977, 40; U.S. Congress, House, Committee on Foreign Affairs, Subcommittee on Inter-American Affairs, *Impact of Cuban-Soviet Ties in the Western Hemisphere, Spring 1980*, 96th Cong., 2nd sess., 1980, 82; Lawrence Theriot, "U.S.-Cuba Trade: Question Mark," *Commerce America*, 24 April 1978, 3.

36. Carter Speech to the OAS, 14 April 1977, *PPP*, 614; U.S. Congress, Senate, Committee on Foreign Relations, *Delusions and Reality: The Future of United States–Cuba Relations*, 95th Cong., 1st sess., October 1977, 7–8. Castro's "sense of morals" comment occurred during an interview with Bill Moyers broadcast on CBS News, 9 February 1977. For McGovern's briefing for President Carter on his 1977 trip, see "Merits and Tactics of Partially Lifting the Cuban Embargo," 19 April 1977, Folder "Cuba, 5–10/77," Box 13, CF, National Security Affairs, ZBC.

37. Pastor to Brzezinski, "Cuban Terrorists," 20 July 1997, Folder "Cuba, 5–10/79," Box 13, RNSA; Walters, "Interview with Fidel Castro," 36.

38. Speech, Havana, 17 December 1975; Press Conference, Dar es Salaam, Tanzania, 21 March 1977, in *Granma*, weekly English ed., 27 March 1977, 1. Carter's comments are 20 May, 30 May 1977, *PPP*, 947, 1043.

39. Castro Press Conference, 21 November 1978, in *Granma*, 22 November 1978, 2; Section 101, PL 94-265, 13 April 1976.

40. "Maritime Boundary: Modus Vivendi between the United States of America and Cuba, Effected by Exchange of Letters Signed at Havana April 27, 1977," 28 *UST* 5285; U.S. Congress, House, *Governing International Fishery Agreement with Cuba, Message from the President of the United States*, House Doc. 95-157, 95th Cong., 1st sess., 17 May 1977. For the negotiating sequence, see "Cuban-U.S. Relations Chronology (January–July, 1977)," Folder "Meetings—PRC 29: 8/3/77," Box 24, Subject File, ZBC.

41. "Exchange of Notes," 30 *UST* 2101; *Washington Post*, 29 April 1977, A1 (Todman). The chiefs of the interests sections were designated "counselors" in the Swiss and Czech embassies.

42. U.S. Congress, House, Committee on House Administration, *Presidential Campaign 1976*, 1:685; Donald Rumsfeld to President, "The Cuban Presence in Angola," 11 October 1976, enclosing Interagency Intelligence Memorandum NIO IIM 76-037-C, "Angola: Cuban Intentions and Changes in Cuban Personnel Strength," Folder "Cuba (7)," Box 4, National Security Affairs, Presidential CFs for Latin America, 1974–77, GRFL.

43. *London Times*, 7 August 1890, 6.

44. The Katangan gendarmes had been organized by European mercenaries and fought under Tshombe for an independent Katanga. See Gerald J. Bender, "Angola, the Cubans,

and American Anxieties," *Foreign Policy* 31 (Summer 1978): esp. 18; Raymond L. Garthoff, *Détente and Confrontation: American-Soviet Relations from Nixon to Reagan*, rev. ed. (Washington, D.C.: Brookings Institution, 1994), esp. 687–88.

45. Ball and JFK discussion, 29 August 1962, in *John F. Kennedy: The Great Crises: The Presidential Recordings*, ed. Philip Zelikow and Timothy Naftali (New York: Norton, 2001), 1:643; Don Bonker: U.S. Congress, House, Committee on International Relations, Subcommittee on Africa, *United States–Angolan Relations*, 95th Cong., 2nd sess., 25 May 1978, 31; Stansfield Turner, *Secrecy and Democracy: The CIA in Transition* (Boston: Houghton Mifflin, 1985), 86.

46. Castro Interview with French Weekly *Afrique-Asie*, May 1977, LANIC; Walters, "Interview with Fidel Castro," 40 ("We Cubans have neither trained, nor armed, nor had anything to do with that question of Zaire"); Cyrus Vance, *Hard Choices: Critical Years in America's Foreign Policy* (New York: Simon and Schuster, 1983), 90.

47. Conversation with Erich Honecker, Berlin, 3 April 1977, Folder "USSR-US Conference, 3/95: Briefing Book I," Box 117, Vertical File, JCL; Piero Gleijeses, "Truth or Credibility: Castro, Carter, and the Invasions of Shaba," *International History Review* 18 (February 1996): esp. 99–100.

48. U.S. Congress, House, Committee on International Relations, *Foreign Assistance Legislation 1978*, 9 (Vance); Carter Statements, 24 March 1977, *PPP*, 502, 22 April 1977, *PPP*, 703.

49. U.S. Congress, House, Committee on International Relations, *Foreign Assistance Legislation 1978*, 3; Colin L. Powell with Joseph E. Persico, *My American Journey* (New York: Random House, 1995), 415.

50. Carter Press Conference, 22 April 1977, *PPP* 703; Castro Speech, Moscow, 5 April 1977.

51. English-language transcript of the televised portion of Walters's 19 May 1977 interview, Folder "CO38 7/1/77–8/31/77," Box CO-20, WHCF, Subject File, Countries, JCL; Unsigned State Department or NSC Memorandum, "Shaba, Castro, and the Evidence," 6 June 1978, Folder "Cuba, 3–9/78," Box 13, RNSA; Castro Speech, Havana, 19 April 1976, in *Granma*, 20 April 1976, 2.

52. U.S. Congress, House, Committee on House Administration, *Presidential Campaign 1976*, 1:544, 685–86, 989.

53. Thirty-six thousand is the figure Fidel Castro gave East German premier Erich Honecker (Conversation with Erich Honecker, Berlin, 3 April 1977, Folder "USSR-US Conference, 3/95: Briefing Book I," Box 117, Vertical File, JCL); for the U.S. estimate, see Response to Presidential Review Memorandum 36, "Soviet/Cuban Presence in Africa," 18 August 1978, 12, Folder "Presidential Review Memoranda 36–47," Box 105, Vertical File, JCL; U.S. Congress, House, Committee on Foreign Affairs, Subcommittee on Inter-American Affairs, *Impact of Cuban-Soviet Ties in the Western Hemisphere, Spring 1979*, 96th Cong., 1st sess., April 1979, 11; U.S. Congress, House, Committee on Foreign Affairs, Subcommittee on Inter-American Affairs, *Impact of Cuban-Soviet Ties, Spring 1980*, 13, 122. For the president's view, see Carter, *Keeping Faith*, 256.

54. In February 1977, Cubans told Representative Jonathan Bingham that the number of Cuban troops had declined to twenty thousand; for Bingham's report to President Carter, see Folder "CO 38 1/20/77–1/20/81," Box CO-20, WHCF, Subject File, JCL; Conversation with Erich Honecker, Berlin, 3 April 1977, Folder "USSR-US Conference, 3/95: Briefing Book I," Box 117, Vertical File, JCL.

55. Pastor to David Aaron, "Cuban Statements about Cuba's Involvement in Africa," 7 August 1978, Folder "Cuba, 3–9/78," Box 13, National Security Affairs, CF, ZBC; Castro Press Conference, Dar es Salaam, Tanzania, 21 March 1977, in *Granma*, weekly English ed., 27 March 1977, 1.

56. Conversation with Erich Honecker, Berlin, 3 April 1977, Folder "USSR-US Conference, 3/95: Briefing Book I," Box 117, Vertical File, JCL; Carter Interview, 11 November 1977, *PPP*, 2011; Raúl Castro Speech, Angola, in *Granma*, weekly English ed., 18 December 1977, 2; Fidel Castro Speech, Havana, 24 December 1977, in *Granma*, weekly English ed., 1 January 1978, 2–4.

57. Fidel Castro Speech, Havana, 24 December 1977, in *Granma*, weekly English ed., 1 January 1978, 2–4.

58. Brzezinski to President, "The Soviet Union and Ethiopia: Implications for U.S.-Soviet Relations," 3 March 1978, Folder "Meetings—SCC61: 3/2/78," Box 28, ZBC; see also Peter Bourne to Warren Christopher, "Cuba to Supply Medical Personnel for Work in Iraq," 27 February 1978, DDRS; Brzezinski, *Power and Principle*, 178, 181–82. Brzezinski later downplayed the Horn's significance (Oral History, 13 June 1997, NSA).

59. CIA Intelligence Information Cable, "Increased Support for Ethiopia by the USSR and Cuba . . . ," 14 December 1977, DDRS.

60. Web page of George "Zazz" Sasadil, http://www.geozass.com, updated 6 March 2002. See Michela Wrong, *I Didn't Do It for You: How the World Betrayed a Small African Nation* (London: Fourth Estate, 2005), esp. chap. 10; "Ethiopia—Kagnew Station and Military Assistance, NSDM 231, 14 August 1973, NSSM 233, 23 October 1975, Box 2, National Security Decision Memoranda and Study Memoranda, GRFL; Paul B. Henze to Brzezinski, "Closing Kagnew," 31 March 1977, DDRS.

61. Tom J. Farer, *War Clouds on the Horn of Africa: The Widening Storm*, 2nd rev. ed. (New York: Carnegie Endowment for International Peace, 1979), 12; Walters, "Interview with Fidel Castro," 41; Odd Arne Westad, *Global Cold War* (New York: Cambridge University Press, 2005), esp. 253–87; Donald Levine, *Greater Ethiopia: The Evolution of a Multi-Ethnic Society* (Chicago: University of Chicago Press, 1974); Jeffrey Lefebvre, *Arms for the Horn: U.S. Security Policy in Ethiopia and Somalia, 1953–1991* (Pittsburgh: University of Pittsburgh Press, 1991); Tekeste Hegash and Kjetil Tronvoll, *Brothers at War: Making Sense of the Eritrean-Ethiopian War* (London: Currey, 2000).

62. "Summary of Conclusions," Policy Review Committee, 25 August 1977, DDRS; Carter Interview, 10 June 1977, and Press Conference, 13 June 1977, *PPP*, 1091, 1109; "Excerpts from Your Earlier Letters," a summary of correspondence between Moscow and Havana, [early March 1978], Folder "Meetings—SSC61: 3/2/78," Box 28, ZBC. Helpful guides to this conflict are Fred Halliday and Maxine Molyneux, *The Ethiopian Revolution* (London: Verso and NLB, 1981); Garthoff, *Détente and Confrontation*.

63. "INR Afternoon Analysis: Castro's Visit to the USSR," 11 April 1977, Folder "Cuba, 1–4/77," Box 13, National Security Affairs, CF, ZBC; Memcon, M. A. Manasov and Commandante Raúl Valdes Vivo, 7 May 1979, NSA; "Record of Conference btw Fidel Castro and Soviet Ambassador to Cuba V. I. Vorotnikov," 25 June 1979, *Cold War International History Project Bulletin* 8–9 (Winter 1996): 190; Piero Gleijeses, "Cuba and the Cold War, 1959–1980," in *Cambridge History of the Cold War*, ed. Melvyn Leffler and Odd Arne Westad (London: Cambridge University Press, forthcoming).

64. Minutes, NSC Meeting, Subject: The Horn of Africa, 23 February 1978, DDRS; Minutes, Special Coordination Committee, Subject: The Horn of Africa, 22 February 1978, Folder "Meetings—SSC 59A: 2/22/78," Box 28, Subject File, ZBC.

65. Henze to Brzezinski, "Possible Actions to Drive Home to the Soviets and Cubans the Need to Moderate their Intervention in the Horn," 1 March 1978, DDRS; Pastor to Brzezinski, "U.S. Policy to Cuba: SCC Meeting on Horn of Africa," 23 March 1978, "SSC Meeting—March 23, 1978, Cuba's Role in Africa: US Responses," 23 March 1978, both in Folder "Meetings—SCC 68: 3/27/78," Box 28, Subject File, ZBC.

66. Turner: Minutes, "SSC Meeting on Horn of Africa, 2 March 1978, 12:50–2:15 P.M., White House Situation Room," Folder "Meetings—SSC61: 3/2/78," Box 28, Subject File, ZBC. The interview notes by Thomas Hughes, the former State Department official, are attached to Peter Tarnoff to Brzezinski, "Tom Hughes' Memorandum of Conversation on His Talk with the Cuban Vice President," 22 March 1978, Folder "Cuba 2/78–4/78," Box 10, Geographic File, ZBC.

67. Summary of Conclusions, Special Coordination Committee Meeting, "Horn of Africa," 27 March 1978, Folder "Meetings—SCC77: 5/15/78," Box 28, Subject File, ZBC; David Aaron Exit Interview, 15 December 1980, DDRS.

68. Lyle Lane to Secretary of State, "Fidel Castro Denies Cuban Involvement in Shaba," 18 May 1978, Folder "Cuban Troops in Zaire, 5/78–6/78," Box 55, Staff Office Files, Press Office, Powell, JCL. See also unsigned State Department or NSC Memorandum, "Shaba, Castro, and the Evidence," 6 June 1978, Folder "Cuba, 3–9/78," Box 13, RNSA.

69. Secretary of State to USINT, "Message for Foreign Minister Malmierca," 19 May 1978, reply from Havana with same title and date, both in Folder "Cuban Troops in Zaire, 5/78–6/78," Box 55, Staff Office Files, Press Office, Powell, JCL. For the State Department's accusation that Castro was not telling the truth, see "The White House News Summary, Wednesday, June 14, 1978," Folder "Cuban Troops in Zaire, 5/78–6/78," Box 55, Staff Office Files, Press Office, Powell, JCL. For Carter Press Conferences, 25 May, 14 June 1978, see *PPP*, 973, 1092–93; Lane to Secretary of State, "Response to Secretary's Message," 19 May 1978, Folder "Cuban Troops in Zaire, 5/78–6/78," Box 55, Staff Office Files, Press Office, Powell, JCL.

70. Wayne S. Smith, *Closest of Enemies*, 140; Gleijeses, "Truth or Credibility," 97; unsigned State Department or NSC Memorandum, "Shaba, Castro, and the Evidence," 6 June 1978, Folder "Cuba, 3–9/78," Box 13, RNSA.

71. Gleijeses, "Truth or Credibility," 102. But Gleijeses also notes that "the role of the *Angolan* government in the two invasions of Shaba remains murky. Probably it was aware of the Katangans' plans and allowed them to proceed, and probably it gave them some help" (99; emphasis added).

72. Brzezinski, *Power and Principle*, 209 (emphasis added); *Meet the Press*, 28 May 1978, *DOSB*, July 1978, 26 (emphasis added).

73. Lane to Secretary of State, "Solarz Meets with Fidel Castro," 13 June 1978, Folder "Cuban Troops in Zaire, 5/78–6/78," Box 55, Staff Office Files, Press Office, Powell, JCL. For a more detailed report on this nine-hour meeting, see Folder "Cuba—5/78–8/78," Box 10, Geographic File, ZBC.

74. Memcon, "US/Cuban Relations, December 3–4, 1978," Havana, [early December 1978], Brzezinski to President, "Conversations in Havana," [early December 1978], both in

"Cuba: President Carter's Trip, May 12–17, 2002," Vertical File, JCL; for Vaky's 14 December 1978 speech, see *DOSB*, March 1979, 64–67.

75. On the specific nature of U.S. support, see Odom to Aaron, "SSC Working Group Meeting on Zaire—Friday, May 19, 1978," Folder "Meetings—SSC 80: 5/26/78," Box 28, Subject File, ZBC.

76. Carter Speech, Winston-Salem, North Carolina, 17 March 1978, *PPP*, 531–32; U.S. Congress, House, Committee on International Relations, *Foreign Assistance Legislation 1979*, pt. 1, 95th Cong., 2nd sess., February–March 1978, 61 (Fascell).

77. Carter's Remarks, 12 May 1978, Press Conference, 25 May 1978, both in *PPP*, 904, 975. First offered as Senate Concurrent Resolution 91, the Senate measure became Senate Unprinted Amendment 1379, *Congressional Record*, 28 June 1978, 19260–65. For earlier opposition see Senator Bob Dole to President, 7 February 1978, Folder "Cuba, 11/77–2/78," Box 13, National Security Affairs, CF, ZBC.

78. Senator Church to President, "Visit to Cuba," 12 August 1977, Folder "CO 38 1/20/77–1/20/81," WHCF, Subject File, JCL; Smith: U.S. Congress, House, Committee on International Relations, Subcommittee on Inter-American Affairs, *Impact of Cuban-Soviet Ties in the Western Hemisphere*, 95th Cong., 2nd sess., March–April 1978, 61; Wayne Smith Interview; *Washington Post*, 25 May 1978, A3; Brzezinski to President, "Conversations in Havana," [early December 1978], in "Cuba: President Carter's Trip, May 12–17, 2002," Vertical File, JCL.

79. Handwritten "Memo To: Dr. Z.B. From: Dr..B. Benes," 24 March 1978, Brzezinski to David Aaron, "Cuba," 27 March 1978, both in Folder "Cuba, 2/78–4/78," Box 10, ZBC.

80. Pastor to Brzezinski, "My Conversation with [redacted]," 11 January 1978, Folder "CO 38 1/20/77–1/20/81," Box CO-20, WHCF, Subject File, JCL.

81. Carlucci to Brzezinski, "Message from Fidel Castro," 22 March 1978, Folder "Cuba 2/78–4/78," Box 10, Geographic File, ZBC.

82. "Memo To: Dr. Z.B. From: Dr. B. Benes," 24 March 1978, Folder "Cuba 1/78–4/78," Box 10, Geographic File, ZBC; for Carter and Castro's letters carried by Paul Austin, 7, 26 February 1978, respectively, see Folder "Cuba 2/78–4/78," Box 10, Geographic File, ZBC.

83. Kissinger to President Ford, 15 March 1976, Folder "March 15, 1976—Ford, Kissinger," Box 18, National Security Affairs, Memoranda of Conversations, 1973–77, GRFL.

84. Aaron to Brzezinski, "Meeting with Cubans in New York," 13 April 1978, Folder "Cuba 2/78–4/78," Box 10, Geographic File, ZBC.

85. U.S. Congress, Senate, Committee on Foreign Relations, *Vance Nomination*, 99; Castro Speech, Havana, 24 December 1977, in *Granma*, weekly English ed., 1 January 1978, 2–4. The Cuban leader had said the same thing to Barbara Walters during a May 1977 interview (*Bohemia*, 1 July 1977, 67). For President Carter's 1977 comments on Cuban political prisoners, see *PPP*, 222, 1043, 1046.

86. Wayne S. Smith, *Closest of Enemies*, 147; "Memorandum of Conversation, Meeting Held on June 15, 1978, St. Regis Hotel, New York City, 9:30 A.M.," Folder "Cuba—5/78–8/78," Box 10, Geographic File, ZBC.

87. "Memorandum of Conversation, Meeting Held on June 15, 1978, St. Regis Hotel, New York City, 9:30 A.M.," Folder "Cuba—5/78–8/78," Box 10, Geographic File, ZBC; "Summary of Conversation between U.S. and Cuban Officials," 5 July 1978, Vance to President, "Further Contact with Castro's Representative, Jose Luis Padron," 7 July 1978, both in Folder "Cuba—Alpha Channel: 6/78–10/78," Box 10, Subject File, ZBC.

88. U.S. Congress, Senate, Committee on Foreign Relations, *Delusions and Reality*, 7.

89. U.S. Congress, House, Committee on International Relations, Subcommittee on Inter-American Affairs, *Impact of Cuban-Soviet Ties* (1978), 50. For a list of ten dual nationals held in Cuban jails for counterrevolutionary activities, see John T. Wainwright to President, "Status of U.S. Citizens Imprisoned in Cuba on Political Charges; and Efforts to Improve U.S.-Cuban Relations," 22 February 1977, Folder "CO38 1/20/77–3/31/77," Box CO-20, WHCF, Subject File, JCL. On Everett Jackson, see U.S. Congress, House, Committee on Foreign Affairs, *Caribbean Nations: Assessments of Conditions and U.S. Influence*, 96th Cong., 1st sess., July 1979, 44–45, for the Swiss diplomat's observation of the trial.

90. U.S. Congress, House, Committee on Foreign Affairs, *Caribbean Nations*, 25n; Memcon, "US/Cuban Relations, December 3–4, 1978, Havana," [early December 1978], "Cuba: President Carter's Trip, May 12–17, 2002," Vertical File, JCL.

91. Pastor to Brzezinski and David Aaron, "Lolita Lebron," 26 September 1978, Pastor to Brzezinski, "Letter to Townsend Hoopes," 31 August 1978, both in DDRS; Lawrence K. Lunt, *Leave Me My Spirit* (Tempe, Ariz.: Affiliated Writers of America, 1990), 2. On Lunt, see Folder "Cuba—Lawrence Lunt Case," Box 11, John Marsh Files, 1974–77, GRFL; Folder "Cuba, 5/76–10/76," Box 9, Issues Office—Stuart Eizenstat, Jimmy Carter Pre-Presidential Papers, JCL; Brzezinski to Hamilton Jordan, "A Presidential Meeting with Cuban Political Prisoners," 18 September 1979, Folder "CO38 7/1/79–1/20/81," Box CO-21, WHCF, Subject File, JCL. For U.S. prisoners in 1980, most apprehended while transporting illegal drugs, see U.S. Congress, House, Committee on Foreign Affairs, Subcommittee on Inter-American Affairs, *Impact of Cuban-Soviet Ties, Spring 1980*, 71, 87.

92. Vance to President, "Contact with Castro's Representative, Jose Luis Padron," 19 June 1978, Brzezinski to President, "Contact with Castro's Representative Jose Luis Padron," [after 19 June 1978], both in Folder "Cuba—Alpha Channel: 6/78–10/78," Box 10, Subject File, ZBC.

93. "Memorandum of Conversation, Meeting Held on June 15, 1978, St. Regis Hotel, New York City, 9:30 A.M.," Folder "Cuba—5/78–8/78," Box 10, Geographic File, ZBC.

94. For the 8 August meeting in Atlanta, see Warren Christopher to President, 9 August 1978, Folder "State Department Evening Reports, 8/78," Box 39, Plains File, JCL.

95. Gates to Aaron, 27 September 1978, Folder "Cuba 9/78–10/78," Box 10, Subject File, ZBC.

96. Walters Interview, *Bohemia*, 1 July 1977, 61; Wayne S. Smith, *Closest of Enemies*, 119–20; INR—William G. Bowdler to Secretary, "Cuban Motives on Puerto Rico," 14 September 1978, Folder "Cuba, 3–9/78," Box 13, RNSA.

97. Christopher and Brzezinski to President, "Discussions with the Cubans," 19 October 1978, Brzezinski to President, "Private Talks with the Cubans," 24 October 1978, both in Folder "Cuba—Alpha Channel: 6/78–10/78," Box 10, Subject File, ZBC.

98. Aaron to President, "Private Meeting with the Cubans," 30 October 1978, Folder "Cuba—Alpha Channel: 6/78–10/78," Box 10, Subject File, ZBC; for Pastor's growing concern, see Pastor to Aaron, "Cuba and Nickel," 20 October 1978, Folder "Cuba 9/78–9/79," Box 10, Geographic File, ZBC.

99. "Memorandum of Conversation, Meeting Held on June 15, 1978, St. Regis Hotel, New York City, 9:30 A.M.," Folder "Cuba—5/78–8/78," Box 10, Geographic File, ZBC; Tarnoff to

Brzezinski, "Castro Appeals to the Cuban-American Community," 13 September 1978, Folder "Cuba, 3–9/78," Box 13, RNSA.

100. Warren Christopher to President, 7 September 1978, Folder "Department Evening Reports, 9/78," Box 39, Plains File, JCL.

101. Press Conference, Havana, 21 November 1978, in *Granma*, 22 November 1978, 2–3; Bernardo Benes and Alfredo Duran to Phil Wise, White House, "The Issuance of Parole Visas to 5,000 Ex-Political Prisoners of Cuba," and Bernardo Benes to Mary King, 21 September 1979, both enclosed with Brzezinski to Jordan, "A Presidential Meeting with Cuban Political Prisoners," 18 September 1979, Folder "CO38 7/1/79–1/20/81," Box CO-21, WHCF, Subject File, JCL. For indispensable coverage of the Benes initiative, see Robert M. Levine, *Secret Missions to Cuba: Fidel Castro, Bernardo Benes, and Cuban Miami* (New York: Palgrave Macmillan, 2001); Wayne S. Smith, *Closest of Enemies*, 146–69; Mirta Ojito, *Finding Mañana: A Memoir of a Cuban Exodus* (New York: Penguin, 2005), 37–56.

102. Vance to President, 13 November 1978, Folder "State Department Evening Reports, 11/78," Box 39, Plains File, JCL; Pastor to Brzezinski, "Castro and Political Prisoners: Your Request for My Reaction," 4 May 1979, Folder "Cuba, 5/79," Box 13, RNSA; USINT (Smith) to Secretary of State, "Political Prisoners Parole Program," 31 July 1979, Folder "Cuba, 7–8/79," Box 14, RNSA. For the Immigration and Naturalization Service foot-dragging, see Special Coordination Committee Meeting, "Cuba after the Summit," 20 July 1979, NSA; Brzezinski to President, "Cuban Political Prisoner Program," n.d., President Carter to Griffin Bell, 10 August 1979, Benjamin R. Civiletti to President, "Cuban Political Prisoner Program," 16 August 1979, all in Folder "Cuba, 7–8/79," Box 14, RNSA.

103. Smith's comment reported in Memcon, Peter Tarnoff, Robert Pastor, and Wayne Smith with José Luis Padrón, Ricardo Alarcón, and José Antonio Arbesú, Havana, 17 June 1980, "Cuba: President Carter's Trip, May 12–17, 2002," Vertical File, JCL.

104. Rowland Evans and Robert Novak, "Cuba's Mig23s," *Washington Post*, 15 November 1978, A19. Two weeks earlier, in late October, someone in the Department of Defense had leaked this news to the Associated Press, which ran the story on 30 October, but it received little media attention: on 31 October, the *Post* ran the story in a small article at the bottom of p. 16.

105. Huntington to Brzezinski, "Cuban Missile Crisis: Offensive Weapons," 22 November 1978, Folder "Cuba, 10–11/78," Box 13, National Security Affairs, CF, ZBC; Raymond L. Garthoff, "American Reaction to Soviet Aircraft in Cuba, 1962 and 1978," *Political Science Quarterly* 95 (Fall 1980): 429–35; DOS, "White Paper on the Presence of Soviet Troops in Cuba," 28 September 1979, DDRS.

106. Gloria Duffy, "Crisis Prevention in Cuba," in *Managing U.S.-Soviet Rivalry: Problems of Crisis Prevention*, ed. Alexander L. George (Boulder, Colo.: Westview, 1983), 296; without citing his sources, Garthoff insisted that Moscow shipped both versions of the MiG-23 to Cuba ("American Reaction to Soviet Aircraft in Cuba," 439).

107. Castro Press Conference, 21 November 1978, in *Granma*, 22 November 1978, 2–3; Carter Press Conference, 30 November 1978, *PPP*, 2101.

108. Press Conference, 9 December 1978, in *Granma*, 11 December 1978, 2–3.

109. John McCone, "Discussions with President Johnson on the Johnson Ranch on Friday, December 27th," 29 December 1963, Folder "Meetings with the President 23 November

1963–27 December 1973," John McCone Memoranda, Meetings with the President, LBJL; Odom Interview.

110. [Captain Elmo Zumwalt?], Department of Defense, "General Pressures to Create a Contingency," 11 March 1963, Folder 9, Box 6, Joseph Califano Papers, JFKL. For evidence of the Johnson administration's awareness of how much the overflights—up to three a week— annoyed the Cubans, see the collection of Cuba's public statements in Foreign Broadcast Information Service, "Report on Cuban Propaganda—No. 16. Castro and Khrushchev on Overflights," FBIS Research Series RS 71, 30 June 1964, Folder "Cuba Overflights Volume 1, 1/64–1/65," Box 29, NSFJ, CF, Cuba (see also Folder "Cuban Overflights Volume II, 3/64– 7/65"); Chase, "Meeting with the President, November 19, 1964—Cuba," Folder "Miscellaneous Meetings, Vol. I," Box 18, Files of McGeorge Bundy, NSFJ. On the flight frequencies and the general tenor of U.S. policy, see "Summary Record of National Security Council Meeting No. 531, May 5, 1964, 12:00 noon—Laos and Overflights of Cuba," "National Security Council Record of Actions," 5 May 1964, both in Folder "NSC Meetings, Vol. 2 Tab 3 5/5/64," NSFJ, NSC Meetings File.

111. Chase to Bundy, "Legal Rationale for Cuban Overflights," 14 July 1964, Folder "Cuba Overflights Volume II, 3/64–7/64," Box 20, NSFJ, CF, Cuba; Henze to Brzezinski, "SR-71 Flights over Cuba," 2 November 1979, DDRS. For State Department opposition, see Summary of Conclusions, Special Coordination Committee Meeting, "Horn of Africa," 27 March 1978, Folder "Meetings—SCC 77: 5/15/78," Box 28, Subject File, ZBC.

112. Memcon, "US/Cuban Relations, December 3–4, 1978, Havana," [early December 1978], Brzezinski to President, "Conversations in Havana," [early December 1978], Tarnoff and Pastor, "Memorandum of Conversation," Havana, 2–3 December 1978, all in "Cuba: President Carter's Trip, May 12–17, 2002," Vertical File, JCL.

113. Presidential Review Memorandum 36, "Soviet/Cuban Presence in Africa," 18 August 1978, DDRS; Castro Interview by Robert MacNeil, February 1985, LANIC.

114. USINT to Secretary of State, "Castro Takes Pessimistic Line on U.S. Relations," 11 December 1978, "Cuba: Carter's Trip 2002," Vertical File, JCL; for Brzezinski Cover Memo forwarding the reports of Pastor and Tarnoff, see Brzezinski to President, "Conversations in Havana," [19 or 20 December 1978?], "Cuba: Carter's Trip 2002," Vertical File, JCL; Castro Speech, Havana, 1 January 1979, in *Granma*, 2 January 1979, 2–3.

115. Speech, Havana, 1 January 1979, in *Granma*, 2 January 1979, 2–3.

116. Pastor to Brzezinski and Aaron, "Cuba Conversation," 19 December 1978, "Cuba: Carter's Trip 2002," Vertical File, JCL.

117. *NYT*, 13 July 1979, 1.

118. Speech, 15 July 1979, *PPP*, 1235–41.

119. Brzezinski to President, "NSC Weekly Report #83," 28 December 1978, DDRS; Joseph Kraft, "Vance's Role," *Washington Post*, 22 June 1978, A27; "Rapping for Carter's Ear," *Time*, 12 June 1978, 18; "Remarks and a Question-and-Answer Session," at Fort Worth, Texas, 23 June 1978, *PPP*, 1159–60. Promptly leaked to the press, Brzezinski's memo was reprinted in *The Nation*, 24 June 1978, 749.

120. Brzezinski to President, "NSC Weekly Report #104," 27 July 1979, Folder "Weekly Reports to the President, 102–120: 7/79–12/79," Box 42, Subject File, ZBC. The sentence "Cy Vance is reluctant" is redacted from the Carter Library's copy; with privileged access, Brzezinski includes it in his memoir, *Power and Principle*, 565.

121. Vance Press Conference, 5 September 1979, Folder "Soviet Troops in Cuba, 9/79," Box 79, Staff Office Files, Press Office, Powell, JCL; Brzezinski, *Power and Principle*, 428.

122. U.S. Congress, Senate, Committee on Foreign Relations, *Hearings on EX.Y, 96-1, Part 2*, 96th Cong., 1st sess., July 1979, 178–79. For Brzezinski's concerns about the Castro-Torrijos friendship, see Brzezinski to President, "Weekly National Security Report #6," 25 March 1977, DDRS.

123. U.S. Congress, Senate, Committee on Foreign Relations, *Hearings on EX.Y, 96-1, Part 2*, 179–80; Wayne S. Smith, *Closest of Enemies*, 183.

124. Stone to President, 24 July 1979, Vance to Stone, 27 July 1979, both in Folder "CO38 7/1/79–1/20/81," Box CO-21, WHCF, Subject File, JCL; Odom Interview. See also Interagency Intelligence Memorandum, "Updated Report on Soviet Ground Forces Brigade in Cuba," 18 September 1979, Folder "Cuba-USSR Brigade," Box 34, Chief of Staff, Jordan, JCL.

125. Odom Interview; Brzezinski, *Power and Principle*, 246.

126. A State Department synopsis reported that the Soviet unit was "unassociated with the presence of Cuban units or personnel" ("White Paper on the Presence of Soviet Troops in Cuba," 28 September 1978, DDRS).

127. Turner, *Secrecy and Democracy*, 232–34; Turner, foreword to David D. Newsom, *The Soviet Brigade in Cuba: A Study in Political Diplomacy* (Bloomington: Indiana University Press, 1987), viii, ix–x; see also 21–22. Another explanation offered by an involved State Department official (Garthoff, *Détente and Confrontation*, 920) is that the agency simply needed a term to distinguish the brigade from advisory or logistical units—"that term ['combat'] was not intended to designate its purpose, which remained unknown." See also Gloria Duffy, "Crisis Mangling and the Cuban Brigade," *International Security* 8 (Summer 1983): 75–6.

128. Radio Commentary, 9 October 1977, in *Reagan on Cuba: Selected Statements by the President* (n.p.: Cuban American National Foundation, 1986), 15.

129. Senator Church's 30 August news conference was reported on the front page of the *Washington Post*, 31 August and 6 September 1979; Secretary of State to U.S. Mission NATO and Others, "Soviet Ground Unit in Cuba," 31 August 1979, NSA; David Reuther to P, S/M and others, "Press Guidance," 28 July 1979, NSA; "Statement of David D. Newsom," 5 September 1979, in *The Cuban Missile Crisis, 1962: A National Security Archive Document Set*, ed. Laurence Chang (Alexandria, Va.: Chadwyck-Healey, 1990), document 3293.

130. U.S. Congress, Senate, Committee on Foreign Relations, *Delusions and Reality*, 2–8. For the criticism of Church, see Carter, *Keeping Faith*, 262–63; Newsom, *Soviet Brigade in Cuba*, 3, 50, 56–58; Vance, *Hard Choices*, 361; Brzezinski, *Power and Principle*, 347.

131. Vance to President, "Senator McGovern's Memorandum on Cuba," 23 April 1977, Brzezinski to President, "Your Request for Comments on Senator McGovern's Memorandum on Cuba," 27 April 1977, both in Folder "Cuba, 5-10/77," Box 13, RNSA.

132. *Congressional Record*, 11 May 1977, 14343 (Helms); *Congressional Record*, 6, 10 June 1977, 17640–42, 18436–37 (Dole); Radio Address, 16 May 1977, in *Reagan on Cuba*, 10, 13–14 (Reagan).

133. Brzezinski to President, "Your Request for Comments on Senator McGovern's Memorandum on Cuba," 27 April 1977, Pastor to Brzezinski, "Cuba Policy—PRC Meeting," 8 March 1977, Pastor to Brzezinski, "Clarification Requested on Your Memorandum to the President on the McGovern Amendment to Lift the Embargo on Cuba," 2 May 1977, all in "Cuba: President Carter's Trip, May 12–17, 2002," Vertical File, JCL; Odom Interview.

134. *Congressional Record*, 16 June 1977, 19438. Section 123 of PL 95-88, 3 August 1977, repealed Section 620(a)(1) and Section 620 (a)(3) of the Foreign Assistance Act of 1961. The first had been added in August 1962 (PL 87-565, 76 *Stat.* 255), the second in December 1963 (PL 88-205, 77 *Stat.* 386).

135. *DOSB*, October 1979, 63; a transcript of the State Department's daily press briefing for 31 August 1979 is reprinted as appendix A in Newsom, *Soviet Brigade in Cuba*. Brzezinski had informed President Carter months earlier that about two thousand Soviet military personnel were stationed in Cuba and that "we have no basis under the 1962 agreements to object to them" (Brzezinski to President, "NSC Weekly Report #98," 25 May 1979, DDRS). The State Department took the same position: the 1962 Kennedy-Khrushchev exchanges "do not address the question of Soviet ground forces" (Cyrus Vance to President, "Your Forthcoming Appearance with Senator Stone," 29 August 1979, enclosed with Henry Owen to President, "Possible Talks with Senator Stone Thursday, August 30, 1979," DDRS).

136. "White Paper on the Presence of Soviet Troops in Cuba," 28 September 1979, DDRS; see also Brzezinski to President, "Soviet Brigade in Cuba—The Kennedy Years," 12 September 1979, Folder "Cuba 9/78–9/79," Box 10, Geographic File, ZBC; Vance to President, "Summary of the 1962 and 1970 Understandings," 11 October 1979, Folder "Cuba: Soviet Brigade, 10/2/79–5/80," Box 16, RNSA.

137. Press Conference, 5 September 1979, Folder "Soviet Troops in Cuba, 9/79," Box 79, Staff Office Files, Press Office, Powell, JCL; Statement to the Press, 7 September 1979, *PPP*, 1602–3.

138. Brzezinski Interview with Editors, 21 September 1979, in *NYT*, 23 September 1979, A4; Carter Question-and-Answer Sessions, 21, 25 September 1979, *PPP*, 1714, 1754–57.

139. Press Conference, 28 September 1979, LANIC.

140. Ibid. Two days later, Castro repeated his comments to CBS News correspondent Dan Rather (transcript in Folder "Soviet Troops in Cuba, 9/79," Box 78, Staff Office Files, Press Office, Powell, JCL). Castro further reiterated the point to two U.S. envoys in January 1980 and to the Cuban public in his 1980 May Day speech (Memcon, Fidel Castro with Peter Tarnoff, Robert Pastor, and Wayne Smith, 16 January 1980, in "Cuba: President Carter's Trip, May 12–17, 2002," Vertical File, JCL).

141. Marshall Brement to Brzezinski, "VBB: The Soviet Brigade in Cuba—Where Do We Go from Here?," 12 September 1979, Folder "Meetings—Vance/Brown/Brzezinski: 8/79–9/79," Box 42, Subject File, ZBC. The U.S. negotiating position is outlined in the Mini-Special Coordination Committee Meeting, "Summary of Conclusions," 29 August 1979, Folder "Cuba 9/78–9/79," Box 10, Geographic File, ZBC; Gromyko's 5 September 1979 statement is quoted in Newsom, *Soviet Brigade in Cuba*, 45–46.

The Soviet position carried the day over Cuba's opposition, as Fidel Castro explained to East German premier Erich Honecker: "We were of the opinion that it should be termed a brigade. But after explaining all of this in the Soviet Union, it was determined that it would be a study [training] center. Of course, the Soviet comrades did not want to heat up the international situation, and since SALT II was still pending before the Senate, we had no other choice than to call it a study center. This was now the name of the brigade, Study Center No. 2. Once this had been said we had to stick with this term" (Minutes of Meeting between Erich Honecker and Fidel Castro, Havana, 28 May 1980, Folder "USSR-US Conference, 3/95: Briefing Book (II)," Box 117, Vertical File, JCL).

142. "Interim Report by the Preparedness Investigating Subcommittee, Appointed under Senate Resolution 75 of the 88th Congress, on the Cuban Military Buildup," 9 May 1963; *Congressional Record*, 2 October 1979, 27032–36; JFK Press Conference, 20 August 1963, *PPP*, 636.

143. Memcon, Fidel Castro with Peter Tarnoff, Robert Pastor, and Wayne Smith, 16 January 1980, in "Cuba: President Carter's Trip, May 12–17, 2002," Vertical File, JCL; Interagency Intelligence Memorandum, "Updated Report on Soviet Ground Forces Brigade in Cuba," 18 September 1979, Folder "Cuba-USSR Brigade," Box 34, Chief of Staff, Jordan, JCL; Jorge I. Domínguez, "Cuba as Superpower: Havana and Moscow, 1979," *Cold War International History Project Bulletin* 8–9 (Winter 1996): 216.

144. For the evolving estimates during 1963, see McCone, "Memorandum for the Record," 9 January 1963, *FRUS* 1961–63, vols. 10–12, microfiche supplement, document 592; JFK Press Conferences, 24 January 1963, 7, 21 February, 3 April 1963, *PPP*, 93, 154, 207, 305; "Soviet Forces in Cuba," 5 February 1963, *FRUS* 1961–63, vols. 10–12, microfiche supplement, document 612; "Department of Defense, Special Briefing by Honorable Robert S. McNamara, Secretary of Defense, State Department Auditorium, 5:00 P.M. February 6, 1963," Folder "Cuba, 9/79–5/80," Box 70, Staff Office Files, Counsel, Cutler, JCL; see also aide-mémoire, 18 February 1963, Folder "Cuba General, 2/63," Box 37A, NSFK; McCone, "Memorandum on Cuban Policy," 25 April 1963, *FRUS* 1961–63, vols. 10–12, microfiche supplement, document 670; *CINCLANT Historical Account of the Cuban Crisis—1963* (Norfolk, Va.: Atlantic Command, 1963), 6; "Annex 3. C. Soviet Forces in Cuba," 18 April 1963, Folder "Cuba General, Standing Committee 4/63," Box 38, NSFK; "Investigation of the Preparedness Program," Interim Report by Preparedness Subcommittee of the Committee on Armed Services, United States Senate, . . . on the Cuban Military Buildup," 9 May 1963, Folder "Defense, Armed Services Committee, Interim Report on the Cuban Military Build-Up," Box 78, POF; CIA, NIE 85-63, "Situation and Prospects in Cuba," 14 June 1963, *FRUS* 1961–63, vols. 10–12, microfiche supplement, document 687; the August estimate is *FRUS* 1961–63, 11:857; "Draft State-Defense Contingency Plan for a Coup in Cuba," 26 September 1963, Folder 5, Box 6, Joseph Califano Papers, National Archives and Records Administration, Washington, D.C.; DIA to McNamara, 8 October 1963, Memcon, Gromyko, JFK, and others, 10 October 1963, both in *FRUS* 1961–63, 11:874–75; DIA to Secretary of Defense, 24 October 1963, *FRUS* 1961–63, vols. 10–12, microfiche supplement, document 716; John McCone, "Discussions with President Johnson on the Johnson Ranch on Friday, December 27th," 29 December 1963, Folder "Meetings with the President 23 November 1963–27 December 1973," John McCone Memoranda, Meetings with the President, LBJL. This was repeated by separate CIA and DIA memoranda on 18 December ("no identifiable Soviet ground combat units remain on the island") and 20 December ("no organized Soviet ground combat units remain in Cuba"), respectively. At President Johnson's first Cuba briefing, NSC staffer Gordon Chase said that the four to seven thousand Soviet military personnel were "mostly advisers and technicians" and noted that "a net outflow appears to be continuing." Joint CIA-DIA Memorandum, "Assessment of Soviet Military Personnel in Cuba," 20 December 1963, DDRS; CIA, "The Situation in Cuba," 18 December 1963, *FRUS* 1961–63, vols. 10–12, microfiche supplement, document 731; DIA memo, 20 December 1963, *FRUS* 1961–63, vols. 10–12, microfiche supplement, document 734; Gordon Chase, "Memorandum for the President, Meeting on Cuba—December 19, 1963, Folder "Chron. File 8/63–12/63," Box 1, Gordon Chase Papers, JFKL.

145. The Nixon-era estimate is NSSM 32—Cuba, 2 July 1969, NSA; McGeorge Bundy, "The Brigade's My Fault," *NYT*, 23 October 1979, A23.

146. Reagan Speech, 18 September 1979, in *Reagan on Cuba*, 18; Humphrey in *Congressional Record*, 27 September 1979, 26419.

147. On 29 September, Brzezinski received mixed advice from an "Alumni Panel" of former foreign policy officials. Among the hawks, Henry Kissinger suggested that the administration assert that the Soviet brigade was intended to heighten regional instability in the Caribbean and Central America, and former CIA director John McCone urged the administration, "Don't accept the training unit version." George Ball, Sol Linowitz, Clark Clifford, and Averell Harriman all seemed to agree with McGeorge Bundy, who told Brzezinski that Castro was "nearer the truth on the facts" regarding the brigade. Everyone agreed that neither the president nor Vance should have said "the status quo is not acceptable" (Memorandum Containing Verbatim Notes of the Meeting, Brzezinski to President, 29 September 1979, DDRS).

148. Marshall Brement to Brzezinski and Aaron, "Foreign Reaction to the Brigade Issue," 14 September 1979, Folder "Presidential Interviews, 5/77–5/80," Box 50, Collection #7, RNSA; Nick Platt to Brzezinski and Aaron, "Letter to Japanese Prime Minister on President's Decision on the Soviet Brigade," 1 October 1979, Folder "Platt Chron. File, 10/79," Box 68, Collection #26, National Security Affairs, Staff Material, Far East—Platt, JCL; Gromyko at United Nations quoted in Newsom, *Soviet Brigade in Cuba*, 45–46.

149. Carter to General Secretary Leonid Brezhnev, 25 September 1979, L. Brezhnev to James E. Carter, 27 September 1979, both in DDRS. For the minutes of the Soviet Politburo meeting discussing Carter's letter and the Soviet response, see Folder "USSR-US Conference, 3/95: Briefing book (II)," Box 117, Vertical File, JCL.

150. Address, 1 October 1979, *PPP*, 1802–6. In a background sheet handed to reporters just minutes before the president's speech, the State Department admitted, "We do not know what they're doing" (DOS, "Background on the Question of Soviet Troops in Cuba," Press Release 92, 1 October 1979, *DOSB*, November 1979, 9–11).

151. Brzezinski to President, "NSC Weekly Report #100," Folder "Weekly Reports to the President, 102–120 (7/79–12/79)," Box 42; Brzezinski to President, "Different Outcomes for the Cuban Problem—And Their International and Domestic Consequences," 17 September 1979, Folder "Cuba 9/78–9/79," Box 10, Geographic File, both in ZBC.

152. *Congressional Record*, 2 October 1979, 27031–32 (Helms), 27037–39 (Baker), 27040 (Hatch), 3 October 1979, 27113–14 (Pell), 27114 (Tower); see also the criticism by moderate Republicans such as John Chafee and liberal Democrats such as Alan Cranston, 27115, 27116. For Kennedy's comment, see *NYT*, 29 January 1980, A12.

153. Schlesinger, *Journals*, 474; *Congressional Record*, 2 October 1979, 27039; *NYT*, 18 September 1979, A12; *Baltimore Sun*, 3 October 1979 (reprinted in *Congressional Record*, 3 October 1979, 27117); *Washington Post*, 16 October 1979, A14.

154. Carter, *Keeping Faith*, 264; Vance, *Hard Choices*, 364; William Attwood, *The Twilight Struggle: Tales of the Cold War* (New York: Harper and Row, 1987), 364; *Washington Post*, 28 October 1979, A4 (Byrd). Brzezinski agreed that the brigade issue undermined public confidence in Carter's leadership but argued that Soviet-Cuban activity in the Horn of Africa was more important: "SALT lies buried in the sands of the Ogaden" (Brzezinski, *Power and Principle*, 189, 514). One powerful vote lost by the brigade was that of Louisiana's Russell Long

("Long Says He Opposes SALT, Cites Unverifiability, Soviet Troops in Cuba," *Washington Post*, 13 September 1979, A1).

155. The committee's 2 November vote to approve the understanding was 13–2 (Senators McGovern and Pell); the 9–6 vote to approve the treaty came on 9 November.

156. Newsom, *Soviet Brigade in Cuba*, 59; Brzezinski to President, "NSC Weekly Report #112," 12 October 1979, Folder "Weekly Reports to the President, 102–120 (7/79–12/79)," Box 42, ZBC. The CIA's Stansfield Turner later agreed that "Brzezinski publicly inflamed this issue at the same time the Secretary of State was trying to damp it down" (foreword to Newsom, *Soviet Brigade in Cuba*, xii). For their differing views on the episode, see Vance, *Hard Choices*, 362–64; Brzezinski, *Power and Principle*, 349–52.

157. "We have had good relations with the Sandinistas for twenty years," Castro said (Memcon, Peter Tarnoff, Robert Pastor, and Wayne Smith, 16 January 1980, in "Cuba: President Carter's Trip, May 12–17, 2002," Vertical File, JCL). For the DIA's assessment of Cuban assistance to the Sandinista effort to overthrow Somoza, see U.S. Congress, House, Committee on Foreign Affairs, Subcommittee on Inter-American Affairs, *Impact of Cuban-Soviet Ties, Spring 1980*, esp. 12, 19, 28, 40.

158. U.S. Congress, House, Committee on Foreign Affairs, Subcommittee on Inter-American Affairs, *Impact of Cuban-Soviet Ties, Spring 1979*, 28, 36–37; CIA, Directorate of Operations, Intelligence Information Cable, "Comments of Senior Cuban Official Raul Valdes Vivo on . . . the Positive Potential for Revolution in Latin America in the 1980's," 28 February 1979, DDRS.

159. Pastor to Brzezinski and Aaron, "Time to Reassess U.S. Policy to Grenada and the Caribbean: Second-Generation Surrogates," 14 April 1979, DDRS.

160. U.S. Congress, House, Committee on Foreign Affairs, Subcommittee on Inter-American Affairs, *Impact of Cuban-Soviet Ties* (1978), 12, 40, 129 (DIA), 59–63 (Smith); Pastor to Brzezinski and Aaron, "A Systematic Strategy for Dealing with Cuba's Increasing Involvement in Africa: The NAM," 24 April 1978, Folder "Meetings—SCC 77: 5/15/78," Box 28, Subject File, ZBC.

161. In September, Castro announced, "There have been some Cubans there. There have been some Cubans to give some aid and modest assistance." When asked if he was speaking of military aid, Castro responded, "Yes, yes" (Press Conference, 28 September 1979, LANIC).

162. The 14 January 1980 vote on Resolution ES-6/2 condemning the invasion was 104–18, with 18 abstentions and 12 absences. For the roll call, see United Nations, *Index to Proceedings of the General Assembly, Sixth Emergency Special Session—1980* (ST/LIB/SER.B/A.32), 58–60. For the DIA and State Department comments, see U.S. Congress, House, Committee on Foreign Affairs, Subcommittee on Inter-American Affairs, *Impact of Cuban-Soviet Ties, Spring 1980*, 31, 87; for similar warnings about Cuban activities elsewhere in the Caribbean, see CIA, "Cuban and Soviet Influence in the Caribbean and Central America," 2 November 1979, DDRS; CIA, "Growth and Prospects of Leftist Extremists in El Salvador," 21 January 1980, DDRS.

163. Robert Pastor, *Condemned to Repetition: The United States and Nicaragua* (Princeton: Princeton University Press, 1987), esp. photo caption on unnumbered page following 206.

164. U.S. Congress, House, Committee on Appropriations, Subcommittee on Foreign Operations and Related Programs, *Foreign Assistance and Related Programs Appropriations*

for 1980, pt. 7, 96th Cong., 1st sess., 11 September 1979, 94; see also 44, 53. For Bauman, see *Congressional Record*, 6 September 1979, 23363. On this period of U.S.-Nicaraguan relations, see William M. LeoGrande, *Our Own Backyard: The United States in Central America, 1977–1992* (Chapel Hill: University of North Carolina Press, 1998), 27–32.

165. "Memorandum of Conversation," Tarnoff, Pastor, and Wayne Smith with Fidel Castro, Carlos Rafael Rodríguez, and José Luis Padrón, Havana, 16 January 1980, in "Cuba: President Carter's Trip, May 12–17, 2002," Vertical File, JCL; Castro Speech, Havana, 8 March 1980, in *Granma*, 10 March 1980, 4.

166. U.S. Congress, House, Committee on Foreign Affairs, Subcommittee on Inter-American Affairs, *Impact of Cuban-Soviet Ties, Spring 1980*, 46; for the State Department's similar view, see 58; for the Pentagon's warning about Cuban involvement, see Harold Brown to Brzezinski, "Memorandum for the Assistant to the President for National Security Affairs," 22 January 1980, DDRS.

167. Theriot, "U.S.-Cuba Trade," 3–4; Richard Turits, "Trade, Debt, and the Cuban Economy," *World Development* 15 (January 1987): 165; Carmelo Mesa-Lago, *The Economy of Socialist Cuba: A Two-Decade Appraisal* (Albuquerque: University of New Mexico Press, 1981), 183; Jorge F. Pérez-López, *Measuring Cuban Economic Performance* (Austin: University of Texas Press, 1987).

168. Carmelo Mesa-Lago, "The First Five-Year Plan: Success or Failure?," in *Cuba: Internal and International Affairs*, ed. Jorge I. Domínguez (Beverly Hills, Calif.: Sage, 1982), table 3.4, 121; CIA, National Foreign Assessment Center, *The Cuban Economy: A Statistical Review*, Report ER 81-10052, March 1981, table 21, 23.

169. Speech, Havana, 24 December 1977, in *Granma*, weekly English ed., 1 January 1978, 2–4; Speech, Havana, 30 June 1978, LANIC; Speech, Havana, 2 December 1978.

170. Speech to the Closing Session of the Asamblea Nacional del Poder Popular, Havana, 27 December 1979 (Jorge Pérez-López kindly provided a transcript of this difficult-to-locate speech); Raúl Castro Speech, Santiago de Cuba, 30 November 1979, in *Granma*, 1 December 1979, 2.

171. U.S. Congress, House, Committee on Foreign Affairs, Subcommittee on Inter-American Affairs, *Impact of Cuban-Soviet Ties* (1978), 6, 59; Roa in United Nations, *Index to Proceedings*, 14 January 1980, 96–97.

172. Speech to the U.N. General Assembly, 12 October 1979.

173. For the public accusation, see "Report to the Second Congress of the Communist Party of Cuba," Havana, 17 December 1980, in *Granma*, weekly English ed., 28 December 1980, 15; for the private comment, see Memcon, Tarnoff, Pastor, and Wayne Smith with Fidel Castro, Carlos Rafael Rodríguez, and José Luis Padrón, Havana, 16–17 January 1980, "Cuba: President Carter's Trip, May 12–17, 2002," Vertical File, JCL. (Castro's somber mood during the envoys' visit was no doubt reinforced by a personal loss: Celia Sánchez had lost her battle against cancer five days earlier.)

In his 17 December 1980 speech to the Second Congress of the Cuban Communist Party, Castro said that "the USSR had to help save the process and preserve the victories of the April 1978 [Afghan] revolution" (in *Granma*, weekly English ed., 28 December 1980, 14). At the congress's closing session three days later, Castro went out of his way to refer to "our dear and inseparable Soviet Union" and to insist that "our ties with the Soviet Union will never be broken. Never!" (in *Granma*, 22 December 1980, 2).

174. For DIA estimates of these two Soviet subsidies, see U.S. Congress, House, Committee on Foreign Affairs, Subcommittee on Inter-American Affairs, *Impact of Cuban-Soviet Ties* (1978), 23; see also CIA, National Foreign Assessment Center, *Cuban Economy*, tables 32, 35, 36, 39; Mesa-Lago, "First Five-Year Plan," table 3.3, 120. Sugar purchases had an exceptionally heavy influence on these estimates; the subsidy was calculated by subtracting the "world" price of sugar from the price paid by Moscow. The utility of using this world price was questionable: in the 1970s, about 75 percent of all sugar was consumed in its country of origin, and about half of the remaining 25 percent was shipped under preferential arrangements. Only about 12 percent of the world's supply of sugar was sold on the residual world market, often at distress prices and often reflecting the owners' decisions to stop paying storage costs and obtain something rather than nothing.

175. For the "freest" comment, see Barbara Walters, "Interview with Fidel Castro," 46; for the "bite the hand" comment, see Speech, Havana, 1 January 1979, in *Granma*, 2 January 1979, 2–3; for the subsidies, see U.S. Congress, House, Committee on Foreign Affairs, *Caribbean Nations*, 21–22 (for 1979); for sugar prices, see CIA, National Foreign Assessment Center, *Cuban Economy*, 31.

176. Speech, Havana, 2 December 1978, LANIC; Pastor to Brzezinski and Aaron, "The Trip to Cuba: Some Impressions," 19 December 1978, in "Cuba: President Carter's Trip, May 12–17, 2002," Vertical File, JCL.

177. U.S. Congress, House, Committee on Foreign Affairs, Subcommittee on Inter-American Affairs, *Impact of Cuban-Soviet Ties, Spring 1980*, 8–9; Castro Speech, Havana, 27 December 1979.

178. Emphasis added. The U.S. Refugee Act of 1980 (PL 96-212, Sec. 201) accepted this definition.

179. Brzezinski to President, "NSC Weekly report #137," 18 April 1980, DDRS; Benjamin R. Civiletti to President, "Hijacking of Cuban Vessels," 9 June 1980, Folder "Cuba, 7–8/80," Box 15, RNSA.

180. Speech, Havana, 8 March 1980, in *Granma*, 10 March 1980, 4.

181. Speech, Havana, 1 May 1980; Remarks at a White House Reception, 9 April 1980, *PPP*, 626.

182. *Granma*, 21 April 1980, 1; *Granma*, 22 April 1980, 1.

183. Office of the Vice President, "Meeting on Cuban Refugees, Roosevelt Room, the White House, April 26, 1980, 11:00 A.M.," 25 April 1980, DDRS; Jack Watson to President, "Cuban Refugees—a Status Report," 2 May 1980, Folder "Cuban Refugees [1]," Box 178, Staff Office Files, Domestic Policy Staff/Eizenstat, JCL; Speech to the League of Women Voters, 5 May 1980, *PPP*, 834.

184. DOS, "Agenda for a Meeting at the White House, 22 April 1980, DDRS; Office of the Vice President, "Meeting on Cuban Refugees, Roosevelt Room, the White House, April 26, 1980, 11:00 A.M.," 25 April 1980, DDRS; Jack Watson to President, "Cuban Refugees—A Status Report," 2 May 1980, Folder "Cuban Refugees [1]," Box 178, Staff Office Files, Domestic Policy Staff/Eizenstat, JCL; Announcement to the Press, 14 May 1980, Folder "Cuban Refugees, 1980," Box 1, Staff Offices, Hispanic Affairs—Rendon, JCL. (Watson was cabinet secretary until June, when he became White House chief of staff.) On the legal issues of transporting unauthorized entrants, see Paul W. Schmidt to David Crosland, "Possible Violations Being Committed by Individuals Who Bring Cubans to the United States without Government Per-

mission," 25 April 1980, Folder "Refugees—Cubans and Haitians [8]," Box 23, Staff Office Files, Domestic Policy Staff/Civil Rights and Justice—White, JCL.

185. Office of the Vice President, "Meeting on Cuban Refugees, Roosevelt Room, the White House, April 26, 1980, 11:00 A.M.," 25 April 1980, DDRS; Carter Speech, Washington, D.C., 5 May 1980, *PPP*, 833–34; Pastor to Brzezinski et al., "Necessary Decisions on Cuban Refugees—Inadequacies in U.S. Policy and in Existing Laws," 9 May 1980, Folder "Cuban Refugees [1]," Box 178, Staff Office Files, Domestic Policy Staff/Eizenstat, JCL. At that time, U.S. authorities had seized only 4 of the 711 boats arriving from Cuba. The State Department's Coordinator for Refugee Affairs agreed with Watson: "The Carter speech was a disaster because it showed how much confusion there was." This and the Watson quotation are from David W. Engstrom, *Presidential Decision Making Adrift: The Carter Administration and the Mariel Boatlift* (Lanham, Md.: Rowman and Littlefield, 1997), 87.

186. USINT to Secretary of State, "U.S. Posture on Refugees in USINT," 8 May 1980. I am indebted to Professor David Engstrom for sharing this document and others he obtained through a FOIA request. See also USINT (Smith) to Secretary of State, "Neighborhood Violence and Beatings of Cuban Refugees and Families," 7 May 1980, Folder "Cuba, 5/80," Box 14, RNSA; Tarnoff to Brzezinski, "Letter to President Carter from USINT Refugees, Havana," 19 July 1980, Folder "Cuba, 7–8/80," Box 15, RNSA. For sensitive coverage of the Peruvian embassy situation, see Ojito, *Finding Mañana*, 97–133.

187. Eizenstat in Engstrom, *Presidential Decision Making*, 70.

188. Press Release, 14 May 1980, Folder "Cuban Refugees, 1980," Box 1, Staff Offices, Hispanic Affairs—Rendon, JCL. Part of the strengthened enforcement was a mid-May revision of the Cuban Assets Control Regulations to target transportation to and from Cuba: 45 *FR* 32671, 19 May 1980; Alarcón Interview.

189. Memcon, Peter Tarnoff, Robert Pastor, and Wayne Smith with José Luis Padrón, Ricardo Alarcón, and José Antonio Arbesú, Havana, 17 June 1980, "Cuba: President Carter's Trip, May 12–17, 2002," Vertical File, JCL.

190. Tarnoff and Pastor to President, "Cuban Discussions, June 17, 1980—Summary and Next Steps," [June 1980], DDRS.

191. Speech, Havana, 1 May 1980; USINT (Smith) to Secretary of State, "Call on Rafael Rodríguez," 3 July 1980, Folder "Cuba, 7–8/80," Box 15, RNSA. Some Cubans left the Interests Section immediately, while others trickled out slowly, with the final eleven departing on 23 September 1980, ending the 144-day ordeal after Smith had negotiated a promise from the Cuban government to permit all of them to depart for the United States. None was harmed, and with the exception of a handful who changed their minds, the embassy's temporary residents and their immediate relatives—about fifteen hundred people—eventually went into exile. The final departures did not occur until the mid-1980s, however. For the tortured negotiations, see Wayne S. Smith, *Closest of Enemies*, esp. 234, 263, 276.

192. Office of the Vice President, "Meeting on Cuban Refugees, Roosevelt Room, the White House, April 26, 1980, 11:00 A.M.," 25 April 1980, DDRS.

193. John M. Harmon, Assistant Attorney General, to Stuart Eizenstat, 27 May 1980, Folder "Cuban Refugees [1]," Box 178, Staff Office Files, Domestic Policy Staff/Eizenstat, JCL; Larry M. Eig, *Cuban Migration: Legal Basics*, CRS Report 94-692A, 1 September 1994, esp. 3–4. Carter Press Conference, 14 May 1980, *PPP*, 904–5. The Refugee Act is PL 96-212, 17 March 1980, 94 *Stat.* 102. On the dissimilar treatment of Haitian and Cuban arrivals, see

Folder "Refugees—Cuban & Haitian [7]," Box 23, Staff Office Files, Domestic Policy Staff/Civil Rights and Justice—White, JCL, with an especially illuminating undated comparative chart entitled "Handling of Arrivals"; on pressure from the Congressional Black Caucus, see Folder "Refugees—Cuban and Haitian [9]," Box 23, Staff Office Files, Domestic Policy Staff/Civil Rights and Justice—White, JCL.

194. Eizenstat, Watson, and Brzezinski to President, "Cuban Boat People—8 A.M. Meeting Wednesday, May 14," 13 May 1980, Folder "Refugees—Cubans & Haitians [4]," Box 22, Domestic Policy Staff/Civil Rights and Justice—White, JCL; for Carter's statement, see *PPP*, 912–16; Reagan quoted in *NYT*, 17 May 1980, 10. On the administration's keen awareness of the domestic political implications, see Jack Watson to President, "Cuban Refugees—A Status Report," 2 May 1980, Folder "Cuban Refugees [1]," Box 178, Staff Office Files, Domestic Policy Staff/Eizenstat, JCL.

195. Eizenstat quoted in *NYT*, 31 March 1985, 30; Brzezinski to President, "Guantanamo," [23 September 1980?], "Cuba: President Carter's Trip, May 12–17, 2002," Vertical File, JCL.

196. *NYT*, 31 March 1985, 30. About 16 percent of the arrivals had been incarcerated at some time in Cuba, but many had been imprisoned for ambiguous offenses such as refusing to cut sugarcane, buying goods on the black market, or evading military service (Robert L. Bach, Jennifer B. Bach, and Timothy Triplett, "The Flotilla 'Entrants': Latest and Most Controversial," *Cuban Studies* 11–12 [January 1981–January 1982]: 45).

197. Folder "Security," Folder "Reports to the Secretary of Health and Human Services," both in Box 8, Subject File, Records of the Cuban-Haitian Task Force, Record Group 220, JCL; James Conaway, "Unwanted Immigrants: Cuban Prisoners in America," *Atlantic Monthly*, February 1981, 75–76; James A. Baker III with Thomas M. DeFrank, *The Politics of Diplomacy: Revolution, War and Peace, 1989–1992* (New York: Putnam's, 1995), esp. 89.

198. Secretary of State to USINT, "U.S. Note Protesting Mariel and Announcing U.S. Will Exclude Cuban Criminals to Cuba," 7 June 1980, FOIA; DOS (William T. Lake and Others) to Lloyd Cutler, White House, "Possible Recourse against Cuban Refusal to Readmit Criminal Expatriates," 7 June 1980, Folder "Cuban Refugees, 6/80," Box 70, Staff Office Files, Counsel, Cutler, JCL; Brzezinski to President, "NSC Weekly Report #149," 7 August 1980, DDRS; Frank White to Stu Eizenstat, "Your 2:30 Meeting re Return of Undesirable Cubans," Folder "Cuban Refugees [1]," Box 178, Staff Office Files, Domestic Policy Staff/Eizenstat, JCL.

199. Castro Interview Broadcast on Cuban Television, 10 February 1989, LANIC; for the official U.S. tally of Mariel departures, see *DOSB*, February 1985, 44; Kenneth N. Skoug Jr., *The United States and Cuba under Reagan and Shultz: A Foreign Service Officer Reports* (Westport, Conn.: Praeger, 1996), 4.

200. William E. Odom Interview by Author, Washington, D.C., 7 April 2005; Pastor to Brzezinski and Aaron, "Trip to Guantanamo, September 19–20, 1980," 23 September 1980, Folder "Cuba 9–10/80," Box 15, RNSA; Vance, *Hard Choices*, 358; Wayne Smith was far harsher: *Closest of Enemies*, 285.

Chapter 11

1. *60 Minutes* (CBS) interview with Dan Rather, recorded 26 January 1980, audio CD, Ronald Reagan Presidential Library, Simi Valley, California. Reagan's "game of dominoes" comment was reported by the *Wall Street Journal*, 3 June 1980, 1. President Carter's comment

came during an interview for ABC-TV *World News Tonight*, 31 December 1979, videotape, JCL.

2. Speech, Georgetown University, Washington, D.C., 28 January 1980, in *NYT*, 29 January 1980, A12.

3. Speech, in *NYT*, 29 February 1980, B4. Reagan also repeatedly attacked the Cuban government in his weekly pre-presidential radio addresses: 20 December 1976, 16 May 1977, 25 June–15 July 1977, 19 September–7 October 1977, 8 October 1977, all in *Reagan on Cuba* (n.p.: Cuban American National Foundation, 1986).

4. Eugene V. Rostow, "Rearming America," *Foreign Policy* 39 (Summer 1980): 8; Charles Tyroler II, ed., *Alerting America: The Papers of the Committee on the Present Danger* (Washington, D.C.: Pergamon-Brassey's, 1984), xv–xvi, 3.

5. Castro Report to the Second Congress of the Cuban Communist Party, Havana, 17 December 1980, in *Granma*, weekly English ed., 28 December 1980, 13–16; Reagan Press Conference, 29 January 1981, *PPP*, 57; Interview, 3 March 1981, *PPP*, 193.

6. Speech to Evangelicals, 8 March 1983, *PPP*, 362–68; George Kennan, "Reflections: Breaking the Spell," *New Yorker*, 30 October 1983, 44, 49.

7. Committee of Santa Fe, *A New Inter-American Policy for the Eighties* (Washington, D.C.: Council for Inter-American Security, 1980), 3, 9, 46. The most cogent neoconservative statement on U.S.-Cuban relations was Hugh Thomas, *Coping with Cuba* (Washington, D.C.: Coalition for a Democratic Majority, 1980).

8. Speech, Santiago, 26 July 1983.

9. William E. Odom Interview by Author, Washington, D.C., 7 April 2005.

10. Jeane J. Kirkpatrick, "U.S. Security and Latin America," in *Rift and Revolution: The Central American Imbroglio*, ed. Howard J. Wiarda (Washington, D.C.: American Enterprise Institute, 1984), 353; Jeane J. Kirkpatrick, "U.S. Security and Latin America," *Commentary* 71 (January 1981): 34.

11. Interview with CBS News, 3 March 1981, *PPP*, 196; see also the Reagan-Carter Debate, 28 October 1980, *PPP*, 2488.

12. Kirkpatrick, "U.S. Security and Latin America," *Commentary*, 34–35; Reagan Press Conference, Los Angeles, 14 October 1980, *NYT*, 15 October 1980, 24; see also Press Conference, Washington, D.C., 31 March 1982, *PPP*, 400; Speech, Washington, D.C., 10 March 1983, *PPP*, 372; Speech, Miami, 20 May 1983, *PPP*, 743; Speech, Tampa, 12 August 1983, *PPP*, 1153; Ronald Reagan, *An American Life* (New York: Simon and Schuster, 1990), 472, 474.

13. Alexander M. Haig Jr. Interview by Author, Arlington, Virginia, 16 December 2004; U.S. Congress, Senate, Committee on Foreign Relations, *Nomination of Alexander M. Haig, Jr.*, 97th Cong., 1st sess., 1981, 72; Alexander M. Haig Jr., *Caveat: Realism, Reagan, and Foreign Policy* (New York: Macmillan, 1984), 30, 96, 108, 122, 129, 221, 278.

14. Kirkpatrick Speech, Miami, 22 October 1982, reprinted as *Cuba and the Cubans* (n.p.: Cuban American National Foundation, 1983), 4; Jeane J. Kirkpatrick, *The Reagan Phenomenon and Other Speeches on Foreign Policy* (Washington, D.C.: American Enterprise Institute for Public Policy Research, 1983), 13, 195; U.S. Department of Defense, *Annual Report to the Congress, Caspar W. Weinberger, Secretary of Defense, Fiscal Year 1983* (Washington, D.C.: U.S. Government Printing Office, 1982), II-23; Elliott Abrams Speech, Center for Strategic and International Studies, Washington, D.C., 6 October 1983, reprinted in *Current Policy*, no. 518, 3.

15. Caspar W. Weinberger, *Fighting for Peace: Seven Critical Years in the Pentagon* (New York: Warner, 1990), 29–31. In 2004, Haig had no detailed recall of this early meeting, but when shown Weinberger's statement, he replied, "What Cap writes is hogwash" (Haig Interview).

16. U.S. Congress, Senate, Committee on Foreign Relations, *Nomination of Haig*, 150; John Crimmins Oral History, 10 May 1989, PC; Gerald S. Strober and Deborah H. Strober, *Nixon: An Oral History of His Presidency* (New York: HarperCollins, 1994), 285; Robert C. McFarlane with Zofia Smardz, *Special Trust* (New York: Cadell and Davies, 1994), 177–78.

17. NATO Briefing, 17 February 1981, *NYT*, 21 February 1981, 1, 6; Meese on *Issues and Answers* (ABC News), 22 February 1981.

18. CBS Interview, 3 March 1981, *PPP*, 192–93; McFarlane quoting his memo to Haig in McFarlane with Smardz, *Special Trust*, 179.

19. McFarlane with Smardz, *Special Trust*, 179–80; Haig Interview.

20. Haig Interview.

21. In 1982, President Reagan wrote in his diary, "It's amazing how sound he can be on complex international matters but how utterly paranoid with regard to the people he must work with" (Reagan, *American Life*, 271). "Hell, I worked for Nixon," was Haig's reply when these words were read to him. "I knew the White House then, and it wasn't a nice place, but it wasn't the den of iniquity that Ronald Reagan had" (Haig Interview).

22. Tad Szulc, "Confronting the Cuban Nemesis," *New York Times Magazine*, 5 April 1981, 40; Nancy Reagan with William Novak, *My Turn: The Memoirs of Nancy Reagan* (New York: Random House, 1989), 242; Haig, *Caveat*, 77, 129.

23. *NYT*, 28 February 1981, 1; for similar instances, see U.S. Congress, Senate, Committee on Foreign Relations, *Foreign Assistance Authorization for Fiscal Year 1982*, 97th Cong., 1st sess., 1981, 13; U.S. Congress, Senate, Committee on Appropriations, *Foreign Assistance and Related Programs Appropriations Fiscal Year 1982*, pt. 1, 97th Cong., 1st sess., 1981, 24. Castro Speech, Havana, 19 April 1981.

24. Carter Telegram, 12 September 1980, Folder "CO38 7/1/79–1/20/81," Box CO-21, White House Central Files, Subject File, JCL; *Washington Post*, 10 January 1981, A3; *NYT*, 13 July 1981, 5. In 1984, Eduardo Arocena was found guilty of twenty-five federal charges, including the murder of the U.N. official, and sentenced to life in prison plus thirty-five years.

25. Castro focused on Task 33 of Operation Mongoose, whose declassified documents he quoted: "to incapacitate Cuban sugar workers during the harvest through the employment of warlike chemical agents" (Speech, Las Tunas, 26 July 1981).

26. The 1980 U.S. census listed 803,226 people of "Cuban origin or descent," a number that did not include the Mariel arrivals since the census was taken on 1 April. On the pitfalls of comparing these census data with earlier or later censuses, see Lisandro Pérez, "The Cuban Population in the United States: The Results of the 1980 U.S. Census of Population," *Cuban Studies* 15 (Summer 1985): esp. 1, 17. On the Cuban American community's apolitical stance during the 1970s, see Francisco Raimundo Wong, "The Political Behavior of Cuban Migrants" (Ph.D. diss., University of Michigan, 1974), 93, 105. On the founding of CANF, see Patrick J. Haney and Walt Vanderbush, "The Role of Ethnic Interest Groups in U.S. Foreign Policy: The Case of the Cuban American National Foundation," *International Studies Quarterly* 43 (June 1999): 341–61. An especially insightful introduction to the politics of the Cuban American community is Félix R. Masud-Piloto, *From Welcomed Exiles to Illegal*

Immigrants: Cuban Migration to the U.S., 1959–1995 (Lanham, Md.: Rowman and Littlefield, 1988).

27. Video Address to CANF Dinner, Miami, 20 May 1983; see *Reagan on Cuba*, 32, and *PPP* 1983, 774.

28. Press Conference, 29 January 1981, *PPP*, 59; *Cold War International History Project Bulletin* 8–9 (Winter 1996): 202–3 (Castro-Honecker). Castro held Manley responsible for his own defeat, complaining to Honecker that Manley government officials "act like the Chileans [in 1970–73]. They simply are too democratic."

29. Jorge I. Domínguez, *To Make a World Safe for Revolution: Cuba's Foreign Policy* (Cambridge: Harvard University Press, 1989), 230–32.

30. Julio Scherer García, "No es ciencia ficción: la guerra total y definitiva, posibilidad real, dice Fidel Castro," *Proceso*, 21 September 1981, 9–10.

31. DOS, INR, "The Mexico Summit: Sign of a New Era in North-South Negotiations?," 22 June 1981, DDRS; Castro Speech, Havana, 15 September 1981, LANIC.

32. Speeches, Havana, 16 April 1981, Las Tunas, 14 June 1980, Bayamo, 26 July 1982.

33. Speech, Havana, 16 April 1981; see also Speech, Las Tunas, 14 June 1980; Speech, Bayamo, 26 July 1982; for the price changes, see CIA, Directorate of Intelligence, *The Cuban Economy: A Statistical Review*, Report ALA 89-10009, April 1989, 35; Jorge F. Pérez-López, *The Economics of Cuban Sugar* (Pittsburgh: University of Pittsburgh Press, 1991), 126; for the continued dependence on sugar, see Jorge F. Pérez-López, "Sugar and Structural Change in the Cuban Economy," *World Development* 17 (October 1989): 1643.

34. U.S. Congress, Joint Economic Committee, *Soviet Economy in a Time of Change*, 96th Cong., 1st sess., 10 October 1979, 2:565; Richard Turits, "Trade, Debt, and the Cuban Economy," *World Development* 15 (January 1987): 165; Lawrence H. Theriot and JeNelle Matheson, "Soviet Economic Relations with Non-European CMEA: Cuba, Vietnam, and Mongolia," in U.S. Congress, Joint Economic Committee, *Soviet Economy in a Time of Change*, 557; U.S. Department of Commerce, Domestic and International Business Administration, Bureau of East-West Trade, *United States Commercial Relations with Cuba: A Survey* (Washington, D.C.: Department of Commerce, 1975), 8. In 1969, Cuba's debt to Western sources was $291 million, rising to $580 million by 1973 and then skyrocketing to $2.2 billion by 1977.

35. CIA, National Intelligence Council, "Castro Agonistes: The Mounting Dilemmas and Frustrations of Cuba's Caudillo," November 1981, FOIA.

36. Kenneth N. Skoug Jr., *The United States and Cuba under Reagan and Shultz: A Foreign Service Officer Reports* (Westport, Conn.: Praeger, 1996), 26. For the still-classified instructions from the administration's National Security Planning Group, see "U.S. Policy in Central America and Cuba through F.Y. '84: Summary Paper," leaked and reprinted in full, *NYT*, 7 April 1983, 16. For the nickel ban, see Dennis M. O'Connell to Richard J. Davis, "Use of Cuban Nickel in Specialty Steel by Creusot-Loire," 26 September 1980, Robert D. Blackwill and Timothy Deal to Brzezinski, "MBB: Creusot-Loire," 16 October 1980, both in Folder "Meetings—Muskie/Brown/Brzezinski: 10/80–1/81," Box 24, Subject File, ZBC.

37. Skoug, *United States and Cuba*, 28, 38.

38. 47 *FR* 4385, 25 January 1982; 50 *FR* 5753, 12 February 1985. The original May 1981 instruction to seize Cuban literature had not been codified (a process that ends with publication of new rules in the *Federal Register* as a change in the Code of Federal Regulations);

instead, under the powers granted by the Trading with the Enemy Act, Treasury's Office of Foreign Assets Control had simply instructed another part of the Department of the Treasury, the Customs Service, to seize the literature. The 1982 instruction to resume delivery of single copies of books and periodicals was codified, but the Customs Service interpreted that to mean literature mailed to U.S. recipients and continued to confiscate publications carried by U.S. travelers. For Customs Service implementation between 1982 and 1985, see Kitty Stewart, "Welcome Back to the Free World," *CubaTimes* 5 (November–December 1984): 9–11.

39. Primarily the result of work by Representative Howard Berman, the Trading with the Enemy Act amendment is Sec. 2502(1) of the Omnibus Trade and Competitiveness Act, PL 100-418, 23 August 1988, 102 *Stat.* 1371. For the narrow interpretation, see 54 *FR* 5229, 2 February 1989. For the lifting of the ban on paintings, sculpture, and other artwork, see 56 *FR* 13284, 1 April 1991.

40. For the reinstatement of the travel ban, see 47 *FR* 17030, 20 April 1982; 47 *FR* 32060, 23 July 1982.

41. U.S. Congress, Senate, Committee on the Judiciary, Subcommittee on Security and Terrorism, *The Role of Cuba in International Terrorism and Subversion*, 97th Cong., 2nd sess., 1982, 238.

42. International Emergency Economic Powers Act, Title II of PL 95-223, 91 *Stat.* 1625, 28 December 1977.

43. 46 U.S. 222, 104 S.Ct. 3026.

44. Banco Nacional de Cuba, *Economic Report*, February 1985, 24, 41. A facsimile of this leaked report was published as an occasional paper by the Cuban American National Foundation. On earlier debt servicing, see Pastor to Aaron, "Prospects for U.S.-Cuban Trade," 14 April 1978, Folder "Cuba 2/78–4/78," Box 10, Geographic File, ZBC.

45. DOS, "Communist Interference in El Salvador," Special Report 80, 23 February 1981, *DOSB*, April 1981, 13–20; for Secretary Haig's March 1981 accusation, see U.S. Congress, Senate, Committee on Foreign Relations, *Foreign Assistance Authorization*, 3.

46. Speech to the Sixty-eighth Inter-Parliamentary Union, Havana, 15 September 1981, LANIC; Scherer García, "No es ciencia ficción," 9–11; Castro made similar comments in speeches on 15 September 1981 and 19 April 1986. For a Cuban view of what Castro meant, see Francisco López Segera, "La política del imperialismo yanqui hacia Cuba de Eisenhower a Reagan," *Casa de las Américas* 22 (March–April 1982): 22–33.

47. Haig, *Caveat*, 96, 129.

48. Press Conference, 10 November 1981, *PPP*, 1031–32; *U.S. News and World Report*, 6 April 1981, 20–22; *NYT*, 5 November 1981, 1, 8; 6 November 1981, 1.

49. Address to the Twenty-sixth Congress of the Communist Party of the Soviet Union, Moscow, 23 February 1981, in *Granma*, 24 February 1981, 1; Secretary of State to Amembassy Rome et al., "Information on Cuba, Nicaragua, and El Salvador," 18 February 1982, DDRS.

50. The edited interview was shown as segments on PBS stations on 11–13 February 1985. Cuban television showed the unedited interview on 16 February; this quotation is taken from the Cuban broadcast. See also *NYT*, 5 November 1981, 1, 8; 6 November 1981, 1, 13; 12 November 1981, 4; *Washington Post*, 18 November 1981, A37. Responding to a congressional query, Haig had said that "there is some evidence" of Cuban advisers in El Salvador, but he

was careful not to sound certain, adding that "there have been reports of Cuban advisers, not a large number" (U.S. Congress, Senate, Committee on Appropriations, *Foreign Assistance and Related Programs Appropriations*, 34).

51. Lawrence A. Pezzullo Oral History, 24 February 1989, NSA; for typical press reports, see *NYT*, 30 October 1981, 20; 31 October 1981, 20; 6 November 1981, 1, 9; Reagan, *American Life*, 254, 360; Reagan Exchange with Reporters, 29 October 1981, *PPP*, 1000.

52. Wayne S. Smith, *The Closest of Enemies: A Personal and Diplomatic Account of U.S.-Cuban Relations since 1957* (New York: Norton, 1987), 294, cites two still-classified cables: Smith to Secretary of State, "Assessment of Internal Conditions in Cuba," 25 March 1981, Smith to Secretary of State, "Cuban Foreign Policy: Recapitulation and Assessment," 10 April 1981. See also Wayne S. Smith, "Dateline Havana: Myopic Diplomacy," *Foreign Policy* 48 (Fall 1982): 161.

53. Peter Kornbluh, "A 'Moment of Rapprochement': The Haig-Rodriguez Secret Talks," *Cold War International History Project Bulletin* 8–9 (Winter 1996): 218.

54. For Haig on Mexican assistance, see *Caveat*, 133.

55. After introducing the two men, Castañeda had left them alone with a Cuban translator, who clearly taped the discussion. These and the quotations that follow are from a thirty-eight-page Spanish-language stenographic transcript that the Cubans provided to the Soviet Union and that the Soviet Union subsequently declassified. The English-language translation is published in *Cold War International History Project Bulletin* 8–9 (Winter 1996): 207–15. The U.S. version of this meeting remains classified.

56. State of the Union Address, 26 January 1982, *PPP*, 77.

57. Vernon Walters Oral History, 21 April 1970, DDEL; for the authoritarian/totalitarian distinction, see Vernon A. Walters, *Silent Missions* (Garden City, N.Y.: Doubleday, 1978), 389.

58. Vernon Walters, *The Mighty and the Meek: Dispatches from the Front Line of Diplomacy* (London: St. Ermin's, 2001), 150–51; Haig, *Caveat*, 132–33.

59. Walters, *Mighty and the Meek*, 150–51.

60. Speeches, Las Tunas, 26 July 1981, Havana, 1 May 1980; Speech, Havana, 8 March 1980, in *Granma*, 10 March 1980, 4; Speech, Moscow, 23 February 1981, in *Granma*, 24 February 1981, 1.

61. Alfonso Chardy, *Miami Herald*, 18 December 1983, 21M; James Chace, "The Turbulent Tenure of Alexander Haig," *NYT*, 22 April 1984, BR21.

62. Walters, *Mighty and the Meek*, 153.

63. 17 April 1982, *PPP*, 484 (Reagan); William M. LeoGrande, *Our Own Backyard: The United States in Central America, 1977–1992* (Chapel Hill: University of North Carolina Press, 1998), 150.

64. Directorate of Intelligence, CIA, "Cuba: Tactics and Strategy for Central America [redacted word]," August 1982, DDRS.

65. Myles R. R. Frechette, "Letter to the Editor," *Foreign Policy* 48 (Fall 1982): 175–76; U.S. Congress, House, Committee on Foreign Relations, Subcommittees on International Economic Policy and Trade and on Inter-American Affairs, *Issues in United States–Cuban Relations*, 97th Cong., 2nd sess., 14 December 1982, 5; Reagan Interview, 11 February 1985, *PPP*, 159.

66. *NYT*, 8 September 1982, A26; Wayne S. Smith, *Closest of Enemies*, 256, 260. For an example of the type of dispatch that convinced Reagan officials that Smith was unsympathetic

to their views of Cuba and Central America, see his cable, "CUBECJHF [*sic*] Shipments to El Salvador and Nicaragua," 4 February 1982, NSA.

67. CIA, "Cuban International Activities Inimical to U.S. Interests," 9 November 1982, NSA; CIA, "Memorandum: Possible Soviet Military Activity in the Caribbean Basin," 15 June 1983, DDRS; Thomas Enders in U.S. Congress, Senate, Committee on the Judiciary, Sub-committee on Security and Terrorism, *Role of Cuba*, 147; Casey Speeches, Washington, 18 September 1986, Washington, 25 June 1986, Atlanta, 8 November 1986, all in DDRS.

68. CIA, Directorate of Intelligence, "Cuban International Activities Inimical to U.S. Interests," 9 November 1982, NSA; Reagan Interview, 30 April 1982, *PPP*, 540; Castro Speech, Cienfuegos, 26 July 1984.

69. Haig Interview.

70. Ibid.

71. For the comments about Allen, Clark, Nancy Reagan, and Deaver, see ibid. See also Haig, *Caveat*, 129–30; Alexander M. Haig Jr. with Charles McCarry, *Inner Circles: How America Changed the World* (New York: Warner, 1992), 546–47.

72. George Shultz, *Turmoil and Triumph: My Years as Secretary of State* (New York: Scrib-ner's, 1993), 305, 308; Shultz, "Human Rights and the Moral Dimension of U.S. Foreign Policy," Speech to the Creve Coeur Club, Peoria, Illinois, 22 February 1984, in *DOSB*, April 1984, 15–18.

73. Kenneth Skoug Jr. Interview by Author, Alexandria, Virginia, 3 March 2005; U.S. Con-gress, Senate, Committee on Foreign Relations, *Nomination of George Shultz*, 97th Cong., 2nd sess., 13–14 July 1982, 70–71, 181–82, 44; "U.S. Relations with the USSR," National Security Decision Directive 75, 17 January 1983, DDRS; George Shultz, "New Realities and New Ways of Thinking," *Foreign Affairs* 63 (Spring 1985): 713; *Face the Nation* (CBS), 5 September 1982, reprinted in *DOSB*, October 1982, 13.

74. Memorandum, CIA, "El Salvador: Military Prospects," 2 January 1981, Folder "Meet-ings—Muskie/Brown/Brzezinski: 10/80–1/81," Box 24, Subject File, ZBC; Reagan radio broadcast recorded in March and scheduled for broadcast in March and April 1979, in Ronnie Dugger, *On Reagan: The Man and His Presidency* (New York: McGraw-Hill, 1983), 518.

75. Pezzullo Oral History (quoting Enders); Skoug Interview; Victor Johnson Interview by Author, Washington, D.C., 10 May 1983.

76. Thomas O. Enders, "Building the Peace in Central America," *DOS Current Policy* 144 (20 August 1982): 4; CIA, "Nicaraguan Military Buildup," 1 January 1982, DDRS; CIA, National Foreign Assessment Center, "The Sandinistas and the Creation of a One-Party State: An Intelligence Assessment," 11 April 1981, DDRS; INR, "Developing Soviet-Nicaraguan Rela-tions," 24 June 1981, NSA.

Two declassified versions currently exist of the 1 December 1981 presidential finding. One, heavily redacted, is available from the National Security Archive; the other, also heavily redacted, nonetheless contains the words quoted here as part of an unsigned CIA memoran-dum to "Members of the National Security Planning Group," 24 March 1983, DDRS. See also the CIA memos, "Scope of CIA Activities under the Nicaragua Finding," 12 July 1982, "Scope of CIA Activities under the Nicaragua Finding," 19 September 1983, both in NSA.

77. CIA, National Foreign Assessment Center, "Patterns of International Terrorism, 1980: A Research Paper," June 1981, DDRS; Reagan Speech, Washington, D.C., 24 February 1982, *PPP*, 214; CIA, "Nicaraguan Military Buildup," 22 March 1982, DDRS, which was not a new

analysis: "NSC Weekly Report #111," 5 October 1979, Folder "Weekly Reports to the President, 102–120 (7/79–12/79)," Box 42, ZBC.

78. William D. Rogers and Jeffrey A. Meyers, "The Reagan Administration and Latin America: An Uneasy Beginning," *Caribbean Review* 11 (Spring 1982): 15; Robert White, "There Is No Military Solution in El Salvador," *Center* 14 (July–August 1981): 8; U.S. Congress, House, Committee on Foreign Affairs, Subcommittee on Inter-American Affairs, *Presidential Certification on El Salvador*, 97th Cong., 2nd sess., 1982, 1:135, 228; Helms: U.S. Congress, Senate, Committee on Foreign Relations, *Nomination of Robert E. White*, 96th Cong., 2nd sess., 1980, 3–5; Author's Notes on Helms Speech to Rotary Club, Asheville, North Carolina, 30 April 1983.

79. Speech, Hollywood, Florida, 18 July 1983, *PPP*, 1044.

80. The 41–39 vote was to table Amendment 1348 to a bill authorizing a new ceiling on the national debt. The accompanying debate provides a perfect outline of existing divisions: *Congressional Record*, April 1982, 6376–6823, resolution on 6379, vote on 6823. The missile crisis resolution was Senate Joint Res. 230, PL 87-733, 76 *Stat.* 697, 3 October 1962.

81. "Kissinger and Moynihan: Five Years Later," *Public Opinion* 6 (April–May 1983): 54.

82. Mas Canosa quoted in *Washington Post*, 10 September 1983, A5; LeoGrande, *Our Own Backyard*, 238.

83. DIA: U.S. Congress, House, Committee on Foreign Affairs, Subcommittee on Inter-American Affairs, *Impact of Cuban-Soviet Ties in the Western Hemisphere, Spring 1980*, 96th Cong., 2nd sess., 1980, 31, 87; CIA, "Cuban and Soviet Influence in the Caribbean and Central America," 2 November 1979, DDRS. A helpful memoir on the Carter administration's perspective is Robert A. Pastor, "Does the United States Push Revolutions to Cuba?: The Case of Grenada," *Journal of Interamerican Studies and World Affairs* 28 (Spring 1986): 1–35. For the Carter administration's hostility, see U.S. Congress, House, Committee on Foreign Affairs, Subcommittee on Inter-American Affairs, *United States Policy toward Grenada*, 97th Cong., 2nd sess., 15 June 1982, 91.

84. The two 20 December 1980 speeches are in *Granma*, 22 December 1980, 4.

85. Address, 23 March 1983, *PPP*, 440.

86. AID: U.S. Congress, Senate, Committee on Foreign Relations, *The Situation in Grenada*, 98th Cong., 1st sess., 1983, 46 (AID); U.S. Congress, House, Committee on Foreign Affairs, Subcommittee on Inter-American Affairs, *United States Policy toward Grenada*, 7, 47; Jonathan T. Howe (PM) to Secretary of State, "The Strategic Importance of Cuban Activities on Grenada," 29 October 1983, CIA, "Cuba-USSR-Grenada: Military Cooperation," 29 January 1983, 3, both in DDRS; CIA, "Cuban International Activities Inimical to U.S. Interests," 9 November 1982, FOIA; Constantine C. Menges, *Inside the National Security Council: The True Story of the Making and Unmaking of Reagan's Foreign Policy* (New York: Simon and Schuster, 1988), 63; National Security Decision Directive 75, 17 January 1983, NSA; McFarlane with Smardz, *Special Trust*, 257–58.

87. U.S. Congress, House, Committee on Foreign Affairs, Subcommittee on Inter-American Affairs, *United States Policy toward Grenada*, 12–13.

88. Ibid., 39.

89. Statement in Barbados, 8 April 1982, *PPP*, 448; CIA, "This Week's Briefing on Grenada," 5 February 1983, DDRS; CIA, "Grenada: Status Report of Airport Project," 20 May 1983, DDRS; U.S. Congress, Senate, Committee on Foreign Relations, *Situation in Grenada*,

12; U.S. Congress, House, Committee on Foreign Affairs, Subcommittee on Inter-American Affairs, *United States Policy toward Grenada*, 47; [redacted] to Director of Central Intelligence, "Grenadian Documents/Meeting between Maurice Bishop and Andre [*sic*] Gromyko," 1 May 1984, DDRS.

90. Timothy J. Christmann, "TacAir in Grenada," *Naval Aviation*, November–December 1985, 8–9.

91. Castro's order is reported in CIA, "Grenada Situation Report, 0700 Hours—26 October 1983," FOIA; for two views of who fired first, see USINT (Ferch) to Secretary of State, "Castro Responds to USG Approach," 26 October 1983, Secretary of State to USINT, "Arrangements for Cuban Withdrawal," 26 October, 1983, both DDRS.

92. USINT (Ferch) to Secretary of State, "Cuban Reaction to Latest U.S. Note—Great Bitterness," 26 October 1983, DDRS; John Ferch Interview by Author, Fairfax, Virginia, 17 February 2005; Skoug Interview; Ricardo Alarcón Interview by Author, Havana, 11 March 2005.

93. *Congressional Record*, 27 October 1983, 29550–52, 29 October 1983, 29823; Secretary of State to USINT, 29 October 1983, DDRS; see also Secretary of State to U.S. Embassy, Moscow, "Evacuation of Soviet Embassy in Grenada," 3 November 1983, DDRS. For good coverage of the Cuba-Grenada relationship, see Jorge I. Domínguez, *To Make a World Safe for Revolution: Cuba's Foreign Policy* (Cambridge: Harvard University Press, 1989), 162–71.

94. Address, 27 October 1983, *PPP*, 1521; *NYT*, 20 November 1983, 60–61; Speech, 19 March 1984, *PPP*, 371; Reagan, *American Life*, 457–58; DOS Press Release 40, 8 February 1984, in possession of the author; John Poindexter to Langhorne A. Motley, "NSC Suggestions for the Grenadan Implementation Plan—State Draft of November 9, 1983," 10 November 1983, DDRS.

95. Ferch Interview.

96. *Report of the President's National Bipartisan Commission on Central America* (New York: Macmillan, 1984), 2, 109; Reagan Speech to Central American Leaders, Washington, D.C., 19 March 1984, *PPP*, 371.

97. Press Release, Office of Senator Jesse Helms, 7 February 1984, in possession of the author; Lagomarsino in U.S. Congress, House, Committee on Foreign Affairs, *Foreign Assistance Legislation for Fiscal Year 1985*, pt. 8, 98th Cong., 2nd sess., 1984, 172; Reagan, *American Life*, 482.

98. For the 1984 party platforms, see www.presidency.ucsb.edu/platforms.php.

99. Skoug, *United States and Cuba*, 7, 40; for the distribution by holding facility in late 1982, see U.S. Congress, House, Committee on Foreign Relations, Subcommittees on International Economic Policy and Trade and on Inter-American Affairs, *Issues in United States–Cuban Relations*, 97th Cong., 2nd sess., 14 December 1982, 20.

100. The "dregs" comment came in a speech during the crisis on 1 May 1980; see also Speeches, 17 December 1980, 21 April 1980, 14 December 1984, Castro Interview by Robert MacNeil, February 1985, all in LANIC.

101. Haig Interview; Memcon, Peter Tarnoff, Robert Pastor, and Wayne Smith with José Luis Padrón, Ricardo Alarcón, and José Antonio Arbesú, Havana, 17 June 1980, in "Cuba: President Carter's Trip, May 12–17, 2002," Vertical File, JCL; Skoug, *United States and Cuba*, 6–7; Skoug Interview; Haig, *Caveat*, 127; Governor Robert Graham to President Ronald Reagan, 18 July 1984, FOIA.

102. Kenneth Skoug, "U.S. Efforts to Negotiate the Return to Cuba of the Mariel Excludables," 2 May 1984, FOIA.

103. Castro Televised Speech, 15 December 1984, LANIC; Skoug Interview.

104. Skoug Interview; Ferch Interview.

105. On the Cuban desire to put off talks until after the U.S. election, see Tony Motley to Michael Armacost, "Human Rights and Cuba Policy," 29 May 1984, FOIA; Skoug, *United States and Cuba*, 13; *DOSB*, May 1988, 76–81.

106. DOS, "Opening Statement," 12 July 1984, FOIA; Skoug Interview. Asked about the disparity in rank, John Ferch commented that "it just shows again what I was saying—Cubans think of us all the time; we barely bother with them" (Ferch Interview). Alarcón had a different explanation: "I meet with anyone. It's our style. You will never understand a thing about Cuba if you don't understand that we are informal, particularly when Fidel Castro is involved. It's a guerrilla style" (Alarcón Interview).

107. Alarcón Interview.

108. Speech, Cienfuegos, 26 July 1984, LANIC.

109. Ferch Interview; John Ferch, "Fencing with Fidel and Other Tales of Life in the Foreign Service: A Selective Memoir," 181-page unpublished typescript, n.d., 161–62, courtesy of John Ferch.

110. The first New York meeting had occurred on 12–13 July, followed by a second round of talks on 31 July–2 August, summarized in J. A. Ritchie, "Mariel Talks," 21 November 1984, FOIA; "Agreement on Immigration Procedures and the Return of Cuban Nationals," 14 December 1984, *TIAS* 11057, *ILM* 24 (1985), 32–37; *DOSB*, February 1985, 44–45; DOS, "Minute of Implementation," 4 December 1984, FOIA. Discussions stopped during the U.S. political campaign and resumed with a third meeting in New York from 28 November to 5 December. A fourth and final meeting occurred on 13–14 December.

111. For the Cuban note canceling the agreement, 19 May 1985, see *Granma*, 20 May 1985, 1.

112. Minutes of NSC Meeting, 7 July 1960, and attached memo, James S. Lay Jr. to NSC, "U.S. Policy toward Cuba and the Dominican Republic," 12 July 1960, Folder "Cuba (May 1959–September 1960)(3)," Box 4, WHOF, Office of the Special Assistant for National Security Affairs: Records, 1952–61, NSC Series, Subject Subseries. On Mundt's proposal, see Samuel E. Belk to Gordon Gray, 31 March 1960, Folder "Cuban Situation (1) 1959–60," Box 6, WHOF, Office of the Special Assistant for National Security Affairs: Records, 1952–61, NSC Series, Subject Subseries; Proceedings of the Forty-second National Convention of the American Legion, Miami Beach, Florida, 18–20 October 1960.

For facsimiles of the basic documents, see the carefully annotated collection by Jon Elliston, *Psywar on Cuba: The Declassified History of U.S. Anti-Castro Propaganda* (Melbourne, Australia: Ocean, 1999); for the history, see John Spicer Nichols, "The U.S. View of Radio Interference," in *Subject to Solution: Problems in Cuban-U.S. Relations*, ed. Wayne S. Smith and Esteban Morales Domínguez (Boulder, Colo.: Rienner, 1988), 122–44; Lawrence C. Soley and John S. Nichols, *Clandestine Radio Broadcasting: A Study of Revolutionary and Counterrevolutionary Electronic Communication* (New York: Praeger, 1987), 187–89; Howard H. Frederick, *Cuban-American Radio Wars: Ideology in International Telecommunications* (Norwood, N.J.: Ablex, 1986).

113. CIA, "Types of Covert Action against the Castro Regime," 8 November 1961, *FRUS*

1961–63, 10:675; [Gordon Chase?], "U.S. Policy towards Cuba April to November, 1964," 22 March 1964, DDRS. See also USIA director Edward R. Murrow to the CIA's John McCone, 10 December 1962, reproduced in Elliston, *Psywar on Cuba*, 154–55.

The three commercial stations were WGBS Miami, WKWF Key West, and WWL New Orleans. The shift to AM was important, since at the time there were only about 150,000 shortwave sets in Cuba. One trade publication incorrectly described the CIA's Cuban Freedom Committee as "a small group of American citizens who buy the time for the programs and provide the professional staff. . . . The committee's money comes from various private foundations and several large corporations" (*Broadcasting* 62 [4 June 1962]: 70–71); Lansdale to Special Group (Augmented), "Review of Operation Mongoose," 25 July 1962, *FRUS* 1961–63, 10:881; Wilson (USIA) to Edward G. Lansdale, "Broadcasting to Cuba," 11 September 1962, Folder "Special Group (Augmented) General 9/62," Box 319A, NSFK; "Memorandum of Discussion at the 441st Meeting of the National Security Council, Washington, April 14, 1960," *FRUS* 1958–60, 6:894; Wilson to Lansdale, "The Technical Feasibility of Medium Wave Broadcasting to Cuba," 3 August 1962, Folder "Special Group (Augmented) General 9/62," Box 319A, NSFK.

114. "Memorandum of the Discussion at the 441st Meeting of the National Security Council, Washington, April 14, 1960," *FRUS* 1958–60, 6:894–95. The North American Regional Broadcasting Agreement (55 *Stat.* 1005) was negotiated in 1937 but is occasionally cited as a 1941 agreement because that is the year it was ratified by the U.S. Senate. Wilson to Lansdale, "Broadcasting to Cuba," 11 September 1962, Folder "Special Group (Augmented) General 9/62," Box 319A, NSFK, contains an explanation of the international agreements the United States was violating by broadcasting to Cuba. For an example of U.S. interest in these agreements, see the 1942 U.S. complaint that a Cuban station was using so much power that it interfered with two U.S. stations (U.S. Embassy to Minister of State, Cuba, 9 December 1942, Folder "Correspondence Diplomatic 1942 M–R," Box 9, Spruille Braden Papers, Columbia University, New York).

115. For the station owners' complaints, see Donald M. Wilson to Ralph A. Dungan, 14 October 1963, Folder "Cuba General 10/63," Box 39, NSFK; for the relationship between farmers and radio stations in the Eisenhower era, see U.S. Congress, Senate, Committee on Foreign Relations, *North American Regional Broadcasting Agreement*, 83rd Cong., 1st sess., July 1953. An interesting survey of station managers is Mary Lou Cornette, "Cuban Interference with Commercial United States Amplitude Modulated Radio Stations" (master's thesis, Colorado State University, 1984).

116. Hurwitch to Martin, "Observations on Operational Potential with Respect to Cuba," 15 August 1962, *FRUS* 1961–63, 10:937–38; George C. Denny Jr. (INR) to Crimmins (CCA), "Cuba: Possible Courses of Action," 25 July 1963, Folder "Cuba, Subjects, Policy, 5/63–8/63," Box 55, NSFK.

117. Dorothy Dillon (USIA) to Edward S. Little (ARA), "VOA Program Cita Con Cuba," 4 June 1974, Folder "Cuba—Political, Military (1)," Box 2, NSA, NSC Latin American Affairs Staff: Files, 1974–77, GRFL; Edward S. Little to Shlaudeman, "Attached USIA Memorandum on 'Cita Con Cuba,'" 7 June 1974, Folder "Cuba—Political, Military (1)," Box 2, NSA, NSC Latin American Affairs Staff: Files, 1974–77, GRFL. Other memoranda in this folder detail the State Department and USIA capitulation.

118. U.S. Congress, House, Committee on International Relations, Subcommittee on

Inter-American Affairs, *Impact of Cuban-Soviet Ties in the Western Hemisphere*, 95th Cong., 2nd sess., March–April 1978, 40 (Fascell); Henze to Brzezinski, "Cuban Refugees—Situation in Cuba," 15 May 1980, Henze to Pastor, "Harold Brown to ZB Memo on Cuban Broadcasting," 22 May 1980, both in Folder "5/80," Box 5, Collection #27, National Security Affairs, Staff Material, Horn/Special, JCL.

119. *Congressional Record*, 16 June 1980, 14840; U.S. Interests Section [Smith] to Secretary of State, "Call on Rafael Rodriguez," 3 July 1980, in "Cuba: President Carter's Trip, May 12–17, 2002," Vertical File, JCL.

120. Executive Order 12323, 22 September 1981, 46 *FR* 47207. The Presidential Commission was abolished in late 1982 (48 *FR* 379) and replaced in May 1984 by a congressionally mandated [Sec. 5(a), PL 98-111, 4 October 1983] Advisory Board for Radio Broadcasting to Cuba, with Mas Canosa as its chair. The report of the Committee on Government Operations is House Report 97-298, 11 December 1981.

121. *Broadcasting* 101 (21 December 1981): 30; *NYT*, 1 September 1982, A11, 3 September 1982, B6; CIA, "Radio Jamming Policy in the East Bloc," 13 August 1981, in Elliston, *Psywar on Cuba*, 217.

122. U.S. Congress, House, Committee on Foreign Affairs, *Radio Broadcasting to Cuba (Radio Marti)*, 97th Cong., 2nd sess., March 1982, 132–43; U.S. Congress, Senate, Committee on Foreign Relations, *Radio Broadcasting to Cuba*, pt. 1, 97th Cong., 2nd sess., 1982.

123. *Congressional Record*, 29 September 1983, 26453–54, 26456–57, 13 September 1983, 23748–94.

124. PL 98-111, 6 October 1983, 97 *Stat.* 749; National Security Decision Directive 170, 20 May 1985, in Elliston, *Psywar on Cuba*, 228–30.

125. Reagan Speech to the American Bar Association, 8 July 1985, *PPP*, 898; Castro Press Conference, 10 July 1985, LANIC.

126. The job-loss study by John Kaminarides of Arkansas State University is reprinted in U.S. Congress, House, Committee on Foreign Affairs, *Cuba and the United States: Thirty Years of Hostility and Beyond*, 101st Cong., 1st sess., August–September 1989, 425–28; *NYT*, 14 February 1985, 31.

127. Turits, "Trade, Debt, and the Cuban Economy," 171; Banco Nacional de Cuba, *Economic Report*, February 1984, 1, 43; A. R. M. Ritter, "Cuba's Convertible Currency Debt Problem," *CEPAL Review* 36 (December 1988): 117; Carmelo Mesa-Lago, *Market, Socialist, and Mixed Economies: Comparative Policy and Performance—Chile, Cuba, and Costa Rica* (Baltimore: Johns Hopkins University Press, 2000), 243.

128. Speech to the Third Congress of the Cuban Communist Party, Havana, 4 February 1986, in *Granma*, 5 February 1986, 3.

129. Lawrence H. Theriot and JeNelle Matheson, "Soviet Economic Relations with Non-European CMEA: Cuba, Vietnam, and Mongolia," in U.S. Congress, Joint Economic Committee, *Soviet Economy in a Time of Change*, 558; Jorge F. Pérez-López, "The Cuban Economic Crisis of the 1990s and the External Sector," *Cuba in Transition* 8 (1998): 386–413; Mesa-Lago, *Market, Socialist, and Mixed Economies*, esp. 242–43; Ritter, "Cuba's Convertible Currency Debt Problem"; Turits, "Trade, Debt, and the Cuban Economy."

130. Jorge F. Pérez-López, "Cuban Hard-Currency Trade and Oil Reexports," in *Socialist Cuba: Past Interpretations and Future Challenges*, ed. Sergio G. Roca (Boulder, Colo.: Westview, 1988), 129, tables 131, 140; Jorge F. Pérez-López, "Cuban Oil Reexports: Significance

and Prospects," *Energy Journal* 8, no. 1 (1987): 1–16; George Grayson, "Energy Crisis Tests Revolution," *Petroleum Economist* 59 (September 1992): esp. 12; Turits, "Trade, Debt, and the Cuban Economy," 175; Ritter, "Cuba's Convertible Currency Debt Problem," 126. Between 1983 and 1985, the Banco Nacional (*Economic Report*, February 1984, 31) placed the value of oil reexports at 1.4 billion pesos, or about 40 percent of total convertible currency exports and twice the value of sugar sales to non–Council for Mutual Economic Assistance countries.

131. Castro Speeches, 19 April 1986, in *Granma*, 21 April 1986, 2–7, 26 July 1986, Sancti Spirtus, in *Granma*, 29 July 1986, 4; Ritter, "Cuba's Convertible Currency Debt Problem," 138; Banco Nacional de Cuba, *Economic Report*, February 1984, 2. In early 1985, Cuba placed its convertible currency debt at 3.03 billion pesos, or $3.26 billion (Banco Nacional de Cuba, *Economic Report*, February 1984, 41).

132. Speech, Havana, 2 December 1986.

133. Speech, Santiago, 26 July 1988; on the 1988 debt/export ratio, see Ritter, "Cuba's Convertible Currency Debt Problem," esp. 118, 139. For the Soviet Union's apparent unwillingness to help, see two CIA reports: "Cuba: Economic Realities Prompt Policy Changes," 8 February 1985, and "USSR-Cuba: Holding Tight on Economic Aid," 15 June 1985, both in FOIA.

134. Speech, Sancti Spirtus, 26 July 1986, in *Granma*, 29 July 1986, 4; Speech to the Closing Session of the Third Party Congress, Havana, 2–3 December 1986, LANIC.

135. Speech, Santiago, 26 July 1988. Cubans had been informed of the National Assembly's belt-tightening in *Granma*, 27 December 1986, 1. For an analysis, see Ritter, "Cuba's Convertible Currency Debt Problem," 134; on the difficulty of using Cuban data during this period, when the government was shifting its bookkeeping from gross domestic product to gross social product, see Pérez-López, "Sugar and Structural Change," 1631; Jorge F. Pérez-López, *Cuba's Second Economy: From Behind the Scenes to Center Stage* (New Brunswick, N.J.: Transaction, 1995), 51, 121.

136. Report to the Second Congress of the Cuban Communist Party, Havana, 17 December 1980, in *Granma*, weekly English ed., 18 December 1980, 13. Raúl Castro had strongly criticized Cuban workers for the "irresponsibility, self-serving behavior, negligence, and a buddy system" (Speech, Santiago, 30 November 1979, in *Granma*, 1 December 1980, 2). Overviews of rectification include Jorge Pérez-López, "The Cuban Economy: Rectification in a Changing World," *Cambridge Journal of Economics* 16 (March 1992): 113–26; Carmelo Mesa-Lago, "Cuba's Economic Counter-Reform (Rectificación): Causes, Policies, and Effects," *Journal of Communist Studies* 5 (December 1989): 98–139; Mesa-Lago, *Market, Socialist, and Mixed Economies*, 264–88.

137. Speech to the Third Congress of the Cuban Communist Party, Havana, 4 February 1986, in *Granma*, 5 February 1986, 3–4; for the full report, see *Granma*, 5–7 February 1986.

138. Castro Interview by MacNeil; Jonathan Rosenberg, "Cuba's Free-Market Experiment: Los Mercados Libres Campesinos, 1980–1986," *Latin American Research Review* 27, no. 3 (1992): 70; see also Carmen Diana Deere and Mieke Meurs, "Markets, Markets Everywhere: Understanding the Cuban Anomaly," *World Development* 20 (June 1992): 825–39.

139. Speech, Havana, 19 April 1986, in *Granma*, 21 April 1986, 2–7. Also closed were the artisan markets that had sprung up alongside the free peasant markets.

140. Speech to the Plenary of the Central Committee of the Cuban Communist Party,

Havana, 19 July 1986, paraphrased in *Granma*, 22 July 1986, 1; Speech to the Closing Session of the Third Congress of the Cuban Communist Party, Havana, 2 December 1986; Speech, Santiago, 26 July 1988.

141. Speech, Havana, 2 December 1978; Banco Nacional de Cuba, *Economic Report*, February 1984, 15, 37; U.S. Department of Commerce, Bureau of Foreign Commerce, *Investment in Cuba: Basic Information for United States Businessmen* (Washington, D.C.: U.S. Government Printing Office, 1956), 143; Lawrence Theriot, "U.S.-Cuba Trade: Question Mark," *Commerce America*, 24 April 1978, 5.

142. Banco Nacional de Cuba, *Economic Report*, February 1984, 15, 37, 62; Discussion with Reporters, Varadero, 27 September 1988, LANIC; Speech, Santiago, 26 July 1988; Interview, Caracas, [3, 4, or 5 February 1989], broadcast on Venezuelan television on 10 February 1989, LANIC; Speech, Havana, 28 September 1990, in *Granma*, 1 October 1990, 3–6; Speech, Santiago, 26 July 1988.

143. Jonathan G. Clarke and William Ratliff, *Report from Havana: Time for a Reality Check on U.S. Policy toward Cuba*, Policy Analysis 418 (Washington, D.C.: Cato Institute, 2001), 10; *NYT*, 28 December 2004, A6.

144. Andres Oppenheimer, *Castro's Final Hour: The Secret Story behind the Coming Downfall of Communist Cuba* (New York: Simon and Schuster, 1992), 24. The door to the visa section in Havana had remained open for the immediate relatives (spouses, parents, and unmarried minor children) of U.S. citizens, including naturalized Cuban immigrants, but Washington's response to Cuba's refusal to continue accepting the excludables was to close completely the door for the relatives of noncitizen permanent residents of the United States. As an added expression of dissatisfaction, in early October the administration issued a presidential proclamation (5377, 4 October 1985, 50 *FR* 41329) prohibiting nonimmigrant travel to the United States by Cuban government employees, which in Cuba included nearly everyone, including Cuban academics.

145. Until all the relevant documents are declassified, the best coverage of this trip by Kennedy aide Gregory Craig and of the U.S. perspective of the ensuing Mexico City negotiations is Kenneth Skoug's memoir, *United States and Cuba*, 122–27, and his 9 March 1988 speech reprinted in *DOSB*, May 1988, 76–81. Castro's favorable comment about the 1984 agreement came in his 4 February 1986 speech, in *Granma*, 7 February 1986, 3.

146. Skoug Interview; Skoug, *United States and Cuba*, 125–26.

147. The Mexico City meeting occurred on 8–9 July 1986; presidential proclamation 5517 was issued on 22 August 1986 (51 *FR* 30470). The logic behind the proclamation is explained in National Security Decision Directive 235, "Strengthening U.S. Policy toward Cuba," 18 August 1986, NSA.

148. U.S. Congress, House, Committee on Foreign Affairs, Subcommittee on Human Rights and International Organizations, *Cuban Political Prisoners*, 99th Cong., 2nd sess., 24 September 1986, 2.

149. Ibid., 13; Skoug Interview.

150. Skoug, *United States and Cuba*, 173, 192; Skoug Interview. Formal agreement had to wait while the diplomats checked with their principals; the final agreement was reached at a meeting in Mexico City on 19 November. For the process of resuming normal visa processing, see Paul Schott Stevens, "Review of National Security Decision Directive 235," 23 December 1987, National Security Decision Directive 299, 26 January 1988, both in NSA.

151. Skoug Interview.

152. María Cristina García, *Havana USA: Cuban Exiles and Cuban Americans in South Florida, 1959–1994* (Berkeley: University of California Press, 1996), 156; U.S. Congress, House, Committee on Foreign Affairs, *Cuba and the United States*, 312; Skoug, *United States and Cuba*, 167, 202. Operation Exodus ended in 1993.

153. On the difficulties of returning the excludables, see J. E. Donoghue and C. Barry, "Mariel Implementation Working Group, Topics for Meeting No. 2," 7 February 1985, Secretary of State to USINT, "Implementation of Mariel Agreement—Return of Excludables," 8 February 1985, Ken Skoug to Michel, "Alleged Return of 'Minor Criminals' to Cuba," 20 March 1985, Secretary of State to USINT, "Return of Mariel Excludables," 22 March 1985, all FOIA.

154. James Cason Interview by Author, Havana, 8 March 2005; Michael Parmly Interview by Author, Havana, 18 January 2008; *Clark v. Martínez*, consolidated with *Benítez v. Rozos*, 12 January 2005, 543 U.S. 371 (2005). For a helpful overview, see Gastón A. Fernández, *The Mariel Exodus: Twenty Years Later* (Miami: Ediciones Universal, 2002).

155. On the National Endowment for Democracy funding of Cuban Americans, see the endowment's annual reports beginning with Fiscal Year 1984, available online at http://www.ned.org; Secretary of State to U.S. Embassies, "National Endowment for Democracy Funded Programs," 25 February 1988, DDRS.

156. Elliott Abrams, "The Cuban Revolution and Its Impact on Human Rights," Address to the Center for Security and International Studies, Washington, D.C., 6 October 1983, reprinted in *Current Policy*, no. 518; Skoug, *United States and Cuba*, 134; Abrams, September 1986, in U.S. Congress, House, Committee on Foreign Affairs, Subcommittee on Human Rights and International Organizations, *Cuban Political Prisoners*, 14; for Reagan's Human Rights Day messages, see *PPP* 1985, 1459, *PPP* 1986, 1638, *PPP* 1988, 1598.

157. Human Rights Watch and Lawyers Committee for Human Rights, *Critique: Review of the Department of State's Country Reports on Human Rights Practices for 1987* (New York: Human Rights Watch and the Lawyers Committee for Human Rights, 1988), 28–29, 32.

158. For Abrams's 1983 estimate, see Abrams, "Cuban Revolution"; in 1986, Abrams told Congress that "only the Cuban Government knows the exact number of political prisoners in Cuba" (U.S. Congress, House, Committee on Foreign Affairs, Subcommittee on Human Rights and International Organizations, *Cuban Political Prisoners*, 37); Castro Interview by MacNeil; Castro Interview, *Proceso*, 21 September 1981, 8.

159. Vernon Walters, Statement before the Forty-third Session of the U.N. Commission on Human Rights, Geneva, 5 March 1987, in *Current Policy*, no. 954. "President's call to [Colombian President Virgilio] Barco this afternoon will be important," wrote the State Department officials coordinating the lobbying effort (Herman J. Cohen and José S. Sorzano to Colin L. Powell, "Cuba at Human Rights Commission: Update," 8 March 1988, DDRS); Skoug, *United States and Cuba*, 152, 196.

160. Reagan, 10 December 1985, *PPP*, 1479; *El Mercurio*, 24 February 1985, D1; Castro Interview by MacNeil. On Pinochet, Assistant Secretary of State Langhorne Motley continued, "The Western democracies owe a debt of gratitude to the Chilean people and government for what they did in 1973, not only for their own benefit, but also for the West, in the sense of the stability of the Hemisphere in which we live."

161. U.S. Congress, House, Committee on Foreign Affairs, Subcommittee on Human

Rights and International Organizations, *Cuban Political Prisoners*, 21. A month later, Senator Edward Kennedy completed a family obligation by obtaining the release of Ramón Conte Hernández, the last of the imprisoned Bay of Pigs veterans.

162. U.S. Congress, House, Committee on Foreign Affairs, Subcommittee on Western Hemisphere Affairs, *Soviet Posture in the Western Hemisphere*, 99th Cong., 1st sess., 28 February 1985, 6.

163. In mid-1988, for example, CANF enlisted the help of Miami representative Claude Pepper to insert Section 1911 into the complex Omnibus Trade and Competitiveness Act of 1988. It instructed "all relevant agencies [to] prepare appropriate recommendations for improving the enforcement of restrictions on the importation of articles from Cuba." The result was a slight tightening of the embargo during Reagan's final weeks in the White House (PL 100-418, 100 *Stat.* 1107, 23 August 1988; 53 *FR* 47526, 23 November 1988; see also 53 *FR* 44397, 3 November 1988, which enlarged the existing list [51 *FR* 44459, 10 December 1986] of "Specially Designated Cuban Nationals"—Cuban-controlled companies and individuals based in third countries—with which transactions were prohibited).

164. Skoug Interview; Skoug, *United States and Cuba*, 208.

Chapter 12

1. James A. Baker III with Thomas M. DeFrank, *The Politics of Diplomacy: Revolution, War and Peace, 1989–1992* (New York: Putnam's, 1995), 50–52; Lawrence A. Pezzullo Oral History, 24 February 1989, NSA. At Aronson's confirmation hearing, Senator Christopher Dodd offered praise: "I understand that you have diligently gone about learning Spanish over the last several months" (U.S. Senate, Committee on Foreign Relations, *Nomination of Assistant Secretary of State for Inter-American Affairs*, 19 May 1989, 6).

2. DOS to All American Republic Diplomatic Posts, "Cuban Support for Subversion in Latin America," 13 February 1989, NSA. The telegram indicated that "the following draft report . . . will be used to brief the incoming assistant secretary."

3. U.S. Congress, House, Committee on Foreign Affairs, *Cuba and the United States: Thirty Years of Hostility and Beyond*, 101st Cong., 1st sess., August–September 1989, 175 (Crockett), 108, 158, 168, 170 (Kozak), 32 (Domínguez), 52 (Falk).

4. National Security Decision Directive 75, 17 January 1983, NSA; Charles W. Freeman Jr., "The Angola/Namibia Accords," *Foreign Policy* 68 (Summer 1989): esp. 133, 136; CIA, "Cuban International Activities Inimical to US Interests," 9 November 1982, NSA.

5. Secretary of State to Amembassy Mexico City [and] Contadora Collective, "Meeting of U.S. and Mexican Delegations during President's Visit to Mexicali, Mexico, January 3, 1986," 3 January 1986, DDRS.

6. A useful outline of what became the Reagan State Department's approach is L. Paul Bremer III (by Charles Hill) to William Clark, "Update on the Southern Africa Negotiations," 24 March 1983, DDRS. Assistant Secretary of State Chester Crocker's principal deputy, Freeman, discusses the details of the agreement in "Angola/Namibia Accords," 126–41.

7. Baker with DeFrank, *Politics of Diplomacy*, 599. Candidate and then Vice President Bush regularly repeated the surrogate charge. See *Bush on Cuba: Selected Statements of the President* (Washington, D.C.: Cuban American National Foundation, 1991), 7–8, 11, 12, 19, 22, 27.

8. CIA, "Gorbachev's Policy toward the United States, 1986–88," Special NIE 11-9-86, September 1986, 23–24; Castro Speech, Havana, 5 December 1988.

9. Interview, Caracas, 4 February 1989; Interview, Caracas, [3, 4 or 5 February 1989], broadcast 10 February 1989, LANIC.

10. Speech Introducing Mikhail Gorbachev to the National Assembly, Havana, 4 April 1989, Joint Press Conference, Havana, 4 April 1989, LANIC.

11. Comments to Reporters, 5 April 1989, LANIC.

12. Speech, Camagüey, 26 July 1989.

13. Bush Interview with French Television, 24 May 1990, *PPP*, 724; Castro Speech, Havana, 7 December 1989.

14. Speech, Havana, 28–29 January 1990; for Cuba's position at the CMEA meeting, see the speech by Vice President Carlos Rafael Rodríguez, in *Granma*, 10 January 1990, 4. For a helpful overview, see Mervyn J. Bain, *Soviet-Cuban Relations, 1985 to 1991: Changing Perceptions in Moscow and Havana* (Lanham, Md.: Lexington Books, 2007).

15. Bush Speech, Miami, 19 December 1991, *PPP*, 1647; Castro Speeches, Havana, 28–29 January, 3 April 1990, LANIC.

16. Television Interview, Caracas, broadcast 10 February 1989; Speech, Camagüey, 26 July 1989; Speech, Havana, 7 December 1989; Speech, Cienfuegos, 5 September 1992, LANIC.

17. These bills included a requirement that the Soviets end aid to Cuba before receiving U.S. bilateral aid or U.S. support for Soviet access to multilateral lending agencies. Other punitive legislation not aimed specifically at the Soviets included a bill to deny most-favored nation status to China unless it significantly cut its aid to Cuba, another required a reduction in U.S. aid to any country purchasing Cuban sugar, and a third prohibited the use of U.S. ports by third-country vessels that traded with Cuba. None of the bills became law.

18. Press Conference, 28 November 1989, *PPP*, 1592, 1594; Bush quoting Gorbachev in George Bush and Brent Scowcroft, *A World Transformed* (New York: Knopf, 1998), 165; Press Conferences, 3, 4 December 1989, *PPP*, 1637, 1651.

19. Bush and Scowcroft, *World Transformed*, 275 (Scowcroft), 277, 287 (Bush).

20. Bush Press Conference, Houston, 11 July 1990, *PPP*, 995; see also Question-and-Answer Session with Reporters, 13 June 1990, *PPP*, 724; Press Conferences in Alabama, 20 June 1990, Washington, D.C., 29 June 1990, London, 6 July 1990, *PPP*, 845, 886–87, 969; Baker in U.S. Congress, Senate, Committee on Foreign Relations, Subcommittee on European Affairs, *The Future of Europe*, 101st Cong., 2nd sess., 12 June 1990, 647–48. German Chancellor Helmut Kohl also carried the message to the Soviet leader: "I told him if he wants to improve relations with the U.S., he would have to change his policy on Cuba," and "I think he realizes that Cuba is important for the U.S. and for George Bush and that there is a connection to U.S. assistance" (Memorandum of Telephone Conversation, President Bush and Chancellor Helmut Kohl, 17 July 1990, DDRS).

21. Castro Speech, Havana, 26 July 1990.

22. Bush Press Conference, London, 17 July 1991, *PPP*, 909; Remarks in Moscow, 30 July, 2 August 1991, *PPP*, 980, 1017; see also Bush and Scowcroft, *World Transformed*, 507.

23. Press Conference, Kennebunkport, 2 September 1991, *PPP*, 1102.

24. Baker with DeFrank, *Politics of Diplomacy*, 528–29.

25. *Granma*, 14 September 1991, 1; Castro Speech, Matanzas, 26 July 1991.

26. *Congressional Record*, 17 June 1992, 4672–73.

27. Kozak to Congress, August 1989, in U.S. Congress, House, Committee on Foreign Affairs, *Cuba and the United States*, 94. The International Monetary Fund put loans at $2.3 billion and nonrepayable Soviet subsidies at $2 billion per year in 1986–90, for a total of $4.3 billion, or 15 percent of Cuba's gross domestic product at the official exchange rate and much more if converted at the market exchange rate. Ernesto Hernández-Catá, *The Fall and Recovery of the Cuban Economy in the 1990s: Mirage or Reality?*, Working Paper WP/01/48 (Washington, D.C.: IMF, 2001); Jorge F. Pérez-López, "The Cuban Economic Crisis of the 1990s and the External Sector," *Cuba in Transition* 8 (1998): 394; Carmelo Mesa-Lago, *Are Economic Reforms Propelling Cuba to the Market?* (Miami: North-South Center, University of Miami, 1994), 3–6.

In addition to the trade subsidies, Moscow was funding three major economic aid projects in Cuba at the time of Soviet Union's dissolution: a nuclear power plant at Juraguá, a nickel refinery at Camarioca, and an upgraded oil refinery at Cienfuegos. On the three projects, see *Granma*, 27 October 2001, 1; Víctor Alvarez Marco, "Cuba-URSS: cooperación para el desarrollo," *Economía y Desarrollo* 89 (July–August 1989): 166–71; Yuri Pavlov, *Soviet-Cuban Alliance: 1959–1991* (New Brunswick, N.J.: Transaction, 1994).

28. CIA, National Intelligence Daily, 3 July 1991, FOIA; Castro Speech, Santiago, 10 October 1991.

29. William M. LeoGrande and Julie M. Thomas, "Cuba's Quest for Economic Independence," *Journal of Latin American Studies* 24 (May 2002): 325–63, estimates Cuba's debt to Russia at between $18 and $20 billion. See also Archibald R. M. Ritter (*Cuba's Economic Performance and the Challenges Ahead*, Background Briefing RFC-02-1, [Ottawa: Canadian Foundation for the Americas, 2002], 5), which suggests that the debt may be as high as $27 billion or, as Cuba claims, zero.

30. Bush, 17 October 2001, *PPP*, 1259; the Cuban "Nota Oficial," 17 October 2001, in *Granma*, 18 October 2001, 1.

31. Castro Speech, Santiago, 26 July 1988; Speech, Camagüey, 26 July 1989; Speech, Havana, 26 July 1990; Speech, Matanzas, 26 July 1991; Speech, Cienfuegos, 5 September 1992. (In 1992, Castro was in Spain attending the Ibero-American summit on 26 July, and the Cienfuegos speech was the delayed celebration.)

32. For CMEA trade data, see Elena Alvarez González and María Antonia Fernández Mayo, *Dependencia externa de la economía cubana* (Havana: Instituto de Investigaciones Económicas, 1992); for the precollapse view of how Cuba benefited from this trade, see Anatoli Bekarévich, "Cuba y CAME: el camino de la integración," in Academia de Ciencias de la URSS, Instituto de América Latina, *Cuba: 25 años de construcción del socialismo* (Moscow: Redacción Ciencias Sociales Contemporáneas, 1986), 115–32; on the socialist international division of labor, see Zoila González Maicas and Julio A. Díaz-Vázquez, "Los convenios de especialización agrícola de Cuba con los países miembros del CAME," *Economía y Desarrollo* 88 (1988): 145–55. On the terms of trade, see José Alvarez and Lázaro Peña Castellanos, *Cuba's Sugar Industry* (Gainesville: University Press of Florida, 2001), 45; Archibald R. M. Ritter and John M. Kirk, eds., *Cuba in the International System: Normalization and Integration* (New York: St. Martin's, 1995), 24; Alvarez González and Fernández Mayo, *Dependencia externa*, 8.

33. U.S. Congress, Joint Economic Committee, Subcommittee on International Trade, Finance, and Security Economics, *The Political Economy of the Western Hemisphere: Selected Issues for U.S. Policy*, 97th Cong., 1st sess., 18 September 1981, 120; U.S. Congress, House,

Committee on Foreign Affairs, Task Force on International Narcotics Control, *Cuban Involvement in International Narcotics Trafficking*, 101st Cong., 1st sess., July 1989, 66.

34. Speeches, Havana, 5 December 1988, 2 January 1989: "That is why, let us say louder than ever, 'Socialism or Death!' 'Marxism-Leninism or Death!'" Castro did not use "Socialism or Death" again until December 1989, after which it became a regular feature at the end of each speech.

35. Speeches, Havana, 7 December 1989, 28–29 January 1990.

36. Speech, Havana, 13 March 1990, LANIC; Speech to FMC, Havana, 7 March 1990, in *Granma*, 10 March 1990, special supplement; Speech, Havana, 26 July 1990. The origin of "Patria o muerte" (Fatherland or Death) dates to a 27 March 1960 speech. "Patria o muerte" subsequently began to appear regularly (e.g., 1 May) and then invariably.

37. *Granma*, 29 August 1990, 1; Speeches, Havana, 28 September 1990, 28–29 January 1990; Speech, Havana, 7 March 1990, in *Granma*, 10 March 1990, special supplement.

38. William Kast, "Cuba's Agriculture: Collapse and Economic Reform," *USDA Agricultural Outlook*, October 1998, 26; Carmen Diana Deere, Niurka Pérez, and Ernel González, "The View from Below: Cuban Agriculture in the 'Special Period in Peacetime,'" *Journal of Peasant Studies* 21 (January 1994): 194–234; Jorge F. Pérez-López, "Waiting for Godot: Cuba's Stalled Reforms and the Continuing Economic Crisis," *Problems of Post-Communism* 48 (November–December 2001): 44–46; Pérez-López, "Cuban Economic Crisis"; Louis A. Pérez Jr., *To Die in Cuba: Suicide and Society* (Chapel Hill: University of North Carolina Press, 2005), esp. 353; Jorge Domínguez, "The Political Impact on Cuba of the Reform and Collapse of Communist Regimes," in *Cuba after the Cold War*, ed. Carmelo Mesa-Lago (Pittsburgh: University of Pittsburgh Press, 1993), 99–132; CIA, "Cuba: The Outlook for Castro and Beyond," NIE 93-30, August 1993; Sergio Díaz-Briquets and Jorge F. Pérez-López, "Cuba's Labor Adjustment Policies during the Special Period," in *Cuba at a Crossroads*, ed. Jorge F. Pérez-López (Gainesville: University Press of Florida, 1994), 118–46; Sonia Sánchez, "Obreros interruptos, pero no desocupados," *Trabajadores*, 2 December 1991, 9.

On the difficulty of assessing Cuba's economy, see Jorge F. Pérez-López, *Measuring Cuban Economic Performance* (Austin: University of Texas Press, 1987); Carmelo Mesa-Lago and Jorge Pérez-López, *A Study of Cuba's Material Product System, Its Conversion to the System of National Accounts, and Estimation of Gross Domestic Product Per Capita and Growth Rates*, World Bank Staff Working Paper 770 (Washington, D.C.: World Bank, 1985).

39. Castro Speech, Havana, 7 March 1990, in *Granma*, 10 March 1990, special supplement.

40. For Bush comments, see 10 May, 17 July, 2, 26 August, 20, 30 September, 20 November, 19, 26 December 1991, 525, 909, 1017, 1089, 1197, 1233, 1495, 1647, 1658; 4 March, 18 April, 20 May, 23 October 1992, *PPP*, 377, 615, 805, 1950; for Aronson, see U.S. Congress, House, Committee on Foreign Affairs, Subcommittees on Europe and the Middle East and on Western Hemisphere Affairs, *Cuba in a Changing World: The United States–Soviet–Cuban Triangle*, 102nd Cong., 1st sess., April–July 1991, 116; see also U.S. Congress, Senate, Committee on Foreign Relations, Subcommittee on Western Hemisphere and Peace Corps Affairs, *The Cuban Democracy Act of 1992, S. 2918*, 102nd Cong., 2nd sess., 5 August 1992, 26; Santiago Aroca, *Fidel Castro: el final del camino* (Barcelona: Planeta, 1992), esp. 309; Andres Oppenheimer, *Castro's Final Hour: The Secret Story behind the Coming Downfall of Communist Cuba* (New York: Simon and Schuster, 1992).

41. U.S. Southern Command, "Cuba's Possible Entry into the International Arms Market—An Effort to Continue to Keep Regional Insurgents in Arms and to Provide Cuba Necessary Hard Currency," 10 April 1989, NSA.

42. Bush and Scowcroft, *World Transformed*, 134–35.

43. For the transcript of Mas Canosa's 27 September 1991 radio commentary, see *Jorge Mas Canosa: en busca de una Cuba libre, edición completa de sus discursos, entrevistas y declaraciones, 1962–1997*, comp. Rolando Bonachea (Miami: North-South Center Press, University of Miami, 2003), 2:1126.

44. Philip Brenner, "The Thirty-Year War," *NACLA Report on the Americas* 24 (November 1990): 19; Bush Speech, Miami, 16 August 1989, *PPP*, 1093.

45. U.S. Congress, House, Committee on Foreign Affairs, *Consideration of the Cuban Democracy Act of 1992*, 102nd Cong., 2nd sess., 1992, 167–68.

46. In CANF's first year, 1981–82, Mas Canosa and his wife contributed thirty-three thousand dollars to various political candidates, and that number rose steadily during the 1980s and 1990s (Patrick J. Kiger, *Squeeze Play: The United States, Cuba, and the Helms-Burton Act* [Washington, D.C.: Center for Public Integrity, 1997], 28).

47. 13 June 1988 in *Bush on Cuba*, 32; 16 August 1989, *PPP*, 1019; 23 October 1992, *PPP*, 1939.

48. U.S. Congress, House, Committee on Foreign Affairs, Subcommittee on Western Hemisphere Affairs, *Recent Developments in Cuba Policy: Telecommunications and Dollarization*, 103rd Cong., 1st sess., 4 August 1993, 5 (Ros-Lehtinen); John Ferch Interview by Author, Fairfax, Virginia, 17 February 2005.

49. "Once again, as always, we appreciate what you and what the Foundation do for our efforts in foreign affairs," said Florida's Democratic representative Larry Smith (U.S. Congress, House, Committee on Foreign Affairs, Task Force on International Narcotics Control, *Cuban Involvement*, 147). "You are always welcome before this committee, and I thank you for your very thoughtful statement," said New Jersey's Torricelli (U.S. Congress, House, Committee on Foreign Affairs, Subcommittees on Europe and the Middle East and on Western Hemisphere Affairs, *Cuba in a Changing World*, 169).

50. Ann Louise Bardach, *Cuba Confidential: Love and Vengeance in Miami and Havana* (New York: Random House, 2002), xviii; Kenneth Skoug Jr. Interview by Author, Alexandria, Virginia, 3 March 2005; Ferch Interview.

51. A facsimile of Mas Canosa's curriculum vitae is reproduced in Jon Elliston, *Psywar on Cuba: The Declassified History of U.S. Anti-Castro Propaganda* (Melbourne, Australia: Ocean, 1999), 223 (emphasis added); Ann Louise Bardach, "Our Man in Havana—Mas Canosa: Mobster and Megalomaniac," *New Republic*, 3 October 1994, 20–25. Added by the magazine's editor, the "Mobster and Megalomaniac" subtitle triggered Mas Canosa's unsuccessful libel suit. Americas Watch, *Dangerous Dialogue: Attacks on Freedom of Expression in Miami's Cuban Exile Community* (New York: Americas Watch, August 1992).

52. *NYT*, 20 February 1990, A1, A14; "Report of the Commission on a Free Cuba," June 1990, 15, in possession of the author.

53. U.S. Congress, House, Committee on Foreign Affairs, Subcommittees on International Operations and on Western Hemisphere Affairs, *Foreign Policy Implications of TV Marti*, 100th Cong., 2nd sess., 22 September 1988, 61 (Smith), 58 (Mas).

54. Memorandum of the Discussion at the 441st Meeting of the NSC, Washington, D.C.,

14 April 1960, *FRUS* 1958–60, 6:893–97. For how television broadcasts would violate international telecommunications agreements, see GAO, *TV Martí: Costs and Compliance with Broadcast Standards and International Agreements*, GAO/NSIAD-92-199, May 1992.

55. USIA (Morrow) to President, "Airborne Television Capability," 3 December 1962, Folder "1/62–12/62," Box 91, POF, Departments and Agencies, USIA; Edwin M. Martin, "Stratovision—TV Broadcasts to Cuba from Aircraft," enclosed with William H. Brubeck to Arthur Schlesinger Jr., "Stratovision—TV Broadcasts to Cuba from Aircraft," 25 May 1962, Folder "Cuba General 1/62–8/62," Box 36, NSFK; Donald M. Wilson to Brigadier General Edward G. Lansdale, "Broadcasting to Cuba," 11 September 1962, Folder "Special Group (Augmented) General 9/62," Box 319A, NSFK.

56. PL 100-202, 101 *Stat.* 1337, 22 December 1987; Minutes of a meeting of the Advisory Board for Radio Broadcasting to Cuba, 17 November 1988, U.S. Advisory Panel on Radio Martí and TV Martí, Summary of "Technical Session: February 17, 1994," both in Elliston, *Psywar*, 243–44, 262–64.

57. U.S. Congress, House, Committee on Foreign Affairs, Subcommittees on International Operations and on Western Hemisphere Affairs, *Foreign Policy Implications*, 1, 3, 42; the Executive Summary of the "Television Marti Feasibility and Background Studies," May 1988, is 73–91. See also U.S. Congress, Senate, *International Telecommunication Convention (Nairobi, 1982): Message from the President of the United States Transmitting the International Telecommunications Convention*, Treaty Doc. 99-6, 99th Cong., 1st sess., 15 May 1985, 203 (United States), 198 (Cuba).

58. U.S. Congress, House, Committee on Foreign Affairs, Subcommittees on International Operations and on Western Hemisphere Affairs, *Foreign Policy Implications*, 61–64, 70.

59. For the start-up appropriation, see Title V of PL 100-459, 102 *Stat.* 2186, 1 October 1988; Bush Speech, Washington, D.C., 22 May 1989, *PPP*, 591; *Bush on Cuba*, 19; U.S. Congress, Senate, Committee on Foreign Relations, *Nomination of James A. Baker III*, 101st Cong., 1st sess., 17–18 January 1989, 85; U.S. Congress, House, Committee on Foreign Affairs, *Cuba and the United States*, 105.

60. Manuel Gómez, "Pull the Plug on TV Martí," *NYT*, 9 June 1989, A31; Lieberman in *NYT*, 24 June 1989, A22. CANF had supported Lieberman to defeat liberal Republican Lowell Weicker, who had been a major advocate of détente with Cuba. "Joe's been great for us," CANF spokesperson José Cárdenas told journalist Ann Louise Bardach; "one of our great successes was getting rid of Lowell Weicker" (Bardach, "Our Man in Havana," 22).

61. The act is Title II of PL 101-246, 104 *Stat.* 15. Section 247(b) required the president to certify that TV Martí "will not cause objectionable interference with the broadcasts of incumbent domestic licensees." U.S. Advisory Board for Cuba Broadcasting, *Special Report by the Advisory Board for Cuba Broadcasting on TV Martí: Presented to President George Bush, January, 1991* (Washington, D.C.: Advisory Board for Cuba Broadcasting, 1991). President Bush's 26 August 1990 certification, Presidential Determination 90-35, is 55 *FR* 38659.

62. GAO, *TV Martí*, 11–12; Castro Speech, Havana, 28–29 January 1990, LANIC; see also Speeches, Havana, 13 March, 3 April 1990, LANIC.

63. *Broadcasting* 118 (2 April 1990): 50.

64. The monitoring reports are reproduced in Elliston, *Psywar*, 258–61.

65. GAO, "Broadcasts to Cuba: TV Marti Surveys Are Flawed," Report GAO/NSIAD-90-252,

August 1990, 1–3; "Letter to Hon. Howard L. Berman and Hon. John F. Kerry regarding Radio Martí Broadcast Standards," GAO/NSIAD-93-126R, 17 February 1993; "Radio Martí, Program Review Processes Need Strengthening," GAO/NSIAD-94-265, September 1994; "U.S. Information Agency, Issues Related to Reinvention Planning in the Office of Cuba Broadcasting," GAO/NSIAD-96-110, May 1996. For other assessments, see DOS, Office of the Inspector General, "Review of Policies and Procedures for Ensuring that Radio Martí Broadcasts Adhere to Applicable Requirements," 99-IB-010, June 1999; Advisory Panel on Radio Martí and TV Martí, "Report of the Advisory Panel on Radio Martí and TV Martí," 3 vols., March 1994, which is a report required by law: Title V, PL 103-121. Vol. 3 (*Classified Appendices*) remains classified, but vol. 1 (*Findings and Conclusions*) and a very useful vol. 2 (*Statements to the Panel*) are available in *Latin America: Special Studies, 1995–1997 Supplement*, ed. Robert E. Lester (Bethesda, Md.: University Publications of America, 1999), reel 6; the affidavit by Kristin Juffer is reproduced in Elliston, *Psywar*, 297–301.

66. A summary of the advisory panel report is contained in Susan B. Epstein and Mark Sullivan, *Radio and Television Broadcasting to Cuba: Background and Current Issues*, Report 94-636F (Washington, D.C.: CRS, 1994). The Advisory Panel was created by PL 103-121, 107 *Stat.* 1192, 27 October 1993; *Washington Post*, 4 August 1992, A17; *NYT*, 4 August 1992, A7.

67. For a survey of 486 visa applicants at the U.S. Interests Section during a week in April 1998 that placed viewership at 1.5 percent during the previous week and 6 percent during the previous year, see David Burke (chair, Broadcasting Board of Governors) to Representative David E. Skaggs, 15 April 1998 (facsimile in Elliston, *Psywar*, 266–68).

68. Article II of the original 1903 Guantánamo base lease (Treaty Series 418), extended in 1934, gives the United States the right "to do any and all things necessary to fit the premises for use as coaling or naval stations only, and for no other purpose." For the Pentagon's position, see Elliston, *Psywar*, 262; James Cason Interview by Author, Havana, 8 March 2005.

69. Sec. 107, PL 104-135, 110 *Stat.* 1321, 25 April 1996; Daniel W. Fisk, "Cuba: The End of an Era," *Washington Quarterly* 24 (Winter 2001): 104.

70. This schedule is for the antenna broadcasts for the week of 15 January 2005, when TV Martí was broadcasting 4.5 hours per day on UHF channels 18, 50, and 64 via Cudjoe Key and on VHF channel 13 via airborne C-130s. A repetitive but somewhat broader variety of TV programming was available twenty-four hours a day via Hispasat and Web streaming.

71. U.S. Congress, Senate, Committee on Foreign Relations, *Nomination of James A. Baker III*, 171; U.S. Congress, House, Committee on Foreign Affairs, *Cuba and the United States*, 167.

72. Michael Krinsky and David Golove, *United States Economic Measures against Cuba: Proceedings in United Nations and International Law Issues* (Northampton, Mass.: Aletheia, 1993), 113–14; Gordon Chase to Bundy, "Imposition of Blocking Controls on Cuba," 11 June 1963, G. D'Andelot Belin to McGeorge Bundy, "Blocking of Cuban Dollar Accounts with Canadian Banks," 29 July 1963, both in Folder "Cuba Subjects Blocking Documents 6/1/63–8/15/63," Box 45, NSFK.

73. These figures are for the dollar value of licenses, not actual Cuban imports, which were always significantly less. There are no data about precisely how much less, but in the mid-1990s, one expert estimated that only about 15 percent of licensed trade actually occurred. U.S. Congress, House, Committee on Ways and Means, Subcommittee on Trade, *Cuban Democracy Act of 1992; and Withdrawal of MFN Status from the Federal Republic of Yugo-*

slavia, 102nd Cong., 2nd sess., 10 August 1992, 105; Ritter and Kirk, *Cuba in the International System*, 255 n. 1, 27, 104, 108, 240; U.S. Congress, House, Committee on Foreign Affairs, *Cuba and the United States*, 125–26, 143–45. On the Mack proposal, see *Congressional Record*, 20 July 1989, 15484–85, for an amendment to S. 1160; 5 April 1990, 7104–6 for S. 2444; 13 September 1990, 24348–49, for S. 2929, which became H.R. 4653, An Act to Reauthorize the Export Administration Act of 1979, passed by Congress on 26 October 1990, only to be pocket vetoed in November.

74. U.S. Congress, House, Committee on Foreign Affairs, Subcommittees on Europe and the Middle East and on Western Hemisphere Affairs, *Cuba in a Changing World*, 128 (Aronson), 154–55 (Mas Canosa).

75. U.S. Congress, House, Committee on Foreign Affairs, *Consideration of the Cuban Democracy Act*, 42.

76. Ibid., 26–28.

77. Ibid., 359.

78. Statement on Actions to Support Democracy in Cuba, 18 April 1992, *PPP*, 615–16. The two new regulations consisted of one stick (closure of U.S. ports to ships carrying Cuban goods) and one carrot (family-to-family shipments of food, medicine, toiletries, and other "humanitarian" items via charter flights from Miami). The shipments could not be valued at more than one hundred dollars, could be sent no more often than once per month, and could not contain more than two bottles of medicine (57 *FR* 15216, 24 April 1992).

79. 23 April 1992, reported in *Miami Herald*, 24 April 1992, 1, 15.

80. U.S. Congress, House, Committee on Foreign Affairs, *Consideration of the Cuban Democracy Act*, 851, 446, 464.

81. Ibid., 28–29, 47. The Committee on Foreign Affairs had primary responsibility in the House for the Cuban Democracy Act, but five other committees had partial responsibility for the complex legislation, and none was as one-sided in its choice of hearing witnesses.

82. U.S. Congress, House, Committee on Foreign Affairs, *Consideration of the Cuban Democracy Act*, 420.

83. U.S. Congress, Senate, Committee on Foreign Relations, Subcommittee on Western Hemisphere and Peace Corps Affairs, *Cuban Democracy Act of 1992*, 117, 125; U.S. Congress, House, Committee on Ways and Means, Subcommittee on Trade, *Cuban Democracy Act of 1992*, 265, 295–96; Cargill's statement (265–71) captures especially well the sentiment of U.S. businesses seeking to trade with Cuba. See also U.S. Congress, House, Committee on Foreign Affairs, *Cuba and the United States*, 335–37.

84. The Cuban Democracy Act is Title 17 of the National Defense Authorization Act for Fiscal Year 1993, PL 102-484, 106 *Stat.* 2315, 23 October 1992. President Bush's Miami Remarks, 23 October 1992, *PPP*, 1940. The Clinton and Bush letters to House speaker Thomas Foley are reprinted in *Congressional Record*, 22 September 1992, 26914; U.S. Congress, House, Committee on Foreign Affairs, Subcommittees on Economic Policy, Trade, and Environment; on Western Hemisphere Affairs; and on International Operations, *U.S. Policy and the Future of Cuba: The Cuban Democracy Act and U.S. Travel to Cuba*, 103rd Cong., 1st sess., 18 November 1993.

85. This was the codification of an April 1992 regulation closing U.S. ports to third-country vessels carrying goods or passengers to or from Cuba (57 *FR* 15216, 24 April 1992). For an earlier version of this proposal, see *Congressional Record*, 19 May 1987, 12969–71.

86. U.S. Congress, House, Committee on Foreign Affairs, *Consideration of the Cuban Democracy Act*, 382–86; U.S. Congress, House, Committee on Foreign Affairs, *Cuban Democracy Act of 1991*, House Report 102-615, 102nd Cong., 2nd sess., 25 June 1992, 12.

87. The Bush administration had previously announced additional restrictions to curb the travel-related flow of money to Cuba, and as a final move in mid-November 1992 a lame-duck President Bush narrowed the definition of a general license for travel for "professional research" to stipulate that it must be "generally of a noncommercial, academic nature." Sec. 628, PL 103-393, 106 *Stat.* 1729, 6 October 1992. The three additional restrictions were (1) a first-ever limit of five hundred dollars on the amount that could be sent to Cuba for fees to permit a Cuban to visit relatives in the United States; (2) a similar first-ever limit of five hundred dollars on the amount of money that a U.S. national of Cuban birth could spend to obtain a Cuban passport (as the Cuban government required) to visit family in Cuba; and (3) a flat prohibition on Cuban visitors to the United States returning to the island with more hard currency than they had brought with them. At the same time, the administration reduced from five hundred dollars to three hundred dollars the amount of money Cuban Americans could remit to the household of a close relative every three months. 54 *FR* 49246, 2 October 1991; 57 *FR* 53997, 16 November 1992.

88. *Congressional Record*, 22 September 1992, 26914.

89. Edwin M. Martin to Alexis Johnson, "Track Two," 12 October 1962, *FRUS* 1961–63, 11:22–25; U.S. Congress, House, Committee on Foreign Affairs, *Cuban Democracy Act of 1991*, 1, 35 (Mas Canosa).

90. Sections 1707 and 1708 of PL 102-484; Aronson address to CANF's 10th Anniversary Meeting, Miami, 20 May 1991, *DOS Dispatch* 2 (27 May 1991), 378; see also a similar comment to Congress ("We have no desire to order Cuba's internal affairs") reprinted in *DOS Dispatch* 2 (5 August 1991), 581.

91. *Granma*, 24 May 1991, 6; Castro Speech, Havana, 19 April 1991.

92. Press Conference, 19 December 1991, *PPP*, 1647; Speech at the Republican National Convention, 20 August 1992, *PPP*, 1381.

93. Speech, Cienfuegos, 5 September 1992.

Chapter 13

1. The Democratic platform promised "to resist oppression in Cuba." The Republicans promised to "continue to strive toward the day when the alien ideology of communism and Fidel Castro's regime will be purged from Cuba," added a specific promise to support Radio and TV Martí, and congratulated the people of El Salvador and Nicaragua, "whose bravery and blood thwarted communism and Castro despite the inconstancy of congressional Democrats." Both platforms available at www.presidency.ucsb.edu/platforms.php.

2. For the elder Díaz-Balart's passionately antirevolution testimony to Congress in 1960, see U.S. Congress, Senate, Committee on the Judiciary, Subcommittee to Investigate the Administration of the Internal Security Act and Other Internal Security Laws, *Communist Threat to the United States through the Caribbean*, 86th–92nd Congresses, pt. 7, May 1960, 347–63.

3. U.S. Congress, Senate, Committee on Foreign Relations, *Nomination of Warren M. Christopher to be Secretary of State*, 103rd Cong., 1st sess., 14 January 1993, 140–43.

4. Anthony Lake, "Confronting Backlash States," *Foreign Affairs* 73 (March–April 1994): 45.

5. U.S. Congress, Senate, Select Committee on Intelligence, *Prospects for Democracy in Cuba*, 103rd Cong., 1st sess., 29 July 1993, 9; U.S. Congress, House, Committee on Foreign Affairs, Subcommittees on Economic Policy, Trade and Environment; on Western Hemisphere Affairs; and on International Operations, *U.S. Policy and the Future of Cuba: The Cuban Democracy Act and U.S. Travel to Cuba*, 103rd Cong., 1st sess., 18 November 1993, 16, 22–23. For Clinton, see 13, 23 March, 20 May, 28 July, 30 August 1993, *PPP*, 290, 340, 709, 1221, 1412, 20 March 1994, *PPP*, 504.

6. U.S. Congress, Senate, Select Committee on Intelligence, *Prospects for Democracy*, 1 (Warner), 20 (Chafee), 2 (Graham), 3 (DeConcini), 4 (Kerrey).

7. H.R. 2229, 20 May 1993; U.S. Congress, House, Committee on Foreign Affairs, Subcommittee on Western Hemisphere Affairs, *The Free and Independent Cuba Assistance Act of 1993*, 103rd Cong., 2nd sess., 24 March 1994, 9.

8. *Red Lion Broadcasting v. FCC*, 395 U.S. 367, 390 (1969).

9. Christopher to Berman, 7 June 1993, quoted in U.S. Congress, House, Committee on Foreign Affairs, Subcommittees on Economic Policy, Trade and Environment; on Western Hemisphere Affairs; and on International Operations, *U.S. Policy and the Future of Cuba*, 101; see also 107–13. Berman's proposal, H.R. 1579, was introduced on 1 April 1993. The rewritten regulations are 58 *FR* 34709, 29 June 1993. See also Mark Sullivan, *Cuba: U.S. Restrictions on Travel and Legislative Initiatives*, CRS Report RL31139C (Washington, D.C.: CRS, 2003), esp. 3.

The full policy review promised to Representative Berman was not completed until February 1994, when Senator John Kerry, prodded by his Massachusetts constituents, in turn prodded the administration by proposing a nonbinding resolution (S. 1281) asserting that the president should not restrict travel for informational, educational, religious, or humanitarian exchanges, including travel to any country for public performances or exhibitions (Amendment 1354, *Congressional Record*, 1 February 1994, 710). A few days later, the promised review had been completed, and travel restrictions were lightened for all countries except North Korea and Cuba. That decision made no sense to many members of Congress, who approved a law that included Senator Kerry's nonbinding resolution (Sec. 525, PL 103-236, 108 *Stat.* 382, 30 April 1994).

10. U.S. Congress, House, Committee on Foreign Affairs, Subcommittees on Economic Policy, Trade and Environment; on Western Hemisphere Affairs; and on International Operations, *U.S. Policy and the Future of Cuba*, 2 (Gejdenson), 2–3 (Ros-Lehtinen), 6 (Díaz-Balart), Hernández (49). The subcommittees were chaired by Howard Berman (D-Calif.), Sam Gejdenson (D-Conn.), and Robert Torricelli (D-N.J.).

11. Ibid., 52–53. Díaz-Balart denied any involvement. On the threats by Alpha 66, see *NYT*, 6 November 1993, 9.

12. Comment about Mitterand, 12 November 1993, *PPP*, 1973; Clinton was aware of similar opposition voiced by the U.N. Security Council (13 March 1993, *PPP*, 290); the Caricom countries (30 August 1993, *PPP*, 1411), Mexico (12 November 1993, *PPP*, 1973), Spain (6 December 1993, *PPP*, 2131), and the Summit of the Americas (11 December 1994, *PPP*, 2178); Comment during the October 1996 Presidential Debate, *PPP*, 1767; for the Ibero-American summit, including Fidel Castro's 15 July speech, see *Granma*, 16 July 1993, 1.

13. For Helms's Juraguá comment, see U.S. Congress, Senate, Committee on Foreign Relations, *Nomination of Warren M. Christopher*, 141; Castro announced the unfinished plant's closure in a speech at Cienfuegos, 5 September 1992, LANIC; DOS, "Patterns of Global Terrorism, 1995," 30 April 1996. See also "Patterns of Global Terrorism, 1996," 30 April 1997, and the Clinton administration's final report, "Patterns of Global Terrorism, 2000," 30 April 2001, where the section on Cuba is a single sentence: "Cuba continued to provide safehaven to several terrorists and US fugitives and maintained tics to state sponsors and Latin American insurgents." Clinton: *PPP*, 4 April 1993, 400; CIA: 29 July 1993, in U.S. Congress, Senate, Select Committee on Intelligence, *Prospects for Democracy*, 14; U.S. Navy, Office of Naval Intelligence, "DNI Posture Statement," 1994, NSA; on Cuba's military budget cuts, see CIA, "Cuba: The Outlook for Castro and Beyond," NIE 93-30, August 1993, 3, 15; Hal C. Klepak, *Cuba's Military, 1990–2005: Revolutionary Soldiers during Counter-Revolutionary Times* (New York: Palgrave Macmillan, 2005).

14. DIA, "The Cuban Threat to U.S. National Security," 6 May 1998.

15. Brian Latell, *After Fidel: The Inside Story of Castro's Regime and Cuba's Next Leader* (New York: Palgrave Macmillan, 2002), 191; Montes's statement in U.S. District Court, Washington, D.C., 16 October 2002, reported in *Miami Herald*, 17 October 2002; Scott W. Carmichael, *True Believer: Inside the Investigation and Capture of Ana Montes, Cuba's Master Spy* (Annapolis, Md.: Naval Institute Press, 2007).

16. U.S. Congress, House, Committee on Foreign Affairs, Task Force on International Narcotics Control, *Cuban Involvement in International Narcotics Trafficking*, 101st Cong., 1st sess., 25 July 1989, 7; CIA, "National Intelligence Daily," 12 August 1989, FOIA.

17. *PPP*, 2 December 1996, 2162; see also *PPP*, 22 February 1996, 318. The administration reached the same conclusion a year later (*PPP*, 9 November 1997, 1529), and this estimate continued until the end of Clinton's presidency: *PPP*, 4 December 1998, 2134–35; *PPP*, 10 November 1999, 2057–59; *PPP*, 1 November 2000, 2411; McCaffrey Speech to the Director's Forum, Woodrow Wilson International Center for Scholars, Washington, D.C., 7 May 1999, in possession of the author; *Congressional Record*, 12 May 1999, 9387 (Díaz-Balart).

18. For the 1999 State Department report, see U.S. Congress, House, Committee on Government Reform, Subcommittee on Criminal Justice, Drug Policy, and Human Resources, *Cuba's Link to Drug Trafficking*, 106th Cong., 1st sess., 17 November 1999, 26.

19. Interview, *Die Woche* (Hamburg), 22 December 1993, 24, translated from the German by LANIC; see also Ann Louise Bardach, "El último revolucionario," *Elle* (Spanish ed.), June 1994, 64; *NYT*, 16 June 1993, A10 (Ernesto Meléndez), 29 June 1993, A9 (Robaina).

20. Clinton: 15 June 1993, *PPP*, 853; Gelbard: U.S. Congress, House, Subcommittee on Western Hemisphere Affairs, *Recent Developments in Cuba Policy: Telecommunications and Dollarization*, 103rd Cong., 1st sess., 4 August 1993, 14, 24. Section 1705(e)(2) of the Cuban Democracy Act instructed the executive branch "to provide efficient and adequate telecommunications service between the United States and Cuba," and the president, in turn, instructed executive branch agencies "to take all appropriate measures" to implement this provision (Executive Order 12854, 4 July 1993, 58 *FR* 36587). Direct-dial service began in November 1994.

21. *Jorge Mas Canosa: En busca de una Cuba libre: edición completa de sus discursos, entrevistas y declaractiones, 1962–1997*, comp. Rolando Bonachea (Miami: North-South Center, University of Miami, 2003), 2:1209; Susan Kaufman Purcell, "Collapsing Cuba," *Foreign Af-*

fairs 71 (Winter 1991–1992): 130; Carlos Alberto Montaner, *Víspera del final* (Buenos Aires: Marymar, 1993).

22. American Public Health Association, *The Impact of the U.S. Embargo on the Health of the Cuban People* (Washington, D.C.: American Public Health Association, 1993); Cuba Neuropathy Field Investigation Team, "Epidemic Optic Neuropathy in Cuba: Clinical Characterization and Risk Factors," *New England Journal of Medicine* 333 (2 November 1995): 1176–82; Katherine Tucker and Thomas R. Hedges, "Food Shortages and an Epidemic of Optic and Peripheral Neuropathy in Cuba," *Nutrition Reviews* 51 (December 1993): 349–57. For the performance of the Cuban economy during this period, see Comisión Económica para América Latina y el Caribe, *La economía cubana: reformas estructurales y desempeño en los noventa* (Mexico City: Fondo de Cultura Económica, 1997), esp. table A.1, which indicates a drop of 24.8 percent in gross domestic product in 1990–92 with a further drop of 14.2 percent in 1993. An English translation of the second Spanish edition is *The Cuban Economy: Structural Reforms and Economic Performance in the 1990s*, LC/mEX/R.746/Rev.1 (Mexico City: ECLAC, 2001).

23. Soledad Cruz, "Todavía responde la esperanza," *Juventud Rebelde*, 20 June 1993, 10; Rosa Miriam Elizalde and Amado del Pino, "'Flores' de 5th Avenida," *Juventud Rebelde*, 23 January 1994, 6–7; "Lucha contra el delito: caso Ruta 84," *Granma*, 4 September 1993, 2; "La tranquilidad ciudadana, una conquista irrenunciable," *Granma*, 8 September 1993, 8. On the black market, see Carmen Diana Deere in U.S. Congress, House, Committee on Agriculture, Subcommittee on Foreign Agriculture and Hunger, *Agricultural Implications of Renewed Trade with Cuba*, 103rd Cong., 2nd sess., 19 May 1994, 18; Andrew Zimbalist, "Teetering on the Brink: Cuba's Current Economic and Political Crisis," *Journal of Latin American Studies* 24 (May 1992): 412.

24. CIA, "Cuba: The Outlook for Castro and Beyond," NIE 93-30, August 1993; U.S. Congress, House, Committee on Foreign Affairs, Subcommittees on Economic Policy, Trade and Environment; on Western Hemisphere Affairs; and on International Operations, *U.S. Policy and the Future of Cuba*, 16; Richard Gott, *Cuba: A New History* (New Haven: Yale University Press, 2004), esp. chap. 8.

25. Jorge F. Pérez-López, "The Cuban Economic Crisis of the 1990s and the External Sector," *Cuba in Transition* 8 (1998): 408; Gabriel Fernández, "Cuba's Hard Currency Debt," *Cuba in Transition* 6 (1996): 44–49.

26. Speech, Heredia Theater, Santiago, 26 July 1993. For the government's explanation of the indoor celebration, see *Granma*, 22 June 1993, 1. The implementing legislation, Decreto-Ley 140 (*Gaceta Oficial*, 13 August 1993), revoked the part of Article 235 of the Código Penal that made it unlawful to possess or use foreign currency. Carlos Lage Dávila, "Comments to a Conference on 'La Nación y la Emigración,'" typescript, Havana, 22–24 April 1994, in possession of the author; Castro, Report [Speech] to the Fifth Congress of the Communist Party of Cuba, Havana, 8 October 1997, in possession of the author.

27. Decreto-Ley 141, 8 September 1993, reprinted with a list of the 117 occupations in *Granma*, 9 September 1992, 4–5. Handicraft markets were authorized in October, as were eighteen more occupations, including bicycle taxis, florists, and jewelry repair, and in mid-1995 another nineteen occupations were added, plus permission to open family-operated restaurants.

28. On the pre-reform structure of Cuban agriculture, see Carmen Diana Deere, Mieke

Meurs, and Niurka Pérez Rojas, "Toward a Periodization of the Cuban Collectivization Process: Changing Incentives and Peasant Response," *Cuban Studies* 22 (1992): 119–49; Lauren A. Burnhill, *The Private Sector in Cuban Agriculture: A Socio-Economic Study*, Occasional Paper 8 (Baltimore: Central American and Caribbean Program, School of Advanced International Studies, Johns Hopkins University, 1985). For the 1993–94 reforms, see Pérez-López, "Cuban Economic Crisis"; Philip Peters, *Survival Story: Cuba's Economy in the Post-Soviet Decade* (Washington, D.C.: Lexington Institute, 2002). For the UBPCs, see the law enacting them (Decreto-Ley 142, *Gaceta Oficial*, 20 September 1993, 15); Angel Bu Wong, "La cooperativización: su desarrollo en Cuba," *Cuba: Investigación económica* 4 (January–March 1998): 95–109; George Carriazo, "Cambios estructurales en la agricultura cubana: la cooperativización," in *Economía y reforma económica en Cuba*, ed. Dietmar Dirmoser and Jaime Estay (Caracas: Editorial Nueva Sociedad, 1997), 189–202; Santiago Rodríguez Castellón, "El sector agropecuario en 1996," in *Evolución de la economía cubana* (Havana: Centro de Estudios de la Economía Cubana, Universidad de la Habana, 1997), 68–78; Niurka Pérez Rojas, Ernel González, Miriam García Aguiar, and Miguel Valdés Pérez, *UBPC: Desarrollo rural y participación*, 2nd ed. (Havana: Universidad de la Habana, 1998); José Alvarez, *Cuba's Agricultural Sector* (Gainesville: University Press of Florida, 2004), esp. 75–96; William A. Messina Jr., "Agricultural Reform in Cuba: Implications for Agricultural Production, Markets and Trade," *Cuba in Transition* 9 (1999): 433–42.

29. Castro Speeches, Matanzas, 26 July 1991, Santiago, 26 July 1993. On the policy shift, see Archibald R. M. Ritter and John M. Kirk, eds., *Cuba in the International System: Normalization and Integration* (New York: St. Martin's, 1995), 103; Pérez-López, "Cuban Economic Crisis," 398; William M. LeoGrande and Julie M. Thomas, "Cuba's Quest for Economic Independence," *Journal of Latin American Studies* 34 (May 2002): 325–63; Debra Evenson, *Law and Society in Contemporary Cuba*, 2nd ed. (The Hague: Kluwer Law International, 2003), 250–60.

30. U.S. Congress, House, Committee on Foreign Affairs, Subcommittee on Western Hemisphere Affairs, *Free and Independent Cuba Assistance Act*, 1. First-term Representative Robert Menéndez agreed (3, 30–31, 34); his proposal (HR 2758, 27 July 1993) eventually became Title II of the 1996 Helms-Burton Act.

31. U.S. Congress, House, Committee on Ways and Means, Subcommittees on Select Revenue Measures and on Trade, *H.R. 2229, Free Trade with Cuba Act*, 103rd Cong., 2nd sess., 17 March 1994, 84 (Serrano), 8 (Shaw).

32. Ibid., 75 (Díaz Balart), 82 (Rangel).

33. Ibid., 345–48 (Institute for International Economics), 447 (Otis Elevators), 268 (aviation), 199–201, 291 (telecommunications).

34. Ibid., 215 (Mas Canosa), 220 (Jackson).

35. Speech, Miami, 21 March 1994, *PPP*, 517.

36. CIA, Directorate of Intelligence, "Cuba: Impact of Soviet Change," 10 September 1991, FOIA.

37. U.S. Congress, House, Committee on Foreign Affairs, Subcommittee on Western Hemisphere Affairs, *Recent Developments: Telecommunications and Dollarization*, 16; Carmelo Mesa-Lago, "Cuba's Raft Exodus of 1994: Causes, Settlement, Effects, and Future," *North-South Agenda Papers* 12 (April 1995): 2; U.S. Congress, House, Committee on Foreign Affairs, Subcommittee on Western Hemisphere Affairs, *Recent Developments in United States–Cuban*

Relations: Immigration and Nuclear Power, 102nd Cong., 1st sess., 5 June 1991, 21; Larry M. Eig, *Cuban Migration: Legal Basics*, CRS Report 94-692A (Washington, D.C.: CRS, 1994). The 1990 census (U.S. Summary, table 1, p. 7) reported 754,716 foreign-born Cubans living in the United States, 50.3 percent of whom had become citizens, and the Cuban Americans who had become citizens were disproportionately from the earlier waves of immigrants and therefore less likely to have immediate family members still living in Cuba. By 2000, the percentage of Cuban Americans who had become citizens had risen to 60.6 percent (U.S. Summary, table 1, p. 8).

38. *Department of State Dispatch* 2 (5 August 1991): 582; U.S. Congress, House, Committee on Foreign Affairs, Subcommittees on Europe and the Middle East and on Western Hemisphere Affairs, *Cuba in a Changing World: The United States–Soviet–Cuban Triangle*, 102nd Cong., 1st sess., April–July 1991, 230–31; Ruth Ellen Wasem, *Cuban Migration to the U.S.: Trends and Policy Issues*, CRS Report 93-259EPW (Washington, D.C.: CRS, 1993), 4, esp. estimates of overstayers; U.S. Congress, House, Committee on Foreign Affairs, Subcommittee on Western Hemisphere Affairs, *Recent Developments: Immigration and Nuclear Power*, 33.

39. Castro Press Conference, Havana, 5 August 1994, LANIC; CIA, Directorate of Intelligence, *Cuba Trends*, vol. 5, issue 1, January 1994, 4, FOIA.

40. *Agresión Migratoria*, Declaración de la Comisión Permanente de Relaciones Internacionales de la Asamblea Nacional del Poder Popular, 26 December 1993, in possession of the author; U.S. Congress, House, Committee on Foreign Affairs, Subcommittee on Western Hemisphere Affairs, *Recent Developments: Telecommunications and Dollarization*, 17. For the INS interpretation of the Cuban Adjustment Act at this time, see U.S. Congress, House, Committee on Foreign Affairs, Subcommittee on Western Hemisphere Affairs, *Recent Developments in United States–Cuban Relations: Immigration and Nuclear Power*, 11, 46. On the rafters, see Michael H. Erisman, *Cuba's Foreign Relations in a Post-Soviet World* (Gainesville: University Press of Florida, 2000), 176; Alfredo A. Fernández, *Adrift: The Cuban Raft People* (Houston: Arte Público, 2000).

41. CIA, Directorate of Intelligence, Office of African and Latin American Analysis, "Cuba: The Rising Specter of Illegal Migration," 11 May 1994, 5, 7, FOIA.

42. House Concurrent Resolution 279 was submitted on 5 August 1994, debated on 3 October, passed on 4 October, and then referred to the Senate Committee on Foreign Relations, which took no action. The House debate (*Congressional Record*, 27320–30) is indicative of the prevailing mood in Washington. For Burton, see U.S. Congress, House, Committee on International Relations, *Shoot Down of U.S. Civilian Aircraft by Castro Regime*, 104th Cong., 2nd sess., 29 February 1996, 1–2. For State Department, see U.S. Congress, Senate, Committee on Foreign Relations, Subcommittee on Western Hemisphere and Peace Corps Affairs, *Cuban Liberty and Democratic Solidarity Act*, 104th Cong., 1st sess., May–June 1995, 169; Castro Television Interview, 5 August 1994, Press Conference, 11 August 1994, both in LANIC.

43. Castro, Television Interviews, 5, 6 August 1994, Press Conference, 11 August 1994, all in LANIC.

44. Bill Clinton, *My Life* (New York: Knopf, 2004), 282, 615; on the 1980 contest, see Jonathan C. Smith, "Foreign Policy for Sale?: Interest Group Influence on President Clinton's Cuba Policy, August 1994," *Presidential Studies Quarterly* 28 (Winter 1998): 207–20.

45. Mesa-Lago, "Cuba's Raft Exodus."

46. Clinton Press Conference, 19 August 1994, *PPP*, 1477–84.

47. Bush Interview, 20 November 1991, *PPP*, 1494.

48. Alfredo A. Fernández, *Adrift: The Cuban Raft People*, trans. Susan Giersbach Rascón (Houston: Arte Público, 2000); Milagros Martínez, *Los balseros cubanos: un estudio a partir de las salidas ilegales* (Havana: Editorial de Ciencias Sociales, 1996); Holly Ackerman and Juan Clark, *The Cuban Balseros: Voyage of Uncertainty* (Miami: Cuban American National Council, 1995).

49. Press Conference, 19 August 1994, *PPP*, 1480; *The Gallup Poll, 1994* (New York: Random House, 1994), 228–33.

50. *Jorge Mas Canosa*, 3:1892–93, 1896. The new Clinton regulations were announced in "Statement on Cuba," 20 August 1994, *PPP*, 1487, and published in 59 *FR* 44884–86, 30 August 1994, which permitted specific travel licenses for educational and religious activities, for human rights investigations, for telecommunications installations, for professional research, and for the import or export of informational materials.

51. For Clinton, see 25 August 1994, *PPP*, 1504; for Castro, see 25 August 1994, LANIC.

52. The 9 September 1994 "Joint Communique on Migration" is 35 *ILM* 329; see also *Department of State Dispatch* 5 (12 September 1994): 603.

53. *Granma*, 16 November 1994, 2.

54. Clinton: 7 October 1994, *PPP*, 1721; 7 April 1995, *PPP*, 483; U.S. Congress, House, Committee on International Relations, Subcommittee on the Western Hemisphere, *The Clinton Administration's Reversal of U.S. Immigration Policy toward Cuba*, 104th Cong., 1st sess., 18 May 1995, 41.

55. Ricardo Alarcón Interview by Author, Havana, 11 March 2005. Earlier September talks in New York had been between Alarcón and deputy assistant secretary of state Michael Skol.

56. The 2 May 1995 Joint Statement is 35 *ILM* 327 (1996). The fifteen thousand visas would be credited against the twenty thousand per year commitment at the rate of five thousand per year for three years. The actual transfer was much quicker: the last of the Cubans left Guantánamo eight months later. On the Tarnoff-Alarcón negotiations, see U.S. Congress, House, Committee on International Relations, Subcommittee on the Western Hemisphere, *Clinton Administration's Reversal*; U.S. Congress, Senate, Committee on Foreign Relations, Subcommittee on Western Hemisphere and Peace Corps Affairs, *Cuban Liberty and Democratic Solidarity Act*, esp. 174.

57. *Congressional Record*, 2 May 1995, 11604.

58. U.S. Congress, House, Committee on International Relations, Subcommittee on the Western Hemisphere, *Cuba and U.S. Policy*, 104th Cong., 1st sess., 23 February 1995, 1–2 (Burton), 103 (Mas Canosa), 119 (Ros-Lehtinen).

59. U.S. Congress, House, Committee on International Relations, Subcommittee on the Western Hemisphere, *Clinton Administration's Reversal*, 55–56, 127.

60. U.S. Congress, House, Committee on International Relations, Subcommittee on the Western Hemisphere, *Clinton Administration's Reversal*, 36, 55–56, 122, 127; Videotaped Remarks to the Cuban American Community, 7 June 1995, *PPP*, 953–55.

61. *Washington Post*, 8 September 1994, A19.

62. U.S. Congress, House, Committee on International Relations, Subcommittee on the

Western Hemisphere, *Cuba and U.S. Policy*, 1–3, 11, 14 (Burton), 6 (Ros-Lehtinen), 10 (Díaz-Balart), 15–16, 20, 88–90 (Hall of Shame list).

63. S. 381, introduced 9 February 1995; *Congressional Record*, 9 February 1995, 4238. On 14 February, Representative Burton introduced a nearly identical companion measure, H.R. 927.

64. *Congressional Record*, 28 October 1987, 29620 (smoking on airliners), 15 December 1987, 18145 (Trojan horse).

65. Ibid., *Congressional Record*, 15 December 1987, 35612–17, 12 October 1995, 27721–23.

66. Sánchez's Miami law firm issued a press release boasting of his work in "drafting and commenting" on the bill (*Miami Herald*, 17 July 1995, 1C). For the drafting and negotiating of Helms-Burton, see Patrick J. Kiger, *Squeeze Play: The United States, Cuba, and the Helms-Burton Act* (Washington, D.C.: Center for Public Integrity, 1997).

67. H.R. 927, Sec. 303(b). On Cuban Americans' desire to become certified claimants, see, for example, U.S. Congress, Senate, Committee on Foreign Relations, Subcommittee on Western Hemisphere and Peace Corps Affairs, *Cuban Liberty and Democratic Solidarity Act*, 202–5, 217–18.

68. *Congressional Record*, 5 March 1996, 3580; U.S. Congress, Senate, Committee on Foreign Relations, Subcommittee on Western Hemisphere and Peace Corps Affairs, *Cuban Liberty and Democratic Solidarity Act*, 214–16. Headquartered at the Connecticut offices of Lone Star Industries, which had lost its cement plant at Mariel, the committee had been created in 1975 when the Ford administration's brief opening to Cuba made compensation seem possible. At its peak in the late 1970s, the committee represented fifty-eight claimants, including Allied Chemical and Woolworth.

Although no reliable estimate exists of the number of claims that could have been advanced by Cuban Americans who were Cuban nationals at the time their property was expropriated, in 1996 the State Department placed the number at between seventy-five thousand and two hundred thousand, and the dollar amount "could run easily into the tens of billions of dollars" (Barbara Larkin, Department of State, to Senator Jesse Helms, 27 September 1996; I thank the office of Senator Helms for providing a copy of this letter).

69. U.S. Congress, Senate, Committee on Foreign Relations, Subcommittee on Western Hemisphere and Peace Corps Affairs, *Cuban Liberty and Democratic Solidarity Act*, 165, 217, 202–5; PL 104-114, Secs. 302(b), 303(b).

70. U.S. Congress, House, Committee on International Relations, Subcommittee on the Western Hemisphere, *The Cuban Liberty and Democratic Solidarity (Libertad) Act of 1995*, 104th Cong., 1st sess., 16 March 1995, 14–15, 17–18, 160, 165.

71. Dole to Helms, 13 June 1995, reprinted in U.S. Congress, Senate, Committee on Foreign Relations, Subcommittee on Western Hemisphere and Peace Corps Affairs, *Cuban Liberty and Democratic Solidarity Act*, 51.

72. *Congressional Record*, 20 September 1995, 25930.

73. Speech, 6 October 1995, *PPP*, 1459; the revised regulations are 60 *FR* 54194, 20 October 1995. Until this speech, President Clinton had repeatedly gone out of his way to emphasize that no change of any kind was envisioned (6 December 1993, *PPP*, 2131; 11 December 1994, *PPP*, 2179; 15 April, 27 June 1995, *PPP*, 533–34, 953–55). For identical language by other senior officials, see U.S. Congress, House, Committee on International Relations, Subcom-

mittee on the Western Hemisphere, *The Cuban Liberty and Democratic Solidarity (Libertad) Act of 1995*, 21; U.S. Congress, Senate, Committee on Foreign Relations, Subcommittee on Western Hemisphere and Peace Corps Affairs, *Cuban Liberty and Democratic Solidarity Act*, 24.

74. CIA, Directorate of Intelligence, Office of African and Latin American Analysis, "Cuba: The Rising Specter of Illegal Migration," 11 May 1994, 4, FOIA.

75. Castro Speech, Havana, 7 February 1997, in *Granma*, 11 February 1997, 6. For Tarnoff, see U.S. Congress, House, Committee on International Relations, *Shoot Down*, 18. On other warnings to Bill Richardson and former ambassador Robert White, see Carl Nagin, "Annals of Diplomacy: Backfire," *New Yorker*, 26 January 1998, 33; *Time*, 11 March 1996, 36–38. For Basulto's background as "a veteran of the violent anti-Castro resistance based in Miami," which included firing at a suburban Havana hotel with a twenty-millimeter cannon, see Jefferson Morley, "Shoot Down," *Washington Post Magazine*, 25 May 1997, 8–13, 23–31.

76. International Civil Aviation Organization, "Report on the Shooting Down of Two U.S.-Registered Civil Aircraft by Cuban Military Aircraft on 24 February 1996," C-WP/10441, 20 June 1996, in U.N. Security Council, S/1996/509, 1 July 1996, 20. Both the 26 July 1996 Security Council debate and Resolution 1967 (1996) are in the lengthy Security Council Press Release SC/6247, 27 July 1996, in possession of the author; Inter-American Commission: Report 86/99 on Case 11.589, 29 September 1999, in possession of the author; Castro Speech, Havana, 7 February 1997, in *Granma*, 11 February 1997, 6. For an example of the warning press coverage, see *St. Petersburg Times*, 15 July 1995, 6A.

77. Clinton Statements, 24, 26 February 1996, *PPP*, 331–32, 339; "Notice to the Congress of the United States," 1 March 1996, *PPP*, 350. Brothers to the Rescue continued its flights in international waters but ceased operations in 2003 after the George W. Bush administration continued the Clinton policy of returning interdicted rafters.

78. For a flavor of the post-shoot-down consensus, see *Congressional Record*, 27 February 1996, 2851 (Dole), 5 March 1996, 3597 (Coverdell), 6 March 1996, 3791 (Clinton); U.S. Congress, House, Committee on International Relations, *Shoot Down*, 2 (Burton), 5, 15 (Ros-Lehtinen), 35 (Díaz-Balart).

79. U.S. Congress, House, Committee on International Relations, *Shoot Down*, 2, 6, 16. A consultant to Torricelli's Foreign Affairs Subcommittee from mid-1991 to mid-1993, Nuccio had then moved to the Clinton State Department and in mid-1995 had been appointed special adviser to the president and to the secretary of state for Cuba. His later attempt to distance himself from responsibility includes an assertion that "the president, on some bad advice from some of his close advisors, signed Helms-Burton when I don't think he needed to or should have" (Richard Nuccio Interview, *Common Ground* [radio program], 22 December 1998, transcript in possession of the author). U.S. Congress, House, Committee on International Relations, Subcommittee on the Western Hemisphere, *Clinton Administration's Reversal*, 118.

80. Press Conference, 19 August 1994, *PPP*, 1482.

81. Andreas F. Lowenfeld, "Agora: The Cuban Liberty and Democratic Solidarity (Libertad) Act," *American Journal of International Law* 90 (July 1996): 429.

82. PL 104-114, 110 *Stat.* 785, 12 March 1996; "Statement on Signing the Cuban Liberty and Democratic Solidarity (Libertad) Act of 1996," 12 March 1996, *PPP*, 434.

83. William M. LeoGrande, "Enemies Evermore: U.S. Policy towards Cuba after Helms-Burton," *Journal of Latin American Studies* 29 (February 1997): 214; Richard A. Nuccio, "Cuba: A U.S. Perspective," in *Transatlantic Tensions: The United States, Europe, and Problem Countries*, ed. Richard N. Haass (Washington, D.C.: Brookings Institution Press, 1999), 27 n. 9; Nagin, "Annals of Diplomacy," 34; Clinton: 11 April, 1 May 1997, *PPP*, 429, 521–25; Clinton, *My Life*, 701; Helms: *Congressional Record*, 5 March 1996, 3598.

84. National Association of Manufacturers, *Catalog of New U.S. Unilateral Economic Sanctions for Foreign Policy Purposes* (Washington, D.C.: National Association of Manufacturers, 1997), 8. For State Department warnings to both houses of Congress, see U.S. Congress, House, Committee on International Relations, Subcommittee on the Western Hemisphere, *Clinton Administration's Reversal*, 16; U.S. Congress, Senate, Committee on Foreign Relations, Subcommittee on Western Hemisphere and Peace Corps Affairs, *Cuban Liberty and Democratic Solidarity Act*, 160, 166. For Helms, see *Congressional Record*, 12 October 1995, 27722. For Nicolás Gutiérrez, see *The Economist*, 13 April 1996, 36. For a legal brief supporting the Helms position, see Brice M. Clagett, "Title III of the Helms-Burton Act Is Consistent with International Law," *American Journal of International Law* 90 (July 1996): 434–40; Brice M. Clagett, "A Reply to Professor Lowenfeld," *American Journal of International Law* 90 (October 1996): 641–44. For the Act of State doctrine underlying the opposition to Helms-Burton, see Helen Kim, "The Errand Boy's Revenge: Helms-Burton and the Supreme Court's Response to Congress's Abrogation of the Act of State Doctrine," *Emory Law Journal* 38 (Winter 1999): 305–36.

85. 23 May, 16, 29 August, 20, 22 October 1996, *PPP*, 808, 1299, 1415, 1872, 1902; Clinton, *My Life*, 727.

86. Dole Speech, Miami, 19 May 1996, in *NYT*, 20 May 1996, B7; Presidential Debate, 6 October 1996, *PPP*, 1766–67.

87. U.S. Congress, Senate, Committee on Foreign Relations, *Nomination of Secretary of State*, 105th Cong., 1st sess., 8 January 1997, 97.

88. U.S. Interests Section Interviews by Author with Susan Archer, 7 January 2003; James Cason, 8 March 2005; Michael Parmly, 27 January 2006, 19 January 2008, Havana.

89. Speech, Havana, 8 October 1997. The hijackers received prison terms ranging from eight to twenty years.

90. *PPP*, 11 April 1997, 429–30.

91. Philip Brenner, "Washington Loosens the Knot (Just a Little)," *NACLA Report on the Americas* 32 (March–April 1999): 45.

92. For the State Department warning, see U.S. Congress, Committee on Foreign Affairs, *Consideration of the Cuban Democracy Act of 1992*, 102nd Cong., 2nd sess., 8 April 1992, 403.

93. Castro Speech, Havana, 1 May 1961; CIA, Directorate of Plans, "Study on the Churches in Cuba," 8 September 1969, DDRS; CIA, Directorate of Intelligence, "Castro's Cuba Today," 30 September 1966, FOIA.

94. Transcript of Meeting between Castro and Honecker, Havana, 25 May 1980, Memorandum of Conversation between Raúl Castro and Soviet Ambassador V. I. Vorotnikov, 1 September 1979, both in *Cold War International History Project Bulletin* 8–9 (Winter 1996): 202, 192.

95. Castro Press Interview, Caracas, 4 February 1989, LANIC. The constitution's Article 8

reads, "The state recognizes, respects and guarantees religious freedom. In the Republic of Cuba, religious institutions are separate from the state. The various beliefs and religions enjoy equal consideration."

96. For the pastoral letter, see U.S. Congress, House, Committee on International Relations, Subcommittee on the Western Hemisphere, *The Visit of His Holiness Pope John Paul II to Cuba: An Assessment of Its Impact on Religious Freedom in Cuba*, 105th Cong., 2nd sess., 4 March 1998, 208–14; Lorenzo Albacete, "The Poet and the Revolutionary," *New Yorker*, 26 January 1998, 36–41.

97. U.S. Congress, House, Committee on International Relations, Subcommittee on the Western Hemisphere, *Visit*, 215–20.

98. *PPP*, 21 January 1998, 90; see also 11 April, 9 November 1997, *PPP*, 429–30, *PPP*, 1519; 20 January 1998, *PPP*, 80–81.

99. U.S. Congress, House, Committee on International Relations, Subcommittee on the Western Hemisphere, *Visit*, 21.

100. The 20 March 1998 changes are codified in 63 *FR* 27347–49, 18 May 1998.

101. George S. Vest to C. Fred Bergsten, 10 October 1978, Folder "Cuba 78/79," Box 14, RNSA.

102. Chargé d'affaires Michael Kergin to Sam M. Gibbons, Chair, Subcommittee on Trade, Committee on Ways and Means, 6 August 1992, in U.S. Congress, House, Committee on Ways and Means, Subcommittee on Trade, *Cuban Democracy Act of 1992; and Withdrawal of MFN Status from the Federal Republic of Yugoslavia*, 102nd Cong., 2nd sess., 10 August 1992, 264. According to the Foreign Extraterritorial Measures (United States) Order, 1992, SOR/92-584, 9 October 1992 (in possession of the author), "No Canadian corporation and no director, officer, manager or employee in a position of authority of a Canadian corporation shall, in respect of any trade or commerce between Canada and Cuba, comply with an extraterritorial measure of the United States."

103. Kim Campbell, "Helms-Burton: The Canadian View," 25 January 1977, reprinted in *Hastings International and Comparative Law Review* 20 (Fall 1997): 799–800; *Hansard*, 20 September 1996, 4508; John M. Kirk, "Unravelling the Paradox: The Canadian Position on Cuba," in *Cuba in the International System*, ed. Ritter and Kirk, 145–58; Beverly L. Campbell, "Helms-Burton: Checkmate or Challenge for Canadian Firms Doing Business in Cuba?" *Cuba in Transition* 6 (1996): 496–501; Cristina Warren, "Canada's Policy of Constructive Engagement with Cuba: Past, Present and Future," Background Briefing RFC-03-01, Canadian Foundation for the Americas, May 2003, in possession of the author.

104. *Hansard*, 20 September 1996, 4509–18. Bilateral negotiations had already failed: Canada had requested consultations under NAFTA's dispute settlement procedures immediately after President Clinton signed Helms-Burton, and fruitless talks were held on 26 April and 28 May. The amended Canadian law is 36 *ILM* 111 (1997). The quotation is from Section 7.1 of the 9 October 1996 amendment. Section 8.1 also allowed a Canadian firm to use Canadian courts to recover damages if a Helms-Burton decision led to the seizure of Canadian assets in the United States. Section 3 prohibited any Canadian from cooperating with any foreign tribunal if it "is likely to adversely affect significant Canadian interests in relation to international trade." See Christine L. Quickenden, "Helms-Burton and Canadian-American Relations at the Crossroads: The Need for an Effective, Bilateral Cuban Policy," *American University Journal of International Law and Policy* 12, no. 4 (1997): 733–67.

105. For Helms, see *Congressional Record*, 5 March 1996, 3597; for Clinton, see 8 April 1997, *PPP*, 403–4; for an overview, see John M. Kirk and Peter McKenna, *Canada-Cuba Relations: The Other Good Neighbor Policy* (Gainesville: University Press of Florida, 1997).

106. Ricardo Pascoe Pierce, *En el filo: historia de una crisis diplomática, Cuba 2001–2002* (Mexico City: Ediciones Sin Nombre, 2004), 95; Clinton-Zedillo Press Conference, 10 October 1995, *PPP*, 1564; the Mexican government's 28 August 1996 statement on Helms-Burton is reprinted in *Hastings International and Comparative Law Review* 20 (Fall 1997): 809–14. The Juridical Committee's 23 August 1996 opinion on Helms-Burton is reprinted in the 1996 *Informe Anual del Comité Jurídico Interamericano a la Asamblea General* and in OAS document CJI/SO/II/doc.67/96 rev.5.

107. "Resolution on the Restrictions on International Trade Imposed by the United States (Cuban Democracy Act)," B3-1692, etc., 17 December 1992, *Official Journal of the European Communities, Information and Notices* 36 (25 January 1993): C21/156; "Resolution on the Embargo against Cuba and the Torricelli Act," A3-0243/93, 16 September 1993, *Official Journal of the European Communities, Information and Notices*, 36 (4 October 1993): C268/153; see also C268/14.

108. The 5 March 1996 démarche is 35 *ILM* 397 (1996); Donna Rich Kaplowitz, "U.S. Foreign Subsidiary Trade with Cuba: Before and after the Cuban Democracy Act," in *Cuba in the International System*, ed. Ritter and Kirk, esp. 244–45.

109. Clinton: 12 June, 15, 16 July 1996, *PPP*, 902–4, 1126, 1137. Section 306 of the Helms-Burton Act stipulated that Title III would become effective on 1 August 1996 unless the president notified Congress that he was suspending the title for a period of not more than six months. Thereafter, Title III could be waived indefinitely, but only for six months at a time.

110. European Council Regulation 2271/96, 22 November 1996, *Official Journal of the European Communities, Legislation* 39 (29 November 1996): L309/1–7 (see 1–4 for the regulation and 7 for the council's resolution). See also *Bulletin of the European Union*, 4-1996, 75, 79; Jürgen Huber, "The Blocking Statute of the European Union," *Fordham International Law Journal* 20 (March 1997): 699–716.

111. Clinton Press Conference, 16 December 1996, *PPP*, 2211, 2213. For the Common Position adopted 2 December 1996, see *EU Official Journal*, 12 December 1996: 1. On this issue and Helms-Burton generally, see Joaquín Roy, *Cuba, the United States, and the Helms-Burton Doctrine: International Reactions* (Gainesville: University Press of Florida, 2000).

112. The original (1947) and revised (1994) GATT agreement provided that "nothing in this agreement shall be construed . . . to prevent any contracting party from taking any action which it considers necessary for the protection of its national security" but restricted the use of this proviso to matters related to fissionable materials, arms trade or when "taken in a time of war or other emergency in international relations." The national security argument was never openly announced; the closest the administration came is U.S. Congress, House, Committee on International Relations, Subcommittee on International Economic Policy and Trade, *World Trade Organization—Dispute Settlement Body*, 105th Cong., 2nd sess., 30 March 1998, 2, 11.

113. European Commission, "Understanding between the European Union and the United States on U.S. Extraterritorial Legislation," 11 April 1997, in possession of the author.

114. Blair at News Conference with President Clinton, 18 May 1998, *PPP*, 791–92; DOS

Press Release, "Statement by Secretary of State Albright," London, 18 May 1998, in possession of the author. The agreement is reprinted in *Americas Trade* 5 (28 May 1998): 18–22.

115. U.S. Congress, House, Committee on International Relations, *Economic Sanctions and U.S. Policy Interests*, 105th Cong., 2nd sess., 3 June 1998, 11–12, 85.

116. Author's notes on David Wallace, Joint Committee on Cuban Claims, at Policy Forum of the Institute for U.S.-Cuba Relations, Washington, D.C., 23 July 1998.

117. U.S. Congress, House, Committee on International Relations, *Economic Sanctions*, 22.

118. 12 March 1996, *PPP*, 434.

119. European Union, "Understanding between the European Union and the United States on U.S. Extraterritorial Legislation," 11 April 1997, in possession of the author.

120. Clinton: 16 January 1998, *PPP*, 75. Penalized during the Clinton administration were Canada's Sherritt International, Israel's BM Group, and Mexico's Grupo Domos, which regained its entry privileges after disinvesting. Its investment was assumed by an Italian telecommunications company, STET International, which avoided sanctions by paying twenty-five million dollars to U.S.-based ITT for use of its confiscated property.

121. Author's notes on Alan Larson, Speech at the Institute for U.S.-Cuba Relations, Washington, D.C., 23 July 1998, *European Union News*, May 1998. A letter to Secretary Albright insisting on seven changes in the U.S.-EU agreement, sent by the chair of the House Committee on International Relations, Benjamin Gilman, and the chair of the Senate Committee on Foreign Relations, Jesse Helms, is reprinted in *Americas Trade* 5 (25 June 1998): 9–10. Jamaica's SuperClubs was the one entity penalized by the George W. Bush administration. It promptly dropped its investment in two Cuban hotels. On Title IV during the George W. Bush administration, see Commission for Assistance to a Free Cuba, *CAFC I Implementation Highlights Fact Sheet* (Washington, D.C.: Department of State, 20 July 2006). On the U.S.-EU agreement, see Stefaan Smis and Kim Van der Borght, "The EU-U.S. Compromise on the Helms-Burton and D'Amato Acts," *American Journal of International Law* 93 (January 1999): 227–36.

122. Author's notes on Assistant Secretary of State Alan Larson, Speech at the Institute for U.S.-Cuba Relations, Washington, D.C., 23 July 1998; Joaquín Roy, "The Helms-Burton Law: Development, Consequences, and Legacy for Inter-American and European-U.S. Relations," *Journal of Interamerican Studies and World Affairs* 39 (Fall 1977): 101 nn. 14, 15.

123. American Public Health Association, *Impact*; for Deere, see U.S. Congress, House, Committee on Agriculture, Subcommittee on Foreign Agriculture and Hunger, *Agricultural Implications*, 10–11; for Fontaine, see U.S. Congress, House, Committee on Ways and Means, Subcommittees on Select Revenue Measures and on Trade, *H.R. 2229*, 363; Roger Fontaine and William Ratliff, *A Strategic Flip-Flop in the Caribbean: Lift the Embargo on Cuba* (Stanford, Calif.: Hoover Institution Press, 2000).

124. U.S. Congress, House, Committee on International Relations, Subcommittee on the Western Hemisphere, *Clinton Administration's Reversal*, 83–84.

125. For Schlesinger, see *NYT*, 26 February 1997, A22; for Sánchez, see *NYT*, 22 April 1997, A21.

126. Bernard W. Aronson and William D. Rogers, *U.S.-Cuban Relations in the 21st Century: Report of an Independent Task Force Sponsored by the Council on Foreign Relations* (New York: Council on Foreign Relations Press, 1999), 10. A moderate Democrat, Rogers had been a

longtime champion of engagement, was central to the 1974–75 opening to Cuba, and was a key member of the 1973–74 Linowitz Commission. The only clearly identifiable task force liberal was historian Franklin Knight, and he was heavily outnumbered by conservatives Dan Fisk, the primary author/arranger of Helms-Burton; Peter Rodman of the Nixon Center; Mark Falcoff of the American Enterprise Institute; Susan Kaufmann Purcell of the Council of the Americas; and Adrian Karatnycky of Freedom House.

127. The letters are reprinted in *Congressional Record*, 20 October 1998, 27167–68.

128. Jorge Mas Santos, "Aim at Cuba's Freedom, Not Money," *Miami Herald*, 30 November 1998, A13; the 13 October 1998 letter from Ileana Ros-Lehtinen, Robert Menéndez, and Lincoln Díaz-Balart is reprinted in *Americas Trade* 5 (29 October 1998): 9.

129. Albright's statement, 5 January 1999, is reprinted in Aronson and Rogers, *U.S.-Cuban Relations*, 57–59; for the president's announcement, see *PPP*, 7–8; for the implementing regulations, see 64 *FR* 25807–20, 13 May 1999; State Department Press Briefing by Peter Romero, 5 January 1999. For an insightful Cuban perspective on the Clinton "please everyone" style, see Soraya M. Castro Mariño, "U.S.-Cuban Relations during the Clinton Administration," *Latin American Perspectives* 29 (July 2002): 47–76.

130. *Granma*, 9 January 1999, 5. Fearing mail bombs, Cuba nixed regular postal service.

131. U.S. Congress, House, Committee on International Relations, Subcommittee on the Western Hemisphere, *U.S.-Cuba Relations: Where Are We and Where Are We Heading?*, 106th Cong., 1st sess., 24 March 1999, 1 (Ros-Lehtinen), 27 (Mas Santos), 28 (Reich). The Baltimore team's owner, Peter Angelos, a major contributor to the Democratic Party, had requested permission to play the Cuban team as early as 1995. Cuba won the rematch in Baltimore a month later.

132. U.S. Congress, House, Committee on Agriculture, Subcommittee on Foreign Agriculture and Hunger, *Agricultural Implications of Renewed Trade with Cuba*, 101 (oilseeds), 31 (rice), 33 (pork). Agricultural economist William Messina noted (14–15) that other large potential markets included cereal grains, cotton, potatoes, fertilizer, pesticides, animal feed and agricultural machinery. For data on prerevolutionary rice exports to Cuba, see U.S. Congress, House, Committee on Agriculture, *Review of U.S. Agricultural Trade with Cuba*, 109th Cong., 1st sess., 16 March 2005, 57.

133. "Report to the Speaker of the House Mandated by the Export Administration Act of 1979 (PL 96-72)," 29 December 1979, *PPP*, 2296; *Wall Street Journal*, 26 August 1994, A10; "Curbing Castro," *The Economist*, 28 October 1995, 17–18; "Isolating Cuba Hasn't Worked," *Chicago Tribune*, 23 August 1994, 14; Barbara Walters, "An Interview with Fidel Castro," *Foreign Policy* 28 (Fall 1977): 31; U.S. Congress, House, Committee on Agriculture, Subcommittee on Foreign Agriculture and Hunger, *Agricultural Implications of Renewed Trade with Cuba*, 39–40, 42, 117.

134. *Denial of Food and Medicine: The Impact of the U.S. Embargo on Health and Nutrition in Cuba* (Washington, D.C.: American Association for World Health, March 1997), with quotation from Executive Summary, n.p. For assessments of the report, see *Cuba in Transition* 8 (1998): 216–29.

135. Bourne to Pastor, "Cuba Embargo and Pharmaceutical Products," 3 October 1977, Folder "Cuba—List of Drugs, 10/7/77–4/2/79," Box 32, Staff Office Files—Bourne, JCL; USINT to Secretary of State, "Visit of U.S. Surgeon-General to Cuba," 2 April 1979, Folder "Cuba—List of Drugs, 10/7/77–4/2/79," Box 32, Staff Office Files—Bourne, JCL. Humani-

tarian exports of food, medicine, and medical supplies were exempted in JFK's February 1962 embargo proclamation, although the regulations were changed in May 1964 (29 *FR* 6381) to require a specific license. For JFK's original policy, see *DOSB*, 11 May 1964, 738–39.

136. The issue of humanitarian medicine and food shipments received some consideration during the first Bush administration when Representative Mickey Leland (D-Texas) proposed legislation (H.R. 1853) exempting medicine and medical supplies from the embargo. When Leland died, the bill's sponsorship was picked up by three Democratic House members (Torricelli, Weiss, and Crockett) with the support of the editor of *Conservative Digest*, who told Congress in 1989 that "it is wrong in every instance to withhold medical supplies or medical equipment as an instrument of foreign policy." Torricelli added food. U.S. Congress, House, Committee on Foreign Affairs, *Cuba and the United States: Thirty Years of Hostility and Beyond*, 101st Cong., 1st sess., August–September 1989, 381, 343.

137. U.S. Congress, Senate, Committee on Foreign Relations, *Nomination of Warren M. Christopher*, 133–34; Watson in U.S. Congress, House, Committee on Foreign Affairs, Subcommittees on Economic Policy, Trade and Environment; on Western Hemisphere Affairs; and on International Operations, *U.S. Policy and the Future of Cuba*, 17; Mark Falcoff, "Is It Time to Rethink the Cuban Embargo?," *American Enterprise Institute Latin American Outlook*, 1 March 1998, 2; George Grayson, "Energy Crisis Tests Revolution," *Petroleum Economist* 59 (September 1992): 11n; U.S. Congress, House, Committee on International Relations, Subcommittee on the Western Hemisphere, *U.S.-Cuba Relations*, 6.

138. American Association for World Health, "Denial of Food and Medicine"; Anthony F. Kirkpatrick, "The U.S. Attack on Cuba's Health," *Canadian Medical Association Journal* 157 (1 August 1997): 281; Robin C. Williams, "In the Shadow of Plenty, Cuba Copes with a Crippled Health Care System," *Canadian Medical Association Journal* 157 (1 August 1997): 291–93; Richard Garfield and Sarah Santana, "The Impact of the Economic Crisis and the U.S. Embargo on Health in Cuba," *American Journal of Public Health* 87 (January 1997): 15–20; Elizardo Sánchez, *NYT*, 22 April 1997, A21; U.S. Congress, House, Committee on International Relations, Subcommittee on the Western Hemisphere, *Visit*, 40.

139. *Congressional Record*, 15 July 1998, 15557–59 (Torricelli); National Association of Manufacturers, *Catalog*; Andreas, Interview by Patrick J. Kiger, 1996, Decatur, Illinois, courtesy of Kiger; quotation is from Kiger, *Squeeze Play*, 40; William Kost, "Cuba's Agriculture: Collapse and Economic Reform," *USDA Agricultural Outlook*, October 1998, 30; U.S. International Trade Commission, *The Economic Impact of U.S. Sanctions with Respect to Cuba*, Investigation 332-413, Publication 3398 (2001), xxv–xxvi.

140. *Congressional Quarterly Weekly Report*, 27 March 1999, 767; *Congressional Record*, 11 February 1999, 2330, 3 August 1999, 19139.

141. U.S. Congress, House, Committee on International Relations, Subcommittee on the Western Hemisphere, *U.S.-Cuba Relations*, 1 (Ros-Lehtinen), 8 (Catholic Church), 10 (Horowitz), 15 (Reich), 18, 20 (Mas Santos).

142. U.S. Congress, House, Committee on Agriculture, *Economic Sanctions and the Effect on U.S. Agriculture*, 106th Cong., 1st sess., 9 June 1999, 52–53 (Farm Bureau), 45 (corn producers), 41, 50 (Farmland Industries), 46–47 (rice producers), 3 (Stenholm). The rice growers estimated that they could supply rice for about half the price Cuba was paying to its Asian providers. For an estimate of the savings on shipping costs, see U.S. International Trade

Commission, *U.S. Agricultural Sales to Cuba: Certain Economic Effects of U.S. Restrictions*, Investigation 332-489, Publication 3932 (2007), 2–5.

143. *Congressional Record*, 3 August 1999, 19144. This was the Senate's only roll-call vote on the Food and Medicine for the World Act, which was then adopted by voice vote (p. 19150). As an indicator of agribusiness strength, a measure to lift the travel ban failed at about the same time, 55–43, with almost all the switch votes by farm-state senators (*Congressional Record*, 30 June 1999, 14859–72).

144. Bo Cooper, General Counsel, INS, to Doris Meissner, Commissioner, "Elian Gonzalez," 3 January 2000, in possession of the author.

145. 6 April, 25 January 2000, *PPP*, 651, 117–18.

146. *NYT*, 23 April 2000, A1. On the effect of the Elián affair, see Lillian Guerra, "Elián González and the 'Real Cuba' of Miami: Visions of Identity, Exceptionality, and Divinity," *Cuban Studies* 38 (2007): 1–25; William M. LeoGrande, "A Politics-Driven Policy: Washington's Cuba Agenda Is Still in Place—For Now," *NACLA Report on the Americas* 34 (November–December 2000): 39; Philip Brenner, Patrick J. Haney, and Walter Vanderbush, "The Confluence of Domestic and International Interests: U.S. Policy toward Cuba, 1998–2001," *International Studies Perspectives* 3 (May 2002): 199; Jorge I. Domínguez, "Your Friend, Fidel: A Letter from Cuba," *Harvard Magazine*, July–August 2000, 35–36, 39.

147. *Congressional Record*, 24 May 2000, 9117.

148. Ibid., 20 July 2000, 15747–48. On this division within the Republican Party, see Daniel Erickson, "The New Cuba Divide," *National Interest* 67 (Spring 2002): 65–71.

149. U.S. Congress, Senate, Committee on Foreign Relations, *2000 Foreign Policy Overview and the President's Fiscal Year 2001 Foreign Affairs Budget Request*, 106th Cong., 2nd sess., 23 March 2000, 440, 457.

150. *Congressional Record*, 20 July 2000, 15736–61.

151. The Act was Title IX of the FY2001 agriculture appropriations act, PL 106-387, 114 Stat. 1549, 28 October 2000. The implementing regulations are 66 *FR* 36676, 12 July 2001; see also *PPP*, 28 October 2001, 2359.

152. *Congressional Record*, 18 October 2000, 23112 (Durbin), 23102 (Dodd).

153. 21 March 1994, *PPP*, 517; 21 January 1998, *PPP*, 90; 5 November 1999, *PPP*, 1988–92; 18 January 2000, *PPP*, 71–78.

154. 4 November 2000, *PPP*, 2500–2501.

Chapter 14

1. Bill Clinton, *My Life* (New York: Knopf, 2004), 906; Castro Speech, San José de las Lajas, 27 January 2001.

2. *Miami Herald*, 30 April 1993, B2; *NYT*, 5 October 2000, A29.

3. For the 2000 party platforms, see www.presidency.ucsb.edu/platforms.php.

4. Speech, Pinar del Río, 5 August 2000; see also Speech, San José de las Lajas, 27 January 2001, where Castro dismissed both candidates as "boring and insipid" ("dos candidatos tan aburridos e insípidos").

5. U.S. Congress, Senate, Committee on Foreign Relations, *Challenges for U.S. Policy toward Cuba*, 108th Cong., 1st sess., 2 October 2003, 69. On the Pedro Pan exodus of about

fourteen thousand unaccompanied children in the early 1960s, see María de los Angeles Torres, *The Lost Apple: Operation Pedro Pan, Cuban Children in the U.S., and the Promise of a Better Future* (Boston: Beacon, 2003); Carlos M. N. Eire, *Waiting for Snow in Havana: Confessions of a Cuban Boy* (New York: Free Press, 2003).

6. Oscar Arias, "A Nominee Who Stands for War," *Los Angeles Times*, 29 April 2001, M1; Comptroller General to Representatives Jack Brooks and Dante Fascell, 30 September 1987, NSA.

7. Author's notes on Reich Speech, Center for Strategic and International Studies, Washington, D.C., 12 March 2002; William Finnegan, "Castro's Shadow: America's Man in Latin America, and His Obsession," *New Yorker*, 14–21 October 2002, 101–13; NSA Electronic Briefing Book, "Public Diplomacy and Covert Propaganda: The Declassified Record of Ambassador Otto Juan Reich," NSA. For Noriega, see U.S. Congress, Senate, Committee on Foreign Relations, *Foreign Assistance Oversight*, 108th Cong., 2nd sess., 2 March 2004, 58.

8. Colin L. Powell with Joseph E. Persico, *My American Journey* (New York: Random House, 1995), 436; U.S. Congress, Senate, Committee on Foreign Relations, *Nomination of Colin L. Powell to Be Secretary of State*, 107th Cong., 1st sess., 17 January 2001, 25, 61.

9. Republican Margin of Victory in Florida:

1980	625,319	55.5 percent
1984	1,280,431	65.3
1988	960,746	60.9
1992	100,130	40.9 (Ross Perot 20 percent; Bill Clinton 39 percent)
1996	(302,644)	42.3
2000	537	48.8

Data from Florida Department of State, Division of Elections, Tallahassee.

10. Most studies of Cuban American voting relied on ecological data that presumed a high level of precinct homogeneity, which was not the case by 2000, when Miami's Cuban American enclaves such as Little Havana were experiencing a rapid influx of other Hispanic groups. Survey data also presented problems. The 2000 exit poll conducted by the Voter News Service was clearly unreliable; it indicated that the two candidates evenly split Florida's Cuban American vote, perhaps because it polled only 25 (weighted) Cuban Americans in a sample of 1,089 voters. A 2004 poll (*Washington Post*, 16 October 2004, A1) indicated that 81 percent of Florida's Cuban American voters favored George W. Bush.

I am indebted to Professors Guillermo Grenier and Darío Moreno of Florida International University, whose useful surveys of South Florida Cuban Americans have been conducted regularly since 1991. The 2007 FIU poll indicated that 65 percent of respondents were U.S. citizens and that 91 percent of citizens were registered to vote. Sixty-six percent were registered Republicans, 18 percent Democrats, and 15 percent were independents.

11. Daniel W. Fisk, "Cuba: The End of an Era," *Washington Quarterly* 24 (Winter 2001): 93; see also Daniel Fisk and Stephen Johnson, "How to Help the People of Cuba, Not the Regime," *Heritage Foundation Backgrounder*, 6 July 2001, n.p. The proposed legislation included:

H.R. 173 to allow for financing of agricultural sales
H.R. 174 to lift the embargo

H.R. 796/S. 401 to normalize trade relations

H.R. 797/S. 402 to further exempt agricultural and medical goods

H.R. 798/S. 400 to lift the embargo

H.R. 2138/S. 1017 to ease restrictions on the sale of food/medicine and travel and to · provide scholarships to Cubans

H.R. 2590/S. 1398 to prohibit enforcement of travel regulations

H.R. 2662 to lift the embargo

S. 171 to repeal travel restrictions

S. 239 to ease restrictions on agricultural trade

H.R. 2646/S. 1731 to repeal restrictions on private financing of agricultural sales.

12. Texas State Senate Concurrent Resolution 54/House Concurrent Resolution 274, 24 May 2001.

13. Jonathan G. Clarke and William Ratliff, *Report from Havana: Time for a Reality Check on U.S. Policy toward Cuba*, Policy Analysis 418 (Washington, D.C.: Cato Institute, 2001), 18; Mark A. Groombridge, *Missing the Target: The Failure of the Helms-Burton Act*, Trade Briefing Paper 12 (Washington, D.C.: Cato Institute, 2001), executive summary, 7.

14. TSRA, secs. 906, 908; for the Department of Commerce's extraordinarily complex licensing regulations, see 66 *FR* 36676–92, 12 July 2001.

15. U.S. Congress, Senate, Committee on Commerce, Science and Transportation, Subcommittee on Consumer Affairs, Foreign Commerce and Tourism, *U.S. Trade Policy with Cuba*, 107th Cong., 2nd sess., 21 May 2002, 40. For the estimate of one hundred million dollars, see Remy Jurenas, *Exempting Food and Agriculture Products from U.S. Economic Sanctions: Status and Implementation*, CRS Report IB 10061 (Washington, D.C.: CRS, 2006), 10; for two other estimates, both larger, see U.S. Congress, House, Committee on Agriculture, *Review of U.S. Agricultural Trade with Cuba*, 109th Cong., 1st sess., 16 March 2005, 27; U.S. International Trade Commission, *U.S. Agricultural Sales to Cuba: Certain Economic Effects of U.S. Restrictions*, Investigation 332-489, Publication 3932 (2007), 2–5.

16. S. 1731, Sec. 335, 27 November 2001.

17. Farm Security and Rural Investment Act of 2002, PL 107-171, 116 *Stat.* 134, 13 May 2002.

18. "Bush's Cuba Pickle," *Wall Street Journal*, 9 May 2002, A14; U.S. Congress, Senate, Committee on Commerce, Science and Transportation, Subcommittee on Consumer Affairs, Foreign Commerce and Tourism, *U.S. Trade Policy*, 2–3. On the financial benefits of agricultural trade, see James E. Ross, "The Impact of Potential Changes in U.S.-Cuba Relations on Midwest Agribusiness and Investment," *Journal of Transnational Law and Contemporary Problems* 14 (Fall 2004): 743–800; for a commodity-by-commodity breakdown, see U.S. International Trade Commission, *U.S. Agricultural Sales*, chap. 4.

19. U.S. Congress, Senate, Committee on Foreign Relations, Subcommittee on the Western Hemisphere, Peace Corps, and Narcotics Affairs, *Bridges to the Cuban People Act of 2001, S. 1017*, 107th Cong., 2nd sess., 19 June 2002, 39.

20. Question-and-Answer Session, Irvine, California, 24 April 2006, *PPP*, 777–78.

21. Dave Beattie to Assignment Editors and Producers, "Views of Miami-Dade County Cubans," 9 July 2003, in possession of the author; *Miami Herald*, 10 July 2003, B3; Jorge I. Domínguez, *Latinos and U.S. Foreign Policy*, Working Paper 06-05 (Cambridge: Weatherhead

Center for International Affairs, Harvard University, 2006), 14; María Cristina García, "Hard-liners v. 'Dialogueros': Cuban Exile Political Groups and United States–Cuba Policy," *Journal of American Ethnic History* 17 (Summer 1998): 3–29.

22. *Congressional Record*, 27 February 2002, 2133–34 (Specter), 23 July 2002, 14124–25 (Snyder); U.S. Congress, Senate, Committee on Commerce, Science, and Transportation, Subcommittee on Consumer Affairs, Foreign Commerce, and Tourism, *U.S. Trade Policy*, 5 (Boxer).

23. Carter Speech, University of Havana, 14 May 2002, Press Conference, Havana, 17 May 2002, both in *President Carter's Trip Report* (Atlanta: Carter Center, 21 May 2002), n.p.; Bush Speech, Miami, 20 May 2002, *PPP*, 822–28.

24. Meg Scott Phipps, "Lift Ban on Trade with Cuba," 24 October 2002; for Phipps's similar published commitment "to do everything possible to support lifting agricultural trade and travel restrictions," see North Carolina's *State Government News* 45 (November–December 2002), 31; Mark Sullivan, *Cuba: U.S. Restrictions on Travel and Remittances*, CRS Report RL 31139 (Washington, D.C.: CRS, 2005), 22.

25. Moran's Amendment 554 was to H.R. 5120; the veto threat was made in the president's 20 May 2002 Miami speech, *PPP*, 828.

26. *Congressional Record*, 13 February 2003, 4057–58.

27. The agriculture appropriations bill, which included the general license amendment (S. 1427, Sec. 760), was twinned with a House bill (H.R. 2673) that had no such provision. The Senate provision was stripped from a FY2004 consolidated appropriations act, PL 108-199, 23 January 2004. The FY2005 agricultural appropriations (Sec. 776 of S. 2803) and FY2005 transportation-treasury appropriations (Sec. 649 of H.R. 5025) were both merged in the FY2005 consolidated appropriations act, PL 108-447, 8 December 2004.

28. U.S. Congress, Senate, Committee on Appropriations, Subcommittee on Treasury and General Government, *Restrictions on Travel to Cuba*, 107th Cong., 2nd sess., 11 February 2002, 24; U.S. Congress, Senate, Committee on Foreign Relations, Subcommittee on the Western Hemisphere, Peace Corps, and Narcotics Affairs, *Bridges*, 52–54; U.S. Congress, Senate, Committee on Foreign Relations, *Challenges*, 76; U.S. Congress, House, Committee on Government Reform, Subcommittee on Human Rights and Wellness, *Castro's Cuba: What Is the Proper U.S. Response to Ongoing Human Rights Violations in Our Hemisphere?*, 108th Cong., 1st sess., 16 October 2003, 71. OFAC was authorized to issue fines of up to $55,000, but the fine generally was $7,500 for a first offense and was almost always negotiated down even further. In 2005, the average penalty was $1,157. U.S. Congress, Senate, Committee on Appropriations, Subcommittee on Treasury and General Government, *Restrictions*, 38.

29. *Aptheker v. Secretary of State*, 378 U.S. 500, 520 (1964); *Congressional Record*, 23 July 2002, 14124, 14128 (Flake); Treasury and General Government Appropriations Act, Fiscal Year 2002, PL 107-67, 115 *Stat.* 514, 12 November 2001, which began as H.R. 2590 and S. 1398; *Congressional Record*, 19 September 2001, 17237 (Dorgan). Flake's proposal was Sec. 648 of H.R. 2590. The conference report (H. Rept. 107-253) did not contain Sec. 648.

30. The Brattle Group, *The Impact on the U.S. Economy of Lifting Restrictions on Travel to Cuba* (Washington, D.C.: Brattle Group, 2002); Carter Speech, University of Havana, 14 May 2002.

31. Bush Speech, Miami, 20 May 2002, *PPP*, 828 (veto pledge). For the 262–167 House vote on H. Amdt. 552 to H.R. 5120, see *Congressional Record*, 23 July 2002, 14136; U.S. Con-

gress, Senate, Committee on Appropriations, Subcommittee on Treasury and General Government, *Restrictions*, 6.

32. *Congressional Record*, 30 April 2003, 10205; U.S. Congress, Senate, Committee on Appropriations, Subcommittee on Treasury and General Government, *Restrictions*, 51 (OFAC director). Responding to this criticism, in 2003 OFAC twice published its guidelines and schedules of civil penalties (68 *FR* 4422–29, 29 January 2003; 68 *FR* 53640–61, 11 September 2003), and OFAC's director reported (U.S. Congress, House, Committee on Government Reform, Subcommittee on Human Rights and Wellness, *Castro's Cuba*, 63) that case-by-case information on penalty proceedings was available at the agency's Web site. He also reported that 15 percent of his staff was enforcing the Cuba embargo while 20 percent was tracking down sources of terrorist financing (U.S. Congress, Senate, Committee on Foreign Relations, *Challenges*, 76).

33. 68 *FR* 14141–48, 24 March 2003. Family visits had previously been restricted to two degrees of relationship, and since most mortals did not understand this concept, tax dollars were used to pay the salary of someone to explain: "Your mother's cousin is your close relative for the purposes of this section, because you are both no more than three generations removed from your great-grandparents, who are the ancestors you have in common. Similarly, your husband's great-grandson is your close relative for the purposes of this section, because he is no more than three generations removed from you. Your daughter's father-in-law is not your close relative for the purposes of this section, because you have no common ancestor."

34. For Enzi proposal, S. 950, see *Congressional Record*, 30 April 2003, 10203–6; for Flake proposal, H.R. 2071, see *Congressional Record*, 13 May 2003, 11229.

35. U.S. Congress, Senate, Committee on Foreign Relations, *Challenges*, 21, 42 (Noriega); Author's notes on Flake Speech to "Freedom to Travel Forum and Day of Action," Washington, D.C., 15 July 2003. The 1999 vote is *Congressional Record*, 30 June 1999, 14872. In 1995 the Senate (*Congressional Record*, 18 October 1995, 28290) had defeated a move to lift the travel ban by an even-larger margin, 73–25. For the 2003 House and Senate votes, see *Congressional Record*, 9 September 2003, 21551, 23 October 2003, 22597. Flake regularly used an instrumental Track 2 argument: "Fidel Castro is still around. He is still a thug. He is still very much a bad guy. We will all stipulate that. The question is how do we best remove him?" (*Congressional Record*, 23 July 2002, 14124, 14128).

36. *Congressional Record*, 9 December 2003, 16109–10. The transportation-treasury appropriations bill was eventually rolled into the Consolidated Appropriations Act for FY2004, PL 108-199, 23 January 2004. The two bills were identical except for one point: the Senate version provided an effective date of one day after the bill's enactment, while the House version had no such stipulation.

37. *Miami El Nuevo Herald*, 3 August 2003, A24.

38. Remarks on Cuba, 10 October 2003, *PPP*, 1292–95. The commission, which included only members of the executive branch, was to be chaired by Secretary of State Powell and housing secretary Mel Martínez, but Martínez soon resigned to launch his Senate bid, leaving Powell to continue as the sole chair. He gave principal responsibility to Assistant Secretary Noriega, and Noriega in turn handed most of the job to deputy Dan Fisk.

39. *Congressional Record*, 30 June 1999, 14866, 14871 (Kerry); in an 18 April 2004 appearance on NBC's *Meet the Press*, Kerry said he "wouldn't just give something for nothing but

I would begin to encourage travel." For the 2004 party platforms, see www.presidency.ucsb.edu/platforms.php.

40. Bush Remarks, Miami, 27 August 2004, *WCPD*, 1718; Coral Gables, 23 April 2004, *WCPD*, 683; Tampa, 16 July 2004, *WCPD*, 1311. After passage of the Victims of Trafficking and Violence Protection Act (PL 106-386, 114 *Stat.* 1464, 28 October 2000), the State Department was required to produce an annual "Trafficking in Persons Report," which classified the world's countries on three "Tiers," from Tier 1 (no problem), to Tier 2 (some problems), to Tier 3 (does not comply with minimum standards). Cuba was not included in the first two reports but became a Tier 3 country in 2003 and thereafter.

41. U.S. Congress, House, Committee on Agriculture, *Review*, 2, 10, 29. The new definition is 70 *FR* 9225-26, 25 February 2005.

42. U.S. Congress, House, Committee on Agriculture, *Review*, 40; Pedro Alvarez, Teleconference Presentation to the U.S.-Cuba Trade Association, 27 April 2005, in possession of the author. On the 1961 lard shipment, see *Hispanic American Report* 14 (September 1961): 606.

43. For the compromise and its details, see Jurenas, *Exempting Food and Agriculture Products*.

44. Jurenas, *Exempting Food and Agriculture Products*. On potential sales of fish products, see U.S. International Trade Commission, *U.S. Agricultural Sales*, 4–29.

45. Press Conference, Monterrey, 22 March 2002, *PPP*, 478.

46. Press Conference, Havana, 22 April 2002. For Mexico-Cuba relations during the Fox years (2000–2006), see Georgina Sánchez, "Mexican-Cuban Relations: Between Interests and Principles," in *Redefining Cuban Foreign Policy: The Impact of the "Special Period,"* ed. H. Michael Erisman and John M. Kirk (Gainesville: University Press of Florida, 2006), 260–79.

47. Speech to the Heritage Foundation, Washington, D.C., 6 May 2002.

48. U.S. Congress, Senate, Committee on Foreign Relations, Subcommittee on Western Hemisphere, Peace Corps and Narcotics Affairs, *Cuba's Pursuit of Biological Weapons: Fact or Fiction?*, 107th Cong., 2nd sess., 5 June 2002, 7, 9, 36; U.S. Congress, Senate, Committee on Foreign Relations, Subcommittee on the Western Hemisphere, Peace Corps, and Narcotics Affairs, *Bridges*, 42.

49. For Castro's denials, see Speeches, Havana, 10 May 2002, 1 May 2003, 26 July, 17 November 2005, Sancti Spiritus, 25 May 2002; U.S. President, "The National Security Strategy of the United States of America," September 2002, in possession of the author; Wilkerson: Statement to the Senate Committee on Finance, 11 December 2007, typescript, in possession of the author; Reich: U.S. Congress, Senate, Committee on Commerce, Science and Transportation, Subcommittee on Consumer Affairs, Foreign Commerce and Tourism, *U.S. Trade Policy*, 9; Noriega: U.S. Congress, Senate, Committee on Foreign Relations, *Challenges*, 39; Mark Sullivan, *Cuba and the State Sponsors of Terrorism List*, CRS Report RL 32251 (Washington, D.C.: CRS, 12 May 2005), 7 (Bolton). The "unclear" comment is DOS, "Adherence to and Compliance with Arms Control, Nonproliferation and Disarmament Agreements and Commitments," August 2005, 19–20, in possession of the author.

50. Speech, University of Havana, 14 May 2002.

51. For Cuba's response to the 9/11 terrorist attacks, see Soraya Castro Mariño, "The Cuba–United States Conflict: Notes for Reflection in the Context of the War against Terror-

ism," in *Foreign Policy toward Cuba: Isolation or Engagement?*, ed. Michele Zebich-Knos and Heather N. Nicol (Lanham, Md.: Lexington Books, 2005), esp. 195–96.

52. Castro speech, Havana, 11 September 2001; Bush Speech to Joint Session of Congress, 20 September 2001, *PPP*, 1142; Castro Speech, Havana, 22 September 2001.

53. DOS, *Country Reports on Terrorism*, May 2002 (for 2001) and April 2006 (for 2005), in possession of the author; Castro, Open Letter to President Bush, 21 June 2004, Speech, University of Havana, 17 November 2005; on Guantánamo, see Ministry of Foreign Relations, "Statement by the Government of Cuba to the National and International Public Opinion," 11 January 2002, in possession of the author.

54. James Cason Interview by Author, Havana, 8 March 2005.

55. U.S. Congress, Senate, Committee on Foreign Relations, *Challenges*, 53.

56. "La Patria Es de Todos," 27 June 1997.

57. *Essential Measures?: Human Rights Crackdown in the Name of Security* (New York: Amnesty International, June 2003), 45. In 2001, the *New York Times* had published a public statement rejecting U.S. financial support written by Palacios and another of the seventy-five, Pedro Alvarez Ramos, "Aid We Would Rather Not Receive," *NYT*, 18 June 2001, A29.

58. Pérez Roque Press Conference, Havana, 18 April 2003, transcript excerpts in possession of the author. In 2005, the U.S.-government funded National Endowment for Democracy (NED) had given CubaNet two hundred thousand dollars to support more than two dozen Cuba-based writers, and AID was funding CubaNet under its program rubric, "Giving Voice to Cuba's Independent Journalists."

59. Pérez Roque Press Conference, 9 April 2003, transcript excerpts in possession of the author.

60. "Nota Oficial," *Granma*, 19 March 2003, 1; Castro Speech, Havana, 1 May 2003.

61. U.S. Congress, Senate, Committee on Foreign Relations, *Challenges*, 40 (Noriega); for the kiss-of-death argument, see William M. LeoGrande, "The United States and Cuba," in *Cuba, the United States, and the Post–Cold War World: The International Dimensions of the Washington-Havana Relationship*, ed. Morris Morley and Chris McGillion (Gainesville: University Press of Florida, 2005), 44.

62. Cuba Policy Foundation Press Statement, 23 April 2003; U.S. Congress, House, Committee on International Relations, Subcommittees on Africa, Global Human Rights and International Operations, and the Western Hemisphere, *Year Two of Castro's Brutal Crackdown on Dissidents*, 109th Cong., 1st sess., 3 March 2005, 3 (Powell); see also the secretary's unusual op-ed article prepared for the first anniversary of the arrests of the seventy-five dissidents: "Cuba: Condemn Castro Regime's Abuses," *Miami Herald*, 19 March 2004; *Congressional Record*, 30 April 2003, 10205 (Baucus); House vote on H. Res. 197: *Congressional Record*, 8 April 2003, 8802. The foundation was led by former undersecretary of state William D. Rogers.

63. *Essential Measures?*; U.S. Congress, Senate, Committee on Foreign Relations, *Challenges*, 54.

64. Hilda Puerta Rodríguez, "El acuerdo de Cotonou y el posible ingreso de Cuba," *Revista de Estudios Europeos*, no. 60 (2002): 3–24; Joaquín Roy, "Cuba and the European Union: Chronicle of a Dead Agreement Foretold," in *Redefining Cuban Foreign Policy*, ed. Erisman and Kirk, 98–120. In early 2005, the European Council suspended the measures adopted in mid-2003.

65. Speech, Santiago, 26 July 2003.

66. Pérez Roque Press Conference, 18 April 2003, in *Granma*, 22 April 2003; Castro Speech, Havana, 1 May 2003.

67. Wilkerson quoted in Wil S. Hylton, "Casualty of War," *Gentlemen's Quarterly*, June 2004, 236. In 2007 Wilkerson, now a private citizen, told Congress that "Republican or Democrat, presidents and their congresses are too cowed by the prospect of losing the Florida vote to take any ameliorative action. And so this feckless, stupid and failed policy persists" (Statement to the Senate Committee on Finance, 11 December 2007, in possession of the author).

68. "Progress Report on Cuba," 17 August, 8 September 1960, Folder "Cuba (May 1959–September 1960)(6)," Box 4, White House Office Files, Office of the Special Assistant for National Security Affairs: Records, 1952–61, NSC Series, Subject Subseries, DDEL; DOS, "Preliminary Outline Contingency Plan Covering U.S. Assistance to Post-Castro Cuban Government," 1 September 1960, *FRUS* 1958–60, 6:1065–69.

69. Sec. 1703(10), PL 102-484, 106 *Stat.* 2315, 23 October 1992.

70. U.S. Congress, House, Committee on Foreign Affairs, Subcommittee on Western Hemisphere Affairs, *Free and Independent Cuba Assistance Act of 1993*, 103rd Cong., 2nd sess., 24 March 1994, 87. The academic study, edited by Lisandro Pérez, was published as *Transition in Cuba: New Challenges for U.S. Policy* (Miami: Cuban Research Institute, Florida International University, 1993). For a conservative critique, see Antonio de la Cova, *Academic Espionage: U.S. Taxpayer Funding of a Pro-Castro Study* (Washington, D.C.: Institute for U.S. Cuba Relations, 1993).

71. CANF, *Transition Program for a Post-Castro Cuba, Outline* (Miami: CANF, 1993).

72. Sec. 202(a)(1), PL 104-114, 110 *Stat.* 785, 12 March 1996: "The President shall develop a plan for providing economic assistance to Cuba." *Support for Democratic Transition in Cuba* (Washington, D.C.: AID, 28 January 1997); *PPP*, 28 January 1997, 88–89. The distribution claim came in a speech by coordinator for Cuban affairs Michael Ranneberger, Tulane University, 9 November 1998, in possession of the author.

73. Alarcón in CBS/TeleNoticias Debate, 5 September 1996, reprinted as *Debate between Jorge Mas Canosa and Ricardo Alarcón*, Cuba Paper Series 14 (Miami: Endowment for Cuban Studies, 1996); Castro Speech, Havana, 7 February 1997, in *Granma*, 11 February 1997, 3–6.

74. *Congressional Presentation for FY 2000* (Washington, D.C.: AID, February 1999); U.S. Congress, House, Committee on International Relations, Subcommittee on the Western Hemisphere, *U.S.-Cuba Relations: Where Are We and Where Are We Heading?*, 106th Cong., 1st sess., 24 March 1999, 17; *USAID/Cuba Program* (Washington, D.C.: AID, August 1999). The Pentagon's National Defense Research Institute also paid the RAND Corporation to produce a transition plan: Edward González and Kevin F. McCarthy, eds., *Cuba after Castro: Legacies, Challenges, and Impediments*, RAND Report TR-131-RC (Santa Monica, Calif.: RAND, 2004).

75. *Report to the President* (Washington, D.C.: U.S. Commission for Assistance to a Free Cuba, May 2004), xiii, xxv, xxi.

76. *WCPD*, 6 May 2004, 799–800.

77. Castro Proclamation, 14 May 2004; Speech, University of Havana, 17 November 2005.

78. For the new regulations, see 69 *FR* 33768–74, 16 June 2004; Noriega in U.S. Congress, House, Committee on International Relations, Subcommittees on Africa, Global Human

Rights and International Operations, and the Western Hemisphere, *Year Two*, 42; on Cuban Americans' expenditures in Cuba, see *Report to the President*, 28, 36–37.

79. *Report to the President*, 30; *Congressional Record*, 22 September 2004, H7338 (Lee).

80. *Report to the President*, 35–36.

81. The amount that could be carried had only recently been increased from three hundred dollars to three thousand dollars (68 *FR* 14141–48, 24 March 2003); *Report to the President*, 34–35; Castro, Open Letter to President Bush, 4 July 2004.

82. *Report to the President*, 52.

83. Remarks, Miami, 27 August 2004, *WCPD*, 1718. In 2005, Congress appropriated ten million dollars for TV Martí to purchase its own aircraft (PL 109-108, 119 *Stat.* 2290, 22 November 2005; H. Rept. 109-272, 196).

84. Churchill Roberts, Ernesto Betancourt, Guillermo Grenier, and Richard Scheaffer, *Measuring Cuban Public Opinion: Project Report*, AID Contract LAG-G-00-98-00021-01 (Gainesville: University of Florida, 1999), vii, viii, 11; U.S. Congress, House, Committee on International Relations, Subcommittees on Africa, Global Human Rights and International Operations, and the Western Hemisphere, *Year Two*, 22.

Although limited to Havana and Santiago, in 2006 a highly unusual independent poll of Cuban public opinion by the Costa Rican affiliate of the Gallup organization indicated that Cubans had confidence in the country's health care system (75 percent) and were satisfied with Cuba's educational system (78 percent) but were overwhelmingly critical of several other aspects of Cuban life—only 25 percent were satisfied with their freedom to choose what to do with their lives, for example. Forty-seven percent approved of Cuba's leadership, 40 percent disapproved, and 13 percent had no opinion (Gallup World Poll, "The Gallup Organization's Cuba ThinkForum," September 2006, in possession of the author).

85. Clinton Announcement, 6 October 1995, *PPP*, 1459. Of AID's forty Cuba grants between 1996 and 2005, the agency modified twenty-eight to extend completion dates, increase funding, or both, increasing the grants' value from $5.9 million to $50.1 million and extending the completion date by an average of three years (GAO, *Foreign Assistance: U.S. Democracy Assistance for Cuba Needs Better Management and Oversight*, GAO Report 07-147 [2006], 17).

86. *Congressional Presentation, FY2000* (Washington, D.C.: AID, February 1999); *USAID Cuba Program* (Washington, D.C.: AID, 30 November 2005). The Creighton Report is Patrick Borchers, Michael J. Kelly, Erika Moreno, Richard C. Witmer, James S. Wunsch, and Arthur Pearlstein, *Report on the Resolution of Outstanding Property Claims between Cuba and the United States* (Omaha, Neb.: Creighton University Press, 2007). For an earlier analysis of the compensation issue, see David A. Gantz to Harry W. Shlaudeman, "Agreement with Cuba on Resumption of Diplomatic Relations and Claims," 17 March 1975, NSA.

AID: $5 million in FY2001 and FY2002, $6 million in FY2003, $21.4 million in FY2004 (in reprogrammed funds to implement the Commission's report), $8.9 million in FY 2005, and $10.9 million in FY2006. NED: $765,000 in FY2001, $841,000 in FY2002, $1.14 million in FY2003, $1.15 million in FY2004, and $2.4 million in FY2005 (Mark Sullivan, *Cuba: Issues for the 109th Congress*, CRS Report RL 32730 [Washington, D.C.: CRS, 2006]; U.S. Congress, Senate, Committee on Foreign Relations, *Challenges*, 75).

While the NED is technically not a U.S. government organization, since its creation in 1983, virtually all of its funds (98.8 percent in 2000, a typical year) have come from a federal government appropriation. Acutely aware of the hand that feeds it, the endowment was among the first to fund CANF's International Coalition for Human Rights in Cuba (in 1991); between 1984 and 2005, NED funded 158 grants worth $13.3 million to promote democracy in Cuba (GAO, *Foreign Assistance*, 15).

87. GAO, *Foreign Assistance*, 4, 36–37; Flake Press Conference, Washington, D.C., 15 November 2006, transcript in possession of the author.

88. U.S. Congress, House, Committee on International Relations, Subcommittee on the Western Hemisphere, *Overview of Radio and Television Martí*, 108th Cong., 1st sess., 11 June 2003, 62. In 2002, the Voice of America launched a new Sunday evening shortwave program to Cuba, *Ventana a Cuba*, a resuscitation of the old *Cita con Cuba* program that had gone off the air in 1974.

89. Dana Doo-Soghian (AID) to Associate Dean Andy S. Gómez (University of Miami), 29 June 2000, enclosing contract LAG-A-00-00-00013-00, AID FOIA. See also the university's proposal, "Developing Civil Society in Cuba," 14 January 2000, Suchlicki to David Mutchler (AID), 26 February 2002, both AID FOIA.

90. Public affairs officer Colette Christian Interview by Author, U.S. Interests Section, Havana, 8 March 2005. The number of radios is from GAO, *Foreign Assistance*, 20; cf. AID's claim to have distributed 120,000 in U.S. Congress, House, Committee on International Relations, Subcommittees on Africa, Global Human Rights and International Operations, and the Western Hemisphere, *Year Two*, 72.

91. The Cuban government's diplomatic note is reprinted in *Granma*, 26 April 2003, 1; Castro Speech, Havana, 3 January 2004.

92. Cason Interview.

93. The third witness, René Gómez Manzano, characterized Cuba as a "big jail" (U.S. Congress, House, Committee on International Relations, Subcommittees on Africa, Global Human Rights and International Operations, and the Western Hemisphere, *Year Two*, 21, 28, 30).

94. "President Carter's Cuba Trip Report," 21 May 2002, Carter Center, Atlanta, Georgia. Sánchez and Gutierrez-Menoyo as reported by Reuters, 10 May 2004; Payá and Cuesta Morúa as reported by Inter-Press Service, 11 May 2004. In a book whose publication must have been approved by the Cuban government, Sánchez was said to be an agent of Cuban state security (Arleen Rodríguez and Lázero Barredo, *El camaján* [Havana: Política, 2003]).

95. Michael Parmly Speech, 10 December 2005, in possession of the author.

96. "Sueño con que un día esta nación se levante"; "El comunismo no funciona porque a la gente le gusta tener cosas"; "No temen que pierdan sus casas despúes de la transición; no es cierto"; "En un país libre no hostigan los que intentaron de emigrar; no se conoce el apartheid turismo; es Cuba un país libre?" Interests Section *letrero* for 16, 27–29, 31 January, 2 February 2006, in possession of the author.

97. Michael Parmly Interview by Author, Havana, 27 January 2006.

98. Castro Television Speech, 22 January 2006.

99. *Washington Post*, 15 December 2006; 6 November 1959, *FRUS* 1958–60, 6:659 (Bonsal); Remarks at Newport, Rhode Island, 28 June 2007, *WCPD*, 2 July 2007, 881–82.

100. "Todos los cubanos deben saber que su mejor amigo es Estados Unidos de América." 5, 7 August 2007, in possession of the author; Bush Speech to the Council of the Americas, Washington, D.C., 7 May 2008, *WCPD*, 12 May 2008, 667.

Conclusion

1. William H. Taft, "Some Recent Instances of National Altruism," *National Geographic*, July 1907, 438; George H. W. Bush Press Conference, 19 December 1991, *PPP*, 1647.

2. *In Defense of National Sovereignty: Cuba Replies to the U.S.A. Note* (Havana: Public Relations Department, Ministry of State, Republic of Cuba, 1959); Lisa Howard, Message from Fidel Castro to President Johnson, 12 February 1964, *FRUS* 1964–68, 32:592–93; Memcon, Peter Tarnoff and Robert Pastor, "U.S./Cuban Relations, December 3–4, 1978, Havana," in "Cuba: President Carter's Trip, May 12–17, 2002," Vertical File, JCL. Another of the few instances of the message being heard is Embassy (Braddock) to DOS, 5 December 1960, *FRUS* 1958–60, 6:1144.

3. Roosevelt Speech to the Harvard Union, 23 February 1907, in Theodore Roosevelt, *Presidential Addresses and State Papers*, 8 vols. (New York: Review of Reviews, 1910), 6:1178–79; Bush Speech to the Council of the Americas, Washington, D.C., 7 May 2008, *WCPD*, 12 May 2008, 667; Memcon, Peter Tarnoff and Robert Pastor, "U.S./Cuban Relations, December 3–4, 1978, Havana," in "Cuba: President Carter's Trip, May 12–17, 2002," Vertical File, JCL.

4. Castro Speech, Havana, 1 May 1961; Nixon Speeches, Detroit, 24 August 1960, Springfield, Missouri, 21 September 1960, reprinted in U.S. Congress, Senate, *Freedom of Communications: Final Report of the Committee on Commerce, United States Senate*, pt. 2, *The Speeches, Remarks, Press Conferences, and Study Papers of Vice President Richard M. Nixon, August 1 through November 7, 1960*, 87th Cong., 1st Sess., 1961, 30, 219.

5. Minutes, National Security Planning Group, 11 September 1984, NSA.

6. William Howard Taft, "Some Recent Instances of National Altruism," *National Geographic*, July 1907, 438; Speech of Provisional Governor William Howard Taft, Opening Day Exercises of the National University of Havana, 1 October 1906, reprinted in *Annual Reports of the War Department for the Fiscal Year Ended June 30, 1906* (Washington, D.C.: U.S. Government Printing Office, 1906), 541.

7. Wood to Senator Foraker, 11 January 1901, Box 30, Leonard Wood Papers, LC.

8. "The wine, of plantain. And if it turns out to be bitter—it's *our* wine!" José Martí, "Nuestra América," January 1891, in *Obras Completas* (Havana: Editorial Nacional de Cuba, 1963), 6:20; Marvin R. Shanken, "A Conversation with Fidel," *Cigar Aficionado*, Summer 1994, 57; Castro Speech, Cienfuegos, 5 September 1992.

9. "Statement on Signing the Cuban Liberty and Democratic Solidarity (Libertad) Act of 1996," 12 March 1996, *PPP*, 434 (Clinton); "Message on the Observance of Cuban Independence Day," 18 May 2007, *WCPD*, 20 May 2007, 659; Bush Speech to the Council of the Americas, Washington, D.C., 7 May 2008, *WCPD*, 12 May 2008, 667.

10. *WCPD*, 6 May 2004, 799–800.

11. Senator Allen J. Ellender Diary, 14 December 1958, *FRUS* 1958–60, 6:288; Embassy to Department of State, 22 October 1958, 611.37/10-2258, RG59; Southcom Intelligence Summary, 2 January 1959, PC.

12. Hunter S. Thompson, *Fear and Loathing in Las Vegas* (New York: Random House, 1971), 67; see also Richard E. Welch Jr., *Response to Revolution: The United States and the Cuban Revolution, 1959–1961* (Chapel Hill: University of North Carolina Press, 1985), 13.

13. Embassy to Department of State, 6 November 1959, *FRUS* 1958–60, 6:659; Herter to

Foreign Secretary Selwyn Lloyd, 5 November 1959, Cable 2335, AK 1233/88, FO371/139474, PRO; Sir H. Caccia to Secretary of State, 24 November 1959, Cable 2455, NSA.

14. Herbert L. Matthews to Publisher, 17 August 1960, Box 2, Herbert Matthews Papers, Columbia University, New York.

15. James M. Lambie Jr., "Notes on Legislative Leadership Meeting August 16, 1960," 16 August 1960, Folder "Legislative Leaders 1960 (4)," Box 3, Legislative Meetings Minutes, AWF ("great difficulty"); CIA, "Increasing Opposition to Castro/Shortage of Consumer Goods/ Lack of Currency," Report 00-A3177796, [late January] 1961, PC.

16. Memcon, Meeting with President, 19 February 1964, *FRUS* 1964–68, 31:11; CIA, Directorate of Intelligence, "Castro's Cuba Today," 30 September 1966, FOIA.

17. CIA, National Intelligence Council, "Castro Agonistes: The Mounting Dilemmas and Frustrations of Cuba's Caudillo," November 1981, FOIA.

18. CIA, "Cuba: The Outlook for Castro and Beyond," NIE 93-30, August 1993, iii, FOIA; President Bush: 20 November 1991, *PPP*, 1495; see also 20, 30 September, 19, 26 December 1991, *PPP*, 1197, 1233, 1647, 1658; 4 March, 18 April, 20 May, 23 October 1992, *PPP*, 377, 615, 805, 1940, 1950.

19. Deputy Assistant Secretary of State Robert Gelbard in U.S. Congress, Senate, Committee on Foreign Relations, Subcommittee on Western Hemisphere and Peace Corps Affairs, *The Cuban Democracy Act of 1992, S. 2918*, 102nd Cong., 2nd sess., 5 August 1992, 26; U.S. Congress, House, Committee on Foreign Affairs, Subcommittees on Europe and the Middle East and on Western Hemisphere Affairs, *Cuba in a Changing World: The United States–Soviet–Cuban Triangle*, 102nd Cong., 1st Sess., July 1991, 116 (State Department); Secretary of Defense Richard Cheney, 11 September 1991, quoted in *NYT*, 12 September 1999, A12; Senator Jesse Helms in *Congressional Record*, 5 March 1996, 3598; Representative Robert Torricelli in U.S. Congress, House, Committee on Foreign Affairs, Subcommittee on Western Hemisphere Affairs, *The Free and Independent Cuba Assistance Act of 1993*, 103rd Cong., 2nd sess., 24 March 1994, 1; Senator John Ashcroft in *Congressional Record*, 17 September 1997, 19219.

20. President Bush, 10 October 2003, *PPP*, 1294; *Report to the President* (Washington, D.C.: U.S. Commission for Assistance to a Free Cuba, May 2004), 2; James Cason, "Fostering Democracy in Cuba: Lessons Learned," Speech, University of Miami, 12 September 2005, in possession of the author; Adolfo Franco, Speech, University of Iowa, 6 February 2004, in possession of the author; AID in U.S. Congress, House, Committee on International Relations, *Castro's Brutal Crackdown on Dissidents*, 108th Cong., 1st sess., 16 April 2003, 25; Richard Lugar in U.S. Congress, Senate, Committee on Foreign Relations, *Challenges for U.S. Policy toward Cuba*, 108th Cong., 1st Sess., 2 October 2003, 2; John Negroponte to *Washington Post* editors, 14 December 2006, in *Washington Post*, 15 December 2006, A23; Brian Latell, "The End of an Era," *Miami Herald*, 10 December 2006, 5L.

See also the speech by Secretary of Commerce Carlos M. Gutiérrez to the Council of the Americas, Washington, D.C., 2 May 2007, in possession of the author: "It's just a matter of time before the regime crumbles." For Congress, see also Senator Mel Martínez ("We are reaching a decisive moment in Cuba, given the age of the dictator Castro"), interview in *El País* (Madrid), 19 February 2006, 8; Senator Christopher Dodd ("The transition, when it comes—and I think it will come sooner rather than later") in U.S. Congress, Senate, Committee on Foreign Relations, *Nomination of Colin L. Powell to Be Secretary of State*, 107th Cong., 1st Sess., 17 January 2001, 98. For the Office of the Director of National Intelligence, see also the statement by spokesperson Ross Feinstein, *Miami Herald*, 6 January 2007, 11A: "The bottom line: He is terminally ill."

21. Castro Speech, Havana, 16 April 1981; Clinton Press Interview, 4 November 2000, *PPP*, 2500–2501; Bush Remarks at the Naval War College, Newport, Rhode Island, 28 June 2007, *WCPD*, 2 July 2007, 882.

22. Kleberg to Johnson, 25 June 1959, Folder "Foreign Relations Cuba," Box 68, Subject File, LBJA, LBJL.

23. Allen Dulles, "My Answer to the Bay of Pigs," n.d., page headed "Outline I Communism & Cuba in 1960," Allen Dulles Papers, Princeton University. See introduction, n. 16, for an explanation of this sixty-six-page undated handwritten manuscript.

24. John Ferch Interview, Fairfax, Virginia, 17 February 2005; Dwayne Andreas Interview (1996) in Patrick J. Kiger, *Squeeze Play: The United States, Cuba, and the Helms-Burton Act* (Washington, D.C.: Center for Public Integrity, 1997), 40.

25. Wood to Roosevelt, 12 April 1901, Theodore Roosevelt Papers, LC.

26. Wilson's famous comment—that his policy was "to teach the South American Republics to elect good men"—may be apocryphal. It comes to us fourthhand from the biographer of Wilson's ambassador to Great Britain. See Burton J. Hendrick, ed., *The Life and Letters of Walter Hines Page*, 3 vols. (Garden City, N.Y.: Doubleday, Page, 1923–25), 1:204; for a firsthand letter expressing the same idea, see Woodrow Wilson to William Tyrrell, 22 November 1913, Woodrow Wilson Papers, LC.

27. Magoon to Roosevelt, 16 April 1908, Roosevelt Papers.

28. Morrow to Crowder, 26 May 1922, Dwight Morrow Papers, Amherst College, Amherst, Massachusetts.

29. Castro Speech, Havana, 23 April 1961.

30. Martí, "Nuestra América," 22; Castro Speech, Havana, 23 April 1961; Castro Interview, 1974, published as Frank Mankiewicz and Kirby Jones, "Conversation with Fidel Castro," *Oui*, January 1975, 114.

INDEX